American Casebook Series
Hornbook Series and Basic Legal Texts
Nutshell Series

of

WEST PUBLISHING COMPANY
P.O. Box 64526
St. Paul, Minnesota 55164–0526

ACCOUNTING

Faris' Accounting and Law in a Nutshell, 377 pages, 1984 (Text)

Fiflis, Kripke and Foster's Teaching Materials on Accounting for Business Lawyers, 3rd Ed., 838 pages, 1984 (Casebook)

Siegel and Siegel's Accounting and Financial Disclosure: A Guide to Basic Concepts, 259 pages, 1983 (Text)

ADMINISTRATIVE LAW

Davis' Cases, Text and Problems on Administrative Law, 6th Ed., 683 pages, 1977 (Casebook)

Gellhorn and Boyer's Administrative Law and Process in a Nutshell, 2nd Ed., 445 pages, 1981 (Text)

Mashaw and Merrill's Cases and Materials on Administrative Law–The American Public Law System, 2nd Ed., 976 pages, 1985 (Casebook)

Robinson, Gellhorn and Bruff's The Administrative Process, 3rd Ed., 978 pages, 1986 (Casebook)

ADMIRALTY

Healy and Sharpe's Cases and Materials on Admiralty, 2nd Ed., 876 pages, 1986 (Casebook)

Maraist's Admiralty in a Nutshell, about 362 pages, 1988 (Text)

Schoenbaum's Hornbook on Admiralty and Maritime Law, Student Ed., 692 pages, 1987 (Text)

Sohn and Gustafson's Law of the Sea in a Nutshell, 264 pages, 1984 (Text)

AGENCY—PARTNERSHIP

Fessler's Alternatives to Incorporation for Persons in Quest of Profit, 2nd Ed., 326 pages, 1986 (Casebook)

AGENCY—PARTNERSHIP—Cont'd

Henn's Cases and Materials on Agency, Partnership and Other Unincorporated Business Enterprises, 2nd Ed., 733 pages, 1985 (Casebook)

Reuschlein and Gregory's Hornbook on the Law of Agency and Partnership, 625 pages, 1979, with 1981 pocket part (Text)

Selected Corporation and Partnership Statutes and Forms, 621 pages, 1987

Steffen and Kerr's Cases and Materials on Agency-Partnership, 4th Ed., 859 pages, 1980 (Casebook)

Steffen's Agency-Partnership in a Nutshell, 364 pages, 1977 (Text)

AGRICULTURAL LAW

Meyer, Pedersen, Thorson and Davidson's Agricultural Law: Cases and Materials, 931 pages, 1985 (Casebook)

ALTERNATIVE DISPUTE RESOLUTION

Kanowitz' Cases and Materials on Alternative Dispute Resolution, 1024 pages, 1986 (Casebook)

Riskin and Westbrook's Dispute Resolution and Lawyers, 223 pages, 1987 (Coursebook)

Riskin and Westbrook's Dispute Resolution and Lawyers, Abridged Ed., 223 pages, 1988 (Coursebook)

Teple and Moberly's Arbitration and Conflict Resolution, (The Labor Law Group), 614 pages, 1979 (Casebook)

AMERICAN INDIAN LAW

Canby's American Indian Law in a Nutshell, 288 pages, 1981 (Text)

Getches and Wilkinson's Cases on Federal Indian Law, 2nd Ed., 880 pages, 1986 (Casebook)

List current as of January, 1988

T7202—1g

I

ANTITRUST LAW

Gellhorn's Antitrust Law and Economics in a Nutshell, 3rd Ed., 472 pages, 1986 (Text)

Gifford and Raskind's Cases and Materials on Antitrust, 694 pages, 1983 with 1985 Supplement (Casebook)

Hovenkamp's Hornbook on Economics and Federal Antitrust Law, Student Ed., 414 pages, 1985 (Text)

Oppenheim, Weston and McCarthy's Cases and Comments on Federal Antitrust Laws, 4th Ed., 1168 pages, 1981 with 1985 Supplement (Casebook)

Posner and Easterbrook's Cases and Economic Notes on Antitrust, 2nd Ed., 1077 pages, 1981, with 1984–85 Supplement (Casebook)

Sullivan's Hornbook of the Law of Antitrust, 886 pages, 1977 (Text)

See also Regulated Industries, Trade Regulation

ART LAW

DuBoff's Art Law in a Nutshell, 335 pages, 1984 (Text)

BANKING LAW

Lovett's Banking and Financial Institutions in a Nutshell, 409 pages, 1984 (Text)

Symons and White's Teaching Materials on Banking Law, 2nd Ed., 993 pages, 1984, with 1987 Supplement (Casebook)

BUSINESS PLANNING

Painter's Problems and Materials in Business Planning, 2nd Ed., 1008 pages, 1984 with 1987 Supplement (Casebook)

Selected Securities and Business Planning Statutes, Rules and Forms, about 475 pages, 1987

CIVIL PROCEDURE

American Bar Association Section of Litigation—Reading on Adversarial Justice: The American Approach to Adjudication, edited by Landsman, about 204 pages, 1988 (Coursebook)

Casad's Res Judicata in a Nutshell, 310 pages, 1976 (text)

Cound, Friedenthal, Miller and Sexton's Cases and Materials on Civil Procedure, 4th Ed., 1202 pages, 1985 with 1987 Supplement (Casebook)

Ehrenzweig, Louisell and Hazard's Jurisdiction in a Nutshell, 4th Ed., 232 pages, 1980 (Text)

Federal Rules of Civil-Appellate Procedure—West Law School Edition, 596 pages, 1987

Friedenthal, Kane and Miller's Hornbook on Civil Procedure, 876 pages, 1985 (Text)

Kane's Civil Procedure in a Nutshell, 2nd Ed., 306 pages, 1986 (Text)

CIVIL PROCEDURE—Cont'd

Koffler and Reppy's Hornbook on Common Law Pleading, 663 pages, 1969 (Text)

Marcus and Sherman's Complex Litigation—Cases and Materials on Advanced Civil Procedure, 846 pages, 1985 (Casebook)

Park's Computer-Aided Exercises on Civil Procedure, 2nd Ed., 167 pages, 1983 (Coursebook)

Siegel's Hornbook on New York Practice, 1011 pages, 1978 with 1987 Pocket Part (Text)

See also Federal Jurisdiction and Procedure

CIVIL RIGHTS

Abernathy's Cases and Materials on Civil Rights, 660 pages, 1980 (Casebook)

Cohen's Cases on the Law of Deprivation of Liberty: A Study in Social Control, 755 pages, 1980 (Casebook)

Lockhart, Kamisar, Choper and Shiffrin's Cases on Constitutional Rights and Liberties, 6th Ed., 1266 pages, 1986 with 1987 Supplement (Casebook)—reprint from Lockhart, et al. Cases on Constitutional Law, 6th Ed., 1986

Vieira's Civil Rights in a Nutshell, 279 pages, 1978 (Text)

COMMERCIAL LAW

Bailey's Secured Transactions in a Nutshell, 2nd Ed., 391 pages, 1981 (Text)

Epstein, Henning and Nickles' Basic Uniform Commercial Code Teaching Materials, 3rd Ed., about 720 pages, 1988 (Casebook)

Henson's Hornbook on Secured Transactions Under the U.C.C., 2nd Ed., 504 pages, 1979 with 1979 P.P. (Text)

Murray's Commercial Law, Problems and Materials, 366 pages, 1975 (Coursebook)

Nickles, Matheson and Dolan's Materials for Understanding Credit and Payment Systems, 923 pages, 1987 (Casebook)

Nordstrom, Murray and Clovis' Problems and Materials on Sales, 515 pages, 1982 (Casebook)

Nordstrom, Murray and Clovis' Problems and Materials on Secured Transactions, 594 pages, 1987 (Casebook)

Selected Commercial Statutes, 1527 pages, 1987

Speidel, Summers and White's Teaching Materials on Commercial Law, 4th Ed., 1448 pages, 1987 (Casebook)

Speidel, Summers and White's Commercial Paper: Teaching Materials, 4th Ed., about 578 pages, 1987 (Casebook)—reprint from Speidel, et al. Commercial Law, 4th Ed.

Speidel, Summers and White's Sales: Teaching Materials, 4th Ed., 804 pages, 1987 (Casebook)—reprint from Speidel, et al. Commercial Law, 4th Ed.

LAW SCHOOL PUBLICATIONS—Continued

COMMERCIAL LAW—Cont'd

Speidel, Summers and White's Secured Transactions—Teaching Materials, 4th Ed., 485 pages, 1987 (Casebook)—reprint from Speidel, et al. Commercial Law, 4th Ed.

Stockton's Sales in a Nutshell, 2nd Ed., 370 pages, 1981 (Text)

Stone's Uniform Commercial Code in a Nutshell, 2nd Ed., 516 pages, 1984 (Text)

Uniform Commercial Code, Official Text with Comments, 994 pages, 1978

UCC Article 9, Reprint from 1962 Code, 128 pages, 1976

UCC Article 9, 1972 Amendments, 304 pages, 1978

Weber and Speidel's Commercial Paper in a Nutshell, 3rd Ed., 404 pages, 1982 (Text)

White and Summers' Hornbook on the Uniform Commercial Code, 3rd Ed., 1988 (Text)

COMMUNITY PROPERTY

Mennell and Boykoff's Community Property in a Nutshell, about 475 pages, 1988 (Text)

Verrall and Bird's Cases and Materials on California Community Property, 4th Ed., 549 pages, 1983 (Casebook)

COMPARATIVE LAW

Barton, Gibbs, Li and Merryman's Law in Radically Different Cultures, 960 pages, 1983 (Casebook)

Glendon, Gordon and Osakive's Comparative Legal Traditions: Text, Materials and Cases on the Civil Law, Common Law, and Socialist Law Traditions, 1091 pages, 1985 (Casebook)

Glendon, Gordon, and Osakwe's Comparative Legal Traditions in a Nutshell, 402 pages, 1982 (Text)

Langbein's Comparative Criminal Procedure: Germany, 172 pages, 1977 (Casebook)

COMPUTERS AND LAW

Maggs and Sprowl's Computer Applications in the Law, 316 pages, 1987 (Coursebook)

Mason's An Introduction to the Use of Computers in Law, about 275 pages, 1988 (Text)

CONFLICT OF LAWS

Cramton, Currie and Kay's Cases-Comments-Questions on Conflict of Laws, 4th Ed., 876 pages, 1987 (Casebook)

Scoles and Hay's Hornbook on Conflict of Laws, Student Ed., 1085 pages, 1982 with 1986 P.P. (Text)

Scoles and Weintraub's Cases and Materials on Conflict of Laws, 2nd Ed., 966 pages, 1972, with 1978 Supplement (Casebook)

CONFLICT OF LAWS—Cont'd

Siegel's Conflicts in a Nutshell, 469 pages, 1982 (Text)

CONSTITUTIONAL LAW

Barron and Dienes' Constitutional Law in a Nutshell, 389 pages, 1986 (Text)

Engdahl's Constitutional Federalism in a Nutshell, 2nd Ed., 411 pages, 1987 (Text)

Lockhart, Kamisar, Choper and Shiffrin's Cases-Comments-Questions on Constitutional Law, 6th Ed., 1601 pages, 1986 with 1987 Supplement (Casebook)

Lockhart, Kamisar, Choper and Shiffrin's Cases-Comments-Questions on the American Constitution, 6th Ed., 1260 pages, 1986 with 1987 Supplement (Casebook)—abridgment of Lockhart, et al. Cases on Constitutional Law, 6th Ed., 1986

Manning's The Law of Church-State Relations in a Nutshell, 305 pages, 1981 (Text)

Miller's Presidential Power in a Nutshell, 328 pages, 1977 (Text)

Nowak, Rotunda and Young's Hornbook on Constitutional Law, 3rd Ed., Student Ed., 1191 pages, 1986 (Text)

Rotunda's Modern Constitutional Law: Cases and Notes, 2nd Ed., 1004 pages, 1985, with 1987 Supplement (Casebook)

Williams' Constitutional Analysis in a Nutshell, 388 pages, 1979 (Text)

See also Civil Rights, Foreign Relations and National Security Law

CONSUMER LAW

Epstein and Nickles' Consumer Law in a Nutshell, 2nd Ed., 418 pages, 1981 (Text)

Selected Commercial Statutes, 1527 pages, 1987

Spanogle and Rohner's Cases and Materials on Consumer Law, 693 pages, 1979, with 1982 Supplement (Casebook)

See also Commercial Law

CONTRACTS

Calamari & Perillo's Cases and Problems on Contracts, 1061 pages, 1978 (Casebook)

Calamari and Perillo's Hornbook on Contracts, 3rd Ed., 904 pages, 1987 (Text)

Corbin's Text on Contracts, One Volume Student Edition, 1224 pages, 1952 (Text)

Fessler and Loiseaux's Cases and Materials on Contracts, 837 pages, 1982 (Casebook)

Friedman's Contract Remedies in a Nutshell, 323 pages, 1981 (Text)

Fuller and Eisenberg's Cases on Basic Contract Law, 4th Ed., 1203 pages, 1981 (Casebook)

Hamilton, Rau and Weintraub's Cases and Materials on Contracts, 830 pages, 1984 (Casebook)

LAW SCHOOL PUBLICATIONS—Continued

CONTRACTS—Cont'd

Jackson and Bollinger's Cases on Contract Law in Modern Society, 2nd Ed., 1329 pages, 1980 (Casebook)

Keyes' Government Contracts in a Nutshell, 423 pages, 1979 (Text)

Schaber and Rohwer's Contracts in a Nutshell, 2nd Ed., 425 pages, 1984 (Text)

Summers and Hillman's Contract and Related Obligation: Theory, Doctrine and Practice, 1074 pages, 1987 (Casebook)

COPYRIGHT

See Patent and Copyright Law

CORPORATE FINANCE

Hamilton's Cases and Materials on Corporate Finance, 895 pages, 1984 with 1986 Supplement (Casebook)

CORPORATIONS

Hamilton's Cases on Corporations—Including Partnerships and Limited Partnerships, 3rd Ed., 1213 pages, 1986 with 1986 Statutory Supplement (Casebook)

Hamilton's Law of Corporations in a Nutshell, 2nd Ed., 515 pages, 1987 (Text)

Henn's Teaching Materials on Corporations, 2nd Ed., 1204 pages, 1986 (Casebook)

Henn and Alexander's Hornbook on Corporations, 3rd Ed., Student Ed., 1371 pages, 1983 with 1986 P.P. (Text)

Jennings and Buxbaum's Cases and Materials on Corporations, 5th Ed., 1180 pages, 1979 (Casebook)

Selected Corporation and Partnership Statutes, Regulations and Forms, 621 pages, 1987

Solomon, Schwartz' and Bauman's Materials and Problems on Corporations: Law and Policy, 2nd Ed., about 900 pages, 1988 (Casebook)

CORRECTIONS

Krantz's Cases and Materials on the Law of Corrections and Prisoners' Rights, 3rd Ed., 855 pages, 1986 with 1988 Supplement (Casebook)

Krantz's Law of Corrections and Prisoners' Rights in a Nutshell, 2nd Ed., 386 pages, 1983 (Text)

Popper's Post-Conviction Remedies in a Nutshell, 360 pages, 1978 (Text)

Robbins' Cases and Materials on Post Conviction Remedies, 506 pages, 1982 (Casebook)

CREDITOR'S RIGHTS

Bankruptcy Code, Rules and Forms, Law School Ed., 792 pages, 1988

Epstein's Debtor-Creditor Law in a Nutshell, 3rd Ed., 383 pages, 1986 (Text)

CREDITOR'S RIGHTS—Cont'd

Epstein, Landers and Nickles' Debtors and Creditors: Cases and Materials, 3rd Ed., 1059 pages, 1987 (Casebook)

LoPucki's Player's Manual for the Debtor-Creditor Game, 123 pages, 1985 (Coursebook)

Riesenfeld's Cases and Materials on Creditors' Remedies and Debtors' Protection, 4th Ed., 914 pages, 1987 (Casebook)

White's Bankruptcy and Creditor's Rights: Cases and Materials, 812 pages, 1985, with 1987 Supplement (Casebook)

CRIMINAL LAW AND CRIMINAL PROCEDURE

Abrams', Federal Criminal Law and its Enforcement, 882 pages, 1986 (Casebook)

Carlson's Adjudication of Criminal Justice, Problems and References, 130 pages, 1986 (Casebook)

Dix and Sharlot's Cases and Materials on Criminal Law, 3rd Ed., 846 pages, 1987 (Casebook)

Federal Rules of Criminal Procedure—West Law School Edition, 567 pages, 1987

Grano's Problems in Criminal Procedure, 2nd Ed., 176 pages, 1981 (Problem book)

Israel and LaFave's Criminal Procedure in a Nutshell, 4th Ed., about 500 pages, 1988 (Text)

Johnson's Cases, Materials and Text on Criminal Law, 3rd Ed., 783 pages, 1985 (Casebook)

Johnson's Cases on Criminal Procedure, 859 pages, 1987 (Casebook)

Kamisar, LaFave and Israel's Cases, Comments and Questions on Modern Criminal Procedure, 6th Ed., 1558 pages, 1986 with 1987 Supplement (Casebook)

Kamisar, LaFave and Israel's Cases, Comments and Questions on Basic Criminal Procedure, 6th Ed., 860 pages, 1986 with 1987 Supplement (Casebook)—reprint from Kamisar, et al. Modern Criminal Procedure, 6th ed., 1986

LaFave's Modern Criminal Law: Cases, Comments and Questions, 2nd Ed., about 1000 pages, 1988 (Casebook)

LaFave and Israel's Hornbook on Criminal Procedure, Student Ed., 1142 pages, 1985 with 1987 P.P. (Text)

LaFave and Scott's Hornbook on Criminal Law, 2nd Ed., Student Ed., 918 pages, 1986 (Text)

Langbein's Comparative Criminal Procedure: Germany, 172 pages, 1977 (Casebook)

Loewy's Criminal Law in a Nutshell, 2nd Ed., 321 pages, 1987 (Text)

Saltzburg's American Criminal Procedure, Cases and Commentary, 3rd Ed., about 1200 pages, 1988 (Casebook)

CRIMINAL LAW AND CRIMINAL PROCEDURE—Cont'd

Uviller's The Processes of Criminal Justice: Investigation and Adjudication, 2nd Ed., 1384 pages, 1979 with 1979 Statutory Supplement and 1986 Update (Casebook)

Uviller's The Processes of Criminal Justice: Adjudication, 2nd Ed., 730 pages, 1979. Soft-cover reprint from Uviller's The Processes of Criminal Justice: Investigation and Adjudication, 2nd Ed. (Casebook)

Uviller's The Processes of Criminal Justice: Investigation, 2nd Ed., 655 pages, 1979. Soft-cover reprint from Uviller's The Processes of Criminal Justice: Investigation and Adjudication, 2nd Ed. (Casebook)

Vorenberg's Cases on Criminal Law and Procedure, 2nd Ed., 1088 pages, 1981 with 1987 Supplement (Casebook)

See also Corrections, Juvenile Justice

DECEDENTS ESTATES

See Trusts and Estates

DOMESTIC RELATIONS

Clark's Cases and Problems on Domestic Relations, 3rd Ed., 1153 pages, 1980 (Casebook)

Clark's Hornbook on Domestic Relations, 2nd Ed., Student Ed., about 1100 pages, 1988 (Text)

Krause's Cases and Materials on Family Law, 2nd Ed., 1221 pages, 1983 with 1986 Supplement (Casebook)

Krause's Family Law in a Nutshell, 2nd Ed., 444 pages, 1986 (Text)

Krauskopf's Cases on Property Division at Marriage Dissolution, 250 pages, 1984 (Casebook)

ECONOMICS, LAW AND

Goetz' Cases and Materials on Law and Economics, 547 pages, 1984 (Casebook)

See also Antitrust, Regulated Industries

EDUCATION LAW

Alexander and Alexander's The Law of Schools, Students and Teachers in a Nutshell, 409 pages, 1984 (Text)

Morris' The Constitution and American Education, 2nd Ed., 992 pages, 1980 (Casebook)

EMPLOYMENT DISCRIMINATION

Jones, Murphy and Belton's Cases on Discrimination in Employment, 1116 pages, 1987 (Casebook)

Player's Cases and Materials on Employment Discrimination Law, 2nd Ed., 782 pages, 1984 (Casebook)

EMPLOYMENT DISCRIMINATION—Cont'd

Player's Federal Law of Employment Discrimination in a Nutshell, 2nd Ed., 402 pages, 1981 (Text)

Player's Hornbook on the Law of Employment Discrimination, Student Ed., about 650 pages, 1988 (Text)

See also Women and the Law

ENERGY AND NATURAL RESOURCES LAW

Laitos' Cases and Materials on Natural Resources Law, 938 pages, 1985 (Casebook)

Rodgers' Cases and Materials on Energy and Natural Resources Law, 2nd Ed., 877 pages, 1983 (Casebook)

Selected Environmental Law Statutes, about 654 pages, 1987

Tomain's Energy Law in a Nutshell, 338 pages, 1981 (Text)

See also Environmental Law, Oil and Gas, Water Law

ENVIRONMENTAL LAW

Bonine and McGarity's Cases and Materials on the Law of Environment and Pollution, 1076 pages, 1984 (Casebook)

Findley and Farber's Cases and Materials on Environmental Law, 2nd Ed., 813 pages, 1985 (Casebook)

Findley and Farber's Environmental Law in a Nutshell, 343 pages, 1983 (Text)

Rodgers' Hornbook on Environmental Law, 956 pages, 1977 with 1984 pocket part (Text)

Selected Environmental Law Statutes, 654 pages, 1987

See also Energy Law, Natural Resources Law, Water Law

EQUITY

See Remedies

ESTATES

See Trusts and Estates

ESTATE PLANNING

Kurtz' Cases, Materials and Problems on Family Estate Planning, 853 pages, 1983 (Casebook)

Lynn's Introduction to Estate Planning, in a Nutshell, 3rd Ed., 370 pages, 1983 (Text)

See also Taxation

EVIDENCE

Broun and Meisenholder's Problems in Evidence, 2nd Ed., 304 pages, 1981 (Problem book)

Cleary and Strong's Cases, Materials and Problems on Evidence, 3rd Ed., 1143 pages, 1981 (Casebook)

EVIDENCE—Cont'd

Federal Rules of Evidence for United States Courts and Magistrates, 370 pages, 1987

Graham's Federal Rules of Evidence in a Nutshell, 2nd Ed., 473 pages, 1987 (Text)

Kimball's Programmed Materials on Problems in Evidence, 380 pages, 1978 (Problem book)

Lempert and Saltzburg's A Modern Approach to Evidence: Text, Problems, Transcripts and Cases, 2nd Ed., 1232 pages, 1983 (Casebook)

Lilly's Introduction to the Law of Evidence, 2nd Ed., about 600 pages, 1987 (Text)

McCormick, Sutton and Wellborn's Cases and Materials on Evidence, 6th Ed., 1067 pages, 1987 (Casebook)

McCormick's Hornbook on Evidence, 3rd Ed., Student Ed., 1156 pages, 1984 with 1987 P.P. (Text)

Rothstein's Evidence, State and Federal Rules in a Nutshell, 2nd Ed., 514 pages, 1981 (Text)

Saltzburg's Evidence Supplement: Rules, Statutes, Commentary, 245 pages, 1980 (Casebook Supplement)

FEDERAL JURISDICTION AND PROCEDURE

Currie's Cases and Materials on Federal Courts, 3rd Ed., 1042 pages, 1982 with 1985 Supplement (Casebook)

Currie's Federal Jurisdiction in a Nutshell, 2nd Ed., 258 pages, 1981 (Text)

Federal Rules of Civil-Appellate Procedure—West Law School Edition, 596 pages, 1987

Forrester and Moye's Cases and Materials on Federal Jurisdiction and Procedure, 3rd Ed., 917 pages, 1977 with 1985 Supplement (Casebook)

Redish's Cases, Comments and Questions on Federal Courts, 878 pages, 1983 with 1986 Supplement (Casebook)

Vetri and Merrill's Federal Courts, Problems and Materials, 2nd Ed., 232 pages, 1984 (Problem Book)

Wright's Hornbook on Federal Courts, 4th Ed., Student Ed., 870 pages, 1983 (Text)

FOREIGN RELATIONS AND NATIONAL SECURITY LAW

Franck and Glennon's United States Foreign Relations Law: Cases, Materials and Simulations, 941 pages, 1987 (Casebook)

FUTURE INTERESTS

See Trusts and Estates

HEALTH LAW

See Medicine, Law and

IMMIGRATION LAW

Aleinikoff and Martin's Immigration Process and Policy, 1042 pages, 1985, with 1987 Supplement (Casebook)

Weissbrodt's Immigration Law and Procedure in a Nutshell, 345 pages, 1984 (Text)

INDIAN LAW

See American Indian Law

INSURANCE

Dobbyn's Insurance Law in a Nutshell, 281 pages, 1981 (Text)

Keeton's Cases on Basic Insurance Law, 2nd Ed., 1086 pages, 1977

Keeton and Wydiss' Insurance Law, Student Ed., about 1024 pages, 1988 (Text)

Wydiss and Keeton's Case Supplement to Keeton and Wydiss Insurance Law, 425 pages, 1988 (Casebook)

York and Whelan's Cases, Materials and Problems on Insurance Law, 715 pages, 1982, with 1985 Supplement (Casebook)

INTERNATIONAL LAW

Buergenthal and Maier's Public International Law in a Nutshell, 262 pages, 1985 (Text)

Folsom, Gordon and Spanogle's International Business Transactions – a Problem-Oriented Coursebook, 1160 pages, 1986, with Documents Supplement (Casebook)

Henkin, Pugh, Schachter and Smit's Cases and Materials on International Law, 2nd Ed., 1517 pages, 1987 with Documents Supplement (Casebook)

Jackson and Davey's Legal Problems of International Economic Relations, 2nd Ed., 1269 pages, 1986, with Documents Supplement (Casebook)

Kirgis' International Organizations in Their Legal Setting, 1016 pages, 1977, with 1981 Supplement (Casebook)

Weston, Falk and D'Amato's International Law and World Order—A Problem Oriented Coursebook, 1195 pages, 1980, with Documents Supplement (Casebook)

Wilson's International Business Transactions in a Nutshell, 2nd Ed., 476 pages, 1984 (Text)

INTERVIEWING AND COUNSELING

Binder and Price's Interviewing and Counseling, 232 pages, 1977 (Text)

Shaffer and Elkins' Interviewing and Counseling in a Nutshell, 2nd Ed., 487 pages, 1987 (Text)

INTRODUCTION TO LAW STUDY

Dobbyn's So You Want to go to Law School, Revised First Edition, 206 pages, 1976 (Text)

LAW SCHOOL PUBLICATIONS—Continued

INTRODUCTION TO LAW STUDY—Cont'd

Hegland's Introduction to the Study and Practice of Law in a Nutshell, 418 pages, 1983 (Text)

Kinyon's Introduction to Law Study and Law Examinations in a Nutshell, 389 pages, 1971 (Text)

See also Legal Method and Legal System

JUDICIAL ADMINISTRATION

Nelson's Cases and Materials on Judicial Administration and the Administration of Justice, 1032 pages, 1974 (Casebook)

JURISPRUDENCE

Christie's Text and Readings on Jurisprudence—The Philosophy of Law, 1056 pages, 1973 (Casebook)

JUVENILE JUSTICE

Fox's Cases and Materials on Modern Juvenile Justice, 2nd Ed., 960 pages, 1981 (Casebook)

Fox's Juvenile Courts in a Nutshell, 3rd Ed., 291 pages, 1984 (Text)

LABOR LAW

Atleson, Rabin, Schatzki, Sherman and Silverstein's Collective Bargaining in Private Employment, 2nd Ed., (The Labor Law Group), 856 pages, 1984 (Casebook)

Gorman's Basic Text on Labor Law—Unionization and Collective Bargaining, 914 pages, 1976 (Text)

Grodin, Wollett and Alleyne's Collective Bargaining in Public Employment, 3rd Ed., (the Labor Law Group), 430 pages, 1979 (Casebook)

Leslie's Labor Law in a Nutshell, 2nd Ed., 397 pages, 1986 (Text)

Nolan's Labor Arbitration Law and Practice in a Nutshell, 358 pages, 1979 (Text)

Oberer, Hanslowe, Andersen and Heinsz' Cases and Materials on Labor Law—Collective Bargaining in a Free Society, 3rd Ed., 1163 pages, 1986 with Statutory Supplement (Casebook)

See also Employment Discrimination, Social Legislation

LAND FINANCE

See Real Estate Transactions

LAND USE

Callies and Freilich's Cases and Materials on Land Use, 1233 pages, 1986 (Casebook)

Hagman's Cases on Public Planning and Control of Urban and Land Development, 2nd Ed., 1301 pages, 1980 (Casebook)

LAND USE—Cont'd

Hagman and Juergensmeyer's Hornbook on Urban Planning and Land Development Control Law, 2nd Ed., Student Ed., 680 pages, 1986 (Text)

Wright and Gitelman's Cases and Materials on Land Use, 3rd Ed., 1300 pages, 1982, with 1987 Supplement (Casebook)

Wright and Wright's Land Use in a Nutshell, 2nd Ed., 356 pages, 1985 (Text)

LEGAL HISTORY

Presser and Zainaldin's Cases on Law and American History, 855 pages, 1980 (Casebook)

See also Legal Method and Legal System

LEGAL METHOD AND LEGAL SYSTEM

Aldisert's Readings, Materials and Cases in the Judicial Process, 948 pages, 1976 (Casebook)

Berch and Berch's Introduction to Legal Method and Process, 550 pages, 1985 (Casebook)

Bodenheimer, Oakley and Love's Readings and Cases on an Introduction to the Anglo-American Legal System, 2nd Ed., about 165 pages, 1988 (Casebook)

Davies and Lawry's Institutions and Methods of the Law—Introductory Teaching Materials, 547 pages, 1982 (Casebook)

Dvorkin, Himmelstein and Lesnick's Becoming a Lawyer: A Humanistic Perspective on Legal Education and Professionalism, 211 pages, 1981 (Text)

Greenberg's Judicial Process and Social Change, 666 pages, 1977 (Casebook)

Kelso and Kelso's Studying Law: An Introduction, 587 pages, 1984 (Coursebook)

Kempin's Historical Introduction to Anglo-American Law in a Nutshell, 2nd Ed., 280 pages, 1973 (Text)

Kimball's Historical Introduction to the Legal System, 610 pages, 1966 (Casebook)

Murphy's Cases and Materials on Introduction to Law—Legal Process and Procedure, 772 pages, 1977 (Casebook)

Reynolds' Judicial Process in a Nutshell, 292 pages, 1980 (Text)

See also Legal Research and Writing

LEGAL PROFESSION

Aronson, Devine and Fisch's Problems, Cases and Materials on Professional Responsibility, 745 pages, 1985 (Casebook)

Aronson and Weckstein's Professional Responsibility in a Nutshell, 399 pages, 1980 (Text)

Mellinkoff's The Conscience of a Lawyer, 304 pages, 1973 (Text)

Mellinkoff's Lawyers and the System of Justice, 983 pages, 1976 (Casebook)

LEGAL PROFESSION—Cont'd

Pirsig and Kirwin's Cases and Materials on Professional Responsibility, 4th Ed., 603 pages, 1984 (Casebook)

Schwartz and Wydick's Problems in Legal Ethics, 2nd Ed., about 330 pages, 1988 (Casebook)

Selected Statutes, Rules and Standards on the Legal Profession, 449 pages, 1987

Smith's Preventing Legal Malpractice, 142 pages, 1981 (Text)

Wolfram's Hornbook on Modern Legal Ethics, Student Edition, 1120 pages, 1986 (Text)

LEGAL RESEARCH AND WRITING

Child's Materials and Problems on Drafting Legal Documents, about 276 pages, 1988 (Text)

Cohen's Legal Research in a Nutshell, 4th Ed., 450 pages, 1985 (Text)

Cohen and Berring's How to Find the Law, 8th Ed., 790 pages, 1983. Problem book by Foster, Johnson and Kelly available (Casebook)

Cohen and Berring's Finding the Law, 8th Ed., Abridged Ed., 556 pages, 1984 (Casebook)

Dickerson's Materials on Legal Drafting, 425 pages, 1981 (Casebook)

Felsenfeld and Siegel's Writing Contracts in Plain English, 290 pages, 1981 (Text)

Gopen's Writing From a Legal Perspective, 225 pages, 1981 (Text)

Mellinkoff's Legal Writing—Sense and Nonsense, 242 pages, 1982 (Text)

Ray and Ramsfield's Legal Writing: Getting It Right and Getting It Written, 250 pages, 1987 (Text)

Rombauer's Legal Problem Solving—Analysis, Research and Writing, 4th Ed., 424 pages, 1983 (Coursebook)

Squires and Rombauer's Legal Writing in a Nutshell, 294 pages, 1982 (Text)

Statsky's Legal Research and Writing, 3rd Ed., 257 pages, 1986 (Coursebook)

Statsky and Wernet's Case Analysis and Fundamentals of Legal Writing, 2nd Ed., 441 pages, 1984 (Text)

Teply's Programmed Materials on Legal Research and Citation, 2nd Ed., 358 pages, 1986. Student Library Exercises available (Coursebook)

Weihofen's Legal Writing Style, 2nd Ed., 332 pages, 1980 (Text)

LEGISLATION

Davies' Legislative Law and Process in a Nutshell, 2nd Ed., 346 pages, 1986 (Text)

Eskridge and Frickey's Cases on Legislation, 937 pages, 1987 (Casebook)

Nutting and Dickerson's Cases and Materials on Legislation, 5th Ed., 744 pages, 1978 (Casebook)

LEGISLATION—Cont'd

Statsky's Legislative Analysis and Drafting, 2nd Ed., 217 pages, 1984 (Text)

LOCAL GOVERNMENT

McCarthy's Local Government Law in a Nutshell, 2nd Ed., 404 pages, 1983 (Text)

Reynolds' Hornbook on Local Government Law, 860 pages, 1982, with 1987 pocket part (Text)

Valente's Cases and Materials on Local Government Law, 3rd Ed., 1010 pages, 1987 (Casebook)

MASS COMMUNICATION LAW

Gillmor and Barron's Cases and Comment on Mass Communication Law, 4th Ed., 1076 pages, 1984 (Casebook)

Ginsburg's Regulation of Broadcasting: Law and Policy Towards Radio, Television and Cable Communications, 741 pages, 1979, with 1983 Supplement (Casebook)

Zuckman, Gaynes, Carter and Dee Mass Communications Law in a Nutshell, 3rd Ed., 538 pages, 1988 (Text)

MEDICINE, LAW AND

Furrow, Johnson, Jost and Schwartz' Health Law: Cases, Materials and Problems, 1005 pages, 1987 (Casebook)

King's The Law of Medical Malpractice in a Nutshell, 2nd Ed., 342 pages, 1986 (Text)

Shapiro and Spece's Problems, Cases and Materials on Bioethics and Law, 892 pages, 1981 (Casebook)

Sharpe, Fiscina and Head's Cases on Law and Medicine, 882 pages, 1978 (Casebook)

MILITARY LAW

Shanor and Terrell's Military Law in a Nutshell, 378 pages, 1980 (Text)

MORTGAGES

See Real Estate Transactions

NATURAL RESOURCES LAW

See Energy and Natural Resources Law

NEGOTIATION

Edwards and White's Problems, Readings and Materials on the Lawyer as a Negotiator, 484 pages, 1977 (Casebook)

Peck's Cases and Materials on Negotiation, 2nd Ed., (The Labor Law Group), 280 pages, 1980 (Casebook)

Williams' Legal Negotiation and Settlement, 207 pages, 1983 (Coursebook)

OFFICE PRACTICE

Hegland's Trial and Practice Skills in a Nutshell, 346 pages, 1978 (Text)

Strong and Clark's Law Office Management, 424 pages, 1974 (Casebook)

LAW SCHOOL PUBLICATIONS—Continued

OFFICE PRACTICE—Cont'd

See also Computers and Law, Interviewing and Counseling, Negotiation

OIL AND GAS

Hemingway's Hornbook on Oil and Gas, 2nd Ed., Student Ed., 543 pages, 1983 with 1986 P.P. (Text)

Kuntz, Lowe, Anderson and Smith's Cases and Materials on Oil and Gas Law, 857 pages, 1986, with Forms Manual (Casebook)

Lowe's Oil and Gas Law in a Nutshell, 443 pages, 1983 (Text)

See also Energy and Natural Resources Law

PARTNERSHIP

See Agency—Partnership

PATENT AND COPYRIGHT LAW

Choate, Francis and Collins' Cases and Materials on Patent Law, 3rd Ed., 1009 pages, 1987 (Casebook)

Miller and Davis' Intellectual Property—Patents, Trademarks and Copyright in a Nutshell, 428 pages, 1983 (Text)

Nimmer's Cases on Copyright and Other Aspects of Entertainment Litigation, 3rd Ed., 1025 pages, 1985 (Casebook)

PRODUCTS LIABILITY

Fischer and Powers' Cases and Materials on Products Liability, about 700 pages, 1988 (Casebook)

Noel and Phillips' Cases on Products Liability, 2nd Ed., 821 pages, 1982 (Casebook)

Phillips' Products Liability in a Nutshell, 3rd Ed., about 350 pages, 1988 (Text)

PROPERTY

Bernhardt's Real Property in a Nutshell, 2nd Ed., 448 pages, 1981 (Text)

Boyer's Survey of the Law of Property, 766 pages, 1981 (Text)

Browder, Cunningham and Smith's Cases on Basic Property Law, 4th Ed., 1431 pages, 1984 (Casebook)

Bruce, Ely and Bostick's Cases and Materials on Modern Property Law, 1004 pages, 1984 (Casebook)

Burke's Personal Property in a Nutshell, 322 pages, 1983 (Text)

Cunningham, Stoebuck and Whitman's Hornbook on the Law of Property, Student Ed., 916 pages, 1984, with 1987 P.P. (Text)

Donahue, Kauper and Martin's Cases on Property, 2nd Ed., 1362 pages, 1983 (Casebook)

Hill's Landlord and Tenant Law in a Nutshell, 2nd Ed., 311 pages, 1986 (Text)

Kurtz and Hovenkamp's Cases and Materials on American Property Law, 1296 pages, 1987 (Casebook)

PROPERTY—Cont'd

Moynihan's Introduction to Real Property, 2nd Ed., 239 pages, 1988 (Text)

Uniform Land Transactions Act, Uniform Simplification of Land Transfers Act, Uniform Condominium Act, 1977 Official Text with Comments, 462 pages, 1978

See also Real Estate Transactions, Land Use

PSYCHIATRY, LAW AND

Reisner's Law and the Mental Health System, Civil and Criminal Aspects, 696 pages, 1985, with 1987 Supplement (Casebooks)

REAL ESTATE TRANSACTIONS

Bruce's Real Estate Finance in a Nutshell, 2nd Ed., 262 pages, 1985 (Text)

Maxwell, Riesenfeld, Hetland and Warren's Cases on California Security Transactions in Land, 3rd Ed., 728 pages, 1984 (Casebook)

Nelson and Whitman's Cases on Real Estate Transfer, Finance and Development, 3rd Ed., 1184 pages, 1987 (Casebook)

Nelson and Whitman's Hornbook on Real Estate Finance Law, 2nd Ed., Student Ed., 941 pages, 1985 (Text)

Osborne's Cases and Materials on Secured Transactions, 559 pages, 1967 (Casebook)

REGULATED INDUSTRIES

Gellhorn and Pierce's Regulated Industries in a Nutshell, 2nd Ed., 389 pages, 1987 (Text)

Morgan, Harrison and Verkuil's Cases and Materials on Economic Regulation of Business, 2nd Ed., 666 pages, 1985 (Casebook)

See also Mass Communication Law, Banking Law

REMEDIES

Dobbs' Hornbook on Remedies, 1067 pages, 1973 (Text)

Dobbs' Problems in Remedies, 137 pages, 1974 (Problem book)

Dobbyn's Injunctions in a Nutshell, 264 pages, 1974 (Text)

Friedman's Contract Remedies in a Nutshell, 323 pages, 1981 (Text)

Leavell, Love and Nelson's Cases and Materials on Equitable Remedies and Restitution, 4th Ed., 1111 pages, 1986 (Casebook)

McCormick's Hornbook on Damages, 811 pages, 1935 (Text)

O'Connell's Remedies in a Nutshell, 2nd Ed., 320 pages, 1985 (Text)

York, Bauman and Rendleman's Cases and Materials on Remedies, 4th Ed., 1029 pages, 1985 (Casebook)

LAW SCHOOL PUBLICATIONS—Continued

REVIEW MATERIALS

Ballantine's Problems
Black Letter Series

SECURITIES REGULATION

Hazen's Hornbook on The Law of Securities Regulation, Student Ed., 739 pages, 1985, with 1988 P.P. (Text)

Ratner's Securities Regulation: Materials for a Basic Course, 3rd Ed., 1000 pages, 1986 (Casebook)

Ratner's Securities Regulation in a Nutshell, 3rd Ed., about 335 pages, 1988 (Text)

Selected Securities and Business Planning Statutes, Rules and Forms, 493 pages, 1987

SOCIAL LEGISLATION

Hood and Hardy's Workers' Compensation and Employee Protection Laws in a Nutshell, 274 pages, 1984 (Text)

LaFrance's Welfare Law: Structure and Entitlement in a Nutshell, 455 pages, 1979 (Text)

Malone, Plant and Little's Cases on Workers' Compensation and Employment Rights, 2nd Ed., 951 pages, 1980 (Casebook)

SPORTS LAW

Schubert, Smith and Trentadue's Sports Law, 395 pages, 1986 (Text)

TAXATION

Dodge's Cases and Materials on Federal Income Taxation, 820 pages, 1985 (Casebook)

Dodge's Wills, Trusts and Estate Planning, 700 pages, 1988 (Casebook)

Garbis, Struntz and Rubin's Cases and Materials on Tax Procedure and Tax Fraud, 2nd Ed., 687 pages, 1987 (Casebook)

Gelfand and Salsich's State and Local Taxation and Finance in a Nutshell, 309 pages, 1986 (Text)

Gunn's Cases and Materials on Federal Income Taxation of Individuals, 785 pages, 1981 with 1985 Supplement (Casebook)

Hellerstein and Hellerstein's Cases on State and Local Taxation, 4th Ed., 1041 pages, 1978 with 1982 Supplement (Casebook)

Kahn and Gann's Corporate Taxation and Taxation of Partnerships and Partners, 2nd Ed., 1204 pages, 1985 (Casebook)

Kaplan's Federal Taxation of International Transactions: Principles, Planning and Policy, about 600 pages, 1988 (Casebook)

Kragen and McNulty's Cases and Materials on Federal Income Taxation: Individuals, Corporations, Partnerships, 4th Ed., 1287 pages, 1985 (Casebook)

TAXATION—Cont'd

McNulty's Federal Estate and Gift Taxation in a Nutshell, 3rd Ed., 509 pages, 1983 (Text)

McNulty's Federal Income Taxation of Individuals in a Nutshell, 3rd Ed., 487 pages, 1983 (Text)

Pennell's Cases and Materials on Income Taxation of Trusts, Estates, Grantors and Beneficiaries, 460 pages, 1987 (Casebook)

Posin's Hornbook on Federal Income Taxation of Individuals, Student Ed., 491 pages, 1983 with 1987 pocket part (Text)

Rose and Chommie's Hornbook on Federal Income Taxation, 3rd Ed., about 875 pages, 1988 (Text)

Selected Federal Taxation Statutes and Regulations, 1399 pages, 1988

Solomon and Hesch's Cases on Federal Income Taxation of Individuals, 1068 pages, 1987 (Casebook)

TORTS

Christie's Cases and Materials on the Law of Torts, 1264 pages, 1983 (Casebook)

Dobbs' Torts and Compensation—Personal Accountability and Social Responsibility for Injury, 955 pages, 1985 (Casebook)

Green, Pedrick, Rahl, Thode, Hawkins, Smith, and Treece's Advanced Torts: Injuries to Business, Political and Family Interests, 2nd Ed., 544 pages, 1977 (Casebook)

Keeton, Keeton, Sargentich and Steiner's Cases and Materials on Tort and Accident Law, 1360 pages, 1983 (Casebook)

Kionka's Torts in a Nutshell: Injuries to Persons and Property, 434 pages, 1977 (Text)

Malone's Torts in a Nutshell: Injuries to Family, Social and Trade Relations, 358 pages, 1979 (Text)

Prosser and Keeton's Hornbook on Torts, 5th Ed., Student Ed., 1286 pages, 1984, with 1988 pocket part (Text)

See also Products Liability

TRADE REGULATION

McManis' Unfair Trade Practices in a Nutshell, 444 pages, 1982 (Text)

Oppenheim, Weston, Maggs and Schechter's Cases and Materials on Unfair Trade Practices and Consumer Protection, 4th Ed., 1038 pages, 1983 with 1986 Supplement (Casebook)

See also Antitrust, Regulated Industries

TRIAL AND APPELLATE ADVOCACY

Appellate Advocacy, Handbook of, 2nd Ed., 182 pages, 1986 (Text)

Bergman's Trial Advocacy in a Nutshell, 402 pages, 1979 (Text)

LAW SCHOOL PUBLICATIONS—Continued

TRIAL AND APPELLATE ADVOCACY—Cont'd

Binder and Bergman's Fact Investigation: From Hypothesis to Proof, 354 pages, 1984 (Coursebook)

Goldberg's The First Trial (Where Do I Sit?, What Do I Say?) in a Nutshell, 396 pages, 1982 (Text)

Haydock, Herr and Stempel's, Fundamentals of Pre-Trial Litigation, 768 pages, 1985 (Casebook)

Hegland's Trial and Practice Skills in a Nutshell, 346 pages, 1978 (Text)

Hornstein's Appellate Advocacy in a Nutshell, 325 pages, 1984 (Text)

Jeans' Handbook on Trial Advocacy, Student Ed., 473 pages, 1975 (Text)

Martineau's Cases and Materials on Appellate Practice and Procedure, 565 pages, 1987 (Casebook)

McElhaney's Effective Litigation, 457 pages, 1974 (Casebook)

Nolan's Cases and Materials on Trial Practice, 518 pages, 1981 (Casebook)

Parnell and Shellhaas' Cases, Exercises and Problems for Trial Advocacy, 171 pages, 1982 (Coursebook)

Sonsteng, Haydock and Boyd's The Trialbook: A Total System for Preparation and Presentation of a Case, Student Ed., 404 pages, 1984 (Coursebook)

See also Civil Procedure

TRUSTS AND ESTATES

Atkinson's Hornbook on Wills, 2nd Ed., 975 pages, 1953 (Text)

Averill's Uniform Probate Code in a Nutshell, 2nd Ed., 454 pages, 1987 (Text)

Bogert's Hornbook on Trusts, 6th Ed., Student Ed., about 794 pages, 1987 (Text)

Clark, Lusky and Murphy's Cases and Materials on Gratuitous Transfers, 3rd Ed., 970 pages, 1985 (Casebook)

McGovern, Rein and Kurtz' Hornbook on Wills, Trusts and Estates, 1988 (Text)

TRUSTS AND ESTATES—Cont'd

McGovern's Cases and Materials on Wills, Trusts and Future Interests: An Introduction to Estate Planning, 750 pages, 1983 (Casebook)

Mennell's Wills and Trusts in a Nutshell, 392 pages, 1979 (Text)

Simes' Hornbook on Future Interests, 2nd Ed., 355 pages, 1966 (Text)

Turano and Radigan's Hornbook on New York Estate Administration, 676 pages, 1986 (Text)

Uniform Probate Code, Official Text With Comments, 615 pages, 1982

Waggoner's Future Interests in a Nutshell, 361 pages, 1981 (Text)

Waterbury's Materials on Trusts and Estates, 1039 pages, 1986 (Casebook)

WATER LAW

Getches' Water Law in a Nutshell, 439 pages, 1984 (Text)

Sax and Abram's Cases and Materials on Legal Control of Water Resources, 941 pages, 1986 (Casebook)

Trelease and Gould's Cases and Materials on Water Law, 4th Ed., 816 pages, 1986 (Casebook)

See also Energy and Natural Resources Law, Environmental Law

WILLS

See Trusts and Estates

WOMEN AND THE LAW

Kay's Text, Cases and Materials on Sex-Based Discrimination, 2nd Ed., 1045 pages, 1981, with 1986 Supplement (Casebook)

Thomas' Sex Discrimination in a Nutshell, 399 pages, 1982 (Text)

See also Employment Discrimination

WORKERS' COMPENSATION

See Social Legislation

CRIMINAL LAW
CASES AND MATERIALS
Third Edition

By

George E. Dix

A.W. Walker Centennial Chair in Law, University of Texas

M. Michael Sharlot

Wright C. Morrow Professor of Criminal Law,
University of Texas

AMERICAN CASEBOOK SERIES

WEST PUBLISHING CO.
ST. PAUL, MINN.,
1987

Library of Congress Cataloging in Publication Data

Dix, George E.
  Criminal law.

  (American casebook series)
  Includes bibliographies and index.
  1. Criminal law—United States—Cases.
I. Sharlot, M. Michael. II. Title. III. Series.
KF9218.D5 1987   345.73   87–2017
                          347.305

  ISBN 0–314–35159–0

Dix & Sharlot, Cs. Crim.Law 3rd Ed. ACB
1st Reprint—1988

Preface to the Third Edition

This book reflects our continued belief in the importance of the substantive criminal law in the law school curriculum. Substantive criminal law, more than any other subject in law school curricula, poses the great questions of the relationship of the individual to the state. The goals of the criminal law and the unending debate over how they can best be achieved and at what cost to the values of our society should be part of the intellectual life of every thinking citizen and most especially every lawyer. Thus, something more than a vehicle by which the student may be familiarized with the law of crimes is essential to any meaningful criminal law course.

This book is designed to facilitate inquiry into the broadest issues involved in the decision to employ the state's ultimate sanction to coerce conduct. As with the earlier editions, an attempt has been made to select cases and materials which are likely to evoke the interest of the students. Fact situations likely to spark emotional responses which must then be filtered through the requirements of the law and its underlying rationales may be found throughout the book. Insights from other fields of intellectual endeavor into the nature of human behavior are integrated with the case material and the notes, particularly in Chapters II and XII.

In revising the second edition of this book, we have been guided by several criteria which, we believe, are mutually reinforcing. The goal of producing an effective teaching vehicle has provided the major criterion for the selection and retention of cases and materials. Our own experience and that of many colleagues who have used the book over the years has identified those cases and materials which are most helpful in achieving this aim. In addition, however, we have given preference to more recent cases. Contemporary discussions often provide a review of recent changes in criminal jurisprudence. They also serve as an implicit illustration of the continuing importance of the subject matter. We have attempted to include insofar as possible the relevant significant discussions of substantive criminal law issues by the United States Supreme Court. Even when the Court's opinions are not rested on Constitutional grounds, they are likely to both reflect and affect the thinking of other American courts with respect to the area under review. Finally, we have attempted to select material illustrating some of the special concerns regarding the criminal law's impact on women, as reflected in the "battered wife" defense and the marital exemption to the crime of rape.

In addition to the many new cases which have been included, this revision involves significant changes in organization and format. The materials have been divided into a larger number of discrete units. These divisions will, we hope, allow teachers to more easily select the areas of special interest to them, as well as offering students a greater sense of progress and organization. A totally new division, Chapter XI, has been created to focus attention on the role of attendant circumstances in defining liability and assessing punishment. The chapter uses sexual assault as a vehicle for examining attendant circumstances, in much the same way as Chapter VII uses homicide to examine the relationship between state of mind and death in determining the level of liability. Another change is to be found in the more extensive use of introductory notes preceding each subdivision of the book. The aim of these notes is to aid the student's examination of the case and materials which follow by providing an overview that often involves the historical and jurisprudential context of the subject area. We have also tried to avoid any significant increase in the size of the book through the use of only one principal case for each area, stringent editing, and the elimination of notes which are more appropriate to a treatise than a casebook. The deletions do not affect the integrity of the book's design. Moreover, the size should make it possible for teachers to cover virtually all the materials in a single course. Certainly, a relatively traditional course may be taught using Chapters II–XII with, if the instructor desires, Chapter I, or even I–III, being assigned as background reading.

Chapter I, the introductory portion, deals with the general framework of criminal law. Editorial notes provide the major vehicle for addressing the scope of criminal activity, the modern debate over sentencing and the "reforms" which have ensued, and the procedure for processing a criminal case. The material on sentencing examines "determinant" and "indeterminant" institutionalization, but the death penalty is left to be treated in Chapter III which deals with some special Constitutional limitations on the substantive criminal law. Chapter I continues with material, including an introductory note and the most significant Supreme Court pronouncements concerning several procedural matters which we consider essential to an understanding of the context in which criminal law issues are raised and resolved. A textual note in this section defines many traditional crimes in summary fashion to provide the student with a general background in the law of crimes.

Chapter II presents the issues of what is meant by punishment and how it is to be justified. Students are introduced to the age-old debate over the functions and justifications for the use of the criminal sanction. A final subsection addresses the propriety of the use of the criminal law to reflect and enforce morality.

The limits placed on criminalization and punishment by the Constitution are examined in Chapter III. Three basic problem areas are reviewed through the use of introductory notes, recent and sharply contested decisions of the Supreme Court, and supplemental notes. These areas include the vagueness doctrine, proportionality in punishment both capital and imprisonment, and the right of privacy as presented by the Georgia sodomy case of the United States Supreme Court's most recent term.

The remaining chapters present the substantive criminal law. A brief introductory chapter, Chapter IV, presents the general scheme of analysis which serves as the conceptual basis for the organization of the remainder of the material. This is followed by Chapters V, VI, VIII and IX, in which the meaning and appropriateness of various requirements of specific substantive crimes are dealt with in the context of the general principles governing the elements of act, state of mind, results and attendant circumstances. It includes, where applicable, cases posing the possible constitutional implications of excluding an act or a state of mind from the definition of crimes. The material permits discussion of the differences in terms of act, state of mind and attendant circumstances that exist among traditional property crimes, as well as the acts which are required for certain non-property crimes. Chapter VI makes a special effort to help students unravel the troublesome distinction between general and specific intents, and also examines the operation of strict liability offenses. Those "defenses" that involve challenging the existence of an element of the offense charged are covered here along with the underlying requirements they "disprove". Chapter IX, dealing with attendant circumstances, is new. We hope it will focus needed attention on attendant circumstances, which are often conflated with other aspects of the actus reus.

Homicide provides the vehicle, in Chapter VII, for examining the relationship between state of mind and the grading of criminally-caused death. Chapter X covers the inchoate offenses including RICO as a modern supplement to traditional conspiracy doctrine. The principles governing liability on the basis of attribution of the harms caused by others, including the special rule of liability for co-conspirators, and liability for accessories after the fact, are examined in Chapter XI. Matters of justification and excuse, including "defenses" relating to the offender's psychological abnormality are the subject of Chapter XII. These matters are dealt with by a mix of cases and, with respect to entrapment and psychological impairment, editorial notes which, it is hoped, will aid the students' comprehension of these difficult matters.

We express our appreciation to the numerous authors and publishers who have given us permission to reproduce their materials. A special note of gratitude must go to the American Law Institute which kindly granted permission to reprint extensive portions of their copyrighted Model Penal Code (and the various tentative drafts and commentary thereto). In editing the materials reprinted in this book, we have left out citations and footnotes without any specific indication of such omissions. Footnotes retained from the original material are indicated by numbers. We have chosen not to renumber the footnotes that have been retained; consequently, the numbers appearing in the material are those assigned by the original authors. Footnotes indicated by letters are those we have inserted.

The introductory and following notes contain many references to outside reading that may enrich or clarify the particular sections of the book where they appear. More generally, students may be well advised to take advantage of the second edition of the hornbook, Handbook on Criminal Law, published in 1986 by Professor Wayne R. LaFave and based on the enormous efforts of himself and the late Professor Austin W. Scott, Jr. Another recent publication representing the efforts of many prominent scholars, which offers great aid through thoughtful articles on a great variety of subjects relevant to an understanding of the substantive criminal law is the four volume work, The Encyclopedia of Crime and Justice (1983), edited by Professor Sanford H. Kadish. In terms of historical impact on the development of the substantive criminal law in the United States, no work is comparable to the commentary to the drafts of the American Law Institute's Model Penal Code. The drafts and commentary are especially useful now that they have been revised and republished in two Parts; Part II in three volumes was published in 1980, and Part I in two volumes appeared in 1985. Excerpts from these volumes have been included but, of course, these are but the barest sampling of the thoughtful discussions contained therein. Also of significant aid, although less elaborate, are the two volumes of Working Papers of the ill-fated National Commission on Reform of the Federal Criminal Laws, published in 1970.

The best single source of information about the actual operation of the criminal justice system and recommendations for its improvement remains, despite being somewhat outdated, The Challenge of Crime in a Free Society, A Report by the President's Commission on Law Enforcement and Administration of Justice, published in 1967, and the many Task Force Reports produced by the Commission. A thought-provoking discussion of the jurisprudential aspects of the substantive criminal law with frequent reference to comparative approaches in other nations is Professor George Fletcher's Rethinking Criminal Law, published in 1978. Another provocative but very different examination of the problems of dealing with crime in society is Crime and Human Nature, published in 1983 by Professors James Q. Wilson and Richard J. Herrnstein. This reviews the many theories of the etiology of crime and the empirical data offered in their support. Finally, no finer short overview of the problems of the criminal law can be recommended than the late Professor Herbert Packer's short volume, The Limits of the Criminal Sanction, published in 1968.

GED
MMS

January, 1987

Summary of Contents

Table of Contents

References to the Proposed Federal Criminal Code

*

References to the Model Penal Code

Table of Cases

The principal cases are in bold type. Cases cited or discussed in the text are roman type. References are to pages. Cases cited in principal cases and within other quoted materials are not included.

Chapter I

INTRODUCTION

Contents

1

Patterson v. New York.
Notes and Questions.
Model Penal Code § 1.12 and Comments.

The subject of this book is substantive criminal law, not criminology (the study of criminal behavior) or criminal procedure. But identification, evaluation, and resolution of substantive criminal law issues requires some consideration of these related matters. Providing some general background of this sort is the purpose of this chapter.

Resolution of substantive criminal law issues may be affected by the perception of the amount of and changes in serious criminal behavior, especially as compared with the situation in what might be regarded as similar countries. Information on these matters is presented in Section A. Throughout the book, issues concerning particular criminal offenses will be explored, but a preliminary overview of traditional serious crimes is useful as an introduction. This is provided by Section B.

Substantive criminal law is today largely a matter of statutory coverage. In most jurisdictions, moderately comprehensive criminal codes address the area. The background of these codes and the model formulations often used in their drafting is considered in Section C. Sentencing provisions of these codes are of special importance in substantive criminal law. In many cases, the only disputed issue is not whether an accused is guilty of an offense but rather which offense most appropriately applies to his conduct. This, in turn, is of significance primarily because the choice from among offenses may bring into play different penalty provisions. Penalty provisions of modern codes, then, are explored in Section D.

Given the need to study substantive criminal law issues through the written opinions of appellate courts, it is important to understand how criminal law issues arise in trial courts and how those issues are presented to appellate tribunals. Section E considers these matters. Allocating the burdens of proof and of producing evidence is a matter of special importance and sometimes confusion in criminal litigation, explored in that section. Its complexity is increased, however, by federal constitutional limits on the manner in which these burdens can be placed on accused persons. These federal constitutional concerns are consequently considered more extensively in Section F.

A. THE AMERICAN "CRIME PROBLEM"

Editors' Note: The American "Crime Problem"

As background to an examination of issues of substantive criminal law, it is useful to consider the amount of serious criminal activity in the country, trends with regard to such activity, and how questions of substantive criminal law might relate to these matters. In some sense, of course, any crime is too much crime. But decisions with regard to a number of issues may depend, in part at least, upon the nature and seriousness of the "crime problem," which in turn depends in part upon the amount of crime and the nature and rate of changes in criminal activity.

The major traditional source of information on criminal activity has been the Federal Bureau of Investigation's Uniform Crime Reporting Program. Based on information provided by local and state law enforcement programs, the Bureau estimates the total number of certain "index offenses" known to law enforcement agencies. Yearly publications titled *Crime in the United States* contain the results of this process together with a crime index. Table 1 combines statistical information concerning crimes rates per 100,000 persons for the years 1960 through 1985. Property crimes rates have been decreasing since 1980, and violent crimes have shown a similar although somewhat more complicated decline.

In light of evidence that many—and with regard to some offenses, most—crimes are not reported to law enforcement authorities, the reliability of this sort of information has been questioned. These concerns led to the development of the Justice Department's National Crime Survey, which uses interviewing techniques to obtain information concerning victimization by criminal activity. This information has been collected only since 1973 and addresses fewer offenses than do the Uniform Crime Reports. Table 2 summarizes victimization rates for the period 1973–1984. Note that the rates are per 1,000 persons age 12 and over (or households) and therefore the figures in table 2 cannot be compared directly with those in table 1. Again, however, this measure of criminal activity indicates a recent decrease in the rate of the measured criminal conduct.

Insofar as attention is properly devoted to that criminal conduct which generates the most apprehension in Americans, however, the information from both of these sources may be too broad. The President's Commission on Law Enforcement and the Administration of Justice noted in 1967 that "the fear of crimes of violence is * * *, at bottom, a fear of strangers." *The Challenge of Crime in a Free Society* 52 (1967). This may be an oversimplification. Despite the American tradition of defining rape in terms of a sexual assault upon a victim not related to the attacker, it is clear that the problem of sexual and other assaults upon spouses is a widespread and serious one. These matters are addressed in Chapter XI of this book. On the assumption that stranger crime is a problem of unusual severity, however the National Crime Survey has inquired of crime victims as to their prior acquaintance, if any, with the perpetrator of the violent crimes of which they were victims. Recently it reported that the resulting pattern remained stable for the period 1973–79. During that time, 59 percent of all violent crime was committed by strangers to the victim. In regard to specific offenses, rapes were perpetrated by strangers in 65 per cent of

Table 1. United States Crime Rate (Offenses Known to Police) Per 100,000 Inhabitants: 1960–1985

Year	Crime Index total	Violent crime A	Property crime B	Murder and non-negligent homicide	Forcible rape	Robbery	Aggravated assault	Burglary	Larceny-theft	Motor vehicle theft
1960	1,887.2	160.9	1,726.3	5.1	9.6	60.1	86.1	508.6	1,034.7	183.0
1961	1,906.1	158.1	1,747.9	4.8	9.4	58.3	85.7	518.9	1,045.4	183.6
1962	2,019.8	162.3	1,857.5	4.6	9.4	59.7	88.6	535.2	1,124.8	197.4
1963	2,180.3	168.2	2,012.1	4.6	9.4	61.8	92.4	576.4	1,219.1	216.6
1964	2,388.1	190.6	2,197.5	4.9	11.2	68.2	106.2	634.7	1,315.5	247.4
1965	2,449.0	200.2	2,248.8	5.1	12.1	71.7	111.3	662.7	1,329.3	256.8
1966	2,670.8	220.0	2,450.9	5.6	13.2	80.8	120.3	721.0	1,442.9	286.9
1967	2,989.7	253.2	2,736.5	6.2	14.0	102.8	130.2	826.6	1,575.8	334.1
1968	3,370.2	298.4	3,071.8	6.9	15.9	131.8	143.8	923.3	1,746.6	393.0
1969	3,680.0	328.7	3,351.3	7.3	18.5	148.4	154.5	984.1	1,930.9	436.2
1970	3,984.5	363.5	3,621.0	7.9	18.7	172.1	164.8	1,084.9	2,079.3	456.8
1971	4,164.7	396.0	3,768.8	8.6	20.5	188.0	178.8	1,163.5	2,145.5	459.8
1972	3,961.4	401.0	3,560.4	9.0	22.5	180.7	188.8	1,140.8	1,993.6	426.1
1973	4,154.4	417.4	3,737.0	9.4	24.5	183.1	200.5	1,222.5	2,071.9	442.6
1974 C	4,850.4	461.1	4,389.3	9.8	26.2	209.3	215.8	1,437.7	2,489.5	462.2
1975	5,298.5	487.8	4,810.7	9.6	26.3	220.8	231.1	1,532.1	2,804.8	473.7
1976	5,287.3	467.8	4,819.5	8.8	26.6	199.3	233.2	1,448.2	2,921.3	450.0
1977	5,077.6	475.9	4,601.7	8.8	29.4	190.7	247.0	1,419.8	2,729.9	451.9
1978	5,140.3	497.8	4,642.5	9.0	31.0	195.8	262.1	1,434.6	2,747.4	460.5
1979	5,565.5	548.9	5,016.6	9.7	34.7	218.4	286.0	1,511.9	2,999.1	505.6
1980	5,950.0	596.6	5,353.3	10.2	36.8	251.1	298.5	1,684.1	3,167.0	502.2
1981	5,858.2	594.3	5,263.9	9.8	36.0	258.7	289.7	1,649.5	3,139.7	474.7
1982	5,603.6	571.1	5,032.5	9.1	34.0	238.9	289.2	1,488.8	3,084.8	458.8
1983	5,175.0	537.7	4,637.4	8.3	33.7	216.5	279.2	1,337.7	2,868.9	430.8
1984	5,031.3	539.2	4,492.1	7.9	35.7	205.4	290.2	1,263.7	2,791.3	437.1

A. Violent crimes include murder, forcible rape, robbery, and aggravated assault.
B. Property crimes include burglary, larceny-theft and motor vehicle theft.
C. Data for the years 1975–1985 was adjusted for certain reporting problems that were not accommodated in the data for 1960–1974.
Source: U.S. Dept. of Justice, Federal Bureau of Investigation, Uniform Crime Reports for the United States, for years 1969–1985.

the cases, robberies in 76 per cent, aggravated assaults in 56 per cent and simple assaults in 53 per cent. *Violent Crimes by Strangers* 1 (U.S. Dept. of Justice, Bureau of Justice Statistics, Bulletin, undated). The Survey does not collect information on homicides, but the report noted that according to the Uniform Crime Reports, in 1979 the relationship between murderers and their victims was unknown in over one third of

Table 2. Victimization rates for personal and household crimes, 1973–84

	Victimization rates per 1,000 population age 12 and over or per 1,000 households											
	1973	1974	1975	1976	1977	1978	1979	1980	1981	1982	1983	1984
Personal crimes												
Crimes of violence	32.6	33.0	32.8	32.6	33.9	33.7	34.5	33.3	35.3	34.3	31.0	31.0
Rape	1.0	1.0	0.9	0.8	0.9	1.0	1.1	0.9	1.0	0.8	0.8	0.9
Robbery	6.7	7.2	6.8	6.5	6.2	5.9	6.3	6.6	7.4	7.1	6.0	5.8
Assault	24.9	24.8	25.2	25.3	26.8	26.9	27.2	25.8	27.0	26.4	24.1	24.3
Aggravated assault	10.1	10.4	9.6	9.9	10.0	9.7	9.9	9.3	9.6	9.3	8.0	8.7
Simple assault	14.8	14.4	15.6	15.4	16.8	17.2	17.3	16.5	17.3	17.1	16.2	15.5
Crimes of theft	91.1	95.1	96.0	96.1	97.3	96.8	91.9	83.0	85.1	82.5	76.9	71.8
Personal larceny with contact	3.1	3.1	3.1	2.9	2.7	3.1	2.9	3.0	3.3	3.1	3.0	2.8
Personal larceny without contact	88.0	92.0	92.9	93.2	94.6	93.6	89.0	80.0	81.9	79.5	74.0	69.1
Household crimes												
Household burglary	91.7	93.1	91.7	88.9	88.5	86.0	84.1	84.3	87.9	78.2	70.0	64.1
Household larceny	107.0	123.8	125.4	124.1	123.3	119.9	133.7	126.5	121.0	113.9	105.2	99.4
Motor vehicle theft	19.1	18.8	19.5	16.5	17.0	17.5	17.5	16.7	17.1	16.2	14.6	15.2

NOTE: Detail may not add to total shown because of rounding.
Source: U.S. Dept. of Justice, *Criminal Victimization 1984* 3 (Bureau of Justice Statistics Bulletin, Oct. 1985).

the cases. In the remaining cases, however, in only 20 per cent of the cases were the victim and the murderer strangers. Id.

Differences in data development makes comparative analysis difficult. But there is widespread agreement that the United States, as compared to other arguably similar countries, has an especially serious crime problem. In 1979, for example, the American homicide rate was 9.7 per 100,000 population; that of England was 1.16 and the Canadian rate was 2.7. P. Brantingham and P. Brantingham, Patterns in Crime 139 (1984). Analysis of crimes reported to law enforcement in the United States and Canada for 1964 through 1974 indicates that the United States has a much higher crime rate and that a larger portion of American crime is violent. The American violent crime rate was about four times the Canadian rate. Id., at 136–37.

As might be imagined, there is substantial dispute with regard to the causes of crime and its increase as well as what impact various social or governmental actions or policies might have upon the amount of or increase in serious criminal activity. Whether those matters at issue in this book—so-called "substantive criminal law" problems—can reasonably be expected to affect crime is especially problematic. In some ways the substantive criminal law obviously has such effects. At the most basic level, no conduct is "criminal", and thus counted in statistical studies, unless and until it is so defined by an appropriate authority. Property crimes are often categorized as felonies or misdemeanors by the value of the items misappropriated: theft of property valued at $50 or more may be defined as a felony. Even if the total number of thefts per 100,000 persons remains constant, therefore, economic inflation means that there will be an ever-increasing rate of felony thefts unless the monetary standard for felony theft specified by the applicable statute is periodically adjusted.

A more significant effect might result from a legislative decision to criminalize or decriminalize conduct which had not been so treated in the past. If, for example, the possession and sale of heroin were decriminalized, the amount of crime to be counted would be reduced. It would obviously do so directly by removing this activity from the statute books and statistical studies. It would do so indirectly insofar as legalization might reduce the price and thus the need for other criminal conduct to obtain funds for its purchase. Finally, decriminalization of this conduct would release police, prosecutorial, judicial, and correctional resources which might then be applied to the struggle against other crimes and thereby, possibly, reduce their incidence. Of course, any such action might involve costs to society in terms of increased use, lowered productivity, and other anti-social conduct. All of this suggests that in considering particular issues, it is well to ask whether the need to affect the amount of criminal activity strongly argues in favor of some rather than other resolutions. Perhaps substantive criminal law issues are best resolved on the basis of other considerations.

B. TRADITIONAL CRIMINAL OFFENSES

Editors' Note: Traditional Criminal Offenses

Although crimes are today almost entirely statutory, most have deep historical roots in the English common law. Specific issues concerning the elements of liability under some of these offenses will be dealt with later, but it is necessary at this point to take a preliminary look at the major criminal offenses. Understanding of the law's approach to defining criminal liability requires at least a basic knowledge of the major traditional offenses. Because of the wide variations among the manner in which various jurisdictions define different offenses, this summary must necessarily be quite general and may not correspond to the law of any particular jurisdiction.

Crimes are generally grouped according to the interest protected: security of the person, security of the habitation, security of rights in property, public health, safety, and morals, and public authority.

Offenses Against the Security of the Person

The major common law offense protecting the security of the person was, of course, homicide. At common law, unlawful homicides were either murder or manslaughter. A killing was murder if it was committed with "malice aforethought." As the subsequent material develops, the definition of the state of mind described by the term "malice aforethought" presents a variety of important issues. No degrees of murder were recognized at common law, although many subsequent codifications of the law of homicide have so divided murder. Manslaughter was of two types: voluntary and involuntary. Voluntary manslaughter was an intentional killing committed in a heat of passion induced by adequate provocation. Involuntary manslaughter consisted of an unintentional killing resulting from negligence or the commission of an unlawful act.

The crime of assault, a misdemeanor at common law, has been defined in a wide variety of ways. Some jurisdictions define the offense as an attempt to commit a battery. Under such a definition, the defendant must intend to commit a battery and engage in some activity designed to effectuate that intent. If, as is sometimes the case, the definition also requires the present ability to commit a battery, it is also necessary that there have been no inherent impediment to success. But under this definition, the reaction of the victim is of no legal significance. Probably a majority of jurisdictions include in the definition of assault threatening conduct engaged in with intent to injure or frighten the victim which does create in the victim a reasonable apprehension of immediate physical harm.

A battery is a successful assault, consisting of any application of force to the person of another. Modern American jurisdictions often distinguish between "simple" assaults and batteries and "aggravated" crimes of that nature. The latter consist of assaults and batteries performed under specified circumstances and carry a higher penalty.

Mayhem or maim at common law consisted of a violently inflicted injury rendering the victim less able to fight or annoy his enemy. Except where it took the form of castration, it was a misdemeanor. This offense is often retained in contemporary codes, although it is no longer restricted to injuries affecting the victim's ability to defend himself.

Rape consists, as it did at common law, of an act of intercourse with a woman not the wife of the perpetrator against her will and accomplished by actual or constructive force. At common law, a girl under the age of ten was legally incapable of consenting to intercourse, so any such act with her constituted rape. Modern statutes defining the crime of "statutory" rape generally set a significantly higher age at which a girl may give legally effective consent to intercourse. Also, the marital rape exemption is being rejected or limited by an increasing number of jurisdictions. At common law rape was a felony, and it is also under contemporary statutes.

False imprisonment at common law consisted of any unlawful restraint upon a person's liberty and was a misdemeanor. It is retained in this form in most modern codes.

The common law misdemeanor of kidnapping consisted of the forcible abduction of another and the transportation of the victim to another country. Current statutes have greatly modified this offense in several ways. First, the seriousness of the crime has been increased. In many jurisdictions, at least some forms of kidnapping are categorized with the most serious felonies. Second, the extent to which the victim must be affected has been modified. Transportation to another country is not required; movement of any sort is often sufficient. In some jurisdictions, mere detention (if done with the requisite intent) is sufficient. Finally, some forms of kidnapping have been formulated so as to require detention or movement of the victim for certain specific purposes, such as the infliction of bodily harm, the obtaining of money or property, or the commission of some sexual offense.

Offenses Against the Security of the Habitation

Two common law felonies were designed to protect the interest of the security of the habitation. Arson was committed by the malicious burning of a dwelling (or some building used in connection with it) belonging to or occupied by another. Modern criminal codes generally retain the offense in this form, although many have expanded it to cover the burning of structures other than residential dwellings.

Burglary consisted of a breaking and entry of the dwelling of another in the nighttime with the intent to commit a felony in the dwelling. Modern statutes often modify the crime of burglary by removing the requirement of a breaking, expanding the type of buildings protected, and eliminating the requirement that the offense be committed in the nighttime. The intent to commit even misdemeanor theft is often made a sufficient intent for the offense.

Offenses Against the Security of Interests in Property

The common law offenses related to the acquisition of property have an interesting historical development demonstrating an increasing willingness of the law to protect interests in personal property. In some jurisdictions the various offenses have to some extent been consolidated under the general title of "theft," but even such codifications often retain elements of the common law distinctions.

Robbery is an offense against both the security of the person and of interests in property. It consists of the taking and asportation of personal property from the person or the presence of another against his will by means of violence or placing the other in fear of personal safety with the intent to permanently deprive him of his interest in the property. It was apparently the initial common law property offense, although it was defined somewhat more narrowly.

Larceny, a felony at common law, consisted of a taking and asportation of personal property in the possession of another accomplished against the will of the other and by means of a trespass with the intent to permanently deprive the other of his interests in the property. Modern codes generally retain the offense as defined at common law, either as the separate offense of larceny or as one form of theft. Embezzlement was not a common law offense but was made a crime by early English statute. It is committed when one who has possession of another's property by virtue of a trust relationship fraudulently appropriates that property to a use inconsistent with the trust. The limited common law offense of cheating by use of false tokens was developed by early statutes into the crime of obtaining property by false pretenses. Under the early definitions, this offense required fraudulently causing another to part with ownership of property by means of false representations of fact known to be false. The statutory crime of "false pretenses" thus covered much of the gap left by the relatively restricted definitions of larceny and embezzlement.

Extortion was a misdemeanor at common law consisting of the unlawful collection by an official of an unlawful fee under color of his office. Thus it was an offense against the administration of justice. But in modern codes extortion has often been expanded (sometimes under the label of blackmail) to include obtaining property by means of a threat not sufficient to constitute robbery, including threats to do future (i.e., not immediate) bodily injury, to injure property, to accuse the victim of a crime, or to reveal certain types of information concerning the victim.

Several other offenses against property frequently found in modern criminal codes may have had their origin in common law. Forgery, clearly a misdemeanor at common law, consisted of a material false making or alteration of a writing or document of some legal significance with the intent to defraud. Current statutes often contain similar definitions. It is less clear whether receipt of stolen goods was a common law crime. It is, however, an offense in contemporary codes and requires a taking of possession of property which had been stolen knowing that it had been acquired in a manner constituting larceny (or theft). Similar doubt exists as to the origin of malicious mischief, which consists of malicious destruction of or injury to property of another.

Offenses Against the Public Health, Safety, Morals and Peace

There is a wide variety of offenses with roots in early English law that have in common only the fact that all are defined as crimes because the conduct prohibited has been viewed as infringing the broad interest of the state in maintaining the general public health, safety, and morality.

The misdemeanor of common nuisance consisted of creating a condition prejudicial to the health, safety, comfort, sense of decency, or property of the citizens at large by an act not warranted by law or by neglect of a duty imposed by law. It remains a criminal offense in some jurisdictions. Fornication—usually defined as intercourse between a man and woman not lawfully married—was not a common law offense, although the common law did prohibit any open and notorious lewdness and indecency, including open and notorious cohabitation. Incest—sexual relations between individuals related within the degrees of consanguinity or affinity within which marriage is prohibited—was not a common law offense, although there is dispute as to whether adultery—usually defined as illicit sexual relations in which at least one of the persons is married to someone other than the sexual partner—was such a crime. Bigamy, the marriage of another by one with a spouse living, was made criminal by statute in 1604. Contemporary criminal codes are tending to abandon fornication, adultery, incest, and bigamy.

Any willful and unjustifiable disturbance of the public peace was a common law misdemeanor, and is presently an offense in all American jurisdictions. The problem of mob action was dealt with by three offenses, consisting of progressive group activity. Unlawful assembly consisted of three or more persons assembled with intent to carry out any purpose by open force or in any manner such as would cause reasonable apprehension of a breach of the peace. Rout consisted of an unlawful assembly which had begun the accomplishment of the common objective. Riot was the execution of the unlawful purpose, that is, the accomplishment of the objective in a riotous manner. These offenses are retained to varying extents in modern codes.

Offenses Against Public Authority and the Administration of Justice

Treason was a common law offense but its definition was apparently quite uncertain. Later development of the offense by statute was significantly different in America than in England. Article 3, section 3 of the United States Constitution specifically provides that "treason against the United States shall consist only of levying war against them or in adhering to their enemies, giving them aid and comfort." State criminal codes often contain similar crimes, often expanded to prohibit treason against the state as well as the federal government.

Perjury, a misdemeanor at common law, is generally defined as the giving of testimony known to be false which is material to the proceeding and is given in a proceeding in which sworn testimony is permitted. Subornation of perjury is simply the procuring by one person of another to commit perjury.

C. MODERN CRIMINAL CODES

Editors' Note: Modern Criminal Codes

The last 25 years have seen a significant movement towards comprehensive revision of statutory provisions governing substantive criminal law matters. Both the impetus for this revision and the substance of the revised provisions can be traced in large part to the development of the Model Penal Code by the American Law Institute. The Institute approved the final draft of the Code in May of 1962.

Prior to the revision movement, state and federal statutes often addressed substantive criminal law matters but seldom in a comprehensive manner. Often, the statutes did little but specify the penalties for particular offenses. Even here, the legislative approach was often haphazard. Penalties were often assigned with little view towards uniformity or consistency. No effort was made in the statutes to define the various offenses but instead common law and sometimes more recent judicial formulations of the elements of these crimes was presumably incorporated. Even less legislative attention was developed to defensive matters, such as responsibility, justification and the like, so these areas were left largely or entirely to judicial development. See generally, Wechsler, The Challenge of a Model Penal Code, 65 Harv.L. Rev. 1097, 1100–01 (1952).

The Model Penal Code

In the development of the Model Penal Code, initial formulations were drafted by the reporters. Professor Herbert Wechsler of Columbia University Law School was Chief Reporter. These were reviewed by a multidisciplinary Advisory Committee and by the Council of the American Law Institute. Tentative Drafts were then prepared for review, discussion, and approval of the entire Institute membership. These tentative drafts—ultimately 13 in number—included extensive "Comments" on the proposed provisions. A proposed final draft was developed in 1962 and was approved by the membership of the Institute the same year. No "Official Draft" was published at that time, however. As a result, scholarly and judicial references (including some references in this book) to the Institute's final action have generally been to the proposed official draft, often in the following form: Model Penal Code § 1.10 (P.O.D. 1962). Revised and expanded commentaries were prepared as a later Institute project. In 1980, a three volume set consisting of the text of and revised commentaries to Part II of the Code—dealing with the definition of particular offenses—was published. Another three volume set consisting of the text and revised commentaries of Part I—dealing with general matters—was published in 1985. In the course of this work, "it became evident that a final, official publication of the complete text of the Model Penal Code would be of value." Wechsler, Foreward, Model Penal Code xii (Official Draft and Explanatory Notes, 1985). Such a version was prepared under the guidance of Professor R. Kent Greenawalt of Columbia University Law School and published in 1985. Id. This contains Explanatory Notes drafted in the course of preparing the revised commentaries. The final drafts, tentative drafts and commentary in the tentative drafts still constitute a major source of academic discussion on American substantive criminal law matters.

Several major thrusts of the Model Penal Code can be identified. First, it addresses "general" matters—that is, matters other than the definition of particular criminal offenses—much more extensively than was usual under traditional statutory provisions. See Wechsler, Revision and Codification of Penal Law in the United States, 7 Dalhousie L.J. 219, 224 (1983). General principles are set out with regard to the conduct and state of mind necessary for criminal liability. "Defensive" matters, in addition, are addressed in some detail. This is in contrast with traditional statutory provisions which often emphasized or addressed only the existence and definition of the particular offenses.

Second, the Code attempts to comprehensively and carefully address those matters covered. Rather than using traditional terms with some assumed meaning, the Code attempted to address specifically and completely all matters on which the existence or nonexistence of criminal liability will depend. This includes both the elements of particular criminal offenses as well as those things—loosely regarded as "defenses"—that may prevent liability. The elements of various offenses and defenses were defined in specific terms and the drafting was done in a manner that tended to emphasize the different elements so as to reduce the risk of confusion among them.

A third major theme of the Code is the organization of the penalty schemes. Rather than providing for penalties on a crime-by-crime basis, the Model Penal Code proposed the creation of a number of categories of both felonies, Model Penal Code § 6.01 (P.O.D. 1962) (three degrees of felonies) and misdemeanors, id., at § 1.04(3)–(4) (petty misdemeanors and misdemeanors). Penalties were then authorized for each category. E.g., id., at 6.06(1) (first degree felonies punishable by a sentence of imprisonment with a minimum of not less than one year nor more than ten years and a maximum of life).

A major substantive contribution of the Model Penal Code is its offered provisions regarding "criminal intent." These are considered at length in Chapter VI, infra. At this point, however, it is useful to note that the Code's drafters reaffirmed the traditional notion that *mens rea* is central to criminal liability. In addition, however, they proposed a framework for consistent analysis of what mental states are required for liability for various offenses and relating this to various "defensive" matters, such as intoxication and self-defense. See Packer, The Model Penal Code and Beyond, 63 Colum.L.Rev. 594–95 (1963). Perhaps unfortunately, the Code uses the term "culpability" to refer to the mental states required for criminal liability. E.g., Model Penal Code § 2.02 (P.O.D. 1962) ("General Requirements of Culpability"). This use of a term which in ordinary usage refers to the more comprehensive notion of "blameworthiness," however, serves to emphasize the importance which the Model Penal Code placed upon the mental element in defining and grading criminal liability.

The Model Penal Code has not received uniformly favorable reviews. A member of the staff of the District Attorney of New York County, for example, criticized the Code's provisions addressing the mental elements of criminal liability:

> [S]ome provisions of the Code * * * confuse because of the draftmen's too fertile and too fully-expressed imagination. Today, for instance, in instructing a jury as to culpability, a judge is likely to inform the jurors that criminal intent is necessary, and to further instruct them that a person is presumed to intend the natural consequences of his acts. Such instructions are simple enough, and I know of no reason to believe that they are either poor law or have caused any confusion in the minds of jurors. * * * Although medieval scholars have not been spotted on the Advisory Committee, the Institute has fashioned a section on culpability that would, I venture, be the envy of those monastics whose hitherto favorite pastime had been debating the number of angels who might dance on the head of a pin.

Kuh, A Prosecutor Considers the Model Penal Code, 63 Colum.L.Rev. 608, 621 (1963).

Post-Model Penal Code Statutory Revision

Whatever its merits, the Model Penal Code has been a major source of reference for the extensive legislative activity in criminal law after 1962. Professor Wechsler recently noted that 34 legislative substantive criminal law revisions, of varying thoroughness, occurred between 1962 and 1983 and that all were influenced to some degree by the Model Penal Code. More revisions were under consideration by some state legislatures at the time of his writing. Wechsler, Foreward to Model Penal Code and Commentaries Part I (Official Draft and Rev. Comments 1985).

One additional legislative effort deserves special mention. Although no comprehensive revision of federal criminal law has passed

Congress, proposals have been developed for this purpose. In 1966, Congress created the National Commission on Reform of Federal Criminal Laws. The Commission was chaired by Edmund G. Brown, former San Francisco District Attorney and eight-year governor of California. A "study draft" of a revision, with comments, was published in 1970. National Commission on Reform of Federal Criminal Laws, Study Draft of a New Federal Criminal Code (1970). At the same time, the Commission published a compilation of consultants' reports and staff memoranda that were used in development of the study draft. National Commission of Reform of Federal Criminal Laws, Working Papers of the National Commission on Reform of Federal Criminal Laws (1970). The next year a final report, consisting of a proposed new federal criminal code and comments, was published. National Commission on Reform of Federal Criminal Laws, Final Report of the Commission on Reform of Federal Criminal Laws (1971). This report recommended revision of Title 18 of the United States Code, which contains most federal crimes, so as to provide the sort of comprehensive statutory coverage of federal substantive criminal law as was being developed in the states.

Legislation seeking such comprehensive reform of the federal statutes was introduced into Congress and gave rise to considerable academic discussion. See Symposiums, 72 J.Crim.L. & Criminology 381 (1981) (including bibliography); 47 Geo.Wash.L.Rev. 451 (1979). Congressional views differed sharply. See, for example, Eisenberg, Congress and the Criminal Code * * * a legislative adventure, 36 nlada briefcase 145 (1979). In large part because of the controversy generated by particular provisions, no Congressional action was taken. When, in 1982, supporters of the Criminal Code Reform Act of 1981 gave up on their bill, Senator Strom Thurmond explained this action in terms of the Senate's reluctance to vote on such controversial matters as the death penalty and gun control in an election year. See, Senate Fails to Act on Criminal Code, 13 C. Justice Newsletter (No. 9) at page 1 (May 10, 1982).

In 1984, Congress passed the Comprehensive Crime Control Act of 1984, which included some of the features of earlier efforts at federal criminal code reform. Several aspects of this legislation are discussed at various points in this book. The sentencing scheme provided for federal prosecutions is considered at pages 24–26, infra. Congressional specification of a criterion for determining whether those charged with federal crimes are to be acquitted on insanity grounds is addressed in Chapter XII at pages 791, 799, infra. The 1984 legislation has been called "the culmination of an 11–year effort to make major changes in the federal criminal code." Cohodas, Enactment of Crime Package Culmination of 11–Year Effort, 42 Cong.Q.W.Rep. 2752 (1984). See also, Melone, The Politics of Criminal Code Revision: Lessons for Reform, 15 Capital U.L.Rev. 191 (1986). But unlike many of the earlier unsuccessful efforts, this legislation did not comprehensively revise Title 18 of the United States Code along the lines of the Model Penal

Code and as recommended by the Brown Commission. Federal substantive criminal law has not, then, undergone the sort of extensive revision and recodification that the Model Penal Code stimulated in many of the states.

To the extent that American jurisdictions have developed more comprehensive criminal codes, does this reduce the power of the judiciary in developing the substantive criminal law? It seems likely that enactment of these codes does represent, to some extent, an assumption by the legislatures of responsibility for developing substantive criminal law that previously was exercised largely by the courts. Some, and perhaps many, of the code provisions, however, use quite general phraseology. This appears to leave to the judiciary substantial responsibility for defining as well as applying substantive criminal law doctrines. But in exercising that responsibility, the courts may now have a duty to refer to the codes and look to them for indications of legislative policy which, if found, should be binding on or at least influential with the courts. Cf. State v. Tate, 102 N.J. 64, 68, 505 A.2d 941, 943 (1986).

"Strict" and Other Construction of Penal Codes and Statutes

There is more widespread agreement that courts should approach the task of applying modern criminal codes with a somewhat different attitude than has traditionally been taken towards penal statutes. Application of penal statutes has been subject to the principle that that criminal statutes are to be strictly construed and its "identical twin," Sedima, S.P.R.L. v. Imrex, Inc., ___ U.S. ___, ___ n. 10, 105 S.Ct. 3275, 3283 n. 10, 87 L.Ed.2d 346, 357 n. 10 (1985), the "rule of lenity":

"[A]mbiguity concerning the ambit of criminal statutes should be resolved in favor of lenity." Rewis v. United States, 401 U.S. 808, 812, 91 S.Ct. 1056, 1059, 28 L.Ed.2d 493 (1971). In various ways over the years, we have stated that "when choice has to be made between two readings of what conduct Congress has made a crime, it is appropriate, before we choose the harshest alternative, to require that Congress should have spoken in language that is clear and definite." United States v. Universal C.I.T. Credit Corp., 344 U.S. 218, 221–22, 73 S.Ct. 227, 229, 97 L.Ed. 260 (1952). This principle is founded on two policies that have long been part of our tradition. First, "a fair warning should be given to the world in language that the common world will understand, of what the law intends to do if a certain line is passed. To make the warning fair, so far as possible the line should be clear." McBoyle v. United States, 283 U.S. 25, 27, 51 S.Ct. 340, 341, 75 L.Ed. 816 (1931) (Holmes, J.). Second, because of the seriousness of criminal penalties, and because criminal punishment represents the moral condemnation of the community, legislatures and not courts should define criminal activity. This policy embodies "the instinctive distastes against men languishing in prison unless the lawmaker has clearly said they should." H. Friendly, Mr. Justice Frankfurter and the Reading of Statutes in Benchmark 196, 209 (1967). Thus, where there is ambiguity in a criminal statute, doubts are resolved in favor of the defendant.

United States v. Bass, 404 U.S. 336, 347–48, 92 S.Ct. 515, 522–23, 30 L.Ed.2d 488, 496–97 (1971).

Neither this approach nor the rationale is new. Early in our history Chief Justice Marshall observed:

> The rule that penal laws are to be construed strictly, is perhaps not much less old than construction itself. It is founded on the tenderness of the law for the rights of individuals; and on the plain principle that the power of punishment is vested in the legislature, not in the judicial department. It is the legislature, not the Court, which is to define a crime and ordain its punishment.

United States v. Wiltberger, 18 U.S. (5 Wheat.) 76, 95, 5 L.Ed. 37 (1820).

The reduction in the severity of penalties for criminal offenses— and particularly the limitation of capital punishment to a relatively small class of murders—arguably weakens somewhat a major impetus for the rule of lenity. For this or perhaps other reasons, this approach is sometimes applied sparingly. In Callanan v. United States, 364 U.S. 587, 81 S.Ct. 321, 5 L.Ed.2d 312 (1961), for example, the Supreme Court commented:

> [The rule of lenity,] as is true of any guide to statutory construction, only serves as an aid for resolving an ambiguity; it is not to be used to beget one. * * * The rule comes into operation at the end of the process of construing what Congress has expressed, not at the beginning as an overriding consideration of being lenient to wrongdoers.

364 U.S. at 596, 81 S.Ct. at 326, 5 L.Ed.2d at 319.

Perhaps the care with which modern criminal codes have been drafted and the comprehensive nature of the provisions has removed the justification for the traditional approach. This seems to have been the position of the drafters of the Model Penal Code, which provides:

> The provisions of this Code shall be construed according the the fair import of their terms but when the language is susceptible to differing constructions it shall be interpreted to further the general purposes states in this Section and the special purposes of the particular provisio involved.

Model Penal Code § 1.02(3) (Official Draft 1985). Among the "general purposes of the provisions governing the definition of offenses" are "to give fair warning of the nature of conduct declared to constitute an offense." Id., at § 1.02(1)(d). But the relevant section also emphasizes the purpose "to forbid and prevent conduct that unjustifiably and inexcusably inflicts or threatens substantial harm to individual or public interest." Id., at § 1.02(1)(a). The Explanatory Note indicates that the rule of construction set out in § 1.02(3) is intended to replace the traditional rule that penal statutes are to be strictly construed. Model Penal Code, Explanatory Note to § 1.02, at 4 (Official Draft 1985).

A number of legislatures have adopted provisions along the lines of that in the Model Penal Code. See Cal.Penal Code § 4 ("The rule of the common law, that penal statutes are to be strictly construed, has no application to this Code. All its provisions are to be construed according to the fair import of their terms, with a view to effect its objects and to promote justice."); N.Y.Penal Law § 5.00 (provisions of Penal Law to be interpreted "according to the fair import of their terms to promote justice and effect the objects of the law"); Texas Penal Code § 1.05. What effect should such provisions have? The New York Court of Appeals recently commented:

> [The statutory directive summarized above] obviously does not justify the imposition of criminal sanctions for conduct that falls beyond the scope of the Penal Law, but it does authorize a court to dispense with hypertechnical or strained interpretations of the statute.

People v. Ditta, 52 N.Y.2d 657, 660, 439 N.Y.S.2d 855, 857, 422 N.E.2d 515, 517 (1981).

The ambiguity which triggers judicial invocation of the rule of lenity or strict construction may sometimes be avoided by the tradition of courts to "interpret common law terminology in statutes according to its common law meaning rather than its everyday meaning." W. LaFave and A. Scott, Criminal Law 79 (2nd ed. 1986). For an example of such interpretation, see Morissette v. United States, 342 U.S. 246, 72 S.Ct. 240, 96 L.Ed. 288 (1952), reprinted at page 309, infra. Also, compare Dowling v. United States, 473 U.S. 207, 105 S.Ct. 3127, 87 L.Ed.2d 152 (1985) with Bell v. United States, 462 U.S. 356, 103 S.Ct. 2398, 76 L.Ed.2d 638 (1983).

D. SENTENCING PROVISIONS OF MODERN CRIMINAL CODES

Editors' Note: Sentencing Provisions

There is no doubt that the selection of penalties for offenders is as significant a task as those of formulating and applying the definitions of various crimes and defenses to criminal liability. In most criminal cases, there is no serious doubt as to the provable guilt of the accused and the only "issue" in the case is the penalty to be imposed. Modern criminal codes virtually always establish the basic framework for the disposition of convicted criminals—or sentencing—and these statutory provisions have undergone substantial recent revision. Perhaps the single most significant change is the Sentencing Reform Act of 1984, codified primarily as 18 U.S.C.A. §§ 3551–3580, which dramatically changes the sentencing procedures for federal criminal cases.

The following discussion focuses on punishment for felonies. The traditional distinction recognized in virtually all American jurisdictions is that felony is used to refer to more serious crimes which carry the possibility of a prison term of a year or more, while misdemeanors are those punishable by a year or less in the county jail. Although many more misdemeanors than felonies are committed and punished each year, the latter are more interesting to examine. This is because the longer sentences associated with felonies sharpen the concerns and debates concerning how the length and nature of punishment should be determined and by whom. Also, although many of these same considerations apply to misdemeanor punishment more complex institutions have been developed to deal with felonies; parole, for example, only applies to felony sentences.

Much of the difficulty in developing a satisfactory legal framework for criminal sentencing comes from the difficulty in reconciling two basic approaches to sentencing. One would have the seriousness of the penalty determined exclusively or primarily by how the legislature has categorized the offense committed. The legislature's ordering of offenses reflects a proper judgment as to society's relative need to pursue prevention by imposing severe penalties. To the extent that sentencing should serve retributive functions, the seriousness of the offense provides an objective measure of the seriousness of the offender's violation. Emphasizing the offense avoids the difficult task of attempting to consistently tailor sentences to the circumstances presented by specific offenders. It also minimizes the danger that discretion in sentencing may be employed to the disadvantage of members of disfavored groups.

A second approach, on the other hand, would encourage the individualization of sentences by accommodating particular circumstances of the offense and particular characteristics of the offender. No legislature can, in its definition of crimes and defenses, provide for the extraordinary variety of offenders and the means of commission of crimes. Mitigating considerations that do not, under the law, justify acquittal or even affect the degree of the offense of which the person is guilty might nevertheless be accommodated in determining the severity of the appropriate penalty. Just as criminal guilt should be based only on morally blameworthy behavior, the severity of the penalty should depend upon the blameworthiness of the specific offender. In fact, substantive criminal law doctrines often fail to take into account frequently-existing mitigating considerations on the ground that these considerations are more appropriately used to determine the severity of the penalty. On a somewhat different line, the circumstances of some cases will demonstrate that a severe penalty is not necessary to accomplishing some of the objectives of criminal liability. The circumstances under which some crimes are committed, for example, demonstrate that the offenders do not require prolonged incarceration in order to incapacitate them from further criminal activity, even though others committing the same offense pose sufficient risks to justify long-term incarceration.

Developing a framework for criminal sentencing, then, requires that two basic decisions be made. First, how much leeway should be created for individualizing penalties to fit the facts of particular cases? Second, to the extent that individualization should take place, who should have how much discretion to individualize sentencing? If it is decided to provide for some individualization, the authority to do this must be distributed among the legislature, sentencing judges, and—in some systems—correctional authorities such as parole boards. But the realities of day-to-day criminal justice administration are that prosecutors have substantial power—either directly or indirectly—over the disposition of convicted offenders. Analysis of any sentencing framework, then, must include consideration of the extent to which it permits prosecutors to affect the severity of penalties imposed in particular cases.

Until the late nineteenth century, American jurisdictions tended to follow a definite-sentence system, under which specific terms of imprisonment were specified by the legislature for various offenses. Judges had little or no discretion in determining the length of sentence. See Tappan, Sentencing Under the Model Penal Code, 23 L. & Cont.Prob. 528, 529 (1958). Little effort was made to individualize criminal penalties and legislatures themselves retained the authority to make the basic decisions as to the severity of penalties to be imposed upon conviction of particular crimes. But the subsequent history of criminal sentencing in the United States reflects efforts to make a somewhat more accommodating resolution of the conflicting considerations.

Indeterminate Sentencing Movement

In the late nineteenth century, there was widespread perception that the time a convicted offender spent in incarceration should be related to the offender's conduct during incarceration and to expert assessments concerning when the offender was least likely to commit additional offenses if released. An offender who, by his conduct during imprisonment or otherwise, demonstrated that he was "rehabilitated" should be released sooner than other offenders, even if all had committed the same offense. Moreover, since these considerations were not present at the time of original sentencing, the decision concerning the length of incarceration could not be made at the original sentencing proceeding because it depended upon information which was not then available. This entire approach, of course, was closely tied to acceptance of the notion that the "rehabilitation" of offenders was a realistic goal of imprisonment and that the "corrections" process—including sentencing—should be structured so as to facilitate pursuit of that goal.

The result was the development of parole and, to implement parole, the indeterminate sentence. Administrative authorities, often members of a "parole board," were frequently authorized to release convicted offenders before the expiration of their term. The offenders were released from imprisonment, but were subject to supervision during the remainder of the term and, upon a showing of further misbehavior, to reincarceration to serve the remainder of the term in prison. Since the sentence imposed by the sentencing court did not necessarily determine the length of actual incarceration which would be imposed upon the offender, the period of imprisonment was necessarily rendered some-what "indeterminate" by the availability of parole.

The underlying assumption was that imprisonment could rehabili-tate or change many offenders and that parole authorities could deter-mine whether particular offenders had been sufficiently changed so that they no longer posed a risk to society and therefore could safely be released. The converse was, of course, that parole authorities could also accurately determine when an offender had *not* changed and therefore whose continued imprisonment was necessary for the protec-tion of society. If an offender's release was inevitable (as where the indeterminacy of the sentence was subject to a maximum term at the expiration of which the offender had to be released; see below), the assumption was that parole authorities could identify the point at which the offender posed as low a risk to society as he would ever pose during his sentence. To incarcerate him further, it was assumed, would increase the risk of his reoffending; to release him earlier, on the other hand, would sacrifice the opportunity to achieve maximum change.

Legislative unwillingness to completely trust parole authorities has undoubtedly been a factor in discouraging development of a completely indeterminate sentencing system, in which all offenders would be subject to imprisonment until and unless parole authorities determined that release was appropriate. In many American jurisdictions, the result is legislation that gives a sentencing judge considerable discre-tion to impose a minimum term, before which the offender cannot be paroled, and a maximum term, upon completion of which the offender has to be released regardless of parole authorities' views. Minimums offer some assurance to the public that the convicted offender will pay some price for his violation. Maximums operate to restrain possible cruelty in the exercise of discretion by correctional authorities. They also maintain some order in the legislatively-created hierarchy of crimes by perceived seriousness.

The sentencing judge's discretion, however, is often limited by legislation mandate. Thus a statutory provision might provide that upon conviction of crime X a person is subject to

> a term of imprisonment the minimum of which shall be fixed by the court at not less than one year nor more than five years and the maximum of which shall be fixed by the court at not less than ten nor more than fifty years.

Provisions of this sort reflect a quite complex allocation of responsibili-ty. The legislature, of course, assured that convicted offenders would serve at least one year but not more than fifty years. Sentencing judges can exercise substantial discretion in determining how long an offender must, as matter of certainty, remain incarcerated (by setting the minimum between one and five years) and in determining the time at which the offender must be released (by setting the maximum between ten and fifty years). Within the limits imposed by the sentencing judge, parole authorities have discretion to determine how long specific offenders will in fact remain imprisoned.

Even these provisions are subject to further influences. Since prosecutors have virtually unlimited control over charges to be brought, they can often exercise substantial power over sentencing by choosing among alternative charges. As a matter of informal plea bargaining practice, moreover, prosecutors' recommendations as to how trial judges might exercise their discretion are often influential. In some jurisdictions, prosecutors are authorized—subject to court approval—to enter into enforceable agreements with defendants, pursuant to which a particular sentence is to be imposed in return for the defendant's willingness to plead guilty.

In addition, parole discretion is affected by "good time" credit, awarded to offenders for acceptable behavior during imprisonment. The effect of such good time" varies widely; it may reduce the minimum term (thus permitting but not requiring earlier parole), the maximum (thus requiring earlier release but not affecting parole eligibility) or some combination of these.

Legislative limits on sentencing judges' authority often leaves very broad discretion in the trial judges. Legislation was often framed with the "worst cases" in mind. Dawson, Book Review, 88 Yale L.J. 440, 442 (1978). Thus the legislative maximum was often set sufficiently high so that trial judges could impose a sufficiently severe sentence upon the worst possible person who might be convicted of the crime involved.

Additional flexibility is also created by the availability of probation. Probation differs from parole in that probation is supervised liberty in the community without preliminary service of a prison sentence. Authority to impose probation is often somewhat limited; statutes frequently make probation unavailable upon conviction for certain serious offenses such as the highest degree of criminal homicide, rape or sexual assault, and sometimes other offenses as well. W. LaFave and J. Israel, Criminal Procedure 942 (1985). Trial judges nevertheless have very broad discretion as to whether to eschew any prison sentence and instead impose a period of probation. In many cases, then, the discretionary decision as to the length of a period of imprisonment need be made only after the sentencing judge has made the preliminary and similarly discretionary decision as to whether or not to impose a sentence of incarceration.

Sentencing schemes are further complicated by the inclusion of provisions for what are sometimes called "extended terms." One common type of statute provides that upon proof that an offender to be sentenced had been convicted of prior offenses, the trial court is authorized to impose a more severe penalty. The increased severity may differ depending upon how many prior convictions are shown. For obvious reasons, these are often called "habitual offender" statutes. Other provisions for extended terms in unusual cases were sometimes made. In some jurisdictions, for example, so-called "sex psychopath" provisions authorized inquiry into whether certain convicted offenders were mentally abnormal and, if so, dangerous; upon a determination that offenders were abnormal and dangerous, extended terms are authorized, sometimes in psychiatric facilities rather than correctional institutions. The sex psychopath provisions have largely been abandoned, Dix, Special Dispositional Alternatives for Abnormal Offenders: Developments in the Law, in Mentally Disordered Offenders (J. Monahan & H. Steadman eds. 1983), but the habitual criminal provisions remain part of many modern sentencing frameworks. Constitutional problems posed by these provisions are explored at pages 125–36, infra.

The Model Penal Code proposed a sentencing framework that embodied the limited indeterminate sentencing approach. See Model Penal Code § 6.06 (P.O.D. 1962). Its formulation, however, would give sentencing judges discretion with regard to the minimum term only; the maximum would be automatically fixed by statute. Thus a person convicted of a second degree felony would have to receive a maximum term of ten years but the trial judge could set the minimum at any period not less than one year nor more than three years. Id., at § 6.06(2). This gave the court an important role in sentencing by permitting it to greatly affect the offender's eligibility for parole. But it limited the discretion of both the court and the parole authorities by providing for a legislatively fixed maximum. It also assured that there would be a substantial difference between the minimum and maximum terms, thus assuring that parole authorities would have a substantial opportunity for the exercise of their discretion.

Despite the superficial simplicity of the concept of "indeterminate" sentencing, statutory frameworks for such sentencing tended to become quite complex. Generally speaking, however, they provided for allocation of authority to make quite discretionary decisions concerning the length of incarceration. Parole authorities acted within limits set by sentencing judges. Sentencing judges acted within limits set by the legislature. But nevertheless the amount of time particular offenders actually spent in prison was greatly affected by essentially discretionary decisions made by both sentencing judges and parole authorities.

Release of offenders on parole, to some extent, disturbed those who sought severe punishment as a means of crime control. But to a great extent, the indeterminate sentencing approach and its reliance upon rehabilitation avoided some hard choices. The need for parole authorities to have substantial discretion argued for long sentences. This suggested that objectives other than rehabilitation might be pursued without interfering with the presumed rehabilitative aspect of imprisonment. Imposition of long sentences could be viewed as sufficient to provide deterrence to others, an opportunity to incapacitate the particular offender, and to uphold the moral integrity of the law. Rehabilitation could occur during the implementation of a long sentence of imprisonment that also served other purposes. Cf. Rothman, Sentencing Reforms in Historical Perspective, 29 Crime & Delinquency 631, 635 (1983).

The Movement for Sentencing Reform

In the 1960's, substantial dissatisfaction arose with the indeterminate sentencing systems. Empirical evidence demonstrated inconsistencies in sentencing practices and results that were difficult or impossible to justify as legitimate "individualization" of sentences. See, e.g., S. Frankel, The Sentencing Morass and a Suggestion for Reform, 3 Crim.L.Bull. 365 (1967). The difficulties encountered by a conscientious federal district judge in attempting to live up to the expectations of individualized sentencing were graphically presented in Judge Marvin Frankel's book, *Criminal Sentences: Law Without Order* (1972). As a result, there developed a widespread perception that sentencing judges and parole authorities exercised their substantial discretion in an arbitrary manner, with the result that no reasonable basis existed for the differences in the periods of incarceration which particular offenders were required to serve. Among the published works influential in the reform movement were the 1971 report prepared for the American Friends Service Committee, *Struggle for Justice: A Report on Crime and Punishment in America,* and two later reports, Committee for the Study of Incarceration (A. von Hirsch) *Doing Justice: The Choice of Punishments* (1976) and Twentieth Century Fund Task Force on Criminal Sentencing, *Fair and Certain Punishment* (1976).

To a large extent, this dissatisfaction with indeterminate sentencing was based upon increasing suspicion that some or all of the assumptions of individualized and indeterminate sentencing were simply incorrect. Sentencing situations may present such a variety of situations that no way exists to consistently give effect in sentencing to individual variations in blameworthiness or future dangerousness. Imprisonment may not actually rehabilitate offenders. Or, if offenders do change during (and perhaps because of) imprisonment, parole authorities may be unable to identify when any particular offender has been sufficiently changed so that his release poses minimum threats of future criminal conduct by the offender. Moreover, there was some concern that parole might be withheld because of an inmate's independent spirit, or political views or other factors not shown to correlate with recidivism. In addition, from more conservative quarters, there was undoubtedly some concern that individualization too often meant only reduction of sentences and that parole release was too freely granted. Consequently, the individualized and indeterminate features of criminal sentencing provided insufficient assurance that society's interests would be pursued.

Since rehabilitative considerations and the blameworthiness of particular offenders could not serve as a basis for determining penalty severity, many reformers urged, attention should be turned to the seriousness of the offense of which the defendant was convicted. Reliance upon the offense in determining the severity of penalty, it was urged, would provide a relatively objective criterion for determining sentence length that would reduce or eliminate the unjustified disparities that resulted from traditional indeterminate sentencing. Moreover, such a criterion would serve appropriate goals. Generally speaking, retributive notions suggested that the more serious the offense, the more severe the penalty that should be imposed. Deterrence and preventive considerations similarly suggested that as the seriousness of the offense increased, social objectives required a more severe penalty to discourage future offenses of this sort and to incapacitate the offender from committing future offenses of this sort in the future.

The sentencing reform movement resulted in a variety of changes in many jurisdictions. Several different aspects of the changes can usefully be distinguished, although it is necessary to keep in mind that some reforms incorporated more than one.

Recent Reform: "Determinate" Sentencing

In response to the concerns outlined above, a number of jurisdictions—beginning with Maine in 1976, closely followed by California—adopted so-called "determinate" sentencing schemes. Under these provisions, discretionary parole is abolished. The sentence imposed by the trial judge is "determinate" in the sense that it determines when the offender will be released from incarceration.

The federal Sentencing Reform Act of 1984 incorporates a determinate feature. A convicted offender sentenced to imprisonment is to be released upon the expiration of his sentence less any time credited to him for "satisfactory behavior." 18 U.S.C.A. § 3624(a). At the time of sentencing, however, the trial court may impose both a sentence of imprisonment and a term of "supervised release" to begin upon the offender's release from incarceration. Id., at § 3583. The offender can be required to observe certain specified conditions during the period of supervised release. This is, in some ways, much like traditional parole. Unlike traditional parole, however, this feature does not affect the timing of the offender's release from imprisonment. Nor does a violation of the conditions of the supervised release subject the offender to a requirement that some "remainder" of his sentence be served in prison. But an offender on supervised release who violates the terms of that release can be found in contempt of the trial court. Id., at 3583(e)(3). Other jurisdictions also retain this form of "parole." See Cal.Penal Code § 3000(a) (all offenders released from imprisonment to have period of parole not to exceed three years, unless this is waived by board).

Adoption of determinate features of sentencing obviously responds only to the concerns regarding the exercise of discretion by parole authorities. Trial judges may still, of course, have and exercise substantial discretion in selecting an appropriate length for particular determinate sentences. Nor do determinate features of the sentencing framework affect the ability of prosecutors to influence sentencing by choice of charge and behavior during plea bargaining. The problems posed by multiple charges, convictions, and punishments for related activity are also left largely untouched by these reforms; these problems are considered in Section D of Chapter V of this book at pages 242–62, infra.

Recent Reform: "Presumptive" Sentencing

A number of recent reforms in sentencing frameworks have incorporated what is sometimes called a "presumptive" approach. Under this approach, a specific sentence is specified and the legislative intent is that it be applied as a general rule. Trial judges are, it might be said, directed by the legislature to "presume" that this sentence is appropriate. But trial judges are authorized to impose a more severe penalty or a more lenient one if the facts of a specific case are shown to justify this.

The California scheme provides a useful illustration. Penalty provisions generally specify three periods. Robbery, for example, is punishable by two, three or five years imprisonment. Cal.Penal Code § 213. A sentencing court is directed to impose the middle term, unless circumstances in aggravation justify the higher term or circumstances in mitigation justify the lower term. If the middle term is not imposed, the trial judge is to set forth on the record the facts and reasons for imposing the upper or lower term. Id., at § 1170(b). Some jurisdictions specifically list possible aggravating or mitigating considerations that might justify deviation from the "presumptively" appropriate sentence. E.g., Ind.Code Ann. § 35–38–1–7.

These presumptive features of some sentencing frameworks are obviously aimed at limiting and controlling the exercise of sentencing discretion by judges. To some extent, they reduce the discretion available to the judge. Insofar as discretion remains, however, the schemes attempt to structure the exercise of that discretion and to provide some mechanism for review. The record which a trial judge must make under the California scheme, for example, permits appellate review of the trial judge's decision to deviate from the middle term. Underlying this, of course, is the hope that the discretion will be exercised more carefully and with more consistent results. Obviously, it also creates one more point for review on appeal.

Recent Reform: "Guideline" Sentencing

Another approach to modifying the traditionally unlimited sentencing discretion of judges under frameworks where such discretion is retained is the development of sentencing "guidelines." These guidelines are to be used by judges both to determine whether to impose a sentence of imprisonment and to determine the length of the sentence of either imprisonment or probation. See P. O'Donnell, M. Churgin, and D. Curtis, Towards a Just and Efficient Sentencing System: Agenda for Legislative Reform (1971).

This is the approach taken in the federal Sentencing Reform Act of 1984. This legislation created the United States Sentencing Commission, and gave the Commission the task of promulgating guidelines to be used by federal courts in determining the sentences to be imposed in criminal cases, 28 U.S.C.A. § 994(a)(1). Categories of offenses and defendants are to be developed. For each category a range of offenses is to be specified; this range is to be such that the maximum does not exceed the minimum by more than 25 per cent. Sentencing judges are to impose sentences within the guidelines "unless the court finds that an aggravating or mitigating circumstance exists what was not adequately taken into consideration by the Sentencing Commission in formulating the guidelines and that should result in a sentence different from that described. If a sentence is outside the guidelines, the court is to state the specific reason for deviating from the guidelines." Id., at § 3553. Either side may appeal a sentence and obtain appellate review of—among other issues—a judge's decision to impose a sentence deviating from the guidelines. Id., at § 3742.

Other jurisdictions have taken a similar approach. The Minnesota agency has developed a grid containing various sentences to be determined by the seriousness of the offense and the defendant's "criminal history score." The score is determined by the defendant's criminal history, including felony convictions, misdemeanor convictions, and juvenile offenses committed after the offender's sixteenth birthday. See Minn.Stat.Ann. § 244.09.

The guideline approach, like presumptive sentences, is aimed at trial court discretion. Unlike the presumptive sentencing approach, guideline systems tend to confer authority on a nonlegislative body to develop the "substantive" rules which trial judges will be encouraged to follow. This may permit the development of more elaborate rules than could be developed in the legislative forum. Is it possible, however, that the rules' nonlegislative origin may reduce the willingness of trial judges to follow them?

Impact of the Reforms

Despite reforms, some of the traditional characteristics of sentencing frameworks have often been retained. Provisions for extending the terms of "habitual" offenders, for example, remain available in many jurisdictions. Efforts to address the discretionary decision as to the length of prison terms assessed convicted offenders sometimes do not address the preliminary decision as to whether to impose any prison sentence at all. Imprisoned offenders' release dates are often still affected by "good time" earned during incarceration. Nevertheless, the reforms often constitute a major change in the legal framework for penalizing convicted criminal defendants.

Whether the sentencing reforms have or will live up to expectations is and will be difficult to determine because of the varying expectations held. There was widespread agreement—or hope—that the reforms would increase uniformity, that is, that offenders convicted of the same offense would spend more closely equal times in imprisonment. But beyond this expectations varied.

The law enforcement community supported the California reforms on the general ground that it constituted an implicit legislative directive to toughen sentencing policies and on the specific ground that short and predictable sentences would encourage judges to send marginal offenders to prison and thus increase the courts' use of imprisonment. Casper, Brereton and Neal, The California Determinate Sentence Law, 19 Crim.L.Bull. 405, 415 (1983). Will the reforms have any effect upon the time convicted offenders spend in prison? The effect of a presumptive feature on time spent in incarceration might well turn on the sentence terms designated as the presumptively applicable ones. In some jurisdictions, the legislatures chose sentence times that were longer than terms generally served under pre-reform law, so that the reforms were expected by some to increase the amount of time served by convicted offenders sentenced to imprisonment. Rothman, supra, at 643.

How much and in what ways will reforms affect which offenders are imprisoned and for how long? A recent study by researchers of the Rand Corporation suggested that the use of sentencing guidelines may increase the likelihood that blacks and other minorities will receive prison sentences rather than probation and, when prison sentences are received, will be given more severe sentences than whites. Sentencing guidelines, the study explained, rely heavily upon such criteria as the offender's juvenile and criminal record, whether the offender was on probation or parole at the time of the offense, and whether the offense involved violence. These criteria sometimes correlate positively with race. J. Petersilia and S. Turner, Guideline-Based Justice: The Implications for Racial Minorities (Rand Corp.1985).

E.   SUBSTANTIVE CRIMINAL LAW ISSUES IN THEIR PROCEDURAL CONTEXT

Editors' Note: The Procedural Context

The material in this casebook consists largely of appellate judicial decisions in criminal litigation. Perhaps unfortunately, the appellate courts seldom address directly many of the substantive criminal law issues with which the casebook is concerned. Because of the division of functions between trial and appellate courts, in other words, appellate tribunals are seldom called upon to determine whether, on particular facts, a criminal accused is or is not guilty of a particular crime. Since substantive criminal law issues arise in a complex procedural context, some preliminary understanding of this procedural context may be useful in reading and evaluating the decisions reprinted in this case-book.

Substantive criminal law issues may arise in trial litigation in a number of ways. Usually the issues will find their way to an appellate court only if the defendant is convicted and appeals from that conviction. But in other situations, the issue may get to the appellate tribunal in other ways.

Matters in Issue and "Burdens"

What matters are in issue in any criminal trial is determined by interaction among the applicable substantive criminal law, the pleadings of the parties, and the evidence introduced by the parties. It is universally agreed in the United States that in a criminal trial, the prosecution bears the extraordinarily high burden of proof beyond a reasonable doubt. But it is not always clear what this means.

It is necessary as preliminary matter to distinguish several different trial burdens which might be placed upon the prosecution. One the burden of persuasion. This, of course, is the duty to convince the trier of fact of the matter at issue. A second is the burden of proceeding or coming forward with—or production of—evidence. This is, in effect, the duty to produce a certain amount of evidence on a matter in order to make that matter an issue in the case. A third is the burden of pleading. This is the duty to address a matter in the pleadings.

Pleading matters will be discussed below and the burdens of persuasion and coming forward with evidence will also be developed. At this point, however, these matters can be distinguished by considering the following District of Columbia abortion statute at issue in United States v. Vuitch, 402 U.S. 62, 91 S.Ct. 1294, 28 L.Ed.2d 601 (1971):

> Whoever, by means of any instrument, medicine, drug or other means whatever, procures or produces, or attempts to procure or produce an abortion or miscarriage on any woman, unless the same were done as necessary for the preservation of the mother's life or health and under the direction of a competent licensed practioner of medicine, shall be imprisoned in the penitentiary not less than one year or not more than ten years * * *

D.C.Code Ann. § 22–201. This criminalized conduct which is now constitutionally protected under the Supreme Court's more recent case law restricting on federal constitutional grounds the extent to which abortions may be prohibited; see Roe v. Wade, 410 U.S. 113, 93 S.Ct. 705, 35 L.Ed.2d 147 (1973); Doe v. Bolton, 410 U.S. 179, 93 S.Ct. 739, 35 L.Ed.2d 201 (1973). But the statute and its application in *Vuitch* are useful illustrations of certain substantive and procedural law issues.

It is clear from the terms of the statute that under the substantive criminal law, the necessity of an abortion to preserve the woman's life or health *might* be issue in a prosecution under the statute. If it is an issue, this will require that evidence on the matter be introduced by someone and will require that the trier of fact address the matter. What must be done to make what can be called "medical necessity" an issue in a particular prosecution?

It might be regarded as in issue in all prosecutions under the statute. The prosecution might be required to plead in each case that no medical necessity existed. This would, in effect, make the lack of medical necessity an element of the offense which the prosecution must allege and prove in each case. Or, it might be regarded as in issue only if the defense raised it by an appropriate pleading. The defense, for example, might be required to file some sort of responsive pleading alleging that the abortion alleged in the prosecution's charging instrument was medically necessary within the meaning of the statute. Or, the matter might be regarded in issue only if the defense, during trial, produced some evidence indicating that the particular abortion at issue was medically necessary.

Once it is determined that medical necessity is an issue in the case, it is then necessary to determine who has the burden of persuasion on that matter. It could, of course, be regarded—once raised—as part of the prosecution's case and thus the prosecution might be required to prove the lack of medical necessity by its usual burden, beyond a reasonable doubt. Or, it could be regarded as a matter that the defense must establish. If, therefore, the prosecution proves that an abortion was produced or procured by the defendant, this could be regarded as justifying conviction *unless* the defendant established that this abortion was medically necessary within the meaning of the statute. If the latter course was chosen, the defense's burden might be the usual "civil" burden of a preponderance of the evidence, it might be the prosecution's criminal burden of proof beyond a reasonable doubt, or some intermediate standard, such as proof by "clear and convincing" evidence.

Pleading Sufficiency

The basic pleading in a criminal case is the formal charge against the defendant; this is usually an indictment returned by a grand jury or an information filed by the prosecutor. There is substantial variation among jurisdictions as to how detailed and specific a criminal pleading must be. In many jurisdictions, however, it is necessary for the indictment or information to allege sufficient facts so that those facts, if proved, will establish the defendant's guilt. Rule 7(c)(1) of the Federal Rules of Criminal Procedure, for example, provides: "The indictment or information shall be a plain, concise, and definite written statement of the essential facts constituting the offense charged." Often the requirement is met by simply using the language of the statute creating the crime with specific references for such details as the name of the victim. See W. LaFave and J. Israel, Criminal Procedure 714 (1985). But the general rule is that if, at trial, the prosecution has to prove a fact to secure the defendant's conviction, that fact must—in a general way, at least—be pleaded in the indictment or information.

If an indictment or information does not allege sufficient facts, it must—upon motion of the defense—be dismissed as failing to charge an offense.

If the defense moves before trial to dismiss a charging instrument on these grounds, the motion to dismiss may raise issues of substantive criminal law. Whether particular facts need to be alleged obviously turns upon the substantive criminal law defining the crime which is charged. In deciding whether to dismiss an indictment, then, a trial judge must often identify the elements of the crime charged and determine whether the indictment alleges facts constituting all such elements. Dismissal before trial because of insufficiency of the charge does not preclude the prosecution from seeking a new indictment or filing a new information. This is because the defendant is not regarded as having been placed in jeopardy so as to have the Double Jeopardy Clause of the Constitution apply and bar a new prosecution.

If a defense motion to dismiss is overruled, no appeal may ordinarily be taken unless and until the defendant is ultimately convicted. On an appeal from a conviction, the trial court's improper failure to dismiss the indictment may constitute reversible error. But if the motion to dismiss is granted and the indictment dismissed, the prosecution is sometimes authorized to appeal from the order dismissing the charge.

Generally, no specific pleading is required of a criminal defendant. At the arraignment, the defendant is asked for a plea. But if the defendant refuses to plead, a plea of not guilty is entered for him. There are some exceptions. A few jurisdictions demand that the defense disclose before trial the general nature of any defenses it will raise at trial. W. LaFave and J. Israel, Criminal Procedure 747 (1985). And in most jurisdictions, a defendant who intends to raise the defense of insanity (see pages 786–821, infra) must provide the prosecution with pretrial notice of this. Sometimes this requirement also requires the defense to give pretrial notice of an intention to introduce at trial expert testimony that because of mental impairment the defendant did not have the criminal intent required by the crime charged. Id., at 745–46.

Some of the facts of United States v. Vuitch, supra, can be used to illustrate how substantive criminal law issues can arise in the context of criminal pleadings. Vuitch was charged with a violation of the District of Columbia abortion statute by means of an indictment along the following lines:

UNITED STATES DISTRICT COURT
FOR THE DISTRICT OF COLUMBIA

Criminal No. 1043-68

Violation: D.C. Code 201
(Abortion)

The United States of American
v.
Milan Vuitch

The Grand Jury Charges:

On or about February 1, 1968, within the District of
Columbia, Milan Vuitch, by means of instruments, medicines,
drugs and substances, a more particular description of which is
unknown to the Grand Jury, did procure and produce an abortion
and miscarriage of Inez M. Fradin, she being then and there
pregnant.

Mary Smith
Attorney of the United States
in and for the District of
Columbia

A TRUE BILL: ___*Lany Jones*___
Foreman

Although the major issues in *Vuitch* did not involve pleading or
proof, the defense could reasonably have moved to dismiss the indictment on the ground that the Government failed to allege that the
abortion and miscarriage was not "done as necessary for the preservation of the mother's life or health and under the direction of a
competent licensed practitioner of medicine." This, of course, would
have raised the question of whether the inapplicability of the statutory
exception is an element of the offense which the prosecution must
allege. It is widely agreed that "defenses" created by case law or
statutes other than those defining the charged crime need not be
negated in criminal pleadings. Thus the existence of an insanity
defense does not require that in each indictment the prosecution allege
that that the defendant was not insane. But where there is an
exception to liability created by the statute defining the crime, there is
less agreement.

The matter is, in the first instance at least, one of construing legislative intent. In *Vuitch*, the Supreme Court indicated that a reasonable construction of the statute placed upon the Government the obligations both to negate in its charge applicability of the statutory exception and to prove at trial that the exception did not apply. First, the Court emphasized the location of the statutory language creating the exception:

> It is a general guide to the interpretation of criminal statutes that when an exception is incorporated in the enacting clause of a statute, the burden is on the prosecution to plead and prove that the defendant is not within the exception.

402 U.S. at 70, 91 S.Ct. at 1298, 28 L.Ed.2d at 608. Turning to other indicators of legislative intent, the Court noted that the statute creating the offense enlarged the situations in which abortions could be caused without creating criminal liability:

> It would be highly anomalous for a legislature to authorize abortions necessary for life or health and then to demand that a doctor, upon pain of one to ten years' imprisonment, bear the burden of proving that an abortion he performed fell within that category. Placing such a burden of proof on a doctor would be peculiarly inconsistent with society's notions of the responsibilities of the medical profession. Generally, doctors are encouraged by society's expectations, by the strictures of malpractice law and by their own professional standards to give their patients such treatment as is necessary to preserve their health. We are unable to believe that Congress intended that a physician be required to prove his innocence.

402 U.S. at 70–71, 91 S.Ct. at 1298–99, 28 L.Ed.2d at 608–09. Allocation of the burden of persuasion, at least, has significant federal constitutional ramifications. These are discussed in the next section of the present Chapter.

Another issue might have been raised in *Vuitch* by a defense attack upon the indictment. The statute itself contains no *mens rea* or intent element. Despite this, however, judicial construction of the statute may nevertheless impose a requirement of mens rea; see generally Chapter VI, infra. If intent must be proved in order to convict a defendant under the statute, it is arguable that this intent must be pleaded in the indictment. See W. LaFave & J. Israel, Criminal Procedure 714 (1985). The defense, then, might have moved to dismiss the indictment on the ground that the crime charged requires criminal intent and since this is not alleged in the indictment the indictment fails to allege all elements of the crime. In order to rule on this motion, the trial court would have to address and resolve the substantive criminal law question as to what criminal intent, if any, is required by the District's abortion statute.

In *Vuitch*, the actual issue before the Supreme Court was whether the abortion statute was unconstitutionally vague; see Section A of Chapter III, infra. This had been raised by a defense motion to dismiss the indictment, which claimed that the statute was unconstitutionally vague and therefore unenforceable and consequently that no prosecution could be brought under it. The trial judge dismissed the indictment on this ground and the Government appealed. As *Vuitch* itself indicates, pretrial attacks upon the validity of the statute defining the crime may require both the trial court and appellate tribunals to address, before trial, the issues raised in these materials.

Admissibility of Evidence

During trial, objections may be made to the admissibility of evidence offered by either side. Resolving objections to evidence may require addressing issues of substantive criminal law. If a conviction is appealed, the defendant may offer errors in the admissibility of evidence as grounds for reversing the conviction.

Suppose, for example, that a defendant charged with murder seeks to establish the defense of insanity. In support of this defense, he offers the testimony of a psychiatrist. If permitted to testify, the psychiatrist will say that at the time the defendant killed the victim, the defendant was mentally ill and, because of that illness, he was unable to control his behavior. Suppose further that the prosecution objects to this evidence. As a general matter, evidence is admissible only if it is relevant to some issue in the case. The evidence here is relevant only to the defendant's ability to exercise conscious control over his behavior at the time of the crime. Whether his ability to control his behavior is a possible issue in the case depends in part upon the substantive law defining the crime charged and defenses to that crime.

In this example, the trial judge must, in ruling on the objection to the testimony of the psychiatrist, determine the criterion for insanity in the jurisdiction. If insanity is defined so as to make it a defense that the defendant was unable to control his conduct, the offered evidence is relevant to insanity and probably admissible. If, on the other hand, insanity is defined so that a defense is established only if the defendant proves that he was unable to "understand" that his conduct was contrary to the law, the offered testimony may not be relevant. It may not, in other words, tend to show insanity as the law defines it. It is important to note that in ruling on the evidence objection, the trial judge must make a substantive criminal law determination—what is "insanity" for purposes of the insanity defense.

If the trial judge excludes the evidence, the defendant is convicted, and an appeal is taken, the defendant may seek reversal of the conviction on the ground that the psychiatrist's testimony was erroneously excluded at trial. To determine whether the trial court's action was error, the appellate court must resolve the substantive criminal law issue of the content of the insanity defense.

Evidential Sufficiency

In a trial, of course, the ultimate question is the sufficiency of the evidence to prove the defendant guilty. If trial is to a jury, this is—generally speaking—a matter for the jury to determine. Even in a jury trial, however, the sufficiency of the evidence may be subjected to a preliminary test before the jury has an opportunity to evaluate it. The defense may move for a directed verdict of acquittal. If this motion is granted, the court's action has the effect of taking the case from the jury and acquitting the defendant without the need for jury consideration. Principles of double jeopardy and defendants' right to trial by jury mean that the acquittal is final; the prosecution cannot appeal and cannot try the defendant again for the offense. Because the prosecution has no recourse from a directed verdict and since guilt-or-innocence is generally to be determined by a jury, it is clear that trial judges are to be quite reluctant to grant defense motions for directed verdicts.

A defendant's right to jury trial means that a defendant has a complete right to have a jury decide guilt or innocence. This right exists no matter how conclusive the prosecution's evidence. Therefore, the trial judge cannot grant a prosecution's motion for a directed verdict of guilty.

In determining evidential sufficiency, federal constitutional considerations as well as local law in all American jurisdictions require that the prosecution establish the defendant's guilt by proof that reaches the extraordinarily high level of "proof beyond a reasonable doubt." Generally, this means that each element of the charged offense must be identified and the prosecution must prove each element beyond a reasonable doubt.

But as a criminal trial develops, issues may arise concerning matters other than proof of the elements of the charged offense. Allocating the burden of proof concerning these matters is a complex task. The next section of this Chapter presents the case law creating federal constitutional limitations upon the extent to which the prosecution can be relieved of the burden of proving by its usual high burden its position on all issues controlling the fact or degree of guilt or the severity of punishment. Basically, there are two major positions that are taken concerning the burden of proof on issues other than the elements of the charged offense.

One position is that the defendant bears the burden of proof. In the murder situation discussed earlier, for example, it is clear that the prosecution must prove that the defendant caused the victim's death and the defendant did so with the state of mind required for murder. These matters are all elements of the crime of murder. But the defendant's claim of insanity may be viewed as imposing upon the defense the burden of proving that the defendant was insane within the meaning given that term by the criminal law. Of course, the jury should not reach the question of whether the defendant has met this burden unless it first finds the state has proven, beyond a reasonable doubt, all elements of the offense charged. If it finds the state has met its burden, however, it might appropriately convict the defendant unless it finds the defense has proven the "elements" of a "defense" of insanity.

The major alternative approach would distinguish between assignment of the burden of "production," on the one hand, and the burden of "persuasion," on the other. The defendant may, under this approach, have the burden of raising an issue by producing a certain amount of evidence bearing upon that issue. But when the defendant does this and the issue is "raised," the prosecution then has the burden of persuasion.

Under this approach, no issue of insanity would be regarded as present unless the defendant produced a certain—usually a rather small—amount of evidence suggesting that he was insane. Producing this evidence would have the effect of raising the issue. Once it is raised, the burden of persuasion is on the prosecution. Thus, once the issue of insanity is raised by defense evidence, the prosecution must negate it by proof beyond a reasonable doubt. It must, in other words, prove beyond a reasonable doubt that the defendant was sane at the time of the offense. But this burden does not arise *until and unless* the defendant meets the burden of production on that issue.

Under this second approach, the following issues are presented: Did the state prove the elements of murder beyond a reasonable doubt? If so, did the defendant produce sufficient evidence to raise the issue of insanity? If so, did the prosecution produce sufficient evidence on the issue of insanity, i.e., did it produce evidence showing beyond a reasonable doubt that the defendant was not insane?

Terminology differs among jurisdictions. But a common pattern is to characterize some matters as "affirmative defenses." These are matters on which the defense has the burden of persuasion. Other matters are characterized as simply "defenses." These tend to be matters on which the prosecution has the burden of persuasion *if* the defendant raises the matter by sufficient evidence.

These matters are closely tied to the question of whether the trial judge was obligated to instruct the jury on matters other than the elements of the charged offense. This is considered below.

Jury Instructions

In a criminal case tried to a jury, it is, as a general rule, necessary to adequately instruct the jury on all issues raised by the charge against the defendant and the evidence introduced at trial. This involves two significantly different although interrelated questions: When must the jury be instructed on an issue? What is necessary for instructions on an issue to be sufficient?

On the first question, it is clear that the jury must always be informed with regard to the elements of the crime charged and told that the prosecution must prove each element beyond a reasonable doubt. Upon proper request, the jury must be similarly instructed concerning any other offense of which the defendant might be convicted. Generally speaking, of course, a defendant can be convicted only of that offense (or those offenses) charged in the indictment. A defendant charged with burglary, for example, cannot at trial be convicted of robbery, even if the prosecution's evidence undeniably shows the defendant guilty of robbery rather than burglary.

There is an important "exception," however. A defendant may be convicted of offenses other than those charged in the indictment if those offenses are "lesser included offenses" of an offense charged. An offense is a lesser included offense of a charged offense if it is established by some of the same but less than all of the evidence necessary to prove the charged, "greater," offense. The "lesser" offense, in other words, must require for its proof no evidence not required for proof of the "greater."

Suppose, for example, a defendant is charged with the felony of burglary. In the jurisdiction, burglary is defined as an entry into another's dwelling with the intent therein to commit a felony, where the entry is made without the other person's effective consent. The jurisdiction also prohibits as a misdemeanor what is labeled "criminal trespass." This is defined as entry onto the property of another without effective consent. It is quite likely that criminal trespass is a lesser included offense of burglary. Burglary requires proof of everything that is required for criminal trespass, plus something further: that at the time of the entry, the accused had the intent to commit a felony. Or, to put the matter another way, criminal trespass is established by proof of some but not all of the facts necessary to show burglary, and no other facts.

Again speaking generally, a defendant charged with and tried for burglary will be entitled to have the jury instructed on criminal trespass if it is clear that criminal trespass is a lesser included offense of burglary *and* there is some basis in the proof at trial for the jury to conclude that he is guilty of only criminal trespass. If, for example, there is some evidence that the defendant did enter the premises without consent but at the time lacked the intent to commit a felony, then the jury should be instructed on criminal trespass as well as the charged offense of burglary.

If the jury is "charged on" criminal trespass, the instructions should tell the jury the elements of both it and burglary. They should further tell the jury to first consider whether the prosecution has proved beyond a reasonable doubt the defendant's guilt of the charged offense of burglary. But, the instructions should make clear, if the jury concludes the prosecution has not met its burden on the charged offense, the jury should then consider whether the prosecution has proved beyond a reasonable doubt all elements of criminal trespass. If the jury concludes that the prosecution has done so, the instructions should make clear, the defendant should be convicted of criminal trespass but not burglary.

Of course, the prosecution may seek, and the defendant may resist, having the jury instructed on a lesser included offense. See, for example, State v. Carson, 292 Or. 451, 640 P.2d 586 (1982), in which Carson had been charged with attempted murder and convicted of attempted voluntary manslaughter. On appeal, he urged that the evidence was insufficient to support a verdict of attempted voluntary manslaughter and therefore the judge erred in submitting that possibility to the jury. Carson, in other words, argued that he was entitled to have the jury given an all-or-nothing choice—either he was guilty of attempted murder as charged or he was not guilty of any criminal offense related to the homicide. In such a situation, the standard is generally the same. The prosecution is entitled to an instruction on a lesser included offense if, but only if, the evidence provides a basis for the jury to conclude that the defendant is not guilty of the charged offense but is guilty of the lesser included offense.

As the discussion above made clear, criminal litigation often presents more complicated questions as to whether or not a jury should be "instructed on" defensive "issues." If evidence introduced by the defense merely casts doubt upon the sufficiency of the prosecution's evidence to show one or more elements of the crimes at issue, ordinarily no specific instruction is necessary. Suppose, for example, a defendant is charged with rape, which is defined as sexual intercourse by a man with a woman without the woman's effective consent. At trial, the defense introduces medical testimony that the defendant was, at the time of the alleged offense, impotent. Is the defendant entitled to have the jury instructed specifically on the "issue" of impotency? Probably not. The defense evidence challenges the sufficiency of the prosecution's evidence to establish one element of the offense—the act of sexual intercourse. If the defendant was impotent and therefore incapable of the act, it necessarily follows that he did not engage in intercourse. If the evidence shows the defendant did not engage in intercourse, it also shows he did not commit rape as defined. Generally speaking, it is assumed in criminal litigation that this is made sufficiently clear to the jury by instructions that convey to the jurors that the prosecution must prove beyond a reasonable doubt all elements of the offense, including that element consisting of an act of intercourse.

But other "issues" in criminal litigation consist of matters that go beyond challenging the prosecution's proof of all elements of the crime. Whether or not the jury must be instructed concerning these presents more difficult issues. Suppose in the rape prosecution above the defense also introduces evidence—consisting of testimony by the defendant's brother—that the defendant was crazy and that this may have affected his ability to refrain from engaging in intercourse with the victim. In the jurisdiction, there is a "defense" of insanity and insanity is defined as mental abnormality that renders a person unable to control his actions. As a general matter, it should be clear that insanity is not a matter that challenges the sufficiency of the prosecution's evidence concerning the elements of the crime. The accused's ability to control his conduct is not something the prosecution must prove in each case and, generally speaking, juries are not told in rape prosecutions that the prosecution must prove beyond a reasonable doubt that the defendant was able to, but chose not to, avoid raping the victim. If insanity exists, it consists of additional evidence (that is, evidence not tending to prove or disprove any element of the crime) that is given the effect of requiring acquittal *despite* the sufficiency of the evidence to prove, beyond a reasonable doubt, each element of the crime.

If the jury is "instructed on" insanity, it will usually be told that insanity is a defense and that insanity consists of a condition in which the defendant is, because of mental illness, unable to control his action. The instructions should tell the jury that it should consider insanity only if it first finds that the prosecution has proven each element of the charged offense—rape—beyond a reasonable doubt. If the jury finds the evidence sufficient on these matters, it should then but only then consider insanity. If it finds the defendant insane, the instruction should make clear, the jury is to acquit the defendant despite its earlier conclusion that the prosecution's evidence sufficiently established each element of the offense.

Generally speaking, a jury needs to be instructed on defensive issues such as insanity only if they are "raised by the evidence." And the instructions should make clear to the jury who has the burden of proof or "persuasion" on the defensive issue and what that burden is. Normally, a defensive issue is raised only if some evidence has been introduced from which the jury might find that the "defense" has been established. In the rape example discussed above, whether the defense of insanity has been so "raised" is arguable. The defense introduced no expert testimony. Whether "lay" testimony that the defendant was sufficiently crazy to be "insane" in the legal sense is sufficient to "raise" the issue of insanity and thus to require a jury instruction is a matter of legitimate debate.

As a general matter, a defensive matter is "raised" if some evidence has been introduced which, if believed, would mean that a defense exists. If, for example, the defendant takes the witness stand and testifies to a version of the facts which, if accepted, mean that the defendant had a defense for the conduct constituting the crime, the matter should go to the jury. See, e.g., Brown v. State, 698 P.2d 671, 674 (Alaska App.1985) (jury should be instructed on self-defense even if only evidence supporting that theory was defendant's own testimony). That the evidence supporting the defense version of the facts is weak and unlikely to be believed by the jury is not a legitimate basis for refusing to submit the issue to the jury. Defendants' right to jury trial means that they have the right to have the jury, under proper instruction, evaluate the credibility or "believability" of testimony supporting their version of the events on which the prosecution is based. The matter can become quite complex. In United States v. Bailey, 444 U.S. 394, 100 S.Ct. 624, 62 L.Ed.2d 575 (1980), reprinted in part at page 720, infra, the members of the Supreme Court were divided not on the issue of the substantive criminal law—under what circumstances is duress or necessity a defense to charge of prison escape—but rather on whether the defense testimony raised a jury issue on that defense in the particular cases before the Court.

If an instruction is required because the issue has been "raised," what the jury is told concerning the burden of persuasion depends—as was discussed—upon local law relating to the particular defensive matter at issue. The defendant may have the burden of persuasion on insanity and this burden may be one of a "preponderance of the evidence," by proof "beyond a reasonable doubt," or some intermediate one, as by "clear and convincing" evidence. Or, once the defendant has "raised" the issue of insanity by evidence sufficient to require a jury instruction, the prosecution may have the burden of proving—probably by proof beyond a reasonable doubt—that the accused was "sane" at the time of the events constituting the crime. In any case, the jury instructions must make clear to the jury what the burden of proof on the defensive issue is and upon which party that burden rests.

In addition, jury instructions must adequately inform the jury as to "the law" relating to all matters that must be addressed. Obviously, the sufficiency of jury instructions in this regard presents numerous substantive criminal law issues. When jury instructions are erroneous in content presents some of the most difficult questions in criminal law and procedure.

Many American jurisdictions have developed so-called "pattern" instructions for criminal as well as civil cases. Thus a trial judge's task, with the help of both the prosecutor and defense counsel, is to identify on what matters the jury must be instructed and then to choose and give the portions of the pattern instructions relating to those matters. As a result, however, the instructions are obviously drafted in a general fashion and are not "individualized" for particular cases.

Jury instructions in criminal cases have recently come under substantial attack, especially by social scientists. See Perlman, Pattern Jury Instructions: The Application of Social Science Research, 65 Neb. L.Rev. 520 (1986). A major consideration in drafting instructions, these critics claim, is the need to avoid reversal on appeal for legal inaccuracies in the instructions. As a result, the instructions tend to use "safe" language found in statutes or in old judicial opinions. While such language may survive scrutiny by appellate courts, the critics suggest, it is often ineffective in helping jurors to understand "the law" that they are called upon to apply. Severance, Greene and Loftus, Towards Criminal Jury Instructions that Jurors Can Understand, 75 J.Crim.L. & Crim. 198, 201 (1984), note that a 1950 book of approved jury instructions contained the following comment:

> The one thing an instruction must do above all else is correctly state the law. This is true regardless of who is capable of understanding it.

Severance and Loftus, Improving the Ability of Jurors to Comprehend and Apply Criminal Jury Instructions, 17 L. & Soc.Rev. 153 (1982), studied a series of criminal trials in which deliberating juries had specifically asked the trial judge for additional information or guidance. They concluded that these requests showed that despite the trial judge's instructions, juries experienced confusion concerning the elements of the crime that needed to be proved and, in particular, were uncertain concerning the intent that was necessary for guilt. Id., at 170–71.

Argument of Counsel

Substantive criminal law issues may also arise in disputes concerning jury arguments made by either or both defense counsel or prosecutors. Generally speaking, lawyers' arguments are limited to the facts in evidence and the law applicable to cases of this sort. Lawyers may not—to put the matter negatively—argue on the basis of information not in evidence or propositions of law contrary to the jurisdiction's law. In the rape cases hypothesized above, for example, the prosecutor could not properly argue to the jury that they should convict the defendant of rape even if they find that because of impotence he did not engage in intercourse with the victim. Since the jurisdiction's substantive law defining rape probably requires that the defendant have achieved penetration, the prosecutor may not urge the jury to apply a different definition of the charged offense. Defense counsel is similarly limited. If under the jurisdiction's definition of legal insanity loss of control does not amount to insanity, defense counsel cannot urge that the jury acquit the defendant on the ground that the evidence shows he was unable to control his conduct at the time of the incident.

If objection is made to a lawyer's argument on the basis that it goes beyond or is inconsistent with the applicable law or with the evidence that has been introduced, the trial judge must, in ruling on the objection, often make a substantive criminal law determination. Thus substantive criminal law issues can arise in the procedural context of objections to argument of counsel.

Appellate Review

Although procedures exist for the prosecution, under some circumstances, to obtain appellate review of trial court decisions, most appeals in criminal cases are appeals taken by convicted defendants from their convictions. Many American jurisdictions have so-called "two tier" appellate court structures. In such structures, convicted defendants have a virtually absolute right to appeal to the first—or "intermediate"—appellate court. When that appellate court has acted, the highest appellate court—often, in the state context, the state "supreme court"—has the authority but not the obligation to review the decision of the intermediate appellate court. This often means that the party losing before the intermediate appellate court—whether that party is the convicted defendant or the prosecution—may seek review by the higher court. Whether or not to undertake review, however, is discretionary with that tribunal; neither party has a "right" to review by the highest court. Schemes of this sort are often subject to exceptions in cases of maximum severity, i.e., those in which the death penalty has been imposed. Defendants sentenced to death often are absolutely entitled to review of their convictions and sentence by the jurisdiction's highest appellate court.

The general public often has the perception that appellate tribunals "release" convicted defendants with some frequency and for mere "technicalities." This is, however, unlikely to be true. A recent study, Davies, Affirmed: A Study of Criminal Appeals and Decision-Making Norms in a California Court of Appeals, 1982 Am.Bar Ass. Research J. 543 (1982), carefully studied criminal appeals in one state intermediate appellate court. In only 14 percent of criminal cases did the appellate court give an appealing defendant some relief. In contrast, 31 percent of appellants in civil litigation were, to some extent, successful before the appellate court. Id., at 573. Even those defendants who secured some relief on appeal often obtained only some modification of their situation, such as a reduction in sentence or a reversal of some but not all convictions from which they appealed. In only 4.8 percent of the cases did the appellate court reverse all convictions and therefore require that the appealing defendant either be released or retried. Id., at 575. In terms of convictions obtained, Davies estimated that about 2.6 convictions in every thousand (or 0.26 percent) were reversed on appeal. Id., at 577.

Convicted defendants can appeal on a variety of grounds, but most defendant appeals fall into one of two categories. In both categories, the role of the appellate court is limited and this helps explain the low reversal rate. First, defendants may argue that there was insufficient evidence to convict. Davies' study reported that about 24 percent of appeals raised issues of this sort, id., at 564, but that relief was seldom granted on this ground. Appellate courts, generally speaking, have no authority to address directly whether the evidence presented at trial proves guilt beyond a reasonable doubt. They may, however, depending upon local law, subject the evidence to scrutiny of two sorts. This is of special importance, because of the double jeopardy implications of an appellate ruling on evidential sufficiency. If an appellate court finds that the evidence is insufficient to support a conviction, this is—for double jeopardy purposes—the equivalent of acquittal. It means that the appellate court cannot remand the case for a new trial but must instead see that the defendant is acquitted. Burks v. United States, 437 U.S. 1, 98 S.Ct. 2141, 57 L.Ed.2d 1 (1978). Under double jeopardy doctrine, an acquittal bars a defendant from being again prosecuted for the offense of which he was acquitted.

The standard for appellate review of evidential sufficiency is designed to require appellate courts to accord great deference to the trier of fact, whether a jury or, when the defendant has waived a jury trial, the judge. As a result, the issue for the appellate court on an appeal from a conviction is usually only whether there is some evidence in the record on each matter which the prosecution was obligated to establish from which a reasonable trial judge or jury could conclude that guilt was shown beyond a reasonable doubt. If such evidence exists, a conviction should be affirmed against an insufficient evidence attack, even if the appellate judges would—had they been the trial judge or jurors—have acquitted.

Some jurisdictions, however, authorize appellate courts to engage in a more rigorous scrutiny of the evidence than is permissible under the "insufficient evidence" standard. Under this approach, an appellate court can grant relief if the court determines that the verdict of guilty is against "the weight of the evidence." Moreover, the double jeopardy clause of the federal constitution permits a state to enable its appellate courts to direct a new trial rather than an acquittal upon determinations that the record of case contains sufficient evidence to support the conviction but also that the verdict of guilty was contrary to the weight of the evidence presented at trial. Tibbs v. Florida, 457 U.S. 31, 102 S.Ct. 2211, 72 L.Ed.2d 652 (1982). Application of the second criterion obviously gives the appellate tribunal greater authority to consider the evidence. The Supreme Court explained in *Tibbs:*

> [A] conviction rests upon insufficient evidence when, even after viewing the evidence in the light most favorable to the prosecution, no rational factfinder could have found the defendant guilty beyond a reasonable doubt. A reversal based on the weight of the evidence, on the other hand, draws the appellate court into questions of credibility. The "weight of the evidence" refers to "a determination [by] the trier of fact that a greater amount of credible evidence supports one side of an issue or cause than the other."

457 U.S. at 37, 102 S.Ct. at 2216, 72 L.Ed.2d at 658–59.

Defendants can also attack convictions on grounds in a second category. This category consists of trial errors. Davies found that various issues of this sort were raised in appeals to the court he studied with the following frequency: evidence improperly admitted under the rules of evidence law (raised in 39.7 percent of cases); evidence improperly admitted because of invalid searches (27.8 percent of cases); improper jury instructions (25.9 percent of cases); improper argument or comments by prosecutor (22.6 percent of cases); evidence offered by the defense improperly excluded (15.6 percent of cases). Id., at 564. A conviction may be reversed for trial error of this sort, of course, even if the evidence to support the conviction is sufficient.

But appellate courts' role in reviewing errors in this second category is affected by widespread acceptance in criminal litigation of what is often called the "harmless error" rule. Under this doctrine, an error in a criminal trial does not justify reversal of the conviction if it is "harmless." Sometimes the rule is put otherwise—trial error constitutes reversible error requiring that a conviction be invalidated only if it is "prejudicial." Whether an error was "prejudicial" or "harmless" within the meaning of this rule generally turns upon whether the appellate court determines that there is a sufficiently high risk that it affected the outcome of the trial, i.e., that it "caused" or contributed to the conviction. No significant interests are served, the reasoning goes, by reversal of a conviction for an error if it is sufficiently certain that the error did not affect the outcome of the trial. See generally, W. LaFave and J. Israel, Criminal Procedure 995–96 (1985).

Whether an error is harmless or not often involves a complex inquiry that depends in large part upon the nature of the error found. A conclusion that the record shows that the defendant is clearly guilty, of course, does not automatically mean that the conviction should be upheld despite the occurrence of error in the trial. But in many cases the sufficiency of the evidence supporting the defendant's guilt is a relevant consideration. The stronger the evidence showing guilt, the more likely it is that a procedural error in the trial did not affect the outcome. Overwhelming evidence of guilt, in other words, often indicates that had the trial been conducted without the error, the defendant would nevertheless have been convicted.

In any event, appellate court opinions constitute a major source of the substantive criminal law area, as is true in other areas of law. In evaluating the significance of appellate holdings and discussions, however, it is necessary to consider carefully the manner in which the substantive criminal law issue arose in the trial court. It is also necessary to consider what is often the limited role of the appellate tribunal in reviewing a conviction from which a defendant appeals. Seldom does an appellate court have occasion to address whether on particular evidence a defendant is or is not guilty of a particular offense.

F. ALLOCATING THE PROCEDURAL BURDENS IN CRIMINAL LITIGATION: DUE PROCESS CONSIDERATIONS

Editors' Introduction: The Prosecution's Burden

How the various procedural obligations in criminal litigation are to be distributed between the parties raises constitutional as well as policy issues. There has long been agreement that as a matter of local procedural law the prosecution must prove the guilt of the defendant beyond a reasonable doubt. But not until In re Winship, 397 U.S. 358, 90 S.Ct. 1068, 25 L.Ed.2d 368 (1970), did the Supreme Court hold that the federal constitutional requirement of due process demanded this. In *Winship,* Justice Brennan's opinion for the Court explained:

> The reasonable-doubt standard plays a vital role in the American scheme of criminal procedure. It is a prime instrument for reducing the risk of convictions resting on factual error. The standard provides concrete substance for the presumption of innocence—that bedrock "axiomatic and elementary" principle whose "enforcement lies at the foundation of the administration of our criminal law." Coffin v. United States, [156 U.S. 432, 453, 15 S.Ct. 394, 403, 39 L.Ed. 481 (1895)]. As the dissenters in the New York Court of Appeals [below] observed, and we agree, "a person accused of crime * * * would be at a severe disadvantage, a disadvantage amounting to a lack of fundamental fairness, if he could be adjudged guilty and imprisoned for years on the strength of the same evidence as would suffice in a civil case." 24 N.Y.2d, at 205, 299 N.Y.S.2d, at 422, 247 N.E.2d, at 259.

> The requirement of proof beyond a reasonable doubt has this vital role in our criminal procedure for cogent reasons. The accused during a criminal prosecution has at stake interest of immense importance, both because of the possibility that he may lose his liberty upon conviction and because of the certainty that he would be stigmatized by the conviction. Accordingly, a society that values the good name and freedom of every individual should not condemn a man for commission of a crime when there is reasonable doubt about his guilt. As we said in Speiser v. Randall, [357 U.S. 513, 525–26, 78 S.Ct. 1332, 1343, 2 L.Ed. 2d 1460 (1958)]: "There is always in litigation a margin of error, representing error in factfinding, which both parties must take into account. Where one party has at stake an interest of transcending value—as a criminal defendant his liberty—this margin of error is reduced as to him by the process of placing on the other party the burden of * * * persuading the factfinder at the conclusion of the trial of his guilt beyond a reasonable doubt. Due process commands that no man shall lose his liberty unless the Government has borne the burden of * * * convincing the factfinder of his guilt." To this end, the reasonable-doubt standard is indispensable, for it "impresses on the trier of fact the necessity of reaching a subjective state of certitude on the facts in issue." Dorsen & Resnick, In re Gault and the Future of Juvenile Law, 1 Family Law Quarterly, No. 4, at 26 (1967).

> Moreover, use of the reasonable doubt standard is indispensable to command the respect and confidence of the community in application of the criminal law. It is critical that the moral force of the criminal law not be diluted by a standard of proof that leaves people in doubt whether innocent men are being condemned. It is also important in our free society that every individual going about his ordinary affairs have confidence that his government cannot adjudge him guilty of a criminal offense without convincing a proper factfinder of his guilt with utmost certainty.

> Lest there remain any doubt about the constitutional stature of the reasonable-doubt standard, we explicitly hold that the Due Process Clause protects the accused against conviction except upon proof be-

yond a reasonable doubt of every fact necessary to constitute the crime with which he is charged.

397 U.S. at 363–64, 90 S.Ct. at 1072–73, 25 L.Ed.2d at 375.

The apparent simplicity of the due process requirement was misleading, however, as became clear in Mullaney v. Wilbur, 421 U.S. 684, 95 S.Ct. 1881, 44 L.Ed.2d 508 (1975). Wilbur was charged with murder under Maine law; the facts indicated that he had killed the victim following homosexual advances by the victim. Under Maine law, two types of criminal homicide were recognized: murder and manslaughter. Both required proof that the killing was unlawful—neither justifiable nor excusable—and intentional. The difference between them was that "malice aforethought" was an element of murder. If the facts of a case showed that an intentional killer acted in the heat of passion on sudden provocation, malice aforethought was absent. The trial judge instructed the jury in part as follows:

> Malice aforethought is presumed to be present in all homicides until the contrary appears from the circumstances of alleviation to be made out by the defendant, or arising out of the evidence produced in the case. * * * So * * * if you find that there was an unlawful killing of the victim by the defendant, then malice aforethought is implied unless it has been proven to you that the act was done upon sudden provocation in the heat of passion without malice aforethought. * * * [F]rom all of the evidence in the case [the defendant] must be able to satisfy you by a fair preponderance of the evidence that * * * he killed in the heat of passion upon sudden provocation * * *.

Mullaney v. Wilbur, Appendix, at 44–45.

A unanimous Supreme Court held that the instructions violated due process. The State of Maine argued that *Winship* should require that the prosecution prove beyond a reasonable doubt only those facts which, if not proved, would wholly exonerate the defendant. It should not, the state continued, apply to those facts that merely determine the specific offense a defendant has committed and for which he should be punished. Rejecting this, the Court reasoned:

> This analysis fails to recognize that the criminal law * * * is concerned not only with guilt or innocence in the abstract but also with the degree of criminal culpability. * * * The safeguards of due process are not rendered unavailing simply because a determination may already have been reached that would stigmatize the defendant and that might lead to a significant impairment of personal liberty. The fact remains that the consequences resulting from a verdict of murder, as compared with a verdict of manslaughter, differ significantly. * * *

> Moreover, if *Winship* were limited to those facts that constitute a crime as defined by state law, a State could undermine many of the interests that decision sought to protect without effecting any substantive changes in its law. It would only be necessary to redefine the elements that constitute different crimes, characterizing them as fac-

tors that bear solely on the extent of punishment. * * * Maine
could impose a life sentence for any felonious homicide * * * unless
the *defendant* was able to prove that his act was neither intentional
nor criminally reckless.

Winship is concerned with substance rather than this kind of
formalism. The rationale of that case requires an analysis that looks
to the "operation and effect of the law as applied and enforced by the
state" and to the interests of both the State and the defendant as
affected by the allocation of the burden of proof. * * * These
interests are implicated to a greater degree in this case than they were
in *Winship* itself. * * * [Wilbur] faces a differential in sentencing
ranging from a nominal fine to a mandatory life sentence. * * * [I]n
one respect the protection afforded [the relevant] interests is less here.
In *Winship* the ultimate burden of persuasion remained with the
prosecution, although the standard had been reduced to proof by a fair
preponderance of the evidence. In this case, by contrast, the State has
affirmatively shifted the burden of proof to the defendant. The result,
in a case such as this one where the defendant is required to prove the
critical fact in dispute, is to increase further the likelihood of an
erroneous murder conviction.

421 U.S. at 697–701, 95 S.Ct. at 1889–91, 44 L.Ed.2d at 519–20. Rejecting Maine's argument that the difficulties of proving a negative—
that a killing was not committed in the heat of passion—justify a shift
in the burden, the Court noted that many jurisdictions require the
prosecution to prove the absence of such provocation beyond a reasonable doubt. Further:

Nor is the requirement of proving a negative unique in our system
of criminal jurisprudence. Maine itself requires the prosecution to
prove the absence of self-defense beyond a reasonable doubt. Satisfy-
ing this burden imposes an obligation that, in all practical effect, is
identical to the burden involved in negating the heat of passion on
sudden provocation. Thus, we discern no unique hardship on the
prosecution that would justify requiring the defendant to carry the
burden of proving a fact so critical to criminal culpability.

421 U.S. at 702, 95 S.Ct. at 1891, 44 L.Ed.2d at 521–22.

Mullaney seemed to some to encourage attacks on all of the many
affirmative defenses and presumptions in the criminal law, despite
their often ancient pedigrees. Do the post-*Mullaney* cases provide a
clear and satisfactory method of identifying when the prosecution need
not prove a matter beyond a reasonable doubt and when the defendant
can be required to assume the burden of persuasion?

PATTERSON v. NEW YORK

Supreme Court of the United States, 1977.
432 U.S. 197, 97 S.Ct. 2319, 53 L.Ed.2d 281.

MR. JUSTICE WHITE delivered the opinion of the Court.

* * *

I

After a brief and unstable marriage, the appellant, Gordon Patterson, Jr., became estranged from his wife, Roberta. Roberta resumed an association with John Northrup, a neighbor to whom she had been engaged prior to her marriage to appellant. On December 27, 1970, Patterson borrowed a rifle from an acquaintance and went to the residence of his father-in-law. There, he observed his wife through a window in a state of semiundress in the presence of John Northrup. He entered the house and killed Northrup by shooting him twice in the head.

Patterson was charged with second-degree murder. In New York there are two elements of this crime: (1) "intent to cause the death of another person"; and (2) "caus[ing] the death of such person or of a third person." N.Y. Penal Law § 125.25 (McKinney 1975). Malice aforethought is not an element of the crime. In addition, the State permits a person accused of murder to raise an affirmative defense that he "acted under the influence of extreme emotional disturbance for which there was a reasonable explanation or excuse."

New York also recognizes the crime of manslaughter. A person is guilty of manslaughter if he intentionally kills another person "under circumstances which do not constitute murder because he acts under the influence of extreme emotional disturbance." Appellant confessed before trial to killing Northrup, but at trial he raised the defense of extreme emotional disturbance.

The jury was instructed as to the elements of the crime of murder. Focusing on the element of intent, the trial court charged:

> "Before you, considering all of the evidence, can convict this defendant or anyone of murder, you must believe and decide that the People have established beyond a reasonable doubt that he intended, in firing the gun, to kill either the victim himself or some other human being. * * *

The jury was further instructed, consistently with New York law, that the defendant had the burden of proving his affirmative defense by a preponderance of the evidence. The jury was told that if it found beyond a reasonable doubt that appellant had intentionally killed Northrup but that appellant had demonstrated by a preponderance of the evidence that he had acted under the influence of extreme emotional disturbance, it had to find appellant guilty of manslaughter instead of murder.

The jury found appellant guilty of murder. Judgment was entered on the verdict, and the Appellate Division affirmed. While appeal to the New York Court of Appeals was pending, this Court decided Mullaney v. Wilbur * * *. In the Court of Appeals appellant urged that New York's murder statute is functionally equivalent to the one struck down in Mullaney and that therefore his conviction should be reversed.

The Court of Appeals rejected appellant's argument, holding that the New York murder statute is consistent with due process. 39 N.Y. 2d 288, 383 N.Y.S.2d 573, 347 N.E.2d 898 (1976). The Court distinguished Mullaney on the ground that the New York statute involved no shifting of the burden to the defendant to disprove any fact essential to the offense charged since the New York affirmative defense of extreme emotional disturbance bears no direct relationship to any element of murder. * * * We affirm.

II

It goes without saying that preventing and dealing with crime is much more the business of the States than it is of the Federal Government and that we should not lightly construe the Constitution so as to intrude upon the administration of justice by the individual States. Among other things, it is normally "within the power of the State to regulate procedures under which its laws are carried out, including the burden of producing evidence and the burden of persuasion," and its decision in this regard is not subject to proscription under the Due Process Clause unless "it offends some principle of justice so rooted in the traditions and conscience of our people as to be ranked as fundamental." Speiser v. Randall, 357 U.S. 513, 523, 78 S.Ct. 1332, 1341, 2 L.Ed.2d 1460 (1958).

In determining whether New York's allocation to the defendant of proving the mitigating circumstances of severe emotional disturbance is consistent with due process, it is therefore relevant to note that this defense is a considerably expanded version of the common-law defense of heat of passion on sudden provocation and that at common law the burden of proving the latter, as well as other affirmative defenses—indeed, "all * * * circumstances of justification, excuse or alleviation"—rested on the defendant. This was the rule when the Fifth Amendment was adopted, and it was the American rule when the Fourteenth Amendment was ratified.

In 1895 the common-law view was abandoned with respect to the insanity defense in federal prosecutions. Davis v. United States, 160 U.S. 469, 16 S.Ct. 353, 40 L.Ed. 499 (1895). This ruling had wide impact on the practice in the federal courts with respect to the burden of proving various affirmative defenses, and the prosecution in a majority of jurisdictions in this country sooner or later came to shoulder the burden of proving the sanity of the accused and of disproving the facts constituting other affirmative defenses, including provocation. Davis was not a constitutional ruling, however, as Leland v. Oregon, [343 U.S. 790, 72 S.Ct. 1002, 96 L.Ed. 1302 (1952)] made clear.

At issue in Leland v. Oregon was the constitutionality under the Due Process Clause of the Oregon rule that the defense of insanity must be proved by the defendant beyond a reasonable doubt. Noting that Davis "obviously establish[ed] no constitutional doctrine," the Court refused to strike down the Oregon scheme, saying that the burden of proving all elements of the crime beyond a reasonable doubt, including the elements of premeditation and deliberation, was placed on the State under Oregon procedures and remained there throughout the trial. To convict, the jury was required to find each element of the crime beyond reasonable doubt, based on all the evidence, including the evidence going to the issue of insanity. Only then was the jury "to consider separately the issue of legal sanity per se. * * * " This practice did not offend the Due Process Clause even though among the 20 States then placing the burden of proving his insanity on the defendant, Oregon was alone in requiring him to convince the jury beyond a reasonable doubt.

In 1970, the Court declared that the Due Process Clause "protects the accused against conviction except upon proof beyond a reasonable doubt of every fact necessary to constitute the crime with which he is charged." In re Winship. * * *

* * *

III

We cannot conclude that Patterson's conviction under the New York law deprived him of due process of law. The crime of murder is defined by the statute, which represents a recent revision of the state criminal code, as causing the death of another person with intent to do so. The death, the intent to kill, and causation are the facts that the State is required to prove beyond a reasonable doubt if a person is to be convicted of murder. No further facts are either presumed or inferred in order to constitute the crime. The statute does provide an affirmative defense—that the defendant acted under the influence of extreme emotional disturbance for which there was a reasonable explanation—which, if proved by a preponderance of the evidence, would reduce the crime to manslaughter, an offense defined in a separate section of the statute. * * *

* * *

In convicting Patterson under its murder statute, New York did no more than Leland * * * permitted it to do without violating the Due Process Clause. * * * once the facts constituting a crime are established beyond a reasonable doubt, based on all the evidence including the evidence of the defendant's mental state, the State may refuse to sustain the affirmative defense of insanity unless demonstrated by a preponderance of the evidence.

The New York law on extreme emotional disturbance follows this pattern. This affirmative defense, which the Court of Appeals described as permitting "the defendant to show that his actions were caused by a mental infirmity not arising to the level of insanity, and that he is less culpable for having committed them," does not serve to negative any facts of the crime which the State is to prove in order to convict of murder. * * *

[E]ven if we were to hold that a State must prove sanity to convict once that fact is put in issue, it would not necessarily follow that a State must prove beyond a reasonable doubt every fact, the existence or nonexistence of which it is willing to recognize as an exculpatory or mitigating circumstance affecting the degree of culpability or the severity of the punishment. Here, in revising its criminal code, New York provided the affirmative defense of extreme emotional disturbance, a substantially expanded version of the older heat-of-passion concept; but it was willing to do so only if the facts making out the defense were established by the defendant with sufficient certainty. The State was itself unwilling to undertake to establish the absence of those facts beyond a reasonable doubt, perhaps fearing that proof would be too difficult and that too many persons deserving treatment as murderers would escape that punishment if the evidence need merely raise a reasonable doubt about the defendant's emotional state. It has been said that the new criminal code of New York contains some 25 affirmative defenses which exculpate or mitigate but which must be established by the defendant to be operative. The Due Process Clause, as we see it, does not put New York to the choice of abandoning those defenses or undertaking to disprove their existence in order to convict of a crime which otherwise is within its constitutional powers to sanction by substantial punishment.

The requirement of proof beyond a reasonable doubt in a criminal case is "bottomed on a fundamental value determination of our society that it is far worse to convict an innocent man than to let a guilty man go free." Winship, 397 U.S., at 372, 90 S.Ct., at 1077 (Harlan, J., concurring). The social cost of placing the burden on the prosecution to prove guilt beyond a reasonable doubt is thus an increased risk that the guilty will go free. While it is clear that our society has willingly chosen to bear a substantial burden in order to protect the innocent, it is equally clear that the risk it must bear is not without limits; and Mr. Justice Harlan's aphorism provides little guidance for determining what those limits are. Due process does not require that every conceivable step be taken, at whatever cost, to eliminate the possibility of convicting an innocent person. Punishment of those found guilty by a jury, for example, is not forbidden merely because there is a remote possibility in some instances that an innocent person might go to jail.

It is said that the common-law rule permits a State to punish one as a murderer when it is as likely as not that he acted in the heat of passion or under severe emotional distress and when, if he did, he is guilty only of manslaughter. But this has always been the case in those jurisdictions adhering to the traditional rule. It is also very likely true that fewer convictions of murder would occur if New York were required to negative the affirmative defense at issue here. But in each instance of a murder conviction under the present law, New York will have proved beyond a reasonable doubt that the defendant has intentionally killed another person, an act which it is not disputed the State may constitutionally criminalize and punish. If the State nevertheless chooses to recognize a factor that mitigates the degree of criminality or punishment, we think the State may assure itself that the fact has been established with reasonable certainty. To recognize at all a mitigating circumstance does not require the State to prove its nonexistence in each case in which the fact is put in issue, if in its judgment this would be too cumbersome, too expensive, and too inaccurate.

We thus decline to adopt as a constitutional imperative, operative countrywide, that a State must disprove beyond a reasonable doubt every fact constituting any and all affirmative defenses related to the culpability of an accused. Traditionally, due process has required that only the most basic procedural safeguards be observed; more subtle balancing of society's interests against those of the accused have been left to the legislative branch. We therefore will not disturb the balance struck in previous cases holding that the Due Process Clause requires the prosecution to prove beyond a reasonable doubt all of the elements included in the definition of the offense of which the defendant is charged. Proof of the nonexistence of all affirmative defenses has never been constitutionally required; and we perceive no reason to fashion such a rule in this case and apply it to the statutory defense at issue here.

This view may seem to permit state legislatures to reallocate burdens of proof by labeling as affirmative defenses at least some elements of the crimes now defined in their statutes. But there are obviously constitutional limits beyond which the States may not go in this regard. "[I]t is not within the province of a legislature to declare an individual guilty or presumptively guilty of a crime." McFarland v. American Sugar Rfg. Co., 241 U.S. 79, 86, 36 S.Ct. 498, 500, 60 L.Ed. 899 (1916). The legislature cannot "validly command that the finding of an indictment, or mere proof of the identity of the accused, should create a presumption of the existence of all the facts essential to guilt." Tot v. United States, 319 U.S. 463, 469, 63 S.Ct. 1241, 1246, 87 L.Ed. 1519 (1943). * * *

* * *

Mullaney surely held that a State must prove every ingredient of an offense beyond a reasonable doubt, and that it may not shift the burden of proof to the defendant by presuming that ingredient upon proof of the other elements of the offense. This is true even though the State's practice, as in Maine, had been traditionally to the contrary. Such shifting of the burden of persuasion with respect to a fact which the State deems so important that it must be either proved or presumed is impermissible under the Due Process Clause.

It was unnecessary to go further in Mullaney. The Maine Supreme Judicial Court made it clear that * * * a killing became murder in Maine when it resulted from a deliberate, cruel act committed by one person against another, "suddenly without any, or without a considerable provocation." * * * [M]alice, in the sense of the absence of provocation, was part of the definition of that crime. Yet malice, i.e., lack of provocation, was presumed and could be rebutted by the defendant only by proving by a preponderance of the evidence that he acted with heat of passion upon sudden provocation. In Mullaney we held that however traditional this mode of proceeding might have been, it is contrary to the Due Process Clause as construed in Winship.

As we have explained, nothing was presumed or implied against Patterson; and his conviction is not invalid under any of our prior cases. The judgment of the New York Court of Appeals is affirmed.

MR. JUSTICE REHNQUIST took no part in the consideration or decision of this case.

MR. JUSTICE POWELL, with whom MR. JUSTICE BRENNAN and MR. JUSTICE MARSHALL join, dissenting.

In the name of preserving legislative flexibility, the Court today drains In re Winship of much of its vitality. Legislatures do require broad discretion in the drafting of criminal laws, but the Court surrenders to the legislative branch a significant part of its responsibility to protect the presumption of innocence.

I

An understanding of the import of today's decision requires a comparison of the statutes at issue here with the statutes and practices of Maine struck down by a unanimous Court just two years ago in Mullaney v. Wilbur.

A

Maine's homicide laws embodied the common-law distinctions along with the colorful common-law language. * * *

* * *

New York's present homicide laws had their genesis in lingering dissatisfaction with certain aspects of the common-law framework that this Court confronted in Mullaney. Critics charged that the archaic language tended to obscure the factors of real importance in the jury's decision. Also, only a limited range of aggravations would lead to mitigation under the common-law formula, usually only those resulting from direct provocation by the victim himself. It was thought that actors whose emotions were stirred by other forms of outrageous conduct, even conduct by someone other than the ultimate victim, also should be punished as manslaughterers rather than murderers. Moreover, the common-law formula was generally applied with rather strict objectivity. Only provocations that might cause the hypothetical reasonable man to lose control could be considered. And even provocations of that sort were inadequate to reduce the crime to manslaughter if enough time had passed for the reasonable man's passions to cool, regardless of whether the actor's own thermometer had registered any decline.

The American Law Institute took the lead in moving to remedy these difficulties. As part of its commendable undertaking to prepare a Model Penal Code, it endeavored to bring modern insights to bear on the law of homicide. The result was a proposal to replace "heat of passion" with the moderately broader concept of "extreme mental or emotional disturbance." * * *

At about this time the New York Legislature undertook the preparation of a new criminal code, and the Revised Penal Law of 1967 was the ultimate result. The new code adopted virtually word for word the ALI formula for distinguishing murder from manslaughter. * * *

* * *

B

Mullaney held invalid Maine's requirement that the defendant prove heat of passion. The Court today, without disavowing the unanimous holding of Mullaney, approves New York's requirement that the defendant prove extreme emotional disturbance. The Court manages to run a constitutional boundary line through the barely visible space that separates Maine's law from New York's. It does so on the basis of distinctions in language that are formalistic rather than substantive.

This result is achieved by a narrowly literal parsing of the holding in Winship: "[T]he Due Process Clause protects the accused against conviction except upon proof beyond a reasonable doubt of every fact necessary to constitute the crime with which he is charged." The only "facts" necessary to constitute a crime are said to be those that appear on the face of the statute as a part of the definition of the crime. Maine's statute was invalid, the Court reasons, because it "defined [murder] as the unlawful killing of a human being 'with malice aforethought, either express or implied.'" "[M]alice," the Court reiterates, "in the sense of the absence of provocation, was part of the definition of that crime." Winship was violated only because this "fact"—malice— was "presumed" unless the defendant persuaded the jury otherwise by showing that he acted in the heat of passion. New York, in form presuming no affirmative "fact" against Patterson, and blessed with a statute drafted in the leaner language of the 20th century, escapes constitutional scrutiny unscathed even though the effect on the defendant of New York's placement of the burden of persuasion is exactly the same as Maine's.

* * *

With all respect, this type of constitutional adjudication is indefensibly formalistic. A limited but significant check on possible abuses in the criminal law now becomes an exercise in arid formalities. What Winship and Mullaney had sought to teach about the limits a free society places on its procedures to safeguard the liberty of its citizens becomes a rather simplistic lesson in statutory draftsmanship. Nothing in the Court's opinion prevents a legislature from applying this new learning to many of the classical elements of the crimes it punishes. It would be preferable, if the Court has found reason to reject the rationale of Winship and Mullaney, simply and straightforwardly to overrule those precedents.

The Court understandably manifests some uneasiness that its formalistic approach will give legislatures too much latitude in shifting the burden of persuasion. And so it issues a warning that "there are obviously constitutional limits beyond which the States may not go in this regard." The Court thereby concedes that legislative abuses may occur and that they must be curbed by the judicial branch. But if the State is careful to conform to the drafting formulas articulated today, the constitutional limits are anything but "obvious." This decision simply leaves us without a conceptual framework for distinguishing abuses from legitimate legislative adjustments of the burden of persuasion in criminal cases.

II

It is unnecessary for the Court to retreat to a formalistic test for applying Winship. Careful attention to the Mullaney decision reveals the principles that should control in this and like cases. * * *

* * * The Due Process Clause requires that the prosecutor bear the burden of persuasion beyond a reasonable doubt only if the factor at issue makes a substantial difference in punishment and stigma. The requirement of course applies a fortiori if the factor makes the difference between guilt and innocence. But a substantial difference in punishment alone is not enough. It also must be shown that in the Anglo-American legal tradition the factor in question historically has held that level of importance. If either branch of the test is not met, then the legislature retains its traditional authority over matters of proof. But to permit a shift in the burden of persuasion when both branches of this test are satisfied would invite the undermining of the presumption of innocence, "that bedrock 'axiomatic and elementary' principle whose 'enforcement lies at the foundation of the administration of our criminal law.'" * * *

* * *

III

The Court beats its retreat from Winship apparently because of a concern that otherwise the federal judiciary will intrude too far into substantive choices concerning the content of a State's criminal law. The concern is legitimate, see generally Powell v. Texas, 392 U.S. 514, 533–534, 533–534, 88 S.Ct. 2145, 2154, 20 L.Ed.2d 1254 (1968) (plurality opinion) but misplaced. Winship and Mullaney are no more than what they purport to be: decisions addressing the procedural requirements that States must meet to comply with due process. They are not outposts for policing the substantive boundaries of the criminal law.

* * *

Furthermore, as we indicated in Mullaney, even as to those factors upon which the prosecution must bear the burden of persuasion, the State retains an important procedural device to avoid jury confusion and prevent the prosecution from being unduly hampered. The State normally may shift to the defendant the burden of production, that is, the burden of going forward with sufficient evidence "to justify [a reasonable] doubt upon the issue." If the defendant's evidence does not cross this threshold, the issue—be it malice, extreme emotional distur-bance, self-defense, or whatever—will not be submitted to the jury. Ever since this Court's decision in Davis v. United States, 160 U.S. 469, 16 S.Ct. 353, 40 L.Ed. 499 (1895), federal prosecutors have borne the burden of persuasion with respect to factors like insanity, self-defense, and malice or provocation, once the defendant has carried this burden of production. I know of no indication that this practice has proven a noticeable handicap to effective law enforcement.

* * *

Notes and Questions

1. In Simopoulos v. Virginia, 462 U.S. 506, 103 S.Ct. 2532, 76 L.Ed.2d 755 (1983), a Virginia statute provided:

> Except as provided in other sections of this article, if any person administer to, or cause to be taken by a woman, any drug or other thing, or use means, with intent to destroy her unborn child, or to produce abortion or miscarriage, and thereby destroy such child, or produce such abortion or miscarriage, he shall be guilty of a Class 4 felony.

Va.Code Ann. § 18.2–71. Other sections provided that no criminal liability existed if the abortion was performed during the first trimester, or in a hospital during the second trimester, or if the abortion was necessary to save the woman's life. Dr. Simopoulos was charged with performing a second trimester abortion outside a hospital. No evidence was introduced at trial as to the existence or nonexistence of the "medical necessity" of the abortion the state's evidence showed he facilitated. As construed by the Virginia courts, the statute did not require the state to prove lack of medical necessity unless and until a defendant invoked it as a defense, apparently by introducing at least some evidence that medical necessity existed. Finding no violation of due process, the Court cited Mullaney v. Wilbur and stated, "Placing upon the defendant the burden of going forward with evidence on an affirmative defense is normally permissible." 462 U.S. at 510, 103 S.Ct. at 2535, 76 L.Ed.2d at 760.

2. As *Mullaney* itself suggested, allocation of the burden of proof is sometimes affected or even accomplished by devices called "presumptions." "Presumption" has been characterized as among the slipperiest of legal terms. McCormick on Evidence 965 (3rd ed. 1985). Generally, however, a presumption is a "rule" or an "evidentiary device" relating particular kinds of evidence to particular matters at issue in litigation. If, for example, a party must prove fact A—for example, that the addressee of a letter received it—it may introduce evidence tending to prove fact B—that the letter, properly addressed, was mailed—and ask the trier of fact to infer fact A from fact B. If the law has developed some sort of rule concerning the relationship between fact A and fact B, that rule may be a presump-tion. In a jury case, the jury is often instructed concerning presumptions applicable to the crime or any defenses at issue.

These presumptions, rules or "evidentiary devices" were discussed in general terms in County Court of Ulster County v. Allen, 442 U.S. 140, 99 S.Ct. 2213, 60 L.Ed.2d 777 (1979):

> Inferences and presumptions are a staple of our adversary system of factfinding. It is often necessary for the trier of fact to determine the existence of an element of the crime—that is, an "ultimate" or "elemental" fact—from the existence of one or more "evidentiary" or "basic" facts. * * *

> The most common evidentiary device is the entirely permissive inference or presumption, which allows—but does not require—the trier of fact to infer the elemental fact from proof by the prosecutor of the basic one and which places no burden of any kind on the defendant. In that situation, the basic fact may constitute prima facie evidence of the elemental fact. * * *

> A mandatory presumption is a far more troublesome evidentiary device. * * * [I]t tells the trier that he or they *must* find the elemental fact upon proof of the basic fact, at least unless the defendant has come forward with some evidence to rebut the presumed connection between the two facts. * * *

442 U.S. at 157, 99 S.Ct. at 2224–25, 60 L.Ed.2d at 791–92. In Francis v. Franklin, 471 U.S. 307, 105 S.Ct. 1965, 85 L.Ed.2d 344 (1985), the Court explained further:

> A mandatory presumption may be either conclusive or rebuttable. A conclusive presumption removes the presumed element from the case once the State has proven the predicate facts giving rise to the presumption. A rebuttable presumption does not remove the presumed element from the case but nevertheless requires the jury to find the presumed element unless the defendant persuaded the jury that such a finding is unwarranted.

471 U.S. at 313 n. 2, 105 S.Ct. at 1971 n. 2, 85 L.Ed.2d at 353 n. 2. Another distinction was also drawn in *Allen:*

> [M]andatory [rebuttable] presumptions can be subdivided into two [types]: presumptions that merely shift the burden of production to the defendant, following the satisfaction of which the ultimate burden of persuasion returns to the prosecution; and presumptions that entirely shift the burden of proof to the defendant. * * *

> To the extent that a presumption imposes an extremely low burden of production—e.g., being satisfied by "any" evidence—it may well be that its impact is no greater than that of a permissive inference * * *.

442 U.S. at 157 n. 16, 99 S.Ct. at 2224–25 n. 16, 60 L.Ed.2d at 702 n. 16.

Allen, Francis, and Sandstrom v. Montana, 442 U.S. 510, 99 S.Ct. 2450, 61 L.Ed.2d 39 (1979), make clear that use of presumptions may intrude upon defendants' due process right to have the prosecution prove guilt beyond a reasonable doubt.

In *Allen,* three adult males and a 16 year old girl—referred to as "Jane Doe"—were jointly tried on charges that they possessed two loaded handguns, a loaded machinegun and a pound of heroin. The group's car had been stopped for speeding; the girl was the front seat passenger. The handguns were found in an open handbag positioned on either the front floor or front seat of the car. The machinegun and heroin were found in the trunk. According to the girl's admission, the handbag was hers. The trial judge instructed the jury that each defendant was to be presumed innocent, that the prosecution had the burden to prove guilt beyond a reasonable doubt, and that guilt required proof of possession. Further, he explained:

> [P]ossession means actual physical possession, just as having the drugs or weapons in one's hand, one one's home or other place under one's exclusive control, or constructive possession which may exist without personal domination over the drugs or weapons but with the intent and ability to retain such control or dominion.

He also instructed the jury pursuant to a statutory presumption:

> Our Penal Law * * * provides that the presence in an automobile of any machine gun or of any handgun or firearm which is loaded is presumptive evidence of their unlawful possession.

> In other words, * * * upon proof of the presence of the machine gun and the hand weapons, you may infer and draw a conclusion that such prohibited weapon was possessed by each of the defendants who occupied the automobile at the time when such instruments were found. The presumption * * * is effective only so long as there is no substantial evidence contradicting the conclusion flowing from the presumption, and the presumption is said to disappear when such contradictory evidence is adduced.

> The presumption * * * need not be rebutted by affirmative proof or affirmative evidence but may be rebutted by any evidence or lack of evidence in the case.

The jury convicted all four defendants of possession of the items found in the passenger compartment and acquitted all four of possession of the items found in the trunk. All three adult male defendants challenged before the Supreme Court the use of the presumption in their prosecution. In general terms, the Court noted:

> The * * * validity [of various evidentiary devices] vary from case to case * * * depending on the strength of the connection between the particular basic and elemental facts involved and on the degree to which the device curtails the factfinder's freedom to assess the evidence independently. Nonetheless, in criminal cases, the ultimate test of any device's constitutional validity in a given case remains constant: the device must not undermine the factfinder's responsibility at trial, based on evidence adduced by the State, to find the ultimate facts beyond a reasonable doubt.

442 U.S. at 156, 99 S.Ct. at 2224, 60 L.Ed.2d at 791.

The trial judge's instructions, concluded the court, concerned only a "permissive inference." It was made clear to the jury that it could ignore the presumption even if no evidence was offered by the defense in rebuttal. The Court continued:

When reviewing this type of device, the Court has required the party challenging it to demonstrate its invalidity as applied to him. Because this permissible presumption leaves the trier of fact free to credit or reject the inference and does not shift to the burden of proof, it affects the application of the "beyond a reasonable doubt" standard only if, under the facts of the case, there is no rational way the trier could make the connection permitted by the inference. For only in that situation is there any risk that an explanation of the permissive inference to a jury, or its use by a jury, as caused the presumptively rational factfinder to make an erroneous determination.

442 U.S. at 157, 99 S.Ct. at 2224–25, 60 L.Ed.2d at 792. The due process standard by which such presumptions are tested was found in Leary v. United States, 395 U.S. 6, 36, 89 S.Ct. 1532, 1548, 23 L.Ed.2d 57, 82 (1969):

[A] criminal statutory presumption must be regarded as * * * unconstitutional, unless it can at least be said with substantial assurance that the presumed fact is more likely than not to flow from the proved fact on which it is made to depend.

See also, Francis v. Franklin, 471 U.S. 307, 313, 105 S.Ct. 1965, 1971, 85 L.Ed.2d 344, 353–54 (1985) ("A permissive inference violates the Due Process Clause only if the suggested conclusion is not one that reason and common sense justify in light of proven facts before the jury."). Continuing in *Allen,* the Court reasoned:

As applied to the facts of this case, the presumption of possession is entirely rational. * * * [T]he jury would have been entirely reasonable in rejecting the suggestion * * * that the handguns were in the sole possession of Jane Doe. Assuming the jury did reject it, the case is tantamount to one in which the guns were lying on the floor or the seat of the car in plain view of the three other occupants of the automobile. In such a case, it is surely rational to infer that each of the respondents was fully aware of the presence of the guns and had both the ability and the intent to exercise dominion and control over the weapons. The application of the statutory presumption in this case therefore comports with the [due process] standard * * *. For there is a "rational connection" between the basic facts the prosecution proved and the ultimate fact presumed, and the latter is "more likely than not to flow from" the former.

442 U.S. at 163–65, 99 S.Ct. at 2228–29, 60 L.Ed.2d at 795–97.

3. In Sandstrom v. Montana, 442 U.S. 510, 99 S.Ct. 2450, 61 L.Ed.2d 39 (1979), Sandstrom was charged with deliberate murder under a statute requiring proof that the defendant "purposely or knowingly" killed the victim. At trial, he admitted killing the victim but contested that he had done it with the requisite state of mind. Expert testimony was introduced from which the jury might have concluded that because of a personality disorder and consumption of alcohol, Sandstrom did not kill the victim purposely or knowingly. Over Sandstrom's objection, the jury was instructed that "[t]he law presumes that a person intends the ordinary consequences of his voluntary acts." The Supreme Court held that this instruction violated Sandstrom's due process rights. Some jurors, the Court acknowledged, might have interpreted the instruction as authorizing them

only to apply a permissive presumption or a mandatory presumption requiring only that the defendant come forward with "some" evidence. But reasonable jurors could also have construed it as directing them to apply either a conclusive or "persuasion-shifting" presumption. Therefore, the instructions must be analyzed as involving presumptions of the latter sorts.

Winship and *Patterson*, the Court continued, provide the appropriate mode of constitutional analysis for the presumption at issue in *Sandstrom*. Under these cases, "the question before before this Court is whether the challenged jury instruction had the effect of relieving the State of the burden of proof enunciated in *Winship* on the critical question of [Sandstrom's] state of mind." 442 U.S. at 521, 99 S.Ct. at 2458, 61 L.Ed.2d at 49. The Court acknowledged that the jury might have construed the instruction in either of two ways, but found that either interpretation would render the instruction constitutionally deficient. First, the jury might have understood the instructions as describing a conclusive presumption. That is, the jurors might have understood that if they found the proof sufficient to show that Sandstrom caused the victim's death, that Sandstrom's acts were "voluntary, and that the victim's death was the "ordinary consequence" of Sandstrom's actions, they were *required* to find that he killed the victim purposely or knowingly. This, the court concluded, would relieve the prosecution of its burden of proving criminal intent and violate the holding of *Winship*.

Second, the jurors might have understood the instruction as merely shifting to Sandstrom the burden of persuasion. Thus the jurors might have concluded that upon proof that Sandstrom, by "voluntary" actions, killed the victim and that the victim's death was the "ordinary consequence" of those actions, they must conclude that Sandstrom acted purposely or knowingly unless he proved to the contrary. This, the court concluded, would violate the holding of Mullaney v. Wilbur.

In Francis v. Franklin, 471 U.S. 307, 105 S.Ct. 1965, 85 L.Ed.2d 344 (1985), a murder case, the instructions included the following:

> The acts of a person of sound mind and discretion are presumed to be the product of the person's will, but the presumption may be rebutted. A person of sound mind and discretion is presumed to intend the natural and probable consequences of his acts, but the presumption may be rebutted.

The Supreme Court rejected the state court's conclusion that this instruction embodied only a permissive inference to be tested under *Allen*. As a mandatory presumption of intent—although a rebuttable one—it was invalid under *Sandstrom*.

4. Under the Pennsylvania Mandatory Minimum Sentencing Act, 42 Pa.Cons.Stat. § 9712, enacted in 1982, a person convicted of any of certain serious crimes—including some murders and sexual assaults, robbery, and aggravated assault—is to be sentenced to a minimum sentence of at least five years if "the person visibly possessed a firearm during the commission of the offense." The Act specifically provides that "[p]rovisions of this section shall not be an element of the crime" and whether the section applies is to be determined by the judge at sentencing. In McMillam v.

Pennsylvania, ___ U.S. ___, 106 S.Ct. 2411, 91 L.Ed.2d 67 (1986), several Pennsylvania defendants challenged the Act on the ground (among others) that it effectively made visible possession of a firearm an element of the offenses but permitted the state to prove this by only a preponderance standard. A majority of the Supreme Court upheld the statute under *Patterson:*

> *Patterson* stressed that in determining what facts must be proved beyond a reasonable doubt the state legislature's definition of the elements of the offense is usually dispositive * * * [.] [T]he Pennsylvania legislature has expressly provided that visible possession of a firearm is not an element of the crimes enumerated in the * * * statute, but instead is a sentencing factor that comes into play only after the defendant has been found guilty of one of those crimes beyond a reasonable doubt. * * *

> As *Patterson* recognized, of course, there are constitutional limits to the State's power in this regard; in certain circumstances *Winship's* reasonable doubt requirement applies to facts not formally identified as elements of the offense charged. * * * While we have never attempted to define precisely the constitutional limits noted in *Patterson,* i.e., the extent to which due process forbids the reallocation or reduction of burdens of proof in criminal cases, and do not do so today, we are persuaded by several factors that Pennsylvania's Mandatory Minimum Sentencing Act does not exceed those limits.

> We note first that the Act plainly does not transgress the limits expressly set out in *Patterson.* * * * [T]he Act * * * does [not] relieve the prosecution of its burden of proving guilt * * *.

> * * * Section 9712 neither alters the maximum penalty for the crime committed nor creates a separate offense calling for a separate penalty; it operates solely to limit the sentencing court's discretion in selecting a penalty within the range already available to it * * *. The statute gives no impression of having been tailored to permit the visible possession finding to be a tail which wags the dog of the substantive offense. Petitioners' claim * * * would have at least more superficial appeal if a finding of visible possession exposed them to greater or additional punishment, cf. 18 U.S.C. § 2113(d) (providing separate and greater punishment for bank robberies accomplished through "use of a dangerous weapon or device"), but it does not.

> * * *

> Finally, we note that the specter raised * * * of States restructuring existing crimes in order to "evade" the commands of *Winship* just does not appear in this case. * * * The Pennsylvania legislature did not change the definition of any existing offense. It simply took one factor that has always been considered by sentencing courts to bear on punishment—the instrumentality used in committing a violent felony—and dictated the precise weight to be given that factor if the instrumentality is a firearm. Pennsylvania's decision to do so has not

transformed against its will a sentencing factor into an "element" of some hypothetical "offense."

___ U.S. at ___, 106 S.Ct. at 2416–19, 91 L.Ed.2d at 75–79.

Justice Stevens expressed disagreement:

[T]he Due Process Clause requires proof beyond a reasonable doubt of conduct which exposes a criminal defendant to greater stigma or punishment, but does not likewise constrain state reductions of criminal penalties * * *. [I]f a state provides that a specific component of a prohibited transaction shall give rise both to a special stigma and to a special punishment, that component must be treated as a "fact necessary to constitute the crime" within the meaning of our holding in *In re Winship*.

___ U.S. at ___, 106 S.Ct. at 2424, 2426, 91 L.Ed.2d at 85, 87 (Stevens, J., dissenting). The democratic process, he urged, provides a practical barrier to abuse of the ability to manipulate mitigating facts. No state would enact or retain a criminal statute making it a serious offense to "be present in any public or private place" but providing for a defense consisting of proof that the accused was not at the time robbing a bank. Since abuse of the ability to manipulate aggravating facts is a greater risk, the distinction would identify and address "genuine constitutional threats." Applying this standard, he continued:

> Pennsylvania's Mandatory Minimum Sentencing Act reflects a legislative determination that a defendant who "visibly possessed a firearm" during the commission of an aggravated assault is more blameworthy than a defendant who did not. A judicial finding that the defendant used a firearm in an aggravated assault places a greater stigma on the defendant's name than a simple finding that he committed an aggravated assault. And not to be overlooked, such a finding with respect to petitioner Dennison automatically mandates a punishment that is more than twice as severe as the *maximum* punishment that the trial judge considered appropriate for his conduct. * * * The finding identifies conduct that the legislature specifically intended to prohibit and to punish by a special sanction.

___ U.S. at ___, 106 S.Ct. at 2426, 91 L.Ed.2d at 87–88.

Justice Marshall, joined by Justices Brennan and Blackmun, also dissented, agreeing with "much in Justice Stevens' dissent" but preferring to delay discussion of how mitigating facts should be analyzed under *Winship*. ___ U.S. at ___, 106 S.Ct. at 2421, 91 L.Ed.2d at 8 (Marshall, J., dissenting).

5. May the burden of persuasion as to some or all traditional "defenses" be placed upon the defendant? Ohio law puts on a defendant both the burden of going forward with the evidence and the burden of persuasion, by a preponderance of the evidence, with regard to affirmative defenses such as self-defense. Ohio Rev.Code § 29.01.05(A). Several recent cases have involved prosecutions for aggravated murder, defined by the following:

(A) No person shall purposely, and with prior calculation and design, cause the death of another.

Ohio Rev.Code § 29.03.01. The majority of a split Ohio Supreme Court has found no violation of *Patterson* in placing on the defendant the burden of proof with regard to self-defense in such prosecutions:

> [T]he burden of proving self-defense does not require the defendant to prove his innocence by disproving an element of the offense with which he is charged. The elements of the crime and the existence of self-defense are separate issues. Self-defense seeks to relieve the defendant from culpability rather than to negate an element of the crime charged.

State v. Martin, 21 Ohio St.3d 91, 94, 488 N.E.2d 166, 168 (1986). But other members of the court disagreed:

> For more than a century, self-defense has been considered to negate the element of unlawfulness which must be present in order to convict a defendant of aggravated murder. See Silvus v. State (1871), 22 Ohio St. 90. Thus, R.C. 2901.05 permits the state to convict a defendant without proving every element of the crime charged, contrary to the principles of *Patterson* * * *.

21 Ohio St.3d at 97, 488 N.E.2d at 171 (Brown, J., dissenting). The Supreme Court has commented that a similar argument—that under *Patterson* the state must prove self-defense as part of its task of establishing guilty mens rea, voluntariness and unlawfullness—"states a colorable constitutional claim." Engle v. Isaac, 456 U.S. 107, 122, 102 S.Ct. 1558, 1569, 71 L.Ed.2d 783, 797 (1982). Review was granted by the Supreme Court in *Martin,* apparently to resolve the issue. ___ U.S. ___, 106 S.Ct. 1634, 90 L.Ed.2d 180 (1986).

6. Issues concerning presumptions and burdens of proof are also treated at other points in these materials. Presumptions sometimes applied in prosecutions for killings with "malice aforethought," for example, are discussed in Chapter VII.

7. For discussion of these issues, see generally, Allen, The Restoration of In re Winship: A Comment on Burdens of Persuasion in Criminal Cases After Patterson v. New York, 76 Mich.L.Rev. 30 (1977); Jeffries and Stephen, Defenses, Presumptions and the Burden of Proof in the Criminal Law, 88 Yale L.J. 1325 (1979); Nesson, Reasonable Doubt and Permissive Inferences: The Value of Complexity, 92 Harv.L.Rev. 1187 (1979); Saltzberg, Burden of Persuasion in Criminal Cases: Harmonizing the Views of the Justices, 20 Am.Crim.L.Rev. 383 (1983); Underwood, The Thumb on the Scales of Justice: Burdens of Persuasion in Criminal Cases, 86 Yale L.J. 1299 (1977).

MODEL PENAL CODE *
(Official Draft, 1985).

Section 1.12. Proof Beyond a Reasonable Doubt; Affirmative Defenses; Burden of Proving Fact When Not an Element of an Offense; Presumptions.

(1) No person may be convicted of an offense unless each element of such offense is proved beyond a reasonable doubt. In the absence of such proof, the innocence of the defendant is assumed.

(2) Subsection (1) of this Section does not:

(a) require the disproof of an affirmative defense unless and until there is evidence supporting such defense; or

(b) apply to any defense which the Code or another statute plainly requires the defendant to prove by a preponderance of evidence.

(3) A ground of defense is affirmative, within the meaning of Subsection (2)(a) of this Section, when:

(a) it arises under a section of the Code which so provides; or

(b) it relates to an offense defined by a statute other than the Code and such statute so provides; or

(c) it involves a matter of excuse or justification peculiarly within the knowledge of the defendant on which he can fairly be required to adduce supporting evidence.

MODEL PENAL CODE, COMMENTS
TO § 1.13, 110–11 **
(Tent. Draft No. 4, 1955).

No single principle can be conscripted to explain when these shifts of burden to defendants are defensible, even if the burden goes no further than to call for the production of some evidence. Neither the logical point that the prosecution would be called upon to prove a negative, nor the grammatical point that the defense rests on an exception or proviso divorced from the definition of the crime is potently persuasive, although both points have been invoked. * * * What is involved seems rather a more subtle balance which acknowledges that a defendant ought not be required to defend until some solid substance is presented to support the accusation but, beyond this, perceives a point where need for narrowing the issues, coupled with the relative accessibility of evidence to the defendant, warrants calling upon him to present his defensive claim. No doubt this point is reached more quickly if, given the facts the prosecution must establish, the normal probabilities are against the defense, but this is hardly an essential factor. Given the mere fact of an intentional homicide, no one can estimate the probability that it was or was not committed in self-defense. The point is rather that purposeful homicide is an event of such gravity to society, and the basis for a claim of self-defense is so specially within the cognizance of the defendant, that it is fair to call on him to offer evidence if the defense is claimed. * * *

Chapter II

CRIMINALIZATION POLICY

Contents

This chapter looks very briefly at two basic issues: First, what is distinctive about criminalization as a societal institution? Second, how do we justify the use of this technique which invariably involves the intentional infliction of harm on another human being? This harm can take the form of an economic sanction such as a fine or order of restitution, a loss of freedom whether by incarceration or the restrictions of probation, or even death. Both questions are of more than theoretical significance. The first, which can also be understood as

65

what do we mean when we say we are "punishing" someone, can have important practical consequences because "punishment" requires that certain procedural protections be afforded the subject. The second plays an important role in public policy debates over the propriety of criminalizing certain conduct. Unless the wellspring of the conduct are seen as comporting with the premises underlying a particular justification for punishment, criminalization will appear to involve pointless cruelty.

A. THE NATURE OF CRIMINAL LIABILITY

All societies classify some conduct as undesirable and develop techniques to minimize its occurrence. There is enormous congruence among cultures separated by history and geography as to the conduct which is subject to disapproval. It is difficult to imagine a society which does not condemn unprovoked aggression towards a group member or intrusions upon recognized property interests—although there may be great differences among societies as to those persons considered "group members" and what is subject to protected ownership. There is also great variation among societies as to conduct prohibited. Some might make the raising of pigs a crime, while others prohibit the public display of a woman's face or the sale of property in other than state-controlled stores. In our own country, the proper scope of the criminal law is the subject of much debate. As is commonplace here, this debate often takes on Constitutional dimensions. The argument is most heated in connection with so-called victimless crimes: obscenity, prostitution, public intoxication, possession or sale of "dangerous" drugs and similar matters. Some constitutional aspects of this debate are addressed in Section C of Chapter III, infra.

The single most important means for preventing the disapproved behavior is perhaps the process of acculturation that begins in the home and is carried on by the particular society's formal or informal system of education and socialization. For most people the key values of their society are, through these processes, internalized. This means that most people, most of the time, control their own behavior in a manner consistent with the requirements of their culture. They exercise personal control even though there may be no threat of immediate apprehension or sanction, so that there might be at least short term net psychological or financial benefits, or both, from ignoring the societally-sanctioned claims of another to the integrity of person or property. The socialization process is reinforced by formal strictures as to behavioral requirements. In complex modern societies these strictures will take the form of laws and regulations. Some of these will reflect basic cultural values. Others will be directives as to how persons are to act or refrain from acting so as to facilitate the operation of an urbanized, bureaucratic, and highly technological society. Rules such as those concerning traffic flow and parking, the making of cheese, or the retailing of tobacco are examples of strictures of the latter sort.

Sometimes persons fail to behave in accord with societal norms. Various responses to such lapses are available. Herbert Packer, in his fine volume, The Limits of the Criminal Sanction (1968), has categorized the basic techniques as *regulation, compensation, treatment* and *punishment*. *Regulation* represents an effort to control future conduct for the general good. In the event that its directives—e.g., prescribed standards of cleanliness in a dairy—are violated, society may subject the responsible party to some "penalty" without regard to whether any one has been injured by the "violation". If, however, someone had been made ill by this failure to observe the rules of sanitation, she might be authorized to compel the dairy to compensate her for the injuries attributable to this breach of duty owed her by the dairy. Such *compensation* is thought to both redress the harm caused the specific individual and to encourage greater care on the part of the actor in the future.

What if the adulteration of the dairy's products was attributable to a psychotic employee who, due to a delusional state, believed floor sweepings were butterfat? Regulations might require retrieval and destruction of the adulterated product as well as a fine for the employer dairy. Any person damaged by ingestion of that product might seek compensation from the dairy. But what would be done with the employee? He would seem to be a prime candidate for *treatment*. He might be seized, examined, adjudicated mentally ill and a danger to himself or others, and involuntarily committed to a mental hospital until such time as he achieved an adequate level of recovery. The focus of the process would be on the condition of the individual rather than any specific acts he committed, although the latter might be crucial to reaching a satisfactory level of certainty as to the former. The deprivation of freedom is primarily premised on the possibility of benefit to the individual although in the event of sufficient danger the person might be incarcerated despite the absence of any effective therapy.

Punishment is the technique of behavioral control which is the subject of this course. It obviously shares the same instrumental premise as do the other techniques, that is, that society can bring the behavior of the targeted groups and individuals into greater conformity with group norms. It differs, however, in very important ways from the other techniques which have been mentioned. Packer attempted to define punishment as involving the infliction of pain or other unpleasantness on an individual who has done something in violation of a rule previously prescribed by the authority which now punishes the infraction. That violation will usually, although not invariably, be morally blameworthy. The punishment will be imposed in order to prevent future offenses against those legal norms or to exact retribution, or both. The concern is for the good of society in general. The crucial factor which distinguishes punishment is its purpose. Packer, supra at 21–31.

In reading the following excerpt from the work of Henry M. Hart, Jr., consider whether his point about the distinguishing feature of punishment differs from Packer. Consider also whether there can be any system of sanctions which either Hart or Packer would consider as involving punishment which was not predicated on the existence of free will.

HENRY M. HART, JR., THE AIMS OF THE CRIMINAL LAW

23 Law and Contemporary Problems 401, 402–06 (1958).

What do we mean by "crime" and "criminal"? * * *

A great deal of intellectual energy has been misspent in an effort to develop a concept of crime as "a natural and social phenomenon" abstracted from the functioning system of institutions which make use of the concept and give it impact and meaning. But the criminal law, like all law, is concerned with the pursuit of human purposes through the forms and modes of social organization, and it needs always to be thought about in that context as a method or process of doing something.

What then are the characteristics of this method?

1. The method operates by means of a series of directions, or commands, formulated in general terms, telling people what they must or must not do. Mostly, the commands of the criminal law are "must-nots," or prohibitions, which can be satisfied by inaction. "Do not murder, rape, or rob." But some of them are "musts," or affirmative requirements, which can be satisfied only by taking a specifically, or relatively specifically, described kind of action. "Support your wife and children," and "File your income tax return."

2. The commands are taken as valid and binding upon all those who fall within their terms when the time comes for complying with them, whether or not they have been formulated in advance in a single authoritative set of words. They speak to members of the community, in other words, in the community's behalf, with all the power and prestige of the community behind them.

3. The commands are subject to one or more sanctions for disobedience which the community is prepared to enforce.

Thus far, it will be noticed, nothing has been said about the criminal law which is not true also of a large part of the noncriminal, or civil, law. The law of torts, the law of contracts, and almost every other branch of private law that can be mentioned operate, too, with general directions prohibiting or requiring described types of conduct, and the community's tribunals enforce these commands. What, then, is distinctive about the method of the criminal law?

Can crimes be distinguished from civil wrongs on the ground that they constitute injuries to society generally which society is interested in preventing? The difficulty is that society is interested also in the due fulfillment of contracts and the avoidance of traffic accidents and most of the other stuff of civil litigation. The civil law is framed and interpreted and enforced with a constant eye to these social interests. Does the distinction lie in the fact that proceedings to enforce the criminal law are instituted by public officials rather than private complainants? The difficulty is that public officers may also bring many kinds of "civil" enforcement actions—for an injunction, for the recovery of a "civil" penalty, or even for the detention of the defendant by public authority. Is the distinction, then, in the peculiar character of what is done to people who are adjudged to be criminals? The difficulty is that, with the possible exception of death, exactly the same kinds of unpleasant consequences, objectively considered, can be and are visited upon unsuccessful defendants in civil proceedings.

If one were to judge from the notions apparently underlying many judicial opinions, and the overt language even of some of them, the solution of the puzzle is simply that a crime is anything which is *called* a crime, and a criminal penalty is simply the penalty provided for doing anything which has been given that name. So vacant a concept is a betrayal of intellectual bankruptcy. Certainly, it poses no intelligible issue for a constitution-maker concerned to decide whether to make use of "the method of the criminal law." Moreover, it is false to popular understanding, and false also to the understanding embodied in existing constitutions. By implicit assumptions that are more impressive than any explicit assertions, these constitutions proclaim that a conviction for crime is a distinctive and serious matter—a something, and not a nothing. What is that something?

4. What distinguishes a criminal from a civil sanction and all that distinguishes it, it is ventured, is the judgment of community condemnation which accompanies and justifies its imposition. As Professor Gardner wrote not long ago, in a distinct but cognate connection:

> The essence of punishment for moral delinquency lies in the criminal conviction itself. One may lose more money on the stock market than in a court-room; a prisoner of war camp may well provide a harsher environment than a state prison; death on the field of battle has the same physical characteristics as death by sentence of law. It is the expression of the community's hatred, fear, or contempt for the convict which alone characterizes physical hardship as punishment.

If this is what a "criminal" penalty is, then we can say readily enough what a "crime" is. It is not simply anything which a legislature chooses to call a "crime." It is not simply antisocial conduct which public officers are given a responsibility to suppress. It is not simply any conduct to which a legislature chooses to attach a "criminal" penalty. It is conduct which, if duly shown to have taken place, will incur a formal and solemn pronouncement of the moral condemnation of the community.

5. The method of the criminal law, of course, involves something more than the threat (and, on due occasion, the expression) of community condemnation of antisocial conduct. It involves, in addition, the

threat (and, on due occasion, the imposition) of unpleasant physical consequences, commonly called punishment. But if Professor Gardner is right, these added consequences take their character as punishment from the condemnation which precedes them and serves as the warrant for their infliction. Indeed, the condemnation plus the added consequences may well be considered, compendiously, as constituting the punishment. Otherwise, it would be necessary to think of a convicted criminal as going unpunished if the imposition or execution of his sentence is suspended.

In traditional thought and speech, the ideas of crime and punishment have been inseparable; the consequences of conviction for crime has been described as a matter of course as "punishment." The Constitution of the United States and its amendments, for example, use this word or its verb form in relation to criminal offenses no less than six times. Today, "treatment" has become a fashionable euphemism for the older, ugly word. This bowdlerizing of the Constitution and of conventional speech may serve a useful purpose in discouraging unduly harsh sentences and emphasizing that punishment is not an end in itself. But to the extent that it dissociates the treatment of criminals from the social condemnation of their conduct which is implicit in their conviction, there is danger that it will confuse thought and do a disservice.

At least under existing law, there is a vital difference between the situation of a patient who has been committed to a mental hospital and the situation of an inmate of a state penitentiary. The core of the difference is precisely that the patient has not incurred the moral condemnation of his community, whereas the convict has.

Note

The analysis of whether particular conduct has been, should be, and can—constitutionally—be criminalized begins with an examination of legislative intent. On several occasions the Supreme Court has addressed the issue of whether a particular sanction constitutes criminal punishment. This was important because, as previously noted, under our constitution certain protections must be afforded the subject before a criminal penalty can be imposed. In Kennedy v. Mendoza-Martinez, 372 U.S. 144, 83 S.Ct. 554, 9 L.Ed.2d 644 (1963), the appellees contended that depriving them of their citizenship for having left the country to evade the military draft constituted punishment and, as such, could not be inflicted without a prior criminal trial with all procedural safeguards. The Court announced a series of tests which it said were to be applied in order to decide whether Congress had intended the statute to be:

> penal or regulatory in character, even though in other cases this problem has been extremely difficult and elusive of solution. Whether the sanction involves an affirmative disability or restraint, whether it has historically been regarded as a punishment, whether it comes into play only on a finding of *scienter*, whether its operation will promote the traditional aims of punishment—retribution and deterrence,

whether the behavior to which it applies is already a crime, whether an alternative purpose to which it may rationally be connected is assignable for it, and whether it appears excessive in relation to the alternative purpose assigned are all relevant to the inquiry, and may often point in differing directions.

372 U.S. at 168–69, 83 S.Ct. at 567, 9 L.Ed.2d at 661. The Court concluded, over three dissents, that loss of citizenship under these circumstances had been intended to serve as punishment.

In contrast, in United States v. Ward, 448 U.S. 242, 100 S.Ct. 2636, 65 L.Ed.2d 742 (1980), the penalty was far less draconian than the loss of American citizenship. It was a $500 fine, designated a "civil penalty" which was assessed because oil had escaped from property leased by the defendant driller and had reached a navigable water. The Court held that this fine, per the *Mendoza-Martinez* tests, was intended by Congress as a civil sanction and was not so punitive as to transform that fine into a criminal penalty. The sole dissenter, Justice Stevens, acknowledged that it was a close case but nevertheless concluded that inasmuch as the fine was not calculated to reimburse the Government for the cost of cleaning the spill it was "clearly aimed at exacting retribution * * * [which] leads to the conclusion that the penalty is a criminal sanction rather than a purely regulatory measure." 448 U.S. at 258, 100 S.Ct. at 2646, 65 L.Ed.2d at 755. Given the nature of the offense and the absence of any finding that the defendant intended this spill to occur or was even careless with respect to it, is it reasonable to think, in Henry Hart's terms, that we hate or revile him?

Most recently the Court faced the problem in a context very different from both *Mendoza-Martinez* and *Ward*. In Allen v. Illinois, __ U.S. __, 106 S.Ct. 2988, 92 L.Ed.2d 296 (1986), the question was whether proceedings to determine if the actor is a "sexually dangerous person" were civil or criminal. If they were criminal the actor would be entitled to the Fifth Amendment privilege against self-incrimination so that the testimony of psychiatrists based on information elicited from the actor in alleged violation of the privilege would be inadmissible. The Supreme Court, by a five to four vote, concluded that the Illinois act in issue was designed to identify persons in need of "treatment" not "punishment" and this basic distinction was not altered by the fact that persons so identified would be involuntary committed to a maximum-security institution that also housed convicts needing psychiatric care.

B. JUSTIFICATION AND FUNCTIONS OF CRIMINALIZATION

The justifications for criminalizing conduct are obviously relevant to the basic policy question of what conduct to make criminal. Given the nature of criminal liability, it seems beyond reasonable question that conduct should not be made subject to the criminal sanction in the absence of good reason for this action.

The materials in this section consider the two major theories of justification that might be relied upon in criminalizing and punishing conduct. These are retributionism and utilitarianism. Retributionism rests upon the idea of just deserts. One who violates the strictures of the law (or even, in a broader sense, offends morality) "merits" punishment whether or not the infliction of pain upon the offender can be demonstrated to have any socially desirable effects upon her or upon others. Adherents of this view contend that no society is moral if good goes unrewarded and evil unpunished.

The notion of "deserts" necessarily embodies two crucial premises that limit those circumstances in which punishment can justifiably be imposed. First, no punishment is appropriate unless an evil has been done. Therefore, the offender must have "chosen" to do wrong. One who unavoidably causes harm or, due to infancy or insanity, acts without comprehension, is not a fit subject for punishment. But if the actor is "responsible" for her actions, punishment expresses our society's respect for her as an independent moral agent. The existence of free will, then, is an assumption of just deserts.

Second, the punishment imposed must, in some general sense, be proportionate to the gravity of the offense. Hopes of achieving some desired change in the conduct of many people would not, for a retributionist, justify the infliction of punishment disproportionate to the offense. Gravity of the conduct, then, limits the severity of the punishment that may be imposed.

Utilitarianism, by contrast, is predicated on the notion that the harm which is inherent in the infliction of punishment is justified only if it will be outweighed by the good for society to be achieved thereby. This theory subsumes both specific and general deterrence, rehabilitation, the inculcation of moral values, and the satisfaction of the public's demand for revenge, although these subdivisions are often treated as separate justifications. They are combined here because all are based on the same idea that the minimization of criminal violations—whether through incarceration, fear, treatment, the internalization of the law's commands, or the preclusion of self help—is the only justification for punishment. In reviewing these materials, consider whether, in practice, both major theories are drawn upon to explain who is to be punished and to what degree of severity.

The first two subsections offer a small sampling of materials concerning these justifications. The last subsection presents a debate over the propriety of using criminalization for the enforcement of morality.

H.L.A. HART, MURDER AND THE PRINCIPLES OF PUNISHMENT: ENGLAND AND THE UNITED STATES
52 Nw.U.L.Rev. 433, 448–49 (1957).[a]

[W]e must distinguish two questions commonly confused. They are, first "Why do men in fact punish?" * * * The second question

a. Reprinted by special permission of the Northwestern University Law Review   (Northwestern University School of Law), Copyright © 1958, Vol. 52, No. 4.

* * * is "What justifies men in punishing? Why is it morally good or morally permissible for them to punish?" It is clear that no demonstration that in fact men have punished or do punish for certain reasons can amount *per se* to a justification for this practice unless we subscribe to what is itself a most implausible moral position, namely, that whatever is generally done is justified or morally right * * *.

When this simple point is made clear and the two questions * * * are forced apart, very often the objector to the utilitarian position will turn out to be a utilitarian of a wider and perhaps more imaginative sort. He will perhaps say that what justifies punishment is that it satisfies a popular demand (perhaps even for revenge) and explain that it is good that it satisfies this demand because if it did not there would be disorder in society, disrespect for the law, or even lynching. Such a point of view, of course, raises disputable questions of fact * * *. Nevertheless, this objection itself turns out to be a utilitarian position, emphasizing that the good to be secured by punishment must not be narrowly conceived as simply protecting society from the harm represented by the particular type of crime punished but also as a protection from a wider set of injuries to society.

1. RETRIBUTION

The concept of retributionism has experienced a period of disfavor in our criminal jurisprudence. In 1948 Justice Black, speaking for the United States Supreme Court, announced that "retribution is no longer the dominant objective of the criminal law. Reformation and rehabilitation of offenders have become important goals of criminal jurisprudence." Williams v. New York, 337 U.S. 241, 248, 69 S.Ct. 1079, 1084, 93 L.Ed. 1337, 1343 (1949). In part, at least, this was a function of an increased confidence in the social sciences. Sociology and allied fields strongly urged the view that criminal conduct was properly attributable to the failure of society to provide adequate shelter, nutrition, education, employment and other conditions essential to the formation of law-abiding citizens. The notion of blaming others, an integral part of retributionism, became a source of discomfort. As Professor James White has written: "when enough is sympathetically understood about a person, blaming become impossible, even in the case of the person who commits atrocities or is utterly selfish." White, Making Sense of the Criminal Law, 50 U.Colo.L.Rev. 1, 20 (1978). This tendency to downplay the placement of blame was reinforced by the claimed insights of psychology which, in addition, offered the promise of correcting antisocial behavior through the manipulation of the individual psyche.

More recently there has been a decline in public and professional confidence in the role of sociological and psychological factors in determining crime rates and effecting the rehabilitation of offenders. See Wilson and Herrnstein, Crime and Human Nature 215 ff, 312–15, 324, 335 (1985) and Allen, The Decline of the Rehabilitative Ideal

(1981). Reflecting these changes in the intellectual climate, several members of the Supreme Court recently observed that retribution is neither "a forbidden objective nor one inconsistent with our respect for the dignity of men." Gregg v. Georgia, 428 U.S. 153, 183, 96 S.Ct. 2909, 2930, 49 L.Ed.2d 859, 880 (1976) (opinion of Stewart, Powell, and Stevens, JJ., announcing the judgment of the Court).

Whatever the current acceptability of retributionism as a justification for punishment, consider—after reading the following material—whether Justice Holmes was right when he pronounced that it was "only vengeance in disguise." O. Holmes, The Common Law 45 (1881). More directly, can harming another human being ever be justified in the absence of some reasonable hope that by doing so some greater good will be achieved?

P. BRETT, AN INQUIRY INTO CRIMINAL GUILT
51 (1963).

The retributive theory of punishment can be formulated in a number of ways. Its distinguishing feature is that it asks for no further justification of the right to punish than that the offender has committed a wrong. "Judicial punishment * * * can never serve merely as a means to further *another* good, whether for the offender himself or of society, but must always be inflicted on him for the sole reason that he *has committed a crime.* * * * The law of punishment is a categorical imperative, and woe to him who crawls through the serpentine windings of the happiness theory seeking to discover something which in virtue of the benefit it promises will release him from the duty of punishment or even from a fraction of its full severity." Thus Kant expounded the theory, and he based it upon his view that man must always be treated as an end in himself and never as a means of achieving some other end. Kant's position here is an intuitive one, with which one can only either agree or disagree in the light of one's own intuitions. Other formulations of the retributive theory are likewise intuitive, and occasionally they take on a somewhat mystical tinge, as with Hegel's view that crime is a negation and punishment a negation of that negation.

Note and Question

Insofar as retributive notions provide the justification for criminal punishment, do they also suggest a limitation upon those who may be punished? Consider the following:

The aim of criminal legislation is to prevent the perpetration of acts classified as criminal (because they are regarded as being socially damaging). * * * I can subscribe fully to this premise, and would only add the rider that, if by putting it forward it is sought to suggest, as does Barbara Wooton, that the purpose of penal legislation is *not* retribution for guilt, then the point rests on a misunderstanding. For this is something no one has even claimed. The so-called retributivist theories are not concerned with the *purpose* of penal law (its intended effects) but with the moral basis for sentencing a particular person and for the kind and extent of the punishment imposed. The substance of the retributivist's case is that the guilt requirement sets a moral limitation upon the state's right to pursue its preventive aims.

Ross, The Campaign Against Punishment, 14 Scandinavian Studies in Law 109, 124–25 (1970).

2. UTILITARIANISM

"Utilitarian theories of punishment have dominated American jurisprudence during most of the twentieth century." Greenawalt, Punishment, in 4 Encyclopedia of Crime & Justice 1340 (1983). According to these theories, punishment—or any other conduct—is justifiable only if it promises to promote happiness more than any alternative choice of conduct. Thus, this justification is a form of instrumentalism. The state punishes in order to achieve certain effects. Punishment provides an opportunity to control or alter the behavior of the offender or others. Necessarily the justification fails if either such change cannot be anticipated or if the cost of effecting the change—in terms of human happiness—is greater than the increase in happiness which is likely to be achieved. Moreover, unlike retributionism, utilitarian theories need not presuppose free will. Punishment can serve its posited functions even if the behavior which occasioned its use—or, indeed, all human behavior—was in some sense determined. Under that view, the threat of punishment, or "corrective" measures taken under its aegis, becomes one of the determinants of future conduct for the offender and others.

In reading the materials which follow, consider whether utilitarianism places any limitations on the use of punishment. If human happiness will be increased by the punishment of an innocent person, or by a punishment of a severity disproportionate to the offense, what principle would militate against its use? Or, to put the question another way, do utilitarian justifications invite the use of one person for the benefit of others?

a. Prevention: Deterrence, Moralization and the Like

A belief in the deterrent affect of the threat of punishment seems to be part of the common sense of all. It would be difficult to find anyone who, as a child or a parent, did not experience or employ this theory in practice. Our daily lives are replete with instances in which our conduct is adjusted because of the anticipation of undesirable consequences which may follow from indulging in the satisfaction of our desires. As a simple example, consider how speed limits are observed according, in part, to drivers' estimation of the prospect of apprehension.

Acknowledging the relationship between conduct and a desire to avoid pain offers very little guidance for legislators and judges who are required to decide what conduct should be criminalized, or what level of severity of punishment should be attached to violation of proscriptions in the abstract and in the individual case. Rather, it brings to the fore extraordinarily intractable questions of the extent to which criminalization of conduct will prevent persons from engaging in that conduct.

There are so many variables involved in human decision-making and their interaction is so complex that providing empirical evidence of deterrence is a daunting task. To what extent must the severity of penalties be increased in order to offset a low level of certainty regarding their imposition? To what extent must penalties be adjusted to offset the hypothesized power of the motivation to engage in the prohibited conduct? Is the threat of sanction equally effective to all who would contemplate engaging in the conduct, or does the pain of imprisonment or stigmatization vary with the life circumstances of the individual? If the effect varies, how can those making decisions regarding criminalization and punishment learn of such differences and adjust the system to take account of them? And, inherent in all of these and many other questions in this area, how is a society to calculate when the costs in human happiness incident to prevention are greater than the gains in happiness which may be anticipated from the crime suppressed thereby? These costs must be understood as involving both the diversion of monetary resources from efforts to secure other goods, and the loss in freedom that may follow from the legislative proscription of certain conduct and the efforts to enforce those proscriptions.

The material in this subsection suggests the need to distinguish among a number of different means by which criminalization might have a preventive effect. It also raises the possibility that the extent to which these preventive effects can reasonably be expected to operate may vary among different kinds of activity. To what extent may the law rely upon the demonstrated or suggested preventive effect of criminal punishment in deciding whether or not to criminalize certain conduct? Should criminalization be rejected as a technique of social control in the absence of proof that a preventive effect will be achieved?

ANDENAES, THE GENERAL PREVENTIVE EFFECTS OF PUNISHMENT
114 U.Pa.L.Rev. 949–51 (1966).[b]

In continental theories of criminal law, a basic distinction is made between the effects of punishment on the man being punished—individual prevention or special prevention—and the effects of punishment upon the members of society in general—general prevention. The characteristics of special prevention are termed "deterrence," "reformation" and "incapacitation," and these terms have meanings similar to their meanings in the English speaking world. General prevention, on the other hand, may be described as the *restraining influences emanating from the criminal law and the legal machinery.*

By means of the criminal law, and by means of specific applications of this law, "messages" are sent to members of a society. The criminal law lists those actions which are liable to prosecution, and it specifies the penalties involved. The decisions of the courts and actions by the police and prison officials transmit knowledge about the law, underlining the fact that criminal laws are not mere empty threats, and providing detailed information as to what kind of penalty might be expected for violations of specific laws. To the extent that these stimuli restrain citizens from socially undesired actions which they might otherwise have committed, a general preventive effect is secured. While the effects of special prevention depend upon how the law is implemented in each individual case, general prevention occurs as a result of an interplay between the provisions of the law and its enforcement in specific cases. In former times, emphasis was often placed on the physical exhibition of punishment as a deterrent influence, for example, by performing executions in public. Today it is customary to emphasize the *threat* of punishment as such. From this point of view the significance of the individual sentence and the execution of it lies in the support that these actions give to the law. It may be that some people are not particularly sensitive to an abstract threat of penalty, and that these persons can be motivated toward conformity only if the penalties can be demonstrated in concrete sentences which they feel relevant to their own life situations.

The effect of the criminal law and its enforcement may be *mere deterrence.* Because of the hazards involved, a person who contemplates a punishable offense might not act. But it is not correct to regard general prevention and deterrence as one and the same thing. The concept of general prevention also includes the *moral* or *sociopedagogical* influence of punishment. The "messages" sent by law and the legal processes contain factual information about what would be risked by disobedience, but they also contain proclamations specifying that it is *wrong* to disobey. * * *

The moral influence of the criminal law may take various forms. It seems to be quite generally accepted among the members of society that the law should be obeyed even though one is dissatisfied with it and wants it changed. If this is true, we may conclude that the law as an institution itself to some extent creates conformity. But more important than this formal respect for the law is respect for the values which the law seeks to protect. It may be said that from law and the legal machinery there emanates a flow of propaganda which favors such respect. Punishment is a means of expressing social disapproval. In this way the criminal law and its enforcement supplement and enhance the moral influence acquired through education and other nonlegal processes. Stated negatively, the penalty neutralizes the demoralizing consequences that arise when people witness crimes being perpetrated.

Deterrence and moral influence may both operate on the conscious level. The potential criminal may deliberate about the hazards involved, or he may be influenced by a conscious desire to behave lawfully. However, with fear or moral influence as an intermediate link, it is possible to create unconscious inhibitions against crime, and perhaps to establish a condition of habitual lawfulness. In this case, illegal actions will not present themselves consciously as real alternatives to conformity, even in situations where the potential criminal would run no risk whatsoever of being caught.

General preventive effects do not occur only among those who have been informed about penal provisions and their applications. Through a process of learning and social imitation, norms and taboos may be transmitted to persons who have no idea about their origins—in much the way that innovations in Parisian fashions appear in the clothing of country girls who have never heard of Dior or Lanvin.

Making a distinction between special prevention and general prevention is a useful way of calling attention to the importance of legal punishment in the lives of members of the general public, but the distinction is also to some extent an artificial one. The distinction is simple when one discusses the reformative and incapacitative effects of punishment on the individual criminal. But when one discusses the deterrent effects of punishment the distinction becomes less clear. Suppose a driver is fined ten dollars for disregarding the speed limit. He may be neither reformed or incapacitated but he might, perhaps, drive more slowly in the future. His motivation in subsequent situations in which he is tempted to drive too rapidly will not differ fundamentally from that of a driver who has not been fined; in other words a general preventive effect will operate. But for the driver who has been fined, this motive has, perhaps, been strengthened by the recollection of his former unpleasant experience. We may say that a general preventive feature and special preventive feature here act together.

Notes and Questions

1. Andenaes mentions the possibility that deterrence and moral influence may operate on an unconscious level. Under psychoanalytic theory (or at least under some versions of it), law-abiding persons have an unconscious need to have those who transgress laws punished. The personality's ability to restrain instinctual urges to engage in aggressive and antisocial behavior will remain effective only if it is periodically reinforced by punishment of those who engage in such behavior. Probably the leading presentation of this view is F. Alexander and H. Staub, The Criminal, The Judge, and The Public (1931). This theory explains the "urge to punish": law-abiding persons are unconsciously motivated to

demand punishment of offenders because failure to punish the offenders is likely to weaken the self-control of the law-abiding persons and to lead to the commission of conduct which the law-abiding person will find deeply offensive to values he has unconsciously developed. If accepted, this theory also presents a utilitarian justification for punishment: punishment serves to reinforce the mechanism that keeps most persons from engaging in antisocial behavior.

2. Can the law justifiably rely upon an expectation that criminal punishment will have a general preventive effect? Consider the following from Andenaes, The Morality of Deterrence, 37 U.Chi.L.Rev. 649, 663–64 (1970):

> [I]t is often asserted that there is no scientific proof for the general preventive effects of punishment, and it may be argued that it is morally unjustifiable to inflict punishment on the basis of a belief which is not corroborated by scientific evidence. The burden of proof, it is sometimes said, is on those who would invoke punishment. Others may answer that the burden of proof is on those who would experiment at the risk of society by removing or weakening the protection which the criminal law now provides.
>
> Two points should be made. First, our lack of knowledge of general prevention may be exaggerated. In some areas of criminal law we have experiences which come as close to scientific proof as could be expected in human affairs. In many other areas it seems reasonably safe to evaluate the general preventive effects of punishment on a common sense basis. Modern psychology has shown that the pleasure-pain principle is not as universally valid as is assumed, for instance, in Bentham's penal philosophy. Nevertheless, it is still a fundamental fact of social life that the risk of unpleasant consequences is a very strong motivational factor for most people in most situations.
>
> Second, even in questions of social and economic policy we rarely are able to base our decisions on anything which comes close to strict scientific proof. Generally we must act on the basis of our best judgment. In this respect, the problems of penal policy are the same as problems of education, housing, foreign trade policy, and so on. The development of social science gradually provides a better factual foundation for decisions of social policy, but there is a long way to go. Besides, research always lags behind the rapid change of social conditions.
>
> However, it is undeniable that punishment—the intentional infliction of suffering—is a special category among social policies. It contrasts sharply with the social welfare measures which characterize our modern state. This calls for caution and moderation in its application. I do not think the legal concept of "burden of proof" is very useful in this context. The balance that should be struck between defense of society and humaneness towards the offender can hardly be expressed in a simple formula. The solution of the conflict will depend on individual attitudes. Some people identify more with the values threatened by criminal behavior; others identify more with the law-breaker. But certainly punishment should not be imposed precipitous-

ly. History provides a multitude of examples of shocking cruelty based on ideas of deterrence, often in combination with ideas of just retribution.

3. Sociological researchers have provided some material bearing on the preventive effects of punishment, but it is difficult to evaluate because of complex methodological differences and difficulties. See, e.g., Gibbs, Crime, Punishment and Deterrence, 48 Southwestern Social Science Quarterly 515 (1968) (finding a distinct inverse association between certainty and severity of punishment for homicide and homicide rate); Gray and Martin, Punishment and Deterrence: Another Analysis of Gibbs' Data, 50 Social Science Q. 389 (1969). Economic theory has also been invoked. See Ehrlich, The Deterrent Effect of Capital Punishment: A Question of Life and Death, 65 Am.Economic Rev. 397 (1975). Compare, Peck, The Deterrent Effect of the Death Penalty: Ehrlich and his Critics, 85 Yale L.J. 359 (1976). See generally, Cook, Punishment and Crime: A Critique of Current Findings Concerning the Preventive Effects of Punishment, 41 Law and Contemporary Problems 164 (1977); Secker and Kohlfeld, Crimes, Crime Rates, Arrests, and Arrest Ratios: Implications for Deterrence Theory, 23 Criminology 437 (1985).

Some researchers have focused upon the "incapacitative" effect of punishment, i.e., that impact accomplished simply by keeping offenders imprisoned so that their opportunity to commit crimes is at least minimized. E.g., Van Dine, Dinitz, and Conrad, The Incapacitation of the Dangerous Offender: A Statistical Experiment, 14 J.Research in Crime and Delinquency 22 (1977). But the results are difficult to evaluate, especially in terms of possible "side effects." See, e.g., Phillips, McCleary and Dinitz, The Special Deterrent Effect of Incarceration in Evaluating Performance of Criminal Justice Agencies 237, 259 (Whitaker and Phillips eds., 1983) (incarcerated juvenile offenders seemed to increase their criminal activity following release from incarceration).

In 1975, the Governing Board of the National Research Council, whose members are drawn from the Councils of the National Academy of Science, the National Academy of Engineering, and the Institute of Medicine, approved a project by a group called the Panel of Research on Deterrent and Incapacitative Effects. After undertaking to provide "an objective technical assessment of the studies of deterrent and incapacitative effects of sanctions on crime rates," the panel concluded:

> [W]e cannot yet assert that the evidence warrants an affirmative conclusion regarding deterrence. We believe scientific caution must be exercised in interpreting the limited validity of the available evidence and the number of competing explanations for the results. Our reluctance to draw stronger conclusions does not imply support for a position that deterrence does not exist, since the evidence certainly favors a position supporting deterrence more than it favors one asserting that deterrence is absent.

Deterrence and Incapacitation: Estimating the Effects of Criminal Sanctions on Crime Rates 7 (1978). In regard to the death penalty, the report concluded that "the available studies provide no useful evidence on the deterrent effect of capital punishment." Id., at 9.

b. Prevention: Treatment of Offenders

Rehabilitation as a theoretical justification for punishment has long coexisted with other instrumentalist theories such as specific and general deterrence. Under this view, punishment provides an opportunity to alter the character of the offender so as to prevent future offenses. Consider how this justification may affect decisions as to sentencing. If the object of punishment is the correction of character defects, should the offender remain incarcerated for a period sufficient to allow the beneficent effects of such programs to be achieved? Does this affect the choice between determinant and indeterminant sentencing examined at pages 19–27, supra?

The powerful appeal of the theory of rehabilitation is illustrated in some of the most commonly employed terminology of punishment: "corrections," "reformatory," and "penitentiary." Today the last term summons up images of punitive confinement for purposes of incapacitation and deterrence. The original notion of the penitentiary, however, was very different. Proposals to create such institutions originated in reaction to the harshness of brandings, stocks, floggings, and executions which were thought to brutalize the public as well as the offenders. The penitentiary was conceived of as a place for penitence, where through quiet reflection and religious and moral instruction the offender's character would be altered to that of a productive, law-abiding citizen.

In more modern times, the humane impulse of rehabilitation has found expression in many forms. Probation as a means of avoiding the contagion of criminality perceived to be present in the exclusive association with other offenders is such a technique. (That same concern was dealt with in the earliest penitentiaries by attempting to impose a regime of strict solitary confinement.) Rehabilitative intervention in the lives of offenders who are imprisoned include efforts in two general areas. There are attempts to strengthen ties to institutions—such as families and religions—which are seen to reinforce law-abiding conduct. Prison programs are also designed to address conditions which directly correlate with criminal behavior. Thus efforts are made to reduce illiteracy, lack of employment skills, and alcohol or drug dependence.

Beginning in the 1920s, adherents of psychology and psychiatry offered proposals for rehabilitation through treatment on a medical model. These proposals posited that criminal conduct was attributable to emotional and psychological disabilities which could be both diagnosed and treated. To what extent is this treatment rationale an adequate justification for criminalizing conduct? This subsection presents divergent views concerning the extent to which the law might reasonably rely upon the promise of treatment following conviction. Consider in this connection the difficulty of achieving success where the "patients" are subject to the inherent coercion of imprisonment, and the dangers of invading the autonomy of other human beings in the name of benevolence.

K. MENNINGER, THE CRIME OF PUNISHMENT

253, 257–61 (1968).[c]

The medical use of the word *treatment* implies a program of presumably beneficial action prescribed for and administered to one who seeks it. The purpose of treatment is to relieve pain, correct disability, or combat an illness. Treatment may be painful or disagreeable but, if so, these qualities are incidental, not purposive.

* * *

When the community begins to look upon the expression of aggressive violence as the symptom of an illness or as indicative of illness, it will be because it believes doctors can do something to correct such a condition. At present, some better-informed individuals do believe and expect this. However angry at or sorry for the offender, they want him "treated" in an effective way so that he will cease to be a danger to them. And they know that the traditional punishment, "treatment-punishment," will not effect this.

What *will?* What effective treatment is there for such violence? It will surely have to begin with motivating or stimulating or arousing in a cornered individual the wish and hope and intention to change his methods of dealing with the realities of life. Can this be done by education, medication, counseling, training? I would answer *yes*. It can be done successfully in a majority of cases, if undertaken in time.

The present penal system and the existing legal philosophy do not stimulate or even expect such a change to take place in the criminal. Yet change is what medical science always aims for. The prisoner, like the doctor's other patients, should emerge from his treatment experience a different person, differently equipped, differently functioning, and headed in a different direction from when he began the treatment.

It is natural for the public to doubt that this can be accomplished with criminals. But remember that the public used to doubt that change could be effected in the mentally ill. * * * The average length of time required for restoring a mentally ill patient to health in [one particular] hospital has been reduced from years, to months, to weeks. Four-fifths of the patients living there today will be back in their homes by the end of the year. There are many empty beds, and the daily census is continually dropping.

WHAT IS THIS EFFECTIVE TREATMENT?

If these "incurable" patients are now being returned to their homes and their work in such numbers and with such celerity, why not something similar for offenders? Just what are the treatments used to effect these rapid changes? Are they available for use with offenders?

c. From the Crime of Punishment by Karl Menninger, M.D. Copyright © 1966, 1968 by Jeannette Lyle Menninger. Reprinted by permission of The Viking Press, Inc.

The forms and techniques of psychiatric treatment used today number in the hundreds. Psychoanalysis; electroshock therapy; psychotherapy; occupational and industrial therapy; family group therapy; milieu therapy; the use of music, art, and horticultural activities; and various drug therapies—these are some of the techniques and modalities of treatment used to stimulate or assist the restoration of a vital balance of impulse control and life satisfaction. No one patient requires or receives all forms, but each patient is studied with respect to his particular needs, his basic assets, his interests, and his special difficulties. In addition to the treatment modalities mentioned, there are many facilitations and events which contribute to total treatment effect: a new job opportunity (perhaps located by a social worker) or a vacation trip, a course of reducing exercises, a cosmetic surgical operation or a herniotomy, some night school courses, a wedding in the family (even one for the patient!), an inspiring sermon. Some of these require merely prescription or suggestion; others require guidance, tutelage, or assistance by trained therapists or by willing volunteers. A therapeutic team may embrace a dozen workers—as in a hospital setting—or it may narrow down to the doctor and the spouse. Clergymen, teachers, relatives, friends, and even fellow patients often participate informally but helpfully in the process of readaptation.

All of the participants in this effort to bring about a favorable change in the patient, i.e., in his vital balance and life program, are imbued with what we may call a *therapeutic attitude*. This is one in direct antithesis to attitudes of avoidance, ridicule, scorn, or punitiveness. Hostile feelings toward the subject, however justified by his unpleasant and even destructive behavior, are not in the curriculum of therapy or in the therapist. This does not mean that therapists approve of the offensive and obnoxious behavior of the patient; they distinctly disapprove of it. But they recognize it as symptomatic of continued imbalance and disorganization, which is what they are seeking to change. * * * A patient may cough in the doctor's face or may vomit on the office rug; a patient may curse or scream or even struggle in the extremity of his pain. But these acts are not "punished." Doctors and nurses have no time or thought for inflicting unnecessary pain even upon patients who may be difficult, disagreeable, provocative, and even dangerous. It is their duty to care for them, to try to make them well, and to prevent them from doing themselves or others harm. This requires love, not hate.

This is the deepest meaning of the therapeutic attitude. Every doctor knows this; every worker in a hospital or clinic knows it (or should). * * *

"But you were talking about the mentally ill," readers may interject, "those poor, confused, bereft, frightened individuals who yearn for help from you doctors and nurses. Do you mean to imply that willfully perverse individuals, our criminals, can be similarly reached and rehabilitated? Do you really believe that effective treatment of the sort you visualize can be applied to people *who do not want any help,* who are so willfully vicious, so well aware of the wrongs they are doing, so lacking in penitence or even common decency that punishment seems to be the only thing left?"

Do I believe there is effective treatment for offenders, and that they *can* be changed? *Most certainly and definitely I do.* Not all cases, to be sure; there are also some physical afflictions which we cannot cure at the moment. Some provision has to be made for incurables—pending new knowledge—and these will include some offenders. But I believe the majority of them would prove to be curable. The willfulness and the viciousness of offenders are part of the thing for which they have to be treated. These must not thwart the therapeutic attitude.

Note

The optimism expressed by Dr. Menninger in the selection above has been challenged by a number of recent commentators. Perhaps the most widely quoted is Martinson, What Works? Questions and Answers About Prison Reform, 35 Public Interest 22 (1974). The review article presents the results of a study of research reports on correctional programs published from 1945 through 1967; the material is presented in greater detail in D. Lipton, R. Martinson, and J. Wilks, The Effectiveness of Correctional Treatment (1975). Martinson's "rather bald" summary of the researchers' findings is:

> *With few and isolated exceptions, the rehabilitative efforts that have been reported so far have had no appreciable effect on recidivism.* Studies that have been done since our survey was completed do not represent any major ground for altering that original conclusion.

Martinson, supra, at 25 (emphasis in original). Later, he does acknowledge having found instances of success or partial success, but he describes them as having "been isolated, producing no clear pattern to indicate the efficacy of any particular method of treatment." Id. at 49. The Martinson article was criticized severely in Palmer, Martinson Revisited, 12 J.Research in Crime and Delinquency 133 (1975), which indicated that 48% of the 82 individual studies examined by Martinson reported positive or partly positive results. Id. at 142. Because of Martinson's criteria, Palmer argued, methods of treatment that were proven successful for some offenders but not others were improperly classified as unsuccessful. Id. at 150. Martinson defended his original results in Martinson, California Research at the Crossroads, 22 Crime & Delinquency 180 (1976). In this piece, Martinson summarizes the implications of his earlier essay as follows: "the *addition* of isolated 'treatment' elements to a system (probation, imprisonment, parole) in which a given flow of offenders has generated a gross rate of recidivism has very little effect (and, in most cases, no effect) in making this rate of recidivism better or worse." Id. at 190 (emphasis in original).

At a 1978 workshop, however, Martinson was said to have engaged in a "blistering critique" of his earlier work. Subsequent work in the area, he is reported to have said, had convinced him that in his earlier efforts he needlessly rejected significant pieces of research because of methodological flaws. "Martinson Attacks His Own Earlier Work," Criminal Justice Newsletter, Vol. 9, No. 24, p. 4 (Dec. 4, 1978).

A more recent summary of the reviews of hundreds of sociological studies of the effectiveness of prisons in achieving rehabilitation is Marsden & Orsagh, Prison Effectiveness Measurement, in Evaluating Performance of Criminal Justice Agencies 211 (Whitaker & Phillips, eds. 1983). The authors write: "The result of these and other assessments of prison performance with respect to rehabilitation has been the belief that 'nothing works,' or at least not very well." Id. at 218.

3. CRIMINALIZATION AND PUNISHMENT AS A REFLECTION OF MORALITY

The preceding materials have examined the distinctive qualities of criminalization as a social institution and presented various justifications for punishment of those who violate the criminal law. The question of what conduct should be criminalized is a distinct issue that can be even more difficult to resolve. There is little debate over the propriety of criminalizing conduct which clearly threatens the security of person, place, or property. Such actions violate "rights" that all are thought to enjoy and are regarded as moral wrongs as well as criminal offenses. Yet not all behavior which is morally reprehensible—betraying the confidences of friends, ignoring the needs of aged parents, or exploiting the love of another—are the subject of criminal proscriptions. The criminal law reflects moral values but is not coterminous with them. On what basis is the law justified in making conduct criminal *because* that conduct is viewed as immoral? The materials in this subsection address this question.

A number of subissues may arise. For example, Mill seems to suggest that the immoral nature of conduct should not, in the absence of an adverse impact from the conduct on persons other than the actor, be regarded as justifying the criminalization of that conduct. But is it possible to draw an acceptable line between conduct that is simply immoral and that which is—in addition, perhaps, to being immoral—injurious to persons other than the actor? It may also be relevant to consider what might be accomplished in utilitarian terms by criminalizing conduct because it is viewed as immoral.

Devlin urges that certain concrete effects will flow from causing the criminal law to reflect moral values; Hart, on the other hand, questions this. In this regard, consider whether both parties to the debate are not arguing in utilitarian terms although Devlin may be contending for the use of the criminal law "as a protection from a wider set of injuries to society". See Hart, page 72, supra.

Reconsider the basic question: Even if we cannot reasonably expect specific beneficial effects to flow from the criminalization of immoral conduct, can it be argued that the mere fact that the conduct is immoral justifies its criminalization? Is it appropriate to consider as a beneficial result a possible reduction in the incidence of the conduct due to the moralizing effect of criminalization, i.e., the solemn pronouncement of a society's disapproval? Reconsider the views of Andenaes, from page 76 supra?)

P. DEVLIN, THE ENFORCEMENT OF MORALS
9 (1965).

I think it is clear that the criminal law as we know it is based upon moral principle. In a number of crimes its function is simply to enforce a moral principle and nothing else.

J. MILL, UTILITARIANISM: LIBERTY AND REPRESENTATIVE GOVERNMENT 73 [d]

The sole end for which mankind is warranted, individually or collectively, in interfering with the liberty of action of any of their number is self-protection. That the only purpose for which power can be rightfully exercised over any member of a civilized community, against his will, is to prevent harm to others. His own good, whether physical or moral, is not a sufficient warrant. He cannot rightfully be compelled to do or forbear because it will be better for him to do so, because it will make him happier, because, in the opinion of others, to do so would be wise, or even right. These are good reasons for remonstrating with him, or reasoning with him or persuading him, or entreating him but not for compelling him, or visiting him with any evil in case he do otherwise. To justify that, the conduct from which it is desired to deter him must be calculated to produce evil to some one else. The only part of the conduct of any one, for which he is amenable to society, is that which concerns others. In the part which merely concerns himself, his independence is, of right, absolute.

Note and Question

If Mill's statement set out above is accepted, does this provide a practical method of determining which actions are properly made criminal? What conduct of a person—to adopt Mill's own terms—"merely concerns himself" and what conduct "concerns others?" Nagel, The Enforcement of Morals, The Humanist, May/June 1968, 21 suggests that relatively few if any human actions have no impact upon persons other than the actor. As a result, Nagel argues, Mill's standard can only be applied if there is "a fairly detailed moral philosophy" that permits the identification of those impacts upon others that justify regarding conduct as concerning others. Nagel also argues that even if such a moral philosophy does exist, applying it requires more than appeal to "uncriticized custom" or consideration of conduct in isolation from "the enormously complex field of human rela-

d. From the book Utilitarianism: Liberty and Representative Government by John Stuart Mill. Everyman's Library Edition. Published by E.P. Dutton & Co., Inc. and used with their permission.

tions" in which conduct is frequently embedded. Empirical study of the actual consequences of conduct is essential. Is Nagel correct? If so, does Mill's essay contribute much to the question of what conduct to criminalize?

P. DEVLIN, THE ENFORCEMENT OF MORALS
9–10 (1965).[e]

What makes a society of any sort is a community of ideas, not only political ideas but also ideas about the way its members should behave and govern their lives; these latter ideas are its morals. Every society has a moral structure as well as a political one: or rather, since that might suggest two independent systems, I should say that the structure of every society is made up both of politics and morals. Take, for example, the institution of marriage. Whether a man should be allowed to take more than one wife is something about which every society has to make up its mind one way or the other. In England we believe in the Christian idea of marriage and therefore adopt monogamy as a moral principle. Consequently the Christian institution of marriage has become the basis of family life and so part of the structure of our society. It is there not because it is Christian. It has got there because it is Christian, but it remains there because it is built into the house in which we live and could not be removed without bringing it down. The great majority of those who live in this country accept it because it is the Christian idea of marriage and for them the only true one. But a non-Christian is bound by it, not because it is part of Christianity but because, rightly or wrongly, it has been adopted by the society in which he lives. It would be useless for him to stage a debate designed to prove that polygamy was theologically more correct and socially preferable; if he wants to live in the house, he must accept it as built in the way in which it is.

We see this more clearly if we think of ideas or institutions that are purely political. Society cannot tolerate rebellion; it will not allow argument about the rightness of the cause. Historians a century later may say that the rebels were right and the Government was wrong and a percipient and conscientious subject of the State may think so at the time. But it is not a matter which can be left to individual judgment.

The institution of marriage is a good example for my purpose because it bridges the division, if there is one, between politics and morals. Marriage is part of the structure of our society and it is also the basis of a moral code which condemns fornication and adultery. The institution of marriage would be gravely threatened if individual judgments were permitted about the morality of adultery; on these points there must be a public morality. But public morality is not to be confined to those moral principles which support institutions such as marriage. People do not think of monogamy as something which has to

e. From Morals and the Criminal Law included in The Enforcement of Morals by Lord Devlin, published by Oxford University Press.

be supported because our society has chosen to organize itself upon it; they think of it as something that is good in itself and offering a good way of life and that it is for that reason that our society has adopted it. I return to the statement that I have already made, that society means a community of ideas; without shared ideas on politics, morals, and ethics no society can exist. Each one of us has ideas about what is good and what is evil; they cannot be kept private from the society in which we live. If men and women try to create a society in which there is no fundamental agreement about good and evil they will fail; if, having based it on common agreement, the agreement goes, the society will disintegrate. For society is not something that is kept together physically; it is held by the invisible bonds of common thought. If the bonds were too far relaxed the members would drift apart. A common morality is part of the bondage. The bondage is part of the price of society; and mankind, which needs society, must pay its price.

Common lawyers used to say that Christianity was part of the law of the land. That was never more than a piece of rhetoric * * *[.] What lay behind it was the notion which I have been seeking to expound, namely that morals—and up till a century or so ago no one thought it worth distinguishing between religion and morals—were necessary to the temporal order.

H.L.A. HART, SOCIAL SOLIDARITY AND THE ENFORCEMENT OF MORALITY
35 U.Chi.L.Rev. 1, 8–13 (1967).

If we ask in relation to theories such as Lord Devlin's * * * precisely what empirical claim they make concerning the connection between the maintenance of a common morality and the existence of society, some further disentangling of knots has to be done.

It seems a very natural objection to such theories that if they are to be taken seriously * * * the justification which they attempt to give for the enforcement of social morality is far too general. It is surely both possible and good sense to discriminate between those parts of a society's moral code (assuming it has a single moral code) which are essential for the existence of a society and those which are not. Prima facie, at least, the need for such a discrimination seems obvious even if we assume that the moral code is only to be enforced where it is supported by "sentiments which are strong and precise" * * * or by "intolerance, indignation and disgust" * * *. For the decay of all moral restraint on the free use of violence or deception would not only cause individual harm but would jeopardise the existence of a society since it would remove the main conditions which make it possible and worthwhile for men to live together in close proximity to each other. On the other hand the decay of moral restraint on, say, extramarital intercourse, or a general change of sexual morality in a permissive direction seems to be quite another matter and not obviously to entail any such consequences as "disintegration" or "men drifting apart."

It seems, therefore, worthwhile pausing to consider two possible ways of discriminating within a social morality the parts which are to be considered essential.

(i) The first possibility is that the common morality which is essential to society, and which is to be preserved by legal enforcement, is that part of its social morality which contains only those restraints and prohibitions that are essential to the existence of any society of human beings whatever. Hobbes and Hume have supplied us with general characterisations of this moral minimum essential for social life: they include rules restraining the free use of violence and minimal forms of rules regarding honesty, promise keeping, fair dealing, and property. It is, however, quite clear that * * * Devlin * * * [does not mean] that only those elements, which are to be found in common morality, are to be enforced by law * * *. Quite clearly the argument * * * concerns moral rules which may differ from society to society * * *

(ii) The second possibility is this: the morality to be enforced, while not coextensive with every jot and tittle of an existent moral code, includes not only the restraints and prohibitions such as those relating to the use of violence or deception which are necessary to any society whatever, but also what is essential for a particular society. The guiding thought here is that for any society there is to be found, among the provisions of its code of morality, a central core of rules or principles which constitutes its pervasive and distinctive style of life. Lord Devlin frequently speaks in this way of what he calls monogamy adopted "as a moral principle," and of course this does deeply pervade our society in two principal ways. First, marriage is a *legal* institution and the recognition of monogamy as the sole legal form of marriage carries implications for the law related to wide areas of conduct: the custody and education of children, the rules relating to inheritance and distribution of property, etc. Second, the principle of monogamy is also morally pervasive: monogamous marriage is at the heart of our conception of family life, and with the aid of the law has become part of the structure of society. Its disappearance would carry with it vast changes throughout society so that without exaggeration we might say that it had changed its character.

On this view the morality which is necessary to the existence of society is neither the moral minimum required in all societies (Lord Devlin himself says that polygamous marriage in a polygamous society may be an equally cohesive force as monogamy is in ours), nor is it every jot and tittle of a society's moral code. What is essential and is to be preserved is the central core. On this footing it would be an open and empirical question whether any particular moral rule or veto, e.g., on homosexuality, adultery, or fornication, is so organically connected with the central core that its maintenance and preservation is required as a vital outwork or bastion. There are perhaps traces of some of these ideas in Lord Devlin * * *. But even if we take this to be the position, we are still not really confronted with an empirical claim concerning the connection of the maintenance of a common morality and the prevention of disintegration or "drifting apart." Apart from the point about whether a particular rule is a vital outwork or bastion of the central core, we may still be confronted only with the unexciting tautology depending now on the identification of society, not with the whole of its morality but only with its central core or "character" and this is not the disintegration thesis.

* * *

What is required to convert the last mentioned position into the disintegration thesis? It must be the theory that the maintenance of the core elements in a particular society's moral life is in fact necessary to prevent disintegration, because the withering or malignant decay of the central morality is a disintegrating factor. But even if we have got thus far in identifying an empirical claim, there would of course be very many questions to be settled before anything empirically testable could be formulated. What are the criteria in a complex society for determining the existence of a single recognised morality or its central core? What is "disintegration" and "drifting apart" under modern conditions? I shall not investigate these difficulties but I shall attempt to describe in outline the types of evidence that might conceivably be relevant to the issue if and when these difficulties are settled. They seem to be the following:

(a) Crude historical evidence in which societies—not individuals—are the units. The suggestion is that we should examine societies which have disintegrated and enquire whether their disintegration was preceded by a malignant change in their common morality. This done, we should then have to address ourselves to the possibility of a causal connection between decay of a common morality and disintegration. But of course all the familiar difficulties involved in macroscopic generalisations about society would meet us at this point, and anyone who has attempted to extract generalisations from what is called the decline and fall of the Roman Empire would know that they are formidable. To take only one such difficulty: suppose that all our evidence was drawn from simple tribal societies or closely knit agrarian societies * * *. We should not, I take it, have much confidence in applying any conclusions drawn from these to modern industrial societies. Or, if we had, it would be because we had some well developed and well evidenced theory to show us that the differences betwen simple societies and our own were irrelevant to these issues as the differences in the size of a laboratory can safely be ignored as irrelevant to the scope of the generalisations tested by laboratory experiments.
* * *

(b) The alternative type of evidence must be drawn presumably from social psychology and must break down into at least two subforms according to the way in which we receive the alternatives to the maintenance of a common morality. One alternative is general uniform *permissiveness* in the area of conduct previously covered by the common morality. The lapse, for example, of the conception that the choices between two wives or one, heterosexuality or homosexuality, are more than matters of personal taste. This (the alternative of permissiveness) is what Lord Devlin seems to envisage or to fear when he says: "The enemy of society is not error but indifference," and "Whether the new belief is better or worse than the old, it is the interregnum of disbelief that is perilous." On the other hand the alternative may not be permissiveness but moral *pluralism* involving divergent submoralities in relation to the same area of conduct.

To get off the ground with the investigation of the questions that either of these two alternatives opens up, it would be reasonable to abandon any general criteria for the disintegration of society in favour of something sufficiently close to satisfy the general spirit of the disintegration thesis. It would be no doubt sufficient if our evidence were to show that malignant change in a common morality led to a general increase in such forms of antisocial behaviour as would infringe what seem the minimum essentials: the prohibitions and restraints of violence, disrespect for property, and dishonesty. We should then require some account of the conceivable psychological mechanisms supposed to connect the malignant decay of a social morality with the increase in such forms of behavior. Here there would no doubt be signal differences between the alternatives of permissiveness and moral pluralism. On the permissiveness alternative, the theory to be tested would presumably be that in the "interregnum conditions," without the discipline involved in the submission of one area of life, e.g., the sexual, to the requirements of a common morality, there would necessarily be a weakening of the general capacity of individuals for self control. So, with permissiveness in the area formally covered by restrictive sexual morality, there would come increases in violence and dishonesty and a general lapse of those restraints which are essential for any form of social life. This is the view that the morality of the individual constitutes a seamless web. There is a hint that this, in the last resort, is Lord Devlin's view of the way in which the "interregnum" constitutes a danger to the existence of society: for he replied to my charge that he had assumed without evidence that morality was a seamless web by saying that though "[s]eamlessness presses the simile rather hard," "most men take their morality as a whole." But surely this assumption cannot be regarded as obviously true. The contrary view seems at least equally plausible: permissiveness in certain areas of life (even if it has come about through the disregard of a previously firmly established social morality) might make it easier for men to submit to restraints on violence which are essential for social life.

If we conceive the successor to the "common morality" to be not permissiveness but moral pluralism in some area of conduct once covered by a sexual morality which has decayed through the flouting of its restrictions, the thesis to be tested would presumably be that where moral pluralism develops in this way quarrels over the differences generated by divergent moralities must eventually destroy the minimal forms of restraints necessary for social cohesion. The counter-thesis would be that plural moralities in the conditions of modern large scale societies might perfectly well be mutually tolerant. To many indeed it might seem that the counter-thesis is the more cogent of the two, and that over wide areas of modern life, sometimes hiding behind lip service to an older common morality, there actually are divergent moralities living in peace.

Note

Reconsider the materials in this subsection in connection with Bowers v. Hardwick, reprinted at page 140, infra.

Chapter III

CONSTITUTIONAL LIMITS ON CRIMINALIZATION AND PUNISHMENT

Contents

The imposition of criminal liability and criminal punishments is obviously subject to many federal and state constitutional limitations. Conduct that amounts to an exercise of a person's First Amendment right to free speech, for example, cannot serve as the basis for conviction of a crime. The distinctions drawn in criminal statutes and doctrines may be subject to attack on equal protection grounds. In Michael M. v. Superior Court, 450 U.S. 464, 101 S.Ct. 1200, 67 L.Ed.2d 437 (1981) (discussed in Chapter IX, at page 526, infra), for example, the California "statutory rape" law was upheld against a claim that it impermissibly created an offense that could only be committed by males.

93

This Chapter presents several constitutional doctrines that are—or might be—unusually significant in limiting criminal liability or punishment. First, the due process requirement of precision in the definition of crimes is considered. Second, the demand—generally found in the Eighth Amendment prohibition against cruel and unusual punishment—that criminal penalties not be "disproportionate" is addressed. Finally, attention is turned to the constitutional right of privacy and limitations it might impose upon criminal liability.

Some constitutional issues are covered elsewhere in this book. Limitations which the Eighth Amendment prohibition against cruel and unusual punishment might place on criminalizing "involuntary" actions and "status" offenses, for example, are considered in the discussion of the "act" or conduct required for criminal liability, presented in Chapter V, infra.

A. THE REQUIREMENT OF PRECISION

The United States Supreme Court has repeatedly held that due process prohibits criminal conviction of a person under an insufficiently precise—or a "vague"—criminal offense. In United States v. Harriss, 347 U.S. 612, 74 S.Ct. 808, 98 L.Ed. 989 (1954), the Court explained the content of and the rationale for the rule:

> The constitutional requirement of definiteness is violated by a criminal statute that fails to give a person of ordinary intelligence fair notice that his contemplated conduct is forbidden by the statute. The underlying principle is that no man shall be held criminally responsible for conduct which he could not reasonably understand to be proscribed.

347 U.S. at 618, 74 S.Ct. at 812, 98 L.Ed. at 996.

Early application of the due process requirement was illustrated by Lanzetta v. New Jersey, 306 U.S. 451, 59 S.Ct. 618, 83 L.Ed. 888 (1939). Lanzetta and several others were convicted of violating a New Jersey statute making it a crime, punishable by a fine not exceeding $10,000, imprisonment not exceeding 20 years, or both, to be a gangster. The operative language defining the offense provided:

> Any person not engaged in any lawful occupation, known to be a member of any gang consisting of two or more persons, who has been convicted at least three times of being a disorderly person, or who has been convicted of any crime, in this or any other State, is declared to be a gangster * * *

The Court held that the terms employed by the statute "are so vague, indefinite and uncertain that it must be condemned as repugnant to the due process clause of the Fourteenth Amendment." In explanation, it stated:

> The phrase, "consisting of two or more persons" is all that purports to define "gang." The meaning of that word indicated in dictionaries and in historical and sociological writings are numerous and

varied. Nor is the meaning derivable from the common law, for neither in that field nor anywhere in the language of the law is there definition of the word. * * *

The lack of certainty * * * is not limited to the word "gang" or to its dependent "gangster." Without resolving the serious doubts arising from the generality of the language, we assume that the clause "any person not engaged in any lawful occupation" is sufficient to identify a class of persons to which must belong all capable of becoming gangsters within the terms of the provision. The enactment employs the expression, "known to be a member". It is ambiguous. There immediately arises the doubt whether actual or putative association is meant. If actual membership is required, that status must be established as a fact, and the word "known" would be without significance. If reputed membership is enough, there is uncertainty whether that reputation must be general or extend only to some persons. And the statute fails to indicate what constitutes membership or how one may join a "gang."

306 U.S. at 453–54, 458, 59 S.Ct. at 619, 621, 83 L.Ed. at 890–91, 893.

As the principal case in this section makes clear, the due process requirement remains viable although its rationale and perhaps its content as well may have undergone development since *Harriss* and *Lanzetta.*

KOLENDER v. LAWSON

Supreme Court of the United States, 1983.
461 U.S. 352, 103 S.Ct. 1855, 75 L.Ed.2d 903.

JUSTICE O'CONNOR delivered the opinion of the Court.

This appeal presents a facial challenge to a criminal statute that requires persons who loiter or wander on the streets to provide a "credible and reliable" identification and to account for their presence when requested by a peace officer * * *.[1]

I

Appellee Edward Lawson was detained or arrested on approximately 15 occasions between March 1975 and January 1977 pursuant to Cal. Penal Code § 647(e).[2] Lawson was prosecuted only twice, and was convicted once. The second charge was dismissed.

1. Cal.Penal Code § 647(e) provides:

"Every person who commits any of the following acts is guilty of disorderly conduct, a misdemeanor: * * *. (e) Who loiters or wanders upon the streets or from place to place without apparent reason or business and who refuses to identify himself and to account for his presence when requested by any peace officer to do so, if the surrounding circumstances are such as to indicate to a reasonable man that the public safety demands such identification.

2. The District Court failed to find facts concerning the particular occasions on which Lawson was detained or arrested under § 647(e). However, the trial transcript contains numerous descriptions of the stops given both by Lawson and by the police officers who detained him. For example, one police officer testified that he stopped Lawson while walking on an otherwise vacant street because it was late at night, the area was isolated, and the area was located close to a high crime area. Tr. 266–267. Another officer testified that he

Lawson then brought a civil action in the District Court for the Southern District of California seeking a declaratory judgment that § 647(e) is unconstitutional, a mar⁀atory injunction seeking to restrain enforcement of the statute, and compensatory and punitive damages against the various officers who detained him. * * * The Court of Appeals affirmed the District Court determination as to the unconstitutionality of § 647(e). * * *

II

In the courts below, Lawson mounted an attack on the facial validity of § 647(e). "In evaluating a facial challenge to a state law, a federal court must, of course, consider any limiting construction that a state court or enforcement agency has proffered." *Village of Hoffman Estates v. Flipside, Hoffman Estates*, 455 U.S. 489, 494, 102 S.Ct. 1186, 1191, 71 L.Ed.2d 362 (1982). As construed by the California Court of Appeal,⁴ § 647(e) requires that an individual provide "credible and reliable" identification when requested by a police officer who has reasonable suspicion of criminal activity * * *. *People v. Solomon*, 33 Cal.App.3d 429, 108 Cal.Rptr. 867 (1973). "Credible and reliable" identification is defined by the state Court of Appeal as identification "carrying reasonable assurance that the identification is authentic and providing means for later getting in touch with the person who has identified himself." *Id.*, at 438, 108 Cal.Rptr. 867. In addition, a suspect may be required to "*account for his presence* * * * to the extent that it assists in producing credible and reliable identification * * *." *Ibid.* Under the terms of the statute, failure of the individual to provide "credible and reliable" identification permits the arrest.

III

Our Constitution is designed to maximize individual freedoms within a framework of ordered liberty. Statutory limitations on those freedoms are examined for substantive authority and content as well as for definiteness or certainty of expression.

As generally stated, the void-for-vagueness doctrine requires that a penal statute define the criminal offense with sufficient definiteness

detained Lawson, who was walking at a late hour in a business area where some businesses were still open, and asked for identification because burglaries had been committed by unknown persons in the general area. Tr. 207. The appellee states that he has never been stopped by police for any reason apart from his detentions under § 647(e).

4. In *Wainwright v. Stone*, 414 U.S. 21, 22–23, 94 S.Ct. 190, 192, 38 L.Ed.2d 179 (1973), we held that "[f]or the purpose of determining whether a state statute is too vague and indefinite to constitute valid legislation 'we must take the statute as though it read precisely as the highest court of the State has interpreted it.' *Minnesota ex rel. Pearson v. Probate Court*, 309 U.S. 270, 273 [60 S.Ct. 523, 525, 84 L.Ed. 744] (1940)." The Court of Appeals for the Ninth Circuit noted in its decision that the state intermediate appellate court has construed the statute in *People v. Solomon*, 33 Cal.App.3d 429, 108 Cal.Rptr. 867 (1973), that the state supreme court has refused review, and that *Solomon* has been the law of California for nine years. In these circumstances, we agree with the Ninth Circuit that the *Solomon* opinion is authoritative for purposes of defining the meaning of § 647(e). See 658 F.2d 1362, 1364–1365 n. 3 (1981).

that ordinary people can understand what conduct is prohibited and in a manner that does not encourage arbitrary and discriminatory enforcement. *Smith v. Goguen,* 415 U.S. 566, 94 S.Ct. 1242, 39 L.Ed.2d 605 (1974); *Papachristou v. City of Jacksonville,* 405 U.S. 156, 92 S.Ct. 839, 31 L.Ed.2d 110 (1972). Although the doctrine focuses both on actual notice to citizens and arbitrary enforcement, we have recognized recently that the more important aspect of vagueness doctrine "is not actual notice, but the other principal element of the doctrine—the requirement that a legislature establish minimal guidelines to govern law enforcement." *Smith, supra,* 415 U.S. at 574, 94 S.Ct., at 1247–1248. Where the legislature fails to provide such minimal guidelines, a criminal statute may permit "a standardless sweep [that] allows policemen, prosecutors, and juries to pursue their personal predilections." *Id.,* at 575, 94 S.Ct., at 1248.

Section 647(e), as presently drafted and construed by the state courts, contains no standard for determining what a suspect has to do in order to satisfy the requirement to provide a "credible and reliable" identification. As such, the statute vests virtually complete discretion in the hands of the police to determine whether the suspect has satisfied the statute and must be permitted to go on his way in the absence of probable cause to arrest. An individual, whom police may think is suspicious but do not have probable cause to believe has committed a crime, is entitled to continue to walk the public streets "only at the whim of any police officer" who happens to stop that individual under § 647(e). *Shuttlesworth v. City of Birmingham,* 382 U.S. 87, 90, 86 S.Ct. 211, 213, 15 L.Ed.2d 176 (1965). Our concern here is based upon the "potential for arbitrarily suppressing First Amendment liberties * * *." *Id.,* at 91, 86 S.Ct., at 213. In addition, § 647(e) implicates consideration of the constitutional right to freedom of movement. See *Kent v. Dulles,* 357 U.S. 116, 126, 78 S.Ct. 1113, 1118, 2 L.Ed.2d 1204 (1958); *Aptheker v. Secretary of State,* 378 U.S. 500, 505–506, 84 S.Ct. 1659, 1663–1664, 12 L.Ed.2d 992 (1964).[8]

8. In his dissent, Justice White claims that "[t]he upshot of our cases * * * is that whether or not a statute purports to regulate constitutionally protected conduct, it should not be held unconstitutionally vague on its face unless it is vague in all of its possible applications." *Post,* at 1865. The description of our holdings is inaccurate in several respects. First, it neglects the fact that we permit a facial challenge if a law reaches "a substantial amount of constitutionally protected conduct." *Hoffman Estates v. Flipside,* 455 U.S. 489, 494, 102 S.Ct. 1186, 1191, 71 L.Ed.2d 362 (1982). Second, where a statute imposes criminal penalties, the standard of certainty is higher. See *Winters v. New York,* 333 U.S. 507, 515, 68 S.Ct. 665, 670, 92 L.Ed. 840 (1948). This concern has, at times, led us to invalidate a criminal statute on its face even when it could conceivably have had some valid application. See *e.g., Colautti v. Franklin,* 439 U.S. 379, 394–401, 99 S.Ct. 675, 685–688, 58 L.Ed.2d 596 (1979); *Lanzetta v. New Jersey,* 306 U.S. 451, 59 S.Ct. 618, 83 L.Ed. 888 (1939). The dissent concedes that "the overbreadth doctrine permits facial challenge of a law that reaches a substantial amount of conduct protected by the First Amendment * * *." *Post,* at 1866. However, in the dissent's view, one may not "confuse vagueness and overbreadth by attacking the enactment as being vague as applied to conduct other than his own." *Id.* But we have traditionally viewed vagueness and overbreadth as logically related and similar doctrines. See *e.g., Keyishian v. Board of Regents,* 385 U.S. 589, 609, 87 S.Ct. 675, 687, 17 L.Ed.2d 629 (1967); *NAACP v. But-*

Section 647(e) is not simply a "stop-and-identify" statute. Rather, the statute requires that the individual provide a "credible and reliable" identification that carries a "reasonable assurance" of its authenticity, and that provides "means for later getting in touch with the person who has identified himself." *Solomon, supra,* 33 Cal.App.3d 438, 108 Cal.Rptr. 867. In addition, the suspect may also have to account for his presence "to the extent it assists in producing credible and reliable identification." *Ibid.*

At oral argument, the appellants confirmed that a suspect violates § 647(e) unless "the officer [is] satisfied that the identification is reliable." Tr. of Oral Arg. 6. In giving examples of how suspects would satisfy the requirement, appellants explained that a jogger, who was not carrying identification, could, depending on the particular officer, be required to answer a series of questions concerning the route that he followed to arrive at the place where the officers detained him, or could satisfy the identification requirement simply by reciting his name and address. See *id.,* at 6–10.

It is clear that the full discretion accorded to the police to determine whether the suspect has provided a "credible and reliable" identification necessarily "entrust[s] lawmaking 'to the moment-to-moment judgment of the policeman on his beat.' " *Smith, supra,* 415 U.S., at 575, 94 S.Ct., at 1248 (quoting *Gregory v. City of Chicago,* 394 U.S. 111, 120, 89 S.Ct. 946, 951, 22 L.Ed.2d 134 (1969) (Black, J., concurring)). Section 647(e) "furnishes a convenient tool for 'harsh and discriminatory enforcement by local prosecuting officials, against particular groups deemed to merit their displeasure,' " *Papachristou, supra,* 405 U.S., at 170, 92 S.Ct., at 847–848 (quoting *Thornhill v. Alabama,* 310 U.S. 88, 97–98, 60 S.Ct. 736, 741–742, 84 L.Ed. 1093 (1940)), and "confers on police a virtually unrestrained power to arrest and charge persons with a violation." *Lewis v. City of New Orleans,* 415 U.S. 130, 135, 94 S.Ct. 970, 973, 39 L.Ed.2d 214 (1974) (POWELL, J., concurring).   *   *   *

Appellants stress the need for strengthened law enforcement tools to combat the epidemic of crime that plagues our Nation. The concern of our citizens with curbing criminal activity is certainly a matter requiring the attention of all branches of government. As weighty as this concern is, however, it cannot justify legislation that would other-

---

ton, 371 U.S. 415, 433, 83 S.Ct. 328, 338, 9 L.Ed.2d 405 (1963). See also Note, *The Void-for-Vagueness Doctrine in the Supreme Court,* 109 Pa.L.Rev. 67, 110–113 (1960).

No authority cited by the dissent supports its argument about facial challenges in the arbitrary enforcement context. The dissent relies heavily on *Parker v. Levy,* 417 U.S. 733, 94 S.Ct. 2547, 41 L.Ed.2d 439 (1974), but in that case, we deliberately applied a less stringent vagueness analysis "[b]ecause of the factors differentiating military society from civilian society." *Id.,*

at 756, 94 S.Ct., at 2562. *Hoffman Estates, supra,* also relied upon by the dissent, does not support its position. In addition to reaffirming the validity of facial challenges in situations where free speech or free association are affected, see 455 U.S., at 494, 495, 498–499, 102 S.Ct., at 1191, 1193–1194, the Court emphasized that the ordinance in *Hoffman Estates* "simply regulates business behavior" and that "economic regulation is subject to a less strict vagueness test because its subject matter is often more narrow." *Id.,* at 499, 498, 102 S.Ct., at 1193 (footnote omitted).

wise fail to meet constitutional standards for definiteness and clarity. Section 647(e), as presently construed, requires that "suspicious" persons satisfy some undefined identification requirement, or face criminal punishment. Although due process does not require "impossible standards" of clarity, this is not a case where further precision in the statutory language is either impossible or impractical.

IV

We conclude § 647(e) is unconstitutionally vague on its face because it encourages arbitrary enforcement by failing to describe with sufficient particularity what a suspect must do in order to satisfy the statute. Accordingly, the judgment of the Court of Appeals is affirmed, and the case is remanded for further proceedings consistent with this opinion.

It is so ordered.

[The concurring opinion of JUSTICE BRENNAN is omitted.]

JUSTICE WHITE, with whom JUSTICE REHNQUIST joins, dissenting.

The usual rule is that the alleged vagueness of a criminal statute must be judged in light of the conduct that is charged to be violative of the statute. If the actor is given sufficient notice that his conduct is within the proscription of the statute, his conviction is not vulnerable on vagueness grounds, even if as applied to other conduct, the law would be unconstitutionally vague. None of our cases "suggests that one who has received fair warning of the criminality of his own conduct from the statute in question is nonetheless entitled to attack it because the language would not give similar fair warning with respect to other conduct which might be within its broad and literal ambit. One to whose conduct a statute clearly applies may not successfully challenge it for vagueness." *Parker v. Levy,* 417 U.S. 733, 756, 94 S.Ct. 2547, 2561–2562, 41 L.Ed.2d 439 (1974). The correlative rule is that a criminal statute is not unconstitutionally vague on its face unless it is "impermissibly vague in all of its applications." *Hoffman Estates v. Flipside,* 455 U.S. 489, 497, 102 S.Ct. 1186, 1193, 71 L.Ed.2d 362 (1982).

These general rules are equally applicable to cases where First Amendment or other "fundamental" interests are involved. The Court has held that in such circumstances "more precision in drafting may be required because of the vagueness doctrine in the case of regulation of expression," *Parker v. Levy, supra,* 417 U.S., at 756, 94 S.Ct., at 2561; a "greater degree of specificity" is demanded than in other contexts. *Smith v. Goguen,* 415 U.S. 566, 573, 94 S.Ct. 1242, 1247, 39 L.Ed.2d 605 (1974). But the difference in such cases "relates to how strict a test of vagueness shall be applied in judging a particular criminal statute." *Parker v. Levy, supra,* 417 U.S., at 756, 94 S.Ct., at 2562. It does not permit the challenger of the statute to confuse vagueness and overbreadth by attacking the enactment as being vague as applied to conduct other than his own. See *ibid.* Of course, if his own actions are themselves protected by the First Amendment or other constitutional provision, or if the statute does not fairly warn that it is proscribed, he may not be convicted. But it would be unavailing for him to claim that although he knew his own conduct was unprotected and was plainly enough forbidden by the statute, others may be in doubt as to whether their acts are banned by the law.

The upshot of our cases, therefore, is that whether or not a statute purports to regulate constitutionally protected conduct, it should not be held unconstitutionally vague on its face unless it is vague in all of its possible applications. If any fool would know that a particular category of conduct would be within the reach of the statute, if there is an unmistakable core that a reasonable person would know is forbidden by the law, the enactment is not unconstitutional on its face and should not be vulnerable to a facial attack in a declaratory judgment action such as is involved in this case. Under our cases, this would be true, even though as applied to other conduct the provision would fail to give the constitutionally required notice of illegality.

Of course, the overbreadth doctrine permits facial challenge of a law that reaches a substantial amount of conduct protected by the First Amendment; and, as I have indicated, I also agree that in First Amendment cases the vagueness analysis may be more demanding. But to imply, as the majority does, that the overbreadth doctrine requires facial invalidation of a statute which is not vague as applied to a defendant's conduct but which is vague as applied to other acts is to confound vagueness and overbreadth, contrary to *Parker v. Levy, supra.*

The Court says that its decision "rests on our concern for arbitrary law enforcement, and not on the concern for lack of actual notice." But if there is a range of conduct that is clearly within the reach of the statute, law enforcement personnel, as well as putative arrestees, are clearly on notice that arrests for such conduct are authorized by the law. There would be nothing arbitrary or discretionary about such arrests. If the officer arrests for an act that both he and the law breaker know is clearly barred by the statute, it seems to me an untenable exercise of judicial review to invalidate a state conviction because in some other circumstance the officer may arbitrarily misapply the statute. That the law might not give sufficient guidance to arresting officers with respect to other conduct should be dealt with in those situations. It is no basis for fashioning a further brand of "overbreadth" and invalidating the statute on its face, thus forbidding its application to identifiable conduct that is within the state's power to sanction.

I would agree with the majority in this case if it made at least some sense to conclude that the requirement to provide "credible and reliable identification" after a valid stop on reasonable suspicion of criminal conduct is "impermissibly vague in all of its applications." *Hoffman Estates v. Flipside, supra,* at 495, 102 S.Ct., at 1191. But the statute is not vulnerable on this ground; and the majority, it seems to me, fails to demonstrate that it is. Suppose, for example, an officer requests identification information from a suspect during a valid * * * stop and the suspect answers: "Who I am is just none of your business." Surely the suspect would know from the statute that a refusal to provide any information at all would constitute a violation. It would be absurd to suggest that in such a situation only the unfettered discretion of a police officer, who has legally stopped a person on reasonable suspicion, would serve to determine whether a violation of the statute has occurred.

* * *

[E]ven if as the majority cryptically asserts, the statute here implicates First Amendment interests, it is not vague on its face, however more strictly the vagueness doctrine should be applied. The judgment below should therefore not be affirmed but reversed and appellee Lawson remitted to challenging the statute as it has been or will be applied to him.

The majority finds that the statute "contains no standard for determining what a suspect has to do in order to satisfy the requirement to provide a 'credible and reliable' information." At the same time, the majority concedes that "credible and reliable" has been defined by the state court to mean identification that carries reasonable assurance that the identification is authentic and that provides means for later getting in touch with the person. The narrowing construction given this statute by the state court cannot be likened to the "standardless" statutes involved in the cases cited by the majority. For example, *Papachristou v. City of Jacksonville,* 405 U.S. 156, 92 S.Ct. 839, 31 L.Ed.2d 110 (1972), involved a statute that made it a crime to be a "vagrant." The statute provided:

> "Rogues and vagabonds, or dissolute persons who go about begging, common gamblers, * * * common drunkards, common night walkers, * * * lewd, wanton and lascivious persons, * * * common railers and brawlers, persons wandering or strolling around from place to place without any lawful purpose or object, habitual loafers, * * * shall be deemed vagrants." 405 U.S., at 156, n. 1, 92 S.Ct., at 840, n. 1.

In *Lewis v. City of New Orleans,* 415 U.S. 130, 132, 94 S.Ct. 970, 972, 39 L.Ed.2d 214 (1974), the statute at issue made it a crime "for any person wantonly to curse or revile or to use obscene or opprobrious language toward or with reference to any member of the city police while in the actual performance of his duty." The present statute, as construed by the state courts, does not fall in the same category.

The statutes in *Lewis v. City of New Orleans* and *Smith v. Goguen, supra,* as well as other cases cited by the majority clearly involved threatened infringements of First Amendment freedoms. A stricter test of vagueness was therefore warranted. Here, the majority makes a vague reference to potential suppression of First Amendment liberties, but the precise nature of the liberties threatened are never mentioned. *Shuttlesworth v. City of Birmingham,* 382 U.S. 87, 86 S.Ct. 211, 15 L.Ed. 2d 176 (1965), is cited, but that case dealt with an ordinance making it a crime to "stand or loiter upon any street or sidewalk * * * after having been requested by an police officer to move on," *id.*, at 90, 86 S.Ct., at 213, and the First Amendment concerns implicated by the statute were adequately explained by the Court's reference to *Lovell v. City of Griffin,* 303 U.S. 444, 58 S.Ct. 666, 82 L.Ed. 949 (1938), and *Schneider v. State,* 308 U.S. 147, 60 S.Ct. 146, 84 L.Ed. 155 (1939), which dealt with the First Amendment right to distribute leaflets on city streets and sidewalks. There are no such concerns in the present case.

* * * [The Court] resorts instead to the vagueness doctrine to invalidate a statute that is clear in many of its applications but which is somehow distasteful to the majority. As here construed and applied, the doctrine serves as an open-ended authority to oversee the states' legislative choices in the criminal-law area and in this case leaves the state in a quandary as to how to draft a statute that will pass constitutional muster.

I would reverse the judgment of the Court of Appeals.

Notes and Questions

1. Consider the following comment by Mr. Justice Frankfurter, dissenting in Winters v. New York, 333 U.S. 507, 68 S.Ct. 665, 92 L.Ed. 840 (1948):

[The] requirement of fair notice that there is a boundary of prohibited conduct not to be overstepped is included in the conception of "due process of law." The legal jargon for such failure to give forewarning is to say that the statute is void for "indefiniteness."

But "indefiniteness" is not a quantitative concept. It is not even a technical concept of definite components. It is itself an indefinite concept. There is no such thing as "indefiniteness" in the abstract, by which the sufficiency of the requirement expressed by the term may be ascertained. The requirement is fair notice that conduct may entail punishment. But whether notice is or is not "fair" depends upon the subject matter to which it relates. Unlike the abstract stuff of mathematics, or the quantitatively ascertainable elements of much of natural science, legislation is greatly concerned with the multiform psychological complexities of individual and social conduct. Accordingly, the demands upon legislation, and its responses, are variable and multiform. That which may appear to be too vague and even meaningless as to one subject matter may be as definite as another subject matter of legislation permits, if the legislative power to deal with such a subject is not to be altogether denied. The statute books of every State are full of instances of what may look like unspecific definitions of crime, of the drawing of wide circles of prohibited conduct.

In these matters legislatures are confronted with a dilemma. If a law is framed with narrow particularity, too easy opportunities are afforded to nullify the purposes of the legislation. If the legislation is drafted in terms so vague that no ascertainable line is drawn in advance between innocent and condemned conduct, the purpose of the legislation cannot be enforced because no purpose is defined. It is not

merely in the enactment of tax measures that the task of reconciling
these extremes—of avoiding throttling particularity or unfair generality—is one of the most delicate and difficult confronting legislators.
The reconciliation of these two contradictories is necessarily an empiric
enterprise largely depending on the nature of the particular legislative
problem.

What risks do the innocent run of being caught in a net not
designed for them? How important is the policy of the legislation, so
that those who really like to pursue innocent conduct are not likely to
be caught unaware? How easy is it to be explicitly particular? How
necessary is it to leave a somewhat penumbral margin but sufficiently
revealed by what is condemned to those who do not want to sail close
to the shore of questionable conduct? These and like questions confront legislative draftsmen. Answers to these questions are not to be
found in any legislative manual nor in the work of great legislative
draftsmen. They are not to be found in the opinions of this Court.
These are questions of judgment, peculiarly within the responsibility
and the competence of legislatures. The discharge of that responsibility should not be set at naught by abstract notions about "indefiniteness."

333 U.S. at 524–27, 68 S.Ct. at 674–75, 92 L.Ed. at 854–55. If "indefiniteness" or "vagueness" is not definable as an abstract matter, how should the
judicial decision as to whether, in a specific context, the legislature has
been "too indefinite" or "too vague" be made? Is the question whether,
given the possible justifications for imprecision and the potential costs of
such imprecision, the legislative judgment that the imprecision was worth
the risks was "unreasonable?" If so, what factors—in addition to those
enumerated by Mr. Justice Frankfurter—might be considered? See Note,
The Void-For-Vagueness Doctrine in the Supreme Court, 109 U.Penn.L.
Rev. 67 (1961).

2. In Giaccio v. Pennsylvania, 382 U.S. 399, 86 S.Ct. 518, 15 L.Ed.2d
447 (1966) the Court struck down a statute authorizing the imposition of
court costs upon an acquitted defendant in a nonfelony case "whenever the
jury shall [so] determine." Explaining, the Court stated:

[A] law fails to meet the requirements of Due Process if it is so vague
and standardless that it * * * leaves judges and jurors free to decide,
without any legally fixed standards, what is prohibited and what is not
in each particular case. * * * [The statute at issue] contains no
standards at all, nor does it place any conditions of any kind upon the
jury's power to impose costs upon a defendant who has been found by
the jury to be not guilty of a crime charged against him. * * *
Certainly one of the basic purposes of the Due Process Clause has
always been to protect a person against having the Government impose
burdens upon him except in accordance with the valid laws of the land.
Implicit in this constitutional safeguard is the premise that the law
must be one that carries an understandable meaning with legal standards that courts must enforce. This state Act as written does not
even begin to meet this constitutional requirement.

382 U.S. at 402–03, 86 S.Ct. at 520–21, 15 L.Ed.2d at 450. Is this an indication of another interest that the constitutional requirement of precision is intended to protect? Does not efficient administration of a court system—on both the trial and appellate levels—require that the participants have laws to work with that are reasonably precise? If so, does the constitutional requirement of precision serve the purpose of furthering the administrative efficiency of the judicial system, either expressly or implicitly? Is it important whether or not it does so?

If adequate guidance to the judiciary is part of the rationale for the vagueness doctrine what is the appropriate disposition of a law which authorizes pretrial detention of an accused juvenile delinquent based on a finding that there is a "serious risk" that the child may commit another crime before his next court appearance? Schall v. Martin, 467 U.S. 253, 277–80, 104 S.Ct. 2403, 2417–18, 81 L.Ed.2d 207, 226–27 (1984).

3. In United States v. Powell, 423 U.S. 87, 96 S.Ct. 316, 46 L.Ed.2d 228 (1975), Powell was convicted under a federal statute that prohibited the mailing of firearms "capable of being concealed on the person." At trial, the Government's evidence showed that she mailed a sawed-off shotgun with a barrel length of 10 inches and an overall length of 22⅛ inches. The Court of Appeals held that Powell's conviction had to be reversed because of the vagueness of the statute. The Supreme Court, however, reversed the intermediate tribunal:

> While doubt as to the applicability of the language in marginal fact situations may be conceived, we think that the statute gave [Powell] adequate warning that her mailing of a 22-inch-long sawed-off shotgun was a criminal offense.   *   *   *
>
>   The Court of Appeals questioned whether the "person" referred to in the statute to measure the capability of concealment was to be "the person mailing the firearm, the person receiving the firearm, or, perhaps, an average person, male or female, wearing whatever garb might be reasonably appropriate wherever the place and whatever the season." But we think it fair to attribute to Congress the common-sense meaning that such a person would be an average person garbed in a manner to aid, rather than hinder, concealment of the weapons. Such straining to inject doubt into the meaning of words where no doubt would be felt by the normal reader is not required by the "void for vagueness" doctrine, and we will not indulge in it.

423 U.S. at 93, 96 S.Ct. at 320, 46 L.Ed.2d at 234. The Court of Appeals had observed that requiring Congress to delimit specifically the size of the firearms it intends to declare unmailable would "impose no insurmountable burden upon it." The Supreme Court responded:

> [T]his observation of the Court of Appeals *   *   * seriously misconceives the "void for vagueness" doctrine. The fact that Congress might, without difficulty, have chosen "[c]learer and more precise language" equally capable of achieving the end which it sought does not mean that the statute which it in fact drafted is unconstitutionally vague.

423 U.S. at 94, 96 S.Ct. at 320–21, 46 L.Ed.2d at 235. Is this consistent with the principal case?

4. Parker v. Levy, 417 U.S. 733, 94 S.Ct. 2547, 41 L.Ed.2d 439 (1974), relied upon by the dissent in the principal case, involved an army doctor who had become a strong opponent of the war in Viet-Nam and, despite admonishments from his superiors to desist, had urged enlisted men not to go to fight. He had been convicted by a court martial of violating two provisions of the Code of Military Justice and sentenced to three years at hard labor. One section prohibited "conduct unbecoming an officer and gentleman", the other "all disorders and neglects to the prejudice of good order and discipline". The Supreme Court rejected his claim that these provisions were "void for vagueness" and overbroad in violation of the First Amendment. Although the majority acknowledged that the literal language of these provisions was very broad, its meaning in practice had been significantly narrowed by opinions of various military courts and authorities. Moreover, although his conduct involved expression, Captain Levy could not have reasonably doubted that his behavior was condemned by these prohibitions. He could not, therefore, make a constitutional challenge on behalf of others who might not be given fair warning as to the application of these provisions to their conduct.

As is noted in footnote 8 of the principal case, the decision in *Levy* was strongly influenced by the special needs of the military. Persons who engage in certain occupations or professions or activities may thereby subject themselves to an obligation to observe prohibitions couched in terms more vague than would be constitutionally acceptable if directed to the general public. As the Court has explained:

> The degree of vagueness that the Constitution tolerates—as well as the relative importance of fair notice and fair enforcement—depends in part on the nature of the enactment. Thus economic regulation is subject to a less strict vagueness test because its subject matter is often more narrow, and because businesses, which face economic demands to plan behavior carefully, can be expected to consult relevant legislation in advance of action. Indeed, the regulated enterprise may have the ability to clarify the meaning of the regulation by its own inquiry, or by resort to an administrative process.

Village of Hoffman Estates v. Flipside, Hoffman Estates, 455 U.S. 489 at 498, 102 S.Ct. 1186 at 1193, 71 L.Ed.2d 362 at 371–72 (1982).

B. THE REQUIREMENT OF PROPORTIONALITY

There is little quarrel with the proposition that a criminal penalty should be reasonably related—or "proportional"—to the offense, the offender, or both. But there is substantial dispute as to how much severity or leniency is justified by various characteristics of the crime or the offender or other considerations, such as the need to discourage others from committing similar offenses. There is also dispute as to the extent to which the proportionality of particular sentences should be subject to review beyond the sentencing level.

Insofar as such review occurs, it may be as part of a scheme for appellate review of sentences for excessiveness or disproportionality. But among the most vigorous efforts to secure proportionality review have been ones seeking federal court review of penalties imposed by state courts. These efforts, as the cases in this section make clear, have generally invoked the Eighth Amendment's prohibition against cruel and unusual punishment.

Review of the proportionality of a penalty may be easier—and, for that reason, more appropriate as a constitutional matter—when the penalty at issue is that of death. For that reason, this section treats separately Eighth Amendment review of death penalties from similar review of sentences of imprisonment.

1. THE PENALTY OF DEATH

Editors' Introduction: Eighth Amendment Limits on the Death Penalty

The United States Supreme Court's most extensive use of the Eighth Amendment to limit permissible penalties for offenses has been in the area of the death sentence. Most of the holdings, however, have dealt with the *procedure* necessary for determining which convicted defendants should be put to death. In only a few cases has the Court addressed the *substantive* question of when—assuming all required procedural regularity—the imposition of the sentence of death upon a defendant is impermissible under the Eighth Amendment. These cases are considered in this subsection. But because the procedural concerns that have invoked most attention cannot be separated from the fundamental Eighth Amendment limits upon the penalty of death, these need to be briefly considered as a preliminary matter.

Furman v. Georgia, 408 U.S. 238, 92 S.Ct. 2726, 33 L.Ed.2d 346 (1972), held that the sentences of death there at issue had been imposed in violation of the Eighth Amendment. Although nine opinions were written, none constituted an opinion of the Court and consequently the precise significance of *Furman* was somewhat unclear. There was general agreement, however, that *Furman* precluded the execution of defendants sentenced to death under most if not all of the capital sentencing procedures then in effect. Many states responded with new procedures designed to meet what appeared to be the *Furman* requirement that capital sentencing provide reasonable assurance against inconsistent and arbitrary imposition of the ultimate penalty. Some pursued the task by reducing or eliminating discretion; others attempted to provide for guided discretion.

In 1976, the Court decided five cases challenging capital sentencing procedures enacted after *Furman*. Gregg v. Georgia, 428 U.S. 153, 96 S.Ct. 2909, 49 L.Ed.2d 859 (1976); Profitt v. Florida, 428 U.S. 242, 96 S.Ct. 2960, 49 L.Ed.2d 913 (1976); Jurek v. Texas, 428 U.S. 262, 96 S.Ct. 2950, 49 L.Ed.2d 929 (1976); Woodson v. North Carolina, 428 U.S. 280, 96 S.Ct. 2978, 49 L.Ed.2d 944 (1976); Roberts v. Louisiana, 428 U.S. 325,

96 S.Ct. 3001, 49 L.Ed.2d 974 (1976). Four justices took the position that all five statutes before the Court met Eighth Amendment requirements. Two judges took the opposite view that none of them did. The outcome of the cases, then, turned upon the positions taken by a "plurality" consisting of the remaining three justices, Justices Stewart, Stevens, and Powell, who issued rare joint opinions in all five cases.

Justices Brennan and Marshall expressed the view that the death penalty was inherently "cruel and unusual" within the meaning of the Eighth Amendment. 428 U.S. 227, 96 S.Ct. 2971, 49 L.Ed.2d 904 (Brennan, J.); 428 U.S. at 231, 96 S.Ct. at 2973, 49 L.Ed.2d at 907 (Marshall, J.). The plurality opinions rejected the position. This penalty was accepted at common law and at the time of adoption of the Eighth Amendment. Pre-*Furman* decisions of the Court had specifically recognized its validity. Responding to the argument that the "standard of decency" inherent in the Eighth Amendment had evolved to the point at which death was no longer acceptable, the plurality explained:

> Despite the continuing debate, dating back to the 19th century, over the morality and utility of capital punishment, it is now evident that a large proportion of American society continues to regard it as an appropriate and necessary criminal sanction.
>
> The most marked indication of society's endorsement of the death penalty for murder is the legislative response to *Furman*. The legislatures of at least 35 states have enacted new statutes that provide for the death penalty in at least some crimes that result in the death of another person. And the Congress of the United States, in 1974, enacted a statute providing the death penalty for aircraft piracy that results in death. * * *

428 U.S. at 179–80, 96 S.Ct. at 2928, 49 L.Ed.2d at 878–79. The plurality continued:

> [T]he Eighth Amendment demands more than that challenged punishment be acceptable to contemporary society. The Court also must ask whether it comports with the basic concept of human dignity at the core of the Amendment. * * * [T]he sanction imposed cannot be so totally without penological justification that it results in the gratuitous infliction of suffering.
>
> The death penalty is said to serve two principal social purposes: retribution and deterrence of capital crimes by prospective offenders.
>
> In part, capital punishment is an expression of society's moral outrage at particularly offensive conduct. * * * [T]he decision that capital punishment may be an appropriate sanction in extreme cases is an expression of the community's belief that certain crimes are themselves so grievous an affront to humanity that the only adequate response may be the penalty of death.
>
> Statistical attempts to evaluate the worth of the death penalty as a deterrent to crimes by potential offenders have occasioned a great deal of debate. The results have simply been inconclusive. * * *

The value of capital punishment as a deterrent of crime is a complex factual issue the resolution of which properly rests with the legislatures * * *. [W]e cannot say that the judgment of the Georgia legislature that capital punishment may be necessary in some cases is clearly wrong. * * *

Finally, we must consider whether the punishment of death is disproportionate to the crime for which it is imposed. There is no question that death as a punishment is unique in its severity and irrevocability. When a defendant's life is at stake, the Court has been particularly sensitive to insure that every safeguard is observed. But we are concerned here only with the imposition of capital punishment for the crime of murder, and when a life has been taken deliberately by the offender, we cannot say that the punishment is invariably disproportionate to the crime. * * *

428 U.S. at 182–87, 96 S.Ct. at 2929–32, 49 L.Ed.2d at 880–82.

Turning to procedural questions, the plurality rejected the proposition that *Furman's* requirements could be met by eliminating discretion and consequently voted to hold unconstitutional the North Carolina and Louisiana statutes that required the death penalty upon conviction of defendants for certain offenses. The Georgia, Florida, and Texas statutes were upheld as providing sufficiently guided discretion to avoid the constitutional infirmities *Furman* found in the procedures there at issue. As a result of these cases, the Court has since characterized *Furman* as follows:

A fair statement of the consensus expressed by the Court in *Furman* is that "where discretion is afforded a sentencing body on a matter so grave as the determination of whether a human life should be taken or spared, that discretion must be suitably directed and limited so as to minimize the risk of wholly arbitrary and capricious action." Gregg v. Georgia, 428 U.S. 153, 189, 96 S.Ct. 2909, 2932, 49 L.Ed.2d 859 (1976) (opinion of Stewart, Powell, and Stevens, JJ.).

Zant v. Stephens, 462 U.S. 862, 874, 103 S.Ct. 2733, 2741, 77 L.Ed.2d 235, 248 (1983).

Post-1976 cases have pursued this approach. In Lockett v. Ohio, 438 U.S. 586, 98 S.Ct. 2954, 57 L.Ed.2d 973 (1978), for example, the defendant challenged the Ohio capital sentencing procedure. Under this procedure, following conviction of capital murder, death had to be imposed unless the trial judge determined that (1) the victim had induced or facilitated the killing; (2) there was duress, coercion or strong provocation except for which it was unlikely the defendant would have committed the offense; or (3) the offense was primarily the result of the defendant's psychosis or mental deficiency. This, Lockett urged, barred the sentencing judge from considering as mitigating considerations such factors as her character, prior record, age, lack of specific intent to cause death, and the degree of her participation in the killing. A majority of the Court held Lockett's death sentence, imposed under the statute, constitutionally invalid, but again there was no opinion of the Court. *Lockett* has since been described by the Court as holding that "the sentencer in capital cases must be permitted to consider any relevant mitigating factor," because "a consistency produced by ignoring individual differences is a false consistency." Eddings v. Oklahoma, 455 U.S. 104, 112, 102 S.Ct. 868, 875, 71 L.Ed.2d 1, 9 (1982). In *Eddings,* the Court held that the death sentence at issue was constitutionally invalid because the sentencing judge regarded himself as barred from considering in mitigation evidence that the defendant—who was 16 years of age at the time of the offense—had a troubled background which included excessive physical punishment by his father.

These decisions, however, did not address directly the substantive question of when, if ever, the penalty of death was insufficiently related to the offense, the offender, or the functions of criminal punishment to render the penalty constitutionally unacceptable. This is considered in the principal case.

COKER v. GEORGIA

Supreme Court of the United States, 1977.
433 U.S. 584, 97 S.Ct. 2861, 53 L.Ed.2d 982.

MR. JUSTICE WHITE announced the judgment of the Court and filed an opinion in which MR. JUSTICE STEWART, MR. JUSTICE BLACKMUN, and MR. JUSTICE STEVENS, joined.

Georgia Code Ann. § 26–2001 (1972) provides that "[a] person convicted of rape shall be punished by death or by imprisonment for life, or by imprisonment for not less than one nor more than 20 years." Punishment is determined by a jury in a separate sentencing proceeding in which at least one of the statutory aggravating circumstances must be found before the death penalty may be imposed. Petitioner Coker was convicted of rape and sentenced to death. * * *

I

While serving various sentences for murder, rape, kidnaping, and aggravated assault, petitioner escaped from the Ware Correctional Institution near Waycross, Ga., on September 2, 1974. At approximately 11 o'clock that night, petitioner entered the house of Allen and Elnita Carver through an unlocked kitchen door. Threatening the couple with a "board," he tied up Mr. Carver in the bathroom, obtained a knife from the kitchen, and took Mr. Carver's money and the keys to the family car. Brandishing the knife and saying "you know what's going to happen to you if you try anything, don't you," Coker then raped Mrs. Carver. Soon thereafter, petitioner drove away in the Carver car, taking Mrs. Carver with him. Mr. Carver, freeing himself, notified the police; and not long thereafter petitioner was apprehended. Mrs. Carver was unharmed.

Petitioner was charged with escape, armed robbery, motor vehicle theft, kidnaping, and rape. Counsel was appointed to represent him.

Having been found competent to stand trial, he was tried. The jury returned a verdict of guilty, rejecting his general plea of insanity. A sentencing hearing was then conducted in accordance with the procedures dealt with at length in *Gregg v. Georgia*, 428 U.S. 153, 96 S.Ct. 2909, 49 L.Ed.2d 859 (1976), where this Court sustained the death penalty for murder when imposed pursuant to the statutory procedures. The jury was instructed that it could consider as aggravating circumstances whether the rape had been committed by a person with a prior record of conviction for a capital felony and whether the rape had been committed in the course of committing another capital felony, namely, the armed robbery of Allen Carver. The court also instructed, pursuant to statute, that even if aggravating circumstances were present, the death penalty need not be imposed if the jury found they were outweighed by mitigating circumstances, that is, circumstances not constituting justification or excuse for the offense in question, "but which, in fairness and mercy, may be considered as extenuating or reducing the degree" of moral culpability or punishment. The jury's verdict on the rape count was death by electrocution. Both aggravating circumstances on which the court instructed were found to be present by the jury.

II

Furman v. Georgia, 408 U.S. 238, 92 S.Ct. 2726, 33 L.Ed.2d 346 (1972), and the Court's decisions last Term in *Gregg v. Georgia*, 428 U.S. 153, 96 S.Ct. 2909, 49 L.Ed.2d 859 (1976); *Proffitt v. Florida*, 428 U.S. 242, 96 S.Ct. 2960, 49 L.Ed.2d 913 (1976); *Jurek v. Texas*, 428 U.S. 262, 96 S.Ct. 2950, 49 L.Ed.2d 929 (1976); *Woodson v. North Carolina*, 428 U.S. 280, 96 S.Ct. 2978, 49 L.Ed.2d 944 (1976); and *Roberts v. Louisiana*, 428 U.S. 325, 96 S.Ct. 3001, 49 L.Ed.2d 974 (1976), make unnecessary the recanvassing of certain critical aspects of the controversy about the constitutionality of capital punishment. It is now settled that the death penalty is not invariably cruel and unusual punishment within the meaning of the Eighth Amendment; it is not inherently barbaric or an unacceptable mode of punishment for crime; neither is it always disproportionate to the crime for which it is imposed. It is also established that imposing capital punishment, at least for murder, in accordance with the procedures provided under the Georgia statutes saves the sentence from the infirmities which led the Court to invalidate the prior Georgia capital punishment statute in *Furman v. Georgia, supra*.

In sustaining the imposition of the death penalty in *Gregg*, however, the Court firmly embraced the holdings and dicta from prior cases to the effect that the Eighth Amendment bars not only those punishments that are "barbaric" but also those that are "excessive" in relation to the crime committed. Under *Gregg*, a punishment is "excessive" and unconstitutional if it (1) makes no measurable contribution to acceptable goals of punishment and hence is nothing more than the purposeless and needless imposition of pain and suffering; or (2) is grossly out of proportion to the severity of the crime. A punishment might fail the test on either ground. Furthermore, these Eighth Amendment judgments should not be, or appear to be, merely the subjective views of individual Justices; judgment should be informed by objective factors to the maximum possible extent. To this end, attention must be given to the public attitudes concerning a particular sentence—history and precedent, legislative attitudes, and the response of juries reflected in their sentencing decisions are to be consulted. In *Gregg,* after giving due regard to such sources, the Court's judgment was that the death penalty for deliberate murder was neither the purposeless imposition of severe punishment nor a punishment grossly disproportionate to the crime. But the Court reserved the question of the constitutionality of the death penalty when imposed for other crimes.

III

That question, with respect to rape of an adult woman, is now before us. We have concluded that a sentence of death is grossly disproportionate and excessive punishment for the crime of rape and is therefore forbidden by the Eighth Amendment as cruel and unusual punishment.[4]

A

As advised by recent cases, we seek guidance in history and from the objective evidence of the country's present judgment concerning the acceptability of death as a penalty for rape of an adult woman. At no time in the last 50 years have a majority of the States authorized death as a punishment for rape. In 1925, 18 States, the District of Columbia, and the Federal Government authorized capital punishment for the rape of an adult female. By 1971 just prior to the decision in *Furman v. Georgia,* that number had declined, but not substantially, to 16 States plus the Federal Government. *Furman* then invalidated most of the capital punishment statutes in this country, including the rape statutes, because, among other reasons, of the manner in which the death penalty was imposed and utilized under those laws.

With their death penalty statutes for the most part invalidated, the States were faced with the choice of enacting modified capital punishment laws in an attempt to satisfy the requirements of *Furman* or of being satisfied with life imprisonment as the ultimate punishment for *any* offense. Thirty-five States immediately reinstituted the death penalty for at least limited kinds of crime. *Gregg v. Georgia,* 428 U.S., at 179 n. 23, 96 S.Ct., at 2928. This public judgment as to the

---

4. Because the death sentence is a disproportionate punishment for rape, it is cruel and unusual punishment within the meaning of the Eighth Amendment even though it may measurably serve the legitimate ends of punishment and therefore is not invalid for its failure to do so. We observe that in the light of the legislative decisions in almost all of the States and in most of the countries around the world, it would be difficult to support a claim that the death penalty for rape is an indispensable part of the States' criminal justice system.

acceptability of capital punishment, evidenced by the immediate, post-*Furman* legislative reaction in a large majority of the States, heavily influenced the Court to sustain the death penalty for murder in *Gregg v. Georgia, supra,* at 179–182, 96 S.Ct., at 2928–2929.

But if the "most marked indication of society's endorsement of the death penalty for murder is the legislative response to *Furman," Gregg v. Georgia, supra,* at 179–180, 96 S.Ct., at 2928, it should also be a telling datum that the public judgment with respect to rape, as reflected in the statutes providing the punishment for that crime, has been dramatically different. In reviving death penalty laws to satisfy *Furman's* mandate, none of the States that had not previously authorized death for rape chose to include rape among capital felonies. Of the 16 States in which rape had been a capital offense, only three provided the death penalty for rape of an adult woman in their revised statutes—Georgia, North Carolina, and Louisiana. In the latter two States, the death penalty was mandatory for those found guilty, and those laws were invalidated by *Woodson* and *Roberts.* When Louisiana and North Carolina, responding to those decisions, again revised their capital punishment laws, they reenacted the death penalty for murder but not for rape; none of the seven other legislatures that to our knowledge have amended or replaced their death penalty statutes since July 2, 1976, including four States (in addition to Louisiana and North Carolina) that had authorized the death sentence for rape prior to 1972 and had reacted to *Furman* with mandatory statutes, included rape among the crimes for which death was an authorized punishment.

Georgia argues that 11 of the 16 States that authorized death for rape in 1972 attempted to comply with *Furman* by enacting arguably mandatory death penalty legislation and that it is very likely that, aside from Louisiana and North Carolina, these States simply chose to eliminate rape as a capital offense rather than to *require* death for *each* and *every* instance of rape. The argument is not without force; but 4 of the 16 States did not take the mandatory course and also did *not* continue rape of an adult woman as a capital offense. Further, as we have indicated, the legislatures of 6 of the 11 arguably mandatory States have revised their death penalty laws since *Woodson* and *Roberts* without enacting a new death penalty for rape. And this is to say nothing of 19 other States that enacted nonmandatory, post-*Furman* statutes and chose not to sentence rapists to death.

It should be noted that Florida, Mississippi, and Tennessee also authorized the death penalty in some rape cases, but only where the victim was a child and the rapist an adult. The Tennessee statute has since been invalidated because the death sentence was mandatory. *Collins v. State,* 550 S.W.2d 643 (Tenn.1977). The upshot is that Georgia is the sole jurisdiction in the United States at the present time that authorizes a sentence of death when the rape victim is an adult woman, and only two other jurisdictions provide capital punishment when the victim is a child.

The current judgment with respect to the death penalty for rape is not wholly unanimous among state legislatures, but it obviously weighs very heavily on the side of rejecting capital punishment as a suitable penalty for raping an adult woman.

B

It was also observed in *Gregg* that "[t]he jury * * * is a significant and reliable objective index of contemporary values because it is so directly involved." 428 U.S., at 181, 96 S.Ct., at 2929, and that it is thus important to look to the sentencing decisions that juries have made in the course of assessing whether capital punishment is an appropriate penalty for the crime being tried. Of course, the jury's judgment is meaningful only where the jury has an appropriate measure of choice as to whether the death penalty is to be imposed. As far as execution for rape is concerned, this is now true only in Georgia and in Florida; and in the latter State, capital punishment is authorized only for the rape of children.

According to the factual submissions in this Court, out of all rape convictions in Georgia since 1973—and that total number has not been tendered—63 cases had been reviewed by the Georgia Supreme Court as of the time of oral argument; and of these, 6 involved a death sentence, 1 of which was set aside, leaving 5 convicted rapists now under sentence of death in the State of Georgia. Georgia juries have thus sentenced rapists to death six times since 1973. This obviously is not a negligible number; and the State argues that as a practical matter juries simply reserve the extreme sanction for extreme cases of rape and that recent experience surely does not prove that jurors consider the death penalty to be a disproportionate punishment for every conceivable instance of rape, no matter how aggravated. Nevertheless, it is true that in the vast majority of cases, at least 9 out of 10, juries have not imposed the death sentence.

IV

These recent events evidencing the attitude of state legislatures and sentencing juries do not wholly determine this controversy, for the Constitution contemplates that in the end our own judgment will be brought to bear on the question of the acceptability of the death penalty under the Eighth Amendment. Nevertheless, the legislative rejection of capital punishment for rape strongly confirms our own judgment, which is that death is indeed a disproportionate penalty for the crime of raping an adult woman.

We do not discount the seriousness of rape as a crime. It is highly reprehensible, both in a moral sense and in its almost total contempt for the personal integrity and autonomy of the female victim and for the latter's privilege of choosing those with whom intimate relationships are to be established. Short of homicide, it is the "ultimate violation of self." It is also a violent crime because it normally involves force, or the threat of force or intimidation, to overcome the will and the capacity of the victim to resist. Rape is very often accompanied by physical injury to the female and can also inflict mental and psychological damage. Because it undermines the community's sense of security, there is public injury as well.

Rape is without doubt deserving of serious punishment; but in terms of moral depravity and of the injury to the person and to the public, it does not compare with murder, which does involve the unjustified taking of human life. Although it may be accompanied by another crime, rape by definition does not include the death of or even the serious injury to another person. The murderer kills; the rapist, if no more than that, does not. Life is over for the victim of the murderer; for the rape victim, life may not be nearly so happy as it was, but it is not over and normally is not beyond repair. We have the abiding conviction that the death penalty, which "is unique in its severity and irrevocability," *Gregg v. Georgia,* 428 U.S., at 187, 96 S.Ct., at 2931, is an excessive penalty for the rapist who, as such, does not take human life.

This does not end the matter; for under Georgia law, death may not be imposed for any capital offense, including rape, unless the jury or judge finds one of the statutory aggravating circumstances and then elects to impose that sentence. For the rapist to be executed in Georgia, it must therefore be found not only that he committed rape but also that one or more of the following aggravating circumstances were present: (1) that the rape was committed by a person with a prior record of conviction for a capital felony; (2) that the rape was committed while the offender was engaged in the commission of another capital felony, or aggravated battery; or (3) the rape "was outrageously or wantonly vile, horrible or inhuman in that it involved torture, depravity of mind, or aggravated battery to the victim." [14] Here, the first two of these aggravating circumstances were alleged and found by the jury.

Neither of these circumstances, nor both of them together, change our conclusion that the death sentence imposed on Coker is a disproportionate punishment for rape. Coker had prior convictions for capital felonies—rape, murder, and kidnaping—but these prior convictions do not change the fact that the instant crime being punished is a rape not involving the taking of life.

It is also true that the present rape occurred while Coker was committing armed robbery, a felony for which the Georgia statutes authorize the death penalty. But Coker was tried for the robbery offense as well as for rape and received a separate life sentence for this crime; the jury did not deem the robbery itself deserving of the death penalty, even though accompanied by the aggravating circumstance,

---

14. There are other aggravating circumstances provided in the statute, but they are not applicable to rape.

which was stipulated, that Coker had been convicted of a prior capital crime.

We note finally that in Georgia a person commits murder when he unlawfully and with malice aforethought, either express or implied, causes the death of another human being. He also commits that crime when in the commission of a felony he causes the death of another human being, irrespective of malice. But even where the killing is deliberate, it is not punishable by death absent proof of aggravating circumstances. It is difficult to accept the notion, and we do not, that the rapist, with or without aggravating circumstances, should be punished more heavily than the deliberate killer as long as the rapist does not himself take the life of his victim. The judgment of the Georgia Supreme Court upholding the death sentence is reversed, and the case is remanded to that court for further proceedings not inconsistent with this opinion.

So ordered.

[Justices Brennan and Marshall concurred in the judgment on the grounds that the death penalty is in all circumstances cruel and unusual punishment under the Eighth and Fourteenth Amendments. Neither expressed a view as to how the contents of the Eighth and Fourteenth Amendments should be defined *if* those provisions permitted imposition of the death penalty for deliberate murder. Neither brief opinion, therefore, addressed the appropriate criterion for determining when death was a constitutionally-permissible penalty for rape of an adult woman.

MR. JUSTICE POWELL, concurring in the judgment in part and dissenting in part.

I concur in the judgment of the Court on the facts of this case, and also in the plurality's reasoning supporting the view that ordinarily death is disproportionate punishment for the crime of raping an adult woman. Although rape invariably is a reprehensible crime, there is no indication that petitioner's offense was committed with excessive brutality or that the victim sustained serious or lasting injury. The plurality, however, does not limit its holding to the case before us or to similar cases. Rather, in an opinion that ranges well beyond what is necessary, it holds that capital punishment *always*—regardless of the circumstances—is a disproportionate penalty for the crime of rape.

* * *

Today, in a case that does not require such an expansive pronouncement, the plurality draws a bright line between murder and all rapes—regardless of the degree of brutality of the rape or the effect upon the victim. I dissent because I am not persuaded that such a bright line is appropriate. As noted in *Snider v. Peyton*, 356 F.2d 626, 627 (CA4 1966), "[t]here is extreme variation in the degree of culpability of rapists." The deliberate viciousness of the rapist may be greater than that of the murderer. Rape is never an act committed accidentally. Rarely can it be said to be unpremeditated. There also is wide variation in the effect on the victim. The plurality opinion says that "[l]ife is over for the victim of the murderer; for the rape victim, life may not be nearly so happy as it was, but it is not over and normally is not beyond repair." But there is indeed "extreme variation" in the crime of rape. Some victims are so grievously injured physically or psychologically that life *is* beyond repair.

Thus, it may be that the death penalty is not disproportionate punishment for the crime of aggravated rape. Final resolution of the question must await careful inquiry into objective indicators of society's "evolving standards of decency," particularly legislative enactments and the responses of juries in capital cases. The plurality properly examines these idicia, which do support the conclusion that society finds the death penalty unacceptable for the crime of rape in the absence of excessive brutality or severe injury. But it has not been shown that society finds the penalty disproportionate for all rapes. In a proper case a more discriminating inquiry than the plurality undertakes well might discover that both juries and legislatures have reserved the ultimate penalty for the case of an outrageous rape resulting in serious, lasting harm to the victim. I would not prejudge the issue. To this extent, I respectfully dissent.

MR. CHIEF JUSTICE BURGER, with whom MR. JUSTICE REHNQUIST joins, dissenting.

*   *   *

I accept that the Eighth Amendment's concept of disproportionality bars the death penalty for minor crimes. But rape is not a minor crime; hence the Cruel and Unusual Punishments Clause does not give the Members of this Court license to engraft their conceptions of proper public policy onto the considered legislative judgments of the States. Since I cannot agree that Georgia lacked the constitutional power to impose the penalty of death for rape, I dissent from the Court's judgment.

(1)

On December 5, 1971, the petitioner, Ehrlich Anthony Coker, raped and then stabbed to death a young woman. Less than eight months later Coker kidnaped and raped a second young woman. After twice raping this 16-year-old victim, he stripped her, severely beat her with a club, and dragged her into a wooded area where he left her for dead. He was apprehended and pleaded guilty to offenses stemming from these incidents. He was sentenced by three separate courts to three life terms, two 20-year terms, and one 8-year term of imprisonment. Each judgment specified that the sentences it imposed were to run consecutively rather than concurrently. Approximately 1½ years later, on September 2, 1974, petitioner escaped from the state prison where he was serving these sentences. He promptly raped another 16-year-old woman in the presence of her husband, abducted her from her home, and threatened her with death and serious bodily harm. It is this crime for which the sentence now under review was imposed.

The Court today holds that the State of Georgia may not impose the death penalty on Coker. In so doing, it prevents the State from imposing any effective punishment upon Coker for his latest rape. The Court's holding, moreover, bars Georgia from guaranteeing its citizens that they will suffer no further attacks by this habitual rapist. In fact, given the lengthy sentences Coker must serve for the crimes he has already committed, the Court's holding assures that petitioner—as well as others in his position—will henceforth feel no compunction whatsoever about committing further rapes as frequently as he may be able to escape from confinement and indeed even within the walls of the prison itself. To what extent we have left States "elbowroom" to protect innocent persons from depraved human beings like Coker remains in doubt.

(2)

My first disagreement with the Court's holding is its unnecessary breadth. The narrow issue here presented is whether the State of Georgia may constitutionally execute this petitioner for the particular rape which he has committed, in light of all the facts and circumstances shown by this record. The plurality opinion goes to great lengths to consider societal mores and attitudes toward the generic crime of rape and the punishment for it; however, the opinion gives little attention to the special circumstances which bear directly on whether imposition of the death penalty is an appropriate societal response to Coker's criminal acts: (a) On account of his prior offenses, Coker is already serving such lengthy prison sentences that imposition of additional periods of imprisonment would have no incremental punitive effect; (b) by his life pattern Coker has shown that he presents a particular danger to the safety, welfare, and chastity of women, and on his record the likelihood is therefore great that he will repeat his crime at the first opportunity; (c) petitioner escaped from prison, only a year and a half after he commenced serving his latest sentences; he has nothing to lose by further escape attempts; and (d) should he again succeed in escaping from prison, it is reasonably predictable that he will repeat his pattern of attacks on women—and with impunity since the threat of added prison sentences will be no deterrent.

Unlike the plurality, I would narrow the inquiry in this case to the question actually presented: Does the Eighth Amendment's ban against cruel and unusual punishment prohibit the State of Georgia from executing a person who has, within the space of three years, raped three separate women, killing one and attempting to kill another, who is serving prison terms exceeding his probable lifetime and who has not hesitated to escape confinement at the first available opportunity? Whatever one's view may be as to the State's constitutional power to impose the death penalty upon a rapist who stands before a court convicted for the first time, this case reveals a chronic rapist whose continuing danger to the community is abundantly clear.

MR. JUSTICE POWELL would hold the death sentence inappropriate in *this* case because "there is no indication that petitioner's offense was committed with excessive brutality or that the victim sustained serious or lasting injury." Apart from the reality that rape is inherently one of the most egregiously brutal acts one human being can inflict upon another, there is nothing in the Eighth Amendment that so narrowly limits the factors which may be considered by a state legislature in determining whether a particular punishment is grossly excessive. Surely recidivism, especially the repeated commission of heinous crimes, is a factor which may properly be weighed as an aggravating circumstance, permitting the imposition of a punishment more severe than for one isolated offense. * * * Since the Court now invalidates the death penalty as a sanction for all rapes of adults at all times under all circumstances, I reluctantly turn to what I see as the broader issues raised by this holding.

(3)

The plurality acknowledges the gross nature of the crime of rape. A rapist not only violates a victim's privacy and personal integrity, but inevitably causes serious psychological as well as physical harm in the process. The long-range effect upon the victim's life and health is likely to be irreparable; it is impossible to measure the harm which results. Volumes have been written by victims, physicians, and psychiatric specialists on the lasting injury suffered by rape victims. Rape is not a mere physical attack—it is destructive of the human personality. The remainder of the victim's life may be gravely affected, and this in turn may have a serious detrimental effect upon her husband and any children she may have.

Despite its strong condemnation of rape, the Court reaches the inexplicable conclusion that "the death penalty * * * is an excessive penalty" for the perpetrator of this heinous offense. This, the Court holds, is true even though in Georgia the death penalty may be imposed only where the rape is coupled with one or more aggravating circumstances. * * *

The analysis of the plurality opinion is divided into two parts: (a) an "objective" determination that most American jurisdictions do not presently make rape a capital offense, and (b) a subjective judgment that death is an excessive punishment for rape because the crime does not, in and of itself, cause the death of the victim. I take issue with each of these points.

(A)

The plurality opinion bases its analysis, in part, on the fact that "Georgia is the sole jurisdiction in the United States at the present time that authorizes a sentence of death when the rape victim is an adult woman." Surely, however, this statistic cannot be deemed determinative, or even particularly relevant. As the opinion concedes, two other States—Louisiana and North Carolina—have enacted death penalty statutes for adult rape since this Court's 1972 decision in *Furman v. Georgia,* 408 U.S. 238, 92 S.Ct. 2726, 33 L.Ed.2d 346. If the Court is to rely on some "public opinion" process, does this not suggest the beginning of a "trend"?

More to the point, however, it is myopic to base sweeping constitutional principles upon the narrow experience of the past five years. Considerable uncertainty was introduced into this area of the law by this Court's *Furman* decision. A large number of States found their death penalty statutes invalidated; legislatures were left in serious doubt by the expressions vacillating between discretionary and mandatory death penalties, as to whether this Court would sustain *any* statute imposing death as a criminal sanction. Failure of more States to enact statutes imposing death for rape of an adult woman may thus reflect hasty legislative compromise occasioned by time pressures following *Furman,* a desire to wait on the experience of those States which did enact such statutes, or simply an accurate forecast of today's holding.

In any case, when considered in light of the experience since the turn of this century, where more than one-third of American jurisdictions have consistently provided the death penalty for rape, the plurality's focus on the experience of the immediate past must be viewed as truly disingenuous. Having in mind the swift changes in positions of some Members of this Court in the short span of five years, can it rationally be considered a relevant indicator of what our society deems "cruel and unusual" to look solely to what legislatures have *refrained* from doing under conditions of great uncertainty arising from our less than lucid holdings on the Eighth Amendment? Far more representative of societal mores of the 20th century is the accepted practice in a substantial number of jurisdictions preceding the *Furman* decision.
* * *

Three state legislatures have, in the past five years, determined that the taking of human life and the devastating consequences of rape will be minimized if rapists may, in a limited class of cases, be executed for their offenses. That these States are presently a minority does not, in my view, make their judgment less worthy of deference. * * *

The question of whether the death penalty is an appropriate punishment for rape is surely an open one. It is arguable that many prospective rapists would be deterred by the possibility that they could suffer death for their offense; it is also arguable that the death penalty would have only minimal deterrent effect. It may well be that rape victims would become more willing to report the crime and aid in the apprehension of the criminals if they knew that community disapproval of rapists was sufficiently strong to inflict the extreme penalty; or perhaps they would be reluctant to cooperate in the prosecution of rapists if they knew that a conviction might result in the imposition of the death penalty. Quite possibly, the occasional, well-publicized execution of egregious rapists may cause citizens to feel greater security in their daily lives; or, on the contrary, it may be that members of a civilized community will suffer the pangs of a heavy conscience because such punishment will be perceived as excessive. We cannot know which among this range of possibilities is correct, but today's holding forecloses the very exploration we have said federalism was intended to foster. It is difficult to believe that Georgia would long remain alone in punishing rape by death if the next decade demonstrated a drastic reduction in its incidence of rape, an increased cooperation by rape victims in the apprehension and prosecution of rapists, and a greater confidence in the rule of law on the part of the populace.

* * *

(B)

The subjective judgment that the death penalty is simply disproportionate to the crime of rape is even more disturbing than the "objective" analysis discussed *supra*. The plurality's conclusion on this point is based upon the bare fact that murder necessarily results in the physical death of the victim, while rape does not. However, no Member of the Court explains why this distinction has relevance, much less constitutional significance. It is, after all, not irrational—nor constitutionally impermissible—for a legislature to make the penalty more severe than the criminal act it punishes in the hope it would deter wrongdoing:

Until now, the issue under the Eighth Amendment has not been the state of any particular victim after the crime, but rather whether the punishment imposed is grossly disproportionate to the evil committed by the perpetrator. As a matter of constitutional principle, that test cannot have the primitive simplicity of "life for life, eye for eye, tooth for tooth." Rather States must be permitted to engage in a more sophisticated weighing of values in dealing with criminal activity which consistently poses serious danger of death or grave bodily harm. If innocent life and limb are to be preserved I see no constitutional barrier in punishing by death all who engage in such activity, regardless of whether the risk comes to fruition in any particular instance.

* * *

The Court's conclusion * * * is very disturbing indeed. The clear implication of today's holding appears to be that the death penalty may be properly imposed only as to crimes resulting in death of the victim. This casts serious doubt upon the constitutional validity of statutes imposing the death penalty for a variety of conduct which, though dangerous, may not necessarily result in any immediate death, *e.g.*, treason, airplane hijacking, and kidnaping. In that respect, today's holding does even more harm than is initially apparent. We cannot avoid taking judicial notice that crimes such as airplane hijacking, kidnaping, and mass terrorist activity constitute a serious and increasing danger to the safety of the public. It would be unfortunate indeed if the effect of today's holding were to inhibit States and the Federal Government from experimenting with various remedies—including possibly imposition of the penalty of death—to prevent and deter such crimes.

* * *

Whatever our individual views as to the wisdom of capital punishment, I cannot agree that it is constitutionally impermissible for a state legislature to make the "solemn judgment" to impose such penalty for the crime of rape. Accordingly, I would leave to the States the task of legislating in this area of the law.

Notes and Questions

1. In Eberheart v. State, 232 Ga. 247, 206 S.E.2d 12 (1974), the defendant and several companions abducted the female victim, and beat, sodomized and raped her. In the course of these events, the victim sustained a dislocated jaw, a broken nose, a concussion, numerous lacerations and bruises, and a split lip. Several of her teeth were shorn off. She suffered a loss of hearing in her right ear and received internal injuries to her stomach that "continued for some time." Following his conviction for rape and kidnapping, Eberheart was sentenced to death on each of the charges. Vacating the sentences of death, the Supreme Court tersely explained, "The imposition and carrying out of the death penalty constitutes cruel and unusual punishment in violation of the Eighth and Fourteenth Amendments. Coker v. Georgia, 433 U.S. 584, 97 S.Ct. 2861, 53 L.Ed.2d 982 (1977)." Eberheart v. Georgia, 433 U.S. 917, 97 S.Ct. 2994, 53 L.Ed.2d 1104 (1977) (per curiam).

2. In Enmund v. Florida, 458 U.S. 782, 102 S.Ct. 3368, 73 L.Ed.2d 1140 (1982), the evidence tended to show that Enmund remained in a car while several companions robbed and killed an elderly couple. Under Florida law, his presence nearby in readiness to help his companions escape made him a participant in the robbery and under the felony-murder rule (see pages 428–31 infra) as applied in Florida his participation in the felony rendered him guilty of the deaths directly "caused" by his companions. The death sentence was imposed. A majority of the Supreme Court analyzed the constitutional validity of this penalty in a manner "similar" to that used in *Coker*. Of the thirty-seven jurisdictions authorizing the death penalty, only eight permitted this sentence solely for participation in a robbery in which another robber took life. Sentencing juries in death cases, moreover, have generally rejected the death penalty in such cases. Analysis of the 362 executions since 1954, the majority reported, revealed that in only six cases was a "nontriggerman felony murderer" put to death. Further:

> In Gregg v. Georgia the opinion announcing the judgment observed that "[t]he death penalty is said to serve two principal social purposes: retribution and deterrence of capital crimes by prospective offenders." 428 U.S., at 183, 96 S.Ct., at 2929–30 (footnote omitted). Unless the death penalty when applied to those in Enmund's position measurably contributes to one or both of those goals, it "is nothing more than the purposeless and needless imposition of pain and suffering," and hence an unconstitutional punishment. Coker v. Georgia, supra, 433 U.S., at 592, 97 S.Ct., at 2866. We are quite unconvinced, however, that the

threat that the death penalty will be imposed for murder will measurably deter one who does not kill and has no intention or purpose that life be taken. * * * [I]f a person does not intend that life be taken or contemplate that lethal force will be employed by others, the possibility that the death penalty will be imposed for vicarious felony murder will not "enter into the cold calculus that precedes the decision to act." Gregg v. Georgia, supra, 428 U.S., at 186, 96 S.Ct., at 2981 (footnote omitted).

It would be very different if the likelihood of a killing in the course of a robbery were so substantial that one should share the blame for the killing if he somehow participated in the felony. But competent observers have concluded that there is no basis in experience for the notion that death so frequently occurs in the course of a felony for which killing is not an essential ingredient that the death penalty should be considered as a justifiable deterrent to the felony itself. Model Penal Code § 210.2, Comment, p. 38 and n. 96. This conclusion was based on three comparisons of robbery statistics, each of which showed that only about one-half of one percent of robberies resulted in homicide. The most recent national crime statistics strongly support this conclusion. In addition * * *, the death penalty is rarely imposed on one only vicariously guilty of the murder, a fact which further attenuates its possible utility as an effective deterrence.

As for retribution as a justification for executing Enmund, we think this very much depends on the degree of Enmund's culpability—what Enmund's intentions, expectations, and actions were. * * *

For purposes of imposing the death penalty, Enmund's criminal culpability must be limited to his participation in the robbery, and his punishment must be tailored to his personal responsibility and moral guilt. Putting Enmund's to death to avenge two killings that he did not commit and had no intention of committing or causing does not measurably contribute to the retributive end of ensuring that the criminal gets his just deserts.

458 U.S. at 798–801, 102 S.Ct. at 3377–78, 73 L.Ed.2d at 1152–54. The majority therefore concluded

Because the Florida Supreme Court affirmed the death penalty in this case in the absence of proof that Enmund killed or attempted to kill, and regardless of whether Enmund intended or contemplated that life would be taken, we reverse the judgment upholding the death penalty * * *.

458 U.S. at 801, 102 S.Ct. at 3378–79, 73 L.Ed.2d at 1154.

Justice O'Connor, joined by three other members of the Court, dissented, reasoning in part that "the decision of whether or not a particular punishment serves the admittedly legitimate goal of retribution seems uniquely suited to legislative resolution." 458 U.S. at 826 n. 42, 102 S.Ct. at 3392 n. 42, 73 L.Ed.2d at 1170 n. 42 (O'Connor, J., dissenting). In addition, she reasoned:

[E]xamination of the qualitative factors underlying the concept of proportionality do not show that the death penalty is disproportionate as applied to Earl Enmund. In contrast to the crime in *Coker*, [Enmund's] crime involves the very type of harm that this Court has held justifies the death penalty. * * * [B]ecause of the unique and complex mixture of facts involving a defendant's actions, knowledge, motives, and participation during the commission of a felony murder, I believe the factfinder is best able to assess the defendant's blameworthiness. Accordingly, I conclude that the death penalty is not disproportionate to the crime of felony murder, even though the defendant did not actually kill or intend to kill his victims.

458 U.S. at 826, 102 S.Ct. at 3391–92, 73 L.Ed.2d at 1170.

Implementing the holding in *Enmund*, the Court has held that there is no constitutional necessity that the sentencing judge or jury determine specifically that the defendant had the culpability necessary to make the death penalty constitutionally acceptable. It is only necessary that "at some point in the process"—as, for example, in an appellate court's scrutiny of the sufficiency of the evidence to support the death penalty—"the requisite factual finding as to the defendant's culpability [was] made." Cabana v. Bullock, __ U.S. __, __, 106 S.Ct. 689, 697, 88 L.Ed.2d 704, 717 (1986).

3. In Eddings v. Oklahoma, 455 U.S. 104, 110 n. 5, 102 S.Ct. 868, 874 n. 5, 71 L.Ed.2d 1, 8 n. 5 (1982), the Court noted but did not reach the question of whether the Eighth Amendment prohibits the execution of a murderer who was sixteen years of age at the time of the offense. But lower courts have upheld the death penalty in such situations. E.g., Trimble v. State, 300 Md. 387, 478 A.2d 1143 (1984), cert. denied, __ U.S. __, 105 S.Ct. 1231, 84 L.Ed.2d 368 (1985) (Eighth Amendment does not bar death penalty for all offenders under eighteen at time of offense).

4. Pulley v. Harris, 465 U.S. 37, 104 S.Ct. 871, 79 L.Ed.2d 29 (1984), raised proportionality issues of a somewhat different sort. Harris had been convicted of murder and sentenced to death by the California courts. He attacked the procedure under which his sentence was reviewed on appeal. The Supreme Court noted:

Traditionally, "proportionality" has been used with reference to an abstract evaluation of the appropriateness of a sentence for a particular crime. Looking to the gravity of the offense and the severity of the penalty, to sentences imposed for other crimes, and to sentencing practices in other jurisdictions, this Court has occasionally struck down punishments as inherently disproportionate, and therefore cruel and unusual, when imposed for a particular crime or category of crime [citing, among other cases, *Coker* and *Enmund*]. The death penalty is not in all cases a disproportionate penalty in this sense.

The proportionality review sought by Harris * * * and provided for in numerous state statutes is of a different sort. This sort of proportionality review presumes that the death sentence is not disproportionate to the crime in the traditional sense. It purports to inquire instead whether the penalty is nonetheless unacceptable in a particular case because disproportionate to the punishment imposed on others convicted of the same crime. The issue in this case, therefore, is whether the Eighth Amendment * * * requires a state appellate court, before it affirms a death sentence, to compare the sentence in the case before it with the penalties imposed in similar cases if requested to do so by the prisoner. Harris insists that it does and that this is the invariable rule in every case. * * * We do not agree.

* * *

There is * * * no basis in our cases for holding that comparative proportionality review by an appellate court is required in every case in which the death penalty is imposed and the defendant requests it. * * * We are not persuaded that the Eighth Amendment requires us to take that course.

* * *

Assuming that there could be a capital sentencing scheme so lacking in other checks on arbitrariness that it would not pass constitutional muster without comparative proportionality review, the * * * California statute is not of that sort. [If the state seeks the death penalty, under the California procedure, it specifies in its charge of first degree murder "special circumstances" that it believes exist. If the jury finds the defendant guilty of first degree murder, it must determine whether the alleged special circumstances have been proved beyond a reasonable doubt to be present. If the jury finds such circumstances have been proved, a penalty hearing is held. The jury is then given a list of relevant considerations and is told to determine whether the penalty is to be life imprisonment without parole or death. It is instructed to take into account and be guided by the aggravating and mitigating circumstances in the list. If the jury determines that death is appropriate, it so finds. This is reviewed by the trial judge, who has the power to modify the sentence by imposing life imprisonment. This review is to involve an independent determination of whether the weight of the evidence supports the jury's findings and verdict. The trial judge's reasons for his conclusion are to be placed in the record. If the trial judge does not modify the penalty, appellate review is automatic and the appellate court reviews the evidence relied upon by the trial judge in refusing to modify the jury's determination that death is the appropriate penalty.] On its face, this system, without any requirement or practice of comparative proportionality review, cannot be successfully challenged under *Furman* and our subsequent cases.

Any capital sentencing scheme may occasionally produce aberrational outcomes. Such inconsistencies are a far cry from the major systemic defects identified in *Furman*. As we have acknowledged in the past, "there can be 'no perfect procedure for deciding in which cases governmental authority should be used to impose death.'" Zant v. Stephens, 462 U.S. [862, 884], 103 S.Ct. [2733,] 2747, [77 L.Ed.2d 235 (1983)], quoting Lockett v. Ohio, 438 U.S. 586, 605, 98 S.Ct. 2954, 2965, 57 L.Ed.2d 973 (1977) (plurality opinion). As we are presently informed, we cannot say that the California procedures provided Harris inadequate protections against the evil identified in *Furman*. * * *

465 U.S. at 42–54, 104 S.Ct. at 879–81, 79 L.Ed.2d at 35–42. Does the Supreme Court's holding preclude Harris or others sentenced to death from

specifically attacking *their particular sentences* on the ground those sentences of death are disproportionate to the punishment imposed on others convicted of the same offense?

2. IMPRISONMENT

Eighth Amendment review of the proportionality of criminal sentences may be less appropriate when the issue is the length of a sentence of imprisonment. This was indicated by the Supreme Court's decision in Rummel v. Estelle, 445 U.S. 263, 100 S.Ct. 1133, 63 L.Ed.2d 382 (1980). In 1964, Rummel was convicted in a Texas court of fraudulent use of a credit card to obtain goods or services of a value exceeding $50; he received a sentence of three years' imprisonment. In 1969, he was convicted of passing a forged check in the amount of $28.36; he received a sentence of four years' imprisonment. In 1973, Rummel was charged and convicted of obtaining $120.75 by false pretenses. Proceeding under Texas' recidivist statute, the prosecution alleged and proved his two prior felony convictions. Texas law required, upon proof of two such prior convictions in a felony sentencing, that a life sentence be imposed and this was done in Rummel's case. A majority of the Supreme Court held that this mandatory penalty of life imprisonment did not constitute cruel and unusual punishment:

> [Rummel] might have received more lenient treatment in almost any State other than Texas, West Virginia, or Washington [which all provide mandatory life sentences upon a third felony conviction]. The distinctions, however, are subtle rather than gross. A number of States impose a mandatory life sentence upon conviction of four felonies rather than three. Other States require one or more of the felonies to be "violent" to support a life sentence. Still other States leave the imposition of a life sentence after three felonies within the discretion of a judge or jury.

445 U.S. at 279–80, 100 S.Ct. at 1142, 63 L.Ed.2d at 394. Texas, the Court noted, has a "relatively liberal policy of granting 'good time' credits to its prisoners," with the result that Rummel might become eligible for parole in as little as 12 years. Any comparison of recidivist schemes would be extremely complex. Further:

> Even were we to assume that the statute employed against Rummel was the most stringent found in the 50 States, that severity hardly would render Rummel's punishment "grossly disproportionate" to his offenses or to the punishment he would have received in other States. * * * Penologists themselves have been unable to agree whether sentences should be light or heavy, discretionary or determinate. This uncertainty reinforces our conviction that any "nationwide trend" towards lighter, discretionary sentences must find its source and its sustaining forces in the legislatures, not in the federal courts.

445 U.S. at 281, 283–84, 100 S.Ct. at 1143–44, 63 L.Ed.2d at 395–97.

As the principal case in this subsection indicates, the Supreme Court has not been unqualified in its reluctance to review the proportionality of sentences of imprisonment. Are there meaningful differences between Rummel's sentence and that of the convicted defendant in the principal case?

SOLEM v. HELM

Supreme Court of the United States, 1983.
463 U.S. 277, 103 S.Ct. 3001, 77 L.Ed.2d 637.

JUSTICE POWELL delivered the opinion of the Court.

The issue presented is whether the Eighth Amendment proscribes a life sentence without possibility of parole for a seventh nonviolent felony.

I

By 1975 the State of South Dakota had convicted respondent Jerry Helm of six nonviolent felonies. In 1964, 1966, and 1969 Helm was convicted of third-degree burglary. In 1972 he was convicted of obtaining money under false pretenses. In 1973 he was convicted of grand larceny. And in 1975 he was convicted of third-offense driving while intoxicated. The record contains no details about the circumstances of any of these offenses, except that they were all nonviolent, none was a crime against a person, and alcohol was a contributing factor in each case.

In 1979 Helm was charged with uttering a "no account" check for $100. The only details we have of the crime are those given by Helm to the state trial court:

> " 'I was working in Sioux Falls, and got my check that day, was drinking and I ended up here in Rapid City with more money than I had when I started. I knew I'd done something I didn't know exactly what. If I would have known this, I would have picked the check up. I was drinking and didn't remember, stopped several places.' " *State v. Helm*, 287 N.W.2d 497, 501 (S.D.1980) (Henderson, J., dissenting) (quoting Helm).

After offering this explanation, Helm pleaded guilty.

Ordinarily the maximum punishment for uttering a "no account" check would have been five years imprisonment in the state penitentiary and a $5,000 fine. As a result of his criminal record, however, Helm was subject to South Dakota's recidivist statute:

> "When a defendant has been convicted of at least three prior convictions [*sic*] in addition to the principal felony, the sentence for the principal felony shall be enhanced to the sentence for a Class 1 felony." S.D.Codified Laws § 22–7–8 (1979) (amended 1981).

The maximum penalty for a "Class 1 felony" was life imprisonment in the state penitentiary and a $25,000 fine. Moreover, South Dakota law explicitly provides that parole is unavailable: "A person sentenced to life imprisonment is not eligible for parole by the board of pardons and paroles." S.D. Codified Laws § 24–15–4 (1979). The Governor is authorized to pardon prisoners, or to commute their sentences, S.D.Const.,

Art. IV, § 3, but no other relief from sentence is available even to a rehabilitated prisoner.

Immediately after accepting Helm's guilty plea, the South Dakota Circuit Court sentenced Helm to life imprisonment under § 22–7–8. * * *

After Helm had served two years in the state penitentiary, he requested the Governor to commute his sentence to a fixed term of years. Such a commutation would have had the effect of making Helm eligible to be considered for parole when he had served three-fourths of his new sentence. The Governor denied Helm's request in May 1981.

In November 1981, Helm sought habeas relief in the United States District Court for the District of South Dakota. Helm argued, among other things, that his sentence constituted cruel and unusual punishment under the Eighth and Fourteenth Amendments. Although the District Court recognized that the sentence was harsh, it concluded that this Court's recent decision in *Rummel v. Estelle,* 445 U.S. 263, 100 S.Ct. 1133, 63 L.Ed.2d 382 (1980), was dispositive. It therefore denied the writ.

The United States Court of Appeals for the Eighth Circuit reversed. 684 F.2d 582 (1982). * * *

We granted certiorari to consider the Eighth Amendment question presented by this case. * * *

II

The Eighth Amendment declares: "Excessive bail shall not be required, nor excessive fines imposed, nor cruel and unusual punishments inflicted." The final clause prohibits not only barbaric punishments, but also sentences that are disproportionate to the crime committed.

A

The principle that a punishment should be proportionate to the crime is deeply rooted and frequently repeated in common-law jurisprudence. In 1215 three chapters of Magna Carta were devoted to the rule that "amercements" [8] may not be excessive. And the principle was repeated and extended in the First Statute of Westminster, 3 Edw. I, ch. 6 (1275). These were not hollow guarantees, for the royal courts relied on them to invalidate disproportionate punishments. When prison sentences became the normal criminal sanctions, the common law recognized that these, too, must be proportional. See, *e.g., Hodges v. Humkin,* 2 Bulst. 139, 140, 80 Eng.Rep. 1015, 1016 (K.B. 1615) (Croke, J.) ("imprisonment ought always to be according to the quality of the offence").

---

8. An amercement was similar to a modern-day fine. It was the most common criminal sanction in 13th century England. See 2 F. Pollock & F. Maitland, The History of English Law 513–515 (2d ed. 1909).

The English Bill of Rights repeated the principle of proportionality in language that was later adopted in the Eighth Amendment: "excessive Baile ought not to be required nor excessive Fines imposed nor cruell and unusuall Punishments inflicted." 1 W. & M., sess. 2, ch. 2 (1689). Although the precise scope of this provision is uncertain, it at least incorporated "the longstanding principle of English law that the punishment * * * should not be, by reason of its excessive length or severity, greatly disproportionate to the offense charged." R. Perry, Sources of Our Liberties 236 (1959). Indeed, barely three months after the Bill of Rights was adopted, the House of Lords declared that a "fine of thirty thousand pounds, imposed by the court of King's Bench upon the earl of Devon, was excessive and exorbitant, against magna charta, the common right of the subject, and against the law of the land." *Earl of Devon's Case,* 11 State Trials 133, 136 (1689).

When the Framers of the Eighth Amendment adopted the language of the English Bill of Rights, they also adopted the English principle of proportionality. Indeed, one of the consistent themes of the era was that Americans had all the rights of English subjects. Thus our Bill of Rights was designed in part to ensure that these rights were preserved. Although the Framers may have intended the Eighth Amendment to go beyond the scope of its English counterpart, their use of the language of the English Bill of Rights is convincing proof that they intended to provide at least the same protection—including the right to be free from excessive punishments.

B

The constitutional principle of proportionality has been recognized explicitly in this Court for almost a century. In the leading case of *Weems v. United States,* 217 U.S. 349, 30 S.Ct. 544, 54 L.Ed. 793 (1910), the defendant had been convicted of falsifying a public document and sentenced to 15 years of "cadena temporal," a form of imprisonment that included hard labor in chains and permanent civil disabilities. The Court noted "that it is a precept of justice that punishment for crime should be graduated and proportioned to offense," *id.,* at 367, 30 S.Ct., at 549, and held that the sentence violated the Eighth Amendment. The Court endorsed the principle of proportionality as a constitutional standard, see, *e.g., id.,* at 372–373, 30 S.Ct., at 551, and determined that the sentence before it was "cruel in its excess of imprisonment," *id.,* at 377, 30 S.Ct., at 553, as well as in its shackles and restrictions.

* * *

Most recently, the Court has applied the principle of proportionality to hold capital punishment excessive in certain circumstances. And the Court has continued to recognize that the Eighth Amendment proscribes grossly disproportionate punishments, even when it has not been necessary to rely on the proscription.

C

There is no basis for the State's assertion that the general principle of proportionality does not apply to felony prison sentences. The constitutional language itself suggests no exception for imprisonment. We have recognized that the Eighth Amendment imposes "parallel limitations" on bail, fines, and other punishments, *Ingraham v. Wright* [430 U.S. 651, 664, 97 S.Ct. 1401, 1408, 51 L.Ed.2d 711 (1977)], and the text is explicit that bail and fines may not be excessive. It would be anomalous indeed if the lesser punishment of a fine and the greater punishment of death were both subject to proportionality analysis, but the intermediate punishment of imprisonment were not. There is also no historical support for such an exception. * * *

[W]e hold as a matter of principle that a criminal sentence must be proportionate to the crime for which the defendant has been convicted. Reviewing courts, of course, should grant substantial deference to the broad authority that legislatures necessarily possess in determining the types and limits of punishments for crimes, as well as to the discretion that trial courts possess in sentencing convicted criminals. But no penalty is *per se* constitutional. * * *

III

A

When sentences are reviewed under the Eighth Amendment, courts should be guided by objective factors that our cases have recognized. First, we look to the gravity of the offense and the harshness of the penalty. In *Enmund* [v. Florida, 458 U.S. 782, 102 S.Ct. 3368, 73 L.Ed.2d 1140 (1982)], for example, the Court examined the circumstances of the defendant's crime in great detail. 458 U.S., at 797–801, 102 S.Ct., at 3377. In *Coker* [v. Georgia, 433 U.S. 584, 97 S.Ct. 2861, 53 L.Ed.2d 982 (1977)] the Court considered the seriousness of the crime of rape, and compared it to other crimes, such as murder. 433 U.S., at 597–598, 97 S.Ct., at 2868–2869 (plurality opinion) * * * Of course, a court must consider the severity of the penalty in deciding whether it is disproportionate.

Second, it may be helpful to compare the sentences imposed on other criminals in the same jurisdiction. If more serious crimes are subject to the same penalty, or to less serious penalties, that is some indication that the punishment at issue may be excessive. Thus in *Enmund* the Court noted that all of the other felony murderers on death row in Florida were more culpable than the petitioner there. 458 U.S., at 795–796, 102 S.Ct., at 3376. The *Weems* Court identified an impressive list of more serious crimes that were subject to less serious penalties. 217 U.S., at 380–381, 30 S.Ct., at 554–555.

Third, courts may find it useful to compare the sentences imposed for commission of the same crime in other jurisdictions. In *Enmund* the Court conducted an extensive review of capital punishment statutes and determined that "only about a third of American jurisdictions would ever permit a defendant [such as Enmund] to be sentenced to die." 458 U.S., at 792, 102 S.Ct., at 3374. Even in those jurisdictions, however, the death penalty was almost never imposed under similar circumstances. *Id.*, at 794–796, 102 S.Ct., at 3375. * * *

In sum, a court's proportionality analysis under the Eighth Amendment should be guided by objective criteria, including (i) the gravity of the offense and the harshness of the penalty; (ii) the sentences imposed on other criminals in the same jurisdiction; and (iii) the sentences imposed for commission of the same crime in other jurisdictions.

B

Application of these factors assumes that courts are competent to judge the gravity of an offense, at least on a relative scale. In a broad sense this assumption is justified, and courts traditionally have made these judgments—just as legislatures must make them in the first instance. Comparisons can be made in light of the harm caused or threatened to the victim or society, and the culpability of the offender. Thus in *Enmund* the Court determined that the petitioner's conduct was not as serious as his accomplices' conduct. Indeed, there are widely shared views as to the relative seriousness of crimes. See Rossi, Waite, Bose & Berk, The Seriousness of Crimes: Normative Structure and Individual Differences, 39 Am.Soc.Rev. 224, 237 (1974). For example, as the criminal laws make clear, nonviolent crimes are less serious than crimes marked by violence or the threat of violence.

There are other accepted principles that courts may apply in measuring the harm caused or threatened to the victim or society. The absolute magnitude of the crime may be relevant. Stealing a million dollars is viewed as more serious than stealing a hundred dollars—a point recognized in statutes distinguishing petty theft from grand theft. Few would dispute that a lesser included offense should not be punished more severely than the greater offense. Thus a court is justified in viewing assault with intent to murder as more serious than simple assault. It also is generally recognized that attempts are less serious than completed crimes. Similarly, an accessory after the fact should not be subject to a higher penalty than the principal.

Turning to the culpability of the offender, there are again clear distinctions that courts may recognize and apply. In *Enmund* the Court looked at the petitioner's lack of intent to kill in determining that he was less culpable than his accomplices. 458 U.S., at 798, 102 S.Ct., at 3377. Most would agree that negligent conduct is less serious than intentional conduct. * * * A court, of course, is entitled to look at a defendant's motive in committing a crime. Thus a murder may be viewed as more serious when committed pursuant to a contract.

This list is by no means exhaustive. It simply illustrates that there are generally accepted criteria for comparing the severity of different crimes on a broad scale, despite the difficulties courts face in attempting to draw distinctions between similar crimes.

C

Application of the factors that we identify also assumes that courts are able to compare different sentences. This assumption, too, is justified. The easiest comparison, of course, is between capital punishment and noncapital punishments, for the death penalty is different from other punishments in kind rather than degree. For sentences of imprisonment, the problem is not so much one of ordering, but one of line-drawing. It is clear that a 25–year sentence generally is more severe than a 15–year sentence, but in most cases it would be difficult to decide that the former violates the Eighth Amendment while the latter does not. Decisions of this kind, although troubling, are not unique to this area. The courts are constantly called upon to draw similar lines in a variety of contexts.

IV

It remains to apply the analytical framework established by our prior decisions to the case before us. We first consider the relevant criteria, viewing Helm's sentence as life imprisonment without possibility of parole. We then consider the State's argument that the possibility of commutation is sufficient to save an otherwise unconstitutional sentence.

A

Helm's crime was "one of the most passive felonies a person could commit." *State v. Helm,* 287 N.W.2d, at 501 (Henderson, J., dissenting). It involved neither violence nor threat of violence to any person. The $100 face value of Helm's "no account" check was not trivial, but neither was it a large amount. One hundred dollars was less than half the amount South Dakota required for a felonious theft. It is easy to see why such a crime is viewed by society as among the less serious offenses.

Helm, of course, was not charged simply with uttering a "no account" check, but also with being an habitual offender. And a State is justified in punishing a recidivist more severely than it punishes a first offender. Helm's status, however, cannot be considered in the abstract. His prior offenses, although classified as felonies, were all relatively minor. All were nonviolent and none was a crime against a person. * * *

Helm's present sentence is life imprisonment without possibility of parole. Barring executive clemency, Helm will spend the rest of his life in the state penitentiary. This sentence is far more severe than the life sentence we considered in *Rummel v. Estelle.* Rummel was likely to have been eligible for parole within 12 years of his initial confinement, a fact on which the Court relied heavily. Helm's sentence is the most severe punishment that the State could have imposed on any criminal for any crime. Only capital punishment, a penalty not authorized in South Dakota when Helm was sentenced, exceeds it.

We next consider the sentences that could be imposed on other criminals in the same jurisdiction. When Helm was sentenced, a South Dakota court was required to impose a life sentence for murder, and was authorized to impose a life sentence for treason, first degree manslaughter, first degree arson, and kidnapping. No other crime was punishable so severely on the first offense. * * *

Helm's habitual offender status complicates our analysis, but relevant comparisons are still possible. Under § 22–7–7, the penalty for a second or third felony is increased by one class. Thus a life sentence was mandatory when a second or third conviction was for treason, first degree manslaughter, first degree arson, or kidnapping, and a life sentence would have been authorized when a second or third conviction was for such crimes as attempted murder, placing an explosive device on an aircraft, or first degree rape. Finally, § 22–7–8, under which Helm was sentenced, authorized life imprisonment after three prior convictions, regardless of the crimes.

In sum, there were a handful of crimes that were necessarily punished by life imprisonment: murder, and, on a second or third offense, treason, first degree manslaughter, first degree arson, and kidnapping. There was a larger group for which life imprisonment was authorized in the discretion of the sentencing judge, including: treason, first degree manslaughter, first degree arson, and kidnapping; attempted murder, placing an explosive device on an aircraft, and first degree rape on a second or third offense; and any felony after three prior offenses. Finally, there was a large group of very serious offenses for which life imprisonment was not authorized, including a third offense of heroin dealing or aggravated assault.

Criminals committing any of these offenses ordinarily would be thought more deserving of punishment than one uttering a "no account" check—even when the bad-check writer had already committed six minor felonies. Moreover, there is no indication in the record that any habitual offender other than Helm has ever been given the maximum sentence on the basis of comparable crimes. It is more likely that the possibility of life imprisonment under § 22–7–8 generally is reserved for criminals such as fourth-time heroin dealers, while habitual bad-check writers receive more lenient treatment. In any event, Helm has been treated in the same manner as, or more severely than, criminals who have committed far more serious crimes.

Finally, we compare the sentences imposed for commission of the same crime in other jurisdictions. The Court of Appeals found that "Helm could have received a life sentence without parole for his offense in only one other state, Nevada," 684 F.2d, at 586, and we have no reason to doubt this finding. At the very least, therefore, it is clear that Helm could not have received such a severe sentence in 48 of the 50 States. But even under Nevada law, a life sentence without possibility of parole is merely authorized in these circumstances. See Nev.Rev. Stat. § 207.010(2) (1981). We are not advised that any defendant such as Helm, whose prior offenses were so minor, actually has received the maximum penalty in Nevada. It appears that Helm was treated more severely than he would have been in any other State.

B

The State argues that the present case is essentially the same as *Rummel v. Estelle,* for the possibility of parole in that case is matched by the possibility of executive clemency here. The State reasons that the Governor could commute Helm's sentence to a term of years. We conclude, however, that the South Dakota commutation system is fundamentally different from the parole system that was before us in *Rummel.*

As a matter of law, parole and commutation are different concepts, despite some surface similarities. Parole is a regular part of the rehabilitative process. Assuming good behavior, it is the normal expectation in the vast majority of cases. The law generally specifies when a prisoner will be eligible to be considered for parole, and details the standards and procedures applicable at that time. Thus it is possible to predict, at least to some extent, when parole might be granted. Commutation, on the other hand, is an *ad hoc* exercise of executive clemency. A Governor may commute a sentence at any time for any reason without reference to any standards.

* * *

The Texas and South Dakota systems in particular are very different. In *Rummel,* the Court did not rely simply on the existence of some system of parole. Rather it looked to the provisions of the system presented, including the fact that Texas had "a relatively liberal policy of granting 'good time' credits to its prisoners, a policy that historically has allowed a prisoner serving a life sentence to become eligible for parole in as little as 12 years." 445 U.S., at 280, 100 S.Ct., at 1142. A Texas prisoner became eligible for parole when his calendar time served plus "good conduct" time equaled one-third of the maximum sentence imposed or 20 years, whichever is less. An entering prisoner earned 20 days good-time per 30 days served, and this could be increased to 30 days good-time per 30 days served. Thus Rummel could have been eligible for parole in as few as 10 years, and could have expected to become eligible, in the normal course of events, in only 12 years.

In South Dakota commutation is more difficult to obtain than parole. For example, the board of pardons and paroles is authorized to make commutation recommendations to the Governor, but § 24–13–4 provides that "no recommendation for the commutation of * * * a life sentence, or for a pardon * * *, shall be made by less than the unanimous vote of all members of the board." In fact, no life sentence has been commuted in over eight years, while parole—where authorized—has been granted regularly during that period. Furthermore, even if Helm's sentence were commuted, he merely would be eligible to be considered for parole. Not only is there no guarantee that he would be paroled, but the South Dakota parole system is far more stringent than the one before us in *Rummel.* Helm would have to serve three-fourths of his revised sentence before he would be eligible for parole, and the provision for good-time credits is less generous.

The possibility of commutation is nothing more than a hope for "an *ad hoc* exercise of clemency." It is little different from the possibility of executive clemency that exists in every case in which a defendant challenges his sentence under the Eighth Amendment. Recognition of such a bare possibility would make judicial review under the Eighth Amendment meaningless.

V

The Constitution requires us to examine Helm's sentence to determine if it is proportionate to his crime. Applying objective criteria, we find that Helm has received the penultimate sentence for relatively minor criminal conduct. He has been treated more harshly than other criminals in the State who have committed more serious crimes. He has been treated more harshly than he would have been in any other jurisdiction, with the possible exception of a single State. We conclude that his sentence is significantly disproportionate to his crime, and is therefore prohibited by the Eighth Amendment. The judgment of the Court of Appeals is accordingly

Affirmed.

CHIEF JUSTICE BURGER, with whom JUSTICE WHITE, JUSTICE REHNQUIST, and JUSTICE O'CONNOR join, dissenting.

* * *

Although historians and scholars have disagreed about the Framers' original intentions, the more common view seems to be that the Framers viewed the Cruel and Unusual Punishments Clause as prohibiting the kind of torture meted out during the reign of the Stuarts.

* * *

This Court has applied a proportionality test only in extraordinary cases, *Weems* being one example and the line of capital cases another. See, *e.g., Coker v. Georgia,* 433 U.S. 584, 97 S.Ct. 2861, 53 L.Ed.2d 982 (1977); *Enmund v. Florida,* 458 U.S. 782, 102 S.Ct. 3368, 73 L.Ed.2d 1140 (1982). The Court's reading of the Eighth Amendment as restricting legislatures' authority to choose which crimes to punish by death rests on the finality of the death sentence. Such scrutiny is not required where a sentence of imprisonment is imposed after the State has identified a criminal offender whose record shows he will not conform to societal standards.

The Court's traditional abstention from reviewing sentences of imprisonment to ensure that punishment is "proportionate" to the crime is well founded in history, in prudential considerations, and in traditions of comity. Today's conclusion by five Justices that they are able to say that one offense has less "gravity" than another is nothing other than a bald substitution of individual subjective moral values for those of the legislature. Nor, as this case well illustrates, are we endowed with Solomonic wisdom that permits us to draw principled distinctions between sentences of different length for a chronic "repeater" who has demonstrated that he will not abide by the law.

* * *

Even if I agreed that the Eighth Amendment prohibits imprisonment "disproportionate to the crime committed," I reject the notion that respondent's sentence is disproportionate to his crimes for, if we are to have a system of laws, not men, *Rummel* is controlling.

The differences between this case and *Rummel* are insubstantial. First, Rummel committed three truly nonviolent felonies, while respondent, as noted at the outset, committed seven felonies, four of which cannot fairly be characterized as "nonviolent." At the very least, respondent's burglaries and his third-offense drunk driving posed real risk of serious harm to others. It is sheer fortuity that the places respondent burglarized were unoccupied and that he killed no pedestrians while behind the wheel. * * *

The Court's opinion necessarily reduces to the proposition that a sentence of life imprisonment with the possibility of commutation, but without possibility of parole, is so much more severe than a life sentence with the possibility of parole that one is excessive while the other is not. This distinction does not withstand scrutiny; a well-behaved "lifer" in respondent's position is most unlikely to serve for life.

It is inaccurate to say, as the Court does, that the *Rummel* holding relied on the fact that Texas had a relatively liberal parole policy. In context, it is clear that the *Rummel* Court's discussion of parole merely illustrated the difficulty of comparing sentences between different jurisdictions. However, accepting the Court's characterization of *Rummel* as accurate, the Court today misses the point. Parole was relevant to an evaluation of Rummel's life sentence because in the "real world," he was unlikely to spend his entire life behind bars. Only a fraction of "lifers" are not released within a relatively few years. In Texas, the historical evidence showed that a prisoner serving a life sentence could become eligible for parole in as little as 12 years. In South Dakota, the historical evidence shows that since 1964, 22 life sentences have been commuted to terms of years, while requests for commutation of 25 life sentences were denied. And, of course, those requests for commutation may be renewed.

In short, there is a significant probability that respondent will experience what so many "lifers" experience. Even assuming that at the time of sentencing, respondent was likely to spend more time in prison than Rummel, that marginal difference is surely supported by respondent's greater demonstrated propensity for crime—and for more serious crime at that.

Note and Question

What characteristics of Helm's situation triggered the application of Eighth Amendment proportionality? Was it the nature of the offenses of which he was convicted, the absence of any opportunity for parole, some other consideration, or a combination of these and perhaps other factors? In Seritt v. Alabama, 731 F.2d 728 (11th Cir.1984), cert. denied, 469 U.S. 1062, 105 S.Ct. 545, 83 L.Ed.2d 433 (1985), the defendant, following his conviction for armed robbery, had been sentenced to a mandatory life sentence without parole upon proof of his prior conviction for five separate drug felonies. He challenged the constitutionality of his sentence on, among other grounds, that the "without parole" provision was disproportionate to his crimes and thus violative of the Eighth Amendment prohibition as interpreted in Solem v. Helm. The court rejected this claim. It concluded that *Solem* was sharply distinguishable because it dealt with the absence of parole in the context of nonviolent felonies whereas Seritt's most recent conviction was for a crime of violence.

C. THE RIGHT OF PRIVACY

Editors' Introduction: Federal Constitutional Privacy

Constitutional considerations may impose an absolute prohibition against criminalizing certain conduct or may at least bar criminal conviction for certain conduct engaged in under certain circumstances. As is demonstrated by the arguments of the respondent in the principal case in this section, the federal constitutional right of "privacy" is often invoked as the basis for such limits upon the legislative power to "criminalize."

The right of privacy is most explicitly recognized in Griswold v. Connecticut, 381 U.S. 479, 85 S.Ct. 1678, 14 L.Ed.2d 510 (1965), in which a physician and an officer of a Planned Parenthood League were convicted as "accessories" (see Chapter XI, infra) to the offense of use of contraceptives to prevent conception. Conviction was based upon evidence that the defendants had given advice to married persons as to means of preventing conception. Concluding that the conviction violated federal constitutional standards, the Court—speaking through Justice Douglas—explained:

> [The law of which the defendants were convicted] operates directly on an intimate relation of husband and wife and their physician's role in one aspect of that relationship.
>
> * * *
>
> In NAACP v. State of Alabama, 357 U.S. 449, 462, 78 S.Ct. 1163, 1172, [12 L.Ed.2d 325,] we protected the "freedom to associate and privacy in one's associations," noting that freedom of association was a peripheral First Amendment right. * * * [This and other] cases suggest that specific guarantees in the Bill of Rights have penumbras, formed by emanations from those guarantees that help give them life and substance. * * *

The Fourth and Fifth Amendments were described in Boyd v. United States, 116 U.S. 616, 630, 6 S.Ct. 524, 29 L.Ed. 746, as protection against all governmental invasions "of the sanctity of a man's home and the privacies of life." * * *

The present case * * * concerns a relationship lying within the zone of privacy created by several different fundamental constitutional guarantees. And it concerns a law which, in forbidding the *use* of contraceptives rather than regulating their manufacture or sale, seeks to achieve its goals by means having a maximum destructive impact upon that relationship. Such a law cannot stand in light of the familiar principle, so often applied by this Court, that a "governmental purpose to control or prevent activities constitutionally subject to state regulation may not be achieved by means which sweep unnecessarily broadly and thereby invade the area of protected freedoms." NAACP v. Alabama, 377 U.S. 288, 307, 84 S.Ct. 1302, 1314, 12 L.Ed.2d 325.

381 U.S. at 482–85, 85 S.Ct. at 1680–82, 14 L.Ed.2d at 513–16.

Federal constitutional protection for "privacy" may have been expanded in Stanley v. Georgia, 394 U.S. 557, 89 S.Ct. 1243, 22 L.Ed.2d 542 (1969). An obscene film had been found in Stanley's bedroom during a search for gambling records and items. His conviction for possession of obscene matter was held constitutionally invalid by the Supreme Court:

[Roth v. United States, 354 U.S. 476, 77 S.Ct. 1304, 1 L.Ed.2d 1498 (1957)] and its progeny certainly do mean that the First and Fourteenth amendments recognize a valid governmental interest in dealing with the problem of obscenity. But the assertion of that interest cannot, in every context, be insulated from all constitutional protections. * * *

It is now well established that the Constitution protects the right to receive information and ideas. * * * This right to receive information and ideas, regardless of their social worth, is fundamental to our free society. Moreover, in the context of this case—a prosecution for mere possession of printed or filmed matter in the privacy of a person's own home—that right takes on an added dimension. For also fundamental is the right to be free, except in very limited circumstances, from unwanted governmental intrusions into one's privacy.

"The makers of our Constitution undertook to secure conditions favorable to the pursuit of happiness. They recognized the significance of a man's spiritual nature, of his feelings and of his intellect. * * * They sought to protect Americans in their beliefs, their thoughts, their emotions and their sensations. They conferred, as against the government, the right to be let alone— the most comprehensive of rights and the most valued by civilized man." Olmstead v. United States, 277 U.S. 438, 478, 48 S.Ct. 564, 572, 72 L.Ed. 944 (1928) (Brandeis, J., dissenting).

See Griswold v. Connecticut, [381 U.S. 479, 85 S.Ct. 1678, 14 L.Ed.2d 510 (1965)].

These are the rights that [Stanley] is asserting in the case before us. He is asserting the right to read or observe what he pleases—the right to satisfy his intellectual and emotional needs in the privacy of his home. He is asserting the right to be free from state inquiry into the contents of his library. * * * [W]e think that the mere categorization of these films as "obscene" is insufficient justification for such a drastic invasion of personal liberties guaranteed by the First and Fourteenth Amendments. Whatever may be the justifications for other statutes regulating obscenity, we do not think they reach into the privacy of one's own home. * * *

* * * Georgia asserts that exposure to obscene materials may lead to deviant sexual behavior or crimes of sexual violence. There appears to be little empirical basis for that assertion. But more important, if the State is only concerned about printed or filmed material inducing antisocial conduct, we believe that in the context of private consumption of ideas and information we should adhere to the view that "[a]mong free men, the deterrents ordinarily to be applied to prevent crime are education and punishment for violations of the law * * *." Whitney v. California, 274 U.S. 357, 378, 47 S.Ct. 641, 649, 71 L.Ed. 1095 (1927). Given the present state of knowledge, the State may no more prohibit mere possession of obscene matter on the ground that it may lead to antisocial conduct than it may prohibit possession of chemistry books on the ground that they may lead to the manufacture of homemade spirits.

It is true that in *Roth* this Court rejected the necessity of proving that exposure to obscene material would create a clear and present danger of antisocial conduct or would probably induce its recipients to such conduct. But that case dealt with public distribution of obscene materials and such distribution is subject to different objections. For example, there is always the danger that obscene material might fall into the hands of children or that it might intrude upon the sensibilities or privacy of the general public. No such dangers are present in this case.

Finally, we are faced with the argument that prohibition of possession of obscene materials is a necessary incident to statutory schemes prohibiting distribution. That argument is based on alleged difficulties of proving an intent to distribute or in producing evidence of actual distribution. We are not convinced that such difficulties exist, but even if they did we do not think that they would justify infringement of the individual's right to read or observe what he pleases. Because that right is so fundamental to our scheme of individual liberty, its restriction may not be justified by the need to ease the administration of otherwise valid criminal laws.

We hold that the First and Fourteenth Amendments prohibit making mere private possession of obscene material a crime. * * *

394 U.S. at 563–68, 89 S.Ct. at 1247–49, 22 L.Ed.2d at 548–51. The Court continued:

What we have said in no way infringes upon the power of the State or Federal Governments to make possession of other items, such as narcotics, firearms, or stolen goods, a crime. Our holding * * * turns upon the Georgia statute's infringement of fundamental liberties protected by the First and Fourteenth Amendments. No First Amendment rights are involved in most statutes making mere possession criminal.

394 U.S. at 568 n. 11, 89 S.Ct. at 1249 n. 11, 22 L.Ed.2d at 551 n. 11.

Despite its eloquent words in *Stanley* concerning the constitutional significance of satisfaction of intellectual and emotional needs in the privacy of one's home, the Supreme Court had, prior to the principal case in this section, declined to read *Stanley* as meaning that privacy in the home meant a right to receive items to take into and possess in the home. In United States v. Orito, 413 U.S. 139, 93 S.Ct. 2674, 37 L.Ed.2d 513 (1973), Orito had been charged with transporting obscene matter by interstate common carrier. Holding the prosecution permissible, the Court explained:

[Orito's contention] is that *Stanley* has firmly established the right to possess obscene material in the privacy of the home and that this creates a correlative right to receive it, transport it, or distribute it. We have rejected that reasoning. * * * Given (a) that obscene material is not protected under the First Amendment, (b) that the Government has a legitimate interest in protecting the public commercial environment by preventing such material from entering the stream of commerce, and (c) that no constitutionally protected privacy is involved, we cannot say that the Constitution forbids comprehensive federal regulation of interstate transportation of obscene material merely because such transport may be by private carriage, or because the material is intended for the private use of the transporter. * * * Congress could reasonably determine such regulation to be necessary * * * [to protect against the] risk of ultimate exposure to juveniles or to the public and the harm that exposure would cause.

413 U.S. at 141–44, 93 S.Ct. at 2676–78, 37 L.Ed.2d at 517–18.

The principal case below explores the extent to which "privacy"—as that is protected by the federal constitution—bars the criminalization of certain conduct under various circumstances. As the following note indicates, the reach of the criminal law may be shortened by state law requirements as well as those imposed by the United States Constitution. In considering the content of these privacy limitations on criminalization of conduct, is the material on the functions of and justifications for criminalization—explored in Chapter II, supra—relevant?

BOWERS v. HARDWICK

Supreme Court of the United States, 1986.
—— U.S. ——, 106 S.Ct. 2841, 92 L.Ed.2d 140.

JUSTICE WHITE delivered the opinion of the Court.

In August 1982, respondent was charged with violating the Georgia statute criminalizing sodomy[1] by committing that act with another adult male in the bedroom of respondent's home. After a preliminary hearing, the District Attorney decided not to present the matter to the grand jury unless further evidence developed.

Respondent then brought suit in the Federal District Court, challenging the constitutionality of the statute insofar as it criminalized consensual sodomy.[2] He asserted that he was a practicing homosexual, that the Georgia sodomy statute, as administered by the defendants, placed him in imminent danger of arrest, and that the statute for several reasons violates the Federal Constitution. The District Court granted the defendants' motion to dismiss for failure to state a claim.

   *   *   *

A divided panel of the Court of Appeals for the Eleventh Circuit reversed. 760 F.2d 1202 (1985). * * * Relying on our decisions in *Griswold v. Connecticut,* 381 U.S. 479, 85 S.Ct. 1678, 14 L.Ed.2d 510 (1965), *Eisenstadt v. Baird,* 405 U.S. 438, 92 S.Ct. 1029, 31 L.Ed.2d 349 (1972), *Stanley v. Georgia,* 394 U.S. 557, 89 S.Ct. 1243, 22 L.Ed.2d 542 (1969), and *Roe v. Wade,* 410 U.S. 113, 93 S.Ct. 705, 35 L.Ed.2d 147 (1973), the court [held] that the Georgia statute violated respondent's fundamental rights because his homosexual activity is a private and intimate association that is beyond the reach of state regulation by reason of the Ninth Amendment and the Due Process Clause of the Fourteenth Amendment. The case was remanded for trial, at which, to prevail, the State would have to prove that the statute is supported by a compelling interest and is the most narrowly drawn means of achieving that end.

1. Ga.Code Ann. § 16–6–2 (1984) provides, in pertinent part, as follows:

"(a) A person commits the offense of sodomy when he performs or submits to any sexual act involving the sex organs of one person and the mouth or anus of another. * * *

"(b) A person convicted of the offense of sodomy shall be punished by imprisonment for not less than one nor more than 20 years. * * * "

2. John and Mary Doe were also plaintiffs in the action. They alleged that they wished to engage in sexual activity proscribed by § 16–6–2 in the privacy of their home, App. 3, and that they had been "chilled and deterred" from engaging in such activity by both the existence of the statute and Hardwick's arrest. The District Court held, however, that because they had neither sustained, nor were in immediate danger of sustaining, any direct injury from the enforcement of the statute, they did not have proper standing to maintain the action. The Court of Appeals affirmed the District Court's judgment dismissing the Does' claim for lack of standing and the Does do not challenge that holding in this Court.

The only claim properly before the Court, therefore, is Hardwick's challenge to the Georgia statute as applied to consensual homosexual sodomy. We express no opinion on the constitutionality of the Georgia statute as applied to other acts of sodomy.

* * * We agree with the State that the Court of Appeals erred, and hence reverse its judgment.

This case does not require a judgment on whether laws against sodomy between consenting adults in general, or between homosexuals in particular, are wise or desirable. It raises no question about the right or propriety of state legislative decisions to repeal their laws that criminalize homosexual sodomy, or of state court decisions invalidating those laws on state constitutional grounds. The issue presented is whether the Federal Constitution confers a fundamental right upon homosexuals to engage in sodomy and hence invalidates the laws of the many States that still make such conduct illegal and have done so for a very long time. The case also calls for some judgment about the limits of the Court's role in carrying out its constitutional mandate.

We first register our disagreement with the Court of Appeals and with respondent that the Court's prior cases have construed the Constitution to confer a right of privacy that extends to homosexual sodomy and for all intents and purposes have decided this case. The reach of this line of cases was sketched in *Carey v. Population Services International*, 431 U.S. 678, 685, 97 S.Ct. 2010, 2016, 52 L.Ed.2d 675 (1977). *Pierce v. Society of Sisters*, 268 U.S. 510, 45 S.Ct. 571, 69 L.Ed. 1070 (1925), and *Meyer v. Nebraska*, 262 U.S. 390, 43 S.Ct. 625, 67 L.Ed. 1042 (1923), were described as dealing with child rearing and education; *Prince v. Massachusetts*, 321 U.S. 158, 64 S.Ct. 438, 88 L.Ed. 645 (1944), with family relationships; *Skinner v. Oklahoma ex rel. Williamson*, 316 U.S. 535, 62 S.Ct. 1110, 86 L.Ed. 1655 (1942), with procreation; *Loving v. Virginia*, 388 U.S. 1, 87 S.Ct. 1817, 18 L.Ed.2d 1010 (1967), with marriage; *Griswold v. Connecticut, supra*, and *Eisenstadt v. Baird*, *supra*, with contraception; and *Roe v. Wade*, 410 U.S. 113, 93 S.Ct. 705, 35 L.Ed.2d 147 (1973), with abortion. The latter three cases were interpreted as construing the Due Process Clause of the Fourteenth Amendment to confer a fundamental individual right to decide whether or not to beget or bear a child.

Accepting the decisions in these cases and the above description of them, we think it evident that none of the rights announced in those cases bears any resemblance to the claimed constitutional right of homosexuals to engage in acts of sodomy that is asserted in this case. No connection between family, marriage, or procreation on the one hand and homosexual activity on the other has been demonstrated, either by the Court of Appeals or by respondent. Moreover, any claim that these cases nevertheless stand for the proposition that any kind of private sexual conduct between consenting adults is constitutionally insulated from state proscription is unsupportable. * * *

Precedent aside, however, respondent would have us announce, as the Court of Appeals did, a fundamental right to engage in homosexual sodomy. This we are quite unwilling to do. It is true that despite the language of the Due Process Clauses of the Fifth and Fourteenth Amendments, which appears to focus only on the processes by which life, liberty, or property is taken, the cases are legion in which those Clauses have been interpreted to have substantive content, subsuming rights that to a great extent are immune from federal or state regulation or proscription. * * *

Striving to assure itself and the public that announcing rights not readily identifiable in the Constitution's text involves much more than the imposition of the Justices' own choice of values on the States and the Federal Government, the Court has sought to identify the nature of the rights qualifying for heightened judicial protection. In *Palko v. Connecticut,* 302 U.S. 319, 325, 326, 58 S.Ct. 149, 151, 152, 82 L.Ed. 288 (1937), it was said that this category includes those fundamental liberties that are "implicit in the concept of ordered liberty," such that "neither liberty nor justice would exist if [they] were sacrificed." A different description of fundamental liberties appeared in *Moore v. East Cleveland,* 431 U.S. 494, 503, 97 S.Ct. 1932, 1937, 52 L.Ed.2d 531 (1977) (opinion of POWELL, J.), where they are characterized as those liberties that are "deeply rooted in this Nation's history and tradition." *Id.,* at 503, 97 S.Ct., at 1938 (POWELL, J.).

It is obvious to us that neither of these formulations would extend a fundamental right to homosexuals to engage in acts of consensual sodomy. Proscriptions against that conduct have ancient roots. See generally, Survey on the Constitutional Right to Privacy in the Context of Homosexual Activity, 40 U.Miami L.Rev. 521, 525 (1986). Sodomy was a criminal offense at common law and was forbidden by the laws of the original thirteen States when they ratified the Bill of Rights. In 1868, when the Fourteenth Amendment was ratified, all but 5 of the 37 States in the Union had criminal sodomy laws. In fact, until 1961, all 50 States outlawed sodomy, and today, 24 States and the District of Columbia continue to provide criminal penalties for sodomy performed in private and between consenting adults. Survey, U.Miami L.Rev., *supra,* at 524, n. 9. Against this background, to claim that a right to engage in such conduct is "deeply rooted in this Nation's history and tradition" or "implicit in the concept of ordered liberty" is, at best, facetious.

Nor are we inclined to take a more expansive view of our authority to discover new fundamental rights imbedded in the Due Process Clause. The Court is most vulnerable and comes nearest to illegitimacy when it deals with judge-made constitutional law having little or no cognizable roots in the language or design of the Constitution. That this is so was painfully demonstrated by the face-off between the Executive and the Court in the 1930's, which resulted in the repudiation of much of the substantive gloss that the Court had placed on the Due Process Clause of the Fifth and Fourteenth Amendments. There should be, therefore, great resistance to expand the substantive reach of those Clauses, particularly if it requires redefining the category of rights deemed to be fundamental. Otherwise, the Judiciary necessarily takes to itself further authority to govern the country without express constitutional authority. The claimed right pressed on us today falls far short of overcoming this resistance.

Respondent, however, asserts that the result should be different where the homosexual conduct occurs in the privacy of the home. He relies on *Stanley v. Georgia*, 394 U.S. 557, 89 S.Ct. 1243, 22 L.Ed.2d 542 (1969) * * *.

Stanley did protect conduct that would not have been protected outside the home, and it partially prevented the enforcement of state obscenity laws; but the decision was firmly grounded in the First Amendment. The right pressed upon us here has no similar support in the text of the Constitution, and it does not qualify for recognition under the prevailing principles for construing the Fourteenth Amendment. Its limits are also difficult to discern. Plainly enough, otherwise illegal conduct is not always immunized whenever it occurs in the home. Victimless crimes, such as the possession and use of illegal drugs do not escape the law where they are committed at home. *Stanley* itself recognized that its holding offered no protection for the possession in the home of drugs, firearms, or stolen goods. And if respondent's submission is limited to the voluntary sexual conduct between consenting adults, it would be difficult, except by fiat, to limit the claimed right to homosexual conduct while leaving exposed to prosecution adultery, incest, and other sexual crimes even though they are committed in the home. We are unwilling to start down that road.

Even if the conduct at issue here is not a fundamental right, respondent asserts that there must be a rational basis for the law and that there is none in this case other than the presumed belief of a majority of the electorate in Georgia that homosexual sodomy is immoral and unacceptable. This is said to be an inadequate rationale to support the law. The law, however, is constantly based on notions of morality, and if all laws representing essentially moral choices are to be invalidated under the Due Process Clause, the courts will be very busy indeed. Even respondent makes no such claim, but insists that majority sentiments about the morality of homosexuality should be declared inadequate. We do not agree, and are unpersuaded that the sodomy laws of some 25 States should be invalidated on this basis.[8]

Accordingly, the judgment of the Court of Appeals is

Reversed.

CHIEF JUSTICE BURGER, concurring.

I join the Court's opinion, but I write separately to underscore my view that in constitutional terms there is no such thing as a fundamental right to commit homosexual sodomy.

As the Court notes, the proscriptions against sodomy have very "ancient roots." Decisions of individuals relating to homosexual conduct have been subject to state intervention throughout the history of

8. Respondent does not defend the judgment below based on the Ninth Amendment, the Equal Protection Clause or the Eighth Amendment.

Western Civilization. Condemnation of those practices is firmly rooted in Judaeo-Christian moral and ethical standards. Homosexual sodomy was a capital crime under Roman law. See Code Theod. 9.7.6; Code Just. 9.9.31. See also D. Bailey, Homosexuality in the Western Christian Tradition 70–81 (1975). During the English Reformation when powers of the ecclesiastical courts were transferred to the King's Courts, the first English statute criminalizing sodomy was passed. 25 Hen. VIII, c. 6. Blackstone described "the infamous crime against nature" as an offense of "deeper malignity" than rape, an heinous act "the very mention of which is a disgrace to human nature," and "a crime not fit to be named." Blackstone's Commentaries *215. The common law of England, including its prohibition of sodomy, became the received law of Georgia and the other Colonies. In 1816 the Georgia Legislature passed the statute at issue here, and that statute has been continuously in force in one form or another since that time. To hold that the act of homosexual sodomy is somehow protected as a fundamental right would be to cast aside millennia of moral teaching.

This is essentially not a question of personal "preferences" but rather of the legislative authority of the State. I find nothing in the Constitution depriving a State of the power to enact the statute challenged here.

JUSTICE POWELL, concurring.

I join the opinion of the Court. I agree with the Court that there is no fundamental right—*i.e.*, no substantive right under the Due Process Clause—such as that claimed by respondent, and found to exist by the Court of Appeals. This is not to suggest, however, that respondent may not be protected by the Eighth Amendment of the Constitution. The Georgia statute at issue in this case, Ga.Code Ann. § 16–6–2, authorizes a court to imprison a person for up to 20 years for a single private, consensual act of sodomy. In my view, a prison sentence for such conduct—certainly a sentence of long duration—would create a serious Eighth Amendment issue. Under the Georgia statute a single act of sodomy, even in the private setting of a home, is a felony comparable in terms of the possible sentence imposed to serious felonies such as aggravated battery, first degree arson, and robbery.

In this case, however, respondent has not been tried, much less convicted and sentenced. Moreover, respondent has not raised the Eighth Amendment issue below. For these reasons this constitutional argument is not before us.

JUSTICE BLACKMUN, with whom JUSTICE BRENNAN, JUSTICE MARSHALL, and JUSTICE STEVENS join, dissenting.

* * *

I believe we must analyze respondent's claim in the light of the values that underlie the constitutional right to privacy. If that right means anything, it means that, before Georgia can prosecute its citizens for making choices about the most intimate aspects of their lives, it must do more than assert that the choice they have made is an

" 'abominable crime not fit to be named among Christians.' " *Herring v. State,* 119 Ga. 709, 721, 46 S.E. 876, 882 (1904).

I

* * *

A fair reading of the statute and of the complaint clearly reveals that the majority has distorted the question this case presents.

* * * [T]he Court's almost obsessive focus on homosexual activity is particularly hard to justify in light of the broad language Georgia has used. Unlike the Court, the Georgia Legislature has not proceeded on the assumption that homosexuals are so different from other citizens that their lives may be controlled in a way that would not be tolerated if it limited the choices of those other citizens. Rather, Georgia has provided that "[a] person commits the offense of sodomy when he performs or submits to any sexual act involving the sex organs of one person and the mouth or anus of another." Ga.Code Ann. § 16–6–2(a). The sex or status of the persons who engage in the act is irrelevant as a matter of state law. * * * I therefore see no basis for the Court's decision to treat this case as an "as applied" challenge to § 16–6–2, or for Georgia's attempt, both in its brief and at oral argument, to defend § 16–6–2 solely on the grounds that it prohibits homosexual activity. Michael Hardwick's standing may rest in significant part on Georgia's apparent willingness to enforce against homosexuals a law it seems not to have any desire to enforce against heterosexuals. But his claim that § 16–6–2 involves an unconstitutional intrusion into his privacy and his right of intimate association does not depend in any way on his sexual orientation.

* * *

I believe that Hardwick has stated a cognizable claim that § 16–6–2 interferes with constitutionally protected interests in privacy and freedom of intimate association. * * *

II

"Our cases long have recognized that the Constitution embodies a promise that a certain private sphere of individual liberty will be kept largely beyond the reach of government." *Thornburgh v. American Coll. of Obst. & Gyn.,* ___ U.S. ___, ___, 106 S.Ct. 2169, 2184, 90 L.Ed.2d ___ (1986). In construing the right to privacy, the Court has proceeded along two somewhat distinct, albeit complementary, lines. First, it has recognized a privacy interest with reference to certain *decisions* that are properly for the individual to make. Second, it has recognized a privacy interest with reference to certain *places* without regard for the particular activities in which the individuals who occupy them are engaged. The case before us implicates both the decisional and the spatial aspects of the right to privacy.

A

The Court concludes today that none of our prior cases dealing with various decisions that individuals are entitled to make free of governmental interference "bears any resemblance to the claimed constitutional right of homosexuals to engage in acts of sodomy that is asserted in this case." While it is true that these cases may be characterized by their connection to protection of the family, the Court's conclusion that they extend no further than this boundary ignores the warning in *Moore v. East Cleveland,* 431 U.S. 494, 501, 97 S.Ct. 1932, 1936, 52 L.Ed.2d 531 (1977) (plurality opinion), against "clos[ing] our eyes to the basic reasons why certain rights associated with the family have been accorded shelter under the Fourteenth Amendment's Due Process Clause." We protect those rights not because they contribute, in some direct and material way, to the general public welfare, but because they form so central a part of an individual's life. "[T]he concept of privacy embodies the 'moral fact that a person belongs to himself and not others nor to society as a whole.'" *Thornburgh v. American Coll. of Obst. & Gyn.,* __ U.S., at __, n. 5, 106 S.Ct., at 2187, n. 5 (STEVENS, J., concurring), quoting Fried, Correspondence, 6 Phil. & Pub. Affairs 288–289 (1977). And so we protect the decision whether to marry precisely because marriage "is an association that promotes a way of life, not causes; a harmony in living, not political faiths; a bilateral loyalty, not commercial or social projects." *Griswold v. Connecticut,* 381 U.S., at 486, 85 S.Ct., at 1682. We protect the decision whether to have a child because parenthood alters so dramatically an individual's self-definition, not because of demographic considerations or the Bible's command to be fruitful and multiply. And we protect the family because it contributes so powerfully to the happiness of individuals, not because of a preference for stereotypical households. * * *

Only the most willful blindness could obscure the fact that sexual intimacy is "a sensitive, key relationship of human existence, central to family life, community welfare, and the development of human personality," *Paris Adult Theatre I v. Slaton,* 413 U.S. 49, 63, 93 S.Ct. 2628, 2638, 37 L.Ed.2d 446 (1973). The fact that individuals define themselves in a significant way through their intimate sexual relationships with others suggests, in a Nation as diverse as ours, that there may be many "right" ways of conducting those relationships, and that much of the richness of a relationship will come from the freedom an individual has to *choose* the form and nature of these intensely personal bonds.

In a variety of circumstances we have recognized that a necessary corollary of giving individuals freedom to choose how to conduct their lives is acceptance of the fact that different individuals will make different choices. * * * The Court claims that its decision today merely refuses to recognize a fundamental right to engage in homosexual sodomy; what the Court really has refused to recognize is the fundamental interest all individuals have in controlling the nature of their intimate associations with others.

B

The behavior for which Hardwick faces prosecution occurred in his own home, a place to which the Fourth Amendment attaches special significance. The Court's treatment of this aspect of the case is symptomatic of its overall refusal to consider the broad principles that have informed our treatment of privacy in specific cases. Just as the right to privacy is more than the mere aggregation of a number of entitlements to engage in specific behavior, so too, protecting the physical integrity of the home is more than merely a means of protecting specific activities that often take place there. * * *

The Court's interpretation of the pivotal case of *Stanley v. Georgia*, 394 U.S. 557, 89 S.Ct. 1243, 22 L.Ed.2d 542 (1969), is entirely unconvincing. * * *

The central place that *Stanley* gives Justice Brandeis' dissent in *Olmstead*, a case raising *no* First Amendment claim, shows that *Stanley* rested as much on the Court's understanding of the Fourth Amendment as it did on the First. * * * "The right of the people to be secure in their * * * houses," expressly guaranteed by the Fourth Amendment, is perhaps the most "textual" of the various constitutional provisions that inform our understanding of the right to privacy, and thus I cannot agree with the Court's statement that "[t]he right pressed upon us here has no * * * support in the text of the Constitution[.]" Indeed, the right of an individual to conduct intimate relationships in the intimacy of his or her own home seems to me to be the heart of the Constitution's protection of privacy.

III

The Court's failure to comprehend the magnitude of the liberty interests at stake in this case leads it to slight the question whether petitioner, on behalf of the State, has justified Georgia's infringement on these interests. I believe that neither of the two general justifications for § 16–6–2 that petitioner has advanced warrants dismissing respondent's challenge for failure to state a claim.

First, petitioner asserts that the acts made criminal by the statute may have serious adverse consequences for "the general public health and welfare," such as spreading communicable diseases or fostering other criminal activity. Inasmuch as this case was dismissed by the District Court on the pleadings, it is not surprising that the record before us is barren of any evidence to support petitioner's claim. In light of the state of the record, I see no justification for the Court's attempt to equate the private, consensual sexual activity at issue here with the "possession in the home of drugs, firearms, or stolen goods," to which *Stanley* refused to extend its protection. None of the behavior so mentioned in *Stanley* can properly be viewed as "[v]ictimless;" drugs and weapons are inherently dangerous, and for property to be "stolen," someone must have been wrongfully deprived of it. Nothing in the record before the Court provides any justification for finding the activity forbidden by § 16–6–2 to be physically dangerous, either to the persons engaged in it or to others.[4]

4. Although I do not think it necessary to decide today issues that are not even remotely before us, it does seem to me that a court could find simple, analytically sound distinctions between certain private, consensual sexual conduct, on the one

The core of petitioner's defense of § 16–6–2, however, is that respondent and others who engage in the conduct prohibited by § 16–6–2 interfere with Georgia's exercise of the " 'right of the Nation and of the States to maintain a decent society,' " *Paris Adult Theatre I v. Slaton,* 413 U.S., at 59–60, 93 S.Ct., at 2636, quoting *Jacobellis v. Ohio,* 378 U.S. 184, 199, 84 S.Ct. 1676, 1684, 12 L.Ed.2d 793 (1964) (Warren, C.J., dissenting). Essentially, petitioner argues, and the Court agrees, that the fact that the acts described in § 16–6–2 "for hundreds of years, if not thousands, have been uniformly condemned as immoral" is a sufficient reason to permit a State to ban them today.

I cannot agree that either the length of time a majority has held its convictions or the passions with which it defends them can withdraw legislation from this Court's scrutiny. * * * It is precisely because the issue raised by this case touches the heart of what makes individuals what they are that we should be especially sensitive to the rights of those whose choices upset the majority.

The assertion that "traditional Judeo-Christian values proscribe" the conduct involved, Brief for Petitioner 20, cannot provide an adequate justification for § 16–6–2. That certain, but by no means all, religious groups condemn the behavior at issue gives the State no license to impose their judgments on the entire citizenry. The legitimacy of secular legislation depends instead on whether the State can advance some justification for its law beyond its conformity to religious doctrine. * * *

Nor can § 16–6–2 be justified as a "morally neutral" exercise of Georgia's power to "protect the public environment," *Paris Adult Theatre I,* 413 U.S., at 68–69, 93 S.Ct., at 2641. Certainly, some private behavior can affect the fabric of society as a whole. Reasonable people may differ about whether particular sexual acts are moral or immoral, but "we have ample evidence for believing that people will not abandon morality, will not think any better of murder, cruelty and dishonesty, merely because some private sexual practice which they abominate is not punished by the law." H.L.A. Hart, Immorality and Treason, reprinted in The Law as Literature 220, 225 (L. Blom-Cooper ed. 1961). Petitioner and the Court fail to see the difference between laws that protect public sensibilities and those that enforce private morality.

hand, and adultery and incest (the only two vaguely specific "sexual crimes" to which the majority points, on the other. For example, marriage, in addition to its spiritual aspects, is a civil contract that entitles the contracting parties to a variety of governmentally provided benefits. A State might define the contractual commitment necessary to become eligible for these benefits to include a commitment of fidelity and then punish individuals for breaching that contract. Moreover, a State might conclude that adultery is likely to injure third persons, in particular, spouses and children of persons who engage in extramarital affairs. With respect to incest, a court might well agree with respondent that the nature of familial relationships renders true consent to incestuous activity sufficiently problematical that a blanket prohibition of such activity is warranted. Notably, the Court makes no effort to explain why it has chosen to group private, consensual homosexual activity with adultery and incest rather than with private, consensual heterosexual activity by unmarried persons or, indeed, with oral or anal sex within marriage.

Statutes banning public sexual activity are entirely consistent with protecting the individual's liberty interest in decisions concerning sexual relations: the same recognition that those decisions are intensely private which justifies protecting them from governmental interference can justify protecting individuals from unwilling exposure to the sexual activities of others. But the mere fact that intimate behavior may be punished when it takes place in public cannot dictate how States can regulate intimate behavior that occurs in intimate places.

This case involves no real interference with the rights of others, for the mere knowledge that other individuals do not adhere to one's value system cannot be a legally cognizable interest let alone an interest that can justify invading the houses, hearts, and minds of citizens who choose to live their lives differently.

IV

* * * I can only hope that * * * the Court soon will reconsider its analysis and conclude that depriving individuals of the right to choose for themselves how to conduct their intimate relationships poses a far greater threat to the values most deeply rooted in our Nation's history than tolerance of nonconformity could ever do. Because I think the Court today betrays those values, I dissent.

JUSTICE STEVENS, with whom JUSTICE BRENNAN and JUSTICE MARSHALL join, dissenting.

Like the statute that is challenged in this case, the rationale of the Court's opinion applies equally to the prohibited conduct regardless of whether the parties who engage in it are married or unmarried, or are of the same or different sexes. * * *

Because the Georgia statute expresses the traditional view that sodomy is an immoral kind of conduct regardless of the identity of the persons who engage in it, I believe that a proper analysis of its constitutionality requires consideration of two questions: First, may a State totally prohibit the described conduct by means of a neutral law applying without exception to all persons subject to its jurisdiction? If not, may the State save the statute by announcing that it will only enforce the law against homosexuals? The two questions merit separate discussion.

I

Our prior cases make two propositions abundantly clear. First, the fact that the governing majority in a State has traditionally viewed a particular practice as immoral is not a sufficient reason for upholding a law prohibiting the practice; neither history nor tradition could save a law prohibiting miscegenation from constitutional attack. Second, individual decisions by married persons, concerning the intimacies of their physical relationship, even when not intended to produce offspring, are a form of "liberty" protected by the Due Process Clause of the Fourteenth Amendment. *Griswold v. Connecticut,* 381 U.S. 479, 85 S.Ct. 1678, 14 L.Ed.2d 510 (1965). Moreover, this protection extends to intimate choices by unmarried as well as married persons. *Carey v. Population Services International*, 431 U.S. 678, 97 S.Ct. 2010, 52 L.Ed. 2d 675 (1977); *Eisenstadt v. Baird*, 405 U.S. 438, 92 S.Ct. 1029, 31 L.Ed. 2d 349 (1972).

In consideration of claims of this kind, the Court has emphasized the individual interest in privacy, but its decisions have actually been animated by an even more fundamental concern. As I wrote some years ago:

> "These cases do not deal with the individual's interest in protection from unwarranted public attention, comment, or exploitation. They deal, rather, with the individual's right to make certain unusually important decisions that will affect his own, or his family's, destiny. * * *" *Fitzgerald v. Porter Memorial Hospital*, 523 F.2d 716, 719–20 (CA7 1975) (footnotes omitted), cert. denied, 425 U.S. 916, 96 S.Ct. 1518, 47 L.Ed.2d 768 (1976).

Society has every right to encourage its individual members to follow particular traditions in expressing affection for one another and in gratifying their personal desires. It, of course, may prohibit an individual from imposing his will on another to satisfy his own selfish interests. It also may prevent an individual from interfering with, or violating, a legally sanctioned and protected relationship, such as marriage. And it may explain the relative advantages and disadvantages of different forms of intimate expression. But when individual married couples are isolated from observation by others, the way in which they voluntarily choose to conduct their intimate relations is a matter for them—not the State—to decide. The essential "liberty" that animated the development of the law in cases like *Griswold* * * * surely embraces the right to engage in nonreproductive, sexual conduct that others may consider offensive or immoral.

Paradoxical as it may seem, our prior cases thus establish that a State may not prohibit sodomy within "the sacred precincts of marital bedrooms," *Griswold*, 381 U.S., at 485, 85 S.Ct., at 1682, or, indeed, between unmarried heterosexual adults. *Eisenstadt*, 405 U.S., at 453, 92 S.Ct., at 1038. In all events, it is perfectly clear that the State of Georgia may not totally prohibit the conduct proscribed by § 16–6–2 of the Georgia Criminal Code.

II

If the Georgia statute cannot be enforced as it is written—if the conduct it seeks to prohibit is a protected form of liberty for the vast majority of Georgia's citizens—the State must assume the burden of justifying a selective application of its law. Either the persons to whom Georgia seeks to apply its statute do not have the same interest in "liberty" that others have, or there must be a reason why the State may be permitted to apply a generally applicable law to certain persons that it does not apply to others.

The first possibility is plainly unacceptable. Although the meaning of the principle that "all men are created equal" is not always clear, it surely must mean that every free citizen has the same interest in "liberty" that the members of the majority share. From the standpoint of the individual, the homosexual and the heterosexual have the same interest in deciding how he will live his own life, and, more narrowly, how he will conduct himself in his personal and voluntary associations with his companions. State intrusion into the private conduct of either is equally burdensome.

The second possibility is similarly unacceptable. A policy of selective application must be supported by a neutral and legitimate interest—something more substantial than a habitual dislike for, or ignorance about, the disfavored group. Neither the State nor the Court has identified any such interest in this case. The Court has posited as a justification for the Georgia statute "the presumed belief of a majority of the electorate in Georgia that homosexual sodomy is immoral and unacceptable." But the Georgia electorate has expressed no such belief—instead, its representatives enacted a law that presumably reflects the belief that *all sodomy* is immoral and unacceptable. Unless the Court is prepared to conclude that such a law is constitutional, it may not rely on the work product of the Georgia Legislature to support its holding. For the Georgia statute does not single out homosexuals as a separate class meriting special disfavored treatment.

Nor, indeed, does the Georgia prosecutor even believe that all homosexuals who violate this statute should be punished. This conclusion is evident from the fact that the respondent in this very case has formally acknowledged in his complaint and in court that he has engaged, and intends to continue to engage, in the prohibited conduct, yet the State has elected not to process criminal charges against him. As JUSTICE POWELL points out, moreover, Georgia's prohibition on private, consensual sodomy has not been enforced for decades. The record of nonenforcement, in this case and in the last several decades, belies the Attorney General's representations about the importance of the State's selective application of its generally applicable law.[12]

Both the Georgia statute and the Georgia prosecutor thus completely fail to provide the Court with any support for the conclusion that homosexual sodomy, *simpliciter,* is considered unacceptable conduct in that State, and that the burden of justifying a selective application of the generally applicable law has been met.

III

The Court orders the dismissal of respondent's complaint even though the State's statute prohibits all sodomy; even though that prohibition is concededly unconstitutional with respect to heterosexu-

12. It is, of course, possible to argue that a statute has a purely symbolic role. Since the Georgia Attorney General does not even defend the statute as written, however, the State cannot possibly rest on the notion that the statute may be defended for its symbolic message.

als; and even though the State's *post hoc* explanations for selective application are belied by the State's own actions. At the very least, I think it clear at this early stage of the litigation that respondent has alleged a constitutional claim sufficient to withstand a motion to dismiss.

I respectfully dissent.

Note

Article I, Section 22 of the Alaska Constitution provides:

The right of the people to privacy is recognized and shall not be infringed * * *

In Ravin v. State, 537 P.2d 494 (Alaska 1975), the Alaska Supreme Court held that this provision barred the state from criminalizing the possession of marijuana by adults at home for personal use:

[C]itizens of the State of Alaska have a basic right to privacy in their homes under Alaska's constitution. This right to privacy would encompass the possession and ingestion of substances such as marijuana in a purely personal, non-commercial context in the home unless the state can meet its substantial burden and show that proscription of possession of marijuana is supportable by achievement of a legitimate state interest.

* * *

The justifications offered by the State * * * are generally that marijuana is a psychoactive drug; that it is not a harmless substance; that heavy use has concomitant risks; that it is capable of precipitating a psychotic reaction in at least individuals who are predisposed towards such reaction; and that its use adversely affects the user's ability to operate an automobile. * * * It appears that there is no firm evidence that marijuana, as presently used in this country, is generally a danger to the user or others. But neither is there conclusive evidence to the effect that it is harmless * * * [G]iven the relative insignificance of marijuana consumption as a health problem in our society at present, we do not believe that the potential harm generated by drivers under the influence of marijuana, standing alone, creates a close and substantial relationship between the public welfare and control of ingestion of marijuana or possession of it in the home for personal use. Thus we conclude that no adequate justification for the state's intrusion into the citizen's right to privacy by its prohibition of possession of marijuana by an adult for personal consumption has been shown. * * * [M]ere scientific doubts will not suffice. The state must demonstrate a need based on proof that the public health or welfare will in fact suffer if the controls are not applied.

537 P.2d at 504, 508, 511.

In State v. Erickson, 574 P.2d 1 (Alaska 1978), however, the court held that similar personal possession of cocaine was not protected:

We have found no authorities which state that the effects of cocaine are less harmful than marijuana, and it seems clear that cocaine is substantially more a threat to health and welfare. Unlike marijuana, cocaine can cause death as a direct result of the pharmacological action of the drug.

* * *

We find that there is a sufficiently close and substantial relationship between the means chosen to regulate cocaine and the legislative purpose of preventing harm to health and welfare so as to justify the prohibition against the use of cocaine even in the home. * * *

574 P.2d at 21, 22.

Other courts considering the issue litigated in *Ravin* have rejected the proposition that possession of marijuana in the home is constitutionally protected. E.g., State v. Murphy, 117 Ariz. 57, 570 P.2d 1070 (1977); People v. Williams, 135 Mich.App. 537, 355 N.W.2d 268 (1984); State v. Smith, 93 Wn.2d 329, 610 P.2d 869 (1980).

Chapter IV

GENERAL PRINCIPLES OF CRIMINAL LIABILITY: INTRODUCTION

It is often said that a crime consists of both *mens rea* and *actus reus* or, to abandon "law latin," that a crime consists of a mental state and a physical act. To some extent, however, this may suggest an oversimplified analysis, depending upon how the terms, especially *actus reus,* is defined. *Actus reus* might be defined as simply the physical activity which a person must perform in order to incur liability for a crime. But then the often-repeated statement that *mens rea* and *actus reus* make up a crime ignores the fact that many crimes require proof of other types of matters, such as certain results that must occur (the victim's death in homicide offenses, for example) and attendant circumstances that must exist (such as "nighttime" in burglary).

It is also possible to define *actus reus* as including all nonmental elements—the physical activity, any results that must occur, and any circumstances that must exist. Cohen, Actus Reus, in 1 Encyclopedia of Crime & Justice 15 (1983) ("the actus reus designates all the elements of the criminal offense except the mens rea"). This is the sense in which the term will be used in this book. Thus the "act" required for criminal liability by a particular crime—the physical movement or omission by the defendant—must be distinguished from the *actus reus* of that crime. The "act" is part of, but often not the complete, *actus reus* of the offense.

The Model Penal Code follows a somewhat similar approach, although it does not use the traditional "law latin" terms *actus reus* and *mens rea.* "Act" (or "action") is defined as "a bodily movement whether voluntary or involuntary." Model Penal Code § 1.13(2) (Official Draft 1985). "Conduct," on the other hand, is defined as "an action or omission and its accompanying state of mind." Id., at § 1.13(5). "Elements of an offense" are defined as possibly including—depending upon the particular offense being considered—conduct, attendant circumstances, and results of conduct. Id., at § 1.13(9).

154

It is perhaps best, insofar as can be done, to avoid reference to such terms and instead to adopt as functional an approach as possible. These materials propose a scheme of analysis which is designed to facilitate careful analysis of the issues that might arise in applying a crime to a particular set of facts. Given the widespread trend towards adoption of comprehensive criminal codes often based upon the American Law Institute's Model Penal Code (see the discussion in Section C of Chapter I, supra), this almost always involves consideration and application of statutory provisions creating and defining the offense and providing for defenses to liability. Sometimes, however, the contents of modern statutory provisions and definitions can only be meaningfully established by considering the common law definitions of their predecessors. Even more frequently, reference to early common law and more recent judicial development of defenses and general principles is necessary, given the tendency of American legislation to focus upon the definition of particular offenses rather than general matters.

The analysis proposed here is a three-step process. The first step in the ascertainment of the elements of the offense, that is, those matters which the prosecution must usually plead in the charging instrument and which it must always prove at trial.

For the sake of convenience and clarity, it is valuable to consider elements of offenses in terms of four categories. A particular crime may not contain an element in each category, although to some extent constitutional considerations may require proof of some element in each of the first two categories.

1. The "Act." It is most useful to think of the act required for liability in terms of what physical activities must be shown on the part of the accused. The statute creating and defining the crime may specifically describe (and limit) the type of physical activity which can constitute the crime, as, for example, by requiring that the defendant have been "driving." Or, as in the case with most homicide offenses, the definition of the crime may make no effort to describe the required physical activity. In this case, any action or failure to act that meets general requirements will suffice. Compare the specificity of the act required by 18 U.S.C.A. § 488, with the total absence of definition in Ariz.Rev.Stat. § 13–3613, both of which are reprinted on pages 157–58, infra.

2. The State of Mind. For a number of reasons, the criminal law is deeply concerned with the accused's conscious state of mind at the time of the act constituting the offense. Probably all offenses require that the trier of fact be convinced beyond a reasonable doubt that the accused was, at that time, aware of something. But the state of mind required differs drastically among offenses. Identify the state of mind, if any, required by each of the three statutes reprinted on pages 157–58, infra.

3. Results. A number of offenses require that a particular result be shown to have occurred. When this is the case, the prosecution must also show that there was a causal relationship between the defendant's act and her state of mind, on the one hand, and the occurrence of the result, on the other. In which of the statutes reprinted on pages 157–58, infra is a result required? Why is a result not always a requirement for liability?

4. Attendant Circumstances. Some offenses require a showing that particular circumstances existed at the time of the offense. These differ from results (those elements in the third category described above) in that there is no necessity of a causal relationship between the accused's actions and state of mind, on the one hand, and the attendant circumstances, on the other. Circumstances may serve an important policy purpose in defining or limiting the conduct made criminal. Or, they may be of relatively minor importance. Federal crimes, for example, often require the showing of certain circumstances for the sole purpose of justifying federal jurisdiction over the offense. Frequently, circumstances are included in the definition of a crime to distinguish the offense from less serious crimes and to provide the basis for a more severe penalty. Many jurisdictions have several burglary offenses, for example, which define as a more serious category of burglary (with a more serious penalty) those prohibited entries occurring at a time when the circumstance of "nighttime" existed. Identify any attendant circumstances required by the statutes reprinted on pages 157–58, infra, and consider the function which they may serve.

The second step of the analysis involves the ascertainment of any so-called "defenses" which are really means of disproving one of the elements of the offense. Most often this amounts to disproving the state of mind required for the crime. Proof of a defendant's mistake as to the facts existing at the time of her actions, for example, may serve to raise in the jurors' minds a reasonable doubt as to whether the defendant entertained the requisite state of mind.

The final step in the analysis involves consideration of defenses in the true sense. These are matter which, if established, prevent or reduce liability despite proof of all elements of the offense. One who kills to preserve her own life, for example, will have entertained an awareness that her actions would cause the death of the victim; this suffices (under most statutes) for murder. Yet if in addition the elements of self-defense are established, she is relieved of liability.

The remainder of this book is organized with reference to this analysis. Chapter V deals with problems in identifying the "act" required for liability. Chapter VI addresses state of mind requirements; so-called "defenses" that consist of challenging the adequacy of the prosecution's proof of state of mind are included in this material. "Result" elements and causation problems are considered in Chapter VIII, but only after a brief digression in Chapter VII into the homicide offenses to explore one particular effort to use state of mind requirements to differentiate among identical results—the death of another human being—brought about by the defendants' acts. Matters related to those elements categorized as attendant circumstances are handled in Chapter IX, with special emphasis upon the role of circumstances in defining and applying sexual offenses. Chapters X and XI digress somewhat by exploring the issues raised when liability is sought for an "inchoate" or "preparatory" crime such as attempt, solicitation or conspiracy (Chapter X) or when liability is sought to be imposed upon one defendant for conduct actually committed by another person (Chapter XI). These subjects involve issues concerning elements in a number of different categories. Finally, attention is turned to the "true" defenses—such as self-defense, entrapment, and insanity—in Chapter XII.

No pretense can be made that substantive criminal law may be analyzed "scientifically." It may be helpful, however, to visualize the basic framework of analysis described above through the following formula:

$$\left[\left(\begin{array}{c} \text{Act } + \text{ State} \\ \text{of Mind} \end{array}\right) \xrightarrow{\text{(Causation)}} \text{Results} \; + \; \begin{array}{c}\text{Attendant} \\ \text{Circumstances}\end{array}\right]$$

$$= \text{ Liability}$$

This reflects the need to show for liability the required physical conduct, the necessary state of mind, any required result (and causation between the conduct and intent and that result), and any demanded attendant circumstances. In considering the material which follows, periodically pause to place it within the framework of the above formula. See whether the absence, or a reduction in the importance, of any particular element in the definition of an offense is accompanied by a compensatory increase in the emphasis given another element on the left of the equation or a reduction in the severity of punishment associated with liability. If such reciprocal changes are identified, reflect on why this is the case.

Ariz.Rev.Stat. (1978)

§ 13–3613. Contributing to delinquency and dependency; classification; procedure

A.   A person who by any act, causes, encourages or contributes to the * * * delinquency of a child * * *, or who for any cause is responsible therefore is guilty of a class 1 misdemeanor.

18 U.S.C.A.

§ 488. Making or possessing counterfeit dies for foreign coins

Whoever, within the United States, without lawful authority, makes any die, hub, or mold, or any part thereof * * * in the likeness or similitude, as to the design or the inscription thereon, of any die, hub, or mold designated for the coining of the genuine coin of any foreign government; or

Whoever, without lawful authority, possesses any such die, hub, or mold, or any part thereof, or conceals, or knowingly suffers the same to be used for the counterfeiting of any foreign coin—

Shall be fined not more than $5,000 or imprisoned not more than five years, or both.

Maryland Code Ann. (1976)

Art. 27 § 111A. Opening gate of another's pasture, etc.

Any person who shall willfully and maliciously open the gate of another's field, pasture, or enclosure, enclosing livestock, shall be guilty of a misdemeanor, and upon conviction thereof shall be subject to imprisonment for a period of not more than one year or to a fine of not more than five hundred dollars ($500.00), or to both imprisonment and fine.

Chapter V

GENERAL PRINCIPLES OF CRIMINAL LIABILITY: THE ACT

Contents

A. GENERAL REQUIREMENT OF AN ACT

Editors' Introduction: What Is an Act?

As was explained in Chapter IV, this book will use the term *actus reus* to refer to all the nonmental elements of a crime: the physical activity which the accused must be shown to have performed, the consequences of that activity, and the circumstances under which the activity was performed. This encourages a differentiation of each category of element and forces a more thorough examination of the proof necessary for liability.

There is some basis for contending that the United States Constitution may require proof of some act on the part of the accused. See *Robinson v. California,* page 168, infra, as interpreted by Mr. Justice Marshall in *Powell v. Texas,* page 345, infra.

Aside from any possible constitutional imperative, the act requirement places an obvious restriction on the authority of the state to employ the criminal sanction. Given that it marks an extreme outer limit on the exercise of governmental power, the student should consider whether the requirement is desirable, and why. Consider also whether it is of any practical importance: For purposes of determining whether the state may employ the criminal sanction; for purposes of determining the severity of the sanction which may be employed?

In a recent federal case the defendants were a power company, its legislative lobbyist, a construction company and its president. The government alleged that the defendants had engaged in a scheme in which a percentage of the proceeds paid by the power company for construction projects would be laundered and then used to make improper payments to members of the state legislature. The evidence showed that $15,000 in laundered funds had been assembled and that the lobbyist had told the majority leader of the state house of representatives of his intention to make an illicit payment. Was this sufficient to support a finding that a payment was made? In reversing the conviction the court wrote:

The prosecution's evidence *might* support a conviction for conspiring to make an unreported payment, but that offense was not charged. The government's argument would erase the dividing line between a conspiracy or an attempt, and the substantive offense. * * * Under the government's theory, the planning of a crime would constitute the commission of the crime itself. This result would run counter to a fundamental concept that underlies our criminal justice system. Until an individual actually commits an offense, he is innocent. Thinking about perpetrating a crime is not unlawful. The evil lies in the commission of the illegal act. Prior to the time one actually crosses the line and acts, there is always the possibility that conscience, civic responsibility or plain good judgment will prevail. The Government's evidence * * * is insufficient as a matter of law * * *.

United States v. Washington Water Power Co., 793 F.2d 1079, 1082 (9th Cir.1986). (Note the crucial importance of the crime which the prosecution decided to charge.)

Several of the most basic questions regarding the requirement of an "act" are raised in this section. What is the significance, if any, of the requirement that the "act" be "willed" or "voluntary"? In particular, after becoming familiar with the "state of mind" requirement, Chapter VI, infra, the student should reconsider the *Mercer* case, infra, to decide whether the issues involved there could not have been as effectively analyzed and resolved without any reference whatever to the "act" requirement.

In this regard consider the view of Professor Perkins:

It is sometimes said that no crime has been committed unless the harmful result was brought about by a "voluntary act." Analysis of such a statement will disclose, however, that as so used the phrase "voluntary act" means no more than the mere word "act." An act must be a willed movement or the omission of a possible and legally-required performance. This is essential to the *actus reus* rather than to the *mens rea*. "A spasm is not an act."

* * * A positive act (willed movement) always has a voluntary element and hence the phrase "voluntary act" is merely tautological as so applied. A negative act may be either a forbearance or an unintentional omission of a legally-required performance. The former is voluntary, the latter is not. If a watchman charged with the duty of lowering the gates at a crossing whenever a train is approaching fails to do so on a particular occasion, with fatal consequences to a motorist, the death is due to his (negative) act. But it would be absurd to speak of this act as "voluntary" if he was inattentive and did not know the train was approaching. As his legal duty required him to be attentive in this regard his want of knowledge of the need for immediate action will not excuse him, but it leaves his failure wholly unintentional. Hence the assertion that there is no crime without a "voluntary act" is redundant as to positive action and incorrect as to negative action.

Furthermore, such an assertion invites confusion in two directions—first because the modifier may be improperly extended to the legally-recognized consequences of the act, and second because it may raise a false issue as to the meaning of the word "voluntary." As to the first, assume the unintentional, but fatal, discharge of a weapon which had been pointed unlawfully at the deceased with no thought other than to intimidate him. The intentional pointing of the weapon was an act and the resulting death is imputable to the pointer. It is not improper to hold the slayer guilty of criminal homicide in certain cases of this nature, but to speak of the "shooting" or the "killing" as voluntary or intentional is merely confusion of words. * * * the notion of a "voluntary act" as requisite to criminal guilt may result in the jury's being confused by argument of counsel to the effect that defendant's act was committed under the stress and strain of difficult circumstances and hence was not "voluntary." If the harm was caused by a willed movement of the defendant it was caused by his "act" no matter how much "pressure" he may have been under at the moment. Perkins, Criminal Law 749–50 (1969).

Is the persuasiveness of Professor Perkins' position affected by the time frame within which the defendant's conduct is evaluated? If the relevant "act" of the railroad watchman is the failure to lower the gate just prior to the train's arrival, it would seem, on the facts as assumed by Professor Perkins, inaccurate to describe his failure as "voluntary". However, if the appropriate period in which to evaluate the watchman's conduct encompasses the earlier time when he failed to ensure that he would be alert to the approach of trains—as by setting an alarm, staying awake, or avoiding distractions—it might be quite appropriate to describe that failure as "voluntary".

Professor Perkins' point about the involuntary shooting is more readily understood if one realizes that the actor's liability (the right hand side of the equation on page 157, supra) will be significantly less than if the trigger was pulled voluntarily. That is, the actor is being punished for a voluntary act—pointing the weapon with the requisite state of mind—but the crime thus committed, and the penalty attached thereto, is not as serious as it would be if the second act had also been voluntary. An excellent analysis of just such a problem is to be found in George v. State, 681 S.W.2d 43 (Tex.Crim.App.1984). It was agreed that t'e defendant, in an effort to obtain a dollar from the victim, had cocked the hammer of his pistol short of its locked position and pointed it at the victim's face. The defendant testified that he did not know the gun would go off nor did he intend that it should (he and the victim were friends); its discharge, he testified, was an accident. The intermediate appellate court had agreed with the defendant that the jury in his trial for aggravated assault should have been instructed on the defense of accident or involuntary conduct. The Court of Criminal Appeals rejected this view and reinstated the conviction:

Here the evidence shows that appellant's actions were sufficiently voluntary until "the hammer * * * slipped off [his] thumb," but the court of appeals then turned its focus to the handgun, finding that *it* discharged "involuntarily or by accident." We cannot accept that a mechanical object is capable of volition, and if the court meant to say that appellant was not at that moment doing an "act," we do not agree. If the hammer "slipped off [his] thumb," it had to be that the thumb holding the hammer partially back released just enough pressure for the hammer to "slip" forward. However slight, that is "bodily movement" within the meaning of * * * [the statutory definition], and there is no evidence that it was involuntary. Accordingly, the trial court was correct in refusing the requested charge on "defense of involuntary conduct."

> * * * [F]actually, whether appellant's precise bodily movement that released the hammer * * * was voluntary or involuntary is of little moment. Where the issue is whether an accused recklessly caused bodily injury by shooting with a gun and the evidence shows that the accused voluntarily engaged in conduct that includes, *inter alia,* one or more voluntary acts leading to the actual shooting, we hold as a matter of law the fact that when such conduct also includes a bodily movement of the accused sufficient for the gun to discharge a bullet, without more—such as precipitation by another individual * * *—a jury need not be charged on the matter of whether the accused voluntarily engaged in the conduct with which he is charged.

681 S.W.2d at 47.

Even when it appears that the defendant has voluntarily engaged in the conduct proscribed by the statute, difficulties in interpretation may be posed by the inherent imprecision of language.

18 U.S.C.A. § 1792 provides, in pertinent part: "Whoever conveys * * * from place to place [within a Federal penal institution] any * * * weapon * * * designed to kill, injure or disable any officer, agent, employee or inmate thereof * * * shall be imprisoned not more than ten years." Does a prisoner violate this provision if, while carrying a knife under his clothing, he walks from his cell pursuant to a guard's order? What if he is running a knife across a sander in the prison workshop and, on the approach of his foreman, he drops it to the floor? Should the statute be applied to a prisoner who, in the course of an altercation with another inmate, receives a knife from a third prisoner and uses it to stab his antagonist. He then walked 10 feet to deliver the knife to a correctional officer. Which of the following factors would control the interpretation: the meaning of the verb "convey"; the voluntariness of the conduct; or the purpose of the statute given the fact that mere possession of a knife by an inmate is not defined as criminal, and that there are other provisions—assault and murder, for example—criminalizing harm caused by use of the knife. Compare United States v. Fountain, 642 F.2d 1083 (7th Cir.1981) and United States v. Meador, 456 F.2d 197 (10th Cir.1972) with United States v. Greschner, 647 F.2d 740 (7th Cir.1981) and United States v. Bedwell, 456 F.2d 448 (10th Cir.1972).

To what extent is a failure to act sufficient for liability? To what extent may a defendant be held liable if the acts relied upon are performed by someone other than himself, i.e., to what extent may "vicarious liability" be imposed?

STATE v. MERCER

Supreme Court of North Carolina, 1969.
275 N.C. 108, 165 S.E.2d 328.

Separate indictments charged defendant with the first degree murder on September 14, 1967, of (1) Myrtle R. Mercer, defendant's wife, (2) Ida Mae Dunn, and (3) Jeffrey Lane Dunn, Ida's five-year-old son.

*   *   *

There was evidence tending to show the facts narrated below.

Defendant, a member of the United States Army for 19½ years, was stationed at Fort Benning, Georgia, at the time of the trial.

Defendant and Myrtle Mercer were married in Fayetteville, N. C., in April, 1965. Thereafter, he was stationed at duty posts in and out of the United States. Myrtle Mercer, Ida Mae Dunn, and Jeffrey Lane Dunn, Ida's five-year-old boy, lived together in Wilson, N. C. Defendant visited Myrtle in Wilson from time to time when on leaves. He was thirty-nine; Myrtle was twenty-three.

Marital difficulties developed. Defendant had heard that Myrtle was having affairs with other men. He thought Myrtle's relationship with Ida involved more than normal affection. As time passed, defendant's strong affection for Myrtle was not reciprocated.

On July 6, 1967, defendant received a letter from Myrtle, referred to in the evidence as a "Dear John" letter, in which she told him she was tired of being tied down and wanted to come and go as she pleased. In a letter mailed August 10th from Kentucky (where he was then stationed), defendant wrote Myrtle: "Please don't make me do something that will send both of us to our graves." Also: "I could never see you with another man, and I would die and go to hell before I would see you with some other man, and take myself with you."

In September, 1967, defendant obtained a ten-day leave "to come home and see if he could get straightened out with his wife. *   *   *" Defendant told his first sergeant that "if he did not get straightened out he would not be back."

On September 13, 1967, defendant visited the house in Wilson where Myrtle, Ida, and Jeffrey lived. He talked with Myrtle. However, she would not discuss their marital problems and did not want him to stay at that house.

Defendant stayed at the home of his cousin, Mrs. Mable Owens, in Tarboro. He left there on the morning of September 14, 1967, and arrived at Myrtle's around noon. She would not talk with him. (Note: Defendant testified Myrtle at that time gave him some clothes, a camera and a paper bag containing a pistol he had given to her for her protection.) At the conclusion of this visit, he returned to the home of

Mrs. Owens. Sometime during the day defendant bought a pint of vodka and had two drinks from it.

About 8:30 p.m., Mrs. Owens, at the request of defendant, drove defendant to Myrtle's house in Wilson. The two children of Mrs. Owens accompanied them. Defendant knocked. There was no response. The house was unlighted and apparently no one was there. They left and visited defendant's brother (in Wilson) for some twenty-five or thirty-five minutes. While there, defendant telephoned Myrtle's house. The line was busy. They went back to Myrtle's house. Defendant asked Mrs. Owens if she and her children would go into the house with him. She replied that they would wait in the car.

Defendant went to the front door and knocked several times. There was no answer. Defendant shot at the door twice, pushed it open with his foot and went inside. At that time, a light came on in the front bedroom. Someone said, "Ervin, don't do that." Defendant fired three or four shots killing Myrtle instantly and fatally wounding Ida and Jeffrey. He then left the house. A neighbor called the police.

* * *

Defendant was arrested at the home of his brother in Wilson, a few hours after the fatal shots were fired. He accompanied the officers to a lot behind Myrtle's house where the gun which inflicted the fatal injuries was hidden.

Testimony of defendant, in addition to that referred to above, is set out in the opinion. It tended to show he was completely unconscious of what transpired when Myrtle, Ida and Jeffrey were shot.

In each case, the jury returned a verdict of guilty of murder in the second degree. * * *

BOBBITT, JUDGE.

* * *

The court's final instructions were as follows: "(T)he Court instructs you that the evidence in regard and surrounding the alleged loss of memory by the defendant will be considered by you *on the question of premeditation and deliberation in the charge of murder in the first degree.* * * * if you find from the evidence, not by the greater weight, nor by the preponderance, but if the defendant has satisfied you—merely satisfied you—that he lost consciousness, sufficient consciousness, to the extent that he did not have sufficient time to *premeditate or deliberate,* that is, if he did not have sufficient time to form in his mind the intent to kill, under the definition of *premeditation* and *deliberation,* then it would be your duty to return a verdict of not guilty of murder in the first degree, because the Court has instructed you if the State has failed to satisfy you of the element of *premeditation* or *deliberation,* or if there arises in your minds a reasonable doubt in regard to those two elements or either one of those two elements, it would be your duty to return a verdict of not guilty. And further in regard, when you come to consider those elements of *premeditation* and *deliberation,* if the defendant has satisfied you, not beyond a reasonable doubt, not by the greater weight of the evidence, but has merely satisfied you that he lost consciousness to such an extent that he was unable to *premeditate,* and was unable to *deliberate,* according to the definition of those terms that the law has given you, then he could not be guilty of murder in the first degree, and it would be your duty to return a verdict of not guilty as to murder in the first degree, under those circumstances. Now, *the Court feels that those are the only two elements in the case in which this evidence in regard to his loss of consciousness applies,* and the Court has ruled that there is no element of legal insanity in the evidence." (Our italics.)

Defendant's assignment of error, based on his exception to the foregoing portion of the charge, must be sustained. Defendant testified he was completely unconscious of what transpired when Myrtle, Ida and Jeffrey were shot. The court instructed the jury that this evidence was for consideration *only* in respect of the elements of premeditation and deliberation in first degree murder. This restriction of the legal significance of the evidence as to defendant's unconsciousness was erroneous.

* * *

"If a person is in fact unconscious at the time he commits an act which would otherwise be criminal, he is not responsible therefor. The absence of consciousness not only precludes the existence of any specific mental state, but also excludes the possibility of a voluntary act without which there can be no criminal liability." 1 Wharton's Criminal Law and Procedure (Anderson), § 50, p. 116.

"Unconsciousness is a complete, not a partial, defense to a criminal charge." 21 Am.Jur.2d, Criminal Law § 29, p. 115.

"*Unconsciousness.* A person cannot be held criminally responsible for acts committed while he is unconscious. Some statutes broadly exempt from responsibility persons who commit offenses without being conscious thereof. Such statutes, when construed in connection with other statutes relating to criminal capacity of the insane and voluntarily intoxicated, do not include within their protection either insane or voluntarily intoxicated persons, and are restricted in their contemplation to persons of sound mind suffering from some other agency rendering them unconscious of their acts * * *." 22 C.J.S. Criminal Law § 55, p. 194.

Defendant contends he had no knowledge of and did not consciously commit the act charged in the indictments. He does not contend he was insane. Unconsciousness and insanity are separate grounds of exemption from criminal responsibility.

* * *

There was no evidence defendant was a somnambulist or an epileptic. Nor was there evidence he was under the influence of intoxicants or narcotics. Under cross-examination, defendant testified his only previous "blackout" experience, which was of brief duration, occurred when he received and read the "Dear John" letter.

Upon the present record, defendant was entitled to an instruction to the effect the jury should return verdicts of not guilty if in fact defendant was *completely* unconscious of what transpired when Myrtle, Ida and Jeffrey were shot.

* * *

It should be understood that unconsciousness, although always a factor of legal significance, is not a complete defense under all circumstances. Without undertaking to mark the limits of the legal principles applicable to varied factual situations that will arise from time to time, but solely by way of illustration, attention is called to the following: In California, "unconsciousness produced by voluntary intoxication does not render a defendant incapable of committing a crime." People v. Cox, 67 Cal.App.2d 166, 153 P.2d 362, and cases cited. In Colorado, a person who precipitates a fracas and as a result is hit on the head and rendered semi-conscious or unconscious cannot maintain that he is not criminally responsible for any degree of homicide above involuntary manslaughter, or that he is not criminally responsible at all. Watkins v. People, 158 Colo. 485, 408 P.2d 425. In Oklahoma, a motorist is guilty of manslaughter if he drives an automobile with knowledge that he is subject to frequent blackouts, when his continued operation of the automobile is in reckless disregard to the safety of others and constitutes culpable or criminal negligence. Carter v. State [376 P.2d 351 (Okl.Cr.1962)]; Smith v. Commonwealth [268 S.W.2d 937 (Ky.1954)]. As to somnambulism, see Fain v. Commonwealth [78 Ky. 183 (1879)], and Lewis v. State, 196 Ga. 755, 27 S.E.2d 659.

Notes and Questions

1. The North Carolina Supreme Court expounded further on the defense of automatism in State v. Caddell, 287 N.C. 266, 215 S.E.2d 348 (1975). Automatism, it said, differs in nature from insanity (see Chapter XII, Sec. D.1., infra) in that for automatism the alleged criminal act need not have been the result of a disease or defect of the mind. The distinction seems to turn on how settled is the condition causing the defendant's claimed unconsciousness. Automatism—unlike insanity—might be due to somnambulism, hypnotism, concussion, delirium, shock, or epileptic blackouts. The court also said that there was a consequent difference in the effect of the two defenses. A defendant acquitted by virtue of unconsciousness is not subject to commitment to an asylum.

The court in *Caddell* overruled *Mercer* in one regard, and questioned it in another. It held, contrary to the *Mercer* opinion, that automatism is an affirmative defense so that the defendant would bear the risk of nonpersuasion. It questioned but did not decide whether the uncorroborated and unexplained testimony of Mercer that he had blacked out at the time of the shootings and was now amnesic with respect to those events was sufficient to raise the defense. That is, whether the evidence was enough to justify an instruction to the jury on this defensive theory.

Do the clarifications of the nature and operation of the automatism doctrine found in *Caddell* affect its desirability as a matter of public policy? Is it necessary if there is an insanity defense?

2. Notice how the Court in *Mercer* distinguishes situations in which the defendant's unconsciousness will not be a defense: intoxication or driving with knowledge of the danger of blackouts. Why are the harm-causing acts of these actors regarded as "voluntary" although Mercer's were not? Does it have to do with the time frame within which we consider the defendant's conduct? Do the court's distinctions suggest that the crucial point is our belief concerning the defendant's knowledge at some prior time, deemed relevant to our determination of responsibility, of the risk of harm? If so, is this an "act" problem or one of "state of mind"?

MODEL PENAL CODE *

Official Draft, 1985.

Section 2.01. Requirement of Voluntary Act; Omission as Basis of Liability; Possession as an Act

(1) A person is not guilty of an offense unless his liability is based on conduct which includes a voluntary act or the omission to perform an act of which he is physically capable.

(2) The following are not voluntary acts within the meaning of this Section:

(a) a reflex or convulsion;

(b) a bodily movement during unconsciousness or sleep;

(c) conduct during hypnosis or resulting from hypnotic suggestion;

(d) a bodily movement that otherwise is not a product of the effort or determination of the actor, either conscious or habitual.

*   *   *

(4) Possession is an act, within the meaning of this Section, if the possessor knowingly procured or received the thing possessed or was aware of his control thereof for a sufficient period to have been able to terminate his possession.

ROBINSON v. CALIFORNIA

Supreme Court of the United States, 1962.
370 U.S. 660, 82 S.Ct. 1417, 8 L.Ed.2d 758 (1962), reh. denied, 371 U.S. 905, 83 S.Ct. 202, 9 L.Ed.2d 166 (1962).

MR. JUSTICE STEWART delivered the opinion of the Court.

A California statute makes it a criminal offense for a person to "be addicted to the use of narcotics." This appeal draws into question the constitutionality of that provision of the state law, as construed by the California courts in the present case.

The appellant was convicted after a jury trial in the Municipal Court of Los Angeles. The evidence against him was given by two Los Angeles police officers. Officer Brown testified that he had had occasion to examine the appellant's arms one evening on a street in Los Angeles some four months before the trial. The officer testified that at that time he had observed "scar tissue and discoloration on the inside" of the appellant's right arm, and "what appeared to be numerous needle marks and a scab which was approximately three inches below the crook of the elbow" on the appellant's left arm. The officer also testified that the appellant under questioning had admitted to the occasional use of narcotics.

Officer Lindquist testified that he had examined the appellant the following morning in the Central Jail in Los Angeles. The officer stated that at that time he had observed discolorations and scabs on the appellant's arms, and he identified photographs which had been taken of the appellant's arms shortly after his arrest the night before. Based upon more than ten years of experience as a member of the Narcotic Division of the Los Angeles Police Department, the witness gave his opinion that "these marks and the discoloration were the result of the injection of hypodermic needles into the tissue into the vein that was not sterile." He stated that the scabs were several days old at the time of his examination, and that the appellant was neither under the influence of narcotics nor suffering withdrawal symptoms at the time he saw him. This witness also testified that the appellant had admitted using narcotics in the past.

The appellant testified in his own behalf, denying the alleged conversations with the police officers and denying that he had ever used narcotics or been addicted to their use. He explained the marks on his arms as resulting from an allergic condition contracted during his military service. His testimony was corroborated by two witnesses.

The trial judge instructed the jury that the statute made it a misdemeanor for a person "either to use narcotics, or to be addicted to the use of narcotics * * *. That portion of the statute referring to the 'use' of narcotics is based upon the 'act' of using. That portion of the statute referring to 'addicted to the use' of narcotics is based upon a condition or status. They are not identical. * * * To be addicted to the use of narcotics is said to be a status or condition and not an act. It is a continuing offense and differs from most other offenses in the fact that [it] is chronic rather than acute; that it continues after it is complete and subjects the offender to arrest at any time before he reforms. The existence of such a chronic condition may be ascertained from a single examination, if the characteristic reactions of that condition be found present."

The judge further instructed the jury that the appellant could be convicted under a general verdict if the jury agreed *either* that he was of the "status" *or* had committed the "act" denounced by the statute. "All that the People must show is either that the defendant did use a narcotic in Los Angeles County, or that while in the City of Los Angeles he was addicted to the use of narcotics * * *."

Under these instructions the jury returned a verdict finding the appellant "guilty of the offense charged."

* * *

The broad power of a State to regulate the narcotic drug traffic within its borders is not here in issue. * * *

Such regulation, it can be assumed, could take a variety of valid forms. A State might impose criminal sanctions, for example, against the unauthorized manufacture, prescription, sale, purchase, or possession of narcotics within its borders. In the interest of discouraging the violation of such laws, or in the interest of the general health or welfare of its inhabitants, a State might establish a program of compulsory treatment for those addicted to narcotics. Such a program of treatment might require periods of involuntary confinement. And penal sanctions might be imposed for failure to comply with established compulsory treatment procedures. Or a State might choose to attack the evils of narcotics traffic on broader fronts also—through public health education, for example, or by efforts to ameliorate the economic and social conditions under which those evils might be thought to flourish. In short, the range of valid choice which a State might make in this area is undoubtedly a wide one, and the wisdom of any particular choice within the allowable spectrum is not for us to decide. Upon that premise we turn to the California law in issue here.

It would be possible to construe the statute under which the appellant was convicted as one which is operative only upon proof of the actual use of narcotics within the State's jurisdiction. But the California courts have not so construed this law. Although there was evidence in the present case that the appellant had used narcotics in Los Angeles, the jury were instructed that they could convict him even if they disbelieved that evidence. The appellant could be convicted, they were told, if they found simply that the appellant's "status" or "chronic condition" was that of being "addicted to the use of narcotics." And it is impossible to know from the jury's verdict that the defendant was not convicted upon precisely such a finding.

* * *

This statute, therefore, is not one which punishes a person for the use of narcotics, for their purchase, sale or possession, or for antisocial or disorderly behavior resulting from their administration. It is not a law which even purports to provide or require medical treatment. Rather, we deal with a statute which makes the "status" of narcotic addiction a criminal offense, for which the offender may be prosecuted "at any time before he reforms." California has said that a person can be continuously guilty of this offense, whether or not he has ever used or possessed any narcotics within the State, and whether or not he has been guilty of any antisocial behavior there.

It is unlikely that any State at this moment in history would attempt to make it a criminal offense for a person to be mentally ill, or a leper, or to be afflicted with a venereal disease. A State might determine that the general health and welfare require that the victims of these and other human afflictions be dealt with by compulsory treatment, involving quarantine, confinement, or sequestration. But, in the light of contemporary human knowledge, a law which made a criminal offense oi such a disease would doubtless be universally thought to be an infliction of cruel and unusual punishment in violation of the Eighth and Fourteenth Amendments. * * *

We cannot but consider the statute before us as of the same category. In this Court counsel for the State recognized that narcotic addiction is an illness.[8] Indeed, it is apparently an illness which may be contracted innocently or involuntarily.[9] We hold that a state law which imprisons a person thus afflicted as a criminal, even though he has never touched any narcotic drug within the State or been guilty of any irregular behavior there, inflicts a cruel and unusual punishment in violation of the Fourteenth Amendment. To be sure, imprisonment for ninety days is not, in the abstract, a punishment which is either cruel or unusual. But the question cannot be considered in the abstract. Even one day in prison would be a cruel and unusual punishment for the "crime" of having a common cold.

We are not unmindful that the vicious evils of the narcotics traffic have occasioned the grave concern of government. There are, as we have said, countless fronts on which those evils may be legitimately attacked. We deal in this case only with an individual provision of a particularized local law as it has so far been interpreted by the California courts.

Reversed.

MR. JUSTICE DOUGLAS, concurring.

While I join the Court's opinion, I wish to make more explicit the reasons why I think it is "cruel and unusual" punishment in the sense of the Eighth Amendment to treat as a criminal a person who is a drug addict. * * * [T]he principle that would deny power to exact capital punishment for a petty crime would also deny power to punish a person by fine or imprisonment for being sick. * * *

MR. JUSTICE HARLAN, concurring.

8. In its brief the appellee stated: "Of course it is generally conceded that a narcotic addict, particularly one addicted to the use of heroin, is in a state of mental and physical illness. So is an alcoholic." Thirty-seven years ago this Court recognized that persons addicted to narcotics "are diseased and proper subjects for [medical] treatment." Linder v. United States, 268 U.S. 5, 18, 45 S.Ct. 446, 449, 69 L.Ed. 819.

9. Not only may addiction innocently result from the use of medically prescribed narcotics, but a person may even be a narcotics addict from the moment of his birth. * * *

I am not prepared to hold that on the present state of medical knowledge it is completely irrational and hence unconstitutional for a State to conclude that narcotics addiction is something other than an illness nor that it amounts to cruel and unusual punishment for the State to subject narcotics addicts to its criminal law. * * * Since addiction alone cannot reasonably be thought to amount to more than a compelling propensity to use narcotics, the effect of [the] instruction was to authorize criminal punishment for a bare desire to commit a criminal act.

If the California statute reaches this type of conduct, * * * it is an arbitrary imposition which exceeds the power that a State may exercise in enacting its criminal law. Accordingly, I agree that the application of the California statute was unconstitutional in this case and join the judgment of reversal.

MR. JUSTICE CLARK, dissenting.

* * *

[T]he majority admits that "a State might establish a program of compulsory treatment for those addicted to narcotics" which "might require periods of involuntary confinement." I submit that California has done exactly that. The majority's error is in instructing the California Legislature that hospitalization is the *only treatment* for narcotics addiction—that anything less is a punishment denying due process. California has found otherwise after a study which I suggest was more extensive than that conducted by the Court. Even in California's program for hospital commitment of nonvolitional narcotic addicts—which the majority approves—it is recognized that some addicts will not respond to or do not need hospital treatment. As to these persons its provisions are identical to those of § 11721—confinement for a period of not less than 90 days. Section 11721 provides this confinement as treatment for the volitional addicts to whom its provisions apply, in addition to parole with frequent tests to detect and prevent further use of drugs. The fact that § 11721 might be labeled "criminal" seems irrelevant,* not only to the majority's own "treatment" test but to the "concept of ordered liberty" to which the States must attain under the Fourteenth Amendment. The test is the overall purpose and effect of a State's act, and I submit that California's program relative to narcotic addicts—including both the "criminal" and "civil" provisions—is inherently one of treatment and lies well within the power of a State.

* * *

MR. JUSTICE WHITE, dissenting.

If appellant's conviction rested upon sheer status, condition or illness or if he was convicted for being an addict who had lost his power of self-control, I would have other thoughts about this case. But this

---

* Any reliance upon the "stigma" of a misdemeanor conviction in this context is misplaced as it would hardly be different from the stigma of a civil commitment for narcotics addiction.

record presents neither situation. * * * [T]here was no evidence at all that appellant had lost the power to control his acts. * * * He was an incipient addict, a redeemable user, and the State chose to send him to jail for 90 days rather than to attempt to confine him by civil proceedings under another statute which requires a finding that the addict has lost the power of self-control. In my opinion, on this record, it was within the power of the State of California to confine him by criminal proceedings for the use of narcotics or for regular use amounting to habitual use.

* * *

Notes and Questions

1. The Supreme Court returned to the requirements of the Eighth Amendment in Powell v. Texas, 392 U.S. 514, 88 S.Ct. 2145, 20 L.Ed.2d 1254 (1968). Powell had been convicted under the following Texas statute:

> Whoever shall get drunk or be found in a state of intoxication in any public place, or at any private house except his own, shall be fined not exceeding one hundred dollars.

The charge and proof was that Powell had been found in a state of public intoxication in a public place. The defense was that Powell was a chronic alcoholic and unable therefore to avoid the situation on which his conviction was based. Evidence in support of these contentions was presented. The members of the Court split on the meaning of the Eighth Amendment as applied in *Robinson* as well as on the sufficiency of Powell's showing to bring himself within the *Robinson* holding. This is explored more fully in the opinions reprinted at pages 345–56, infra. For present purposes, however, it is useful to note that in an opinion announcing the judgment of the Court affirming Powell's conviction, Justice Marshall explained:

> The entire thrust of *Robinson's* interpretation of the Cruel and Unusual Punishment Clause is that criminal penalties may be inflicted only if the accused has committed some act, has engaged in some behavior, which society has an interest in preventing, or perhaps in historical common law terms, has committed some *actus reus*.

392 U.S. at 533, 88 S.Ct. 2154–55, 20 L.Ed.2d at 1268. This opinion was joined by Chief Justice Warren and Justices Black and Harlan. Justice Black, in a concurring opinion, amplified the reasons he favored this interpretation of *Robinson*:

> [I believe] our attempt in *Robinson* to limit our holding to pure status crimes, involving no conduct whatever, was a sound one. * * * [Some] problems raised by status crimes are in no way involved when the State attempts to punish for conduct, and these * * * problems were, in my view, the controlling aspects of our decision.
>
> Punishment for a status is particularly obnoxious, and in many instances can reasonably be called cruel and unusual, because it involves punishment for a mere propensity, a desire to commit an offense; the mental element is not simply one part of the crime but may constitute all of it. This is a situation universally sought to be avoided in our criminal law; the fundamental requirement that some

action be proved is solidly established even for offenses most heavily based on propensity, such as attempt, conspiracy, and recidivist crimes.

* * *

The reasons for this refusal to permit conviction without proof of an act are difficult to spell out, but they are nonetheless perceived and universally expressed in our criminal law. Evidence of propensity can be considered relatively unreliable and more difficult for a defendant to rebut; the requirement of a specific act thus provides some protection against false charges. See 4 Blackstone, Commentaries 21. Perhaps more fundamental is the difficulty of distinguishing, in the absence of any conduct, between desires of the day-dream variety and fixed intentions that may pose a real threat to society; extending the criminal law to cover both types of desires would be unthinkable, since "[t]here can hardly be anyone who has never thought evil. When a desire is inhibited it may find expression in fantasy; but it would be absurd to condemn this natural psychological mechanism as illegal." [R. Perkins, Criminal Law 762 (1957)]

In contrast, crimes that require the State to prove that the defendant actually committed some proscribed act involve none of these special problems.

392 U.S. at 542–44, 88 S.Ct. at 2159–60, 20 L.Ed.2d at 1273–74 (Black, J., concurring).

Under this approach, why was not Powell's conviction nevertheless subject to attack under *Robinson?* Did the theory under which Powell was charged and convicted require proof of an "act" or behavior such as to distinguish it from a constitutionally prohibited status offense? Is being found in a public place an act on Powell's part? Justice Marshall offered:

The State of Texas * * * has not sought to punish a mere status, as California did in *Robinson* * * *. Rather, it has imposed upon [Powell] a criminal sanction for public behavior * * *. This seems a far cry from convicting one for being an addict [or for] being a chronic alcoholic * * *.

392 U.S. at 532, 88 S.Ct. at 2154, 20 L.Ed.2d at 1267.

Four members of the Court, in an opinion by Justice Fortas, urged that *Robinson* stands upon:

"a principle which * * * is the foundation of individual liberty and the cornerstone of the relations between a civilized state and its citizens: Criminal penalties may not be inflicted upon a person for being in a condition he is powerless to change."

They further found that Powell had sufficiently proved that he was powerless to avoid the condition upon which his conviction rested and thus his conviction could not stand. 392 U.S. at 567–68, 88 S.Ct. at 2171–72, 20 L.Ed.2d at 1286–87 (Fortas, J., dissenting). Justice White agreed that the Eighth Amendment barred the conviction of a chronic alcoholic even for conduct which, as a result of his alcoholism, he was powerless to avoid. But Justice White further concluded that Powell had not demonstrated that he was unable to avoid being found in public while intoxicated. Therefore, in his view, Powell's conviction was not barred by the Eighth

Amendment. 392 U.S. at 548–49, 88 S.Ct. at 2163–64, 20 L.Ed.2d at 1276–77 (White, J., concurring in the result).

2. As Mr. Justice Marshall makes clear in *Powell* (see note 1 supra, there must be "some act ＊ ＊ ＊ some behavior" before criminal penalties may be imposed. Does that mean that Mercer can't be convicted unless there is proof that he committed some "voluntary" act which caused the death? If so, and if automatism is logically inconsistent with the concept of a voluntary act, can the risk of non-persuasion on that issue be placed on the defendant consistent with the teaching of *Winship, Mullaney,* and *Patterson* (see Chapter I, Sec. C.1. supra)?

3. The Court in *Robinson* explicitly included "possession of narcotics" in its recitation of acts which might properly be criminalized. Is possession an "act"? See Section 2.01 of the Model Penal Code, reprinted at page 168, supra.

4. As is suggested by the definition of possession cited in note 3 supra, the contraband need not be actually possessed in the sense of being on the person of the possessor. The doctrine of "constructive possession" significantly broadens the ambit of possession statutes by extending culpability to situations where the defendant may be found to have been "in a position to exercise dominion or control" over the contraband. United States v. Holland, 445 F.2d 701, 703 (D.C.Cir.1971) and United States v. McCoy, 767 F.2d 395 (7th Cir.1985). A common problem in this area arises where the alleged possession is not only constructive but joint, as where the contraband is found in a car or room occupied by more than one person. See Folk v. State, 11 Md.App. 508, 275 A.2d 184 (1971).

5. Joint, constructive possession of a prohibited drug has not been the minimum "behavior" on which the use of the criminal sanction has been predicated. Prohibitions on the possession of the implements of crime are commonplace. An example is Section 16.01 of the Texas Penal Code which provides:

(a) A person commits an offense if:

(1) he possesses a criminal instrument with intent to use it in the commission of an offense; or

(2) with knowledge of its character and with intent to use or aid or permit another to use in the commission of an offense, he manufactures, adapts, sells, installs, or sets up a criminal instrument.

(b) For the purpose of this section, "criminal instrument" means anything, the possession, manufacture, or sale of which is not otherwise an offense, that is specially designed, made, or adapted for use in the commission of an offense.

(c) An offense under Subsection (a)(1) of this section is one category lower than the offense intended. An offense under Subsection (a)(2) of this section is a felony of the third degree.

Note that to be criminal the possession must be conscious and with a specific criminal intent. It may be relatively easy to infer the existence of such intent where the defendant is shown to have had on his person a collection of lock picks, but what if the instrument is a syringe and the "actor" is a physician? If that is too ambiguous a signal of criminality is it enough that the "narcotics paraphernalia" includes pieces of tinfoil, spoons, syringes and needles" in the possession of a defendant with twenty puncture marks on his arm? Should it be necessary that the paraphernalia contain traces of some prohibited drug? See Crawford v. United States, 278 A.2d 125 (D.C.App.1971).

For an especially ingenious, although ultimately unsuccessful, use of a criminal instruments statute see Universal Amusement Co. v. Vance, 404 F.Supp. 33 (S.D.Tex.1975), vac'd on other grounds, 425 U.S. 262, 96 S.Ct. 1527, 47 L.Ed.2d 774 (1976), aff'd. 587 F.2d 176 (5th Cir.1978), cert. denied, 442 U.S. 929, 99 S.Ct. 2859, 61 L.Ed.2d 296 (1979). There, a local district attorney, as part of his campaign against obscenity, had repeatedly charged the manager of a theater with possession of a criminal instrument, specifically an ordinary 16 millimeter film projector, with intent to use it in the commission of an offense, to wit the projection of *Deep Throat*, an allegedly obscene film. With each arrest and charge both the film and the projector would be seized and held, thereby forcing the theater to obtain another copy and another projector. The federal court enjoined this prosecution (and the seizures) on the grounds that the § 16.01 could not in good faith be stretched to cover the conduct in question.

What is the rationale for criminalizing the possession of instruments or contraband? Why should the authorities not wait until some effort is made to bring about the harm which the instruments or other contraband are thought to threaten?

STATE v. BUGGER

Supreme Court of Utah, 1971.
25 Utah 2d 404, 483 P.2d 442.

TUCKETT, JUSTICE. The defendant was found guilty of a violation of Section 41–6–44, U.C.A.1953, and from that conviction he has appealed to this court.

During the night of July 28, 1969, the defendant was asleep in his automobile which was parked upon the shoulder of a road known as Tippet's Lane in Davis County. The automobile was completely off the traveled portion of the highway and the motor was not running. An officer of the Highway Patrol stopped at the scene and discovered the defendant was asleep. With some effort the officer succeeded in awakening the defendant, at which time the officer detected the smell of alcohol and arrested the defendant for being in actual physical control of the vehicle while under the influence of intoxicating liquor.

The complaint charges the defendant with the violation of the statute above referred to which provides as follows:

It is unlawful and punishable as provided in subsection (d) of this section for any person who is under the influence of intoxicating liquor to drive or be in actual physical control of any vehicle within this state.

The defendant is here challenging the validity of the statute on the grounds of vagueness. However, we need not decide the case upon that ground. That part of the statute which states: "be in actual physical control of any vehicle" has been before the courts of other jurisdictions which have statutes with similar wordings. The word "actual" has been defined as meaning "existing in act or reality; * * * in action or existence at the time being; present; * * *." The word "physical" is defined as "bodily," and "control" is defined as "to exercise restraining or directing influence over; to dominate; regulate; hence, to hold from actions; to curb." The term in "actual physical control" in its ordinary sense means "existing" or "present bodily restraint, directing influence, domination or regulation." It is clear that in the record before us the facts do not bring the case within the wording of the statute. The defendant at the time of his arrest was *not* controlling the vehicle, nor was he exercising any dominion over it. It is noted that the cases cited by the plaintiff in support of its position in this matter deal with entirely different fact situations, such as the case where the driver was seated in his vehicle on the traveled portion of the highway; or where the motor of the vehicle was operating; or where the driver was attempting to steer the automobile while it was in motion; or where he was attempting to brake the vehicle to arrest its motion.

We are of the opinion that the facts in this case do not make out a violation of the statute and the defendant's conviction is reversed. We do not consider it necessary to discuss the other claimed errors raised by the defendant.

CALLISTER, C.J., and HENRIOD and CROCKETT, JJ., concur.

ELLETT, JUSTICE (dissenting).

I dissent.

The statute formerly made it unlawful for a person under the influence of intoxicating liquor to drive any vehicle upon any highway within this state. The amendment added a provision making it unlawful to be in actual physical control of a vehicle while under the influence of intoxicating liquor. It removed the need to be upon a highway before the crime was made out and did away with the necessity of driving before a crime was committed.

The reason for the change is obvious. It is better to prevent an intoxicated person in charge of an automobile from getting on the highway than it is to punish him after he gets on it. The amended statute gives officers a right to arrest a drunk person in the control of an automobile and thus prevent him from wrecking havoc a minute later by getting in traffic, or from injuring himself by his erratic driving.

It does not matter whether the motor is running or is idle nor whether the drunk is in the front seat or in the back seat. His potentiality for harm is lessened but not obviated by a silent motor or a backseat position—provided, of course, that he is the one in control of the car. It only takes a flick of the wrist to start the motor or to engage the gears, and it requires only a moment of time to get under the wheel from the back seat. A drunk in control of a motor vehicle has such a propensity to cause harm that the statute intended to make it criminal for him to be in a position to do so.

Restraining the movement of a vehicle is controlling it as much as moving it is. A person finding a drunk in the back seat of a car parked in one's driveway is likely to learn who is in control of that car if he should attempt to move it. A drunk may maliciously block one's exit, and in doing so he is in control of his own vehicle.

I think the defendant in this case was in control of his truck within the meaning of the statute even though he may have been asleep. He had the key and was the only one who could drive it. The fact that he chose to park it is no reason to say he was not in control thereof.

I, therefore, think that we should consider the question which he raises in his brief as to the validity of the statute.

Cases wherein an attack was made on statutes like ours have been decided in a number of jurisdictions. They hold the statute good.

In the case of State v. Webb, 78 Ariz. 8, 274 P.2d 338 (1954), the defendant was intoxicated and asleep in a truck parked next to some barricades in a lane of traffic. An officer passed by and observed no one in the car. Later he returned and found the defendant "passed out." The statute made it a crime to be in actual physical control of a car while under the influence of intoxicating liquor. The defendant contended that the wording of the statute was not meant to apply to a situation where the car was parked and that it was only concerned with the driving of an automobile and other acts and conduct of a positive nature. In holding that the statute was applicable to the conduct of the defendant, the court said:

> An intoxicated person seated behind the steering wheel of a motor vehicle is a threat to the safety and welfare of the public. The danger is less than that involved when the vehicle is actually moving, but it does exist.

In the case of Parker v. State, 424 P.2d 997 (Okl.Cr.App.1967), the appellant challenged the constitutionality of a statute making it unlawful for "any person who is under the influence of intoxicating liquor to drive, operate, or be in actual physical control of any motor vehicle within this state." There the defendant (appellant) claimed that the statute was unconstitutional in that it was so vague and indefinite that a person charged thereunder would be deprived of due process of law. The court held that the statute did not violate any of appellant's constitutional rights.

Under a similar statute the Montana Supreme Court in State v. Ruona, 133 Mont. 243, 321 P.2d 615 (1958), held that the statute was not void for vagueness, and in doing so said:

> * * * Thus one could have "actual physical control" while merely parking or standing still so long as one was keeping the car in restraint or in position to regulate its movements. Preventing a car

from moving is as much control and dominion as actually putting the car in motion on the highway. Could one exercise any more regulation over a thing, while bodily present, than prevention of movement or curbing movement. As long as one were physically or bodily able to assert dominion, in the sense of movement, then he has as much control over an object as he would if he were actually driving the vehicle.

* * * [I]t is quite evident that the statute in the instant case is neither vague nor uncertain. * * *

The defendant was found guilty in the court below of being in actual physical control of his truck while he was under the influence of intoxicating liquor. He does not dispute that he was drunk. If the statute is good, we should not attempt to overrule the trier of the facts and find that the defendant was not the one actually controlling his truck.

I would affirm the judgment of the trial court.

Note

The majority and the dissent take very different approaches to the problem of interpreting the crucial words describing the prohibited act: "actual physical control". Which is more persuasive? The similar Arkansas statute employs the same language and the Arkansas Supreme Court appears to have used a variety of approaches to its construction. In Wiyott v. State, 284 Ark. 399, 683 S.W.2d 220 (1985), the defendant was found asleep in a car parked in the parking lot of a store. Awakened by the arresting officer banging on the windows, the defendant reached for the key which was in the ignition and attempted to start the car. He was restrained by the officer who opened the door and removed the key from the ignition. In affirming the conviction, Justice Purtle, for the court, reasoned very much like the dissent in *Bugger*. He held that the defendant was in actual physical control of the car because he "was exercising direct influence over his vehicle and had the authority to manage it. At any moment he could have awakened and started the vehicle." Id. at 222. The continuing difficulty with the words "in actual physical control" is illustrated by Dowell v. State, 283 Ark. 161, 671 S.W. 740 (1984), which was not cited in the *Wiyott* opinion. The defendant there was also found asleep in his car in the driveway of a business near the highway. The keys were in the seat by the defendant's side. Justice Purtle, again writing for the court, reversed because the defendant:

> may not have been the person who drove the vehicle to where it was parked. If he drove it to the place where it was found may have become intoxicated later. Criminal laws are to be strictly construed in favor of the accused.

283 Ark. at 162, 671 S.W.2d at 741. Can it be that the placement of the key in the ignition is the crucial distinguishing factor? If so, why wasn't this mentioned in *Wiyott*. There was one other distinctive feature to *Wiyott*. The defendant was found with a male companion in the car, with both in a state of undress.

B. LIABILITY BASED ON FAILURE TO ACT

It is clear that normally a crime must include the element of an act. Can the absence of an act, an omission, ever constitute the equivalent of an act for purposes of holding a person criminally liable? There are two basic situations in which the answer is yes. The first category is easily understood. There are many statutes which impose duties on us to act and employ the criminal sanction if we fail to do so. All owners of cars are under a duty in many states to have them inspected, virtually all adults have a duty to file a tax return, young men of a certain age have a duty to register for a possible draft. Such statutes announce a clearly defined course of conduct and are doctrinally unobjectionable in terms of the act requirement.

Far more problematic are those situations in which some harmful and prohibited result has occurred which can be attributed to a particular person in the sense that it would not have occurred had the accused taken action to prevent it. In Jones v. United States, 113 U.S.App.D.C. 352, 308 F.2d 307 (1962), the defendant was convicted of involuntary manslaughter for the death of a 10 month old infant who had been left in her care by the child's mother. The death was attributed to severe malnutrition and lack of adequate medical care. The issue on appeal was whether the jury could convict without first finding beyond a reasonable doubt that the defendant was under a legal duty to supply food and medical care to the victim. Why should such a finding be required when a helpless infant is shown to have starved to death under the defendant's eyes? Could we live in a world in which criminal penalties might be imposed based upon a failure to succor others despite our knowledge of their needs? In reading the principal case and the materials which follow consider whether it is possible for the criminal law to devise a reasonable middle ground between atomistic individualism and generalized obligations to all the world.

DAVIS v. COMMONWEALTH

Supreme Court of Virginia, 1985.
230 Va. 201, 335 S.E.2d 375.

STEPHENSON, JUSTICE.

In a bench trial, Mary B. Davis was convicted of involuntary manslaughter of her mother, Emily B. Carter, and sentenced to 10 years in the penitentiary. The trial court found that Carter's death resulted from Davis' criminal negligence in failing to provide her mother with heat, food, liquids, and other necessaries.

The principal issues in this appeal are: (1) whether Davis had a legal duty to care for Carter, and if so, (2) whether she breached the duty by conduct constituting criminal negligence. . . .

On November 29, 1983, a paramedic with the Lynchburg Fire Department responded to a call at a house located at 1716 Monroe

Street in the City of Lynchburg. The house was occupied by Davis and Carter. The paramedic arrived about 5:35 p.m. and found Carter lying on a bed. It was a cold day, and there was no heat in Carter's room. The only source of heat was a tin heater, and it was not being used. The only food in the house was two cans of soup, a can of juice, and an open box of macaroni and cheese. Two trash cans were found behind the house. One contained 11 or 12 empty vegetable cans, and the other was full of empty beer cans. An operable stove, a supply of firewood and a color television were found in Davis' upstairs bedroom.

Carter was admitted to a hospital that evening. According to her treating physician, Carter's vital signs were unstable and she was severely ill. A nurse testified that Carter's "pulse was 35; respiration was 18 * * *[,] blood pressure was 148 over nothing * * * and her [body] temperature was 80 degrees." Carter was at least five to seven percent dehydrated. The doctor diagnosed her principal problems to be low body temperature, severe malnutrition, and bilateral pneumonia. She also had a blood stream infection, a skull laceration, and multiple rib fractures. Carter died in the early hours of December 2.

A forensic pathologist with the Chief Medical Examiner's Office conducted an autopsy on Carter's body. He concluded that the causes of death were "pneumonia and freezing to death due to exposure to cold with a chronic state of starvation." He stated that any one of these conditions alone could have caused her death.

Additionally, the pathologist testified that a body temperature of 80 degrees was extremely low and that, except in rare, isolated cases involving children or young people, "no one survives" such a low body temperature. He estimated that it would take nine hours for a dead body to reach a temperature of 82 degrees in a room temperature of 67 degrees and that a living person would require a longer exposure to the cold to reach that temperature.

The pathologist further testified that when a person's dehydration reaches a five to seven percent range, it suggests that she has received no liquids for at least two days. He described Carter's condition as "bone dry." He also testified that Carter's physical condition at the time of the autopsy indicated that she had eaten "no food whatsoever" for at least 30 days.

For a number of years, Carter had been senile and totally disabled. The attending physician testified that Davis said her mother was "not able to feed herself at all; that she was not able to care for her personal needs and that she had to wear diapers and had to have total care." Moreover, Davis informed a number of people that she was responsible for the total care of Carter.

Carter signed a writing naming Davis her authorized representative to apply for, receive, and use her food stamps. Relying on this document, the Department of Social Services awarded Davis additional food stamp benefits of $75 per month and exempted her from the requirement of registering for outside employment as a requisite to receiving these benefits.

Davis also was the representative payee of Carter's social security benefits in the amount of $310 per month. Davis' household expenses were paid exclusively from Carter's social security. Davis also received $23 per month in food stamps for her mother.

* * *

Next, we determine whether, under the facts and circumstances presented, Davis was under a legal duty to care for her mother. This presents an issue which we have not addressed previously.

A legal duty is one either "imposed by law, or by contract." *Pierce v. Commonwealth,* 135 Va. 635, 651, 115 S.E. 686, 691 (1923). When a death results from an omission to perform a legal duty, the person obligated to perform the duty may be guilty of culpable homicide. If the death results from a malicious omission of the performance of a duty, the offense is murder. On the other hand, although no malice is shown, if a person is criminally negligent in omitting to perform a duty, he is guilty of involuntary manslaughter.

Davis acknowledges the accuracy of the foregoing legal principles. She contends, however, that the evidence fails to establish that she had a legal duty to care for her mother, asserting that the evidence proved at most a moral duty. We do not agree.

The evidence makes clear that Davis accepted sole responsibility for the total care of Carter. This became her full-time occupation. In return, Carter allowed Davis to live in her home expense free and shared with Davis her income from social security. Additionally, Carter authorized Davis to act as her food stamp representative, and for this Davis received food stamp benefits in her own right. From this uncontroverted evidence, the trial court reasonably could find the existence of an implied contract. Clearly, Davis was more than a mere volunteer; she had a legal duty, not merely a moral one, to care for her mother.

Finally, we consider whether the evidence is sufficient to support the trial court's finding of criminal negligence. When the sufficiency of the evidence is challenged on appeal, the evidence and all reasonable inferences fairly deducible therefrom shall be viewed in the light most favorable to the Commonwealth, and the court's judgment must be affirmed unless it is plainly wrong or without evidence to support it.

When the proximate cause of a death is simply ordinary negligence, *i.e.,* the failure to exercise reasonable care, the negligent party cannot be convicted of involuntary manslaughter. To constitute criminal negligence essential to a conviction of involuntary manslaughter, an accused's conduct "must be of such reckless, wanton or flagrant nature as to indicate a callous disregard for human life and of the probable consequences of the act." *Lewis v. Commonwealth,* 211 Va. 684, 687, 179 S.E.2d 506, 509 (1971).

Davis contends that she cared for her mother as best she could under the circumstances. She points to the testimony of her four sisters and her boyfriend who stated that everything seemed normal and that they observed nothing to suggest that Carter was being neglected. These witnesses stated that the house always was heated properly and that sufficient food was available at all times.

Against this testimony, however, was the scientific evidence that Carter died of starvation and freezing. The evidence indicates that Carter had received no food for at least 30 days. She lay helpless in bed in an unheated room during cold weather. The trial court, as the trier of fact, determines the weight of the evidence and the credibility of the witnesses. Obviously, the court, as it had the right to do, accepted the Commonwealth's evidence and gave little or no weight to the testimony of the defendant and her witnesses. The court reasonably could conclude that Carter could not have starved or frozen to death unless she had been neglected completely for a protracted period of time.

We hold, therefore, that the evidence supports the trial court's finding that Davis' breach of duty was so gross and wanton as to show a callous and reckless disregard of Carter's life and that Davis' criminal negligence proximately caused Carter's death. Accordingly, we will affirm the judgment of the trial court.

Affirmed.

Notes and Questions

1. Would the result in *Davis* have been different if the house had been that of the defendant rather than of the deceased, and if the defendant had received no financial aid associated with her care of her mother? Should it be different? Why?

2. The enormous increase in the portion of the American population which is aged has heightened concern about their abuse and neglect. A typical expression of this concern is found in Texas Penal Code Section 22.04 which provides:

(a) A person commits an offense if he intentionally, knowingly, recklessly, or with criminal negligence, by act or omission, engages in conduct that causes to a child who is 14 years of age or younger or to an individual who is 65 years of age or older:

(1) serious bodily injury;

(2) serious physical or mental deficiency or impairment;

(3) disfigurement or deformity; or

(4) bodily injury.

(b) An offense under Subsection (a)(1), (2), or (3) of this section is a felony of the first degree when the conduct is committed intentionally or knowingly. When the conduct is engaged in recklessly it shall be a felony of the third degree.

(c) An offense under Subsection (a)(4) of this section is a felony of the third degree when the conduct is committed intentionally or knowingly. When the conduct is engaged in recklessly it shall be a Class A misdemeanor.

(d) An offense under Subsection (a) of this section when the person acts with criminal negligence shall be a Class A misdemeanor.

Would this statute permit the prosecution of Mrs. Davis if, as suggested in Note 1 above, she owned the house and did not receive financial aid for the support of her mother? What if the Mrs. Carter's physical and mental condition, and dependence on Mrs. Davis, was as described in the principle case but she lived alone in another dwelling next to Mrs. Davis? If she lived in another city?

3. Would the following statute be appropriate? What changes might be desirable?

Liability for Omission. A person shall be criminally responsible for a result if he fails to take action to prevent that result, but for his failure to take action the result would not have occurred, and the failure to take action constitutes a substantial deviation from common decency. In determining whether a failure to act constitutes a substantial deviation from common decency the following factors shall be taken into account:

1. the seriousness of the result,

2. the likelihood that the result would occur without action,

3. any burden or risk which taking action would have required the person to assume, and

4. any responsibility of the person for creating the need for action.

Compare this proposal with the following provision of the Texas Penal Code.

Sec. 6.01 (c) A person who omits to perform an act does not commit an offense unless a statute provides that the omission is an offense or otherwise provides that he has a duty to perform the act.

Statutes quite similar to the first proposal are found in European Codes. Feldbrugge, "Good and Bad Samaritans," 14 Am.J.Comp.L. 630 (1966). The Texas statute is typical of the Anglo-American approach to this issue except that its use of "a statute" as the source of the duty is somewhat narrower than the more common reference to duties imposed "by law". See "Vermont Requires Rescue: A Comment," 25 Stan.L.Rev. 51 (1972). Why do you think European Codes are different? Which approach is preferable in dealing with the following problems?

a. A, from the safety of his home, sees a young woman being assaulted by a man on a deserted street in the early hours of the morning. She cries for aid, screaming: "Oh my God, he stabbed me! Please help me!" A shouts at the assailant who stops momentarily but then pursues the victim. A takes no further action and the victim is again struck. The police, responding to a call from B who passes by after the assault has ended, arrive within two minutes after being notified. The victim dies on the way to the hospital.

The above hypothetical is drawn from the 1964 murder of "Kitty" Genovese in Queens, N.Y. More recently the problem of when, if ever, a bystander to a crime should be required to act was posed by a 1983 gang rape in a New Bedford, Massachusetts tavern. Revulsion at the failure of onlookers to intervene in any way moved at least one state legislature to address the issue. R.I.Gen.Laws (Cum.Supp.1985), § 11–37 provides:

> 3.1. Duty to report sexual assault.—Any person, other than the victim, who knows or has reason to know that a first degree sexual assault or attempted first degree sexual is taking place in his/her presence shall immediately notify the state police or the police department of the city or town in which said assault or attempted assault is taking place of said crime.

A knowing failure to make such a report is declared by Section 11–37–3.3 to be a misdemeanor punishable by imprisonment up to one year or a fine of up to $500, or both. Is this a desirable solution? Does it threaten the privacy interests of rape victims? Does it impose undue burdens and dangers on innocent bystanders? What if the bystander misjudges the situation; is she liable to those accused? With respect to this last concern, Section 11–37–3.4 grants civil and criminal immunity to any person making a good faith report.

b. A, a physician who has stopped at a rural restaurant while on vacation, hears a distraught young man announce that his wife is in very painful labor in a car outside. He asks if there is a doctor there or nearby. A does not respond but gets in his car and drives away. For want of proper assistance the woman and child perish.

c. Assume that the young man in "b." is rushing his wife to the hospital when he is involved in a minor accident with A who is at least partly to blame. The young man's car is disabled but A, fearing loss of his license because of prior violations and possible criminal penalties if his involvement is discovered by the police, flees the scene. Because the woman can't be taken to the hospital in time she and the child perish.

d. A, a school-crossing guard, leaves her post to obtain a cup of coffee on a bitterly cold winter day. A first-grader, slightly late for school, dashes across the street and is struck and killed by a car.

e. A group of air traffic controllers call in sick in a wage dispute knowing that there are insufficient replacements. In the course of diverting planes from that area, a mistake is made by an inexperienced substitute and a crash ensues killing all aboard.

3. Can one be convicted of a criminal omission in the absence of knowledge of the duty to act? See Lambert v. California, 355 U.S. 225, 78 S.Ct. 240, 2 L.Ed.2d 228 (1957) reprinted at page 282.

4. The most commonly recognized duty which will provide a basis for liability for omissions is that of parents to minor children. E.g., State v. Clark, 5 Conn.Cir. 699, 261 A.2d 294 (1969). Duties can also be assumed contractually. E.g., Jones v. United States, 113 U.S.App.D.C. 352, 308 F.2d 307 (1962). A duty to act may also arise when the defendant is responsible

for a condition that required assistance that the defendant failed to provide. Thus, in Herman v. State, 472 So.2d 770 (Fla.App.1985), the defendant's conviction for manslaughter was affirmed where the victim, a cocaine addict, died from the hemorrhaging of her nose and mouth due to a cocaine overdose administered by the defendant, who failed to call medical assistance when the victim began convulsing.

Whatever the source of the duty, it is crucial that the victim be unable to take remedial action herself. In Commonwealth v. Konz, 498 Pa. 639, 450 A.2d 638 (1982) the victim's wife and close friend successfully appealed from the Superior Court's reinstatement of their involuntary manslaughter convictions which had been set aside by the trial court. It was agreed that they had failed to call medical aid for the victim when he was stricken with a fatal diabetic crisis brought on by his decision, encouraged by the appellants, to forego taking his insulin in reliance on a belief that God would heal his diabetes. The appellants had strongly discouraged the victim's efforts to obtain insulin and assistance—at one point hiding his insulin; at another struggling to prevent his phoning the police—but ultimately, the court found, it was the victim who failed to seek aid although he was conscious and free to do so. The court feared that the imposition of liability on these facts would create peril of prosecution for a failure of accurate diagnosis, and would be inconsistent with the mutual respect each spouse owes the expressed preferences of the other.

5. Defendant, as secretary-treasurer of a local union, was under a statutory duty to file an annual financial report of the union with the Secretary of Labor. He is charged with willfully violating the statute because, although aware of this duty, he did not file the report. May he defend his failure on the grounds that it was impossible for him to comply? United States v. Spingola, 464 F.2d 909 (7th Cir.1972).

MODEL PENAL CODE *
(Official Draft, 1985).

Section 2.01. * * * Omission as Basis of Liability * * *

* * *

(3) Liability for the commission of an offense may not be based on an omission unaccompanied by action unless:

(a) the omission is expressly made sufficient by the law defining the offense; or

(b) a duty to perform the omitted act is otherwise imposed by law.

* * *

C. SPECIFIC REQUIREMENTS IMPOSED BY PARTICULAR OFFENSES

In the substantive definition of a number of crimes, no attempt is made to define the "act" which the defendant must have committed. In such cases—the homicide offenses are perhaps the best example—any voluntary physical movement or failure to move that meets general requirements is sufficient. The substantive definition of other crimes, however, contains a more limited definition of the "act" which must have been performed.

The importance of statutory definitions of the act requirement and the difficulties which may be posed by them is well illustrated by the case of State v. Decina, 2 N.Y.2d 133, 157 N.Y.S.2d 558, 138 N.E.2d 799 (1956). The defendant had had an epileptic seizure while driving his car. He lost consciousness and the car veered onto a sidewalk striking and killing four schoolgirls. The defendant, who was aware of his susceptibility to such attacks, was charged with negligent vehicular homicide under a statute which declared guilty "a person who operates or drives any vehicle * * * in a reckless or culpably negligent manner, whereby a human being is killed." If defendant was unconscious when the car moved from the roadway, was he operating or driving it? Can one be "reckless" while unconscious? If the recklessness is thought to refer to driving with knowledge of the danger of seizure no matter how carefully he did so while conscious, is the statutory definition of the act required being ignored?

The following material presents cases dealing with such limited definitions in a number of offenses. In regard to each, consider the policy reasons for limiting those acts which will give rise to liability, and the extent to which the specific definition of the required act serves those policies.

1. PROPERTY ACQUISITION OFFENSES

The following cases all involve the misappropriation or attempted misappropriation of property. The first four subsections deal with crimes where the misappropriation threatens only the owner's enjoyment of the property without any threat to the person of another. The last two—robbery and extortion—involve invasions of other interests as well as that inherent in ownership. They illustrate only a handful of the many statutory formulations which, largely as a function of history, attempt to distinguish among various crimes of acquisition: e.g., theft, theft by false pretext, conversion by a bailee, theft from the person, shoplifting, acquisition of property by theft, swindling, embezzlement, extortion, receiving or concealing embezzled or stolen property. The various statutes turn in their application on such niceties as whether or not the accused obtained possession of the property by trespass (larceny as contrasted with embezzlement) or whether the owner in reliance on the accused's misrepresentations of fact delivered mere possession or title (larceny by trick as contrasted with false pretenses). The fine distinctions required in the application of these laws have produced considerable appellate litigation.

a. Larceny

Larceny was the first and only common law theft offense. When it was decided that other forms of property acquisition should be criminalized it was Parliament which created the new crimes. Larceny involved: 1. the taking (caption); 2. by trespass; and 3. carrying away (asportation); 4. of the tangible personal property of another; 5. with the intent to steal. Although different terminology is employed in modern consolidated theft statutes, see pages 205–09, infra, the meaning of the words currently employed is often deeply colored by their common law antecedents.

Each of the terms employed in the above definition can be the basis for contention at trial and on appeal. As is indicated in the principal case, the requirement that the taking have been trespassory—from the owner's possession without her consent—is crucial to larceny as contrasted with other property offenses. Taking and carrying away, as indicated above, have traditionally been viewed as theoretically separate elements. The former refers to the thief's exercise of control over the property, either directly or through an innocent third party. The latter refers to some movement, however slight, of the property. In practice the distinction is seldom of importance today, when the slightest movement will suffice. The issue of what constitutes property which can be the subject of larceny posed many "nice" questions for the common law. The adjective "personal" indicates that real property or things attached thereto were excluded. Thus, growing crops could not be the subject of larceny unless and until they had been harvested by the owner or his agents. The use of "tangible" indicates that at common law intangible personal property, such as checks, could not be the subject of larceny. Although modern codes commonly eliminate these distinctions, new problems have arisen over intellectual and artistic property. This is further discussed in note 2 on page 203, infra. The intent element, which has emerged in modern times as the most significant aspect of this crime, is dealt with in the section on State of Mind, Chapter VI.C.2.

PEOPLE v. OLIVO

Court of Appeals of New York, 1981.
52 N.Y.2d 309, 438 N.Y.S.2d 242, 420 N.E.2d 40.

COOKE, CHIEF JUDGE.

These cases present a recurring question in this era of the self-service store which has never been resolved by this court: may a person be convicted of larceny for shoplifting if the person is caught with goods while still inside the store? For reasons outlined below, it is concluded that a larceny conviction may be sustained, in certain situations, even though the shoplifter was apprehended before leaving the store.

I

In *People v. Olivo*, defendant was observed by a security guard in the hardware area of a department store. Initially conversing with another person, defendant began to look around furtively when his acquaintance departed. The security agent continued to observe and saw defendant assume a crouching position, take a set of wrenches and secret it in his clothes. After again looking around, defendant began walking toward an exit, passing a number of cash registers en route. When defendant did not stop to pay for the merchandise, the officer accosted him a few feet from the exit. In response to the guard's inquiry, denied having the wrenches, but as he proceeded to the security office, defendant removed the wrenches and placed them under his jacket. At trial, defendant testified that he had placed the tools under his arm and was on line at a cashier when apprehended. The jury returned a verdict of guilty on the charge of petit larceny. The conviction was affirmed by Appellate Term.

II

In *People v. Gasparik*, defendant was in a department store trying on a leather jacket. Two store detectives observed him tear off the price tag and remove a "sensormatic" device designed to set off an alarm if the jacket were carried through a detection machine. There was at least one such machine at the exit of each floor. Defendant placed the tag and the device in the pocket of another jacket on the merchandise rack. He took his own jacket, which he had been carrying with him, and placed it on a table. Leaving his own jacket, defendant put on the leather jacket and walked through the store, still on the same floor, by passing several cash registers. When he headed for the exit from that floor, in the direction of the main floor, he was apprehended by security personnel. At trial, defendant denied removing the price tag and the sensormatic device from the jacket, and testified that he was looking for a cashier without a long line when he was stopped. The court, sitting without a jury, convicted defendant of petit larceny. Appellate Term affirmed 102 Misc.2d 487, 425 N.Y.S.2d 936.

III

In *People v. Spatzier*, defendant entered a bookstore on Fulton Street in Hempstead carrying an attaché case. The two co-owners of the store observed the defendant in a ceiling mirror as he browsed through the store. They watched defendant remove a book from the shelf, look up and down the aisle, and place the book in his case. He then placed the case at his feet and continued to browse. One of the owners approached defendant and accused him of stealing the book. An altercation ensured and when defendant allegedly struck the owner with the attaché case, the case opened and the book fell out. At trial, defendant denied secreting the book in his case and claimed that the owner had suddenly and unjustifiably accused him of stealing. The jury found defendant guilty of petit larceny, and the conviction was affirmed by the Appellate Term.

IV

The primary issue in each case is whether the evidence, viewed in the light most favorable to the prosecution, was sufficient to establish the elements of larceny as defined by the Penal Law. To resolve this common question, the development of the common-law crime of larceny and its evolution into modern statutory form must be briefly traced.

Larceny at common law was defined as a trespassory taking and carrying away of the property of another with intent to steal it. The early common-law courts apparently viewed larceny as defending society against breach of the peace, rather than protecting individual property rights, and therefore placed heavy emphasis upon the requirement of a *trespassory taking* (e.g., Fletcher, Metamorphosis of Larceny, 89 Harv.L.Rev. 469; American Law Institute, Model Penal Code [Tent. Draft No. 1], art. 206, app. A, at p. 101; La Fave & Scott, Criminal Law, § 85, at pp. 622–623). Thus, a person such as a bailee who had rightfully obtained possession of property from its owner could not be guilty of larceny (e.g., Glanvill, Treatise on the Laws and Customs of the Realm of England [Hall ed. 1965], pp. 128–130 [Book 10, at pp. 13–14]; see, e.g., *Carrier's Case,* Y B Pasch 13 Edw. IV, f.9, pl 5 [1473]). The result was that the crime of larceny was quite narrow in scope.[1]

Gradually, the courts began to expand the reach of the offense, initially by subtle alterations in the common-law concept of possession (e.g., American Law Institute, Model Penal Code [Tent. Draft No. 1], art. 206, app. A, p. 101). Thus, for instance, it became a general rule that goods entrusted to an employee were not deemed to be in his possession, but were only considered to be in his custody, so long as he remained on the employer's premises (e.g., 3 Holdsworth, A History of English Law [3d ed. 1923], at p. 365).[2] And, in the case of *Chisser* (Raym. Sir.T. 275, 83 Eng.Rep. 142), it was held that a shop owner retained legal possession of merchandise being examined by a prospective customer until the actual sale was made. In these situations, the employee and the customer would not have been guilty of larceny if they had first obtained lawful possession of the property from the owner. By holding that they had not acquired possession, but merely custody, the court was able to sustain a larceny conviction.

As the reach of larceny expanded, the intent element of the crime became of increasing importance, while the requirement of a trespasso-

---

1. One popular explanation for the limited nature of larceny is the "unwillingness on the part of the judges to enlarge the limits of a capital offense" (*Commonwealth v. Ryan,* 155 Mass. 523, 527, 30 N.E. 364; Hall, Theft, Law and Society [2d ed.], at p. 118 *et seq.*). The accuracy of this view is subject to some doubt (see Fletcher, Meta-morphosis of Larceny, 89 Harv.L.Rev. 469, 483–484, n. 64).

2. In 1529, a statute was passed subjecting employees to the law of larceny as to all valuable property entrusted to them by their employers (21 Hen. VIII, ch. 7).

ry taking became less significant. As a result, the bar against convicting a person who had initially obtained lawful possession of property faded. In *King v. Pear* (1 Leach 212, 168 Eng.Rep. 208), for instance, a defendant who had lied about his address and ultimate destination when renting a horse was found guilty of larceny for later converting the horse. Because of the fraudulent misrepresentation, the court reasoned, the defendant had never obtained legal possession. Thus, "larceny by trick" was born.

Later cases went even further, often ignoring the fact that a defendant had initially obtained possession lawfully, and instead focused upon his later intent. The crime of larceny then encompassed, not only situations where the defendant initially obtained property by a trespassory taking, but many situations where an individual, possessing the requisite intent, exercised control over property inconsistent with the continued rights of the owner.[3] During this evolutionary process, the purpose served by the crime of larceny obviously shifted from protecting society's peace to general protection of property rights.[4]

Modern penal statutes generally have incorporated these developments under a unified definition of larceny (see e.g., American Law Institute, Model Penal Code [Tent. Draft No. 1], § 206.1 [theft is appropriation of property of another, which includes unauthorized exercise of control]). Case law, too, now tends to focus upon the actor's intent and the exercise of dominion and control over the property (see, e.g., *People v. Alamo,* 34 N.Y.2d 453, 358 N.Y.S.2d 375, 315 N.E.2d 446.) Indeed, this court has recognized, in construing the New York Penal Law,[5] that the "*ancient* common-law concepts of larceny" no longer strictly apply (*People v. Alamo, supra,* 34 N.Y.2d at p. 459, 358 N.Y.S.2d 375, 315 N.E.2d 446 [emphasis added]).

This evolution is particularly relevant to thefts occurring in modern self-service stores. In stores of that type, customers are impliedly

3. Parliament also played a role in this development. Thus, for example, in 1857 a statute extended larceny to all conversions by bailees (20 & 21 Vict., ch. 54).

4. One commentator has argued that the concept of possessorial immunity—i.e., that one who obtains possession of property by delivery from the owner cannot be guilty of larceny—stems from a general reluctance of the early common law to criminalize acts arising out of private relationships (Fletcher, Metamorphosis of Larceny, 89 Harv.L.Rev. 469, 472–476). Thus, although an owner deprived of property by a bailee could seek a civil remedy in detinue and later trover (Maitland, Equity and the Forms of Action at Common Law, at pp. 356–357, 365), the harm was deemed private and not a matter for societal intervention. Over time, the public-private dichotomy waned and the criminal law increasingly was viewed as an instrument for protecting certain interests and controlling social behavior (Fletcher, at pp. 502–504). As a concomitant development, the criminal law changed its main focus from the objective behavior of the defendant to his subjective intent (*id.,* at pp. 498–518).

5. Section 155.05 of the Penal Law defines larceny: "1. A person steals property and commits larceny when, with intent to deprive another of property or to appropriate the same to himself or to a third person, he wrongfully takes, obtains, or withholds such property from an owner thereof. 2. Larceny includes a wrongful taking, obtaining or withholding of another's property, with the intent prescribed in subdivision one of this section, committed in any of the following ways: (a) By conduct heretofore defined or known as common law larceny by trespassory taking, common law larceny by trick, embezzlement, or obtaining property by false pretenses."

invited to examine, try on, and carry about the merchandise on display. Thus in a sense, the owner has consented to the customer's possession of the goods for a limited purpose. That the owner has consented to that possession does not, however, preclude a conviction for larceny. If the customer exercises dominion and control wholly inconsistent with the continued rights of the owner, and the other elements of the crime are present, a larceny has occurred.[6] Such conduct on the part of a customer satisfies the "taking" element of the crime.

It is this element that forms the core of the controversy in these cases. The defendants argue, in essence, that the crime is not established, as a matter of law, unless there is evidence that the customer departed the shop without paying for the merchandise.

Although this court has not addressed the issue, case law from other jurisdictions seems unanimous in holding that a shoplifter need not leave the store to be guilty of larceny. This is because a shopper may treat merchandise in a manner inconsistent with the owner's continued rights—and in a manner not in accord with that of prospective purchaser—without actually walking out of the store. Indeed, depending upon the circumstances of each case, a variety of conduct may be sufficient to allow the trier of fact to find a taking. It would be well-nigh impossible, and unwise, to attempt to delineate all the situations which would establish a taking. But it is possible to identify some of the factors used in determining whether the evidence is sufficient to be submitted to the fact finder.

In many cases, it will be particularly relevant that defendant concealed the goods under clothing or in a container. Such conduct is not generally expected in a self-service store and may in a proper case be deemed an exercise of dominion and control inconsistent with the store's continued rights. Other furtive or unusual behavior on the part of the defendant should also be weighed. Thus, if the defendant surveys the area while secreting the merchandise or abandoned his or her own property in exchange for the concealed goods, this may evince larcenous rather than innocent behavior. Relevant too is the customer's proximity to or movement towards one of the store's exits. Certainly it is highly probative of guilt that the customer was in possession of secreted goods just a few short steps from the door or moving in that direction. Finally, possession of a known shoplifting device actually used to conceal merchandise, such as a specially designed outer garment or false bottomed carrying case, would be all but decisive.

---

6. Also, required, of course, is the intent prescribed by subdivision 1 of section 155.05 of the Penal Law, and some movement when property other than an automobile is involved. As a practical matter in shoplifting cases the same evidence which proves the taking will usually involve movement.

The movement, or asportation requirement has traditionally been satisfied by a slight moving of the property. This accords with the purpose of the asportation element which is to show that the thief had indeed gained possession and control of the property.

Of course, in a particular case, any one or any combination of these factors may take on special significance. And there may be other considerations, not now identified, which should be examined. So long as its bears upon the principal issue—whether the shopper exercised control wholly inconsistent with the owner's continued rights—any attending circumstance is relevant and may be taken into account.

V

Under these principles, there was ample evidence in each case to raise a factual question as to the defendants' guilt.[7] In *People v. Olivo,* defendant not only concealed goods in his clothing, but he did so in a particularly suspicious manner. And, when defendant was stopped, he was moving towards the door, just three feet short of exiting the store. It cannot be said as a matter of law that these circumstances failed to establish a taking.[8]

In *People v. Gasparik,* defendant removed the price tag and sensor device from a jacket, abandoned his own garment, put the jacket on and ultimately headed for the main floor of the store. Removal of the price tag and sensor device, and careful concealment of those items, is highly unusual and suspicious conduct for a shopper. Coupled with defendant's abandonment of his own coat and his attempt to leave the floor, those factors were sufficient to make out a prima facie case of a taking.

In *People v. Spatzier,* defendant concealed a book in an attaché case. Unaware that he was being observed in an overhead mirror, defendant looked furtively up and down the aisle before secreting the book. In these circumstances, given the manner in which defendant concealed the book and his suspicious behavior, the evidence was not insufficient as a matter of law.

* * *

VII

In sum, in view of the modern definition of the crime of larceny, and its purpose of protecting individual property rights, a taking of property in the self-service store context can be established by evidence that a customer exercised control over merchandise wholly inconsistent with the store's continued rights. Quite simply, a customer who crosses the line between the limited right he or she has to deal with merchandise and the store owner's rights may be subject to prosecution for larceny. Such a rule should foster the legitimate interests and continued operation of self-service shops, a convenience which most members of the society enjoy.

7. In analyzing the proof to determine legal sufficiency, the evidence must be viewed in the light most favorable to the prosecution.

8. As discussed, the same evidence which establishes dominion and control in these circumstances will often establish movement of the property. And, the requisite intent generally may be inferred from all the surrounding circumstances. It would be the rare case indeed in which the evidence establishes all the other elements of the crime but would be insufficient to give rise to an inference of intent.

Accordingly, in each case, the order of the Appellate Term should be affirmed.

JASEN, GABRIELLI, JONES, WACHTLER, FUCHSBERG and MEYER, JJ., concur.

b. Embezzlement

Embezzlement was not a crime at common law. If one came into possession of property with the owner's consent and subsequently absconded with it, no crime was made out because there had not been a trespassory taking. As is indicated by the opinion in *Olivo* the problem thus posed had been dealt with in part by the doctrine of "constructive possession" under which servants normally had only custody of their master's property rather than possession. Owners were also said to retain "constructive possession" of lost property or property delivered to another for very limited purposes. However, these fictions were not applied in the famous case of The King v. Bazeley, 168 Eng.Rep. 117 (1799). Bazeley, a bank clerk, had received money for deposit to the owner's account. Instead of transferring it to the bank's possession by moving it to the cash drawer or vault he pocketed the money. This was held not to be larceny because possession had been willingly surrendered by the owner but never received by the bank. To fill this gap, Parliament, that very year enacted the first embezzlement statute.

Embezzlement requires that the actor, in lawful possession of another's property, fraudulently convert it. The basic meaning of conversion in this context is to act upon the property in a manner seriously inconsistent with the trust relationship underlying the owner's willing transfer of possession.

STATE v. WILLIAMS
Supreme Court of Iowa, 1970.
179 N.W.2d 756.

BECKER, JUSTICE. Defendant was indicted and tried for the crime of embezzlement by bailee, section 710.4, Code of Iowa, 1966.[1] Jury verdict of guilty was returned, defendant's post trial motions were overruled and he was sentenced to the State Penitentiary for term not exceeding five years. He appeals. We reverse.

The embezzlement charge is an outgrowth of a business arrangement between defendant, his father and Liberty Livestock Farms, a partnership owned by Dwaine Clark and Dr. Joe Graham. Both Earl Williams, defendant's father and Dwaine Clark, one of the partners, were deceased at time of trial.

The parties mentioned entered into an agreement under which the partnership was to deliver 35 head of Hampshire open gilt hogs and 2

1. "Embezzlement by bailee. Whoever embezzles or fraudulently converts to his own use, or secrets with intent to embezzle or fraudulently convert to his own use, money, goods, or property delivered to him, or any part thereof, which may be the subject of larceny, shall be guilty of larceny and punished accordingly."

boars to defendant and his father for breeding purposes. Defendant and his father were to keep the hogs long enough to farrow and raise two litters of pigs. Thereafter the partnership was to receive one hog from each litter plus the return of the hogs originally delivered.

The 35 gilts and two boars were delivered as agreed to the farm owned by defendant's father and operated by defendant. Defendant took delivery of the animals.

The contract provided the gilts were to be large enough to breed and the boars large enough for service. One of the State's witnesses notes that he talked to defendant after the hogs were delivered and received complaints that the hogs were too small. Defendant claims the hogs were too small and were returned.

The contract contemplated defendant and his father would have the hogs on their farm for over a year. Delivery was made February 24, 1967. Frank Madera told of visiting defendant's farm and seeing the hogs in early April 1967. Dwaine Clark died May 27, 1967. His son-in-law, Leo Seuferer, took over the management of the partnership, discovered the contract for 35 gilts and two boars in the active file but took no further action until February 3, 1968, when he went to defendant's farm to check on the animals. Neither defendant nor his father was at home. Seuferer looked around the premises but saw no hogs. Two days later he reached defendant on the telephone and asked how the hogs were getting along. Defendant said they were doing fine. Seuferer then said he had been at the farm the previous Saturday and did not see any hogs on the farm. The telephone then went dead and Seuferer could not immediately reestablish connections.

Later the same evening Seuferer again called defendant and said he wanted to pick up the animals belonging to Liberty Livestock Farms. Defendant said he and his father did not have the animals, they had only been on the farm about a week when they were picked up. Defendant said he had been thinking about another deal when Seuferer had called earlier in the evening.

Defendant acknowledges the above telephone calls but denies the substance of the conversation. He denied he hung up on the first conversation and said that during the second conversation he told Seuferer Dwaine Clark had picked up the hogs.

Defendant did not produce the hogs and Seuferer then took the matter to the county attorney. The result was the instant indictment.

The first line of defense was that the State did not generate a jury question on all essential elements of the crime charged. The affirmative portion of the defense was that the hogs were returned to their rightful owners. Defendant contends the hogs were too small for proper breeding when delivered. His father was dissatisfied and called Dwaine Clark. Defendant's wife testified Dwaine Clark and a trucker came and took the hogs away while defendant was working in the fields. She was in the house. Earl Williams, defendant's father, went out and helped load the animals.

Since Dwaine Clark, the manager of the partnership that owned the hogs, died May 1967, shortly after the hogs were delivered and Earl Williams, defendant's father, died July 20, 1968, three weeks before defendant was indicted, the only person active in the contract, and still alive, was defendant. No evidence was produced as to how the partnership kept track of its hogs, what books were kept on financial transactions or what, if any, evidence the partnership papers contained as to whether the hogs in question had or had not been returned. In this regard the sole evidence was by James Clark and Leo Seuferer. Both said to the best of their knowledge no hogs had been returned but they did not know what, if anything, Dwaine Clark might have done about the hogs in April 1967. Seuferer said he found the contract under which the hogs were delivered in the active files maintained by Dwaine Clark at the time of his death in May 1967. Dr. Graham was an inactive partner and knew nothing about the matter.

* * *

Embezzlement was not a crime at common law. In Iowa embezzlement and all other crimes are wholly statutory.

Chapter 710, Code, 1966, deals with embezzlement in several sections which define distinct and separate crimes; i.e., embezzlement by public officers, § 710.1; by bailee, § 710.4; by agents, § 710.9; et cetera. These crimes are similar but not subject to identical rules, State v. Cavanaugh, 214 Iowa 457, 460, 236 N.W. 96.

The different crimes of embezzlement covering different situations are noted here because of a rule laid down in State v. Bryan, 40 Iowa 379, 381, 382:

> "The crime with which the defendant is charged, is that of converting the money which came into his hands as treasurer to his own use. The rule is too well established to require citation of authorities to verify it, that conversion may be shown either by direct proof of the fact of conversion, or by proof of a demand and refusal. Where the fact of conversion is sought to be proved by evidence of a demand and refusal, it may always be met and neutralized by evidence showing an excuse for this refusal; and when the excuse shown is sufficient, then the evidence of a demand and refusal does not establish the fact of conversion. * * *

> "But this doctrine does not apply to the crime of embezzlement as defined by the next section of our statute, (Code, 3909). (Now § 710.5, at that time § 710.3, embezzlement by bailee had not been enacted.) There the doctrine relied upon by appellant's counsel and vindicated by the authorities they cite applies."

The State's brief relies on the above rule: "* * * The State showed that appellant signed an agreement to lease certain hogs, the hogs were delivered to appellant and when the lease expired a demand was made on appellant to return the hogs and the hogs were never returned. Obviously the State sustained its burden in proving the elements of the crime in question and the case was properly submitted to the jury." If the rule applies to embezzlement by bailee there is sufficient evidence for a jury case. This rule, under which the State need only show receipt of the property, demand and refusal to redeliver, is peculiar to embezzlement by public officials. State v. Bryan, supra, so states. Reference to section 710.1 relating to public officials will show the wealth of prohibited acts provided in the section and a rational basis for the rule.

In cases charging embezzlement by persons other than public officials a different rule applies. Ordinarily, fraudulent conversion to defendant's use must be shown. Cf. Footnote 1. See also, 2 Burdick, Law of Crime, § 575, p. 353: " * * * the accused must have fraudulently converted the property; and under most statutes, there must be an intent to defraud."

We have had little occasion in the past to consider the quantum of proof of conversion required necessary in cases of this kind. In similar cases there has always been proof of some overt act of defendant which is inconsistent with the rights of the true owner of the property; State v. Dykes (Iowa 1968) 158 N.W.2d 154 (sale of corn at other than designated elevator); State v. Christiansen, 231 Iowa 525, 1 N.W.2d 623 (admitted collection of monies retained by agent and kept by him); State v. Schumacher, 162 Iowa 231, 143 N.W. 1110 (use of company funds to purchase grain options); State v. Boggs, 166 Iowa 452, 147 N.W. 934 (pledge of nonowned contract as security for personal loan); State v. Rowell, 172 Iowa 208, 154 N.W. 488 (commingling and use of funds by agent. The funds belonged to the principal). Other cases to the same effect could be cited. In each case, where conviction has been sustained there has been some evidence, direct or circumstantial, of wrongful conversion. We can find no such evidence here.

The subject, as it relates to demand and refusal, is best covered by Perkins on Criminal Law, Second Ed., chapter 4(D), p. 293, where he quotes People v. Ward (1901), 134 Cal. 301, 304, 66 P. 372, 373:

> " 'A demand, followed by a refusal *if the other essential facts exist,* is evidence of embezzlement, and sometimes indispensable evidence of it; *but it is the fraudulent and felonious conversion of the money or other property that constitutes the offense,* and that may often be proved without a demand' " (Emphasis supplied.)

Except in the case of public officials our statutes ordinarily require a showing of conversion of the property to the use of the embezzler. This may be done by circumstantial evidence and the State is entitled to all reasonable inferences to be taken from the factual circumstances shown. Here the State relied entirely on circumstantial evidence to prove defendant converted the property to his own use.

* * *

We know of no other case with a similar factual situation; i.e., where the accused defendant was one of two joint bailees either of whom could have disposed of the bailed property. There is no direct evidence that either bailee actually did so act. The possible activity of the deceased father is simply not met as an issue in the State's case. This alone is a fatal weakness under the foregoing rule long recognized in this court.

Nor is there any substantial evidence to eliminate the very real possibility that the bailor Dwaine Clark did not come and take the hogs away. The jury's obvious rejection of defendant's contention in this regard is not enough "to exclude a reasonable doubt that defendant was innocent of the charge". The negative factor of rejection of defendant's story does not relieve the State of its affirmative burden to prove its case. Defendant's evidence is to be considered but here it did not add to the weight of the State's case. There was no effort, beyond the finding of the papers with the "active files", to show the partnership still charged defendant and his father with possession of the hogs at the time of Clark's death.

The books of the partnership may or may not have been sufficiently detailed to show the location and number of hogs to which the partnership claimed ownership. If such evidence was available it was not produced. In the absence of such evidence and because of the death of Mr. Clark, the jury was left to speculate as to what the active partner did or did not do between the date of delivery of the hogs and the date of his death. As in the case of the possible activity of defendant's father, this dearth of evidence constitutes a fatal weakness in the State's case.

The rule applicable to public officials as to demand and nondelivery is inapplicable here. The record is completely silent as to what happened to the hogs. The evidence permits rational hypothesis inconsistent with defendant's guilt. As was asked in State v. Daves, 259 Iowa 584, 591, 144 N.W.2d 879, 884:

> "The evidence is circumstantial. Can we say it is sufficient to allow the jury to find every rational hypothesis of innocence has been negatived as required by the cases?" As in State v. Daves, supra, the answer must be negative under the record made.

What has been said here makes moot the other points relied upon by defendant. The motion for directed verdict made at the close of all the evidence should have been sustained.

Reversed.

MOORE, C.J., and MASON, RAWLINGS, LEGRAND and UHLENHOPP, JJ., concur.

LARSON, STUART and REES, JJ., dissent.

c. *False Pretenses*

As has been noted, the essence of common law larceny was that it involved a trespassory taking. What then of the duplicitous criminal who obtains the tangible personal property of another through the owner's willing transfer of the property on the basis of the actor's false statements? In King v. Pear, 168 Eng.Rep. 208 (1779), the defendant had obtained a horse by telling the owner that he intended to use it for one purpose when he in fact intended to sell it and keep the proceeds. The court adopted the fiction that because of the misrepresentation, the owner retained possession and the subsequent acts of the thief constituted larceny by trick. This expansion of the concept of larceny was undertaken even though Parliament had earlier created a crime which could be seen as covering the conduct of Pear. This was the statutory offense of false pretenses which had been enacted in 1757. For reasons which are unclear, the court in *Pear* treated the statute as being limited to situations in which the actor has obtained title to the property.

Thus, even now it is said that a key theoretical distinction between false pretenses and larceny by trick is whether the thief, through his trickery, acquired title to the property from the owner (false pretenses), or merely possession (larceny by trick) Bell v. United States, 462 U.S. 356, 103 S.Ct. 2398, 76 L.Ed.2d 638 (1983). Traditionally, the owner must have relied upon the actor's knowing misrepresentations of a material past or present fact, and the actor must have acted with an intent to defraud. Although courts and statutes continue to employ the name "false pretenses" they do not always require proof of each of the above elements.

POLLARD v. STATE

Supreme Court of Mississippi, 1971.
244 So.2d 729.

ROBERTSON, JUSTICE. The appellant, Norman Pollard, was indicted, tried and convicted in the Circuit Court of Lee County, of the crime of false pretenses (giving a bad check), and was sentenced to serve a term of three years in the State Penitentiary and to pay a fine of $250.00.[a]

The appellant assigned as error: the granting of State's Instruction No. 1; the refusal to direct a verdict for the defendant * * *

Appellant had a sideline of buying used cars, repairing and improving them, and then selling them at a profit. He was a young married man with no capital and operated on a shoestring. He had been doing business for some months with Ronald Michael and Charles Baxter, of B & M Motors, Inc., Baldwin, Mississippi.

On September 5, 1968, Pollard gave B & M Motors a $2,550.00 check for three used cars. September 5th was on Thursday, and

---

a. Pollard was charged under the following provision of the Mississippi Code:

Section 2153. False pretenses—bad check

If any person, with intent to defraud, shall make, issue and deliver to another person, for value, any check, draft or order on any bank or other depository and thereby obtain from such other person any money, goods or other property of value, and have no funds or have insufficient funds on deposit to his credit in such bank or depository * * *, he shall be guilty of [an offense].

Pollard testified that he asked Ronald Michael to hold the check until the following week. The proof showed that the check was held until the following Tuesday, September 10th, when it was deposited to the account of B & M Motors. Michael explained that B & M Motors was charged a flat exchange fee of $5.00 whether he deposited $1,000.00 or $50,000.00, so he usually waited until after the auction sale on Monday to make his deposit. The $2,550.00 check of Pollard was returned because of insufficient funds.

At the November, 1968, term of Circuit Court, Pollard was indicted for the crime of false pretense, (the giving of a bad check for $2,550.00 and receiving value for the check in the form of three used cars). The one indispensable element of this offense is the receiving of value for the check at the very time it is delivered. In other words, the seiler parts with something of value on the belief that the check is good at that particular time. * * *

The gravamen of the offense was succinctly stated in Jackson v. State, 251 Miss. 529, 170 So.2d 438 (1965):

"So an essential element of the offense under section 2153 is the making and delivering of the check to another person for value, *and thereby obtaining from such other person money, goods, or other property of value.*" (Emphasis added). 251 Miss. at 531, 170 So.2d at 439.

It would appear that the transaction between Pollard and B & M Motors was a credit sale, and not an exchange for value based on the belief that Pollard's check was good at that particular moment.

If Pollard is to be believed, he was doing business on a hold-check basis, received the cars on Thursday and his check was deposited the following Tuesday. This would indicate a credit sale.

If Michael is to be believed, he frequently allowed dealers to take cars one day and mail in a check several days later. He testified that he had followed this practice with Pollard on two or three occasions. This also would indicate a credit sale based on Michael's confidence in the purchaser generally. Michael had followed this procedure with Pollard just a week before. Pollard had taken delivery of two used cars on August 24, 1968, and his check to B & M Motors was dated August 27, 1968. Michael's uncertain testimony about this transaction was:

"A I'm saying it is a possibility that—it's been a long time, Mr. Parker, that he could have bought the cars, come by my place and bought the cars, verbally bought them, and said that when I send after the cars or when somebody brings them to me I'll send the check back or I'll put the check in the mail. There is that possibility, which I do that on numerous occasions.

"Q You have done that for him on numerous occasions, is that right?

"A No, probably a couple of times, but I do that with all of my dealers. *I had no reason to doubt the man wouldn't send me the check.*

"Q In fact you had no reason to doubt that he wouldn't send you the $2550 check?

"A I didn't—

"Q Isn't that a fact?

"A I thought the check was good when he gave it to me, I'll tell that.

"Q You had delivered his cars before that hadn't you?

"A I'm not sure when they delivered the cars on the $2550 check.

"Q That's all my questions.

*   *   *

"A I believe he took those cars that day, Mr. McCreary I believe took those cars down there, I'm not sure." (Emphasis added).

This Court said in Grenada Coca Cola Co. et al. v. Davis, 168 Miss. 826, 151 So. 743 (1934):

"The so-called bad check law does not cover the obtaining of goods where the goods had already been delivered, had passed completely out of the possession of the seller and away from his hands and premises in a previously completed transaction or transactions, *although those transactions may have been at previous hours on the same day. There must be an exchange for the check at the time of delivery.* The bad check law is severe enough without extending it by construction so as to include past deliveries, to say nothing of the question of the constitutional validity of such a statute if it were so construed." (Emphasis added.) 168 Miss. at 832, 151 So. at 744.

In the later case of Broadus v. State, 205 Miss. 147, 38 So.2d 692 (1949), this Court again interpreted the bad check law:

"In the case at bar, the pressing machinery had been delivered to the agent of Broadus and the agent had completely removed them from the possession and premises of Fowler and had departed from Roses Hill for Escatawpa, and had been gone for some thirty minutes before Broadus came up and delivered the check to Fowler in payment for same. When Fowler let the machinery leave his possession and control without demanding and receiving the purchase price, he extended credit for same. Broadus did not obtain the machinery with the check, for he had already, before that time, obtained the machinery. He obtained nothing with the check. The check was given in discharge of a pre-existing debt. The bad check law has no application here." 205 Miss. at 150–151, 38 So.2d at 693.

The court should have directed a verdict for the Defendant Pollard.

*   *   *

Judgment reversed and defendant discharged.

GILLESPIE, P.J., and RODGERS, JONES and INZER, JJ., concur.

Notes and Questions

1. The most distinctive element of larceny is that the taking have been trespassory. As is indicated by *Olivo,* modern theft statutes may use other terminology. In *Olivo* the problem is analyzed in terms of whether the defendants' acts constituted "wrongful takings"—that is, exercises of dominion inconsistent with the rights in the property reserved by the

owner. Under other statutes, such as the Texas Penal Code, the essence of the element of trespass would be examined in terms of whether the defendant's "appropriation" of the property had been "without the owner's effective consent."

It is easy to understand that one who snatches a wallet from the sales counter where it has been placed momentarily and flees with it has committed a trespassory taking—has appropriated our property without our consent. However, economic activities have become increasingly complex, and larceny or theft is now asked to cover actions which do not so clearly announce their criminality. In State v. Langford, 483 So.2d 979 (La.1986), the defendant, denied a loan for $225,000, opened a NOW account at that same bank. A bank employee mistakenly coded the defendant's account—and some 83 other new accounts—as "01". For the computer this designation meant unlimited overdraft privileges. This error was compounded when the "overdraft reports" were not delivered for review and approval to bank officers but rather were discarded. In the meantime the bookkeepers did not raise questions because the "01" designation meant that any overdraft had already been approved. However, the computer automatically generated a notice for each check that overdrew the account. Such a notice advised the drawer of the check of the amount of each check and the total negative balance of the account. It did not include a request that the customer take any action. In 195 days after opening the account the defendant had issued some 213 checks and overdrawn the account by $848,904.39; he had also received 198 overdraft notices.

The defendant responded to a theft charge by claiming that the evidence did not establish that the taking was non-consensual. The Supreme Court of Louisiana rejected this: "The evidence overwhelmingly supports the fact that no human person with the bank ever made a conscious decision to honor defendant's checks notwithstanding the account's overdraft status." 483 So.2d at 983–84. The majority also found it important that, despite the repeated honoring of the checks by the bank, the defendant could not have believed that a bank which had refused him a loan of $225,000 would have consented to his taking of $848,000 as some sort of loan.

Two justices dissented. The Chief Justice acknowledged that Langford might have been guilty of issuing worthless checks but he was not guilty of theft: "The bank knew it was honoring defendant's overdrafts the only way a bank can know anything—by the knowledge of its employees (and machines) gained from the bank's records." Id., at 986.

The issue of when a taking is non-consensual was also the key to Fussell v. United States, 505 A.2d 72 (D.C.App.1986) although the amount taken was minuscule by comparison with Langford's haul. In Fussell the defendant had approached a plainclothes transit officer and offered to sell him a D.C. bus pass for half of its $20.00 value. The officer realized that the pass was bogus but gave the defendant the $10.00 and then arrested him as he pocketed it.

The appellate court reversed the defendant's conviction for taking property without right on the grounds that it cannot be "without right" if "the property is voluntarily surrendered for the purpose of completing a criminal transaction. The essential element of lack of consent is missing". 505 A.2d at 73.

Is *Langford* or *Fussell* more in keeping with the purpose of criminalizing larceny?

2. The nature of property which could be the subject of larceny at common law was far narrower than is true under modern statutes. Massachusetts Gen.Laws Ann.C. 266 § 30(2) recites additions to the notion of property subject to larceny in the following terms:

> The term "property", as used in this section, shall include money, personal chattels, a bank note, bond, promissory note, bill of exchange or other bill, order or certificate, a book of accounts for or concerning money or goods due or to become due or to be delivered, a deed or writing containing a conveyance of land, any valuable contract in force, a receipt, release or defeasance, a writ, process, certificate or title or duplicate certificate * * * a public record, anything which is of the realty or is annexed thereto * * * and any domesticated animal, other than a dog, or a beast or bird which is ordinarily kept in confinement and is not the subject of larceny at common law.

In Commonwealth v. Yourawski, 384 Mass. 386, 425 N.E.2d 298 (1981) the question was whether the defendants who had received unauthorized copies of video cassettes of "Star Wars" had received stolen "property". The court was unanimous in concluding that they had not.

> We do not read the definition of "property" * * * as reaching the property interest that is alleged to have been stolen in this case. Certainly, the images and sounds captured on the cassette tapes are not within any of the items specified § 30(2). We have treated § 30(2)'s definition * * * as all-inclusive, apart from items that were subject to larceny at common law.

The same conclusion was reached in Dowling v. United States, 473 U.S. 207, 105 S.Ct. 3127, 87 L.Ed.2d 152 (1985) (bootlegged Elvis Presley recordings do not constitute stolen "goods, wares, [or] merchandise").

The decisions in *Yourawski* and *Dowling* reflect, in part, the fact that alternatives to theft prosecutions—such as actions under copyright laws—which are more carefully tailored to the defendant's actions may be available. What then should be done where the information or data obtained by the defendant without the owner's permission is not otherwise legally protected? In United States v. DiGilio, 538 F.2d 972 (3d Cir.1976), cert. denied sub nom. Lupo v. United States, 429 U.S. 1038, 97 S.Ct. 733, 50 L.Ed.2d 749 (1977), the defendant and others had arranged for an FBI typist to make unauthorized copies of documents in FBI files relating to an investigation of the named defendant's alleged criminal activities. The charge was that the defendants had converted to their own use the photocopies of the files in violation of 18 U.S.C.A. § 641 which makes it a felony for anyone to covert to his own use "any record, voucher, money, or thing of value of the United States". The defendants argued that their conduct did not deprive the United States of anything—not even the use of the information in the records—and that a copy is not itself a record within the meaning of § 641. The court affirmed the convictions on the ground that the typist had used government time, equipment and supplies in making the copies. What would have been the result if the typist had made the copies on her own time with her own copier? What if she had memorized the contents? If the definition of "property" in § 641 is read to include mere information would it run afoul of the First Amendment? See United States v. Jeter, 775 F.2d 670 (6th Cir.1985) and United States v. Lambert, 446 F.Supp. 890 (D.Conn.1978), aff'd sub nom. United States v. Girard, 601 F.2d 69 (2d Cir.1979), cert. denied, 444 U.S. 871, 100 S.Ct. 148, 62 L.Ed.2d 96 (1979).

The breadth of modern concepts of property subject to larceny can cause more pedestrian difficulties. If the defendant is an employee who uses his employer's computer to keep records of his personal business, has he committed theft? Of what? Does he intend to deprive his employer? Assume that the computer is not operating at full capacity and that the rental cost of the computer is unrelated to the frequency of its use. See State v. McGraw, 480 N.E.2d 552 (1985). If he has committed theft, would it be any different if he kept his records on his own paper, after normal work hours but making use of the employer's furniture, electric lights, and heat or air-conditioning?

3. Why did the prosecutor in *Williams* proceed on embezzlement rather than larceny? What element of larceny was missing? What additional element is required for embezzlement? Is there any justification for differentiating between embezzlement by a public officer and by a bailee?

4. The distinctive feature of embezzlement is the betrayal of the trust imposed in the actor by the owner of the property. If the prosecution proves that betrayal—the conversion of the property with knowledge that this was unauthorized by the owner—the fact that the owner may have benefited by the actor's conduct, or that restitution is subsequently made, will not serve as an excuse. See, e.g., United States v. Stockton, 788 F.2d 210 (4th Cir.1986).

A number of other crimes have been developed which supplement embezzlement by focusing upon the special responsibilities of specific classes of persons who hold property as fiduciaries. Common forms of such statutes are "theft by misapplication" and "misapplication of fiduciary property or property of financial institutions". These crimes will usually not require proof of any intent "to steal" or to "fraudulently convert" and are normally punished less severely than is embezzlement.

In State v. Pleasant Hill Health Facility, Inc., 496 A.2d 306 (Me.1985), the defendant, which operated a nursing home, had been convicted of theft by misapplication based on its handling of the social security checks of its patients. It had deposited those checks into corporate accounts and subsequently would transfer to the patient's personal accounts those amounts not due the corporation for room and board. Sometimes the transfer would take as long as six months, and there were times when the defendant had insufficient funds to cover all legitimate claims by patients regarding their personal accounts. However, at no time was a patient's request for her funds ever denied, and all funds due were ultimately paid. The defendant was charged under a statute which provided that a person who obtains property from another "subject to a known legal obligation to make a specified payment or other disposition" and then "intentionally or recklessly fails to make the required payment or disposition and deals with the property * * * as his own" is guilty of theft. The conviction was upheld because the statute was read to proscribe any commingling of funds for any length of time.

5. Was either larceny or embezzlement a viable alternative for the prosecution in *Pollard*? Why?

6. It should be noted in connection with *Pollard* that "bad check" laws were enacted because of difficulties encountered in fitting this activity within the traditional requirement that in obtaining property by false pretense there must be reliance by the victim on a false representation with respect to a past or present fact. Cf. Chaplin v. United States, 157 F.2d 697 (D.C.Cir.1946). Unlike the statute in *Pollard* most such laws do not require that property be obtained as a result of the check. It is sufficient that the check be given with the requisite state of mind—usually knowledge of insufficient funds and an intent to defraud. In contrast, for theft by false pretense to lie the actor's misrepresentation must have been the decisive influence operating upon the victim's mind in inducing him to part with his property. See State v. Fierson, 146 Ariz. 287, 705 P.2d 1338 (App.1985); People v. Davis, 112 Ill.2d 55, 96 Ill.Dec. 693, 491 N.E.2d 1153 (1986); and Deardorf v. State, 477 N.E.2d 934 (Ind.App.1985). This principle may be an alternative, albeit unenunciated, explanation for the decision in *Fussell* which is discussed in note 1, above.

7. At common law if one by false pretenses obtained possession of property, as where one, by lying, convinced an owner to lend property, the crime of false pretenses did not lie since there title had to have been transferred. Instead, assuming that the actor had converted the property, the charge would have been larceny by trick. Today distinctions based on the nature of the interest transferred have largely been abandoned. See, e.g., State v. Kelly, 75 N.C.App. 461, 331 S.E.2d 227 (1985).

It is still the generally accepted view that, unless specifically changed by statute, the misrepresentations necessary for the crime of false pretenses must be as to a present or existing fact or a past fact or event. Promises or predictions as to the future, no matter how fraudulent when uttered, will not suffice. People v. Cage, 410 Mich. 401, 301 N.W.2d 819 (1981). However, such statutory changes have been frequently adopted. E.g., People v. Emerson, 117 A.D.2d 935, 499 N.Y.S.2d 242 (1986) and State v. Droddy, 702 P.2d 111 (Utah 1985).

d. Theft: Consolidated Acquisition Offenses

Dissatisfaction with hairsplitting such as is illustrated by the immediately preceding notes has led to efforts at consolidating the various theft offenses. An example is the following sections of the Model Penal Code * (Official Draft, 1985).

Section 223.0   Definitions

In this Article, unless a different meaning plainly is required:

(1) "deprive" means: (a) to withhold property of another permanently or for so extended a period as to appropriate a major portion of its economic value, or with intent to restore only upon payment of reward or other compensation; or (b) to dispose of the property so as to make it unlikely that the owner will recover it.

(2) "financial institution" means a bank, insurance company, credit union, building and loan association, investment trust or other organization held out to the public as a place of deposit of funds or medium of savings or collective investment.

(3) "government" means the United States, any State, county, municipality, or other political unit, or any department, agency or subdivision of any of the foregoing, or any corporation or other association carrying out the functions of government.

(4) "movable property" means property the location of which can be changed, including things growing on, affixed to, or found in land, and documents although the rights represented thereby have no physical location; "immovable property" is all other property.

(5) "obtain" means: (a) in relation to property, to bring about a transfer or purported transfer of a legal interest in the property, whether to the obtainer or another; or (b) in relation to labor or service, to secure performance thereof.

(6) "property" means anything of value, including real estate, tangible and intangible personal property, contract rights, choses-in-action and other interests in or claims to wealth, admission or transportation tickets, captured or domestic animals, food and drink, electric or other power.

(7) "property of another" includes property in which any person other than the actor has an interest which the actor is not privileged to infringe, regardless of the fact that the actor also has an interest in the property and regardless of the fact that the other person might be precluded from civil recovery because the property was used in an unlawful transaction or was subject to forfeiture as contraband. Property in possession of the actor shall not be deemed property of another who has only a security interest therein, even if legal title is in the creditor pursuant to a conditional sales contract or other security agreement.

Section 223.1.   Consolidation of Theft Offenses; Grading; Provisions Applicable to Theft Generally

(1) *Consolidation of Theft Offenses.* Conduct denominated theft in this Article constitutes a single offense. [The 1962 Proposed Official Draft included the following language at this point: "embracing the separate offenses heretofore known as larceny, embezzlement, false pretense, extortion, blackmail, fraudulent conversion, receiving stolen

property, and the like."] An accusation of theft may be supported by evidence that it was committed in any manner that would be theft under this Article, notwithstanding the specification of a different manner in the indictment or information, subject only to the power of the Court to ensure fair trial by granting a continuance or other appropriate relief where the conduct of the defense would be prejudiced by lack of fair notice or by surprise.

(2) *Grading of Theft Offenses.*

(a) Theft constitutes a felony of the third degree if the amount involved exceeds $500, or if the property stolen is a firearm, automobile, airplane, motorcycle, motorboat, or other motor-propelled vehicle, or in the case of theft by receiving stolen property, if the receiver is in the business of buying or selling stolen property.

(b) Theft not within the preceding paragraph constitutes a misdemeanor, except that if the property was not taken from the person or by threat, or in breach of a fiduciary obligation, and the actor proves by a preponderance of the evidence that the amount involved was less than $50, the offense constitutes a petty misdemeanor.

(c) The amount involved in a theft shall be deemed to be the highest value, by any reasonable standard, of the property or services which the actor stole or attempted to steal. Amounts involved in thefts committed pursuant to one scheme or course of conduct, whether from the same person or several persons, may be aggregated in determining the grade of the offense.

(3) *Claim of Right.* It is an affirmative defense to prosecution for theft that the actor:

(a) was unaware that the property or service was that of another; or

(b) acted under an honest claim of right to the property or service involved or that he had a right to acquire or dispose of it as he did; or

(c) took property exposed for sale, intending to purchase and pay for it promptly, or reasonably believing that the owner, if present, would have consented.

(4) *Theft From Spouse.* It is no defense that theft was from the actor's spouse, except that misappropriation of household and personal effects, or other property normally accessible to both spouses, is theft only if it occurs after the parties have ceased living together.

Section 223.2. Theft by Unlawful Taking or Disposition

(1) *Movable Property.* A person is guilty of theft if he unlawfully takes, or exercises unlawful control over, movable property of another with purpose to deprive him thereof.

(2) *Immovable Property.* A person is guilty of theft if he unlawfully transfers immovable property of another or any interest therein with purpose to benefit himself or another not entitled thereto.

Section 223.3. Theft by Deception

A person is guilty of theft if he obtains property of another by deception. A person deceives if he purposely:

(1) creates or reinforces a false impression, including false impressions as to law, value, intention or other state of mind; but deception as to a person's intention to perform a promise shall not be inferred from the fact alone that he did not subsequently perform the promise; or

(2) prevents another from acquiring information which would affect his judgment of a transaction; or

(3) fails to correct a false impression which the deceiver previously created or reinforced, or which the deceiver knows to be influencing another to whom he stands in a fiduciary or confidential relationship; or

(4) fails to disclose a known lien, adverse claim or other legal impediment to the enjoyment of property which he transfers or encumbers in consideration for the property obtained, whether such impediment is or is not valid, or is or is not a matter of official record.

The term "deceive" does not, however, include falsity as to matters having no pecuniary significance, or puffing by statements unlikely to deceive ordinary persons in the group addressed.

Section 223.4. Theft by Extortion

A person is guilty of theft if he obtains property of another by threatening to:

(1) Inflict bodily injury on anyone or commit any other criminal offense; or

(2) accuse anyone of a criminal offense; or

(3) expose any secret tending to subject any person to hatred, contempt or ridicule, or to impair his credit or business repute; or

(4) take or withhold action as an official, or cause an official to take or withhold action; or

(5) bring about or continue a strike, boycott or other collective unofficial action, if the property is not demanded or received for the benefit of the group in whose interest the actor purports to act; or

(6) testify or provide information or withhold testimony or information with respect to another's legal claim or defense; or

(7) inflict any other harm which would not benefit the actor.

It is an affirmative defense to prosecution based on paragraphs (2), (3) or (4) that the property obtained by threat of accusation, exposure, lawsuit or other invocation of official action was honestly claimed as restitution or indemnification for harm done in the circumstances to which such accusation, exposure, lawsuit or other official action relates, or as compensation for property or lawful services.

Section 223.7. Theft of Services

(1) A person is guilty of theft if he obtains services which he knows are available only for compensation, by deception or threat, or by false token or other means to avoid payment for the service. "Services" includes labor, professional service, transportation, telephone or other public service, accommodation in hotels, restaurants or elsewhere, admission to exhibitions, use of vehicles or other movable property. Where compensation for service is ordinarily paid immediately upon the rendering of such service, as in the case of hotels and restaurants, refusal to pay or absconding without payment or offer to pay gives rise to a presumption that the service was obtained by deception as to intention to pay.

(2) A person commits theft if, having control over the disposition of services of others, to which he is not entitled, he knowingly diverts such services to his own benefit or to the benefit of another not entitled thereto.

Note

There are, of course, many other offenses against property which are not covered by these provisions, but all of the significant ones involve invasions or threatened invasions of socially valued interests in addition to our interest in protecting the enjoyment of property. Thus arson is generally punished more severely than would be the theft of the same property or its destruction by other means because of the special dangers posed by fire to persons and other property. The distinguishing features of robbery and extortion which are, in a sense, aggravated property offenses, and burglary which is commonly engaged in for purposes of theft, are treated in the materials which follow.

e. Robbery

Robbery, a common law felony, is traditionally defined as a theft aggravated by the fact that the taking of the property is from the person or in the presence of the owner by the use or the threatened imminent use of force. In some modern statutes, such as that involved in State v. Long which follows, any taking of property accompanied by the aggravating conditions will be sufficient whether or not the actor had the intent to steal which is the mental element of theft.

A major issue in the area of robbery is the proximity which must be shown between the use or threatened imminent use of force, the crucial distinguishing element of robbery, and the taking. That is the subject of State v. Long. Note that the idea of the imminence of the threatened use of force is obviously related to the traditional requirement that the taking be from the person or presence of the owner. Unless the owner is physically within reach of the actor's force, it would be difficult to see how the taking of the property was the result of that force, or threat of force. However, the taking might still constitute theft and, as shall be seen, it might also be extortion.

STATE v. LONG

Court of Appeals of Kansas, 1983.
8 Kan.App.2d 733, 667 P.2d 890.

REES, PRESIDING JUDGE:

A jury convicted defendant of robbery (K.S.A. 21–3426). He appeals. His arguments are that the evidence was insufficient and the trial judge erroneously failed to instruct on theft as a lesser included offense.

We accept the State's version of the facts established by the evidence. It is that Margo Wolf and her husband reside in rural Butler County, Kansas, and operate a dairy farm there. As a part of that business they maintain a small sale building in which they stock and refrigerate gallon bottles of milk. This building is open to the public. The Wolfs employ an "honor system" in their business operation at the sale building. It includes the open display of refrigerated milk and a locked, slotted money box mounted on a wall. Customers may enter the sale building, obtain milk and deposit payment in the locked box, thereby eliminating the need for the Wolfs to be present at all times. On the evening of February 17, 1981, Mrs. Wolf was in an adjacent milk barn filling gallon milk bottles in order to replenish the sale building's supply which the day's business had reduced to two bottles. While there, she observed a car drive up to the sale building. Seeing this, she went to the sale building to inform the customer that in a few minutes she would have more milk available. As she opened the door to the sale building, she observed the defendant crouched in front of the money box. It had been pried open. The defendant had his hands in his pockets. Mrs. Wolf saw a dollar bill lying on the floor beneath the forced money box. She positioned herself in the doorway so as to prevent the defendant from leaving the building. She twice asked the defendant what he was doing, to which he made no response. Instead, the defendant walked toward her, shoved her arm out of the way, forcing himself by her, and proceeded to drive away in his car. Mrs. Wolf noted down defendant's license tag number. The money box had approximately $40 to $45 in currency in it prior to Mrs. Wolf's observation of defendant crouched near the box. Immediately after the incident there was nothing in the box except some small change. The defendant admitted that he "brushed by" Mrs. Wolf as he exited the sale building.

K.S.A. 21–3426 defines robbery as "the taking of property from the person or presence of another by threat of bodily harm to his person or the person of another or by force."

Defendant's first argument to us is that the evidence fails to support the conclusion that defendant "did unlawfully * * * take * * * cash from the presence of Margo Wolf by force" as the State charged in its information. The question raised is not whether there was the use of force. That is assumed. The question is whether there was a taking by force. We conclude that upon the authority of *State v. Aldershof,* 220 Kan. 798, 556 P.2d 371 (1976); *State v. Buggs,* 219 Kan. 203, 547 P.2d 720 (1976); and *State v. Miller,* 53 Kan. 324, 36 P. 751 (1894), there was not.

Commission of the crime of robbery is complete when the robber takes possession of the property. In *State v. Buggs,* 219 Kan. at 204–205, 547 P.2d 720, the victim was the operator of a Dairy Queen store. As she was leaving the store at the close of business one evening, with the day's business receipts in a bank money bag in her purse, she was accosted. Under threat of bodily harm she was ordered back into the store where she was asked for "the money." She handed over her purse. Police officers arrived in response to a silent alarm. They confronted and apprehended defendant before he had left the store premises. On appeal, defendant claimed he was erroneously denied an instruction on attempted robbery as a lesser included offense of robbery. The Supreme Court reasoned that attempted robbery occurs only when the proscribed taking is not accomplished. It held at 206, 547 P.2d 720:

> "Here all the evidence is that the bank money bag was 'taken' from [the victim] * * * and later removed * * * to the restroom. * * * The robbery was complete when [the victim] handed over the bag. * * *"

In *State v. Miller,* 53 Kan. 324, 36 P. 751, where a robbery conviction was sustained, the defendant cut the victim's hand contemporaneously with his taking of money from a cash drawer. The physical taking and removal of the money had not been completed; the defendant had not completed the act of obtaining possession of the money until after force was used.

From *State v. Aldershof,* 220 Kan. 798, 556 P.2d 371, we glean the governing principles. Robbery is not committed where possession is obtained without the use of force. Neither is there a robbery where there is no use of force except to resist arrest or escape. To constitute the crime of robbery, it is necessary that the use of force precede or be contemporaneous with the act of obtaining physical possession of the property. The line of cases represented by *People v. Kennedy,* 10 Ill. App.3d 519, 294 N.E.2d 788 (1973), is not in accord with the position taken by Kansas authority and it is distinguished in *Aldershof.*

In the case before us, we assume, for the purpose of our decision, defendant took money from the money box and his shoving of Mrs.

Wolf out of his way when exiting the sale building constituted the use of force. However, the evidence wholly fails to support a conclusion that defendant's use of force preceded or was contemporaneous to defendant's acquisition of possession of money from the money box. The "taking," if it occurred, was accomplished and completed before Mrs. Wolf observed defendant. It neither was preceded by nor occurred contemporaneously with defendant's use of force. Defendant's conviction for robbery must be reversed.

This case should be remanded for a new trial on a charge of theft (K.S.A. 21–3701) only if theft is a lesser included offense when robbery, as defined by K.S.A. 21–3426, is charged. * * *

[The Court of Appeals then concluded that larceny was not a lesser included offense of robbery because under Kansas law the lesser offense must not require the proof of any element not necessary to the greater. Under the Kansas robbery provision the taking need not have been made with the intent to steal, whereas that intent is a crucial element of larceny. Therefore, the court reversed and remanded with instructions that the defendant be discharged.]

STATE v. LONG

Supreme Court of Kansas, 1984.
234 Kan. 580, 675 P.2d 832.

* * * To establish the charge of robbery the State must prove there was a *taking* of the property from the person or presence of the victim and that *such taking* was either by threat of bodily harm or by force. *State v. Aldershof,* 220 Kan. at 800, 556 P.2d 371. In *Aldershof,* 220 Kan. at 803, 556 P.2d 371, this court held:

> [T]o constitute the crime of robbery by forcibly taking money from the person of its owner, it is necessary that the violence to the owner must either precede or be contemporaneous with the taking of the property and robbery is not committed where the thief has gained peaceable possession of the property and uses no violence except to resist arrest or to effect his escape. We believe that the test should be whether or not the taking of the property has been completed at the time the force or threat is used by the defendant.

This position is in accord with the general rule followed in most jurisdictions. See Annot., 58 A.L.R. 656; Annot., 93 A.L.R.3d 643.

The question then is whether the taking of the money from the money box was completed prior to the appellant's exit from the sale building. No established set of guidelines exists which can be readily applied for a quick and easy answer to this question. The court in *Aldershof* stated "[t]his must of necessity be determined from the factual circumstances presented in the particular case before the court." * * *

Prior Kansas cases are not in accord with one another and as such do not provide much assistance in determining when a taking is completed. Some of these cases imply a taking is not complete until the property has been removed from the premises of the owner, whereas others indicate the taking is accomplished at the moment the thief, with the intent to steal, removes the property from its customary location.

In *Aldershof* the defendant snatched two purses from a table in a tavern during a power failure. One of the victims pursued the defendant into the tavern parking lot where the defendant struck her. We held the defendant was a sneak thief and could not be guilty of robbery because "the taking of the property had been completed when the thief snatched the purses *and left the premises of the tavern.*" (Emphasis added.) Any violence used thereafter by the thief in an attempt to prevent the owner from regaining possession of the property could not convert the theft into a robbery. 220 Kan. at 803–04, 556 P.2d 371. However, in *State v. Buggs,* 219 Kan. at 206, 547 P.2d 720, this court rejected the defendant's claim that the taking of the property had not been accomplished because the defendants were apprehended before leaving the owner's premises. As the victim was leaving her place of business at the close of the day, she was ordered back into the store by two "armed" men, where she handed over her purse containing the day's business receipts. The defendant and his accomplice were apprehended by police responding to a silent alarm before they left the store. We held:

> "The completed crime of robbery is thus the 'taking' of property from the person by the proscribed means; an 'attempt' to commit robbery occurs only when the taking is not accomplished. Here all the evidence is that the bank money bag was 'taken' from Mrs. Penner by Perry, and later removed by him to the restroom. There is no evidence to the contrary. *The robbery was complete when Mrs. Penner handed over the bag,* and there was no call for an instruction on an attempt." (Emphasis added.) 219 Kan. at 206, 547 P.2d 720.

Other cases have similarly held the taking was complete prior to the time the defendant left the owner's premises.

* * *

On the other hand, a robbery conviction was sustained in *State v. Miller,* 53 Kan. at 327, 36 P. 751, based upon the court's finding the taking had not been completed when force was used against the victim. The victim had caught the defendant's hand as the defendant grabbed a fistful of money from the victim's money drawer. The defendant then cut the victim's hand with a knife in order to get away. The court determined the defendant had not obtained complete possession of the money before using violence on the victim. The court aptly remarked:

> "Nice questions may and do arise as to just when the possession of the owner of articles not attached to his person, but under his immediate charge and control, is divested, and it may well be doubted whether a thief can be said to have taken peaceable possession of money or other thing of value in the presence of the owner, *when the taking is instantly resisted by the owner, before the thief is able to remove it from*

his premises or from his immediate presence." (Emphasis added.) 53 Kan. at 328, 36 P. 751.

* * *

As these cases demonstrate, inherent difficulties exist in determining when possession attaches to constitute a completed taking for a robbery conviction under K.S.A. 21–3426. Commission of the crime of robbery is complete when the robber takes possession of the property, as the element of asportation is no longer required to complete the crimes of theft or robbery. The defendant takes possession of the property of another when he exercises dominion and control over the property. Earlier cases have recognized the term "possession," as it relates to theft or possession of stolen property, imports more than an innocent handling of property; the term denotes control, or the right to exercise control and dominion, over the property.

C.J.S., Larceny § 6, states:

> "[I]n order to constitute a taking the prospective thief must have obtained at some particular moment the complete, independent, and absolute possession and control of the thing desired adverse to the rights of the owner therein * * *.

* * *

> "If the possession of the would-be taker is imperfect in any degree, or if his control of the thing desired is qualified by any circumstance, however slight, the taking is incomplete and the act is only an attempt."

Did the appellant in the instant case obtain and exercise complete control and dominion over the money removed from the Wolfs' money box prior to the time the appellant was confronted by Mrs. Wolf and used force to flee from the sale building? Under the factual circumstances presented in this case we conclude he did not. Construed in the light most favorable to the prosecution, the facts presented at trial show Mrs. Wolf entered the sale building directly after the appellant had removed the money from the money box and at the precise moment he stuffed the money into his pockets. A dollar bill which had apparently fallen from the appellant's grasp lay below the money box at the appellant's feet. Mrs. Wolf immediately barred the door to prevent the appellant from leaving and demanded to know what he was doing. In this posture, this case differs from *State v. Miller* only in the fact that here the appellant managed to place most of the money in his pocket before being confronted by the victim, whereas in *Miller* the defendant was stopped by the victim after he had grabbed the money from the drawer, but before he could secrete it on his person. Such a slight variance in the factual circumstances of these cases does not warrant a different result in the two cases.

In *Miller* the court expressed doubt as to whether a thief could obtain peaceable possession of money or other property where the taking is instantly resisted by the owner, before the thief is able to remove it from the premises or the owner's immediate presence. The court in *Aldershof* emphasized the taking was complete when the thief left the premises of the tavern with the purse under his control. Based upon these cases and authorities cited we conclude a thief does not obtain the complete, independent and absolute possession and control of money or property adverse to the rights of the owner where the taking is immediately resisted by the owner before the thief can remove it from the premises or from the owner's presence. Accordingly, in the instant case the appellant did not obtain actual possession of the money and the taking was not completed until the appellant by force overcame Mrs. Wolf's efforts to stop him from making his exit from the sales room. The result reached in *State v. Buggs*, 219 Kan. at 206, 547 P.2d 720, is readily distinguishable. There the defendant forcibly removed the victim's purse from her immediate presence and exerted complete and absolute dominion and control over the purse. The taking was therefore complete, as the victim's possession of the purse and its contents was severed by the defendant's actual possession and control, although such control lasted only a short period of time before the defendant and his accomplice were apprehended by police. The issue there was whether the trial court should have instructed on attempted robbery.

* * *

[The Supreme Court then addressed the second issue raised by the defendant—his claimed right to have the jury charged on larceny as a lesser included offense. It agreed that the Court of Appeals was correct as to the difference in the elements required for the proof of each crime. However, it concluded that it could still be a lesser included offense under another statutory definition of "included" offenses as one which is a "lesser degree of the same crime". Here, said the court: "The unlawful taking of the property of another is the gravamen of both offenses. Robbery is the greater * * * as it is characterized as a 'crime against persons' in our criminal code and carries a higher penalty." Nevertheless, a defendant has no right to such an instruction unless there is evidence on which an accused might reasonably be convicted of the lesser. Here the defendant denied he had taken the money at all. In his view, then, he was guilty of robbery or of nothing. Therefore, the decision of the Court of Appeals was reversed and the defendant's conviction was affirmed.]

Notes and Questions

1. Defendant asks a stranger for money in order to get his pregnant wife to the hospital for the delivery. The stranger takes out his wallet and the defendant snatches it from his hand. Is this robbery? Jones v. State, 467 S.W.2d 453 (Tex.Crim.App.1971). What if he seized a woman's bag from her shoulder?

2. Defendant is retained by an 84 year old woman for some repair work to cost $25. He and two other men come to her house, do the work, and present a bill for $600. She pays $300 because, according to her testimony, she was frightened by the demand even though none of the men

were impolite. Is this robbery? Is it any crime? Should it be? Parnell v. State, 389 P.2d 370 (Okl.Crim.App.1964). The defendant in Chase v. State, 541 P.2d 867 (Okl.Crim.App.1975) was convicted, on facts essentially identical to those in *Parnell,* of theft by false pretenses. Should it be necessary that the prosecution prove that the owner's reliance on the defendant's misrepresentation was reasonable? See State v. Schneider, 148 Ariz. 441, 715 P.2d 297 (App.1985) (actual, rather than justifiable, reliance is sufficient).

Why should the law protect those who are unreasonably timid or unreasonably gullible? If the law required that the alleged victim of a robbery have displayed "reasonable courage", or the alleged victim of theft by false pretenses "reasonable skepticism", could we distinguish the burglar or thief who would claim that the owner had been unreasonably careless in leaving her home open, or the keys in her car? In considering these issues do you focus on what the particular facts reveal as to the defendant's criminality, or on the injury suffered by the victim?

3. Robbery is not consolidated into theft in the Model Penal Code, but rather is retained as a separate offense in the following provision:

§ 222.1. Robbery

(1) *Robbery Defined.* A person is guilty of robbery if, in the course of committing a theft, he:

(a) inflicts serious bodily injury upon another; or

(b) threatens another with or purposely puts him in fear of immediate serious bodily injury; or

(c) commits or threatens immediately to commit any felony of the first or second degree.

An act shall be deemed "in the course of committing a theft" if it occurs in an attempt to commit theft or in flight after the attempt or commission.

(2) *Grading.* Robbery is a felony of the second degree, except that it is a felony of the first degree if in the course of committing the theft the actor attempts to kill anyone, or purposely inflicts or attempts to inflict serious bodily injury.

4. Robbery, an aggravated form of larceny, is commonly further aggravated if the offender causes serious bodily harm or employs or threatens to employ a deadly weapon. The language of the various aggravated or armed robbery statutes varies, as do the definitions of terms such as "serious bodily harm" or "deadly weapon". Given that a firearm would normally be included as a "deadly weapon", should a robber be subject to the higher penalty if his gun cannot shoot? See, e.g., McLaughlin v. United States, ___ U.S. ___, 106 S.Ct. 1677, 90 L.Ed.2d 15 (1986) (unloaded firearm is a "dangerous weapon" within meaning of statute) and State v. Joyner, 312 N.C. 779, 324 S.E.2d 841 (1985) (inoperable rifle is a firearm). What if the defendant merely simulates possession of a gun by placing his hand in his coat pocket? Should such a person be treated by the law in the same way as one who actually uses a gun? Is this the same problem as is discussed in note 2 above? See State v. Butler, 89 N.J. 220,

445 A.2d 399 (1982) and State v. Bill, 194 N.J.Super. 192, 476 A.2d 813 (1984). What if the robber carries a gun but does not reveal or suggest its presence. United States v. Wardy, 777 F.2d 101, 105 (2d Cir.1985) (dictum).

5. If, on one occasion, a defendant has taken the personal property of two persons by threat of force, has he committed two robberies? What if he goes to a bank and forces two tellers to give him the contents of their cash drawers; is that two robberies? If there are two employees threatened by the defendant but only one cash drawer? Compare State v. Faatea, 65 Hawaii 156, 648 P.2d 197 (1982) (taking the property of hotel by force from five employees is one theft and therefore one robbery) with Thomas v. Warden, 683 F.2d 83 (4th Cir.1982) (taking of bank's property from three tellers is three robberies), and Commonwealth v. Levia, 385 Mass. 345, 431 N.E.2d 928 (1982). What if the defendant compels the bank teller to turn over his wallet as well as the contents of the cash drawer? Is that two robberies? Compare Lash v. State, 433 N.E.2d 764 (Ind.1982) (yes) with State v. Beaty, 306 N.C. 491, 293 S.E.2d 760 (1982) (no). Do the differing definitions and rationales of theft and robbery provide a principled basis for deciding these issues?

f. Extortion

Robbery and extortion are both aggravated forms of larceny. In the former the taking is from or in the presence of the person by means of violence or intimidation. But where the intimidation is not a threat of immediate harm to the possessor or someone in her company, or is not of physical harm the surrender of the property in response would not constitute robbery. Extortion and blackmail statutes have been created to cover these situations. These very similar offenses have sometimes been distinguished by a statutory requirement that for extortion the accused be a public official, whereas blackmail involves private citizens.

To the extent that the accused has employed threats of violence or of false accusations of crime it is relatively easy to understand why the conduct should be criminalized. However, what if the accused threatens to reveal the truth about the "victim" unless the "victim" acts to the benefit of the accused. Should not all persons have the right to make such truthful revelations? Indeed, some persons—journalists or informers for the Internal Revenue Service—are paid for it. Do not all persons have the right to seek recompense for being of service to others? The case which follows illustrates some of these quandries. For interesting efforts to explain the reason for criminalizing such conduct see Epstein, "Blackmail", 50 U.Chi.L.Rev. 553 (1983) and Lindgren, "Unraveling the Paradox of Blackmail", 84 Columb.L.Rev. 670.

STATE v. HARRINGTON

Supreme Court of Vermont, 1969.
128 Vt. 242, 260 A.2d 692.

HOLDEN, CHIEF JUSTICE. The respondent John B. Harrington has been tried and found guilty of the offense of threatening to accuse

Armand Morin of Littleton, New Hampshire, of the crime of adultery. The indictment charges that the threat was maliciously made with the intent to extort $175,000 and to compel Morin to do an act against his will in violation of 13 V.S.A. § 1701.[b]

At the outset the respondent acknowledges that there is no serious conflict in the material evidence presented to the jury. The main effort of his appeal challenges the jurisdiction and the sufficiency of the evidence to sustain the conviction.

At the time of the alleged offense the respondent was engaged in the general practice of law in a firm with offices in Burlington, Vermont. Early in March, 1968, he was consulted by Mrs. Norma Morin, the wife of the alleged victim, Armand E. Morin. Mrs. Morin had separated from her husband because of his recent and severe physical abuse. Prior to their separation they owned and operated the Continental 93 Motel in Littleton, New Hampshire, where the Morins maintained a residential apartment. The respondent learned the marital estate of the parties had a net value of approximately $500,000. Mrs. Morin reported to the respondent that her husband had also been guilty of numerous marital infidelities with different women at the motel. Mrs. Morin also disclosed that she had been guilty of marital misconduct which apparently had been condoned.

During the first conference the respondent advised Mrs. Morin that, because of her residence in New Hampshire, she could not undertake divorce proceedings in Vermont for at least six months and for her to obtain a divorce in New Hampshire it would be necessary that she obtain counsel from that state. Mrs. Morin indicated she wished to retain Mr. Harrington to represent her.

On one of the subsequent conferences a friend of Mrs. Morin's, who accompanied her to the respondent's office, suggested that an effort should be made to procure corroborative evidence of Mr. Morin's marital misconduct. To this end, the floor plan of the motel was discussed and a diagram prepared. At this time a scheme was designed to procure the services of a girl who would visit the motel in an effort to obtain corroborative evidence of Morin's infidelity.

After some screening, a Mrs. Mazza, who had been suggested by the respondent, was selected to carry out the assignment. The respondent explained to Mrs. Mazza the purpose of her employment and the results she was expected to accomplish and provided her with a "cover story" to explain her registration and presence as a guest at the Continental 93 Motel. Warning Mrs. Mazza against enticement and entrapment, the respondent instructed the employee to be "receptive and available," but not aggressive. The agreement with Mrs. Mazza was that she

---

b. A person who maliciously threatens to accuse another of a crime or offense, or with an injury to his person or property, with intent to extort money or other pecuniary advantage, or with intent to compel the person so threatened to do an act against his will, shall be imprisoned in the state prison not more than two years or fined not more than $500.00.

would be paid one hundred dollars at the time she undertook the assignment and one hundred dollars when her mission was completed.

Mrs. Morin was without funds at the time. A contingent fee agreement was signed by Mrs. Morin and the firm of Harrington and Jackson, by the respondent. The agreement was dated March 5, 1968 and provided that in the event a satisfactory property settlement was obtained, the respondent's firm was to receive twelve and a half percent of the settlement, in addition to reimbursement for expenses advanced by counsel. Electronic listening and recording equipment was ordered and delivered by air.

On the afternoon of March 6 the respondent and two office associates traveled to St. Johnsbury in two vehicles. Mrs. Mazza continued on to Littleton unaccompanied. She registered on arrival at the Continental 93 Motel under the name of Jeanne Raeder. She called the respondent at St. Johnsbury from a public telephone and informed him of her room number and location. Mrs. Mazza later delivered the key to her room to the respondent to enable him to procure a duplicate. The respondent, representing that he was a book salesman, registered at the motel and procured a room directly above that occupied by Mrs. Mazza. He was accompanied by a junior associate and an investigator,—both employed by the respondent's law firm.

During the next day Mrs. Mazza attracted Mr. Morin's attention. The sequence of events which followed led to an invitation by Morin for her to join him at his apartment for a cocktail. Mrs. Mazza accepted. Later she suggested that they go to her room because Mr. Morin's young son was asleep in his quarters. Morin went to Mrs. Mazza's room about midnight. Soon after the appointed hour the respondent and his associates entered the room. With one or more cameras, several photographs were taken of Morin and Mrs. Mazza in bed and unclothed. Morin grabbed for one camera and broke it.

During the time of her stay at the motel Mrs. Mazza carried an electronic transmitter in her handbag. By means of this device, her conversations with Morin were monitored by the respondent and his associates.

The respondent and his companions checked out of the motel at about one in the morning. Before doing so, there was a brief confrontation with Morin. According to Morin's testimony, the respondent demanded $125,000. Morin testified—"at that time I made him an offer of $25,000 to return everything he had, and in a second breath I retracted the offer."

The following day the respondent conferred with Mrs. Morin and reported the events of the trip to New Hampshire. He asked Mrs. Morin to consider reconciliation over the weekend. On March 11, 1968, Mrs. Morin informed the respondent she decided it was too late for reconciliation. With this decision, the respondent dictated, in the presence of Mrs. Morin, a letter which was received in evidence as State's Exhibit 1. The letter was addressed to Armand Morin at

Littleton, New Hampshire, and was placed in the United States mail at Burlington the same day.

The communication is designated personal and confidential. The following excerpts are taken from the full text:

"—Basically, your wife desires a divorce, and if it can be equitably arranged, she would prefer that the divorce be as quiet and as undamaging as possible.

"This letter is being written in your wife's presence and has been completely authorized by your wife. The offer of settlement contained herein is made in the process of negotiation and is, of course, made without prejudice to your wife's rights.

"It is the writer's thinking that for the children's sake, for your sake, and for Mrs. Morin's sake, that neither the courts in New Hampshire nor in Vermont should become involved in this potentially explosive divorce. If a suitable 'stipulation or separation agreement' can be worked out, the writer would recommend a Mexican, Stipulation-Divorce. This divorce would be based upon the catch-all grounds 'Incompatability'. A Mexican divorce of this type can be obtained when both parties have agreed as to terms of separation and have executed certain powers of attorney, etc., which this office can provide. With incompatability as the grounds, it is actually immaterial who goes down for the 48 hour period necessary to obtain the divorce in the State of Chihuahua. Mrs. Morin is willing to go; however, if a settlement can be reached, she has no objection to your going.

"Mrs. Morin is willing to give up the following:

"1. All of her marital rights, including her rights to share in your estate.

"2. All of her right, title, and interest, jointly or by reason of marital status, that she has in and to, any or all property of the marriage, including the Continental 93 Motel, the three (3) farms in Vermont, the capital stock that you own, the house in Lindenville, the joint venture in land in East Burke, all personal property except as is specifically hereinafter mentioned and in short, all rights that she may now have or might acquire in the future, as your wife. Furthermore, any such settlement would include the return to you of all tape recordings, all negatives, all photographs and copies of photographs that might in any way, bring discredit upon yourself. Finally, there would be an absolute undertaking on the part of your wife not to divulge any information of any kind or nature which might be embarrassing to you in your business life, your personal life, your financial life, of your life as it might be affected by the Internal Revenue Service, the United States Customs Service, or any other governmental agency.—"

The letter goes on to specify the terms of settlement required by Mrs. Morin, concerning custody of the minor child, her retention of an automobile and the disposition of certain designated personal effects. It further provides:

"5. Mrs. Morin would waive all alimony upon receipt of One Hundred Seventy Five Thousand Dollars ($175,000)—."

The sum of $25,000 is specified to be paid at the signing of the separation agreement, with the balance due according to a schedule of payments over the period of eighteen months.

The letter continues:

"—At the present time Mrs. Morin is almost without funds. She did have the $200 that you gave her when she left and she does have the $1500 in Canadian bills from the 'found' money. Because of her shortage of money, and, because she is badly missing David, and finally, because she cannot continue for any substantial period of time to live in the present vacuum, the writer must require prompt communication from you with respect to the proposed settlement contained herein. This letter is being dictated on March 11 and you should have it in your possession by March 13, at the latest. Unless the writer has heard from you on or before March 22, we will have no alternative but to withdraw the offer and bring immediate divorce proceedings in Grafton County. This will, of course, require the participation by the writer's correspondent attorneys in New Hampshire. If we were to proceed under New Hampshire laws, without any stipulation, it would be necessary to allege, in detail, all of the grounds that Mrs. Morin has in seeking the divorce. The writer is, at present, undecided as to advising Mrs. Morin whether or not to file for "informer fees' with respect to the Internal Revenue Service and the United States Customs Service. In any event, we would file, alleging adultery, including affidavits, alleging extreme cruelty and beatings, and asking for a court order enjoining you from disposing of any property, including your stock interests, during the pendency of the proceeding.

"The thought has been expressed that you might, under certain circumstances, decide to liquidate what you could and abscond to Canada or elsewhere. The writer would advise you that this would in no way impede Mrs. Morin's action. You would be served by publication and under those circumstances, I am very certain that all property in New Hampshire and in Vermont, would be awarded, beyond any question, to Mrs. Morin.

"With absolutely no other purpose than to prove to you that we have all of the proof necessary to prove adultery beyond a reasonable doubt, we are enclosing a photograph taken by one of my investigators on the early morning of March 8. The purpose of enclosing the photograph as previously stated, is simply to show that cameras and equipment were in full operating order.—"

It was stipulated that the letter was received by Morin in Littleton, New Hampshire, "in the due course of the mail."

Such is the evidence upon which the respondent was found guilty.

* * *

Turning to the other grounds advanced in the motion for acquittal, the respondent maintains his letter (State's Exhibit 1) does not constitute a threat to accuse Morin of the crime of adultery. He argues the implicit threats contained in the communication were "not to accuse of the CRIME of adultery but to bring an embarrassing, reputation-ruining divorce proceeding, in Mr. Morin's county of residence unless a stipulation could be negotiated." (Brief of Respondent-Appellant, p. 13.)

In dealing with a parallel contention in State v. Louanis, 79 Vt. 463, 467, 65 A. 532, 533, the Court answered the argument in an opinion by Chief Judge Rowell. "The statute is aimed at blackmailing, and a threat of any public accusation is as much within the reason of the statute as a threat of a formal complaint, and is much easier made, and may be quite as likely to accomplish its purpose. There is nothing in the statute that requires such a restricted meaning of the word 'accuse'; and to restrict it thus, would well nigh destroy the efficacy of the act."

The letter, marked "personal and confidential," makes a private accusation of adultery in support of a demand for a cash settlement. An incriminating photograph was enclosed for the avowed purpose of demonstrating "we have all the proof necessary to prove adultery beyond a reasonable doubt." According to the writing itself, cost of refusal will be public exposure of incriminating conduct in the courts of New Hampshire where the event took place.

In further support of motion for acquittal, the respondent urges that the totality of the evidence does not exclude the inference that he acted merely as an attorney, attempting to secure a divorce for his client on the most favorable terms possible. This, of course, was the theory of the defense.

* * *

At the time of the writing, the respondent was undecided whether to advise his client to seek "informer fees." One of the advantages tendered to Morin for a "quiet" and "undamaging" divorce is an "absolute undertaking" on the part of the respondent's client not to inform against him in any way. The Internal Revenue Service, the United States Customs Service and other governmental agencies are suggested as being interested in such information. Quite clearly, these veiled threats exceeded the limits of the respondent's representation of his client in the divorce action. Although these matters were not specified in the indictment, they have a competent bearing on the question of intent.

Apart from this, the advancement of his client's claim to the marital property, however well founded, does not afford legal cause for the trial court to direct a verdict of acquittal in the background and context of his letter to Morin. A demand for settlement of a civil action accompanied by a malicious threat to expose the wrongdoer's criminal conduct, if made with intent to extort payment, against his will, constitutes the crime alleged in the indictment.

The evidence at hand establishes beyond dispute the respondent's participation was done with preconceived design. The incriminating evidence which his letter threatens to expose was wilfully contrived and procured by a temptress hired for that purpose. These factors in the proof are sufficient to sustain a finding that the respondent acted maliciously and without just cause, within the meaning of our criminal statutes. The sum of the evidence supports the further inference that the act was done with intent to extort a substantial contingent fee to the respondent's personal advantage.

* * * The evidence of guilt is ample to support the verdict and the trial was free from errors in law.

Judgment affirmed.

Notes and Questions

1. Attorney Harrington was sentenced to serve 10 to 15 months. He served four months at the state prison and then was on work release for six months. After completing his sentence he was disbarred. About six years later he was pardoned and readmitted to the bar. Petition of Harrington, 134 Vt. 549, 367 A.2d 161 (1976). For his role in the Mazza-Morin assignation, Harrington's young associate was suspended from the bar with leave to file for reinstatement after three months. In re Knight, 129 Vt. 428, 281 A.2d 46 (1971).

2. Although extortion and blackmail are distinguishable from the crime of false pretenses inasmuch as there may be neither misrepresentations nor an intent to defraud involved, it has been suggested, see, e.g., Model Penal Code § 223.1 (P.O.D. 1962) (reprinted at page 206), they be included in the consolidation of theft offenses. Does the employment of threats, particularly those of future violence, invade a distinct social interest to the extent that it is more appropriate to treat this crime as equivalent to robbery?

2. OFFENSES AGAINST THE HABITATION

At common law there were two felony offenses designed to protect the special sense of security we place in our dwellings. These were burglary and arson. Other prohibitions such as criminal trespass and malicious mischief may today be employed to protect this same interest but they are not defined in terms of dwellings as the specific object of concern.

The elements of burglary at common law were: (a) a breaking, and (b) entering, of (c) the dwelling of, (d) another, (e) at night, (f) with the intent to commit a felony within. Arson involved: (a) the malicious, (b) burning, of (c) the dwelling of, (d) another. Each of these elements was of importance and the subject of significant litigation addressed to the definition of each. The breaking was of importance in burglary because it could be seen as indicating the strength of the actor's purpose. Entry might be seen as requiring the type of intrusion which might reasonably give rise to the disquiet which the prohibition is designed to minimize. This is also true of the requirement that the entry be in the night. Dwelling was defined for purposes of both burglary and arson to include more than just residences. Outbuildings commonly associated with and in near proximity to the residence were held to be within the meaning of the term. Sometimes it was said that any buildings "within the curtilage"—an expression still employed in the jurisprudence of the search and seizure clause of the Fourth Amendment—could be the object of burglary and arson. However, the basic point was that a dwelling was a place where people commonly slept and the invasion of such an area by a burglar or an arsonist was both especially disturbing and especially dangerous.

As can be seen from a reading of the principal case and the Model Penal Code provision which follows, the elements of burglary have been greatly altered by modern statutes. The result of these changes is often to expand very significantly the behavior covered by the crime.

PEOPLE v. GAUZE

Supreme Court of California, 1975.
15 Cal.3d 709, 125 Cal.Rptr. 773, 542 P.2d 1365.

MOSK, JUSTICE.

Can a person burglarize his own home? That is the quandry which emerges in the case of James Matthew Gauze, who appeals from a judgment of conviction of assault with a deadly weapon and burglary.

Defendant shared an apartment with Richard Miller and a third person and thus had the right to enter the premises at all times. While visiting a friend one afternoon, defendant and Miller engaged in a furious quarrel. Defendant directed Miller to "Get your gun because I am going to get mine." While Miller went to their mutual home, defendant borrowed a shotgun from a neighbor. He returned to his apartment, walked into the living room, pointed the gun at Miller and fired, hitting him in the side and arm. Defendant was convicted of assault with a deadly weapon and burglary; the latter charge was predicated on his entry into his own apartment with the intent to commit the assault.

Common law burglary was generally defined as "the breaking and entering of the dwelling *of another* in the nighttime with intent to commit a felony." (Italics added.) (Perkins on Criminal Law (2d ed. 1969) p. 192.) The present burglary statute, Penal Code section 459, provides in relevant part that "Every person who enters *any* house, room, apartment * * * with intent to commit grand or petit larceny or any felony is guilty of burglary." (Italics added.)

Facially the statute is susceptible of two rational interpretations. On the one hand, it could be argued that the Legislature deliberately revoked the common law rule that burglary requires entry into the building of another. On the other hand, the Legislature may have impliedly incorporated the common law requirement by failing to enumerate one's own home as a possible object of burglary. No cases directly on point have been found. Therefore, in determining which statutory interpretation should be adopted it is necessary to examine the purposes underlying common law burglary and how they may have been affected by the enactment of the Penal Code.

Common law burglary was essentially an offense "against habitation and occupancy." By proscribing felonious nighttime entry into a dwelling house, the common law clearly sought to protect the right to peacefully enjoy one's own home free of invasion. In the law of burglary, in short, a person's home was truly his castle. It was clear under common law that one could not be convicted of burglary for entering his *own* home with felonious intent. This rule applied not only to sole owners of homes, but also to joint occupants. The important factor was occupancy, rather than ownership.

California codified the law of burglary in 1850. That statute and subsequent revisions and amendments preserved the spirit of the common law, while making two major changes. First, the statute greatly expanded the type of buildings protected by burglary sanctions. Not only is a person's home his castle under the statute, but so, inter alia, are his shop, tent, airplane, and outhouse. This evolution, combined with elimination of the requirement that the crime be committed at night, signifies that the law is no longer limited to safeguarding occupancy rights. However, by carefully delineating the type of structures encompassed under section 459, the Legislature has preserved the concept that burglary law is designed to protect a possessory right in property, rather than broadly to preserve any place from all crime.

The second major change effected by codification of the burglary law was the elimination of the requirement of a "breaking": under the statute, every person who *enters* with felonious intent is a burglar. This means, at a minimum, that it no longer matters whether a person entering a house with larcenous or felonious intent does so through a closed door, an open door or a window. The entry with the requisite intent constitutes the burglary.

The elimination of the breaking requirement was further interpreted in People v. Barry (1892) 94 Cal. 481, 29 P. 1026, to mean that trespassory entry was no longer a necessary element of burglary. In *Barry*, this court held a person could be convicted of burglary of a store even though he entered during regular business hours. * * *

Barry and its progeny should not be read, however, to hold that a defendant's right to enter the premises is irrelevant. Indeed, the court in *Barry*, by negative implication, substantiated the importance of determining the right of an accused to enter premises. When the defendant thief in *Barry* argued he had a right to be in the store, the court could have replied that his right to enter the store was immaterial. Instead the court declared, "To this reasoning, we can only say a party who enters with the intention to commit a felony enters without an invitation. He is not one of the public invited, nor is he entitled, to enter. Such a party could be refused admission at the threshold, or ejected from the premises after the entry was accomplished." (Id., 94

Cal. at p. 483, 29 P. at p. 1027.) Thus, the underlying principle of the *Barry* case is that a person has an implied invitation to enter a store during business hours for legal purposes only. The cases have preserved the common law principle that in order for burglary to occur, "The entry must be *without consent.* If the possessor actually invites the defendant, or actively assists in the entrance, e.g., by opening a door, there is no burglary." (1 Witkin, Cal. Crimes (1963) Crimes Against Property, § 457, p. 420.) (Italics in original.)

Thus, section 459, while substantially changing common law burglary, has retained two important aspects of that crime. A burglary remains an entry which invades a possessory right in a building. And it still must be committed by a person who has no right to be in the building.

Applying the foregoing reasoning, we conclude that defendant cannot be guilty of burglarizing his own home. His entry into the apartment, even for a felonious purpose, invaded no possessory right of habitation; only the entry of an intruder could have done so. More importantly defendant had an absolute right to enter the apartment. This right, unlike that of the store thief in *Barry,* did not derive from an implied invitation to the public to enter for legal purposes. It was a personal right that could not be conditioned on the consent of defendant's roommates. Defendant could not be "refused admission at the threshold" of his apartment, or be "ejected from the premises after the entry was accomplished." (People v. Barry (1892) supra, 94 Cal. 481, 483, 29 P. 1026, 1027.) He could not, accordingly, commit a burglary in his own home.

The People argue, however, that a contrary conclusion is compelled by a dictum in. People v. Sears (1965) 62 Cal.2d 737, 44 Cal.Rptr. 330, 401 P.2d 938. In *Sears,* defendant was convicted of felony murder. For three years prior to the murder, defendant had slept in a garage nearby the cottage occupied by his wife. Then the spouses separated and defendant moved to a hotel. Three weeks later, he returned to the cottage, looking for his wife and hiding a reinforced steel pipe under his shirt. In an ensuing struggle, he killed his wife's daughter. This court reversed his conviction because a confession was improperly admitted, but for guidance upon retrial we declared valid a felony-murder instruction based on burglary—entering the cottage with intent to assault his wife—as the felony. In answer to defendant's argument that he could not be guilty of burglary because he had a right to enter the house, the court replied, "One who enters a room or building with the intent to commit a felony is guilty of burglary even though permission to enter has been extended to him personally or as a member of the public. The entry need not constitute a trespass. Moreover, since defendant had moved out of the family home three weeks prior to the crime, he could claim no right to enter the residence of another without permission. Even if we assume that defendant could properly enter the house for a lawful purpose, such an entry still constitutes burglary if accomplished with the intent to commit a felonious assault within it." (Id. at p. 746, 44 Cal.Rptr. at p. 36, 401 P.2d at p. 944.)

As the above quotation indicates, our opinion that Sears could be convicted of burglary was based on two separate considerations. First, Sears had no right to enter his wife's house; that fact alone supported the conviction. Second, even if he had a right to enter, the right was based on former section 157 of the Civil Code (now § 5102), which gave a person the right to enter the *separate* property of his or her spouse, subject to certain conditions. Thus Sears' "right" to enter his wife's house, like the "right" of the felon to enter the store in *Barry,* was at best conditional. An entry for anything but a legal purpose was a breach of his wife's possessory rights, in marked contrast to the entry in the present case.

Only if the *Sears* dictum is read in an expansive manner can it be used to support the prosecution theory that a person can burglarize his own home. Such a reading would be entirely inconsistent with the purposes of section 459. As aptly articulated by the Court of Appeal in People v. Lewis (1969) 274 Cal.App.2d 912, 920, 79 Cal.Rptr. 650, 655, "Burglary laws are based primarily upon a recognition of the dangers to personal safety created by the usual burglary situation—the danger that the intruder will harm the occupants in attempting to perpetrate the intended crime or to escape and the danger that the occupants will in anger or panic react violently to the invasion, thereby inviting more violence. The laws are primarily designed, then, not to deter the trespass and the intended crime, which are prohibited by other laws, so much as to forestall the germination of a situation dangerous to personal safety." Section 459, in short, is aimed at the danger caused by the unauthorized entry itself.

In contrast to the usual burglary situation, no danger arises from the mere entry of a person into his own home, no matter what his intent is. He may cause a great deal of mischief once inside. But no emotional distress is suffered, no panic is engendered, and no violence necessarily erupts merely because he walks into his house. To impose sanctions for burglary would in effect punish him twice for the crime he committed while in the house. In such circumstances it serves no purpose to apply section 459.

* * *

To hold otherwise could lead to potentially absurd results. If a person can be convicted for burglarizing his own home, he could violate section 459 by calmly entering his house with intent to forge a check. A narcotics addict could be convicted of burglary for walking into his home with intent to administer a dose of heroin to himself. Since a burglary is committed upon entry, both could be convicted even if they changed their minds and did not commit the intended crimes.

In positing such hypotheticals, we indulge in no idle academic exercise. The differing consequences are significant, for the punishment for burglary is severe. First degree burglary is punishable by imprisonment for five years to life, while a second degree burglar is subject to imprisonment in the county jail for a one-year maximum or in state prison for one to fifteen years. In contrast, the punishment for assault with a deadly weapon, the underlying crime committed in this case, is less severe: imprisonment in state prison for six months to life or in county jail for a maximum of one year, or a fine.

For the foregoing reasons, we conclude defendant cannot be guilty of burglarizing his own home, and the judgment of conviction for burglary must therefore be reversed.

* * *

Notes and Questions

1. The enormous contemporary increase in marital separations has posed a number of issues under burglary statutes. Does the prolonged departure of one spouse from the marital residence mean that a subsequent, unconsented to, breaking and entry with the requisite intent constitutes a burglary? It has been argued that until the marriage is dissolved or the separation is the subject of legal directives each spouse retains the right of consortium, which includes the right to be in the presence of the other spouse so as to enjoy the other's company and comfort. Under this view even a forcible entry into the other spouse's personal residence could not be deemed nonconsenual since, as in *Gauze,* the actor has the absolute right to enter.

The "consortium" analysis may be somewhat persuasive as a matter of abstract doctrine. It becomes less attractive where the facts involve an angry husband breaking down the door of his estranged wife's apartment in order to beat her. However, a decision that the conduct of such a spouse cannot constitute burglary does not mean that prosecution and punishment for the battery is precluded. If separated spouses can be treated as burglars for entering the premises of the other spouse without permission, will undue discretion be given prosecutors with respect to domestic disputes? See Cladd v. State, 398 So.2d 442 (Fla.1981) holding that such an entry constitutes burglary. The decision was by a vote of four to three, and the several countervailing considerations are discussed in three separate opinions.

In one of the most celebrated modern American murder cases—the defendant was a prominent millionaire—the question of spousal burglary was crucial to the decision of whether the homicide could be charged as a capital murder because committed in the course of a felony. This, in turn, would determine whether the accused could be held without bail. The defendant and his brother owned a home, but it was occupied by his wife pursuant to a temporary court order issued in the course of a pending divorce action. The order also directed the defendant to stay away from the premises. The prosecution's theory was that the defendant, with intent to murder, entered the house without his wife's consent. See Ex Parte Davis, 542 S.W.2d 192 (Tex.Crim.App.1976). It should be noted that Mr. Davis was eventually acquitted of the charges.

2. One of the greatest sources of hairsplitting has been the question of what constitutes an "entry" for purposes of burglary. It is clear that the actor's whole body need not intrude but what if the actor, with the requisite intent, has raised a window (the breaking) is such a manner that his fingers are within the house, or throws a brick through a window, or bores a hole in a corn storehouse so that the corn runs out? On what basis are the distinctions, if any, to be made? See People v. Tragni, 113 Misc.2d 852, 449 N.Y.S.2d 923 (1982) and Russell v. State, 158 Tex.Crim. 350, 255 S.W.2d 881 (1953).

3. The Model Penal Code would provide:

§ 221.0. Definitions

In this Article, unless a different meaning plainly is required:

(1) "occupied structure" means any structure, vehicle or place adapted for overnight accommodation of persons, or for carrying on business therein, whether or not a person is actually present.

(2) "night" means the period between thirty minutes past sunset and thirty minutes before sunrise.

§ 221.1. Burglary

(1) *Burglary Defined.* A person is guilty of burglary if he enters a building or occupied structure, or separately secured or occupied portion thereof, with purpose to commit a crime therein, unless the premises are at the time open to the public or the actor is licensed or privileged to enter. It is an affirmative defense to prosecution for burglary that the building or structure was abandoned.

(2) *Grading.* Burglary is a felony of the second degree if it is perpetrated in the dwelling of another at night, or if, in the course of committing the offense, the actor:

(a) purposely, knowingly or recklessly inflicts or attempts to inflict bodily injury on anyone; or

(b) is armed with explosives or a deadly weapon.

Otherwise, burglary is a felony of the third degree. An act shall be deemed "in the course of committing" an offense if it occurs in an attempt to commit the offense or in flight after the attempt or commission.

(3) *Multiple Convictions.* A person may not be convicted both for burglary and for the offense which it was his purpose to commit after the burglarious entry or for an attempt to commit that offense, unless the additional offense constitutes a felony of the first or second degree.

Notice that the above proposal abandons common law requirements that there be a "breaking", that it be at night and that it be into a dwelling. How would you explain these changes in the definition of the prohibited conduct? Is the resulting expansion of criminalization desirable? Can there be any justification for retaining burglary as a separate offense? Is there any conduct which we wish to deter which could not be punished in the absence of a burglary provision?

There are lesser intrusions into our enjoyment of real property which are considered a proper subject for criminalization. Notice how in the following provision, although no damage is done to the property, distinctions are drawn for purposes of punishment. What interest (or interests) underline these distinctions?

§ 221.2. Criminal Trespass

(1) *Buildings and Occupied Structures.* A person commits an offense if, knowing that he is not licensed or privileged to do so, he enters or surreptitiously remains in any building or occupied structure, or separately secured or occupied portion thereof. An offense under this Subsection is a misdemeanor if it is committed in a dwelling at night. Otherwise it is a petty misdemeanor.

(2) *Defiant Trespasser.* A person commits an offense if, knowing that he is not licensed or privileged to do so, he enters or remains in any place as to which notice against trespass is given by:

(a) actual communication to the actor; or

(b) posting in a manner prescribed by law or reasonably likely to come to the attention of intruders; or

(c) fencing or other enclosure manifestly designed to exclude intruders.

An offense under this Subsection constitutes a petty misdemeanor if the offender defies an order to leave personally communicated to him by the owner of the premises or other authorized person. Otherwise it is a violation.

3. CRIMES AGAINST THE PERSON

Editors' Introduction: The Crimes of Assault and Kidnapping

The most basic purpose of civil society and the criminal law is to protect the bodily integrity of all citizens from illicit aggression. Homicide, the most important of all crimes against the person and, indeed, of all crimes is treated separately and at considerable length in Chapter VII. Rape, another crime of special gravity, together with some sexual offenses, is examined in some detail in Chapter XI. Other crimes traditionally treated under this heading are assault and battery, and kidnapping. Robbery could readily be considered as a crime against the person but is commonly dealt with as an aggravated larceny.

Assault and battery were treated at common law as separate and distinct crimes. A battery was the unlawful application of force to the person of another. Thus, it involved a result brought about by the actor's conduct: an injury or an offensive touching. LaFave & Scott, Criminal Law 685 (2nd Ed. 1986). Assault was more difficult to define. One form of assault was a failed attempt at battery. Another form was where the actor has put another person in fear of a battery. Id., at 692–93. Modern codes commonly treat both assaults and batteries under the title "assault". The definitions often require that although a completed "battery" can be committed recklessly, an "assault" of either type requires that the defendant have acted purposely or with knowledge.

In a minority of jurisdictions an assault of the attempted battery type requires that the defendant have had "present ability" to commit the battery. 1 Encyclopedia of Crime and Justice 89 (1983). Thus, if the accused has pointed a gun at his victim and pulled the trigger but unknown to either the gun is unloaded, there would be no assault. Can such a decision be understood as reflecting doubt on the accused's true purpose when he has selected a means inadequate to the alleged end. This should be considered in connection with the materials on impossibility in "attempt" in Chapter X, Sec. A.3. In a majority of American jurisdictions the pointing of the gun at another would be an assault since it places another in reasonable apprehension of receiving a battery. Should the result be different if the "victim" was unaware of the accused's actions?

Simple assault is normally a misdemeanor as it was at common law. There are also many different forms of aggravated assault of the battery type which are punished as felonies. The aggravation is based on various characteristics of the victim or the results of the accused's actions. Examples of aggravation are where the assault causes serious bodily injury or is committed with a deadly weapon, or is committed against peace officers who are acting in the line of duty, or against a child or an elderly person.

At common law, kidnapping involved the forcible asportation— carrying away—of a person from their own country to another. The crime has evolved in many jurisdictions to prohibit as a very serious felony any malicious and unlawful abduction or confinement of another with the intent to hold for ransom or other benefit, or to facilitate the commission of some other crime. "Abduction" and "confinement" are susceptible to definition in ways which would include a great deal of conduct. As can be seen from the following materials, the breadth of many such statutes has posed problems for courts. Conduct which might or might not, under such modern statutes, constitute kidnapping will, in any case amount to less serious offenses, such as unlawful or false imprisonment. The basic question, then, is when is it appropriate to convert such conduct to the more serious offense of kidnapping. In some situations, the conduct will constitute another offense, such as robbery or rape, that may be as serious as kidnapping. In those cases, the question is often whether that conduct should constitute *both* robbery or rape and, in addition, kidnapping. Among the legitimate concerns in both types of situations is whether the end result will be primarily to confer upon prosecutors the discretion, in situations of the sort at issue, to charge "only" the less serious offense or the underlying robbery or rape or, rather to proceed instead or in addition on a charge of kidnapping.

PEOPLE v. ADAMS

Court of Appeals of Michigan, 1971.
34 Mich.App. 546, 192 N.W.2d 19.

LEVIN, JUDGE. The defendant, Otis L. Adams, appeals his conviction of kidnapping.

Kidnapping is now a statutory, not a common-law crime. The relevant portion of our statute makes it unlawful to "wilfully, maliciously and without lawful authority * * * forcibly or secretly confine or imprison any other person within this state against his will." But every forcible confinement is not the capital offense of kidnapping.

Our kidnapping statute, like most, is so all-encompassing in its literal breadth that unless its operative effect is confined by objective standards it would be void for overbreadth.

Where a kidnapping statute does not in terms require a "carrying away" of the victim, an asportation requirement or, as a substitute, the elements of secrecy, has been judicially read into and made a part of the definition of the crime.

There are two basic kidnapping patterns. In one, the victim is seized and removed to another place; in the other, the victim is confined in the place where he is found. In the first, an asportation or movement of the victim is an essential element; in the second, movement is not an element, but secrecy of the confinement is required.

In this case the people do not charge the victim was secretly confined. The information charged the defendant Otis Adams with "forcibly confining and imprisoning" his victim—the word "secretly" in the statutory phrase "forcibly or secretly confine" was omitted when the charge was drawn.

To save the Michigan kidnapping statute, insofar as it applies to nonsecret confinements, from a declaration of unconstitutionality because of overbreadth we read it as requiring an asportation. A confinement (other than a secret confinement) without a movement of the victim is not kidnapping. And, for reasons which we will spell out, every movement of the victim of an assaultive crime incidental to the commission of that crime is not kidnapping; the asportation must have a significance independent of the assault in order to manifest the capital and separate offense of kidnapping.

In this case the victim, a prison official, was seized in Jackson State Prison by Adams and other inmates and moved from one part of the prison to another. The seizure and movement occurred in the presence of prison guards; the exact location of both the victim and of the defendant Adams was at all times known to prison guards who had the place cordoned off and surrounded by overwhelming armed force. It is not claimed that Adams ever intended to remove his victim from the prison or that he intended to attempt to effect an escape. This is not the usual hostage pattern, nor is it the usual kidnapping pattern.

I.

FACTS

* * *

[In the course of a prison riot, Inspector Joseph Dembosky was seized by defendant Adams and other inmates and forced at knife point to the prison yard and ultimately to the prison hospital about 1500 feet from the place where he was originally seized. During the journey the inmates threatened the tower guards that Dembosky would be killed if they were fired upon. Dembosky and the other guards held captive were released unharmed after about five and one-half hours.]

The reprehensible nature of Adams' action does not alter our duty to determine whether the evidence against him is sufficient to support his conviction for kidnapping Inspector Dembosky.

II.

THE STATUTE AND ITS OVERBREADTH

* * *

What is immediately obvious about the language of our kidnapping statute is the extraordinary range of conduct it might proscribe.

In the phrase "forcible confinement or imprisonment," the word "imprisonment" is clearly a narrower term than "confinement"; every "imprisonment" would be a "confinement." The word "forcible" adds little, if anything, to the word "confine." "Confine," in the sense in which it is used in this statute, clearly speaks of an involuntary restraint of the liberty of the individual, which, of necessity, is brought about by the use of some force. Similarly, as to the words "against his will." If the confinement was voluntary, it would mean that the victim was confined although he was free to leave—an obvious contradiction of terms.

Since "confine" in this context strongly implies force of some kind, the offense is complete when the actor "wilfully, maliciously and without lawful authority" confines the victim. And, since in the ordinary case there is likely to be no question of lawful authority (and besides, lawful authority negatives "malice"), and since the wilfulness required by law does not enlarge the requirement of malice, *violation of the terms of the statute occurs whenever the actor "maliciously confines" any other person.*

"Malice, in its common acceptation, means ill will toward some person. In its legal sense, it applies to a wrongful act committed intentionally against that person, without legal justification or excuse." Bonkowski v. Arlan's Department Store (1970), 383 Mich. 90, 99, 174 N.W.2d 765, 768.

* * *

Accordingly, freed of its tautology, the kidnapping statute, simply put, makes it kidnapping to *intentionally confine another person without legal justification or excuse.*

It will be observed that the statute makes no reference to the duration or circumstances of the confinement. Literally construed, the statute leads to absurd results. The trespasser who momentarily locks a caretaker in his cottage is placed on the same footing as the professional criminal who invades a home, seizes the occupants at gunpoint, transports them to a secret hideout, and holds them for ransom. The robber who orders his victim to stand motionless while his wallet is removed is guilty of the same crime as the robber who forces his victim to drive for miles to a deserted location, where he is terrorized and abandoned. A group of college students who invade a dean's office, wrongfully confining its occupants, commit the same offense as a gang of rapists to seize a woman and remove her from her family to a place of isolation.

Shopkeepers who wrongfully detain suspected shoplifters, cabdrivers who purposely deliver passengers to the wrong destinations, tavernkeepers who bar exits until bar bills have been paid, all may be subject to civil damage actions, but a sensible penology rebels at the classification of such acts as capital offenses.

As emphatically as these examples offend a rational penal code, they scarcely embrace all the varieties of technically culpable, but scarcely menacing, conduct which violates a statutory ban on "intentional confinement" of any other person.

* * *

[The Court's discussion of the problems posed by statute under the void-for-vagueness doctrine (see section III.A. supra) is omitted. The Court concluded that a literal reading of the statute would expose perpetrators of virtually every crime against the person to capital sanctions in the discretion of prosecutors, judges and juries. To avoid such results and thereby preserve the statute the court turned to an analysis of its substance.]

III.

Substantive Law of Kidnapping

At common law, kidnapping required an asportation of the victim out of the country. Kidnapping was a misdemeanor, and was viewed merely as an aggravated form of false imprisonment; the aggravating factor was the removal of the victim from the sovereign's protection.

Kidnapping statutes in the United States have abolished the requirement that a national or a regional boundary be breached.

Modification of the asportation element of the common-law crime was not the only American statutory departure from the common law. Public revulsion against the wave of carefully-planned and often brutal kidnappings for ransom of the 1920's and 1930's resulted in the imposition of heavy penalties, including the death penalty, for kidnappers, and passage of the Federal Kidnapping Act, the so-called Lindbergh Law. It was in 1931 that Michigan imposed a maximum sentence of life imprisonment for kidnapping.

Another characteristic of kidnapping legislation has been its failure to distinguish between the crimes of kidnapping and false imprisonment. Michigan, along with most States, does not have a separate false imprisonment statute.

These matters aside, the principal question that has perplexed American courts in construing kidnapping legislation has been the degree of asportation required to transform an assault, robbery, or other crime into kidnapping. Torn between the common-law rule that a most significant asportation was required, and the obvious legislative intention to broaden the scope of the offense, the courts, virtually without exception, endorsed the idea that any asportation, however slight, was sufficient to constitute kidnapping.

Representative of this formulation were the opinions of the California Supreme Court in People v. Chessman (1951), 38 Cal.2d 166, 192, 238 P.2d 1001, 1017, and People v. Wein (1958), 50 Cal.2d 383, 399, 400, 326 P.2d 457, 466. In *Chessman,* the defendant forced his victim to move 22 feet to his automobile, where he sexually assaulted her. The Court held that, "It is the fact, not the distance, of forcible removal which constitutes kidnapping in this state." In *Wein,* the Court applied the *Chessman* standard to uphold the kidnapping conviction of a defendant who forced his victims to move from room to room in their own homes during a series of robberies and rapes. These holdings came under sharp criticism, but were accurate reflections of the state of the law until quite recently.

The first significant departure from the "any asportation" requirement came in another California case, Cotton v. Superior Court (1961), 56 Cal.2d 459, 464, 15 Cal.Rptr. 65, 68, 364 P.2d 241, 244. A labor dispute led to the invasion of a farm worker's camp by union members. Several braceros were assaulted and dragged about the camp during the ensuing riot. The California Supreme Court ruled that the assailants could not be convicted of kidnapping, saying that "all 'asportation' in the instant case would appear to be only incidental to the assault and rioting." The Court declared that it should avoid "absurd consequences" in the application of the kidnapping laws; it warned that a literal reading of the California statute "could result in a rule that every assault could also be prosecuted for kidnapping." The Court ignored, it did not overrule, *Chessman* and *Wein,* but the significance of *Cotton* was not lost on the commentators.

A few years after *Cotton* was decided, the New York Court of Appeals articulated a new approach to the asportation requirement. In People v. Levy (1965), 15 N.Y.2d 159, 164, 256 N.Y.S.2d 793, 796, 204 N.E.2d 842, 844, the defendants accosted the victims, who had just arrived at their home in an automobile. One of the defendants took the wheel, and the victims, husband and wife, were driven about city streets for twenty minutes, covering twenty-seven blocks. During this journey the victims were robbed of money and jewelry.

The defendants were convicted by a jury of kidnapping under the New York statute, which provided that a person who "confines" another with intent to "cause him ＊ ＊ ＊ to be confined" against his will is guilty of kidnapping. The Court of Appeals reversed. Central to the Court's holding was its concern that the broad statutory definition, "could literally overrun several other crimes, notably robbery and rape, and in some circumstances assault, since detention and sometimes confinement, against the will of the victim, frequently accompany these crimes ＊ ＊ ＊ It is a common occurrence in robbery, for example, that the victim be confined briefly at gunpoint or bound and detained, or moved into and left in another room or place.

> "It is unlikely that these restraints, sometimes accompanied by asportation, which are incidents to other crimes and have long been treated as integral parts of other crimes, were intended by the Legislature in framing its broad definition of kidnapping to constitute a separate crime of kidnapping, even though kidnapping might sometimes be spelled out literally from the statutory words." The Court overruled a contrary prior decision and held that the kidnapping statute was to be limited in its application "to 'kidnapping' in the conventional sense in which that term has now come to have acquired meaning."

Left unresolved in *Levy* was the precise degree of asportation necessary to constitute "kidnapping in the conventional sense." The opinion did, however, revive the requirement that some meaningful asportation must accompany the crime. In a subsequent case the Court of Appeals declared that "the direction of the criminal law has been to limit the scope of the kidnapping statute, with its very substantially more severe penal consequences, to true kidnapping situations and not to apply it to crimes which are essentially robbery, rape or assault and in which some confinement or asportation occurs as a subsidiary incident." People v. Lombardi (1967), 20 N.Y.2d 266, 270, 282 N.Y.S.2d 519, 521, 229 N.E.2d 206, 208. But, in a still more recent case, the Court held that "the more complicated nature of the asportation" pursued in the defendant's efforts to kill the victim, removed the case from the *Levy-Lombardi* rule.

The reasoning of the New York Court of Appeals was not accepted by other courts. Several jurisdictions expressly rejected the idea that a substantial asportation was necessary under broadly-worded kidnapping statutes.

In 1969, by a 6–to–1 decision the California Supreme Court overruled its prior constructions in the *Chessman-Wein* line of cases. People v. Daniels (1969), 71 Cal.2d 1119, 1139, 80 Cal.Rptr. 897, 910, 459 P.2d 225, 238, clearly repudiates the doctrine that any asportation of the victim is sufficient to constitute kidnapping. There the victims had been forced to move about in their apartments during the commission of crimes of robbery and rape. The Court declared:

"We hold that the intent of the Legislature ＊ ＊ ＊ was to exclude from [the statute's] reach not only 'standstill' robberies ＊ ＊ ＊ but also those in which the movements of the victim are merely incidental to the commission of the robbery and do not substantially increase the risk of harm over and above that necessarily present in the crime of robbery itself."

＊ ＊ ＊

IV.

THE ASPORTATION REQUIREMENT AND THE STANDARD BY WHICH IT IS APPLIED

We hold that, except in those relatively rare cases where the victim is intentionally locked in the place where he is found and there secretly isolated and confined, a reasonable construction of our kidnapping statute requires an asportation of the victim before the crime of kidnapping is complete. Still to be answered is the extent of the asportation required.

We believe that the history of kidnapping jurisprudence in this country demonstrates the futility of attempting to calculate the requisite asportation in terms of linear measurement. The harm sought to be prevented is not movement of the victim, but his removal from one place to another and attendant increased risks to the victim. The actual distance the victim is transported does not necessarily correspond with the invasion of his physical interest. An asportation of 50 feet may in some cases expose the victim to precisely those abuses which kidnapping statutes are designed to prevent; in other cases, an asportation of 500 feet may alter the victim's situation not at all.

We have concluded that under the kidnapping statute a movement of the victim does not constitute an asportation unless it has significance independent of the assault. And, unless the victim is removed from the environment where he is found, the consequences of the movement itself to the victim are not independently significant from the assault—the movement does not manifest the commission of a separate crime—and punishment for injury to the victim must be founded upon crimes other than kidnapping.

A comprehensive scheme for dealing with this offense rests within the province of the legislature, not the courts. The standard we apply today does, however, discriminate with some certainty between conduct which ought clearly to be punished under the kidnapping statute and conduct which falls within the scope of other crimes.[36]

36. While, as Judge Gillis points out, this case does not involve movement of a victim incident to a robbery or rape, it does involve movement incident to a felonious assault which, too, is a separate crime.

Indeed, under Michigan law there is little reason to charge kidnapping where the movement is incidental to an armed robbery or a rape because both of those offenses are punishable by life sentences and in Michigan all sentences, with few exceptions, run concurrently. It is only where the other offense is punishable by a sentence less than life that there is likely to be an issue whether movement incidental to the commission of that offense constituted the separate crime of kidnapping.

V.

THE STANDARD APPLIED TO THE FACTS OF THIS CASE

To define "environment" restrictively, e.g., the mere geographic location of the victim, would be to return to the "any movement" concept. The relevant environment is the totality of the surroundings, animate and inanimate.

Applying these criteria to the assault on Inspector Dembosky, we conclude that Adams did not commit the crime of kidnapping. The movement of Inspector Dembosky did not remove him from the prison environment. As his duties customarily took him throughout the entire prison, it cannot be said that moving him from the confused threatening situation in 4-block to the fifth floor hospital was independently significant from the assault.

The purpose of the movement was neither to avoid detection nor to expose Inspector Dembosky to an increased risk of harm. He was moved to reduce the risk of escalation by providing a cooling-off period. When he was first assaulted the inspector asked, "Can't we talk about this?" And, when the group moved off, he suggested that they go to the prison gymnasium. Instead he was required to accompany the assailants to the fifth floor of the prison hospital. This case is not like a case of street assault where the victim is seized on a thoroughfare and pulled into a dark alley or into an automobile to prevent detection so that the assault can be completed in greater privacy; such a movement might have significance independent of the assault.

The evidence does not support a contention that the movement to the fifth floor of the hospital exposed the inspector to an increased risk of harm because it made his rescue more difficult. Adams and the other men were armed with knives. There is no evidence, no reason to suppose or infer that they were less likely to use their knives if a confrontation with rescuers had occurred at 4-block than at the fifth floor landing of the hospital. Might not the presence at 4-block of hundreds of milling men have made rescue there more difficult? Might not one of the three agitated, perhaps still intoxicated and narcotized, assailants reacted mortally on the spur of the moment to a taunting challenge from an unseen voice in the milling throng? Under the circumstances we are satisfied that the evidence does not support a finding that the movement had significance adverse to Inspector Dembosky independent of the continuing assault.[39]

Accordingly, the likelihood is that in Michigan kidnapping will be charged for a street assault most frequently where the assailant failed to consummate his objective, the prosecutorial purpose in charging kidnapping being to aggravate the penalty for the unsuccessful attempt. The degree of asportation that should be required to justify a kidnapping prosecution in such a case is beyond the scope of this opinion.

39. It is important in this case to make clear what we do not decide as well as what we hold so that our opinion is not misread.

The taking of a hostage may be the offense of kidnapping. In the hostage situation, if the victim is removed from the environment where he is found, the removal will generally have significance adverse to the victim independent of the assault

The inspector was seized in Jackson Prison. It is an atypical place, an armed enclosure that no one can enter or leave without passing through guarded entranceways. Movement from one building to another in Jackson Prison, for purposes of the kidnapping statute, is not significantly different than movement from one room to another in a building, especially where, as here, the movement was under surveillance of armed guards who had the enclosure protected and there was no intention on the part of Adams or the other felons themselves to leave or to remove Inspector Dembosky from the prison.

The movement of Inspector Dembosky did not make the apprehension of the felons less likely, nor did the movement make it less likely that the inspector would be released unharmed. It provided a cooling-off period—which Inspector Dembosky himself wisely sought. It provided time for these impetuous, desperate men to reflect and to draw back from worse folly.

Adams' conduct was highly dangerous and indefensible. The prison and prosecutorial authorities are understandably anxious to see that he is severely punished. Prison guards and officials like Inspector Dembosky mingle with frustrated, assaultive desperate men. An assault upon any of them is a serious breach of discipline; punishment should be clear, certain and severe.

Michigan, unlike other jurisdictions, does not have a specific statute making assault by a prisoner on a prison guard or official a crime carrying special penalties. In Michigan, assault upon a prison guard is treated no differently than assault outside of prison walls. The maximum penalties are relatively mild for the kind of aggravated conduct indulged in by Adams and his confederates. That is a good reason for the legislature to amend the penal code to provide adequate sanctions for an assault by a prisoner. It is not a reason for transforming, without legislative authorization, what under present law may be nothing more than a felonious assault, into an offense which carries with it a possible life sentence.

Criminal statutes, in contrast with the common law, may not be expanded to meet new problems beyond the contemplation of the legislature when the statute was enacted.[42]

and the offense of kidnapping will be completed upon his removal from the environment. Even if the victim is not so removed, if the actor intends to remove him from the environment where he is found and commits an overt act going beyond mere preparation, that would be attempted kidnapping. If the victim is seized with intent "to extort money or other valuable thing" or to hold the victim "to service against his will" that too *may* be kidnapping even though there has been no asportation * * *

Nor do we express any opinion as to when a seizure of a person on the street incidental to the commission or attempted commission of another offense (e.g., rape, robbery) becomes the separate offense of kidnapping. * * *

42. * * *

The kidnapping statute is not a catchall, a means of aggravating the penalties—to fill in a gap in the law—so that penalties as those that can be meted out for extortion, armed robbery and kidnapping can be imposed for "extortion" not involving threatened assault on a relative. We may not properly engraft an additional pattern and provide by judicial interpreta-

Reversed.

J.H. GILLIS, PRESIDING JUDGE (dissenting).

Unlike my Colleagues, I am satisfied that there was sufficient evidence from which the jury could lawfully find defendant Adams guilty of kidnapping. Accordingly, I would affirm defendant's conviction.

In my view, the majority misapply the teachings of such cases as People v. Levy, People v. Lombardi and People v. Daniels. And, as a result, the majority reach what I consider to be an absurd result. This case is not one in which the restraint and forcible movement of Inspector Dembosky can be characterized solely as "incident[s] to other crimes and * * * integral parts of other crimes." People v. Levy, 15 N.Y.2d at 164–165, 256 N.Y.S.2d at 796, 204 N.E.2d at 844. This case does not involve movement of the victim incident to robbery (People v. Levy, supra; People v. Daniels, supra); nor does it involve asportation incident to rape (People v. Lombardi, supra; People v. Daniels, supra).

In People v. Miles (1969), 23 N.Y.2d 527, 539, 540, 297 N.Y.S.2d 913, 922, 245 N.E.2d 688, 694, 695, the New York Court of Appeals explained the *Levy-Lombardi* rationale as follows:

> "In the *Levy* and *Lombardi* cases, and especially in the *Levy* case, the restraint and asportation were parts of the crimes ultimately committed. The robbery and the rapes could not be committed in the forms planned without the limited asportations there involved. Indeed, in any robbery, there is a restraint of 'false imprisonment' and in every rape there is a similar restraint and often removal in some limited sense. It is this kind of factual merger with the ultimate crime of the preliminary, preparatory, or concurrent action that the rule is designed to recognize, and thus prevent unnatural elevation of the 'true' crime to be charged.

> * * *

> "Moreover, *the rule has no purpose of ignoring as independent crimes alternative or optional means used in committing another crime which, by the gravity and even horrendousness of the means used, constitute and should constitute a separately cognizable offense.*

> * * *

> "In short, the *Levy-Lombardi* rule was designed to prevent gross distortion of lesser crimes into a much more serious crime by excess of prosecutorial zeal. *It was not designed to merge 'true' kidnappings into*

tion that any detention of a person for the purpose of extracting any advantage whatsoever is kidnapping even though there is no meaningful asportation and no secrecy, or that where "extortion" is involved the quality of the asportation required to establish kidnapping need not be of the kind required where extortion is not present * * *.

An asportation is the gist of the offense of kidnapping. If we sustain a conviction for kidnapping on evidence that the victim of the confinement has been held a "substantial" period of time and exposed to "serious" risk of harm even though there was not an asportation having significance independent of the assault, then most every assaultive crime can be the capital offense of kidnapping if the prosecutor so charges and a jury so finds.

* * *

other crimes merely because the kidnappings were used to accomplish ultimate crimes of lesser or equal or greater gravity.'' (Emphasis supplied.)

Nothing in this record suggests to me an excess of prosecutorial zeal. Accordingly, the *Levy-Lombardi* rule is inapposite. In my view, Adams' conduct could lawfully be considered "true" kidnaping.

In People v. Congdon (1889), 77 Mich. 351, 354, 43 N.W. 986, the Michigan Supreme Court noted that the gist of the offense under the kidnaping statute is the involuntariness of the seizure. Similarly, the United States Supreme Court has stated that "the involuntariness of seizure and detention * * * is the very essence of the crime of kidnaping." Chatwin v. United States (1946), 326 U.S. 455, 464, 66 S.Ct. 233, 237, 90 L.Ed. 198, 203. On the facts as recited in the majority opinion, it clearly appears that the jury could find that Inspector Dembosky had been involuntarily seized.

Moreover, "the gravity and even horrendousness", People v. Miles, 23 N.Y.2d at 539, 297 N.Y.S.2d at 922, 245 N.E.2d at 694, of Adams' conduct serves to distinguish this case from mere false imprisonment. Inspector Dembosky was confined against his will for a substantial period of time. He was exposed to serious risk of harm. Thus, Inspector Dembosky was subjected to the very abuses the kidnaping statute is intended to prevent. It follows that we should not, as a matter of law, refuse to characterize defendant Adams' conduct as kidnaping. At least, on this record, the jury should be permitted to so find.

* * *

Defendant's other contentions are without merit. His conviction should be affirmed.

Note and Question

The decision of the Michigan Court of Appeals was affirmed in part and reversed in part by the Supreme Court of Michigan. People v. Adams, 389 Mich. 222, 205 N.W.2d 415 (1973). The Supreme Court agreed that it was necessary to read in an asportation requirement to save the statute. It disagreed, however, with Judge Levin's formulation as to when movement would constitute asportation sufficient to sustain kidnapping in the case before it. It rejected the notion that the victim must be removed from the environment in which he was found. It noted: "in one sense you can change the environment of the smallest room by intruding a criminal with a weapon, although in another sense it is still the same room." 389 Mich. at 236, 205 N.W.2d at 421–22. It agreed that the movement is insufficient if merely incidental to a lesser underlying crime, but indicated that if the underlying crime involves taking a hostage, movement incidental thereto is generally sufficient to establish a kidnapping. This, of course, is in recognition that the paradigmatic kidnapping involves the holding of a person in order to exact ransom or some other advantage. (See Mobley v. State, 409 So.2d 1031 (Fla.1982).) Thus, a properly charged jury could have found that Adams had kidnapped Dembosky in that his movement was incidental to Adams' attempt to extort redress of the prisoners' grievances through use of Dembosky as a hostage.

The major concern of the courts in *Adams* was the danger that lesser crimes would be converted to the greater one of kidnapping solely on the basis of movement having no independent significance. Judge Levin thought there would be little reason to charge kidnapping when the movement was incidental to a crime such as rape which is punished as severely as is kidnapping. (See footnote 36 supra.) But in People v. Barker, 411 Mich. 291, 307 N.W.2d 61 (1981) the court expressed the fear that "overly zealous" prosecutors might use such movement to create two crimes where there should be only one. Therefore the Court held that in cases of "co-equal" offenses the jury must be satisfied that the asportation was for the purpose of the kidnapping.

It is a commonplace that robbers and rapists may move their victims short distances to facilitate the commission of the crime, or tie them up to facilitate escape. Is the "asportation" requirement a useful device for distinguishing between defendants who are "merely" robbers or rapists and those who are also kidnappers? See, e.g., State v. Jackson, 703 S.W.2d 30 (Mo.App.1985).

D. ONE "ACT" OR RELATED ACTIVITY AS MORE THAN ONE CRIME

Editors' Introduction: Should Limits be Placed on Multiple Punishment Assessed for One "Act" or "Episode?"

In 1305, William Wallace, a notorious traitor, was "drawn for treason, hanged for robbery and homicide and disembowelled for sacrilege, beheaded as an outlaw and quartered for divers depredations." 2 Pollack and Maitland, History of English Law 501 (2nd ed. 1905). Although the practical effect of such multiple punishment on Wallace may have been minimal, the problem of imposing multiple liability and punishment for related or identical activity has today become of greater significance. This is true for at least two reasons. The first is a function of the movement to rationalize punishment. This movement tried to order crimes by the severity of the punishment attached to each crime and has tended to reduce punishment for any particular offense. This notion of proportionality is seen as threatened with violation by cumulative liability or punishment for what is, in some sense, the same conduct. Second, the number of separate offenses with considerable overlapping application has increased and therefore the matter arises more frequently. This subsection considers this problem.

The situations raising the problem can be divided into a number of fact situation categories. One consists of those situations in which the accused has committed what is clearly a single physical act which arguably constitutes several crimes. Those crimes may consist of different violations of the same statutory provision, as where several persons die as the result of one shot fired by the defendant. Or they may consist of violations of different statutory provisions, as where one shot fired by the defendant results in the death of one person and injury of another. Another category of situations arises when different crimes are committed by what can be—in a physical sense—regarded as different physical acts of the defendant but these acts are related in time, purpose, and perhaps other characteristics. Thus a defendant may enter a dwelling with intent to steal money therein, and thus commit burglary, and then actually take the money, thus committing theft. Although the act of "entry" and that of "taking" the money are distinguishable, they may have occurred within moments of each other and arguably they both were motivated by a single "purpose." Whether distinguishing between these categories is helpful in resolving the underlying issues is unclear.

As the principal case in this section demonstrates, several legal doctrines may impose limits upon multiple convictions or punishments in some or all of these situations. These limits may be found in the federal constitutional prohibition against double jeopardy, or somewhat equivalent provisions in state constitutions. The definitions of particular offenses may affect how many of those offenses can be identified in a particular situation. State statutory provisions of general applicability may limit multiple convictions or punishment; some are presented in note 2 following the principal case. Or, as the principal case indicates, judicially-developed nonconstitutional doctrines—such as "merger"—may be available.

In evaluating the issue, consider the extent to which various objectives of imposing criminal liability ought to be regarded as influential or controlling in the resolution of the matter. Should the law's objective be to permit the imposition of cumulative liability or punishment where, but only where, that can be expected to have some preventive effect? Should the objective be to avoid situations where the total punishment imposed is disproportionate to the offender's conduct? If the latter, how should the conduct be evaluated for this purpose? Should, for example, the total punishment be compared to the harm caused by the offender (as, for example, the number of deaths), the offender's "intention" in some sense (as, for example, whether the offender had multiple criminal objectives in mind), or perhaps something else.

Even if multiple punishments are seldom actually imposed, there may be legitimate concern regarding prosecutors' ability to bring multiple charges. Defending against a multiplicity of charges may exhaust a defendant and prevent her from effectively raising defenses. Multiple charges may strengthen unduly prosecutors' position in plea bargaining.

Are any formal limitations on liability or punishment necessary? Cannot reliance be had upon prosecutors' discretion not to seek an inappropriate number of convictions and sentencing judges' discretion not to inappropriately cumulate punishments?

Commentators have provided extensive discussions of the matter. E.g., Blair, Constitutional Limitations on the Lesser Included Offense Doctrine, 21 Am.Crim.L.Rev. 445 (1984); Horack, The Multiple Consequences of a Single Criminal Act, 21 Minn.L.Rev. 805 (1937); Westen and Drubel, Towards a General Theory of Double Jeopardy, 1978 Sup. Ct.Rev. 81 (1979); Note, Double Jeopardy: Multiple Prosecutions Arising from the Same Transaction, 15 Am.Crim.L.Rev. 259 (1978); Note, Twice in Jeopardy, 75 Yale L.J. 262 (1965).

COMMONWEALTH v. WILLIAMS

Superior Court of Pennsylvania, 1985.
344 Pa.Super. 108, 496 A.2d 31.

CIRILLO, JUDGE:

This case was certified to the Court en banc to address problems arising under the doctrine of merger of offenses for sentencing.

I

Leon Williams was tried by jury and convicted of aggravated assault, possession of a prohibited offensive weapon, carrying a firearm on a public street in Philadelphia, and resisting arrest. The charges stemmed from an incident that occurred on an evening in February, 1976, in the City of Philadelphia. Officers Moriarity and Winchester of the Philadelphia Police Department were on highway patrol; near the intersection of Belmont and Westminster Avenues they spotted two men by a row of parked cars. One of the men had a suspicious large bulge under his jacket, so the officers got out of their car to investigate. Officer Winchester approached the man with the bulge, who turned out to be Michael Jefferson. The bulge turned out to be a fourteen-inch mallet. Officer Moriarity approached the other man, appellant Leon Williams, and asked to see identification. After showing the officer an ID card, Williams began to shake and tremble, then suddenly jumped back and crouched. Instinctively, Moriarity yelled out "He has a gun" and dove for cover. In the same instant a blast emanated from the sawed-off shotgun Williams had produced from under his clothing. The officers returned fire as Williams stood behind a nearby car pointing the shotgun at both officers and warning them to stay back or he would shoot. Williams then fled down the street with Moriarity in pursuit on foot and Winchester giving chase in the squad car. Moriarity had to take cover several times when Williams turned and waved the shotgun at him. Eventually Williams discarded the gun, ran into an abandoned housing complex, and disappeared.

About three days later, a New York policeman stopped an automobile driven by Williams headed north on a highway in upstate New York. The Philadelphia authorities, however, were unable to catch up with Williams until April of 1977, when he was brought back to stand trial on charges arising from the shotgun incident. After a jury found him guilty of the previously mentioned charges, Williams was sentenced in the Philadelphia Court of Common Pleas to consecutive, maximum prison terms for each offense.

II

Williams appealed to this Court, alleging that he

was unlawfully and duplicitously sentenced to consecutive maximum terms of imprisonment for assault, resisting arrest, possessing a prohibited offensive weapon, and carrying a firearm on a public street, since all of these convictions resulted from the single unlawful act of firing a sawed-off shotgun, and they thus merge for sentencing purposes.

* * *

[W]e now hold that the firearms and weapons offenses merge with each other for sentencing purposes, but that the aggravated assault and resisting arrest charges do not merge with each other, nor do they merge with the other violations.

The doctrine of merger is at best a confusing area of the law to approach. As Mr. Justice Pomeroy frankly admitted, speaking for the Supreme Court of Pennsylvania, "Our decisions on the doctrine of merger are not altogether harmonious." *Commonwealth v. Sparrow,* 471 Pa. 490, 503, 370 A.2d 712, 718 (1977). Superior Court decisions on sentencing merger exhibit little consistency in rationale of their own. The confusion surrounding merger stems in part from its dual origins in constitutional and common law. To curtail this trend of confusion, we strongly urge courts deciding sentencing merger issues in the future to keep both of these roots firmly in mind.

III

A

CONSTITUTIONAL LIMITATIONS ON MULTIPLE PUNISHMENTS

One of the guarantees found in the Double Jeopardy Clause of the United States Constitution is protection against more than one punishment for the "same offence." U.S.Const. amend. V; *Ex parte Lange,* 85 U.S. (18 Wall.) 163, 21 L.Ed. 872 (1874). The Fifth Amendment proscription on multiple punishments for the same offense has of late been made binding on the State governments by virtue of the Fourteenth Amendment, U.S.Const. amend. XIV. *See North Carolina v. Pearce,* 395 U.S. 711, 89 S.Ct. 2072, 23 L.Ed.2d 656 (1969).

Pennsylvania has its own constitutional provision making it unlawful for any person to be twice put in jeopardy for the "same offense." Pa.Const. art. 1, § 10. As our State Supreme Court recently reaffirmed, however, in the multiple punishments context the double jeopardy guarantee contained in Article 1, § 10 is coextensive with its counterpart in the Fifth Amendment. *Commonwealth v. Goldhammer,* ___ Pa. ___, ___ n. 4, 489 A.2d 1307, 1313 n. 4 (1985). Thus, in determining whether multiple punishments have been unconstitutionally inflicted for the same offense, our State courts simply apply the rules used to effectuate the Fifth Amendment guarantee against double jeopardy.

In *Blockburger v. United States,* 284 U.S. 299, 304, 52 S.Ct. 180, 182, 76 L.Ed. 306, 309 (1932), the Supreme Court set forth the definitive test for determining when conduct in violation of more than one statute must be treated as the "same offense" for double jeopardy purposes: "The applicable rule is that where the same act or transaction constitutes a violation of two distinct statutory provisions, the test to be applied to determine whether there are two offenses or only one, is whether each provision requires proof of a fact which the other does not." That is, more than one offense may be found and punished in any given act or transaction only where each offense requires proof of an element not contained in the other(s). *Id.*

The *Blockburger* "same offense" test is the same one that traditionally has been used to determine whether one offense is a "constituent" or "lesser included" offense of another. The test depends solely on a comparison of the elements of the crimes charged, not on the similarity or even the identity of the evidence introduced at trial to establish their commission. *See United States v. Woodward,* 469 U.S. __, 105 S.Ct. 611, 83 L.Ed.2d 518 (1985). Only when all the elements of one crime are also elements of the other may they be classified as the "same offense." *See, e.g., Harris v. Oklahoma,* 433 U.S. 682, 97 S.Ct. 2912, 53 L.Ed.2d 1054 (1977).

Although it is frequently overlooked, it cannot be overemphasized that the "same offense" test of double jeopardy does not prohibit cumulating punishments at a single trial for multiple statutory offenses simply because they all arise from the same act or transaction. Even a single, indivisible act may support more than one punishment under separate statutory provisions if each provision requires proof of a fact that the other does not. Thus, in *Woodward, supra,* a unanimous Supreme Court held that the defendant's solitary act of checking off the "no" box on a customs form supported double punishments for making a false statement to a federal agency and failing to report currency, because each statutory offense required proof of an element not contained in the other. * * *

Classic examples of one offense being necessarily included in another are the greater and lesser offenses of rape and fornication, and robbery and theft. To use another example that has recently come to prominence, in a felony-murder prosecution the underlying felony is a lesser included offense of, and therefore the "same offense" as, the felony-murder itself, because proof of felony-murder ipso facto proves all the elements of the underlying felony; indeed, proof of the underlying felony is necessary to establish that a killing was in fact felony-murder.

The final principle of double jeopardy law which must be stated here is that the Double Jeopardy Clause does not restrict the *legislature's* ability to prescribe more than one punishment for the same offense. It serves only to restrain courts from imposing and prosecutors from seeking more than one punishment under a particular legislative enactment, and to prevent the court from exceeding its legislative authorization by imposing more than one punishment for the same offense. For double jeopardy purposes, the *Blockburger* "same offense" test is merely a rule of statutory construction to be employed where the legislature has not explicitly authorized separate punishments for a single offense. "The assumption underlying the rule is that Congress *ordinarily* does not intend to punish the same offense under two different statutes. Accordingly, where two statutory provisions proscribe the 'same offense,' they are construed not to authorize cumulative punishments *in the absence of a clear indication of contrary legislative intent.*" *Whalen v. United States,* 445 U.S. 684, 691–92, 100 S.Ct. 1432, 1437–38, 63 L.Ed.2d 715, 723–24 (1980) (emphasis added).

> Where * * * a legislature specifically authorizes cumulative punishment under two statutes, *regardless of whether those two statutes proscribe the "same" conduct under Blockburger,* a court's task of statutory construction is at an end and the prosecutor may seek and the trial court or jury may impose cumulative punishment under such statutes in a single trial.

Missouri v. Hunter, 459 U.S. 359, 368–69, 103 S.Ct. 673, 679, 74 L.Ed.2d 535, 544 (1983) (emphasis added).

Thus, in *Hunter,* * * * *supra,* where a legislative intention to do so was clearly spelled out, cumulative punishments could be imposed for a felony and for the use of a firearm in commission of that felony, even though one was necessarily involved in the other and both therefore amounted to the "same offense" as defined in *Blockburger.*

B

DOUBLE JEOPARDY APPLIED

Bearing in mind the *Blockburger* "same offense" test as a constitutionally established rule of statutory construction, we turn to examine whether it was a violation of double jeopardy for appellant to receive separate sentences for aggravated assault, resisting arrest, prohibited offensive weapons, and carrying a firearm on the streets of Philadelphia. We conclude that it was not.

The aggravated assault charge was submitted to the jury under 18 Pa.C.S. § 2702*(a)*(1) & (2). These provisions state in pertinent part: *"(a) Offense defined.—*A person is guilty of aggravated assault if he: (1) attempts to cause serious bodily injury to another * * * *(2) attempts to cause * * * serious bodily injury to a police officer making or attempting to make a lawful arrest. * * *"* (Emphasis ours). The crime of resisting arrest of which appellant was found guilty is defined at *id.* § 5104:

> A person commits a misdemeanor of the second degree if, with the intent of preventing a public servant from effecting a lawful arrest or discharging any other duty, the person creates a substantial risk of

bodily injury to the public servant or anyone else, or employs means justifying or requiring substantial force to overcome the resistance.

Initially, a comparison of the elements of these two crimes reveals that each requires proof of a fact that the other does not. The aggravated assault charge lodged against appellant required proof that he attempted to cause *serious bodily injury* to Officer Moriarity. "Serious bodily injury" is defined in the Crimes Code as "Bodily injury which creates a substantial risk of death or which causes serious, permanent disfigurement, or protracted loss or impairment of the function of any bodily member or organ." *Id.* § 2301. To prove this element of the assault, the Commonwealth had to prove the actual intentional discharging of the shotgun at Moriarity. This particular fact was not crucial to the resisting arrest charge. Resisting arrest does not require an attempt to cause serious bodily injury to a police officer. Here, evidence that appellant brandished the shotgun, threatened the officers with it, and used it to escape would alone have been sufficient to prove that he created "a substantial *risk* of bodily injury" (defined as "impairment of physical condition or substantial pain," *id.*), or that he put up resistance requiring a policeman to use "substantial force" to overcome it. Any of these lesser degrees of force employed by appellant in turn would have sufficed to prove resisting arrest.

* * *

The firearms offenses appellant committed are defined at 18 Pa. C.S. § 908 ("Prohibited offensive weapons") and *id.* § 6108 ("Carrying firearms on public streets or public property in Philadelphia"). As pertinent here, the crime of prohibited offensive weapons was made out by appellant's simple use or possession of a specific weapon, a sawed-off shotgun, whereas the firearms offense under Section 6108 required proof that appellant carried a firearm in the City of Philadelphia. Precisely the same act on Williams's part established both crimes; nevertheless they are not the "same offense" for double jeopardy purposes because each requires proof of a fact that the other does not.

The charge of carrying a firearm in Philadelphia required proof that appellant possessed the firearm in a particular location, namely, on a public street in Philadelphia. This element of location was not relevant to a conviction under Section 908, which proscribes the possession anywhere of a certain class of prohibited weapons.

To prove a violation of Section 908, on the other hand, the Commonwealth had to establish that a particular type of weapon belonging to the prohibited class was involved. This element was established here by proof that the firearm in appellant's possession was indeed a *sawed-off shotgun.* 18 Pa.C.S. § 908(c). Proof of the exact type of weapon was not necessary under Section 6108, which was satisfied once the Commonwealth proved that appellant carried *any* "firearm, rifle or shotgun" in Philadelphia.

Each firearms offense, therefore, was a discrete offense under the Double Jeopardy Clause. From the foregoing discussion of the elements of the various crimes charged, it is also apparent that the firearms charges were not constitutionally the "same offense" as aggravated assault or resisting arrest. Thus, there was no double jeopardy violation in sentencing appellant separately for each offense.

IV

A

COMMON LAW MERGER DOCTRINE

Our inquiry has not ended, however, for we have yet to delve into the common law doctrine of merger, which in this State can be traced at least as far back as *Harman v. Commonwealth*, 12 Serg. & Rawle 69 (Pa.1824). We must recognize at the outset that the doctrine is to a large extent coterminous with the double jeopardy protection against multiple punishments. Thus, it has been said that merger raises essentially the same question as the doctrine of lesser included offenses. The test of merger is also said to be whether one crime "necessarily involves" another. Often merger is invoked side by side with double jeopardy principles as the grounds upon which "duplicitous" sentences may be vacated.

Indeed, one former member of the Pennsylvania Supreme Court offered the following explanation for the existence of Pennsylvania's merger doctrine:

> The doctrine of merger was adopted by this Court because the double jeopardy clause of the Pennsylvania constitution has traditionally been applied only to capital offenses. The double jeopardy clause of the United States Constitution, of course, had not yet been applied to the states.

Commonwealth v. Carter, 482 Pa. 274, 280 n. 3, 393 A.2d 660, 663 n. 3 (1978) (Pomeroy, J., dissenting, joined by O'Brien, J.).

As it has developed in this jurisdiction, however, the doctrine of sentencing merger is actually broader and more flexible than the double jeopardy protection against multiple punishments for the "same offense." The doctrine acts to limit the multiplicity of sentences which may be meted out for what is, in practical effect, a single criminal act, even when a comparison of the elements of the various crimes charged does not reveal that any of those crimes is necessarily included in any other. "Thus, in merger of sentences cases, we focus not only on the similarity of the elements of the crimes but also, and primarily, on the facts proved at trial, for the question is whether those facts show that in practical effect the defendant committed *a single criminal act.* * * *" *Commonwealth v. Crocker*, 280 Pa.Super. 470, 475, 421 A.2d 818, 820–21 (1980) (emphasis added). * * *

The difficulty in applying this doctrine is how to determine, practically speaking, when the facts disclose but one offense. This inquiry demands special attention to the "unique facts" of each case. However, the merger doctrine is not and cannot be so fluid that it permits absolute discretion in the judiciary to decide on the facts of each case whether or not two statutory crimes were "essentially the same criminal act." *Commonwealth v. Watson,* 311 Pa.Super. 89, 92, 457 A.2d 127, 128 (1983). * * *

If anything is settled in sentencing law, it is that the legislature has the exclusive power to define criminal offenses and set the punishments to be imposed on them. A punishment, even if it constitutes a duplicitous punishment, is not illegal if the legislature has authorized it. The only principle that can therefore justify the merger doctrine is that, just like the Double Jeopardy Clause, it provides a rule of statutory construction for determining what the legislature intended.

The difference is that the merger doctrine does not ask us to adhere rigidly to a "same offense" test in searching for legislative intent. Nor, on the other hand, is it concerned exclusively with the physical facts that must be proven to make out various crimes. Instead, it obliges us to take a broader view of the purposes of criminal legislation and the diverse evils which particular enactments were meant to protect against. "Analysis of duplicitous sentence questions has traditionally revolved around the concept of injury to the sovereign, in this case the Commonwealth. * * * Therefore, in order to support the imposition of two sentences . . ., it must be found that [the defendant's] conduct constituted two injuries to the Commonwealth." *Commonwealth v. Walker,* 468 Pa. 323, 331–32, 362 A.2d 227, 231 (1976).

In order to find that separate statutory offenses merge, we must therefore determine not only that the crimes arose out of the same criminal act, transaction, or episode, but also that the statutes defining the crimes charged were directed to substantially the same harm or evil. If we do not take both of these steps, we fail in our duty to effectuate the legislative mandate in carrying out statutory punishments.

Obviously if a defendant has committed several discrete criminal acts, he may be punished separately for each of them despite their close relationship in a single criminal episode, as long as each act is a separate injury in itself. If there are separate criminal acts, the first condition for application of the merger doctrine does not exist. Once a defendant commits an original crime, he is not permitted to compound the injuries he inflicts and then escape liability for additional crimes under the guise that they all were done in the same criminal transaction. *See, e.g., Commonwealth v. Gray,* 339 Pa.Super. 385, 489 A.2d 213 (1985) (defendant could be sentenced for two robberies arising from the same transaction involving two victims).

Even if the defendant's criminal conduct consists of a single physical act, however, the merger doctrine does not bar separate punishments if there are substantially different interests of the Commonwealth at stake and the defendant's act has injured each interest. *See Commonwealth v. Lawton,* 272 Pa.Super. 40, 414 A.2d 658 (1979) (single act of swinging fist into crowd supported separate sentences for simple assault on one person and reckless endangerment of another).

* * *

Suppose a defendant robs his victim, and wantonly injures or tries to kill him as well; such a case raises a legitimate question whether the defendant has actually done two substantially different injuries to the peace and dignity of the Commonwealth. Sometimes to prove that a theft was robbery it is necessary to prove an aggravated assault; if so the same facts will prove both robbery and assault and they will merge. The legislative intention to punish the defendant only once for the robbery would be apparent in such a case since the robbery statute has a built-in prohibition against inflicting serious bodily injury in the course of stealing property. *See* 18 Pa.C.S. § 3701(a)(1). On the other hand, if an aggravated assault were not "necessarily involved" in the robbery and the prosecutor could prove each without proving the other, then maybe two separate offenses in fact were committed. A robbery can be carried out by the infliction of serious injury, but it can also be accomplished by mere threats of force ("terroristic threats") or simple assault; the commission of robbery by these or any means does not give the robber carte blanche to engage in as many repeated attempts on the life or well-being of the victim as the circumstances allow. If a court were nevertheless to merge the offenses of robbery and aggravated assault as a matter of routine, it might defeat whatever legislative purpose there was in identifying the taking of property by force and the doing of physical harm to persons as two separate and distinct means of injuring the Commonwealth. It might also permit the defendant to escape liability for one of two separate and distinct crimes which he has committed and should justly pay for. We cannot allow our merger doctrine to act as an open invitation to violent assailants to go ahead and perpetrate actual physical injury on their victims after having robbed or raped them by putting them in fear of such injury. This would clearly be an abuse of a doctrine whose salutary purpose is to prevent the imposition of multiple sentences on a single criminal offense.

B

"SINGLE ACT/SINGLE INJURY" THEORY REJECTED

Amicus next argues that it is an unsupportable and erroneous extension of the merger doctrine which holds that the "same act" may never eventuate in more than one punishment. Our decision of this issue is important to a proper disposition of this case because appellant makes a point of arguing that all four of his convictions stem from the same act. Thus, once the prosecution proved that appellant stood in a street in Philadelphia and fired a shotgun at Officer Moriarity, it had proven all the facts necessary to establish aggravated assault, resisting arrest, possession of a prohibited offensive weapon, and carrying a firearm in Philadelphia. Appellant contends that because all four offenses were comprised in a "single act," the offenses merged for sentencing purposes.

* * *

The single act/single injury theory is predicated in part on *Commonwealth v. Walker, supra,* wherein the Supreme Court said, " '[w]here there is but one act of cause of injury, or death of a number of persons, there is but one injury to the Commonwealth, but where the acts or causes are separate, they are separate injuries to the peace and dignity of the Commonwealth.' " 468 Pa. at 331, 362 A.2d at 231. The Court also stated that "it is beyond the power of a court imposing sentence to impose multiple sentences on a defendant for a *single act.*" 468 Pa. at 330 n. 3, 362 A.2d at 230 n. 3 (emphasis added). These statements were supported in the text of the opinion by a line of Pennsylvania Superior Court cases holding that a single act resulting in multiple deaths could support only one conviction for involuntary manslaughter.

Walker was a case where dual punishments had been imposed for rape and statutory rape arising out of a single act of forcible sexual intercourse. Under the applicable statutes as they read at the time, statutory rape was a *consensual* act of intercourse with a female under the age of sixteen, whereas rape was sexual intercourse with a victim of any age procured through force. Thus, the crimes were mutually exclusive by definition, and the Court correctly found in the case before it that only one injury, forcible invasion of the female's person, had been accomplished by the defendant's "single act." Although the Court therefore vacated the statutory rape sentence as "duplicitous," the "single act/single injury" language quoted above simply was not necessary to the holding.

* * *

* * * [L]ast year the Supreme Court explicitly overruled the quoted portion of *Walker* in *Commonwealth v. Frisbie,* 506 Pa. 461, 485 A.2d 1098 (1984). *Frisbie* held that nine separate sentences for reckless endangerment could be imposed on a defendant for a single act that injured nine people. The Court stated that "in resolving the issue of whether a single act which injures multiple victims can be the basis for multiple sentences, our task is simply to determine whether the legislature intended that each injury constitute a separate offense." *Id.* at 466, 485 A.2d at 1100. Upon examining the language of the reckless endangerment statute, the Court concluded that the Legislature clearly intended to prescribe separate punishment for each individual endangered by the single act of a defendant. The Court therefore reversed the holding of the Superior Court which had relied on the "single act/ single injury" theory.

* * *

C

SUMMARY

To summarize, in applying rules of merger courts should remember that the test is a flexible, fact-based tool for determining how many offenses against the Commonwealth have actually been committed. Despite the repeated and varied attempts of judges to state one "true test" of merger, the question of merger will often turn on an appraisal of the precise facts of the case. However, in the interest of promoting as much uniformity as possible in the application of merger rules, we emphasize that merger of offenses does not depend solely on a finding that there has been only one act or succession of acts. It also depends fundamentally and ultimately on the *different* finding that there has been only one injury to the Commonwealth.

We hold that separate punishments may be imposed for a single, indivisible act where the act includes conduct proscribed by separate statutes each of which seeks to prevent a substantially different harm or evil. *See* 18 Pa.C.S. § 110(1)(iii)(A). Our holding is in harmony with the purpose of the merger doctrine to effectuate legislative intent in the sentencing of offenders. *See id.* § 104(1) ("The general purposes of this title are: (1) to forbid and prevent conduct that unjustifiably inflicts or threatens harm to individual or public interest * * *."). In determining how many different "evils" are present in a given criminal act, the sentencing court should devote close attention to the language the Legislature has used and the scheme it has followed in defining offenses in the Crimes Code and other penal statutes. The court must also approach the question with a heavy dose of common sense.

VI

Turning to the charges at hand, we find that when Mr. Williams discharged a shotgun at Officer Moriarity, and by the same or related acts resisted the officers' attempts to perform their duties, he violated two separate and distinct interests which inure to the peace and dignity of this Commonwealth. By assaulting the officer, he endangered that precious and irreplaceable interest which all right-thinking citizens share in the life and safety of every person in the Commonwealth, whether police officer or civilian. By resisting arrest, Williams threatened that time-tested yet fragile social balance whereby our elected representatives provide laws for the good of society, and public officers to execute and enforce them, and under which respect and obedience shown to officers discharging their lawful duties are as essential to the orderly administration of justice as the laws themselves.

In deciding that the aggravated assault and resisting arrest statutes protect different interests of the Commonwealth, we have considered not only the language and evident purpose of each statute, but also that the Legislature has classified them separately under "Offenses Involving Danger to the Person" (Title 18, Part II, art. B), and "Offenses Against Public Administration" (*id.* art. E). Compare *Common-*

wealth v. Nelson, 452 Pa. 275, 305 A.2d 369 (1973), which held that assault and battery merged with resisting arrest, but so held under a previous statute defining the latter crime as, inter alia, *"assault[ing] or beat[ing]* any officer * * * making a lawful arrest. * * *" Act of June 24, 1939, P.L. 872, § 314.

We have little difficulty concluding that Williams's conviction for carrying a firearm in Philadelphia did not merge with aggravated assault, for merger is a rule of statutory construction and the Legislature has specifically provided that a conviction under the Uniform Firearms Act shall not merge with a violent offense. 18 Pa.C.S. § 6103. Nor is there any valid reason why the UFA violation should merge with resisting arrest, even though the illegal gun undoubtedly was instrumental in facilitating Williams's acts of resistance and escape. The interests of the Commonwealth in compelling the submission of arrestees to police officers, and in discouraging people from carrying unlicensed firearms around on the streets of Philadelphia, are so clearly distinct that we can say without further discussion that the conduct involved affronted two separate sources of public peace and dignity.

However, the firearms offense and the prohibited offensive weapons charge merged. We can conceive that the statutes defining these crimes *theoretically* might protect different interests of the Commonwealth; the firearms statute is particularly directed against the possession of guns in public places in Philadelphia, a practice which would cause alarm among the people of that heavily populated city if left unchecked; the prohibited weapons statute, on the other hand, is clearly directed against those types of weapons which have no legitimate purpose and are universally found to be used only in the commission of crime. Nevertheless where as here possession of the same gun in the same circumstances is proof of both crimes, they "necessarily involve" one another on the facts of the case, and the Commonwealth interests protected by the two statutes are not sufficiently diverse to allow the conclusion that two separate harms have been done. We will vacate the sentence for prohibited offensive weapons due to the clearly expressed legislative intention to punish the UFA violation separately where a firearm was used in a violent crime.

We need not remand for resentencing on the other convictions because the sentence imposed for prohibited offensive weapons could not have affected the maximum sentences which the court imposed on the other charges.

Sentence for prohibited offensive weapons vacated; otherwise judgment affirmed.

Notes and Questions

1. When cumulative convictions are sought by means of successive prosecutions instead of in one proceeding, other interests are involved. Accuseds' interests in being free from successive proceedings are more

rigorously protected by the Double Jeopardy clause of the Fifth Amendment. Therefore, subsequent prosecutions are barred in some situations where multiple prosecutions, convictions, and punishments would be constitutionally acceptable if sought in one action. In Brown v. Ohio, 432 U.S. 161, 97 S.Ct. 2221, 53 L.Ed.2d 187 (1977), Brown was prosecuted, convicted and sentenced for the offense of "joyriding" (taking, driving or operating a motor vehicle without the consent of the owner) under Ohio law. He was then, in a new proceeding over his claim of former jeopardy, prosecuted, convicted and sentenced for auto theft (stealing any motor vehicle) of the same car. The underlying facts showed that Brown took the car in East Cleveland on November 29, 1973 and was caught driving it in Wickliffe on December 8 of the same year. An Ohio appellate court affirmed. It concluded that joyriding was a lesser included offense of theft but held that for Brown's plea of former jeopardy to be meritorious he was required also to show that the two prosecutions were based on the same "operative act" or transaction. It upheld the theft conviction on the ground that the theft conviction rested on his original taking of the car and the joyriding conviction rested on his driving of the car in Wickliffe eight days later; he failed to meet the second requirement for a successful plea of former jeopardy. Brown v. State, No. 34,316 (Court of Appeals of Ohio, Eighth District, filed Dec. 11, 1975). The Supreme Court of Ohio refused to consider the case, but it was taken by the United States Supreme Court which reversed. It posed the issue as whether the two convictions rested on the "same offense" within the meaning of the Fifth Amendment. On this issue, the *Blockburger* test, discussed in *Williams,* was regarded as controlling:

> Applying the *Blockburger* test, we agree * * * that joyriding and auto theft * * * constitute "the same statutory offense" within the meaning of the Double Jeopardy Clause. For it is clearly *not* the case that "each [statute] requires proof of a fact which the other does not." As is invariably true of a greater and lesser included offense, the lesser offense—joyriding—requires no proof beyond that which is required for conviction of the greater—auto theft. The greater offense is therefore by definition the "same" for purposes of double jeopardy as any lesser offense included in it.

> This conclusion merely restates what has been this Court's understanding of the Double Jeopardy Clause at least since In re Nielson [, 131 U.S. 176, 9 S.Ct. 672, 33 L.Ed. 118 (1889),] was decided in 1889. In that case the Court endorsed the rule that

>> "where * * * a person has been tried and convicted for a crime which has various incidents included in it, he cannot be a second time tried for one of those incidents without being twice put in jeopardy for the same offence." 131 U.S., at 188, 9 S.Ct., at 676.

> Although in this formulation the conviction of the greater precedes the conviction of the lesser. The opinion makes it clear that the sequence is immaterial. * * * Whatever the sequence may be, the Fifth Amendment forbids successive prosecution and cumulative punishment for a greater and lesser included offense.

432 U.S. at 168, 97 S.Ct. at 2226–27, 53 L.Ed.2d at 195–96. Rejecting the Ohio court's holding that both convictions were proper "because the charges against him focused on different parts of his 9-day joyride," the Court explained:

> The Double Jeopardy Clause is not such a fragile guarantee that prosecutors can avoid its limitations by the simple expedient of dividing a single crime into a series of temporal or spatial units. * * * Brown's offense * * * was * * * only one offense under Ohio law. Accordingly, the specification of different dates in the two charges on which Brown was convicted cannot alter the fact that he was placed twice in jeopardy for the same offense in violation of the Fifth and Fourteenth Amendments.

432 U.S. at 169–70, 97 S.Ct. at 2227, 53 L.Ed.2d at 196–97. Justice Blackmun, joined by the Chief Justice and Justice Rehnquist, dissented:

> I am unable to ignore as easily as the Court does * * * the specific finding of the Ohio Court of Appeals that the two prosecutions at issue here were based on [Brown's] separate and distinct acts committed, respectively, on November 29 and December 8, 1973.
>
>   * * *
>
> Nine days elapsed between the two incidents that are the basis of [Brown's] convictions. During that time the automobile moved from East Cleveland to Wickliffe. It strains credulity to believe that [Brown] was operating the vehicle every minute of those nine days. A time must have come when he stopped driving the car. When he operated it again nine days later in a different community, the Ohio courts could properly find, consistently with the Double Jeopardy Clause, that the acts were sufficiently distinct to justify a second prosecution. Only if the Clause requires the Ohio courts to hold that the allowable unit of prosecution is the course of conduct would the Court's result here be correct. On the facts of this case, no such requirement could be inferred, and the state courts should be free to construe Ohio's statute as they did.

432 U.S. at 171–72, 97 S.Ct. at 2228, 53 L.Ed.2d at 197–98.

What values were being protected by the Court's insistence that joyriding was a lesser included offense of auto theft? Would the Court have found Brown's conviction and punishment for both offenses violative of the Double Jeopardy Clause if they had been obtained and imposed in a single trial?

2. Some jurisdictions have attempted to address the matter of multiple punishment by statute. Consider the following efforts:

Cal. Penal Code

§ 654. Offenses punishable in different ways by different provisions

       * * *

An act or omission which is made punishable in different ways by different provisions of this code may be punished under either of such

provisions, but in no case can it be punished under more than one
* * *.

An Arizona statute is similar except that it provides that such acts or
omissions "may be punished under both [provisions], but in no event may
sentences be other than concurrent." Ariz.Rev.Stat. § 13–116.

Ohio Rev.Code

§ 2941.25. Multiple counts

(A) Where the same conduct by the defendant can be construed to
constitute two or more allied offenses of similar import, * * * the
defendant may be convicted of only one.

(B) Where the defendant's conduct constitutes two or more offenses of dissimilar import, or where his conduct results in two or more
offenses of the same or similar kind committed separately and with a
separate animus as to each, * * * the defendant may be convicted of
all of them.

3. If formal limitations on liability or punishment are appropriate,
should they bar multiple convictions or, as in the case of the merger
doctrine applied by the *Williams* court, only cumulative punishment?

The Supreme Court has held that when multiple convictions are
precluded by virtue of legislative intent, the defendant has a right to have
one conviction vacated even though the sentence for that conviction is to
run concurrently with that for another, legitimate, conviction. The separate conviction, apart from any sentence, is seen as having potentially
adverse effects. These include the possible delay of eligibility for parole or
the increase of sentence under a recidivist statute for some future offense.
The additional conviction can be used to impeach the defendant's credibility as a witness, and carries an additional societal stigma. Thus, it must be
vacated. Ball v. United States, 470 U.S. 856, ___, 105 S.Ct. 1668, 1673–74,
84 L.Ed.2d 740, 748 (1985).

4. Should the double jeopardy clauses of the United States or state
constitutions be construed so as to impose limits upon legislatures' power to
permit multiple convictions or punishments in a single trial for identical or
related criminal activity? Perhaps any such limitation would have to rest
upon penological or other assumptions too unsettled to be regarded as
embodied in any particular form in constitutional double jeopardy provisions. And perhaps any such limitation as might be imposed would be so
readily circumvented as to deprive it of any real meaning. In Gore v.
United States, 357 U.S. 386, 78 S.Ct. 1280, 2 L.Ed.2d 1405 (1958), Gore had
been convicted of offenses defined by different federal statutory provisions
as consisting of (1) sale of drugs not in pursuance of a written order of the
person to whom the drugs had been sold; (2) sale and distribution of the
drugs not in or from the original stamped package; and (3) facilitating
concealment of drugs with knowledge that the drugs had been unlawfully
imported. The offenses were committed in one sale. Although under
Blockburger these multiple convictions were appropriate, Gore urged that
the double jeopardy clause of the United States Constitution be given a

broader reading so as to bar those multiple convictions. Rejecting this, the Court explained:

> Suppose Congress, instead of enacting the three provisions before us, had passed an enactment substantially in this form: "Anyone who sells drugs except from the original stamped package and who sells such drugs not in pursuance of a written order of the person to whom the drug is sold, and who does so by way of facilitating the concealment and sale of drugs knowing the same to have been unlawfully imported, shall be sentenced to not less than fifteen years' imprisonment: Provided, however, That if he makes such sale in pursuance of a written order of the person to whom the drug is sold he shall be sentenced to only ten years' imprisonment: Provided further, That if he sells such drugs in the original stamped package he shall also be sentenced to only ten years' imprisonment: And provided further, That if he sells such drugs in pursuance of a written order and from a stamped package, he shall be sentenced to only five years' imprisonment." Is it conceivable that such a statute would not be within the power of Congress? And is it rational to find such a statute constitutional but to strike down [the application of the three provisions before us] as violative of the double jeopardy clause?

> In effect, we are asked to enter the domain of penology, and more particularly that tantalizing aspect of it, the proper apportionment of punishment. Whatever views may be entertained regarding severity of punishment, * * * these are peculiarly questions of legislative policy * * *

357 U.S. at 392–93, 78 S.Ct. at 1284–85, 2 L.Ed.2d at 1410.

5. There is widespread agreement that a defendant who, by one act or related acts, injures or kills several victims may be convicted and punished consecutively for as many offenses as there are victims. In State v. Myers, ___ W.Va. ___, 298 S.E.2d 813 (1982), the West Virginia Supreme Court held that two involuntary manslaughter offenses are committed when the defendant engages in a single act of negligent driving that causes two deaths. It explained:

> Our holding today is given * * * support by Justice Miller's reasoning in State ex rel. Watson v. Ferguson, W.Va., 274 S.E.2d 440, 446 (1980), where he wrote:

> > There can be little doubt that one function of a criminal justice system is to enable those individuals who have been victimized by the criminal acts of another to find some individual vindication of the harm done to each. Certainly, the degree of culpability, and as a consequence the degree of punishment, must bear some proportion not only to the magnitude of the crime but also to the number of victims involved. These are fundamental considerations that society expects from a criminal justice system.

> As Justice Miller, noted, it is consistent with the goals of our criminal justice system that both society as whole and the relatives of victims individually be able to attain some sense of vindication by

punishing the appellant separately for each outrageous consequence of his negligent actions. * * *

298 S.E.2d at 816. Compare Wilkoff v. Superior Court, 38 Cal.3d 345, 211 Cal.Rptr. 742, 696 P.2d 134 (1985).

6. Often the question is the "unit of the crime" or the "unit of prosecution" as determined by the substantive definition of the crime. In Commonwealth v. Donovan, 395 Mass. 20, 478 N.E.2d 727 (1985), for example, Donovan and his codefendant Grant had a false bank night deposit box constructed and, one evening, attached it to the bank's regular box so that deposits made would fall into the false box rather than the regular one. The false box was removed before morning but not until after seven customers had made deposits totaling $37,000 in the false box. Donovan was convicted of seven larcenies under a fairly standard definition of that crime. Holding this impermissible, the Massachusetts court explained:

> The issue before us turns on whether the Legislature intended to authorize more than a single conviction for the larcenous scheme at issue here. The statute is silent with respect to situations such as this. We have held, however, that criminal statutes must be construed strictly against the Commonwealth. * * *

> In Commonwealth v. Stasiun, 349 Mass. 38, 45, 206 N.E.2d 672 (1965), this court recognized that "where it appears that successive takings are actuated by a single, continuing criminal impulse or intent or are pursuant to the execution of a general larcenous scheme, such successive takings constitute a single larceny, regardless of the extent of the time which may have elapsed between each taking." We conclude that the case before us controlled by this principle. The evidence shows that Donovan and Grant hatched a single plan to place a phony night deposit box on the wall of a single bank. The box was only placed on the wall for a single time, on a single evening. Thus the defendants executed a single larcenous scheme pursuant to a "single, continuing criminal impulse or intent." Commonwealth v. Stasiun, supra. Consequently, their conduct constitutes only a single crime.

> The Commonwealth contends that the principle set forth in Commonwealth v. Stasiun, supra, is inapplicable where, as here, property has been taken from seven different depositors. Consistent with the overwhelming weight of authority in other jurisdictions, we disagree, and conclude that, in the circumstances here, only a single crime has been committed even though the larcenous scheme involves the taking of property from a number of owners. In State v. Myers, 407 A.2d 307, 309 (Me.1979), the defendant stole money from a single cash box which contained funds belonging to several different towns. He was indicted for four counts of larceny, a separate count for each of the towns which had deposited cash in the box. The Supreme Judicial Court of Maine held that * * * "The stealing of property from different owners at the same time and at the same place constitutes but one larceny." * * *

We emphasize that nothing in this opinion signals a retreat from our holding in Commonwealth v. Levia, 385 Mass. 345, 351, 431 N.E.2d 928 (1982), where we affirmed the convictions of a defendant who had robbed two individuals in the course of a single criminal episode. Whenever a single criminal transaction gives rise to crimes of violence which are committed against several victims, then multiple indictments (and punishments) are appropriate. As the Supreme Court of Michigan recently held, though the "appropriate 'unit' of prosecution" for larceny is the taking at a single time and place without regard to the number of items taken; the appropriate 'unit of prosecution' for armed robbery is the person assaulted and robbed." People v. Wakeford, 418 Mich. 95, 112, 341 N.W.2d 68 (1983).

395 Mass. at 28, 478 N.E.2d at 734–35.

Is there any principle for distinguishing between the interest of each robbery victim in being free from fear of injury and the interest of each larceny victim in the continued possession of her property?

7.   Where an offense lends itself to characterization as a "continuing offense," the "unit of prosecution" is likely to be defined differently. In State v. Williams, 211 Neb. 650, 319 N.W.2d 748 (1982), the court held that possession of a firearm by a felon on two different days is only one offense in the absence of any evidence that the weapon was out of his possession between those days. The underlying question is "whether the idea of 'possession,' within a criminal statute of this nature, contemplates a continuing offense as opposed to a single incident." Then:

While the word "possess" is not a word of precise definition, it is clear that "possess," when used in a criminal statute, means something more than momentary control. * * *

It would seem to follow that the crime of "possession" may be brief, if complete, or it may extend over a period of time, if uninterrupted. To hold otherwise would make it near impossible to determine when the "possession" commenced and when it terminated. Absent a statute to the contrary, the ability to determine when a criminal act commenced and when it terminated appears essential in order to determine when a subsequent crime occurs. Certainly an arrest and indictment would be sufficient to interrupt possession so that a subsequent possession would constitute another crime. * * * In the instant case, the court must either declare that a given unit of time constitutes a separate offense or arbitrarily establish a period of time which constitutes each separate offense. There appears no basis for doing so. If the Legislature desires to take such action, it is at liberty to do so, but the courts * * * are not.

211 Neb. at 655–57, 319 N.E.2d at 751–53. See also, Bruce v. United States, 471 A.2d 1005 (D.C.App.1984) (multiple convictions for carrying an unlicensed pistol in the absence of evidence of a break in the act of carrying between the two incidents are objectionable because this threatens punishment disproportionate to the offense).

8.   It must be recognized that multiplication of charges with their inherent dangers of multiple convictions and punishment is not merely a

function of the increase in the number of separate yet overlapping criminal prohibitions. Nor is it merely the result of prosecutorial vindictiveness.

Cumulative pressures lead prosecutors to multiply the individual counts in an indictment or information. There is a high degree of uncertainty at the time of charge as to just what the proof at trial will be. The speed which is essential to a humane and efficient system of criminal administration compounds this uncertainty, for a prosecutor often must draw the charge very shortly after the crime or arrest and is not free to engage in extensive discovery and investigation while the defendant is in custody awaiting trial.

The sixth amendment right to a grand jury indictment has been understood severely to restrict the prosecutor's right to amend indictments, and this combines with the rules concerning variance to place a heavy penalty on the prosecutor who does not plead to cover every contingency of proof at trial. Returning to the hypothetical concerning the forgery of the social security check, reliance solely upon a forgery charge is likely to lead to disaster if, as is too often sadly the case, the expert handwriting witness lacks credibility or the person who accepted the check proves a weak identification witness at trial. In such a situation, however, it is likely that the theft of the instrument from the mail or its possession by the defendant can be independently proved without these weak witnesses.

Rules of criminal pleading also lead a prosecutor to break down his charge into as many counts of individual offenses as possible. The prosecutor is justifiably apprehensive of violating the hypertechnical rules of multiplicity and duplicity which are said to be related to the defendant's sixth amendment right to be specifically informed of the precise charges against him. A parallel pressure is exerted by the prosecutor's desire to present the judge and jury with narrow, clear issues of fact.

The dynamics of criminal justice administration also contribute to the multiplication of charges. Most criminal charges are disposed of by a plea of guilty, which often is the product of explicit or tacit negotiations between prosecutor and defense counsel. The multiplication of charges provides both lawyers with leverage for negotiation, even when as a practical matter there can be only one conviction or sentence and the likelihood of consecutive sentences is remote. Often a defendant can be persuaded to plead guilty to one charge on the assurance that the remaining 27 counts will be dismissed. Some judges express resentment when a prosecutor presents a 1 count indictment or information, complaining that this unduly restricts their sentencing flexibility.

Finally, the impact of the multiplicity of charges on proof at trial must be recognized. Some judges will not allow proof of similar acts not charged in the indictment and sometimes a prosecutor will be limited in showing the entire transaction if it includes other criminal offenses not charged. All of these pressures to charge as large a number of offenses as possible tend to be aggravated by the prosecutor's perception of himself as the avenging agent of society. Certainly there is often more emotion than sense in the 100 count indictment, but the existing rules provide few countervailing pressures, or even escapes, through which the prosecutor can avoid the multiplication of charges.

Rosett, Arthur I. and Green, Richard A., Working Papers of the National Commission on Reform of Federal Criminal Laws, Vol. I, at 335–36 (1970).

Chapter VI

GENERAL PRINCIPLES OF CRIMINAL LIABILITY: THE STATE OF MIND

Contents

COWAN, TOWARDS AN EXPERIMENTAL DEFINITION OF CRIMINAL MIND

In Philosophical Essays in Honor of Edgar Arthur Singer, Jr.
163 (F. Clarke and M. Nahm eds. 1942).

In the 17th year of the reign of Edward IV, Brian pronounced his celebrated dictum that a man is responsible only for his words and deeds and not for his thoughts, because "the devil himself knoweth not the mind of man." What the learned judge apparently took to be an axiomatic rule of evidence has become a part of the substantive law of contracts in the form of the doctrine of objective intent. Contract law is now taken to be concerned only with intent as outwardly manifested by the conduct of the parties.

Similarly, the law of torts is almost exclusively occupied with the external behavior of the parties. Only in the case of intentional wrongs does it purport to refer to states of mind as qualifying responsibility. The great body of non-intentional torts applies what are called "objective standards." In determining negligence, for instance, the law does not inquire whether the harmful act was accompanied by a culpable state of mind. On the contrary, it merely decides whether the defendant failed to conform to external standards of reasonably expectable conduct. His state of mind is immaterial. Anglo-American *civil* law, therefore, has from the earliest times indicated that, with certain few exceptions, objective intent is the only kind of intent with which it is prepared to deal.

The theory of the *criminal* law is different. Here it is still felt necessary to investigate a man's secret thought, or absence of thought, whenever intention, or malice, or even negligence is an element of the crime in question.

Notes

1. The so-called subjective theory of criminal liability assumes that state of mind and therefore "mind" itself as ascertainable. This underlying assumption has been called into question on both practical and theoretical grounds.

The practical ground is based upon difficulty of proof. If there is such a "thing" as state of mind, it is nevertheless so subjective and difficult of proof that it is unrealistic to believe that an individual's state of mind at a past time can generally be reliably determined. Thus, it is argued, the criminal law should not attempt to make criminal liability turn on state of mind.

The theoretical ground is more basic. This view holds that "mind" is a mere abstraction and therefore it is artificial to treat states of mind as if they actually existed. Rather than waste time attempting to infer an offender's state of mind from his behavior, this view holds that the law would better serve its purposes if it regarded the so-called mind as the criminal behavior itself rather than using the behavior as evidence from which to infer "mind". See T. Cowan, Towards an Experimental Definition of Criminal Mind, in Philosophical Essays in Honor of Edgar Arthur Singer, Jr. (F. Clarke and M. Nahm eds. 1942); Cowan, A Critique of the Moralistic Conception of Criminal Law, 97 U.Pa.L.Rev. 502, 510 (1949). In fact, Cowan represents, the law in fact does this by procedural devices such as the presumption that a person "intends" the natural consequences of his act. Inserting the concept of "state of mind", he concludes, merely serves to confuse analysis. (Reconsider the discussion of this "presumption" in note 3, page 58, supra.)

2. The historical development of the criminal law's emphasis upon an alleged offender's state of mind (the mens rea requirement) is traced in the following portions of Sayre, Mens Rea, 45 Harv.L.Rev. 974, 981–83, 988–89, 993–94 (1932): [a]

> [S]tudy of the early law seems to show that up to the twelfth century the conception of *mens rea* in anything like its present sense was nonexistent. In certain cases at least criminal liability might attach irrespective of the actor's state of mind. But because the old records fail to set forth a *mens rea* as a general requisite of criminality one must not reach the conclusion that even in very early times the mental element was entirely disregarded. The very nature of the majority of the early offenses rendered them impossible of commission without a criminal intent. Waylaying and robbery are impossible without it; so is rape; and the same is roughly true of housebreaking.
>
> * * *
>
> Furthermore, the intent of the defendant seems to have been a material factor, even from the very earliest times, in determining the extent of punishment.

a. Reprinted from 45 Harvard Law Review 974 (1932).

By the end of the twelfth century two influences were making themselves strongly felt. One was the Roman law[;] * * * the Roman law conceptions of *dolus* and *culpa* required careful consideration of the mental element in crime.

A second influence, even more powerful, was the canon law, whose insistence upon moral guilt emphasized still further the mental element in crime. * * * Henceforth, the criminal law of England, developing in the general direction of moral blameworthiness, begins to insist upon a *mens rea* as an essential element of criminality. * * *

We can trace the changed attitude in the new generalizations concerning the necessity of an evil intent which are found scattered through the Year Books in the remarks of judges and counsel * * *. We sense it in the growing insistence upon more and more sharply defined mental requisites as essentials of the common-law felonies. We find it fermenting in the form of new defenses which show the absence of an evil mind and therefore of criminal liability-defenses such as infancy or insanity or compulsion.

* * *

By the second half of the seventeenth century, it was universally accepted law that an evil intent was as necessary for felony as the act itself. * * *

At the outset when the *mens rea* necessary for criminality was based on general moral blameworthiness, the conception was an exceedingly vague one. As a result of the slow judicial process of discriminating one case from another and "talking of diversities," much sharper and more precise lines gradually came to be drawn as to the exact mental requisites for various crimes. Since each felony involved different social and public interests, the mental requisites for one almost inevitably came to differ from those of another.

REMINGTON AND HELSTAD, THE MENTAL ELEMENT IN CRIME—A LEGISLATIVE PROBLEM

1952 Wis.L.Rev. 644, 678.

If the problem of the mental element in crime is difficult and confused, that is due in large part to the fact that it is comparatively a neglected area in the law. While the scope of the criminal law is continually being expanded through legislative enactment, little attention has been given to broad aspects such as the mental state required. * * * The problem is not easy. In fact it is perhaps as difficult as any in the law, but the need for improvement is imperative and with some effort much improvement can be made. The solution requires * * * awareness of the problem, a willingness to face squarely the policy determinations that must be made, and once those determinations are made, careful attention to the drafting [and interpretation] of criminal statutes so as to assure that the basis of liability is clearly expressed.

A. STATE OF MIND ANALYSIS AND TYPES OF MENTAL STATES

Editors' Introduction: Defining the Terms Used in Describing the Mental Elements of Crimes

Despite longstanding agreement that the actor's state of mind is of major, if not critical, importance in determining whether criminal liability exists for an act, and, where appropriate, the gradation of liability, the precise state of mind requirements demanded for conviction of particular crimes remains amazingly unclear. Even less certainty exists concerning some general terms often used in judicial and textual discussions of criminal intent, particularly the phrases "general intent" and "specific intent."

These terms are widely used in formulating what are often regarded as generally accepted "rules." For example, the "defenses" of voluntary intoxication and diminished capacity are often defined as available only where the crime at issue requires proof of a "specific" intent. See the discussions in State v. Stasio, p. 357, and Chapter XII, Section D.2., infra. A "mistake of fact" is often required to be "reasonable" as well as honestly entertained *unless* it shows the lack of a "specific" intent required by the crime charged; see the discussion in Chapter VI. Section E.1., infra.

In view of this widespread use of the terms, it is suprising that there is not more widespread agreement on their meaning. The United States Supreme Court recently observed:

> At common law, crimes generally were classified as requiring either "general intent" or "specific intent." This venerable distinction, however, has been the source of a good deal of confusion. As one treatise explained:
>
>> "Sometimes 'general intent' is used in the same way as 'criminal intent' to mean the general notion of *mens rea*, while 'specific intent' is taken to mean the mental state required for a particular crime. Or, 'general intent' may be used to encompass all forms of the mental state requirement, while 'specific intent' is limited to the one mental state of intent. Another possibility is that 'general intent' will be used to characterize an intent to do something on an undetermined occasion, and 'specific intent' to denote an intent to do that thing at a particular time and place." W. LaFave & A. Scott, Handbook on Criminal Law § 28, pp. 201–02 (1972) (footnotes omitted).

This ambiguity has led to a movement away from the traditional dichotomy of intent [between "specific" and "general" intent] and towards an alternative analysis of *mens rea*. This new approach, exemplified in the American Law Institute's Model Penal Code, is based on two principles. First, the ambiguous and elastic term "intent" is replaced with a hierarchy of culpable states of mind. The different levels in this hierarchy are commonly identified, in descending order of culpability, as purpose, knowledge, recklessness, and negligence. * * *

[Second,] there is another ambiguity inherent in the traditional distinction between specific intent and general intent. Generally, even time-honored common-law crimes consist of several elements, and complex statutorily defined crimes exhibit this characteristic to an even greater degree. Is the same state of mind required of the actor for each element of the crime, or may some elements require one state of mind and some another. * * * [T]he American Law Institute stated: "[C]lear analysis requires that the question of the kind of culpability required to establish the commission of an offense be faced separately with respect to each material element of the crime. MPC Comments 123.

United States v. Bailey, 444 U.S. 394, 403–06, 100 S.Ct. 624, 631–32, 62 L.Ed.2d 575, 586–88 (1980).

The analysis of mental states embodied in the Model Penal Code has been widely followed in legislative criminal code revision, see pages 13–15, supra, and constitutes one of the major contributions of the Code to the development of American substantive criminal law. Because of its prominence in contemporary substantive criminal law, the Model Penal Code's approach is a major focus of this Chapter.

This analysis suggests and perhaps requires that the states of mind required for criminal liability be considered with regard to two dimensions. First, it is necessary to identify what the state of mind must concern. This might usefully be characterized as the "object dimension." Second, it is necessary to identify what state of mind concerning that object is required. This might usefully be characterized as the "level" dimension. As the Supreme Court's *Bailey* discussion indicates, a single crime may require mental states that differ in "level" depending upon which "object" they concern.

The federal statute at issue in United States v. Feola, 420 U.S. 671, 95 S.Ct. 1255, 43 L.Ed.2d 541 (1975) provides an example:

Whoever forcibly assaults * * * any person designated [a federal officer] while engaged in * * * the performance of his official duties, shall be fined not more than $5,000 or imprisoned not more than three years, or both.

18 U.S.C.A. § 111. The nonmental elements of this crime can be identified as follows:

1. forcibly assault[ing];

2. a person designated a federal officer;

3. who is, at the time, engaged in the performance of his official duties.

A mental state might be required concerning each of these matters or, in the terminology used above, concerning each of these "objects." But if a decision is made to require a mental state with regard to each of these objects, those mental states might differ with regard to—again

in the terminology used above—their level. For example, it might well
be regarded as appropriate to require that a defendant act with at least
knowledge concerning element 1, that is, that the defendant at least be
aware that he is, depending upon the applicable definition of assault
injuring another person, putting him in apprehension of injury, or
touching him in an offensive way without his consent. But with regard
to elements 2 and 3, it may equally well be determined that recklessness or perhaps even negligence should be sufficient, that is, that the
defendant need only have been aware (or that he should have been
aware) of a substantial and unjustifiable risk that his victim is a federal
officer and that the federal officer was, at the time, engaged in the
performance of his official duties. Indeed, no state of mind at all might
be required as to either or both of these elements.

In any case, such mental states would all concern "objects" that are
themselves elements of the offense. Congress might, however, have
concluded that liability for this offense should require proof that the
actor had a state of mind concerning matters other than the act of
assault and the attendant circumstances of the victim's federal identity
and activity. For example, it is not necessary under § 111 for the
Government to prove that a defendant's conduct impeded the victim's
performance of his official duties. But Congress might have determined that such assaults should constitute a federal offense only if they
were made with the intent to impede the federal officer's performance
of his official duties. Such a conclusion could have been embodied in a
somewhat different version of § 111:

> Whoever forcibly assaults * * * any person designated [a federal
> officer] while engaged in * * * the performance of his official duties,
> with the purpose of impeding the officer's performance of those duties,
> shall be fined not more than $5,000 or imprisoned not more than three
> years, or both.

Now, by the precise terms of the offense, one element of the crime is a
mental state concerning an object—impediment of the victim's performance of his official duties—that need not itself be proved to establish
guilt. The quality of that mental state is "purpose," that is, the
defendant must—using the distinctions of the Model Penal Code—have
had the conscious objective of impeding the officer's performance of his
duties.

This distinction, then, is between states of mind that concern or
have as their objects matters—acts, circumstances, or results—that are
themselves nonmental elements of the crime, and other states of mind
that concern matters not elements of the offense.

Is this distinction useful? There is some reason to believe that it
may assist in understanding what at least some courts mean when they
use the term, "general intent." Although, as the *Bailey* discussion
above suggested, use of this terminology has been inconsistent, many
courts appear to use the phrase "general intent" to refer to the mental
state or states required by the crime which have as their object or

objects the defendant's acts or, perhaps, other matters which are elements of the offense. See State v. McVey, 376 N.W.2d 585, 586 (Iowa 1985) (theft by exercising control over stolen goods is only general intent crime because it does not require proof of any intent beyond the voluntary act of exercising the prohibited control over property the accused knows to have been stolen); Dean v. State, 668 P.2d 639, 642 (Wyo.1983) (arson defined as willfully and maliciously burning a house was not a specific intent crime but revised statute defining crime as maliciously starting a fire with intent to damage occupied structure would create specific intent offense)."

Is there any utility in continuing to use the terms specific and general intent? Given the inconsistencies in the meaning given the terms, it is arguable that they contribute little but further confusion to an already uncertain area. Of course, to the extent that courts and legislatures use them, they cannot be ignored.

The distinction drawn by the definition suggested above, however, may have some analytical value. It is useful in careful analysis to distinguish and address separately two points with regard to particular crimes. First, what mental states ought to be required with regard to those matters that are themselves part of the "actus reus" of the crime (that is, what "general intent" in the terminology discussed above ought to be required)? Second, what mental states ought to be required with regard to other matters (that is, what "specific intent" ought to be required)? Since different considerations may apply to the issues posed by these inquiries, analysis that separates them will encourage independent resolution of the issues.

Given the rationales for stressing the actor's state of mind in deciding whether criminal liability ought to exist, it is arguable that—as a general rule—some level of mental state ought to be required with regard to each part of the *actus reus* of the offense. This is the position taken in Section 2.02 of the Model Penal Code, reprinted in this section.

But other mental states—or "specific intents"—may not, as a general rule, be suggested by basic principles of criminal liability. Perhaps they should be imposed only where a specifically identifiable function would be served. Also, proving a specific intent may pose special difficulties for the prosecution and may trigger the operation of so-called "defenses" such as intoxication. Therefore, given these considerations, perhaps courts willing to find requirements of "general intent" even in the absence of statutory language requiring this should be more reluctant to find specific intents required by crimes where the legislative language does not impose such requirements.

"Specific intent," then, may usefully be regarded as meaning mental states that have as their objects matters which are not elements of the crime. Cf. W. LaFave & A. Scott, Criminal Law 389–90 (2nd ed. 1986) (in caselaw discussing intoxication, specific intent sometimes means intent in addition to the intent to do the physical act which the crime requires); R. Perkins & R. Boyce, Criminal Law 832 (3rd ed. 1982).

The example considered above provides an opportunity for an illustrative example. Those states of mind, if any, required by § 111 that concern the three nonmental elements of the offense—forcible assault, that the victim be a federal officer, and that the victim be engaged in the performance of official duties—would constitute the "general intent" required by the offense. As actually embodied in the federal code, § 111 would not require any "specific intent." But the further intent demanded by the hypothetical version of the statute, above, would require a such a specific intent, because it would require a mental state concerning a matter—impediment of the victim's performance of his official duties—that is not itself an element of the offense.

As so defined, the characterization of mental states does not depend on their level within the hierarchy of mental states. The fact that the specific intent required by the hypothetical version of § 111 demands "purpose" does not, in itself, make that a specific intent.

It is important to stress that there is not general agreement on this use of the terminology. In *Bailey,* for example, the Supreme Court observed that, "In a general sense, 'purpose' corresponds loosely with the common-law concept of specific intent, while 'knowledge' corresponds loosely with the concept of general intent." 444 U.S. at 405, 100 S.Ct. at 632, 62 L.Ed.2d at 587. Under the definition of the terms used above, of course, this is simply not the case.

This and the next several sections of this Chapter assume that this distinction between "general" and "specific" intents—as so defined—has analytical value and use this distinction as basis for the subdivision of the Chapter. This section reprints those portions of the Model Penal Code that define and distinguish among various states of mind according to what was above characterized as their level. Section B deals with "general intent" as defined above—the state of mind required concerning those matters that are part of the actus reus of the crime. Section C, in contrast, concerns what under these definitions would be specific intents. In particular, attention is addressed to the specific intents required by the property acquisition offenses. Section D, on the other hand, addresses those situations in which a decision is or may be made that even "general intent" is not appropriately required.

MODEL PENAL CODE *
(Official Draft, 1985).

Section 2.02. General Requirements of Culpability

* * *

(2) *Kinds of Culpability Defined.*

(a) *Purposely.*

A person acts purposely with respect to a material element of an offense when:

(i) if the element involves the nature of his conduct or a result thereof, it is his conscious object to engage in conduct of that nature or to cause such a result; and

(ii) if the element involves the attendant circumstances, he is aware of the existence of such circumstances or he believes or hopes that they exist.

(b) *Knowingly.*

A person acts knowingly with respect to a material element of an offense when:

(i) if the element involves the nature of his conduct or the attendant circumstances, he is aware that his conduct is of that nature or that such circumstances exist; and

(ii) if the element involves a result of his conduct, he is aware that it is practically certain that his conduct will cause such a result.

(c) *Recklessly.*

A person acts recklessly with respect to a material element of an offense when he consciously disregards a substantial and unjustifiable risk that the material element exists or will result from his conduct. The risk must be of such a nature and degree that, considering the nature and purpose of the actor's conduct and the circumstances known to him, its disregard involves a gross deviation from the standard of conduct that a law-abiding person would observe in the actor's situation.

(d) *Negligently.*

A person acts negligently with respect to a material element of an offense when he should be aware of a substantial and unjustifiable risk that the material element exists or will result from his conduct. The risk must be of such a nature and degree that the actor's failure to perceive it, considering the nature and purpose of his conduct and the circumstances known to him, involves a gross deviation from the standard of care that a reasonable person would observe in the actor's situation.

B. THE STANDARD STATE OF MIND REQUIREMENT FOR CRIMINAL LIABILITY: "GENERAL INTENT"

Under the approach suggested in the Editors' Introduction to Section A of this Chapter, analysis most usefully begins with consideration of what state of mind is required concerning each element of the crime charged. Thus it is necessary to consider whether a defendant must have entertained purpose, knowledge, recklessness, or perhaps negligence with regard to the act constituting the crime, any result required, and any circumstances that the crime requires be proved. This is the subject of the present section.

Those portions of the Model Penal Code defining and distinguishing the different levels of state of mind were reprinted in Section A, supra, at page 272. This section begins with the provisions of the Code governing the application of those definitions to particular criminal offenses. The principal case presents the task of implementing a somewhat similar statutory structure with regard to a particular crime. As the Texas statute being applied in that case suggests, the approach of the Model Penal Code has been widely used as a model for actual legislation, but it has sometimes been modified. Consider the wisdom of such modifications.

The application of state of mind requirements to those elements that constitute "circumstances" and, specifically, to the circumstances required by many major sexual offenses is considered in Chapter XI, infra.

MODEL PENAL CODE *
(Official Draft, 1985).

Section 2.02. General Requirements of Culpability

(1) *Minimum Requirements of Culpability.* Except as provided in Section 2.05, a person is not guilty of an offense unless he acted purposely, knowingly, recklessly or negligently, as the law may require, with respect to each material element of the offense.

* * *

(3) *Culpability Required Unless Otherwise Provided.* When the culpability sufficient to establish a material element of an offense is not prescribed by law, such element is established if a person acts purposely, knowingly or recklessly with respect thereto.

(4) *Prescribed Culpability Requirement Applies to All Material Elements.* When the law defining an offense prescribes the kind of culpability that is sufficient for the commission of an offense, without distinguishing among the material elements thereof, such provision shall apply to all the material elements of the offense, unless a contrary purpose plainly appears.

(5) *Substitutes for Negligence, Recklessness and Knowledge.* When the law provides that negligence suffices to establish an element of an offense, such element also is established if a person acts purposely, knowingly or recklessly. When recklessness suffices to establish an element, such element also is established if a person acts purposely or

knowingly. When acting knowingly suffices to establish an element, such element also is established if a person acts purposely.

(6) *Requirement of Purpose Satisfied if Purpose Is Conditional.* When a particular purpose is an element of an offense, the element is established although such purpose is conditional, unless the condition negatives the harm or evil sought to be prevented by the law defining the offense.

(7) *Requirement of Knowledge Satisfied by Knowledge of High Probability.* When knowledge of the existence of a particular fact is an element of an offense, such knowledge is established if a person is aware of a high probability of its existence, unless he actually believes that it does not exist.

(8) *Requirement of Wilfulness Satisfied by Acting Knowingly.* A requirement that an offense be committed wilfully is satisfied if a person acts knowingly with respect to the material elements of the offense, unless a purpose to impose further requirements appears.

(9) *Culpability as to Illegality of Conduct.* Neither knowledge nor recklessness or negligence as to whether conduct constitutes an offense or as to the existence, meaning or application of the law determining the elements of an offense is an element of such offense, unless the definition of the offense or the Code so provides.

(10) *Culpability as Determinant of Grade of Offense.* When the grade or degree of an offense depends on whether the offense is committed purposely, knowingly, recklessly or negligently, its grade or degree shall be the lowest for which the determinative kind of culpability is established with respect to any material element of the offense.

Notes and Questions

1. The definitional section of the Code further specifies:

(10) "material element of an offense" means an element that does not relate exclusively to the statute of limitations, jurisdiction, venue, or to any other matter similarly unconnected with (i) the harm or evil, incident to conduct, sought to be prevented by the law defining the offense, or (ii) the existence of a justification or excuse for such conduct.

Model Penal Code § 1.13 (Official Draft 1985).

2. The position of the Model Penal Code—that in the absence of a specific indication to the contrary with respect to any material element of an offense a culpability of at least "recklessness" would be required—was defended by the drafters of the Model Penal Code as representing "what usually is regarded as the common law position." Model Penal Code, Comments to § 2.02, 244 (Official Draft 1985). It also, according to the comments, "represents the most convenient norm for drafting purposes. When purpose or knowledge is required, it is conventional to be explicit. And since negligence is an exceptional basis of liability, it should be excluded as a basis unless explicitly prescribed." Id.

ALVARADO v. STATE

Court of Criminal Appeals of Texas, 1986.
704 S.W.2d 36.

CLINTON, JUDGE.

[Appellant Amelia Alvarado was charged with injury to a child in violation of § 22.04 of the Texas Penal Code:

(a) A person commits an offense if he intentionally, knowingly, recklessly or with criminal negligence engages in conduct that causes serious bodily injury * * * to a child who is 14 years of age or younger.

The indictment alleged that appellant "intentionally and knowingly * * * caused serious bodily injury [to the child] by * * * placing him in a tub of hot water." At trial, appellant testified in her own behalf. She acknowledged that she had been angry with the victim for resisting his bath and refusing to disrobe and that she placed him, fully clothed, into the water without first testing it. She denied, however, that she knew the water was hot enough to cause burning as serious bodily injury is defined.

The Texas Penal Code also provides:

§ 6.02 Requirements of Culpability

(a) Except as provided in Subsection (b) of this section, a person does not commit an offense unless he intentionally, knowingly, recklessly, or with criminal negligence engages in conduct as the definition of the offense requires.

(b) If the definition of an offense does not prescribe a culpable mental state, a culpable mental state is nevertheless required unless the definition plainly dispenses with any mental element.

(c) If the definition of an offense does not prescribe a culpable mental state, but one is nevertheless required under Subsection (b) of this section, intent, knowledge, or recklessness suffices to establish criminal responsibility.

* * *

Another provision of the Code, Section 6.03, defines the various mental states in terms somewhat similar to those used in the Model Penal Code; see page 272, supra. "Intentionally," however, is used instead of "purposely." Moreover, both recklessness and negligence are defined only with respect to "circumstances surrounding [the actor's] conduct or the results of his conduct." Texas Penal Code §§ 6.03(c), 6.03(d). No definition is provided for recklessness or negligence concerning the nature of the actor's conduct.

On original submission, a panel of the court affirmed the judgment of conviction. Appellant was granted leave to file a motion for rehearing.]

[At trial,] appellant argued the focus of the pertinent culpable mental states in the statute, is on the "result of conduct," here, "serious bodily injury." [2] She accordingly requested that the trial court limit the definitions of the culpable mental states to that which relates in each to the "result" of the offense as follows:

"A person acts intentionally, or with intent, *with respect to a result* of his conduct when it is his conscious objective or desire to cause the result."

"A person acts knowingly, or with knowledge, *with respect to a result* of his conduct when he is aware that his conduct is reasonably certain to cause the result."

The trial judge denied these charges because they "lack everything that is in the definition in the Code," and instead charged the jury [:

"A person acts intentionally, or with intent, with respect to the nature of her conduct *or* to a result of her conduct *when it is her conscious objective or desire to engage in the conduct* or cause the result."

"A person acts knowingly, or with knowledge, with respect to the nature of her conduct or to circumstances surrounding her conduct *when she is aware of her conduct* or that the circumstances exist. A person acts knowingly, or with knowledge, with respect to a result of her conduct when she is aware that her conduct is reasonably certain to cause the result."]

In his final argument to the jury, defense counsel stressed the fact that in order to find his client guilty * * * the jury must find it was her conscious objective or desire to cause serious bodily injury to the child or that she was aware that putting the child in the water was reasonably certain to cause serious bodily injury to the child. In response, the district attorney pointed out to the jury that what defense counsel had said was a misstatement of the court's charge; he urged the jury to read the charge and observed that a finding that appellant had engaged in the conduct of putting the child in "hot water" knowingly or intentionally was sufficient for a conviction.

On appeal, the * * * panel asserted that the language of § 22.04, supra, (which includes the phrase "engages in conduct,") "clearly focuses on the conduct *and* the result of that conduct" [emphasis original]. However, without addressing the contention that the court's charge allowed conviction if appellant had requisite culpability as to *either* the result *or* the conduct alone, the panel overruled * * * appellant's ground of error.

* * *

[A]ll the culpable mental states do not apply to all possible "elements of conduct." Section 22.04 provides an offense is committed if a person intentionally, knowingly, *recklessly or with criminal negligence*

2. [* * * (All emphasis is supplied throughout by the writer of this opinion unless otherwise indicated.)]

causes injury to a child, but, as was acknowledged in *Lugo-Lugo,* [v. State, 650 S.W.2d 72, 77 (Tex.Crim.App.1983)] "[a] person cannot be reckless or negligent with respect to the 'nature of conduct.'" See §§ 6.03(c) and (d).[5] The only "element of conduct" which can be the object of all four of the culpable mental states is, "result of conduct." See §§ 6.03(a), (b), (c) and (d). Indeed, experience teaches that when all four culpable mental states have been prescribed by the Legislature in defining an offense, it is a strong indication that the offense is a "specific result" type of crime.

    *   *   * [I]t is usually a simple matter to look at a penal proscription and determine whether the Legislature intended to punish "specified conduct" as opposed to a "specified result." For example, before 1983 amendments, V.T.C.A. Penal Code, § 21.02(a) prohibited a person from "having sexual intercourse with a female" when certain "circumstances surrounding" the intercourse were extant. By specifying the "nature of the conduct" prohibited (having sexual intercourse) the Legislature indicated rape is a "nature of conduct" crime and the required culpability must go to that element of conduct.

By contrast, the injury to a child statute, like the homicide and other assaultive proscriptions, does not specify the "nature of conduct." Clearly then, the "nature of conduct" in these offenses is inconsequential (so long as it includes a voluntary act) to commission of the crimes. What matters is that the conduct (whatever it may be) is done with the required culpability to effect the *result* the Legislature has specified.

On original submission the panel stated that even if the trial court erred in refusing appellant's request, no harm was apparent because appellant made "what amounted to a confession on the witness stand." The panel then cited other evidence, presumably from which the jury could have inferred scienter on the part of appellant.

Our reading of the record, however, discloses the appellant steadfastly denied through the trial that she knew the water was hot enough to cause burning as serious bodily injury is defined, even though she admitted she was angry at the child for resisting his bath and refusing to disrobe, and placed him, fully clothed, into the water, without first testing it. In other words, the issue of appellant's mental culpability was contested.

But the court's charge permitted the jury to convict appellant if they found she knowingly or intentionally placed the child in "a tub of hot water," without requiring a finding that she intended or knew serious bodily injury would result.

No matter how incredible appellant's defense may have appeared to the panel, the accused was entitled to have the jury properly instructed on all matters affecting that defense. And in view of her specially requested instructions, the trial court's failure to limit its

---

5. Thus, under the rationale of the panel—that the pertinent culpable mental state goes to the "nature of conduct"— neither "recklessly" or "with criminal negligence" could be utilized.

charge on the applicable culpable mental states to those appropriate to this case, constituted reversible error.

Accordingly, this cause is reversed and remanded to the trial court.

ONION, P.J., and W.C. DAVIS and McCORMICK, JJ., dissent.

Notes and Questions

1. On retrial, should the defendant be convicted? Has the state proven beyond a reasonable doubt that she acted with the state of mind required by the crime charged as construed by the appellate court? Under the statute, either recklessness or negligence is a sufficient level of culpability, but since the state in this case pleaded that the defendant acted either knowingly or intentionally it was precluded from relying on either of these levels of culpability. If negligence is sufficient, has the state met its burden of proof? If recklessness is sufficient?

2. Would the analysis have been easier if Section 6.02 of the Texas Penal Code had used the language of Section 2.02(4) of the Model Penal Code?

3. In 1976, Orlando Letelier, the former Chilean Ambassador to the United States, and Ronni Moffitt, an American associate, were mortally wounded when a bomb attached to the car in which they were riding in Washington, D.C. was detonated by remote control. The defendants were convicted of, among other things, the first degree murder of each. On appeal, they contended that the conviction for the murder of Moffitt had to be reversed because of a lack of evidence that they intended to kill her. The appellate court rejected this claim on the basis of the doctrine of "transferred intent". It explained the doctrine by quoting from the 1576 English case of Regina v. Saunders, 2 Plowd. 473, 474a, 75 Eng.Rep. 706, 708:

> [I]t is every man's business to foresee what wrong or mischief may happen from that which he does with an ill-intention, and it shall be no excuse for him to say that he intended to kill another, and not the person killed. (c) For if a man of malice prepense shoots an arrow at another with an intent to kill him, and a person to whom he bore no malice is killed by it, this shall be murder in him for when he shot the arrow he intended to kill, and inasmuch as he directed his instrument of death at one, and thereby has killed another, it shall be the same offence in him as if he had killed the person he aimed at * * *.

United States v. Sampol, 636 F.2d 621, 674 (D.C.Cir.1980). Is this doctrine preserved in Section 2.02 of the Model Penal Code?

4. Under the specific terms of the statute involved in *Alvarado*, negligence is a sufficient level of culpability. The position of the Model Penal Code—and to some extent of Section 6.02(c) of the Texas Penal Code—is that negligence is and ought to be "an exceptional basis of liability." Model Penal Code Comments to § 2.02, 127 (Tent.Draft No. 4, 1955). Why should negligence be an exceptional basis of liability, presumably to be used only where specific and important reasons for reducing the required level of culpability exist? Are there sufficient reasons for regard-

ing the offense created by the statute at issue in *Alvarado* as coming within this exception? Consider the following:

Since negligence involves no *mens rea,* the question is raised as to the advisability of punishing negligent conduct with criminal sanctions. Professor Edwin Keedy responded to this question as follows: "If the defendant, being mistaken as to the material facts, is to be punished because his mistake is one an average man would not make, punishment will sometimes be inflicted *when the criminal mind does not exist.* Such a result is contrary to fundamental principles, and is plainly unjust, for a man should not be held criminal because of lack of intelligence." [10] This argument is persuasive, especially when considered in conjunction with the traditional concepts and goals of criminal punishment.

The concept of criminal punishment is based on one, or a combination, of four theories: deterrence, retribution, rehabilitation and incapacitation.

The deterrence theory of criminal law is based on the hypotheses that the prospective offender knows that he will be punished for any criminal activity, and, therefore, will adjust his behavior to avoid committing a criminal act. This theory rests on the idea of "rational utility," i.e., prospective offenders will weigh the evil of the sanction against the gain of the contemplated crime. However, punishment of a negligent offender in no way implements this theory, since the negligent harm-doer is, by definition, unaware of the risk he imposes on society. It is questionable whether holding an individual criminally liable for acts the risks of which he has failed to perceive will deter him from failing to perceive in the future.

The often-criticized retributive theory of criminal law presupposes a "moral guilt," which justifies society in seeking its revenge against the offender. This "moral guilt" is ascribed to those forms of conduct which society deems threatening to its very existence, such as murder and larceny. However, the negligent harm-doer has not actually committed this type of morally reprehensible act, but has merely made an error in judgment. This type of error is an everyday occurrence, although it may deviate from a normal standard of care. Nevertheless, such conduct does not approach the moral turpitude against which the criminal law should seek revenge. It is difficult to comprehend how retribution requires such mistakes to be criminally punished.

It is also doubtful whether the negligent offender can be rehabilitated in any way by criminal punishment. Rehabilitation presupposes a "warped sense of values" which can be corrected. Since inadvertence, and not a deficient sense of values, has caused the "crime," there appears to be nothing to rehabilitate.

The underlying goal of the incapacitation theory is to protect society by isolating an individual so as to prevent him from perpetrating a similar crime in the future. However, this approach is only

---

10. Keedy, Ignorance and Mistake in the Criminal Law, 22 Harv.L.Rev. 75, 84 (1908) (Emphasis added.)

justifiable if less stringent methods will not further the same goal of protecting society. For example, an insane individual would not be criminally incarcerated, if the less stringent means of medical treatment would afford the same societal protection. Likewise, with a criminally negligent individual, the appropriate remedy is not incarceration, but "to exclude him from the activity in which he is a danger."

The conclusion drawn from this analysis is that there appears to be no reasonable justification for punishing negligence as a criminal act under any of these four theories. It does not further the purposes of deterrence, retribution, rehabilitation or incapacitation; hence, there is no rational basis for the imposition of criminal liability on negligent conduct.

This view, favoring exclusion of negligence from the criminal law, is not without support. The chief exponent of this position is Professor Jerome Hall, who maintains that there are persuasive historical, ethical and scientific reasons to support the exclusionary argument.[16]

Hall's historical ground rests upon a continuing trend toward restricting criminal negligence in many Anglo-American legal systems. In addition, the same trend can be noted in civil law systems, where negligence is not criminally punishable absent a specific provision to that effect. Such provisions are very few. While Hall recognizes that history is often a dubious ground upon which to support a thesis, he argues that a long and sustained movement, such as that limiting the applicability of criminal negligence, places the burden of retention upon the proponents of penalization. This burden, Hall maintains, has not been carried.

Professor Hall's ethical argument is based on the premise that, throughout the long history of ethics, the essence of fault has been voluntary harm-doing. He maintains that this requirement of voluntary action becomes even more persuasive in the penal law, because no one should be criminally punished unless he has clearly acted immorally, by voluntarily harming someone. Negligence, of course, cannot be classified as voluntary harm-doing. Therefore, no fault is involved and accordingly no punishment is justified.

In addition, Hall suggests scientific arguments for the exclusion of negligence from penal liability. One contention is that the incorporation of negligence into the penal law imposes an impossible function on judges, namely, to determine whether a person, about whom very little is known, had the competence and sensitivity to appreciate certain dangers in a particular situation when the facts plainly indicate that he did not exhibit that competence. Also, Hall maintains that "the inclusion of negligence bars the discovery of a scientific theory of penal law, i.e., a system of propositions interrelating variables that have a realistic foundation in fact and values."

16. Hall, Negligent Behavior Should be Excluded from Penal Liability, 63 Colum.L. Rev. 632 (1963).

Comment, Is Criminal Negligence A Defensible Basis for Penal Liability?, 16 Buffalo L.Rev. 749, 750–52 (1967).* See also Fletcher, The Theory of Criminal Negligence: A Comparative Analysis, 119 U.Pa.L.Rev. 401 (1971); Note, Negligence and the General Problem of Criminal Liability, 81 Yale L.J. 949 (1972).

C. STATE OF MIND BEYOND "GENERAL INTENT"

Editors' Introduction: "Specific Intents"

Once it is determined what if any state of mind is required by a crime concerning those matters that are themselves elements of the offense, it is useful to address whether an additional mental state must be proved for guilt to be established. In the terms proposed for convenient usage in the introduction to Section A of this Chapter, these mental states would be identified as "specific intents." Again, however, it is important to note that this use of the term does not coincide with the manner in which some courts define "general" and "specific" intents.

At this point, it may be useful to reconsider the formula presented in Chapter IV at page 157, supra, as an aid in visualizing the framework of analysis described in that chapter. As presented at that point, the formula oversimplifies the state of mind issues that may arise in determining the requirements imposed by a particular offense. A more refined and complete formula would be:

$$\left[\left(\text{act} + \frac{\text{mental}}{\text{state}}\right) \xrightarrow{\text{causation}} \left(\text{result} + \frac{\text{mental}}{\text{state}}\right)\right] +$$

$$\left(\frac{\text{attendant}}{\text{circumstances}} + \frac{\text{mental}}{\text{state}}\right) + \frac{\text{specific}}{\text{intent}} = \text{Liability}$$

The first subsection that follows addresses the extent to which the prosecution is required, in particular situations, to prove that the accused was aware of the law defining the offense. In the second, attention is turned to the states of mind required by the traditional property crimes—the intent to permanently deprive the owner of the property at issue.

Notes and Questions

Consider the following offenses in the Texas Penal Code. What reasons might be urged in support of the decisions as to the state of mind requirements of these offenses?

§ 38.13. Hindering Proceedings by Disorderly Conduct

(a) A person commits an offense if he intentionally hinders an official proceeding by noise or violent or tumultuous behavior or disturbance.

* Copyright © 1967 by Buffalo Law Review. Reprinted with permission.

(b) A person commits an offense if he recklessly hinders an official proceeding by noise or violent or tumultuous behavior or disturbance and continues after explicit official request to desist.

(c) An offense under this section is a Class A misdemeanor.

§ 42.05. Disrupting Meeting or Procession

(a) A person commits an offense if, with intent to prevent or disrupt a lawful meeting, procession, or gathering, he obstructs or interferes with the meeting, procession, or gathering by physical action or verbal utterance.

(b) An offense under this section is a Class B misdemeanor.

1. What is the difference between the state of mind required for conviction under § 38.13(a) and that required for conviction under § 38.13(b)? Inasmuch as the punishment is the same for violations of either subsection) what function, if any, is served by the different levels of culpability?

2. In a prosecution under § 38.13(b) should the state be required to plead and prove that the defendant had any state of mind with respect to the notice to desist? Or should it be sufficient that it proves that the required "explicit official request" was made? Why?

3. In a prosecution under § 38.13 should the state be required to plead and prove that the defendant had any state of mind with respect to the circumstance that this was an "official proceeding"? Or should it be sufficient that the existence of that required circumstance is proven? Is § 42.05 relevant to the decision?

1. AWARENESS OF THE LAW CREATING AND DEFINING THE OFFENSE

Generally speaking, the prosecution in a criminal case need not prove that the defendant was aware of the existence and meaning of the statute or case law creating and defining the offense at issue. But in some situations this may be necessary. As the first principal case in this subsection suggests, proof relating to the defendant's awareness of this "law," or at least relating to the likelihood that the defendant was aware of it, may be constitutionally required for conviction.

LAMBERT v. CALIFORNIA

Supreme Court of the United States, 1957.
355 U.S. 225, 78 S.Ct. 240, 2 L.Ed.2d 228.

MR. JUSTICE DOUGLAS delivered the opinion of the Court.

Section 52.38(a) of the Los Angeles Municipal Code defines "convicted person" as follows:

"Any person who, subsequent to January 1, 1921, has been or hereafter is convicted of an offense punishable as a felony in the State of California, or who has been or who is hereafter convicted of any offense in any place other than the State of California, which offense, if committed in the State of California, would have been punishable as a felony."

Section 52.39 provides that it shall be unlawful for "any convicted person" to be or remain in Los Angeles for a period of more than five days without registering; it requires any person having a place of abode outside the city to register if he comes into the city on five occasions or more during a 30-day period; and it prescribes the information to be furnished the Chief of Police on registering.

Section 52.43(b) makes the failure to register a continuing offense, each day's failure constituting a separate offense.

Appellant, arrested on suspicion of another offense, was charged with a violation of this registration law. The evidence showed that she had been at the time of her arrest a resident of Los Angeles for over seven years. Within that period she had been convicted in Los Angeles of the crime of forgery, an offense which California punishes as a felony. Though convicted of a crime punishable as a felony, she had not at the time of her arrest registered under the Municipal Code. At the trial, appellant asserted that § 52.39 of the Code denies her due process of law and other rights under the Federal Constitution, unnecessary to enumerate. The trial court denied this objection. The case was tried to a jury which found appellant guilty. The court fined her $250 and placed her on probation for three years. Appellant, renewing her constitutional objection, moved for arrest of judgment and a new trial. This motion was denied. On appeal the constitutionality of the Code was again challenged. The Appellate Department of the Superior Court affirmed the judgment, holding there was no merit to the claim that the ordinance was unconstitutional. The case is here on appeal. * * * The case having been argued and reargued, we now hold that the registration provisions of the Code as sought to be applied here violate the Due Process requirement of the Fourteenth Amendment.

The registration provision, carrying criminal penalties, applies if a person has been convicted "of an offense punishable as a felony in the State of California" or, in case he has been convicted in another State, if the offense "would have been punishable as a felony" had it been committed in California. No element of willfulness is by terms included in the ordinance nor read into it by the California court as a condition necessary for a conviction.

We must assume that appellant had no actual knowledge of the requirement that she register under this ordinance, as she offered proof of this defense which was refused. The question is whether a registration act of this character violates due process where it is applied to a person who has no actual knowledge of his duty to register, and where no showing is made of the probability of such knowledge.

We do not go with Blackstone in saying that "a vicious will" is necessary to constitute a crime, 4 Bl.Comm. 21, for conduct alone without regard to the intent of the doer is often sufficient. There is wide latitude in the lawmakers to declare an offense and to exclude elements of knowledge and diligence from its definition. * * * But we deal here with conduct that is wholly passive—mere failure to register. It is unlike the commission of acts, or the failure to act under circumstances that should alert the doer to the consequences of his deed. * * * The rule that "ignorance of the law will not excuse" is deep in our law, as is the principle that of all the powers of local government, the police power is "one of the least limitable." District of Columbia v. Brooke, 214 U.S. 138, 149, 29 S.Ct. 560, 563, 53 L.Ed. 941. On the other hand, due process places some limits on its exercise. Engrained in our concept of due process is the requirement of notice. Notice is sometimes essential so that the citizen has the chance to defend charges. Notice is required before property interests are disturbed, before assessments are made, before penalties are assessed. Notice is required in a myriad of situations where a penalty or forfeiture might be suffered for mere failure to act. [citations omitted] These cases involved only property interests in civil litigation. But the principle is equally appropriate where a person, wholly passive and unaware of any wrongdoing, is brought to the bar of justice for condemnation in a criminal case.

Registration laws are common and their range is wide. * * * Many such laws are akin to licensing statutes in that they pertain to the regulation of business activities. But the present ordinance is entirely different. Violation of its provisions is unaccompanied by any activity whatever, mere presence in the city being the test. Moreover, circumstances which might move one to inquire as to the necessity of registration are completely lacking. At most the ordinance is but a law enforcement technique designed for the convenience of law enforcement agencies through which a list of the names and addresses of felons then residing in a given community is compiled. The disclosure is merely a compilation of former convictions already publicly recorded in the jurisdiction where obtained. Nevertheless, this appellant on first becoming aware of her duty to register was given no opportunity to comply with the law and avoid its penalty, even though her default was entirely innocent. She could but suffer the consequences of the ordinance, namely, conviction with the imposition of heavy criminal penalties thereunder. We believe that actual knowledge of the duty to register or proof of the probability of such knowledge and subsequent failure to comply are necessary before a conviction under the ordinance can stand. As Holmes wrote in The Common Law, "A law which punished conduct which would not be blameworthy in the average member of the community would be too severe for that community to bear." Id., at 50. Its severity lies in the absence of an opportunity either to avoid the consequences of the law or to defend any prosecution brought under it. Where a person did not know of the duty to register and where there was no proof of the probability of such knowledge, he may not be convicted consistently with due process. Were it otherwise, the evil would be as great as it is when the law is written in print too fine to read or in a language foreign to the community.

MR. JUSTICE BURTON, dissents because he believes that, as applied to this appellant, the ordinance does not violate her constitutional rights.

MR. JUSTICE FRANKFURTER, whom MR. JUSTICE HARLAN and MR. JUSTICE WHITTAKER join, dissenting.

The present laws of the United States and of the forty-eight States are thick with provisions that command that some things not be done and others be done, although persons convicted under such provisions may have had no awareness of what the law required or that what they did was wrongdoing. The body of decisions sustaining such legislation, including innumerable registration laws, is almost as voluminous as the legislation itself. The matter is summarized in United States v. Balint, 258 U.S. 250, 252, 42 S.Ct. 301, 302, 66 L.Ed. 604: "Many instances of this are to be found in regulatory measures in the exercise of what is called the police power where the emphasis of the statute is evidently upon achievement of some social betterment rather than the punishment of the crimes as in cases of *mala in se*."

Surely there can hardly be a difference as a matter of fairness, of hardship, or of justice, if one may invoke it, between the case of a person wholly innocent of wrongdoing, in the sense that he was not remotely conscious of violating any law, who is imprisoned for five years for conduct relating to narcotics, and the case of another person who is placed on probation for three years on condition that she pay $250, for failure, as a local resident, convicted under local law of a felony, to register under a law passed as an exercise of the State's "police power." Considerations of hardship often lead courts, naturally enough, to attribute to a statute the requirement of a certain mental element—some consciousness of wrongdoing and knowledge of the law's command—as a matter of statutory construction. Then, too, a cruelly disproportionate relation between what the law requires and the sanction for its disobedience may constitute a violation of the Eighth Amendment as a cruel and unusual punishment, and, in respect to the States, even offend the Due Process Clause of the Fourteenth Amendment.

But what the Court here does is to draw a constitutional line between a State's requirement of doing and not doing. What is this but a return to Year Book distinctions between feasance and nonfeasance— a distinction that may have significance in the evolution of common-law notions of liability, but is inadmissible as a line between constitutionality and unconstitutionality. * * *

If the generalization that underlies, and alone can justify, this decision were to be given its relevant scope, a whole volume of the United States Reports would be required to document in detail the legislation in this country that would fall or be impaired. I abstain from entering upon a consideration of such legislation, and adjudications upon it, because I feel confident that the present decision will turn out to be an isolated deviation from the strong current of precedents—a derelict on the waters of the law. Accordingly, I content myself with dissenting.

Note

The response of the California courts to the United States Supreme Court's decision was to grant a new trial. Mrs. Lambert sought a writ of prohibition enjoining such retrial, primarily on the ground that the Supreme Court decision held that the ordinance was invalid. The trial court refused to issue the writ and this was first reversed by the District Court of Appeal. Lambert v. Municipal Court, 174 Cal.App.2d 601, 345 P.2d 98 (1959). Upon rehearing, however, the District Court of Appeal vacated its initial opinion and order and affirmed. Lambert v. Municipal Court, 343 P.2d 81 (Cal.App.1959). In the second opinion the court noted that the prosecution's brief asserted that the records established that Mrs. Lambert was advised by a deputy probation officer to register with the Los Angeles Police Department in accordance with the city's regulation. On appeal to the California Supreme Court, the judgment of the District Court of Appeal was reversed and the trial court was ordered to issue the writ on the authority of another case holding such municipal ordinances void as encroaching upon an area preempted by state legislation. Lambert v. Municipal Court, 53 Cal.2d 690, 3 Cal.Rptr. 168, 349 P.2d 984 (1960).

LIPAROTA v. UNITED STATES

Supreme Court of the United States, 1985.
471 U.S. 419, 105 S.Ct. 2084, 85 L.Ed.2d 434.

JUSTICE BRENNAN delivered the opinion of the Court.

The federal statute governing food stamp fraud provides that "whoever knowingly uses, transfers, acquires, alters, or possesses coupons or authorization cards in any manner not authorized by [the statute] or the regulations" is subject to a fine and imprisonment. 7 U.S.C. § 2024(b). The question presented is whether in a prosecution under this provision the Government must prove that the defendant knew that he was acting in a manner not authorized by statute or regulations.

I

Petitioner Frank Liparota was the co-owner with his brother of Moon's Sandwich Shop in Chicago, Illinois. He was indicted for acquiring and possessing food stamps in violation of § 2024(b). The Department of Agriculture had not authorized petitioner's restaurant to accept food stamps. At trial, the Government proved that petitioner on three occasions purchased food stamps from an undercover Department of Agriculture agent for substantially less than their face value. On the first occasion, the agent informed petitioner that she had $195 worth of food stamps to sell. The agent then accepted petitioner's offer of $150 and consummated the transaction in a back room of the restaurant with petitioner's brother. A similar transaction occurred one week later, in which the agent sold $500 worth of coupons for $350. Approximately one month later, petitioner bought $500 worth of food stamps from the agent for $300.

In submitting the case to the jury, the District Court rejected petitioner's proposed "specific intent" instruction, which would have instructed the jury that the Government must prove that "the defendant knowingly did an act which the law forbids, purposely intending to violate the law." Concluding that "[t]his is not a specific intent crime" but rather a "knowledge case," the District Court instead instructed the jury as follows:

"When the word 'knowingly' is used in these instructions, it means that the Defendant realized what he was doing, and was aware of the nature of his conduct, and did not act through ignorance, mistake, or accident. Knowledge may be proved by defendant's conduct and by all of the facts and circumstances surrounding the case."

The District Court also instructed that the Government had to prove that "the Defendant acquired and possessed food stamp coupons for cash in a manner not authorized by federal statute or regulations" and that "the Defendant knowingly and wilfully acquired the food stamps." Petitioner objected that this instruction required the jury to find merely that he knew that he was acquiring or possessing food stamps; he argued that the statute should be construed instead to reach only "people who knew that they were acting unlawfully." The judge did not alter or supplement his instructions, and the jury returned a verdict of guilty.

Petitioner appealed his conviction to the Court of Appeals for the Seventh Circuit. * * * The Court of Appeals rejected petitioner's arguments. * * * We reverse.

II

The controversy between the parties concerns the mental state, if any, that the Government must show in proving that petitioner acted "in any manner not authorized by [the statute] or the regulations." The Government argues that petitioner violated the statute if he knew that he acquired or possessed food stamps and if in fact that acquisition or possession was in a manner not authorized by statute or regulations. According to the Government, no *mens rea,* or "evil-meaning mind," *Morissette v. United States,* 342 U.S. 246, 251, 72 S.Ct. 240, 244, 96 L.Ed. 288 (1952), is necessary for conviction. Petitioner claims that the Government's interpretation, by dispensing with *mens rea,* dispenses with the only morally blameworthy element in the definition of the crime. To avoid this allegedly untoward result, he claims that an individual violates the statute if he knows that he has acquired or possessed food stamps *and* if he also knows that he has done so in an unauthorized manner. Our task is to determine which meaning Congress intended.

The definition of the elements of a criminal offense is entrusted to the legislature, particularly in the case of federal crimes, which are solely creatures of statute. *United States v. Hudson,* 7 Cranch 32, 3

L.Ed. 259 (1812).[6] With respect to the element at issue in this case, however, Congress has not explicitly spelled out the mental state required. Although Congress certainly intended by use of the word "knowingly" to require *some* mental state with respect to *some* element of the crime defined in § 2024(b), the interpretations proffered by both parties accord with congressional intent to this extent. Beyond this, the words themselves provide little guidance. Either interpretation would accord with ordinary usage.[7] The legislative history of the statute contains nothing that would clarify the congressional purpose on this point.

Absent indication of contrary purpose in the language or legislative history of the statute, we believe that § 2024(b) requires a showing that the defendant knew his conduct to be unauthorized by statute or regulations. "The contention that an injury can amount to a crime only when inflicted by intention is no provincial or transient notion. It is as universal and persistent in mature systems of law as belief in freedom of the human will and a consequent ability and duty of the normal individual to choose between good and evil." *Morissette v. United States, supra,* 342 U.S., at 250, 72 S.Ct., at 243. Thus, in *United States v. United States Gypsum Co.,* 438 U.S. 422, 438, 98 S.Ct. 2864, 2874, 57 L.Ed.2d 854 (1978), we noted that "[c]ertainly far more than the simple omission of the appropriate phrase from the statutory definition is necessary to justify dispensing with an intent requirement" and that criminal offenses requiring no *mens rea* have a "generally disfavored status." Similarly, in this case, the failure of Congress explicitly and unambiguously to indicate whether *mens rea* is required does not signal a departure from this background assumption of our criminal law.

This construction is particularly appropriate where, as here, to interpret the statute otherwise would be to criminalize a broad range of apparently innocent conduct. For instance, § 2024(b) declares it criminal to use, transfer, acquire, alter, or possess food stamps in any manner not authorized by statute or regulations. The statute provides further that "[c]oupons issued to eligible households shall be used by them only to purchase food in retail food stores which have been

---

6. Of course, Congress must act within any applicable constitutional constraints in defining criminal offenses. In this case, there is no allegation that the statute would be unconstitutional under either interpretation.

7. One treatise has aptly summed up the ambiguity in an analogous situation:

"Still further difficulty arises from the ambiguity which frequently exists concerning what the words or phrases in question modify. What, for instance, does 'knowingly' modify in a sentence from a 'blue sky' law criminal statute punishing one who 'knowingly sells a security without a permit' from the securities commissioner? To be guilty must the seller of a security without a permit know only that what he is doing constitutes a sale, or must he also know that the thing he sells is a security, or must he also know that he has no permit to sell the security he sells? As a matter of grammar the statute is ambiguous; it is not at all clear how far down the sentence the word 'knowingly' is intended to travel—whether it modifies 'sells,' or 'sells a security,' or 'sells a security without a permit.' " W. LaFave & A. Scott, Criminal Law § 27 (1972).

approved for participation in the food stamp program *at prices prevail-ing in such stores.*" 7 U.S.C. § 2016(b). This seems to be the *only* authorized use. A strict reading of the statute with no knowledge of illegality requirement would thus render criminal a food stamp recipi-ent who, for example, used stamps to purchase food from a store that, unknown to him, charged higher than normal prices to food stamp program participants. Such a reading would also render criminal a nonrecipient of food stamps who "possessed" stamps because he was mistakenly sent them through the mail due to administrative error, "altered" them by tearing them up, and "transferred" them by throw-ing them away. Of course, Congress *could* have intended that this broad range of conduct be made illegal, perhaps with the understanding that prosecutors would exercise their discretion to avoid such harsh results. However, given the paucity of material suggesting that Con-gress did so intend, we are reluctant to adopt such a sweeping interpre-tation.

In addition, requiring *mens rea* is in keeping with our longstanding recognition of the principle that "ambiguity concerning the ambit of criminal statutes should be resolved in favor of lenity." *Rewis v. United States,* 401 U.S. 808, 812, 91 S.Ct. 1056, 1059, 28 L.Ed.2d 493 (1971). Application of the rule of lenity ensures that criminal statutes will provide fair warning concerning conduct rendered illegal and strikes the appropriate balance between the legislature, the prosecutor and the court in defining criminal liability. * * * Although the rule of lenity is not to be applied where to do so would conflict with the implied or expressed intent of Congress, it provides a time-honored interpretive guideline when the congressional purpose is unclear. In the instant case, the rule directly supports petitioner's contention that the Government must prove knowledge of illegality to convict him under § 2024(b).

* * *

The Government advances two additional arguments in support of its reading of the statute. First, the Government contends that this Court's decision last Term in *United States v. Yermian,* 468 U.S. ___, 104 S.Ct. 2936, 82 L.Ed.2d 53 (1984), supports its interpretation. *Yermi-an* involved a prosecution for violation of the federal false statement statute, 18 U.S.C. § 1001. All parties agreed that the statute required proof at least that the defendant "knowingly and willfully" made a false statement. Thus, unlike the instant case, all parties in *Yermian* agreed that the Government had to prove the defendant's *mens rea.* The controversy in *Yermian* centered on whether the Government also had to prove that the defendant knew that the false statement was made in a matter within the jurisdiction of a federal agency. With respect to this element, although the Court held that the Government did not have to prove actual knowledge of federal agency jurisdiction, the Court explicitly reserved the question whether *some* culpability was necessary with respect even to the jurisdictional element. 468 U.S., at ___, n. 14, 104 S.Ct., at 2943, n. 14. In contrast, the Government in the instant case argues that *no mens rea* is required with respect to any element of the crime. Finally, *Yermian* found that the statutory language was unambiguous and that the legislative history supported its interpretation. The statute at issue in this case differs in both respects.

Second, the Government contends that the § 2024(b) offense is a "public welfare" offense, which the Court defined in *United States v. Morissette,* 342 U.S., at 252–253, 72 S.Ct., at 244–245, to "depend on no mental element but consist only of forbidden acts or omissions." Yet the offense at issue here differs substantially from those "public welfare offenses" we have previously recognized. In most previous instances, Congress has rendered criminal a type of conduct that a reasonable person should know is subject to stringent public regulation and may seriously threaten the community's health or safety. Thus, in *United States v. Freed,* 401 U.S. 601, 91 S.Ct. 1112, 28 L.Ed.2d 356 (1971), we examined the federal statute making it illegal to receive or possess an unregistered firearm. In holding that the Government did not have to prove that the recipient of unregistered hand grenades knew that they were unregistered, we noted that "one would hardly be surprised to learn that possession of hand grenades is not an innocent act." *Id.,* at 609, 91 S.Ct., at 1118. Similarly, in *United States v. Dotterweich,* 320 U.S. 277, 284, 64 S.Ct. 134, 138, 88 L.Ed. 48 (1943), the Court held that a corporate officer could violate the Food and Drug Act when his firm shipped adulterated and misbranded drugs, even "though consciousness of wrongdoing be totally wanting." The distinctions between these cases and the instant case are clear. A food stamp can hardly be compared to a hand grenade, see *Freed,* nor can the unauthorized acquisition or possession of food stamps be compared to the selling of adulterated drugs, as in *Dotterweich.*

III

We hold that in a prosecution for violation of § 2024(b), the Government must prove that the defendant knew that his acquisition or possession of food stamps was in a manner unauthorized by statute or regulations. This holding does not put an unduly heavy burden on the Government in prosecuting violators of § 2024(b). To prove that petitioner knew that his acquisition or possession of food stamps was unauthorized, for example, the Government need not show that he had knowledge of specific regulations governing food stamp acquisition or possession. Nor must the Government introduce any extraordinary evidence that would conclusively demonstrate petitioner's state of mind. Rather, as in any other criminal prosecution requiring *mens rea,* the Government may prove by reference to facts and circumstances surrounding the case that petitioner knew that his conduct was unauthorized or illegal.[17]

17. In this case, for instance, the Government introduced evidence that petitioner bought food stamps at a substantial dis- count from face value and that he conducted part of the transaction in a back room of his restaurant to avoid the pres-

Reversed.

JUSTICE POWELL took no part in the consideration or decision of this case.

JUSTICE WHITE, with whom THE CHIEF JUSTICE joins, dissenting.

Forsaking reliance on either the language or the history of § 2024(b), the majority bases its result on the absence of an explicit rejection of the general principle that criminal liability requires not only an *actus reus,* but a *mens rea.* In my view, the result below is in fact supported by the statute's language and its history, and it is the majority that has ignored general principles of criminal liability.

I

The Court views the statutory problem here as being how far down the sentence the term "knowingly" travels. Accepting for the moment that if "knowingly" does extend to the "in any manner" language today's holding would be correct—a position with which I take issue below—I doubt that it gets that far. The "in any manner" language is separated from the litany of verbs to which "knowingly" is directly connected by the intervening nouns. We considered an identically phrased statute last Term in *United States v. Yermian,* 468 U.S. __, 104 S.Ct. 2936, 82 L.Ed.2d 53 (1984). The predecessor to the statute at issue in that case provided: " '[W]hoever shall knowingly and willfully * * * make * * * any false or fraudulent statements or representations * * * in any matter within the jurisdiction of any department or agency of the United States * * * shall be fined.' " *Id.,* at __, n. 6, 104 S.Ct., at 2940, n. 6. We found that under the "most natural reading" of the statute, "knowingly and willfully" applied only to the making of false or fraudulent statements and not to the fact of jurisdiction. 468 U.S., at __, n. 6, 104 S.Ct., at 2940, n. 6. By the same token, the "most natural reading" of § 2024(b) is that knowingly modifies only the verbs to which it is attached.

In any event, I think that the premise of this approach is mistaken. Even accepting that "knowingly" does extend through the sentence, or at least that we should read § 2024(b) as if it does, the statute does not mean what the Court says it does. Rather, it requires only that the defendant be aware of the relevant aspects of his conduct. A requirement that the defendant know that he is acting in a particular manner, coupled with the fact that that manner is forbidden, does not establish a defense of ignorance of the law. It creates only a defense of ignorance or mistake of fact. Knowingly to do something that is unauthorized by law is not the same as doing something knowing that it is unauthorized by law.

ence of the other patrons. Moreover, the Government asserts that food stamps themselves are stamped "nontransferable." Brief for United States 34. A jury could have inferred from this evidence that petitioner knew that his acquisition and possession of the stamps was unauthorized.

This point is demonstrated by the hypothetical statute referred to by the majority, which punishes one who "knowingly sells a security without a permit." See *ante*, at 2088, n. 7. Even if "knowingly" does reach "without a permit," I would think that a defendant who knew that he did not have a permit, though not that a permit was required, could be convicted.

Section 2024(b) is an identical statute, except that instead of detailing the various legal requirements, it incorporates them by proscribing use of coupons "in any manner not authorized" by law. This shorthand approach to drafting does not transform knowledge of illegality into an element of the crime. * * *

The Court's opinion provides another illustration of the general point: someone who used food stamps to purchase groceries at inflated prices without realizing he was overcharged. I agree that such a person may not be convicted, but not for the reason given by the majority. The purchaser did not "knowingly" use the stamps in the proscribed manner, for he was unaware of the circumstances of the transaction that made it illegal.

The majority and I would part company in result as well as rationale if the purchaser knew he was charged higher than normal prices but not that overcharging is prohibited. In such a case, he would have been aware of the nature of his actions, and therefore the purchase would have been "knowing." I would hold that such a mental state satisfies the statute. Under the Court's holding, as I understand it, that person could not be convicted because he did not know that his conduct was illegal.[3]

* * *

II

The broad principles of the Court's opinion are easy to live with in a case such as this. But the application of its reasoning might not always be so benign. For example, § 2024(b) is little different from the basic federal prohibition on the manufacture and distribution of controlled substances. 21 U.S.C. § 841(a) provides:

"Except as authorized by this subchapter, it shall be unlawful for any person knowingly or intentionally—

3. The appropriate prosecutorial target in such a situation would of course be the seller rather than the purchaser. I have no doubt that every prosecutor in the country would agree. The discussion of this hypothetical is wholly academic.

For similar reasons, I am unmoved by the spectre of criminal liability for someone who is mistakenly mailed food stamps and throws them out, see *ante*, at 2088–2089, and do not think the hypothetical offers much of a guide to congressional intent. We should proceed on the assumption that Congress had in mind the run-of-the-mill situation, not its most bizarre mutation. Arguments that presume wildly unreasonable conduct by government officials are by their nature unconvincing, and reliance on them is likely to do more harm than good. No rule, including that adopted by the Court today, is immune from such contrived defects.

"(1) to manufacture, distribute, or dispense, or possess with intent to manufacture, distribute or dispense, a controlled substance. * * *"

I am sure that the members of the majority would agree that a defendant charged under this provision could not defend on the ground that he did not realize his manufacture was unauthorized or that the particular substance was controlled. See *United States v. Balint*, 258 U.S. 250, 42 S.Ct. 301, 66 L.Ed. 604 (1922). On the other hand, it would be a defense if he could prove he thought the substance was something other than what it was. By the same token, I think, someone in petitioner's position should not be heard to say that he did not know his purchase of food stamps was unauthorized, though he may certainly argue that he did not know he was buying food stamps. I would not stretch the term "knowingly" to require awareness of the absence of statutory authority in either of these provisions.

* * *

III

In relying on the "background assumption of our criminal law" that *mens rea* is required, the Court ignores the equally well-founded assumption that ignorance of the law is no excuse. It is "the conventional position that knowledge of the existence, meaning or application of the law determining the elements of an offense is not an element of that offense. * * *" Model Penal Code, at 130.

This Court's prior cases indicate that a statutory requirement of a "knowing violation" does not supersede this principle. For example, under the statute at issue in *United States v. International Minerals & Chemical Corp.*, 402 U.S. 558, 91 S.Ct. 1697, 29 L.Ed.2d 178 (1971), the Interstate Commerce Commission was authorized to promulgate regulations regarding the transportation of corrosive liquids, and it was a crime to "knowingly violat[e] any such regulation." 18 U.S.C. § 834(f) (1970 ed.). Viewing the word "regulations" as "a shorthand designation for specific acts or omissions which violate the Act," 402 U.S., at 562, 91 S.Ct., at 1700, we adhered to the traditional rule that ignorance of the law is not a defense. The violation had to be "knowing" in that the defendant had to know that he was transporting corrosive liquids and not, for example, merely water. *Id.*, at 563–564, 91 S.Ct., at 1700–1701. But there was no requirement that he be aware that he was violating a particular regulation. Similarly, in this case the phrase "in any manner not authorized by" the statute or regulations is a shorthand incorporation of a variety of legal requirements. To be convicted, a defendant must have been aware of what he was doing, but not that it was illegal.

In *Boyce Motor Lines, Inc. v. United States*, 342 U.S. 337, 72 S.Ct. 329, 96 L.Ed. 367 (1952), the Court considered a statute that punished anyone who "knowingly violates" a regulation requiring trucks transporting dangerous items to avoid congested areas where possible. In rejecting a vagueness challenge, the Court read "knowingly" to mean not that the driver had to be aware of the regulation, see *id.*, at 345, 72 S.Ct., at 333 (Jackson, J., dissenting), but that he had to know a safer alternative route was available.   *   *   *

In each of these cases, the statutory language lent itself to the approach adopted today if anything more readily than does § 2024(b).[6] I would read § 2024(b) like those statutes, to require awareness of only the relevant aspects of one's conduct rendering it illegal, not the fact of illegality.   This reading does not abandon the "background assumption" of *mens rea* by creating a strict liability offense,[7] and is consistent with the equally important background assumption that ignorance of the law is not a defense.

IV

I wholly agree that "[t]he contention that an injury can amount to a crime only when inflicted by intention is no provincial or transient notion."   *Morissette v. United States,* 342 U.S. 246, 250, 72 S.Ct. 240, 243, 96 L.Ed. 288 (1952).   But the holding of the court below is not at all inconsistent with that longstanding and important principle.   Petitioner's conduct was intentional; the jury found that petitioner "realized what he was doing, and was aware of the nature of his conduct, and did not act through ignorance, mistake, or accident" (trial court's instructions).   Whether he knew which regulation he violated is beside the point.

2. STATE OF MIND REQUIRED BY THE PROPERTY ACQUISITION OFFENSES

Editors' Introduction: The "Intent to Steal"

The earlier discussion of property crimes in Section C.1. of Chapter V, supra, focused on the significance of some of the intricacies concerning the nature of the property involved, the relationship of the accused

---

6. The Court distinguishes these as "public welfare offense" cases involving inherently dangerous articles of commerce whose users should have assumed were subject to regulation.   But see *United States v. Freed,* 401 U.S., at 612, 91 S.Ct., at 1119 (Brennan, J., concurring in judgment).   Apart from the fact that a reasonable person would also assume food stamps are heavily regulated and not subject to sale and exchange, this distinction is not related to the actual holdings in those cases.   The Court's opinion in *Boyce* and the concurrence in *Freed* do not discuss this consideration.   And the Court's references to the dangerousness of the goods in *International Minerals* were directed to possible due process challenges to convictions without notice of criminality.   402 U.S., at 564–565, 91 S.Ct., at 1701–1702. As today's majority acknowledges, there is no constitutional defect with the holding of

the court below.   The only issue here is one of congressional intent.

7. Under a strict liability statute, a defendant can be convicted even though he was unaware of the circumstances of his conduct that made it illegal.   To take the example of a statute recently before the Court, a regulation forbidding hunting birds in a "baited" field can be read to have a scienter requirement, in which case it would be a defense to prove that one did not know the field was baited, or not, in which case someone hunting in such a field is guilty even if he did not know and could not have known that it was baited.   See *Catlett v. United States,* 471 U.S. ___, 105 S.Ct. 2153, 84 L.Ed.2d ___ (1985) (White, J., dissenting from denial of certiorari).   I do not argue that the latter approach should be taken to this statute, nor would the statutory language allow it.

to the property, and the accused's behavior with respect to the property. It has been strenuously argued that the many fine distinctions concerning the elements of larceny generated by the common law courts were aimed at ensuring that only persons whose conduct manifested their criminality were to be punished. (Another important reason for some of these distinctions was the fact that all theft offenses were capital crimes. A judge faced with an accused whose conduct varied from the paradigm of theft might be reluctant to find the crime had been committed if it would place the defendant in jeopardy of the gallows.) Over the centuries, courts and legislatures have moved from assigning crucial importance to the "act" and "circumstances" elements of these crimes to increasing emphasis on the actor's state of mind. Fletcher, "The Metamorphosis of Larceny", 89 Harv.L.Rev. 469 (1976). An interesting and rewarding exchange between Professors Fletcher and Weinreb concerning the persuasiveness of the historical evidence for these contentions can be found at 90 Yale L.J. 294, 319 (1980).

Whatever the importance of the act requirement in the past, it is clear that today the accused's state of mind is central to a determination of whether conduct is criminal and, if so, at what level. The requisite larcenous intent at common law was the intent to steal. Section 223.0(1) of the Model Penal Code's version of a modern consolidated theft statute proposes retention of the following version of this intent:

> [The purpose] (a) to withhold property of another permanently or for so extended a period as to appropriate a major portion of its economic value, or with intent to restore only upon payment of reward or other compensation; or (b) to dispose of the property so as to make it unlikely that the owner will recover it.

Consolidated theft statutes are commonly written so as to encompass the crimes of embezzlement, and false pretense, as well as larceny and many other property offenses. The state of mind required at common law for embezzlement and false pretense was not the intent to steal but rather that the actor "fraudulently" converts in the case of the former, and "knowingly" misleads with the "intent to defraud" as to the latter. In essence, the embezzler acts on another's property which has been entrusted to her in a manner she knows to be inconsistent with the trust relationship. Under the Model Penal Code Consolidated Theft Statute the requisite state of mind would be the intent to deprive, defined as set forth above, with respect to movable property, and the intent purposely to benefit herself with respect to immovable property. See Section 223.2, reprinted at page 207, supra. The state of mind required by the Model Penal Code for what would have been false pretense at common law is that she purposely obtain the property of another by deception. See Section 223.3, at page 208, supra.

These distinctions, retained even in modern codes, reflect the historical evolution of the various property crimes and continuing recognition of the differences in the nature of the interests protected by these prohibitions. One who purposely lies to inveigle another into the transfer of an interest in property may easily be thought to have given an adequate signal of criminality without regard to the actor's intent regarding that property. In contrast, the exercise of control over the property of another, whether or not that property is lawfully within the actor's possession, is readily susceptible to interpretations other than crime. The requirement that the prosecution establish that the control was exercised with the "intent to deprive" offers reassurance that the actor has been appropriately identified as a fit subject for the criminal sanction.

The various state of mind distinctions are, if anything, even more significant with respect to modern statutes derived more directly from the common law than with regard to those based upon the Model Penal Code model. This is especially true of many property crimes found in the United States Code, inasmuch as recent efforts to modernize the language, definitions, and design of the federal criminal laws have yet to achieve success.

STATE v. GORDON

Supreme Judicial Court of Maine, 1974.
321 A.2d 352.

[Defendant was convicted by a jury of armed robbery and appeals from this conviction.]

One Edwin Strode, and defendant had escaped in Vermont from the custody of the authorities who had been holding them on a misdemeanor charge. In the escape defendant and Strode had acquired two hand guns and also a blue station wagon in which they had fled from Vermont through New Hampshire into Maine. Near Standish, Maine, the station wagon showed signs of engine trouble, and defendant and Strode began to look for another vehicle. They came to the yard of one Franklin Prout. In the yard was Prout's 1966 maroon Chevelle and defendant, who was operating the station wagon, drove it parallel to the Prout Chevelle. Observing that the keys were in the Chevelle, Strode left the station wagon and entered the Chevelle. At this time Prout came out of his house into the yard. Strode pointed a gun at him, and defendant and Strode then told Prout that they needed his automobile, were going to take it but they "would take care of it and see he [Prout] got it back as soon as possible." With defendant operating the station wagon and Strode the Chevelle, defendant and Strode left the yard and proceeded in the direction of Westbrook. Subsequently, the station wagon was abandoned in a sand pit, and defendant and Strode continued their flight in the Chevelle. A spectacular series of events followed—including the alleged assault (with intent to kill) upon Westbrook police officer, Stultz, a shoot-out on Main Street in Westbrook, and a high speed police chase, during which the Chevelle was driven off the road in the vicinity of the Maine Medical Center in Portland where it was abandoned, Strode and defendant having commandeered another automobile to resume their flight.   Ultimately, both the defendant and Strode were apprehended, defendant having been arrested on the day following the police chase in the vicinity of the State Police Barracks in Scarborough.

* * * [D]efendant maintains that the evidence clearly established that (1) defendant and Strode had told Prout that they "would take care of * * * [the automobile] and see [that] he [Prout] got it back as soon as possible" and (2) defendant intended only a temporary use of Prout's Chevelle.   Defendant argues that the evidence thus fails to warrant a conclusion beyond a reasonable doubt that defendant had the specific intent requisite for "robbery."   (Hereinafter, reference to the "specific intent" necessary for "robbery" signifies the "specific intent" incorporated into "robbery" as embracing "larceny.")

Although defendant is correct that robbery is a crime requiring a particular specific intent,[2] defendant wrongly apprehends its substantive content.

A summarizing statement appearing in defendant's brief most clearly exposes his misconception of the law.   Acknowledging that on all of the evidence the jury could properly

"* * * have inferred * * * that [defendant and Strode] * * * intended to get away from the authorities by going to New York or elsewhere *where they would abandon* the car * * *", (emphasis supplied)

defendant concludes that, nevertheless, the State had failed to prove the necessary specific intent because it is

"* * * entirely irrational to conclude * * * that the defendant himself intended at the time he and Strode took the car, *to keep the car in their possession for any length of time.*"   (emphasis supplied)

Here, defendant reveals that he conceives as an essential element of the specific intent requisite for "robbery" that the wrongdoer must intend: (1) an advantageous relationship between himself and the property wrongfully taken, and (2) that such relationship be permanent rather than temporary.

Defendant's view is erroneous.   The law evaluates the "animus furandi" of "robbery" in terms of the detriment projected to the legally protected interests of the owner rather than the benefits intended to accrue to the wrongdoer from his invasion of the rights of the owner.

* * * [M]any of the earlier decisions reveal language disagreements, as well as conflicts as to substance, concerning whether a

---

2. It is generally required that the necessary specific intent exist simultaneously with the wrongful taking of the property. State v. McKeough, supra, (n. 4, 300 A.2d at p. 757) makes clear that, as noted in State v. Boisvert, Me., 236 A.2d 419 (1967):

"Maine is one of the jurisdictions which has recognized as an exception to the simultaneous intent rule the principle that if the property is taken from the owner against his will, by a trespass or fraud, a *subsequently* formed intent * * * [of the requisite content] will constitute larceny."

defendant can be guilty of "robbery" without specifically intending a gain to himself (whether permanent or temporary), so-called "lucri causa." In the more recent cases, there is overwhelming consensus that "lucri causa" is not necessary. * * *

* * *

We now decide, in confirmatory clarification of the law of Maine, that "lucri causa" is not an essential element of the "animus furandi" of "robbery." [T]he specific intent requisite for "robbery" is defined solely in terms of the injury projected to the interests of the property owner:—specific intent "to deprive permanently the owner of his property."

The instant question thus becomes: on the hypothesis, arguendo, that defendant here actually intended to use the Prout automobile "only temporarily" (as he would need it to achieve a successful flight from the authorities), is defendant correct in his fundamental contention that this, *in itself,* negates, *as a matter of law,* specific intent of defendant to deprive permanently the owner of his property? We answer that defendant's claim is erroneous.

Concretely illustrative of the point that a wrongdoer may intend to use wrongfully taken property "only temporarily" and yet, without contradiction, intend that the owner be deprived of his property permanently is the case of a defendant who proposes to use the property only for a short time and then to destroy it. At the opposite pole, and excluding (as a matter of law) specific intent to deprive permanently the owner of his property, is the case of a defendant who intends to make a temporary use of the property and then by his own act to return the property to its owner. Between these two extremes can lie various situations in which the legal characterization of the wrongdoer's intention, as assessed by the criterion of whether it is a specific intent to deprive permanently the owner of his property, will be more or less clear and raise legal problems of varying difficulty.

In these intermediate situations a general guiding principle may be developed through recognition that a "taking" of property is *by definition* "temporary" only if the possession, or control, effected by the taking is relinquished. Hence, measured by the correct criterion of the impact upon the interests of the owner, the wrongdoer's "animus furandi" is fully explored for its true legal significance only if the investigation of the wrongdoer's state of mind extends beyond his anticipated *retention* of possession and includes an inquiry into his contemplated manner of *relinquishing* possession, or control, of the property wrongfully taken.

On this approach, it has been held that when a defendant takes the tools of another person with intent to use them temporarily and then to leave them wherever it may be that he finishes with his work, the factfinder is justified in the conclusion that defendant had specific intent to deprive the owner permanently of his property. State v. Davis, 38 N.J.L. 176 (1875).

Similarly, it has been decided that a defendant who wrongfully takes the property of another intending to use it for a short time and then to relinquish possession, or control, in a manner leaving to chance whether the owner recovers his property is correctly held specifically to intend that the owner be deprived permanently of his property. State v. Smith, 268 N.C. 167, 150 S.E.2d 194 (1966).

The rationale underlying these decisions is that to negate, as a matter of law, the existence of specific intent to deprive permanently the owner of his property, a wrongful taker of the property of another must have in mind not only that his retention of possession, or control, will be "temporary" but also that when he will relinquish the possession, or control, he will do it in some manner (whatever, particularly, it will be) he regards as having affirmative tendency toward getting the property returned to its owner.[4] In the absence of such thinking by the defendant, his state of mind is fairly characterized as *indifference* should the owner *never* recover his property; and such indifference by a wrongdoer who is the moving force separating an owner from his property is appropriately regarded as his "willingness" that the owner *never* regain his property. In this sense, the wrongdoer may appropriately be held to entertain specific intent that the deprivation to the owner be permanent.

* * *

On this basis, the evidence in the present case clearly presented a jury question as to defendant's specific intent. Although defendant may have stated to the owner, Prout, that defendant

"would take care of * * * [the automobile] and see [that] * * * [Prout] got it back as soon as possible",

defendant himself testified that

"[i]n my mind it was just to get out of the area. * * * Just get out of the area and leave the car and get under cover somewhere."

This idea to "leave the car" and "get under cover somewhere" existed in defendant's mind as part of an uncertainty about where it would happen. Because defendant was " * * * sort of desperate during the whole day", he had not "really formulated any plans about destination."

Such testimony of defendant, together with other evidence that defendant had already utterly abandoned another vehicle (the station wagon) in desperation, plainly warranted a jury conclusion that defendant's facilely uttered statements to Prout were empty words, and it

4. Since we are here dealing with specific intent of the wrongdoer, the legal criterion is in subjective terms: whether or not defendant actually has in his mind the thought of relinquishing possession, or control, of the wrongfully taken property in a manner which will, *as defendant thinks of it,* be an affirmative step toward a recovery of the property by its owner. Whether the manner in which defendant *in fact* relinquishes his possession, or control, has, or has not, a reasonable tendency in all the circumstances (objectively) to assist in a recovery of the property by the owner may be *evidence* of defendant's actual state of mind. Evidence, however, must be distinguished from the ultimate fact legally required to be proved by evidence.

was defendant's true state of mind to use Prout's Chevelle and abandon it in whatever manner might happen to meet the circumstantial exigencies of defendant's predicament—without defendant's having any thought that the relinquishment of the possession was to be in a manner having some affirmative tendency to help in the owner's recovery of his property. On this finding the jury was warranted in a conclusion that defendant was indifferent should the owner, Prout, *never* have back his automobile and, therefore had specific intent that the owner be deprived permanently of his property.

UNITED STATES v. ADAMSON

United States Court of Appeals, Fifth Circuit, Unit B, en banc, 1983.
700 F.2d 953.

R. LANIER ANDERSON, III, CIRCUIT JUDGE:

The appellant, John R. Adamson, III, and three others were indicted under 18 U.S.C.A. §§ 656,[1] 1005, 1014, and 2 (West 1976) in connection with several loans made by the First Augusta Bank and Trust Company. After a jury trial, appellant was convicted of one count of willful misapplication of bank funds in violation of § 656 * * *. A panel of this court affirmed the convictions under §§ 656 and 1014, but reversed the conviction under § 1005. *United States v. Adamson*, 665 F.2d 649 (5th Cir.1982). Rehearing en banc was granted, * * *.

The only issues presented to the en banc court relate to the propriety of the jury instructions under §§ 656 and 1005. We conclude that the jury instructions improperly lowered the mens rea standard under § 656 to mere "recklessness." Consequently, we reverse appellant's conviction on the willful misapplication count under § 656. However, we conclude that the error did not taint the jury charge with respect to § 1005, and therefore we affirm appellant's conviction on that false entry count.

I. FACTS AND POSTURE OF THE ISSUES

This case arises out of a series of events which contributed to the failure of the First Augusta State Bank of Augusta, Georgia. The bank was insured by the Federal Deposit Insurance Corporation. During the times covered by the indictment, appellant Adamson was the president and a director of the bank. He also served as a lending officer and was a member of the bank's Loan and Investment Committee. Two of Adamson's co-defendants, Glenn Bertrand Hester and R. Eugene Holley, also were convicted on both the § 656 count and the § 1005 count. Hester was a major stockholder of the bank, a member of the bank's executive committee, and the attorney for the bank. Holley, a close

---

1. 18 U.S.C.A. § 656 provides in pertinent part:

Whoever, being an officer, director, agent or employee of * * * any Federal Reserve Bank, member bank, national bank or insured bank, * * * willfully misapplies any of the moneys, funds or credits of such bank * * * shall be fined not more than $5,000 or imprisoned not more than five years, or both.
* * *

friend, business associate and law partner of Hester, was also a major borrower from the bank. * * *

The two counts presented to the en banc court involve a substantial loan which appellant Adamson authorized and which ostensibly was made to Island Summit, Inc., a corporation either wholly owned by or under the control of Hester. The actual beneficiaries of the loan were co-defendants Hester and Holley, who signed the note as guarantors. The evidence permitted a finding by the jury that the corporation was inactive and financially unable to repay the loan. Further, the defendants admitted that no one expected the corporation to repay the loan; rather, the loan was made on the strength of the net worth of the actual beneficiaries of the loan, Hester and Holley. At trial, the government's theory of the case was that appellant Adamson authorized a sham loan to a nominal corporate borrower in order to conceal an illegal and potentially unsafe concentration of bank loans to a single debtor. The evidence justified a finding that the loan would have violated the bank's legal aggregate lending and unsecured loan limits if it had been made directly to Holley. The evidence also permitted a finding that the loan was structured in a way which made detection difficult and which tended to deceive the bank and the bank examiners about the true state of affairs. The jury found appellant guilty of willful misapplication of bank funds (§ 656) and a false entry in the bank's records (§ 1005) in connection with this loan.

With respect to § 656, appellant contends that the jury instructions erroneously defined the requisite mental state that the accused must have in order to commit willful misapplication of bank funds. In particular, the appellant objects to the charge that:

> A reckless disregard of the interest of the bank is the equivalent of the intent to injure or defraud the bank.

> * * *

> I charge you that the element of criminal intent necessary for conviction for a willful misapplication of bank funds is not fulfilled by a mere showing of indiscretion or foolhardiness on the part of the bank officer. His conduct must amount to reckless disregard of the bank's interests * * *

> * * *

> The word "willful" is also employed to characterize a thing done without ground for believing it is lawful, or conduct marked by a reckless disregard, whether or not one has the right to so act.

If the proper mens rea for § 656 is knowledge, and if the jury instructions as a whole either equate recklessness with knowledge or substitute recklessness for knowledge, then *Sandstrom v. Montana,* 442 U.S. 510, 99 S.Ct. 2450, 61 L.Ed.2d 39 (1979), compels the conclusion that the charge is erroneous. Neither the government nor the dissenting judges dispute this. *Sandstrom* found error in a charge under which the requisite mens rea was merely presumed. Here there was more than a presumption; the charge actually equated the lesser recklessness mens rea with the higher mens rea of knowledge.

To resolve the issues raised by appellant, we first must determine the appropriate mens rea for a § 656 conviction (Part II). Then we must decide whether the jury instructions as a whole erroneously permitted the jury to apply a lower recklessness mens rea standard to the § 656 count (Part III). * * *

II. Mens Rea for § 656

A. Background

* * * [A] previous Fifth Circuit case, *United States v. Welliver,* 601 F.2d 203 (5th Cir.1979), held that a defendant's reckless disregard for the interests of the bank was sufficient to satisfy the intent requirement of § 656. If the rule as stated in *Welliver* is correct, then the instant charge which permitted a finding of guilt based on a mens rea of recklessness would not be erroneous. * * *

B. The Predecessor Statute

The predecessor to § 656 was 12 U.S.C. § 592 (Rev.Stat. § 5209), which utilized language substantially the same as that of the current statute.[5] The Supreme Court,[6] the Fifth Circuit, and other circuits had held that knowledge or purpose was the required mens rea for the predecessor statute. The legislative history of § 656 makes it clear that no change of substance or meaning was intended. * * *

C. The Positions of Other Circuit Courts of Appeal

The Fifth Circuit's rule permitting a conviction under § 656 based on a reckless disregard of a bank's interest stands alone. Cases in the other circuits uniformly state that knowledge is the proper mens rea standard for § 656.

One of the leading cases in the area is the First Circuit's decision in *United States v. Gens,* 493 F.2d 216 (1st Cir.1974). There the defendant, Gens, helped two other defendants, Porter and Carleton, gain control of a Massachusetts bank. Porter and Carleton were officers and directors of the bank, and Gens was a director. After Gens reached his loan

---

5. The primary difference is the omission in the current statute of the language "with intent to injure or defraud." However, courts almost uniformly have judicially imposed the element of intent to injure or defraud, noting that the legislative history indicates that § 656 was not intended to change the meaning or substance of the preexisting law.

6. *Evans v. United States,* 153 U.S. 584, 592, 594, 14 S.Ct. 934, 938, 38 L.Ed. 830 (1894) ("The criminality really depends upon the question whether there was, at the time of the discount, a *deliberate purpose* on the part of the defendant to defraud the bank of the amount" and "the gravamen of the offense consists in the *evil design* with which the misapplication is made * * *.") (emphasis added); *United States v. Britton,* 108 U.S. 193, 199, 2 S.Ct. 526, 531, 27 L.Ed. 701 (1883) (The defendant's conduct "might be an act of maladministration on the part of the defendant. It might show neglect of official duty, indifference to the interests of the association or breach of trust, and subject the defendant to the severest censure and to removal from office; but to call it a criminal misapplication by him of the moneys and funds of the association would be to stretch the words of this highly penal statute beyond all reasonable limits.").

limit with the bank, he arranged for eight additional loans to other borrowers, who then turned the loan proceeds over to Gens. Among the named borrowers on the eight loans were Gens' business partner and two attorneys who did substantial legal work for Gens. Another loan was made to a neighbor and close friend of Gens who was asked to sign the note alone, in part because Gens had borrowed up to his limit and despite the fact that the proceeds were to be used for a joint investment for the friend and the three defendants. The First Circuit reversed the § 656 convictions of the three defendants, in part because the jury instructions erroneously permitted a finding of guilty if the jury found no more than that the defendants granted loans to named debtors knowing that the proceeds would be turned over to Gens. Noting that a bank official innocently and properly could make loans to a financially capable party, even though the officer may know that the named borrower plans to turn around and lend the proceeds to a third party, the court held that more is required before there is a violation of § 656. The court held that there could be criminal responsibility in three situations: (1) where the bank official *knows* that the named debtor is either fictitious or wholly unaware that his name is being used; (2) where the banker *knows* that the named debtor is financially incapable of repaying the loan whose proceeds are being passed on to a third party; and (3) where the banker assures the named debtor, regardless of his financial capabilities, that the bank would look for repayment only to the third party who actually receives the proceeds. In other words, there must be *knowing participation* in a loan which is de facto to the third party to whom the bank would be unwilling to make a formal loan. *See* 493 F.2d at 221–22. The jury instructions in *Gens* permitted a finding of guilty *merely* upon the jury's finding that the defendant bankers knew that the loan proceeds would be turned over to Gens. Holding that criminal responsibility under § 656 *also* requires *knowledge* that the named borrowers were financially incapable of repaying the loan or *knowing participation* in a deceptive scheme, the court reversed. Thus, with respect to the mens rea issue before us, the *Gens* opinion establishes the First Circuit position as requiring *knowing* participation in a deceptive arrangement.

* * *

[The majority's review of the decisions of other circuits is omitted]

In summary, we believe that a careful reading of the cases from other circuits reveals a uniform rule that the appropriate mens rea standard for § 656 is *knowledge*. The Eighth Circuit has explicitly rejected the lower recklessness standard. The First, Sixth and Ninth Circuits have adopted knowledge as the proper mens rea, expressly placing recklessness in its proper role as evidence from which intent may be inferred. The Second, Third, Fourth and Tenth Circuits have all either stated or held, without discussion, that knowledge is the proper mens rea standard. Further, although imprecise language occasionally has led to confusion, courts generally recognize that the proper role of recklessness is that it may justify an inference of intent to injure or defraud. Such a reading of the case law is buttressed by the government's brief in this case which, after surveying a number of cases, states:

> It is nowhere suggested that "recklessness" is the standard of intent under any element of § 656. Rather, "reckless disregard" has always been used * * * to describe the kind of activity the jury must find from the facts before considering whether to make the permissible inference that such activity demonstrated an intent to injure or defraud the bank.

Brief of Appellee at 13. Thus, by the government's own admission, the Fifth Circuit's rule, as stated in the outline of cases leading up to *Welliver*, is inconsistent with the case law of the other circuits. Moreover, as discussed below, numerous other Fifth Circuit cases cast considerable doubt upon the rule.

D. Previous Fifth Circuit Cases

The *Welliver* Court cited two former Fifth Circuit decisions, *United States v. Wilson*, 500 F.2d 715 (5th Cir.1974), *cert. denied sub nom.*, *White v. United States*, 420 U.S. 977, 95 S.Ct. 1403, 43 L.Ed.2d 658 (1975), and *United States v. Reynolds*, 573 F.2d 242 (5th Cir.1978), to support its holding that recklessness is sufficient to satisfy the intent requirement of § 656. *See United States v. Welliver*, 601 F.2d at 210. Both of the cited cases contain the following language: "[R]eckless disregard of the interest of a bank is, for the purpose of 'willful misapplication,' the equivalent of intent to injure or defraud." Although the evolution of the rule is thus understandable, we now believe that a careful examination of the issues and authorities discussed in *Wilson* and *Reynolds* reveals that we erred when we held in *Welliver* that a jury is properly charged that recklessness is the equivalent of intent to injure or defraud.

* * *

For the reasons discussed above, we conclude that the appropriate mens rea standard for § 656 is knowledge. In order to convict a defendant for willfully misapplying funds with intent to injure or defraud a bank, the government must prove that the defendant *knowingly* participated in a deceptive or fraudulent transaction. The trier of fact may infer the required intent, *i.e.*, knowledge, from the defendant's reckless disregard of the interest of the bank; however, jury instructions should not equate recklessness with intent to injure or defraud.
* * *

III. The § 656 Jury Instructions

Having determined that knowledge is the proper mens rea standard for § 656, we must decide whether the charge in this case erroneously permitted the jury to apply the lower recklessness standard to the element of willful misapplication with intent to defraud. If the jury charge did equate reckless disregard with the required higher standard of knowledge, *Sandstrom v. Montana*, 442 U.S. 510, 99 S.Ct.

2450, 61 L.Ed.2d 39 (1979), mandates a reversal of appellant's § 656 conviction.

Appellant took exception to the jury instructions, asserting that they improperly equated recklessness with the requisite mens rea element of the crime. Appellant pointed specifically to the following charge:

A reckless disregard of the interest of the bank is the equivalent of intent to injure or defraud the bank.

The dissenting judges argue that the instructions considered as a whole fairly and accurately state the law. It is true, of course, that a jury charge must be judged as a whole. * * *

It might be argued that the following three passages from the jury charge properly informed the jury that a higher mens rea than recklessness was required:

"[I]ntent to defraud" means to act with intent to deceive or cheat.

To act with intent to defraud means to act willfully and with a specific intent to deceive or cheat.

I charge you that a thing is done willfully if it is done voluntarily and purposefully and with a specific intent to fail to do what the law requires, that is to say, with an evil motive or a bad purpose, whether to disobey or disregard the law.

* * * [It] is inescapable that the jury could reasonably have thought that, while an intent to deceive or a bad purpose would suffice, it *also* would be sufficient to find recklessness.

* * *

We conclude that reasonable jurors could have interpreted, and indeed most likely did interpret, the instructions in this case to establish the erroneous recklessness mens rea standard for the element of willful misapplication with intent to injure or defraud. Accordingly, appellant's conviction on the § 656 count must be reversed.

* * *

RONEY and FAY, CIRCUIT JUDGES, with whom JAMES C. HILL and HATCHETT, CIRCUIT JUDGES, join dissenting in part:

Most respectfully we dissent as to the reversal of the 18 U.S.C.A. § 656 conviction for two reasons. * * * Reading the instruction as a whole, we believe the jury was not misled as to *mens rea* required, even under the highly technical, semantic analysis of the Court's opinion. Although the district court used the words "reckless disregard" and stated that "a reckless disregard of the interest of the bank is the equivalent of intent to injure or defraud the bank," read as a whole, we think the instruction adequately conveyed to the jury the high standard of proof of intent required and the proper options available to the jury in this case.

Second, it seems to us that with all that is said in the Court's opinion, there is a level of reckless disregard that translates immutably into the precise intent espoused by the majority, with which we have no substantial quarrel. 18 U.S.C.A. § 656 deals with a very limited special group of people. By its very terms this section deals only with officers, directors, agents or employees of covered banks. These individuals have an affirmative duty to protect the funds and assets placed in their care.

As stated by Judge Morgan in *United States v. Wilson,* 500 F.2d at 720:

> It should be remembered above all else that this statute was enacted to preserve the FDIC from loss and to preserve and protect the assets of banks having a federal relationship.

Keeping the legislative history in mind, we have no difficulty in understanding how and why the Fifth Circuit arrived at the point where "a reckless disregard of the interest of the bank is the equivalent of the intent to injure or defraud the bank." The *en banc* court is now changing the law of our Circuit, so that these words cannot be used in a § 656 instruction, no matter what other words are also used. It is a subtle change, however, that in our opinion will probably make no difference in the outcome of any trial and would have made no difference in this one. If applied prospectively, we would not even dissent. We should not, however, reverse a conviction on such a technicality.

As we read the Court's opinion, it will be proper for trial judges to instruct a jury to the effect that in determining whether the defendant is guilty of a willful misapplication of bank funds, it may (or may not) infer such from a reckless disregard of the bank's interest, if such existed. Then on appeal in determining the sufficiency of the evidence and whether the government has established the necessary intent to injure or defraud the bank, a showing of conduct amounting to a reckless disregard of the bank's interest will meet this requirement. The distinction between instructing a jury that reckless disregard is the equivalent of the requisite *mens rea* and instructing it that the requisite *mens rea* may be inferred from evidence of reckless disregard is so tenuous as to be more meaningful in the classroom than the courtroom.

The Court properly holds that the appropriate *mens rea* is knowledge. By law a bank officer must know the applicable statutes, rules and regulations controlling the bank's operations. If such an officer (or official covered by the statute) makes a loan with the level of reckless disregard of those rules and the interests of the bank as defined in the instructions in this case, he has acted knowingly in a manner contemplated by Congress to fall within the ambit of knowing and willful misapplication of the bank's funds or credit.

This is not mere recklessness or mere disregard. Tying the two words together, coupled with the strong instructions on the intent required, properly conveyed to the jury the level of knowing and willful conduct required. It seems to us that *Welliver* was correctly decided and that the panel opinion in this matter was equally correct. When we get a case with a charge of "mere recklessness," defined as little more than negligence, then might be the time for the decision in this case. But here, the instruction was at best correct, at worst contained incorrect words that were harmless when read in context, and the jury's verdict of guilty should be affirmed.

*   *   *

D. STATE OF MIND LESS THAN "GENERAL INTENT": THE "STRICT LIABILITY" OFFENSES

As was indicated by the majority opinion in Lambert v. California, page 282, supra, *mens rea* is of central importance to the substantive criminal law. *Lambert* is an expression of *mens rea* as the embodiment of a basic ethical concept about the minimal prerequisites to the employment of the criminal sanction. That ethical principle is that one should not be punished where there was no opportunity to avoid violating the law. Nevertheless, just as some crimes require proof of more than "general intent," others require less. These are the so-called "strict liability" crimes.

In covering the material in this Section, consider in regard to each case whether the issue is whether any state of mind is required for guilt of the offense at issue, or rather whether there is no state of mind required concerning one or more but less than all elements of the crime. When, as a matter of policy, should legislatures dispense with the state of mind requirement, at least concerning some elements of a crime? If legislative intent is not clear, when should courts interpret a crime as imposing liability without a showing of a culpable state of mind? To what extent does the Federal Constitution preclude the imposition of such "strict liability?"

UNITED STATES v. BALINT
Supreme Court of the United States, 1922.
258 U.S. 250, 42 S.Ct. 301, 66 L.Ed. 604.

MR. CHIEF JUSTICE TAFT delivered the opinion of the Court.

* * * The indictment charged [the defendants] with unlawfully selling to another a certain amount of a derivative of opium and a certain amount of a derivative of coca leaves, not in pursuance of any written order on a form issued in blank for that purpose by the Commissioner of Internal Revenue, contrary to the provisions of section 2 of the [Narcotic Act of December 17, 1914] * * * The defendants demurred to the indictment on the ground that it failed to charge that they had sold the inhibited drugs knowing them to be such. The statute does not make such knowledge an element of the offense. The District Court sustained the demurrer and quashed the indictment. The correctness of this ruling is the question before us.

While the general rule at common law was that the scienter was a necessary element in the indictment and proof of every crime, and this was followed in regard to statutory crimes even where the statutory definition did not in terms include it (Rex v. Sleep, 8 Cox, 472), there has been a modification of this view in respect to prosecutions under statutes the purpose of which would be obstructed by such a requirement. It is a question of legislative intent to be construed by the court. It has been objected that punishment of a person for an act in violation of law when ignorant of the fact making it so, is an absence of due process of law. But that objection is considered and overruled in Shevlin-Carpenter Co. v. Minnesota, 218 U.S. 57, 69, 70, 30 S.Ct. 663, 666, 54 L.Ed. 930, in which it was held that, in the prohibition or punishment of particular acts, the state may in the maintenance of a public policy provide "that he who shall do them shall do them at his peril and will not be heard to plead in defense good faith or ignorance." Many instances of this are to be found in regulatory measures in the exercise of what is called the police power where the emphasis of the statute is evidently upon achievement of some social betterment rather than the punishment of the crimes as in cases of mala in se. * * *

So, too, in the collection of taxes, the importance to the public of their collection leads the Legislature to impose on the taxpayer the burden of finding out the facts upon which his liability to pay depends and meeting it at the peril of punishment. Again where one deals with others and his mere negligence may be dangerous to them, as in selling diseased food or poison, the policy of the law may, in order to stimulate proper care, require the punishment of the negligent person though he be ignorant of the noxious character of what he sells.

The question before us, therefore, is one of the construction of the statute and of inference of the intent of Congress. The Narcotic Act has been held by this court to be a taxing act with the incidental purpose of minimizing the spread of addiction to the use of poisonous and demoralizing drugs. * * * It is very evident from a reading of [section 2 of the Narcotics Act] that the emphasis of the section is in securing a close supervision of the business of dealing in these dangerous drugs by the taxing officers of the Government and that it merely uses a criminal penalty to secure recorded evidence of the disposition of such drugs as a means of taxing and restraining the traffic. Its manifest purpose is to require every person dealing in drugs to ascertain at his peril whether that which he sells comes within the inhibition of the statute, and if he sells the inhibited drug in ignorance of its character, to penalize him. Congress weighed the possible injustice of subjecting an innocent seller to a penalty against the evil of exposing innocent purchasers to danger from the drug, and concluded that the latter was the result preferably to be avoided. Doubtless considerations as to the opportunity of the seller to find out the fact and the difficulty of proof of knowledge contributed to this conclusion. We think the demurrer to the indictment should have been overruled.

Judgment reversed.

MORISSETTE v. UNITED STATES

Supreme Court of the United States, 1952.
342 U.S. 246, 72 S.Ct. 240, 96 L.Ed. 288.

MR. JUSTICE JACKSON delivered the opinion of the Court.

This would have remained a profoundly insignificant case to all except its immediate parties had it not been so tried and submitted to the jury as to raise questions both fundamental and far-reaching in federal criminal law, for which reason we granted certiorari.

On a large tract of uninhabited and untilled land in a wooded and sparsely populated area of Michigan, the Government established a practice bombing range over which the Air Force dropped simulated bombs at ground targets. * * * At various places about the range signs read "Danger—Keep Out—Bombing Range." Nevertheless, the range was known as good deer country and was extensively hunted.

Spent bomb casings were cleared from the targets and thrown into piles "so that they will be out of the way." They were not stacked or piled in any order but were dumped in heaps, some of which had been accumulating for four years or upwards, were exposed to the weather and rusting away.

Morissette, in December of 1948, went hunting in this area but did not get a deer. He thought to meet expenses of the trip by salvaging some of these casings. He loaded three tons of them on his truck and took them to a nearby farm, where they were flattened by driving a tractor over them. After expending this labor and trucking them to market in Flint, he realized $84.

Morissette, by occupation, is a fruit stand operator in summer and a trucker and scrap iron collector in winter. An honorably discharged veteran of World War II, he enjoys a good name among his neighbors and has had no blemish on his record more disreputable than a conviction for reckless driving.

The loading, crushing and transporting of these casings were all in broad daylight, in full view of passers-by, without the slightest effort at concealment. When an investigation was started, Morissette voluntarily, promptly and candidly told the whole story to the authorities, saying that he had no intention of stealing but thought the property was abandoned, unwanted and considered of no value to the Government. He was indicted, however, on the charge that he "did unlawfully, wilfully and knowingly steal and convert" property of the United States of the value of $84, in violation of 18 U.S.C. § 641, 18 U.S.C.A. § 641, which provides that "whoever embezzles, steals, purloins, or knowingly converts" government property is punishable by fine and imprisonment. Morissette was convicted and sentenced to imprisonment for two months or to pay a fine of $200. The Court of Appeals affirmed, one judge dissenting.

On his trial, Morissette, as he had at all times told investigating officers, testified that from appearances he believed the casings were cast-off and abandoned, that he did not intend to steal the property, and took it with no wrongful or criminal intent. The trial court, however, was unimpressed, and ruled: "[H]e took it because he thought it was abandoned and he knew he was on government property. * * * That is no defense. * * * I don't think anybody can have the defense they thought the property was abandoned on another man's piece of property." The court stated: "I will not permit you to show this man thought it was abandoned. * * * I hold in this case that there is no question of abandoned property." The court refused to submit or to allow counsel to argue to the jury whether Morissette acted with innocent intention. It charged: "And I instruct you that if you believe the testimony of the government in this case, he intended to take it. * * * He had no right to take this property. * * * [A]nd it is no defense to claim that it was abandoned, because it was on private property. * * * And I instruct you to this effect: That if this young man took this property (and he says he did), without any permission (he says he did), that was on the property of the United States Government (he says it was), that it was of the value of one cent or more (and evidently it was), that he is guilty of the offense charged here. If you believe the government, he is guilty. * * * The question on intent is whether or not he intended to take the property. He says he did. Therefore, if you believe either side, he is guilty." Petitioner's counsel contended "But the taking must have been with a felonious intent." The court ruled, however: "That is presumed by his own act."

The Court of Appeals suggested that "greater restraint in expression should have been exercised", but affirmed the conviction because "As we have interpreted the statute, appellant was guilty of its violation beyond a shadow of doubt, as evidenced even by his own admissions." Its construction of the statute is that it creates several separate and distinct offenses, one being knowing conversion of government property. The court ruled that this particular offense requires no element of criminal intent. This conclusion was thought to be required by the failure of Congress to express such a requisite and this Court's decisions in United States v. Behrman, 258 U.S. 280, 42 S.Ct. 303, 66 L.Ed. 619, and United States v. Balint, 258 U.S. 250, 42 S.Ct. 301, 66 L.Ed. 604.

I.

In those cases this Court did construe mere omission from a criminal enactment of any mention of criminal intent as dispensing with it. If they be deemed precedents for principles of construction generally applicable to federal penal statutes, they authorize this conviction. Indeed, such adoption of the literal reasoning announced in those cases would do this and more—it would sweep out of all federal crimes, except when expressly preserved, the ancient requirement of a culpable state of mind. We think a résumé of their historical background is convincing that an effect has been ascribed to them more comprehensive than was contemplated and one inconsistent with our philosophy of criminal law.

The contention that an injury can amount to a crime only when inflicted by intention is no provincial or transient notion. It is as universal and persistent in mature systems of law as belief in freedom of the human will and a consequent ability and duty of the normal individual to choose between good and evil. A relation between some mental element and punishment for a harmful act is almost as instinctive as the child's familiar exculpatory "But I didn't mean to," and has afforded the rational basis for a tardy and unfinished substitution of deterrence and reformation in place of retaliation and vengeance as the motivation for public prosecution. Unqualified acceptance of this doctrine by English common law in the Eighteenth Century was indicated by Blackstone's sweeping statement that to constitute any crime there must first be a "vicious will." * * *

Crime, as a compound concept, generally constituted only from concurrence of an evil-meaning mind with an evil-doing hand, was congenial to an intense individualism and took deep and early root in American soil. As the states codified the common law of crimes, even if their enactments were silent on the subject, their courts assumed that the omission did not signify disapproval of the principle but merely recognized that intent was so inherent in the idea of the offense that it required no statutory affirmation. Courts, with little hesitation or division, found an implication of the requirement as to offenses that were taken over from the common law. The unanimity with which they have adhered to the central thought that wrongdoing must be conscious to be criminal is emphasized by the variety, disparity and confusion of their definitions of the requisite but elusive mental element. However, courts of various jurisdictions, and for the purposes of different offenses, have devised working formulae, if not scientific ones, for the instruction of juries around such terms as "felonious intent," "criminal intent," "malice aforethought," "guilty knowledge," "fraudulent intent," "wilfulness," *"scienter,"* to denote guilty knowledge, or *"mens rea,"* to signify an evil purpose or mental culpability. By use or combination of these various tokens, they have sought to protect those who were not blameworthy in mind from conviction of infamous common-law crimes.

However, the Balint and Behrman offenses belong to a category of another character, with very different antecedents and origins. The crimes there involved depend on no mental element but consist only of forbidden acts or omissions. This, while not expressed by the Court, is made clear from examination of a century-old but accelerating tendency, discernible both here and in England, to call into existence new duties and crimes which disregard any ingredient of intent. The industrial revolution multiplied the number of workmen exposed to injury from increasingly powerful and complex mechanisms, driven by

freshly discovered sources of energy, requiring higher precautions by
employers. Traffic of velocities, volumes and varieties unheard of came
to subject the wayfarer to intolerable casualty risks if owners and
drivers were not to observe new cares and uniformities of conduct.
Congestion of cities and crowding of quarters called for health and
welfare regulations undreamed of in simpler times. Wide distribution
of goods became an instrument of wide distribution of harm when those
who dispersed food, drink, drugs, and even securities, did not comply
with reasonable standards of quality, integrity, disclosure and care.
Such dangers have engendered increasingly numerous and detailed
regulations which heighten the duties of those in control of particular
industries, trades, properties or activities that affect public health,
safety or welfare.

While many of these duties are sanctioned by a more strict civil
liability,[13] lawmakers, whether wisely or not,[14] have sought to make
such regulations more effective by invoking criminal sanctions to be
applied by the familiar technique of criminal prosecutions and convictions. This has confronted the courts with a multitude of prosecutions,
based on statutes or administrative regulations, for what have been
aptly called "public welfare offenses." These cases do not fit neatly
into any of such accepted classifications of common-law offenses, such
as those against the state, the person, property, or public morals.
Many of these offenses are not in the nature of positive aggressions or
invasions, with which the common law so often dealt, but are in the
nature of neglect where the law requires care, or inaction where it
imposes a duty. Many violations of such regulations result in no direct
or immediate injury to person or property but merely create the danger
or probability of it which the law seeks to minimize. While such
offenses do not threaten the security of the state in the manner of

---

13. The development of strict criminal
liability regardless of intent has been
roughly paralleled by an evolution of a
strict civil liability for consequences regardless of fault in certain relationships, as
shown by Workmen's Compensation Acts,
and by vicarious liability for fault of others
as evidenced by various Motor Vehicle
Acts.

14. Consequences of a general abolition
of intent as an ingredient of serious crimes
have aroused the concern of responsible
and disinterested students of penology. Of
course, they would not justify judicial disregard of a clear command to that effect
from Congress, but they do admonish us to
caution in assuming that Congress, without clear expression, intends in any instance to do so.

Radin, Intent, Criminal, 8 Encyc.Soc.Sci.
126, 130, says, " * * * as long as in popular belief intention and the freedom of the
will are taken as axiomatic, no penal system that negates the mental element can

find general acceptance. It is vital to retain public support of methods of dealing
with crime." * * *

Sayre, Public Welfare Offenses, 33 Col.L.
Rev. 55, 56, says: "To inflict substantial
punishment upon one who is morally entirely innocent, who caused injury through
reasonable mistake or pure accident, would
so outrage the feelings of the community
as to nullify its own enforcement."

Hall, Prolegomena to a Science of Criminal Law, 89 U. of Pa.L.Rev. 549, 569, appears somewhat less disturbed by the
trend, if properly limited, but, as to so-
called public welfare crimes, suggests that
"There is no reason to continue to believe
that the present mode of dealing with
these offenses is the best solution obtainable, or that we must be content with this
sacrifice of established principles. *The
raising of a presumption of knowledge
might be an improvement.*" (Italics added.)

* * *

treason, they may be regarded as offenses against its authority, for their occurrence impairs the efficiency of controls deemed essential to the social order as presently constituted. In this respect, whatever the intent of the violator, the injury is the same, and the consequences are injurious or not according to fortuity. Hence, legislation applicable to such offenses, as a matter of policy, does not specify intent as a necessary element. The accused, if he does not will the violation, usually is in a position to prevent it with no more care than society might reasonably expect and no more exertion than it might reasonably exact from one who assumed his responsibilities. Also, penalties commonly are relatively small, and conviction does no grave damage to an offender's reputation. Under such considerations, courts have turned to construing statutes and regulations which make no mention of intent as dispensing with it and holding that the guilty act alone makes out the crime. This has not, however, been without expressions of misgiving.

* * *

After the turn of the Century, a new use for crimes without intent appeared when New York enacted numerous and novel regulations of tenement houses, sanctioned by money penalties. Landlords contended that a guilty intent was essential to establish a violation. Judge Cardozo wrote the answer: "The defendant asks us to test the meaning of this statute by standards applicable to statutes that govern infamous crimes. The analogy, however, is deceptive. The element of conscious wrongdoing, the guilty mind accompanying the guilty act, is associated with the concept of crimes that are punished as infamous. * * * Even there it is not an invariable element. * * * But in the prosecution of minor offenses there is a wider range of practice and of power. Prosecutions for petty penalties have always constituted in our law a class by themselves. * * * That is true, though the prosecution is criminal in form." Tenement House Department of City of New York v. McDevitt, 1915, 215 N.Y. 160, 168, 109 N.E. 88, 90.

Soon, employers advanced the same contention as to violations of regulations prescribed by a new labor law. Judge Cardozo, again for the court, pointed out, as a basis for penalizing violations whether intentional or not, that they were punishable only by fine "moderate in amount", but cautiously added that in sustaining the power so to fine unintended violations "we are not to be understood as sustaining to a like length the power to imprison. We leave that question open." People ex rel. Price v. Sheffield Farms-Slawson-Decker Co., 1918, 225 N.Y. 25, 32–33, 121 N.E. 474, 476, 477.

* * *

Before long, similar questions growing out of federal legislation reached this Court. Its judgments were in harmony with this consensus of state judicial opinion, the existence of which may have led the Court to overlook the need for full exposition of their rationale in the context of federal law. In overruling a contention that there can be no conviction on an indictment which makes no charge of criminal intent but alleges only making of a sale of a narcotic forbidden by law, Chief Justice Taft, wrote: "While the general rule at common law was that the *scienter* was a necessary element in the indictment and proof of every crime, and this was followed in regard to statutory crimes even where the statutory definition did not in terms include it * * *, there has been a modification of this view in respect to prosecutions under statutes the purpose of which would be obstructed by such a requirement. It is a question of legislative intent to be construed by the court. * * *" United States v. Balint, supra, 258 U.S. 251–252, 42 S.Ct. 302.

* * *

Of course, the purpose of every statute would be "obstructed" by requiring a finding of intent, if we assume that it had a purpose to convict without it. Therefore, the obstruction rationale does not help us to learn the purpose of the omission by Congress. * * *

* * *

Neither this Court nor, so far as we are aware, any other has undertaken to delineate a precise line or set forth comprehensive criteria for distinguishing between crimes that require a mental element and crimes that do not. We attempt no closed definition, for the law on the subject is neither settled nor static. The conclusion reached in the Balint and Behrman cases has our approval and adherence for the circumstances to which it was there applied. A quite different question here is whether we will expand the doctrine of crimes without intent to include those charged here.

Stealing, larceny, and its variants and equivalents, were among the earliest offenses known to the law that existed before legislation; they are invasions of rights of property which stir a sense of insecurity in the whole community and arouse public demand for retribution, the penalty is high and, when a sufficient amount is involved, the infamy is that of a felony, which, says Maitland, is " * * * as bad a word as you can give to man or thing." State courts of last resort, on whom fall the heaviest burden of interpreting criminal law in this country, have consistently retained the requirement of intent in larceny-type offenses. If any state has deviated, the exception has neither been called to our attention nor disclosed by our research.

Congress, therefore, omitted any express prescription of criminal intent from the enactment before us in the light of an unbroken course of judicial decision in all constituent states of the Union holding intent inherent in this class of offense, even when not expressed in a statute. Congressional silence as to mental elements in an Act merely adopting into federal statutory law a concept of crime already so well defined in common law and statutory interpretation by the states may warrant quite contrary inferences than the same silence in creating an offense new to general law, for whose definition the courts have no guidance except the Act. Because the offenses before this Court in the Balint and Behrman cases were of this latter class, we cannot accept them as authority for eliminating intent from offenses incorporated from the common law. * * *

The Government asks us by a feat of construction radically to change the weights and balances in the scales of justice. The purpose and obvious effect of doing away with the requirement of a guilty intent is to ease the prosecution's path to conviction, to strip the defendant of such benefit as he derived at common law from innocence of evil purpose, and to circumscribe the freedom heretofore allowed juries. Such a manifest impairment of the immunities of the individual should not be extended to common-law crimes on judicial initiative.

The spirit of the doctrine which denies to the federal judiciary power to create crimes forthrightly admonishes that we should not enlarge the reach of enacted crimes by constituting them from anything less than the incriminating components contemplated by the words used in the statute. And where Congress borrows terms of art in which are accumulated the legal tradition and meaning of centuries of practice, it presumably knows and adopts the cluster of ideas that were attached to each borrowed word in the body of learning from which it was taken and the meaning its use will convey to the judicial mind unless otherwise instructed. In such case, absence of contrary direction may be taken as satisfaction with widely accepted definitions, not as a departure from them.

We hold that mere omission from § 641 of any mention of intent will not be construed as eliminating that element from the crimes denounced.

II.

It is suggested, however, that the history and purposes of § 641 imply something more affirmative as to elimination of intent from at least one of the offenses charged under it in this case. The argument does not contest that criminal intent is retained in the offenses of embezzlement, stealing and purloining, as incorporated into this section. But it is urged that Congress joined with those, as a new, separate and distinct offense, knowingly to convert government property, under circumstances which imply that it is an offense in which the mental element of intent is not necessary.

Congress has been alert to what often is a decisive function of some mental element in crime. It has seen fit to prescribe that an evil state of mind, described variously in one or more such terms as "intentional," "wilful," "knowing," "fraudulent" or "malicious," will make criminal an otherwise indifferent act, or increase the degree of the offense or its punishment. Also, it has at times required a specific intent or purpose which will require some specialized knowledge or design for some evil beyond the common-law intent to do injury. The law under some circumstances recognizes good faith or blameless intent as a defense, partial defense, or as an element to be considered in mitigation of punishment. And treason—the one crime deemed grave enough for definition in our Constitution itself—requires not only the duly witnessed overt act of aid and comfort to the enemy but also the mental element of disloyalty or adherence to the enemy. In view of the care that has been bestowed upon the subject, it is significant that we have not found, nor has our attention been directed to, any instance in which Congress has expressly eliminated the mental element from a crime taken over from the common law.

* * *

We find no grounds for inferring any affirmative instruction from Congress to eliminate intent from any offense with which this defendant was charged.

III.

As we read the record, this case was tried on the theory that even if criminal intent were essential its presence (a) should be decided by the court (b) as a presumption of law, apparently conclusive, (c) predicated upon the isolated act of taking rather than upon all of the circumstances. In each of these respects we believe the trial court was in error.

Notes and Questions

1. The Supreme Court has addressed itself to the question of the necessity for the state of mind element on a number of occasions since *Morissette*. Three are of particular interest.

In United States v. Park, 421 U.S. 658, 95 S.Ct. 1903, 44 L.Ed.2d 489 (1975), the defendant, president of a major supermarket chain, was charged with violating the Federal Food, Drug and Cosmetic Act because the firm's warehouse contained rats which resulted in the introduction into interstate commerce of contaminated food. He was convicted by a jury which, over defendant's objection, was instructed, in effect, that it was to find him guilty if he "had a responsible relation to the situation, even though he may not have participated personally * * * [and] did not consciously do wrong" and "by virtue of his position * * * had * * * authority and responsibility to deal with the situation." Defendant was fined $50 on each of five counts.

Relying on the nature and purpose of the statute, the Supreme Court held, 6–3, that this did not offend the Constitution. The only defense permitted such a defendant, said the Court, was to produce evidence that he was powerless to prevent or correct the violation.

Mr. Park was faced with minor penalties in the context of a business in which he was a knowledgeable and responsible actor. However, in United States v. Freed, 401 U.S. 601, 91 S.Ct. 1112, 28 L.Ed.2d 356 (1971), the defendants were subject to penalties of a $10,000 fine and imprisonment for ten years for possessing hand grenades not registered under the National Firearms Act. The issue was whether there was a *mens rea* requirement with respect to the fact of registration. Mr. Justice Douglas, for the Court, wrote that there was a continuum of statutes posing this issue, from the larceny provision in *Morissette* with its common law history of *mens rea* to that in *Lambert* where there was nothing about the defendant's conduct which would have given notice of a duty to act. The Firearms Act was said to pose neither difficulty to the imposition of strict liability. It was a regulatory measure, akin to the statute in *Balint,* and "premised on the theory that one would hardly be surprised to learn that possession of hand grenades is not an innocent act." Should it matter whether Freed was a gun dealer or a one-time purchaser?

The conviction in *Freed* required proof beyond a reasonable doubt of a mental element with respect to the fact of possession and the item possessed. Moreover, the statute, despite its substantial penalties, closely resembled other regulatory or public welfare offenses. This was arguably not the case in United States v. Feola, 420 U.S. 671, 95 S.Ct. 1255, 43 L.Ed. 2d 541 (1975), where the defendants had agreed to sell heroin to their victims but intended to substitute a form of sugar for the drug. If the ruse failed, they intended to simply rob the buyers of the purchase money. During the transaction, a fight broke out and the victims—who turned out to be undercover agents of the Bureau of Narcotics and Dangerous Drugs— arrested the defendants. The defendants were charged with assault upon federal officers, under 18 U.S.C.A. § 111. At trial, the trial court instructed the jury that in order to convict the defendants, it was not necessary to find that at the time of the assault the defendants were aware that the victims were federal officers. In considering the propriety of this interpretation of the statute, the Supreme Court saw the issue as related to the purpose of the crime:

> If the primary purpose is to protect federal law enforcement personnel, that purpose could well be frustrated by the imposition of a strict scienter requirement. On the other hand, if § 111 is seen primarily as an anti-obstruction statute [intended to prevent hinderance to the execution of federal duties and to protect federal officers only as incidental to that aim] it is likely that Congress intended criminal liability to be imposed only when a person acted with the specific intent to impede enforcement activities.

420 U.S. at 678, 95 S.Ct. at 1261, 43 L.Ed.2d at 549. After reviewing the legislative history of the statute, the Court concluded that Congress intended the statute to serve both purposes. It then reasoned that the Congressional purpose of giving federal officers maximum protection by making prosecutions for assault upon such officers cognizable in federal courts precluded an interpretation of the statute that would require awareness that the victim of the assault was a federal officer. "A contrary conclusion," the Court explained, "would give insufficient protection to the agent enforcing an unpopular law, and none to the agent acting under cover." 420 U.S. at 684, 95 S.Ct. at 1264, 43 L.Ed.2d at 553. Defending this result on policy grounds, the Court continued:

> This interpretation poses no risk of unfairness to defendants. It is no snare for the unsuspecting. Although the perpetrator of a narcotics 'rip-off', such as the one involved here, may be surprised to find that his intended victim is a federal officer in civilian apparel, he nonetheless knows from the very outset that his planned course of conduct is wrongful. The situation is not one where legitimate conduct becomes

unlawful solely because of the identity of the individual or agency affected. In a case of this kind the offender takes the victim as he finds him. The concept of criminal intent does not extend so far as to require that the actor understand not only the nature of his act but also its consequences for the choice of a judicial forum.

420 U.S. at 685, 95 S.Ct. at 1264, 43 L.Ed.2d at 553. The defendants were also convicted of conspiracy to assault federal officers; the Supreme Court's treatment of the state of mind required for the conspiracy charge is discussed in the note on page 640, infra.

The Court's readiness to accept "strict liability" in each of the cases discussed above should be contrasted with its opinion in Smith v. California, 361 U.S. 147, 80 S.Ct. 215, 4 L.Ed.2d 205 (1959). Smith was the owner of a bookstore who was charged with possession of obscene matter for sale under a statute imposing strict liability. All of the justices were troubled by this feature of the statute. The state had argued and the court below had concluded, that this was like other penal statutes, exemplified by food and drug legislation, which dispense with the requirement of knowledge on the part of the accused. Justice Brennan, for the majority, wrote:

"The usual rationale for such statutes is that the public interest in the purity of its food is so great as to warrant the imposition of the highest standard of care on distributors—in fact an absolute standard which will not hear the distributor's pleas as to the amount of care he has used. Cf. United States v. Balint. His ignorance of the character of the food is irrelevant. There is no specific constitutional inhibition against making the distributors of food the strictest censors of their merchandise, but the constitutional guarantees of the freedom of speech and of the press stand in the way of imposing a similar requirement on the bookseller. By dispensing with any requirement of knowledge of the contents of the book on the part of the seller, the ordinance tends to impose a severe limitation on the public's access to constitutionally protected matter. For if the bookseller is criminally liable without knowledge of the contents * * * he will tend to restrict the books he sells to those he has inspected; and thus the State will have imposed a restriction upon the distribution of constitutionally protected as well as obscene literature.

361 U.S. at 152–53, 80 S.Ct. at 218, 4 L.Ed.2d at 210–211.

2. Is "strict liability" appropriate or defensible in regard to those "regulatory offenses" as to which it has traditionally been imposed? Consider the following comments from Mueller, Mens Rea and the Law Without It, 58 W.Va.L.Rev. 34, 37–38, 50, 59–60 (1955):

The reasons for * * * [imposing strict liability in regard to such offenses] have been variously stated: If "mens rea" were required, (1) the enforcement of the statute would be impeded; or (2) the courts would be overburdened; or (3) justice would be hampered; or (4) fraudulent defenses could be fabricated, etc. Prima facie such claims can be just as easily made as refuted. The often stated reason here listed under (1), for instance, seems to be nothing more than a * * * "because", and proves no more.

(2) supra, is a little more specific. It is certainly true that there is hardly any aspect of human activity which has escaped control by the law. When we eat, the (pure food and drug) law eats with us; when we walk, the (traffic) law walks with us; and even the health and soundness of our sleep is regulated by law. To litigate every one of the regulated problems of daily life would surely hamper the administration of justice. But what good will it do to punish indiscriminately, regardless of guilt or innocence, merely to save the time it would take to determine the validity of a defense? And what of the deterrent effect of such a frustrating law? Would it not ease the burden on the court and reduce the length of the court calendar much more if, for instance, in January we would prosecute only blond culprits, in February only bald ones, in March brunettes, etc.? That would at least deter some of the culprits some of the time, whereas absolute criminal liability is totally without deterrent effect. * * *

Ad (3) it might be answered that absolute criminal liability surely is not the vehicle to unhamper criminal justice. If anything, it does away with justice altogether by distributing penalties indiscriminately. *Ad* (4) it will suffice to ask: what crime is there which is not subject to the interposition of fraudulent defenses? Surely the temptation for tricking one's way out of a jam is much greater in crimes threatening serious consequences than it is in petty offenses.

* * *

[It has been feared that the enforcement of the regulatory schemes would bog down if strict liability were not imposed.]

Now then, how can a law deter anybody which inflicts punishment for the mere doing of the outward act? Is it not manifest that a law which punishes without caring about the factual and moral blamelessness of a defendant thereby frustrates him and the community at large? Why should the citizen bother to use care if the courts do not bother whether or not he used care, inflicting punishment in any event? Punishment which befalls the innocent and the guilty alike, like hay fever, hail or hurricane, can have no good effect at all, except perhaps for insurance companies, for whom it creates a new insurable interest.

* * *

[It has also been argued that unless strict liability were imposed, "many unscrupulous persons would not hesitate to fabricate such facts as would be needful to accomplish" the assertion of a defense of mistake of fact.]

The ease of manufacturing surreptitious or fraudulent defenses is, as any lawyer knows, not confined to such cases. * * * Since the temptation to fabricate defenses is even greater in prosecutions in which the stakes are higher, for instance in murder prosecutions, why then not dispense with "mens rea" altogether and make every act, e.g., the killing of a human being, conclusive evidence of a criminal intent to do the act, e.g., killing a human being conclusive evidence of a criminal intent, thus murder?

* * * All other arguments in favor of absolute criminal liability failing, it has sometimes been reasoned that the raising of issues in defense of regulatory violations would require dealing with collateral and irrelevant issues. Hence, too much time, in proportion to the slightness of the offense, would have to be devoted to the matter if the defendant were permitted to present an elaborate defense, or, indeed, any defense. It has been said that courts would never be able to clear their calendars if in this vast mass of petty offenses a judge, or a jury, were to try all defensive facts. Speediness of "justice" is said to be the compelling reason for absolute criminal liability.

If this were truly the only, or major, reason for resort to absolute criminal liability, then it would be sheer folly to dispense with the "mens rea" and nevertheless to consider all defensive arguments for the purpose of possibly mitigating the punishment * * *. Of course, this only goes to show that the "speediness of justice" argument is absurd. The choice does not lie between speedy justice and slow justice, but between speedy injustice and justice of whatever celerity we can achieve by whatever court reform may be necessary. Justice ought to be speedy, but absolute criminal liability is not apt to achieve it.

* * *

[It has also been argued in support of strict liability that "as the penalty is slight, no great injustice is perpetrated by enforcing this type of statute regardless of knowledge".]

Are we compelled to prefer small injustice over justice? I do not think that the writer regarded this point as a major reason for the imposition of absolute criminal liability. But even as collateral support it fails miserably. Such reasoning may be appropriate in a country where absolutism and dictatorial utility sacrifice life, liberty and property to the Moloch state, but not here.

For a very different view see the excellent student Note, Criminal Liability Without Fault: A Philosophical Perspective, 75 Columb.L.Rev. 1517 (1975).

3. For discussions of "strict" liability offenses, see Starrs, The Regulatory Offense in Historical Perspective, in Essays in Criminal Science (G. Mueller ed. 1961); Packer, Mens Rea and the Supreme Court, 1962 Sup.Ct. Rev. 107; Borre, Public Welfare Offenses: A New Approach, 52 J.Crim.L.C. & P.S. 418 (1961); Sayre, Public Welfare Offenses, 33 Colum.L.Rev. 55 (1933); Wasserstrom, Strict Liability in the Criminal Law, 12 Stan.L.Rev. 731 (1960); Comment, Liability Without Fault: Logic and Potential of a Developing Concept, 1970 Wis.L.Rev. 1201.

E. "DEFENSES" CONSISTING OF "DISPROOF" OF STATE OF MIND

What is the major importance of the decision as to whether a particular crime requires proof of a state of mind? For the defendants in *Morissette*, presented in the preceding section, it lies not in the burden thus imposed upon the prosecution in making out the basic case against the defendants. Rather, it is significant because it provides the defendant an opportunity to persuade judges and juries that the required state of mind was in fact not present.

Matters such as this are not "defenses" in the normal sense of the word, because the burden remains on the prosecution to establish the existence of the required state of mind. "True defenses," which are discussed in Chapter XII, normally involve the defendant's acknowledgment that all elements of the crime were present but under circumstances which justify or excuse. *Wilson*, reprinted in the first subsection that follows, suggests that the burden of persuasion with regard to these matters cannot constitutionally be placed on the defendant. But consider the possibility that as a practical matter, the burden is on the defense to persuade the trier of fact that the defendant did not have the state of mind that a reasonable person would have had under the circumstances.

This section deals with three matters: ignorance or mistake concerning matters of "fact," ignorance or mistake concerning "law," and intoxication. Given the general requirement that crimes require a culpable state of mind and in the absence of any specific doctrine applicable to mistake of, ignorance or intoxication, a defendant can obviously challenge the sufficiency of the prosecution's evidence on the basis that the facts, considered as a whole, including any proof tending to show ignorance, mistake, or intoxication, does not prove beyond a reasonable doubt that the defendant acted with the requisite state of mind. This approach to some extent limits defendants' ability to use these "defenses" to escape liability. For example, ignorance or mistake of law are in theory unavailing with respect to a strict liability crime inasmuch as there is no mental state to be negated. Is this treatment consistent with the requirements of due process?

Current law sometimes imposes additional limits upon the ability of defendants to use the opportunities provided by this approach. Intoxication is sometimes excluded from consideration entirely, although more commonly its use is limited to "specific intent" crimes. A mistake of fact may be given effect only if reasonable. Consider the desirability of these limits. Should defendants be convicted if the prosecution's proof fails to establish the state of mind required for the crime, if it is clear that the reason the defendant lacked the requisite state of mind was an unreasonable mistake of fact or voluntary intoxication?

Might it be desirable to create opportunities for defendants to use mistake or intoxication defensively even if there is no question that the prosecution can prove the necessary state of mind existed? For example, should a defendant be entitled to acquittal because he mistakenly believed that his actions were not in violation of the criminal law, if he establishes that this mistaken belief rested upon what appears to be an extraordinarily reasonable basis? The query is answered affirmatively by Section 2.04(3) of the Model Penal Code, reprinted at page 323, infra, and statutes based upon this model.

1. IGNORANCE OR MISTAKE

As a general rule, a defendant's failure to address a matter or an erroneous conclusion regarding a matter addressed has been relevant to criminal liability only under limited circumstances:

It is a commonplace of criminal law that an honest "mistake of fact" negates criminal intent, when the defendant's acts would not constitute a crime if the facts were as he supposed them to be. Conversely, a "mistake of law" is generally held not to excuse the commission of an offense, even though the defendant was unaware his action was prohibited. The frequent difficulty of distinguishing "law" from "fact," as well as the reluctance of modern courts to hold individuals criminally liable when they acted with honest and innocent purpose, however, has led to some erosion of the principle that "everybody is presumed to know the law." When presented with a mistake on the borderline between law and fact, or a case in which the imposition of strict liability would be particularly unjust, the courts have tended either to characterize the defendant's error as factual in nature or to find a way to declare an exception to the "mistake of law" doctrine.

* * *

* * * An error as to the legality of a particular activity, even if based upon the assurance of a government official, has always been treated as a mistake of law in Anglo-Saxon jurisdictions. * * * [T]raditionally a defendant has been allowed a mistake of fact defense only when he was in possession of facts, albeit erroneous, about his activity which, if true, would have rendered it legal. If he is not in the possession of such facts, but relies instead entirely on the erroneous assertion of a government official or private individual as to the legality of the activity, his mistake is one of law.

United States v. Barker, 514 F.2d 208, 264–65 (D.C.Cir.1975) (Wilkey, J., dissenting), cert. denied, 421 U.S. 1013, 95 S.Ct. 2420, 44 L.Ed.2d 682 (1975).

To some extent, this is an oversimplification. Some "mistakes" are held to preclude criminal liability only if, in addition to being "honestly" held, they are found to have been "reasonable" ones. And, as Judge Wilkey indicated, there is some, perhaps a growing, tendency to find "exceptions" that bar criminal conviction because of ignorance or mistake whether or not criminal intent has been "negated" or "disproved." In examining the following material, consider whether the situations presented are appropriately handled by providing defendants with the opportunity to show lack of criminal intent. Consider also the extent to which the fact-law distinction described by Judge Wilkey is an appropriate way of limiting defendants' ability to raise these matters.

The Model Penal Code proposes treatment of mistake or ignorance regarding "fact" and "law" in a single provision, reprinted following this note. But because these matters are so frequently distinguished carefully in judicial discussions, they are treated in separate subsections that follow.

For general discussions of both mistakes of fact and law, see Haddad, The Mental Attitude Requirement in Criminal Law—and Some Exceptions, 59 J.Crim.L., C. & P.S. 4, 11–21 (1968); Hall, Ignorance and Mistake in Criminal Law, 33 Ind.L.J. 1, 2–14 (1957); Hall and Seligman, Mistake of Law and Mens Rea, 8 U.Chi.L.Rev. 641 (1941); Keedy, Ignorance and Mistake in the Criminal Law, 22 Harv.L. Rev. 81–88 (1908); Mueller-Rappard, The Mistake of Law as a Defense, 36 Temple L.Q. 261 (1963); Perkins, Ignorance and Mistake in Criminal Law, 88 U.Pa.L.Rev. 35, 54–65 (1939); Ryu and Silving, Error Juris: A Comparative Study, 24 U.Chi.L.Rev. 421 (1957).

MODEL PENAL CODE *
(Official Draft, 1985).

Section 2.04. Ignorance or Mistake.

(1) Ignorance or mistake as to a matter of fact or law is a defense if:

(a) the ignorance or mistake negatives the purpose, knowledge, belief, recklessness or negligence required to establish a material element of the offense; or

(b) the law provides that the state of mind established by such ignorance or mistake constitutes a defense.

(2) Although ignorance or mistake would otherwise afford a defense to the offense charged, the defense is not available if the defendant would be guilty of another offense had the situation been as he supposed. In such case, however, the ignorance or mistake of the defendant shall reduce the grade and degree of the offense of which he may be convicted to those of the offense of which he would be guilty had the situation been as he supposed.

(3) A belief that conduct does not legally constitute an offense is a defense to a prosecution for that offense based upon such conduct when:

(a) the statute or other enactment defining the offense is not known to the actor and has not been published or otherwise reasonably made available prior to the conduct alleged; or

(b) he acts in reasonable reliance upon an official statement of the law, afterward determined to be invalid or erroneous, contained in (i) a statute or other enactment; (ii) a judicial decision, opinion or judgment; (iii) an administrative order or grant of permission;

or (iv) an official interpretation of the public officer or body chargd by law with responsibility for the interpretation, administration or enforcement of the law defining the offense.

(4) The defendant must prove a defense arising under Subsection (3) of this Section by a preponderance of evidence.

a. Ignorance or Mistake of "Fact"

A defendant who offers a "defense" of reasonable ignorance or mistake of fact is, in effect, claiming that he was not even reckless with respect to the particular element of the crime to which his ignorance or mistake related. Normally, a defendant who produces some evidence— even if only his own testimony—to suggest the existence of such ignorance or mistake has the right to have the jury instructed on it. This, of course, presupposes that some state of mind is required to be established by the prosecution with respect to the element to which the mistake related. If it is determined that the crime imposes strict liability with respect to that element, the defendant will fail inasmuch as there is nothing to be negated by the ignorance or mistake.

A defendant who claims to have operated under a mistake of fact which may not have been "reasonable" is, in effect, contending that he cannot be convicted unless the prosecution can show subjective fault with regard to the element to which the mistake related. If the mistake was honestly but unreasonably held, it may be understood, in Model Penal Code terms, as constituting negligence. But if at least recklessness is required by the offense charged, this mistake is inconsistent with the state of mind which the prosecution must show existed.

As a practical matter, therefore, a defendant's claim of mistake or ignorance ordinarily involves an inquiry into (1) whether, as a matter of logic and evidence, his claimed mistake would have been inconsistent with the state of mind required by the crime charged; and (2) the allocation of the burdens of raising and proving the issues presented.

WILSON v. TARD

United States District Court, District of New Jersey, 1984.
593 F.Supp. 1091.

STERN, DISTRICT JUDGE.

Christopher Wilson petitions for issuance of a writ of habeas corpus pursuant to 28 U.S.C. § 2254, alleging that the jury instructions given in his manslaughter trial prejudiced his constitutional right to be presumed innocent until the state had proven every element of the crime with which he was charged beyond a reasonable doubt.

*   *   *

FACTS

Petitioner was indicted by a Union County Grand Jury on charges of aggravated manslaughter [1]. * * * He pleaded not guilty to both counts and was tried before the Honorable A. Donald McKenzie, J.S.C., and a jury from March 9–12, 1981. Petitioner was charged in connection with the October 15, 1980, shooting death of his friend Rodney Brown while they and two other men were discussing which of them should be the first to use some heroin in their possession. Petitioner did not dispute that he had shot Brown, but at trial he raised as a defense an alleged mistake of fact.[2] Petitioner contended that he had pointed the gun at his friend in a joking attempt to frighten him. He testified that he had removed the magazine of bullets from the gun before he aimed it, and contended that because of his unfamiliarity with the weapon he believed he had disarmed it. However, one bullet remained in the chamber of the gun; when petitioner aimed the gun at his friend and pulled the trigger, it discharged and fatally injured the victim. Petitioner argued, however, that his belief that the gun was unloaded when he pulled the trigger was a reasonable mistake under the circumstances, and that therefore he did not possess the level of mental culpability, recklessness, necessary to find him guilty of manslaughter.

In his instructions to the jury, the trial court stressed that since the cause of Brown's death was not disputed, determination of petitioner's state of mind was critical to the state's proof of the offense of manslaughter. After first stating that the burden of proving each element of the offense beyond a reasonable doubt lay on the prosecution, the judge instructed the jury that the defense of mistake which the defendant had raised was an exception to the state's burden of proving all elements of the crime. After summarizing New Jersey's statute on mistake, he told the jury that the burden lay on the defendant to "prove by a preponderance of the evidence" that he was mistaken in his belief that the gun was not loaded, and that "he arrived at the conclusion reasonably." He stated that the mistake would be a

---

1. New Jersey law provides that aggravated manslaughter occurs "when the actor recklessly causes death under circumstances manifesting extreme indifference to human life," § 2C:11–4a, N.J.Stat.Ann. "Simple" manslaughter occurs when homicide is committed "recklessly." § 2C:11–4b.

Section 2C:2–2, N.J.Stat.Ann., defines "recklessly" in the following way:

A person acts recklessly with respect to a material element of an offense when he consciously disregards a substantial and unjustifiable risk that the material element exists or will result from his conduct. The risk must be of such a nature and degree that, considering the nature

and purpose of the actor's conduct and the circumstances known to him, its disregard involves a gross deviation from the standard of conduct that a reasonable person would observe in the actor's situation.

2. In relevant part, § 2C:2–4a provides that

Ignorance or mistake as to a matter of fact or law is a defense if the defendant reasonably arrived at the conclusion underlying the mistake and: 1) It negatives the culpable mental state required to establish the offense; or 2) The law provides that the state of mind established by such ignorance or mistake constitutes a defense.

defense if the jury could find that "the defendant reasonably arrived at that conclusion underlying the mistake and it negates the culpable mental state required to establish the offense."

The judge further explained that if the jury concluded that defendant's mistake did negate the culpable mental state for manslaughter it should consider, pursuant to § 2C:2–4b, N.J.Stat.Ann., whether the defendant was guilty of aggravated assault.[3]

The jury returned after one hour and forty-five minutes of deliberation and said it was "unclear about the definition of mistake as it pertains to a reduction in charge from simple manslaughter to aggravated assault." The jury was reinstructed, but it returned forty-five minutes later for another explanation of "defensive mistake." After a further hour and fifteen minutes of deliberation, the jury returned a verdict finding defendant not guilty of aggravated manslaughter but guilty of the lesser-included charge of simple manslaughter, as well as guilty of the possession of a handgun charge.

* * *

Petitioner appealed his conviction to the Superior Court of New Jersey, Appellate Division, on several grounds. Among them was his contention that the burden of proof for the defense of mistake of fact had been misallocated to him in the jury charge. On April 14, 1983, the Appellate Division affirmed petitioner's conviction. As to petitioner's argument that the jury charge was in error, the court stated: "One who deliberately aims and discharges a firearm directly at another human being, thereby causing the latter's death, cannot, as a matter of law, be found to have been reasonable in his mistaken belief that the gun was unloaded or to have acted other than recklessly. The defense in question should not even have been submitted to the jury." *State of New Jersey v. Christopher Wilson,* Nos. A–3703–80T4, A–3704–80T4, April 14, 1983 (Superior Court of New Jersey, Appellate Division, *Per Curiam*) at 3.

* * *

I.

We turn first to the decision of the Appellate Division, which amounts to a holding that one who aims a gun at another person and deliberately pulls the trigger has acted recklessly *per se*; in other words, petitioner's mental state is to be presumed from the act itself. By concluding that petitioner's mistake of fact defense should not even

---

3. N.J.Stat.Ann. § 2C:2–4b states that

Although ignorance or mistake would otherwise afford a defense to the offense charged, the defense is not available if the defendant would be guilty of another offense had the situation been as he supposed. In such case, however, the ignorance or mistake of the defendant shall reduce the grade and degree of the offense of which he may be convicted to those of the offense of which he would be guilty had the situation been as he supposed.

Aggravated assault is defined by § 2C:12–1b(4), N.J.Stat.Ann., as "knowingly under circumstances manifesting extreme indifference to the value of human life point(ing) a firearm" at another "whether or not the actor believes it to be loaded."

have been submitted to the jury, the Appellate Division drew a conclusive presumption from petitioner's acts, which amounts to "an irrebuttable direction by the court" to the factfinder to find that petitioner acted recklessly "once (it is) convinced of the facts triggering the presumption." *See Sandstrom v. Montana*, 442 U.S. 510, 517, 99 S.Ct. 2450, 2456, 61 L.Ed.2d 39 (1979).

* * *

Such a presumption, relieving the state from having to prove an element of the crime, conflicts with the principle, set out by the Supreme Court in *In re Winship*, 397 U.S. 358, 364, 90 S.Ct. 1068, 1073, 25 L.Ed.2d 323 (1970) that "the Due Process Clause protects the accused against conviction except upon proof beyond a reasonable doubt of every fact necessary to constitute the crime with which he is charged."

It is clear that the New Jersey statute makes the existence of the mental state of recklessness an essential element of the crime of manslaughter. In fact, it was the only element of the offense at issue in petitioner's trial, since he admitted to causing the death of the victim. Therefore, by directing a finding of recklessness based upon petitioner's acts, the Appellate Division would deny petitioner a necessary constitutional protection. Its reasoning cannot stand.

II.

Since we find that the Appellate Division erred in the grounds it stated in denying petitioner's challenge to the jury instructions, it is necessary for us to consider whether, in those instructions, the trial court erred in assigning the burden of persuasion as to mistake to the defendant and, if so, whether such an error was of constitutional dimension. We now hold that the trial judge's instruction, allocating the burden of proving the mistake of fact defense to petitioner, constitutes a violation of due process.

In *Mullaney v. Wilber*, 421 U.S. 684, 95 S.Ct. 1881, 44 L.Ed.2d 508 (1975), the Supreme Court held that the requirement of *Winship*—that the prosecution prove all elements of the crime beyond a reasonable doubt—necessarily barred the state from shifting to the defendant the burden of disproving any element of the crime charged. * * *

Applying the holding of *Mullaney v. Wilber* to this case, we conclude that, in shifting the burden of proof to petitioner to establish a defense of mistake, the trial court improperly shifted to him the burden of disproving a material element of the offense.

* * *

It is clear that under New Jersey law recklessness and mistake of fact have a mirror relationship * * * they are "two inconsistent things; thus by proving the latter the defendant would negate the former," 421 U.S. 684 at 686–87, 95 S.Ct. 1881 at 1883–1884. A showing that the actor made a reasonable mistake would establish that he did not act recklessly.

In the case before us, in advancing the argument that he had reasonably believed that the gun was unloaded when he pulled its trigger, petitioner had raised a defense whose proof would negate the mental element necessary to constitute manslaughter. Thus, under *Mullaney* he should have borne only the burden of raising the issue, not that of proving it. The state was required to refute this defense beyond a reasonable doubt as an inseparable part of proving beyond a reasonable doubt that petitioner had acted recklessly and thus was guilty of manslaughter. By shifting to petitioner the burden of proving his defense by a preponderance of the evidence, the trial court unconstitutionally relieved the state of its burden of proving all the elements of the crime beyond a reasonable doubt.

This violation of his constitutional rights entitles petitioner to a new trial. The writ of habeas corpus shall issue.

Notes and Questions

1. Suppose the *Wilson* jury had concluded that Wilson in fact mistakenly believed that the gun was unloaded but that a reasonable person in the situation would nevertheless not have been confident that this was the case and therefore would not have pointed the gun at another person and pulled the trigger. The New Jersey statute, like many other formulations of the "doctrine" of defense or ignorance of fact, limits the rule to those situations in which the accused entertained a "reasonable" mistake. Would this present an actual (and perhaps "honest") but unreasonable mistake of fact? Logically, if the jury concluded Wilson entertained such an unreasonable perception, could it logically conclude that the prosecution had proved beyond a reasonable doubt that he acted recklessly? The trial judge's instructions told the jury to convict Wilson in such a situation. Did this aspect of the instructions violate the *Winship* requirement that the prosecution prove each element of the offense beyond a reasonable doubt?

2. Howard, The Reasonableness of Mistake in the Criminal Law, 4 U.Queens L.J. 45 (1961), suggests that the disagreement concerning whether a mistake need be reasonable results from a failure to distinguish mistake as a defense to a crime requiring "general intent" and mistake offered as a defense to a crime for which negligence is sufficient. In the former case, he suggests, no reasonableness is necessary; in the latter, only a reasonable mistake logically bars liability. If a jurisdiction has adopted the general position that negligence will constitute sufficient culpability only in exceptional situations, can it also accept a rule—such as that embodied in the New Jersey statute—that mistakes of fact must, as a general matter, be reasonable? Perhaps the existence of such a statute indicates that despite indications elsewhere to the contrary, the jurisdiction has not really adopted a requirement that more than negligence is generally required for criminal liability.

3. If Wilson did mistakenly and reasonably believe the gun was unloaded and therefore cannot be convicted of either aggravated or simple manslaughter under New Jersey law, could he be convicted of aggravated

assault? Would a conviction of aggravated assault be permissible if the crime was defined as "recklessly causing serious bodily injury to another?"

4. A sexual assault defendant's claim of a mistaken belief that the victim consented is addressed in Chapter IX, infra.

b. Ignorance or Mistake of "Law"

As Judge Wilkey's discussion (see page 322, supra) indicates, ignorance of or mistake concerning "law" is often said not to affect criminal liability; in other words, "ignorance of the law is no excuse." This, of course, is consistant with the notion that ignorance or mistake should affect criminal liability only if it shows the lack of criminal "intent." Generally, the prosecution need not allege or prove that the defendant knew, or even that the defendant should have known, of the existence and meaning of the law under which she is being prosecuted. Lambert v. California, reprinted at page 282, supra, however, stands for the proposition that at least in some extraordinary circumstances this may not be true.

But as Judge Wilkey also noted, the distinction between mistakes of "fact" and those of "law" is not always clear. Sometimes, it is possible that the existence or meaning of a statute, constitutional rule, or proposition of common law may be a "fact" within the meaning of the rule that ignorance or mistake of fact may negate criminal intent. The drafters of the Model Penal Code observed:

> [T]he general principle that ignorance or mistake of law is no excuse is usually greatly overstated; it has no application when the circumstances made material by the definition of the offense include a legal element. * * * The law involved is not the law defining the offense; it is some other legal rule that characterizes the attendant circumstances that are material to the offense.

Model Penal Code, Comment to § 2.02, p. 131 (Tent. Draft No. 4, 1955).

Moreover, there is some tendency on the part of legislatures and courts to provide for limited defenses of ignorance or mistake of law, when that mistake or ignorance does not logically indicate the absence of the state of mind required by the crime charged.

While considering the following cases, consider specifically which approach is taken by the courts involved. Which approach is preferable?

UNITED STATES v. BURTON

United States Court of Appeals for the Fifth Circuit, 1984.
737 F.2d 439.

PATRICK E. HIGGINBOTHAM, CIRCUIT JUDGE:

Eventius Burton appeals his conviction by a jury on two counts of failing to file income tax returns and four counts of filing false withholding forms, contrary to 26 U.S.C. §§ 7203,[1] 7205.[2] Burton argues that the district court effectively withheld the essential element of willfulness from the jury by instructing them that his alleged good faith belief that wages were not taxable income was not a defense. * * * We are persuaded that the instruction regarding Burton's good faith was incorrect * * *. We reverse and remand for a new trial.

I

Evidence at trial established that Burton failed to file required income tax returns and filed withholding forms stating that he was exempt from paying taxes. Burton testified to his good faith belief that wages were not income, and proffered evidence that at relevant times he did not know that the law defined wages as income and consequently did not have the requisite intent to violate the law. Of course if he had no income Burton had no obligation to file a return and his statements to his employers that he was exempt would have been true.

Over Burton's objection the district court instructed the jury that:

> The court has ruled as a matter of law that a good faith belief that wages are not income is not a defense to the charges in this case.

Later he instructed the jury that:

> The test for willfulness under these counts is whether the Defendant intentionally failed to file tax returns under the charged years when he knew the law required him to do so.

* * *

II

Both the failure to file and false filing offenses require that an accused have acted "willfully," that is, intentionally in violation of a known legal duty. *United States v. Pomponio,* 429 U.S. 10, 12, 97 S.Ct. 22, 23, 50 L.Ed.2d 12 (1976). This "implements the pervasive intent of Congress to construct penalties that separate the purposeful tax violator from the well-meaning, but easily confused, mass of taxpayers." *United States v. Bishop,* 412 U.S. 346, 361, 93 S.Ct. 2008, 2017, 36 L.Ed. 2d 941 (1973). Similarly, "Congress did not intend that a person by reason of a bona fide misunderstanding as to his liability for the tax * * * should become a criminal by his mere failure to measure up to the prescribed standard of conduct." *United States v. Murdock,* 290 U.S. 389, 396, 54 S.Ct. 223, 226, 78 L.Ed. 381 (1933).

---

1. Section 7203 provides in pertinent part:

Any person required under this title to pay any estimated tax or tax, or required by this title or by regulations made under authority thereof to make a return * * * who willfully fails to pay such estimated tax or tax, [or] make such return * * * shall * * * be guilty of a misdemeanor * * *.

2. Section 7205 provides in pertinent part:

Any individual required to supply information to his employer under section 3402 who willfully supplies false or fraudulent information * * * shall * * * upon conviction thereof, be fined not more than $500, or imprisoned not more than 1 year, or both.

A bona fide misunderstanding of the tax laws can negate the essential element of willfulness and in this sense is a "defense." There is no question but that the district court's instructions took Burton's alleged bona fide misunderstanding of the taxability of wages out of the definition of willfulness. Nor is there any dispute but that such instructions would ordinarily be error, as a supplanting of the jury's role as fact finder with respect to defendant's state of mind. But the government argues that such a claim of subjective innocence must be "objectively reasonable." In short, the government urges us to conclude that it is the judge who first decides whether a defendant's claim is sufficiently credible to be considered by the jury. Persuaded that a limit of objective reasonableness improperly diminishes the jury's role, we reject the argument.

Beyond dispute, wages are income. Equally so, a defendant's specific intent is an essential element of the crimes alleged. Yet, as far-fetched as it may be, Burton's claim that he did not know that the tax laws included wages in taxable income was for the jury because the government is never entitled to a directed verdict in a criminal jury trial. *United States v. Johnson,* 718 F.2d 1317 (5th Cir.1983) (*en banc*).

We have previously allowed the jury to decide whether the taxpayer held a good faith belief that wages were not taxable income. Courts have also allowed the jury to decide the defendant's credibility when he claims he believed that to be taxable dollars must be paid in gold. *See United States v. Ware,* 608 F.2d 400 (10th Cir.1979). Similarly, we have vacated bench convictions where the defendant had a good faith, although indisputably wrong, belief that he was not required to file quarterly business returns if he didn't have the money to pay the tax owed. In the context of whether the defendant willfully violated the tax laws because he did not think his conduct would result in an understatement of income, we held that it was plain error for the trial court to invite the jury to consider what other people similarly situated would have reasonably realized. *Mann v. United States,* 319 F.2d 404, 409 (5th Cir.1963), *cert. denied,* 375 U.S. 986, 84 S.Ct. 520, 11 L.Ed.2d 474 (1964). We explained:

> The crime of income tax evasion must be accompanied by a specific intent on the part of the accused to defeat or evade the tax, which must be proved by independent evidence. Under the instruction here involved, the jury is invited to speculate as to what any other person similarly situated to Dr. Mann and with his knowledge, would reasonably have expected to be the consequences of the conduct under consideration as shown by the evidence. The test is whether Dr. Mann *himself* willfully attempted to evade or defeat the tax.

Id. (emphasis added). *See also Gaunt v. United States,* 184 F.2d 284, 291 (1st Cir.1950), *cert. denied,* 340 U.S. 917, 71 S.Ct. 350, 95 L.Ed. 662 (1951), approving a jury instruction providing that even gross negligence could not defeat a good faith claim.

The government, seeking support for its "objectively reasonable" limitation on good faith misunderstandings of the law defenses, relies on decisions holding that it is not a defense to a willful violation of the Revenue Code for the defendant to act out of disagreement with the law or out of a belief that the law is unconstitutional. It is immediately apparent that the premise of these decisions is that in each case the defendant *knew* of the tax law and was not uncertain about the duty Congress meant to impose.

Those who refuse to pay taxes as a protest against governmental policies are not asserting any misapprehension of the duty imposed by the statute; their violation of the statutory command is thus willful, and they must suffer the penalties attending their act of civil disobedience. Those who believe, even in good faith, that the income tax law is unconstitutional are similarly willful violators of the tax law if they understand the obligations the statute purports to impose upon them. One who believes a statute to be unconstitutional is entitled to challenge it in court, but disobeys it only at the risk of criminal penalties should the constitutionality of the statute be upheld. The defendant's good faith belief that the statute is unconstitutional does not negate the willfulness of his defiance of the statute, and such a defendant is not entitled to a jury instruction that his belief in the statute's unconstitutionality shields him from liability for willful violation of the statute.

Thus, we agree with the government that there is a difference between willful defiance of a statute and ignorance of a statute's existence or meaning. These distinctions, while arbitrary at their edges, distinguish citizens who simply choose not to obey a known duty from those who act out of ignorance or misunderstanding. Although the jury must, in any event, determine whether the defendant willfully violated the statute, these distinctions will control whether or not the defendant's good faith beliefs will provide a defense to the criminal charge as to which the jury should be instructed. Thus, when this issue is raised by the evidence, the jury can be told that in deciding whether the government has met its burden of proving that the defendant acted willfully, they may draw the inference that the defendant was aware of his legal obligation from acts taken in protest or to express a political view, even though made with conviction and sincerity of purpose. Such inquiries into a defendant's state of mind, while not a quest for a quantifiable and neatly measurable existence, are standard fare for juries. They are the essence of "black box" decisions.

There is a temptation for judges to decide that a defendant's claim is too incredible. This temptation is reinforced by concern that a defendant is being allowed to escape the reach of settled legal rules by erroneous arguments to a jury in an abuse of the roles of counsel and the court. Moreover, there may be concern that such objective limitations by the judge are necessary to prevent confusing "proofs" of law as an evidentiary fact. Each such concern is understandable but unfounded. The quick answer is that, apart from constitutional strictures explained in *United States v. Johnson,* such limitations upon defendants serve no practical purpose, for they will not materially affect the nature of the trial evidence or the trial. A jury is the ultimate discipline to a silly argument. Here the district court was understandably frustrated by the implausibility of Burton's contention, but he ought not have taken the question from the jury.

Nor do *United States v. Moore,* 627 F.2d 830, 833 (7th Cir.1980), *cert. denied,* 450 U.S. 916, 101 S.Ct. 1360, 67 L.Ed.2d 342 (1981), and *United States v. Ware,* 608 F.2d at 405, give much comfort to the government. In both cases the defendants claimed that they believed Federal Reserve Notes were not income. In *Ware* the trial judge specifically instructed that a good faith misunderstanding of the law did constitute a defense. 608 F.2d at 705. By contrast, the jury here was not left to conclude that it could find Burton innocent if it reasonably doubted that he was truly aware that wages were taxable. The *Moore* court did in dicta suggest that a good faith mistake must be objectively reasonable. 627 F.2d at 833. But *Moore's* alleged good faith belief stemmed not from a misunderstanding of the tax laws but from the belief that the income tax and Federal Reserve Notes were unconstitutional. *Id.* at 833. Regardless, this circuit has not adopted a rule that a defendant's claim of ignorance or good faith belief must be objectively reasonable and we decline to do so here.

* * *

Reversed and Remanded.

Notes and Questions

1. Under the case law, a defendant's belief—even if based upon a mistaken view as to some aspect of property or contract law—that he has a legal right to possession of property often is regarded as showing the lack of the "specific intent" required for the property acquisition offenses. E.g., Richardson v. United States, 403 F.2d 574, 576 (D.C.Cir.1968) ("If the jury finds that the defendant believed himself entitled to the money, it cannot properly find that he had the requisite specific intent for robbery."). But some courts appear to search for rationales to avoid applying this rule. In State v. Self, 42 Wn.App. 654, 713 P.2d 142 (1986), the defendant was charged with robbery. He claimed that he had taken the victim's property as compensation for the unpaid wages the victim admittedly owed a former employee who had hired Self to collect the debt. Self was refused a jury instruction that:

> It is a defense to a charge of theft that the property * * * was appropriated openly * * * under a good faith claim of title, even thought the claim be untenable.

The appellate court agreed that under Washington law such a good faith belief in ownership and entitlement to the property would negate the essential element of intent to steal. However, it continued, this defense "is available only where self-help is used to recover *specific* property." 42 Wn. App. at ___, 713 P.2d at 144 (emphasis in original). Here, there was no evidence that either the accused or his principle had a claim to the specific property—cash, a wallet, keys—taken from the victim by force.   In the absence of such evidence, no error was committed by the refusal to give the instructions.   The court concluded:

> Even if we were not constrained by decisions in this jurisdiction clearly contrary to Self's position, the cases cited by Self do not strike us as sensible policy in light of the purposes behind Washington's criminal code * * * [which] is "to forbid and prevent conduct that inflicts or threatens substantial harm to individual or public interests * * *." Further, we recognize as did the court in State v. Larsen, [23 Wn.App. 218, 596 P.2d 1089 (1979),] that violent resolutions of creditor-debtor disputes is contrary to public policy.   When confronted with an argument similar to Self's, the Larsen court said * * *:

>> In our view, the proposition not only is lacking in sound reason and logic, but it is utterly incompatible with and has no place in an ordered and orderly society such as ours, which eschews self-help through violence.   Adoption of the proposition would be one short step short of accepting lawless reprisal as an appropriate means of redressing grievances, real or fancied.   We reject it out of hand.

Larson, 23 Wash.App. at 219–20, 596 P.2d at 1089.

42 Wn.App. at ___, 713 P.2d at 145.   In Richardson, the defendant had taken money from the victim's wallet, but testified that this was an effort to collect a gambling debt owed by the victim.   The victim testified that Richardson used a gun; Richardson denied this.   The court responded to the argument that the rule applied "would encourage violent takings and * * * frustrate the policy of the law that a successful gambler may not recover his winnings from the loser" by saying:

> But "The taking and carrying away of the property of another in the District of Columbia without right to do so" is a misdemeanor.   D.C. Code (1967 ed.) § 22–1211.   Since this section can be violated without specific intent, it provides a deterrent to self-help by a winning gambler without rejecting the principle that specific intent turns on the actor's state of mind and not upon an objective fact.

403 F.2d at 576.   If a jurisdiction has no such offense, would a person like Richardson still be guilty of assault despite his belief that he had a legal right to take the property?   Is liability for such offenses a sufficient deterrent to action of the sort involved, or does society's interest demand that such persons be regarded as guilty of robbery?   Can the concerns expressed by the Self court be entrusted to the good judgment of jurors?

If the Self court is correct that, in general, a good faith belief in ownership and entitlement to the property taken negates the intent to steal, why should that rule be limited to situations in which self-help is used to recover "specific" property?   What would Self have to have shown to bring himself within the rule?   Is the limitation applied by the Self court based on the proposition that only evidence of a claim of ownership and entitlement to the "specific" property adequately tends to show the required belief to justify jury submission?   If so, is this an appropriate allocation of responsibility between judge and jury?

2. In United States v. Merkt, 764 F.2d 266 (5th Cir.1985), the defendant, a worker at a South Texas center for Central American refugees, was convicted of transporting two illegal aliens knowing that they were in the country in violation of the law and in willful furtherance of the alien's violation of the law. Ms. Merkt admitted having transported the aliens but claimed she did so without the requisite knowledge. This lack of knowledge was due in part, she claimed, to her belief that they were political refugees entitled to be in the country under the provisions of the 1980 Refugee Act.

She had requested that the trial judge instruct the jury that they were to acquit unless they found that she knew that the Act did not entitle them to reside lawfully in the United States. The judge refused and instead told the jury that her belief was based on a mistake of law which could not constitute a defense. A majority of the Court of Appeals panel, although reversing on other grounds, agreed because although a mistake of fact might be a defense a mistake of law could not be.

Judge Rubin disagreed on this point. He explained:

The aphorism that imputes knowledge of the law to all is not applicable if a mistaken belief concerning how the law would treat a situation negatives the existence of the *mens rea* essential to the crime charged. If an "apparent 'mistake of law' was actually a 'mistake of fact' in that the mistake pertained to a question of legal status which was determined by a law other than the one under which the defendant was prosecuted," such a mistake constitutes a valid defense. [United States v. Currier, 621 F.2d 7, 9 n. 1 (1st Cir.1980)]

* * * The statute does not penalize the transportation of any alien who has not lawfully been admitted to the United States by a person who is not aware of the alien's illegal status. The defendant's knowledge of the alien's illegal status is an essential element of the offense, which the government is required to prove. This status, in turn, can be determined only by reference to a law separate from the one defining the crime Merkt allegedly committed."

Id., at 275 (Rubin, J., concurring in the result and dissenting in part from the opinion).

OSTROSKY v. STATE

Court of Appeals of Alaska, 1985.
704 P.2d 786.

COATS, JUDGE.

This case raises the question of the extent to which a defendant can rely on mistake of law as a defense to a fish and game violation.

Harold Ostrosky and his two daughters were convicted of fishing without a valid limited entry permit in 1979. Ostrosky's daughters moved for post-conviction relief, contending that the Limited Entry Act violated equal protection. Judge Victor D. Carlson found the act unconstitutional and vacated the convictions on August 14, 1981. Ostrosky was allowed to join in the action, and his conviction was set aside on August 25, 1981. The state appealed. This court certified the case to the supreme court, and the supreme court accepted the case for decision.

On July 3, 1983, Ostrosky was fishing with a drift gill net in open waters off Naknek. Trooper Gary Folger, acting as a fish and wildlife protection officer, boarded Ostrosky's boat and checked it for fish. Despite Ostrosky's admission that he had no permit, the trooper did not arrest Ostrosky or try to stop him from fishing.

On July 7, 1983, while the state's appeal in Ostrosky's earlier case was still pending, the state filed an emergency request with the supreme court for a stay of the effect of Judge Carlson's ruling in that case, pursuant to Appellate Rule 504. The request alleged that "irreparable harm" would result if the stay were not granted, because Ostrosky had continued to fish the waters of Bristol Bay without a permit, creating a "serious potential for violence" in the area and "undermining the fishermen's confidence in the limited entry system." * * * Chief Justice Edmond Burke, acting as a single justice, entered an order granting the stay pending the announcement by the supreme court of a decision in Ostrosky's case. The order states, "the intent of this order is to permit the continued enforcement of the Limited Entry Act pending this court's decision on the merits." On July 8, 1983, Trooper Folger cited Ostrosky for fishing without a permit on that date, for fishing without permit on July 3, and for illegal possession of salmon.

On July 19, 1983, the Alaska Supreme Court reversed Judge Carlson's ruling and upheld the Limited Entry Act. After the supreme court's decision, Ostrosky filed a motion to dismiss in the present case alleging that, at the time he was charged with violating the Limited Entry Act, the Act had been declared unconstitutional in a case in which he was a party. Ostrosky argued that he was entitled to rely on Judge Carlson's ruling. Judge Carlson ruled that Ostrosky had no right to rely on his earlier decision and that by fishing, Ostrosky had taken the risk that the earlier decision would be reversed by the supreme court.

Ostrosky then asked the court to instruct the jury that reasonable reliance on a judicial decision was a defense to this prosecution. Judge Carlson denied this request. He also ruled that Ostrosky could not present testimony concerning reasonable reliance on a judicial decision since that testimony would be irrelevant. Ostrosky at this point made an offer of proof that he would testify that at the time he was fishing he believed that he was fishing legally. He represented that he relied on Judge Carlson's decision declaring the Limited Entry Act unconstitutional and that he had read an article in the *Fisherman's Journal* which reported that a magistrate in Kenai had also ruled that the Limited Entry Act was unconstitutional. He also indicated that after Judge Carlson's ruling declaring the Limited Entry Act to be unconstitutional, Ostrosky had talked to his attorney who had assured him that he would not be arrested for fishing without a permit during the 1983 season.

After Judge Carlson ruled Ostrosky's defense of mistake of law was irrelevant and that he would not give a jury instruction on this defense, Ostrosky agreed to a court trial on the condition that his objection to this ruling would be preserved for appeal. Ostrosky was convicted following a court trial. He now appeals to this court.

The defense of reasonable reliance on a statute or judicial decision is discussed in W. LaFave and A. Scott, *Criminal Law* § 47, at 366–67 (1972):

An individual should be able reasonably to rely upon a statute or other enactment under which his conduct would not be criminal, so that he need not fear conviction if subsequent to his conduct the statute is declared invalid. A contrary rule would be inconsistent with the sound policy that the community is to be encouraged to act in compliance with legislation. Thus, just as it is no defense that the defendant mistakenly believed the statute under which he was prosecuted to be unconstitutional, it is a defense that he reasonably relied upon a statute permitting his conduct though it turned out to be an unconstitutional enactment.

For essentially the same reason, the better view is that it is a defense that the defendant acted in reasonable reliance upon a judicial decision, opinion or judgment later determined to be invalid or erroneous. The clearest case is that in which the defendant's reliance was upon a decision of the highest court of the jurisdiction, later overruled, whether the first decision involved the constitutionality of a statute, the interpretation of a statute, or the meaning of the common law. A contrary rule, whereby the subsequent holding would apply retroactively to the defendant's detriment, would be as unfair as ex post facto legislation.

Under the majority view, reasonable reliance upon a decision of a lower court is likewise a defense. Thus, if the lower court has found a repealer statute constitutional, has declared the relevant criminal statute unconstitutional, or has enjoined enforcement of the statute, there may be a basis for reasonable reliance. However, in the case of lower court decisions there is more likely to arise a question of whether the reliance is reasonable. It has been suggested, for example, that reliance should not be a defense when it was known that the decision of the lower court was on appeal.

We note also that the Model Penal Code provides for mistake of law as an affirmative defense. [See Section 2.04(3) reprinted at page 323, supra.]

* * *

We note that the revised criminal code, which appears to attempt to codify defenses to criminal acts, does not provide for a defense of mistake of law. AS 11.81.620(a) provides:

(a) Knowledge, recklessness, or criminal negligence as to whether conduct constitutes an offense, or knowledge, recklessness, or criminal negligence as to the existence, meaning, or application of the provision of law defining an offense, is not an element of an offense unless the provision of law clearly so provides. Use of the phrase "intent to commit a crime", "intent to promote or facilitate the commission of a crime", or like terminology in a provision of law does not require that the defendant act with a culpable mental state as to the criminality of the conduct that is the object of the defendant's intent.

The commentary to the code indicates that this section is intended to codify "the universal principal that ordinarily ignorance of the law is not a defense." In tracing AS 11.81.620(a) * * * we discover [it] * * * is derived from * * * from New York Penal Law § 15.20(1). New York Penal Law § 15.20 provides for a defense of reasonable mistake of law. Therefore, it appears probable that the drafters of the revised criminal code were aware of the New York provision and did not include it in the revised criminal code. This could mean that the legislature did not intend to allow a mistake of law defense in the revised code. It could also mean that the legislature overlooked the provision or wanted to leave the defense of mistake of law for later court determination. Since the commentary is silent, it is difficult for us to ascertain the legislative intent.

Furthermore, even if we were to conclude that the legislature rejected a defense of reasonable mistake of law in the revised code, that would not mean that the legislature intended that rejection to apply to fish and game offenses. AS 11.81.620(a) only applies to those offenses set forth in Title 11.

The state concedes that "most courts and commentators recognize that a person should be able to rely upon a judicial decision, even if that decision is later overruled." However, the state argues that we should hold that the defense of reasonable reliance on a court decision should be limited to decisions by the state appellate courts or the United States Supreme Court.

In the absence of any statutory or case law establishing or rejecting such a defense, we conclude that a concern for due process of law requires us to establish at least a limited defense. Fish and game laws regulate legitimate activity. Violations of those regulations are *malum prohibitum*, not *malum in se*. As the court stated in *Kratz v. Kratz,* 477 F.Supp. 463, 481 (E.D.Pa.1979):

> It would be an act of "intolerable injustice" to hold criminally liable a person who had engaged in certain conduct in reasonable reliance upon a judicial opinion instructing that such conduct is legal. Indeed, the reliance defense is required by the constitutional guarantee of due process as illuminated by the Supreme Court in *Marks v. United States,* 430 U.S. 188, 97 S.Ct. 990, 51 L.Ed.2d 260 (1977), *Cox v. Louisiana,* 379 U.S. 559, 85 S.Ct. 476, 13 L.Ed.2d 487 (1965) and *Raley v. Ohio,* 360 U.S. 423, 79 S.Ct. 1257, 3 L.Ed.2d 1344 (1959). [Footnotes omitted.]

However, we believe that the defense of reasonable mistake of law must be a limited defense in light of the fact that the general rule of law is that mistake of law is not a defense. The policy behind this rule is to encourage people to learn and know the law; a contrary rule would reward intentional ignorance of the law. The traditional rule of law that mistake of law is not a defense is based upon the fear "that its absence would encourage and reward public ignorance of the law to the detriment of our organized legal system, and would encourage universal pleas of ignorance of the law that would constantly pose confusing and, to a great extent, insolvable issues of fact to juries and judges, thereby bogging down our adjudicative system." *United States v. Barker,* 546 F.2d 940, 954 (D.C.Cir.1976) (Merhige, District J., concurring).

Model Penal Code § 2.04(4) (Proposed Official Draft 1962) provides:

(4) The defendant must prove a defense arising under Subsection (3) [quoted above] of this Section by a preponderance of evidence.

An earlier version of this subsection contained similar language but added:

The reasonableness of the belief claimed to constitute the defense shall be determined as a question of law by the Court.

§ 2.04(4) (Tentative Draft No. 4, 1955). We believe that the 1955 Tentative Draft provision sets forth a reasonable procedure for a trial court to follow in deciding whether a defense of mistake of law has been established.

We hold that a defense of mistake of law is an affirmative defense which the defendant must prove to the court by a preponderance of the evidence. We believe that this procedure will allow a defendant in a criminal case to obtain relief in cases where it would be unfair to hold him to knowledge of the law. Making the defense an affirmative defense argued to the court should protect against abuses of the defense and should ultimately make the law in this area more uniform as judges make decisions concerning what is a reasonable mistake of law. The determination of whether the defense applies requires a legal, technical application of due process considerations, a task within the judicial function. This determination will often depend on an understanding of the legal precedential value of decisions of courts at various levels, and of the appeals process. There is great potential for confusion and distraction if the jury were required, for instance, to determine whether it was reasonable to rely on a superior court decision reversing a district court decision (but in accord with the decisions of another district judge) which is being appealed to the supreme court.

The state would have us rule as a matter of law that it was unreasonable for Ostrosky to rely on Judge Carlson's decision that the Limited Entry Act was unconstitutional. The state argues that since the decision was a trial court decision it was not binding on other courts and, since the decision was on appeal, Ostrosky should have been aware that the decision could be reversed. There is support in the cases and commentary on this issue which suggests that normally it might be unreasonable to rely on a decision of a trial court which is on appeal. However, the question of whether a person's reliance on a lower court decision is reasonable or not is in the first instance a question for the trial court. *See id.; Kratz v. Kratz,* 477 F.Supp. at 481 n. 47 (E.D.Pa. 1979). We are not prepared to rule, as a matter of law, that in every case it would be unreasonable to rely on a lower court decision which is on appeal.

We note that in this case Ostrosky does not just represent that he relied on the ruling of the superior court. The court ruling involved was a case in which Ostrosky was a party. He also claims that his attorney assured him that the decision meant that he could fish.[2] When Ostrosky started fishing, Trooper Folger did not cite him or warn him not to fish. Furthermore, the papers filed with the courts by the Department of Law in July of 1983, taken on their face, indicate that the Department of Law was operating under the assumption that it needed to stay Judge Carlson's decision in order to enforce the Limited Entry Act. If we look at these factors alone, in the light most favorable to Ostrosky, it appears that he has a sufficient claim of reasonable mistake of law to at least allow him to have a hearing on this issue. We therefore remand the case to allow Ostrosky to develop his defense of reasonable mistake of law at a hearing.

* * *

BRYNER, CHIEF JUDGE, dissenting.

* * * In light of the revised criminal code's treatment of defenses and affirmative defenses and in light of the express provisions of AS 11.81.620(a) and the legislative history of that statutory provision I think it reasonably clear that the legislature rejected mistake of law as a defense to criminal responsibility. The majority's decision to create such a defense is therefore unsound.[1]

2. The drafters of the Model Penal Code did not provide for a mistake of law defense based solely upon the advice of an attorney, and we are not today recognizing such a defense. We hold only that when a defendant is seeking to establish the defense of reasonable reliance on a judicial decision, the fact that he consulted an attorney and was told that the decision meant he could embark on a contemplated course of conduct is probative evidence of the reasonableness of the reliance.

1. In any event, if a reasonable mistake of law defense is to be created, I see no justification whatsoever for taking the factual issues involved in that defense away from the jury. There is nothing in the Model Penal Code to suggest that the defense should not be decided by the jury. Nor has the majority found any other juris-

diction permitting a defense of reasonable mistake of law to be raised but treating it as an issue exclusively for the court.

The reasonableness of a defendant's beliefs as to surrounding circumstances is a question resolved by juries in numerous and varied contexts. To suggest that the issue should be taken from the jury in this situation simply because it is potentially confusing betrays a profound mistrust of juries, which is both entirely unwarranted and fundamentally at odds with our traditional system of justice. I perceive utterly no connection between the type of factual issues that the majority's opinion in this case would remove from the jury's consideration and the type of extrinsic policy considerations involved in the entrapment defense.

Moreover, the defense created by the majority is unnecessary: it is a cumbersome and potentially confusing general rule adopted solely to dispose of the specific problem in this case. The problem is susceptible of a far more limited cure.

The crucial facts here are not disputed. Ostrosky challenged the constitutional validity of the limited entry permit system and won in the superior court. The state could have moved immediately for a stay pending appeal but did not. Having personally obtained a favorable judgment from a court of general jurisdiction in a case in which he was himself the plaintiff,[2] and no stay pending appeal having been sought by the state, Ostrosky resumed fishing. No prior Alaska judicial decision addressed the question whether, under the circumstances, Ostrosky was legally entitled to rely on the superior court's ruling.

It seems clear from the record that the Office of the Attorney General initially believed Ostrosky was entitled to fish unless a stay was issued. The state so represented in the motion for a stay that it filed with the supreme court after realizing that Ostrosky had resumed fishing. Similarly, the supreme court justice who granted the state's motion for a stay apparently believed a stay was necessary to prevent Ostrosky from relying on the superior court ruling. To hold that Ostrosky could subsequently be prosecuted for sharing this same view seems, under the circumstances, preposterous. I would, accordingly, simply hold that in the peculiar factual setting of this case, it would be fundamentally unfair, and violative of the Alaska Constitution's guarantee of due process, to permit Ostrosky to be convicted for a limited entry violation committed after the superior court's ruling but before issuance of the stay pending appeal.

Since I believe Ostrosky's conviction must be reversed and the prosecution dismissed as a matter of law, I dissent.

Notes and Questions

1. The majority in *Ostrosky* gave very limited significance to the defendant's claim that his attorney had assured him that his contemplated action would not be criminal. It has been stated that the cases "uniformly hold" that such advice from a private counsel does not constitute a defense. W. LaFave and A. Scot, Criminal Law 419–20 (2nd ed. 1986). But the discussion of the court in Long v. State, 44 Del. (5 Terry) 262, 65 A.2d 489 (1949) suggests that in some such cases, at least, the defendant has "made a bona fide, diligent effort, adopting a course and resorting to sources and means at least as appropriate as any afforded under our legal system, to ascertain and abide by the law," and consequently should be excused. The Delaware court expressed the view that a defendant might appropriately be excused on the advice of counsel where, but only where:

2. An integral part of my conclusion that this case can be resolved as *sui generis* is that Ostrosky was a party in the litigation in which the judgment he relied on was rendered. I do not mean to suggest that, in the absence of a reasonable mistake of law defense, other individuals, who were not parties to Ostrosky's action, would be on similar footing.

he made a full disclosure to the attorney of the relevant circumstances as well as of what he proposed to do, and * * * he had no substantial reason to believe that the advice he received as ill-founded, such as circumstances reasonably indicating that the attorney was incompetent to give advice about the matter, or had not given the question sufficient consideration, or that the advice was lacking in candor.

44 Del. (5 Terry) at 282, 65 A.2d at 498–99. Would such a rule encourage ignorance of the law or would it encourage desirable—and often or sometimes successful—efforts to ascertain it? Would it create a substantial danger of collusion between defendants and attorneys pursuant to which attorneys would falsely testify that they had been consulted and had advised that the contemplated conduct was not criminal?

2. To what extent should defendants be permitted to avoid criminal liability by showing a belief that their actions were authorized by a governmental official or employee? This was presented in a number of prosecutions arising out of the famous "Watergate break-ins," which led to the resignation of then-president Richard Nixon. In United States v. Barker, 514 F.2d 208 (D.C.Cir.1975), cert. denied, 421 U.S. 1013, 95 S.Ct. 2420, 44 L.Ed.2d 682 (1975), Barker and other so-called "footsoldiers" of the break-in entered guilty pleas to seven charges related to the activities. They then unsuccessfully sought to withdraw those pleas. This was sought on the ground that if permitted to plead not guilty, the defendants would have a valid defense based upon their belief that the break-ins were authorized by one Howard Hunt, whom the defendants believed to be acting for the United States government. On appeal, the court held that regardless of the merits of the defendants' claims of innocence, the trial judge did not abuse his discretion in refusing to permit them to withdraw their pleas. Several members of the court, however, expressed views as to the merits of the defendants' claim to a defense. Judge MacKinnon urged that the defendants be regarded as having made a mistake of "fact"—"a mistake as to the fact that all necessary authorization for their activities had been obtained"—and under prevailing doctrine be afforded a defense on this basis. 514 F.2d at 241 (MacKinnon, J., dissenting). Judge Wilkey, on the other hand, acknowledged that the mistake was most properly characterized as one of "law"—that the break-ins were lawful because authorized by Hunt. But he further urged that at least in the context before the court (involving a citizen who participates in an operation at the request of one believed to be a police officer or agent) a defense be made available upon a showing that the defendants honestly and reasonably believed the operation was lawful:

We should be most reluctant criminally to prosecute the public-spirited citizen who freely performs his civic duty—especially in a day when noninvolvement appears the watchword of citizens at the scene of a crime. This does not mean that protection need be afforded every person who asserts a belief, however irrational, that he acted at the behest of an officer of the law. A balance may be struck here by requiring that the citizen's mistake as to the officer's authority be reasonable. All the circumstances surrounding the incident in question would enter into such a determination, including the kind of operation the citizen was asked to take part in and, in cases where the "officer" was not such in reality, the objective manifestations of his office. * * *

There is a wealth of evidence in this case that the appellants honestly and reasonably believed they were engaged in a top-secret national security operation lawfully authorized by a government intelligence agency. According to their affidavits, Hunt was widely known in Miami's Cuban-American community as a CIA agent; indeed he was Barker's "supervisor" for the Bay of Pigs invasion. Martinez has long been on CIA retainer, and Sturgis has taken part in the Bay of Pigs affair and other "clandestine operations" against the Castro regime. Gonzales was fully apprised of his colleagues' CIA operations. Further, Hunt had an office at the White House. He engaged Barker (along with Martinez and Liddy) for the Ellsberg break-in, which apparently had official authorization, in order to gather information on "a traitor to this country who had been giving information to the Russian Embassy." They used CIA tools and equipment for the operation. Subsequently Hunt arranged to have the appellants stand guard at the casket of former FBI Director J. Edgar Hoover. As to the Watergate break-in, they were told that its purpose was to seek "financial information * * * indicating Cuban communist money was going to the Democratic campaign." Hunt said he had information to that effect. If true, this was clearly an important national security matter. The appellants had no reason to doubt Hunt's authority, or the reliability of his information. * * * He was employed by the Executive, had inside information concerning government affairs, and had supervised clandestine operations in the past. Certainly a juror could find that the appellants' mistake of law was reasonable under these circumstances.

514 F.2d at 268–69 (Wilkey, J., dissenting).

Some of the same "footsoldiers" also participated in another burglary under the leadership of Howard Hunt. They had broken into the office of a psychiatrist in an effort to obtain evidence which might discredit a prominent opponent of the Viet Nam war and, as a result, were convicted for violating the doctor's civil rights. These convictions were overturned on appeal. United States v. Barker, 546 F.2d 940 (D.C.Cir.1976). Two of the three members of the court agreed that reversal was required but each wrote separate opinions. Judge Wilkey urged that the jury should have been instructed that a defense exists if the defendants acted in objectively reasonable reliance upon the authority of a government official who requested the action. 546 F.2d at 949. Judge Merhige, on the other hand, urged that the defense be limited to situations in which the defendants acted in reasonable reliance upon a conclusion or statement of the law issued by an official charged with interpretation, administration or enforcement responsibilities in the relevant field:

The reasonableness of the reliance may dissipate if one depends on nonenforceable advisory opinions of minor officials * * *. * * * [T]he defense [therefore] does not extend to reliance on individuals, who although employed in an official capacity, have no interpretative or administrative responsibilities in the area associated with the legal concepts involved in the mistaken opinion or decision.

546 F.2d at 956. Further, Judge Merige argued, the person relied upon must actually be an appropriate official; no defense is therefore available to one who relies—although reasonably—upon "a stranger to public office" erroneously believing that person to be a public official. Id. On the facts of the case, he continued:

> A jury may well find that John Erlichman, then Assistant to the President for Domestic Affairs, expressed or implied that the break-in of Dr. Fielding's office was legal under a national security rationale, and that Hunt, as an executive official in a go-between capacity, passed the position on to the defendants, which they, acting as reasonable men, relied upon in performing the break-in.

Id., at 957. Erlichman was convicted for his role in the same burglary but was unsuccessful in his efforts to seek reversal. The court rejected his claim of a good faith belief in the legality of the break-in. This was because he was unable to offer evidence of any actual authorization or that any superior had misled him. United States v. Erlichman, 546 F.2d 910 (D.C.Cir.1976), cert. denied 429 U.S. 1120, 97 S.Ct. 1155, 57 L.Ed.2d 570 (1977).

3. As the opinion in *Burton* makes clear, an erroneous but good faith belief in the unconstitutionality of a statute will not be accepted as a defense. Courts have similarly rejected defenses based on claims, no matter how sincerely held, that the conduct in question is required or legitimated by some "higher" law. See United States v. Berrigan, 283 F.Supp. 336 (D.Md.1968), convictions aff'd 417 F.2d 1002, 1009 (4th Cir. 1969), cert. denied 397 U.S. 909, 90 S.Ct. 907, 25 L.Ed.2d 90 (1969). There the defendants, charged with willfully injuring the property of the United States (draft records) claimed, *inter alia,* that they could not have the requisite state of mind because of their belief that the Viet Nam war was illegal under international law. In Gaetano v. United States, 406 A.2d 1291 (D.C.App.1979) the defendants were charged with tresspassing at an abortion clinic. They claimed that they had the right to do this in order to save the lives of fetuses whom they believed to be persons. The defense contentions in both *Berrigan* and *Gaetano* were rejected. Why should such presumably well-motivated people be subjected to punishment?

2. INTOXICATION

Given the frequently-encountered coincidence between consumption of intoxicants and criminal activity, the effect of intoxication upon criminal liability is at least a potentially important issue. Indeed, the implications of having a constitutional rule on the effect of intoxication on criminal responsibility are enormous. Powell v. Texas, which was first considered in section V. A. (see note 1, page 173, supra) for its implications on the requirement of an "act", is here presented at greater length. It represents an effort to grapple seriously with the problem of creating constitutional rules in this area when there are such uncertainties concerning the effect of the ingestion of alcohol and the nature of alcoholism. These considerations appear to have played an important role in the reluctance of some members of the Court to read Robinson v. California (reprinted at page 168, supra), as broadly as other Justices and many others thought appropriate. It has been widely assumed that *Powell* rejects a broad reading of *Robinson* as announcing a constitutionally-required defense that otherwise criminal conduct cannot be punished if it was attributable to the defendant's "involntary" consumption of intoxicants. Thus it is left to the states to formulate their individual rules on the legal effect of intoxication, and this has continued to be an area of considerable theoretical, if not practical, variation. But if the positions of the various Justices in *Powell* are carefully considered, what is the "holding" of the case? What are its implications?

The contending positions in *Powell* represent a major stage in the ongoing struggle between criminal law traditionalists and those who would have the teachings of the behavioral sciences play a larger role. In reading the various opinions consider, in particular, the position of Mr. Justice White as to the meaning of *Robinson*. Is he closer to Mr. Justice Marshall or Mr. Justice Fortas?

Following *Powell,* a state case, State v. Stasio, is offered in which the court rejects one commonly asserted limitation on the use of voluntary intoxication as a defense: that it can be used only to "prove" the absence of a specific intent if one is required by the crime charged.

The majority in *Stasio* finds no sound basis for distinguishing between a defendant charged with rape and one charged with assault with intent to rape, for purposes of allowing him to try to persuade the trier of fact that due to his intoxication, he did not possess the requisite intent to commit the crime charged. Is there a need to discourage consumption of intoxicants, especially by those prone to commit crimes, and will this goal be furthered by such a limitation on the defense? If so, why should a claim of voluntary intoxication ever be permitted? Given the widespread knowledge in our society concerning the effects of intoxication, is it inappropriate to say that anyone who voluntarily puts himself in that condition has shown the requisite culpability to justify conviction? Does that theory of "substituted" intent work as well where the crime requires proof of, in Model Penal Code terms, purpose or knowledge as where it is satisfied by negligence or recklessness?

POWELL v. TEXAS

Supreme Court of the United States, 1968.
392 U.S. 514, 88 S.Ct. 2145, 20 L.Ed.2d 1254.

MR. JUSTICE MARSHALL announced the judgment of the Court and delivered an opinion in which THE CHIEF JUSTICE, MR. JUSTICE BLACK, and MR. JUSTICE HARLAN join.

In late December 1966, appellant was arrested and charged with being found in a state of intoxication in a public place, in violation of

Vernon's Ann.Texas Penal Code, Art. 477 (1952), which reads as follows:

> "Whoever shall get drunk or be found in a state of intoxication in any public place, or at any private house except his own, shall be fined not exceeding one hundred dollars."

Appellant was tried in the Corporation Court of Austin, Texas, found guilty, and fined $20. He appealed to the County Court at Law No. 1 of Travis County, Texas, where a trial *de novo* was held. His counsel urged that appellant was "afflicted with the disease of chronic alcoholism," that "his appearance in public [while drunk was] * * * not of his own volition," and therefore that to punish him criminally for that conduct would be cruel and unusual, in violation of the Eighth and Fourteenth Amendments to the United States Constitution.

The trial judge in the county court, sitting without a jury, made certain findings of fact, * * * but ruled as a matter of law that chronic alcoholism was not a defense to the charge. He found appellant guilty, and fined him $50. There being no further right to appeal within the Texas judicial system, appellant appealed to this Court * * *.

I.

The principal testimony was that of Dr. David Wade, a Fellow of the American Medical Association, duly certificated in psychiatry. His testimony consumed a total of 17 pages in the trial transcript. Five of those pages were taken up with a recitation of Dr. Wade's qualifications. In the next 12 pages Dr. Wade was examined by appellant's counsel, cross-examined by the State, and re-examined by the defense, and those 12 pages contain virtually all the material developed at trial which is relevant to the constitutional issue we face here. Dr. Wade sketched the outlines of the "disease" concept of alcoholism; noted that there is no generally accepted definition of "alcoholism"; alluded to the ongoing debate within the medical profession over whether alcohol is actually physically "addicting" or merely psychologically "habituating"; and concluded that in either case a "chronic alcoholic" is an "involuntary drinker," who is "powerless not to drink," and who "loses his self-control over his drinking." He testified that he had examined appellant, and that appellant is a "chronic alcoholic," who "by the time he has reached [the state of intoxication] * * * is not able to control his behavior, and [who] * * * has reached this point because he has an uncontrollable compulsion to drink." Dr. Wade also responded in the negative to the question whether appellant has "the willpower to resist the constant excessive consumption of alcohol." He added that in his opinion jailing appellant without medical attention would operate neither to rehabilitate him nor to lessen his desire for alcohol.

On cross-examination, Dr. Wade admitted that when appellant was sober he knew the difference between right and wrong, and he responded affirmatively to the question whether appellant's act in taking the first drink in any given instance when he was sober was a "voluntary exercise of his will." Qualifying his answer, Dr. Wade stated that "these individuals have a compulsion, and this compulsion, while not completely overpowering, is a very strong influence, an exceedingly strong influence, and this compulsion coupled with the firm belief in their mind that they are going to be able to handle it from now on causes their judgment to be somewhat clouded."

Appellant testified concerning the history of his drinking problem. He reviewed his many arrests for drunkenness; testified that he was unable to stop drinking; stated that when he was intoxicated he had no control over his actions and could not remember them later, but that he did not become violent; and admitted that he did not remember his arrest on the occasion for which he was being tried. On cross-examination, appellant admitted that he had had one drink on the morning of the trial and had been able to discontinue drinking.

* * *

Following this abbreviated exposition of the problem before it, the trial court indicated its intention to disallow appellant's claimed defense of "chronic alcoholism." Thereupon defense counsel submitted, and the trial court entered, the following "findings of fact":

"(1) That chronic alcoholism is a disease which destroys the afflicted person's will power to resist the constant, excessive consumption of alcohol.

"(2) That a chronic alcoholic does not appear in public by his own volition but under a compulsion symptomatic of the disease of chronic alcoholism.

"(3) That Leroy Powell, defendant herein, is a chronic alcoholic who is afflicted with the disease of chronic alcoholism."

Whatever else may be said of them, those are not "findings of fact" in any recognizable, traditional sense in which that term has been used in a court of law; they are the premises of a syllogism transparently designed to bring this case within the scope of this Court's opinion in Robinson v. State of California, 370 U.S. 660, 82 S.Ct. 1417, 8 L.Ed.2d 758 (1962). Nonetheless, the dissent would have us adopt these "findings" without critical examination; it would use them as the basis for a constitutional holding that "a person may not be punished if the condition essential to constitute the defined crime is part of the pattern of his disease and is occasioned by a compulsion symptomatic of the disease." * * *

The difficulty with that position * * * is that it goes much too far on the basis of too little knowledge. In the first place, the record in this case is utterly inadequate to permit the sort of informed and responsible adjudication which alone can support the announcement of an important and wide-ranging new constitutional principle. We know very little about the circumstances surrounding the drinking bout which resulted in this conviction, or about Leroy Powell's drinking problem, or indeed about alcoholism itself. The trial hardly reflects the sharp legal and evidentiary clash between fully prepared adversary litigants which is traditionally expected in major constitutional cases. The State put on only one witness, the arresting officer. The defense put on three—a policeman who testified to appellant's long history of arrests for public drunkenness, the psychiatrist, and appellant himself.

Furthermore, the inescapable fact is that there is no agreement among members of the medical profession about what it means to say that "alcoholism" is a "disease." * * *

Nor is there any substantial consensus as to the "manifestations of alcoholism." * * *

The trial court's "finding" that Powell "is afflicted with the disease of chronic alcoholism," which "destroys the afflicted person's will power to resist the constant, excessive consumption of alcohol" covers a multitude of sins. Dr. Wade's testimony that appellant suffered from a compulsion which was an "exceedingly strong influence," but which was "not completely overpowering" is at least more carefully stated, if no less mystifying. * * *

Dr. Wade did testify that once appellant began drinking he appeared to have no control over the amount of alcohol he finally ingested. Appellant's own testimony concerning his drinking on the day of the trial would certainly appear, however, to cast doubt upon the conclusion that he was without control over his consumption of alcohol when he had sufficiently important reasons to exercise such control. However that may be, there are more serious factual and conceptual difficulties with reading this record to show that appellant was unable to abstain from drinking. Dr. Wade testified that when appellant was sober, the act of taking the first drink was a "voluntary exercise of his will," but that this exercise of will was undertaken under the "exceedingly strong influence" of a "compulsion" which was "not completely overpowering." Such concepts, when juxtaposed in this fashion, have little meaning.

* * *

It is one thing to say that if a man is deprived of alcohol his hands will begin to shake, he will suffer agonizing pains and ultimately he will have hallucinations; it is quite another to say that a man has a "compulsion" to take a drink, but that he also retains a certain amount of "free will" with which to resist. It is simply impossible, in the present state of our knowledge, to ascribe a useful meaning to the latter statement. This definitional confusion reflects, of course, not merely the undeveloped state of the psychiatric art but also the conceptual difficulties inevitably attendant upon the importation of scientific and medical models into a legal system generally predicated upon a different set of assumptions.

II.

Despite the comparatively primitive state of our knowledge on the subject, it cannot be denied that the destructive use of alcoholic beverages is one of our principal social and public health problems. The lowest current informed estimate places the number of "alcoholics" in America (definitional problems aside) at 4,000,000, and most authorities are inclined to put the figure considerably higher. The problem is compounded by the fact that a very large percentage of the alcoholics in this country are "invisible"—they possess the means to keep their drinking problems secret, and the traditionally uncharitable attitude of our society toward alcoholics causes many of them to refrain from seeking treatment from any source. Nor can it be gain-said that the legislative response to this enormous problem has in general been inadequate.

There is as yet no known generally effective method for treating the vast number of alcoholics in our society. Some individual alcoholics have responded to particular forms of therapy with remissions of their symptomatic dependence upon the drug. But just as there is no agreement among doctors and social workers with respect to the causes of alcoholism, there is no consensus as to why particular treatments have been effective in particular cases and there is no generally agreed-upon approach to the problem of treatment on a large scale. Most psychiatrists are apparently of the opinion that alcoholism is far more difficult to treat than other forms of behavioral disorders, and some believe it is impossible to cure by means of psychotherapy; indeed, the medical profession as a whole, and psychiatrists in particular, have been severely criticised for the prevailing reluctance to undertake the treatment of drinking problems. Thus it is entirely possible that, even were the manpower and facilities available for a full-scale attack upon chronic alcoholism, we would find ourselves unable to help the vast bulk of our "visible"—let alone our "invisible"—alcoholic population.

However, facilities for the attempted treatment of indigent alcoholics are woefully lacking throughout the country. It would be tragic to return large numbers of helpless, sometimes dangerous and frequently unsanitary inebriates to the streets of our cities without even the opportunity to sober up adequately which a brief jail term provides. Presumably no State or city will tolerate such a state of affairs. Yet the medical profession cannot, and does not, tell us with any assurance that, even if the buildings, equipment and trained personnel were made available, it could provide anything more than slightly higher-class jails for our indigent habitual inebriates. Thus we run the grave risk that nothing will be accomplished beyond the hanging of a new sign—reading "hospital"—over one wing of the jailhouse.

One virtue of the criminal process is, at least, that the duration of penal incarceration typically has some outside statutory limit; this is universally true in the case of petty offenses, such as public drunkenness, where jail terms are quite short on the whole. "Therapeutic civil commitment" lacks this feature; one is typically committed until one is "cured." Thus, to do otherwise than affirm might subject indigent alcoholics to the risk that they may be locked up for an indefinite period of time under the same conditions as before, with no more hope than before of receiving effective treatment and no prospect of periodic "freedom."

Faced with this unpleasant reality, we are unable to assert that the use of the criminal process as a means of dealing with the public aspects of problem drinking can never be defended as rational. The picture of the penniless drunk propelled aimlessly and endlessly through the law's "revolving door" of arrest, incarceration, release and re-arrest is not a pretty one. But before we condemn the present practice across-the-board, perhaps we ought to be able to point to some clear promise of a better world for these unfortunate people. Unfortunately, no such promise has yet been forthcoming. If, in addition to the absence of a coherent approach to the problem of treatment, we consider the almost complete absence of facilities and manpower for the implementation of a rehabilitation program, it is difficult to say in the present context that the criminal process is utterly lacking in social value. This Court has never held that anything in the Constitution requires that penal sanctions be designed solely to achieve therapeutic or rehabilitative effects, and it can hardly be said with assurance that incarceration serves such purposes any better for the general run of criminals than it does for public drunks.

Ignorance likewise impedes our assessment of the deterrent effect of criminal sanctions for public drunkenness. The fact that a high percentage of American alcoholics conceal their drinking problems, not merely by avoiding public displays of intoxication but also by shunning all forms of treatment, is indicative that some powerful deterrent operates to inhibit the public revelation of the existence of alcoholism. Quite probably this deterrent effect can be largely attributed to the harsh moral attitude which our society has traditionally taken toward intoxication and the shame which we have associated with alcoholism. Criminal conviction represents the degrading public revelation of what Anglo-American society has long condemned as a moral defect, and the existence of criminal sanctions may serve to reinforce this cultural taboo, just as we presume it serves to reinforce other, stronger feelings against murder, rape, theft, and other forms of antisocial conduct.

Obviously, chronic alcoholics have not been deterred from drinking to excess by the existence of criminal sanctions against public drunkenness. But all those who violate penal laws of any kind are by definition undeterred. The long-standing and still raging debate over the validity of the deterrence justification for penal sanctions has not reached any sufficiently clear conclusions to permit it to be said that such sanctions are ineffective in any particular context or for any particular group of people who are able to appreciate the consequences of their acts. Certainly no effort was made at the trial of this case, beyond a monosyllabic answer to a perfunctory one-line question, to determine the effectiveness of penal sanctions in deterring Leroy Powell in particular or chronic alcoholics in general from drinking at all or from getting drunk in particular places or at particular times.

III.

Appellant claims that his conviction on the facts of this case would violate the Cruel and Unusual Punishment Clause of the Eighth Amendment as applied to the States through the Fourteenth Amendment. The primary purpose of that clause has always been considered, and properly so, to be directed at the method or kind of punishment imposed for the violation of criminal statutes; the nature of the conduct made criminal is ordinarily relevant only to the fitness of the punishment imposed.

*   *   *

Appellant, however, seeks to come within the application of the Cruel and Unusual Punishment Clause announced in Robinson v. State of California, 370 U.S. 660, 82 S.Ct. 1417, 8 L.Ed.2d 758 (1962), which involved a state statute making it a crime to "be addicted to the use of narcotics." This Court held there that "a state law which imprisons a person thus afflicted [with narcotic addiction] as a criminal, even though he has never touched any narcotic drug within the State or been guilty of an irregular behavior there, inflicts a cruel and unusual punishment *   *   *." Id., at 667, 82 S.Ct., at 1420–1421.

On its face the present case does not fall within that holding, since appellant was convicted, not for being a chronic alcoholic, but for being in public while drunk on a particular occasion. The State of Texas thus has not sought to punish a mere status, as California did in *Robinson;* nor has it attempted to regulate appellant's behavior in the privacy of his own home. Rather, it has imposed upon appellant a criminal sanction for public behavior which may create substantial health and safety hazards, both for appellant and for members of the general public, and which offends the moral and esthetic sensibilities of a large segment of the community. This seems a far cry from convicting one for being an addict, being a chronic alcoholic, being "mentally ill, or a leper *   *   *." Id., at 666, 82 S.Ct., at 1420.

Robinson so viewed brings this Court but a very small way into the substantive criminal law. And unless *Robinson* is so viewed it is difficult to see any limiting principle that would serve to prevent this Court from becoming, under the aegis of the Cruel and Unusual Punishment Clause, the ultimate arbiter of the standards of criminal responsibility, in diverse areas of the criminal law, throughout the country.

It is suggested in dissent that *Robinson* stands for the "simple" but "subtle" principle that "[c]riminal penalties may not be inflicted upon a person for being in a condition he is powerless to change." In that view, appellant's "condition" of public intoxication was "occasioned by a compulsion symptomatic of the disease" of chronic alcoholism, and thus, apparently, his behavior lacked the critical element of *mens rea*. Whatever may be the merits of such a doctrine of criminal responsibility, it surely cannot be said to follow from *Robinson*. The entire thrust of *Robinson's* interpretation of the Cruel and Unusual Punishment Clause is that criminal penalties may be inflicted only if the accused has committed some act, has engaged in some behavior, which society has an interest in preventing, or perhaps in historical common law terms, has committed some *actus reus*. It thus does not deal with the question of whether certain conduct cannot constitutionally be punished because it is, in some sense, "involuntary" or "occasioned by a compulsion."

* * *

Ultimately, then, the most troubling aspects of this case, were *Robinson* to be extended to meet it, would be the scope and content of what could only be a constitutional doctrine of criminal responsibility. In dissent it is urged that the decision could be limited to conduct which is "a characteristic and involuntary part of the pattern of the disease as it afflicts" the particular individual, and that "[i]t is not foreseeable" that it would be applied "in the case of offenses such as driving a car while intoxicated, assault, theft, or robbery." That is limitation by fiat. In the first place, nothing in the logic of the dissent would limit its application to chronic alcoholics. If Leroy Powell cannot be convicted of public intoxication, it is difficult to see how a State can convict an individual for murder, if that individual, while exhibiting normal behavior in all other respects, suffers from a "compulsion" to kill, which is an "exceedingly strong influence," but "not completely overpowering." Even if we limit our consideration to chronic alcoholics, it would seem impossible to confine the principle within the arbitrary bounds which the dissent seems to envision.

It is not difficult to imagine a case involving psychiatric testimony to the effect that an individual suffers from some aggressive neurosis which he is able to control when sober; that very little alcohol suffices to remove the inhibitions which normally contain these aggressions, with the result that the individual engages in assaultive behavior without becoming actually intoxicated; and that the individual suffers from a very strong desire to drink, which is an "exceedingly strong influence" but "not completely overpowering." Without being untrue to the rationale of this case, should the principles advanced in dissent be accepted here, the Court could not avoid holding such an individual constitutionally unaccountable for his assaultive behavior.

Traditional common-law concepts of personal accountability and essential considerations of federalism lead us to disagree with appellant. We are unable to conclude, on the state of this record or on the current state of medical knowledge, that chronic alcoholics in general, and Leroy Powell in particular, suffer from such an irresistible compulsion to drink and to get drunk in public that they are utterly unable to control their performance of either or both of these acts and thus cannot be deterred at all from public intoxication. * * *

* * *

Affirmed.

MR. JUSTICE BLACK, whom MR. JUSTICE HARLAN joins, concurring.

While I agree that the grounds set forth in MR. JUSTICE MARSHALL's opinion are sufficient to require affirmance of the judgment here, I wish to amplify my reasons for concurring.

* * *

The rule of constitutional law urged by appellant is not required by Robinson v. State of California, 370 U.S. 660, 82 S.Ct. 1417, 8 L.Ed.2d 758 (1962). In that case we held that a person could not be punished for the mere status of being a narcotics addict. We explicitly limited our holding to the situation where no conduct of any kind is involved * * *[.] The argument is made that appellant comes within the terms of our holding in *Robinson* because being drunk in public is a mere status or "condition." Despite this many-faceted use of the concept of "condition," this argument would require converting *Robinson* into a case protecting actual behavior, a step we explicitly refused to take in that decision.

A different question, I admit, is whether our attempt in *Robinson* to limit our holding to pure status crimes, involving no conduct whatever, was a sound one. I believe it was. Although some of our objections to the statute in *Robinson* are equally applicable to statutes that punish conduct "symptomatic" of a disease, any attempt to explain *Robinson* as based solely on the lack of voluntariness encounters a number of logical difficulties. Other problems raised by status crimes are in no way involved when the State attempts to punish for conduct, and these other problems were, in my view, the controlling aspects of our decision.

Punishment for a status is particularly obnoxious, and in many instances can reasonably be called cruel and unusual, because it involves punishment for a mere propensity, a desire to commit an offense; the mental element is not simply one part of the crime but may constitute all of it. This is a situation universally sought to be avoided in our criminal law; the fundamental requirement that some action be proved is solidly established even for offenses most heavily based on propensity, such as attempt, conspiracy, and recidivist crimes. * * *

The reasons for this refusal to permit conviction without proof of an act are difficult to spell out, but they are nonetheless perceived and universally expressed in our criminal law. Evidence of propensity can be considered relatively unreliable and more difficult for a defendant to rebut; the requirement of a specific act thus provides some protection against false charges. See 4 Blackstone, Commentaries 21. Perhaps more fundamental is the difficulty of distinguishing, in the absence of any conduct, between desires of the day-dream variety and fixed intentions that may pose a real threat to society; extending the criminal law to cover both types of desire would be unthinkable, since "[t]here can hardly be anyone who has never thought evil. When a desire is inhibited it may find expression in fantasy; but it would be absurd to condemn this natural psychological mechanism as illegal."

In contrast, crimes that require the State to prove that the defendant actually committed some proscribed act involve none of these special problems. * * *

MR. JUSTICE WHITE, concurring in the result.

If it cannot be a crime to have an irresistible compulsion to use narcotics, Robinson v. State of California, 370 U.S. 660, 82 S.Ct. 1417, 8 L.Ed.2d 758, rehearing denied 371 U.S. 905, 83 S.Ct. 202, 9 L.Ed.2d 166 (1962), I do not see how it can constitutionally be a crime to yield to such a compulsion. Punishing an addict for using drugs convicts for addiction under a different name. Distinguishing between the two crimes is like forbidding criminal conviction for being sick with flu or epilepsy but permitting punishment for running a fever or having a convulsion. Unless *Robinson* is to be abandoned, the use of narcotics by an addict must be beyond the reach of the criminal law. Similarly, the chronic alcoholic with an irresistible urge to consume alcohol should not be punishable for drinking or for being drunk.

Powell's conviction was for the different crime of being drunk in a public place. Thus even if Powell was compelled to drink, and so could not constitutionally be convicted for drinking, his conviction in this case can be invalidated only if there is a constitutional basis for saying that he may not be punished for being in public while drunk. * * *

The trial court said that Powell was a chronic alcoholic with a compulsion not only to drink to excess but also to frequent public places when intoxicated. Nothing in the record before the trial court supports the latter conclusion which is contrary to common sense and to common knowledge. The sober chronic alcoholic has no compulsion to be on the public streets; many chronic alcoholics drink at home and are never seen drunk in public. Before and after taking the first drink, and until he becomes so drunk that he loses the power to know where he is or to direct his movements, the chronic alcoholic with a home or financial resources is as capable as the nonchronic drinker of doing his drinking in private, of removing himself from public places and, since he knows or ought to know that he will become intoxicated, of making plans to avoid his being found drunk in public. For these reasons, I cannot say that the chronic alcoholic who proves his disease and a compulsion to drink is shielded from conviction when he has knowingly failed to take feasible precautions against committing a criminal act, here the act of going to or remaining in a public place. On such facts the alcoholic is like a person with smallpox, who could be convicted for being on the street but not for being ill, or, like the epileptic, who would be punished for driving a car but not for his disease.

* * *

It is unnecessary to pursue at this point the further definition of the circumstances or the state of intoxication which might bar conviction of a chronic alcoholic for being drunk in a public place. For the purposes of this case, it is necessary to say only that Powell showed nothing more than that he was to some degree compelled to drink and that he was drunk at the time of his arrest. He made no showing that he was unable to stay off the streets on the night in question.

Because Powell did not show that his conviction offended the Constitution, I concur in the judgment affirming the Travis County court.

MR. JUSTICE FORTAS, with whom MR. JUSTICE DOUGLAS, MR. JUSTICE BRENNAN, and MR. JUSTICE STEWART join, dissenting.

* * *

I.

The issue posed in this case is a narrow one. There is no challenge here to the validity of public intoxication statutes in general or to the Texas public intoxication statute in particular. * * *

* * * Nor does [this case] concern the responsibility of an alcoholic for criminal *acts*. We deal here with the mere *condition* of being intoxicated in public.[2]

* * * The questions for this Court are not settled by reference to medicine or penology. Our task is to determine whether the principles embodied in the Constitution of the United States place any limitations upon the circumstances under which punishment may be inflicted, and, if so, whether, in the case now before us, those principles preclude the imposition of such punishment.

It is settled that the Federal Constitution places some substantive limitation upon the power of state legislatures to define crimes for which the imposition of punishment is ordered. In Robinson v. State of California, 370 U.S. 660, 82 S.Ct. 1417, 8 L.Ed.2d 758 (1962), the Court considered a conviction under a California statute making it a criminal offense for a person "[t]o be addicted to the use of narcotics." * * *

This Court reversed Robinson's conviction on the ground that punishment under the law in question was cruel and unusual, in violation of the Eighth Amendment of the Constitution as applied to the States through the Fourteenth Amendment. * * *

Robinson stands upon a principle which, despite its subtlety, must be simply stated and respectfully applied because it is the foundation of

2. It is not foreseeable that findings such as those which are decisive here— namely that the appellant's being intoxicated in public was a part of the pattern of his disease and due to a compulsion symptomatic of that disease—could or would be made in the case of offenses such as driving a car while intoxicated, assault, theft, or robbery. Such offenses require independent acts or conduct and do not typically flow from and are not part of the syndrome of the disease of chronic alcoholism. If an alcoholic should be convicted for criminal conduct which is not a characteristic and involuntary part of the pattern of the disease as it afflicts him, nothing herein would prevent his punishment.

individual liberty and the cornerstone of the relations between a civilized state and its citizens: Criminal penalties may not be inflicted upon a person for being in a condition he is powerless to change. In all probability, Robinson at some time before his conviction elected to take narcotics. But the crime as defined did not punish this conduct. The statute imposed a penalty for the offense of "addiction"—a condition which Robinson could not control. Once Robinson had become an addict, he was utterly powerless to avoid criminal guilt. He was powerless to choose not to violate the law.

In the present case, appellant is charged with a crime composed of two elements—being intoxicated and being found in a public place while in that condition. The crime, so defined, differs from that in *Robinson*. The statute covers more than a mere status. But the essential constitutional defect here is the same as in *Robinson*, for in both cases the particular defendant was accused of being in a condition which he had no capacity to change or avoid. The trial judge sitting as trier of fact found upon the medical and other relevant testimony, that Powell is a "chronic alcoholic." He defined appellant's "chronic alcoholism" as "a disease which destroys the afflicted person's will power to resist the constant, excessive consumption of alcohol." He also found that "a chronic alcoholic does not appear in public by his own volition but under a compulsion symptomatic of the disease of chronic alcoholism." I read these findings to mean that appellant was powerless to avoid drinking; that having taken his first drink, he had "an uncontrollable compulsion to drink" to the point of intoxication; and that, once intoxicated, he could not prevent himself from appearing in public places.

Article 477 of the Texas Penal Code is specifically directed to the accused's presence while in a state of intoxication, "in any public place, or at any private house except his own." This is the essence of the crime. Ordinarily when the State proves such presence in a state of intoxication, this will be sufficient for conviction, and the punishment prescribed by the State may, of course, be validly imposed. But here the findings of the trial judge call into play the principle that a person may not be punished if the condition essential to constitute the defined crime is part of the pattern of his disease and is occasioned by a compulsion symptomatic of the disease. This principle, narrow in scope and applicability, is implemented by the Eighth Amendment's prohibition of "cruel and unusual punishment," as we construed that command in *Robinson*. It is true that the command of the Eighth Amendment and its antecedent provision in the Bill of Rights of 1689 were initially directed to the type and degree of punishment inflicted. But in *Robinson* we recognized that "the principle that would deny power to exact capital punishment for a petty crime would also deny power to punish a person by fine or imprisonment for being sick." 370 U.S., at 676, 82 S.Ct., at 1425 (MR. JUSTICE DOUGLAS, concurring).

* * *

I would reverse the judgment below.

Notes and Questions

1. Would the dissenters in *Powell* think that one who, due to intoxication, falls asleep at the wheel of his car and kills a pedestrian is entitled to the defense because he is unable to control his conduct while asleep? If not, is it because they would expand the time frame within which the ability to control conduct, and therefore the actor's culpability, would be evaluated? What is the appropriate time frame for evaluating Leroy Powell's conduct?

2. If the dissenters in *Powell* had prevailed could a constitutional law of excuses have been avoided? That is, in any situation in which the defendant could show an inability to control his behavior would he not be able to demand acquittal? Or would it be limited to cases in which the lack of control was causally related to a "disease"? If the latter were the case would the scope of this "limitation" be dependent upon the ability of medicine, particularly psychiatry, to discover such diseases? Would defenses based on a lack of ability to control be predicated on a belief that such defendants are not morally blameworthy, or that they cannot be deterred? Does it matter?

3. Could strict liability crimes, see Section D, supra, be constitutional if *Robinson* were taken to mean that the state cannot punish one who could not have done better than he did? Indeed, on that standard could liability be constitutionally predicated on negligence? For an excellent, thorough and provocative article examining many of the questions raised by *Powell*, see Greenawalt, "Uncontrollable" Actions and the Eighth Amendment: Implications of *Powell v. Texas,* 69 Colum.L.Rev. 927 (1969).

4. The dissenters in *Powell* would, presumably, consider the persons acquitted by virtue of their view of *Robinson* as "sick" not "bad". People who are thought afflicted by diseases which threaten harm to others (here non-culpable anti-social conduct) are normally thought to be appropriate subjects for treatment rather than punishment. If it were certain that alcoholism is a disease, should the appropriate disposition of a claim such as Powell's be affected by the ability or inability of doctors or other therapists to "treat" this disease? If treatment, whatever its form, is dependent upon the "victim's" decision to seek and follow a treatment regime, is punishment an inappropriate instrument to encourage such decisions? What would the dissenters in *Powell* do with a "compelled" actor who refused to accept "treatment" and, for example, continued to drive? For a powerful attack on the "disease" approach to alcoholism and its implications for the dignity and freedom of individuals, see Szasz, Alcoholism: A Socio-Ethical Perspective, 6 Washburn L.J. 255 (1967).

STATE v. STASIO
Supreme Court of New Jersey, 1979.
78 N.J. 467, 396 A.2d 1129.

SCHREIBER, J.

The major issue on this appeal is whether voluntary intoxication constitutes a defense to a crime, one element of which is the defendant's intent. Defendant Stasio was found guilty by a jury of assault with intent to rob, in violation of *N.J.S.A.* 2A:90–2, and of assault while being armed with a dangerous knife, contrary to *N.J.S.A.* 2A:151–5. The trial court sentenced the defendant to three to five years on the assault with intent to rob count and a concurrent term of one to two years on the second count. The prison term was suspended and the defendant was placed on probation for three years. The Appellate Division reversed the convictions and ordered a new trial. We granted the State's petition for certification. 75 *N.J.* 613, 384 *A.*2d 843 (1978).

The scene of this incident was the Silver Moon Tavern located at 655 Van Houten Avenue, Clifton. The date was October 7, 1975. The defendant having presented no evidence, what occurred must be discerned from the testimony of three witnesses for the State: Peter Klimek, a part owner of the Silver Moon; Robert Colburn, a patron; and Robert Rowan, a member of the Clifton police force.

Robert Colburn had frequented the Silver Moon Tavern not only for its alcoholic wares but also to engage in pool. On October 7, Colburn arrived at the Tavern about 11:00 a.m. and started to play pool. Sometime before noon the defendant joined him. They stayed together until about 3:00 p.m. when the defendant left the bar. Though the defendant had been drinking during this period, in Colburn's opinion the defendant was not intoxicated upon his departure. Neither the defendant's speech nor his mannerisms indicated drunkenness.

Peter Klimek arrived at the Tavern shortly before 5:00 p.m. and assumed his shift at tending bar. There were about eight customers present when, at approximately 5:40 p.m., the defendant entered and walked in a normal manner to the bathroom. Shortly thereafter he returned to the front door, looked around outside and approached the bar. He demanded that Klimek give him some money. Upon refusal, he threatened Klimek. The defendant went behind the bar toward Klimek and insisted that Klimek give him $80 from the cash register. When Klimek persisted in his refusal, the defendant pulled out a knife. Klimek grabbed the defendant's right hand and Colburn, who had jumped on top of the bar, seized the defendant's hair and pushed his head toward the bar. The defendant then dropped the knife.

Almost immediately thereafter Police Officer Rowan arrived and placed the defendant in custody. He testified that defendant responded to his questions with no difficulty and walked normally. Klimek also stated that defendant did not appear drunk and that he had not noticed any odor of alcohol on defendant's breath.

At the conclusion of the State's case, the defendant elected not to take the stand. He made this decision because of an earlier conference in chambers at which defense counsel had advised the court that his defense would be that defendant had been so intoxicated that he was incapable of forming the intent to rob. The trial court responded by stating that it would charge that "voluntary intoxication was not a defense to any act by the defendant in this matter." The defendant on a *voir dire* made it clear that his decision not to testify was predicated upon the trial court's position. It might be noted that the defendant had no record of prior convictions.

Holding that the trial court's declaration in view of the defendant's proffer of proof was erroneous, the Appellate Division reversed the convictions and ordered a new trial. The Appellate Division reasoned that specific intent is an essential element of the crime of an assault with intent to rob and that voluntary intoxication may be shown to negate that element of the offense.

This Court last considered the culpability of an individual who had committed an illegal act while voluntarily under the influence of a drug or alcohol in *State v. Maik,* 60 *N.J.* 203, 287 *A.*2d 715 (1972). There the defendant *Maik* had been charged with the first degree murder of his friend, a fellow college student. The defense was insanity at the time of the killing. Evidence at the trial had suggested that the defendant was schizophrenic and that a psychotic episode may have been triggered by the defendant's voluntary use of LSD or hashish. The trial court had charged the jury that if it found that the underlying psychosis had been activated by the voluntary use of either narcotic, the defense of insanity would not stand.

On appeal Chief Justice Weintraub, writing for a unanimous Court, began by discussing generally the concept of criminal responsibility. After pointing out that although there was a difference in the treatment of sick and bad offenders, he noted that notwithstanding that difference "the aim of the law is to protect the innocent from injury by the sick as well as the bad." 60 *N.J.* at 213, 287 *A.*2d at 720. It was in that context that a decision would have to be made whether the voluntary use of alcoholic beverages or drugs should support a viable defense. He then stated the generally accepted proposition that criminal responsibility was not extinguished when the offender was under the influence of a drug or liquor and the reasons for that rule:

> It is generally agreed that a defendant will not be relieved of criminal responsibility because he was under the influence of intoxicants or drugs voluntarily taken. This principle rests upon public policy, demanding that he who seeks the influence of liquor or narcotics should not be insulated from criminal liability because that influence impaired his judgment or his control. The required element of badness can be found in the intentional use of the stimulant or depressant. Moreover, to say that one who offended while under such influence was sick would suggest that his sickness disappeared when he sobered up and hence he should be released. Such a concept would hardly protect others from the prospect of repeated injury. [60 *N.J.* at 214, 287 *A.*2d at 720]

The Chief Justice set forth four exceptions to the general rule. First, when drugs being taken for medication produce unexpected or bizarre results, no public interest is served by punishing the defendant since there is no likelihood of repetition. Second, if intoxication so impairs a defendant's mental faculties that he does not possess the wilfulness, deliberation and premeditation necessary to prove first degree murder, a homicide cannot be raised to first degree murder. Under this exception the influence of liquor "no matter how pervasive that influence may be, will not lead to an acquittal. It cannot reduce the crime below murder in the second degree, and this because of the demands of public security." *State v. Maik, supra,* 60 *N.J.* at 215, 287 *A.*2d at 721. Third, a felony homicide will be reduced to second degree murder when intoxication precludes formation of the underlying felonious intent. Parenthetically, it may be noted that since voluntary intoxication does not eliminate responsibility for the felony, it could be contended that the defendant should remain liable for first degree felony murder. On the other hand, considerations of fairness indicate that such a defendant should be treated the same as one charged with ordinary first degree homicide requiring premeditation. Fourth, the defense of insanity is available when the voluntary use of the intoxicant or drug results in a fixed state of insanity after the influence of the intoxicant or drug has spent itself. Since the defense in *Maik* may have fallen into the fourth category, the charge as given was erroneous and the cause was remanded for a new trial on the issue of whether the defendant had been insane at the time of the killing and whether that condition continued thereafter.

A difference of opinion has been expressed in the Appellate Division as to the meaning of Chief Justice Weintraub's discussion of intoxication in *Maik*. In *State v. Del Vecchio,* 142 *N.J.Super.* 359, 361 *A.*2d 579 (App.Div.), certif. den. 71 *N.J.* 501, 366 *A.*2d 657 (1976), a conviction for breaking and entering with intent to steal was reversed on the ground that the jury had improperly been charged that voluntary intoxication was not a defense to a crime requiring a specific intent. The Appellate Division reasoned that, when a specific intent was an element of an offense, voluntary intoxication may negate existence of that intent. Since intoxication may have prevented existence of that specific intent, an acquittal might be in order. The Appellate Division also held that the only principle to be derived from *Maik* was the proposition that voluntary intoxication may be relevant in determining whether a murder may be raised to first degree. In contrast, Judge Allcorn's dissent in *State v. Atkins,* 151 *N.J.Super.* 555, 573, 377 *A.*2d 718 (App.Div.1977), rev'd 78 *N.J.* 454, 396 *A.*2d 1122 (1979), expresses the opinion that *Maik* stands for the proposition that voluntary intoxication is not a defense to any criminal offense irrespective of whether a specific or general intent is an element of the offense.

In our opinion the Chief Justice in *Maik* enunciated a principle applicable generally to all crimes and, unless one of the exceptions to the general rule is applicable, voluntary intoxication will not excuse criminal conduct. The need to protect the public from the prospect of repeated injury and the public policy demanding that one who voluntarily subjects himself to intoxication should not be insulated from criminal responsibility are strongly supportive of this result. We reject the approach adopted by *Del Vecchio* because, although it has surface appeal, it is based on an unworkable dichotomy, gives rise to inconsistencies, and ignores the policy expressed in *Maik*.

Del Vecchio would permit the intoxication defense only when a "specific" as distinguished from a "general" intent was an element of the crime. However, that difference is not readily ascertainable. * * * Professor Hall has deplored the attempted distinction in the following analysis:

> The current confusion resulting from diverse uses of "general intent" is aggravated by dubious efforts to differentiate that from "specific intent." Each crime * * * has its distinctive *mens rea, e.g.* intending to have forced intercourse, intending to break and enter a dwellinghouse and to commit a crime there, intending to inflict a battery, and so on. It is evident that there must be as many *mentes reae* as there are crimes. And whatever else may be said about an intention, an essential characteristic of it is that it is directed towards a definite end. To assert therefore that an intention is "specific" is to employ a superfluous term just as if one were to speak of a "voluntary act." [*J. Hall, General Principles of Criminal Law* 142 (2d ed. 1960)]

For a similar analysis see *People v. Hood,* 1 *Cal.*3d 444, 456–457, 82 *Cal.Rptr.* 618, 625–626, 462 *P.*2d 370, 377–378 (1969). The same point is made in *G. Williams, Criminal Law—The General Part* (2d ed. 1961):

> The adjective "specific" seems to be somewhat pointless, for the intent is no more specific than any other intent required in criminal law. The most that can be said is that the intent is specifically referred to in the indictment. There is no substantive difference between an intent specifically mentioned and one implied in the name of the crime. [*Id.* at 49]

The undeniable fact is "that neither common experience nor psychology knows any such actual phenomenon as 'general intent' that is distinguishable from 'specific intent.'" Hall, "Intoxication and Criminal Responsibility," 57 *Harv.L.Rev.* 1045, 1064 (1944).

Moreover, distinguishing between specific and general intent gives rise to incongruous results by irrationally allowing intoxication to excuse some crimes but not others. In some instances if the defendant is found incapable of formulating the specific intent necessary for the crime charged, such as assault with intent to rob, he may be convicted of a lesser included general intent crime, such as assault with a deadly weapon. *N.J.S.A.* 2A:90–3. In other cases there may be no related general intent offense so that intoxication would lead to acquittal. Thus, a defendant acquitted for breaking and entering with intent to steal because of intoxication would not be guilty of any crime—breaking and entering being at most under certain circumstances the disorderly persons offense of trespass. *N.J.S.A.* 2A:170–31. Similarly, if the specific intent to rob were not demonstrated because of intoxication, then the defendant may have no criminal responsibility since assault with intent to rob would also be excused.

Finally, where the more serious offense requires only a general intent, such as rape, see *J. Hall, General Principles of Criminal Law* 143 (2d ed. 1960), and sources cited, intoxication provides no defense, whereas it would be a defense to an attempt to rape, specific intent being an element of that offense. Yet the same logic and reasoning which impels exculpation due to the failure of specific intent to commit an offense would equally compel the same result when a general intent is an element of the offense.

One commentator summed up the situation in the following way:

* * * [T]he intoxicated offender may be denied exculpation, receive partial exculpation, or receive total exculpation, depending upon the nature of the crime with which he is charged. As one commentator concludes: "It is thus apparent that the criminal liability of the grossly intoxicated offender depends upon the crime fortuitously committed while incapacitated." Note, *Volitional Fault and the Intoxicated Criminal Offender*, 36 U.Cin.L.Rev. 258, 276 (1967). [Comment, 61 *Minn.L. Rev.* 901, 904 n. 14 (1977)]

The *Del Vecchio* approach may free defendants of specific intent offenses even though the harm caused may be greater than in an offense held to require only general intent. This course thus undermines the criminal law's primary function of protecting society from the results of behavior that endangers the public safety. This should be our guide rather than concern with logical consistency in terms of any single theory of culpability, particularly in view of the fact that alcohol is significantly involved in a substantial number of offenses.[3] The demands of public safety and the harm done are identical irrespective of the offender's reduced ability to restrain himself due to his drinking. "[I]f a person casts off the restraints of reason and consciousness by a voluntary act, no wrong is done to him if he is held accountable for any crime which he may commit in that condition. Society is entitled to this protection." *McDaniel v. State*, 356 *So.*2d 1151, 1160–1161 (Miss.1978).

Until a stuporous condition is reached or the entire motor area of the brain is profoundly affected,[5] the probability of the existence of

---

3. See Wilentz, "The Alcohol Factor in Violent Deaths," 12 *Am.Pract.Digest* 829 (1961); Goodwin, Crane & Guze, "Felons Who Drink," 32 *Q.J.Stud.Alc.* 136 (1971); McGeorge, "Alcohol and Crime," 3 *Med. Sci. & L.* 27 (1963). A study in 77 rape cases reflected that 50% of the offenders had been drinking. Rada, "Alcoholism and Forcible Rape," 132 *Am.J.Psychiatry* 4 (1975). Analysis of many studies reflects a high ratio of offenders who have imbibed to those who have not in violent crimes. See K. Pernanen, "Alcohol and Crimes of Violence," in 4 *The Biology of Alcoholism* 351 (B. Kissin & H. Begleiter eds. 1976).

5. There is some evidence that at 0.20% of alcohol in the blood, the typical individu-

al would normally fall into that category. Greenberg, "Intoxication and Alcoholism: Physiological Factors," 315 *Annals Am. Acad.Pol. & Soc.Sci.* 22, 27 (1958). The motor vehicle statute presumes a driver is under the influence of liquor if the percentage is 0.10% or more. *N.J.S.A.* 39:4–50.1(3). Of course, the precise effects of a particular concentration of alcohol in the blood varies from person to person depending upon a host of other factors. See generally Perr, "Blood Alcohol Levels and 'Diminished Capacity'," 3 (No. 4) *J.Legal Med.* 28–30 (April 1975).

intent remains. The initial effect of alcohol is the reduction or removal of inhibitions or restraints. But that does not vitiate intent. The loosening of the tongue has been said to disclose a person's true sentiments—"*in vino veritas.*" One commentator has noted:

> The great majority of moderately to grossly drunk or drugged persons who commit putatively criminal acts are probably aware of what they are doing and the likely consequences. In the case of those who are drunk, alcohol may have diminished their perceptions, released their inhibitions and clouded their reasoning and judgment, but they still have sufficient capacity for the conscious mental processes required by the ordinary definitions of all or most specific *mens rea* crimes. For example, a person can be quite far gone in drink and still capable of the conscious intent to steal, which is an element of common !aw larceny. [Murphy, "Has Pennsylvania Found a Satisfactory Intoxication Defense?", 81 *Dick.L.Rev.* 199, 208 (1977) (citations omitted)]

When a defendant shows that he was comatose and therefore could not have broken and entered into the home or committed some other unlawful activity, such stage of intoxication may be relevant in establishing a general denial. But short of that, voluntary intoxication, other than its employment to disprove premeditation and deliberation in murder, should generally serve as no excuse. In this fashion the opportunities of false claims by defendants may be minimized and misapplication by jurors of the effect of drinking on the defendant's responsibility eliminated.

The significance of the common law approach to voluntary intoxication should not be overlooked. Our criminal law is grounded in large measure in the common law because of its incorporation by our constitutions and statutes.

* * *

At common law voluntary intoxication was not a defense. The earliest pronouncement is found in *Reniger v. Fogossa,* 1 *Plow.* 1, 19, 75 *Eng.Rep.* 1, 31 (Exch.Ch.1551), which reads:

> But where a man breaks the words of the law by involuntary ignorance, there he shall not be excused. As if a person that is drunk kills another, this shall be felony, and he shall be hanged for it, and yet he did it through ignorance, for when he was drunk he had no understanding nor memory; but inasmuch as that ignorance was occasioned by his own act and folly, and he might have avoided it, he shall not be privileged thereby. And Aristotle says, that such a man deserves double punishment, because he has doubly offended, viz. in being drunk to the evil example of others, and in committing the crime of homicide. And this act is said to be done *ignoranter,* for that he is the cause of his own ignorance: and so the diversity appears between a thing done *ex ignorantia,* and *ignoranter.* [citations omitted]

See Singh, "History of the Defence of Drunkenness in English Criminal Law," 49 *L.Q.Rev.* 528, 530 (1933). * * * Our holding today adheres to the central theme of that principle modified only by contemporary circumstances including scientific data on physiological effects of alcohol and our notions of fairness and rightness.

It might be suggested with some justification that we should adhere to the policy expressed in the new Code of Criminal Justice, effective September 1, 1979, *N.J.S.A.* 2C:98–4. However, the Deputy Attorney General implied at oral argument that the Legislature would be requested to modify the provisions dealing with intoxication and, in view of the possibility that the Legislature might act, in the interim we prefer to adhere to the principle enunciated in *Maik.* We note that in Arkansas, a law based on the Model Penal Code's provision for a defense of voluntary intoxication was repealed less than two years after it was enacted. *Ark.Stat.Ann.* § 41–207 (1977). The repealing legislation was made effective immediately by a finding of emergency which read in part "that the defense of voluntary intoxication is detrimental to the welfare and safety of the citizens of this State in that criminals are at times excused from the consequences of their criminal acts merely because of their voluntary intoxication * * *." 1977 *Ark. Acts,* No. 101, § 3. Similarly, Pennsylvania first enacted but then repealed a voluntary intoxication defense which was substantially the same as in the Model Penal Code.

The new Code of Criminal Justice provides that a person is not guilty of an offense unless he acted purposely, knowingly, recklessly or negligently, as the law may require. *N.J.S.A.* 2C:2–2. It also states that intoxication is not a defense "unless it negatives an element of the offense," *N.J.S.A.* 2C:2–8(a), and that "[w]hen recklessness establishes an element of the offense, if the actor, due to self-induced intoxication, is unaware of a risk of which he would have been aware had he been sober, such unawareness is immaterial." *N.J.S.A.* 2C:2–8(b). These provisions were taken from the Model Penal Code of the American Law Institute, § 2.08 (Prop.Off.Draft 1962). The American Law Institute Committee has explained that in those instances when the defendant's purpose or knowledge is an element of a crime, proof of intoxication may negate the existence of either. Tent.Draft No. 9 at 2–9 (1959). The distinction between specific and general intent has been rejected. *Id.* at 4.

Purpose or knowledge has been made a component of many offenses so that voluntary intoxication will be an available defense in those situations. Thus, voluntary intoxication may be a defense to aggravated assaults consisting of attempts to cause bodily injury to another with a deadly weapon. Intoxication could exonerate those otherwise guilty of burglaries and criminal trespass. It would be an available defense to arson, robbery, and theft. It could reduce murder to manslaughter, and excuse shoplifting. The Code would also permit the incongruous result of permitting intoxication to be a complete defense to an attempted sexual assault (rape), but not of a completed sexual assault. * * *

Our holding today does not mean that voluntary intoxication is always irrelevant in criminal proceedings.[7] Evidence of intoxication may be introduced to demonstrate that premeditation and deliberation have not been proven so that a second degree murder cannot be raised to first degree murder or to show that the intoxication led to a fixed state of insanity. Intoxication may be shown to prove that a defendant never participated in a crime. Thus it might be proven that a defendant was in such a drunken stupor and unconscious state that he was not a part of a robbery. See *State v. Letter,* 4 *N.J.Misc.* 395, 133 *A.* 46 (Sup.Ct.1926). His mental faculties may be so prostrated as to preclude the commission of the criminal act. Under some circumstances intoxication may be relevant to demonstrate mistake. However, in the absence of any basis for the defense, a trial court should not in its charge introduce that element. A trial court, of course, may consider intoxication as a mitigating circumstance when sentencing a defendant.

Although the evidence in the record demonstrates that the defendant assaulted Klimek while possessed with a knife and that his mental faculties were not prostrated, we are disturbed by the trial court's ruling which precluded the defendant from taking the stand. Defense counsel's proffer of proof that the defendant had been in the tavern between 7:00 a.m. and 5:30 p.m., that he had been drinking most of the day, and that he did not remember anything about the offense could possibly lead to the conclusion that he did not commit the assault. In that event the effect of the voluntary intoxication would demonstrate a denial of the assault. However, if the attack did occur, then the voluntary intoxication would not serve as a defense, even though the defendant could not remember the event. It would have been far better practice for the trial court not to have made its ruling at some unrecorded conference in chambers. The court should have waited until the issue was reached at trial when evidence of intoxication was offered. Permitting defendants to withhold evidence because of an expected jury instruction focuses the trial on appellate review rather than on producing the evidence at the trial. * * * Under the circumstances here, we are constrained to grant the defendant a new trial.

* * *

The judgment of the Appellate Division is affirmed.

7. While we recognize that the rule we announce here is at odds with the rule in a number of other jurisdictions, see Annot., 8 *A.L.R.*3d 1236 (1966), it is in accord with the holding in several other states. See *McDaniel v. State,* 356 *So.*2d 1151 (Miss. 1978) (armed robbery; court made rule); *State v. Vaughn,* 268 *S.C.* 119, 232 *S.E.*2d 328 (1977) (house-breaking and assault with intent to ravish; court made rule); *Commonwealth v. Geiger,* 475 *Pa.* 249, 380 *A.*2d 338 (1977) (by statute); *McKenty v.* *State,* 135 *Ga.App.* 271, 217 *S.E.*2d 388 (1975) (by statute); *State v. Cornwall,* 95 *Idaho* 680, 518 *P.*2d 863 (1974) (by statute); *Rodriquez v. State,* 513 *S.W.*2d 594 (Tex.Cr. App.1974) (by statute); *State v. Richardson,* 495 *S.W.*2d 435 (Mo.1973) (second degree murder; court made rule); *Chittum v. Commonwealth,* 211 *Va.* 12, 174 *S.E.*2d 779 (1970) (kidnapping and attempted rape; court made rule). See also *Ark.Stat.Ann.* § 41–207 (1977), discussed *supra.*

CLIFFORD and HANDLER, JJ., concurring in the result and PASHMAN, J., concurring in the result and dissenting.

HANDLER, J., concurring.

If a defendant's state of mind is a material factor in determining whether a particular crime has been committed—and if a degree of intoxication so affects the defendant's mental faculties as to eliminate effectively a condition of the mind otherwise essential for the commission of a crime—intoxication should be recognized as a defense in fact.

When dealing with the issue of intoxication, the focus at trial should be upon the mental state which is required for the commission of the particular crime charged. This should not ordinarily call for desiccated refinements between general intent and specific intent.
*   *   *

                 *   *   *

*   *   * I do not think it follows, however, that if the separation between so-called specific and general intent crimes is rejected, voluntary intoxication as a factual defense must also be rejected.

The majority of this Court repudiates the intoxication defense on grounds of general deterrence and a ubiquitous need to protect society from drunken criminals. This approach mirrors a commendable impulse, which I share. But, it fails to consider that enforcement of the criminal law must be fair and just, as well as strict and protective.

The criminal laws need not be impotent or ineffective when dealing with an intoxicated criminal. The question should always be whether under particular circumstances a defendant ought to be considered responsible for his conduct. This involves a factual determination of whether he has acted with volition. Intoxication, in this context, would constitute a defense if it reached such a level, operating upon the defendant's mind, so as to deprive him of his will to act. I would accordingly require, in order to generate a reasonable doubt as to a defendant's responsibility for his acts, that it be shown he was so intoxicated that he could not think, or that his mind did not function with consciousness or volition. *   *   *

I disagree therefore with the suggestion by the Court that if voluntary intoxication is recognized as a defense, as it is under the recently enacted New Jersey Code of Criminal Justice, *N.J.S.A.* 2C:2–8, it will serve to excuse criminal conduct with respect to which purpose or knowledge is a component. I do not share the pessimism of the Court that voluntary intoxication as a recognized defense will wreak havoc in criminal law enforcement under the New Jersey Criminal Justice Code. The fear of condoning criminals, who are also drunks, can be addressed, I respectfully suggest, by imposing a heavy burden of proof upon defendants to show a degree of intoxication capable of prostrating the senses. Drunkenness which does not have this effect does not diminish responsibility and should not serve to excuse criminality. *   *   *

* * * The facts, which are fully set forth in the Court's opinion, reveal that defendant engaged in volitional, purposeful activity—he assaulted his victim with a knife and at the same time unmistakably expressed his purpose by demanding that his victim turn over $80 from the cash register. He had the requisite *mens rea* for affixing criminal responsibility. The evidence of defendant's drinking during the day and before the assault is relevant, of course, to the question of whether he was intoxicated when he committed this crime. But, in light of his unequivocal assault on the bartender with a knife and his loud and clear demand for money from the cash register, the evidence of intoxication was palpably insufficient to negate the volitional character of the defendant's behavior. Juxtaposed against such overwhelming and clear evidence of purposeful criminal conduct, only intoxication which prostrated the defendant's faculties or deprived him of will would justify his acquittal.

Was defendant nevertheless entitled to have the jury consider the evidence of intoxication as a factor relevant to his commission of the charged crime? Evidence of intoxication, which may under some circumstances be inferred from prolonged, continuous, heavy drinking, should ordinarily entitle a defendant to a charge of intoxication as a factual defense bearing upon his mental state and whether he acted without purpose or volition. The charge on intoxication, however, should explain to the jury that unless defendant's intoxication was sufficiently extreme so as to have deprived him of his will to act and ability to reason, and prevented him in fact from having a purpose to rob the bartender, he would not, on this ground, be entitled to an acquittal. The jury, moreover, should be admonished to consider and weigh the evidence of intoxication with great caution.

* * *

JUSTICE CLIFFORD joins in this opinion.

PASHMAN, J., concurring in result only and dissenting.

* * * [T]he majority rules that a person may be convicted of the crimes of assault *with intent* to rob and breaking and entering *with intent* to steal even though he never, in fact, intended to rob anyone or steal anything. The majority arrives at this anomalous result by holding that voluntary intoxication can never constitute a defense to any crime other than first-degree murder even though, due to intoxication, the accused may not have possessed the mental state specifically required as an element of the offense. This holding not only defies logic and sound public policy, it also runs counter to dictates of prior caselaw and the policies enunciated by our Legislature in the new criminal code. I therefore dissent from that holding although I agree that the defendant is entitled to a new trial.

[Judge Pashman's argument over the correct reading of *Maik* and related cases is omitted]

* * *

In order to compensate for the lack of contemporary caselaw supporting its view, the majority resurrects the common law rule that voluntary intoxication is not a defense to any crime. It is well settled, however, that common law principles are to be solely a guide and then only when they reflect current notions of proper jurisprudence. *State v. Toscano*, 74 *N.J.* 421, 378 *A.*2d 755 (1977). As shown above, our caselaw has rejected the common law position. Further, it must be noted that this common law policy originated at a time when public drunkenness was itself a crime. It is perhaps understandable that courts in an earlier day would not allow an accused to utilize one criminal act as a defense to another. In 1975, however, our Legislature decriminalized public intoxication and adopted a broad policy of affording treatment. *N.J.S.A.* 26:2B–7 *et seq.* The Legislature specifically declared that:

> [i]t is the policy of the State of New Jersey that alcoholics and intoxicated persons may not be subjected to criminal prosecution because of their consumption of alcoholic beverages, but rather should be afforded a continuum of treatment in order that they may lead normal lives as productive members of society. [*N.J.S.A.* 26:2B–7]

The foregoing evidences the Legislature's recognition that alcoholism is a disease and should be dealt with through rehabilitation and treatment rather than imprisonment. The Legislature has thus abandoned the common law's premise that one who becomes intoxicated necessarily harbors an "evil" intent.

II

Today's holding by the majority not only departs from precedent, it also stands logic on its head. This Court and the Legislature have long adhered to the view that criminal sanctions will not be imposed upon a defendant unless there exists a " 'concurrence of an evil-meaning mind with an evil-doing hand.' " *State v. Williams*, 29 *N.J.* 27, 41, 148 *A.*2d 22, 29 (1959). The policies underlying this proposition are clear. A person who intentionally commits a bad act is more culpable than one who engages in the same conduct without any evil design. The intentional wrongdoer is also more likely to repeat his offense, and hence constitutes a greater threat to societal repose. A sufficiently intoxicated defendant is thus subject to less severe sanctions not because the law "excuses" his conduct but because the circumstances surrounding his acts have been deemed by the Legislature to be less deserving of punishment.

It strains reason to hold that a defendant may be found guilty of a crime whose definition includes a requisite mental state when the defendant actually failed to possess that state of mind. Indeed, this is the precise teaching of cases allowing the intoxication defense in first-degree murder prosecutions. To sustain a first-degree murder conviction, the State must prove that the homicide was premeditated, willful, and deliberate. If the accused, due to intoxication, did not in fact possess these mental attributes, he can be convicted of at most second-degree murder. That offense, however, can be sustained on a mere showing of recklessness, and the necessary recklessness can be found in the act of becoming intoxicated.

Just as the lack of premeditation, willfulness, or deliberation precludes a conviction for first-degree murder, so should the lack of intent to rob or steal be a defense to assault and battery with intent to rob, or breaking and entering with intent to steal. The principle is the same in both situations. If voluntary intoxication negates an element of the offense, the defendant has not engaged in the conduct proscribed by the criminal statute, and hence should not be subject to the sanctions imposed by that statute.

III

The majority ultimately grounds its conclusions on public policy considerations. It professes to be concerned with protecting society from drunken offenders. There are several problems with this approach. First, the majority's opinion is not even internally consistent. Although intoxication is not to be given the status of a defense, the majority states that it can be considered to "buttress the affirmative defense of reasonable mistake." It is difficult to comprehend why the public would be less endangered by persons who become intoxicated and, as a result, commit alcohol-induced "mistakes" which would otherwise be criminal offenses, than by persons who get so intoxicated that they commit the same acts without any evil intent. In fact, it appears highly likely that the first group would encompass a larger number of persons and hence constitute a greater menace to society.

Second, the majority's opinion is not likely to deter the commission of alcohol-induced crimes. It is unrealistic to expect that before indulging in intoxicants people will consider the extent of their criminal responsibility for acts they might commit. In this respect, therefore, today's holding will not add to the public's safety.

The most important consideration, however, is that the standards for establishing the defense are extremely difficult to meet. Contrary to the implications contained in the majority opinion, it is not the case that every defendant who has had a few drinks may successfully urge the defense. The mere intake of even large quantities of alcohol will not suffice. Moreover, the defense cannot be established solely by showing that the defendant might not have committed the offense had he been sober. *See Final Report of the New Jersey Criminal Law Revision Commission,* Vol. II, Commentary (1971) at 68. What is required is a showing of such a great prostration of the faculties that the requisite mental state was totally lacking. That is, to successfully invoke the defense, an accused must show that he was so intoxicated that he did not have the intent to commit an offense. Such a state of affairs will likely exist in very few cases. I am confident that our judges and juries will be able to distinguish such unusual instances.

IV

The majority and the commentators have criticized as elusive the "specific intent-general intent" dichotomy. *See, e.g.,* LaFave & Scott, *Criminal Law* (1972) § 45 at 344; Note, "Intoxication as a Criminal Defense," 55 *Colum.L.Rev.* 1210, 1218 (1955). The majority's difficulty in distinguishing the various mental states should not, however, be sufficient reason to mandate that *all* intoxicated defendants be incarcerated. The proper approach is to try and outline a more rational rule for applying the defense. I believe that such a rule is that enunciated in our new Code of Criminal Justice, effective September 1, 1979, which provides that intoxication will be a defense whenever it negates an element of an offense. *N.J.S.A.* 2C:98–4. The Act defines four mental states—purpose, knowledge, recklessness and negligence—one of which is necessary to establish guilt depending on the particular offense involved. *N.J.S.A.* 2C:2–2. Purpose and knowledge may be negated by intoxication, whereas recklessness and negligence may not. Moreover, the elements of recklessness or negligence may, where required by the definition of the crime, be satisfied by the recklessness implicit in becoming voluntarily intoxicated.

Although our current criminal law does not neatly compartmentalize *mens rea* into four such categories, the same type of analysis can be applied. Whenever a defendant shows that he was so intoxicated that he did not possess the requisite state of mind, he may not be convicted. Intoxication would not be a defense, however, to criminal offenses which may be established by recklessness or negligence as the carelessness in getting intoxicated would of itself supply the necessary mental state. This analysis would leave intact the long-standing rule that intoxication is not a defense to second-degree murder as that crime may be established by showing recklessness. *State v. Gardner,* 51 *N.J.* 444, 458, 242 *A.*2d 1 (1968).

Although the distinction between specific intent and general intent would be erased by the rule enunciated herein, this does not mean that the different mental states implicit in our criminal law would become irrelevant. Some crimes—battery, for example—only require that the defendant intend the act that he has committed, while others—such as assault and battery with intent to kill—require that he also intend to bring about certain consequences. Certainly it would take a greater showing of intoxication to convince one that defendant had no intent to strike the victim than to show that he did not intend to kill. In the former case, one might well conclude that he must have intended his act unless he was unconscious. Indeed, this is the main reason why the "specific intent/general intent" dichotomy was first formulated.

Inasmuch as defendants in these two cases were charged with crimes requiring intent to rob or intent to steal, their convictions must be reversed and a new trial ordered at which they can attempt to persuade the jury that they lacked those mental states. We must respect the legislative judgment, made explicit in the new Criminal

Code, that those persons who, due to intoxication, act without the intent required by law as an element of the crime, are not to be treated as are those who willfully commit the same acts. Accordingly, I would affirm the judgment of the Appellate Division * * *.

Notes and Questions

1. From a purely tactical point of view, should evidence of voluntary intoxication be introduced by a defendant? Is it likely to be successful if the standard for exculpation is that "a stuporous condition is reached or the entire motor area of the brain is profoundly affected"? (See note 5 and accompanying text of *Stasio,* supra at page 362.) Indeed, practical problems are present even when the announced rule is that a defendant "can offer a defense of voluntary intoxication to any crime." Terry v. State, 465 N.E.2d 1085, 1088 (Ind.1984). The *Terry* court commented:

> The potential of this defense should not be confused with the reality of the situation. It is difficult to envision a finding of not guilty by reason of intoxication when the acts committed require a significant degree of physical or intellectual skills. As a general proposition, a defendant should not be relieved of responsibility when he was able to devise a plan, operate equipment, instruct the behavior of others or carry out acts requiring physical skill.

Ibid.

Under such a standard, is it a wise tactical decision to place evidence of intoxication before the trier of fact? Might the jury employ the evidence for some purpose other than evaluating its effect on the existence of the requisite state of mind?

2. To what extent would the relevance of intoxication to liability for serious criminal acts be simplified by enactment of the following statute:

Dangerous Intoxication.

> A person is guilty of an offense if he takes or permits to be administered to him intoxicating substances while aware of a substantial and unjustifiable risk that he will become intoxicated and, while intoxicated, commit acts that except for his intoxication would be crimes.

What penalty should be assigned to the offense of "dangerous intoxication?" Should the penalty be related to the penalty assigned to the crime which the offender was aware he might commit? Should it be related to the number of crimes the offender was aware he might commit? The number actually committed? For a discussion of a German statute similar to this proposal and suggested English legislation, see Daly, Intoxication and Crime: A Comparative Approach, 27 Inter. & Comp.L.Q. 378 (1978).

3. It is generally held that intoxication from substances other than alcohol have the same effect upon criminal liability as alcohol intoxication. Is this appropriate? Consider the following from Commonwealth v. Campbell, 445 Pa. 388, 284 A.2d 798, 801 (1971):

> Defendant contends that the law with respect to voluntary intoxication is [as it is] because human experience has shown the effects of

taking alcohol are predictable, but not predictable with LSD [and therefore LSD intoxication should be permitted to result in complete acquittal]. The expert testimony in this case (if believed * * *) showed * * * that LSD produces widely varying results among different persons and even different results with the same person on different occasions. This distinction of nonpredictability of effect on the human body is devoid of any adequate legal justification based upon legal precedent, or reason, or policy considerations for a radical change and departure from our law of criminal responsibility. The very fact that the effects of a voluntary, nonmedical use of a hallucinogenic drug are predictably unforeseeable should require Courts to decide in the public interest that this is not legally sufficient to completely exculpate a person from murder or any criminal act.

4. What arguments could be made for or against the enactment of the following statute:

Effect of Intoxication Upon Criminal Liability.

    (a) Except under the circumstances described in subsection (b), no person shall be convicted of an offense committed while intoxicated if it is found that [Alternative A: except for such intoxication he would not have committed the offense.] [Alternative B: his intoxication so reduces his culpability that given general community standards of accountability and blameworthiness he should not be held liable.]

    (b) If a person, contemplating the commission of an offense, becomes intoxicated as a means of causing or enabling himself to commit the offense, he shall be liable for that offense without regard to subsection (a).

5. As is indicated by Note 7 of the *Stasio* opinion, page 365, supra, not all American jurisdictions permit evidence of voluntary intoxication to be used to negate even "specific" intents. One example is a Pennsylvania statute:

Neither voluntary intoxication nor voluntary drugged condition is a defense to a criminal charge, nor may evidence of such conditions be introduced to negative the element of intent of the offense, except that evidence of such intoxication or drugged condition * * * may be offered * * * whenever it is relevant to reduce murder from a higher degree to a lower degree of murder.

18 Pa.Cons.Stat. § 308. An even more sweeping prohibition is imposed by Texas Penal Code § 8.04, which provides that evidence of intoxication can be considered *only* in mitigation of penalty and then *only* if it has caused temporary insanity.

In Chittum v. Commonwealth, 211 Va. 12, 174 S.E.2d 779 (1970), the court held that the jury need not have been instructed to consider the defendant's voluntary intoxication in determining whether he had been capable of forming the states of mind required for the crimes charged, kidnapping and attempted rape. The defendant later applied for federal habeas corpus relief, arguing that the trial court's refusal to instruct the jury on intoxication rendered his convictions invalid. The federal district court, although acknowledging that the Virginia position may well be the "minority view," found nothing in the Federal Constitution that would require the state to adopt a rule permitting juries to consider intoxication as bearing upon whether defendants had the specific intents required by the crimes with which they were charged. Chittum v. Cunningham, 326 F.Supp. 87 (D.C.Va.1971). Accord United States ex rel. Goddard v. Vaughn, 614 F.2d 929, 935 (3d Cir.1980) (defense of voluntary intoxication is not required by Constitution). Is this correct? Can a state impose a state of mind requirement and then refuse to permit a defendant to show that because of his intoxication the prosecution failed to prove that state of mind?

6. In some situations, even voluntary intoxication may give rise to a "defense" rather than merely constitute evidence that a defendant can use to challenge the adequacy of the prosecution's showing of intent. A Maryland court summarized the area as follows:

Lord Hale, in 1 Pleas of the Crown, Ch. IV, pp. 29–33 (1847) recognized three types of "idiocy, madness and lunacy" under the general name of "dementia". The third type was "dementia affectata, namely drunkenness".

"This vice doth deprive men of the use of reason, and puts many men into a perfect, but temporary phrenzy; and therefore, according to some Civilians, such a person committing homicide, shall not be punished simply for the crime of homicide, but shall suffer for his drunkenness answerable to the nature of the crime occasioned thereby; so that yet the formal cause of his punishment is rather the drunkenness, than the crime committed in it: but by the laws of England such a person shall have no privilege by this voluntary contracted madness, but shall have the same judgment as if he were in his right senses. But yet there seems to be two allays to be allowed in this case. 1. That if a person by the unskillfulness of his physician, or by the contrivance of his enemies, eat or drink such a thing as causeth such a temporary or permanent phrenzy, as aconitum or nux vomica, this puts him into the same condition, in reference to crimes, as any other phrenzy, and equally excuseth him. 2. That although the simplex phrenzy occasioned immediately by drunkenness excuse not in criminals, yet if by one or more such practices, an habitual or fixed phrenzy be caused, though this madness was contracted by the vice and will of the party, yet this habitual and fixed phrenzy thereby caused puts the man into the same condition in relation to crimes, as if the same were contracted involuntarily at first." pp. 31–33.

Thus Hale, as the law does today, distinguished between temporary insanity caused by voluntary drunkenness and that caused by involuntary drunkenness and he recognized that permanent insanity, even though caused by voluntary drinking, excused the commission of a crime.

The rule of law with respect to responsibility for criminal conduct as affected by voluntary intoxication which has been consistently followed by the majority of courts in the United States is substantially that stated by Lord Hale. Regardless of what test is applicable to determining insanity, the majority distinguish between (1) the mental effect of voluntary intoxication which is the immediate result of a particular alcoholic bout; and (2) an alcoholic psychosis resulting from long continued habits of excessive drinking. The first does not excuse responsibility for a criminal act; the second may. In other words, if a person drinks intoxicating liquor and is sane both prior to drinking and after the influences of the intoxicant has worn off, but is insane by the applicable test while under the influence of the intoxicant, he comes under the first category. If he is insane whether or not he is directly under the influence of an intoxicant, even though that insanity was caused by voluntary drinking, he comes under the second category. The cases usually refer to the first category as a "temporary" insanity and the second category as a "permanent", "fixed" or "settled" insanity. These terms may be an oversimplification. What "permanent", "fixed" or "settled" means within the frame of reference is that the insanity not only existed while a person was under the influence of intoxicating spirits as an immediate result of imbibing, but existed independent of such influence, even though the insanity was caused by past imbibing. So if a person while in the throes of delirium tremens which may meet the test for insanity, commits a crime, he is not responsible for his criminal conduct, although such defect, resulting remotely from excessive drinking is only a temporary toxic state. It would seem that the distinction, notwithstanding the language of the cases, is not so much between temporary and permanent insanity as it is one between the direct results of drinking, which are voluntarily sought after, and its remote and undesired consequences. We adopt the majority view.

Parker v. State, 7 Md.App. 167, 177, 254 A.2d 381, 387 (1969).

MODEL PENAL CODE *
(Official Draft, 1985).

Section 2.08. Intoxication

(1) Except as provided in Subsection (4) of this Section, intoxication of the actor is not a defense unless it negatives an element of the offense.

(2) When recklessness establishes an element of the offense, if the actor, due to self-induced intoxication, is unaware of a risk of which he would have been aware had he been sober, such unawareness is immaterial.

(3) Intoxication does not, in itself, constitute mental disease within the meaning of Section 4.01 [providing for the defense of insanity].

(4) Intoxication which (a) is not self-induced or (b) is pathological is an affirmative defense if by reason of such intoxication the actor at the time of his conduct lacks substantial capacity either to appreciate its

criminality [wrongfulness] or to conform his conduct to the requirements of law.

(5) *Definitions.* In this Section unless a different meaning plainly is required:

(a) "intoxication" means a disturbance of mental or physical capacities resulting from the introduction of substances into the body;

(b) "self-induced intoxication" means intoxication caused by substances which the actor knowingly introduces into his body, the tendency of which to cause intoxication he knows or ought to know, unless he introduces them pursuant to medical advice or under such circumstances as would afford a defense to a charge of crime;

(c) "pathological intoxication" means intoxication grossly excessive in degree, given the amount of the intoxicant, to which the actor does not know he is susceptible.

Notes and Questions

1. Probably the most difficult issue posed by the Model Penal Code as well as by other statutory formulations relates to the question of whether intoxication should be permitted to "disprove" recklessness when that is sufficient for culpability. The drafters of the Model Penal Code assert that their position—that intoxication should not be permitted to show lack of recklessness—is in accord with prevailing law. Noting that the usual statement of the rule is that intoxication can be used to disprove a "specific" intent but not to disprove "general intent," they explain that the "obscure, unanalyzed distinction between specific and general intent" creates difficulty in applying this distinction. Model Penal Code, Comments to § 2.08, pp. 4–5 (Tent.Draft No. 9, 1959). The actual results of judicial decisions, they conclude, is that recklessness is generally sufficient for *mens rea* and intoxication is generally inadmissible to "disprove" it. But when purpose or knowledge, as defined in § 2.02, is required, such evidence is generally held usable. W. LaFave and A. Scott, Criminal Law 389, 392–93 (2nd ed.1986) find this to be the present majority approach.

As the discussion of "specific intent" earlier in this Chapter indicates, see pages 267–71, supra, this is inconsistent with some definitions of the terms "specific" and "general" intent. LaFave and Scott urge that these concepts be avoided in consideration of the effect of intoxication upon a defendant's liability. Id., at 390.

As to the basic decision of whether defendants should be able to use intoxication to show the absence of recklessness, the commentary to the Model Penal Code defends the Code's position as follows:

Those who oppose a special rule [making intoxication unavailable to "disprove" recklessness] draw strength initially from the presumptive disfavor of any special rules of liability. * * * [They] draw further strength from the proposition that it is precisely the awareness of the risk in recklessness that is the essence of its moral culpability—a culpability dependent on the magnitude of the specific risk advertently created. When that risk is greater in degree than that which the actor perceives at the time of getting drunk, as is frequently the case, the result of a special rule is bound to be a liability disproportionate to culpability. * * *

The case thus made is worthy of respect, but there are strong considerations on the other side. We mention first the weight of the prevailing law * * *. Beyond this, there is the fundamental point that awareness of the potential consequences of excessive drinking on the capacity of human beings to gauge the risks incident to their conduct is by now so dispersed in our culture that we believe it fair to postulate a general equivalence between the risks created by the conduct of the drunken actor and the risks created by his conduct in becoming drunk. Becoming so drunk as to destroy temporarily the actor's power of perception and of judgment is conduct which plainly has no affirmative social value to counterbalance the potential danger. The actor's moral culpability lies in engaging in such conduct. Added to this are the impressive difficulties posed in litigating the foresight of any particular actor at the time when he imbibes and the relative rarity of cases where intoxication really does engender unawareness as distinguished from imprudence. These considerations lead us to propose, on balance, that the Code declare that unawareness of a risk of which the actor would have been aware had he been sober be declared immaterial.

Model Penal Code § 2.08, comment (Tent.Draft No. 9, 1959).

2. Another problem is presented where intoxication is treated as automatically constituting recklessness. Section 19.05(a) of the Texas Penal Code which defines the crime of involuntary manslaughter provides:

A person commits an offense if he:

(1) recklessly causes the death of an individual; or

(2) by accident or mistake when operating a motor vehicle while intoxicated and, by reason of such intoxication, causes the death of an individual.

This statute appears to make intoxication under these circumstances a substitute for recklessness rather than merely barring evidence of intoxication offered to negate the existence of recklessness. Indeed, Section (a)(2) has been interpreted as relieving the prosecution of any obligation to establish a culpable mental state. Hardie v. State, 588 S.W.2d 936, 938 (Tex.Crim.App.1979).

Is this consistent with the "presumption" that *mens rea* is required for all serious crimes? Would a defendant have the right to an instruction that she is to be acquitted if the jury has a reasonable doubt that the defendant, for reasons unrelated to her intoxication, was not aware of the risks posed by her conduct? Cf. St. John v. State, 715 P.2d 1205, 1207 (Alaska App.1986) (jury may not be instructed that intoxication while driving establishes recklessness for purposes of manslaughter). Or is this problem avoided by the fact that the Texas statute requires proof that the intoxication caused the death?

Chapter VII

HOMICIDE: GRADING THE CRIMINAL CAUSATION OF DEATH

Contents

3. Killings by Resisting Victims or Pursuing Police Officers.
    State v. Canola.
    Notes and Questions.

The homicide offenses present an almost unique situation in the criminal law. All, of course, are based upon defendants' liability for the death of the victims. But the existence of several (or more) different crimes all based upon the fact of causing death reflects perception of a need to distinguish among killings according to varying degrees of culpability of the killer and perhaps according to the danger that the killer presents of future additional killings or assaultive criminal acts. In order to accomplish this, virtually all jurisdictions recognize several homicide offenses which differ from each other in terms of the state of mind required and to some extent by the presence of certain circumstances. While grading offenses according to culpability and dangerousness and doing this by carefully defining state of mind requirements and attendant mitigating circumstances is not unique to homicide, the perceived need to create so many different offenses constituting in effect graded degrees of criminal liability for the single "crime" of killing another person has made homicide law stand out as posing an especially difficult task for the law.

The need to distinguish among the homicide offenses may have been somewhat reduced by recently-imposed constitutional limits on capital punishment. The creation of a separate offense of first degree murder was motivated in large part by what was seen as the need to identify those killings for which death would be the appropriate and sometimes mandatory penalty. See McGautha v. California, 402 U.S. 183, 198, 91 S.Ct. 1454, 1462–63, 28 L.Ed.2d 711, 721 (1971). But it is now clear that the Eighth Amendment prohibition against cruel and unusual punishment prohibits a mandatory penalty of death for any particular homicide crime, Woodson v. North Carolina, 428 U.S. 280, 96 S.Ct. 2978, 49 L.Ed.2d 944 (1976), Roberts v. Louisiana, 428 U.S. 325, 96 S.Ct. 3001, 49 L.Ed.2d 974 (1976), and that the death penalty may be imposed only if the sentencing authority is permitted to consider a wide variety of possibly mitigating considerations relating to the offense and the offender, Lockett v. Ohio, 438 U.S. 586, 98 S.Ct. 2954, 57 L.Ed.2d 973 (1978). See the material at pages 106–25, supra. Thus there may be less need to use the definition of the homicide crimes to identify those killers deserving maximum harshness.

Although homicide law is to a large extent a matter of statute in most jurisdictions, many statutes retain to a greater or lesser extent the flavor and substance of common law distinctions. This section first presents several typical statutory schemes for grading criminal homicide. It then examines the traditional distinctions among murder, premeditated murder, voluntary manslaughter, and involuntary manslaughter. In examining the way in which the law has made these distinctions, consider how the cases would come out under different statutory schemes. Consider which method of distinguishing among the offenses best serves the purposes of the criminal law.

A. STATUTORY FORMULATIONS

As in most areas, statutory homicide schemes vary from jurisdiction to jurisdiction. Moreover, there is a discernible difference between modern schemes and more traditional ones which embody with varying degrees of specificity old common law concepts and terminology. This section presents one scheme of each sort.

1. THE CALIFORNIA PENAL CODE: A TRADITIONAL APPROACH

In this subsection those sections of the California Penal Code creating and defining homicide offenses are reprinted. Amendments, primarily in 1981, added to several of these sections language designed to eliminate or minimize the "defense" of diminished capacity as that had developed in the California case law. The diminished capacity case law is discussed and the responsive portions of Sections 188 and 189 of the California Penal Code are discussed in Chapter XII, at pages 834–37, infra.

CALIFORNIA PENAL CODE

§ 187. Murder defined; death of fetus

(a) Murder is the unlawful killing of a human being, or a fetus, with malice aforethought.

(b) This section shall not apply to any person who commits an act which results in the death of a fetus if any of the following apply:

(1) The act complied with the Therapeutic Abortion Act * * *.

(2) The act was committed by a holder of a physician's and surgeon's certificate * * * in a case where, to a medical certainty, the result of a childbirth would be death of the mother of the fetus or where her death from childbirth, although not medically certain, would be substantially certain or more likely than not.

(3) The act was solicited, aided, abetted, or consented to by the mother of the fetus.

(4) Subdivision (b) shall not be construed to prohibit the prosecution of any person under any other provision of law.

§ 188. Malice, express malice, and implied malice defined

Malice Defined. Such malice may be express or implied. It is express when there is manifested a deliberate intention unlawfully to take away the life of a fellow creature. It is implied, when no considerable provocation appears, or when the circumstances attending the killing show an abandoned and malignant heart.

§ 189. Murder; degrees

All murder which is perpetrated by means of a destructive device or explosive, poison, lying in wait, torture, or by any other kind of willful, deliberate, and premeditated killing, or which is committed in the perpetration of, or attempt to perpetrate, arson, rape, robbery, burglary, mayhem, or any act punishable under Section 288 [prohibiting "any lewd or lascivious act * * * upon or with the body, or any part or member thereof, of a child under the age of fourteen years, with the intent of arousing, appealing to, or gratifying the lust or passions or sexual desires of such person or of such child * * *"], is murder of the first degree; and all other kinds of murders are of the second degree.

§ 190. Murder; punishment; discretion of jury

Every person guilty of murder in the first degree shall suffer death, confinement in state prison for life without possibility of parole, or confinement in state prison for life. * * * Every person guilty of murder in the second degree is punishable by imprisonment in the state prison for five, six, or seven years.

§ 192. Manslaughter; voluntary, involuntary, and in driving a vehicle defined; construction of section

Manslaughter is the unlawful killing of a human being, without malice. It is of three kinds:

1. Voluntary—upon a sudden quarrel or heat of passion.

2. Involuntary—in the commission of an unlawful act, not amounting to felony; or in the commission of a lawful act which might produce death, in an unlawful manner, or without due caution and circumspection; provided that this subdivision shall not apply to acts committed in the driving of a vehicle.

3.   In the driving of a vehicle—

(a) In the commission of an unlawful act, not amounting to felony, with gross negligence; or in the commission of a lawful act which might produce death, in an unlawful manner, and with gross negligence.

(b) In the commission of an unlawful act, not amounting to felony, without gross negligence; or in the commission of a lawful act which might produce death, in an unlawful manner, but without gross negligence.

This section shall not be construed as making any homicide in the driving of a vehicle punishable which is not a proximate result of the commission of an unlawful act, not amounting to felony, or of the commission of a lawful act which might produce death, in an unlawful manner.

§ 193. Manslaughter; punishment

Manslaughter is punishable by imprisonment in the state prison for two, three or four years, except that a violation of subsection 3 of Section 192 of this code is punishable as follows: In the case of a violation of subdivision (a) of said subsection 3 the punishment shall be either by imprisonment in the county jail for not more than one year or in the state prison, and in such case the jury may recommend by their verdict that the punishment shall be by imprisonment in the county jail; in the case of a violation of subdivision (b) of said subsection 3, the punishment shall be by imprisonment in the county jail for not more than one year. In cases where, as authorized in this section, the jury recommends by their verdict that the punishment shall be by imprisonment in the county jail, the court shall not have authority to sentence the defendant to imprisonment in the state prison, but may nevertheless place the defendant on probation as provided in this code.

2. THE MODEL PENAL CODE: A MODERN STATUTORY APPROACH

The homicide provisions of the Model Penal Code, reprinted in this subsection, have provided the basis for many modern statutory revisions.

MODEL PENAL CODE *
(Official Draft 1985).

ARTICLE 210. CRIMINAL HOMICIDE

Section 210.0. Definitions

In Articles 210–213, unless a different meaning plainly is required:

(1) "human being" means a person who has been born and is alive;

(2) "bodily injury" means physical pain, illness or any impairment of physical condition;

(3) "serious bodily injury" means bodily injury which creates a substantial risk of death or which causes serious, permanent disfigurement, or protracted loss or impairment of the function of any bodily member or organ;

(4) "deadly weapon" means any firearm, or other weapon, device, instrument, material or substance, whether animate or inanimate, which in the manner it is used or is intended to be used is known to be capable of producing death or serious bodily injury.

Section 210.1. Criminal Homicide

(1) A person is guilty of criminal homicide if he purposely, knowingly, recklessly or negligently causes the death of another human being.

(2) Criminal homicide is murder, manslaughter or negligent homicide.

Section 210.2. Murder

(1) Except as provided in Section 210.3(1)(b), criminal homicide constitutes murder when:

(a) it is committed purposely or knowingly; or

(b) it is committed recklessly under circumstances manifesting extreme indifference to the value of human life. Such recklessness and indifference are presumed if the actor is engaged or is an accomplice in the commission of, or an attempt to commit, or flight after committing or attempting to commit robbery, rape or deviate sexual intercourse by force or threat of force, arson, burglary, kidnapping or felonious escape.

(2) Murder is a felony of the first degree [but a person convicted of murder may be sentenced to death, as provided in Section 210.6].

Section 210.3. Manslaughter

(1) Criminal homicide constitutes manslaughter when:

(a) it is committed recklessly; or

(b) a homicide which would otherwise be murder is committed under the influence of extreme mental or emotional disturbance for which there is reasonable explanation or excuse. The reasonableness of such explanation or excuse shall be determined from the viewpoint of a person in the actor's situation under the circumstances as he believes them to be.

(2) Manslaughter is a felony of the second degree.

Section 210.4. Negligent Homicide

(1) Criminal homicide constitutes negligent homicide when it is committed negligently.

(2) Negligent homicide is a felony of the third degree.

Notes

1. Traditionally, homicide occurred only when the death of a "person" was caused. A fetus was not a person; homicide was committed only if a fetus was born alive and expired as a result of injuries sustained either before or after birth. See People v. Bolar, 109 Ill.App.3d 384, 64 Ill.Dec. 919, 440 N.E.2d 639 (1982). In those jurisdictions following the traditional rule, no homicide occurs even if the defendant intentionally destroyed the fetus. See Hollis v. Commonwealth, 652 S.W.2d 61 (Ky.1983), in which the

defendant, announcing he did not want a baby, forced his hand into his wife's body and destroyed the fetus. When a fetus has been born alive may present a difficult question. In *Bolar,* the fetus was removed and regular but faint heartbeats were heard. After several minutes of resuscitation efforts, the heartbeats stopped and the fetus or child was pronounced dead. The trial court's determination that the fetus had been born alive was upheld on appeal as within the discretion of the trial court. In some jurisdictions, the common law rule has been judicially modified. The South Carolina Supreme Court, for example, has held:

> [A]n action for homicide may be maintained * * * when the state can prove beyond a reasonable doubt the fetus was viable, i.e., able to live separately and apart from its mother without the aid of artificial support.

State v. Horne, 282 S.C. 444, 447, 319 S.E.2d 703, 704 (1984). Those portions of Section 187 of the California Penal Code that deal with killing a fetus are a legislative reaction to Keeler v. Superior Court, 2 Cal.3d 619, 87 Cal.Rptr. 481, 470 P.2d 617 (1970), applying the common law rule. Is § 187 a more appropriate resolution of the matter than the common law rule? than the holding in *Horne?*

2. When does death occur for purposes of homicide analysis? Suppose the following situation: Defendant inflicts wound on victim. Victim's physician, after treating victim, decides that because victim's brain evidences no electrical activity victim is dead despite the fact that victim's heart and lungs are functioning because of respirator. Physician then removes victim from respirator and, as a result, victim's heart and lungs cease functioning. When did victim die or, to put the question in different terms, did defendant "cause" death of victim or did physician? The traditional definition of death defined it in terms of cessation of heartbeat and respiration. But courts have indicated a willingness to accept a definition of death in terms of an absence of brain activity, i.e., "brain death." See Commonwealth v. Golston, 373 Mass. 249, 366 N.E.2d 744 (1977); People v. Saldana, 47 Cal.App.3d 954, 121 Cal.Rptr. 243 (1975). For general discussions, see Charron, Death: A Philosophical Perspective on the Legal Definition, 1975 Wash.U.L.Q. 979; Capron & Kass, A Statutory Definition of Standards for Determining Human Death: An Appraisal and a Proposal, 121 U.Pa.L.Rev. 87 (1972); Halley & Harvey, Medical vs. Legal Definitions of Death, 204 J.A.M.A. 423 (1968).

3. The common law rule was that a person could not be convicted of murder unless the victim died within a year and a day from the time the fatal blow was given or the cause of death administered. See, e.g., Louisville E. & St. L. R. Co. v. Clarke, 152 U.S. 230, 239, 14 S.Ct. 579, 581, 38 L.Ed. 422, 424 (1894). Many American jurisdictions still follow this rule. State v. Minster, 302 Md. 240, 486 A.2d 1197 (1985). Some courts, however, will not apply the rule to prosecutions for manslaughter. State v. Hefler, 310 N.C. 135, 310 S.E.2d 310 (1984). But the rule has sometimes been judicially abandoned. In Commonwealth v. Ladd, 402 Pa. 164, 166 A.2d 501 (1960), for example, the Pennsylvania Supreme Court read the requirement as designed to prevent prosecutions in which the passage of time before the victim's death would create unacceptable difficulty in ascertain-

ing the cause of death. Advances in crime detection and medicine, it reasoned, have now rendered the rigid rule unnecessary. Accuracy is sufficiently assured, it continued by requiring "proof of causation of conventional quality" at trial. Justice Musmanno dissented, arguing that despite advances in crime detention and medicine the absence of the traditional rule would create a real danger of unjustified prosecutions. He pointed specifically to the facts of the case as demonstrating the difficulties the rule was designed to withdraw from courts' consideration; the victim had died of pneumonia thirteen months after being assaulted by the defendant. Other courts have also abolished the rule. Commonwealth v. Lewis, 381 Mass. 411, 409 N.E.2d 771 (1980), cert. denied 450 U.S. 929, 101 S.Ct. 1386, 67 L.Ed.2d 360 (1981); People v. Stevenson, 416 Mich. 383, 331 N.W.2d 143 (1982). Legislative enactment of a comprehensive criminal code that does not include the year and a day rule has been construed as legislative abandonment of the rule. State v. Hudson, 56 Or.App. 462, 642 P.2d 331 (1982), review denied. Some legislatures have retained the rule but expanded the time limit. As a result of a 1969 amendment, § 194 of the California Penal Code provides, "To make the killing either murder or manslaughter, it is requisite that the party die within three years and a day after the stroke received or the cause of death administered. ＊ ＊ ＊"

4. For general treatments of the law of homicide, see R. Moreland, Law of Homicide (1952); Danforth, The Model Penal Code and Degrees of Homicide, 11 Am.U.L.Rev. 147 (1962); Parker, The Evolution of Criminal Responsibility, 9 Alberta L.Rev. 47 (1970); Perkins, The Law of Homicide, 36 J.Crim.L. & C. 391 (1946); Wechsler and Michael, A Rationale of the Law of Homicide, 37 Colum.L.Rev. 701, 1261 (1937). For a discussion emphasizing Canadian law, see Hooper, Some Anomalies and Developments in the Law of Homicide, 3 U.B.C.L.Rev. 55 (1967). English law is covered in Royal Commission on Capital Punishment 1949–1953, Report 25–72 (1953).

B. KILLINGS WITH "MALICE AFORETHOUGHT"

Editors' Introduction: "Malice Aforethought"

Murder—traditionally, a killing with "malice aforethought"—is the basic homicide offense and analysis of a criminal homicide situation will ordinarily begin with an inquiry into the possibility of the killing being murder. Unfortunately, the traditional definition of the crime leaves some uncertainty as to the state of mind required. Consider the following comments from People v. Morrin, 31 Mich.App. 301, 310–18, 187 N.W.2d 434, 438–43 (1971):

> A person who kills another is guilty of the crime of murder if the homicide is committed with malice aforethought. Malice aforethought is the intention to kill, actual or implied, under circumstances which do not constitute excuse or justification or mitigate the degree of the offense to manslaughter. The intent to kill may be implied where the actor actually intends to inflict great bodily harm or the natural tendency of his behavior is to cause death or great bodily harm. (The

common-law felony-murder rule is an example of implied intent or implied malice aforethought.)

Thus, as "malice aforethought" is now defined, a killing may be murder even though the actor harbored no hatred or ill will against the victim and even though he "acted on the spur of the moment." Whatever may be the philological origin of the words "malice aforethought," today "each word has a different significance in legal usage than in ordinary conversation."

The nature of malice aforethought is the source of much of the confusion that attends the law of homicide. The cause of this confusion has been the evolution of malice aforethought from an independently significant element of murder to a "term of art" whose significance is largely historical and procedural.

The precise roots of malice aforethought are uncertain. Common-law courts spoke of "malice prepense" as early as the 13th century. The requirement that malice aforethought be established in all murder prosecutions represented the common law's recognition that a rational legal system will punish certain homicides (for example, those that are intentional) while excusing others (accidental homicides, for example).

From the beginning malice aforethought was defined principally in functional terms. We know what it did; it both distinguished criminal from innocent homicide and murder from manslaughter. Yet what it was, the precise state of mind which it described, eluded symmetrical definition.

The common-law courts were faced with a difficult problem: malice aforethought was a requisite element of murder, but one so elusive that in many cases it resisted direct proof. Their solution was to create a presumption of malice. As early as the 16th century proof that the accused person killed the victim gave rise to a "presumption" that the act was done with malice aforethought. Once it was established that the accused killed the victim, the burden was upon the accused to prove circumstances of justification, excuse, or mitigation.

This rule, firmly rooted in English law, has taken hold in a great many American jurisdictions * * *.

The merits of the rule are that it relieves the prosecution from the necessity of proving the nonexistence of circumstances of excuse, justification, and mitigation—frequently an impossible burden—and instead allocates the burden of proving such circumstances to the defendant, who, arguably, has greater ability to do so than the prosecution.

* * *

There is also, however, a grave drawback to this presumptive device. This defect arises in connection with jury instructions, to instruct a jury that malice is presumed from the fact of killing is to invite confusion concerning the ultimate burden of proof in the trial. The prosecution must always prove the defendant guilty beyond a reasonable doubt; a rule of law that shifts the burden of proof with respect to "malice" tends to cloud the dimensions of the prosecution's ultimate burden.

It was this danger which led the House of Lords in 1935 to repudiate instructions that charged jurors that they are to presume malice from the mere fact of killing.[21] Speaking of the presumption of innocence as a "golden thread" running through the common law, the Court rejected a formulation that required the jurors to find a defendant guilty unless he discharged his burden of rebutting the presumption of malice.

The Court did not rule that malice must be proved by evidence independent of the killing itself. The fact of homicide still *permits* the jury to find malice aforethought. But it in no sense *compels* such a finding, even absent any evidence of excuse, justification or mitigation on the part of the defendant.

> "All that is meant is that if it is proved that the conscious act of the prisoner killed a man and nothing else appears in the case, there is evidence upon which the jury may, not must, find him guilty of murder." Woolmington v. The Director of Public Prosecutions, [1935] AC 462, 480.

But other authorities have undertaken the elusive task of defining with some precision the state of mind required by malice aforethought. The British Royal Commission on Capital Punishment concluded:

> "Malice aforethought" is simply a comprehensive name for a number of different mental attitudes which have been variously defined at different stages in the development of the law, the presence of any one of which in the accused has been held by the courts to render a homicide particularly heinous and therefore to make it murder. These states of mind have been variously expressed by various authorities, but the statement of the modern law most commonly cited as authoritative is that given in 1877 by Sir James Stephen in his *Digest of the Criminal Law:* [4]

> > "Malice aforethought means any one or more of the following states of mind preceding or co-existing with the act or omission by which death is caused, and it may exist where that act is unpremeditated.

> > *(a)* An intention to cause the death of, or grievous bodily harm to, any person, whether such person is the person actually killed or not;

> > *(b)* knowledge that the act which causes death will probably cause the death of, or grievous bodily harm to, some person, whether such person is the person actually killed or not, although such knowledge is accompanied by indifference whether death or grievous bodily harm is caused or not, or by a wish that it may not be caused;

> > *(c)* an intent to commit any felony whatever;

---

21. Woolmington v. The Director of Public Prosecutions, [1935] A.C. 462, 472.

4. 9th ed. (1950), Art. 264, pp. 211 ff.

* * *

> *(d)* an intent to oppose by force any officer of justice on his way to, in, or returning from the execution of the duty of arresting, keeping in custody, or imprisoning any person whom he is lawfully entitled to arrest, keep in custody, or imprison, or the duty of keeping the peace or dispersing an unlawful assembly, provided that the offender has notice that the person killed is such an officer so employed.
>
> The expression 'officer of justice' in this clause includes every person who has a legal right to do any of the acts mentioned, whether he is an officer or a private person.
>
> Notice may be given, either by words, by the production of a warrant or other legal authority, by the known official character of the person killed, or by the circumstances of the case."

Stephen himself, however, elsewhere expressed doubt whether *(c)* was not too widely stated * * *. As Stephen put it, "the loose term 'malice' was used, and then when a particular state of mind came under their notice the Judges called it 'malice' or not according to their view of the propriety of hanging particular people. That is, in two words, the history of the definition of murder".[6] There can be no doubt that the term now covers, and has for long covered, all the most heinous forms of homicide, as well as some cases—those of "constructive murder"—whose inclusion in the category of murder has often been criticised.

Thus the following propositions are commonly accepted[7]:

(i) It is murder if one person kills another with intent to do so, without provocation or on slight provocation, although there is no premeditation in the ordinary sense of the word.

(ii) It is murder if one person is killed by an act intended to kill another.

(iii) It is murder if a person is killed by an act intended to kill, although not intended to kill any particular individual, as if a man throws a bomb into a crowd of people.

(iv) It is murder if death results from an act which is intended to do no more than cause grievous bodily harm. An early example may be found in the case of *Grey*,[8] where a blacksmith, who had had words with an apprentice, struck him on the head with an iron bar and killed him. It was held that it "is all one as if he had run him through with a sword" and he was found guilty of murder.

(v) It is murder if one person kills another by an intentional act which he knows to be likely to kill or to cause grievous bodily harm, although he may not intend to kill or to cause grievous bodily harm and may either be recklessly indifferent as to results of his act or may even desire that no harm should be caused by it. Two examples may be given. A woman may be guilty of murder if

---

6. Minutes of Evidence of the Royal Commission on Capital Punishment, 1866; Q. 2110.

7. Stephen's Digest, 9th ed., pp. 211–6 * * *.

8. R. v. Grey (1666) Kel. 64.

she exposes a helpless infant in circumstances where there is not a reasonable expectation that it will be found and preserved by someone else.[9] A man was convicted of murder when he had killed a number of persons in the street by exploding a barrel of gunpowder against the wall of a prison, although his purpose was only to enable a prisoner to escape. Lord Cockburn, L.C.J., told the jury that such an act was murder, quite apart from the fact that it was committed in the prosecution of a felony.[10]

Royal Commission on Capital Punishment 1949–1953 Report, 27–28 (1953). Some modern statutes, such as the California statutory scheme reprinted at pages 379–81, supra, define homicide offenses in terms that differ little from those used by the early common law courts in homicide discussions. Other modern statutes, including those based upon the Model Penal Code's proposals reprinted at pages 381–82, supra, employ different terminology and, sometimes, different categories, but these schemes often embody requirements and distinctions similar or identical to those used in early common law homicide analysis.

To the extent that the common law terminology is still used, it presents some important questions concerning how juries should be instructed and what instructions may violate federal constitutional requirements. In Engle v. Koehler, 707 F.2d 241 (6th Cir.1983), the defendant was charged with first degree murder under Michigan law. The offense requires that the killing be murder, defined as a killing with malice aforethought, and, in addition, that it be "willful, deliberate and premeditated." At trial, the judge charged the jury in part as follows:

> Malice is used in a technical sense, including not only anger, hatred and revenge but every other unlawful and unjustifiable motive. It is not confined to particular ill will to the deceased but is intended to denote an action flowing from any wicked and corrupt motive, where the fact has been attended with such circumstances as to carry in them the plain indication of a heart, regardless of social duty and fatally bent upon mischief and, therefore, *malice is implied from any deliberate and cruel act against another person,* however sudden. ＊ ＊ ＊
>
>   We, of course, do not have the power to look into a person's mind to tell what that person is thinking at any particular time, *but the law gives us a rule of thumb that a person is presumed to intend the natural consequences of his acts.* ＊ ＊ ＊

Engle was convicted and sought federal habeas corpus relief on the ground that the instruction, and particularly the emphasized portions, relieved the prosecution of its burden of proving guilt beyond a reasonable doubt. As a result, he urged, his rights under Sandstrom v. Montana, 442 U.S. 510, 99 S.Ct. 2450, 61 L.Ed.2d 39 (1979) (discussed at

   9. R. v. Walters (1841) C. & Mar. 164.

   10. R. v. Desmond, Barrett and others, The Times, April 28, 1868.

page 58, supra) were violated. The Court of Appeals agreed. A reasonable juror, it concluded, could have thought that the instructions required findings of malice and intent absent proof to the contrary by the defendant. 707 F.2d at 245. The United States Supreme Court granted review, but Justice Marshall did not participate in the decision of the case. In a one-sentence per curiam opinion, the Court announced, "The judgment is affirmed by an equally divided court." Koehler v. Engle, 466 U.S. 1, 104 S.Ct. 1673, 80 L.Ed.2d 1 (1984) (per curiam).

Did the *Engle* instruction adequately convey to the jury the substance of the definition of the crime charged? the burden upon the prosecution to prove Engle's guilt? Perhaps the common law terminology is too specialized to be readily translatable into meaningful jury instructions. Perhaps, unless modified by "presumptions" or "permissible inferences," there is a risk that it imposes an undesirably difficult burden on the prosecution. But the presumptions or inferences necessary to reduce this burden may be too complex to translate into jury instructions that avoid obsuring the prosecution's ultimate burden of proving guilt beyond a reasonable doubt.

"Intentional killings"—those accomplished with the conscious purpose of causing death—are universally murder under modern statutory schemes, at least in the absence of considerations which excuse, justify or mitigate. Murder of this type raises few conceptual problems, although the inquiries as to whether particular murder defendants in fact intended to kill sometimes pose difficult tasks. What aids should—or may—the prosecution be given in proving intent to kill? In Womble v. State, 618 S.W.2d 59, 64 (Tex.Crim.App.1981), the court commented, in analyzing the sufficiency of the evidence to support a conviction, "where a deadly weapon is fired at close range and death results the law presumes an intent to kill." Is this appropriate? If so, should trial juries be told this? If so, how should the instructions be worded?

Killings accomplished with the intent to cause grievous bodily harm—those in category "iv" of the Royal Commission's analysis—seldom give rise to judicial discussion. Some difficulty is posed by the question of what sort of injuries to the victim must have been intended by the defendant. See People v. Geiger, 10 Mich.App. 339, 159 N.W.2d 383 (1968), suggesting that the defendant must have intended injury of a very serious nature, naturally and commonly involving loss of life or "grievous mischief."

Killings in the course of criminal acts present special problems, as the Royal Commission acknowledged. These killings and the so-called "felony murder" doctrine are considered in Section F of this Chapter.

Those killings potentially falling within category "v" used by the Royal Commission have presented continuing difficulty. Many modern statutes provide for such killings—often referred to as "depraved mind" killings—to be murder, although the statutory language varies in content and specificity. Compare Section 210.02(1)(b) of the Model

Penal Code, at page 382, supra, and Section 188 of the California Penal Code.

In Waters v. State, 443 A.2d 500 (Del.1982), the jury was instructed in terms of § 635, Del.Code.Ann., which provides that a person is guilty of second degree murder if the person:

> recklessly causes the death of another person under circumstances which manifest a cruel, wicked and depraved indifference to human life * * *.

He argued that the failure to define "cruel, wicked and depraved indifference to human life" left the jurors without sufficiently objective (and constitutional) standards for determining whether he was guilty of second degree murder. The appellate court noted that instructions of the sort at issue had been used as early as 1903 and concluded:

> [T]he words "cruel, wicked and depraved indifference to human life" are words with a commonly accepted meaning, time-honored in this State's jurisprudence. Over the years, instructions [involving this language] have been given to innumerable juries in this State. Apparently, they have been able to understand and apply the concepts inherent therein to the facts before them. With this long history in mind, we find no vagueness problem, rising to constitutional levels, created by the instant charge.

443 A.2d at 506.

PEOPLE v. MAGLIATO

New York Supreme Court, Appellate Division, 1985.
110 A.D.2d 266, 494 N.Y.S.2d 307.

BLOOM, JUSTICE:

The issue before us is whether the evidence adduced at the trial warranted a jury finding that defendant, under circumstances evincing a "depraved indifference to human life" recklessly engaged in conduct which created a grave risk of death to another person and thereby caused his death (Penal Law, Section 125.25, subd. 2). We hold that it did not. Accordingly, we reduce the conviction to that of manslaughter in the second degree, vacate the sentence imposed and remand for resentence.

The circumstances leading to the tragedy were relatively simple. On August 6, 1983, the day following Labor Day Donald Schneider, a New Jersey resident, decided to mark the summer's end with a trip to Washington Square Park. Together with his friend Anthony Giani, the deceased, they drove to the park. After a short stay, they started home. As they proceeded west on Houston Street, a red Ferrari driven by Frank Magliato, the defendant, came on the scene. Apparently, the station wagon driven by Schneider clipped the rear of the Ferrari. Whatever the reason, Schneider did not stop. Defendant followed the station wagon until it stopped for a traffic light behind a truck. Defendant got out of his car. As he did so, Giani emerged from the station wagon carrying a nightstick. Initially, both men stood by their vehicles, facing each other and hurling epithets. Giani then started toward defendant. Uttering some of the choicest profanities, he threatened to kill defendant and directed him to "get out of here". Magliato returned to his car. In the interim the light had changed and Schneider drove off to find a parking spot, leaving Giani behind. Defendant followed the station wagon. His passenger, Edward Klaris, recorded its vehicle registration number. After Schneider had parked his vehicle at West Broadway and Broome Street, defendant drove past it and continued on toward Spring Street where he spied Giani, who, apparently, was searching for Schneider. Defendant drove his car past Giani, barely missing him.

Defendant then went looking for a police officer. Failing to find one, he drove to his home, parked the car and went to his apartment, leaving Klaris in the vehicle. He returned shortly. Now, however, he was wearing a holstered gun.

Magliato drove back to where the Schneider vehicle was parked and stopped across the street, near a phone booth. While Klaris called 911, defendant left his car and started toward the station wagon, again shouting profanities. Giani emerged from the station wagon, holding the nightstick in a threatening position. According to the prosecution, the two men faced each other across a distance of some forty five feet. Suddenly, defendant cocked his weapon and assumed a firing position, crouching with both feet planted apart and arms outstretched. The gun in his hand, he took deliberate aim and fired at Giani striking him in the forehead and causing such massive brain damage that he died two days later.

The defense version differs somewhat. Defendant did not dispute that he drew his weapon and cocked it. However, he contended that his weapon could fire under the slightest pressure and that immediately prior to the firing of the weapon, a car passed close to Giani, brushing him back. This incident so unnerved defendant that he accidentally exerted pressure on the trigger sufficient to discharge the weapon.

Immediately after shooting Giani, defendant walked back to his Ferrari and, together with Klaris, drove the car to a garage across the street from his Mercer Street apartment and so positioned it as to secrete it.

A day or two later the police located Klaris through the 911 phone call which he was in the process of making at the time of the shooting. Initially, he refused to cooperate. However, after the police had left he called defendant and informed him that he was ready to tell the police "the whole truth". Defendant then consulted an attorney and six days after the shooting surrendered to the police. His attorney, who accompanied him, turned two guns, both owned by defendant, over to the police. A ballistics test indicated that the bullet which had killed Giani had been fired from one of them, a Colt .38 Detective Special.

I

Defendant was indicted in a two-count indictment charging intentional homicide (Penal Law, Section 125.25, subd. 1) and "depraved indifference" murder (Penal Law Section 125.25, subd. 2). [Under subdivision 2 of Section 125.25, a person commits second degree murder when:

> Under circumstances indicating a depraved indifference to human life, he recklessly engages in conduct which creates a grave risk of death to another person, and thereby causes the death of another person * * *.]

At the conclusion of the evidence, the Trial Court submitted both counts to the jury. It also submitted manslaughter in the first degree [which consists of an intentional killing under the influence of "extreme emotional disturbance"] with respect to the count charging intentional murder, and manslaughter in the second degree [consisting of recklessly causing the death of another person] and criminally negligent homicide with respect to the depraved indifference count, as lesser included counts. In each instance, the charge correctly noted that the lesser included counts were not to be considered by the jury unless it first acquitted on the higher count.

* * *

II

On the record before us it is clear that the jury could have found defendant guilty of either an intentional crime or a crime the central element of which was recklessness. They determined that the act which led to Giani's death was a reckless one. We do not quarrel with their holding. We note only that having determined on recklessness they correctly acquitted on the charges of intentional homicide, for the two are mutually exclusive.

Thus, the primary—indeed the sole—question before us is whether defendant's recklessness was such that it evinced "a depraved indifference to human life" creating "a grave risk of death to another person" and thereby caused the death of another person.

Traditionally, this "highest crime of *reckless* homicide" is "very similar to a former Penal Law offense classified as first degree murder (§ 1044[2]). Each version embraces extremely dangerous and fatal conduct performed without specific homicidal intent but with a depraved kind of wantonness: for example, shooting into a crowd, placing a time bomb in a public place, or opening the door of the lions' cage in the zoo [citations omitted]." (Hechtman, Practice Commentary to Penal Law Section 125.25, McKinney's Penal Law, Vol. 1, p. 399). Other illustrations include the random firing of shots into a house in which several persons are present, resulting in death (*People v. Jernatowski*, 238 N.Y. 188, 144 N.E. 497) and the firing of a gun in a crowded bar which brought about the death of a person in the bar (*People v. Register*, 60 N.Y.2d 270, 469 N.Y.S.2d 599, 457 N.E.2d 704). Essential to the prosecution's case was proof that "defendant's act was imminently dangerous and presented a very high risk of death to others and that *it was committed under circumstances which evidenced a wanton indifference to human life or a depravity of mind* [citations omitted]". (*People v. Register, supra,* 60 N.Y.2d 270, 274, 469 N.Y.S.2d 270, 457 N.E.2d 704; emphasis added). To constitute depraved indifference murder, the action must rise above mere recklessness. It must be " 'so wanton, so deficient in a moral sense of concern, so devoid of regard of the life or lives of others, and so blameworthy as to warrant the same criminal liability as that which the law imposes upon a person who intentionally causes the death of another.' " (*People v. Fenner,* 61 N.Y.2d 971, 973, 475 N.Y.S.2d 276, 463 N.E.2d 617). Recklessness there must be, but there must be something more. There must be an unmotivated wickedness so great as to be indicative of depravity.

While we agree that the jury was justified in finding that defendant was guilty of reckless conduct, we cannot agree that the conduct was so gross, so wanton and so callously indifferent to human life as to constitute a depraved indifference to human life. The defendant's ballistics expert testified that the weapon with which Giani was shot was a double action revolver and could be fired in either of two ways. If the weapon were not cocked it could be fired simply by pulling the trigger. In such event a minimum of ten pounds of pressure would be necessary, first to cock the weapon and then to move the trigger forward so that the firing pin contained in the trigger mechanism would strike the bullet and set in motion its propulsion. If, however, the trigger were manually cocked, only four and one-half pounds of pressure would be needed to set the process in motion. Defendant testified that the weapon was cocked and that when Giani was brushed back by a passing car he became so rattled that he accidentally exerted the minimum pressure necessary to fire the weapon. This evidence was credited by the jury, for only by crediting it could it find recklessness rather than intent. These facts do not warrant the conclusion that defendant's action was so mindless of consequences as to constitute a depraved indifference to human life.

Nor does the presence of others nearby raise the degree of recklessness to the point where it can be construed as depraved indifference. If, as the jury obviously concluded, the actual firing of the weapon was accidental, the reckless act of defendant in placing himself in the position where this could happen did not rise to the point where it was the equivalent of murder in the second degree.

* * *

Accordingly, the judgment of the Supreme Court, New York County (Thomas R. Sullivan, J.) rendered November 1, 1984, convicting defendant of murder in the second degree is modified on the law (and the facts), to reduce the conviction to manslaughter in the second degree and the matter is remanded to the Supreme Court, New York County, for resentence.

* * *

All concur except Murphy, P.J., and Asch, J., who dissent in an opinion by Asch, J.

Asch, Justice (dissenting):

The majority asserts that defendant's testimony, "credited by the jury," that he "accidentally * * * exerted the minimum pressure necessary to fire the weapon," does not warrant the conclusion that his action was so mindless of consequences as to constitute a depraved indifference to human life. I disagree and would affirm.

When defendant went into a shooter's crouch, cocked and aimed the gun at Giani's head, he was acting in such a reckless manner as to evidence a depraved indifference to life. Defendant's own witnesses testified that once the Colt .38 was cocked, even the slightest movement over a distance as short of .012 inch would cause the gun to fire. The owner's manual for this gun warns that cocking the gun is extremely dangerous since it can easily be accidentally discharged. Defendant's experts also testified that they had witnessed or investigated numerous incidents where an accidental application of a very light touch discharged this gun. One of the witnesses even testified that this risk is so serious that numerous law-enforcement agencies, including the New York City Police Department and the Secret Service, do not allow officers to fire in this fashion.

The evidence before the jury showed that defendant was aware of the substantial and unjustifiable risk in cocking his gun and consciously disregarded that risk (Penal Law § 15.05[3]). He had access to the owner's manual and underwent individual training, although brief, from a professional instructor in handling, firing and safety. He had practiced at least half a dozen times on the firing range with the same Colt .38, usually with the weapon cocked. Thus, defendant must have been aware that when he cocked and aimed the gun, there was a grave risk of the gun discharging with the slightest pressure exerted on its hair trigger. He consciously disregarded that grave risk. This conduct evinced a depraved indifference to human life.

* * *

It was well within the jury's province to find a depraved indifference to human life in the factual setting presented.

Notes and Questions

1. Is it significant whether the extreme risk which the defendant creates concerns only the death of one person? The Alabama statutes provide that a person commits murder if:

> Under circumstances manifesting extreme indifference to human life, he recklessly engages in conduct which creates a gave risk of death to a person other than himself, and thereby causes the death of another person.

Ala. Code § 13A–6–2(a)(2). In Northington v. State, 413 So.2d 1169 (Ala. Crim.App.1981), writ quashed as improvidently granted, 413 So.2d 1172

(1982), the evidence showed that the defendant withheld food and medical care from her five month old daughter, causing the daughter's death. She was convicted of murder under the provision set out above. This statute, the appellate court reasoned, restates prior Alabama law under which first degree murder included homicides perpetrated by conduct greatly danger-ous to the lives of others and evincing a depraved mind regardless of human life. The doctrine of "depraved heart murder" is intended to embrace those situations in which the perpetrator harbors a disregard for human life generally. Thus it is necessary that the perpetrator have no deliberate intent to injure or kill any particular individual. Here, the evidence indicated that the defendant's actions and omissions were specifi-cally directed towards the daughter and no others:

> [W]hile the defendant's conduct did indeed evidence an extreme indif-ference to the life of her child, there was nothing to show that the conduct displayed an extreme indifference to human life generally.

413 So.2d at 1172. Reversing the conviction, the court continued:

> The function of this section is to embrace those homicides caused by such acts as driving an automobile in a grossly wanton manner, shooting a firearm into a crowd or moving train, and throwing a timber from a roof onto a crowded street. Napier [v. State, 357 S.2d 1001 (Ala.Crim.App.1977)].

In McCormack v. State, 431 So.2d 1336 (Ala.Crim.App.1982), the state's evidence showed that the defendant struck the deceased while the deceased was riding a bicycle. This caused the deceased to swerve into the path of an oncoming truck and he was struck and killed by the truck. Upholding the conviction, the Court of Criminal Appeals held:

> [T]he appellant, by propelling an innocent person into a public thor-oughfare, created an obstacle which endangered all motorists in the vicinity, as well as the deceased individually. * * * [W]e find conduct distinguishable from that which creates a purposeful or know-ing risk to one individual only. While a risk to the deceased in particular was created by appellant's conduct, the conduct showed an indifference to human life generally by the grave risk created to all those who might occupy the highway. * * * Certainly it was foreseeable that many persons in addition to the victim were potential-ly endangered by such an act.

431 So.2d at 1339. The Alabama Supreme Court, on further review, held that the holding of the Court of Criminal Appeals conflicted with *North-ington* and that the trial judge erred in permitting the murder count to go to the jury:

> The State of Alabama presented no evidence that this petitioner engaged in conduct "manifesting extreme indifference to human life generally."

Ex parte McCormack, 431 So.2d 1340, 1341 (Ala.1983).

The New York statute at issue in *Magliato,* however, has not been given that construction. See People v. LeGrand, 61 A.D.2d 815, 815, 402 N.Y.S.2d 209, 211 (1978) (liability need not be based on conduct which places many persons in danger).

2. When can the causing of death by the operation of an automobile give rise to "depraved mind" murder? Is it significant that the use of automobiles has great social utility and that the risks involved appear to be widely accepted? In People v. Gomez, 104 A.D.2d 303, 478 N.Y.S.2d 638 (1984), aff'd, 65 N.Y.2d 9, 489 N.Y.S.2d 156, 478 N.E.2d 759 (1985), the evidence showed that the defendant drove his automobile on the sidewalk for two blocks at a high rate of speed and without applying his brakes. Two persons were killed. Affirming a conviction under the New York statute, the Court of Appeals commented, "The depraved conduct cannot be excused by the inherent social utility of the object or instrumentality used to cause death." 65 N.Y.2d at 12, 489 N.Y.S.2d at 159, 478 N.E.2d at 762.

In United States v. Fleming, 739 F.2d 945 (4th Cir.1984), cert. denied, 469 U.S. 1193, 105 S.Ct. 970, 83 L.Ed.2d 973 (1985), Fleming, while intoxicated, drove on the George Washington Memorial Parkway in Virginia at speeds between 70 and 100 miles per hour. The speed limit was 45 mph. To avoid traffic, he sometimes swerved into the lanes for oncoming traffic; that traffic had to move out of his way to avoid a collision. After he lost control, his car hit the curb on the opposite side of the parkway and struck the car driven by the victim. She was killed. Finding a conviction for murder supported by the facts, the court explained:

> In the vast majority of vehicular homicides, the accused has not exhibited such wanton and reckless disregard for human life as to indicate the presence of malice on his part. In the present case, however, the facts show a deviation from established standards of regard for life and the safety of others that is markedly different in degree from that found in most vehicular homicides. In the average drunk driving homicide, there is not proof that the driver has acted while intoxicated with the purpose of wantonly and intentionally putting the lives of others in danger. Rather, his driving abilities were so impaired that he recklessly put others in danger simply by being on the road and attempting to do the things that any driver would do. In the present case, however, danger did not arise only by defendant's determination to drive while drunk. Rather, in addition to being intoxicated while driving, defendant drove in a manner that could be taken to indicate depraved disregard for human life, *particularly* in light of the fact that *because he was drunk* his reckless behavior was all the more dangerous.

739 F.2d at 948 (emphasis in original).

Did the court consider Fleming's state of intoxication as tending to show that he had the state of mind necessary for murder? Why shouldn't this intoxication be regarded as tending to show the absence of this mental state? Reconsider the material on intoxication from Chapter VI, at pages 344–76, supra.

C. PREMEDITATED KILLINGS: FIRST DEGREE MURDER

The common law crime of murder was not divided into degrees and premeditation was not an element of the single offense of murder.

American statutes, however, often created different offenses of first and second degree murder; the California statute, reprinted at page 380, supra, is reasonably typical. Under this approach, among the distinguishing features is the premeditation requirement for one type of first degree murder.

Under this approach, second degree murder is often any killing with malice aforethought (or a more modern version of it) that does not come within any of the specific situations sufficient to "raise" it to first degree murder. Second degree murder can, under this approach, be committed other than by an intentional killing. Can premeditation raise a nonintentional murder (such as a "depraved mind" murder) to first degree murder? The Michigan court has held not. People v. Dykhouse, 418 Mich. 488, 345 N.W.2d 150 (1984).

As the following case illustrates, the reported appellate decisions most often address the appellate review process, i.e., when does the evidence support a conviction for first degree murder when a properly instructed jury has convicted a defendant of that offense? Consider also, however, how juries should be instructed. On a more general level, consider whether it is sound policy to separate out premeditated killings for the imposition of more severe penalties than are imposed for other murders.

STATE v. BINGHAM

Court of Appeals of Washington, 1985.
40 Wn.App. 553, 699 P.2d 262.

WORSWICK, CHIEF JUDGE.

We are asked to decide whether the time to effect death by manual strangulation is alone sufficient to support a finding of premeditation in the absence of any other evidence supporting such a finding.
* * *

Leslie Cook, a retarded adult living at the Laurisden Home in Port Angeles, was raped and strangled on February 15, 1982. Bingham was the last person with whom she was seen. The two of them got off the Port Angeles—Sequim bus together at Sequim about 6 p.m. on February 15. They visited a grocery store and two residences. The last of these was Enid Pratt's where Bingham asked for a ride back to Port Angeles. When he was refused, he said they would hitchhike. They took the infrequently travelled Old Olympic Highway. Three days later, Cook's body was discovered in a field approximately ¼ mile from the Pratt residence.

At trial, the State's expert testified that, in order to cause death by strangulation, Cook's assailant would have had to maintain substantial and continuous pressure on her windpipe for 3–5 minutes. The State contended that this alone was enough to raise an inference that the murder was premeditated. The trial judge agreed * * *. Therefore, it allowed the issue of premeditation to go to the jury. The jury convicted Bingham of aggravated first degree murder, rape being the aggravating circumstance. On appeal, counsel for Bingham concedes that a finding of guilty of murder was justified; he challenges only the finding of premeditation, contending that the evidence was insufficient to support it. We agree.

Premeditation is a separate and distinct element of first degree murder. It involves the mental process of thinking over beforehand, deliberation, reflection, weighing or reasoning for a period of time, however short, after which the intent to kill is formed. The time required for manual strangulation is sufficient to permit deliberation. However, time alone is not enough. The evidence must be sufficient to support the inference that the defendant not only had the time to deliberate, but that he actually did so. To require anything less would permit a jury to focus on the method of killing to the exclusion of the mental process involved in the separate element of premeditation.

The concept of premeditation had a slow but sure beginning in Anglo-American legal history. More than 500 years ago, English jurists arrived at the not surprising conclusion that the worst criminals—and those most deserving of the ultimate punishment—were those who planned to kill and then did so. Thus began the movement toward classification of homicides that resulted in restriction of the death penalty to those involving "malice prepensed" or "malice afore-thought." When Washington's first criminal code was enacted in 1854, the Territorial Legislature abandoned this archaic language and used the phrase "deliberate and premeditated malice" in defining first degree murder. It thereby made a clear separation between a malicious intent and the process of deliberating before arriving at that intent.

Our Supreme Court recognized the need for evidence of both time for and fact of deliberation in *State v. Arata,* 56 Wash. 185, 189, 105 P. 227 (1909). Although it reversed a first degree murder conviction because a portion of an instruction was erroneous, it approved the remainder of the instruction, saying:

> In the case at bar, the court said, in substance, the law knows no specific time; if the man reflects upon the act a moment antecedent to the act, it is sufficient; the time of deliberation and premeditation need not be long; if it furnishes room for reflection *and the facts show that such reflection existed,* then it is sufficient deliberation, and closed the instruction upon this point with the statement: "There need be no appreciable space of time between the formation of the intention to kill and the killing." By these few last words the court destroyed at once all that was good in the entire statement, and gave the jury a rule which this court has frequently held was erroneous. This was reversible error.

(Italics ours.)

Arata, 56 Wash. at 189, 105 P. 227. This analysis seems implicitly to have been recognized, although imperfectly expressed, in more recent cases as well.

The subject of premeditation appears frequently in Washington cases. However, it is seldom discussed in a way that affords clear, objective guidance to trial judges in determining the sufficiency of the evidence to support it. Nevertheless, review of these cases reveals that in each one where the evidence has been found sufficient, there has been some evidence beyond time from which a jury could infer the fact of deliberation. This evidence has included, *inter alia,* motive, acquisition of a weapon, and planning directly related to the killing.

Unless evidence of both time for and fact of deliberation are required, premeditation could be inferred in any case where the means of effecting death requires more than a moment in time. For all practical purposes, it would merge with intent; proof of intent would become proof of premeditation. However, the two elements are separate. Premeditation cannot be inferred from intent.

Premeditation can be proved by direct evidence, or it can be proved by circumstantial evidence where the inferences drawn by the jury are reasonable and the evidence supporting the jury's findings is substantial. There was no such evidence here, either direct or circumstantial.

There was no evidence that Bingham had known Cook before February 15 or that he had a motive to kill her. By chance, they took the same bus. When Cook's companion on the bus refused to go to Sequim with her, Bingham offered to see that Cook got back to the Laurisden Home later. That was apparently still his intention when he asked for a ride at the Pratt residence. It could be inferred that between there and the field ¼ mile away, he decided to rape her. A reasonable jury could not infer from this beyond a reasonable doubt that he also planned to kill her. There is no other evidence to support a finding of premeditation. The fact of strangulation, without more, leads us to conclude that the jury only speculated as to the mental process involved in premeditation. This is not enough. The premeditation finding cannot stand.

There remains the difficult question of how to dispose of this case. Counsel for Bingham concedes that Bingham is at least guilty of second degree murder. The jury was instructed on second degree murder as a lesser included offense and necessarily found the requisite elements in order to reach the verdict it did. * * *

Reversed. Remanded for entry of judgment and sentence for second degree murder.

PETRICH, J., concur.

ALEXANDER, JUDGE (dissenting).

* * *

I believe that where the evidence shows that death was caused slowly by manual strangulation in circumstances such as we have here, a rational trier of fact could be convinced beyond a reasonable doubt that the perpetrator intentionally caused death after deliberation and premeditation.

Contrary to the majority view, the law on this issue is unclear and unsettled. Washington case law and statutes do not provide a precise definition of premeditation, forcing us to examine the nature of the crime and the relationship between the concepts of intent and premeditation. "Premeditated" encompasses the mental process of thinking beforehand, deliberation, reflection, weighing or reasoning for a period of time, however short. RCW 9A.32.020(1) provides:

> (1) As used in this chapter the premeditation required in order to support a conviction of the crime of murder in the first degree must involve *more that a moment in point of time.*

(Italics mine.)

Premeditation may be proved by circumstantial evidence, where the inferences drawn by the jury from that evidence are reasonable. A jury may infer premeditation from the facts of the crime when the defendant had an appreciable time in which to deliberate the intent to kill, though such time may be very short.

Time, then, may literally be of the essence. A number of cases have held that the element of premeditation is properly inferable from evidence of the lapse of time to death. * * *

In *State v. Harris,* 62 Wash.2d at 868, 385 P.2d 18, our Supreme Court found the evidence of premeditation to be sufficient in a case where the victim was struck on the head several times with a blunt instrument, struck in the face, and then strangled with a vacuum cleaner cord. The strangling was the immediate cause of death. The court held that the jury could infer premeditation from the circumstances of the killing even though the killing was unwitnessed and defendant did not testify. The "appreciable period" was the time that "elapsed between the first blow of the beating and the choking [causing death] to permit the perpetrator to form the intent to kill. * * *"
* * *

The majority seem to suggest that for a jury to find premeditation or deliberation it must have preceded the formation of intent to kill. In other words, they seem to hold, if the intent to kill is formed impulsively there can be no premeditation. Neither logic nor case law leads me to concur with that conclusion. The fact of deliberation for the requisite time is the key ingredient of premeditation. If there is opportunity for deliberation before death is caused, the jury may find that the death is not the result of an impulsive act. It is not very productive, therefore, to engage in analysis or speculation over which occurred first, formation of intent to kill or reflection on that intent. Common sense suggests that premeditation exists as much if one is reflecting on an already formed intent to kill as it does when one is deliberating whether or not to kill. In either case, reflection and deliberation are present, if the deliberation is for an appreciable time. If the killing follows this process of reflection, then it is a premeditated killing.

In this case, uncontroverted evidence was presented to the jury that it takes 3 to 5 minutes to effect death by manual strangulation. The jury was, therefore, justified in concluding that an appreciable period of time elapsed from the time the defendant first placed his hand or hands on the victim's throat, regardless of what his intent might then have been, until the act of strangulation caused her death. A jury would further be justified in concluding from the circumstances of this case, as it must have done, that the defendant would necessarily have his attention riveted during this period of time on what effect the application of pressure might have on the windpipe of this "child-like" woman. It is significant that the defendant was a large man and there was little sign of struggle at the scene of the killing. These facts indicate that the death was not the result of an impulsive or spontaneous act flowing from an attempt to overcome resistance or to effect sexual contact. In short, the evidence of time-lapse and of the crime scene compels the conclusion that the defendant had ample opportunity to deliberate and premeditate on what he intended to achieve by choking his victim. The fact that he ultimately caused her death by strangulation justifies the conclusion that he intended to kill after reflecting on the deed for the requisite time.

* * *

The majority seem concerned that permitting the jury to infer premeditation in a case such as this would allow the jury to focus on the method of the killing to the exclusion of evidence concerning the mental process involved in the element of premeditation. I disagree. I do not suggest that a jury should be allowed to exclude evidence of mental process. On the other hand, they should not be precluded from considering the method of killing if its very nature provides clues to the mental process of the perpetrator.

I can only assume the Legislature must have intended by distinguishing between first and second degree murder, establishing greater penalties for first degree murder, to discourage killing when one has an opportunity to think about it. The time period during which one continuously exerts sufficient pressure on a victim's throat to block breathing which, in turn, causes unconsciousness and then death, affords a person a significant opportunity for a change of heart. If a person consciously rejects the opportunity to lessen the pressure in that period, the person may be found to have deliberated. The more time required, the greater the probability that even a slow thinker had time to reflect.

The majority correctly observes that in this case there is no evidence of prior planning. The defendant did not testify at trial and thus the jury did not know his mental state except as he revealed it to investigating officers. What a person thinks or intends is always difficult to determine in any case because we cannot pry into the mind. However, what a person does is often the best gauge of his or her thinking. The fact finder is called upon to determine whether a defendant premeditated from the facts surrounding the killing. Here, the jury concluded, as well they might, that this defendant took this mentally retarded young woman to a secluded area of Clallam County, raped her, strangled her with little difficulty for 3 to 5 minutes until she was dead, and then proceeded to bite her dead body. From this evidence a rational trier of fact could conclude beyond a reasonable doubt that the defendant was capable of reflecting and did reflect on his deed sufficiently to cause him to be guilty of premeditated murder in the first degree. The evidence supports the verdict and I would affirm.

Notes and Questions

1. The California Supreme Court has attempted to devise a more structured analysis for determining whether a jury verdict finding premeditation is supported by the evidence. People v. Anderson, 70 Cal.2d 15, 73 Cal.Rptr. 550, 447 P.2d 942 (1968). It noted three categories of evidence tending to establish premeditation:

> (1) facts about how and what defendant did *prior* to the actual killing which show that the defendant was engaged in activity directed toward, and explicable as intended to result in, the killing—what may be characterized as "planning" activity; (2) facts about the defendant's *prior* relationship and/or conduct with the victim from which the jury could reasonably infer a "motive" to kill the victim, which inference of motive, together with facts of type (1) or (3), would in turn support an inference that the killing was the result of "a pre-existing reflection" and "careful thought and weighing of considerations" rather than "mere unconsidered or rash impulse hastily executed" * * *; (3) facts about the nature of the killing from which the jury could infer that the *manner* of killing was so particular and exacting that the defendant must have intentionally killed according to a "preconceived design" to take his victim's life in a particular way for a "reason" which the jury can reasonably infer from facts or type (1) or (2).

70 Cal.2d at 26–27, 73 Cal.Rptr. at 557, 447 P.2d at 949. A verdict of guilty of premeditated murder will be sustained, the court concluded, when the record contains evidence of all three kinds, when there is "extremely strong" evidence of type (1), or evidence of type (2) in conjunction with other evidence of either type (1) or (3). Is this analysis reasonable? Is it likely to accomplish its intended purpose?

2. Where the evidence tends to show provocation (although insufficient to reduce the killing to manslaughter) or concern by the defendant for his safety (although insufficient to constitute a complete defense), appellate courts seem willing to reverse convictions for premeditated murder. In State v. Corn, 303 N.C. 293, 278 S.E.2d 221 (1981), Melton and a companion entered Corn's home and found him lying on a sofa. Melton was intoxicated and said something—it may have been an accusation that Corn was homosexual—to which Corn responded, "You son-of-a-bitch, don't accuse

me of that." He then jumped off the sofa, grabbed a nearby rifle, and shot Melton several times in the chest. Reversing a conviction for premeditated murder, the court explained:

> There is no evidence that defendant acted in accordance with a fixed design or that he had sufficient time to weigh the consequences of his actions. Defendant did not threaten Melton before the incident or exhibit any conduct which would indicate that he formed any intent to kill him prior to the incident in question. There was no significant history of arguments or ill will between the parties. Although defendant shot deceased several times, there is no evidence that any shots were fired after he fell or that defendant dealt any blows to the body once the shooting ended.

> All the evidence tends to show that defendant shot Melton after a quarrel, in a state of passion, without aforethought or calm consideration. * * *

303 N.C. at 298, 278 S.E.2d at 224.

3. Does—or should—premeditation require a "calm" or perhaps "normal" process? In People v. Hamm, 120 Mich.App.388, 328 N.W.2d 51 (1982), Hamm killed a psychiatrist, Dr. Hoyt, who had treated him during hospitalization. Hoyt had become a focal point of Hamm's delusions and Hamm was obsessed with the false belief that Hoyt was conspiring with local physicians to keep Hamm from obtaining treatment for what he believed to be arsenic poisoning. Several hours before the killing, Hamm attempted to get some shells for his gun, explaining that he wanted them "to kill Dr. Hoyt." A friend attempted to calm him down and the two discussed Hamm's problem and several options open to him, such as having his father help him, or going to the police or prosecuting attorney.

On appeal from his conviction for premeditated murder, Hamm urged that his mental illness and delusion precluded him from *adequately* considering "rational, viable alternatives" to killing so as to be guilty of first degree murder. The court first found no authority for construing premeditation as requiring this sort of consideration. But it continued:

> In any event, there was ample evidence to suggest that defendant considered several alternatives to killing Dr. Hoyt. Defendant had considered going to his father for help, suing Dr. Hoyt in a civil action, calling the police or prosecuting attorney, or shooting Dr. Hoyt in the legs and making him "confess" to defendant's father. Therefore, under the defendant's standard for determining deliberation, there was sufficient evidence to sustain a conviction.

120 Mich.App. at 393, 328 N.W.2d at 53. Is it likely that Hamm's consideration of these alternatives was affected by his delusional beliefs? If so, did Hamm engage in the sort of mental process that justifies treating his act of intentionally killing Hoyt as more serious than second degree murder?

4. As was pointed out in the introduction to this chapter, premeditated murders were originally distinguished from other murders for purposes of separate classification in large part to identify those killings for which the death penalty should be required or at least available. As a result of

the Supreme Court's application of the Eighth Amendment in the death penalty context (see pages 106–09, supra), a number of jurisdictions have revised their homicide classification schemes to distinguish in what is regarded as a more appropriate—and constitutionally acceptable—manner those situations in which the death penalty will be available. Some of these jurisdictions have rejected the pattern in which murder is divided into degrees and rather have created the offense of "capital murder" for which death may be imposed. E.g., Texas Penal Code § 19.03; Miss.Code Ann. § 97–3–19; Virginia Code § 18.2–31. The definitions of capital murder sometimes incorporate the premeditation requirement. Under the Virginia statute, for example, capital murder is defined as "the willful, deliberate and premeditated killing" of another if the victim was a law enforcement officer killed for the purpose of interfering with the officer's official duties, the killing was "for hire," more than one person was killed as a part of the same transaction, or the killing was related to the commission of rape, abduction, or robbery. Virginia Code § 18.2–31.

Other jurisdictions limit the death penalty to those situations in which the defendant has been convicted of a specified homicide offense and, in addition, "special" or "aggravating" circumstances are shown by the prosecution to exist. Illinois, for example, make a defendant eligible for the death penalty if the conviction is for murder and any one of eight aggravating factors is shown. Ill.Stat.Ann. ch. 38, § 9–1(b). California permits imposition of the death penalty upon conviction of first degree murder (see page 380, supra) and a finding by the jury that at least one of nineteen "special circumstances" is found to be true. Cal.Penal Code § 190.2(a). Among those special circumstances are:

(1) The murder was intentional and carried out for financial gain.

(2) The defendant was previously convicted of murder in the first or second degree. * * *

* * *

(5) The murder was committed for the purpose of avoiding or preventing a lawful arrest or to perfect, or attempted to perfect an escape from lawful custody.

* * *

(7) The victim was a peace officer * * * who, while engaged in the course of the performance of his duties was intentionally killed, and such defendant knew or reasonably should have known that such victim was a police officer engaged in the performance of his duties; or the victim was a peace officer * * * and was intentionally killed in retaliation for the performance of his official duties.

* * *

(10) The victim was a witness to a crime who was intentionally killed for the purpose of preventing his testimony in any criminal proceeding, and the killing was not committed during the commission, or attempted commission [of] the crime to which he was a witness; or the victim was a witness to a crime and was intentionally killed in retaliation for his testimony in any criminal proceeding.

* * *

(14) The murder was especially heinous, atrocious, or cruel, manifesting exceptional depravity, as utilized in this section, the phrase especially heinous, atrocious or cruel manifesting exceptional depravity means a consciousless, or pitiless crime which is unnecessarily torturous to the victim.

(15) The defendant intentionally killed the victim while lying in wait.

(16) The victim was intentionally killed because of his race, color, religion, nationality or country of origin.

(17) The murder was committed while the defendant was engaged in or was an accomplice in the commission of, or attempted commission of, or the immediate flight after committing or attempting to commit the following felonies:

(i) Robbery * * *.

(ii) Kidnapping * * *.

(iii) Rape * * *.

(iv) Sodomy * * *.

(v) The performance of a lewd or lascivious act upon the person of a child under the age of 15 * * *.

(vi) Oral copulation * * *.

(vii) Burglary in the first or second degree * * *.

(viii) Arson * * *.

(ix) Train wrecking.

(18) The murder was intentional and involved the infliction of torture. For purpose of this section torture requires proof of the infliction of extreme physical pain no matter how long its duration.

(19) The defendant intentionally killed the victim by the administration of poison.

Id. The making of the requisite finding of the truth of the allegation that a special circumstance exists does not require the imposition of the death sentence, but triggers further proceedings to determine whether death or life imprisonment is the appropriate penalty; see page 108, supra.

Are these alternative methods of identifying those offenses for which the maximum penalty should be available more appropriate than the traditional approach under which premeditated—and usually first degree—murders are among those for which death may be imposed?

5. Is premeditation, under any definition, an appropriate criterion with which to select those cases in which the maximum penalty—whatever it is—may be imposed? Consider the following:

The Significance of Deliberation and Impulse

Whether and to what extent homicidal behavior was preceded by deliberation is plainly of evidential value in determining what the actor knew and intended when he acted. The more extensive the deliberation, the more probable it is that at least the more palpable risks created by the homicidal act were clearly perceived, and at least its more immediate consequences intended. From this point of view, however, gradations in homicidal behavior from the purely impulsive to the completely deliberate bear directly upon the question whether the actor created the homicidal risk inadvertently or advertently and, if advertently, whether or not he intended to kill, and only indirectly upon his character. The difficult question is whether the impulsiveness or deliberateness of his behavior has direct and independent significance in relation to his character. Assuming that other factors indicative of his character, such as knowledge, intent and motive are the same, of what additional importance is it that his act was the product of or was preceded by more or less deliberation? It may be argued that the more carefully considered and the less impulsive the act is, the more it indicates basic perversion of the actor's conceptions of good and evil. But it is surely not self-evident that the man who acts on wrong principles is a more dangerous man than one who acts without considering what is good. There are, moreover, other objections to this view of the significance of deliberation. In the first place, it ignores that passion may influence deliberation as well as lead to action without deliberation, so that deliberate as well as impulsive action may be contrary to the actor's real notions of good and evil. In the second place, it does not embrace either deliberation about means rather than ends or acts which are preceded by but are not in accord with the results of deliberation. And yet it is extremely difficult in most cases to discover in what terms the actor deliberated or what was the relationship between deliberation and act. These objections are not avoided by stating the significance of deliberation in another way. Thus it may be said that reflection prior to action indicates that the actor lacks the sort of desires that will prevent such an act, since reflection is the opportunity to bring such desires into play, an opportunity which, by hypothesis, is not afforded by impulsive action; whereas action without reflection does not permit of that inference because if the actor had deliberated he might not have acted as he did. But in order to draw from these premises the conclusion that the man who acts deliberately is more dangerous than the man who acts impulsively, it must be asserted that the probability that the former's deliberations will result in wrong judgments is greater than the probability that the latter will not reflect before acting. This proposition also requires proof. The truth is, we think, that deliberation has no independent significance in relation to character and that the importance usually accorded it properly belongs to other factors which are its concomitants such, for example, as lapse of time, or to still other factors which it evidences, such as knowledge and intent. When the matter is viewed in that way, no difficulty is experienced in dealing with cases in which deliberation itself results in the intensification of passion, as it may when the enormity of an injury done the actor or the value of an end to be served by a homicidal act becomes apparent only after thought.

Wechsler and Michael, A Rationale of the Law of Homicide, 37 Colum.L. Rev. 701, 1261, 1282–84 (1937).

D. PROVOKED KILLINGS: VOLUNTARY MANSLAUGHTER

Homicide law has been characterized by a willingness to give some significance to provoking circumstances that are generally agreed to be insufficient to justify relieving the defendant of all criminal responsibility for the killing. Traditionally, this has been accomplished by providing that a killing will be reduced from murder to manslaughter if the facts show "adequate provocation."

But this tradition has also included substantial concern that juries might abuse the power to mitigate a killing on provocation grounds. As a result, much of the law in this area has addressed the power of the trial judge to characterize provocation as inadequate "as a matter of law" and consequently neither instruct the jury on voluntary manslaughter nor given them that offense as a possible verdict choice.

Modern statutes often retain the traditional approach, even if manslaughter is not formally subdivided between "voluntary" and "involuntary" manslaughter. But both modern statutes and recent judicial decisions reflect discomfort with the traditional limits upon the situations in which juries will be permitted to determine whether provocation is sufficient to mitigate a killing. This is addressed in the following case.

The murder-manslaughter distinction has created significant confusion concerning the desirable—and constitutionally permissible—allocations of the burden of proof or persuasion on the issue of provocation. Reconsider in light of the material in this section Patterson v. New York, 432 U.S. 197, 97 S.Ct. 2319, 53 L.Ed.2d 281 (1977), reprinted at page 46, supra.

PEOPLE v. WALKER
New York Supreme Court, Appellate Division, 1984.
100 A.D.2d 220, 473 N.Y.S.2d 460.

MURPHY, PRESIDING JUSTICE:

The principal issue presented upon this appeal is whether the trial court erroneously refused to submit manslaughter in the first degree to the jury upon the theory that defendant acted under the influence of "extreme emotional disturbance" (PL § 125.20 subd. 2). [The relevant portion of the statute provides as follows:

§ 125.20 Manslaughter in the first degree

A person is guilty of manslaughter in the first degree when:

* * *

2. With intent to cause the death of another person, he causes the death of such person or a third person under circumstances which do not constitute murder because he acts under the influence of extreme

emotional disturbance, as defined in paragraph (a) of subdivision one of section 125.25. * * *.

Section 125.25, subdivision one provides that it is an affirmative defense to an intentional killing that:

> (a) the person acted under the influence of extreme emotional disturbance for which there was a reasonable explanation or excuse, the reasonableness of which is to be determined from the viewpoint of a person in the defendant's situation under the circumstances as the defendant believed them to be. * * *]

The defendant was convicted after trial of murder in the second degree (PL § 125.25 subd. 1) and criminal possession of a weapon in the second degree (PL § 265.03).

Defendant Robert Walker was charged with shooting William Edmunds in the Madrid Bar on November 24, 1980. The Madrid Bar was located on Seventh Avenue between 115th and 116th Streets; it was frequented by high-level drug dealers. According to Lavonia Edmunds, the decedent's sister, defendant had received a consignment of marijuana from her brother, William. The defendant, however, never repaid decedent for this $4,500 consignment. The defendant claimed that he had been robbed of the marijuana. Lavonia had denied defendant's request that she intercede with her brother on defendant's behalf so that he would be given additional consignments.

On the evening of November 24, 1980, William Edmunds encountered defendant in the Madrid Bar. According to witness Warren Hayes, an acquaintance of both individuals, William Edmunds asked defendant for the money owed to him. The defendant maintained that he had no money. Edmunds then asked how defendant could eat in the Madrid Bar if he did not have any money. The defendant continued the argument by stating that Edmunds was not going to obtain his money and that Edmunds could give his money to the defendant. Edmunds countered by stating that the only "dough" the defendant would obtain was in the bread on the table. At that point, Edmunds apparently placed his hands on defendant's plate.

According to Hayes and Annibell Carithers, a waitress, defendant stood up and shot Edmunds three times. Stacey Garner, a drug seller and a drug addict, was standing outside the Madrid Bar. After the shooting, she saw the defendant exit the Bar; he was holding a gun that was partially covered by a jacket. The defendant walked down Seventh Avenue toward 115th Street.

The trial court was not required to charge the affirmative defense based upon "extreme emotional disturbance" (PL § 125.25 subd. 1(a)) unless the evidence sufficiently established the elements of that affirmative defense. At trial, the defense attorney argued that defendant had acted in anger because he had been embarrassed by the decedent. Upon this appeal, an alternative argument is made that defendant shot the decedent because the latter had "cut off" the former from the drug trade. Upon this record, many other motives might be advanced for defendant's action. For example, immediately prior to the occurrence, he asked decedent for his money. It could be argued that defendant's request was a veiled attempt to rob the decedent.

It is possible that defendant acted in anger or for revenge. It is also possible that he shot decedent very calmly and unemotionally. In that regard, it should be stressed that the defendant "walked" rather than "ran" from the Bar after the incident. Anger, revenge and other emotions may serve as a "reasonable explanation" for the presence of an "extreme emotional disturbance". However, it does not follow that defendant was influenced by an "extreme emotional disturbance" merely because he may have acted in anger or for revenge.

Moreover, there was no specific evidence submitted at trial that established that the defendant was influenced by an "extreme emotional disturbance". The defendant himself did not testify. He did not call any psychiatrist or psychologist to prove his affirmative defense. None of the witnesses even described his physical, emotional and mental state at the time of the shooting.

In sum, the trial court properly denied the defense request to charge an affirmative defense under PL § 125.25 subd. 1(a) together with a reduced charge on manslaughter in the first degree under PL § 125.20 subd. 2. The evidence was not sufficient to warrant such a charge. The jury would have been impermissibly asked to find that defendant was influenced by an "extreme emotional disturbance" in the absence of any specific proof of that affirmative defense. The other trial evidence would have merely permitted the jury to speculate as to defendant's motivation in shooting. Speculation of that sort would have been improper. In any event, even if it were assumed that defendant acted in anger or for revenge, it did not follow that he was in any way influenced by an "extreme emotional disturbance". The defendant did not show that he lost "self-control" or that his action was caused by a "mental infirmity" not rising to the level of insanity.

* * *

SANDLER, JUSTICE (dissenting in part).

* * *

The issue presented on this appeal is an important one. The facts developed at the trial raise fundamental questions as to the meaning and application of PL § 125.25(1)(a) and the counterpart language in PL § 125.20(2), defining one form of manslaughter in the first degree. More precisely the issue is whether the courts will give effect to the significant change in law explicitly intended to have been brought about by the distinguished scholars who drafted § 210.3(1)(b) of the Model Penal Code, which formulation was adopted by the Legislature in the enactment of § 125.25(1)(a), with the single substantial distinction that the New York statute placed the burden of proof on this issue upon the defendant.

The character of the change intended to be brought about was set forth by the authors of the Model Penal Code section clearly and in detail, and it cannot be doubted that those responsible for the enactment of the Model Penal Code formulation in the statutory law of this State were fully aware of that which was intended. The concern of the draftsmen of Model Penal Code § 210.3(1)(b) was to change significantly the rules of law that had developed under the traditional common-law rule that defined homicide, even if intentional, as manslaughter "if committed in the heat of passion upon adequate provocation." Model Penal Code and Commentaries, Part II, § 210.3, p. 44. The central purpose was to avoid "the strictures of early precedents" and "to abandon preconceived notions of what constitutes adequate provocation and to submit that question to the jury's deliberation", Model Penal Code and Commentaries, *supra*, at 61.

This change was intended to be achieved in essentially two ways. First, the words "heat of passion" were replaced by the phrase "under the influence of extreme mental or emotional disturbance" so as to expand the concept to include, not only that which had been embraced previously under "heat of passion", but also consideration as a basis for mitigation of events which traditionally were regarded as having been sufficiently distant in time from the homicide to permit the defendant a cooling-off period. See Model Penal Code and Commentaries, *supra*, at 59.

Secondly, in replacing the traditional formula of adequate provocation by the words "under the influence of extreme mental or emotional disturbance for which there is reasonable explanation or excuse * * * to be determined from the viewpoint of a person in the defendant's situation", it was intended to sweep away "the rigid rules that limited provocation to certain defined circumstances." See Model Penal Code and Commentaries, *supra*, at 61. As here pertinent, it was explicitly intended to discard the general rule at common law "that words alone, no matter how insulting, could not amount to adequate provocation." See Model Penal Code and Commentaries, *supra*, at 58; see also Insulting Words as Provocation of Homicide or as Reducing the Degree Thereof, Ann. 2 A.L.R.3d 1292.

In declining to charge the affirmative defense in this case the trial court may well have applied correctly the traditional rule that had prevailed in the courts of this country. Quite understandably, since the legislative background appears not to have been called to the trial court's attention, the court failed to appreciate that the rule it was attempting to follow was one of those intended to be discarded in favor of the central principle that where there is evidence of extreme emotional disturbance "it is for the trier of fact to decide, in light of all the circumstances of the case, whether there exists a reasonable explanation or excuse for the actor's mental condition." See Model Penal Code and Commentaries, *supra*, at 61.

* * *

The New York Court of Appeals addressed at length issues arising out of PL § 125.25(1)(a) in * * * *People v. Casassa*, 49 N.Y.2d 668, 427

N.Y.S.2d 769, 404 N.E.2d 1310. * * * I believe the analysis in *Casassa* is dispositive. * * * *Casassa* was an appeal by a defendant who had been convicted after a non-jury trial in which the judge considered the issue presented by the affirmative defense and concluded that it was not established under the circumstances of the case. After a brief period of casual dating between the deceased and Casassa, she informed the defendant that she was not in love with him and undertook to terminate the relationship. This rejection of the defendant's advances precipitated a "bizarre series of actions on the part of defendant" climaxed by the fatal assault. The totality of his actions was claimed by the defense to demonstrate the existence of extreme emotional disturbance. Conflicting psychiatric testimony was presented.

The trial court rejected the affirmative defense on the essential ground that defendant's emotional reaction at the time of the commission of the crime was so peculiar to him that it could not be considered reasonable so as to reduce the conviction to manslaughter in the first degree.

In sustaining the judgment of conviction, the Court of Appeals carefully reviewed the circumstances surrounding the adoption of the Model Penal Code formulation into the law of this State. It noted that the Model Penal Code formulation "represented a significant departure from the prior law of this State" and that the "new formulation is significantly broader in scope than the 'heat of passion' doctrine which it replaced". It noted specifically the demise of the prior requirement that the defendant's action must be an immediate response to the claimed provocation.

The Court went on to consider carefully the Comments to the Model Penal Code, at that time embodied in Tentative Draft No. 9. From that study, the Court concluded that the first requirement of the formulation, extreme emotional disturbance, "is wholly subjective—i.e., it involves a determination that the particular defendant did in fact act under extreme emotional disturbance, that the claimed explanation as to the cause of his action is not contrived or sham".

The Court further noted:

> The second component is more difficult to describe—i.e., whether there was a reasonable explanation or excuse for the emotional disturbance. It was designed to sweep away "the rigid rules that have developed with respect to the sufficiency of particular types of provocation, such as the rule that words alone can never be enough" * * * and "avoids a merely arbitrary limitation on the nature of the antecedent circumstances that may justify a mitigation." * * * "The ultimate test, however, is objective; there must be 'reasonable' explanation or excuse for the actor's disturbance".

From the foregoing analysis of the Comments to the Model Penal Code, the Court of Appeals concluded:

> In light of these comments and the necessity of articulating the defense in terms comprehensible to jurors, we conclude that the deter-

mination whether there was reasonable explanation or excuse for a particular emotional disturbance should be made by viewing the subjective, internal situation in which the defendant found himself and the external circumstances as he perceived them at the time, however inaccurate that perception may have been, and assessing from that standpoint whether the explanation or excuse for his emotional disturbance was reasonable, so as to entitle him to a reduction of the crime charged from murder in the second degree to manslaughter in the first degree. We recognize that even such a description of the defense provides no precise guidelines and necessarily leaves room for the exercise of judgmental evaluation by the jury. This, however, appears to have been the intent of the draftsmen. "The purpose was explicitly to give full scope to what amounts to a plea in mitigation based upon a mental or emotional trauma of significant dimensions, with the jury asked to show whatever empathy it can." (Wechsler, Codification of Criminal Law in the United States: The Model Penal Code, 68 Col.L. Rev. 1425, 1446.)

The Court of Appeals held in *Casassa* that it could not say as a matter of law that the trial court erred in its judgment that the murder was "the result of defendant's malevolence rather than an understandable human response deserving of mercy". Significantly, nothing in the court's opinion in *Casassa* suggests that the issue had not been an appropriate one for the factual consideration of the trier of the facts. Indeed, the thrust of the opinion is that the evidence in *Casassa* presented a factual issue for the trier of the facts, in that case a judge, and that he did not err as a matter of law in rejecting the affirmative defense.

Turning to the facts presented in this case, the threshold issue clearly is whether there is evidence that the defendant "acted under the influence of extreme emotional disturbance". As we have been instructed by the Court of Appeals in *Casassa*, this requirement "is wholly subjective". From the evidence presented at the trial the jury could reasonably have found that the defendant killed the deceased in a burst of anger, that a smouldering sense of grievance had been ignited by insulting and contemptuous words and actions.

Indeed I find it difficult to see how a jury could have reasonably reached any other conclusion as to the defendant's state of mind. The evidence that would justify the jury's conclusion that the defendant acted during a moment of violent anger is "evidence of extreme emotional disturbance" more than sufficient to have required the submission of that issue, a subjective one, to the jury for its determination.

I am unable to discern in the statutory language, the detailed comments of the authors of the Model Penal Code, the legislative history surrounding the enactment of PL § 125.25, or the several reported opinions dealing with issues relating to that section, any shred of support for the perplexing suggestion in the Court's opinion that "evidence of extreme emotional disturbance" sufficient to make that subjective issue a jury question requires that the defendant testify, or present psychiatric testimony, or that lay witnesses testify that the defendant appeared angry or upset at the time of the homicidal event. It does not follow from the fortuitous presence of one or more such circumstances in the few cases that became the subject of reported opinions that the presence of any one or more such circumstances has become a legal precondition to submitting to the jury what on the facts of this case is manifestly a jury question.

In an effort to avoid what understandably is felt to be an undesirable result in an unsympathetic case, an opinion has been developed that distorts radically and fundamentally the clear meaning and intent of PL § 125.25, and reintroduces into this area of law "preconceived notions" and "rigid rules" similar to those that the statutory section was so carefully and painstakingly designed to sweep away. * * *

Once it is determined that there was "evidence of extreme emotional disturbance", the controlling rule is clear, and indeed not disputed in the majority memorandum: " * * * it is for the trier of fact to decide, in light of all the circumstances of the case, whether there exists a reasonable explanation or excuse for the actor's mental condition * * * " Model Penal Code and Commentaries, *supra,* at 61.

"In the end, the question is whether the actor's loss of self-control can be understood in terms that arouse sympathy in the ordinary citizen. Section 210.3 faces this issue squarely and leaves the ultimate judgment to the ordinary citizen in the function of a juror assigned to resolve the specific case * * * " Model Penal Code and Commentaries, *supra,* at 63.

This is not a sympathetic case. The plight of a narcotics dealer cut off from his source of supply, and then subjected to insulting and contemptuous words and actions by his former supplier, is not likely to evoke widespread feelings of acute compassion. Nevertheless, it is clear that the controlling statutory sections were carefully designed to permit the essential judgment on the kind of issue presented here to be made by jurors on the basis of all the circumstances, and not by the trial judge as a matter of law.

PEOPLE v. WALKER

Court of Appeals of New York, 1984.
64 N.Y.2d 741, 485 N.Y.S.2d 978, 475 N.E.2d 445.

MEMORANDUM.

The order of the Appellate Division should be affirmed.

The evidence showed that the defendant, in the culmination of a long-standing disagreement, shot and killed the victim in a bar after an argument over money, which the victim claimed was owed him, and after the victim placed his hand on the defendant's plate of food. Under these circumstances the trial court was not obligated to charge the affirmative defense to murder in the second degree that the defendant "acted under the influence of extreme emotional disturbance" (Penal Law, § 125.25, subd. 1, par. [a]).

In order for a defendant to be entitled to a charge on "extreme emotional disturbance" there must be evidence sufficient for a jury to find, by a preponderance of the evidence, that the elements of this affirmative defense were established. Here there was no evidence which suggested the presence of "extreme emotional disturbance" (cf. ALI Model Penal Code, § 210.3, Comment, p. 61) and thus charging the affirmative defense would have invited the jury to impermissibly speculate as to the defendant's state of mind at the time of the shooting. At most, the evidence at trial showed that the defendant acted out of anger or embarrassment, or both. While these emotions might sometimes serve as the "reasonable explanation" for the presence of "extreme emotional disturbance" they are not equivalent to the loss of self-control generally associated with that defense, and are not necessarily indicative of the "mental infirmity", not rising to the level of insanity * * *; (see *People v. Casassa,* 49 N.Y.2d 668, 677–678, 427 N.Y.S.2d 769, 404 N.E.2d 1310).

Order affirmed in a memorandum.

Notes and Questions

1. The traditionally rigid rule that "mere words" cannot give rise to provocation has, to some extent, been modified by some courts. In Washington v. State, 249 Ga. 728, 292 S.E.2d 836 (1982), for example, Washington's son had been severely cut in the neck by the deceased several days before the killing at issue. When Washington confronted the deceased, the deceased began cursing and telling Washington what he would do if charges brought by Washington's son were not dropped. Washington killed the deceased. Finding that a failure to charge on voluntary manslaughter was error, the court rejected the argument that the only provocation was the injury to the son which had been followed by a sufficient "cooling period." Relying upon the deceased's oral communication to Washington immediately before the killing, the court reasoned:

> While words and threats alone are generally not sufficient provocation, the issue of whether a reasonable person acts as the result of an irresistible passion may be raised by words which are connected to provocative conduct by the victim.

249 Ga. at 731, 292 S.E.2d at 839.

Another limitation was applied in Sells v. State, 98 N.M. 786, 653 P.2d 162 (1982). Sell's wife revealed to him the existence of a boyfriend and her sexual relationship with that boyfriend, including a trip taken to be with him and him as the cause for the extremely large long distance telephone bill. Sells killed her. At his murder trial, no instructions on voluntary manslaughter were given. The New Mexico Court of Appeals affirmed in reliance on the "mere words" rule. Overruling any cases to the contrary, New Mexico Supreme Court reversed:

The fact that words were used in this case is not dispositive. It is well recognized that informational words, as distinguished from mere insulting words, may constitute adequate provocation. 2 C. Wharton's Criminal Law Section 156 (14 ed. 1979). Accordingly, "a sudden disclosure of an event (the event being recognized in the law as adequate) may be the equivalent of the events presently occurring." Id. at 249.

98 N.M. at 788, 653 P.2d at 164.

2. In *Sells,* the court assumed that adultery of a spouse could be an adequate provocation. Should the result be the same if no marital relationship exists? Most courts assume that adequate provocation arises only if the defendant and the "unfaithful" person were married. If the disclosure in *Sells* had occurred before the Sells were married, then, Sells could not have reasonably been provoked into killing by the relationship of his fiancee and another man. See Tripp v. State, 36 Md.App. 459, 374 A.2d 384 (1977). Is this appropriate? Why, or why not?

3. Traditionally, a killing is not reduced to voluntary manslaughter if an objectively-sufficient "cooling period" occurred between the provocation and the killing. In State v. Lassiter, 197 N.J.Super. 2, 484 A.2d 13 (1984), for example, the deceased, Josephine Branch, had worked for Lassiter as a prostitute. In an effort to terminate the relationship, she ran off. He found her at 4:00 A.M. sharing a bed with a male companion in the man's apartment. Lassiter beat her with a shovel and left her. Later, he picked her up at the hospital where she had been treated and took her to the apartment of another former "employee." About 6:00 A.M., Lassiter returned to the apartment and killed Branch. Finding no error in failing to instruct the jury on voluntary manslaughter despite Lassiter's having found Branch with another man, the court held:

> Branch was discovered with the other man at 4:00 on the morning of July 17. The homicide occurred more than twenty-four hours later. The "heat of passion" defense presupposes that the defendant acted upon a great provocation "before a time sufficient to permit reason to resume its sway had passed." State v. King, 37 N.J. 285, 300, 181 A.2d 158 (1962).

197 N.J.Super. at 13–14, 484 A.2d at 19. In Flores v. State, 654 S.W.2d 14 (Tex.App.—Corpus Christi 1983), PDR dismissed as improvidently granted, 676 S.W.2d 364 (1984), Flores and the deceased engaged in argument and fight in bar. Flores left bar, obtained a gun from his truck, and waited about 15 minutes until deceased appeared at door of bar; he then shot and killed deceased. The jury was instructed on voluntary manslaughter but found Flores guilty of murder. On appeal, this was upheld, on ground that jury could have concluded in light of 15 minute break that defendant's anger had cooled and that he did not act under the immediate influence of sudden passion.

In Commonwealth v. Voytko, 349 Pa.Super. 320, 503 A.2d 20 (1986), the facts were as follows:

> [A]pproximately seven weeks prior to the shooting, Voytko had found his wife, Michelle, in bed with Robert Cole at the latter's home. Six

weeks later, about a week before the shooting, Voytko and Cole became involved in a fight. About the same time, Voytko and his wife had an argument, and she left the marital home to return to the home of her parents. On May 23, 1983, at or about 5:00 a.m., Cole returned Michelle to her parents' home following a date. As Cole was parking his truck, Voytko pulled in behind him, stopped and walked over to the truck. He screamed that his wife should get out of the truck. When Cole opened the door on the driver's side of the truck, Voytko shot Cole in the head with a shotgun. * * * Cole died later the same day.

503 A.2d at 21. Other evidence showed that four days before the shooting, police had been summoned to the parents' home and found Voytko in a wooded area behind the home. When asked what he was doing, Voytko explained that he was checking up on his wife because of marital problems. Id., at 22. The jury was instructed on voluntary manslaughter. What factors could be considered, however, in determining whether adequate provocation existed? Given the seven week gap between the discovery of the victim in bed with his wife and the killing, could that be considered? Should the fight be regarded as relevant? Perhaps any "cooling" that should have occurred between the discovery of the couple in bed or the fight and the events on the morning of May 23, 1983 was offset or negated by the events immediately preceding the killing. The trial judge refused a defense request to instruct the jury that in determining what constitutes adequate provocation, "reliance may be placed upon the cumulative impact of a series of related events." This was held error, under Commonwealth v. McCusker, 448 Pa. 382, 292 A.2d 286 (1972). In *McCusker,* the Pennsylvania Supreme Court had reaffirmed "the well-settled principle that 'preceeding events' may have a 'final culmination'" which in combination may constitute adequate provocation. 448 Pa. at 389 n. 8, 292 A.2d at 290 n. 8.

3. In determining whether provocation would have the requisite effect upon a reasonable person, to what extent should the reasonable person be assumed to have characteristics of the defendant? English courts traditionally refused to attribute any of the defendant's characteristics to the reasonable person. See the review of the cases in The Queen v. McGregor, [1962] N.Z.L.R. 1069. In Bedder's Case [1954] 1 W.L.R. 1119, [1954] 2 All E.R. 801, the defendant, who was apparently impotent, killed a prostitute who jeered and hit him when he tried unsuccessfully to have intercourse with her. The House of Lords rejected the defendant's argument that the provocation should be evaluated according to its likely impact upon a reasonable impotent man. The decision was based in part upon what the lords saw as the impossibility of giving the reasonable person some but not all of the defendant's characteristics; to attribute all of the defendant's characteristics to the reasonable person would, the lords felt, destroy the objective nature of the standard. Compare the New Zealand Crimes Act 1961, § 169(2)(a), which directs the evaluation of offered provocation according to its impact upon "a person having the power of self-control of an ordinary person, but otherwise having the characteristics of the offender." See generally, Milligan, Provocation and the Subjective Test, 1967 N.Z.L.J. 19.

In 1978, however, the House of Lords reversed its position. D.D.P. v. Camplin, [1978] 2 All E.R. 168 involved a 15–year-old youth who had killed an older man after the man had sexually molested the youth and then mocked him. The trial judge instructed the jury that they should consider the adequacy of the victim's provocation according to the impact that it would have upon a reasonable adult. Relying heavily upon the Homicide Act of 1957 (which prohibited trial judges from determining that provocation was inadequate "as a matter of law"), the House determined that the jury should not have been directed to ignore the fact that the defendant was only 15 in determining whether the provocation was adequate. A contrary position, it was reasoned, would amount to almost the same as holding such provocation inadequate as a matter of law, a procedure clearly disallowed by the Act. Generalizing, Lord Diplock concluded:

> [A] proper direction to a jury * * * would * * * explain to them that the reasonable man referred to in the question is a person having the power of self-control to be expected of an ordinary person of the sex and age of the accused, but in other respects sharing such of the accused's characteristics as they think would affect the gravity of the provocation to him, and that the question is not merely whether such a person would in like circumstances be provoked to lose his self-control but also would react to the provocation as the accused did.

Id. at 175. The case is discussed in Wells, The Death Penalty for Provocation?, 1978 Crim.L.R. 662 (1978).

What would be the result in such cases under § 210.3 of the Model Penal Code? (See page 382, supra.) The comment to that section explained it as follows:

> Though it is difficult to state a middle ground between a standard which ignores all individual peculiarities and one which makes emotional distress decisive regardless of the nature of its cause, we think that such a statement is essential. For surely if the actor had just suffered a traumatic injury, if he were blind or were distraught with grief, if he were experiencing an unanticipated reaction to a therapeutic drug, it would be deemed atrocious to appraise his crime for purposes of sentence without reference to any of these matters. They are material because they bear upon the inference as to the actor's character that it is fair to draw upon the basis of his act. * * *
>
> We submit that the formulation in the [section] affords sufficient flexibility to differentiate between those special factors in the actor's situation which should be ignored. * * * The question in the end will be whether the actor's loss of self-control can be understood in terms that arouse sympathy enough to call for mitigation.

Model Penal Code § 210.3, comment (Tent.Draft No. 9, 1959). Does § 210.3 do what the authors of the comment say it does?

In determining the reasonableness of provocation or the sufficiency of an "extreme mental or emotional disturbance," should the matter be viewed from the perspective of an intoxicated person, if there was evidence that the defendant was intoxicated? If the defendant had an emotional or personality disorder that increased his sensitivity to various matters, should the matter be viewed from the perspective of a reasonable person with such a disorder? What if there is evidence that the defendant was merely unusually sensitive? In State v. Ott, 297 Or. 375, 686 P.2d 1001 (1984), the court reviewed the legislative history of Oregon's "extreme emotional disturbance" manslaughter provision. The legislature, it concluded, intended that the adequacy of a disturbance be considered from the view of a person with the defendant's "personal" characteristics but not the "personality traits" of the defendant. To otherwise construe the language, it commented, "would permit the acquittal of a bad-tempered person of murder and conviction of an even-tempered person of murder in 'precisely the same situation and circumstances.'" This, it found, would be unacceptable. 297 Or. at 396, 686 P.2d at 1014.

But in State v. Dumlao, ___ Hawaii ___, 715 P.2d 822 (App.1986), Dumlao shot the victim, Pacita (Dumlao's mother-in-law), during an altercation arising out of Dumlao's suspicions that his wife was having sexual relations with her brothers. Trial evidence included expert testimony by a psychiatrist that Dumlao suffered from a "paranoid personality disorder." Among the symptoms of this disorder were hypersensitivity and extreme suspiciousness of his wife's fidelity. On the night of the shooting, according to defense testimony, Dumlao perceived that his brother-in-law "looked at him" in a way indicating that the brother-in-law was having sexual relations with Dumlao's wife and that his wife's family was "talking about him." Although an ordinary individual might not have perceived a threat in this situation, according to the psychiatrist, Dumlao did and felt the need to "counterattack." The trial judge refused to instruct the jury that it could find Dumlao guilty only of manslaughter on the basis of "extreme mental or emotional disturbance for which there is a reasonable excuse." Under the Hawaii statute defining manslaughter, "The reasonableness of the explanation shall be determined from the view-point of a person in the defendant's situation under the circumstances as he believed them to be." Hawaii Rev.Stat. § 707–702(2). The statutory definition of this type of manslaughter is, of course, almost identical to Section 210.3(b) of the Model Penal Code. After reviewing the evidence, the appellate court concluded that the Model Penal Code provision on which the Hawaii statute was based is flexible enough to "grow in the direction of taking account of mental abnormalities that have been recognized in the developing law of diminished responsibility." 715 P.2d at 830. Unlike the prior law setting out an objective standard, the Model Penal Code formulation "merges the two concepts of heat of passion and diminished capacity." Id., at 829. Considering, among other things, the defense testimony concerning Dumlao's perception of his wife's relationship with male members of her family and Dumlao's paranoid personality disorder, concluded the court, there was evidence of extreme emotional disturbance and a reasonable explanation. While a jury might reject the defense position, the court commented, under the expanded definition of manslaughter Dumlao was entitled to have the jury consider the issue. Id., at 832.

4. The cases frequently speak of "mutual combat" as adequate provocation to reduce a killing from murder to manslaughter. Mutual combat arises where the victim and the defendant intend to fight and are ready to do so, and the defendant acts in the "heat of blood" engendered by the

situation. It is not necessary that blows have actually been struck
mutual combat to exist, but if any blows have been struck it is not mate
which participant struck the first blow or that the deceased may h
struck no blows at all. See Whitehead v. State, 9 Md.App. 7, 262 A.2d
(1970). But see also United States v. Hardin, 443 F.2d 735, 738 n. 6 (D.C.
Cir.1970): "[M]utual combat alone is not a true alternative ground for
mitigating a murder to manslaughter; it is merely one of the circumstances from which the jury could find adequate provocation." If this is
accurate, under what circumstances should mutual combat constitute adequate provocation? The court in Whitehead v. State, supra, noted that in
that case "the [trial] court did not find that an unfair advantage was taken
by appellant at the outset of the combat or that at the commencement of
the contest they did not start on equal terms." Is this relevant? controlling?

5. For a general discussion, see Dressler, Rethinking Heat of Passion:
A Defense in Search of a Rationale, 73 Nw.U.L.Rev. 421 (1982).

E. RECKLESS AND NEGLIGENT KILLINGS: INVOLUNTARY MANSLAUGHTER AND NEGLIGENT HOMICIDE

As the principal case in this Section indicates, killings with "criminal" negligence have traditionally been regarded as involuntary manslaughter. When a defendant's negligence is sufficient to give rise to
criminal liability has presented the major difficulty in applying this
body of law. Judicial descriptions of the sort of negligence necessary
for criminal liability are often colorful but almost equally often of little
guidance. A Florida court, for example, has stated:

> Culpable negligence * * * means action of such a gross and flagrant
> character that it evidences a reckless disregard for human life or safety
> equivalant to an intentional violation of the rights of others.

Dominique v. State, 435 So.2d 974, 974 (Fla.App.1983).

The negligence necessary for such liability must, of course, be
distinguished from the state of mind sufficient to make a killing a
"depraved mind" murder, as was discussed in Section B of this Chapter.

GOODEN v. COMMONWEALTH

Supreme Court of Virginia, 1984.
226 Va. 565, 311 S.E.2d 780.

Before CARRICO, C.J., and COCHRAN, POFF, COMPTON, STEPHENSON,
RUSSELL and THOMAS, JJ.

COMPTON, JUSTICE.

Howard Richard Gooden was found guilty in a bench trial of
involuntary manslaughter. He was sentenced to six months in jail and
ordered to pay a fine of $1,000.00. Execution of the sentence was
suspended upon condition defendant pay the fine and not hunt with a
firearm or have a firearm in his possession under any circumstances for

five years. The issue on appeal is whether the evidence is sufficient to support the August 1982 judgment of conviction.

The facts basically are undisputed, although they are susceptible to conflicting inferences. Applying settled principles, we will state the evidence in the light most favorable to the Commonwealth, the party prevailing below.

On November 16, 1981, the first day of hunting season, the victim, James Everette Wyant, and his 13–year-old brother-in-law, Robert Eugene Sipe, were hunting deer in Rockingham County. Near 5:00 p.m., they were standing together "on top of a knoll" in the "clear" upon a north-south power line easement, which runs generally parallel to and one-half mile east of Route 340. There was no precipitation, but "it was getting close to dark."

Sipe and the victim were facing west, Sipe being two or three feet to Wyant's right side. Sipe was wearing an orange hat and coat. Wyant wore a red hat and red bandannas pinned to the front and back of his jacket.

Suddenly, as Wyant looked "over into the thickets," thinking he heard a deer, he was shot and fell to the ground. According to Sipe, Wyant "hollered, 'Don't shoot no more,'" as he went to his knees and "just laid down." Sipe testified he heard "about five" shots, two or three before Wyant yelled and two after the shout. One of the last shots "went past" Sipe's ear. Sipe answered "no" to a question by the trial court whether he saw "any deer anywhere close to" him in the minute or so before the firing or while he was hearing the shots.

When the firing began, Sipe dropped to the ground, where he remained for "a couple minutes" to determine "if they'd quit shooting." Sipe stood up and immediately sought help, shouting, "Somebody shot my buddy." He ran in the direction of Larry Shiflett, who was about 175 yards south of where the victim fell and to the east of the right-of-way.

Shiflett had been hunting in the area during that afternoon with two brothers. He had observed "too many" hunters along the easement and told his brothers to "get off the power line here a little bit," fearing "somebody might get shot." After Shiflett moved away from the easement and had been "sitting there maybe a half an hour," he heard Sipe shouting. Shiflett and Sipe ran back to Wyant. Shiflett determined "there was no pulse" and that Wyant was dead.

Wyant died from a single bullet wound. The fatal shot entered the right upper chest, travelling from right to left backward without significant upward or downward deviation. The shell exited at the posterior aspect of the left upper arm, lodging between the undershirt and the skin.

After Shiflett determined Wyant was dead, he and Sipe observed two unidentified individuals "take off and start running" from a position in a "hollow" along the power-line easement. This position was approximately 390 yards north of and downhill from the point where Wyant fell. Shiflett observed the individuals move first in a northerly direction. Next, they turned and moved south toward where Shiflett and Sipe were standing. Fearing "trouble," Shiflett and Sipe left the area in the opposite direction and reported the incident to police.

The Sheriff of Rockingham County arrived at the scene near 6:00 p.m. and found Wyant's body where he had fallen on the knoll, "right on the edge of a trail" that the Sheriff considered to be the power company's right-of-way.

Two days after the incident, Detective Daniel Comer of the Rockingham County Sheriff's Department interviewed the defendant twice in Chesterfield County. Defendant, a resident of Chesterfield County but a native of Rockingham County, had been hunting on the day in question in the area where Wyant was shot. Comer "believed that either [defendant] or someone in his hunting party may have known something about the death of the victim."

During the first interview, conducted in the morning at the Chesterfield Police Department in the presence of defendant's attorney, defendant indicated he had been hunting during the afternoon in question along the right-of-way with his brother-in-law. Evidence presented by defendant at the trial showed defendant was downhill and north of the victim's position, at a distance of approximately 636 yards. According to the officer, defendant stated "he had seen a deer cross the Vepco right-of-way, the cleared right-of-way, about a hundred yards south of where he was standing sometime before 5:00 P.M., and that he had shot at the deer with a rifle." Defendant told Comer the rifle was a .30–caliber carbine.

During the second interview, conducted in the afternoon in the office of Gooden's attorney, defendant revealed that when he "fired at the deer that he saw crossing the right-of-way, that he had actually been carrying and had fired two different rifles." Defendant stated "he was about fifty yards west of the—or generally west of the right-of-way in the brushy area when he fired at the deer." He told Comer he was carrying a lever-action rifle and fired at the deer once with that weapon. Defendant said "he dropped that * * * rifle, and shot at the deer additionally three or four times with the thirty caliber carbine." Defendant stated "he felt that he had not hit the deer and that he did not know that he had hit anything."

During the second interview, defendant surrendered the lever-action weapon, a Marlin .30–.30 Winchester rifle. Defendant had delivered the other rifle to a Chesterfield detective on the day after the shooting. Comer also obtained possession of that weapon, a U.S. Military, auto-loading, .30–caliber, M1 carbine. Defendant explained to Comer that he initially did not volunteer information about two weapons because he was afraid he had violated the hunting laws by use of more than one rifle.

According to subsequent laboratory analysis, the bullet that killed Wyant was fired from the .30–.30 Winchester.

Within a week of the homicide, four shell casings were found "very close together" and "a couple of feet" from the right-of-way. They were located approximately 430 yards north of the point where Wyant was shot. Laboratory analysis revealed that the shells had been fired in defendant's M1 carbine.

At trial, defendant presented the testimony of Gary A. Judd, a Harrisonburg surveyor. Defendant had accompanied the surveyor to the scene and pointed out where he had been standing as he shot at the deer. Judd had been advised of the place where the victim's body was found.

From a plat drawn by Judd, as well as from aerial and ground-level police photographs of the entire scene, the following facts appear. The pertinent area of the right-of-way follows a straight line and is approximately 60 feet wide. Photos taken six days after the incident show the easement to be relatively clear of high brush on both sides of utility poles that stand in the center of the right-of-way.

The plat contains a profile of the land. The terrain southwardly, from the point where defendant told Judd he was standing when he shot, slopes gradually downhill for about 140 yards to a stream. The land becomes level for about 220 more yards and then rises 20 feet vertically on the south side of a gully, continuing gradually uphill for approximately 276 yards to the point where Wyant was shot. According to the survey, the difference in elevation between the points where defendant and Wyant were standing was 41.9 feet. The plat shows that defendant told the surveyor he shot at the deer from a point on the western edge of the right-of-way as the deer was on the eastern edge, approximately 70 yards south of defendant.

At the May 1982 trial, defendant, age 40, testified he had hunted regularly for 25 to 30 years. He stated that on the day in question at about 4:00 p.m., he went to the right-of-way with a hunting companion because it was "pretty much" a popular place to hunt. The pair had entered the area by truck from Route 340 along a dirt road. Defendant observed approximately 10 or 15 vehicles, apparently belonging to hunters, as he moved to the right-of-way. The companion went in a northerly direction and defendant proceeded to the point illustrated on the plat.

Defendant testified he "had no more and got there * * * on the edge of the power line" when he saw a deer "coming out" onto the right-of-way approximately 75 yards to the south. He stated that he shot once with the .30–.30 lever-action Winchester diagonally across the easement. The deer "took off," moving east to west. He said that he laid the gun down, took the M1 carbine, and shot approximately three or four times "at the deer when he run through here." Testifying all the shooting took place in 15 or 20 seconds, defendant said he walked a short distance looking for the deer. Defendant stated that because the hour was late, he then proceeded to his truck, still looking along the way for the deer. When he arrived at the truck, parked about 200 yards from the power line, defendant met his companion and they left the area. Defendant testified he was "on" the right-of-way about "ten or fifteen minutes."

On cross-examination, when asked to explain his statement to Detective Comer that he was 50 yards west of the easement when he fired, defendant answered he was "guessing" at that earlier time. He testified that "since then I went back to the area and I found it was more like fifty feet rather than fifty yards." When reminded that he just had testified he was on the "edge of the power line" when he began shooting, defendant denied saying "edge" and stated that he was "back into the brush just a little." He said he actually was "counting" from the power line and that he was positioned 50 feet from the line of the power poles. Finally, on re-direct examination, defendant testified there was "no way" he could know "for sure" his exact location when he shot.

The trial court decided the defendant's version of the tragedy was "incredible" and found the Commonwealth had established beyond a reasonable doubt that Gooden was guilty of criminal negligence. Concluding the defendant shot "blindly" and failed to exercise slight care to ascertain that he could fire his weapons safely, the court found that the defendant demonstrated a callous disregard for the life of other persons who were in the woods on the day in question.

Involuntary manslaughter is defined as the accidental killing of a person, contrary to the intention of the parties, during the prosecution of an unlawful, but not felonious, act, or during the improper performance of some lawful act. The "improper" performance of the lawful act, to constitute involuntary manslaughter, must amount to an unlawful commission of such lawful act, not merely a negligent performance. The negligence must be criminal negligence. The accidental killing must be the proximate result of a lawful act performed in a manner "so gross, wanton, and culpable as to show a reckless disregard of human life." *King v. Commonwealth*, 217 Va. 601, 607, 231 S.E.2d 312, 316 (1977).

Stated differently, reckless conduct must amount to unlawful conduct in order to sustain a charge of involuntary manslaughter. And it is immaterial whether the unlawful act was unlawful in its inception, that is, an inherently unlawful act, such as discharging a deadly weapon into a crowded street, or became unlawful after it was begun, such as lawfully operating a vehicle in a public street but so accelerating its speed that it may cause death or serious bodily harm to persons in that street. The present case is of the second category; conduct not inherently unlawful, but done without requisite caution, in an unlawful manner.

Defendant contends the trial court found him guilty by imposing erroneously a standard of strict liability. Conceding the court properly could disregard his testimony of firing at a deer 75 yards away, defendant argues there was, nonetheless, no evidence of actions by him that would support a finding of criminal negligence, unless the court relied improperly on a theory of strict liability. We disagree.

On appeal of a conviction, we must not only view the evidence in the light most favorable to the Commonwealth, but we must accord to the evidence all reasonable inferences fairly deducible therefrom. In addition, the judgment of a trial court sitting without a jury is entitled to the same weight as a jury verdict; it will not be disturbed on appeal unless plainly wrong or without evidence to support it. We hold the evidence, with all reasonable inferences properly drawn from the evidence, supports the conclusion of the trial court.

As the trial judge aptly stated, defendant's account of the incident is "incredible;" the event could not have occurred in the manner described by the accused. The evidence is undisputed that the victim was killed by a bullet from defendant's gun. That fact, of course, places defendant at the scene of the crime at the time in question. Yet the defendant, in effect, alleges that he shot at a deer, claimed to be 75 yards away, and that he mistakenly struck the victim, who was at a point 636 yards to the south. But the defendant's evidence shows that he was shooting downgrade, at an angle undisclosed by the evidence. Manifestly, a bullet from a weapon aimed downhill would not have hit an object that was elevated, according to the evidence, 41.9 feet above the horizontal at an angle of 27 degrees.

Discarding defendant's testimony about the manner in which he shot, we must examine the evidence remaining, cognizant of the uncontradicted fact that defendant fired the fatal bullet. The record shows that defendant, a hunter of considerable experience, entered the area in question on a day when he knew there were a number of other persons in the immediate vicinity; there were "too many" hunters along the right-of-way. The visibility was reduced due to the time of day. The victim was wearing bright-colored garments and was next to a companion similarly dressed.

Whether defendant was standing 636 yards from the victim, as he contends, or whether he was about 390 yards from Wyant, where Shiflett and Sipe observed the two unidentified persons, is unimportant. Parenthetically, the evidence indicates that if defendant was positioned where the four shell cases were found, a horizontal shot south from that point probably would have hit the steep bank of the gulley. Important, however, is that defendant, from a point on or immediately adjacent to the unobstructed easement, fired a weapon capable of inflicting serious bodily harm or death directly at two persons who were likewise standing in the right-of-way. This is not a case of a hunter who made an identification of game, fired, and because of poor aim struck a human being. Given defendant's incredible testimony, such a theory is eliminated by Sipe's testimony that he saw no deer "anywhere close to" the victim either immediately before the shots were fired or during the shooting. Nor is this a case of mistaken identity in which a hunter, exercising due caution, shot at a human, thinking the human was an animal.

In this case, the defendant either failed to look, or if he looked, he failed to do so with requisite caution within the distance he should have known was the range of the weapon he was discharging. Together, the failure to identify adequately and the subsequent shooting constitute the reckless and unlawful conduct. The act of hunting was not inherently unlawful; rather the shooting was an improper performance of a lawful act. Reasonably inferred from all the circumstances is that defendant fired blindly and wildly from a position on the easement, perhaps at movement or a flash of color on the knoll, in utter disregard of the safety of others.

Accordingly, we cannot say that the trial court's finding of conduct so gross, wanton, and culpable as to show a reckless disregard of human life was plainly wrong or without evidence to support it. Thus, the judgment of conviction will be

Affirmed.

Cochran, Justice, dissenting.

* * *

I do not agree that Sipe's testimony that he saw no deer nearby before or after the shooting eliminates the theory that Gooden may have fired inaccurately at a deer and struck Wyant. Nor do I think the Commonwealth's evidence shows that Gooden did not in the exercise of due caution shoot a human mistaking him for a deer.

The majority find that Gooden "fired a weapon capable of inflicting serious bodily harm or death *directly at two persons* * * *." (Emphasis added.) There is no direct evidence supporting this conclusion, and the finding cannot be justified by any reasonable or fair inference to which the Commonwealth is entitled.

No one can deny that this was a tragic accident. But Gooden was engaged in the lawful pursuit of a form of recreation sponsored by the Commonwealth. He was not required to insure the safety of all other hunters within the range of his weapons. The devotees of this sport are aware of a certain inherent risk of danger where high-powered weapons may lawfully be used. To convict Gooden of manslaughter, under the most favorable view of the evidence, is in effect to impose a rule of strict liability. We have not approved such a rule in civil litigation and we are not justified in applying it in a criminal prosecution. Although the evidence is sufficient to establish ordinary negligence, I do not agree that it is sufficient to establish criminal negligence. Therefore, I would reverse the judgment of the trial court.

Carrico, C.J., and Stephenson, J., join in this dissent.

Notes and Questions

1. Is it clear from the court's discussion in *Gooden* whether the defendant must have in fact been actually aware of the risk of death? Where the matter is not specifically addressed by statute, courts have often left the matter unresolved. See W. LaFave and A. Scott, Criminal Law 586 (1972). Would it make any difference?

2. What led the majority in *Gooden* to conclude that the facts showed "criminal negligence?" Sipes testified that he saw no deer close to the scene of the shooting. But does this conclusively demonstrate that there was no deer at which Gooden might have been aiming? Was there adequate reason to conclude, based on Shifless's testimony, that Gooden fled from the scene of the shooting? During his first interview with Detective Comer, Gooden did not reveal the existence of the .30–.30 Winchester that killed the victim. At trial, Gooden testified to a version of the events that the trial judge found "incredible." Might these considerations have entered into the court's conclusion that the record supported Gooden's guilt? If so, should they have done so?

3. Is it, or should it be, relevant to the analysis that Gooden was engaged—as the dissenters emphasize—in a type of recreation "sponsored" by the state? That the victim was engaged in the same recreational activity? That the victim might well have been aware of the risks involved in this activity and nevertheless chose to participate in the activity? If any of these considerations are or should be relevant, how should they be considered? Perhaps they bear upon the degree of risk that should be required before disregard of that risk (or the failure to perceive the risk) creates criminal liability.

4. Under the Virginia statutory scheme, the only question posed was whether Gooden was guilty of manslaughter. Suppose, however, the Virginia statute followed the pattern of the Model Penal Code (see page 382, supra), under which criminally negligent homicide is a lesser included offense of reckless manslaughter. How should Gooden's potential liability under such a scheme be analyzed? Should he have been convicted of manslaughter, criminally negligent homicide, or of no criminal offense at all?

5. In Edgmon v. State, 702 P.2d 643 (Alaska App.1985), Edgmon had been convicted of manslaughter based upon proof that he had caused the deaths of two persons in the course of driving while intoxicated. Alaska law recognized the offenses of reckless manslaughter and criminally negligent homicide. Further, Alaska applied the quite common rule that voluntary intoxication cannot be used to show the absence of recklessness. Consequently, Edgmon urged on appeal, no meaningful difference exists between the two offenses. The intoxication rule destroys whatever distinction might otherwise exist, that is, the difference between a risk actually perceived and a failure to perceive that risk that should have been recognized. Therefore, equal protection was violated by his conviction of the more serious crime. The court, however, responded that the voluntary intoxication rule "does not totally destroy the distinction between criminal negligence and recklessness." It explained:

The state is still obligated [in a prosecution for reckless manslaughter] to prove that Edgmon, given his facilities, his education, his expertise, and his intelligence, would have perceived the risk but for his intoxication. In contrast, peculiarities of a given individual—his or her intelligence, experience, and physical capabilities—are irrelevant in determining criminal negligence since the standard is one of a reasonably prudent person.

702 P.2d at 645.

6. Homicide convictions based upon proof of criminal negligence were affirmed on appeal in the following cases:

Evidence showed that Narrarro, who was "knowledgable about firearms," placed a loaded clip into the magazine of a .45 caliber automatic pistol, pulled back the side and released it, and then pulled the trigger of the gun to "test fire" it. His girlfriend, with whom he had recently argued, had just walked into the room and was struck and killed by the shot. Narrarro's conviction for manslaughter was affirmed on the ground that these facts showed the necessary "culpable negligence." Nararro v. State, 433 So.2d 1011 Fla.App.1983), review denied, 447 So. 2d 887 (1984).

Dealy failed to seek medical help for his two-week old child during a two day period, despite the child's loss of heartbeat and need for mouth-to-mouth resuscitation ten or fifteen times during that period. This caused the child's death. These facts were held on appeal sufficient to show gross negligence necessary for involuntary manslaughter. People v. Sealy, 136 Mich.App. 168, 356 N.W.2d 614 (1984).

Corker threw a brick at a woman with whom he had argued; the woman was holding a baby. The brick hit and killed the baby. This was held on appeal sufficient to support Corker's conviction for negligence homicide. Corker v. State, 691 S.W.2d 744 (Tex.App.—Dallas 1985).

7. In People v. Erby, 97 A.D.2d 380, 467 N.Y.S.2d 588 (1983), Erby had confronted the victim, Rush, in a park concerning an apparently imagined insult rendered by Rush's girlfriend. When Rush disclaimed any knowledge of the matter, Erby punched him in the face. Rush fell to the ground and hit his head on concrete. He was able to "stagger" home but the next morning he was found dead in his apartment. Death resulted from the injury caused by the fall to the concrete. Reversing a conviction for criminally negligent homicide, the appellate court noted that Erby's actions were quite likely assault. Criminal negligence, however, was not shown with regard to the death of Rush:

That there was a risk is obvious from the fact that a death in fact occurred, but it was not "of such a nature and degree" that a reasonable person would be under a duty to perceive it.

97 A.D.2d at 380, 467 N.Y.S.2d at 589.

F. DEATHS CAUSED IN THE PERPETRATION OF CRIMES: FELONY MURDER AND MISDEMEANOR MANSLAUGHTER

Editors' Introduction: The Felony Murder Rule

As Sir James Stephen's discussion of malice aforethought, see page 386, supra, made clear, there was authority for the proposition that any death caused by conduct engaged in with the intent to commit a felony was, for that reason alone, murder. This is the felony murder rule. A somewhat corresponding rule provided that causing death in the perpetration of an unlawful act not a felony constituted misdemeanor manslaughter; this is the misdemeanor manslaughter rule. Few criminal law doctrines have given rise to more discussion and debate than these rules, although the harsh consequences of a murder conviction caused most discussion to focus upon the felony murder rule.

The significance of the felony murder rule is increased when it is combined with the doctrine making all members of a conspiracy liable for the crimes committed by other members of the conspiracy, at least where those crimes are committed in furtherance of the conspiracy and are a foreseeable result of it. Combination of the two doctrines means, of course, that in jointly-committed felonies, all of the participants may be liable for the felony murder committed by one of their number. The impact of this is illustrated by People v. Friedman, 205 N.Y. 161, 98 N.E. 471 (1912), in which Friedman stood guard while Kuhn, his cofelon, entered a store to rob it. In a struggle, Kuhn killed the victim and Friedman was charged and convicted of felony murder. On appeal, the court held that the trial judge properly refused the following instruction requested by Friedman:

> If * * * the scope and plan of execution of [the] unlawful enterprise did not involve the use of force or violence which might result in the taking of human life, then the defendant is not responsible for the act of Kuhn in taking human life * * *.

Explaining, the court reasoned that the trial court had properly left to the jury the task of deciding whether the killing was a "natural and probable consequence" of the joint undertaking:

> If the natural and probable consequence of the common enterprise was the killing of Mr. Schuchart in case of resistance on his part, the defendant was liable for murder * * *, although he did not do the actual killing. The request assumes that, if the appellant did not fire the fatal shot, he could escape liability unless the conspiracy expressly contemplated the use of force or violence as might cause death. This is an erroneous view of the law. An express agreement by intending robbers not to kill in carrying out a plan of robbery would not save any of the conspirators from responsibility for a homicide by one of them in committing or attempting to commit the robbery, if such killing was

the natural and probable result of the robbery or attempt to rob in such a contingency as actually occurred in this case.

205 N.Y. at 165–66, 98 N.E. at 473.

A recent judicial discussion considered the origin and traced the general history of the felony murder rule:

> Lord Coke's statement of the felony-murder rule [was as follows]:

> "If the act be unlawful it is murder. As if A. meaning to steale a deere in the park of B., shooteth at the deer, and by the glance of the arrow killeth a boy that is hidden in a bush: this is murder, for that the act was unlawfull, although A. had no intent to hurt the boy, nor knew not of him. But if B. the owner of the park had shot at his own deer, and without any ill intent had killed the boy by the glance of his arrow, this had been homicide by misadventure, and no felony.

> "So if one shoot at any wild fowle upon a tree, and the arrow killeth any reasonable creature afar off, without any evill intent in him, this is *per infortunium* [misadventure]: for it was not unlawful to shoot at the wilde fowle: but if he had shot at a cock or hen, or any tame fowle of another mans, and the arrow by mischance had killed a man, this had been murder, for the act was unlawfull." [22]

> The above excerpt from Coke is * * * most often cited as the origin of the felony-murder doctrine. Unfortunately, Coke's statement has been criticized as completely lacking in authority. * * *

> At early common law, the felony-murder rule went unchallenged because at that time practically all felonies were punishable by death. It was, therefore, "of no particular moment whether the condemned was hanged for the initial felony or for the death accidentally resulting from the felony." [34] Thus * * * no injustice was caused directly by application of the rule at that time.

> * * *

> Case law of Nineteenth-Century England reflects the efforts of the English courts to limit the application of the felony-murder doctrine. * * *, culminating in Regina v. Serne, 16 Cox, Crim.Cas. 311 (1887). In the latter case, involving a death resulting from arson, Judge Stephen instructed the jury as follows:

> "[I]nstead of saying that any act done with intent to commit a felony and which causes death amounts to murder, it should be reasonable to say that any act known to be dangerous to life and likely in itself to cause death, done for the purpose of committing a felony which causes death, should be murder."

> In this century, the felony-murder doctrine was comparatively rarely invoked in England and in 1957 England abolished the felony-murder rule. Section 1 of England's Homicide Act, 1957, 5 & 6 Eliz. 2,

22. Coke, Third Institutes (1797), p. 56.

34. Commonwealth v. Redline, 391 Pa. 486, 494, 137 A.2d 472, 476 (1958). * * *

c. 11, § 1, provides that a killing occurring in a felony-murder situation will not amount to murder unless done with the same malice afore-thought as is required for all other murder.

* * *

While only a few states have followed the lead of Great Britain in abolishing felony murder, various legislative and judicial limitations on the doctrine have effectively narrowed the scope of the rule in the United States. Perkins states that the rule is "somewhat in disfavor at the present time" and that "courts apply it where the law requires, but they do so grudgingly and tend to restrict its application where circumstances permit".

* * *

Some courts, recognizing the questionable wisdom of the rule, have refused to extend it beyond what is required. "[W]e do want to make clear how shaky are the basic premises on which [the felony murder rule] rests. With so weak a foundation, it behooves us not to extend it further and indeed, to restrain it within the bounds it has always known." Commonwealth ex rel. Smith v. Myers, 438 Pa. 218, 227, 261 A.2d 550, 555 (1970).

* * *

Many state legislatures have also been active in restricting the scope of felony murder by imposing additional limitations.

People v. Aaron, 409 Mich. 672, 692–703, 299 N.W.2d 304, 309–14 (1980). The misdemeanor manslaughter rule has been somewhat simi-larly limited and perhaps more frequently abandoned, although this has been done with less fanfare.

To the extent that the felony murder and misdemeanor manslaugh-ter rules create liability for causing death without regard to whether the defendant intended or contemplated that death result, they obvi-ously deviate from the general approach that criminal liability should attach only for contemplated results. What social interests might be served by this deviation? Several rationales or justifications for the felony murder rule have been offered. In State v. Goodseal, 220 Kan. 487, 493, 553 P.2d 279, 286 (1976), the Kansas Supreme Court explained that the rationale of the felony murder rule is "to furnish an added deterrent to the perpetration of felonies * * *." A somewhat differ-ent explanation was offered in People v. Washington, 62 Cal.2d 777, 781, 44 Cal.Rptr. 442, 445, 402 P.2d 130, 133 (1965): "The purpose of the felony-murder rule is to deter felons from killing negligently or acciden-tally by holding them strictly responsible for killings they commit." A recent discussion of felony murder offered the following:

Felony murder reflects a societal judgment that an intentionally com-mitted robbery that causes the death of a human being is qualitatively more serious than an identical robbery that does not * * * [and] that a robbery that causes death is more closely akin to murder than to robbery. If this conclusion accurately reflects social attitudes, and if classification of crimes is to be influenced by such attitudes in order to avoid depreciation of the seriousness of the offense and to encourage respect for the law, then the felony murder doctrine is an appropriate classificatory device.

There is impressive empirical evidence that this classification does indeed reflect widely shared societal attitudes. Recently, the Bureau of Justice Standards of the United States Department of Justice released a national survey of public evaluations of the seriousness of 204 hypothetical legal events, ranging from the heinous to the trivial. [Bureau of Justice Statistics of the United States Department of Justice, Report to the Nation on Crime and Justice: The Data 4–5 (1983).] Respondents assigned widely differing scores to various differences in result, without reference to mens rea. Although the events were not described in terms making them unambiguously felony murders or express-malice murders, many were described so as to make intentional killing impossible. Some such ostensible felony murders were ranked by the respondents as more serious than other, apparently intentional killings; in particular, rape- or robbery-homicides were graded far more severely than express-malice family killings.

Jurors provide another index of the public's attitude towards felony murder. Kalven and Zeisel [The American Jury 443 n. 18 (1966)] were surprised to find that jurors faced with actual felony murder cases agreed with the doctrine. *   *   *

Crump and Crump, In Defense of The Felony Murder Doctrine. 9 Harv.J.L. & Public Policy 359, 363–65 (1985).

Given the increasing number of statutes defining homicide offenses and the variety of approaches taken under these statutes, generalizations concerning the felony murder rule are difficult. Quite commonly, however, statutory schemes—like the California one, see page 379, supra—that divide murder into degrees and defines second degree murder and traditional malice aforethought terms are read as creating a general rule that killings in the course of felonies are second degree murder. Some statutes—like Section 189 of the California Penal Code, see page 380, supra—specifically provide for certain felony murders to be first degree murders.

The recent history of the felony murder rule, on which this section focuses, has been one of increasing restriction. In deciding what limitations to impose on felony murder and how to develop those limitations, what policy considerations should be emphasized? More specifically, what functions should the rule be regarded as serving and how effectively should the rule be regarded as pursuing those functions?

1. BASIC LIMITATIONS ON THE FELONY MURDER RULE

While it is somewhat difficult to identify how "basic" various limitations upon the felony murder rule are, there are several matters that are arguably of major significance. The two cases in this subsection present quite different approaches for imposing quite pervasive limitations upon the doctrine. Is one approach preferable to the other? Perhaps both should be imposed.

STATE v. AARSVOLD

Court of Appeals of Minnesota, 1985.
376 N.W.2d 518.

LESLIE, JUDGE.

The State of Minnesota appeals from a pretrial order of the district court dismissing for lack of probable cause a charge of felony murder in which the predicate felony was sale of cocaine. We affirm.

FACTS

During the late evening of September 2, 1984, and the early morning of September 3, respondent was at a party with several people, including Craig Schweiger. At the request of Schweiger, respondent obtained and sold Schweiger a quantity of cocaine. Schweiger, respondent, and others administered to themselves a portion of the cocaine by injection. There was conflicting testimony during the grand jury proceedings as to whether respondent had assisted Schweiger with an injection. Soon after the injection, Schweiger collapsed and was taken to a nearby hospital where he was pronounced dead.

The amended indictment charges respondent with felonious sale of cocaine, felonious distribution of cocaine by injection, second-degree felony murder with distribution by injection as the predicate felony, and second-degree felony murder with sale of cocaine as the predicate felony.

Respondent moved to dismiss the charge of felony murder predicated on sale of cocaine. The trial court granted the motion.

* * *

[Prior to its revision in 1981, Minn.Stat. § 609.195 provided:

Whoever, without intent to effect the death of any person, causes the death of another by * * * the following means, is guilty of murder in the third degree and may be sentenced to imprisonment for not more than 25 years:

* * *

(2) Commits or attempts to commit a felony upon or affecting the person whose death was caused or another * * *.]

In State v. Nunn, 297 N.W.2d 752 (Minn.1980), Nunn had been convicted under the statute. Trial evidence showed that he and two other young men had broken into an estate carriage house in which the estate groundskeeper lived. When the groundskeeper appeared, the three severely beat him. Although the beating would not have caused the death of a healthy person, it did precititate a fatal heart attack in the victim. On appeal, Nunn urged that the underlying felony on which his conviction was based, burglary of a dwelling accompanied by an assault, was not "a felony upon or affecting the person" within the meaning of the statute. Rejecting this and affirming the conviction, the court explained:

> The Advisory Committee Comment to the statute explains the phrase, "upon or affecting the person whose death was caused" as limiting the application of the felony-murder rule and then states as an example that "death resulting from the commission of a purely property crime would not fall within the clause." * * *

> The purpose of the statutory language in question is to isolate for special treatment those felonies that involve some special danger to human life. * * *

> There are two basic approaches that could be taken in determining what felonies are covered by the phrase "upon or affecting the person whose death was caused." One would be to determine from the elements of each offense in the abstract whether it inherently involved some special danger to human life. The other approach would be to consider not just the elements of the felony in the abstract but the facts of the particular case and the circumstances under which the felony was committed to determine whether the felony-murder rule should be applied. W. LaFave & A. Scott, Handbook on Criminal Law, 547 (1972).

> The latter approach is preferable and is the one that we have implicitly followed in our cases. Thus, in State v. Forsman, 260 N.W. 2d 160, 164, 165 (Minn.1977), we upheld the application of the felony-murder rule when the underlying crime was unlawful distribution of narcotics in which the unlawful distribution consisted of injecting the narcotic into the individual. Similarly, in State v. Hansen, 286 Minn. 4, 174 N.W.2d 697 (1970), we upheld a felony-murder conviction when the underlying felony was arson, which is classified in the criminal code in the section entitled, "Damage or Trespass to Property."

> The underlying felony in this case was a burglary of a dwelling with any accompanying assault upon the resident of the dwelling. As committed, the offense obviously involved a special danger to human life. Indeed, even viewed in the abstract, a burglary of a dwelling—while classified in the criminal code under the heading, "Damage or Trespass to Property"—should not be deemed a purely property offense because * * * such an offense always carries with it the possibility of violence and therefore some special risks to human life.

297 N.W.2d at 753–54.

Minn.Stat. § 609.19 (1984) [now] reads in pertinent part as follows:

Whoever does either of the following is guilty of murder in the second degree and may be sentenced to imprisonment for not more than 40 years:

* * * * * * * * *

(2) Causes the death of a human being, without intent to effect the death of any person, while committing or attempting to commit a felony offense other than criminal sexual conduct in the first or second degree with force or violence.

Although the language of this felony-murder statute appears on its face to apply to all felonies, this does not prohibit the use of common law rules to aid in statutory construction and interpretation. Minn.Stat. § 609.015, subd. 1 (1984); *State v. Cantrell*, 220 Minn. 13, 18, 18 N.W.2d 681, 684 (1945).

Broadly construed, the common law felony-murder rule holds that any death occurring during the commission of a felony is chargeable against the felon as murder. 4 W. Blackstone, *Commentaries on the Laws of England* 201 (1769). The common law felonies included homicide, mayhem, rape, arson, robbery, burglary, larceny, prison breach, and rescue of a felon. The basic premises underlying the rule and its various modifications have long been debated by scholars, judges, and legislators. Adlerstein, *Felony-Murder in the New Criminal Codes*, 4 Am.J.Crim.L. 249 (1975–76). Its critics have protested the absolute liability that results from labeling accidental deaths as murder, and proponents of the rule have argued that its harshness is a deterrent for the use of violence in the commission of crimes. *See id.* at 249–50.

* * *

The Minnesota Supreme Court has held that the purpose of the felony-murder rule is "to isolate for special treatment those felonies that involve some special danger to human life." *In re Welfare of M.D.S.*, 345 N.W.2d 723, 729–30 (Minn.1984) (quoting *State v. Nunn*, 297 N.W.2d 752, 753 (Minn.1980)). Shortly before a 1981 amendment to the statute,[4] the supreme court explained its rationale for limiting the application of the rule as follows:

> [T]he statute treats as third-degree murder certain felonious conduct that would otherwise be treated as manslaughter, the rationale being that certain felonious conduct carries with it an especially increased risk that people may be killed as a result and that when a killing occurs as a result of this conduct it is not unfair to punish the person responsible for murder rather than just manslaughter.

Nunn, 297 N.W.2d at 754. The supreme court has since stated that a "typical felony-murder * * * probably is an unintentional killing that occurs in the course of robbery or some other crime against the person." *State v. Back*, 341 N.W.2d 273, 276 (Minn.1983).

It is an established rule of common law that penal statutes are to be construed strictly, with any reasonable doubt to be interpreted in favor of the defendant. *State v. Corbin*, 343 N.W.2d 874 (Minn.Ct.App. 1984). It is with this principle in mind that we seek to determine whether the sole act of selling cocaine is a felony that involves some special danger to human life.

4. * * * The amended statute imposed the stiffer penalty of second-degree murder in reaction to several incidents of violent robberies of convenience stores, in which innocent customers and store employees were severely injured or killed. Report to the Senate Judiciary Committee, April 23, 1981.

Courts in other jurisdictions have held that the act of selling heroin does not fall within the scope of a felony-murder statute. *See State v. Dixon,* 109 Ariz. 441, 511 P.2d 623 (1973) (sole act of selling heroin to a purchaser who voluntarily and out of the presence of the seller injects the quantity and dies as a result does not constitute second degree murder); *Commonwealth v. Bowden,* 456 Pa. 278, 309 A.2d 714 (1973) (element of malice necessary to support a second-degree murder conviction would not be implied from the defendant's act of injecting the decedent, a fellow drug addict, with heroin because although heroin is a dangerous drug, its reaction does not generally cause death); *Sheriff, Clark County v. Morris,* 99 Nev. 109, 659 P.2d 852 (1983) (felony-murder rule would not apply to a situation involving a sale only or a sale with a nonlethal dosage ingested in the defendant's presence).

We conclude that the sole act of selling cocaine does not fall within the scope of the felony-murder statute, Minn.Stat. § 609.19(2). The legislature did not create the felony of sale of cocaine because of any inherent life-threatening qualities. Rather, it was created by the legislature because cocaine has a high potential for abuse and may lead to psychological dependence. Thus, although cocaine is admittedly a substance with an adverse effect on a person's health, use of cocaine, even when injected, does not generally cause death. *See People v. Pinckney,* 65 Misc.2d 265, 317 N.Y.S.2d 416 (1971) (injection of heroin into the body does not generally in itself cause death). Because the sale of cocaine alone does not justify the assumption that the purchaser is incurring a substantial and unjustified risk of death, we hold that sale alone is not a proper felony upon which to predicate a charge of felony murder. To hold otherwise would give the felony-murder statute a broader scope than this court will impute in the absence of clear legislative intent to effectuate that meaning.[5]

Furthermore, the State has failed to show a direct causal relationship between the sale of cocaine and the subsequent death of the buyer. *See* Minn.Stat. § 609.19(2). The Kansas Supreme Court, in *State v. Mauldin,* 215 Kan. 956, 529 P.2d 124 (1974), addressed this issue in a case in which the defendant's only connection to the victim's death was the act of selling him heroin. The court concluded that because the felony of selling heroin was completed upon consummation of the sale,

5. We recognize that respondent will stand trial under the indictment for felonious distribution of cocaine by injection. In *State v. Forsman,* 260 N.W.2d 160, 162 (Minn.1977), the supreme court held that the distribution of heroin by direct injection into the body of another was a felony "upon or affecting the person whose death was caused" and was punishable under the earlier felony-murder rule. (*See supra* n. 4). The court did not reach the issue of whether direct injection of heroin by the defendant into the deceased at the deceased's request was an inherently dangerous felony because the statutory language applied directly to the act for which defendant was convicted. In a footnote, however, the State admitted that "distribution by other means, absent the tactile quality found present here, would present a different issue." *Id.* at 164, n. 7. This is precisely the issue here, suggesting that this court should hesitate before finding an inherent danger to human life from the sale or gift of a controlled substance that does not encompass the tactile qualities of a direct injection.

the resulting death did not fall within the scope of a felony murder. Similarly, in this case, once the exchange of money was complete, the collateral felony of selling cocaine had terminated. Because the death of Craig Schweiger did not occur "while committing or attempting to commit a felony offense," Minn.Stat. § 609.19(2) does not apply.

* * *

Affirmed.

PARKER, JUDGE (dissenting).

In adopting an absolute rule that sale of a controlled substance cannot be an appropriate felony upon which to predicate a charge of felony murder, the majority opinion ignores the facts offered to be proved in this case, and misreads the language and intent of our felony murder statute. Accordingly, I respectfully dissent.

While no transcript of the proceedings below has been prepared, at oral argument before this court the state declared that it had made an offer of proof to the trial court that this particular sale of cocaine was made with knowledge that the deceased intended to take the drug by injection. Respondent did not disagree with this statement. * * * Despite these facts, the majority insists that this case presents nothing more than "the sole act of selling cocaine" as a predicate felony for felony murder.

As the majority notes, the legislature amended Minn.Stat. § 609.19(2) in 1981. * * *

The majority holds that even though the present felony murder statute unambiguously applies to all felony offenses, there still exists a requirement that, in order to be an appropriate predicate offense, a felony must "involve some special danger to human life." *Nunn*, 297 N.W.2d at 753. It is not at all certain that this requirement exists under the present statute.

The majority determines that no sale of cocaine could ever involve special danger to human life asserting, without any evidence whatsoever, that "use of cocaine, even when injected, does not generally cause death." As authority for its position, the majority cites a case which is inapposite,[3] a case the holding of which is directly contrary to Minnesota law[4] and *Sheriff, Clark County v. Morris,* 99 Nev. 109, 659 P.2d 852 (1983), a case where the actual holding is that felonious sale of chloral hydrate with presence of seller during the consumption by buyer of a lethal dose is a proper predicate for felony murder. The majorities' assertions and its proffered authority are less than persuasive.

Minnesota law already considers some sales of cocaine to be felonies involving "special danger to human life." In *State v. Vernon,* 283

3. In *State v. Dixon,* 109 Ariz. 441, 511 P.2d 623 (1973), the purchaser of the heroin injected the drug *out of the presence of* the seller.

4. *Commonwealth v. Bowden,* 456 Pa. 278, 309 A.2d 714 (1973) conflicts with the

holding of *State v. Forsman,* 260 N.W.2d 160 (Minn.1977) where distribution of heroin by injection was determined to be an appropriate predicate felony.

N.W.2d 516 (Minn.1979), the Minnesota Supreme Court upheld the classification of cocaine as a Schedule II controlled substance. In reaching its conclusion, the supreme court examined evidence relevant to the physiological effect of cocaine and found that cocaine "can be fatal when taken with narcotics, or *injected into the blood,* or ingested orally in large quantities." *Vernon* at 518 (emphasis added).

Further, "[t]he statutory testing of cocaine in Schedule II carries, by implication, legislative findings that it has a high potential for abuse * * * " *id* at 518. It is suggested that the statutory listing of cocaine in Schedule II also carries, by implication, legislative findings that the sale of cocaine presents a great "risk to public health" inasmuch as the Board of Pharmacy is required to consider that factor in classifying controlled substances under Minn.Stat. § 152.02, subd. 8 (1984).

In addition, the penalties imposed for selling cocaine are severe, including imprisonment for not more than 15 years and/or a fine of not more than $40,000 for a first violation, and for a subsequent violation, imprisonment for not less than 1 year nor more than 30 years and/or a fine of not more than $50,000. Minn.Stat. § 152.15, subd. 1 (1984).

The Supreme Court of Virginia recently held that unlawful distribution of cocaine with knowledge that the drug was to be injected constituted an appropriate predicate felony upon which to base a charge of felony murder. *Heacock v. Commonwealth,* 228 Va. 397, 323 S.E.2d 90 (1984). *See also Sheriff of Clark County v. Morris,* 99 Nev. 109, 659 P.2d 852 (1983) (felonious sale of drugs and presence during consumption of lethal dose appropriate predicate felony). If the majority wishes to hold that sale of cocaine cannot ever be an appropriate predicate felony, it should address *State v. Randolph,* 676 S.W.2d 943 (Tenn.1984) (sale of heroin with no participation or presence during injection constituted malice for first degree murder charge) and *People v. Taylor,* 11 Cal.App.3d 57, 89 Cal.Rptr. 697 (1970) (furnishing heroin with no participation or presence during injection appropriate predicate felony).

The majority has fallen into the trap of "determin[ing] from the elements of each felony *in the abstract* whether it inherently involved some special danger to human life," instead of examining the facts of the particular case and the circumstances under which the felony was committed. The facts of this particular case and the circumstances under which this sale was committed compel the conclusion that this sale, where there was knowledge that the cocaine was to be taken by injection, involved special danger to human life. This sale of cocaine, therefore, should be held to be a proper predicate felony to prosecute a charge under Minn.Stat. § 609.19(2).

Finally, the majority misreads the felony murder statute and holds that if a felony "terminates" before the death of the victim the offense cannot be a predicate felony. No Minnesota decision is cited for this proposition. Our felony murder statute requires the actor only to *cause* the death while committing the crime, not that the death has to occur while the actor is committing the offense. *See M.D.S.*, 345 N.W.2d 723 (victim died in hospital after actor feloniously aided in discharge of gun at victim's residence). Even the old felony murder statute demanded only that "the felony and the killing [be] parts of one continuous transaction." *Kochevar v. State*, 281 N.W.2d at 686. Nothing in the 1981 amendment changed this rule.

Here, the predicate felony offered to be proved was sale of cocaine with the defendant allegedly knowing that the drug was to be taken in a potentially fatal manner, i.e. by injection. The injection took place in respondent's presence, presumably within a few minutes of the sale. The sale and the injection, therefore, are part of one continuous transaction, and if it can be shown that Schweiger died as a result of the cocaine injection, there would exist a strong causal connection between the felonious act and the death. Our statute requires no more. *See also Heacock*, 228 Va. at 401, 323 S.E.2d at 92.

The majority opinion precludes any "completed" felonious sale of any controlled substance under any circumstances from being a proper predicate felony upon which to base a charge of felony murder under § 609.19(2). The issue is more appropriately addressed on a case-by-case basis, examining the facts and circumstances underlying each particular sale.

WOZNIAK, JUDGE (dissenting).

I join in the dissent of Judge Parker.

Notes and Questions

1. If Aarsvold cannot be prosecuted for felony murder, could a murder conviction be sought on any other theory? The Michigan Supreme Court has commented that the availability of felony murder "should have little effect on the results of the majority of cases," because in many of the cases in which it has been applied "the use of the doctrine was unnecessary because the other types of malice could have been inferred from the evidence." People v. Aaron, 409 Mich. 672, 729, 299 N.W.2d 304, 327 (1980).

Consider Kruse v. Commonwealth, 704 S.W.2d 192 (Ky.1985). Under Kentucky law, the felony murder rule has been legislatively abolished. Murder, however, is committed if one "wantonly engages in conduct which creates a grave risk of death to another person and thereby causes the death of another person." Ky.Rev.Stat. § 507.020. In *Kruse*, the court summarized the facts as follows:

Michael Kruse and Paul Kordenbrock entered a Western Auto Store in Florence, Kruse remaining at the front of the store. Kordenbrock pulled a pistol from a shoulder holster and forced the store owner, William Thompson, and an employee, Stanley Allen, to lie on the floor at the rear of the store. Kruse, after pretending to be an employee while a customer wandered into the store, broke into the gun counter. Kordenbrock shot both prostrate victims in the head, killing Allen and wounding Thompson. The two robbers then placed numerous guns into a cardboard box and fled the scene.

* * * [O]n each of the two days preceding the robbery, Kruse and Kordenbrock had been in the same store, on the first occasion asking about woodcutting tools and on the second evincing an interest in guns. Kruse's father further testified that Michael told him that he and Kordenbrock had planned the robbery before entering the store. There was evidence introduced that both men had consumed a considerable quantity of alcohol and quaaludes prior to the robbery.

704 S.W.2d at 192–93. Upholding Kruse's conviction for the murder of Allen, the Kentucky Supreme Court noted that the statutory homicide scheme abandons the felony murder doctrine as an independent basis for establishing an offense of homicide. It continued:

The culpability of Michael Kruse for the killing of the deceased must now be measured by the degree of wantonness or recklessness reflected by the extent of his participation in the underlying robbery rather than by the implication of intent to murder from the intent to participate in the robbery.

* * *

In this case, with the evidence that the appellant participated in the planning of an armed robbery in which a .357 Magnum was used, that for two days the participants "cased" the store to determine the number of employees, customer frequency, location of the weapons to be stolen, etc.; with the testimony there was a plan to steal those weapons, all coupled with the use of drugs and alcohol immediately prior to the robbery, it is clear there was sufficient "circumstances surrounding the felony" to submit this case to the jury under proper instructions of the court. It is equally clear that the determination of wanton murder by the jury under these circumstances was not contrary to the evidence.

Id., at 195.

2. The California Supreme Court has been among the more rigorous adherents to the approach that the felony murder rule should be limited to those felonies that are inherently dangerous to human life. People v. Phillips, 64 Cal.2d 574, 51 Cal.Rptr. 225, 414 P.2d 353 (1966). It has explained the rationale for this approach:

If the felony is not inherently dangerous, it is highly improbable that the potential felon will be deterred; he will not anticipate that injury or death might arise solely from the fact that he will commit the felony.

People v. Burroughs, 35 Cal.3d 824, 829, 201 Cal.Rptr. 319, 322, 678 P.2d 894, 897 (1984). In *Burroughs,* the victim, Lee Swatsenbarg, had been diagnosed as suffering from terminal lukemia. Burroughs treated him with methods that included administration of a unique "lemonade," exposure to colored lights, and vigorous massage. But Swatsenbarg ultimately died from a massive hemorrhage caused by Burroughs' massage. Under the facts, Burroughs might well have been guilty of the felony of practicing medicine without a license, prohibited by the following statute:

Any person, who willfully, under circumstances or conditions which cause or create a risk of great bodily harm, serious physical or mental illness, or death, practices * * * any mode of treating the sick * * * without at the time having a valid * * * certificate as provided in this chapter * * * is punishable by imprisonment in the county jail for not exceeding one year or in the state prison.

Finding that the trial court erred in giving a felony murder instruction to the trial jury, the California Supreme Court concluded that under the statute one could commit the offense of felony practicing medicine without a license and not necessarily endanger human life. It is sufficient under the statute that a risk is created of "great bodily harm," "serious physical * * * illness," or "serious * * * mental illness." Given the purpose of the statute, it is unlikely that the legislature intended to permit felony conviction for practicing without a license only when the patient's life was placed in danger. Further:

> [O]ur analysis of precedent in this area reveals that the few times we have found an underlying felony inherently dangerous (so that it would support a conviction of felony murder), the offense has been tinged with malevolence totally absent from the facts of this case. In People v. Mattison (1971) 4 Cal.3d 177, 93 Cal.Rptr. 185, 481 P.2d 193, we held that poisoning food, drink or medicine with intent to injure was inherently dangerous. The willful and malicious burning of an automobile (located in a garage beneath an occupied home) was ruled inherently dangerous in People v. Nickols (1970) 3 Cal.3d 150, 162–163, 89 Cal.Rptr. 721, 474 P.2d 673. Finally, we held kidnapping to be such an offense in People v. Ford, [60 Cal.2d 772, 36 Cal.Rptr. 620, 388 P.2d 892 (1964)].

> * * *

> Finally, the underlying purpose of the felony-murder rule, to encourage felons to commit their offenses without perpetrating unnecessary violence which might result in a homicide, would not be served by applying the rule to the facts of this case. Defendant was or should have been aware he was committing a crime by treating Swatsenbarg in the first place. Yet, it is unlikely he would have been deterred from administering to Lee in the manner in which he did for fear of a prosecution for murder, given his published beliefs on the efficacy of massage in the curing of cancer. Indeed, nowhere it is claimed that defendant attempted to perform any action with respect to Swatsenbarg other than to heal him—and earn a fee for doing so.

35 Cal.3d at 832–33, 201 Cal.Rptr. at 324–25, 678 P.2d at 900. Justice Richardson dissented, characterizing the majority's distinctions between the risk of death and great bodily harm, serious physical and mental injury as "hypertechnical and irrelevant." Apparently viewing the purpose of the felony murder rule as providing an additional deterrent to the commission of certain felonies, he reasoned that the nature of the felony at issue— because it required the risk of serious harm to the victim—was one which society has a special need to prevent. As a result, applying the felony murder rule to provide an additional deterrent to commission of the offense

would be appropriate. 35 Cal.3d at 854–57, 201 Cal.Rptr. at 340–42, 678 P.2d at 915–17 (Richardson, J., dissenting).

3. On what level should the "inherent" dangerousness of an offense be considered? If a robbery with a firearm is "armed robbery" regardless of whether the firearm is loaded or not, should the fact that a felony murder defendant believed that the robbery was to be committed with an unloaded weapon be considered? In Commonwealth v. Carter, 396 Mass. 234, 484 N.E.2d 1340 (1985), the court apparently considered the offense to be evaluated as "armed robbery with an unloaded gun" but nevertheless found it inherently dangerous:

> Where an unarmed felon knows that his accomplice in a robbery is carrying a gun, even if he believes the gun is unloaded and his accomplice has no ammunition, that robbery is inherently dangerous to human life. The use of a gun, even if it is unloaded, may provoke violent resistence from the intended victim or may spur others, such as police officers, to intervene with deadly force. Contrary to an unarmed felon's expectation, a gun may come to be loaded in the course of events and, as occurred here, it may be used to cause death.

396 Mass. at ___, 484 N.E.2d at 1342–43.

4. If death was caused in the commission of a felony which, under the approaches discussed above, is not sufficient for felony murder, it may invoke what is often—but inappropriately—called the misdemeanor manslaughter rule. People v. Burroughs, 35 Cal.3d 824, 835–36, 201 Cal.Rptr. 319, 326–27, 678 P.2d 894, 900–02 (1984). Under this rule, a death caused in the commission of an unlawful act is involuntary manslaughter.

But just as the felony murder rule has been limited, so has the misdemeanor—"unlawful act" doctrine been restricted. Some courts limit the rule to those unlawful acts that are malum in se, that is, where the unlawful act is something wrong in itself. If the act—although a criminal offense—is "wrong" only because prohibited by law, a manslaughter conviction requires proof of criminal negligence as well as the causing of death in the course of the unlawful act. See Bartlett v. State, 569 P.2d 1235 (Wyo. 1977), holding that a death caused without criminal negligence but in the course of the misdemeanor of driving over the speed limit is not manslaughter, because speeding is only malum prohibitum. Other courts have limited the rule to those criminal acts insufficient to give rise to felony murder that are dangerous to others. United States v. Walker, 380 A.2d 1388 (D.C.App.1977).

5. The majority indicates that the facts fail to show a sufficiently direct causal relationship between Aarsvold's actions and the victim's death. But generally courts have agreed that the felony murder rule is not rendered inapplicable simply because the felony was technically completed before the fatal harm was done to the victim. E.g., State v. Rinck, 303 N.C. 551, 564, 280 S.E.2d 912, 922 (1981). The North Carolina court generalized in *Rinck* that "a killing is committed in the perpetration of a felony when there is no break in the chain of events leading from the initial felony to the act causing death." Id. Most of the cases involve robberies. In *Rinck*, the robbers left the victim who called police and reported the robbery. Before officers arrived, however, the robbers returned and killed the victim,

apparently to prevent him from identifying them. This killing was held to have been in the perpetration of the robbery. Killings caused during "immediate flight" from a robbery are generally regarded as felony murders because of the robbery. People v. Hickam, 684 P.2d 228, 231 (Colo.1984). The California courts have tended to define a robbery as continuing until the robbers reach a place of temporary safety. E.g., People v. Mothershed, 146 Cal.App.3d 553, 194 Cal.Rptr. 824, 832 (1983) cert. denied, 467 U.S. 1228, 104 S.Ct. 2682, 81 L.Ed.2d 877 (1984). In *Mothershed,* this was explained: "The risk that the robber will carry out his armed threat continues until there is an alleviation of that threat by the robber reaching a place of temporary safety." Id. Mothershed robbed a convenience store and left on foot. About an hour later, an officer saw him three miles from the store and stopped him because the officer recognized that he resembled the description of the perpetrator. Mothershed killed the officer. Finding that this was properly felony murder with the robbery as the predicate felony, the court explained:

> [D]efendant was walking from the area of the scene of the robbery, but had not reached a point where his person was outside the area of search for the fleeing felon. Further, although defendant's parents lived within two miles of the robbery, he chose to continue from the scene to a point three miles away. The defendant thus continued to flee and attempt to elude any pursuers. The officer was in "pursuit" of this fleeing robber.

194 Cal.Rptr. at 832.

Should it make any difference that the *Aarsvold* court was applying a statute that required proof that the defendants caused death "while committing" the felony? In Davis v. State, 477 N.E.2d 889 (Ind.1985), the Indiana Supreme Court, applying a similarly-phrased statute, held that deaths were caused "while committing" child molesting even though the sexual acts had been completed before the victims were killed. It explained:

> [W]hen there is a close proximity in terms of time and distance between the underlying felony and homicide and there is no break in the chain of events from the inception of the felony to the time of the homicide, we treat the two events as part of one continuous transaction.

477 N.E.2d at 894. If this approach had been applied in *Aarsvold,* would the result have been different?

STATE v. NOREN

Court of Appeals of Wisconsin, 1985.
125 Wis.2d 204, 371 N.W.2d 381, review denied, 126 Wis.2d 519, 378 N.W.2d 292 (1985).

Before CANE, P.J., and DEAN and LaROCQUE, JJ.

CANE, PRESIDING JUDGE.

Monte Noren appeals a judgment convicting him of second-degree murder, sec. 940.02(2), Stats. The jury found that Noren killed Joseph Lebakken as a natural and probable consequence of the commission of a felony. The underlying felony was robbery. Noren argues that the evidence was insufficient to prove beyond a reasonable doubt that Lebakken's death was the natural and probable consequence of the robbery. * * *

We review the evidence in the light most favorable to the verdict. Applying this standard, the record shows that Noren struck Lebakken on the head three times during a robbery. He struck the blows with his closed fist, causing his knuckles to bleed. A witness to the crime was concerned that Noren's blows would kill Lebakken. Lebakken was extremely drunk at the time of the robbery. His blood alcohol content was .38% and his urine alcohol content was .48% at the time of death. Noren knew that Lebakken was very drunk.

Noren's blows caused Lebakken to lose consciousness and to become comatose. His extreme intoxication contributed to the loss of consciousness. Lebakken suffered from a preexisting respiratory disease that impeded the removal of mucus from his lungs. This condition, in association with the coma, caused death by asphyxiation. Noren did not know about Lebakken's respiratory disease.

NATURAL & PROBABLE CONSEQUENCE

The state prosecuted Noren for second-degree murder under sec. 940.02(2). The statute provides that whoever causes death as a natural and probable consequence of the commission of a felony is guilty of second-degree murder. This is known as the felony-murder rule. Noren contends that death is not a natural and probable consequence of striking a person's head with a fist.

The phrase "natural and probable" has not been defined under the felony-murder statute. The parties concede that to be a natural consequence of a felony, death must be proximately caused by the defendant's conduct. The test of cause is whether the defendant's conduct was a substantial factor in causing the death. It is undisputed on appeal that Noren's conduct caused Lebakken's death. The critical issue therefore is whether death was a probable consequence of striking Lebakken's head.

Although the parties agree that "probable" relates to the foreseeability of death, they disagree about how foreseeable death must be. We agree that foreseeability requires different degrees of certainty in different contexts. To constitute negligence, harm must be probable rather than merely possible. Negligent homicide requires that conduct create a high probability of death or great bodily harm. *Hart v. State,* 75 Wis.2d 371, 383, 249 N.W.2d 810, 815 (1977). "High probability" is defined as a probability that the ordinary person, having in mind all the circumstances, including the seriousness of the consequences, would consider unreasonable. It does not mean that the mathematical probability of the consequences must be greater than fifty percent. *Id.* at 383–84 n. 4, 249 N.W.2d at 815 n. 4. Death caused by conduct evincing a depraved mind, sec. 940.02(1), Stats., requires that the defendant's conduct be imminently dangerous to human life. "Imminently dangerous" means that the conduct is dangerous in and of itself; it must have been inherently, apparently, and consciously dangerous to life and not such as might casually produce death by misadventure. *Balistreri v. State,* 83 Wis.2d 440, 455, 265 N.W.2d 290, 296 (1978). No Wisconsin appellate decision has addressed the certainty required for death to be foreseeable under the present felony-murder statute.

The statutory requirement that death be a probable consequence of a felony is intended to limit felony-murder liability to situations where the defendant's conduct creates some measure of foreseeable risk of death. *See* Model Penal Code § 201.2 Comment 4C at 37 (Tent. Draft No. 9, 1959). Under the predecessor felony-murder statute, a defendant committed murder when death resulted from the commission of any felony. *Pliemling v. State,* 46 Wis. 516, 519, 1 N.W. 278, 279 (1879). This rule was modified because it imposed severe criminal sanctions without considering the moral culpability of the defendant. *See Commonwealth v. Matchett,* 386 Mass. 492, 436 N.E.2d 400, 409 (1982).

Because felony-murder is a Class B felony, we conclude that the level of foreseeability should be the same as for depraved mind murder, which is also a Class B felony. Under this test, the acts causing death must be inherently dangerous to life. We apply this test to felony-murder because it requires a high degree of foreseeability, thereby implicitly requiring greater culpability than lesser grades of homicide. Our supreme court applied this standard under the predecessor felony-murder statute when it stated that the act constituting the felony must be in itself dangerous to life. *Pliemling,* 46 Wis. at 521, 1 N.W. at 281.

Our conclusion is supported by the fact that most other jurisdictions apply the inherently dangerous test in felony murder cases. *State v. Underwood,* 228 Kan. 294, 615 P.2d 153, 160 (1980). In *State v. Harrison,* 90 N.M. 439, 564 P.2d 1321, 1324 (1977), the New Mexico Supreme Court adopted the "natural and probable" test, which it defined as the "inherently or foreseeably dangerous to human life test." Most courts that have recognized the inherently dangerous test have relied on language from an English case, *Regina v. Serne,* 16 Cox Crim. Cases 311 (Central Crim.Ct.1887), as stating the basis of the modern felony-murder rule. In *Regina,* 16 Cox Crim. Cases at 313, the court stated:

> [I]nstead of saying that any act done with intent to commit a felony and which causes death amounts to murder, it would be reasonable to say that any act known to be dangerous to life, and likely in itself to cause death, done for the purpose of committing a felony which causes death, should be murder.

We are persuaded that Wisconsin's felony-murder statute originates from this case and that the inherently dangerous test applies.

SUFFICIENCY OF THE EVIDENCE

The trial court correctly instructed the jury in this case that the acts constituting the robbery must have been "in and of themselves dangerous to the life of Joseph Lebakken." Whether Noren's conduct was inherently dangerous must be determined from the conduct itself and the surrounding circumstances. Whether the conduct was inherently dangerous is not determined by considering only the abstract qualities of the underlying felony. We review the evidence to determine whether a reasonable jury could be convinced beyond a reasonable doubt that Noren's conduct was inherently dangerous. If more than one reasonable inference can be drawn from the evidence, we must accept the inference supporting the verdict.

Noren argues that striking a person's head three times with a fist is not inherently dangerous. He relies on *Beauregard v. State*, 146 Wis. 280, 289, 131 N.W. 347, 351 (1911), where our supreme court stated that striking a person's head with a gun barrel generally would not cause death. The state argues that striking a very intoxicated person who has a respiratory disease is inherently dangerous. According to this argument, the specific traits of the victim must be considered when deciding whether conduct is dangerous. The state also argues that one who commits a violent crime takes his victim as he finds him.

We agree that generally death is not the natural and probable result of a blow with a hand. *See* 40 Am.Jur.2d *Homicide* § 268 (1968). Our inquiry is not complete, however, because the particular traits of the victim also must be considered. Conduct that is unlikely to cause the death of a healthy adult may be dangerous to others. Only special attributes that the defendant was aware of may be considered. Conduct does not become inherently dangerous on the basis of latent danger. The truism that a defendant takes his victim as he finds him, therefore, does not apply to this case. The proposition applies in tort law when assessing damages. It also applies in criminal law when deciding the issue of causation. The unknown qualities of a victim, however, are irrelevant to the issue of foreseeability of death.

Applying the inherently dangerous test to this case, we conclude that sufficient evidence supports Noren's conviction. Although Lebakken's respiratory disease was irrelevant to the issue of inherent danger, his extreme intoxication was a factor that distinguished him from a healthy adult. Striking an intoxicated person exposes him to familiar risks that a sober person would not face. He may fall and fatally strike his head. He also may asphyxiate from vomit while unconscious. Although Lebakken did not die from either of these causes, the jury could consider such possibilities when determining whether Noren's conduct was inherently dangerous. We conclude that a reasonable jury could have been convinced beyond a reasonable doubt that his conduct was inherently dangerous.

* * *

Judgment affirmed.

Notes and Questions

1. Noren apparently challenged on appeal only the sufficiency of the evidence to support his conviction. No question was raised as to the jury

instructions. How should the jury have been instructed to determine whether Lebakken's death was "a natural and probable consequence" of the robbery committed by Noren? Specifically, must Lebakken have been aware of (a) the degree of the risk of death created by the robbery; and (b) the likelihood of Lebakken's death occurring by virtue of aggravation of Lebakken's respiratory disease?

In regard to (a), the court discusses the matter before it as "foreseeability." Does this mean that the only question is whether a reasonable person would have foreseen the required risk of death? In its analysis, the court notes that "depraved mind" murder under § 940.02(1) requires that the conduct have been "consciously dangerous to life." Does this mean that for liability to exist under this theory, the state must show both that the risk was high enough and that the defendant was aware of this risk? If so, did the court mean to suggest that the same awareness would be required when liability was sought under § 940.02(2) on a felony murder theory? Perhaps the court was drawing upon depraved mind murder only for purposes of determining the requisite risk of death occurring. But if death must reach a certain (and the same) degree of foreseeability under either theory, is there any sound reason why depraved mind murder but not felony murder should require actual awareness of that risk?

With regard to (b), the court considers Noren's awareness of Lebakken's intoxication in concluding that a jury could find that Noren's conduct was inherently dangerous. It assumes Noren was unaware of Lebakken's respiratory condition, and this assumption does not prevent the appellate court from upholding the jury determination. Perhaps the court is saying that inherent dangerousness is proven if those circumstances known to the defendant establish that a reasonable person with awareness of those circumstances would recognize the required risk of death. Once it is shown that the defendant's conduct was inherently dangerous and that "but for" the defendant's conduct the victim would not have died, it is of no significance—at least to the foreseeability or inherent danger analysis—that the manner in which death occurred involved contribution from unknown circumstances—such as Lebakken's preexisting respiratory condition. The significance of the involvement of such unknown (and perhaps unforeseeable) circumstances may be relevant only to "causation" analysis. In that context, the court comments, the "truism" that "a defendant takes his victim as he finds him" does apply.

2. Although it is frequently said that a felon is not liable for murder if during the felony he causes a death in an unforeseeable manner because the felonious activity is not the "proximate cause" of the death, e.g., W. LaFave and A. Scott, Criminal Law 264 (1972), American case law support for this proposition is sparse. Most of the support is dicta in cases holding defendants liable for what is determined to have been a foreseeable death. E.g., State v. Glover, 330 Mo. 709, 50 S.W.2d 1049 (1932) (defendant who set fire to drug store to collect insurance liable for felony-murder of fireman killed fighting the blaze on the ground that he had reason to anticipate that members of the fire department would endanger themselves fighting the fire). See Ward v. State, 109 S.W.2d 207 (Tex.Crim.App.1937), in which the defendant caused fire to be set to a building; a person in an upper room

was killed in the fire. "The testimony," concluded the court, "excludes the idea that the principals knew, or should have known, that any person was in the building at the time the arson was consummated." Defendant also denied any knowledge of this fact. He was charged with murder under a statute in the arson section of the penal code providing that "Where death is occasioned by any offense described in this * * * chapter the offender is guilty of murder." The conviction was upheld, although the court commented that in the absence of the statute it would have grave doubt that the defendant would be liable for murder "unless the death in question was the natural and reasonable consequence of [the] arson * * *." Should the existence of such a statute preclude application of a "proximate cause" requirement of foreseeability?

3. Should more than the foreseeability of death required by the Wisconsin court be necessary for application of the felony murder rule? In Commonwealth v. Matchett, 386 Mass. 492, 436 N.E.2d 400 (1982), the court noted that for the felony murder rule to apply, "[w]e require * * * that a homicide committed in the course of a felony or attempted felony, be the natural and probable consequence of the act." The felony murder rule is based on the theory that the intent to commit the felony is equivalent to the malice aforethought required for murder. This is tenable when the felony is a common law inherently dangerous felony such as arson, rape, burglary and robbery, or a statutory inherently dangerous felony such as breaking and entering with intent to put a person in fear. But when the felony is a statutory felony which is less serious than the common law felonies that gave rise to the rule and which has "no natural tendency to cause death," such as the extortion offense at issue in case before the court, the reasoning cannot stand. As a result, in order to render the continued application of the felony murder rule acceptable in such contexts:

> We hold today that when a death results from the perpetration or attempted perpetration of the statutory felony of extortion, there can be no conviction of felony-murder * * * unless the jury finds that the extortion involved circumstances demonstrating the defendant's conscious disregard to the risk to human life.

386 Mass. at 508, 436 N.E.2d at 410. If such a finding is necessary when felony murder is based upon felonies such as extortion, why is it not necessary in all cases?

A similar but more broadly applicable limitation on felony murder has been imposed by the Michigan Supreme Court. The Michigan statutes do not specifically define murder. A statute defining first degree murder, similar to the California provision reprinted at page 380, supra, provides that murders occurring in the course of certain enumerated felonies constitute first degree murder. Mich.Comp.Laws § 750.316. Another statute simply provides, "All other kinds of murder shall be murder of the second degree * * *." Id., § 750.317. In People v. Aaron, 409 Mich. 672, 299 N.W.2d 304 (1980), the Michigan Supreme Court considered whether the definition of "murder" included the traditional felony murder rule. Expressing doubt as to whether the Michigan case law defining murder had ever embraced the felony murder rule, the court nevertheless decided to reject the felony murder rule on its merits. Explaining, the court continued:

> Accordingly, we hold today that malice is the intention to kill, the intention to do great bodily harm, or the wanton and willful disregard of the likelihood that the natural tendency of defendant's behavior is to cause death or great bodily harm. We further hold that malice is an essential element of any murder, as that term is judicially defined, whether the murder occurs in the course of a felony or otherwise.
>
> * * *
>
> Abrogation of [the felony murder] rule does not make irrelevant the fact that a death occurred in the course of a felony. A jury can properly *infer* malice from evidence that a defendant intentionally set in motion a force likely to cause death or great bodily harm. Thus, whenever a killing occurs in the perpetration or attempted perpetration of an inherently dangerous felony, in order to establish malice the jury may consider the "nature of the underlying felony and the circumstances surrounding its commission". If the jury concludes that malice existed, they can find murder and, if they determine that the murder occurred in the perpetration or attempted perpetration of one of the enumerated felonies, by statute the murder would become first-degree murder.
>
> The difference is that the jury may not find malice from the intent to commit the underlying felony alone. The defendant will be permitted to assert any of the applicable defenses relating to *mens rea* which he would be allowed to assert if charged with premeditated murder.
>
> * * *

409 Mich. at 728–30, 299 N.W.2d at 326–27.

4. A number of courts have refused to find or apply a requirement of either actual apprehension of a risk of death or even of the foreseeability of death. These cases often involve deaths immediately resulting from heart attacks attributable to offenses such as robbery, even if trial evidence showed that the victim's health was bad and the felons neither knew nor could reasonably have known of the victim's susceptibility to heart problems. See, for example, People v. Stamp, 2 Cal.App.3d 203, 82 Cal.Rptr. 598 (1969), cert. denied, 400 U.S. 819, 91 S.Ct. 36, 27 L.Ed.2d 46 (1969), in which no shots were fired during the armed robbery. The victim was among those required to lie on the floor and to remain there so that no one would "get hurt." After the robbers left, the victim got up but soon collapsed from a fatal heart attack. Rejecting arguments that "causation" requirements precluded liability for felony murder, the court reasoned:

> The [felony murder doctrine] is not limited to those deaths which are foreseeable. Rather a felon is held strictly liable for *all* killings committed by him or his accomplices in the course of the felony. As long as the homicide is the direct causal result of the robbery, the felony-murder rule applies whether or not the death was a natural or probable consequence of the robbery. So long as a victim's predisposing physical condition, regardless of the cause, is not the *only* substantial factor bringing about his death, that condition, and the robber's ignorance of it, in no way destroys the robber's criminal responsibility

for the death. So long as life is shortened as a result of the felonious act it does not matter that the victim might have died soon anyway. In this respect, the robber takes his victim as he finds him.

2 Cal.App.2d at 210–11, 82 Cal.Rptr. at 603. Is liability for deaths caused by robbery-induced heart attacks more appropriate if some violence occurred during the robbery? Liability was found in Durden v. State, 250 Ga. 325, 297 S.E.2d 237 (1982), where gunshots were exchanged (and the felon but not the victim was wounded) and in Thomas v. State, 436 N.E.2d 1109 (Ind.1982), where the victim, his wife, and his daughter were bound and the wife and daughter were "slapped and shoved" in an effort to persuade them to reveal the location of a safe.

5. Must there be a causal relationship of some sort between the felonious aspect of the defendant's conduct and the death of the victim? See Moynahan v. State, 140 Tex.Crim.R. 540, 146 S.W.2d 376 (1941), in which the defendant was charged with felony murder for a death arising out of an automobile accident which occurred while the defendant allegedly was driving while intoxicated. Driving while intoxicated was a felony under state law. The conviction was reversed on the basis of the prosecutor's following argument to the jury: "It makes no difference how carefully the defendant was driving his car; he could have been driving it five miles an hour, and he was drunk at the time of the collision he is guilty of murder." The "correct statement of the settled law of the state," the court held, was embodied in the trial court's instruction that the defendant "would not be guilty of murder if he was operating the [car] in the same manner that it would be operated by one not under the influence of intoxicating liquor."

6. Consider the following holdings and what limitations upon felony murder they impose or apply. In Commonwealth v. Burrell, 389 Mass. 804, 452 N.E.2d 504 (1983), Burrell and two others were beating the victim in the course of a robbery. A crowd of about thirty people gathered and some members of the crowd began to participate in the beating. Someone in the crowd said, "Move out of the way." Perry, one of the original three robbers, stepped aside. Someone in the crowd then shot the victim, killing him. Burrell's conviction for felony murder could not stand, "[s]ince the Commonwealth did not produce any evidence that the murder was a natural and probable consequence of the robbery, or that the defendant associated himself or acted in concert with the slayer * * *." 389 Mass. at 808, 452 N.E.2d at 506.

In Bryant v. State, 412 So.2d 347 (Fla.1982), Bryant agreed to help one Jackson burglarize an apartment. When they entered, they found the occupant bound. Bryant assisted in tying the victim more securely and then left. Jackson later engaged in sexual acts on the bound victim and, in the course of this, apparently strangled the victim. Bryant knew that Jackson had previously engaged in homosexual activities. But the Florida Supreme Court agreed that this did not necessarily mean that Bryant was guilty of felony murder:

[I]f the jury finds that the death was not caused or materially contributed to by any acts committed during the perpetration of the robbery but rather was caused solely by acts committed during the perpetration of sexual battery, and if the jury finds that the sexual battery was an independent act of another and not a part of Jackson and Bryant's common scheme or design, then it may not find Bryant guilty of first-degree felony murder.

412 So.2d at 350. Because the jury was not adequately instructed on the "independent act" matter, the conviction was reversed.

2. THE "MERGER" DOCTRINE

An important limitation upon the felony murder rule in many jurisdictions is the requirement that the predicate felony be one in some senses "independent" of the homicide. Where a felony lacks such independence, it is often said to "merge" into the homicide, with the effect that it is unavailable for use as a predicate felony. As the principal case makes clear, determining whether particular offenses should so merge into a resulting homicide has not always been an easy task.

PEOPLE v. SMITH

Supreme Court of California, 1984.
35 Cal.3d 798, 201 Cal.Rptr. 311, 678 P.2d 886.

MOSK, JUSTICE.

Defendant appeals from a judgment convicting her of second degree murder felony child abuse, and child beating. The court sentenced her to imprisonment for 15 years to life on the murder count and stayed service of sentence on the 2 remaining counts * * *. The principal issue on appeal is whether felony child abuse may serve as the underlying felony to support a conviction of second degree murder on a felony-murder theory. We conclude that because the acts constituting such child abuse in the present case were an integral part of the homicide, the offense merged into the homicide; it was therefore error to give a felony-murder instruction, and the judgment must be reversed insofar as it convicts defendant of second degree murder.

Defendant and her two daughters, three-and-a-half-year-old Bethany (Beth) and two-year-old Amy, lived with David Foster. On the day Amy died, she refused to sit on the couch instead of the floor to eat a snack. Defendant became angry, took Amy into the children's bedroom, spanked her and slapped her in the face. Amy then went towards the corner of the bedroom which was often used for discipline; defendant hit her repeatedly, knocking her to the floor. Foster then apparently joined defendant to "assist" in Amy's discipline. Beth testified that both Foster and defendant were striking Amy, who at that point had been at least partially undressed by defendant. Defendant and Foster used both their hands and a paddle on the child, and were also biting her. In addition, Beth testified that Foster put a wastebasket on Amy's head and hit her on the head with his fist. Eventually, defendant knocked the child backwards and she fell, hitting her head on the closet door.

Amy stiffened and went into respiratory arrest. Defendant and Foster took her to the hospital, where defendant admitted that she "beat her too hard." She also stated that Foster had not come home until after the incident. Amy died that evening. Her injuries were consistent with compressive force caused by numerous blows by hands, fists, and a paddle. The severe head injury that was the direct cause of death occurred within an hour before the child was brought to the hospital.

* * *

The court gave the jury the standard instructions defining murder, malice aforethought, second degree murder, second degree felony murder, and manslaughter. The second degree felony-murder instruction informed the jury that an unlawful killing, whether intentional, unintentional, or accidental, is second degree murder if it occurs during the commission of a felony inherently dangerous to human life, and that felony child abuse is such a crime. Defendant contends that on the facts of this case the crime of felony child abuse was an integral part of and included in fact within the homicide, and hence that it merged into the latter under the rule of *People v. Ireland* (1969) 70 Cal.2d 522, 538–540, 75 Cal.Rptr. 188, 450 P.2d 580. We agree.

Our opinions have repeatedly emphasized that felony murder, although the law of this state, is a disfavored doctrine: "We have recognized that the rule is much censured 'because it anachronistically resurrects from a bygone age a "barbaric" concept that has been discarded in the place of its origin' ([*People v. Phillips* (1966) 64 Cal.2d 574, 583, fn. 6, 51 Cal.Rptr. 225, 414 P.2d 353]) and because 'in almost all cases in which it is applied it is unnecessary' and 'it erodes the relation between criminal liability and moral culpability' (*People v. Washington* (1965) 62 Cal.2d 777, 783, 44 Cal.Rptr. 442, 402 P.2d 130)." (*People v. Dillon* (1983) 34 Cal.3d 441, 463, 194 Cal.Rptr. 390, 668 P.2d 697.) Accordingly, we have reiterated that this "highly artificial concept" (*Phillips,* supra, 64 Cal.2d at p. 582, 51 Cal.Rptr. 225, 414 P.2d 353) "should not be extended beyond any rational function that it is designed to serve." (*Washington,* supra, 62 Cal.2d at p. 783, 44 Cal. Rptr. 442, 402 P.2d 130.) "Applying this principle to various concrete factual circumstances, we have sought to insure that the [doctrine] * * * be given the narrowest possible application consistent with its ostensible purpose—which is to deter those engaged in felonies from killing negligently or accidentally" (*People v. Satchell* (1971) 6 Cal.3d 28, 34, 98 Cal.Rptr. 33, 489 P.2d 1361).

In accord with this policy, we restricted the scope of the felony-murder rule in *Ireland* by holding it inapplicable to felonies that are an integral part of and included in fact within the homicide. In that case the defendant and his wife were experiencing serious marital difficulties which eventually culminated in defendant's drawing a gun and killing his wife. The jury was instructed that it could find the defendant guilty of second degree felony murder if it determined that the homicide occurred during the commission of the underlying felony of assault with a deadly weapon. Like all felony-murder instructions, this instruction had the "effect of 'reliev[ing] the jury of the necessity of finding one of the elements of the crime of murder' [citation] to wit, malice aforethought." (*People v. Ireland,* supra, 70 Cal.2d at p. 538, 75 Cal.Rptr. 188, 450 P.2d 580.) We reasoned that "the utilization of the felony-murder rule in circumstances such as those before us extends the operation of that rule 'beyond any rational function that it is designed to serve.' [Citation.] To allow such use of the felony-murder rule would effectively preclude the jury from considering the issue of malice aforethought in all cases wherein homicide has been committed as a result of a felonious assault—a category which includes the great majority of all homicides. This kind of bootstrapping finds support neither in logic nor in law. We therefore hold that *a second degree felony-murder instruction may not properly be given when it is based upon a felony which is an integral part of the homicide and which the evidence produced by the prosecution shows to be an offense included in fact within the offense charged.*" (*Id.* at p. 539, 75 Cal.Rptr. 188, 450 P.2d 580; italics added.)

Very soon after *Ireland* we again had occasion to consider the question of merger in *People v. Wilson* (1969) 1 Cal.3d 431, 82 Cal.Rptr. 494, 462 P.2d 22. There the defendant forcibly entered his estranged wife's apartment carrying a shotgun. Once inside the apartment, he fatally shot a man in the living room and proceeded to break into the bathroom where he killed his wife. The jury was instructed on second degree felony murder based on the underlying felony of assault with a deadly weapon, and convicted the defendant of second degree murder of the man. We determined that the predicate felony was a "necessary ingredient of the homicide" and reversed under *Ireland,* which explicitly prohibited use of the felony-murder rule in such circumstances. (*Id.* at p. 438, 82 Cal.Rptr. 494, 462 P.2d 22.)

The defendant was also convicted of the first degree murder of his wife, and we reversed that conviction on similar grounds. The jury was instructed on first degree felony murder on the theory that the homicide was committed in the course of a burglary because the defendant had entered the premises with intent to commit a felony, i.e., assault with a deadly weapon. We held that the felony-murder rule cannot apply to burglary-murder cases in which "the entry would be nonfelonious but for the intent to commit the assault, and the assault is an integral part of the homicide and is included in fact in the offense charged * * *." (*Id.* at p. 440, 82 Cal.Rptr. 494, 462 P.2d 22.) Because under *Ireland* the "elements of the assault were necessary elements of the homicide" (*id.* at p. 441, 82 Cal.Rptr. 494, 462 P.2d 22), the felony of burglary based on an intent to commit assault was included in fact in the homicide. We reasoned that "Where a person enters a building with an intent to assault his victim with a deadly weapon, he is not deterred by the felony-murder rule. That doctrine can serve its purpose only when applied to a felony independent of the homicide." (*Id.* at p. 440, 82 Cal.Rptr. 494, 462 P.2d 22.) We concluded that an instruction telling the jury that "the intent to assault makes the entry burglary and that the burglary raises the homicide resulting from the assault to first degree murder without proof of malice aforethought and premeditation" used the same bootstrap reasoning we condemned in *Ireland.* (*Id.* at p. 441, 82 Cal.Rptr. 494, 462 P.2d 22.)

In *People v. Sears* (1970) 2 Cal.3d 180, 84 Cal.Rptr. 711, 465 P.2d 847, we followed *Wilson* in a slightly different factual situation. There the defendant entered a cottage with the intent to assault his estranged wife. In the course of the assault, her daughter intervened and was killed by the defendant. The People argued that this situation was distinguishable on the ground that the felony of burglary with intent to assault the wife was "independent of the homicide" of the daughter and therefore the felony-murder rule could apply. We rejected the theory, holding that "It would be anomalous to place the person who intends to attack one person and in the course of the assault kills another inadvertently or in the heat of battle in a worse position than the person who from the outset intended to attack both persons and killed one or both. [¶] Where a defendant assaults one or more persons killing one, his criminal responsibility for the homicide should not depend upon which of the victims died but should be the greatest crime committed viewing each victim of the attack individually and without regard to which in fact died. This result is reached in application of existing principles of transferred intent, and it is unnecessary to resort to the felony-murder rule." (*Id.* at p. 189, 84 Cal.Rptr. 711, 465 P.2d 847.) *Sears* thus reiterated our view that the felony-murder rule should be applied narrowly rather than expansively.

In addition to the offenses of assault with a deadly weapon and burglary with intent to assault, the felony of discharging a firearm at an inhabited dwelling (§ 246) has also been held to merge into a resulting homicide; thus, application of the felony-murder rule in this situation is similarly prohibited. (*People v. Wesley* (1970) 10 Cal.App.3d 902, 907, 89 Cal.Rptr. 377.) The *Wesley* court reasoned that because "The discharge of the firearms by the defendants was the means by which the homicide was committed and was *in fact* an 'integral part' and a 'necessary element' of the homicide," the felony was not independent of the homicide. (*Ibid.*)

Cases in which the second degree felony-murder doctrine has withstood an *Ireland* attack include those in which the underlying felony was furnishing narcotics (Health & Saf.Code, § 11501; *People v. Taylor* (1970) 11 Cal.App.3d 57, 89 Cal.Rptr. 697); driving under the influence of narcotics (Veh.Code, § 23105; *People v. Calzada* (1970) 13 Cal.App.3d 603, 606, 91 Cal.Rptr. 912); poisoning food, drink or medicine (§ 347; *People v. Mattison* (1971) 4 Cal.3d 177, 185–186, 93 Cal.Rptr. 185, 481 P.2d 193); armed robbery (§ 211; *People v. Burton* (1971) 6 Cal.3d 375, 387, 99 Cal.Rptr. 1, 491 P.2d 793); kidnapping (§ 207; *People v. Kelso* (1976) 64 Cal.App.3d 538, 542, 134 Cal.Rptr.

364); and finally, felony child abuse by malnutrition and dehydration (§ 273a, subd. (1); *People v. Shockley* (1978) 79 Cal.App.3d 669, 145 Cal. Rptr. 200) and felony child endangering by beating (§ 273a, subd. (1); *People v. Northrop* (1982) 132 Cal.App.3d 1027, 182 Cal.Rptr. 197). With the exception of *Northrop,* however, none of these decisions involved an underlying felony that has as its principal purpose an assault on the person of the victim.

In *People v. Burton,* supra, we refined the *Ireland* rule by adding the caveat that the felony-murder doctrine may nevertheless apply if the underlying offense was committed with an "independent felonious purpose." (6 Cal.3d at 387, 99 Cal.Rptr. 1, 491 P.2d 793.) Even if the felony was included within the facts of the homicide and was integral thereto, a further inquiry is required to determine if the homicide resulted "from conduct for an independent felonious purpose" as opposed to a "single course of conduct with a single purpose" (*ibid.*). In cases like *Ireland,* the "purpose of the conduct was the very assault which resulted in death"; on the other hand, "in the case of armed robbery, as well as the other felonies enumerated in section 189 of the Penal Code, there is an independent felonious purpose, namely in the case of robbery to acquire money or property belonging to another." (*Ibid;* italics deleted.)

Our task is to apply the foregoing rules to the offense at issue here—felony child abuse defined by section 273a, subdivision (1).[4] We recognize that a violation of its terms can occur in a wide variety of situations: the definition broadly includes both active and passive conduct, i.e., child abuse by direct assault and child endangering by extreme neglect. Two threshold considerations, however, govern all types of conduct prohibited by this law: first, the conduct must be willful; second, it must be committed "under circumstances or conditions likely to produce great bodily harm or death." Absent either of these elements, there can be no violation of the statute.

The language of *Ireland, Wilson* and *Burton* bars the application of the felony-murder rule "where the purpose of the conduct was the very assault which resulted in death." (*People v. Burton,* supra, 6 Cal.3d at p. 387, 99 Cal.Rptr. 1, 491 P.2d 793.) In cases in which the violation of section 273a, subdivision (1), is a direct assault on a child that results in death (i.e., causing or permitting a child to suffer or inflicting thereon unjustifiable physical pain), it is plain that the purpose of the child abuse was the "very assault which resulted in death." It would be wholly illogical to allow this kind of assaultive child abuse to be

---

4. Section 273a, subdivision (1), provided: "Any person who, under circumstances or conditions likely to produce great bodily harm or death, willfully causes or permits any child to suffer, or inflicts thereon unjustifiable physical pain or mental suffering, or having the care or custody of any child, willfully causes or permits the person or health of such child to be injured, or willfully causes or permits such child to be placed in such situation that its person or health is endangered, is punishable by imprisonment in the county jail not exceeding 1 year, or in the state prison for not less than 1 year nor more than 10 years."

bootstrapped into felony murder merely because the victim was a child rather than an adult, as in *Ireland.*

In the present case the homicide was the result of child abuse of the assaultive variety. Thus, the underlying felony was unquestionably an "integral part of" and "included in fact" in the homicide within the meaning of *Ireland.* Furthermore, we can conceive of no independent purpose for the conduct, and the People suggest none; just as in *Ireland,* the purpose here was the very assault that resulted in death. To apply the felony-murder rule in this situation would extend it "beyond any rational function that it is designed to serve." (*People v. Washington,* supra, 62 Cal.2d 777, 783, 44 Cal.Rptr. 442, 402 P.2d 130.) We reiterate that the ostensible purpose of the felony-murder rule is not to deter the underlying felony, but instead to deter negligent or accidental killings that may occur in the course of committing that felony. When a person *willfully* inflicts unjustifiable physical pain on a child under these circumstances, it is difficult to see how the assailant would be further deterred from killing negligently or accidentally in the course of that felony by application of the felony-murder rule.

In *Ireland,* we reasoned that one who violates section 245 is not deterred by the felony-murder rule. The elements of section 245 and the offense here are strikingly similar; the principal difference is that the assault prohibited by section 273a is committed on a child. Accordingly, despite our deep abhorrence of the crime of child abuse, we see no escape from our duty to apply the merger doctrine we carefully enunciated in *Ireland* and its progeny. * * *

The People argue that the present case is controlled by *People v. Shockley,* supra, 79 Cal.App.3d 669, 145 Cal.Rptr. 200, but that decision is distinguishable on its facts. In *Shockley,* the death followed from malnutrition and dehydration; by contrast, the cause of death here was unquestionably a severe beating. The *Shockley* court envisaged this very distinction when it stated that "Where the underlying felony is based on an independent felony *not related to the assault causing the murder,* a different result follows." (Id. at p. 676, 145 Cal.Rptr. 200; italics added.) Here the death of the child was directly caused by an assault that in turn was the basis of the charge of felony child abuse; on these facts, *Ireland* compels application of the merger rule.[7]

It was therefore error to give a felony-murder instruction in this case. The People cannot show that no juror relied on the erroneous instruction as the sole basis for finding defendant guilty of murder. In these circumstances it is settled that the error must be deemed prejudicial. Because we reverse on this ground, we need not reach defendant's alternate claim that felony child abuse is not a felony inherently

7. Because of this factual distinction we need not address the question whether the merger doctrine applies when the defendant is guilty of felony child abuse of the non-assaultive variety, e.g., by extreme neglect—as in *Shockley*—or by failure to intervene when a child in his care or custody is placed in life-endangering situation.

dangerous to human life within the meaning of the second degree felony-murder rule * * *.

* * *

Reversed.

Notes and Questions

1. A few jurisdictions reject the merger rule, that is, the rule that certain felonies "merge" into a subsequent homicide and thus cannot serve as the predicate for felony murder. Some explain this on the ground that the terminology, structure, or history of the state's homicide statutes indicates legislative abandonment of the rule. See State v. Beeman, 315 N.W.2d 770 (Iowa 1982), upholding a first degree felony murder instruction based on the predicate felony of "willful assault." First degree murder is defined as, among other things, killing another "while participating in a forcible felony." "Forcible felony," in turn, is defined as including "any felonious assault." See also, State v. Reams, 292 Or. 1, 636 P.2d 913 (1981) (given terms of statute, burglary did not merge into killing); State v. Jackson, 346 N.W.2d 634, 636 (Minn.1984) (legislative revision of statute without changing prior case law rejecting merger rule constituted legislative rejection of merger analysis).

2. The Georgia Supreme Court has rejected the merger rule on other grounds. Given narrow statutory definitions of manslaughter, it reasoned, deaths caused by assaultive acts but without malice could not be manslaughter. A death caused by an aggravated assault, then, "is either malice murder or felony murder, or else it is not punishable as a homicide." To avoid this result, it rejected the merger limitation on felony murder, Baker v. State, 236 Ga. 754, 758, 225 S.E.2d 269, 271–72 (1976), and has adhered to that position, Sheridan v. State, 253 Ga. 712, 324 S.E.2d 472 (1985) (felony murder conviction upheld on ground that defendant killed victim during assault with deadly weapon).

3. In People v. Jackson, 172 Cal.App.3d 1005, 218 Cal.Rptr. 637 (1985), Jackson, enraged at his child's refusal to undress, beat the child with an 18 inch long wooden dowel and killed him. He was convicted of second degree murder on the theory that death was caused during the commission of the felony of inflicting cruel or inhuman corporal punishment on a child. On appeal, this was upheld despite *Smith*. Jackson, the court reasoned, had an intent to chastise the child as well as the intent to inflict bodily harm upon him. This "collateral felonious intent" meant that the merger doctrine did not apply. The California Supreme Court denied review but ordered that the opinion of the intermediate appellate court not be officially published. 218 Cal.Rptr. at 637 n. *.

3. KILLINGS BY RESISTING VICTIMS OR PURSUING POLICE OFFICERS

Courts have had special difficulty applying the felony murder rule in situations where the "direct" or "immediate" cause of the deceased's death was an action—almost always a gunshot—of the victim of the felony or a police officer seeking to prevent the felony or pursuing the felons. Should the felony murder rule apply in these situations? Should it make any difference whether the deceased was one of the felons, a bystander, or someone else?

STATE v. CANOLA

Supreme Court of New Jersey, 1977.
73 N.J. 206, 374 A.2d 20.

CONFORD, P.J.A.D., Temporarily Assigned.

Defendant, along with three confederates, was in the process of robbing a store when a victim of the robbery, attempting to resist the perpetration of the crime, fatally shot one of the co-felons. The sole issue for our resolution is whether, under N.J.S.A. 2A:113–1, defendant may be held liable for felony murder. * * *

The facts of this case * * * may be summarized as follows. The owner of a jewelry store and his employee, in an attempt to resist an armed robbery, engaged in a physical skirmish with one of the four robbers. A second conspirator, called upon for assistance, began shooting, and the store owner returned the gunfire. Both the owner and the felon, one Lloredo, were fatally shot in the exchange, the latter by the firearm of the owner.

Defendant and two others were indicted on two counts of murder, one count of robbery and one count of having been armed during the robbery. The murder counts were based on the deaths, respectively, of the robbery victim and the co-felon. After trial on the murder counts defendant was found guilty on both and was sentenced to concurrent terms of life imprisonment. * * * Conventional formulations of the felony murder rule would not seem to encompass liability in this case. * * * A recent study of the early formulations of the felony murder rule by such authorities as Lord Coke, Foster and Blackstone and of later ones by Judge Stephen and Justice Holmes concluded that they were concerned solely with situations where the felon or a confederate did the actual killing. Comment, 24 Rutgers L.Rev. 591, 600–601 (1970); and see Commonwealth v. Redline, 391 Pa. 486, 13 A.2d 472, 480 (Sup.Ct.1958). * * *

The precise issue in the present case is whether a broader concept than the foregoing—specifically, liability of a felon for the death of a co-felon effected by one resisting the felony—is required by the language of our statute applicable to the general area of felony murder. N.J.S.A. 2A:113–1. This reads:

> If any person, in committing or attempting to commit arson, burglary, kidnapping, rape, robbery, sodomy or any unlawful act against the peace of this state, of which the probable consequences may be bloodshed, kills another, *or if the death of anyone ensues from the committing or attempting to commit any such crime or act * * * then such person so killing is guilty of murder.* (emphasis added).

* * *

Before attempting, through analysis of the statutory language itself, a resolution of the contrasting views of the statute entertained below, it will be helpful to survey the progress of the pertinent law in the other American jurisdictions. * * *

It is clearly the majority view throughout the country that, at least in theory, the doctrine of felony murder does not extend to a killing, although growing out of the commission of the felony, if directly attributable to the act of one other than the defendant or those associated with him in the unlawful enterprise. * * * This rule is sometimes rationalized on the "agency" theory of felony murder.[2]

A contrary view, which would attach liability under the felony murder rule for *any* death proximately resulting from the unlawful activity—even the death of a co-felon—notwithstanding the killing was by one resisting the crime, does not seem to have the present allegiance of any court. See Johnson v. State, 386 P.2d 336 (Okl.Cr.App.1963); Miers v. State, 157 Tex.Cr.R. 572, 251 S.W.2d 404 (Cr.App.1952); and Hornbeck v. State, 77 So.2d 876 (Fla.Sup.Ct.1955), in all of which either an officer or other innocent person was killed. * * *

At one time the proximate cause theory was espoused by the Pennsylvania Supreme Court, Commonwealth v. Moyer, 357 Pa. 181, 53 A.2d 736 (Sup.Ct.1947) (murder conviction for death of gas station attendant in exchange of gunfire during robbery, without proof that a felon fired fatal shot); Commonwealth v. Almeida, 362 Pa. 596, 68 A.2d 595 (Sup.Ct.1949); cert. den. 339 U.S. 924, 70 S.Ct. 614, 94 L.Ed. 1346, reh. den. 339 U.S. 950, 70 S.Ct. 798, 94 L.Ed. 1364, cert. den. 340 U.S. 867, 71 S.Ct. 83, 95 L.Ed. 633 (1950).[3] The reasoning of the *Almeida* decision, involving the killing of a policeman shot by other police attempting to apprehend robbers, was distinctly circumvented when the question later arose whether it should be applied to an effort to inculpate a defendant for the killing of his co-felon at the hands of the victim of the crime. Commonwealth v. Redline, 391 Pa. 486, 137 A.2d 472 (Sup.Ct.1958). The court there held against liability. Examining the common-law authorities relied upon by the *Almeida* majority, the *Redline* court concluded:

> As already indicated, *Almeida* was, itself, an extension of the felony-murder doctrine by judicial decision and is not to be extended in its application beyond facts such as those to which it was applied.

2. The classic statement of the theory is found in an early case applying it in a context pertinent to the case at bar, Commonwealth v. Campbell, 89 Mass. (7 Allen) 541, 544 (Sup.Jud.Ct.1863), as follows:

No person can be held guilty of homicide unless the act is either actually or constructively his, and it cannot be his act in either sense unless committed by his own hand or by someone acting in concert with him or in furtherance of a common object or purpose.

3. Criticized in the leading commentary supporting adherence to the agency theory of felony murder, Morris, "The Felon's Responsibility For The Lethal Acts Of Others", 105 U.Pa.L.Rev. 50 (1956); in accord with such criticism, see also Ludwig, "Foreseeable Death In Felony Murder", 18 U.Pitt.L.Rev. 51 (1956); Comment, 71 Harv.L.Rev. 1565 (1958); Comment, 106 U.Pa.L.Rev. 1176 (1958).

137 A.2d at 482. The court then held that *"in order to convict for felony-murder, the killing must have been done by the defendant or by an accomplice or confederate or by one acting in furtherance of the felonious undertaking."* 137 A.2d at 476 (emphasis in original). The court refused, however, actually to overrule the *Almeida* decision, thereby creating a distinction (although the opinion indicates it was a halfhearted one; 137 A.2d at 483) between the situation in which the victim was an innocent party and the killing therefore merely "excusable" and that in which the deceased was a felon and the killing thus "justifiable".[4] Twelve years later the Pennsylvania court did overrule *Almeida* in a case involving Almeida's companion, Smith. (Commonwealth ex rel. Smith v. Myers, 438 Pa. 218, 261 A.2d 550 (Sup.Ct.1970)). The court noted, inter alia, the harsh criticism leveled against the common-law felony rule, its doubtful deterrent effect, the failure of the cases cited in *Almeida* to support the conclusions reached therein, the inappropriateness of tort proximate-cause principles to homicide prosecution, and the "will-of-the-wisp" distinction drawn by the *Almeida* court between justifiable and excusable homicides. 261 A.2d at 553–558. It concluded, "beyond a shadow of a doubt * * * *Almeida* and *Thomas* [Commonwealth v. Thomas, 382 Pa. 639, 117 A.2d 204] constituted iberrations [sic] in the annals of Anglo-American adjudicature." Id. at 553.

* * *

To be distinguished from the situation before us here, and from the generality of the cases discussed above, are the so-called "shield" cases. The first of these were the companion cases of Taylor v. State, 41 Tex. Cr.R. 564, 55 S.W. 961 (Cr.App.1900) aff'd 63 S.W. 330 (Cr.App.1901), and Keaton v. State, 41 Tex.Cr.R. 621, 57 S.W. 1125 (Cr.App.1900). In attempting to escape after robbing a train, defendants thrust the brakeman in front of them as a shield, as a result of which he was fatally shot by law officers. The court had no difficulty in finding defendants guilty of murder. * * * In *Keaton,* the court said defendant would be responsible for the "reasonable, natural and probable result of his act" of placing deceased in danger of his life. 57 S.W. at 1129. The conduct of the defendants in cases such as these is said to reflect "express malice", justifying a murder conviction.

This review of the development in this country of the felony murder rule in relation to culpability for lethal acts of non-felons shows that, despite its early limitation to deadly acts of the felons themselves or their accomplices, the rule has undergone several transformations and can no longer be stated in terms of universal application. As one commentator noted, it appears from the reported cases that up until 1922 all cases in the general field denied liability; the period from 1922 to 1935 was one of vacillation; and cases from 1935 * * * to 1956

---

4. Although * * * this distinction survives in a few jurisdictions, it has been criticized in principle, since, *inter alia,* the criminal immunity or liability of the third person killer is irrelevant to the criminal culpability of the accused felon. See Comment, 71 Harv.L.Rev. 1565, 1566 (1958). * * *

tended to impose liability on the grounds of proximate causation where the defendant knew that forceful resistance could be expected. *Morris,* supra, 105 U.Pa.L.Rev. at 57, note 40. But when the Pennsylvania court in *Redline,* supra, overruled its prior holding of liability, in apparent return to the original position of the common law, a number of other jurisdictions followed suit, and the trend since has been towards nonliability; see Annot., cit. supra (56 A.L.R.3d 237).

Reverting to our immediate task here, it is to determine whether our own statute necessarily mandates the proximate cause concept of felony murder * * *. [T]he view of the Appellate Division was that the "ensues clause" of N.J.S.A. 2A:113–1 must be deemed to have expanded the culpability of the felon to killings by others not confederated with him, if proximately related to the felonious enterprise, else the clause would be meaningless surplusage in the act. However, other plausible motivations for the ensues clause can be postulated consistent with a legislative intent to adhere to the traditional limitations of the felony murder doctrine.

Judge Handler, dissenting below, suggested that the purpose of the clause might have been to expand the class of victims of the felon's acts to cover all killings within the res gestae of the felony, even if they formerly would have been considered too distant to be connected therewith, so long as in furtherance of the felony. 135 N.J.Super. at 238, 343 A.2d 110. This view is also advanced by the Comment in Rutgers L.Rev., op.cit. supra (24 Rutgers L.Rev. at 606). It seems to us, moreover, that the ensues clause could well have been intended to ensure effectuation of either or both of the following concomitants of the traditional felony murder rule: (a) that accidental or fortuitous homicides "ensuing" from the felony were contemplated for inclusion, the purpose of the statutory language being to repel the inference of a requisite of intent to kill, normally associated with the unqualified word "kill" as used in the initial clause of the section; and (b) that liability extend to acts of or participation by the accomplice of the killer-felon, as well as those of the killer himself.

* * *

Finally, it is inescapable that the ensues clause is connected with the conclusion of the section, "then such person so killing is guilty of murder". This fortifies the view that even as to a death which "ensues" from the commission or attempt to commit the felony, liability for murder is intended to be restricted to the person "so killing", i.e., the felon or his agents, not third persons, conformably with the limitation of the Pennsylvania *Redline* doctrine.

* * *

With such background, and assuming the statute is facially susceptible of the interpretation here advocated by the State, it is appropriate to consider the public policy implications of the proposed doctrine as an extension of prior assumptions in this State as to the proper limitations of the felony murder rule.

Most modern progressive thought in criminal jurisprudence favors restriction rather than expansion of the felony murder rule. A leading text states: "The felony murder rule is somewhat in disfavor at the present time. The courts apply it when the law requires, but they do so grudgingly and tend to restrict its application where the circumstances permit." Perkins on Criminal Law (2d ed. 1969) 44. It has frequently been observed that although the rule was logical at its inception, when all felonies were punishable by death, its survival to modern times when other felonies are not thought to be as blameworthy as premeditated killings is discordant with rational and enlightened views of criminal culpability and liability. Id. at 44; Comments to A.L.I. Model Penal Code, Tentative Draft No. 9 (1959), Section 201.2, p. 37 * * *.

The final report of the New Jersey Criminal Law Revision Commission was, however, unwilling totally to reject the felony murder rule, concluding instead:

> It is true that we have no way of knowing how many of the homicides resulting in felony murder convictions were committed purposefully, knowingly or recklessly and how many were negligent or accidental. But it is our belief that this rule of law does lead some to refuse to assume a homicidal risk in committing other crimes. Vol. II Commentary, New Jersey Penal Code, p. 158.

The proposed New Jersey Penal Code * * * confines the rule to deaths caused by the felon or his co-felons "in the course of and in furtherance of [the felony]." New Jersey Penal Code § 2C:11–3 (Final Report 1971). This is standard "agency theory" formulation and would seem intended to exclude liability for acts of persons other than felons or co-felons though generally arising out of the criminal episode.

In view of all of the foregoing, it appears to us regressive to extend the application of the felony murder rule beyond its classic common-law limitation to acts by the felon and his accomplices, to lethal acts of third persons not in furtherance of the felonies scheme. The language of the statute does not compel it, and, as indicated above, is entirely compatible with the traditional limitations of the rule. Tort concepts of foreseeability and proximate cause have shallow relevance to culpability for murder in the first degree. Gradations of criminal liability should accord with degree of moral culpability for the actor's conduct. See the compelling thesis for rejection of the proximate cause theory of felony murder by Professor Morris in the article cited above, 105 U.Pa. L.Rev., esp. at 67–68.

It is our judgment that if the course of the law as understood and applied in this State for almost 200 years is to be altered so drastically, it should be by express legislative enactment.

The judgment of the Appellate Division is modified so as to strike the conviction and sentencing of defendant for murder of the co-felon Lloredo.

SULLIVAN, J. (concurring in result only).

The practical result of the majority holding is that even though some innocent person or a police officer be killed during the commission of an armed robbery, the felon would bear no criminal responsibility of any kind for that killing as long as it was not at the hand of the felon or a confederate. The legislative intent, as I see it, is otherwise.

The thrust of our felony murder statute, N.J.S.A. 2A:113–1, is to hold the criminal liable for any killing which ensues during the commission of a felony, even though the felon, or a confederate, did not commit the actual killing. The only exception I would recognize would be the death of a co-felon, which could be classified as a justifiable homicide and not within the purview of the statute.

The Legislature should act promptly to clarify the situation resulting from the majority opinion. If it does not extend the felony murder statute to encompass a killing during the commission of a felony not at the hand of the felon or confederate, it should, at least, provide that the felon be chargeable with manslaughter for such killing (in addition to liability for the felony).

I therefore concur in the result but only for the reason stated above.

HUGHES, C.J., dissenting.

I respectfully dissent from the opinion of the majority here, and would affirm the decision of the Appellate Division, 135 N.J.Super. 224, 343 A.2d 110, for the precise reasons stated in its majority opinion. I certainly believe that what was there referred to as the "ensues clause" can have no other logical or legislatively intended meaning than to extend criminal liability, in a causative sense, to death which ensues or is proximately caused by initiation and furtherance of the felony. This on the concept stated by the Appellate Division:

> The proximate cause theory, simply stated, is that when a felon sets in motion a chain of events which were or should have been within his contemplation when the motion was initiated, the felon, and those acting in concert with him, should be held responsible for any death which by direct and almost inevitable consequences results from the initial criminal act. [State v. Canola, 135 N.J.Super. 224, 235, 343 A.2d 110, 116 (1975)].

Resistance whether by victim or police, and even unintended or accidental deaths which occur in the confused res gestae of violent felony, can hardly be deemed outside the contemplation of the initiator of such criminal violence.

Notes and Questions

1. The courts remain split as to the applicability of the felony murder rule to this situation. Several courts have followed what they have identified as the trend towards or an existing majority approach imposing no felony murder liability. State v. Crane, 247 Ga. 779, 279 S.E.2d 695 (1981) (resisting burglary victim shot and killed one of burglars); Campbell

v. State, 293 Md. 438, 444 A.2d 1034 (1982) (cab driver and police officer shot at two men attempting to rob cab driver; facts unclear as to which shots killed one of robbers). *Crane* was applied to preclude felony murder liability where a police officer's return gunfire struck and killed a bystander. Hill v. State, 250 Ga. 277, 295 S.E.2d 518 (1982), cert. denied, 460 U.S. 1056, 103 S.Ct. 1508, 75 L.Ed.2d 936 (1983). See also, Wooden v. Commonwealth, 222 Va. 758, 284 S.E.2d 811 (1981) (no liability where resisting robbery victim shot and killed one robber). But the Missouri Supreme Court found felony murder liability where a patron in a bar being robbed resisted and killed one of the robbers. State v. Moore, 580 S.W.2d 747 (Mo. 1979), overruling State v. Majors, 237 S.W.2d 486 (Mo.1922). See also, State v. O'Dell, 684 S.W.2d 453 (Mo.App.1984) (where victim of felonious assault returned fire and killed one of those assaulting him, one of deceased's co-felons liable for felony murder).

2. Might persons like Canola be guilty of murder because of the death of their cofelons on some theory other than felony murder? The California Supreme Court held in People v. Washington, 62 Cal.2d 777, 44 Cal.Rptr. 442, 402 P.2d 130 (1965), that the felony murder rule could not be invoked to hold one felon liable for the death of his cofelon occasioned by resistance to the underlying robbery by the victim. It noted, however:

> Defendants who initiate gun battles may also be found guilty of murder if their victims resist and kill. Under such circumstances, "the defendant for a base, anti-social motive and with wanton disregard for human life, does an act that involves a high degree of probability that it will result in death" * * *, and it is unnecessary to imply malice by invoking the felony-murder doctrine.

62 Cal.2d at 782, 44 Cal.Rptr. at 446, 402 P.2d at 134. This possibility was developed in Taylor v. Superior Court, 3 Cal.3d 578, 91 Cal.Rptr. 275, 477 P.2d 131 (1970) (Taylor I). Taylor waited outside a liquor store while his companions, Smith and Daniels, went in to rob it. Smith pointed a gun at the proprietors, Mr. and Mrs. West. According to the Wests' testimony, Daniels "chattered insanely," saying to Mr. West, "Put the money in the bag. * * * Don't move or I'll blow your head off. * * * Don't move or we'll have an execution right here." Mrs. West testified that Smith appeared "intent," "apprehensive," and as if "waiting for something to happen"; his apparent apprehension and nervousness were manifested by the manner in which he stared at Mr. West. As Smith and Daniels were forcing the Wests to lie on the floor, the Wests obtained weapons and shot at the robbers. Smith was fatally wounded. Taylor (and Daniels) were charged with murder. At a preliminary hearing the magistrate found probable cause to believe them guilty of murder. The magistrate's action was challenged by means of an application for a writ of prohibition. The California Supreme Court denied the writ, finding that evidence supported the magistrate's finding of probable cause. Noting that Taylor, as an accomplice to the robbery, would be vicariously responsible for any killing attributable to the intentional acts of his associates committed with "conscious disregard for life, and likely to cause death," the court concluded:

> [T]he evidence * * * discloses acts of provocation on the parts of Daniels and Smith from which the trier of fact could infer malice,

including Daniels' coercive conduct towards Mr. West and his repeated threats of "execution," and Smith's intent and nervous apprehension as held Mrs. West at gunpoint. The foregoing conduct was sufficiently provocative of lethal resistance to lead a man of ordinary caution and prudence to conclude that Smith "initiated" the gun battle, or that such conduct was done with conscious disregard for human life and with natural consequences dangerous to life.

3 Cal.3d at 584, 91 Cal.Rptr. at 279, 477 P.2d at 135. Prior to Taylor's trial on the merits of the charge, however, Daniels was tried; he was convicted of robbery but acquitted of murder. Taylor was nevertheless tried and convicted of both robbery and murder. On appeal, the conviction for murder was reversed on the ground that the state was collaterally estopped by Daniels' acquittal from obtaining Taylor's conviction for murder on the theory that Taylor was vicariously liable for a murder committed by Daniels. People v. Taylor, 12 Cal.3d 686, 117 Cal.Rptr. 70, 527 P.2d 622 (1974) (Taylor II).

If a defendant may be convicted under the *Washington-Taylor I* theory, is the offense first or second degree murder under the California statutory scheme (see page 379, supra)? In Pizano v. Superior Court, 21 Cal.3d 128, 145 Cal.Rptr. 524, 577 P.2d 659 (1978), the court made clear that a conviction of first degree murder would be permissible. The majority reasoned that Section 189 of the Penal Code made any murder "committed in the perpetration of, or attempt to perpetrate" the enumerated felonies first degree murder. This was held controlling, even though the theory on which the killing was murder was not first degree felony murder but rather "implied malice." 21 Cal.3d at 139 n. 4, 145 Cal.Rptr. at 530–31 n. 4, 577 P.2d at 665 n. 4. The dissenters would limit those killings raised to first degree murder by the language quoted above to felony murders based upon felonies enumerated in the statute. 21 Cal.3d at 142–43, 145 Cal.Rptr. at 533, 577 P.2d at 668.

The rule was somewhat limited in People v. Antick, 15 Cal.3d 79, 123 Cal.Rptr. 475, 539 P.2d 43 (1975). According to the prosecution's evidence, Antick and Bose had been involved in a burglary. When they were questioned by a police officer, Bose drew a gun and fired at the officer. The officer returned the fire, killing Bose. Antick was convicted of first degree murder, on the *Washington-Taylor I* theory; he did not personally participate in the gun battle and thus could not be found liable on the basis of his own acts. On appeal, the California Supreme Court reversed, reasoning that Antick could be vicariously liable under the *Washington-Taylor I* rule only if there was a cofelon who himself was—or could be—criminally responsible for the killing. Heavy reliance was placed on *Taylor II*. The court explained:

In order to predicate defendant's guilt upon this theory, it is necessary to prove that Bose committed a murder * * *, in other words, that he caused the death of another human being [and] that he acted with malice. * * *

It is well settled that Bose's conduct in initiating a shootout with police officers may establish the requisite malice. * * * However, Bose's malicious conduct did not result in the unlawful killing of another human being, but rather in Bose's own death. The only homicide which occurred was the justifiable killing of Bose by the police officer. Defendant's criminal liability certainly cannot be predicated upon the actions of the officer. As Bose could not be found guilty of murder in connection with his own death, it is impossible to base defendant's liability for this offense upon his vicarious responsibility for the crime of his accomplice.

15 Cal.3d at 90–91, 123 Cal.Rptr. at 482, 539 P.2d at 50.

The *Washington-Taylor I* approach was reaffirmed by the California court in People v. Caldwell, 36 Cal.3d 210, 203 Cal.Rptr. 433, 681 P.2d 274 (1984). A robbery defendant's conviction of "depraved mind" murder for the death of a cofelon was upheld on a similar theory by the New York Court of Appeals. People v. Brathwaite, 63 N.Y.2d 839, 482 N.Y.S.2d 253, 472 N.E.2d 29 (1984). But this approach was rejected by the Nevada Supreme Court in Sheriff, Clark County v. Hicks, 89 Nev. 78, 506 P.2d 766 (1973), relying in part upon the trial judge's comment that, "A rose, the felon[y] murder rule, is still a rose by any other name * * *." In *Caldwell,* Chief Justice Bird criticized the California Supreme Court's application of the *Washington-Taylor I* analysis. The majority's willingness to find sufficiently provoking conduct to show "implied malice" murder, she suggested, "seriously undermine[s] the well-established principle that the felony-murder rule does not apply to killings committed by persons other than the felons themselves." 36 Cal.3d at 266, 203 Cal.Rptr. at 443, 681 P.2d at 284 (Bird, C.J., dissenting).

3. As the court in *Canola* indicates, the "shield" cases can be resolved without reference to felony murder. But the felony aspect of these cases may nevertheless present problems. In Pizano v. Superior Court, 21 Cal.3d 128, 145 Cal.Rptr. 524, 577 P.2d 659 (1978), Pizano and Esquivel were interrupted by Cuna, a private citizen, during the robbery of Vaca. Pizano opened the door of the house and ran out, followed by Esquivel who forced Vaca at gunpoint to precede him. Without realizing Vaca was present, Cuna opened fire with his gun; Vaca was killed. Pizano was charged with murder and sought dismissal of the charge. He acknowledged that Esquivel's actions in using Vaca as a shield or hostage were acts from which malice could be implied. But he argued that it is necessary that the killing be attributable to those actions of the defendant which evidence the disregard for life from which malice is implied. Since Cuna opened fire without realizing that Esquivel was using Vaca as a shield, he urged, the killing of Vaca cannot be said to be attributable to the acts of the defendants from which malice is implied. Cuna fired solely to prevent the robbery, and a death caused by such action is insufficient to create liability for murder. The California Supreme Court denied relief. For the killing to be murder, it reasoned, the use of the victim as a shield rather than the felony itself must have proximately caused the victim's death. Whether the shot was fired in response to the felony alone or in response to the defendants' malicious acts is not controlling, and on the facts of the case a trier of fact could properly conclude that Vaca's death was proximately caused by Esquivel's malicious conduct in using him as a shield.

See also, Jackson v. State, 286 Md. 430, 408 A.2d 711 (1979) (fleeing armed robbers may be convicted of first degree felony murder for the accidental killing of a hostage by officer seeking to apprehend robbers who were holding hostages at gunpoint).

Chapter VIII

GENERAL PRINCIPLES OF CRIM-INAL LIABILITY: RESULTS AND THE REQUIREMENT OF CAUSATION

Contents

Editors' Introduction: "Results" and "Causation" in Criminal Liability

A number of crimes, including but by no means restricted to the homicide offenses, require proof of the occurrence of a result and of a causal relationship between the defendant's acts and that result. Problems of causation—especially of so-called "proximate" causation—present some of the most perplexing matters with which the substantive criminal law must deal. These problems will, almost always, involve questions of grading rather than responsibility. That is, a negative answer to the question of whether the accused was the "cause" of the harm will seldom leave the accused totally exculpated. In some cases, the accused will have intended or been reckless or negligent with respect to some other criminal act or result. In many cases, a finding of no causation will have no effect upon the accused's liability for attempt.

Enormous effort has been devoted to trying to resolve issues of causation, not only in the criminal law but also, of course, for purposes of torts. A landmark effort to address these questions is Hart and Honore, Causation in the Law (2nd ed. 1985); Chapters XII–XIV are specifically directed to the substantive criminal law. These efforts are expended even though causation issues arise with relative infrequency in criminal cases. The reason for such exertions in addressing seldom-arising issues may be that we are deeply troubled when the particular result which has occurred and provides the basis for the prosecution carries a significantly higher penalty than the defendant's acts and their normal result would carry, or because the connection between the result and the defendant's acts is so attenuated that we are doubtful as to the ethical propriety of imposing the penalty attached to the particular result.

In the reported case law, causation issues are most frequently, and perhaps almost always, presented in the context of criminal homicide. But they may arise in any situation involving an offense that requires proof of an element that is properly characterized as involving a "result." Moreover, modern codes, following the lead of the Model Penal Code, address causation as a general principle rather than as a problem unique to homicide liability. See § 2.03 of the Model Penal Code, reprinted at page 483, infra in this chapter. Given that causation analysis is generally developed in homicide litigation, it may be worth while asking whether principles developed in such litigation adequately serve as a basis for resolving causation issues when they arise in non-homicide contexts.

Under modern criminal codes, the crime of robbery is quite often graded according to—among other considerations—whether harm was inflicted, and an offense consisting of robbery resulting in physical harm may, of course, raise causation problems. Several cases have arisen under the Indiana robbery statute, which provides that robbery is generally a class B or C felony. But it is a class A felony "if it results in either bodily injury or serious bodily injury to any other person." Ind.Code § 35–42–5–1. Consider the following situations arising from the application of this provision:

> Bailey and his companion met Ott and Guyden in a bar. The four left the bar together. Bailey held a knife to Ott's throat, Bailey's companion took Ott's wallet, and Bailey and his companion fled. Ott and Guyden chased them and caught up with them about thirty minutes later and several blocks away. Guyden approached Bailey and in a struggle Bailey wounded Guyden with his knife. Bailey urged that the connection between the robbery and the injury to Guyden had become so attenuated that the robbery did not result in the injury to Guyden within the meaning of the statute and thus the robbery was not a class A felony. Bailey v. State, 274 Ind. 318, 412 N.E.2d 56 (1980).

Moon, carrying a revolver, and a "machete-bearing accomplice," entered the Brookside Market in Indianapolis. Moon fired a shot at the ceiling and demanded money from the cashier. A patron, startled by the shot, bolted down an aisle. Moon's accomplice pursued him. The chase took the duo near a window connecting the store with the owner's living quarters; the owner had been watching the events through the window. As the accomplice prepared to swing his machete at the patron, the owner pushed the window open and fired five shots at the accomplice. One shot hit the accomplice, who—together with Moon—fled the premises. In the aftermath, it was discovered that another of the shots had ricocheted and hit the cashier in the leg. Moon v. State, 275 Ind. 651, 419 N.E.2d 740 (1981).

Larry and his companions fled from the scene of a robbery; police pursued them. Shots were exchanged. Lieutenant Norton and another officer, as a result of radio communications, were attempting to "head off" the robbers. But because of icy conditions, their car slid through the intersection they intended to block. But the officers jumped out and ran to the intersection. As Norton arrived at the intersection on foot, the robbers' car appeared and swerved towards him. In attempting to get out of the way, he slipped and fell on the pavement; the robbers' car barely missed striking him. As a result of the fall, Norton received bruises on his upper legs and buttocks. Larry v. State, 477 N.E.2d 94 (Ind.1985). Suppose Norton had been injured when his vehicle had slid through the intersection? Suppose, as Norton had alighted from his disabled police vehicle, he had been struck by an intoxicated driver?

Can these problems be resolved by application of principles of causation developed in case law arising from homicide situations?

In studying the materials which follow, consider whether the terminology of causation is really helpful to the adequate resolution of the various issues presented. Would it be possible and, if so, more helpful to deal with these issues by application of principles of culpability or state of mind analysis?

WEINREB, COMMENT ON BASIS OF CRIMINAL LIABILITY; CULPABILITY; CAUSATION

In 1 Working Papers of the National Commission On Reform of
Federal Criminal Laws
142–43 (1970).

The principles governing attribution of consequences to a person's conduct for purposes of criminal liability are not ordinarily stated collectively as a coherent body of doctrine. Still less often have such principles been codified.   *   *   *

If anything but for which an event would not have occurred is a cause of the event, there are any number of "causes" of every event. The presence of oxygen in the air and the physical properties of paper are as much causes, in that sense, of the burning of a piece of paper as is touching a lit match to the paper. When we select a cause as *the cause,* the selection is based on some principle that reflects our interests. By making the selection, we focus our attention on some aspect of the situation, usually one which we think is under our control, so that we can assure or prevent a repetition of the occurrence. If someone drops a cup and it breaks, we are more likely to say "You should be more careful," than to say "I wish the floor were not so hard"; but if an infant drops the cup, we are likely to say "We'll have to get him a plastic cup," instead of "He really must not drop things." As a crude and preliminary approximation of ordinary speech and understanding it is fair to say that we distinguish the cause of an event from the (necessary) conditions of an event according to our interests, which usually but not always means that we single out as the "cause" some element of the situation which we can control and describe as "conditions" other necessary elements. Some necessary conditions are taken so much for granted—for example, the presence of oxygen in the air, the physical properties of paper—that unless some curious feature of the situation focuses our attention on them, we do not mention them even as conditions. Without some frame of reference, the question, "What is (are) the cause(s) of X?" is as meaningless as the question, "What are all the conditions but for which X would not have occurred?" Ordinarily the frame of reference is clear and is supplied by commonsense out of common experience.

The inadequacy of principles of causation in the criminal law reflects uncertainty about the basis of criminal liability in situations where results are important to liability. We are not certain whether the assailant who gives the hemophiliac a light blow that causes a bruise from which the hemophiliac dies should be punished for assault or homicide; or whether all the senators should be punished as Caesar's murderers even though any dozen could have stayed away from the Forum on the fateful day without changing the result.

MATTER OF J.N.

District of Columbia Court of Appeals, 1979.
406 A.2d 1275.

NEBEKER, ASSOCIATE JUDGE:

Although these two cases arose from the same occurrence they were tried and were appealed separately. They are here consolidated for disposition. As each defendant raises different issues on appeal, we meet the concerns of each in sequence.

APPELLANT PARKER

Following a jury trial, the defendant was adjudged guilty of murder in the second degree under D.C.Code 1973, § 22–2401 [, apparently on the ground that he killed the victim "without purpose to do so * * * in perpetrating * * * robbery"]. He seeks a new trial on the ground

that the trial judge failed to instruct the jury (1) that, if it concluded
that a doctor's termination of the victim's life support system constituted willful or intentional malpractice or was an "abnormal" response to
the victim's condition, it should find the defendant not guilty; and (2)
that, if it found that the victim would have lived for more than a year
and a day but for the termination of the life support system, it should
find the defendant not guilty. We affirm.

I

On January 13, 1976, the appellant and three others attempted to
snatch a purse from an 85-year-old woman. When the appellant
latched onto the purse, the victim recoiled, whereupon she was struck
from behind by one of the appellant's companions. The blow caused
the victim to fall forward to the sidewalk. The band fled without the
purse. A bystander found the injured woman conscious and able to
talk. By the time the police arrived, she was unable to respond and an
ambulance carried her to a hospital. There she was administered to by
a resident and thereafter by a neurosurgeon. Upon arrival at the
hospital the victim was able to talk. Her condition, however, quickly
degenerated to where she could neither speak nor respond to verbal
commands. After 24 hours in the hospital, she exhibited only primitive
reflexes to stimuli. She failed to improve. Six days later, on January
19, on the basis of the patient's condition and her age, after consultation with other physicians involved in the case and upon agreement by
the victim's son, the neurosurgeon discontinued all "heroic measures." [1]
The woman died fifteen to twenty minutes later.

II

The trial judge properly refused to instruct the jury on the defense's theory that discontinuing the "heroic measures" may have
constituted an "intervening cause" of death [2] so as to insulate the
defendant from homicide liability. Although no specific instruction
was requested, the defendant suggests in his brief that the court could
have properly instructed the jury as follows:

> If you find that the Government has proved beyond a reasonable doubt
> all the other elements of the offense and that the defendant caused [the
> victim's] death, it is your duty to find the defendant guilty of murder.
> If, on the other hand, you find that the Government has failed to prove
> beyond a reasonable doubt that the defendant caused [the victim's]
> death because the actions of [the physician] constituted *intentional or*

---

1. Heroic measures were defined at
trial as

> [m]easures that are other than normal
> supportive care. For example normal
> supportive care would be assuring that
> the patient has food to eat, that they
> have clothing to keep them warm, to
> prevent pneumonia. What I consider
> heroic in this case was infusions of drugs
> in order to reduce the pressure in the

head, maintenance of the patient on a
machine, when there was no obvious response to those measures of therapy in
the sense of improvement in the patient's condition.

2. All agree that under any legally accepted definition of death, the victim was
not dead when the "heroic measures" were
discontinued.

willful malpractice or were an *abnormal response to the situation* caused by the defendant's acts, then you must find the defendant not guilty of murder. [Emphasis added.]

For such an instruction to have been proper, evidence must have been presented (1) to resolve the issue of what constitutes "intentional or willful malpractice" or an "abnormal response," and (2) to demonstrate that the actions of the attending physician breached that standard. *E.g., Haven v. Randolph*, 161 U.S.App.D.C. 150, 152, 494 F.2d 1069, 1070 (1974) (per curiam) * * *. In this case, there is no evidentiary basis for the kind of instruction now proposed.

The situation is analogous to a tort claim for medical malpractice. With one exception, a jury is permitted to find a physician liable in tort for malpractice only when the standard of care has been established by expert testimony. * * *

The medical conduct here involved does not, "as a matter of common knowledge and observation," constitute the requisite malpractice. The exception applies only where "a physician has committed a blunder so egregious that a layman is capable of comprehending its enormity. An example is the case of a surgeon who leaves a sponge in an incision after the removal of a kidney." *Haven v. Randolph, supra* 161 U.S.App.D.C. at 152, 494 F.2d at 1070, *citing Rodgers v. Lawson*, 83 U.S.App.D.C. 281, 284–85, 170 F.2d 157, 160–61 (1948). On facts quite similar to those here, however, an Illinois intermediate appellate court recently ruled that a physician's discontinuance of heroic measures was "reasonable" medical care.

> Defendant's contention that the evidence failed to prove beyond a reasonable doubt that the victim died of the wounds from the gunshot is without merit. When the victim was brought to the hospital, his pulse was minimal. The neurosurgeon who examined him testified that the bullet had damaged a major portion of his brain and that he then exhibited many signs of death. The doctor's decision to withdraw life support measures was reasonable. [*People v. Olson*, 60 Ill.App.3d 535, 538, 18 Ill.Dec. 218, 222, 377 N.E.2d 371, 374–75 (1978).]

We need not hold that the doctor's actions were reasonable because that issue is not before us. It appears clear, however, that they were not so unreasonable, as a matter of common knowledge, as to be grossly negligent or worse.

The legal and medical authorities, cited in the briefs, confirm the conclusion that the facts here do not fall within the exception to the requirement of expert testimony. The government, on one hand, cites authorities to support the proposition that the neurosurgeon's action was reasonable as a matter of law. The defense, on the other hand, quotes from authorities holding the position that it is per se unreasonable for doctors, after consulting with a patient's family, to discontinue artificial life support measures. The lack of consensus among the cited authorities undermines the conclusion that the physician's actions here constituted gross malpractice as a matter of common knowledge.

* * *

The defense * * * contends * * * that no testimony, other than the facts of the physician's action of disconnecting the respirator, would have been necessary to support a verdict based on "superseding cause." Implicit in this argument is the concession that no expert testimony went to establish that the terminating action was anything but reasonable. Consequently, there being no evidentiary predicate for the instruction now proposed, we are unable to conclude that error warranting reversal has been demonstrated. * * *

III

The trial court did not err in failing to instruct the jury as follows:

If you find that with medical care [the victim] would have survived a year and a day, then you may not find him guilty of murder. But if you don't find that she wouldn't [sic] survive for a year and a day, then you may.

The year and a day rule is in force in the District of Columbia, having been adopted under D.C.Code 1973, § 49–301, from the common law. * * * *Louisville, Evansville and St. Louis R.R. v. Clarke*, 152 U.S. 230, 239, 14 S.Ct. 579, 581, 38 L.Ed. 422 (1894) (year and a day rule is in force "in this country" unless statutorily modified). Although the rule has been variously stated, it is essentially that "no person should be adjudged 'by any act whatever to kill another who does not die by it within a year and a day thereafter.'" *Id.* Although this rule is a part of the law of the District, it does not absolve the appellant from liability for murder on the record before us because (1) the victim died within a year and a day of the assault and robbery and (2) there was no evidence upon which a reasonable juror could have concluded that the victim would have lived for a year and a day.

The rule provides for a time beyond which, the courts at common law determined, the prosecution could not, as a matter of law, prove that the unlawful act caused the victim's death. *Id.*, *quoting* 3 Coke, Inst. 53. Under the rule, if the victim expires after the designated time, the defendant is not required to show that the death ensued from something other than his act. His misdeed is per se excluded from the possible causes of death. By its terms and its purpose, however, the rule is inapplicable where the victim dies within a year. Where, as in this case, the victim dies within a year, the defendant may be entitled to an intervening cause instruction, but the time period of a year and a day, and the year and a day rule would be improper subjects of instruction. *See Hopkins v. United States*, 4 App.D.C. 430, 439 (1894) (year and a day rule does not absolve one from liability for "homicide or murder" if death occurs within a year and a day, although proper treatment may have prolonged life beyond that time). Therefore, because the appellant's victim died within a year and a day of the infliction of the wound, this case is without the ambit of the rule, and no reversal is warranted.

The appellant is not prejudiced here by a misunderstanding of the law because, on the record, there was no evidence that the victim would have lived for a year and a day. The only relevant testimony, which the defense attorney elicited from the neurosurgeon and which appears to be dispositive of the defense's contention, is set forth below.[6] The defendant points to the italicized portion as the sole testimony regarding the rule because only it refers explicitly to the year and a day time period. We do not read it so narrowly. No reasonable juror could have concluded, on the basis of this testimony, that the victim would probably have survived for a year and a day.

IV

Our holding in this case is limited. We neither endorse nor condemn the neurosurgeon's actions. No mention has been made of the legal definition of "death" in the District of Columbia. As a matter of law, according to the evidence presented at trial, the defendant was not insulated from homicide culpability. The defendant's conviction is

Affirmed.

APPELLANT J.N.

The appellant has been convicted of attempted robbery under D.C. Code 1973, § 22–2902, and of felony murder under D.C.Code 1973, § 22–2401. He seeks reversal of both convictions because * * * the actions of the physician attending the victim constituted an "intervening cause" that insulates him from liability for murder as a matter of law. We affirm.

*   *   *

6. The following took place during the cross-examination of the neurosurgeon by the defense counsel:

Q. She had a vegetative existence; is that correct?

*   *   *

A. As I explained before, given her age and her clinical appearance at that time, I did not feel the patient would survive.

Q. Had you during the studies of medicine ever heard of anybody surviving, for let us say, a year and a day?

A. *Well, define that. I mean if you take anyone—you could have someone that is five years old. And the answer to that would be yes.*

Q. *All right. In other words, a person could survive for a year and a day in a vegetative condition?*

A. *Depending on their age and various other factors. Yes.*

Q. Now, let us go to the eighty year old level—seventy-five to eighty year old level. Do you have any figures that medical science has compiled that gives statistics for people in that condition at that age that have survived?

A. No. Although, in terms of the getting back to what I was saying before in consultation with colleagues, none of my colleagues or myself have ever heard of an eighty year old, given [the victim's] condition, of surviving.

*   *   *

Q. You are giving no chance of recovery; is that right?

A. That is correct.

Q. Well, when you say no chance of recovery that is no chance of recovery as a normal person?

A. My prognosis was no chance for recovery.

[DEFENSE COUNSEL]: I have no further questions. [Emphasis added.]

＊　＊　＊ The appellant, unlike his companion Parker, touched neither the victim nor her purse. Whereas in *Parker* the issue presented was whether there was any evidence to support a specific suggested intervening cause instruction, we here face the issue of whether the appellant is insulated from liability for murder as a matter of law, the appellant having been tried without a jury. Despite these differences, *Parker* mandates that we reject this contention because there was no expert testimony at trial to support a finding that the attending physician acted inappropriately in disconnecting the life support system.

The success of the appellant's defense of "intervening cause" hinges on his demonstrating that the act, for the commission of which he stands convicted of homicide, was not a "substantial factor" contributing to the victim's death. He attempts the demonstration by defining two forces or acts that impacted upon the deceased. The first act was his, the second was not. It is incumbent on him to establish that the law regards the acts as distinct from one another. *See, e.g., Hamilton v. United States*, 102 U.S.App.D.C. 298, 252 F.2d 862 (1958) (where victim had been rendered unconscious by defendant's blow and had then been left in roadway where she was run over by a taxi, defendant liable for death). If the acts are not separate, the perpetrator of the first is held responsible for the consequences of the second and the appellant's defense fails. *Id.* If the acts are distinct, the law will not punish him except for the first act. *E.g., Hopkins v. United States, supra* at 440. Once the acts are determined to be separate, a second issue arises: whether the first act, standing alone, was a substantial factor contributing to the death.[10] If it was, then liability will attach. An adverse resolution of either of the two issues will lay the defense to rest. While the issues are listed in sequence, they may be resolved also in the reverse order.

Concerning the first issue, whether the law regards the two acts as separate, we hold that the record does not support a conclusion that the acts were separate as a matter of law. The appellant defines the first act as that which resulted in the injury to the victim's head. The discontinuance of extraordinary measures constitutes the second. The second act was performed by medical personnel acting in their role as such. Where the action of such medical personnel is either reasonable or negligent, the law holds the perpetrator of the first act liable also for the consequences of the second. For the law to deem the acts separate, the second act must descend at least below the negligence level. Testimony, establishing that medical treatment is so egregious so as to fall within the category, may generally be elicited only from experts.

10. For example, a defendant may persuade the fact finder that, subsequent to his shooting the victim, the victim was fortuitously shot again by an unknown and unrelated assailant, and that the victim died from the loss of blood from both wounds. Although the defendant may have demonstrated that he is not liable for the consequences of the acts of the second assailant, his defense of intervening cause will nevertheless fail if the wound inflicted by the defendant substantially contributed to the decedent's death.

Parker v. United States, supra. We hold that, on the record in this case, the trial judge could reasonably have concluded that the second act was a reasonable medical procedure because the sole expert testified to this effect.

* * *

Affirmed.

NEWMAN, CHIEF JUDGE, dissenting:

I respectfully dissent. In my view, the issue is, once the evidence established that Mrs. Werlich was alive at the time of removal from the respirator, whether the jury should have been instructed that the government must prove beyond a reasonable doubt that the injury Mrs. Werlich received during the robbery would have caused her to die within a year and a day from the infliction of the wound.

I

In every criminal case the government must prove each element of the offense charged beyond a reasonable doubt. As part of this burden, in a homicide case the government must show that the defendant's conduct is both the actual cause and the legal cause—or proximate cause—of the result. Actual cause means that the defendant's conduct in fact was the cause of death. Legal or proximate cause means that, although intervening occurrences may have contributed to the death, the defendant can still, in all fairness, be held criminally responsible for that death. Thus the two, if proven beyond a reasonable doubt, establish that the defendant's act was the cause of death.

In response to fact situations where two or more actors bring about one death, courts, of necessity, fashioned rules of law to determine which actor is culpable for homicide. These rules reflect an accommodation made by the courts to differing societal interests in punishing certain wrongful acts. Thus, the assailant can be convicted of homicide even though, after inflicting a blow (fatal or nonfatal), (1) the victim fails to receive or accept medical treatment; (2) the victim fails to follow physician's instructions; (3) the victim, because of his injury, takes his own life; (4) a physician administers negligent treatment; (5) or a different or more skillful treatment might have saved the victim's life.

The underlying rationale of these decisions is that the intentional wrongdoer should bear the risk of the victim's death because the aforementioned intervening acts are considered foreseeable and natural consequences of his wrongful act. Implicit in this determination of culpability is a finding that the initial wrongdoer "may fairly be held responsible for the actual result even though it does differ or happens in a different way from the intended or hazarded result." LaFave & Scott, *supra* § 35, at 248.

A more complex issue bearing on allocation of risk and punishment is presented when two or more intentional actors, not in concert, bring about the death of one victim. For example, A seriously wounds B, and, while B is dying, C shoots and kills B instantaneously. Some courts hold that A cannot be liable for homicide because to so hold would necessitate finding that the victim was killed twice. Other courts hold that both A and C can be culpable for homicide because of the combined effects of the wounds, or because the injury inflicted by the first wrongdoer would have also resulted in death without the intervening act. Nevertheless, as a general rule voluntary infliction of harm by a second actor usually suffices to break the chain of legal cause and protects the original actor from, while exposing the second actor to, culpability for the homicide. In sum, when both the original actor and the intervenor inflict harm intentionally, courts differ as to whether the first actor is culpable for homicide, but all agree that the second is culpable. The latter act is considered to have shortened the life of the victim, albeit one who is already dying, and therefore, that act becomes the legal cause of the victim's death.

Likewise, rules have been fashioned to allocate risk and punishment between an intentional wrongful act of one person followed by a grossly negligent act of another. As a general rule, gross negligence by an attending physician, which is the *sole* cause of death, will shield the first wrongful actor from homicide culpability on the theory that the wound inflicted cannot be the legal or proximate cause of death since death results from an unforeseen risk and is not a natural consequence of the wrongful act. Thus, as to the assailant, the causation element of the crime of homicide cannot be proved.

The aforementioned rules concern themselves with fact situations involving intervening acts that are negligent, grossly negligent, or intentional and wrongful. We are faced today with a different kind of intervening act, one not contemplated by courts of earlier ages. Those courts could neither envision the artificial prolongation of life on life-support systems nor contemplate the cessation of that artificially prolonged life by doctors confronted with most difficult decisions pertaining to such prolongation. * * * These are the acts which form the basis of the so-called "pull the plug" cases. These cases require of our jurisprudence an analysis of the principles underlying our legal precedents in this area of the law. We have already noted that courts are generally interested in allocating the risk of the victim's death between the several actors who in some way contribute to the death. If we strictly adhere to the settled rules, we would have to pigeonhole this intentional act in order to allocate that risk. We could term the act negligent, relieve the physician of criminal culpability, and hold the defendant liable for homicide while ignoring the fact that the physician intentionally hastened the victim's death. Alternatively, we could term the act an intentional wrong, hold the physician responsible for death, either solely or in combination with the first intentional actor, and thereby ignore the fact that the physician "is serving a socially better end than the individual risking homicide." *The Law of Homicide: Does it Require a Definition of Death?,* 11 Wake Forest L.Rev. 253, 266 (1975) [hereafter *Definition of Death*]. Clearly, the traditional concepts are not without limitations. To pull the plug on a victim is a unique act. It is an act intentionally done to shorten life. New rules and concepts must be developed not only to protect physicians from an unrealistic application of the law, but also to protect society from assailants who might escape punishment to the full extent of the law for their wrongful acts because of medical advances.

One way to accomplish this end would be to change the definition of death from a cessation of the victim's heart and lungs to a cessation of brain functioning. In this way the physician, with legal immunity, would be able to use the respirator for other patients with some hope of recovery because his conduct of pulling the plug, occurring after death, would bear no legal consequence, while the wrongdoer's conduct would expose him to homicide liability. *Definition of Death, supra* at 262.

Another theory suggests terming the physician's act as *proper* medical treatment necessitated by the injury. The act of removing a patient from a respirator would then be considered a natural consequence of the injury and would play no part in legal causation. The physician escapes liability as long as his act is proper, while the assailant can be found culpable for homicide. The majority appears to adopt a version of this theory.

II

In homicide cases, death must ensue from a mortal wound within a year and a day of its infliction. If death does not take place within that period, the law draws a conclusive presumption that the injury is not the cause of death and that death was due to natural causes. If death occurs after a year and a day there can be no prosecution for homicide. * * * § 191, at 436–37 (1957). Moreover, it is axiomatic that in a criminal case the causation element, as all other elements of the crime, is a matter for the fact finder in all circumstances. Not to allow the jury to determine causation, would be for the court to direct a partial verdict for the government and usurp the role of the jury as fact finder. To avoid this infringement on the jury's function as well as to protect the right of the defendant to a jury determination when a dispute arises concerning the cause of death, "the court may and should instruct the jury fully and clearly on the issue." 41 C.J.S. *Homicide* § 363, at 142 (1944). The refusal to give the instruction becomes reversible error where the evidence presents a theory of defense—that the injury was not the cause of death since the victim might have lived for more than a year and a day—and the court is apprised of this theory and particularly requested to so instruct the jury. *See Levine v. United States,* 104 U.S.App.D.C. 281, 282–83, 261 F.2d 747, 748–49 (1958). This rule "applies as well to situations where special facts present an evidentiary theory which if believed defeats the factual theory of the prosecution." *Id.* at 282. Further, the defendant is entitled to have the theory of defense instruction even if the evidence that forms the foundation for the theory is "weak, insufficient, inconsistent, or of doubtful credibility." *Tatum v. United States,* 88 U.S.App.D.C. 386,

391, 190 F.2d 612, 617 (1951), quoting 53 Am.Jur. *Trial* § 580, at 458 (1945). * * *

III

Having set forth the foregoing legal principles, I proceed to my disagreement with the majority opinion. As I understand its holding, it is this: Where an assailant causes injuries to a victim necessitating "heroic measures" for her treatment and a physician decides to pull the plug on the still alive victim within one year of the inflicting of such injuries, to raise a jury issue, the defendant must present evidence 1) that the doctor's conduct was wrong from a medical standpoint and 2) that the victim would have lived more than 1 year. I respectfully submit that this holding turns the appropriate allocation of the burden of proof on its head. In my view, once evidence is adduced that a conscious, intentional decision was made to terminate life by pulling the plug, it became incumbent that the government be required to prove to the jury, under proper instructions, that this act was not the proximate cause of death and was thus legally irrelevant to appellant's guilt. Stated another way, the government should have been required to prove, under proper instructions, that if the plug had not been pulled, the victim would have died within a year and a day. Whether the jury, with proper instruction, would have resolved this issue adverse to appellant is not for the court to say. No matter how slight the evidence, the jury must, with proper instruction, find that the government proved its whole case, including causation, beyond a reasonable doubt, before the conviction can stand. Since this issue was not properly framed for the jury under proper instructions, I would reverse.

J.N., Jr.

The failure of the majority to appreciate and properly analyze the alleged error committed by the trial court is more apparent in J.N., Jr.'s case where the trial court precluded any testimony bearing on the fact that the victim was alive at the time of removal from the respirator. The record only reveals, from testimony of the treating neurosurgeon, that

> [a]fter seven days, it was determined that the patient's brain function was irreversibly damaged [and that] it was elected not to pursue additional heroic measures, and therefore, that therapy * * * and other variety of operational procedures were not carried out. And, upon that decision, the patient's vital signs ceased to function.

The doctor further testified that the mortality rate in this type of injury after more than seven days was 95%.

The defense had reserved the right to recall the neurosurgeon to cross-examine him after a full reading of Mrs. Werlich's hospital record. From that record, the defense learned that Mrs. Werlich died only after removal from the respirator. It was the defense's contention that "but for the discontinuance, that for pulling the plug, the victim in this case may well still be living today."

The court refused to allow the recall of the neurosurgeon for cross-examination on this issue, though admitted, "[I]f the victim had continued to be physically alive for more than a year and a day following the alleged attack there would be no case of murder before the court. There might be some other charges, but that would not be one."

*   *   *

The appellant should have been given the opportunity of raising a reasonable doubt, whether he was successful or not, that his assault on Mrs. Werlich was not the legal cause of her death—that the injury inflicted would not have caused her to die within a year and a day, and that it was only the doctor's intentional act that assured her death within this period that established appellant's culpability for homicide. *   *   * I dissent.

Notes and Questions

1. The principal case apparently presented the District of Columbia Court of Appeals with considerable difficulty. Approximately three months after the opinion which is reprinted above was issued, rehearing en banc was granted and the opinion vacated. On May 29, 1981, the original judgment was affirmed without a published opinion.

2. The "year and one day" rule and the definition of "death" (including "brain death") are considered in notes 2 and 3, pages 383–84, supra.

3. The accused in Matter of J.N. claimed that the act of the physicians was an "intervening cause" of the victim's death. In more traditional parlance, their claim would be that this constituted a "superceding" cause which, by definition, relieved them of responsibility for the death. See R. Perkins and R. Boyce, Criminal Law 790–804 (3rd ed. 1982). Thus the task, under this terminology, is one of determining when an intervening cause or factor will be regarded as a "superceding" cause.

4. Could the issues in J.N. have been better considered under principles of culpability? Suppose Parker, upon a proper charge of intentional murder, had been proved to have shot the victim in the head as a means of securing her purse, but that she did not die until six days later after her condition deteriorated and the physicians discontinued "heroic measures." It would be reasonable to infer that Parker, when he shot the victim, contemplated that she would die almost immediately from the gunshot wound and did not consciously address the possibility of events developing as they did. Assuming this was Parker's state of mind, can any reasonable argument be made that he lacked the culpability required for intentional murder? Generally speaking, the culpability requirements concern only the defendant's state of mind with regard to the end result—death—and do not require any particular awareness concerning the chain of events between the defendant's actions and that result.

Suppose further that the defense had presented evidence that the physicians' decision to discontinue heroic efforts was, on the facts, "willful malpractice" or at least an "abnormal response to the situation." Under accepted principles of culpability, would Parker have been entitled to an instruction directing the jury to acquit him if the jury found this to be the case? Chief Judge Newman suggests that existing decisions reflect that an intentional wrongdoer is not relieved of liability where "foreseeable and natural consequences of his wrongful act" intervene in the chain of events. Perhaps the instructions proposed by the defense simply identify with somewhat greater precision what particular "consequences" of Parker's wrongful act were "foreseeable and natural." But if so, this goes beyond simple application of general principles of culpability. As noted above, culpability does not require any awareness or contemplation of any particular chain of events between the defendant's conduct and the intended result. Yet the defendant may be relieved of liability, i.e., the chain of causation may be regarded as broken, if the evidence shows that the chain of events from his act to the result were not foreseeable and natural consequences of his actions.

If this functionally states the position applicable to a scenario in which Parker is shown to have acted with intent to cause death, does it apply to the actual case, in which Parker was apparently tried on a felony murder theory? Should it make any difference whether under the applicable felony murder law foreseeability is required, i.e., whether liability exists for felony murder only if the defendant should have been aware of a substantial and unjustifiable risk that his commission of the offense in the intended manner would cause the victim's death?

5. How would *J.N.* be analyzed under Section 2.03 of the Model Penal Code, reprinted at page 483, infra? If the applicable felony murder law requires proof that the death was a foreseeable result of the felony, would that bring the case within Section 2.03(3)? What are the "actual result" and the "probable result" that must be identified and compared for the analysis required by that provision? Perhaps "actual result" means the death of the victim by virtue of the particular chain of events that in fact led to it. "Probable result," then, might mean the death of the victim by virtue of those scenarios or chains of events of which the defendant should have been aware.

6. To what extent should ineffective medical care received by the victim for an assault constitute a "superceding" cause and thus relieve the person who committed the assault of liability for the victim's subsequent death? All members of the *J.N.* court appear to assume that simply ineffective medical care will not affect causation. Some courts have indicated that if ineffective medical care is so inappropriate as to rise to the level of medical malpractice, it may—under some circumstances—break the chain of causation. E.g., State v. Ulin, 113 Ariz. 141, 548 P.2d 19 (1976). In *J.N.*, Judge Newman asserts that liability for homicide is not affected by a showing that "a physician administered negligent treatment" but that "gross negligence by an attending physician, which is the *sole* cause of death," will have that effect. Is this proposition consistent with the defense's proposed instructions? With the analysis of the case by the *J.N.* majority? On what ground can this distinction be defended? Is it because "simple" malpractice is foreseeable but malpractice that is "gross" or somehow aggravated is not?

An English court held that a defendant's conviction for murder (and sentence of death) were unsupported by the evidence where additional information indicated that the victim died not from the perforation of his intestine directly caused by the defendant but rather from pneumonia which resulted from medical treatment which was "palpably wrong" and "not normal." Jordan, 40 Crim.App. 158 (Eng.1956). A critic of *Jordan* has suggested that as a result of the decision, "the courts may find themselves involved in protracted, undesirable, and * * * unnecessary investigations into the medical treatment of victims of homicidal assaults." Camps and Havard, Causation in Homicide—A Medical View, [1957] Crim. L.Rev. (Eng.) 576, 585.

7. Suppose it was determined that the neurosurgeon's action in *J.N.* was action that could relieve the defendant of liability, i.e., that it was "intentional or willful malpractice" or an "abnormal response to the situation." Would it in fact have that effect? The court emphasizes that a second "force" or act—such as the physician's action—will not relieve the defendant of liability if "the first act, standing alone, was a substantial factor contributing to the death." Suppose that the evidence concerning the victim's death established that she died because of the injuries inflicted by the defendant and the absence of life support systems. But, the expert testifies, had the victim not sustained the injury inflicted by the defendant, the absence of heroic measures by the hospital's medical staff would not have caused her death. Under this situation, would the defendants be entitled to acquittal? Consider State v. Hills, 124 Ariz. 491, 605 P.2d 893 (1980), in which the defendant stabbed the victim, who later died. A treating physician had done exploratory surgery to ascertain the extent of the knife wound but failed to discover that the lower intestine had been perforated. As a result of this undiscovered perforation of the lower intestine, the victim developed peritonitis which, in turn, caused his death. Rejecting the argument that this relieved the defendant from liability for the death, the court explained:

> [M]edical malpractice will break the chain of causation and constitute a defense only if death is attributable solely to the medical malpractice and not induced at all by the original wound.
>
> In this case, the original wound gave rise to the peritonitis which ultimately resulted in death. Even if we were to conclude that the failure to find and treat the perforated intestine was malpractice, that would not absolve appellant of guilt because the infection was the direct result of the original wound.

124 Ariz. at 492, 605 P.2d at 894.

8. In People v. Stewart, 40 N.Y.2d 692, 389 N.Y.S.2d 804, 358 N.E.2d 487 (1976), the defendant stabbed the victim. During surgery to treat the stab wound, the surgeon discovered that the victim also had a hernia and decided, after repairing the damage done by the stabbing, to also correct the hernia. During that subsequent part of the surgery, the victim experienced cardiac arrest and died. There was evidence that the cardiac arrest may have been due to the negligence of the anesthesiologist. The New York Court of Appeals reversed a jury verdict finding the defendant guilty of criminal homicide. Is this consistent with the causation law generally applied to homicide cases?

9. Was death a reasonably foreseeable result of a strong-arm robbery of an 85 year old woman by a young man? Reconsider here State v. Noren,

125 Wis.2d 204, 371 N.W.2d 381 (App.1985), review denied, 126 Wis.2d 519, 378 N.W.2d 292 (1985), reprinted at page 442, supra.

MODEL PENAL CODE *
(Official Draft 1985).

Section 2.03. Causal Relationship Between Conduct and Result; Divergence Between Result Designed or Contemplated and Actual Result or Between Probable and Actual Result

(1) Conduct is the cause of a result when:

(a) it is an antecedent but for which the result in question would not have occurred; and

(b) the relationship between the conduct and result satisfies any additional causal requirements imposed by the Code or by the law defining the offense.

(2) When purposely or knowingly causing a particular result is an element of an offense, the elements is not established if the actual result is not within the purpose or the contemplation of the actor unless:

(a) the actual result differs from that designed or contemplated, as the case may be, only in the respect that a different person or different property is injured or affected or that the injury or harm designed or contemplated would have been more serious or more extensive than that caused; or

(b) the actual result involves the same kind of injury or harm as that designed or contemplated and is not too remote or accidental in its occurrence to have a [just] bearing on the actor's liability or on the gravity of his offense.

(3) When recklessly or negligently causing a particular result is an element of an offense, the element is not established if the actual result is not within the risk of which the actor is aware or, in the case of negligence, of which he should be aware unless:

(a) the actual result differs from the probable result only in the respect that a different person or different property is injured or affected or that the probable injury or harm would have been more serious or more extensive than that caused; or

(b) the actual result involves the same kind of injury or harm as the probable result and is not too remote or accidental in its occurrence to have a [just] bearing on the actor's liability or on the gravity of his offense.

(4) When causing a particular result is a material element of an offense for which absolute liability is imposed by law, the element is not established unless the actual result is a probable consequence of the actor's conduct.

Comment

1. *General.* This section is concerned with offenses in which causing a particular result is a material element (e.g., homicide). It defines the causal relationship that is generally required to establish liability for such offenses and deals with the problems that arise when the actual result differs from the result sought or contemplated by the actor, or probable under the circumstances. These problems are currently dealt with as issues of "proximate causation" and present enormous difficulty (especially in homicide) because of the obscurity of that concept. Rather than seeking to systematize the varying and sometimes inconsistent rules in the numerous areas in which the problem has arisen, the section undertakes a fresh approach to the central issues. This approach differs from traditional law both in dealing with this subject in the penal code itself, rather than leaving it exclusively to case law development, and in treating the difficult situations, in which the actual result differs from the expected result, as problems of culpability.

What will usually turn on determinations under this section is not the criminality of the defendant's conduct, but the gravity of his offense. * * *

How far the penal law ought to attribute importance in the grading of offenses to the actual result of conduct, as opposed to results attempted or threatened, presents a significant and difficult issue. Distinctions of this sort are essential, at least when severe sanctions are involved, for it cannot be expected that jurors will lightly return verdicts leading to severe sentences in the absence of the resentment aroused by the infliction of serious injuries. Whatever abstract logic may suggest, a prudent legislator cannot disregard these facts in the enactment of a penal code.

Attributing importance to the actual result does not, moreover, usually detract from the deterrent efficacy of the law, at least in cases of purposeful misconduct. One who attempts to kill, risking the gravest penalty, is unlikely to be influenced in his behavior by the treatment that the law provides for those who fail in such attempts; his expectation is that he will succeed.

2. *But-for Cause and Liability for Unforeseen Consequences.* Subsection (1)(a) treats but-for causation as the causal relationship that is normally sufficient, viewing this as the simple, pervasive meaning of causation in the penal law. When the requirement of "proximate causation" dissociates the actor's conduct from a result of which it is a but-for cause, the reason is always a judgment that the actor's culpability with respect to the result, i.e., his purpose, knowledge, recklessness, or negligence, is such that it would be unjust to permit the result to influence his liability or the gravity of his offense. Consequently, the Code proceeds on the assumption that issues of this sort ought to be

dealt with as problems of the culpability required for conviction and not as problems of "causation."

The Code thus poses an initial factual inquiry, asking whether the conduct of the defendant is an antecedent but for which the result in question would not have occurred. As the law has consistently recognized, some limitation of this broad principle is necessary, and merely qualifying it by normal culpability requirements is not sufficient. For example, if the defendant attempted to shoot his wife, with the result that she retired to her parents' country home and died there from falling off a horse, no one would think that he should be held guilty of murder, though he did intend her death and his attempt to kill her was a but-for cause of her encounter with the horse. Further questions must be asked, and it is the nature of those questions that is critical. The Institute decided that they should not be posed in terms of the encrusted precedents on proximate causation, by reference to doctrines of dependent supervening and independent supervening causes, and so on. The proper inquiry is not merely factual, but concerns the propriety of allowing the result to influence the criminality of the defendant or the gravity of his crime. The question is thus essentially one of culpability, and in Subsections (2) and (3) that question is posed in terms appropriate for submission to the jury.

* * *

[A] preliminary issue is concurrent causation. Suppose two assailants without preconcert attack their victim with intent to kill, and death results because each has simultaneously struck a mortal blow. On the face of it, it appears that neither attack is a but-for cause of death, since the victim's death would have come about as a result of the other assailant's attack, even if one assailant had refrained from attacking. * * *

All who have considered the issue agree that each of the assailants should be liable, and it was the intent of the Institute to make them liable. When assailants act in concert each is, of course, liable for his own actions, and also vicariously liable for the acts of the others under Section 2.06. Since these acts are, taken together, a but-for cause of death, the liability of each participant is clear. The only difficult case is one that arises most infrequently, when the conduct of two actors is completely independent, and each actor's conduct would have been sufficient by itself to produce death or some other forbidden consequence. In such cases the language of Subsection (1)(a) should be assigned a meaning that accords with penal policy. In this context, the result in question should be viewed as including the precise way in which the forbidden consequence occurs. For example, in the illustration of concurrent causation given above, the result should be characterized as "death from two mortal blows." So described, the victim's demise has as but-for causes each assailant's blow.

* * *

3. *Limiting Principles.* As indicated above, Subsections (2) and (3) are based on the theory that but-for causation is the only strictly causal requirement that should be imposed generally, and that the remaining issue is the proper scope of liability in light of the actor's culpability. These subsections assume that liability requires purpose, knowledge, recklessness, or negligence with respect to the result that is an element of the offense, and deal explicitly with variations between the actual result and the intended, contemplated or foreseeable result. Criteria are provided for determining the materiality or immateriality of such variations.

Subsection (2) addresses cases in which the culpability requirement with respect to the result is purpose or knowledge, i.e., cases in which purposely or knowingly causing a specified result is a material element of the offense. If the actual result is not within the purpose or contemplation of the actor, the culpability requirement is not satisfied, except in the circumstances set out in Subsections (2)(a) and (2)(b).

Subsection (2)(a) deals with situations in which the actual result differs from the result designed or contemplated only in that a different person or property was injured or affected, or in that the injury or harm designed or contemplated would have been more serious or extensive than that which actually occurred. Following existing law, the Code makes such differences immaterial.

Subsection (2)(b) deals with situations in which the actual result involves the same kind of injury or harm as that designed or contemplated, but in which the precise injury inflicted was different or occurred in a different way. Here the Code makes no attempt to catalogue the possibilities—intervening or concurrent causes, natural or human; unexpected physical conditions; distinctions between mortal and nonmortal wounds; and so on. It deals only with the ultimate criterion by which the significance of such factors ought to be judged— whether the actual result is too remote or accidental in its occurrence to have a [just] [16] bearing on the actor's liability or the gravity of his offense.

The purpose of this qualification is to exclude situations in which the manner in which the actual result occurs, or the nature of the actual result, is so remote from the actor's purpose or contemplation that it should have no bearing on the gravity of the offense for which he is convicted. In the example given above, in which the actor's wife is killed after falling off a horse, it is clear that both courts and juries

16. The word "just" is in brackets because of disagreement within the Institute over whether it is wise to put undefined questions of justice to the jury. The inclusion of the term has the merit of putting it clearly to the jury that the issue it must decide is whether in light of the remoteness or accidental quality of the occurrence of the actual result, it would be just to accord it significance in determining the actor's liability or the gravity of his offense. Submitting explicit questions involving a broad moral concept like "justice" to the jury is not so different from submitting questions of "unjustifiable risk" and "gross deviation" required by this Code's definition of recklessness and negligence. Section 2.02. *See* ALI Proceedings 72–77 (1962) for the debate over inclusion of the term.

would regard the actual result as "too remote or accidental in its occurrence to have a [just] bearing on the actor's liability or on the gravity of his offense." Similarly, suppose the actor had actually shot his wife, and while hospitalized she had contracted a disease (that was medically unrelated to the wound but related to her presence in the hospital), with death resulting. While her death from the disease may have been rendered substantially more probable by the defendant's conduct, a jury might still regard it as too unusual a result to justify a murder conviction. In general, the infinite variety of contexts in which the issue can arise precludes an advance catalogue of premises that can be used mechanically to deduce a solution. The issue should be put to the jury in terms of a general principle that articulates the ultimate basis of judgment.

It has been argued that this formulation gives insufficient attention to the problem of intervention by a responsible human agent. Consider, for example, the case of a gunshot wound, followed by an operation that brings about the victim's death. Death may have resulted from intentional killing by the surgeon, or from the surgeon's recklessness or negligence, or from the victim's contracting an infection (through no one's fault) in the course of the operation. Even if it is assumed that each of these occurrences is equally probable under the circumstances, Hart and Honoré contend that it is not sufficient in cases of human intervention to put the issue of liability to the jury in terms of whether the result was "too accidental" in its occurrence to have a just bearing on the actor's liability or the gravity of his offense. Rather, relying on what they perceive to be deeply engrained common sense ideas about causality and responsibility, they see the issue as properly turning on the voluntariness of the intervening actor's conduct—to the extent that his intervention is independent and voluntary, the defendant's liability should be diminished.

* * *

The question put to the trier of fact is the same whether the human intervenor acts after the defendant has harmed the victim, as in the example above, or causes the initial injury to the victim in response to some action of the defendant. For example, if one of the participants in a robbery shoots at a policeman with intent to kill and provokes a return of fire by the officer that kills a bystander or an accomplice, the robber who initiated the gunfire could be charged with purposeful murder (*see* Section 210.2(1)(a)). Since his conduct was a but-for cause of death and the actual result (the death of the bystander or accomplice) involved the same kind of injury as that designed or contemplated (the death of the policeman), a jury could convict him if the death of the bystander or accomplice was not deemed too remote or accidental to have a [just] bearing on the gravity of his offense.

Subsection (3) deals with offenses in which recklessness or negligence is the required culpability and in which the actual result is not within the risk of which the actor was aware or, in the case of negligence, of which he should have been aware. The governing principles are the same as in the case of crimes requiring purpose or knowledge. If the actual and probable result differ only in that a different person or property is injured, the variation is immaterial. In other situations, if the actual result involved the same kind of injury or harm as the probable result, the question asked is whether the actual result is too remote or accidental in its occurrence to have a [just] bearing on the actor's liability or the gravity of his offense.

4. *Strict Liability.* Subsection (4) was added in response to criticism of an earlier draft that only required but-for causation in strict liability offenses. * * * [T]he provision is not relevant for most regulatory offenses for which strict liability is imposed, since these typically are not defined in terms of result elements. The most important application may be in jurisdictions in which strict liability continues to play a role in determining the gravity of some offenses. Under the felony-murder rule, for example, a person committing a felony is strictly liable for deaths caused during the felony. The principle of this subsection is that there should be no liability unless the actual result is a probable consequence of the actor's conduct. Thus, suppose the moment a bank robber stepped into the bank, an employee pushing the button for a burglar alarm was electrocuted. The robber would not be liable for the death of the employee.

In general, strict liability is based on a desire to secure extreme care in areas in which it is imposed. This objective is not significantly furthered by finding liability for improbable results, nor would such an approach be just.

WEINREB, COMMENT ON BASIS OF CRIMINAL LIABILITY; CULPABILITY; CAUSATION

In 1 Working Papers of the National Commission on Reform of
Federal Criminal Laws
144–46 (1970).

The only statutory attempt in this country to develop a general explanatory formula of causal relation in criminal cases is that of the Model Penal Code (§ 2.03). As the commentary to the Model Penal Code observes, its formula does not systematize the "variant and sometimes inconsistent rules" that have developed, but "undertakes a fresh approach." The inadequacy of the Code's formulation illustrates the difficulties involved.

The basic provision of the Model Penal Code adopts "but for" causation as the general test; it is both necessary and, unless "additional causal requirements" are specifically imposed, sufficient. This provision does not clearly state the accepted rule or easily lead to the correct result in cases of "concurrent causation."

Even though all of the senators may have intended to kill Caesar and all of them stabbed him, under the Model Penal Code's formulation none would be criminally liable for his death since (so I shall assume) he would have died even though any one of them had held back his knife. Even a senator who stabbed Caesar through the heart would not be liable, since, so Anthony tells us (act 3, scene 2) "sweet Caesar's blood" was streaming from all the wounds.

The Model Penal Code's reliance on "but for" causation as ordinarily enough for liability ignores the cases in which it is not essential to liability. There are situations in which, for purposes of the criminal law, we are properly "interested" in more than one cause of an occurrence, even though none of them alone is necessary or more than one of them are alone sufficient. The paradigm is a situation in which each of two or more persons engages in conduct that fully satisfies the definition of a crime but in which there is only "one" harmful consequence.

> *A* and *B* simultaneously shoot at *X*, both intending to kill him. The bullets enter *X's* body at the same time. Each wound is sufficient to cause death and would alone cause death in the same amount of time. *X* dies from the joint effect of both wounds.

We are just as properly interested if neither of the wounds alone would cause death but the facts are otherwise the same. (Such a set of facts is, of course, hardly likely to occur. It is not so unlikely that, for lack of evidence, a situation should be treated as if it occurred as described.)

This point was discussed during the American Law Institute's discussion of the Model Penal Code. It was concluded that the matter would be clarified in the commentary to the section. In the discussion, Professor Wechsler indicated that he believed the Model Penal Code's statement was acceptable, evidently on the basis that the specific result caused by concurrent causes would not have occurred but for the operation of each. While this is a permissible construction of the language, it is a strain on ordinary usage, which does not attend so carefully to details of this kind in the face of the major fact of a death.

Additional sections of the Model Penal Code's formulation deal with cases in which the actual result is not intended or is not within the risk created by the actor's conduct, by providing that there is no causal relation in such cases unless either the actual and the intended or probable results differ only in respects generally irrelevant to the criminal law (the specific person or property injured; the greater seriousness of the intended or probable harm) or the actual result is similar to ("involves the same kind of injury or harm as") the intended or probable result, and "is not too remote or accidental in its occurrence to have a [just] bearing on the actor's liability or on the gravity of his offense." This formulation breaks down in precisely those cases in which difficulties arise, those covered by the last clause. Of the alternative formulations, that which omits the word "just" states the problem without resolving it (by use of the question-begging word "too"); that which includes the word "just" (in addition to using the word "too") refers to an inapt standard for resolving it—that the connection between a result and conduct but for which the result would not have occurred is remote or accidental does not, unless the words "remote" and "accidental" are given special (question-begging) meaning, affect the justice of holding the actor liable for his conduct.

Illustrative of an alternative to the Model Penal Code's reliance on "but for" causation as the basic test, is the following, drafted for consideration in the Federal Code:

A causal connection between a person's conduct and an occurrence does not exist if:

(a) the person's conduct was not sufficient to cause the occurrence without the cooperation of one or more events or the conduct of one or more persons; and

(b) without the cooperation of the person's conduct, another event or the conduct of another person was sufficient to cause the occurrence.

Such a provision, which does not attempt to state what causation is but only what, in some circumstances, it is not, leads to the correct result in many cases of concurrent causation by providing that a person's conduct is not the cause of a result if someone else's conduct or some other event is both necessary and sufficient to produce the result. Where conduct is not sufficient to cause an occurrence and there is present and identifiable other conduct or some event which is sufficient to cause the occurrence, common understanding would probably regard the latter as the cause. However, the provision, at best, offers no guidance in the case of sequential, as opposed to concurrent causes. (If A shoots X, as a result of which X goes to the hospital, and while he is there (i) the hospital burns down, or (ii) the wound becomes infected, or (iii) a doctor stabs X inadvertently, or (iv) a doctor stabs X deliberately, and X dies, in which of the four cases should A be liable for X's death?) Even though the provision attempts to say only when causation is not present, it is readily perceived as indicating when causation is present. If we understand the provision to refer only to concurrent and not sequential causes, it is only because, without relying on the provision, we have a sense of when an act or event causes an occurrence. (If the provision is not so understood, A would, or at least might, be liable for X's death in all of the cases described, which would surely be the wrong result at least in case (iv) and possibly in others as well.)

The provision gives limited guidance, and even that only because of our independent understanding of the very concept of causation which the provision attempts partially to illuminate.

A final possibility is not to provide what shall or shall not count as a causal relation, but to list factors which shall be relevant to a determination that conduct did or did not cause a result. One might, for example, specify as such factors the extent to which the conduct manifests the danger which is realized in the result or the extent to which the actor's conduct singles him out as the person responsible for the result. All such "factors," however, are either make-weights which collapse on analysis or depend finally on the concept of causation which they are intended to clarify.

Problem

In light of the above what is the appropriate result on the following facts? Defendants had left their very intoxicated robbery victim on the shoulder of an unlit country road without his glasses, coat or shoes, and with his trousers around his ankles. It was done at about 9:30 p.m. with the temperature near zero and visibility obscured by wind-driven fallen snow. A lighted service-station was about a half-mile away. Approximately twenty minutes after the victim had been abandoned, he was struck and killed by a truck being driven at 50 miles per hour in a 40 mph zone. Defendants are charged under a statute declaring a person to be guilty of murder when "under circumstances evincing a depraved indifference to human life, he recklessly engages in conduct which creates a grave risk of death to another person, and thereby causes the death of another person."

How should the jury be instructed? Would a failure to instruct on causation be constitutional error if the trial judge did instruct on the meaning of "recklessly"? See People v. Kibbe, 35 N.Y.2d 407, 362 N.Y.S.2d 848, 321 N.E.2d 773 (1974), which ultimately reached the Supreme Court as Henderson v. Kibbe, 431 U.S. 145, 97 S.Ct. 1730, 52 L.Ed.2d 203 (1977).

PEOPLE v. SCOTT

Court of Appeals of Michigan, 1971.
29 Mich.App. 549, 185 N.W.2d 576.

J.H. GILLIS, PRESIDING JUDGE. Defendant appeals as of right from a conviction by jury of involuntary manslaughter, M.C.L.A. § 750.321 (Stat.Ann.1954 Rev. § 28.553).

The defendant, after engaging in an exchange of verbal hostilities with the occupants of a police patrol car, attempted to force the vehicle off the road. A chase ensued and a radio alert was relayed to other cars in the vicinity. An unmarked patrol car, in pursuit of defendant, collided at an intersection with a DSR bus, killing one of the officers in the patrol car.

The single issue raised on appeal is whether trial court committed reversible error when it instructed the jury that to find the defendant guilty of involuntary manslaughter it must be established that the defendant's negligence was "a" proximate cause of the police officer's death and whether the court further erred in rejecting the defendant's contention that his negligence must constitute "the" proximate cause.

* * *

Michigan courts have traditionally held that a conviction for involuntary manslaughter, especially when committed with an automobile, may be sustained if the trier of fact is

"[Able to] determine [that] the defendant was guilty of gross and culpable negligence in the operation of his motor vehicle and that said gross negligence in the operation of such motor vehicle was the proximate cause of the death of the deceased." People v. Layman (1941), 299 Mich. 141, 145, 146, 299 N.W. 840, 841.

* * *

Defendant stipulates, on appeal, that the speed and manner in which he was operating his car was such as could be deemed wilful and wanton disregard for the safety of others. It is the contention of the people that because the defendant readily admits that his driving was grossly negligent, that that erratic driving then becomes the proximate cause of the death of the police officer. They contend that if the defendant's driving had not been in violation of state law, the police would never have given chase and the death would not have occurred. Further, it is their contention that even if there were another independent cause for the officer's death, the jury could still find the defendant guilty of the offense charged if they found that his gross negligence was "a proximate cause" of the death. We find this logic unacceptable.

The trial judge's charge to the jury defined "proximate cause" to be

"A direct and producing cause of the damage or injury. It doesn't have to be 'the' direct. The reason I say 'a' direct is that there can be more than one proximate cause of the damage or injury complained of * * *. As far as you [the jury] are concerned in this case, it is up to you to determine whether there was a causal connection between the driving of the defendant, if you find there was improper driving, and the end result * * *. There can be more than one proximate cause, as I told you."

* * *

The court, in its definition of "proximate cause," has adopted the civil law definition and applied it to a criminal prosecution.

* * *

If the tort liability concept of proximate cause were applied in criminal homicide prosecutions, the conduct of the decedent would have to be considered. That conduct would be examined not to prove that it was merely an additional proximate cause, but rather to determine whether it amounted to a subsequent wrongful act and thus superseded the original conduct chargeable to defendant. The trial court properly instructed the jury that they could find defendant not guilty if they determined that deceased's conduct was the sole cause of the collision. However, the court did give the instruction that the defendant could be found guilty if it was determined that both defendant and deceased had acted negligently. Such a charge is in opposition to the fundamental principles of criminal responsibility. It is axiomatic that "criminal guilt under our law is personal fault." People v. Sobczak (1955), 344 Mich. 465, 470, 73 N.W.2d 921, 923. "It is the very essence of our deep-rooted notions of criminal liability that guilt be personal and individual." [3] Commentary on Commonwealth v. Redline, 391 Pa. 486, 137 A.2d 472 (1958), reiterates why the tort standard of proximate cause is unacceptable in criminal prosecutions:

> "A closer causal connection between the felony and the killing than the proximate-cause theory normally applicable to tort cases should be required because of the extreme penalty attaching to a conviction for felony murder and the difference between the underlying rationales of criminal and tort law. The former is intended to impose punishment in appropriate cases while the latter is primarily concerned with who shall bear the burden of a loss." [4]

Other states have agreed with the reasoning adopted by Pennsylvania and have compelled their triers of fact, when implementing "proximate causation" in criminal prosecutions, to find that the defendant's act be the proximate cause of the homicide charged. * * *

The people, here, as in People v. Marshall (1961), 362 Mich. 170, 174, 106 N.W.2d 842, actually seek from us an "interpretation of the manslaughter statute which would impose open-ended criminal liability". This we cannot do. It is true as a general rule of law:

> "That a person engaged in the commission of an unlawful act is legally responsible for all of the consequences which may naturally or necessarily flow or result from such unlawful act." People v. Barnes, 182 Mich. 179, 197, 148 N.W. 400, 406 (1914).

But before this principle of law can have any application in this case before us, it must first appear that the defendant's act was grossly negligent and that the resulting homicide was "*the* natural or necessary result of *the act* of [the defendant]." *Barnes,* supra, p. 198, 148 N.W. p. 406. (Emphasis supplied.) * * *

While there are no Michigan cases which are factually similar, there are many Michigan cases dealing with involuntary manslaughter,

> "[W]hich make it clear that to sustain a conviction of manslaughter the conduct of the accused must have been the immediate and direct cause of the death." People v. Ogg (1970), 26 Mich.App. 372, 400, 182 N.W.2d 570, 584, dissent by Danhof, J. and cases cited. See also: People v. Beardsley (1907), 150 Mich. 206, 113 N.W. 1128.

Although neither party is able to cite authority which requires that the defendant's criminally negligent act be the only direct and proximate cause of the ensuing homicide, this Court feels that the reasoning proffered by the Pennsylvania court in Commonwealth v. Root, 403 Pa. 571, 170 A.2d 310 (1961), constitutes the better standard. In criminal prosecutions there must be a more direct causal connection between the criminal conduct of the defendant and the homicide charged than is required by the tort liability concept of proximate cause.

Reversed and remanded for new trial not inconsistent herewith.

---

3. Sayre, "Criminal Responsibility for the Acts of Another," 43 Harvard Law Review 689, 716 (1930).

4. Note, 71 Harvard Law Review 1565, 1566 (1958).

Notes and Questions

1. If it had been Scott's car, rather than that of the pursuing officer, which had crashed and caused a death would there be any doubt as to his culpability? See Tegethoff v. State, 220 So.2d 399 (Fla.Dist.Ct.App.1969). Is this because no other actor intervened or because the crash may be viewed as a natural result of such conduct? Wasn't police pursuit, with its attendant dangers, a natural result of Scott's conduct? Would holding Scott responsible for the results of the officer's mishap serve to deter such flight? Would it violate our sense of fairness? Would holding the officer liable for the results of his apparently reckless pursuit deter such pursuit? Would it violate our sense of fairness?

2. In Pereira v. United States, 347 U.S. 1, 74 S.Ct. 358, 98 L.Ed. 435 (1954), the Supreme Court was faced with the question of whether the appellant had "caused" a check to be mailed pursuant to a scheme to defraud. Writing for a unanimous Court (as to this point) Chief Justice Warren announced: "That question is easily answered. Where one does an act with knowledge that use of the mails will follow in the ordinary course of business, or where such use can reasonably be foreseen, even though not actually intended, then he 'causes' the mails to be used." Id. at 8–9, 74 S.Ct. at 363. If this standard were applied to Scott would the result change? Is there any reason it should not be applied?

3. In Commonwealth v. Feinberg, 433 Pa. 558, 253 A.2d 636 (1969), the defendant owned a small store in the skid-row area of Philadelphia. He commonly sold "Sterno", a jelly-like substance made for use as a fuel and composed primarily of methanol (wood alcohol) and ethanol (grain alcohol) to the local residents knowing that at least some of them would extract the alcohol to drink. The manufacturer changed the formula of the product so that it contained 54% rather than 3.75% of the highly toxic methanol. The cans containing the new product were the same as the old but, in addition to the previous warnings about use only for fuel and the danger of internal consumption, carried a skull and crossbones on the lid and were marked "Poison". The defendant sold approximately 400 cans of the new Sterno which resulted in the death of thirty-one persons in the area due to methanol poisoning. He was charged with thirty-one counts of involuntary manslaughter and convicted on a number of these counts.

On appeal, Feinberg argued, in part, that the causal connection was broken by the victims' voluntary acts in drinking. He sought to rely on the *Root* case (cited in *Scott*) where the Pennsylvania Supreme Court had held that the defendant could not be held criminally responsible for the death of his drag race competitor who was killed when he passed the defendant on a two lane road and collided with a truck. The *Root* court said that there was not a sufficiently direct causal connection between the defendant's act and the death. The court in *Feinberg* held that *Root* was of no aid to the defendant and that the contributory negligence of the victims could not be a defense where the defendant had been reckless.

In Commonwealth v. Atencio, 345 Mass. 627, 189 N.E.2d 223 (1963), the defendants were convicted of manslaughter based upon the self-inflicted death of a companion in the course of a game of "Russian roulette". Both of the defendants had, prior to the fatal shot, examined the revolver, seen that it contained one cartridge, spun the cylinder, pointed at his own head, and pulled the trigger. The court upheld the conviction despite the victim's voluntary involvement in the "game", and without approving the result in *Root* distinguished it on the basis of the skill involved in drag-racing as contrasted with the luck which controlled in Russian roulette.

Is *Atencio* to be distinguished from *Scott* because the chances of a fatal result in Russian roulette are greater than in high speed auto chases? Because of the comparative lack of social utility of the two activities? Because the driving skills of the pursuing officer in *Scott,* or the lack thereof, are a variable for which the defendant should not be held responsible? Is the *Scott* court's reliance on *Root* well-placed given the voluntary participation of the decedent there? Is *Feinberg* distinguishable from *Root* because of our doubts about the voluntary nature of the acts of those who drink Sterno?

Chapter IX

GENERAL PRINCIPLES OF CRIMINAL LIABILITY: ATTENDANT CIRCUMSTANCES

Contents

In the introductory note to the first chapter on the general principles of criminal liability (Chapter IV), attendant circumstances were identified as a separate category of possible elements of particular crimes. Elements in this category are distinct from the act of the defendant, his state of mind with respect to other elements, the result, and any specific intent which might be required. Chapters V through X presented some materials which involved crimes requiring attendant circumstances. Under the traditional definition of larceny, for example, only personal property could be the subject of theft. Burglary statutes often require that for liability, or for an aggravated penalty, the prosecution must prove that the premises invaded were the residence of another. These and countless other crimes involve a legislative decision that proof of the presence of a specified circumstance is essential to identifying the defendant as an appropriate subject for the sanction prescribed by the particular statute.

Complete analysis of a criminal statute necessary to effective prosecution and defense must include identification of any attendant circumstances included within the statutory definition. In addition, a determination must be made of whether any state of mind is required with respect to each particular circumstance, and, if so, at what level. In undertaking this analysis, concepts introduced in other parts of these materials—such as the operation of the doctrine of mistake (see Chapter VI, Section E.1., supra)—must be reviewed and employed.

The materials which follow focus on various aspects of attendant circumstances in the context of the crime of sexual assault. Homicide, the most important of all crimes, was employed as the focus of Chapter VII which analyzed the relationship of state of mind to a particular result. Here, sexual assault, a crime which carries an emotional and intellectual significance even greater than might be suggested by the deplorable frequency of its incidence in our society, is employed as the vehicle for examining the role of a particular category of elements of crime.

As to each required circumstance, several questions emerge. Inasmuch as the requirement of an attendant circumstance increases the state's difficulty in prosecuting, what was the legislative intention in imposing that requirement? How can that purpose be best achieved consistent with any competing values in our society? Is it ever appropriate for liability or the level of liability to turn on the existence of an attendant circumstance without requiring that the prosecution establish a subjective state of mind on the part of the defendant with regard to that element?

Editors' Introduction: "Rape" and Other Sexual Offenses

Although this chapter focuses upon the role played by "attendant circumstances" in sexual offenses, this cannot be considered in isolation from other requirements created by such crimes. Obviously, the legislative decision to require proof of certain circumstances represents only one aspect of a broader decision as to what activity engaged in under what situations should be made criminal. Further, such inquiries often lead to the conclusion that various types of activity should all be criminalized but that distinctions ought to be made among those types. As a result, the legislative decisionmaking process must often progress to consideration of how the prohibited activity should be subdivided in order to provide for penalties of varying seriousness.

In the context of sexual offenses, the decisions involve a variety of subconsiderations. What basic activity should be made criminal? Should this be limited to coitus? Should only conduct upon female victims be encompassed? However the conduct is defined in terms of the sex of the victim, what other limits should be placed upon it? Should it extend to, but no farther than, other penetrations of the victim? Or should it extend as far as mere physical touchings, perhaps of what are regarded as exceptionally personal or private areas of the body?

As part of this process, of course, it is necessary to consider what attendant circumstances to require in particular areas of the offense. Should all aspects of the conduct be regarded as criminal if but only if the victim is shown not to have consented? Should any general requirement of proof of nonconsent be dispensed with upon a showing that the victim was under what is perceived to be some disability, such as youth, mental impairment, or unconsciousness? Or, perhaps even the absence of consent should not be regarded as sufficient unless the prosecution also shows that the act—whether intercourse or something "less"—was accomplished by certain defined types of force or threats.

Most of the conduct at issue—putting aside its sexual aspects—has long constituted a criminal offense of some sort, if nothing more serious than misdemeanor battery or assault. The legislative question is therefore, more accurately, how to describe the activity to be treated together as a distinguishable—and most likely more serious—sexual offense.

Traditionally, the question was posed as how the single offense of rape is appropriately defined. More recently, legislatures have shown a tendency to define degrees of rape. And since the mid-1970s, a number of legislatures have entertained proposals to replace the traditional offense of rape with more broadly-defined offenses often labeled "sexual assault", "criminal sexual conduct" or "sexual contact." See generally, Ireland, Reform in Rape Legislation: A New Standard of Sexual Responsibility, 49 U.Colo.L.Rev. 185 (1978); Note, Recent Statutory Developments in the Definition of Forcible Rape, 61 Va.L.Rev. 1500 (1975). The model for these latter efforts has generally been the Michigan legislation, reprinted at page 503, infra, enacted in 1974. The redefinition of the substantive crime or crimes of which the sexual assaulter might be convicted is only one part of what is often regarded as the reform of "rape laws." Discussion of that reform, however, requires some preliminary consideration of the traditional offense of rape.

It may be useful to consider in connection with the material in this chapter the development in Coker v. Georgia, reprinted at page 109, supra, of the federal constitutional limits upon the availability of death as a punishment for sexual assault.

Traditional Rape Law

At early common law rape was a felony involving unlawful and nonconsensual sexual intercourse with a female. Gradually the law developed a requirement that the prosecution prove both that the defendant employed force or the threat of force and that the female did not consent. This definition led the law to focus on the acts of the victims rather than those of the accused. It also gave rise to the notion that the female had to engage in active resistance for the crime to be made out.   Perkins & Boyce, Criminal Law 198–99, 209–10 (3rd Ed. 1982).   Under this view it was possible that a forceful sexual penetration would not be deemed rape because it was consensual.   According to a leading modern criminal law treatise:

> Obviously a man should not be convicted of this very grave felony where the woman merely put up a little resistance for the sake of "appearance," so to speak, taking care not to resist too much.   The law goes beyond this.   The absence of consent is necessary for this crime. And even where the resistance is genuine and vigorous in the beginning, if the physical contact arouses the passion of the woman to the extent that she willingly yields herself to the sexual act before penetration has been accomplished,—or if she so yields before this time for any other reason—it is not rape.

R. Perkins & R. Boyce, Criminal Law 211 (3rd Ed.1982).

Rape has been fraught with enormous emotional significance for the participants in the processes of criminal justice as well as for the victims.   The investigation and prosecution of rape cases has reflected, according to some commentators, the deep sexism of the law and the criminal justice system.   Estrich, Rape, 95 Yale L.J. 1087, 1090 (1986). As was recently explained by the California Supreme Court:

> The requirement that a woman resist her attacker appears to have been grounded in the basic distrust with which courts and commentators traditionally viewed a woman's testimony regarding sexual assault.   According to the 17th century writings of Lord Matthew Hale, in order to be deemed a credible witness, a woman had to be of good fame, disclose the injury immediately, suffer signs of injury and cry out for help.   (1 Hale, History of the Pleas of the Crown (1st Am. ed. 1847) p. 633.)

> This distrust was formalized in the law in several areas.   For example, juries were traditionally advised to be suspect and cautious in evaluating a rape complainant's testimony, particularly where she was "unchaste."

> In most jurisdictions, corroboration of the complaining witness was necessary for a conviction of rape.   Skeptical of female accusers, the majority of courts and commentators considered it appropriate that the "prosecutrix" in all sexual assault cases undergo psychiatric examination before trial.

People v. Barnes, 42 Cal.3d 284, 298–300, 228 Cal.Rptr. 228, 236–37, 721 P.2d 110, 117–18 (1986).

It is crucial to the crime that the sexual contact be without the victim's consent.   However, this element can, in theory, be established by proof of the accused's use or threatened use of force against the victim or another in the victim's presence, or by proof that the victim was unable to resist due to mental incapacity or unconsciousness, known to the accused, or due to impairment brought about by the accused.   To the extent that the defendant overcomes the victim's lack of consent by means other than the use or threatened use of force, a question can be raised as to whether it is appropriate to treat such conduct as constituting a crime of violence. The Texas Court of Criminal Appeals recently addressed such a contention by reviewing the change in the relevant statutes and in public attitudes:

> A penetration of the victim occurs in all rapes. [This unfortunately ignores sexual assaults committed by "contact"] This act of penetration is a violent act, no matter what the circumstances are which prove that the victim did not consent. This conclusion is reflected in the nature of rapes. Rape is not a sexual offense motivated by a desire for sexual gratification. Rape is primarily a "violent assault motivated by hostility, anger and a need to dominate the victim." [Tchen, Rape Reform and a Statutory Consent Defense, 74 J.Crim.L. & Criminology 1518, 1527 (Winter 1983).] A rape is characterized by the rapist's use of sexuality to express power and anger. "Rape is a psuedo-sexual act, a pattern of sexual behavior that is concerned much more with status, hostility, control and dominance than with sensual pleasure or sexual gratification." A. Goth, Men Who Rape (1979), p. 13. Because it is an assertive violent assault, rape is divorced from consensual sexual activity.

> From both the nature of rape and the effects of rape on its victims, it becomes apparent that rape is an act of violence, anger and power, which is distinguished by its coercive and sometimes brutal nature. The state legislature recognized this fact. We hold that rape is a crime of violence, per se.

Wisdom v. State, 708 S.W.2d 840, 844–45 (Tex.Crim.App.1986).

The fact that nonconsent to the prohibited result is a crucial element of this crime is hardly unique. As was discussed in Section C. 1. of Chapter V, supra, it is essential to larceny and most theft-type crimes derived therefrom, that the taking be trespassory, i.e., without the effective consent of the owner. Similarly, burglary involves an nonconsensual entry, and assault a nonconsensual touching. What is distinct in this regard about rape or, under the more common modern nomenclature, sexual assault or sexual battery, is the frequency with which cases turn on proof of this attendant circumstance. As has been seen, the insistence, historically, on evidence of resistance or an explanation for its absence can be traced to this requirement. This difference may ultimately be attributable to the fact that:

> the law of rape inevitably treads on the explosive ground of sex roles, of male aggression and female passivity, of our understandings of sexuality—areas where differences between a male and a female perspective may be most pronounced.

Estrich, Rape, 95 Yale L.J. 1087, 1091 (1986).

Other Aspects of Rape Law Reform

The modification of the definition of rape or its replacement by some more broadly-defined offense has been only a part—and perhaps a relatively minor part—of efforts to reform the criminal prosecution of sexual offenses. Another aspect of these reform efforts has been the development of limitations upon trial exploration of the victim's prior sexual conduct. Such exploration is widely regarded as exceptionally intrusive into the privacy of the victim, of little relevance to the proper issues in prosecutions; and as creating a significant risk that judges' and juries' attention will be diverted from those issues. The resulting "rape shield" laws have been attacked, however, as impeding defendants' ability to fully develop before juries grounds that may exist for doubting the credibility of the testimony of the victim, which is often the major evidence indicating the defendant's guilt.

Other changes have taken place. The rules which reflected a special distrust of complainants' testimony have been almost entirely rejected. See, e.g., People v. Barnes, 42 Cal.3d 284, 301–302, 228 Cal. Rptr. 228, 238–39, 721 P.2d 110, 120 (1986). In addition, in an effort to encourage the filing of complaints and to ease the prosecution's burden, innovative and sometimes controversial legal practices have evolved in some jurisdictions with respect to the trial of such crimes. One has been the use of expert testimony to the effect that the behavior of the complaining witness after the events in issue was consistent with a "rape trauma syndrome". Such testimony is usually offered to help establish that the intercourse was without consent. It has also been offered to explain the special difficulty—repression engendered by the trauma of the experience—that a rape victim might have in making a positive identification of her assailant. Compare People v. Bledsoe, 36 Cal.3d 236, 203 Cal.Rptr. 450, 681 P.2d 291 (1984) (such testimony is inadmissible) with People v. Marks, 231 Kan. 645, 647 P.2d 1292 (1982) (admissible).

There has also been a widespread movement to authorize children who are complaining witnesses in sexual offense cases to provide their evidence without having to confront their alleged assailants. This is often accomplished by permitting the testimony of such children to be presented in filmed or taped form. However, such laws have been under sharp attack as violative of defendants' right of confrontation under the Sixth Amendment to the United States Constitution. See, e.g., State v. Sheppard, 197 N.J.Super. 411, 484 A.2d 1330 (1984) and Symposium: Child Abuse and the Law, 89 Dickinson L.Rev. 3 (1985).

Also, modern statutes often attempt to give greater emphasis to the culpable conduct of the defendant rather than focusing on the behavior of the victim. This is illustrated by the 1980 amendment of Section 261 of the California Penal Code. The crime had required proof that the victim had resisted but was overcome by force or prevented from resistance by the threat of great and immediate harm. The amendment modified the section to define rape as:

> an act of sexual intercourse accomplished with a person not the spouse of the perpetrator, under any of the following circumstances; * * *

(2) Where it is accomplished against a person's will by means of force or fear of immediate and unlawful bodily injury on the person or another.

How successful have these reforms been? If they have not been adequate, what else is needed? To what extent should reform efforts be focused upon the "substantive" criminal law—as, for example, the definitions of the offenses—rather than procedural matters or perhaps the attitudes of those involved in the processing of cases?

A Task Force on Women in the Courts, appointed by the Chief Judge of the State of New York, recently reported on the administration of New York rape laws. Until recently, the report observed, rape was "virtually unprosecutable" in the state. After examining recent reforms and practice following them, the Task Force found:

1. Until recently, New York's rape law codified the view that women's claims of rape are to be skeptically received. Through a slow process of reform, the most detrimental provisions have been repealed or struck down as unconstitutional

2. The attitudes embodied in the former law and which resisted its reform continue to operate in the minds of some judges, jurors, defense attorneys, and prosecutors.

3. As a result, cultural stigma and myths about rape's perpetrators and victims still narrow the law's protective reach.

   a. Elements of a woman's character unrelated to her powers of observation and veracity—such as her manner of dress, perceived reaction to the crime, and lifestyle—continue to be unfairly deemed relevant to a determination of the defendant's guilt or innocence.

   b. Victims of rape who had any level of past relationship or acquaintanceship with the perpetrator are less likely to see his conviction and appropriate punishment.

4. Certain legislative and prosecutorial measures can offer a more appropriate response to the unique trauma rape victims suffer.

   a. Specialized prosecution units trained to recognize rape victims' psychological trauma and designed to minimize the need for the victim to repeat her story to many individuals and to appear in court have been successfully implemented in a number of counties.

   b. A statute creating victim-rape counsel confidentiality, similar to that applied to communications between psychiatrists and patients, would permit victims to utilize important crisis services without fear that privately related statements would be admitted in court.

Report of the New York Task Force on Women in the Court 89–90 (1986). The Task Force heard testimony that grand juries would be more likely to indict in cases of acquaintance rape if they were offered an option that would categorize such attacks as less serious offenses than attacks by strangers. Id., at 81–82. As a result, the Task Force also recommended that the legislature consider adding one or more additional felony grades to the crime of rape. Id., at 91.

After this note, the provisions of the Michigan statute referred to above as a widely relied upon model for revision of rape offenses are reprinted. The two chapter sections that follow address two aspects of the role of attendant circumstances in defining and applying the substantive crime of rape, sexual assault, or its counterpart. Section A addresses the extent to which it is desirable to define the offense as to require the absence of a spousal relationship between the perpetrator and the victim. To the extent such an attendant circumstance is required, this section considers further how it is best defined. Section B focuses upon the mental state that is or ought to be required with reference to whatever attendant circumstances are determined to be appropriate elements of the offense.

Michigan Penal Code

Sec. 750.520a. As used in sections 520a to 520*l*:

(a) "Actor" means a person accused of criminal sexual conduct.

(b) "Intimate parts" includes the primary genital area, groin, inner thigh, buttock or breast of a human being.

(c) "Mentally defective" means that a person suffers from a mental disease or defect which renders that person temporarily or permanently incapable of appraising the nature of his or her conduct.

(d) "Mentally incapacitated" means that a person is rendered temporarily incapable of appraising or controlling his or her conduct due to the influence of a narcotic, anesthetic, or other substance administered to that person without his or her consent, or due to any other act committed upon that person without his or her consent.

(e) "Physically helpless" means that a person is unconscious, asleep, or for any other reason is physically unable to communicate unwillingness to an act.

(f) "Personal injury" means bodily injury, disfigurement, mental anguish, chronic pain, pregnancy, disease, or loss or impairment of a sexual or reproductive organ.

(g) "Sexual contact" includes the intentional touching of the victim's or actor's intimate parts or the intentional touching of the clothing covering the immediate area of the victim's or actor's intimate parts, if that intentional touching can reasonably be construed as being for the purpose of sexual arousal or gratification.

(h) "Sexual penetration" means sexual intercourse, cunnilingus, fellatio, anal intercourse, or any other intrusion, however slight, of any part of a person's body or of any object into the genital or anal openings of another person's body, but emission of semen is not required.

(i) "Victim" means the person alleging to have been subjected to criminal sexual conduct.

750.520b. (1) A person is guilty of criminal sexual conduct in the first degree if he or she engages in sexual penetration with another person and if any of the following circumstances exists:

(a) That other person is under 13 years of age.

(b) The other person is at least 13 but less than 16 years of age and the actor is a member of the same household as the victim, the actor is related to the victim by blood or affinity to the fourth degree to the victim, or the actor is in a position of authority over the victim and used this authority to coerce the victim to submit.

(c) Sexual penetration occurs under circumstances involving the commission of any other felony.

(d) The actor is aided or abetted by 1 or more persons and either of the following circumstances exists:

(i) The actor knows or has reason to know that the victim is mentally defective, mentally incapacitated or physically helpless.

(ii) The actor uses force or coercion to accomplish the sexual penetration. Force or coercion includes but is not limited to any of the circumstances listed in subdivision (f)(i) to (v).

(e) The actor is armed with a weapon or any article used or fashioned in a manner to lead the victim to reasonably believe it to be a weapon.

(f) The actor causes personal injury to the victim and force or coercion is used to accomplish sexual penetration. Force or coercion includes but is not limited to any of the following circumstances:

(i) When the actor overcomes the victim through the actual application of physical force or physical violence.

(ii) When the actor coerces the victim to submit by threatening to use force or violence on the victim, and the victim believes that the actor has the present ability to execute these threats.

(iii) When the actor coerces the victim to submit by threatening to retaliate in the future against the victim, or any other person, and the victim believes that the actor has the ability to execute this threat. As used in this subdivision, "to retaliate" includes threats of physical punishment, kidnapping, or extortion.

(iv) When the actor engages in the medical treatment or examination of the victim in a manner or for purposes which are medically recognized as unethical or unacceptable.

(v) When the actor, through concealment or by the element of surprise, is able to overcome the victim.

(g) The actor causes personal injury to the victim, and the actor knows or has reason to know that the victim is mentally defective, mentally incapacitated, or physically helpless.

(2) Criminal sexual conduct in the first degree is a felony punishable by imprisonment in the state prison for life or for any term of years.

750.520c.   (1) A person is guilty of criminal sexual conduct in the second degree if the person engages in sexual contact with another person and if any of the following circumstances exists:

(a) That other person is under 13 years of age.

(b) That other person is at least 13 but less than 16 years of age and the actor is a member of the same household as the victim, or is related by blood or affinity to the fourth degree to the victim, or is in a position of authority over the victim and the actor used this authority to coerce the victim to submit.

(c) Sexual contact occurs under circumstances involving the commission of any other felony.

(d) The actor is aided or abetted by 1 or more other persons and either of the following circumstances exists:

(i) The actor knows or has reason to know that the victim is mentally defective, mentally incapacitated or physically helpless.

(ii) The actor uses force or coercion to accomplish the sexual contact. Force or coercion includes but is not limited to any of the circumstances listed in sections 520b(1)(f)(i) to (v).

(e) The actor is armed with a weapon, or any article used or fashioned in a manner to lead a person to reasonably believe it to be a weapon.

(f) The actor causes personal injury to the victim and force or coercion is used to accomplish the sexual contact. Force or coercion includes but is not limited to any of the circumstances listed in section 520b(1)(f)(i) to (v).

(g) The actor causes personal injury to the victim and the actor knows or has reason to know that the victim is mentally defective, mentally incapacitated, or physically helpless.

(2) Criminal sexual conduct in the second degree is a felony punishable by imprisonment for not more than 15 years.

750.520d. (1) A person is guilty of criminal sexual conduct in the third degree if the person engages in sexual penetration with another person and if any of the following circumstances exists:

(a) That other person is at least 13 years of age and under 16 years of age.

(b) Force or coercion is used to accomplish the sexual penetration. Force or coercion includes but is not limited to any of the circumstances listed in section 520b(1)(f)(i) to (v).

(c) The actor knows or has reason to know that the victim is mentally defective, mentally incapacitated, or physically helpless.

(2) Criminal sexual conduct in the third degree is a felony punishable by imprisonment for not more than 15 years.

750.520e. (1) A person is guilty of criminal sexual conduct in the fourth degree if he or she engages in sexual contact with another person and if either of the following circumstances exists:

(a) Force or coercion is used to accomplish the sexual contact. Force or coercion includes but is not limited to any of the circumstances listed in section 520b(1)(f)(i) to (iv).

(b) The actor knows or has reason to know that the victim is mentally defective, mentally incapacitated, or physically helpless.

(2) Criminal sexual conduct in the fourth degree is a misdemeanor punishable by imprisonment for not more than 2 years, or by a fine of not more than $500.00, or both.

*   *   *

750.520i. A victim need not resist the actor in prosecution under sections 520b to 520g.

Note

The provisions above are reprinted as enacted in 1974. 1974 Mich.Pub. Acts No. 266. In 1983, the term "mentally defective" was removed from the statute. "Mentally disabled" was defined as meaning "that a person has a mental illness, is mentally retarded, or has a developmental disability. § 750.520a(e). Definitions of "developmental disability," "mental retardation," and "mentally retarded" were added to § 750.520a. The definition given to "mentally defective" in § 750.520a(c) was retained but applied to the term, "mentally incapable." § 750.520a(f). The definition of "mental illness" was also somewhat modified. § 750.520b, defining criminal sexual conduct in the first degree was modified by substituting "mentally incapable" for "mentally defective" in § 750.520b(g). In addition, § 750.520b was expanded to provide that criminal sexual conduct in the first degree is committed if a person engages in sexual penetration with another person and:

(h) That other person is mentally incapable, mentally disabled, mentally incapacitated, or physically helpless, and any of the following:

(i) The actor is related to the victim by blood or affinity to the fourth degree.

(ii) The actor is in a position of authority over the victim and used this authority to coerce the victim to submit.

§ 750.520b(b) was also rephrased, as was § 750.520c(b). Similar changes were made in § 750.520c, defining criminal sexual conduct in the second degree; criminal sexual conduct was expanded to cover sexual conduct engaged in under those circumstances rendering sexual penetration an offense under § 750.520b(h). See § 750.520c(h). "Mentally incapable" was also substituted for "mentally defective" in §§ 750.520c(g), 750.520d(c), and § 750.520e(b). 1983 Mich.Pub.Acts No. 158.

A. THE ABSENCE OF THE SPOUSAL RELATIONSHIP

A basic decision in the definition of sexual offenses is the extent to which, if at all, the prosecution should be required to show that the victim was not married to the perpetrator. Often the issue is put in terms of whether or to what extent the law should recognize a "marital exemption" from the crime covering spouses of the victims or the extent to which a "marital privilege" should exist. In traditional rape law, the requirement that the act of intercourse be "unlawful" was regarded as demanding the absence of a spousal relationship. R. Perkins and R. Boyce, Criminal Law 202–03 (3rd ed. 1982). The question was sometimes put in terms of whether marriage constitutes irrevocable consent by the wife to sexual intercourse with the husband. Id. As of 1984, some form of marital exemption existed in over 40 states. People v. Liberta, 64 N.Y.2d 152, 163 n. 6, 485 N.Y.S.2d 207, 212 n. 6, 474 N.E.2d 567, 572 n. 6 (1984).

KIZER v. COMMONWEALTH

Supreme Court of Virginia, 1984.
228 Va. 256, 321 S.E.2d 291.

COMPTON, JUSTICE.

In this appeal of a conviction for marital rape, we apply the rule of *Weishaupt v. Commonwealth*, 227 Va. 389, 315 S.E.2d 847 (1984), to the facts of this case. In *Weishaupt*, we held that:

"[A] wife can unilaterally revoke her implied consent to marital sex where . . . she has made manifest her intent to terminate the marital relationship by living separate and apart from her husband; refraining from voluntary sexual intercourse with her husband; and, in light of all the circumstances, conducting herself in a manner that establishes a *de facto* end to the marriage. And, once the implied consent is revoked, even though the parties have not yet obtained a divorce, the husband can be found guilty of raping his wife, if the evidence against him establishes a violation of Code § 18.2–61." *Id.* at 405, 315 S.E.2d at 855.

Applying the foregoing criteria to the circumstances of the present case, we reverse the conviction. [In *Weishaupt* the court concluded that the English courts had never accepted Sir Matthew Hale's statement that a husband cannot rape his wife (1 M. Hale, The History of the Pleas of the Crown 629 (1736)). Rather, marriage carried with it an implied consent to sexual intercourse which could be revoked. The court rejected the English law insofar as it did not permit the wife to revoke her consent unilaterally. The court reached this position by reference to Virginia's no-fault divorce statute. Since that statute contemplates a de facto termination of the marital relationship—it requires that the parties live separate and apart without cohabitation—it would be inconsistent to say that the wife cannot unilaterally withdraw her implied consent to marital sex.]

Indicted for the rape of his wife in violation of Code § 18.2–61, Edward Alan Kizer was found guilty in a bench trial and sentenced on September 9, 1983 to confinement in the penitentiary for a term of 20 years. Execution of 15 years of the sentence was suspended and the defendant was placed on probation for life.

Because the proceedings below in this case were completed before *Weishaupt* was decided, the central issue in the trial court was whether Virginia law permitted a prosecution for rape where the accused, at the time of the alleged offense, was married to the victim. Anticipating the result in *Weishaupt*, the trial court properly answered that question in the affirmative. Likewise anticipating our statement in *Weishaupt* that a wife unilaterally can revoke her implied consent to marital intercourse, the defendant, in an alternative argument, urged the trial court to rule that the Commonwealth's evidence was "insufficient to show a separation of the sort which would be contemplated" by the principles we ultimately adopted in *Weishaupt*. Thus, the trial court, in finding the defendant guilty, implicitly ruled the prosecution carried its burden under *Weishaupt* to establish beyond a reasonable doubt a *de facto* end to the parties' marriage. This was error.

The facts mainly are undisputed. Defendant and his wife, Jeri, were married in June of 1981 in Texas. The couple moved to Norfolk where defendant, age 20, was stationed aboard ship as an enlisted man in the Navy. They occupied rented quarters ashore that were leased in both names. Following the birth of a child, the couple began having marital difficulties. In September of 1982, about six months before the incident in question, the wife returned to Texas briefly. According to her testimony, the purpose of the trip was "to visit" her parents for two weeks; the visit was not "a separation" from her husband.

During the "middle of February" 1983, about three weeks before the alleged offense, the defendant "moved back to the ship." The wife continued to reside in the apartment with the child. According to the wife's testimony, the separation occurred because "[t]he marriage was over and I did not want the marriage to be any longer. * * *" The wife added that she "wanted to be separated and in the process to file for divorce after the legal separation in Virginia." The defendant testified that the parties were not "legally separated" and that he moved to the ship "to avoid any other arguing with my wife * * * in front of our son because we did not want to subject him to arguing between me and my wife, Jeri."

Previously, the wife had left the husband from "about the first of January to about the middle of February" 1983. After the parties "had talked to each other," she returned to the marital home, saying to the husband, "I want to make it work but I do not love you." The defendant had suspected his wife of "fooling around" while he was on duty at sea, but testified that he "still loved the girl" and wanted the marriage "to work."

During the three-week period from the middle of February to the date of the incident, the defendant came to the apartment to visit the child pursuant to an oral agreement with the wife. She estimated he made "a couple" visits. The defendant testified that he "tried" to visit the boy "seven or eight times." The parties had agreed that the defendant would notify the wife in advance of a planned visit so that she would not be in the apartment when he arrived.

On March 5, the day before the incident in question, the defendant came to the apartment without notifying the wife. She refused to allow him to enter the premises during the morning and again during the afternoon. Still later in the day, she permitted him to see the child as the wife, accompanied by a male friend, left the apartment on the friend's motorcycle. She returned to the apartment about five hours later, at 11:30 p.m., but did not remain. The defendant told her he was staying at the marital abode because he did not want to return to the ship due to the lateness of the hour.

The evidence showed that the parties did not engage in sexual intercourse during the period from September 1982, when she visited her parents in Texas, until the date of the incident in question. During a portion of this time, the defendant was aboard ship at sea.

Prior to the alleged offense, the defendant filed a petition in court seeking an award of custody of his child. In addition, the parties decided in February to consult a lawyer "about getting a legal separation." As the parties were en route to an attorney's office, the wife told defendant that she had changed her mind and that she did not want to separate "right now." He said, "Are you sure?" and she responded, "Yes." They returned to their apartment. The wife testified that she decided to discontinue the trip to the attorney because the defendant had just received notification that his father was very ill and she did not want to put more "pressure" on him at that time.

The evidence showed that before the day of the alleged offense, the defendant discussed "the rape laws of Virginia" with a friend. The defendant had said that "he [the defendant] was kind of hard up for sex" and that he thought he "ought to go over there and rip her clothes off of her and take it."

On the day in question, March 6, the defendant had been visiting friends in an apartment "across the hall" from the marital home. He knocked on the door to his apartment about 6:00 p.m. and asked his wife to allow him to use the shower. She refused because she was afraid to be in the premises alone with him. The defendant insisted on gaining entry and, as the wife tried to lock the front door to the apartment, he kicked the door twice. The door "came open and the frame came off the door," according to the wife's testimony. The defendant took the child from the mother's arms and placed him on the floor. The defendant picked up the wife, carried her to the bedroom, ripped off her clothing, and forcibly had sexual intercourse with her. During this time, she was screaming, scratching, kicking, and pulling defendant's hair. At one point during the 45-minute episode, the wife broke away from the defendant and rushed to the bedroom window, screaming for help. After the assault, the wife ran from the apartment and reported the incident to a police officer who was in the area.

The defendant was arrested on a warrant that day about 9:45 p.m., after earlier having confessed to the acts essentially as related by the wife. About three weeks after the incident, and before the rape trial, the defendant was awarded custody of his son following a hearing.

On appeal, the question presented is whether, under this evidence, the Commonwealth established beyond a reasonable doubt the elements necessary to sustain a conviction for marital rape. In such a case, under *Weishaupt*, the prosecution, in addition to establishing a violation of the general rape statute, Code § 18.2–61, must prove beyond a reasonable doubt that the wife unilaterally had revoked her implied consent to marital intercourse. 227 Va. at 405, 315 S.E.2d at 855. The wife's revocation of consent must be demonstrated by a manifest intent "to terminate the marital relationship." *Id.*, 315 S.E.2d at 855. The facts necessary to show this intention to terminate must reveal that the wife: has lived separate and apart from the husband; has refrained from voluntary sexual intercourse with her husband; and, "in light of all the circumstances," has conducted herself "in a manner that establishes a *de facto* end to the marriage." *Id.*, 315 S.E.2d at 855. In this context, "*de facto*" means "in fact," or "actually." Black's Law Dictionary 375 (5th ed. 1979).

In the present case, the evidence shows, first, a violation of the rape statute sufficient to sustain a conviction of the defendant for the rape of a female not his wife. Second, the evidence establishes that the parties lived separate and apart. Third, the proof shows that the wife refrained from voluntary sexual intercourse with the defendant. The evidence fails, however, to show beyond a reasonable doubt the wife conducted herself in a manner that established an actual end to the marriage, in light of all the circumstances.

Significantly, the wife's marital conduct during the six-month period before the assault was equivocal, ambivalent, and ambiguous. Prior to September 1982, the parties had been having domestic difficulties but apparently had been living together as husband and wife. She left Norfolk and went to Texas to "visit" her parents. But she testified that this was not a "separation" in the divorce sense. She returned from Texas and during part of the September-January period, the husband was on shipboard duty at sea. In January, the wife left again but returned after the parties "talked." She stated at the time that she wanted to make the marriage "work." In February, she terminated a planned trip with her husband to a divorce lawyer, advising the husband that she had changed her mind and did not wish to separate "right now." Finally, about three weeks before the alleged offense, the husband began living aboard ship in port. At the time, the wife considered the marriage to be "over."

Evaluating the foregoing circumstances in the light most favorable to the Commonwealth, we think it is apparent that the wife subjectively considered the marriage fractured beyond repair when the parties separated in February. Nevertheless, we cannot say that this subjective intent was manifested objectively to the husband, in view of the wife's vacillating conduct, so that he perceived, or reasonably should have perceived, that the marriage actually was ended.

The facts in *Weishaupt,* upon which the Attorney General relies in urging affirmance, are in sharp contrast to the circumstances of the present case. There, the wife moved out of the marital abode, taking with her the infant child of the parties. At the time of the offense, the parties had been separated continuously for 11 months and had not engaged in sexual relations during the period. There was no contact between the parties during the separation except telephone conversations concerning the child and chance meetings in public. During the period, the wife had consulted a divorce attorney who advised waiting until the parties were separated for a full year before filing suit for divorce. In sum, unlike the present case, the wife's marital conduct in *Weishaupt* during the pertinent period, viewed objectively, was unequivocal, definite, and certain; her conduct manifestly demonstrated that the marriage was in fact at an end and evidenced that the wife unilaterally had revoked her implied consent to marital intercourse. In *Weishaupt,* unlike this case, the Commonwealth proved beyond a reasonable doubt that the husband knew, or reasonably should have known, that the marriage was terminated *de facto*.

Accordingly, the judgment of conviction in this case will be reversed and the indictment will be dismissed.

Reversed and final judgment.

THOMAS, JUSTICE, dissenting.

The victim in this case took a horrible beating. The integrity of her body was brutally invaded by her estranged husband. The facts in this appeal are such that the majority concedes that had the victim not been married to the assailant, the assailant would have been guilty of rape. Nevertheless, in an opinion which fails to give due precedential weight to the Court's recent decision in *Weishaupt,* the majority concludes, in essence, that Edward Kizer had a right to do what he did. The majority opinion marks a retreat from the principles announced in *Weishaupt.*

The majority states that *Weishaupt* requires the proof of three factors before a husband can be convicted of raping his wife. Those factors are that the wife must have

1. lived separate and apart from her husband,

2. refrained from voluntary sexual intercourse with her husband, and

3. in light of all the circumstances, conducted herself in a manner that establishes a *de facto* end to the marriage.

The majority concedes that the Commonwealth proved the first two factors. However, according to the majority, the evidence failed to establish that the wife conducted herself in a manner that established a *de facto* end to the marriage.

In my opinion, the majority's conclusion is wrong. Upon analysis, the majority's error appears to stem from two things: first, the majority has added a condition that was not stated in *Weishaupt;* second, the majority has failed to consider the facts in the light most favorable to the Commonwealth.

According to the majority, before a husband can be found guilty of raping his wife, the wife must make "manifest objectively to the husband" the wife's view that the marriage is at an end. *Weishaupt* nowhere requires that the wife make manifest *to her husband* that the marriage is at an end. *Weishaupt* requires only that the wife make manifest *to an objective observer* "her intent to terminate the marital relationship." The difference is that, under the majority view, the trial court must place itself in the position of the estranged husband to determine whether the husband should have known that his wife considered the marriage over. Under *Weishaupt,* the court was not required to place itself in the husband's shoes; instead, it was called upon to occupy the more traditional posture of looking at the facts from the perspective of an objective observer to determine whether from that perspective the wife conducted herself in a manner that showed the marriage to be over. The perspective from which the facts are reviewed undoubtedly impacts upon the ultimate disposition of the case. The majority opinion works a subtle but important change in the perspective from which the facts are to be considered. This change is apparently designed to make it more difficult for a wife to establish the predicate necessary for conviction in a case of spousal rape.

The majority's modification of *Weishaupt* is less critical to the proper disposition of this appeal than is the majority's failure to consider the facts in the light most favorable to the Commonwealth. Of course, the majority submits that it has properly considered the facts. However, the conclusion it reaches indicates otherwise.

When viewed properly, the evidence shows the following: the couple was married on June 20, 1981. One child was born of the marriage. In September 1982, the couple began to experience marital difficulties. The couple did not engage in voluntary sexual relations from September 1982 through the attack which occurred in March 1983, a period of six months. The husband moved out of the marital abode in the middle of February, 1983. From that time to the attack there was neither sexual nor social contact between the parties. At the time the husband moved out, the parties discussed obtaining a legal separation. They even started on their way to visit a lawyer. The only reason they did not consult with a lawyer at that time was the fact that during the car ride the husband advised his estranged wife that his father was seriously ill. The wife decided to postpone the visit to the lawyer so as not to place an additional emotional burden upon her estranged husband while he tried to handle the problems associated with his father's illness. Further, prior to the attack, the husband filed suit to secure custody of the couple's child.

In my view, the foregoing facts meet either the original *Weishaupt* test or the modified test contained in the majority opinion. The single salient fact among all the facts and circumstances, and the one which makes this a stronger case for conviction than *Weishaupt,* is the husband's attempt to secure the custody of the couple's child. The majority mentions this fact but makes nothing of it, thus glossing over a very critical point.

In the normal course of events, husbands do not file custody suits unless they consider their marriages to be over. It is unrealistic to believe that the husband in this case would have sued for the custody of his child unless he thought the relationship with his wife was at an end. This husband demonstrated by his action in filing a custody suit that it was manifest to him that his marriage was over. The pendency of the custody suit added to the six-month absence of sexual relations and the one-month separation would lead any objective husband or impartial observer to conclude that the marriage in question was at an end.

Thus, in my opinion, the conviction for rape should be affirmed.

CARRICO, C.J., joins in this dissent.

Notes and Questions

1. The opinions in *Kizer* and *Weishaupt* do not examine the arguments which have been offered to justify the marital exemption other than the claim that it was the common law position reflecting the view that the woman was the property of her husband and her legal existence incorporated into his. In People v. Liberta, 64 N.Y.2d 152, 485 N.Y.S.2d 207, 474 N.E.2d 567 (1984), the New York Court of Appeals held that the marital exemption of that state's rape law violated the equal protection clauses of both the United States and the New York Constitutions. Rejecting contemporary justifications for the exemption, it reasoned:

The first [argument advanced in its defense], which is stressed by the People in this case, is that the marital exemption protects against governmental intrusion into privacy and promotes reconciliation of the spouses, and thus that elimination of the exemption would be disruptive to marriages. While protecting marital privacy and encouraging reconciliation are legitimate State interests, there is no rational relationship between allowing a husband to forcibly rape his wife and those interests. The marital exemption simply does not further marital privacy because this right of privacy protects consensual acts, not violent sexual assaults * * *.

Similarly, it is not tenable to argue that elimination of the marital exemption would disrupt marriages because it would discourage reconciliation. Clearly, it is the violent act of rape and not the subsequent attempt of the wife to seek protection through the criminal justice system which "disrupts" a marriage. Moreover, if the marriage has already reached the point where intercourse is accomplished by violent assault it is doubtful that there is anything left to reconcile. This, of course, is particularly true if the wife is willing to bring criminal charges against her husband which could result in a lengthy jail sentence.

Another rationale sometimes advanced in support of the marital exemption is that marital rape would be a difficult crime to prove. A related argument is that allowing such prosecutions could lead to fabricated complaints by "vindictive" wives. The difficulty of proof argument is based on the problem of showing lack of consent. Proving lack of consent, however, is often the most difficult part of any rape prosecution, particularly where the rapist and the victim had a prior relationship. Similarly, the possibility that married women will fabricate complaints would seem to be no greater than the possibility of unmarried women doing so. The criminal justice system, with all of its built-in safeguards, is presumed to be capable of handling any false complaints. * * *

The final argument in defense of the marital exemption is that marital rape is not as serious an offense as other rape and is thus adequately dealt with by the possibility of prosecution under criminal statutes, such as assault statutes, which provide for less severe punishment. The fact that rape statutes exist, however, is a recognition that the harm caused by a forcible rape is different, and more severe, than the harm caused by an ordinary assault. Under the Penal Law, assault is generally a misdemeanor unless either the victim suffers "serious physical injury" or a deadly weapon or dangerous instrument is used. * * * [Many husbands who rape their wives, therefore, could not be charged with a felony], let alone a felony with punishment equal to that for rape in the first degree.

Moreover, there is no evidence to support the argument that marital rape has less severe consequences than other rapes. On the contrary, numerous studies have shown that marital rape is frequently quite violent and generally has more severe, traumatic effects on the victim than other rape.

Among the recent decisions in this country addressing the marital exemption, only one court has concluded that there is a rational basis for it (see People v. Brown, 632 P.2d 1025 [Col.]). [The Colorado Supreme Court ＊ ＊ ＊ stated that the marital exemption "may remove a substantial obstacle to the resumption of normal marital relations" and "averts difficult emotional issues and problems of proof inherent in his sensitive area." 632 P.2d at 1027. We have considered, and rejected, both of these arguments.] We agree with the other courts which have analyzed the exemption, which have been unable to find any present justification for it. ＊ ＊ ＊ [I]t lacks a rational basis, and therefore violates the equal protection clauses ＊ ＊ ＊.

64 N.Y.2d at 164–67, 485 N.Y.S.2d at 213–15, 474 N.E.2d at 574–75.

2. *Weishaupt* and *Kizer* represent a decision to deal with the marital exemption by implying a right to revoke consent. Other jurisdictions have taken different approaches to the problem. Warren v. State, 255 Ga. 151, 336 S.E.2d 221 (1985), for example, held that the Georgia statute contained no such exemption, in part, because "unlawful" was not included in the statute's description of the prohibited conduct.

3. Do the rationales adopted in *Warren* and *Liberta* mean that the difficult factual issues such as those presented in *Kizer* will be avoided? Will it be possible to bring more marital rape prosecutions in Georgia and New York than in Virginia? Are statistically significant differences in the rates of prosecution and of successful prosecutions to be expected based upon these different legal approaches?

4. Does a marital rape defendant in Virginia have to be shown to have a state of mind as to the status of his marriage, or, under the Virginia view, is the crime one of strict liability with respect to this circumstance? If a state of mind is required as to this object, at what level should it be set?

Why should liability for forcible, nonconsensual intercourse turn on the defendant's state of mind with respect to his wife's belief as to the status of their marriage? Is it preferable to hold, as do Georgia and New York, that the marital status of the defendant and the complainant is irrelevant to liability? Consider these questions after covering the material in the next section.

B. MENTAL STATE REGARDING THE ATTENDANT CIRCUMSTANCES OF AGE AND ABSENCE OF CONSENT

Once a decision has been made concerning the attendant circumstances that should be required by a crime, it is then necessary to address what, if any, mental state should be required concerning those circumstances. The principal cases in this section address the mental state required with reference to two circumstances required by two ways of committing the traditional offense of rape. First, State v. Olsen, considers the attendant circumstance of the victim's age. In terms of the incidence with which it is invoked, the most important category of incapacity to consent is where the victim is a minor. Then the crime has usually been treated as a separate offense of non-forcible or statutory rape. The crucial issue in *Olsen* is whether the defendant's claimed belief that the victim was not a minor can serve as a "defense." This, of course, turns on whether the prosecution is required to establish some state of mind on the defendant's part with respect to the element of age. If it is determined that the crime is strict liability with respect to that element, the defendant will fail inasmuch as there is nothing to be negated by the ignorance or mistake. (See Chapter VI, Section E.1., supra.)

Next, the *Morgan* case deals with the consent issue in a highly unusual factual and legal context. There is no dispute that the victim in *Morgan* did not consent. Nor, apparently, is there any claim that the absence of the consent of an adult, competent victim is a strict liability element. The question instead is what level of *mens rea* is required as to this attendant circumstance. A defendant such as *Olsen* claims to have operated under a reasonable mistake as to his partner's age. In Model Penal Code terminology he is saying that he was not even negligent with respect to this matter. This is because to act reasonably means to have remained unconscious of a substantial and unjustifiable risk that the victim was under the prescribed age despite having exercised reasonable care in evaluating the situation and making any inquiries dictated by it. A claim of reasonable mistake thus challenges the existence of even objective fault.

The defendants in *Morgan* go one step further. They contend that they must be acquitted unless the prosecution can show subjective fault. Their claim is to have acted under a mistake which, whether or not reasonable, negates consciousness of risk that the female had not consented. If the mistake was unreasonable, it may be understood, in Model Penal Code terms, as constituting negligence since reasonable persons would have been aware of the danger of nonconsent. Nonetheless, this lack of risk consciousness is inconsistent with recklessness, the lowest level of subjective fault.

Reconsider in light of these issues the approach directed by Section 2.02 of the Model Penal Code, reprinted in Chapter VI at page 273, supra. Under Section 2.02(4), unless otherwise provided, culpability is required with regard to all "material elements" of an offense, presumably including attendant circumstances. But note the limitation in the definition of "material elements" set out in note 1, page 274, supra. How would *Olsen* and *Morgan* be decided under the Model Penal Code? Does the section provide a desirable approach to determining the culpability requirements applicable to attendant circumstances?

PEOPLE v. OLSEN

Supreme Court of California, 1984.
36 Cal.3d 638, 205 Cal.Rptr. 492, 685 P.2d 52.

BIRD, CHIEF JUSTICE.

Is a reasonable mistake as to the victim's age a defense to a charge of lewd or lascivious conduct with a child under the age of 14? [1]

* * *

[The complaining witness, Shawn M. was 13 years and 10 months old on the evening in question. Her testimony was that two young men had entered the camper trailer located in the driveway of her home. However, there were no signs of forced entry despite her testimony that she had locked the door. Employing a knife as a threat one, James Garcia, forced her to have intercourse with the other, Edward Olsen, in his presence. Her father testified that he came to the trailer because he heard male voices within, that he saw three persons on the bed and struggled with Olsen until Garcia stabbed him in the shoulder.

Shawn acknowledged that she knew both men and had been very good friends with Olsen although at the time of the incident considered Garcia her boyfriend. She testified to having previously engaged in intercourse and with having sexual relations short of intercourse with both of these men. She admitted having told both that she was over 16 and that she looked over 16.

Garcia gave a very different version of the event. His claim, supported by the circumstantial evidence of other witnesses, was that he had frequently had intercourse with Shawn and that both had been invited into the trailer for that purpose.]

At the conclusion of the trial, the court found Garcia and appellant guilty of violating section 288, subdivision (a). In reaching its decision, the court rejected defense counsel's argument that a good faith belief as to the age of the victim was a defense to the section 288 charge. Appellant was sentenced to the lower term of three years in state prison. This appeal followed.

Appellant's sole contention on appeal is that a good faith, reasonable mistake of age is a defense to a section 288 charge.

II.

The language of section 288 is silent as to whether a good faith, reasonable mistake as to the victim's age constitutes a defense to a charge under that statute. * * *

---

1. Section 288, subdivision (a) provides in relevant part: "Any person who shall willfully and lewdly commit any lewd or lascivious act * * * upon or with the body, or any part or member thereof, of a child under the age of 14 years, with the intent of arousing, appealing to, or gratifying the lust or passions or sexual desires of such person or of such child, shall be guilty of a felony and shall be imprisoned in the state prison for a term of three, six, or eight years."

All statutory references are to the Penal Code unless otherwise noted.

Twenty years ago, this court in *People v. Hernandez* (1964) 61 Cal. 2d 529, 39 Cal.Rptr. 361, 393 P.2d 673, overruled established precedent,[9] and held that an accused's good faith, reasonable belief that a victim was 18 years or more of age was a defense to a charge of statutory rape.

In *Hernandez,* the accused was charged with statutory rape of a girl who was 17 years and 9 months old, and who had voluntarily engaged in an act of sexual intercourse. The trial court refused to allow the accused to present evidence of his good faith, reasonable belief that the prosecutrix was 18 or over. On appeal, this court held it reversible error to exclude such evidence.

The *Hernandez* court acknowledged that an accused possesses criminal intent when he acts without a belief that his victim is 18 or over. However, the court determined that if one engages in sexual intercourse with a female and reasonably believes she is 18 or over, then the essential element of criminal intent is missing.

Relying on sections 20 [12] and 26 [13] and on *People v. Vogel* (1956) 46 Cal.2d 798, 299 P.2d 850, the court noted that it had recently "given recognition to the legislative declarations" in those two sections when it held in *Vogel* that a good faith belief that a previous marriage had been terminated was a valid defense to a charge of bigamy. (*Hernandez, supra,* 61 Cal.2d at p. 535, 39 Cal.Rptr. 361, 398 P.2d 673.) The court stated, "the reluctance to accord to a charge of statutory rape the defense of a lack of criminal intent has no greater justification than in the case of other statutory crimes [such as bigamy], where the Legislature has made identical provision with respect to intent." (*Ibid.*) Thus, "it cannot be a greater wrong to entertain a bona fide but erroneous belief that a valid consent to an act of sexual intercourse has been obtained." (*Ibid.*) The court went on to hold that a charge of statutory rape is defensible where a criminal intent is lacking unless there is a "legislative direction otherwise." (*Id.,* at p. 536, 39 Cal.Rptr. 361, 393 P.2d 673.)

The *Hernandez* court, however, cautioned that its holding was not "indicative of a withdrawal from the sound policy that it is in the public interest to protect the sexually naive female from exploitation. No responsible person would hesitate to condemn as untenable a claimed good faith belief in the age of consent of an 'infant' female whose obviously tender years preclude the existence of reasonable grounds for that belief." (*Ibid.*) The court then concluded that there was nothing to indicate that "the purposes of the law [could] be better served by foreclosing the defense of a lack of intent." (*Ibid.*)

---

9. *People v. Ratz* (1896) 115 Cal. 132, 46 P. 915 (accused's good faith, mistaken belief as to the victim's age is no defense to statutory rape) * * *.

12. Section 20 provides: "In every crime or public offense there must exist a union, or joint operation of act and intent, or criminal negligence."

13. Section 26 provides in relevant part: "All persons are capable of committing crimes except those belonging to the following classes: * * * [¶] Three—Persons who committed the act or made the omission charged under an ignorance or mistake of fact, which disproves any criminal intent."

* * *

In deciding whether to apply the philosophy of *Hernandez* to the offense of lewd or lascivious conduct with a child under the age of 14, this court is guided by decisions of the Courts of Appeal. The three post-*Hernandez* Court of Appeal decisions which have considered the issue have refused to apply *Hernandez*. (*People v. Gutierrez* (1978) 80 Cal.App.3d 829, 833–836, 145 Cal.Rptr. 823; *People v. Toliver* (1969) 270 Cal.App.2d 492, 494–496, 75 Cal.Rptr. 819, cert. den., 396 U.S. 895, 90 S.Ct. 193, 24 L.Ed.2d 172; *People v. Tober* (1966) 241 Cal.App.2d 66, 72–73, 50 Cal.Rptr. 228.)

In *People v. Tober, supra,* 241 Cal.App.2d 66, 67, 50 Cal.Rptr. 228, the accused was convicted of lewd or lascivious acts on the body of a 10–year-old child. On appeal, the court rejected the premise that lewd or lascivious acts on a 10–year-old child "may be indulged in under a claimed good faith belief that the child is either an adult or has reached the age of 14 years." (*Id.,* at p. 73, 50 Cal.Rptr. 228.) The Court of Appeal explained that "[t]he very refusal to distinguish between a child of tender years and an adult may be said to be characteristic of some of those who engage in the sort of conduct of which defendant has been convicted." (*Ibid.*) The court refused to apply *Hernandez* to section 288 cases, relying on that court's caution that a good faith, mistaken belief as to age is untenable when the victim involved is of " 'tender years.' " (*Ibid.,* quoting *Hernandez, supra,* 61 Cal.2d at p. 536, 39 Cal. Rptr. 361, 393 P.2d 673.)

People v. Toliver, supra, 270 Cal.App.2d 492, 75 Cal.Rptr. 819, also rejected the *Hernandez* rule in the section 288 context. * * *

As *Toliver* explained, *Hernandez* "in effect considered that section 288 is for protection of infants or children as to whom persons commit lewd and lascivious acts at their peril." (270 Cal.App.2d at p. 496, 75 Cal.Rptr. 819.) *Hernandez* points out that consent can be an element of statutory rape, since a male may reasonably believe that a female is older than 18 and, therefore, can consent to an act of intercourse. (*Ibid.*) "On the other hand, [a] violation of section 288 does not involve consent of any sort, thereby placing the public policies underlying it and statutory rape on different footings." (*Ibid.*) The court also found it significant that the Legislature provided harsher penalties for violating section 288 than for statutory rape. (*Ibid.*)

* * *

Another justification for its conclusion was found in a draft of the Penal Code Revision Project. (*Ibid.*) That project had proposed that a reasonable belief that a child is 14 or older is no defense to sex offenses where the crime involves a victim younger than 14. (Joint Legis.Com. for Revision of Pen.Code (Pen.Code Revision Proj.Ten.Draft No. 1, Sept. 1967) § 1600, subd. (4),[16] p. 61.)

---

16. Subdivision (4) provided: "Whenever in this chapter the criminality of conduct depends on a child's being below the age of fourteen, it is no defense that the actor reasonably believed the child to be fourteen or older. Whenever in this chap-

* * *

Moreover, other language in *Hernandez* strongly suggests that a reasonable mistake as to age would not be a defense to a section 288 charge. As *Hernandez* noted, when *People v. Ratz, supra,* 115 Cal. 132, 46 P. 915 was decided, an accused could be convicted of statutory rape only if the victim were under 14. *Hernandez* also found it "noteworthy that the purpose of the rule [announced in *Ratz*] was to afford protection to young females therein described as 'infants.' " (*Hernandez, supra,* 61 Cal.2d at p. 533, 39 Cal.Rptr. 361, 393 P.2d 673.) Thus, an "infant" at the time of *Ratz* was any child under 14. The *Hernandez* court's use of that term, therefore, evidenced a belief that a mistake of age defense would be untenable when the offense involved a child that young.

The language in *Hernandez,* together with the reasoning in *Tober, Toliver* and *Gutierrez,* compel the conclusion that a reasonable mistake as to the victim's age is not a defense to a section 288 charge.

This conclusion is supported by the Legislature's enactment of section 1203.066. (Stats.1981, ch. 1064, § 4, pp. 4095–4096.) Subdivision (a)(3) of that statute renders certain individuals convicted of lewd or lascivious conduct who "honestly and reasonably believed the victim was 14 years old or older" eligible for probation. The Legislature's enactment of section 1203.066, subdivision (a)(3), in the face of a corresponding failure to amend section 288 to provide for a reasonable mistake of age defense, strongly indicates that the Legislature did not intend such a defense to a section 288 charge. To recognize such a defense would render section 1203.066, subdivision (a)(3) a nullity, since the question of probation for individuals who had entertained an honest and reasonable belief in the victim's age would never arise. * * *

* * * Time and again, the Legislature has recognized that persons under 14 years of age are in need of special protection. This is particularly evident from the provisions of section 26. That statute creates a rebuttable presumption that children under the age of 14 are incapable of knowing the wrongfulness of their actions and, therefore, are incapable of committing a crime. A fortiori, when the child is a victim, rather than an accused, similar "special protection," not given to older teenagers, should be afforded. By its very terms, section 288 furthers that goal.

The Legislature has also determined that persons who commit sexual offenses on children under the age of 14 should be punished more severely than those who commit such offenses on children under the age of 18.

* * *

ter the criminality of conduct depends on a child's being below a specified age older than fourteen it is an affirmative defense that the actor reasonably believed the child to be of that age or above."

The tentative draft was never enacted into law.

It is significant that a violation of section 288 carries a much harsher penalty than does unlawful sexual intercourse (§ 261.5), the crime involved in *Hernandez.* Section 261.5 carries a maximum punishment of one year in the county jail or three years in state prison (§ 264), while section 288 carries a maximum penalty of eight years in state prison. The different penalties for these two offenses further supports the view that there exists a strong public policy to protect children under 14.

In recent years, the Legislature has increased the state prison sentence for violations of section 288 without increasing the punishment for unlawful sexual intercourse. * * *

It is true that at common law " ' "an honest and reasonable belief in the existence of circumstances, which, if true, would make the act for which the person is indicted an innocent act, has always been held to be a good defense." ' " (*Hernandez, supra,* 61 Cal.2d at pp. 535–536, 39 Cal. Rptr. 361, 393 P.2d 673, citation omitted.) However, it is evident that the public policy considerations in protecting children under the age of 14 from lewd or lascivious conduct are substantial—far more so than those associated with unlawful sexual intercourse. These strong public policies are reflected in several Penal Code statutes, and they compel a different rule as to section 288.

The legislative purpose of section 288 would not be served by recognizing a defense of reasonable mistake of age. Thus, one who commits lewd or lascivious acts with a child, even with a good faith belief that the child is 14 years of age or older, does so at his or her peril.

* * *

Accordingly, the judgment of conviction is affirmed.

MOSK, KAUS, BROUSSARD, REYNOSO and LUCAS, JJ., concur.

GRODIN, JUSTICE, concurring and dissenting.

I agree that the enactment of Penal Code section 1203.066, which renders eligible for probation persons convicted of lewd or lascivious conduct who "honestly and reasonably believed the victim was 14 years old or older" is persuasive evidence that in the eyes of the Legislature such a belief is not a defense to the crime.[1] What troubles me is the notion that a person who acted with such belief, and is not otherwise shown to be guilty of any criminal conduct, may not only be convicted but be sentenced to prison notwithstanding his eligibility for probation when it appears that his belief did not accord with reality. To me, that smacks of cruel or unusual punishment.

1. I do not agree that legislative intent to eliminate good faith mistake of fact as a defense can be inferred from the imposition of relatively higher penalties for that crime. On the contrary, as this court has stated in connection with the crime of bigamy: "The severe penalty imposed * * * the serious loss of reputation conviction entails, the infrequency of the offense, and the fact that it has been regarded * * * as a crime involving moral turpitude, make it extremely unlikely that the Legislature meant to include the morally innocent to make sure the guilty did not escape." (*People v. Vogel* (1956) 46 Cal.2d 798, 804, 299 P.2d 850.)

I fully accept that "fault" even for purposes of the criminal law, may at times be predicated upon conduct, short of "intentional," which exposes others to substantial and unjustified risks. I recognize also that our legal system includes certain "strict liability" crimes, but generally these are confined to the so-called "regulatory" or "public welfare" offenses, which "do not fit neatly into any of such accepted classifications of common-law offenses, such as those against the state, the person, property, or public morals. * * * Many violations of such regulations result in no direct or immediate injury to person or property but merely create the danger or probability of it which the law seeks to minimize." (*Morissette v. United States* (1952) 342 U.S. 246, 255–256, 72 S.Ct. 240, 245–246, 96 L.Ed. 288.) Moreover, with respect to such crimes, *"The accused, if he does not will the violation, usually is in a position to prevent it with no more care than society might reasonably expect * * * from one who assumed his responsibilities. Also, penalties commonly are relatively small, and conviction does no grave damage to an offender's reputation."* (*Id.*, at p. 256, 72 S.Ct. at p. 246, emphasis added.)

Even in the regulatory context, "judicial and academic acceptance of liability without fault has not been enthusiastic." (Jeffries & Stephan, *Defenses, Presumptions, and Burden of Proof in the Criminal Law* (1979) 88 Yale L.J. 1325, 1373.) And "with respect to traditional crimes, it is a widely accepted normative principle that conviction should not be had without proof of fault. At least when the offense carries serious sanctions and the stigma of official condemnation, liability should be reserved for persons whose blameworthiness has been established." (*Id.*, at pp. 1373–1374, fn. omitted.)

Commentators have suggested that this normative principle has a home in constitutional law (e.g., Dubin, *Mens Rea Reconsidered: A Plea for a Due Process Concept of Criminal Responsibility* (1966) 18 Stan.L. Rev. 322; Hippard, *The Unconstitutionality of Criminal Liability Without Fault: An Argument for a Constitutional Doctrine of Mens Rea* (1973) 10 Houston L.Rev. 1039; Packer, *The Aims of the Criminal Law Revisited: A Plea For a New Look at "Substantive Due Process"* (1971) 44 So.Cal.L.Rev. 490), and decisions of both the United States Supreme Court and this court lend some support to that premise. For example, in *Robinson v. California* (1962) 370 U.S. 660, 666–667, 82 S.Ct. 1417, 1420–1421, 8 L.Ed.2d 758, a California statute making it a misdemeanor punishable by imprisonment for a person to "be addicted to the use of narcotics" even though he had never touched any narcotic drug within the state or been guilty of any irregular behavior there, was held to inflict cruel and unusual punishment in violation of the Fourteenth Amendment. (Cf. *Powell v. Texas* (1968) 392 U.S. 514, 533, 88 S.Ct. 2145, 2154, 20 L.Ed.2d 1254.)

In *Burg v. Municipal Court* (1983) 35 Cal.3d 257, 198 Cal.Rptr. 145, 673 P.2d 732, this court unanimously upheld, against due process constitutional attack, a statute which makes it an offense for "any person who has 0.10 percent or more, by weight, of alcohol in his or her blood to drive a vehicle." (Veh.Code, § 23152, subd. (b).) The heart of that attack, though phrased in familiar terms of "vagueness" and "lack of due notice," was that a person might be unaware that his blood alcohol level exceeds the prescribed limit, and thus might be morally "innocent." In response, we observed that it requires "more than a small amount of alcohol" to produce a .10 blood-alcohol reading, and that readily available and widely disseminated charts "show with reasonable certainty the number of different alcoholic beverages necessary for a particular individual to reach [that level]." (*Burg v. Municipal Court,* supra, 35 Cal.3d at pp. 271–272, 198 Cal.Rptr. 145, 673 P.2d 732.) "The very fact that he has consumed a quantity of alcohol should notify a person of ordinary intelligence that he is in jeopardy of violating the statute." (*Id.,* at p. 271, 198 Cal.Rptr. 145, 673 P.2d 732.) Thus, "[o]ne who drives a vehicle after having ingested sufficient alcohol to approach or exceed the level proscribed is neither 'innocent' * * * nor is he without 'fair warning' * * *. It is difficult to sympathize with an 'unsuspecting' defendant who did not know if he could take a last sip without crossing the line, but who decided to do so anyway." (*Ibid.*)

While upholding the statute's validity, we nevertheless recognized the possibility of constitutional problems arising out of its application in particular cases. Observing that *Burg* involved a facial attack on the statute following overruling of demurrer, we stated: *"We therefore need not consider to what extent in particular cases fundamental notions of due process would permit a defendant to show, for example, that he did not knowingly or voluntarily drive or consume alcohol."* (35 Cal.3d at p. 266, fn. 10, 198 Cal.Rptr. 145, 673 P.2d 732, emphasis added.

The Legislature has itself determined, in section 1203.066, that a person's belief in the victim's age being over 14 may be not only honest but reasonable. No doubt the standard of what is reasonable must be set relatively high in order to accomplish the legislative objective of protecting persons under 14 years of age against certain conduct. Perhaps it is not enough that a person "looks" to be more than 14; perhaps there is a duty of reasonable inquiry besides. At some point, however, the belief becomes reasonable by any legitimate standard, so that one would say the defendant is acting in a way which is no different from the way our society would expect a reasonable, careful, and law-abiding citizen to act.

At that point, it seems to me, the imposition of criminal sanctions, particularly imprisonment, simply cannot be tolerated in a civilized society.

In this case we cannot ascertain from the record on appeal whether the trial court found some merit in defendant's claim that he honestly and reasonably believed the victim to be over 14 years of age. Since the court apparently considered defendant eligible for probation it is possible that the claim was given credence. If so, and defendant's conduct was in other respects that which we would expect of a reasonable, careful, and law-abiding citizen, I would conclude that imposition of a sentence of imprisonment on defendant is impermissible. Inasmuch as the record is inadequate to resolve either question, however, I would remand for a new probation and sentence hearing at which the court, if probation is again denied, should make express findings as to whether defendant honestly and reasonably believed the victim to be over 14 years of age and, if so, whether his conduct with her otherwise reflected that mens rea traditionally accepted as a prerequisite to the imposition of serious penal sanctions.

Notes and Questions

1. The California Supreme Court's decision in *Hernandez,* cited in the principal case, that a reasonable mistake of fact must be permitted as a defense to the charge of statutory rape was followed by the Alaska Supreme Court in State v. Guest, 583 P.2d 836 (Alaska 1978). The court in *Guest* reasoned that it would be unconstitutional to permit conviction in the absence of proof of some criminal intent. However, other courts considering the same issue have rejected the Alaska and California Supreme Courts' conclusions. E.g., State v. Superior Court, 104 Ariz. 440, 454 P.2d 982 (1969); State v. Silva, 53 Hawaii 232, 491 P.2d 1216 (1971); Toliver v. State, 267 Ind. 575, 372 N.E.2d 452 (1978); Eggleston v. State, 4 Md.App. 124, 241 A.2d 433 (1968); People v. Doyle, 16 Mich.App. 242, 167 N.W.2d 907 (1969) ("Current social and moral values make more realistic the California view that a reasonable and honest mistake of age is a valid defense to a charge of statutory rape * * * but this court is bound to follow the law presently in effect."); State v. Moore, 105 N.J.Super. 567, 253 A.2d 579 (1969); State v. Navarrette, 221 Neb. 171, 376 N.W.2d 8 (1985); State v. Fulks, 83 S.D. 433, 160 N.W.2d 418 (1968); Vasquez v. State, 622 S.W.2d 864 (Tex.Crim.App.1981); State v. Randolph, 12 Wn.App. 138, 528 P.2d 1008 (1974). The cases seldom discuss any constitutional issues which might be raised by interpreting statutory rape statutes so as to provide for no defense based upon mistake of age. Why might this be? But see Commonwealth v. Moore, 359 Mass. 509, 269 N.E.2d 636 (1971), in which the defendant was charged with "carnally knowing and abusing" a minor. The victim testified she had an identification card showing her age as eighteen and that she told the defendant she was that age. In addition, the victim had been convicted of prostitution and placed on probation; apparently the police officers, the lawyer representing her, the trial court judge, and the probation officer assumed she was eighteen. Nevertheless, the court held that no affirmative defense of mistake of age was available and that this "strict" liability did not deny the defendant due process of law. See Commonwealth v. Miller, 385 Mass. 521, 432 N.E.2d 463 (1982).

Perhaps no defense is necessary. Rare situations may be presented in which the underage victim is not only a willing or eager participant but is so physically precocious that the actor's belief that the victim is beyond the age covered by statutory rape is reasonable. But it may be, as the Minnesota Supreme Court assumed, that "it is likely that the good judgment of prosecutors and jurors will prevent a miscarriage of justice." State v. Morse, 281 Minn. 378, 385, 161 N.W.2d 699, 703 (1968).

2. Is the position of the majority in *Olsen* persuasive? Do they convincingly distinguish the need for culpability in the statutory rape situation addressed by *Hernandez,* and the absence of such need in the case of Olsen? Is it that in contemporary American society girls under 14 are so obviously inappropriate subjects for sexual contact that all males should know that they should not even come close to the prohibited line? Would that explain the difference in legislative treatment of age and mental incompetency as factors precluding the granting of effective consent to intercourse? As is indicated in note 1, supra, the defense of reasonable mistake as to age has usually been rejected. However, legislatures have commonly required that a defendant charged with rape of a mentally incompetent adult have known of, or been reckless as to, the victim's condition. See e.g., Michigan Penal Code Sec. 750.520d(1)(c) reprinted at page 503, supra.

3. It may be safely assumed that the contention of a defendant such as Olsen would usually be that he reasonably believed that the female was older than fourteen. Is it, as suggested in the preceding note, appropriate that he bear the risk of error because even were he correct he would have been engaging in improper, if not immoral, conduct? In a famous nineteenth century English case a defendant charged with unlawfully taking an unmarried girl of less than sixteen from the possession of her father was found to have reasonably believed she was eighteen. His conviction was, nevertheless, affirmed because at that time fathers had custody of unmarried daughters until 21, so that the defendant, even on the facts as he believed them to be, was committing a civil wrong. Regina v. Prince, L.R. 2 Cr.Cas.Res. 154 (1875). Is that form of reasoning attractive in an age when laws against fornication and adultery have disappeared and the traditional association of out-of-wedlock sexuality with immorality no longer commands a consensus in our society?

4. The age of consent for purposes of rape prosecutions under Anglo-american law has risen significantly since the reign of Queen Elizabeth I when it was set at ten to today when it is often sixteen, seventeen, or eighteen. See Kruger v. State, 623 S.W.2d 386, 387 (Tex.Crim.App.1981) (Clinton, J., dissenting). How is this movement to be explained in light of the apparent steady decline in the age of menarche? Some studies estimate that, in Western Europe, the onset of menarche has declined at about four months per decade since 1850, from above sixteen to below thirteen. Phipps, Long, & Woods, Medical-Surgical Nursing: Concepts and Clinical Practice 220 (Mosby 1983). This means that an increasing percentage of females who are below the legal age of consent are biologically mature and thus more likely to appear to be appropriate subjects for sexual contact. In light of this would it not be more appropriate to require a state of mind as to the female's age? Or is the earlier maturation of females the reason for raising the age of consent while continuing to treat age as a strict liability element?

5. If provision ought to be made for some sort of "defense of mistake as to age" in regard to non-forcible sexual offenses committed upon young

persons, should this be limited? Arizona makes criminal sexual intercourse or oral sexual contact with any person who is under the age of
eighteen and not the actor's spouse. Ariz.Rev.Stat. § 13–1405. But another section provides:

> It is a defense to a prosecution ＊ ＊ ＊ in which the victim's lack of
> consent is based on incapacity to consent because the victim was
> fifteen, sixteen or seventeen years of age, if at the time the defendant
> engaged in the conduct constituting the defense the defendant did not
> know and could not reasonably have known the age of the victim.

Id., at § 13–1407(B).

The Texas Penal Code defines sexual assault as including penetration
of the anus or female sexual organ of a child or oral sexual contact between
the actor and a child. Texas Penal Code § 22.011(a)(2). "Child" is defined
as a person younger than seventeen years of age who is not the spouse of
the actor. Id., at § 22.011(c)(1). The provision continues:

> (d) It is a defense ＊ ＊ ＊ that ＊ ＊ ＊ the child was at the time of
> the offense 14 years of age or older and had prior to the time of the
> offense engaged promiscuously in [the conduct covered by the offense].
>
> (e) It is an affirmative defense ＊ ＊ ＊ that the actor was not more
> than two years older than the victim.

6. If criminal sanctions are appropriate for consensual sexual conduct
involving young persons, is it desirable—or constitutionally acceptable—for
liability to be imposed only on male participants? In Michael M. v.
Superior Court, 450 U.S. 464, 101 S.Ct. 1200, 67 L.Ed.2d 437 (1981), the
Supreme Court considered the argument that California's statutory rape
provision violated the Fourteenth Amendment's requirement of equal protection because it permitted only the conviction of males for having
intercourse with females. A majority rejected the contention and upheld
the statute. Justice Rehnquist's plurality opinion reasoned, first, that the
statute served the legitimate state interest of preventing teenage
pregnancies. Second, the legislative decision to attack that problem by
creating a crime that is not "gender-neutral" was acceptable:

> Because virtually all of the significant harmful and inescapably
> identifiable consequences of teenage pregnancies fall on the young
> female, a legislature acts well within its authority when it elects to
> punish only the participant who, by nature, suffers few of the conse-
> quences of his conduct. It is hardly unreasonable for a legislature
> acting to protect minor females to exclude them from punishment.
> Moreover, the risk of pregnancy itself constitutes a substantial deter-
> rence to young females. No similar sanctions deter males. A criminal
> sanction imposed solely on males thus serves to roughly "equalize" the
> deterrents on the sexes.
>
> ＊　＊　＊
>
> [W]e cannot say that a general-neutral statute would be as effec-
> tive as the statute California has chosen to enact. The State persua-
> sively contends that a gender-neutral statute would frustrate its inter-
> est in effective enforcement. Its view is that a female is surely less
> likely to report violations of the statute if she herself would be subject

to prosecution. In an area already fraught with prosecutorial difficulties, we decline to hold that the Equal Protection Clause requires a legislature to enact a statute so broad that it may well be incapable of enforcement.

450 U.S. at 473–74, 101 S.Ct. at 1206–07, 67 L.Ed.2d at 445.

Whatever the persuasiveness of Justice Rehnquist's rejection of a federal constitutional requirement for gender-neutrality in the context of "statutory rape", should male victims of forcible rape by females be unprotected by the law? This question was addressed by the *Liberta* case, discussed in connection with the "marital exemption" at page 513, supra. The defendant there also challenged his conviction on the grounds that New York's rape law was unconstitutional because, unlike the vast majority of American jurisdictions, it was not gender-neutral. The court agreed that a violation of equal protection was presented. It explained:

> Rape statutes historically applied only to conduct by males against females, largely because the purpose behind the proscriptions was to protect the chastity of women and thus their property value to their fathers or husbands. * * *

> A statute which treats males and females differently violates equal protection unless the classification is substantially related to the achievement of an important governmental objective. * * * [The court then considered and rejected the state's arguments justifying the distinction. The first was that there was no danger of pregnancy.]

> There is no evidence, however, that preventing pregnancies is a primary purpose of the statute prohibiting forcible rape * * *. Rather, * * * its overriding purpose is to protect a woman from an unwanted, forcible, and often violent intrusion into her body. * * *

> [The court then rejected, as reflecting archaic stereotypical attitudes about the sexes, the argument that female victims face unique medical, sociological and psychological problems. Finally, it addressed the claim that the rape of a male was either physiologically impossible or extremely rare. The former was termed simply wrong. As to the latter,] while forcible sexual assaults by females upon males are undoubtedly less common than those by males upon females this numerical disparity cannot by itself make the gender discrimination constitutional. Women may well be responsible for a far lower number of all serious crimes than are men, but such a disparity would not make it permissible for the State to punish only men who commit, for example, robbery.

People v. Liberta, 64 N.Y.2d 152, 167–70, 485 N.Y.S.2d 207, 216–17, 474 N.E.2d 567, 576–77 (1984). The court concluded that the prosecution had failed to meet its burden of justifying the discrimination under the equal protection clause and that the rape law would have to be read as applying to female as well as male assailants. This holding did not, however, require that the defendant's conviction be reversed inasmuch as his conduct had been covered by the law as enacted.

DIRECTOR OF PUBLIC PROSECUTIONS v. MORGAN

House of Lords, 1975.
2 All ER 347.

LORD HAILSHAM OF ST MARYLEBONE. * * * This appeal is concerned with the mental element in rape. It involves two questions at vastly different levels of importance but each strangely illustrative of the other, which were argued before us. The first is a question of great academic importance in the theory of English criminal law, certified for this House by the Court of Appeal, which also gave leave to appeal. The second, which arises only if the first is answered favourably to the appellants, is whether the House can be satisfied that no miscarriage of justice has taken place so as to compel them to apply the proviso to § 2(1) of the Criminal Appeal Act 1968. As I propose to answer these two questions, as to the first favourably, and as the second, unfavourably to the appellants, and thus dismiss the appeals, I will begin this opinion with the facts.[a]

The four appellants were all convicted at the Stafford Crown Court of various offences connected with alleged rapes on the person of Daphne Ethel Morgan of whom the first appellant is, or at the material time was, the husband. The second, third and fourth appellants were convicted each of a principal offence against Mrs. Morgan, and each of aiding and abetting the principal offences alleged to have been committed by each of the other two. The appellant Morgan, who also had connection with his wife allegedly without her consent as part of the same series of events, was not charged with rape, the prosecution evidently accepting and applying the ancient common law doctrine that a husband cannot be guilty of raping his own wife. Morgan was therefore charged with and convicted of aiding and abetting the rapes alleged to have been committed by the other three.

* * * The question certified * * * is:

"Whether, in rape, the defendant can properly be convicted notwithstanding that he in fact believed that the woman consented if such belief was not based on reasonable grounds."

* * *

[The coappellants were all in the Royal Air Force. They had spent the evening drinking together. They had hoped to pick up some women but Mr. Morgan, the oldest and most senior in rank, suggested that they should all come to his house and have sexual intercourse with

---

a. In reading the various opinions which are reproduced here (a small portion of only three of the five issued by the participating Lords), keep in mind that the ultimate disposition by the 3–2 majority is to affirm the conviction. Although the appellants triumphed on the question of law raised by their appeal, the majority concluded, per the proviso to § 2(1) of the Criminal Appeal Act 1968, that the trial judge's error was harmless. That is, the Lords believed that on these facts reasonable jurors, even if properly instructed, could not have believed the defendants' claims.

his wife. The three younger airmen claimed that Morgan said his wife might struggle a bit but this was merely her way of getting "turned on". They all went to the house, invaded Mrs. Morgan's bedroom, shared by her 11 year old son, where she was asleep and seized her. She was then taken by force to another bedroom and, over her most vigorous protests and struggles, had intercourse with her as well as committing various lewd acts. When they were finished, Mrs. Morgan fled to the hospital and immediately complained of being raped.

The testimony of the coappellants and that of Mrs. Morgan as to the events at the house were, for the most part, in agreement. The key difference is that they claimed that after an initial struggle Mrs. Morgan, "not merely consented but took an active and enthusiastic part in a sexual orgy which might have excited unfavourable comment in the courts of Caligula or Nero."]

* * * I mention all these details simply to show, that if, as I think plain, the jury accepted Mrs. Morgan's statement *in substance* there was no possibility whatever of any of the appellants holding any belief whatever, reasonable or otherwise, in their victim's consent to what was being done.

The primary "defence" was consent. I use the word "defence" in inverted commas, because, of course, in establishing the crime of rape, the prosecution must exclude consent in order to establish the essential ingredients of the crime. There is no burden at the outset on the accused to raise the issue.

* * * [I]t is clear that Morgan did invite his three companions home in order that they might have sexual intercourse with his wife and, no doubt, he may well have led them in one way or another to believe that she would consent to their doing so. This, however, would only be matter predisposing them to believe that Mrs. Morgan consented, and would not in any way establish that, at the time, they believed she did consent whilst they were having intercourse.

* * *

* * * The learned judge said:

" * * * The crime of rape consists in having unlawful sexual intercourse with a woman without her consent and by force. By force. Those words mean exactly what they say. It does not mean there has to be a fight or blows have to be inflicted. It means that there has to be some violence used against the woman to overbear her will or that there has to be a threat of violence as a result of which her will is overborne. * * * Further, the prosecution have to prove that each defendant intended to have sexual intercourse with this woman without her consent. * * * Therefore if the defendant believed or may have believed that Mrs. Morgan consented to him having sexual intercourse with her, then there would be no such intent in his mind and he would be not guilty of the offence of rape, but such a belief must be honestly held by the defendant in the first place. He must really believe that. And, secondly, his belief must be a reasonable belief; such a belief as a reasonable man would entertain if he applied his mind and thought about the matter. It is not enough for a defendant to rely upon a belief, even though he honestly held it, if it was completely fanciful; contrary to every indication which could be given which would carry some weight with a reasonable man. * * *"

It is on the second proposition about the mental element that the appellants concentrate their criticism. An honest belief in consent, they contend, is enough. It matters not whether it be also reasonable. No doubt a defendant will wish to raise argument or lead evidence to show that this belief was reasonable, since this will support its honesty. No doubt the prosecution will seek to cross-examine or raise arguments or adduce evidence to undermine the contention that the belief is reasonable, because, in the nature of the case, the fact that a belief cannot reasonably be held is a strong ground for saying that it was not in fact held honestly at all. Nonetheless, the appellants contend, the crux of the matter, the factum probandum, or rather the fact to be refuted by the prosecution, is honesty and not honesty plus reasonableness. In making reasonableness as well as honesty an ingredient in this "defence" the judge, say the appellants, was guilty of a misdirection.

My first comment on this direction is that the propositions described "in the first place" and "secondly" in the above direction as to the mental ingredient in rape are wholly irreconcilable. * * * If it be true, as the learned judge says "in the first place", that the prosecution have to prove that "each defendant intended to have sexual intercourse without her consent. Not merely that he intended to have intercourse with her but that he intended to have intercourse without her consent", the defendant must be entitled to an acquittal if the prosecution fail to prove just that. The necessary mental ingredient will be lacking and the only possible verdict is "not guilty". If, on the other hand, as is asserted in the passage beginning "secondly", it is necessary for any belief in the woman's consent to be "a reasonable belief" before the defendant is entitled to an acquittal, it must either be because the mental ingredient in rape is not "to have intercourse and to have it without her consent" but simply "to have intercourse" subject to a special defence of "honest and reasonable belief", or alternatively to have intercourse without a reasonable belief in her consent. * * *

No doubt it would be possible, by statute, to devise a law by which intercourse, voluntarily entered into, was an absolute offence, subject to a "defence" of belief whether honest or honest and reasonable, of which the "evidential" burden is primarily on the defence and the "probative" burden on the prosecution. But in my opinion such is not the crime of rape as it has hitherto been understood. The prohibited act in rape is to have intercourse without the victim's consent. The minimum mens rea or guilty mind in most common law offences, including rape, is the intention to do the prohibited act, and that is correctly stated in the proposition stated "in the first place" of the judge's direction. * * *

The only qualification I would make to the direction of the learned judge's "in the first place" is the refinement for which, as I shall show, there is both Australian and English authority, that if the intention of the accused is to have intercourse nolens volens, that is recklessly and not caring whether the victim be a consenting party or not that is equivalent on ordinary principles to an intent to do the prohibited act without the consent of the victim.

The alternative version of the learned judge's direction would read that the accused must do the prohibited act with the intention of doing it without an honest and reasonable belief in the victim's consent. * * * In principle, however, I find it unacceptable. I believe that "mens rea" means "guilty or criminal mind", and if it be the case, as seems to be accepted here, that mental element in rape is not knowledge but intent, to insist that a belief must be reasonable to excuse it is to insist that either the accused is to be found guilty of intending to do that which in truth he did not intend to do, or that his state of mind though innocent of evil intent, can convict him if it be honest but not rational. * * * This is to insist on an objective element in the definition of intent, and this is a course which I am extremely reluctant to adopt * * *.

Once one has accepted, what seems to me abundantly clear, that the prohibited act in rape is non-consensual sexual intercourse, and that the guilty state of mind is an intention to commit it, it seems to me to follow as a matter of inexorable logic that there is no room either for a "defence" of honest belief or mistake, or of a defence of honest and reasonable belief and mistake. Either the prosecution proves that the accused had the requisite intent, or it does not. In the former case it succeeds, and in the latter it fails. Since honest belief clearly negatives intent, the reasonableness or otherwise of that belief can only be evidence for or against the view that the belief and therefore the intent was actually held, and it matters not whether * * * "the definition of a crime includes no specific element beyond the prohibited act." * * * Any other view, as for insertion of the word "reasonable" can only have the effect of saying that a man intends something which he does not.

[T]he appellants invited us to overrule the bigamy cases from R. v. Tolson [1] onwards and perhaps also R. v. Prince [2] (the abduction case) as wrongly decided at least insofar as they purport to insist that a mistaken belief must be reasonable. * * * I am content to rest my view of the instant case on the crime of rape by saying that it is my opinion that the prohibited act is and always has been intercourse without consent of the victim and the mental element is and always has been the intention to commit that act, or the equivalent intention of

---

1.   (1889) 23 QBD 168, [1886–90] All ER Rep. 26.

2.   (1875) LR 2 CCR 154, [1874–80] All ER Rep. 881.

having intercourse willy-nilly not caring whether the victim consents or no. A failure to prove this involves an acquittal because the intent, an essential ingredient, is lacking. It matters not why it is lacking if only it is not there, and in particular it matters not that the intention is lacking only because of a belief not based on reasonable grounds. I should add that I myself am inclined to view R. v. Tolson as a narrow decision based on the construction of a statute, which prima facie seemed to make an absolute statutory offence, with a proviso, related to the seven year period of absence, which created a statutory defence. The judges in R. v. Tolson decided that this was not reasonable, and, on general jurisprudential principles, imported into the statutory offence words which created a special "defence" of honest and reasonable belief of which the "evidential" but not the probative burden lay on the defence. I do not think it is necessary to decide this conclusively in the present case. But if this is the true view there is a complete distinction between R. v. Tolson and the other cases based on statute and the present.

* * *

For the above reasons I would answer the question certified in the negative, but would apply the proviso to s 2(1) of the Criminal Appeal Act 1968 on the ground that no miscarriage of justice has or conceivably could have occurred. In my view, therefore these appeals should be dismissed.

LORD SIMON OF GLAISDALE. * * *

The answer to this question, in my view, depends on the following matters: first, a distinction between crimes of basic and of ulterior intent; secondly, a distinction between probative and evidential burdens of proof; thirdly, the interrelationship of these two distinctions; fourthly, ascertainment whether rape is a crime of basic or ulterior intent; and, fifthly, the general policy of the criminal law when the prosecution has provisionally discharged the burden of proving actus reus and mens rea, and the accused then alleges a belief, albeit erroneous, in a state of facts which would, if true, negative the actus reus and the mens rea provisionally proved by the prosecution. After examining these five matters I shall endeavour to determine the reasons for what I believe to be the general policy of the criminal law in such circumstances.

I turn to examine, first, the distinction between crimes of basic and of ulterior intent * * *. By "crimes of basic intent" I mean those crimes whose definition expresses (or, more often, implies) a mens rea which does not go beyond the actus reus. The actus reus generally consists of an act and some consequence. The consequence may be very closely connected with the act or more remotely connected with it; but with a crime of basic intent the mens rea does not extend beyond the act and its consequence, however remote, as defined in the actus reus. * * * For an example of a crime of basic intent where the consequence of the act involved in the actus reus as defined in the crime is less immediate, I take the crime of unlawful wounding. The act is, say, the squeezing of a trigger. A number of consequences (mechanical, chemical, ballistic and physiological) intervene before the final consequence involved in the defined actus reus—namely, the wounding of another person in circumstances unjustified by law. But again here the mens rea corresponds closely to the actus reus. The prosecution must prove that the accused foresaw that some physical harm would ensue to another person in circumstances unjustified by law as a probable (or possible and desired) consequence of his act, or that he was reckless whether or not such consequence ensued.

On the other hand, there are crimes of ulterior intent—"ulterior" because the mens rea goes beyond contemplation of the actus reus. For example, in the crime of wounding with intent to cause grievous bodily harm, the actus reus is the wounding. The prosecution must prove a corresponding mens rea (as with unlawful wounding), but the prosecution must go further: it must show that the accused foresaw that serious physical injury would probably be a consequence of his act, or would possibly be so, that being a purpose of his act. The crime of wounding with intent to cause grievous bodily harm could be committed without any serious physical injury being caused to the victim. This is because there is no actus reus corresponding to the ulterior intent. One of the questions which has to be answered in this appeal is whether rape is a crime of basic or ulterior intent.

A second relevant distinction known to the modern law is that between probative and the evidential burdens of proof. * * * In the criminal law the probative burden of every issue lies on the prosecution (except for the single common law exception of insanity and some statutory exceptions). But the prosecution may adduce evidence sufficient, at a certain stage in the trial, to discharge provisionally the probative burden and thus call for some explanation on behalf of the accused (generally by evidence; though forensic analysis discounting the prosecution's case sometimes suffices): the evidential burden has shifted, though the probative burden remains on the prosecution. Again, the accused may raise a case fit for the consideration of the jury on a fresh issue. For example, although the prosecution may have provisionally discharged the onus of proving an assault, the accused may raise an issue of self-defence in a form fit for the consideration of the jury: if so, the evidential burden of disproving it will shift to the prosecution, which has, of course, also (once the defence is raised in a form fit for the consideration of the jury) the probative burden of disproving it. In this way the evidential burden of proof will often shift backwards and forwards during a trial, the probative burden remaining throughout on the prosecution.

The third matter for consideration is the interaction between these two distinctions—between crimes of basic and of ulterior intent, on the one hand, and between probative and evidential burdens of proof on the other. Such interaction occurs because proof of the actus reus generally raises a presumption of a corresponding mens rea, an act being usually performed with foresight of its probable consequences. I emphasise the words "generally" and "usually"; because the inference may not be a natural one in some circumstances. For example, a different inference as to intention may be drawn from proof that the accused drove his elbow hard into the stomach of a stranger in a crowded train from where it is proved that he did the same act when alone with the stranger in the course of an angry argument. If the crime is one of basic intent, so that the mens rea does not extend beyond the actus reus, proof of the actus reus is therefore, generally, sufficient prima facie proof of the mens rea to shift the evidential burden of proof. Thus, if the prosecution prove that the accused squeezed the trigger of a firearm and thereby wounded a victim, this will often be sufficient proof not only on the actus reus of unlawful wounding but also of the necessary mens rea, i.e., that the accused foresaw the wounding as a likely consequence of his act or was reckless as to whether it ensued, so as to cause the evidential burden to shift and thus to call for some explanation on behalf of the accused. But if the crime is one of ulterior intent, proof of the actus reus tells little about mens rea insofar as it extends beyond the actus reus; so that the evidential burden does not necessarily shift on proof of the actus reus. To prove that A wounded B, even intentionally, does not itself raise a presumption that A thereby intended to cause serious physical injury to B.

This brings me to the fourth question, namely whether rape is a crime of basic or ulterior intent. Does it involve an intent going beyond the actus reus? * * * The actus reus is sexual intercourse with a woman who is not in fact consenting to such intercourse. The mens rea is knowledge that the woman is not consenting or recklessness as to whether she is consenting or not. That it is nothing more can be seen by postulating an offence of rape with an ulterior intent. The offence with which the 4th Earl of Bothwell was popularly charged by his contemporaries was rape with intent to procure marriage. If this were a crime—and several 18th century crimes of abduction are nearby analogous—the crime would be one of ulterior intent. But comparison with such a postulated crime shows that rape itself involves no mens rea going beyond the actus reus.

If this is right, proof of the actus reus in rape—that is, proof of sexual intercourse with a woman who did not consent to it—will generally be sufficient prima facie proof to shift the evidential burden. If the evidential burden shifts in this way, the accused must either prove that his conduct was involuntary (which is irrelevant in the crime of rape) or he must negative the inference as to mens rea which might be drawn from the actus reus. Assuming that the prosecution have proved sexual intercourse with a woman who did not in fact consent to it, in general the only way in which the accused can shift back the evidential burden is by showing a belief in a state of affairs whereby the actus would not be reus. In the context of rape, the accused in such circumstances must, in other words, show that he believed that the woman was consenting. To say that he must show that he believed it "honestly" is tautologous but useful as emphasising a distinction. The question is whether he must show that he believed it reasonably, and, if so, why.

* * *

It remains to consider, why the law requires, in such circumstances, that the belief in a state of affairs whereby the actus would not be reus must be held on reasonable grounds. One reason was given by Bridge, J., in the Court of Appeal:

> "The rationale of requiring reasonable grounds for the mistaken belief must lie in the law's consideration that a bald assertion of belief for which the accused can indicate no reasonable ground is evidence of insufficient substance to raise any issue requiring the jury's consideration."

I agree; but I think there is also another reason. The policy of the law in this regard could well derive from its concern to hold a fair balance between victim and accused. It would hardly seem just to fob off a victim of a savage assault with such comfort as he could derive from knowing that his injury was caused by a belief, however absurd, that he was about to attack the accused. A respectable woman who has been ravished would hardly feel that she was vindicated by being told that her assailant must go unpunished because he believed, quite unreasonably, that she was consenting to sexual intercourse with him. * * *

I would therefore answer the question certified for your Lordships' consideration, Yes. * * *

LORD CROSS OF CHELSEA. * * *

* * * If the words defining an offence provide either expressly or impliedly that a man is not to be guilty of it if he believes something to be true, then he cannot be found guilty if the jury think that he may have believed it to be true, however inadequate were his reasons for doing so. But, if the definition of the offence is on the face of it "absolute" and the defendant is seeking to escape his prima facie liability by a defence of mistaken belief, I can see no hardship to him in requiring the mistake—if it is to afford him a defence—to be based on reasonable grounds. * * * [T]here is nothing unreasonable in the law requiring a citizen to take reasonable care to ascertain the facts relevant to his avoiding doing a prohibited act. To have intercourse with a woman who is not your wife is, even today, not generally considered to be a course of conduct which the law ought positively to encourage and it can be argued with force that it is only fair to the woman and not in the least unfair to the man that he should be under a duty to take reasonable care to ascertain that she is consenting to the intercourse and be at the risk of a prosecution if he fails to take such care. So if the Sexual Offences Act 1956 had made it an offence to have intercourse with a woman who was not consenting to it, so that the defendant could only escape liability by the application of the "Tolson" principle, I would not have thought the law unjust.

But, as I have said, s 1 of the 1956 Act does not say that a man who has sexual intercourse with a woman who does not consent to it commits an offence; it says that a man who rapes a woman commits an offence. * * * Rape, to my mind, imports at least indifference as to the woman's consent. * * *

Notes and Questions

1. In State v. Williams, 696 S.W.2d 809 (Mo.App.1985), the defendant was tried for forcible rape and sodomy of the victim, a seventeen year old female who had accompanied him to his apartment from a tavern. The defendant did not testify. He urged, however, that the prosecution's evidence raised a question as to whether he had mistakenly believed the victim consented and thus that he was entitled to a jury instruction on that issue. This was apparently based in large part upon the victim's failure to leave the apartment after the defendant's first sexual advances. After concluding that the evidence failed to raise a question of reasonable mistake, the court continued:

Appellant broadens his argument to say that he was entitled to an acquittal even if he had recklessly disregarded the victim's opposition and protests and thus unreasonably believed that the victim was consenting. * * * In simple terms, the instruction [requested] would conclude the fact that if an attacker chose to ignore the protests and resistance of a victim and unreasonably believed that the victim was consenting, the accused would be entitled to acquittal. [The appellant's claim is supported by a note within the commentary to our Code] which declares, "all other mental states [*except criminal negligence*] can be negated by a belief (reasonable or not)." Rape and sodomy can be committed recklessly. Fortunately, this is not the law. Our state Supreme Court, in the case of State v. Beishir, 646 S.W.2d 74, 79 (Mo. banc 1983) held, "it is incongruous to define forcible rape and forcible sodomy as being accomplished 'without the person's consent by the use of forcible compulsion' . . . and yet authorize a verdict of not guilty upon the defendant's belief, reasonable or not." * * * The only sensible basis for an instruction upon mistaken belief as to consent and as to its being a special negative defense is if the belief is a reasonable belief.

696 S.W.2d at 813 (emphasis in original).

2. In United States v. Feola, 420 U.S. 671, 95 S.Ct. 1255, 43 L.Ed.2d 541 (1975), the Supreme Court addressed the requirements for liability under 18 U.S.C.A. § 111:

§ 111. Assaulting, resisting, or impeding certain officers or employees.

Whoever forcibly assaults, resists, opposes, impedes, intimidates, or interferes with any person designated in section 1114 of this title [as a federal officer] while engaged in or on account of the performance of his official duties, shall be fined not more than $5,000 or imprisoned not more than three years, or both.

Specifically, it considered whether scienter is required with reference to the victim's identity as a federal officer. This, in turn, was seen by the Court as depending upon Congress' intention in enacting the offense:

> If the primary [Congressional] purpose is to protect federal law enforcement personnel, that purpose could well be frustrated by the imposition of a strict scienter requirement. On the other hand, if § 111 is seen primarily as an anti-obstruction statute, it is likely that Congress intended criminal liability to be imposed only when a person acted with the specific intent to impede enforcement activities.

420 U.S. at 678, 95 S.Ct. at 1261, 43 L.Ed.2d at 549. In the event that Congress intended only the latter, the Court assumed, the required "specific intent" could be present only if the defendant was aware of the identity of his victim as a federal officer. Its review of the legislative history of § 111 convinced the Court that Congress was concerned both with punishing obstruction with federal officers and with providing maximum protection to those officers:

> We conclude * * * that in order to effectuate the congressional purpose of according maximum protection to federal officers by making prosecutions for assaults upon them cognizable in the federal courts, § 111 cannot be construed as embodying an unexpressed requirement that an assailant be aware that his victim is a federal officer. All the statute requires is an intent to assault, not an intent to assault a federal officer. A contrary conclusion would give insufficient protection to the agent enforcing an unpopular law, and none to the agent acting undercover.
>
> This interpretation poses no risk of unfairness to defendants. It is no snare for the unsuspecting. Although the perpetrator of a narcotics "rip-off" * * * may be surprised to find that his intended victim is a federal officer in civilian apparel, he nonetheless knows from the very onset that his planned course of conduct is wrongful. The situation is not one where legitimate conduct becomes unlawful solely because of the identity of the individual or agency affected. In a case of this kind the offender takes his victim as he finds him. The concept of criminal intent does not extend so far as to require that the actor understand not only the nature of his act but also its consequences for the choice of a judicial forum.

420 U.S. at 684–85, 95 S.Ct. at 1264, 43 L.Ed.2d at 552–53. This conclusion led the Court to characterize the requirement that the victim be a federal officer as "jurisdictional only" and therefore as a matter "that need not be in the mind of the actor." 420 U.S. at 676 n. 9, 95 S.Ct. 1260 n. 9, 43 L.Ed. 2d at 548 n. 9. Perhaps *Feola* suggests that, generally speaking, if an attendant circumstance is one required as an element only for jurisdictional or similar purposes, the principles demanding culpability generally do not suggest that culpability should be required with regard to this attendant circumstance.

3.   Compare with *Feola* the reasoning in Mitchell v. United States, 394 F.2d 767 (D.C.Cir.1968), concerning a federal statute, D.C.Code § 22–2206, that provided:

> Whoever shall * * * steal * * * any money, property, or writing, the property of the District of Columbia, shall suffer imprisonment for not exceeding five years or be fined not more than five thousand dollars, or both.

Another statute created the offense of petit larceny and provided a penalty of imprisonment for up to a year, a fine of $200, or both. At issue in *Mitchell* was whether § 22–2206 requires proof that the defendant knew the property was owned by the District of Columbia. In holding that such proof was necessary, the court reasoned as follows:

> [T]he penalties provided for petit larceny * * * are relatively minor. It is quite possible that because of the greater vulnerability of low-valued government property (street lights, refuse containers, park benches, office supplies, etc.), Congress intended to create a greater deterrent to this type of theft * * * and, therefore, enacted § 22–2206 with more severe penalties. Since § 22–2206 would be a greater deterrent only if the potential wrongdoers were aware that the property they were intending to steal belonged to the District of Columbia, the statute would have its intended effect only if construed to require *scienter*. * * * We emphasize, however, that this element of the crime can be shown either by specific knowledge of District of Columbia ownership or by the establishment of sufficient facts to put a reasonable person on notice of the District ownership.

394 F.2d at 773–74. Does 18 U.S.C.A. § 641, creating the offense of stealing property of the United States and at issue in Morissette v. United States, 342 U.S. 246, 72 S.Ct. 240, 96 L.Ed. 288 (1952) (reprinted at page 309, supra), require proof that the defendant knew the property was owned by the United States? See United States v. Baker, 693 F.2d 183, 186 (D.C.Cir. 1982), noting that "[i]t is now well established that the statutory requirement that the stolen property [belong] to the government merely furnishes the basis for federal jurisdiction and that defendant's knowledge of this jurisdictional fact is irrelevant."

4.   Sometimes, as would seem to have been the case in the *Mitchell* case (see note 3, supra), an attendant circumstance is required to differentiate a more serious crime from a lesser offense. Should this make any difference with regard to whether a state of mind is required concerning the circumstance? Section 845a of title 21 of the United States Code makes it a crime to distribute heroin within one thousand feet of any primary or elementary school, and provides for twice the punishment to which the seller would otherwise be liable. In United States v. Falu, 776 F.2d 46 (2d Cir.1985), the defendant argued that the prosecution had to prove that he acted with knowledge of the school's proximity. The court rejected this contention. It held that although *mens rea* is the norm for criminal provisions Congress had dispensed with it here in order to achieve its purpose of protecting school children. The situation, wrote the court, was unlike that in *Liparota* (reprinted at page 286, supra) where the absence of *mens rea* would criminalize apparently innocent conduct. Rather, Falu

was like the defendant in *Feola* (see note 2, supra) in that he knew he was engaged in illicit conduct. 776 F.2d at 50. Is this reasoning persuasive where the presence of the attendant circumstance exposes the actor to twice the maximum punishment—twenty years and $250,000—provided for those who sell drugs further from a school?

The same problem, in less draconian form, is commonly presented by the property acquisition offenses, in which the seriousness of the offense is often determined by the nature of the property, the value of the property, or some combination of these. Where the value of the property make a theft "grand" theft and a felony, should the prosecution be required to prove not only the value of the property but also that the defendant was aware of that value? If the fact that property taken was of a certain sort makes the theft of that property a felony regardless of its value, should the prosecution have to prove that the defendant was aware of the nature of the property?

In regard to the latter, consider People v. Campbell, 63 Cal.App.3d 599, 133 Cal.Rptr. 815 (1976). Campbell was proved to have taken the victim's purse from her car. The purse contained a pistol which was later recovered from a house belonging to a friend of the defendant. Under California theft law, theft of a firearm was a felony without reference to its value and Campbell was convicted of felony theft. On appeal, he urged that the prosecution may have proved his intention to steal the purse but not the pistol because no evidence indicated he knew the pistol was inside the purse. Affirming, the appellate court explained:

> The evidence admits of no doubt that defendant intended to steal *the purse*. In doing so, we are of the view that he intended to steal *the contents* of the purse, in this case the gun.

63 Cal.App.3d at 615, 133 Cal.Rptr. at 824 (emphasis in original). It continued:

> The Attorney General likens this situation to the doctrine of "transferred intent." Under this theory, when a person purposefully attempts to kill one person but by mistake kills another instead, the law transfers the felonious intent from the object of the assault to the actual victim. This theory has some appeal here for it places full responsibility upon the actor who violates the law.

63 Cal.App.3d at 615 n. 11, 133 Cal.Rptr. at 824 n. 11. But should "full responsibility" in this sense be placed upon one who violates the law?

Consider also People v. Magee, 98 A.D.2d 874, 471 N.Y.S.2d 164 (1983). Magee admitted stealing the victim's wallet, removing a $20 bill and some change from it, and discarding the wallet in a garbage container. The wallet contained credit cards, which were found in it when the wallet was recovered. Magee denied knowing that credit cards were in the wallet. Under New York law, theft of the wallet and the money was at most petit larceny given their value, but larceny of property consisting of a credit card is a felony. At his trial for felony theft, is Magee entitled to have the jury instructed that he may be guilty of only petit theft because he lacked the intent required for grand larceny of the credit card? Without further explanation, the appellate court held that no such instruction was necessary because there was no reasonable view of the evidence that would support a finding that Magee was guilty only of petit larceny. See People v. Timmons, 124 Misc.2d 766, 767, 478 N.Y.S.2d 777, 778 (1984), citing *Magee* for the proposition that "a thief who steals a credit card need not even be cognizant of the precise nature of what he has stolen to be charged with the full consequences of his criminal act and with the highest degree of crime committed."

Chapter X

THE INCHOATE CRIMES

Contents

Editors' Introduction: The Inchoate or Preparatory Crimes

The cases and materials on causation and complicity, in Chapters VIII and XI, reveal the special difficulties in imposing liability where, although a harmful and prohibited result has occurred, the manner of its occurrence is bizarre or the defendant's connection therewith is attenuated. Those cases and materials, nevertheless, involved paradigmatic crimes in the sense that the state was required to prove an act, a state of mind, possibly circumstances, and a result. In contrast, this chapter deals with an extensive body of law which has evolved to permit the imposition of punishment in the absence of any result whatever. The offenses of attempt, solicitation, and conspiracy are all "inchoate"—or anticipatory—in the sense that they consist of uncompleted activity directed towards objectives that are almost invariably criminal in nature. Chapter X deals with these three offenses and the defenses specially directed to them.

Conspiracy raises a number of special problems. These are attributable, in large part, to the fact that conspiracy can serve functions other than that of being an inchoate offense. When the prosecution seeks a conviction for conspiracy as well as for the completed offense which was its objective, conspiracy may also serve as a means of aggravating the defendants' actual or potential punishment. Also, as is discussed in Chapter XI, Section B., conspiracy doctrine may be used to attach liability to one individual for the crimes committed by her confederates in a more expansive manner than would be possible under the traditional law of complicity.

Does the "inchoate" nature of these offenses suggest anything concerning the objectives that should be pursued in formulating the substantive law defining these offenses? The drafters of the Model Penal Code offered the following:

> [A]ttempt, solicitation and conspiracy to commit crime [involve] conduct which has in common that it is designed to culminate in the commission of a substantive offense but either has failed to do so in the discrete case or has not yet achieved its culmination because there is something that the actor or another still must do. The offenses are inchoate in this sense.

These, to be sure, are not the only crimes which are so defined that their commission does not rest on proof of the occurrence of the evil that it is the object of the law to prevent; many specific, substantive offenses also have a large inchoate aspect. This is true not only with respect to crimes of risk-creation, such as reckless driving, or specific crimes of preparation, like those of possession with unlawful purpose. It is also true, at least in part, of crimes like larceny, forgery, kidnaping and even arson, not to speak of burglary, where a purpose to cause greater harm than that which is implicit in the actor's conduct is an element of the offense. It may be thought, indeed, that murder is the only crime which by its definition calls for proof that the full evil that the law endeavors to prevent has come to pass. This reservation notwithstanding, attempt, solicitation and conspiracy have such generality of definition and of application as inchoate crimes that it is useful to bring them together in the Code and to confront the common problems they present.

Since these offenses always presuppose a purpose to commit another crime, it is doubtful that the threat of punishment for their commission can significantly add to the deterrent efficacy of the sanction—which the actor by hypothesis ignores—that is threatened for the crime that is his object. There may be cases where this does occur, as when the actor thinks the chance of apprehension low if he succeeds but high if he should fail in his attempt, or when reflection is promoted at an early stage that otherwise would be postponed until too late, which may be true in some conspiracies. These are, however, special situations. Viewed generally, it seems clear that general deterrence is at most a minor function to be served in fashioning provisions of the penal law addressed to these inchoate crimes; that burden is discharged upon the whole by the law dealing with the substantive offenses.

Other and major functions of the penal law remain, however, to be served. They may be summarized as follows:

First: When a person is seriously dedicated to commission of a crime, there is obviously need for a firm legal basis for the intervention of the agencies of law enforcement to prevent its consummation. In determining that basis, there must be attention to the danger of abuse; equivocal behavior may be misconstrued by an unfriendly eye as preparation to commit a crime. It is no less important, on the other side, that lines should not be drawn so rigidly that the police confront insoluble dilemmas in deciding when to intervene, facing the risk that if they wait the crime may be committed while if they act they may not yet have any valid charge.

Second: Conduct designed to cause or culminate in the commission of a crime obviously yields an indication that the actor is disposed towards such activity, not alone on this occasion but on others. There is a need, therefore, subject again to proper safeguards, for a legal basis upon which the special danger that such individuals present may be assessed and dealt with. They must be made amenable to the corrective process that the law provides.

Third: Finally, and quite apart from these considerations of prevention, when the actor's failure to commit the substantive offense is due to a fortuity, as when the bullet misses in attempted murder or when the expected response to solicitation is withheld, his exculpation on that ground would involve inequality of treatment that would shock the common sense of justice. Such a situation is unthinkable in any mature system, designed to serve the proper goals of penal law.

Model Penal Code, Comments to Article 5, 24–26 (Tent.Draft No. 10, 1960).*

One question common to all of the inchoate or "preparatory" crimes is the extent to which they can be combined with each other or with crimes that are intended to prohibit activity regarded as dangerous because it is preparatory to more serious or harmful behavior. If, for example, a jurisdiction has general statutes prohibiting both attempt and conspiracy, may a defendant be convicted of attempted conspiracy to engage in criminal activity? Burglary is traditionally defined as entry into a dwelling with the intent to commit a felony in the structure; may a defendant be convicted of attempted burglary, given that it might be reasonable to regard burglary itself as amounting to an attempt to engage in a felony under particularly dangerous or offensive circumstances? The objection to both attempted conspiracy and attempted burglary, of course, is that the combination of the two crimes may permit persons to be held criminally liable for behavior too far removed from actual harmful conduct. Extending criminal liability this far back from actual commission of substantive crimes may be undesirable on policy grounds, inconsistent with legislative intent in enacting the inchoate crimes, and perhaps even constitutionally impermissible. At least one jurisdiction deals specifically with this problem insofar as it concerns the inchoate crimes themselves. Texas Penal Code § 15.15: "Attempt or conspiracy to commit, or solicitation of, a preparatory offense defined in this chapter [including attempt, solicitation, and conspiracy] is not an offense."

In considering the inchoate crimes covered by this chapter, evaluate the extent to which it should be permissible to combine them with each other and with inchoate-like crimes such as burglary. Might the result properly depend in part upon which of the inchoate crimes is being considered? If, for example, a court were to conclude that attempted burglary is an impermissible combination of preparatory crimes, should it reach the same result concerning conspiracy to commit burglary? Since conspiracy requires an agreement between or among several persons, does the additional danger created by concerted rather than individual pre-crime activity justify holding persons criminally liable for conspiracy to engage in such quasi-inchoate crimes? Does it justify holding them liable for conspiracy to commit an inchoate crime, i.e., conspiracy to solicit another to commit a crime?

A. ATTEMPTS

According to Sayre, Criminal Attempts, 41 Harv.L.Rev. 821 (1928), until quite recently there was no generalized doctrine that attempts to commit crime were, in themselves, criminal. Although some few early convictions for unsuccessful efforts to commit especially heinous crimes are reported, these, according to Professor Sayre, were based on an earlier doctrine that the intention is to be taken for the deed (*voluntas reputabitur pro facto*). The danger of imposing liability upon mere intent was too great to permit resort to this maxim often. Professor Sayre dates the modern doctrine of attempts from Rex v. Scofield, Cald. 397 (1784) where it was declared that "[t]he *intent* may make an act, innocent in itself, criminal; nor is the *completion* of an act, criminal in itself, necessary to constitute criminality." Id., at 400. Many issues vital to the law of attempts seem unsettled and resistant to ready resolution. Perhaps the relative youth of the doctrine explains this; perhaps the difficulties are inherent in efforts to criminalize in the absence of a prohibited result. The drafters of the Model Penal Code have addressed the general policy considerations relevant to the issues presented by attempt:

> The literature and decisions dealing with the definition of a criminal attempt reflect ambivalence as to how far the governing criterion should be found in the dangerousness of the actor's conduct, measured by objective standards, and how far in the dangerousness of the actor, as a person manifesting a firm disposition to commit a crime. Both criteria may lead, of course, to the same disposition of a concrete case. When they do not, we think, for reasons stated in the *Introduction,* that the proper focus of attention is the actor's disposition, and the draft is framed with this in mind. Needless to say, we are in full agreement that the law must be concerned with conduct, not with evil thoughts alone. The question is what conduct, when engaged in with a purpose to commit a crime or to advance towards the attainment of a criminal objective, should suffice to constitute a criminal attempt?

> In fashioning an answer we must keep in mind that in attempt, as distinct from solicitation and conspiracy, it is not intrinsic to the actor's conduct that he has disclosed his criminal design to someone else; nor is there any natural line that is suggested by the situation—like utterance or agreement. The law must deal with the problem presented by a single individual and must address itself to conduct that may fall anywhere upon a graded scale from early preparation to the final effort to commit the crime.

> We think, therefore, that it is useful to begin with any conduct designed to effect or to advance towards the attainment of the criminal objective and to ask when it ought *not* to be regarded as a crime, either because it does not adequately manifest the dangerousness of the actor or on other overriding grounds of social policy.

Model Penal Code, Comment to § 5.01, 26 (Tent.Draft No. 10, 1960).

1. THE ACT: BEYOND MERE PREPARATION

The absence of the requirement of a prohibited result as an element of attempt poses the theoretical danger of punishment for an evil mind without more. Persons might be identified as fit subjects for the criminal sanction on the basis of their evil intentions even though they might never have the character, commitment, or skills to carry out these thoughts. Thus, it is crucial that the defendant be shown to have acted upon his intention; a crucial issue in the law of attempt is the extent of the action which will be deemed sufficient for liability. This is the preparation/attempt dichotomy which is the subject of the principal case.

In reading and reflecting upon the principal case it should be clear that the greater the extent of the conduct required—the closer the defendant must be shown to have approached the harm which is posited as her objective—the fewer convictions will be possible. Thus, persons who, by hypothesis, have the desire to achieve a prohibited result will be free to try again. Moreover, to the extent that convictions for attempt serve as a general deterrent that effect also will be lost. Yet for those who are most concerned about limiting the authority of government, the weaker the conduct requirement, the more expansive the power of the police to intervene at a point distant from the ultimate danger.

UNITED STATES v. JACKSON

United States Court of Appeals, Second Circuit, 1977.
560 F.2d 112, cert. denied, 434 U.S. 941, 98 S.Ct. 434, 54 L.Ed. 301 (1977).

FREDERICK VAN PELT BRYAN, SENIOR DISTRICT JUDGE:

* * * [Robert Jackson, William Scott and Martin Allen were convicted of conspiracy to rob the Manufacturers Hanover Trust branch bank and of attempting to rob this bank on June 14 and June 21, 1976. On appeal, appellants do not contest the sufficiency of the evidence on the conspiracy count but they] assert that, as a matter of law, their conduct never crossed the elusive line which separates "mere preparation" from "attempt." This troublesome question was recently examined by this court in United States v. Stallworth, 543 F.2d 1038 (2d Cir.1976), which set forth the applicable legal principles.

I.

The Government's evidence at trial consisted largely of the testimony of Vanessa Hodges, an unindicted co-conspirator, and of various FBI agents who surveilled the Manufacturers Hanover branch on June 21, 1976. Since the facts are of critical importance in any attempt case, we shall review the Government's proof in considerable detail.

On June 11, 1976, Vanessa Hodges was introduced to appellant Martin Allen by Pia Longhorne, another unindicted co-conspirator. Hodges wanted to meet someone who would help her carry out a plan to rob the Manufacturers Hanover branch located at 210 Flushing

Avenue in Brooklyn, and she invited Allen to join her. Hodges proposed that the bank be robbed the next Monday, June 14th, at about 7:30 A.M. She hoped that they could enter with the bank manager at that time, grab the weekend deposits, and leave. Allen agreed to rob the bank with Hodges, and told her he had access to a car, two sawed-off shotguns, and a .38 caliber revolver.

The following Monday, June 14, Allen arrived at Longhorne's house about 7:30 A.M. in a car driven by appellant Robert Jackson. A suitcase in the back seat of the car contained a sawed-off shotgun, shells, materials intended as masks, and handcuffs to bind the bank manager. While Allen picked up Hodges at Longhorne's, Jackson filled the car with gas. The trio then left for the bank.

When they arrived, it was almost 8:00 A.M. It was thus too late to effect the first step of the plan, *viz.*, entering the bank as the manager opened the door. They rode around for a while longer, and then went to a restaurant to get something to eat and discuss their next move. After eating, the trio drove back to the bank. Allen and Hodges left the car and walked over to the bank. The peered in and saw the bulky weekend deposits, but decided it was too risky to rob the bank without an extra man.

Consequently, Jackson, Hodges, and Allen drove to Coney Island in search of another accomplice. In front of a housing project on 33rd Street they found appellant William Scott, who promptly joined the team. Allen added to the arsenal another sawed-off shotgun obtained from one of the buildings in the project, and the group drove back to the bank.

When they arrived again, Allen entered the bank to check the location of any surveillance cameras, while Jackson placed a piece of cardboard with a false license number over the authentic license plate of the car. Allen reported back that a single surveillance camera was over the entrance door. After further discussion, Scott left the car and entered the bank. He came back and informed the group that the tellers were separating the weekend deposits and that a number of patrons were now in the bank. Hodges then suggested that they drop the plans for the robbery that day, and reschedule it for the following Monday, June 21. Accordingly, they left the vicinity of the bank and returned to Coney Island where, before splitting up, they purchased a pair of stockings for Hodges to wear over her head as a disguise and pairs of gloves for Hodges, Scott, and Allen to don before entering the bank.

Hodges was arrested on Friday, June 18, 1976 on an unrelated bank robbery charge, and immediately began cooperating with the Government. After relating the events on June 14, she told FBI agents that a robbery of the Manufacturers branch at 210 Flushing Avenue was now scheduled for the following Monday, June 21. The three black male robbers, according to Hodges, would be heavily armed with hand and shoulder weapons and expected to use a brown four-door sedan equipped with a cardboard license plate as the getaway car. She told the agents that Jackson, who would drive the car, as light-skinned with a moustache and a cut on his lip, and she described Allen as short, dark-skinned with facial hair, and Scott as 5′9″, slim build, with an afro hair style and some sort of defect in his right eye.

At the request of the agents, Hodges called Allen on Saturday, June 19, and asked if he were still planning to do the job. He said that he was ready. On Sunday she called him again. This time Allen said that he was not going to rob the bank that Monday because he had learned that Hodges had been arrested and he feared that federal agents might be watching. Hodges nevertheless advised the agents that she thought the robbery might still take place as planned with the three men proceeding without her.

At about 7:00 A.M. on Monday, June 21, 1976, some ten FBI agents took various surveilling positions in the area of the bank. At about 7:39 A.M. the agents observed a brown four-door Lincoln, with a New York license plate on the front and a cardboard facsimile of a license plate on the rear, moving in an easterly direction on Flushing Avenue past the bank, which was located on the southeast corner of Flushing and Washington Avenues. The front seat of the Lincoln was occupied by a black male driver and a black male passenger with muttonchop sideburns. The Lincoln circled the block and came to a stop at a fire hydrant situated at the side of the bank facing Washington Avenue, a short distance south of the corner of Flushing and Washington.

A third black male, who appeared to have an eye deformity, got out of the passenger side rear door of the Lincoln, walked to the corner of Flushing and Washington, and stood on the sidewalk in the vicinity of the bank's entrance. He then walked south on Washington Avenue, only to return a short time later with a container of coffee in his hand. He stood again on the corner of Washington and Flushing in front of the bank, drinking the coffee and looking around, before returning to the parked Lincoln.

The Lincoln pulled out, made a left turn onto Flushing, and proceeded in a westerly direction for one block to Waverly Avenue. It stopped, made a U-turn, and parked on the south side of Flushing between Waverly and Washington—a spot on the same side of the street as the bank entrance but separated from it by Washington Avenue. After remaining parked in this position for approximately five minutes, it pulled out and cruised east on Flushing past the bank again. The Lincoln then made a right onto Grand Avenue, the third street east of the bank, and headed south. It stopped halfway down the block, midway between Flushing and Park Avenues, and remained there for several minutes. During this time Jackson was seen working in the front of the car, which had its hood up.

The Lincoln was next sighted several minutes later in the same position it had previously occupied on the south side of Flushing Avenue between Waverly and Washington. The front license plate was now missing. The vehicle remained parked there for close to thirty minutes. Finally, it began moving east on Flushing Avenue once more, in the direction of the bank.

At some point near the bank as they passed down Flushing Avenue, the appellants detected the presence of the surveillance agents. The Lincoln accelerated down Flushing Avenue and turned south on Grand Avenue again. It was overtaken by FBI agents who ordered the appellants out of the car and arrested them. The agents then observed a black and red plaid suitcase in the rear of the car. The zipper of the suitcase was partially open and exposed two loaded sawed-off shotguns, a toy nickel-plated revolver, a pair of handcuffs, and masks. A New York license plate was seen lying on the front floor of the car. All of these items were seized.

* * *

In his memorandum of decision, Chief Judge Mishler * * * characterized the question of whether the defendants had attempted a bank robbery as charged in counts two and three or were merely engaged in preparations as "a close one." After canvassing the authorities on what this court one month later called a "perplexing problem," Chief Judge Mishler applied the following two-tiered inquiry formulated in United States v. Mandujano, 499 F.2d 370, 376 (5th Cir.1974), cert. den. 419 U.S. 1114, 95 S.Ct. 792, 42 L.Ed.2d 812 (1975):

> First, the defendant must have been acting with the kind of culpability otherwise required for the commission of the crime which he is charged with attempting. * * *
>
> Second, the defendant must have engaged in conduct which constitutes a substantial step toward commission of the crime. A substantial step must be conduct strongly corroborative of the firmness of the defendant's criminal intent.

He concluded that on June 14 and again on June 21, the defendants took substantial steps, strongly corroborative of the firmness of their criminal intent, toward commission of the crime of bank robbery and found the defendants guilty on each of the two attempt counts. These appeals followed.

II.

"[T]here is no comprehensive statutory definition of attempt in federal law." United States v. Heng Awkak Roman, 356 F.Supp. 434, 437 (S.D.N.Y.), aff'd 484 F.2d 1271 (2d Cir.1973), cert. den. 415 U.S. 978, 94 S.Ct. 1565, 39 L.Ed.2d 874 (1974). Fed.R.Crim.P. 31(c), however, provides in pertinent part that a defendant may be found guilty of "an attempt to commit either the offense charged or an offense necessarily included therein if the attempt is an offense." 18 U.S.C.A. § 2113(a) specifically makes attempted bank robbery an offense.

* * *

Chief Judge Kaufman, writing for the court [in United States v. Stallworth, supra] selected the two-tiered inquiry of United States v.

Mandujano, supra, "properly derived from the writings of many distinguished jurists," as stating the proper test for determining whether the foregoing conduct constituted an attempt. He observed that this analysis "conforms closely to the sensible definition of an attempt proffered by the American Law Institute's Model Penal Code." * * *

The draftsmen of the Model Penal Code recognized the difficulty of arriving at a general standard for distinguishing acts of preparation from acts constituting an attempt. They found general agreement that when an actor committed the "last proximate act," i.e., when he had done all that he believed necessary to effect a particular result which is an element of the offense, he committed an attempt. They also concluded, however, that while the last proximate act is *sufficient* to constitute an attempt, it is not *necessary* to such a finding. The problem then was to devise a standard more inclusive than one requiring the last proximate act before attempt liability would attach, but less inclusive than one which would make every act done with the intent to commit a crime criminal. *See* Model Penal Code § 5.01, Comment at 38–39 (Tent.Draft No. 10, 1960).

The draftsmen considered and rejected the following approaches to distinguishing preparation from attempt, later summarized in *Mandujano:*

(a) The physical proximity doctrine—the overt act required for an attempt must be proximate to the completed crime, or directly tending toward the completion of the crime, or must amount to the commencement of the consummation.

(b) The dangerous proximity doctrine—a test given impetus by Mr. Justice Holmes whereby the greater the gravity and probability of the offense, and the nearer the act to the crime, the stronger is the case for calling the act an attempt.

(c) The indispensable element test—a variation of the proximity tests which emphasizes any indispensable aspect of the criminal endeavor over which the actor has not yet acquired control.

(d) The probable desistance test—the conduct constitutes an attempt if, in the ordinary and natural course of events, without interruption from an outside source, it will result in the crime intended.

(e) The abnormal step approach—an attempt is a step toward crime which goes beyond the point where the normal citizen would think better of his conduct and desist.

(f) The res ipsa loquitur or unequivocality test—an attempt is committed when the actor's conduct manifests an intent to commit a crime.

499 F.2d at 373 n. 5.

The formulation upon which the draftsmen ultimately agreed required, in addition to criminal purpose, that an act be a substantial step in a course of conduct designed to accomplish a criminal result, and that it be strongly corroborative of criminal purpose in order for it to constitute such a substantial step. The following differences between this test and previous approaches to the preparation-attempt problem were noted:

> First, this formulation shifts the emphasis from what remains to be done—the chief concern of the proximity tests—to what the actor *has already done*. The fact that further major steps must be taken before the crime can be completed does not preclude a finding that the steps already undertaken are substantial. It is expected, in the normal case, that this approach will broaden the scope of attempt liability.

> Second, although it is intended that the requirement of a substantial step will result in the imposition of attempt liability only in those instances in which some firmness of criminal purpose is shown, no finding is required as to whether the actor would probably have desisted prior to completing the crime. Potentially the probable desistance test could reach very early steps toward crime—depending upon how one assesses the probabilities of desistance—but since in practice this test follows closely the proximity approaches, rejection of probable desistance will not narrow the scope of attempt liability.

> Finally, the requirement of proving a substantial step generally will prove less of a hurdle for the prosecution than the *res ipsa loquitur* approach, which requires that the actor's conduct must itself manifest the criminal purpose. The difference will be illustrated in connection with the present section's requirement of corroboration. Here it should be noted that, in the present formulation, the two purposes to be served by the *res ipsa loquitur* test are, to a large extent, treated separately. Firmness of criminal purpose is intended to be shown by requiring a substantial step, while problems of proof are dealt with by the requirement of corroboration (although, under the reasoning previously expressed, the latter will also tend to establish firmness of purpose).

Model Penal Code § 5.01, Comment at 47 (Tent.Draft No. 10, 1960).

The draftsmen concluded that, in addition to assuring firmness of criminal design, the requirement of a substantial step would preclude attempt liability, with its accompanying harsh penalties, for relatively remote preparatory acts. At the same time, however, by not requiring a "last proximate act" or one of its various analogues it would permit the apprehension of dangerous persons at an earlier stage than the other approaches without immunizing them from attempt liability. Id. at 47–48.

* * *

In the case at bar, Chief Judge Mishler anticipated the precise analysis which this Court adopted in the * * * *Stallworth* case. He then found that on June 14 the appellants, already agreed upon a robbery plan, drove to the bank with loaded weapons. In order to carry the heavy weekend deposit sacks, they recruited another person. Cardboard was placed over the license, and the bank was entered and reconnoitered. Only then was the plan dropped for the moment and rescheduled for the following Monday. On that day, June 21, the defendants performed essentially the same acts. Since the cameras had already been located there was no need to enter the bank again, and since the appellants had arrived at the bank earlier, conditions were more favorable to their initial robbery plan than they had been on June 14. He concluded that on both occasions these men were seriously dedicated to the commission of a crime, had passed beyond the stage of preparation, and would have assaulted the bank had they not been dissuaded by certain external factors, *viz.*, the breaking up of the weekend deposits and crowd of patrons in the bank on June 14 and the detection of the FBI surveillance on June 21.

We cannot say that these conclusions which Chief Judge Mishler reached as the trier of fact as to what the evidence before him established were erroneous. As in *Stallworth*, the criminal intent of the appellants was beyond dispute. The question remaining then is the substantiality of the steps taken on the dates in question, and how strongly this corroborates the firmness of their obvious criminal intent. This is a matter of degree. See Model Penal Code § 5.01, Comments at 47 (Tent.Draft No. 10, 1960).

On two separate occasions, appellants reconnoitered the place contemplated for the commission of the crime and possessed the paraphernalia to be employed in the commission of the crime—loaded sawed-off shotguns, extra shells, a toy revolver, handcuffs, and masks— which was specially designed for such unlawful use and which could serve no lawful purpose under the circumstances. Under the Model Penal Code formulation, approved by the *Stallworth* court, either type of conduct, standing alone, was sufficient as a matter of law to constitute a "substantial step" if it strongly corroborated their criminal purpose. Here both types of conduct coincided on both June 14 and June 21, along with numerous other elements strongly corroborative of the firmness of appellants' criminal intent.[8] The steps taken toward a successful bank robbery thus were not "insubstantial" as a matter of law, and Chief Judge Mishler found them "substantial" as a matter of fact. We are unwilling to substitute our assessment of the evidence for his, and thus affirm the convictions for attempted bank robbery * * *.

Notes and Questions

1. The principal case demonstrates quite clearly the movement in the criminal law towards greater subjectivity—an increased emphasis on the

8. After securing the extra man they needed on June 14, the gang returned to the bank with their weapons ready and the car's license plate disguised for the getaway. Hodges' testimony was that they were ready to rob the bank at that time, but eventually postponed the robbery because conditions did not seem favorable. The fact that they then made further preparations by buying the stockings and gloves, an afterthought according to Hodges, does not undercut the firmness of their criminal intent when they were at the bank on June 14. By only postponing execution of the plan, appellants did not renounce their criminal purpose but reaffirmed it. They reflected further upon the plan and embellished it by acquiring the stockings and gloves.

* * *

defendant's state of mind rather than on an objective evaluation of her conduct. Would the convictions in *Jackson* have been affirmed if the court considered itself bound by the older tests for distinguishing between preparation and attempt such as "probable desistence" or "dangerous proximity?" Would we want the police to be required to wait to intervene until the defendants had entered the bank, demanded the funds, or displayed their weapons?

An interesting comparison in approaches to the preparation/attempt distinction may be found in United States v. Rivera-Sola, 713 F.2d 866 (1st Cir.1983) and United States v. Joyce, 693 F.2d 838 (8th Cir.1982). Both cases involved convictions for the attempted possession of illicit drugs with the intent to distribute. Both arose out of "reverse sting" operations in which the police pose as drug sellers. In such "reverse stings", after the sale is made the defendant is immediately arrested and the drugs and purchase money seized. In both of these cases, however, the "target" buyer never completed the transaction—perhaps because each sensed something was amiss with the "seller"—and the question was whether his conduct constituted an attempt. In *Joyce* the defendant had been contacted by an informant and advised of the availability of cocaine. He indicated he had $22,000 available to purchase a pound and was assured that would be sufficient. He flew from Oklahoma City to St. Louis where he met the agent who was posing as the seller. Negotiations proceeded until the agent refused to turn over the cocaine until he saw Joyce's money. Ultimately Joyce left without receiving the cocaine or turning over the money which, upon his arrest, was found in his luggage. The facts of *Rivera-Sola* were almost identical except that the transaction was to be for 100,000 quaaludes, the defendant requested and received 10 pills as a sample, and no funds were found in his possession on his arrest.

On these facts the court in *Joyce* reversed the conviction. It described the events as involving merely preliminary discussions which broke down before the defendant, who it assumed had the necessary intent, had committed any act constituting a substantial step towards possession. In contrast, the court in *Rivera-Sola* affirmed the conviction. It focussed on the defendant's words and actions and was convinced that he had had the intent to possess the drugs and had taken a substantial step. It found his request for and testing of the sample to be particularly significant as being incompatible with innocence.

Is there a substantial danger that the analysis in *Jackson* and *Rivera-Sola* threatens the misidentification of persons as criminals who, if left alone, would never have committed the crimes allegedly attempted? Should a distinction be made between the necessity for earlier intervention in the case of bank robbery than drug distribution? Why? Reconsider *Joyce* in the context of the defense of renunciation, discussed in notes 3 and 4, infra.

2. Legislatures, scholars and commentators have generally assumed the desirability of a general statutory provision prohibiting attempts to commit any criminal offenses. But Glazebrook, Should We Have a Law of Attempted Crime?, 85 L.Q.Rev. 28 (1969), has challenged this view. Rather than including a catch-all attempt provision, he suggests, draftsmen should

select those offenses in regard to which a situation short of the completed offense should give rise to liability and then include this within the definitions of those crimes.

The primary defect in a general attempt statute, as Glazebrook sees the situation, is the inherent vagueness of the preparation/attempt distinction. This, he feels, has permitted courts to impose liability for preparation far beyond the initial legislative intent, as, for example, when an attempt statute is used as the basis for holding a defendant liable for an attempt to solicit. Moreover, the awareness that many of those not coming within the definition of the completed crime will nevertheless come within the definition of attempt causes draftsmen to take less care than is desirable in drafting the definition of the completed crime. Abolition of the general attempt rule would require that statutory crimes be more carefully drafted and thus improve the quality of criminal codes.

Glazebrook also argues that the propriety of distinguishing between acts directed towards the completion of a crime and those amounting to the completed crime differs among the various crimes. Whether or not one who "attempts" but fails should be treated differently than one who achieves success should be decided on a crime-to-crime basis rather than by a generally applicable statute which assumes the appropriateness of such a distinction in all cases. For example, Glazebrook admits the desirability of distinguishing between those who kill and those who merely attempt to kill, but he suggests that there is little to be gained in forcible sexual attack cases by extended inquiries into whether or not penetration was achieved.

Glazebrook argues that the definition of each substantive offense should be expanded so as to cover only those unsuccessful efforts to achieve the offense which the underlying rationale of the offense dictates should be criminalized. Is the problem of encompassing the variety of ways in which men may fail to produce a harmful result as amenable to solution as the problem of defining the offense itself? Is the difficulty of anticipating the diversity of failure a good reason for not attempting it? See Stuart, The Actus Reus in Attempts, [1970] Crim.L.Rev. 505, 513.

In connection with this controversy consider the following statement by Sir James Fitzjames Stephen: "I pass now towards those imperfect crimes which constitute the first steps, so to speak, in criminality. These are—incitement to a crime, conspiracy to commit a crime, and attempts to commit crimes which are not in fact committed. All such preliminary steps towards crime are * * * themselves criminal. The exact point at which they become criminal cannot, in the nature of things, be precisely ascertained, nor is it desirable that such a matter should be made the subject of great precision. There is more harm than good in telling people precisely how far they may go without risking punishment in the pursuit of an unlawful object." A General View of the Criminal Law of England 83 (1890). If Stephen is correct as to the inherent vagueness of the law of attempt why is it not subject to constitutional challenge on that basis? Can this difficulty be resolved by adopting Glazebrook's approach and carefully defining with respect to each substantive offense, those acts which will be penalized even though they fall short of success? Alternatively, or by way of supplementation, we might have statutes criminalizing certain specific forms of preparatory conduct such as those concerning the possession of criminal instruments discussed in note 5, page 175, supra, or prohibiting the use, manufacture, or distribution of combustible or explosive substances with intent to burn property. E.g. Mich.Comp.Laws Ann. § 750.77 (1968) applied in People v. Davis, 24 Mich.App. 304, 180 N.W.2d 285 (1970) (defendant properly convicted where, with intent to burn, he aided others in the manufacture of Molotov cocktails although he did not participate in their use).[a]

To what extent is the desirability of a general attempt statute affected by a decision as to the role of attempt prosecutions in general deterrence? It has been suggested that deterrence is of minor or no consequence in the law of attempts inasmuch as the fact of the attempt establishes that the actor was not deterred by the sanction attached to the substantive offense which it was his object to commit. Nevertheless, it seems reasonable to assume that the more frequently criminal conduct is punished the more likely it is that the rest of us will be conscious of the reality of the existence of the sanction and the greater its deterrent effect. If so, is this a reason to spread the net of attempt as widely as possible consistent with other values in the criminal justice system?

3. Assuming that the defendants did progress far enough to have gone beyond mere preparation, why should they not be absolved of liability because they abandoned or renounced their venture? If on the facts their abandonment does not justify absolution, should abandonment ever constitute a defense to the crime of attempt? If a person is proven to have stolen a car he will not be absolved because he subsequently returns it, nor will one who has committed an assault be exculpated by his willingness to compensate his victim. Should this principle also apply to the law of attempt? That is, where an accused is shown to have gone beyond preparation in pursuit of his criminal purpose what effect, if any, should be given to his renunciation of his activity? The fact that a difference in treatment might be considered can, once again, be traced to the nature of attempt as an inchoate crime. The absence of the forbidden harm reduces the public demand for punishment as well as presenting questions as to the accused's culpability.

The traditional position is that abandonment of an attempt is not a defense. E.g., People v. Staples, 6 Cal.App.3d 61, 85 Cal.Rptr. 589 (1970); Stewart v. State, 85 Nev. 388, 455 P.2d 914 (1969). However, the Model

a. Another and rather more dramatic example of penalizing conduct well removed from an actual attempt is 18 U.S. C.A. § 871 (1970) which provides for a fine of $1,000 and/or not more than five years imprisonment for any person who "knowingly and willfully" makes any threat of bodily harm against the President or any officer in the order of succession to the President. Then Judge Burger has written, in the course of affirming a conviction under this statute—the defendant had publically stated that if required to carry a gun (be drafted) "the first person I want in my sights is LBJ"—that its ultimate purpose was to deter the killing or injuring of the President by deterring such threats, and that there is no requirement that the threat be made with intent to execute it. Watts v. United States, 402 F.2d 676 (D.C. Cir.1968) rev'd on other grounds, per curiam, 394 U.S. 705, 89 S.Ct. 1399, 22 L.Ed.2d 664 (1969). The Supreme Court's reversal was grounded on the view that the statement was mere "political hyperbole". The opinion announces, without discussion, that the statute is facially constitutional, but questions the validity of the Court of Appeals position on the intent required.

Penal Code has inspired many states to permit this defense. Under the Model Penal Code version the defendant would be required to produce evidence that he abandoned his effort or prevented the commission of the offense "under circumstances manifesting a complete and voluntary renunciation of his criminal purpose". See § 5.01(4) reprinted on page 574, infra. Although the Model Penal Code designates this an affirmative defense, it means by that only that the burden of production is shifted to the accused. In some jurisdictions the defense is also designated as "affirmative" but the accused is required to prove abandonment by a preponderance of the evidence.

The creation of this defense is consistent with the emergence of greater subjectivity in the definition of attempt. If less is required by way of conduct where we are satisfied as to the actor's purpose, earlier police intervention is possible and with it the danger of misidentification.

The defense is said to be justified for two reasons. First, it encourages actors to desist and thereby it would reduce the incidence of harm. Second, renunciation is said to tend to negative the dangerousness of the actor. It suggests that his criminal resolve was not firm. Of course, evidence to this point would be relevant to the necessary preliminary inquiry as to the existence of the required specific intent.

To be successful under the Model Penal Code and similar provisions, the defendant must show that his abandonment was "voluntary" in the sense of an almost religious conversion. It cannot have been due to external circumstances such as the threat of imminent apprehension by the authorities or a decision to await a more favorable opportunity. See Thomas v. State, 708 S.W.2d 861 (Tex.Crim.App.1986).

The drafters of the Model Penal Code recognized that the defense was problematical as a matter of theory and practice but weighing the conflicting considerations decided it should be permitted:

It is possible, of course, that the defense of renunciation of criminal purpose may add to the incentives to take the *first* steps toward crime. Knowledge that criminal endeavors can be undone with impunity may encourage preliminary steps that would not be undertaken if liability inevitably attached to every abortive criminal undertaking that proceeded beyond preparation. But this is not a serious problem. First, any consolation the actor might draw from the abandonment defense would have to be tempered with the knowledge that the defense would be unavailable if the actor's purposes were frustrated by external forces before he had an opportunity to abandon his effort. Second, the encouragement this defense might lend to the actor taking preliminary steps would be a factor only where the actor was dubious of his plans and where, consequently, the probability of continuance was not great.

On balance, it is concluded that renunciation of criminal purpose should be a defense to a criminal attempt charge because, as to the early stages of an attempt, it significantly negatives dangerousness of character, and, as to later stages, the value of encouraging desistance outweighs the net dangerousness shown by the abandoned criminal effort. And, because of the importance of encouraging desistance in the final stages of the attempt, the defense is allowed even when the last proximate act has occurred but the criminal result can be avoided, as for example when the fuse has been lit but can still be stamped out. If, however, the actor has gone so far that he has put in motion forces which he is powerless to stop, then the attempt has been completed and cannot be abandoned. In accord with existing law, the actor can gain no immunity for this completed effort, as for example when he fires at the intended victim but misses; all he can do is desist from making a second attempt.

Model Penal Code, Comments to § 5.01(4) 359–60 (Official Draft 1985).*

Under the Model Penal Code formulation, abandonment constitutes a defense rather than a factor in mitigation of sentence. A complete defense was thought necessary in order to provide a sufficient incentive for the actor to desist. However, the Texas Penal code provides that if the defendant fails in his efforts to establish the defense of abandonment, evidence of his efforts to abandon are admissible in mitigation of punishment. Texas Penal Code § 15.04(d). Model Penal Code § 5.05(2), see page 575, infra, authorizes the court in all inchoate crime cases to convict and sentence for a lower degree of crime or even to dismiss the prosecution when the actor's conduct is so inherently unlikely to succeed that neither the conduct nor the actor presents a sufficient danger to justify the normal grading scheme. Although this was inspired primarily by the elimination of impossibility as a defense, it might also be available where there is some evidence of abandonment.

4. In regard to renunciation or abandonment, reconsider United States v. Joyce, discussed in note 1, supra. In reversing the conviction, the appellate court wrote:

> [W]hile we may agree with the government's suggestion that Joyce, who was presumably "street-wise," may have been tipped off that Jones was a DEA undercover agent when Jones refused to open the package, we fail to see how an increased awareness of the risk of apprehension converts what would otherwise be "mere preparation" into an attempt.

693 F.2d at 843.

Although this can be construed as simply a distinction between preparation and attempt, it has also been read as recognizing a defense of abandonment. In United States v. McDowell, 705 F.2d 426 (11th Cir.1983), rehearing en banc denied, 714 F.2d 106 (per curiam) (11th Cir.1983), the facts were quite similar except that McDowell was offered sham rather than real cocaine, and a search of McDowell revealed little cash in comparison to Joyce's $22,000. A panel of the Eleventh Circuit rejected McDowell's claim of "renunciation." Noting that few federal cases deal with renunciation in criminal attempt situations, the court assumed the existence of a defense as proposed by the Model Penal Code. But it found the facts falling short of the required showing:

It appears, and the jury could find, that McDowell spurned the deal not to renounce his criminal intent but because he doubted either the genuineness or quality of the cocaine. McDowell cites no evidence indicating he rejected the cocaine because he had a change of heart.

705 F.2d at 428. Relying upon *Joyce*, McDowell sought rehearing en banc on the grounds that the facts of his case provided an even stronger basis for a finding of abandonment. Nevertheless, the motion was denied.

The Eighth Circuit considered Joyce's refusal to consummate the purchase as an "abandonment," which, as a matter of law, precluded the court from finding that Joyce had taken a substantial step towards commission of the crime. The motivation behind Joyce's refusal was deemed irrelevant.

It seems to us that the defendant's motive is highly relevant. Refusal to purchase because of inability to agree on price, or dissatisfaction about quality, or lack of opportunity to inspect is not necessarily a complete and voluntary renunciation of criminal purpose. *Joyce* would establish a per se rule, and refusal to purchase would preclude an attempt conviction. In our view, *McDowell* permits closer, and more appropriate, analysis. * * * [T]o convict a defendant of attempt his objective acts, without reliance on the accompanying mens rea, must mark his conduct as criminal. This rule requires examination of the totality of objective acts. That totality was sufficient in this case.

714 F.2d at 107.

Given that McDowell, as is true of all targets in these "reverse sting" cases, had indicated a desire to buy cocaine, is it conceivable that such expression of intent was not considered by the trier of fact in concluding that an attempt had occurred? Should the use of the subjective approach of the Model Penal Code require that abandonment be available as a defense? If it is to be available, under either the objective or subjective view, should it have applied to Joyce?

2. THE STATE OF MIND REQUIRED

As has been noted previously, the absence of the result requirement for attempt liability is thought to pose special problems of misidentification. One way to minimize this danger and to restrict the state's power for early intervention is, as has been seen, the requirement of conduct as a clear signal of commitment to the defendant's posited evil intention. The other is to require the prosecution to establish that the defendant acted with a high order of *mens rea*. Consider, for example, that one who causes a death by driving while intoxicated is likely to be held liable for negligent homicide, involuntary manslaughter, or possibly murder. And this is so even though we assume that the defendant was no more than reckless as to the likelihood of causing the death. Does this mean that a reckless defendant who, while intoxicated, starts her car is liable for attempted negligent homicide, involuntary manslaughter, or murder? Such a doctrine would obviously multiply the incidence of serious felonies. Moreover, are persons who do not desire the prohibited harm so dangerous or culpable as to be worthy of the same treatment as those who do have such a purpose? The drafters of the Model Penal Code addressed this problem with great care:

3. *5.01(1). The Requirement of Purpose.* As previously stated, the proposed definition of attempt follows the conventional pattern of limiting this inchoate crime to purposive conduct. In the language of the courts, there must be "intent in fact" or "specific intent" to commit the crime allegedly attempted. Nonetheless a problem of drafting is presented in endeavoring to explain the nature of the requisite purpose.

This section adopts the view that the actor must have for his purpose to engage in the criminal conduct or accomplish the criminal result which is an element of the substantive crime but that his purpose need not encompass all the surrounding circumstances included in the formal definition of the substantive offense. As to them it is sufficient that he acts with the culpability that is required for commission of the crime. Suppose, for example, that it is a federal offense to kill or injure an FBI agent and that recklessness or even negligence with respect to the identity of the victim as an agent suffices for commission of the crime. There would be an attempt to kill or injure such an agent under the present formulation if the actor with recklessness or negligence as to the official position of the victim attempts to kill or injure him. Under paragraph (b) the killing or injuring would be the required purpose; the fact that the victim is an agent would be only a circumstance as to which the actor had "the kind of culpability otherwise required for commission of the crime."

It is difficult to say what the result would be in this kind of case under prevailing principles of attempt liability. However, the proposed formulation imposes attempt liability in a group of cases where the normal basis of such liability is present—purposive conduct manifesting dangerousness—and allows the policy of the substantive crime, respecting recklessness or negligence as to surrounding circumstances, to be applied to the attempt to commit that crime.

* * *

Under paragraph (b), liability for an attempt may be founded upon the actor's belief that his conduct will cause a particular result which is an element of the crime. * * *

It should be emphasized that this extension of paragraph (b) beyond the area of purposive behavior does *not* result in the inclusion of reckless conduct.

Model Penal Code, Comment to § 5.01, 27–30 (Tent.Draft No. 10, 1960).*

PEOPLE v. KROVARZ
Supreme Court of Colorado, 1985.
697 P.2d 378.

DUBOFSKY, JUSTICE.

The Denver District Court acquitted the defendant, Victor Krovarz, of attempted aggravated robbery. The court, relying upon *People v. Frysig*, 628 P.2d 1004 (Colo.1981), ruled that liability for criminal attempt is predicated upon the specific intent to commit the underlying crime and found that the defendant did not possess the requisite intent. The People appeal the district court's ruling as a question of law. We disapprove the ruling of the district court.

[The defendant had put a putty knife to the throat of a store clerk and demanded the money in her register. He was subdued by a customer and subsequently] * * * was charged with attempted aggravated robbery under the second clause of section 18–4–302(1)(b), which requires that the prosecution prove, in addition to the usual elements of robbery, that the defendant "by the use of force, threats, or intimidation with a deadly weapon knowingly put[ ] the person robbed or any other person in reasonable fear of death or bodily injury * * *."

At trial, the defendant's evidence focused on his mental state. A psychologist testified that the defendant had been a patient at the Bethesda Mental Health Center before his transfer to a halfway house in Denver, from which he was released the morning of the robbery. From his examination of the defendant, the psychologist concluded that the defendant was depressed and suicidal that morning, and, rather than intending to take money, the defendant had committed the robbery in the hope of being returned to a mental hospital where he could receive help. On cross-examination, however, the psychologist stated that the defendant did intend to engage in the conduct constituting the attempted robbery, was aware that he thereby placed the victim in reasonable fear of injury, and was aware that he was practically certain to obtain money as a result of his acts. The defendant confirmed the psychologist's testimony.

After hearing the evidence, the district court ruled that *Frysig* required a specific intent to commit the underlying crime before a defendant may be convicted of criminal attempt. The court found that the prosecution had failed to prove specific intent beyond a reasonable doubt and acquitted the defendant. The court added that "if attempt were a knowing offense, my ruling would be different * * *." The People on appeal contend that the culpable mental state for attempt is identical to the culpable mental state required for the underlying crime, and that the district court erred in requiring proof of specific intent to commit the underlying offense of aggravated robbery.

Criminal attempt is defined in section 18–2–101(1), 8 C.R.S. (1978):

A person commits criminal attempt if, acting with the kind of culpability otherwise required for commission of an offense, he engages in conduct constituting a substantial step toward the commission of the offense. A substantial step is any conduct, whether act, omission, or possession, which is strongly corroborative of the firmness of the actor's purpose to complete the commission of the offense * * *.

In *People v. Frysig,* 628 P.2d 1004 (Colo.1981), we analyzed the history and language of the criminal attempt statute and concluded that the General Assembly intended to incorporate the traditional rule that an actor may be found guilty of attempt only if he intends to commit the underlying crime, *i.e.,* if he intends to perform the acts and bring about the results proscribed by statute. 628 P.2d at 1007–10. * * * In reaching this conclusion, we distinguished between the intent necessary to establish a criminal attempt and the culpable mental state of the underlying crime:

> [I]n order to be guilty of criminal attempt, the actor must act with the kind of culpability otherwise required for commission of the underlying offense, and must engage in the conduct which constitutes the substantial step with the further intent to perform acts which, if completed, would constitute the underlying offense.

People v. Frysig, 628 P.2d at 1010.

In the present case, the district court implicitly found that the defendant possessed a culpable mental state of knowledge, which would be sufficient to sustain a conviction for the underlying charge of aggravated robbery. We must determine whether the mental state of knowledge also fulfills the culpable mental state for attempt identified in *Frysig.*

One may be guilty of attempt without having engaged in the harmful conduct or having achieved the harmful result that ordinarily forms the basis for criminal liability; rather, culpability for criminal attempt rests primarily upon the actor's purpose to cause harmful consequences. Enker, *Mens Rea and Criminal Attempt,* 1977 Am.Bar Found.Res.J. 845, 855–56 (Enker). Punishment is justified where the actor intends harm because there exists a high likelihood that his "unspent" intent will flower into harmful conduct at any moment. Enker at 855. The probability of future dangerousness, however, is not confined to actors whose conscious purpose is to perform the proscribed acts or achieve the proscribed results, *i.e.,* those possessing the culpable mental state of specific intent.[7] We believe that this danger is equally present when one acts knowingly.

In analyzing the danger posed by a knowing attempt, we first recognize that the statutory definition of aggravated robbery includes elements of conduct, result and circumstance, and that the definition of

---

7. Section 18–1–501(5), 8 C.R.S. (1978), provides:

All offenses defined in this code in which the mental culpability requirement is expressed as "intentionally" or "with intent" are declared to be specific intent offenses. A person acts "intentionally" or "with intent" when his conscious objective is to cause the specific result proscribed by the statute defining the offense. It is immaterial to the issue of specific intent whether or not the result actually occurred.

the culpable mental state of knowledge differs in relation to each type of element. We therefore examine the mental state of knowledge in relation to each type of element in order to see whether each contains the potential danger that justifies legislative imposition of attempt liability.

With respect to a result, one acts knowingly "when he is aware that his conduct is practically certain to cause the result." When one engages in conduct that is practically certain to cause a prohibited result, with awareness of the likely consequence, one in effect chooses to create that result even though he may not actively desire that it occur.[9] In *Derrera*, we noted that the culpable mental state of knowledge relative to result "approaches the formulation of a specific intent requirement." 667 P.2d at 1368. For this reason, a number of jurisdictions by statute have extended attempt liability to situations where the actor knowingly obtains the forbidden result. The drafters of the Model Penal Code explained that this extension of liability is warranted because

> the manifestation of dangerousness is as great—or very nearly as great—as in the case of purposive conduct. In both instances a deliberate choice is made to bring about the consequence forbidden by the criminal laws, and the actor has done all within his power to cause this result to occur. The absence in one instance of any desire for the forbidden result is not, under these circumstances, a sufficient basis for differentiating between the two types of conduct involved.

Id. § 5.01 comment at 29–30. We agree with this reasoning; a knowing attempt to attain a proscribed result is a sufficient culpable mental state to justify imposition by the legislature of attempt liability.

We next turn to the question of whether a culpable mental state of knowledge relative to the other two types of elements, conduct and circumstances, is a sufficient index of dangerousness to warrant the

---

9. Although we need not decide the question here, we note that this line of reasoning does not necessarily extend to crimes predicated upon a culpable mental state of recklessness. One who acts recklessly "consciously disregards a substantial and unjustifiable risk * * *," § 18–1–501(8); such conscious disregard does not imply that one chooses the result in the same way that one chooses a result he knows to be a practical certainty. Thus, the Model Penal Code, while permitting attempt liability for results obtained knowingly, explicitly excludes results obtained recklessly. In addition, every state court that has considered this question has declined to extend attempt liability to reckless crimes, on the ground that one cannot intend to commit a crime defined as having an unintended result.

Although some * * * cases speak of "specific intent" as a necessary predicate for attempt liability, their analysis is concerned solely with distinguishing intent from recklessness; the cases do not consider whether attempt liability may be based on knowledge, and therefore they are not contrary to the position we adopt today. This is illustrated by the approach of the Indiana Supreme Court. In *Smith v. State*, 422 N.E.2d 1179, 1185 (Ind.1981), the court held that there can be no attempt liability for voluntary manslaughter predicated upon recklessness, declaring that the Indiana attempt statute, identical to that of Colorado, applies exclusively to specific intent crimes. One year later, however, the same court acknowledged the existence of attempted voluntary manslaughter based upon "a knowing or intentional state of mind." *Goodwin v. State*, 439 N.E.2d 595, 599 (Ind.1982).

punishment established by the legislature for criminal attempt. One acts knowingly with respect to statutorily defined conduct and circumstances "when he is aware that his conduct is of such nature or that such circumstance exists." § 18–1–501(6). Acts undertaken with such awareness are the product of deliberate choice. Indeed, the correlation here between knowledge and intention is even closer than it is with regard to result: knowledge with regard to result requires that the actor be "practically certain" of the consequences, while knowledge with regard to conduct and circumstances requires an "awareness" of the nature of the conduct and the presence of the circumstances. Given this awareness, there is no practical difference between knowledge and intention relative to conduct or circumstances. La Fave and Scott, *Handbook on Criminal Law* § 28 at 197 ("an intention to engage in certain conduct or to do so under certain circumstances may * * * be said to exist on the basis of what one knows"); Feinberg, *Toward a New Approach to Culpability: Mens Rea and the Proposed Federal Criminal Code,* 18 Am.Crim.L.Rev. 123, 133 (1980) (both knowing and intentional conduct "involve a conscious undertaking to perform a physical act").

The structure of the Colorado Criminal Code supports our conclusion, so far as criminal attempt is concerned, that there is no practical difference between knowledge and intention relative to conduct or circumstances. The mental state of intention is defined relative to result but not relative to conduct or circumstances; knowledge is the most culpable state attached to either of these latter two types of elements. This scheme indicates a legislative judgment that any definition of intent attaching to either conduct or circumstances is superfluous. At least with regard to conduct, this determination was deliberate. When the culpable mental state requirements of the Code were first adopted, the mental state of intention was defined to include the actor's conscious object of engaging in the proscribed conduct. Based upon the structure and history of the statutory culpable mental state requirements, we conclude that knowledge as to conduct and circumstances is a sufficient index of potential harm to permit the imposition by the legislature of punishment for criminal attempt.

In addition, the attempt statute indicates a legislative intent to permit imposition of attempt liability based upon a culpable mental state of knowledge relative to circumstances. Section 18–2–101(1), 8 C.R.S. (1978) provides in part: "Factual or legal impossibility of committing the offense is not a defense if the offense could have been committed had the attendant circumstances been as the actor believed them to be * * *." This provision permits belief in external circumstances, a mental state of lesser culpability than actual awareness, to establish attempt liability as to circumstances.[11]

11. A number of commentators, arguing that the actor's mental state relative to circumstances is irrelevant to his potential dangerousness, have proposed that the cul- pable mental state attached to the circumstantial elements of the underlying crime should suffice to establish attempt culpability as to such elements. Enker, *Mens*

We hold that a culpable mental state of knowledge suffices to support criminal attempt liability. We recognize that our conclusion that attempt liability may be based on knowing conduct or knowingly attained results conflicts with a plausible reading of *People v. Frysig* that knowledge cannot substitute for intent as a predicate for attempt liability. The precise issue in *Frysig* was whether, in a prosecution for attempted first-degree sexual assault, the trial court erred in failing to instruct the jury that the defendant could be found guilty of attempt only if he intended to commit the underlying crime. The culpable mental state relative to the conduct and result comprised within first-degree sexual assault was, and still is, knowledge. We did not find, however, that the instruction regarding this mental state was an adequate substitute for an instruction on the intent required for attempt; rather, we held that the instruction regarding the "substantial step" necessary for attempt cured the error by referring to "purpose." *Frysig* therefore can be read to imply that knowledge could not substitute for intent as the culpable mental state of attempt. In holding as we do today, we reject such a reading of *Frysig*. The district court erred in requiring a showing of specific intent to commit the underlying crime.

Ruling disapproved.

Notes and Questions

1. Defendant, somewhat inebriated after attending a church festival, was walking with others down a country lane when they came upon a tent containing a lighted lamp. He announced to his companions that he intended to "shoot that God-damned light out". A woman, who occupied the tent with her four children and a servant, admonished him not to do so. Nevertheless, he fired three shots, two of which went through the tent. He was convicted of attempted murder. The conviction was reversed because while his conduct may have been sufficient for attempt liability the evidence did not establish that he shot with the intent to murder the woman. Thacker v. Commonwealth, 134 Va. 767, 114 S.E. 504 (1922).

It seems indisputable that Thacker has shown himself to be a dangerous person who deserves correction. If attempted murder is not possible could the jury have convicted him of attempted manslaughter? If, as is commonly the case, the particular jurisdiction divides manslaughter into voluntary—an intentional but mitigated killing—and involuntary—a reckless killing—neither would seem applicable to Thacker. An attempted voluntary manslaughter is unusual but possible if the prosecution establishes the requisite intent to kill. Taylor v. State, 444 So.2d 931 (Fla.1983). However, in Thacker's case the evidence on intent was insufficient. Attempted involuntary manslaughter is, as explained in footnote 9 of

Rea and Criminal Attempt, 1977 Am.Bar Found.Res.J. 845, 866; Smith, *Two Problems in Criminal Attempts,* 70 Harv.L.Rev. 422, 434–35 (1957); *Model Penal Code* § 5.01 comment at 27–28 (Tent.Draft No. 10, 1960). Because we need analyze here only the culpable mental state of knowledge relative to circumstances, we express no opinion on the propriety of basing attempt liability upon any lesser mental state.

Krovarz, page 562, supra, a logical impossibility; one cannot intend to commit an unintentional killing. State v. Zupetz, 322 N.W.2d 730 (Minn. 1982). For an argument in favor of permitting verdicts of attempted manslaughter where the defendant has acted recklessly or with gross negligence see Stuart, Mens Rea, Negligence and Attempts [1968] Crim.L. Rev. 647.

Could Thacker be convicted of an aggravated assault? This will depend on the statutory formulations of such an offense available to the prosecution. Although recklessness often suffices if there has been injury, assault which merely creates apprehension must commonly be perpetrated with intent or knowledge. Under the formulation presented in *Krovarz,* such a statute might well be applied to Thacker's behavior. Also available to deal with this conduct would be the charge of "reckless endangering". The Texas version of this provides:

(a) A person commits an offense if he recklessly engages in conduct that places another in imminent danger of serious bodily injury.

(b) Recklessness and danger are presumed if the actor knowingly pointed a firearm at or in the direction of another whether or not the actor believed the firearm to be loaded.

Tex.Pen.Code § 22.05. This is a class B misdemeanor punishable by a fine of not more than $1,000, jail for not more than 180 days or both.

2. One effect of the insistence on a high order of intent to sustain an attempted murder is the necessity that the jury be properly charged on that point. In People v. Ratliff, 41 Cal.3d 675, 224 Cal.Rptr. 705, 715 P.2d 665 (1986), the defendant, in the course of a robbery, shot his victim at close range immediately after demanding money and without any struggle which might indicate an accidental shooting or self-defense. His conviction for attempted murder was reversed because the trial court had failed to instruct that a specific intent to kill was required. The Supreme Court of California acknowledged that "it seems clear that the defendant had the *intent to shoot* and thus disable * * * there was no further evidence of a specific *intent to kill* necessary to sustain an attempted murder conviction." 224 Cal.Rptr. at 716, 715 P.2d at 676 (italics in original).

3. Can one be convicted of an attempt to commit a strict liability offense without proof of intent to commit the offense? Cf. Gardner v. Akeroyd, [1952] 2 Q.B. 743 (although a butcher may be held strictly and vicariously liable for the sale of meat at prices in excess of the regulatory maxima, he cannot be held liable for "any act preparatory to the commission" of that offense (prepared but undelivered parcels of meat were found in the shop with tickets showing overcharges) in the absence of mens rea).

3. THE "DEFENSE" OF IMPOSSIBILITY

This topic presents the conflict between subjective and objective approaches to liability more sharply than probably any other in the substantive criminal law. In the cases posing this problem not only need there not have been a prohibited result, as is true of all attempts, but the result intended by the defendant was impossible to achieve.

This exacerbates the concern that attempt doctrine threatens punishment for an evil state of mind without more.

The principal case divides impossibility into two categories: factual and legal. In the former, the defendant's intention is thwarted because of her mistake as to the physical nature of an indispensable instrument or circumstance. Common examples are the shooting of a stump believing it to be one's intended victim, or pulling the trigger of a gun held to the victim's head when, unknown to the defendant, the gun is unloaded, or the picking of an empty pocket. In such cases convictions for attempt are almost uniformly affirmed. Legal impossibility is said to be present when the actions performed by the defendant or set in motion by her, even if fully consummated as she desires, would not constitute the crime. The most common example of this class of cases is where the defendant receives property which had been stolen and which the defendant believes to be stolen but which, unknown to her, has been recovered by the police. Courts have said that once such property has been recovered by the police it has lost its stolen status and hence it cannot be the object of an attempt to receive stolen goods. See, e.g. United States v. Dove, 629 F.2d 325 (4th Cir.1980). Cases such as *Dove* are sometimes described as involving mixed fact and law legal impossibility issues in contrast to "true" legal impossibility. The latter are very rare in courts although not in law review articles. In essence, they involve a person who believes that her objective—smoking cigars in the courthouse—is illegal but no such prohibition exists. Such a defendant has clearly demonstrated a willingness to flout the law but cannot be convicted of even an attempt since to do so would violate the principle of legality which requires that there cannot be punishment without the prior announcement of the prohibition by a duly constituted authority.

Under the subjective approach to legal impossibility the courts look to the defendant's intention—to sell heroin—and if it was to commit a crime and her conduct went beyond preparation, it will constitute an attempt even though the defendant unwittingly possessed a non-controlled substance. Those who stress the importance of objective manifestations of criminality are concerned that the subjective view threatens punishment for evil thoughts since the defendant's conduct—possession of, and attempts to sell the non-controlled substance—will be equivocal signals of criminality. Rather than risk the misidentification of persons as criminals, the objectivists would stress the importance of the defendant's conduct as demonstrating culpability without regard to her intent.

In examining the principal case and the legal impossibility cases (other than those involving "true" legal impossibility) discussed therein, consider when, if ever, it can make sense to absolve such defendants? Why should a person escape punishment when the prosecution has established the requisite intent and shown that the actor has taken substantial steps to effect that intent and which corroborate the firmness of that intent?

PEOPLE v. DLUGASH

Court of Appeals of New York, 1977.
41 N.Y.2d 725, 395 N.Y.S.2d 419, 363 N.E.2d 1155.

JASEN, JUDGE.

The criminal law is of ancient origin, but criminal liability for attempt to commit a crime is comparatively recent. At the root of the concept of attempt liability are the very aims and purposes of penal law. The ultimate issue is whether an individual's intentions and actions, though failing to achieve a manifest and malevolent criminal purpose, constitute a danger to organized society of sufficient magnitude to warrant the imposition of criminal sanctions. Difficulties in theoretical analysis and concomitant debate over very pragmatic questions of blameworthiness appear dramatically in reference to situations where the criminal attempt failed to achieve its purpose solely because the factual or legal context in which the individual acted was not as the actor supposed them to be. Phrased somewhat differently, the concern centers on whether an individual should be liable for an attempt to commit a crime when, unknown to him, it was impossible to successfully complete the crime attempted. For years, serious studies have been made on the subject in an effort to resolve the continuing controversy when, if at all, the impossibility of successfully completing the criminal act should preclude liability for even making the futile attempt. The 1967 revision of the Penal Law approached the impossibility defense to the inchoate crime of attempt in a novel fashion. The statute provides that, if a person engages in conduct which would otherwise constitute an attempt to commit a crime, "it is no defense to a prosecution for such attempt that the crime charged to have been attempted was, under the attendant circumstances, factually or legally impossible of commission, if such crime could have been committed had the attendant circumstances been as such person believed them to be." (Penal Law, § 110.10.) This appeal presents to us, for the first time, a case involving the application of the modern statute. We hold that, under the proof presented by the People at trial, defendant Melvin Dlugash may be held for attempted murder, though the target of the attempt may have already been slain, by the hand of another, when Dlugash made his felonious attempt.

On December 22, 1973, Michael Geller, 25 years old, was found shot to death in the bedroom of his Brooklyn apartment. The body, which had literally been riddled by bullets, was found lying face up on the floor. An autopsy revealed that the victim had been shot in the face and head no less than seven times. Powder burns on the face indicated that the shots had been fired from within one foot of the victim. Four small caliber bullets were recovered from the victim's skull. The victim had also been critically wounded in the chest. * * *

[On December 27, Detective Carrasquillo, who had been assigned to investigate the homicide, contacted the defendant. Dlugash stated that he and his friend Joe Bush had been on a trip and only recently learned of Geller's death. In the course of subsequent interrogations in which he was faced with facts concerning the homicide the defendant altered his story. He claimed he, Bush, and Geller had been out drinking together on the night of December 21. Geller had demanded that Bush pay $100 towards the rent on Geller's apartment where Bush was staying. Bush threatened Geller with "a bullet" unless he "shut up". Back at Geller's apartment, after several hours of further drinking, Geller renewed his demand. Bush drew his .38 pistol and shot Geller several times. After two to five minutes, Dlugash moved to the fallen Geller, drew his .25, and fired about five shots into the victim's head. He claimed that by the time he fired "it looked like Mike Geller was already dead". According to the defendant, he and Bush then left the apartment and Bush disposed of the two weapons. Asked by Carrasquillo three times in the course of the interrogation why he did such a thing, Dlugash finally suggested that "it must have been because I was afraid of Joe Bush." The defendant repeated to a prosecutor the substance of this statement, including his claimed belief that at the time he shot Geller (without mentioning any urgings by Bush) the victim was dead.]

Defendant was indicted by the Grand Jury of Kings County on a single count of murder in that, acting in concert with another person actually present, he intentionally caused the death of Michael Geller. At the trial, there were four principal prosecution witnesses: Detective Carrasquillo, the Assistant District Attorney who took the second admission, and two physicians from the office of the New York City Chief Medical Examiner. For proof of defendant's culpability, the prosecution relied upon defendant's own admissions as related by the detective and the prosecutor. From the physicians, the prosecution sought to establish that Geller was still alive at the time defendant shot at him. Both physicians testified that each of the two chest wounds, for which defendant alleged Bush to be responsible, would have caused death without prompt medical attention. Moreover, the victim would have remained alive until such time as his chest cavity became fully filled with blood. Depending on the circumstances, it might take 5 to 10 minutes for the chest cavity to fill. Neither prosecution witness could state, with medical certainty, that the victim was still alive when, perhaps five minutes after the initial chest wounds were inflicted, the defendant fired at the victim's head.

The defense produced but a single witness, the former Chief Medical Examiner of New York City. This expert stated that, in his view, Geller might have died of the chest wounds "very rapidly" since, in addition to the bleeding, a large bullet going through a lung and the heart would have other adverse medical effects. "Those wounds can be almost immediately or rapidly fatal or they may be delayed in there, in the time it would take for death to occur. But I would say that wounds like that which are described here as having gone through the lungs and the heart would be fatal wounds and in most cases they're rapidly fatal."

The trial court declined to charge the jury, as requested by the prosecution, that defendant could be guilty of murder on the theory that he had aided and abetted the killing of Geller by Bush. Instead, the court submitted only two theories to the jury: that defendant had either intentionally murdered Geller or had attempted to murder Geller.

The jury found the defendant guilty of murder. The defendant then moved to set the verdict aside. He submitted an affidavit in which he contended that he "was absolutely, unequivocally and positively certain that Michael Geller was dead before [he] shot him." Further, the defendant averred that he was in fear for his life when he shot Geller. "This fear stemmed from the fact that Joseph Bush, the admitted killer of Geller, was holding a gun on me and telling me, in no uncertain terms, that if I didn't shoot the dead body I, too, would be killed." This motion was denied.[1]

On appeal, the Appellate Division reversed the judgment of conviction on the law and dismissed the indictment. The court ruled that "the People failed to prove beyond a reasonable doubt that Geller had been alive at the time he was shot by defendant; defendant's conviction of murder thus cannot stand." (51 A.D.2d 974, 975, 380 N.Y.S.2d 315, 317.) Further, the court held that the judgment could not be modified to reflect a conviction for attempted murder because "the uncontradicted evidence is that the defendant, at the time that he fired the five shots into the body of the decedent, believed him to be dead, and * * * there is not a scintilla of evidence to contradict his assertion in that regard".

Preliminarily, we state our agreement with the Appellate Division that the evidence did not establish, beyond a reasonable doubt, that Geller was alive at the time defendant fired into his body. To sustain a homicide conviction, it must be established, beyond a reasonable doubt, that the defendant caused the death of another person. The People were required to establish that the shots fired by defendant Dlugash were a sufficiently direct cause of Geller's death. While the defendant admitted firing five shots at the victim approximately two to five minutes after Bush had fired three times, all three medical expert witnesses testified that they could not, with any degree of medical certainty, state whether the victim had been alive at the time the latter

1. It should be noted that Joe Bush pleaded guilty to a charge of manslaughter in the first degree. At the time he entered his plea, Bush detailed his version of the homicide. According to Bush, defendant Dlugash was a dealer in narcotic drugs and Dlugash claimed that Geller owed him a large sum of money from drug purchases. Bush was in the kitchen alone when Geller entered and threatened him with a shotgun. Bush pulled out his .38 caliber pistol and fired five times at Geller. Geller slumped to the floor. Dlugash then entered, withdrew his .25 caliber pistol and fired five shots into the deceased's face. Bush, however, never testified at Dlugash's trial.

shots were fired by the defendant. Thus, the People failed to prove beyond a reasonable doubt that the victim had been alive at the time he was shot by the defendant. Whatever else it may be, it is not murder to shoot a dead body. Man dies but once.

[The evidence supports the theory that the defendant intentionally aided Bush in killing Geller. Therefore, the trial court erred in refusing to instruct the jury on the prosecution's aiding and abetting theory. But the prosecution cannot appeal from this error and the judgment must stand or fall on the record.]

The procedural context of this matter, a nonappealable but erroneous dismissal of the issue of accessorial conduct, contributes to the unique nature of the attempt issue presented here. Where two or more persons have combined to murder, proof of the relationship between perpetrators is sufficient to hold all for the same degree of homicide, notwithstanding the absence of proof as to which specific act of which individual was the immediate cause of the victim's death. On the other hand, it is quite unlikely and improbable that two persons, unknown and unconnected to each other, would attempt to kill the same third person at the same time and place. Thus, it is rare for criminal liability for homicide to turn on which of several attempts actually succeeded. In the case of coconspirators, it is not necessary to do so and the case of truly independent actors is unlikely. However, procedural developments make this case the unlikely one and we must now decide whether, under the evidence presented, the defendant may be held for attempted murder, though someone else perhaps succeeded in killing the victim.

* * *

The most intriguing attempt cases are those where the attempt to commit a crime was unsuccessful due to mistakes of fact or law on the part of the would-be criminal. A general rule developed in most American jurisdictions that legal impossibility is a good defense but factual impossibility is not. Thus, for example, it was held that defendants who shot at a stuffed deer did not attempt to take a deer out of season, even though they believed the dummy to be a live animal. The court stated that there was no criminal attempt because it was no crime to "take" a stuffed deer, and it is no crime to attempt to do that which is legal. (State v. Guffey, 262 S.W.2d 152 [Mo.App.]; see, also, State v. Taylor, 345 Mo. 325, 133 S.W.2d 336 [no liability for attempt to bribe a juror where person bribed was not, in fact, a juror].) These cases are illustrative of legal impossibility. A further example is Francis Wharton's classic hypothetical involving Lady Eldon and her French lace. Lady Eldon, traveling in Europe, purchased a quantity of French lace at a high price, intending to smuggle it into England without payment of the duty. When discovered in a customs search, the lace turned out to be of English origin, of little value and not subject to duty. The traditional view is that Lady Eldon is not liable for an attempt to smuggle. (1 Wharton, Criminal Law [12th ed.], § 225,

p. 304, n. 9; for variations on the hypothetical see Hughes, One Further Footnote on Attempting the Impossible, 42 N.Y.U.L.Rev. 1005.)

On the other hand, factual impossibility was no defense. For example, a man was held liable for attempted murder when he shot into the room in which his target usually slept and, fortuitously, the target was sleeping elsewhere in the house that night. (State v. Mitchell, 170 Mo. 633, 71 S.W. 175.) Although one bullet struck the target's customary pillow, attainment of the criminal objective was factually impossible. State v. Moretti, 52 N.J. 182, 244 A.2d 499, cert. den. 393 U.S. 952, 89 S.Ct. 376, 21 L.Ed.2d 363, presents a similar instance of factual impossibility. The defendant agreed to perform an abortion, then a criminal act, upon a female undercover police investigator who was not, in fact, pregnant. The court sustained the conviction, ruling that "when the consequences sought by a defendant are forbidden by the law as criminal, it is no defense that the defendant could not succeed in reaching his goal because of circumstances unknown to him." (52 N.J., at p. 190, 244 A.2d, at p. 503.) On the same view, it was held that men who had sexual intercourse with a woman, with the belief that she was alive and did not consent to the intercourse, could be charged for attempted rape when the woman had, in fact, died from an unrelated ailment prior to the acts of intercourse. (United States v. Thomas, 13 U.S.C.M.A. 278.)

The New York cases can be parsed out along similar lines. One of the leading cases on legal impossibility is People v. Jaffe, 185 N.Y. 497, 78 N.E. 169, in which we held that there was no liability for the attempted receipt of stolen property when the property received by the defendant in the belief that it was stolen was, in fact under the control of the true owner. Similarly, in People v. Teal, 196 N.Y. 372, 89 N.E. 1086, a conviction for attempted subornation of perjury was overturned on the theory that the testimony attempted to be suborned was irrelevant to the merits of the case. Since it was not subornation of perjury to solicit false, but irrelevant, testimony, "the person through whose procuration the testimony is given cannot be guilty of subornation of perjury and, by the same rule, an unsuccessful attempt to that which is not a crime when effectuated, cannot be held to be an attempt to commit the crime specified." Factual impossibility, however, was no defense. Thus, a man could be held for attempted grand larceny when he picked an empty pocket.

As can be seen from even this abbreviated discussion, the distinction between "factual" and "legal" impossibility was a nice one indeed and the courts tended to place a greater value on legal form than on any substantive danger the defendant's actions posed for society. The approach of the draftsmen of the Model Penal Code was to eliminate the defense of impossibility in virtually all situations. Under the code provision, to constitute an attempt, it is still necessary that the result intended or desired by the actor constitute a crime. However, the code suggested a fundamental change to shift the locus of analysis to the actor's mental frame of reference and away from undue dependence upon external considerations. The basic premise of the code provision is that what was in the actor's own mind should be the standard for determining his dangerousness to society and, hence, his liability for attempted criminal conduct.

In the belief that neither of the two branches of the traditional impossibility arguments detracts from the offender's moral culpability, the Legislature substantially carried the code's treatment of impossibility into the 1967 revision of the Penal Law. Thus, a person is guilty of an attempt when, with intent to commit a crime, he engages in conduct which tends to effect the commission of such crime. (Penal Law, § 110.00.) It is no defense that, under the attendant circumstances, the crime was factually or legally impossible of commission, "if such crime could have been committed had the attendant circumstances been as such person believed them to be." (Penal Law, § 110.10.) Thus, if defendant believed the victim to be alive at the time of the shooting, it is no defense to the charge of attempted murder that the victim may have been dead.

Turning to the facts of the case before us, we believe that there is sufficient evidence in the record from which the jury could conclude that the defendant believed Geller to be alive at the time defendant fired shots into Geller's head. Defendant admitted firing five shots at a most vital part of the victim's anatomy from virtually point blank range. Although defendant contended that the victim had already been grievously wounded by another, from the defendant's admitted actions, the jury could conclude that the defendant's purpose and intention was to administer the coup de grace. * * * [The defendant did not testify and the jury never learned of his claim that Bush compelled him at gunpoint to shoot Geller. No explanation of his conduct was offered other than his offhand comment to Detective Carrasquillo. Duress was dispelled by his failure to flee Bush after the disposal of the weapons, by his vacation with Bush, and his initial false story in response to police inquiries. His claimed belief that Geller was dead need not have been accepted by the jury inasmuch as he had fired the shots without any instructions from Bush and with an accuracy that not only robbed the victim of any chance of life but demonstrated a callous indifference to the taking of human life. His behavior, during and after the killing, was fully consistent with that of a coperpetrator.] * * * From all of this, the jury was certainly warranted in concluding that the defendant acted in the belief that Geller was yet alive when shot by defendant.

The jury convicted the defendant of murder. Necessarily, they found that defendant intended to kill a live human being. Subsumed within this finding is the conclusion that defendant acted in the belief that Geller was alive. Thus, there is no need for additional fact findings by a jury. Although it was not established beyond a reasonable doubt that Geller was, in fact, alive, such is no defense to attempted murder since a murder would have been committed "had the attendant circumstances been as [defendant] believed them to be." (Penal Law, § 110.10.) The jury necessarily found that defendant believed Geller to be alive when defendant shot at him.

The Appellate Division erred in not modifying the judgment to reflect a conviction for the lesser included offense of attempted murder.

* * *

Note

As indicated in *Dlugash,* Model Penal Code § 5.01 was designed to implement the subjective view of attempt doctrine and thereby largely, albeit implicitly, eliminate the defense of impossibility. This position has been widely adopted. A few states have gone further and adopted statutes which explicitly reject both factual and legal impossibility. Nevertheless, some commentators—and the subject of impossibility has been of special fascination to legal academics—remain concerned about the total abolition of the defense. The fear is that the totally subjective approach poses the danger of convictions being sustained in the absence of conduct that is not strongly corroborative of the actor's purpose, as well as in cases of inherent impossibility. The latter category involves persons who have adopted such ill-suited, inadequate means for the achievement of their criminal purposes—sticking pins in a voodoo doll to bring about another's death or injury—as to suggest that the actor poses no danger to the public. See Robbins, Attempting the Impossible: The Emerging Consensus, Harv.J. Legis. 377, 439–43 (1986) for a proposed statute that would continue the defense in very limited circumstances. For another recent and helpful examination of this area, see Dutile and Moore, Mistake and Impossibility: Arranging a Marriage Between Two Difficult Partners, 74 Nw.U.L.Rev. 166 (1979).

4. THE MODEL PENAL CODE FORMULATION

This subsection reprints the proposed formulation of the law of attempt in the Model Penal Code and the proposed gradation of criminal attempts for purposes of determining penalty.

MODEL PENAL CODE *
(Official Draft, 1985).

Section 5.01. Criminal Attempt

(1) *Definition of Attempt.* A person is guilty of an attempt to commit a crime if, acting with the kind of culpability otherwise required for commission of the crime, he:

> (a) purposely engages in conduct which would constitute the crime if the attendant circumstances were as he believes them to be; or

(b) when causing a particular result is an element of the crime, does or omits to do anything with the purpose of causing or with the belief that it will cause such result without further conduct on his part; or

(c) purposely does or omits to do anything that, under the circumstances as he believes them to be, is an act or omission constituting a substantial step in a course of conduct planned to culminate in his commission of the crime.

(2) *Conduct That May Be Held Substantial Step Under Subsection (1)(c).* Conduct shall not be held to constitute a substantial step under Subsection (1)(c) of this Section unless it is strongly corroborative of the actor's criminal purpose. Without negativing the sufficiency of other conduct, the following, if strongly corroborative of the actor's criminal purpose, shall not be held insufficient as a matter of law:

(a) lying in wait, searching for or following the contemplated victim of the crime;

(b) enticing or seeking to entice the contemplated victim of the crime to go to the place contemplated for its commission;

(c) reconnoitering the place contemplated for the commission of the crime;

(d) unlawful entry of a structure, vehicle or enclosure in which it is contemplated that the crime will be committed;

(e) possession of materials to be employed in the commission of the crime, which are specially designed for such unlawful use or which can serve no lawful purpose of the actor under the circumstances;

(f) possession, collection or fabrication of materials to be employed in the commission of the crime, at or near the place contemplated for its commission, where such possession, collection or fabrication serves no lawful purpose of the actor under the circumstances;

(g) soliciting an innocent agent to engage in conduct constituting an element of the crime.

(3) *Conduct Designed to Aid Another in Commission of a Crime.* A person who engages in conduct designed to aid another to commit a crime that would establish his complicity under Section 2.06 if the crime were committed by such other person, is guilty of an attempt to commit the crime, although the crime is not committed or attempted by such other person.

(4) *Renunciation of Criminal Purpose.* When the actor's conduct would otherwise constitute an attempt under Subsection (1)(b) or (1)(c) of this Section, it is an affirmative defense that he abandoned his effort to commit the crime or otherwise prevented its commission, under circumstances manifesting a complete and voluntary renunciation of his criminal purpose. The establishment of such defense does not,

however, affect the liability of an accomplice who did not join in such abandonment or prevention.

Within the meaning of this Article, renunciation of criminal purpose is not voluntary if it is motivated, in whole or in part, by circumstances, not present or apparent at the inception of the actor's course of conduct, that increase the probability of detection or apprehension or that make more difficult the accomplishment of the criminal purpose. Renunciation is not complete if it is motivated by a decision to postpone the criminal conduct until a more advantageous time or to transfer the criminal effort to another but similar objective or victim.

Section 5.05 Grading of Criminal Attempt * * *; Mitigation in Cases of Lesser Danger; Multiple Convictions Barred

(1) *Grading.* Except as otherwise provided in this Section, attempt * * * [is a crime] of the same grade and degree as the most serious offense that is attempted * * *.

(2) *Mitigation.* If the particular conduct charged to constitute a criminal attempt * * * is so inherently unlikely to result or culminate in the commission of a crime that neither such conduct nor the actor presents a public danger warranting the grading of such offense under this Section, the Court shall exercise its power under Section 6.12 to enter judgment and impose sentence for a crime of lower grade or degree or, in extreme cases, may dismiss the prosecution.

(3) *Multiple Convictions.* A person may not be convicted of more than one offense defined by this Article for conduct designed to commit or to culminate in the commission of the same crime.

B. SOLICITATION

If one person solicits another to commit an offense and the person solicited does in fact commit the offense, the solicitor is liable for the crime under principles of complicity. Similarly, if the person solicited begins actions designed to culminate in the offense and goes far enough to complete an attempt, the solicitor is guilty of that attempt. If, as is discussed in the following section, the solicitor and solicitant agree to the perpetration of the proposed crime and, in jurisdictions which so require, one performs an overt act towards that goal, they can both be convicted of conspiracy. But what if the crime is never committed, nor attempted, nor agreed upon? Should the solicitor, thus frustrated, be liable for any punishment?

The imposition of criminal liability upon such actors represents a further expansion of the state's authority. It permits intervention even more remote from the commission of an offense than is normally true for attempts. And it does so because of the actor's posited evil mind and conduct that may involve no more than mere words. Civil libertarians are likely to be concerned that a general crime of solicitation threatens arrest and conviction for what may only be strident advocacy of unpopular views. However, even if free speech concerns can be allayed, doubts will remain as to whether a solicitor has unequivocally demonstrated her criminality. The very fact that the solicitor has elected to have another perpetrate the object offense is some evidence from which a weak commitment to its achievement might be inferred. It also means that the moral judgments of that other individual stands between the desire of the solicitor and the commission of the offense. Nevertheless, even an unsuccessful effort to hire, or otherwise encourage, another person to commit murder threatens to create apprehension in the community and justifies authorizing the police to intervene. It also suggests that the solicitor is a dangerous person and a fit subject for the criminal sanction.

Since Rex v. Higgins, 102 Eng.Rep 269 (1801), solicitation to commit a felony (and apparently at least some misdemeanors) has been recognized as a common law offense. In most American jurisdictions the balance of countervailing considerations has been struck so as to permit prosecution for solicitation. The Model Penal Code drafters acknowledged that divergent views existed on the question of whether solicitors posed a great enough danger to justify criminalization. They concluded that in some ways the solicitation was more dangerous than a direct attempt. It threatened to bring about cooperative criminal ventures, led by a solicitor "more intelligent and masterful * * * than * * * his hirelings. Comment to § 5.02 of the Model Penal Code 365–66 (1985).

Despite this contention, concern continues as to potential governmental overreaching and the ease with which such a charge can be made given that mere words may suffice. In response to these concerns a number of techniques have been developed to limit the scope of solicitation statutes. State statutes are frequently limited to solicitations to commit extremely serious felonies. E.g., Texas Penal Code § 15.03(a) (solicitation of capital felonies and felonies of the first degree). Another limitation is to require corroboration either by another person or by the circumstances under which the solicitation was committed. E.g., California Penal Code § 653f and Colorado Revised Statutes § 18–2–301(1). Section 1003(1) of the final draft of the ill-fated Proposed Federal Criminal Code would have imposed still another limitation. It would have required that the solicitant commit an overt act in response to the solicitation. This was thought necessary to avoid resting liability upon speech without more. Does such a requirement add to our knowledge of the solicitor's culpability?

MODEL PENAL CODE *

(Official Draft, 1985).

Section 5.02. Criminal Solicitation

(1) *Definition of Solicitation.* A person is guilty of solicitation to commit a crime if with the purpose of promoting or facilitating its commission he commands, encourages or requests another person to engage in specific conduct that would constitute such crime or an attempt to commit such crime or would establish his complicity in its commission or attempted commission.

(2) *Uncommunicated Solicitation.* It is immaterial under Subsection (1) of this Section that the actor fails to communicate with the person he solicits to commit a crime if his conduct was designed to effect such communication.

(3) *Renunciation of Criminal Purpose.* It is an affirmative defense that the actor, after soliciting another person to commit a crime persuaded him not to do so or otherwise prevented the commission of the crime, under circumstances manifesting a complete and voluntary renunciation of his criminal purpose.

Notes and Questions

1. Solicitation, like attempt and conspiracy, would be graded by the Model Penal Code the same as the most serious offense solicited except that: "An attempt, solicitation or conspiracy to commit a [capital crime or a] felony of the first degree is a felony of the second degree." Model Penal Code § 5.05(1) (1985).

2. If a jurisdiction has no general solicitation statute, is it possible that one who solicits another to commit a crime is guilty of an attempt to commit that crime? The courts are in disarray on this issue. In Gervin v. State, 212 Tenn. 653, 371 S.W.2d 449 (1963), the court reversed the defendant's conviction for attempted murder because all he had done was to hire another for this purpose. The court explained:

> To constitute an attempt there must * * * be an act of perpetration. * * * However, solicitation is preparation rather than perpetration. * * * We are reluctant to hold * * * that at the stage of preparation [i.e., solicitation], the attempt will be carried out and that the situation is unequivocal. At this point there are too many contingencies, such as the willingness of the solicitant to carry out the design, to say the [die] is cast. But to hold solicitation an attempt this would be necessary.

212 Tenn. at 658, 371 S.W.2d at 451. The court did indicate that an indictment for the common law misdemeanor of solicitation would lie.

United States v. American Airlines, Inc., 743 F.2d 1114 (5th Cir.1984), involved an alleged attempted monopolization under section 2 of the Sherman Act. At the time the defendant and Braniff Airlines shared the bulk of all air traffic in and out of Dallas-Fort Worth International Airport. The two lines had been engaged in fierce competition as to prices and service. The evidence of the government consisted of a taped phone conversation between the presidents of the two lines in which defendant's president complained bitterly about the effect of the competition. The conversation culminated in the following exchange in which AA represents defendant's president and BA represents Braniff's:

BA: Do you have a suggestion for me?

AA: Yes. I have a suggestion for you. Raise your goddamn fares twenty percent. I'll raise mine the next morning.

BA: Robert, we—

AA: You'll make more money and I will too.

BA: We can't talk about pricing.

AA: Oh bull * * * *, Howard. We can talk about any goddamn thing we want to talk about.

743 F.2d at 1116. Instead of raising his prices Braniff's president turned the tape of the conversation over to the government. The district court had dismissed the complaint on the grounds, inter alia, that an attempt must amount to more than a solicitation. The Court of Appeals reversed:

The district court * * * cited a number of modern cases in support of its conclusion * * * and appellees refer us to others [including *Gervin*, supra]. These cases involving murder, sodomy, and other crimes, however, are not instructive in determining the requirements for attempted monopolization. In the cited cases, an agreement to the solicitation would not result in the completion of the substantive offense at the moment of agreement; other physical acts were required for the completed offense.

The federal courts have generally rejected a rigid or formalistic approach to the attempt offense. * * *

In United States v. May, 625 F.2d 186 (8th Cir.1980), a defendant challenged his conviction for "unlawfully attempt[ing] to cause to have concealed, obliterated, or destroyed" government records * * * on the grounds that his telephone call to the person who controlled certain relevant records constituted only a solicitation and was not an attempt. The Eighth Circuit affirmed * * *.

In United States v. Robles, 185 F.Supp. 82, 85 (N.D.Cal.1960), a solicitation by letter was held to be an attempt to unlawfully import a narcotic.

In sum, we reject appellee's contention that the law in 1890 [the year the Sherman Act was enacted] clearly required more than a solicitation to constitute an attempt. We also conclude that the better reasoned authorities support the view that a highly verbal crime such as attempted monopolization may be established by proof of a solicitation along with the requisite intent.

743 F.2d at 1121.   Do *May* and *Robles,* cited by the Fifth Circuit, support the court's attempted distinction of the authority cited by the appellee?   If not, should the appellee prevail?   Is there any reason why an invitation to monopolize should be subject to sanction but not an invitation to murder?

3.   As mentioned in the introductory note to this section, a major concern about the criminalization of solicitation is its potential use in discouraging the exercise of First Amendment rights, either by direct application or by an indirect "chilling effect."   The Comment to Model Penal Code § 5.02 (Official Draft 1985) mentions that this crime may be an important technique for suppressing the leadership of movements deemed criminal, and cites for that proposition cases involving prosecution for political and labor "agitation."   Id. at page 366 and note 4.   One answer to this concern is to write statutes so as to require that the speaker solicit specific conduct which would constitute the crime.   Moreover, as a constitutional matter, words alleged to be those of solicitation or incitement would be protected if made under circumstances which made it appear abstract and remote from any actual violation.   Brandenburg v. Ohio, 395 U.S. 444, 89 S.Ct. 1827, 23 L.Ed.2d 430 (1969) (per curiam).   Ultimately, however, it may be said that:

> the First Amendment is quite irrelevant if the intent of the actor and the objective meaning of the words used are so close in time and purpose to a substantive evil as to become part of the ultimate crime itself.   In those instances, where speech becomes an integral part of the crime, a First Amendment defense is foreclosed even if the prosecution rests on words alone.

United States v. Freeman, 761 F.2d 549, 552 (9th Cir.1985) (affirming convictions for counseling violations of the tax laws).

4.   Must the solicitation actually be communicated to the solicitant? W. LaFave and A. Scott, Criminal Law 492 (1986)—citing cases decided between 1873 and 1912—say no, but comment that some courts would require that a noncommunicated solicitation be punished as an attempted solicitation.   Compare § 5.02(2) of the Model Penal Code, reprinted at page 577, supra.   Similarly, it can be a solicitation if the actor solicits one person to find someone else to commit the crime.   State v. Furr, 292 N.C. 711, 235 S.E.2d 193 (1977).   (The *Furr* court also held that several requests made to the same solicitant can constitute separate solicitations if the solicitant definitely refuses each.)   Cf. Meyer v. State, 47 Md.App. 679, 425 A.2d 664 (1981), cert. denied, 454 U.S. 865, 102 S.Ct. 327, 70 L.Ed.2d 166 (1981).   In *Meyer* the defendant, while awaiting sentence for two convictions for first degree contract murder which he had arranged, solicited the killing of his wife, the person who had hired him to arrange the two previous murders, and two policemen who had obtained his confession to those crimes.   The solicitant was an undercover police office who recorded their conversations. Meyer was convicted on four counts of solicitation and sentenced to four consecutive twenty-year terms (consecutive to sentences of life and thirty years for the two murders).   These convictions and sentences were upheld on the grounds that they were separate and distinct.   That is, it was not a one-payment mass murder that was contemplated.   Rather the executions

were to occur at different times and places by different means and for separate fees.)

5. Does impossibility of any sort prevent liability for solicitation? Should it? In State v. Keen, 25 N.C.App. 567, 214 S.E.2d 242 (1975), the defendant argued that because the persons he solicited to kill his wife were law enforcement officers and would not have accepted the invitation, his conviction for solicitation was not permissible. Upholding the conviction, the court stated, "The crime of solicitation * * * is complete with the solicitation even though there could never have been an acquiescence in the scheme by the one solicited." 25 N.C.App. at 570, 571, 214 S.E.2d at 244.

6. May one who solicits another to commit an offense escape liability by voluntarily renouncing the venture before the crime is committed by the person solicited? The appellate caselaw is inconclusive. See W. LaFave and A. Scott, Criminal Law 492 (2nd Ed.1986). In People v. Gordon, 47 Cal. App.3d 465, 120 Cal.Rptr. 840 (1975), defendant—an attorney acting on behalf of an undisclosed client—solicited a police officer to plant narcotics on another individual. The next day, she called the police officer and told him that she had decided not to be a party to the scheme, as she did not want to take a chance on ruining her political career. The officer made several subsequent contacts with defendant, but she refused to set up a meeting between her client and the officer. Affirming her conviction for solicitation, the court held: "Since the crime was fully committed * * *, it is no defense that the defendant later withdrew or failed to consummate the crime which was the object of the solicitation." 47 Cal.App.3d at 474, 476, 120 Cal.Rptr. at 845. Consider the Model Penal Code proposal, reprinted at page 577, supra. Compare Ariz.Rev.Stat. § 13–1005(B):

> In a prosecution for solicitation, it is a defense that the defendant, under circumstances manifesting a voluntary and complete renunciation of the defendant's criminal intent completed both of the following acts:
>
> 1. Notified the person solicited.
>
> 2. Gave timely warning to law enforcement authorities or otherwise made a reasonable effort to prevent the conduct or result solicited.

Would the defendant in *Gordon* have had a defense under the Arizona statute?

Chennault v. State, 667 S.W.2d 299 (Tex.App.1984), involved an alleged solicitation of capital murder. The defendant had solicited the murder of an unnamed person who, from defendant's detailed description, was identified as one Lawrence Perry McGinness. It was agreed that the defendant eventually "called off the hit" and he contended that this constituted abandonment under Texas Penal Code § 15.04. On appeal he argued that the following argument by the prosecutor was contrary to the law of abandonment and hence reversible error:

> Let me restate it one more time so there is no confusion.
>
> If you find that he stopped the music and called it off because he did not want Lawrence Perry McGinnes dead, then find him not guilty.

If you believe it's for any other purpose under the sun, then find him guilty.

667 S.W.2d at 303. Is this a misstatement of the law of abandonment? Reconsider Model Penal Code § 5.01(4) reprinted on page 574, supra, and the discussion of this subject in the context of attempt in notes 3 and 4, pages 555–57, supra.

C. CONSPIRACY

Editors' Introduction: Use and Abuse of Conspiracy Law

Conspiracy serves several functions in criminal law. It is, like attempt and solicitation, an inchoate crime for which a defendant may be charged, tried, convicted, and punished even if its criminal purposes are not achieved. But, in addition, it is conceived of as a substantive offense that justifies conviction and punishment in addition to any assessed for any offense committed as the object of the conspiracy. Also, it is sometimes a vehicle for making one person liable for the crimes of other individuals. The so-called Pinkerton Rule discussed in Section B of Chapter XI, infra, provides that under certain circumstances all conspirators are liable for crimes committed by one member of the conspiracy.

Conspiracy prosecutions often involve complex procedural issues that are beyond the scope of direct concern here. But in part because of these procedural aspects of conspiracy—and in part because of the nature of the crime of conspiracy itself—some have expressed serious misgivings regarding the continued vitality of conspiracy doctrine as a part of substantive criminal law. The numerous issues that must be faced in considering conspiracy law should be evaluated in light of these concerns. They were perhaps most effectively put by Mr. Justice Jackson in his concurring opinion in Krulewitch v. United States, 336 U.S. 440, 445–454, 69 S.Ct. 716, 719–723, 93 L.Ed. 790, 795–800 (1949):

This case illustrates a present drift in the federal law of conspiracy which warrants some further comment because it is characteristic of the long evolution of that elastic, sprawling and pervasive offense. Its history exemplifies the "tendency of a principle to expand itself to the limit of its logic." The unavailing protest of courts against the growing habit to indict for conspiracy in lieu of prosecuting for the substantive offense itself, or in addition thereto, suggests that loose practice as to this offense constitutes a serious threat to fairness in our administration of justice.

The modern crime of conspiracy is so vague that it almost defies definition. Despite certain elementary and essential elements, it also, chameleon-like takes on a special coloration from each of the many independent offenses on which it may be overlaid. It is always "predominantly mental in composition" because it consists primarily of a meeting of minds and an intent.

The crime comes down to us wrapped in vague but unpleasant connotations. It sounds historical undertones of treachery, secret plotting and violence on a scale that menaces social stability and the security of the state itself. "Privy conspiracy" ranks with sedition and rebellion in the Litany's prayer for deliverance. Conspiratorial movements do indeed lie back of the political assassination, the *coup d'état,* the *putsch,* the revolution, and seizures of power in modern times, as they have in all history.

But the conspiracy concept also is superimposed upon many concerted crimes having no political motivation. It is not intended to question that the basic conspiracy principle has some place in modern criminal law, because to unite, back of a criminal purpose, the strength, opportunities and resources of many is obviously more dangerous and more difficult to police than the efforts of a lone wrongdoer. It also may be trivialized, as [for example] where the conspiracy consists of the concert of a loathsome panderer and a prostitute to go from New York to Florida to ply their trade and it would appear that a simple Mann Act prosecution would vindicate the majesty of federal law. However, even when appropriately invoked, the looseness and pliability of the doctrine present inherent dangers which should be in the background of judicial thought wherever it is sought to extend the doctrine to meet the exigencies of a particular case.

Conspiracy in federal law aggravates the degree of crime over that of unconcerted offending. The act of confederating to commit a misdemeanor, followed by even an innocent overt act in its execution, is a felony and is such even if the misdemeanor is never consummated. The more radical proposition also is well-established that at common law and under some statutes a combination may be a criminal conspiracy even if it contemplates only acts which are not crimes at all when perpetrated by an individual or by many acting severally.

Thus the conspiracy doctrine will incriminate persons on the fringe of offending who would not be guilty of aiding and abetting or of becoming an accessory, for those charges only lie when an act which is a crime has actually been committed.

* * * [W]e are advised that "The modern crime of conspiracy is almost entirely the result of the manner in which conspiracy was treated by the court of Star Chamber." The doctrine does not commend itself to jurists of civil-law countries, despite universal recognition that an organized society must have legal weapons for combatting organized criminality. Most other countries have devised what they consider more discriminating principles upon which to prosecute criminal gangs, secret associations and subversive syndicates.

* * *

The interchangeable use of conspiracy doctrine in civil as well as penal proceedings opens it to the danger, absent in the case of many crimes, that a court having in mind only the civil sanctions will approve lax practices which later are imported into criminal proceedings. * * *

Of course, it is for prosecutors rather than courts to determine when to use a scatter-gun to bring down the defendant, but there are procedural advantages from using it which add to the danger of unguarded extension of the concept.

An accused, under the Sixth Amendment, has the right to trial "by an impartial jury of the State and district wherein the crime shall have been committed." The leverage of a conspiracy charge lifts this limitation from the prosecution and reduces its protection to a phantom, for the crime is considered so vagrant as to have been committed in any district where any one of the conspirators did any one of the acts, however innocent, intended to accomplish its object. The Government may, and often does, compel one to defend at a great distance from any place he ever did any act because some accused confederate did some trivial and by itself innocent act in the chosen district. Circumstances may even enable the prosecution to fix the place of trial in Washington, D.C., where a defendant may lawfully be put to trial before a jury partly or even wholly made up of employees of the Government that accuses him.

When the trial starts, the accused feels the full impact of the conspiracy strategy. Strictly, the prosecution should first establish *prima facie* the conspiracy and identify the conspirators, after which evidence of acts and declarations of each in the course of its execution are admissible against all. But the order of proof of so sprawling a charge is difficult for a judge to control. As a practical matter, the accused often is confronted with a hodgepodge of acts and statements by others which he may never have authorized or intended or even known about, but which help to persuade the jury of existence of the conspiracy itself. In other words, a conspiracy often is proved by evidence that is admissible only upon assumption that conspiracy existed. The naive assumption that prejudicial effects can be overcome by instructions to the jury all practicing lawyers know to be unmitigated fiction.

The trial of a conspiracy charge doubtless imposes a heavy burden on the prosecution, but it is an especially difficult situation for the defendant. The hazard from loose application of rules of evidence is aggravated where the Government institutes mass trials. * * *

A co-defendant in a conspiracy trial occupies an uneasy seat. There generally will be evidence of wrongdoing by somebody. It is difficult for the individual to make his own case stand on its own merits in the minds of jurors who are ready to believe that birds of a feather are flocked together. If he is silent, he is taken to admit it and if, as often happens, co-defendants can be prodded into accusing or contradicting each other, they convict each other. There are many practical difficulties in defending against a charge of conspiracy which I will not enumerate.

As Justice Jackson makes clear, conspiracy shares the doctrinal problems examined in connection with the other inchoate offenses, attempt and solicitation. There is no necessity that a result be shown. This departure from the model concept of the elements of crime raises questions as to the actor's commitment to the criminal goal and her dangerousness. Conspiracy prosecutions and convictions can be founded on evidence revealing much less corroboration of criminal intent than would suffice for an attempt. This is also true of solicitation but the use of that crime tends to be limited to words and conduct intended to bring about only the most serious of felonies. The criticism of conspiracy is, however, based on more than the theoretical difficulties it shares with other inchoate crimes. The history of its use is an important reason for the bad odor in which it is held in some quarters. Both in England and the United States it has been employed to suppress combinations of workers and political subversives, as well as those of businesses and those seeking more traditional criminal ends.

Given these criticisms how is the continued vitality, indeed the modern efflorescence, of conspiracy to be explained? In part the answer lies in the same considerations which have been seen as justifying liability for attempt and solicitation: it provides a predicate for state intervention without having to await the commission of the object harm; and it reflects our sense of justice which would be offended if the failure of a criminal scheme served to exculpate one whose mens rea and conduct—albeit minimal—identifies her as a danger to the rest of us. In addition there are reasons peculiar to conspiracy itself. The very procedural advantages which disturb civil libertarians serve as powerful weapons which those charged with the duty of crime control are understandably loathe to surrender. Conspiracy also reflects the realities of our more complex society. Modern technology and the enormous increase in our population have resulted in revolutionary changes in the ways in which work, education, leisure and most other human activities have been organized. Parallel changes have occurred in criminal activity. Although the purse snatcher and burglar may continue to operate as individuals, interstate mail fraud, auto theft rings, and, preeminently, international purveyors of illicit drugs reflect the need for elaborate, far flung organizations involving many players. In this connection, it is worthy of note that the federal courts and law enforcement authorities have played the central role in the evolution of conspiracy law. The federal government has assumed a major part of the responsibility for the struggle against certain white collar crimes and organized crime. Both classes are targeted because their activities are so likely to cross state and national boundaries. They are also likely to pose investigative and prosecutorial complexities which may be beyond the resources and expertise of local authorities.

A classic example of the modern use of conspiracy doctrine against a political organization is provided by Dennis v. United States, 341 U.S. 494, 71 S.Ct. 857, 95 L.Ed. 1137 (1951). The petitioners, leaders of the Communist Party of the United States, had been convicted under the Smith Act for, among other things, willfully and knowingly conspiring to teach and advocate the duty and necessity of overthrowing the Government of the United States by force and violence. It might be thought that the prosecution embodied all of the worst aspects of conspiracy doctrine. Yet Justice Jackson concurred in the affirmance of their convictions. He noted that the conspiracy charge was central to the appeal and then addressed the petitioners' constitutional challenge which gained the dissenting votes of Justices Black and Douglas:

> The Constitution does not make conspiracy a civil right. The Court has never before done so and I think it should not do so now. Conspiracies of labor union, trade associations, and news agencies have been condemned, although accomplished, evidenced and carried out, like the conspiracy here, chiefly by letter-writing, meetings, speeches and organization. Indeed, this Court seems, particularly in cases where the conspiracy has economic ends, to be applying its doctrines with increasing severity. While I consider criminal conspiracy a dragnet device capable of perversion into an instrument of injustice in the hands of a partisan or complacent judiciary, it has an established place in our system of law, and no reason appears for applying it only to concerted action claimed to disturb interstate commerce and withholding it from those claimed to undermine our whole Government.

341 U.S. at 572, 71 S.Ct. at 899, 95 L.Ed. at 1185.

Justice Jackson then explained the special dangers posed by persons in criminal concert because of the greater harms which they might bring about. Although he would not permit the punishment of conspiracy to advocate lawful conduct, "it is not forbidden to put down force or violence, it is not forbidden to punish its teaching or advocacy, and the end being punishable, there is no doubt of the power to punish the conspiracy for the purpose." 341 U.S. at 575, 71 S.Ct. at 900, 95 L.Ed. at 1186. He then considered and rejected the contentions that First Amendment freedoms barred the prosecution and required the imposition of a "clear and present danger" test. As to the latter, he wrote:

> In conspiracy cases the Court not only has dispensed with proof of clear and present danger but even of power to create a danger: "It long has been settled, however, that a 'conspiracy to commit a crime is a different offense from the crime that is the object of the conspiracy.' * * * Petitioners, for example, might have been convicted here of a conspiracy to monopolize without ever having acquired the power to carry out the object of the conspiracy. * * * " American Tobacco Co. v. United States, 328 U.S. 781, 789, 66 S.Ct. 1125, 1129, 90 L.Ed. 1575.

341 U.S. at 576, 71 S.Ct. at 901, 95 L.Ed. at 1187.

Justice Jackson, perhaps reflecting his experience as the Chief American Prosecutor at the Nuremburg trials of Nazi war criminals, wrote of the growth of "permanently organized, well-financed, semi-secret and highly disciplined political organizations" of which the Communist Party was one example. He concluded:

> The law of conspiracy has been the chief means at the Government's disposal to deal with the growing problems created by such organizations. I happen to think it is an awkward and inept remedy,

but I find no constitutional authority for taking this weapon from the Government. There is no constitutional right to "gang up" on the Government.

341 U.S. at 577, 71 S.Ct. at 901, 95 L.Ed. at 1187–1188.

In reviewing the material which follows, reflect on the tension between the concerns expressed by Justice Jackson in *Krulewitch* and his acknowledgment in *Dennis* that some concerted criminal activities may require or justify the use of conspiracy doctrine. Can economic crimes such as monopolization or price-fixing be controlled without such a doctrine? Note how principles developed in the context of economic conspiracy cases will be cited in those dealing with traditional crimes (indeed, Justice Jackson in *Dennis* quotes from *American Tobacco*); is this troublesome? Should the crime be abolished or would it be sufficient to modify aspects of the doctrine so as to redress the alleged imbalance between the prosecution and the defense? For an excellent discussion of many of these issues, see Johnson, The Unnecessary Crime of Conspiracy, 61 Calif.L.Rev. 1137 (1973).

1. ELEMENTS OF THE OFFENSE

The two traditional elements of the crime of conspiracy are the agreement between or among the participants and the "intent" or state of mind required concerning the objective of the agreement. Although the performance of an overt act pursuant to the agreement was not an element of the original common law crime of conspiracy, modern statutes impose such a requirement with sufficient frequency that an overt act needs to be considered as a potential additional element in contemporary analysis.

a. Agreement

Editors' Introduction: Agreement and the Overt Act Requirement in Conspiracy Law

The essence of conspiracy is the agreement between or among the parties, although as is developed below, an overt act by one of the parties is sometimes required. The problems raised by the requirement of an agreement are to some extent simply problems of proof—what constitutes sufficient evidence of the agreement required by the crime? In addition, however, traditional law has found "defenses" to charges of conspiracy where the facts are regarded as establishing the logical impossibility of two "guilty" minds having actually met in agreement. This is developed in subsection C.1.a.(3), infra.

Before addressing these matters, it is useful to consider the more basic question of what is necessary to establish that an agreement exists and that a specific person is a party to that agreement. Must the person have made a relatively specific commitment to participate in the scheme that is the subject of the discussion? Consider the following language from Cleaver v. United States, 238 F.2d 766, 771 (10th Cir. 1956), addressing the question of whether one Webster was a member of a conspiracy to commit burglary that the court acknowledges was proved by the prosecution:

> Webster * * * did not participate in the planning or the commission of the burglary, although he was present during a number of the conversations among the various conspirators. Mere knowledge, approval of or acquiescence in the object or purpose of the conspiracy, without an intention and agreement to cooperate in the crime is insufficient to constitute one a conspirator.

The *Cleaver* opinion is correct that "mere presence" at the scene of the planning of a crime will not, without more, support the finding of an agreement which is crucial to a conspiracy conviction. Even knowledge and approval of others' criminal plans does not make one a co-conspirator. If, in *Cleaver,* Webster had been an owner of the premises to be "burgled" and he subsequently filed an inflated insurance claim predicated on the "burglary", would a finding of agreement be precluded? Cf. United States v. Xheka, 704 F.2d 974, 988–89 (7th Cir.1983). What has changed so as to permit the inference of an agreement?

Does the requirement of an agreement, without more, offer sufficient protection from governmental abuse? A major theme of Justice Jackson's attack on conspiracy in *Krulewitch,* see pages 581–83, supra, is that the definition of the offense is too vague. One response to that claim is that the prosecution is required to establish the existence of an agreement. "Conspiracy is an inchoate offense, the essence of which is an agreement to commit an unlawful act." Iannelli v. United States, 420 U.S. 770, 777, 95 S.Ct. 1284, 1289, 43 L.Ed.2d 616, 622 (1975). The agreement, in the view of defenders of conspiracy, is a sufficiently unambiguous act to allay concerns stemming from vagueness. This answer would be more fully reassuring if the agreement requirement could only be satisfied by showing an express meeting of the minds which was formally memorialized. Obviously this is not required for all civil contracts much less those aimed at the achievement of illicit ends. Instead, of necessity, the law permits triers of fact to infer, from circumstantial as well as direct evidence, that the defendant knowingly agreed to join one or more others in a concerted effort to bring about a common end. In practice, this task may prove a small obstacle to the prosecution and, therefore, a minor protection against the dangers claimed to be posed by the vagueness of conspiracy.

The common law crime of conspiracy required no more than that the act of agreement have been completed. But a number of American jurisdictions have required that, in addition to the agreement, the prosecution prove the commission of an overt act by at least one member of the agreement. This is required under the federal criminal conspiracy statute, 18 U.S.C.A. § 371, which requires proof that "one or more of * * * [the] persons [agreeing did an] act to effect the object of the conspiracy." Some statutes imposed a selective requirement. The Arizona statute, for example, requires proof of an overt act except where the object of the conspiracy is to commit burglary while armed, arson of an occupied structure, or any felony upon the person of another.   Ariz.Rev.Stat. § 13–1003.

The Supreme Court summarized the basic law applicable to the overt act requirement under the federal statute as follows:

> It is not necessary that an overt act be the substantive crime charged in the indictment as the object of the conspiracy.   Nor, indeed, need such act, taken by itself, even be criminal in character.   The function of the overt act in a conspiracy prosecution is simply to manifest "that the conspiracy is at work," and is neither a project still resting solely in the minds of the conspirators nor a fully completed operation no longer in existence.

Yates v. United States, 354 U.S. 298, 334, 77 S.Ct. 1064, 1084–85, 1 L.Ed.2d 1356, 1384 (1957).

There are two major issues posed by this aspect of conspiracy law. The first, of course, is whether sound policy dictates that conspiracy be so defined as to include proof of an overt act as well as an agreement. What does an overt act requirement accomplish?   The second issue is related.   What standard should be used to determine whether, under an overt act requirement, specific acts are sufficient?   The relates to the rationale for the overt act requirement.   What criterion for determining the sufficiency of overt acts best accomplishes the intent of this requirement?

As to the first issue it is clear that proponents of an overt act requirement see it as one more way to overcome the danger of misidentification which they believe is inherent in the vagueness of conspiracy. It is an additional manifestation of the actor's purpose which offers some reassurance that the agreement poses a real danger of consummation.   It is also said:

> to allow an opportunity to the conspirators to repent and to terminate the unlawful agreement before any decisive act is done in furtherance of it.   The requirement of the allegation and proof of such an overt act " * * * affords a locus poenitentiae, so that before the act is done either one or all of the parties may abandon their design, and thus avoid the penalty prescribed by the statute."   (United States v. Britton, 108 U.S. 199, 2 S.Ct. 531–34, 27 L.Ed. 698.)

People v. Olson, 232 Cal.App.2d 480, 42 Cal.Rptr. 760, 767 (1965).   A committee proposing that the Illinois conspiracy statute be amended so as to include a requirement of an overt act observed:

> Heretofore, in Illinois, the agreement alone has constituted sufficient conduct to support a charge of conspiracy * * *.   In actuality, however, no case has been found in which some activity pursuant to the agreement has not been present.   This leads to the conclusion that prosecutors find proof of the agreement without subsequent activity too difficult, or consider the agreement alone too inconsequential, to warrant criminal prosecution.

Illinois Criminal Code of 1961, Committee Comments to Section 8–2.   If this is so, what does it say about the wisdom of requiring an overt act in the definition of criminal conspiracy? Perhaps imposing such a requirement would not significantly impede implementation of conspiracy law. But would any such requirement be so easily met that the requirement would serve no actual function? This relates to the second issue introduced above.

As to the second issue, it is clear that where an overt act is required it is a burden easily satisfied. Very minor conduct which is seen as undertaken in furtherance of the conspiracy will be sufficient. What constitutes an act in furtherance can, however, pose some difficulties. It has been held that a payment to a "co-conspirator" to secure his agreement to the conspiracy is not an overt act required by law. People v. Teeter, 86 Misc.2d 532, 382 N.Y.S.2d 938 (1976), aff'd 62 A.D.2d 1158, 404 N.Y.S.2d 210 (1978). On the other hand, if the basic agreement has clearly been achieved mere conversations among the confederates concerning implementation are likely to be sufficient. See United States v. Armone, 363 F.2d 385 (2d Cir.1966), cert. denied, 385 U.S. 957, 87 S.Ct. 391, 17 L.Ed.2d 303 (1966). Certainly the overt act need not itself be criminal. Because so little has been required, some have argued that the requirement should be strengthened so as to require proof that *each* person charged as a conspirator took some significant action in furtherance of the object offense. Such changes would make conspiracy more closely resemble prosecutions under complicity theory.

Finally, it should be noted that overt acts can have significant procedural consequences. For example, venue might be found in any district in which any overt act was performed, a matter which can be of considerable advantage to the prosecution. Similarly, an overt act will extend the statute of limitations which, again, can be advantageous to the government. See People v. Zamora, 18 Cal.3d 538, 134 Cal.Rptr. 784, 557 P.2d 75 (1976).

(1) General Requirement of an Agreement

UNITED STATES v. BROWN

United States Court of Appeals, Second Circuit, 1985.
776 F.2d 397.

FRIENDLY, CIRCUIT JUDGE:

[The defendant and his codefendant, Valentine (a fugitive at the time of trial), were charged with conspiring to distribute heroin and with distribution of heroin. The basis for the prosecution was the purchase by New York City Police Officer William Grimball of a "joint" of "D" (a "joint" is $40 worth of "D" or heroin) while working undercover in Harlem. The jury convicted defendant of conspiracy but was unable to reach a verdict on the substantive count.]

* * *

Officer Grimball was the Government's principal witness. He testified that early in the evening of October 9, 1984, he approached

Gregory Valentine on the corner of 115th Street and Eighth Avenue and asked him for a joint of "D". Valentine asked Grimball whom he knew around the street. Grimball asked if Valentine knew Scott. He did not. Brown "came up" and Valentine said, "He wants a joint, but I don't know him." Brown looked at Grimball and said, "He looks okay to me." Valentine then said, "Okay. But I am going to leave it somewhere and you [meaning Officer Grimball] can pick it up." Brown interjected, "You don't have to do that. Just go and get it for him. He looks all right to me." After looking again at Grimball, Brown said, "He looks all right to me" and "I will wait right here."

Valentine then said, "Okay. Come on with me around to the hotel." Grimball followed him to 300 West 116th Street, where Valentine instructed him, "Sit on the black car and give me a few minutes to go up and get it." Valentine requested and received $40, which had been prerecorded, and then said, "You are going to take care of me for doing this for you, throw some dollars my way?," to which Grimball responded, "Yeah."

Valentine then entered the hotel and shortly returned. The two went back to 115th Street and Eighth Avenue, where Valentine placed a cigarette box on the hood of a blue car. Grimball picked up the cigarette box and found a glassine envelope containing white powder, stipulated to be heroin. Grimball placed $5 of prerecorded buy money in the cigarette box, which he replaced on the hood. Valentine picked up the box and removed the $5. Grimball returned to his car and made a radio transmission to the backup field team that "the buy had went down" and informed them of the locations of the persons involved. Brown and Valentine were arrested. Valentine was found to possess two glassine envelopes of heroin and the $5 of prerecorded money. Brown was in possession of $31 of his own money; no drugs or contraband were found on him. The $40 of marked buy money was not recovered, and no arrests were made at the hotel.

[The prosecution had Grimball qualified as an expert on the basis of several seminars on drug control and his participation in street buys. He then] testified that the typical drug buy in the Harlem area involved two to five people. As a result of frequent police sweeps, Harlem drug dealers were becoming so cautious that they employed

> people who act as steerers and the steerer's responsibility is basically to determine whether or not you are actually an addict or a user of heroin and they are also used to screen you to see if there is any possibility of you being a cop looking for a bulge or some indication that would give them that you are not actually an addict. And a lot of the responsibility relies [sic] on them to determine whether or not the drug buy is going to go down or not.

Officer Grimball was then allowed, over a general objection, to testify that based on his experience as an undercover agent he would describe the role that Ronald Brown played in the transaction as that of a steerer. When asked why, he testified, again over a general objection,

"Because I believe that if it wasn't for his approval, the buy would not have gone down."

[The lengthy discussion of Grimball's qualifications to offer expert testimony is omitted] * * *

SUFFICIENCY OF THE EVIDENCE

In considering the sufficiency of the evidence, we begin with some preliminary observations. One is that, in testing sufficiency, "the relevant question is whether, after viewing the evidence in the light most favorable to the prosecution, *any* rational trier of fact could have found the essential elements of the crime beyond a reasonable doubt." *Jackson v. Virginia*, 443 U.S. 307, 319, 99 S.Ct. 2781, 2789, 61 L.Ed.2d 560 (1979) (emphasis in original). * * * *Jackson*'s emphasis on "*any*," while surely not going so far as to excise "rational," must be taken as an admonition to appellate judges not to reverse convictions because they would not have found the elements of the crime to have been proved beyond a reasonable doubt when other rational beings might do so.

The second observation is that since the jury convicted on the conspiracy count alone, the evidence must permit a reasonable juror to be convinced beyond a reasonable doubt not simply that Brown had aided and abetted the drug sale but that he had agreed to do so. On the other hand, the jury's failure to agree on the aiding and abetting charge does not operate against the Government; even an acquittal on that count would not have done so.

A review of the evidence against Brown convinces us that it was sufficient, even without Grimball's characterization of Brown as a steerer, although barely so. Although Brown's mere presence at the scene of the crime and his knowledge that a crime was being committed would not have been sufficient to establish Brown's knowing participation in the conspiracy, the proof went considerably beyond that. Brown was not simply standing around while the exchanges between Officer Grimball and Valentine occurred. He came on the scene shortly after these began and Valentine immediately explained the situation to him. Brown then conferred his seal of approval on Grimball, a most unlikely event unless there was an established relationship between Brown and Valentine. Finally, Brown took upon himself the serious responsibility of telling Valentine to desist from his plan to reduce the risks by not handing the heroin directly to Grimball. A rational mind could take this as bespeaking the existence of an agreement whereby Brown was to have the authority to command, or at least to persuade. Brown's remark, "Just go and get it for him," permits inferences that Brown knew where the heroin was to be gotten, that he knew that Valentine knew this, and that Brown and Valentine had engaged in such a transaction before.

The mere fact that these inferences were not ineluctable does not mean that they were insufficient to convince a reasonable juror beyond a reasonable doubt. * * * When we add to the inferences that can be reasonably drawn from the facts to which Grimball testified the portion of his expert testimony about the use of steerers in street sales of narcotics, which was clearly unobjectionable once Grimball's qualifications were established, we conclude that the Government offered sufficient evidence, apart from Grimball's opinion that Brown was a steerer, for a reasonable juror to be satisfied beyond a reasonable doubt not only that Brown had acted as a steerer but that he had agreed to do so.[10]

Affirmed.

OAKES, CIRCUIT JUDGE (dissenting):

While it is true that this is another $40 narcotics case, it is also a conspiracy case, and by the majority's own admission one resting on "barely" sufficient evidence. But evidence of what? An agreement—a "continuous and conscious union of wills upon a common undertaking," in the words of Note, *Developments in the Law—Criminal Conspiracy,* 72 Harv.L.Rev. 920, 926 (1959)? Not unless an inference that Brown agreed to act as a "steerer" may be drawn from the fact that he said to Valentine (three times) that Grimball "looks okay [all right] to me," as well as "[j]ust go and get it for him." And the only way that inference may be drawn so as to prove guilt beyond a reasonable doubt is, in my view, with assistance from the "expert" testimony of the ubiquitous Officer Grimball. It could not be drawn from Brown's possession, constructive or otherwise, of narcotics or narcotics paraphernalia, his sharing in the proceeds of the street sale, his conversations with others, or even some hearsay evidence as to his "prior arrangements" with Valentine or "an established working relationship between Brown and Valentine," which are inferences that the majority, Majority Opinion at note 10, believes may reasonably be drawn and which it draws so as to distinguish *United States v. Tyler,* 758 F.2d 66 (2d Cir.1985). There is not a shred of evidence of Brown's "stake in the outcome," *United States v. Falcone,* 109 F.2d 579, 580 (2d Cir.), *aff'd,* 311 U.S. 205, 61 S.Ct. 204, 85 L.Ed. 128 (1940); indeed, Brown was apprehended after leaving the area of the crime with only thirty-one of his own dollars in his

---

10. We do not read *United States v. Tyler,* 758 F.2d 66 (2 Cir.1985), as being to the contrary. The court read the evidence as showing "no more than that Tyler helped a willing buyer find a willing seller." *Id.* at 70. Since there was no basis for inferring a prior contact between Tyler, the introducer, and Bennett, the seller, Tyler could properly be convicted only as an aider or abettor, not as a conspirator. Here a jury could reasonably infer prior arrangements or an established working relationship between Brown and Valentine. * * * Brown's conversation with Valentine in the presence of Grimball establishes that he knew precisely what the transaction was. Finally, the facts in *United States v. Cepeda,* 768 F.2d 1515 (2 Cir.1985) (Oakes, J.), relied upon by the dissent, are not analogous to the situation here. In *Cepeda,* there was no evidence that there had been a sale, or that anyone other than the defendant was involved in the transaction. Thus, two elements of the charged conspiracy were called into question—the agreement with other persons and the intent to distribute. Here, there is no question that a sale occurred, and it is clear that Brown and at least one other person, Valentine, participated in the transaction. Thus, the only further inference required for a conviction—that Brown's participation was pursuant to an agreement with Valentine, with someone else, or with both—is much stronger. * * *.

pocket, and no drugs or other contraband. He did not even stay around for another Valentine sale, though the majority infers, speculatively, that Brown and Valentine had engaged in "such a transaction before."

When * * * numerous other inferences could be drawn from the few words of conversation in which Brown is said to have engaged, I cannot believe that there is proof of *conspiracy,* or Brown's membership in it, beyond a reasonable doubt, within the meaning of *Jackson v. Virginia,* 443 U.S. 307, 99 S.Ct. 2781, 61 L.Ed.2d 560 (1979), unless one gives the Court's emphasis on the word "any"—"*any* rational trier of fact," *id.* at 319, 99 S.Ct. at 2789—such weight that the word "rational" receives little or no significance at all. Until now, as we said in *United States v. Cepeda,* 768 F.2d 1515 (2d Cir.1985), "the court has insisted on proof, whether or not by circumstantial evidence, * * * of a specific agreement to deal."

This case may be unique. It, like *Cepeda,* supports Justice Jackson's reference to the history of the law of conspiracy as exemplifying, in Cardozo's phrase, the " 'tendency of a principle to expand itself to the limits of its logic.' " *Krulewitch v. United States,* 336 U.S. 440, 445, 69 S.Ct. 716, 719, 93 L.Ed. 790 (1949) (Jackson, J., concurring) (footnote omitted). But it also illustrates Cardozo's phrase at work in two other respects—the use of "expert" testimony to prove guilt and the proposition that inconsistent verdicts on different counts are immaterial. Both are carried here to their logical extremes. And the convergence of these three threads in the case of the street sale to Officer Grimball seems to me, again to borrow a phrase from Justice Jackson's *Krulewitch* concurrence, to "constitute[ ] a serious threat to fairness in our administration of justice." *Id.* at 446, 69 S.Ct. at 720. If today we uphold a conspiracy to sell narcotics on the street, on this kind and amount of evidence, what conspiracies might we approve tomorrow? The majority opinion will come back to haunt us, I fear.

*   *   *

As for the rule that "[e]ach count in an indictment is regarded as if it was a separate indictment," *Dunn v. United States,* 284 U.S. 390, 393, 52 S.Ct. 189, 190, 76 L.Ed. 356 (1932) (citations omitted), so that acquittal on a substantive count is not fatal to a conviction for conspiracy, the verdicts in this case carry the rule to the ultimate extreme. Here the only overt act attributed in the indictment to Brown was the same conversation with Valentine that grounded the substantive charge of aiding and abetting, a charge on which Brown was acquitted. The case appears to me to be the very kind of compromise verdict foreseen by Judge Learned Hand in *Steckler v. United States,* 7 F.2d 59, 60 (2d Cir.1925), and by Justice Holmes in *Dunn,* 284 U.S. at 394, 52 S.Ct. at 191. It may be that, in a given case, *see, e.g., Tyler,* 758 F.2d at 71–72, evidence may support a conviction on an aiding and abetting count without supporting a conviction on a conspiracy count. But it is hard to see how, in the case of a completed sale, there can be a conviction of conspiracy but not of aiding and abetting, especially when there is no evidence of a "stake in the outcome."

Although, according to the majority, the admission of "expert" testimony is "rather offensive," the evidence was "sufficient * * * although barely so," and the verdict is both inconsistent and very probably a compromise, the court permits this conspiracy conviction to stand. I fear that it thereby promotes the crime of conspiracy—"that darling of the modern prosecutor's nursery," *Harrison v. United States,* 7 F.2d 259, 263 (2d Cir.1925) (L. Hand, J.)—to a role beyond that contemplated even by Sgt. Hawkins of *Pleas of the Crown* fame. *See* Note, *Developments in the Law—Criminal Conspiracy, supra,* at 923 & n. 14; P. Winfield, *The Chief Sources of English Legal History* 325–26 (1925). Precisely because this is another $40 narcotics case, I would draw the line. This case effectively permits prosecution of everyone connected with a street sale of narcotics to be prosecuted on two counts—a conspiracy as well as a substantive charge. And evidence showing no more than that a defendant was probably aware that a narcotics deal was about to occur will support a conspiracy conviction, our previous cases to the contrary notwithstanding.

Accordingly, I dissent.

Notes and Questions

1. Is the dissent in *Brown* unhappy because reasonable jurors could not have found beyond a reasonable doubt that the defendant had agreed, i.e. conspired, to distribute heroin? Would he have dissented if the activities of Valentine had not culminated in the transfer of the heroin so that there could not be a conviction for distribution or attempted distribution? In the absence of the achievement of, or attempt at, the object offense a conspiracy charge may be the only way in which the police can intervene and the defendant sanctioned. On the other hand, in the absence of the object offense it will often be more difficult to be certain of the intent to join the conspiracy. In United States v. Alvarez, 610 F.2d 1250 (5th Cir. 1980), the defendant was convicted of conspiring to import marijuana. He had driven two conspirators to an airport where they discussed with an undercover DEA agent the arrival of a planeload of marijuana from Columbia. Defendant acquiesced by an affirmative headshake in his identification as someone who would aid in unloading the plane. The plane never arrived and defendant never did anything. Although acknowledging that if the defendant had aided in the unloading it would clearly have constituted aiding and abetting the court reversed the conviction. It wrote:

> To justify a conviction for conspiracy, there must be evidence that Alvarez agreed to join in the unlawful plan. The evidence presented to the jury in this case permits the conclusion only by a long chain of compounded inferences: that Alvarez knew illegal activity was afoot; that Alvarez intended to unload illegal cargo upon the plane's return; that Alvarez, therefore, knew of an agreement between others to import the illegal cargo; and that, consequently, Alvarez must have joined that illegal agreement. There is direct proof only of Alvarez's

intentions. That he knew the activity was criminal is a reasonable inference. The other two conclusions are logical non-sequiturs.

610 F.2d at 1257.

2. Note 1, supra, suggests that the achievement of the object of the alleged conspiracy may make it easier to find the requisite agreement. But if the substantive crime has been committed, is not the justification for a conspiracy count sharply reduced? Should defendants such as Brown and Valentine, who complete a conspiracy, be subject to conviction for both the conspiracy and the completed crime? Should they be subject to consecutive penalties for both offenses? The effect of a rule permitting dual conviction and penalties is, of course, that crimes committed by collective action are punishable by a significantly higher penalty than those committed individually. Is this defensible on policy grounds? In Callanan v. United States, 364 U.S. 587, 81 S.Ct. 321, 5 L.Ed.2d 312 (1961), the Supreme Court rejected an argument that Congress had intended that a defendant who committed conspiracy to obstruct commerce by extorting money and the substantive crime of obstructing commerce by extorting money should be punishable for only one of those offenses created by the Hobbs Anti-Racketeering Act. Explaining the apparent legislative reasoning, the Court stated:

> [C]ollective criminal agreement—partnership in crime—presents a greater potential threat to the public than individual delicts. Concerted action both increases the likelihood that the criminal object will be successfully attained and decreases the probability that the individuals involved will depart from their paths of criminality. Group association for criminal purposes often, if not normally, makes possible the attainment of ends more complex than those which one criminal could accomplish. Nor is the danger of a conspiratorial group limited to the particular end towards which it has embarked. Combination in crime makes more likely the commission of crimes unrelated to the original purpose for which the group was formed. In sum, the danger which a conspiracy generates is not confined to the substantive offense which is the immediate aim of the enterprise.

364 U.S. at 593–94, 81 S.Ct. at 325, 5 L.Ed.2d at 317. Is the Court (or Congress) correct? If so, does this justify a rule that permits conviction for both conspiracy and the completed crime in all cases? The Model Penal Code embraces the "minority" view that conviction for both an offense and conspiracy to commit only that offense should not be permitted. See Model Penal Code § 1.07(1)(b) (Official Draft 1985).

3. Conspiracy doctrine permits the state to intervene long before the defendants have taken any action which brings them close to the achievement of their criminal purpose. It permits this intervention on the basis of conduct, other than the agreement, which may be extremely equivocal as an expression of criminal purpose. Therefore, it is clear that the establishment of an agreement is essential to the rationale for conspiracy prosecutions. The existence of the agreement presumably allays any concerns we might have about possible misidentification of the accused. It has been asserted that:

> * * * The act of agreeing with another to commit a crime
> * * * is concrete and unambiguous; it does not present the infinite

degrees and variations possible in the general category of attempts. The danger that truly equivocal behavior may be misinterpreted as preparation to commit a crime is minimized; purpose must be relatively firm before the commitment involved in agreement is assumed.

Wechsler, Jones & Korn, The Treatment of Inchoate Crimes in the Model Penal Code of The American Law Institute: Attempt, Solicitation, and Conspiracy, 61 Colum.L.Rev. 957, 958 (1961). How consistent is this position with that of the Arkansas Supreme Court:

> Appellant seems to take the position that there must be direct evidence of a conspiracy, common design or purpose, and of the intent of the conspirators or joint actors to engage therein. In this he is mistaken. We have long recognized * * * that it is not necessary that an unlawful combination, conspiracy or concert of action to commit an unlawful act be shown by direct evidence, and that it may be proved by circumstances. * * * It may be inferred, even though no actual meeting among the parties is proved, if it be shown that two or more persons pursued by their acts the same unlawful object, each doing a part, so that their acts, though apparently independent, were in fact connected.

Griffin v. State, 248 Ark. 1223, 1225, 455 S.W.2d 882, 884 (1970).

Would this formulation be acceptable unless the criminal object has been achieved as in United States v. Brown, supra? Should the presence of a substantive offense permit a more relaxed view of what will satisfy the agreement requirement?

Given the obvious difficulties of proving an agreement for criminal purposes isn't it necessary that the state be permitted considerable leeway in how it may establish this element? This view has clearly been expressed in Interstate Circuit v. United States, 306 U.S. 208, 59 S.Ct. 467, 83 L.Ed. 610 (1939). There, defendant motion picture distributors and exhibitors were charged with conspiring, in violation of the Sherman Antitrust Act, to restrain trade by restricting the minimum prices that could be charged by exhibitors. The appellants argued, inter alia, that the finding of conspiracy was not supported by the evidence because all that had been shown was separate agreements between each of the exhibitor defendants and each of the distributor defendants, not acting in concert with any other distributors, to impose restrictions necessary to the protection of their mutual interests in copyright rewards. Mr. Justice Stone, writing for the Court responded:

> As is usual in cases of alleged unlawful agreements to restrain commerce, the Government is without the aid of direct testimony that the distributors entered into any agreement with each other to impose the restrictions upon subsequent-run exhibitors. In order to establish agreement it is compelled to rely on inferences drawn from the course of conduct of the alleged conspirators.

> The trial court drew the inference of agreement from the nature of the proposals made on behalf of Interstate and Consolidated; from the manner in which they were made; from the substantial unanimity of action taken upon them by the distributors; and from the fact that

appellants did not call as witnesses any of the superior officials who negotiated the contracts with Interstate or any official who, in the normal course of business, would have had knowledge of the existence or non-existence of such an agreement among the distributors. * * * We think this inference of the trial court was rightly drawn from the evidence. * * * [F]rom the beginning each of the distributors knew that the proposals were under consideration by the others. Each was aware that all were in active competition and that without substantially unanimous action with respect to the restrictions for any given territory there was risk of a substantial loss of the business and good will of the subsequent-run and independent exhibitors, but that with it there was the prospect of increased profits. There was, therefore, strong motive for concerted action, full advantage of which was taken by Interstate and Consolidated in presenting their demands to all in a single document.

There was risk, too, that without agreement diversity of action would follow. * * * It taxes credulity to believe that the several distributors would, in the circumstances, have accepted and put into operation with substantial unanimity such far-reaching changes in their business methods without some understanding that all were to join, and we reject as beyond the range of probability that it was the result of mere chance.

* * *

While the District Court's finding of an agreement of the distributors among themselves is supported by the evidence, we think that in the circumstances of this case such agreement for the imposition of the restrictions upon subsequent-run exhibitors was not a prerequisite to an unlawful conspiracy. It was enough that, knowing that concerted action was contemplated and invited, the distributors gave their adherence to the scheme and participated in it. Each distributor was advised that the others were asked to participate; each knew that cooperation was essential to successful operation of the plan. They knew that the plan, if carried out, would result in a restraint of commerce, which, we will presently point out, was unreasonable within the meaning of the Sherman Act, and knowing it, all participated in the plan. The evidence is persuasive that each distributor early became aware that the others had joined. With that knowledge they renewed the arrangement and carried it into effect for the two successive years.

It is elementary that an unlawful conspiracy may be and often is formed without simultaneous action or agreement on the part of the conspirators. Acceptance by competitors, without previous agreement, of an invitation to participate in a plan, the necessary consequence of which, if carried out, is restraint of interstate commerce, is sufficient to establish an unlawful conspiracy under the Sherman Act.

306 U.S. at 221–27, 59 S.Ct. at 472–74, 83 L.Ed. at 617–20. Is there any reason why these principles should not be equally applicable to conspiracies to commit traditional crimes?

4. As the material in subsection A.3. of this chapter, supra, indicates, "legal" but not "factual" impossibility may be a defense to a charge of attempt. It seems clear that factual impossibility is unlikely to be accepted as a defense to conspiracy. United States v. Brantley, 777 F.2d 159, 164 (4th Cir.1985) (defendant, a South Carolina sheriff, could be convicted of conspiracy to commit extortion in violation of Hobbs Act even though the bribe he accepted to permit the operation of a high stakes gambling club for nonresidents came from an undercover FBI agent and there was never any chance that interstate commerce might thereby be affected). There is some authority that legal or inherent impossibility precludes conviction for conspiracy. Ventimiglia v. United States, 242 F.2d 620 (4th Cir.1957). But most courts hold that impossibility—whether legal or factual as those terms are used in attempt law discussions—has no effect on guilt of conspiracy. E.g., United States v. Rosner, 485 F.2d 1213, 1228–29 (2d Cir. 1973), cert. denied, 417 U.S. 950, 94 S.Ct. 3080, 41 L.Ed.2d 672 (1974); State v. Palumbo, 137 N.J.Super. 13, 347 A.2d 535 (1975). In State v. Moretti, 52 N.J. 182, 244 A.2d 499 (1968), cert. denied, 393 U.S. 952, 89 S.Ct. 376, 21 L.Ed.2d 363 (1968), the court offered the following explanation for the different treatment accorded impossibility in attempt and conspiracy:

> [A] conspiracy charge focuses primarily on the *intent* of the defendants, while in an attempt case the primary inquiry centers on the defendants' *conduct* tending towards the commission of the substantive crime. The crime of conspiracy is complete once the conspirators, having formed the intent to commit a crime, take any step in preparation; mere preparation, however, is an inadequate basis for an attempt conviction regardless of the intent. Thus, the impossibility that the defendants' conduct will result in the consummation of the contemplated crime is not as pertinent in a conspiracy case as it might be in an attempt prosecution.

52 N.J. at 186–188, 244 A.2d at 502.

English law, interestingly, runs counter to the general American approach. In Director of Public Prosecutions v. Nock, [1978] 2 All E.R. 654, the House of Lords considered an appeal from a conviction for conspiracy to produce cocaine. The facts established that the defendants had agreed to extract cocaine from a substance, lignocaine hydrochloride, which they mistakenly believed could be made to yield cocaine. Characterizing the agreement as limited to "a specific course of conduct which could not result in the commission of the * * * offense," the Lords applied attempt impossibility doctrine and reversed the conviction. The only difference the Lords would find between attempt and conspiracy was that conspiracy permitted earlier intervention into a course of conduct leading towards an offense:

> But [this] distinction has no relevance in determining whether the impossibility of committing the substance offense should be a defense. Indeed * * *, logic and justice would seem to require that the question as to the effect of the impossibility * * * be answered in the same way, whether the crime charged be conspiracy or attempt.

[1978] All E.R. at 661.

5. Should withdrawal be a defense to a charge of conspiring to commit a crime? If so, what should be required for an effective withdrawal? Traditionally, withdrawal has not been a defense. The following quote from United States v. Read, 658 F.2d 1225, 1232–33 (7th Cir.1981), provides a good explanation of the traditional view:

> Withdrawal marks a conspirator's disavowal or abandonment of the conspiratorial agreement. Hyde v. United States, 225 U.S. 347, 369, 32 S.Ct. 793, 803, 56 L.Ed. 1114 (1912). By definition, after a defendant withdraws, he is no longer a member of the conspiracy and the later acts of the conspirators do not bind him. The defendant is still liable, however, for his previous agreement and for the previous acts of his co-conspirators in pursuit of the conspiracy. Withdrawal is not, therefore, a complete defense to the crime of conspiracy. Withdrawal becomes a complete defense only when coupled with the defense of the statute of limitations. A defendant's withdrawal from the conspiracy starts the running of the statute of limitations as to him. If the indictment is filed more than five years after a defendant withdraws, the statute of limitations bars prosecution for his actual participation in the conspiracy. He cannot be held liable for acts or declarations committed in the five years preceding the indictment by other conspirators because his withdrawal ended his membership in the conspiracy. It is thus only the interaction of the two defenses of withdrawal and the statute of limitations which shields the defendant from liability.

If, however, a jurisdiction requires an overt act by one of the conspirators before the crime of conspiracy is complete, a withdrawal by one of the actors before the commission of the overt act would seem to preclude liability. See Developments in the Law—Criminal Conspiracy, 72 Harv.L. Rev. 922, 957 (1959).

As to what is required for an effective withdrawal, it has been said that the defendant:

> must abandon the illegal enterprise in a manner reasonably calculated to reach coconspirators. Mere cessation of participation in the conspiracy is not enough. However, a defendant need not take action to stop, obstruct or interfere with the conspiracy in order to withdraw from it.

United States v. Lowell, 649 F.2d 950, 957 (3d Cir.1981).

Contrast the positions of *Read* and *Lowell* with that expressed in Section 5.03(6) of the Model Penal Code (reprinted at page 644, infra) and Texas Penal Code § 15.04, both of which provide for a defense of renunciation. The latter provides:

> It is an affirmative defense to prosecution [for criminal conspiracy] that under circumstances manifesting a voluntary and complete renunciation of his criminal objective the actor * * * withdrew from the conspiracy before commission of the object offense and took further affirmative action that prevented the commission of the object offense.

Note that Texas makes this an affirmative defense, i.e., the defendant bears the burden of persuasion by a preponderance of the evidence. In contrast, the court in *Read* held that inasmuch as withdrawal negates an essential element of the crime—membership—to place any burden on the defendant other than that of going forward with evidence of withdrawal would violate due process per In re Winship and Mullaney v. Wilbur (see the discussion of these cases in Section I.F., supra). 658 F.2d at 1232–36. Another point of difference lies in the apparent requirement of the statute that the defendant have prevented the commission of the object crime. Suppose a conspirator withdraws and, for reasons unrelated to his withdrawal or subsequent activity, the other members of the group fail to commit the object crime? Is the withdrawal effective? Are these different requirements explicable by the great difference in the limited effect of withdrawal under the *Lowell/Read* view and the total defense afforded by Tex.Pen. Code § 15.04.

Another effect of withdrawal is that declarations of one conspirator made during and in furtherance of the conspiracy but after a conspirator's withdrawal cannot be offered against him under a well-established exception to the hearsay rule. United States v. Mardian, 546 F.2d 973, 978 n. 5 (D.C.Cir.1976). Perhaps most significantly, an effective withdrawal prevents a conspirator from being held liable for substantive crimes committed by other members of the scheme. This is discussed in Section XI.B., infra.

(2) Number of Agreements

Complex multiparty situations giving rise to conspiracy charges may require careful analysis to determine whether they present a single, large conspiracy or rather a number of smaller, perhaps overlapping, conspiracies. This may be important for a number of reasons. If the evidence shows a different number or pattern of agreements than was alleged in the charging instrument, there may be a fatal variance between the instrument and the prosecution's proof at trial; the defendants may consequently be entitled to acquittal. It may be important to determine whether a defendant was a member of the same conspiracy as another person to resolve such matters as the admissibility against the defendant of declarations by the other person, the defendant's liability for crimes committed by the other person (see Section XI.B., infra), whether the other person's recent overt acts will prevent the defendant from successfully claiming that the period of limitations has run concerning the conspiracy of which he is a member, or—if the jurisdiction requires proof of an overt act—whether the other person's action constitutes the requisite overt act that completes the conspiracy of which the defendant is a member. If the facts present several overlapping conspiracies, one or more persons may be members of more than one and thus subject to several charges of conspiracy rather than only one.

Disputes over the number of conspiracies shown by the evidence at trial are among the most commonly raised points on appeal. The normal pattern in practice is, as illustrated by the principal case, that the prosecution alleges a single conspiracy and the defendants claim that, if anything, more than one has been established. Presumably the prosecution favors a single conspiracy because it binds more defendants together in a way which will make the acts and words of each more readily admissible against all others. In those relatively rare instances in which the prosecution alleges multiple conspiracies—perhaps in an effort to obtain multiple sentences—the defendants may claim that there was only one.

Whether the indictment alleges one or more conspiracies, the ultimate resolution turns, in theory, on the nature of the required agreement. Each individual defendant must be shown to have agreed to participate in the concerted effort to achieve the specified object offenses. Of course, as has been discussed by the material in the preceding section, an express agreement is not required. It can be, and normally is, inferred from the nature of the criminal enterprise. Where the prosecution shows that the defendant joined an illicit scheme of obvious complexity it will readily be inferred that he must have realized that others, their identities albeit unknown to him, must be participating. His participation in only one aspect of a complex criminal operation will not mean that the activities of the unknown others in other aspects in furtherance of the overall scheme constitute a separate conspiracy. Blumenthal v. United States, 332 U.S. 539, 556–57, 68 S.Ct. 248, 256, 92 L.Ed. 154 (1947). The resolution of these issues is peculiarly a function of the facts of the individual cases. Further explication of this area can be found in the Model Penal Code Comment to § 5.03(1), which is reprinted at pages 606–10, infra.

UNITED STATES v. JACKSON

United States Court of Appeals, Eighth Circuit, 1982.
696 F.2d 578.

HEANEY, CIRCUIT JUDGE:

[During 1977–78 in Kansas City, Missouri, the defendants allegedly operated an arson for profit ring. Four dwellings—identified by the street where located, Agnes, 51st, Troost, and Indiana—were burned due to arson. Five persons were indicted and charged with conspiracy to commit mail fraud. The claim was that the defendants had conspired with Morgan, an unindicted confederate, to burn the premises in order to defraud insurers. Some of the defendants were also indicted for substantive mail fraud] * * *

All five defendants were jointly tried, despite repeated severance motions by each defendant. The government's chief witness at trial was Charles Morgan, the self-proclaimed "torch" for the four fires. Morgan testified that in August, 1977, Scroggins entered into a contract with him to burn the residence on Agnes Street that Scroggins was renting from Edmunds. Morgan claimed that Edmunds played no part in his scheme. Morgan further testified that Edmunds introduced him to appellant Jackson, and that one or two months after the introduction, Morgan and Jackson agreed that Morgan would torch the 51st Street property. Three weeks after the 51st Street fire, Morgan and Jackson negotiated a "package deal" for the destruction of four more properties: the Troost apartments, the Indiana house and two houses that were never burned. Morgan testified that Dancy [the owner of 51st St. premises] was the "money man" behind Jackson in the arson dealings and directly implicated Edmunds in at least the Troost fire dealings. Morgan stated that he did not know JoAnn Murray, and that he dealt only with Jackson in regard to the burning of the Indiana house owned by Murray.

At the conclusion of its evidence, the government dismissed its charges against Murray. The jury found Scroggins guilty of conspiracy, the only count on which he was charged. The jury convicted Jackson of conspiracy, and on three of the four mail fraud counts relating to the 51st Street fire * * *. [The other dispositions are omitted.]

The most troublesome issue in this appeal is raised by both Scroggins and Jackson. They contend that the government failed as a matter of law to prove the existence of the single conspiracy alleged in the indictment, and that the proof at most showed that two separate conspiracies were in operation: one involving the Agnes fire, and another aimed at executing the Indiana, Troost and 51st Street fires. Scroggins and Jackson argue that this variance between the government's pleading and its proof prejudiced their right to a fair trial. * * * We agree that the government failed to prove the single conspiracy alleged and find that Scroggins and Jackson's conspiracy convictions must be reversed. We conclude, however, that Jackson's convictions on the three substantive mail fraud counts were unaffected by this error.

To resolve the question of whether the government's proof showed that a single conspiracy existed involving at least Scroggins and Jackson, we must determine "whether there was 'one overall agreement' to perform various functions to achieve the objectives of the conspiracy." *United States v. Zemek,* 634 F.2d 1159, 1167 (9th Cir.1980), *cert. denied,* 452 U.S. 905, 101 S.Ct. 3031, 69 L.Ed.2d 406 (1981). The agreement need not be express or formal, and its existence may be inferred from the actions of the parties.

Viewing the evidence in the light most favorable to the verdict, we find that no jury could reasonably conclude that Scroggins and Jackson were parties to a single overall agreement to commit acts of arson and mail fraud. The existence of a single agreement could have been inferred if the evidence had revealed that the alleged participants shared "a common aim or purpose." *United States v. Bertolotti,* 529 F.2d 149, 154 (2d Cir.1975). No such evidence was offered, however. There was testimony from which the jury could conclude that Scroggins had agreed with Morgan that the latter would burn Scroggins' rented dwelling and be compensated with a portion of the fraudulently obtained insurance proceeds. There is no evidence, however, from which the jury could infer that Scroggins had any intention of fostering illegal activity beyond the burning of his own dwelling. Similarly, the jury could have found that Jackson joined forces with Morgan, Dancy and others to execute a number of fires—but the Agnes fire was not one of them. The absence of a common aim or purpose is further revealed by the fact that, as the government admits, Scroggins in no way profited from the later fires and Jackson received no proceeds from the Agnes fire. In sum, the evidence did not reveal "the common purpose of a single enterprise;" at most, it showed "similar purposes of * * * separate adventures of like character." *Kotteakos v. United States*, 328 U.S. 750, 769, 66 S.Ct. 1239, 1250, 90 L.Ed. 1557 (1946).

Further, there is no evidence of "mutual dependence and assistance" among Scroggins and the other prosecuted coconspirators. See *United States v. Bertolotti, supra*, 529 F.2d at 154. Scroggins did not help plan or execute the 51st Street, Troost or Indiana fires; in fact, there is no evidence that he even knew about their occurrence. The government concedes that neither Jackson nor Dancy had anything to do with the Agnes fire, and points to no evidence that they were aware of it.

Relatedly, we cannot infer "from the nature and scope of the operation, that each actor was aware of his part in a larger organization where others performed similar roles equally important to the success of the venture." *United States v. Bertolotti, supra*, 529 F.2d at 154. Scroggins did not, as the government contends, "establish a structure that became a continuing focal point of crime." Scroggins' alleged scheme was a simple one, involving only two actors. The success or failure of the venture depended solely on Morgan's incendiary finesse and on Scroggins' ability to convince the insurance company that his claim was legitimate. Although the later alleged fraudulent scheme was a more elaborate one that involved multiple fires, it is clear from the record that Jackson and Dancy knew the precise scope of their "operation" and that its scope did not encompass Scroggins or any other unidentified minions.

The government concedes, as it must, that the fact that Scroggins, Jackson and Dancy retained the same "torch"—Morgan—does not alone make them confederates. *See Kotteakos v. United States, supra*, 328 U.S. at 755, 66 S.Ct. at 1243. It argues instead that the activities of Samuel Edmunds provide a sufficient nexus between Scroggins' fraud and the multiple-fire scheme of Jackson and Dancy to show the existence of a "single overall agreement."

The government primarily relies on evidence that sometime in the summer of 1977, Edmunds introduced Morgan to Jackson. The government argues that Edmunds thereby opened up the Scroggins' "conspiracy" to include the activities of Jackson and Dancy occurring thereafter. The fallaciousness of this argument is readily apparent. Morgan testified that the purpose of the introduction was to induce Jackson, acting on behalf of his nonprofit organization, to serve as a tax-exempt conduit for a "donation" of property that Edmunds wished to make to Morgan. Morgan's uncontradicted testimony was that this introduction was unrelated to the arson activities of Scroggins, or of Jackson and Dancy, and that his negotiations with Jackson regarding the 51st Street fire occurred a month or two later. There is no evidence that Scroggins even knew about the Morgan-Jackson introduction, much less that he fostered it or benefited in some way from their subsequent relationship.

The government also relies on two conversations that Morgan had with Edmunds shortly before the Agnes fire. One week before the fire, Morgan, who had known Edmunds for some time, asked Edmunds whether he had insurance on the Agnes house. Morgan told Edmunds that he had been hired by Scroggins to burn the dwelling. According to Morgan's uncontradicted testimony, Edmunds replied that "he wanted nothing to do with it," but that his interest was insured. Three days before the burning, Morgan asked Edmunds to lend him a ladder so that he could work around the Agnes dwelling and get the neighbors used to seeing him there; Edmunds apparently lent him the ladder.

Neither of these conversations raise an inference that a single conspiracy was operating in this case. As to the fact that Edmunds was informed of the intended fraud, it is sufficient to note that "[k]nowledge of the existence or acquiescence in a conspiracy does not serve to render one a part of the conspiracy. There must exist some element of affirmative cooperation or at least an agreement to cooperate." *United States v. Williams,* 604 F.2d 1102, 1118 (8th Cir.1979) (quoting *United States v. Collins,* 552 F.2d 243, 245 (8th Cir.), *cert. denied,* 434 U.S. 870, 98 S.Ct. 214, 54 L.Ed.2d 149 (1977)). Edmunds' alleged loan to Morgan of the ladder might be considered a sufficient "element of affirmative cooperation" to render him part of a conspiracy, but the jury's acquittal of Edmunds leaves that factor a very slender reed for the government to hang on. More importantly, both these conversations at most could give rise to an inference that Edmunds was somehow involved with Scroggins' and Morgan's dealings regarding the Agnes fire. That evidence does not provide what is notably lacking here: proof of some interaction among the participants toward a common goal from which we can infer that a *single* overall agreement unified the parties.

Where, as here, a single conspiracy is alleged in the indictment but the proof at trial tended to show that multiple conspiracies were in existence, the error of variance has occurred. An accused's rights may be affected in such cases by the introduction of "substantial evidence of crimes unrelated to the defendant." *United States v. Read,* 658 F.2d 1225, 1230 (7th Cir.1981).

When the proof at trial reveals the existence of more than one conspiracy, "the adequacy of the trial judge's instructions are of critical importance in evaluating the likelihood [that] confusion or prejudice" resulted from transference of guilt from one conspiracy to another. *United States v. Johnson,* 515 F.2d 730, 735 (7th Cir.1975). In *Kotteakos,* the trial court's jury charge was substantially the same as the one given in the present case: the jury was instructed that in order to convict a defendant, he had to be a member of the single conspiracy charged in the indictment and not some other separate conspiracy. The Supreme Court stated that an unfortunate effect of charging the jury that a single conspiracy must be found is that it "prevent[s] the court from giving a precautionary instruction such as would be appropriate, *perhaps required*, in cases where related but separate conspiracies are tried together * * *, namely, that the jury should take care to consider the evidence relating to each conspiracy separately from that relating to each other conspiracy charged." *Kotteakos v. United States, supra,* 328 U.S. at 769–770, 66 S.Ct. at 1250 (emphasis added). The Supreme Court added that the trial court "was careful to caution the jury to consider each defendant's case separately, in determining his participation in 'the scheme' charged. But this obviously does not, and could not, go to keeping distinct conspiracies distinct[.]" *Id.,* at 770, 66 S.Ct. at 1250.

The Seventh Circuit has adopted the rule suggested by the Supreme Court, holding that

> where, at the close of testimony, it is clear * * * that a jury could not find a single overall conspiracy as a matter of law, the defendant is not only entitled to a multiple conspiracies instruction but also to an instruction that evidence relating to the other conspiracy or conspiracies disclosed may not be used against him under any circumstances.

United States v. Lindsey, 602 F.2d 785, 787 (7th Cir.1979).

* * *

The requirement that juries be specifically instructed, where appropriate, to carefully compartmentalize evidence of separate conspiracies is of particular importance because in most cases where single conspiracies are alleged and multiple conspiracies proven, the conspiracy count provided the only justification for the joinder of multiple defendants in the single trial. Although the courts have ruled that the absence of such a unifying count in the indictment necessitates severance of the misjoined defendants, they have not similarly ruled that when proof of the single conspiracy count fails as a matter of law, the defendants are entitled to severance. Thus, members of separate conspiracies jointly tried must rely on the trial court's exercise of its discretion under Rule 14 to grant a severance when prejudice from the joint trial has been shown. The courts' refusal to recognize "retroactive misjoinder" has occurred despite acknowledgement that "misjoinder of defendants is inherently prejudicial." *United States v. Bledsoe,* 674 F.2d 647, 654 (8th Cir.1982). Accordingly, the participants in separate, but jointly tried conspiracies should at least be afforded the protection of explicit limiting instructions. And, when such instructions have not been given, this Court on appeal should give heightened scrutiny to the defendants' claim that the jury erroneously "transfer[red] guilt from one to another and [found] defendants guilty of an overall conspiracy." *United States v. Varelli,* [407 F.2d 735, 747 (7th Cir.1969), *cert. denied,* 405 U.S. 1040, 92 S.Ct. 1311, 31 L.Ed.2d 581 (1972).]

At the conclusion of the government's evidence in this case, the court specifically found that for purposes of the admissibility of evidence, one conspiracy existed and all the defendants were members of that conspiracy. Consistent with its conclusion that one conspiracy existed, the court instructed the jurors at the conclusion of the evidence that they were to determine whether a single conspiracy was shown and which defendants were members of that conspiracy. The court did admonish the jury that "proof of several separate conspiracies is not proof of the single, overall conspiracy charged in the indictment," and that each defendant's participation in a single conspiracy must be separately determined. In light of the fact, however, that as a matter of law a single overall conspiracy could not be found on this record, the defendants were entitled to an instruction to that effect. And, if the evidence of the defendants' alleged involvement in separate conspiracies was to be given to that jury at all, the jury should have been explicitly admonished that evidence of Scroggins' wrongdoing was not to be considered when determining the guilt of Jackson and Dancy and, similarly, that Scroggins' guilt was not to be determined with regard to any evidence of Jackson's and Dancy's activities. In the absence of such instructions, on this record, we "cannot say, with fair assurance, after pondering all that happened without stripping the erroneous action from the whole, that the judgment was not substantially swayed by the error" of variance committed in this case. *Kotteakos v. United States, supra*, 328 U.S. at 765, 66 S.Ct. at 1248. Accordingly, the conspiracy convictions of Scroggins and Jackson are reversed. They, of course, may be tried again on the conspiracy charges if the government decides to pursue that course of action.

* * *

MODEL PENAL CODE, COMMENT TO
§ 5.03(1), 119–24 *
(Tent. Draft No. 10, 1960).

The Draft relies upon the combined operation of Subsections (1), (2) and (3) to delineate the identity and scope of a conspiracy. All three provisions focus upon the culpability of the individual actor. Subsections (1) and (2) limit the scope of his conspiracy (a) in terms of its criminal objects, to those crimes which he had the purpose of promoting or facilitating and (b) in terms of parties, to those with whom he agreed, except where the same crime that he conspired to commit is, to his knowledge, also the object of a conspiracy between one of his coconspirators and another person or persons. Subsection (3) provides that his conspiracy is a single one despite a multiplicity of criminal objectives so long as such crimes are the object of the same agreement or continuous conspiratorial relationship.

2. *Party and Object Dimensions.* The operation of these provisions may be illustrated by considering some of the typical cases of complex criminal networks that have caused difficulty in the courts. The relationships in these networks are sometimes analogized to a wheel (or circle) and a chain. In the former, communication and cooperation exist primarily between a central figure (the "hub") and each individual member (the "spokes"), and not between the spokes themselves. In the chain relationship, there is successive communication and cooperation between A and B, B and C, C and D, and so on, frequently with regard to the distribution from manufacturer to ultimate consumer of such contraband commodities as narcotics, illicit whiskey or counterfeit money.

United States v. Bruno [98] involved both types of relationships. In that case, 88 defendants were indicted for a conspiracy to import, sell and possess narcotics. The proof showed a vast operation extending over a long period of time, which included smugglers who brought narcotics into New York City, middlemen who paid the smugglers and distributed to retailers, and two groups of retailers selling to addicts— one in New York and the other in Texas and Louisiana. There was no evidence of cooperation or communication between the smugglers and either group of retailers or between the two widely separated groups of retailers. The relationship between the smugglers, the middlemen and each group of retailers consequently was a typical chain, with communication as well as narcotics passing from smuggler to middleman to retailer. The two groups of retailers, on the other hand, may be considered separate spokes of a wheel whose hub was the middlemen, since they communicated and cooperated only with the middlemen and not with each other.

The appellants argued that the evidence may have established several separate conspiracies but not the single one alleged. The court held that the jury could have found a single large conspiracy "whose object was to smuggle narcotics into the Port of New York and distribute them to addicts both in [New York] and in Texas and Louisiana." This required, the court reasoned, the cooperation of all the various groups—smugglers, middlemen and the two groups of retailers.

> "[T]he smugglers knew that the middlemen must sell to retailers, and the retailers knew that the middlemen must buy of importers of one sort or another. Thus the conspirators at one end of the chain knew that the unlawful business would not, and could not, stop with their buyers; and those at the other end knew that it had not begun with their sellers. That being true, a jury might have found that all the accused were embarked upon a venture, in all parts of which each was a participant, and an abettor in the sense that the success of that part with which he was immediately concerned, was dependent upon the success of the whole." [99]

98. 105 F.2d 921 (2d Cir.1939).   **99.** Id. at 922.

The only possible basis mentioned in the opinion for a finding of separate conspiracies was the fact that there was apparently "no privity" between the two separate groups of retailers. To the argument that there were consequently two conspiracies—one including the smugglers, the middlemen and the New York retailers, and the other the smugglers, the middlemen and the Texas and Louisiana retailers—the court replied:

> "Clearly, quoad the smugglers, there was but one conspiracy, for it was of no moment to them whether the middlemen sold to one or more groups of retailers, provided they had a market somewhere. So too of any retailer; he knew that he was a necessary link in a scheme of distribution, and the others, whom he knew to be convenient to its execution, were as much parts of a single undertaking or enterprise as two salesmen in the same shop." [100]

The Draft would require a different approach to a case such as *Bruno* and might produce different results.

Since the overall operation involved separate crimes of importing by the smugglers and possession and sale by each group—smugglers, distributors and retailers—the question as to each defendant would be whether and with whom he conspired to commit *each* of these crimes, under the criteria set forth in Subsections (1) and (2). The conspiratorial objective for the purpose of this inquiry could not be characterized in the manner of the *Bruno* court, as "to smuggle narcotics into the Port of New York and distribute them to addicts both in [New York] and in Texas and Louisiana." This is indeed the overall objective of the entire operation. It may also be true of *some* of the participants that they conspired to commit all of the crimes involved in the operation: under Subsection (3) of the Draft as under prevailing law they would be guilty of only one conspiracy if all these crimes were the object of the same agreement or continuing conspiratorial relationship, and the objective of *that* conspiracy or relationship could fairly be phrased in terms of the overall operation. But this multiplicity of criminal objectives affords a poor referent for testing the culpability of each individual who is in any manner involved in the operation.

With the conspiratorial objectives characterized as the particular crimes and the culpability of each participant tested separately, it would be possible to find in a case such as *Bruno*—considering for the moment only each separate chain of distribution—that the smugglers conspired to commit the illegal sales of the retailers but that the retailers did not conspire to commit the importing of the smugglers. Factual situations warranting such a finding may easily be conceived: the smugglers might depend upon and seek to foster their retail markets while the retailers might have many suppliers and be indifferent to the success of any single source. The court's approach in *Bruno* does not admit of such a finding, for in treating the conspiratorial objective as the entire series of crimes involved in smuggling, distribut-

100. Id. at 923.

ing and retailing it requires either a finding of no conspiracy or a single conspiracy in which all three links in the chain conspired to commit all of each other's crimes.

It would also be possible to find, with the inquiry focused upon each individual's culpability as to each criminal objective, that some of the parties in a chain conspired to commit the entire series of crimes while others conspired only to commit some of these crimes. Thus the smugglers and the middlemen in *Bruno* may have conspired to commit, promote or facilitate the importing and the possession and sales of all of the parties down to the final retail sale; the retailers might have conspired with them as to their own possession and sales but might be indifferent to all the steps prior to their receipt of the narcotics. In this situation, a smuggler or a middleman might have conspired with all three groups to commit the entire series of crimes, while a retailer might have conspired with the same parties but to commit fewer criminal objectives. Such results are conceptually difficult to reach under existing doctrine not only because of the frequent failure to focus separately upon the different criminal objectives, but because of the traditional view of the agreement as a bilateral relationship between each of the parties, congruent in scope both as to its party and its objective dimensions.

Of course, the major difficulty in finding any conspiracy which includes as parties both the smugglers and the retailers is the absence of direct communication or cooperation between them. Despite such absence an agreement may be inferred from mutual facilitation and evidence of a mutual purpose. Subsection (1) of the Draft would not preclude the inference, though it is more specific than the present law on the purpose requirement. But the present concept of agreement and even the more specific criteria embodied in Subsection (1) tend to become somewhat ambiguous when applied to a relationship that involves no direct communication or cooperation. Consequently, Subsection (2) of the Draft has been designed to facilitate the inquiry in such cases.

Subsection (2) extends the party dimension of a defendant's conspiracy beyond those with whom he agreed but at the same time preserves the basic limitation that the defendant must have conspired with someone to pursue the particular objective within the meaning of subsection (1). He must have agreed with someone with the purpose of promoting or facilitating the commission of a particular crime; if to his knowledge others have conspired with his coconspirator to commit the *same* crime he is also guilty of conspiring with them to commit that crime. In each chain of the *Bruno* case, for example, where actual cooperation and communication were established only between the smugglers and the middlemen and between the middlemen and the retailers, separate conspiracies might easily be found under Subsection (1) between each of these pairs of groups; and the objectives of each such conspiracy might consist of any or all of the crimes directly committed by its members. The smugglers and the retailers could then be drawn into a single conspiracy under Subsection (2) only as to objectives common to both such conspiracies, if each had knowledge of the other's conspiracy with the middlemen to commit these crimes. Absent such knowledge on the part of, say, the retailers, it would be possible for the smugglers to have conspired with the retailers through the middlemen to commit these crimes while the retailers conspired only with the middlemen. In this case there would be separate conspiracies congruent as to objective but differing as to parties.

The Draft also affords more helpful and precise criteria than existing doctrine in considering the wheel aspect of the *Bruno* case—the relationship between the two separate groups of retailers. The court recognized that these groups presented the greatest obstacle to a finding of a comprehensive conspiracy including all of the parties and all of the criminal objectives. The preceding discussion has indicated the possible conclusions regarding the guilt of a member of one group of retailers for a conspiracy not involving the other retailing group—i.e., a conspiracy with the smugglers or the middlemen to commit any or all of the series of crimes involved in funneling the narcotics to him and his sales. It would generally be more difficult to connect him with any conspiracy that includes the other retailing group as parties or that includes the other group's possession and sales as objectives.

As to any conspiracy including the other group as parties, there is the difficulty of lack of direct communication or cooperation between the two groups. A finding that they were both parties to a single conspiracy to commit any crime would have to rest on the communication and concert of each of them with the middlemen. They could be connected under Subsection (2) in a conspiracy to commit any objective that they each conspired with the middlemen to commit, to the knowledge of the other. With regard to the crimes involved in the middlemen's and the smugglers' operations—assuming each so conspired with the middlemen to the others' knowledge—the problems would be similar to those in the simple chain relationship; the smugglers and the retailers would probably have to be connected under Subsection (2). With regard to a conspiracy including the other retailing group's possession and sales as objectives, however, there would be the additional difficulty of proving the requisite purpose to promote or facilitate such crimes; since those crimes are not a part of the series that funnels the narcotics to him, his interest in promoting them will, as a general matter, probably be more difficult to prove than his interest in the crimes of the smugglers and middlemen.

Notes and Questions

1. In *Bruno,* which is discussed at some length above, a single conspiracy was upheld which included the retailers in New York and those in Louisiana and Texas. There was no evidence of cooperation or even

communication between the two retail groups. Does this make sense in terms of any of the justifications for conspiracy?

It may well be that a Texas retailer must know that the heroin comes from abroad and that his efforts to sell support and encourage the efforts of the smugglers and wholesalers. In light of the inference that he has knowingly agreed to further this goal it would be appropriate to hold the defendant retailer "responsible" for: the out-of-court declarations of other conspirators in furtherance of the conspiracy; the conspiracy itself; and possibly for any substantive offenses which were the object of the agreement or which the defendant should reasonably have anticipated being committed in pursuit of the object offense. Yet in what way has the Texas retailer associated himself with the efforts (and crimes) of the New York retailer? He may not know of the latter's existence but even if he does, how would the Texan's efforts effect the fortunes of the New Yorker, and vice versa?

The alternative position that there were two conspiracies in *Bruno*— one involving smugglers, wholesalers, and New York retailers, and the other involving smugglers, wholesalers and Louisiana/Texas retailers—is not free from difficulty. Under that view would there be a separate conspiracy for each distinct group of retailers? Why not a separate conspiracy for the smugglers, wholesalers, and each *individual* retailer in the absence of evidence of a meaningful mutual dependence among the retailers? The potential multiplication of liability—the possibility of multiple prosecutions, convictions, and sentences—poses very serious problems. See United States v. Cerro, 775 F.2d 908, 38 Cr.L.Rptr. 2170 (7th Cir.1985).

2. *Bruno* represents a classic example of the "party dimension" of agreements to conspire. Braverman v. United States, 317 U.S. 49, 63 S.Ct. 99, 87 L.Ed. 23 (1942), is an excellent illustration of the "object dimension" of this problem. The defendants were charged with seven conspiracies each having as its objective the violation of a different provision of the Internal Revenue laws. The evidence revealed a long-standing collaboration among the defendants to manufacture, transport and distribute distilled spirits. The defense moved, at the beginning and end of the trial, to require the Government to elect one of the seven counts of the indictment upon which to proceed, contending that the proof could not establish more than one agreement. The Government and the lower courts were of the view that a single conspiracy to commit several offenses permitted conviction and punishment of the defendants for conspiracy as to each contemplated offense. The Supreme Court reversed. Mr. Chief Justice Stone wrote: "the precise nature and extent of the conspiracy must be determined by reference to the agreement which embraces and defines its objects. Whether the object of a single agreement is to commit one or many crimes, it is in either case that agreement which constitutes the conspiracy which the statute punishes. The one agreement cannot be taken to be several agreements and hence several conspiracies because it envisages the violation of several statutes rather than one." 317 U.S. at 53, 63 S.Ct. at 102, 87 L.Ed. at 28.

Almost forty years later the petitioners in Albernaz v. United States, 450 U.S. 333, 101 S.Ct. 1137, 67 L.Ed.2d 275 (1981), relied on *Braverman* in seeking relief. They had entered an agreement to import marihuana and to distribute it. They were charged, and convicted, and received consecutive sentences for a conspiracy to import marihuana (21 U.S.C.A. § 963) and a conspiracy to distribute it (21 U.S.C.A. § 841). The Supreme Court distinguished *Braverman* on the ground that although the agreement there had multiple objectives it violated a single statute (the general federal conspiracy provision, 18 U.S.C.A. § 37). Here, the Congress had created two distinct conspiracy provisions which are directed at separate evils posed by drug trafficking. " 'Importation' and 'distribution' of marihuana impose diverse societal harms, and * * * Congress has in effect determined that a conspiracy to import drugs and to distribute them is twice as serious to do either object singly." 450 U.S. at 343, 101 S.Ct. at 1144, 67 L.Ed.2d at 284. This decision was within the constitutional authority of the Congress. (See the discussion of the general problem of multiple prosecutions and convictions for a "single act" in Section D of Chapter V, supra.)

(3) Defenses Based on the Requirement of an Agreement

The "essence" of conspiracy is agreement. Some courts consider this requirement of a meeting of guilty minds so important that situations regarded as inconsistent with a union of "criminal" minds will be held to preclude conviction for conspiracy or even to invalidate a conviction already obtained. Issues arising under this aspect of conspiracy law generally involve the assertion that the disposition of actual or potential charges against other members of an alleged conspiracy requires acquittal of the remaining member, because the disposition of the charges against the other members is logically inconsistent with the existence of a criminal agreement involving the remaining member.

REGLE v. STATE

Court of Special Appeals of Maryland, 1970.
9 Md.App. 346, 264 A.2d 119.

MURPHY, CHIEF JUDGE. On September 28, 1968, Sergeant Frank Mazzone, a Maryland State Police officer working under cover, was advised by other police officers that Michael Isele, a police informer, had informed them that he had been invited by the appellant Regle to participate in a robbery. Mazzone immediately contacted Isele, whom he previously knew, and together they went to see the appellant. Isele introduced Mazzone to the appellant as a prospective participant in the planned robbery. After some discussion, the appellant invited Mazzone to participate in the robbery. While appellant did not then specify the place to be robbed, he indicated to Mazzone that Richard Fields had been involved with him in planning the robbery, and that he would also participate in the crime. Appellant, Mazzone, and Isele then met with Fields and the robbery plan was outlined by appellant and Fields. The need for guns was discussed and appellant and Fields spoke of the necessity of killing two employees at O'Donnell's restaurant, the situs of the proposed robbery. The four men then drove in Isele's car to appellant's home where appellant phoned Kent Chamblee for the purpose of purchasing a shotgun. Thereafter, the men drove to Chamblee's home, purchased the gun from him, and tested it in his presence. While Chamblee knew that the shotgun was to be used "for a job," he did not accompany the others when they then drove to the restaurant to perpetrate the robbery. Upon arriving there, Mazzone told appellant that he first wanted to "case" the restaurant. This being agreed, Mazzone and Isele went into the restaurant while appellant and Fields went to a nearby bar to await their return. Once inside the restaurant, Mazzone contacted police headquarters and requested assistance. Thereafter, he and Isele left the restaurant and rejoined appellant and Fields. While several police cars promptly responded to the scene, Mazzone found it necessary, in the interim, to reveal his identity as a police officer and to arrest appellant and Fields at gunpoint. At the same time he also arrested Isele in order "to cover him." After the arrest, appellant made an incriminating statement to the effect that he and Fields had planned the robbery and that he had invited Isele to participate in the crime.

Appellant, Fields, and Chamblee were thereafter jointly indicted for conspiracy to rob with a dangerous and deadly weapon and for carrying a deadly weapon openly with intent to injure. Appellant was separately tried by a jury, found guilty on both counts, and sentenced to twenty years on the conspiracy charge, and two years, concurrent, on the weapons offense.

The docket entries indicate that the conspiracy indictment against Chamblee was *nol prossed* prior to appellant's trial. It also appears that at his trial appellant established through the testimony of a police officer that Fields had been examined by State psychiatrists at the Clifton Perkins State Hospital and found "not guilty by reason of being insane at the time of the alleged crime." The State did not rebut the officer's testimony, although the record indicates that two of the State psychiatrists who had examined Fields were then present in court.

Against this background, appellant contends that since the indictment against Chamblee was *nol prossed*, only he and Fields were charged as conspirators; and that because Fields was found insane at the time of the commission of the crime and thus was not a person legally capable of engaging in a criminal conspiracy, his own conviction cannot stand since one person alone cannot be guilty of the crime of conspiracy.

Conspiracy—a common law misdemeanor in Maryland—is defined as a combination by two or more persons to accomplish a criminal or unlawful act, or to do a lawful act by criminal or unlawful means. The gist of the offense is the unlawful combination resulting from the agreement, rather than the mere agreement itself, and no overt act is required to constitute the crime. In other words, as succinctly stated by the Supreme Court of New Jersey in State v. Carbone, 10 N.J. 329,

91 A.2d 571, 574, the "gist of the offense of conspiracy lies, not in doing the act, nor effecting the purpose for which the conspiracy is formed, nor in attempting to do them, nor in inciting others to do them, but in the forming of the scheme or agreement between the parties." Concert in criminal purpose, it is said, is the salient factor in criminal conspiracy. Criminal conspiracy is a partnership in crime—"It is the coalition of manpower and human minds enhancing possibilities of achievement aimed at the objective that present a greater threat to society than does a lone offender." Clark and Marshall Crimes (6th Edition) Section 9.00. In short, it is *the existence* of the conspiracy which creates the danger.

As one person cannot conspire or form a combination with himself, it is essential in proving the existence of a criminal conspiracy to show "the consent of two or more minds," Bloomer v. State, 48 Md. 521, 536, viz., it must be shown that at least two persons had a meeting of the minds—a unity of design and purpose—to have an agreement. A formal agreement need not, however, be established; it is sufficient if the minds of the parties meet understandingly, so as to bring about an intelligent and deliberate agreement to do the acts contemplated. As the crime of conspiracy is one requiring a specific intent, and necessarily involves at the least two guilty parties, the required criminal intent must exist in the minds of two or more parties to the conspiracy.

In view of these principles, it is the well settled general rule that one defendant in a prosecution for conspiracy cannot be convicted where all of his alleged coconspirators, be they one or more, have been acquitted or discharged under circumstances that amount to an acquittal. * * * The rationale underlying the rule appears clear: that it is illogical to acquit all but one of a purported partnership in crime; that acquittal of all persons with whom a defendant is alleged to have conspired is repugnant to the existence of the requisite corrupt agreement; and that regardless of the criminal animus of the one defendant, there must be someone with whom he confected his corrupt agreement, and where all his alleged coconspirators are not guilty, a like finding as to him must be made. But "It is only where one is convicted and another or others are acquitted, resulting in a repugnancy upon the record, that the convicted conspirator may be discharged." Berry v. State, 202 Ind. 294, 173 N.E. 705 * * *.

Generally speaking, it would appear that so long as the disposition of the case against a coconspirator does not remove the basis for the charge of conspiracy, a single defendant may be prosecuted and convicted of the offense, even though for one reason or another his coconspirator is either not tried or not convicted. Consistent with this rule, the authorities all agree that the death of one conspirator does not of itself prevent the conviction of the other, where the conspiracy between them is shown by the evidence. In Hurwitz v. State, [200 Md. 578, 92 A.2d 575], a case in which all but one of the conspirators were granted immunity from prosecution on a ground not inconsistent with their participation in the conspiracy, the court held that such grant of immunity was not equivalent to acquittal and would not require reversal of the conviction of the one remaining conspirator. The same rule has been applied where one of two conspirators enjoyed diplomatic immunity and therefore could not be prosecuted for the conspiracy. Farnsworth v. Zerbst, 98 F.2d 541 (5th Cir.). In Adams v. State, 202 Md. 455, 97 A.2d 281, it was held that conviction of one defendant in a conspiracy case was proper despite failure to convict of any of the other conspirators where it was alleged and shown that there were persons unknown to the prosecution with whom the convicted defendant had conspired. And while the cases are generally divided on the question whether the entry of a *nolle prosequi* as to one of two alleged conspirators compels an acquittal of the remaining conspirator, the better reasoned view would appear to support the proposition that it does not, at least where the *nolle prosequi* was not entered without the coconspirator's consent after the trial had begun (which then would have amounted to an acquittal and precluded reindictment). In *Hurwitz*, it was held that the entry of a "stet" to a coconspirator's indictment was not tantamount to an acquittal and did not compel the discharge of the only remaining conspirator.[1]

Some cases suggest that the rule that acquittal of all save one of the alleged conspirators results in the acquittal of all applies only to acquittals on the merits. See Farnsworth v. Zerbst, supra. Other cases—while recognizing that acquittals are not always tantamount to a declaration of innocence—nevertheless conclude that an acquittal is in effect a judicial determination, binding on the State, that the acquitted defendant was not a participant in a criminal conspiracy. The State urges that where the acquittal of one of the alleged conspirators is based solely on the fact that he was insane at the time of the crime, the remaining conspirator should nonetheless be held responsible for the offense. The State relies on Jones v. State, 31 Ala.App. 504, 19 So.2d 81, a case in which the defendant, convicted of murder, maintained that the actual killing was done by his brother and that because his brother was insane at the time of the crime, and hence innocent of the offense, he (the defendant) must likewise be exonerated. The court, after characterizing the defendant as "a co-conspirator and an aider and abettor in the homicide," said (p. 83):

"* * * the insanity [of appellant's brother] would not exculpate the appellant if he conspired with the principal or aided or abetted him in the killing of deceased * * *. If appellant so conspired or aided or abetted in the homicide, the mental irresponsibility of [his brother] could not be invoked to exonerate said appellant. One may or could use an insane person as the agent of destruction—or conspire with such person to accomplish the homicide—just as guilty as with a person of sound mind. The fact, if true, that the coconspirator or principal in the crime is not amenable to justice because of mental irresponsibility does not exempt the other from prosecution."

1. By the Maryland stet procedure, the prosecutor indicates that he does not choose *at that time* to further prosecute the indictment.

We think the cases relied upon by the *Jones* court to support its conclusion stand for the proposition that it is no defense to one who participates either as a principal or aider or abettor in the actual commission of the substantive criminal offense that the principal offender was insane at the time of the crime. The principle would appear similar to the rule that a coconspirator may be convicted of any crime committed by any member of a conspiracy to do an illegal act if the act is done in furtherance of the purpose of the conspiracy. The conspiracy being established, the fact that the member who committed the crime was insane at the time would thus not exonerate the others from complicity in the commission of the substantive offense.

We do not find these cases controlling of the primary question before us, namely, whether *under an indictment for conspiracy,* one conspirator may be convicted of the offense where the only other conspirator was shown to be insane at the time the agreement between them was concluded. Conspiracy to commit a crime is a different offense from the crime that is the object of the conspiracy. One necessarily involves joint action; the other does not. By its nature, conspiracy is a joint or group offense requiring a concert of free wills, and the union of the minds of at least two persons is a prerequisite to the commission of the offense. The essence of conspiracy is, therefore, a mental confederation involving at least two persons; the crime is indivisible in the sense that it requires more than one guilty person; and where the joint intent does not exist, the basis of the charge of conspiracy is necessarily swept away. In short, the guilt of both persons must concur to constitute that of either. It is upon this premise that the authorities all agree that if two persons are charged as conspirators and one is an entrapper, or merely feigns acquiescence in the criminal intent, there is no punishable conspiracy because there was no agreement on the part of the one to engage in a criminal conspiracy.[2] For like reasons, we hold that where only two persons are implicated in a conspiracy, and one is shown to have been insane at the time the agreement was concluded, and hence totally incapable of committing any crime, there is no punishable criminal conspiracy, the requisite joint criminal intent being absent.

The evidence in the record before us plainly shows that appellant and Fields planned to commit a robbery at O'Donnell's restaurant. There is some evidence in the record to suggest that Chamblee may also have been a conspirator although the State made little effort at the trial to establish his involvement in the conspiracy. Since an insane person is mentally incapable of forming a criminal intent, it is clear that if Fields was actually insane at the time of the offense, he could not be found guilty of engaging in a criminal conspiracy. It does not appear however, that Fields was ever tried and acquitted of the conspiracy charge. But the only evidence in the record—the testimony of the police officer—is that Fields was found by State psychiatrists upon

2. This would not be true, however, if after elimination of the alleged entrapper, there are at least two other parties to the conspiracy.

examination to have been insane at the time of the commission of the offense. While such testimony is hardly the equivalent of the expert medical evidence required to prove insanity, the trial judge, in his charge to the jury, stated as a fact that Fields "was found to be insane." Assuming this to be the true situation, it is unlikely that Fields will ever be brought to trial on the conspiracy charge.

As to Chamblee, the docket entries indicate the entry of a *nolle prosequi* to his conspiracy indictment. We cannot ascertain, therefore, whether, in the circumstances in which it was entered, the *nolle prosequi* operated as an acquittal or not. It appears, however, from colloquy between counsel and with the court that Chamblee was permitted to plead to a lesser offense than conspiracy, possibly with the understanding that he would not thereafter be charged with that offense.

In his advisory instructions to the jury, the trial judge, after fully defining the crime of conspiracy, stated that under Maryland law where only two parties are involved in the alleged conspiracy, and one is found not guilty, "the other could not be tried because one person cannot conspire except with another to commit a crime." He further advised the jury that there has to be "an outright finding of not guilty" but such was not the case with Fields who was merely found to be insane and for that reason not brought to trial. With reference to Chamblee, the trial judge instructed that he had not been found not guilty of conspiracy; that he did not believe that Chamblee had been prosecuted for that offense.

While appellant made no objection to the court's instructions, on the state of the record before us we think they constituted "plain error * * * material to the rights of the accused" under Maryland Rule 756g. See Parker v. State, 4 Md.App. 62, 241 A.2d 185. We thus deem it essential in the interest of justice that appellant's conspiracy conviction be reversed and that the State be afforded the opportunity to retry the case in light of the principles of law which we consider relevant and controlling. If, upon retrial, the State intends to charge only Fields and appellant as conspirators, and the evidence properly shows that Fields was legally insane at the time the agreement to perpetrate the robbery was concluded, then even though Fields has not been acquitted of the offense of conspiracy by a judicial determination that he was insane, nevertheless the requisite *joint* criminal intent being absent, appellant cannot properly be convicted of engaging with Fields in a criminal conspiracy. If Fields is shown so to be insane, but the facts show that the conspiracy indictment against Chamblee was not *nol prossed* under circumstances amounting to an acquittal, then the State may undertake to adduce evidence showing that Chamblee was a conspirator, with appellant, in the plan to commit the robbery.

Notes and Questions

1. Assume that Fields was the only other alleged conspirator in *Regle*. Would the reversal of Regle's conviction comport with the rationales of the

crime of conspiracy? How does the insanity of an alleged co-conspirator lessen the dangers which conspiracy doctrine is designed to avoid? Is there any reason why one cannot work in concert with an insane person, or be emboldened by his apparent support? If the answer is yes to these questions, should the conviction nevertheless be reversed because an insane person cannot "agree" in a way which would be binding for purposes of a civil contract? What is achieved by excusing the sane "conspirator" on these facts?

Is the case for reversing Regle's conviction stronger if the only other alleged conspirator was a government agent who never intended to carry out the criminal objective? This appears to be the position of the federal courts which have faced this issue. See United States v. Escobar de Bright, 742 F.2d 1196 (9th Cir.1984) and the cases cited therein. Accord State v. Joles, 485 So.2d 212 (La.App.1986) (relying upon federal cases). The *de Bright* court argued that a conspiracy charge was inappropriate in such circumstances for both formal and policy reasons. It argued, as did the *Regle* court, that there cannot be the required agreement unless at least two persons have a meeting of the minds as to the achievement of the illicit objective. On the policy front it contended that the dangers of group criminality—increased probability of success, future criminal acts of the group, and difficulty of detection—are non-existent where the alleged other conspirator is a government agent. Finally, the judges in *de Bright* expressed a special concern that another rule would encourage the government to "manufacture" conspiracies in a manner condemned by the defense of entrapment. 742 F.2d at 1200.

As to entrapment, consider Section C. of Chapter XII, infra, which suggests how extraordinarily difficult it is for that defense to be successfully invoked. As to the other policy reasons for insisting on a "bilateral" approach to conspiracy consider whether the behavior and state of mind of one who "agrees" with an undercover agent is distinguishable in terms of culpability from the acts and intent of one who "agrees" with a sincere co-conspirator? How is one who "agrees" with the agent distinguishable from an actor who "attempts" a crime by a means which, unknown to him, is ineffective or insufficient? Reconsider the material on impossibility, note 4, page 598, supra.

2. Sometimes the problems discussed in *Regle* and note 1, supra, are posed in the context of modern statutory formulations of the crime of conspiracy. One common source of such formulations is Section 5.03 of the Model Penal Code which is reprinted at page 643, infra. Would the result in *Regle* be the same under the Model Penal Code? Consider the following portions of the Comment to Section 5.03(1):

> *Unilateral Approach of the Draft.* The definition of the Draft departs from the traditional view of conspiracy as an entirely bilateral or multilateral relationship, the view inherent in the standard formulation cast in terms of "two or more persons" agreeing or combining to commit a crime. Attention is directed instead to each individual's culpability by framing the definition in terms of the conduct which suffices to establish the liability of any given actor, rather than the

conduct of a group of which he is charged to be a part—an approach which in this comment we have designated "unilateral."

One consequence of this approach is to make it immaterial to the guilt of a conspirator whose culpability has been established that the person or all of the persons with whom he conspired have not been or cannot be convicted. Present law frequently holds otherwise, reasoning from the definition of conspiracy as an agreement between two or more persons that there must be at least two guilty conspirators or none.

Model Penal Code, Comment to § 5.03(1), 102 (Tent.Draft No. 10, 1960).

In some states which have adopted language drawn from the Model Penal Code with its shift in emphasis to the individual's culpability, the courts have upheld convictions for "unilateral" conspiracies. E.g., State v. Marian, 62 Ohio St.2d 250, 405 N.E.2d 267 (1980), and State v. St. Christopher, 305 Minn. 226, 232 N.W.2d 798 (1975). But the commitment to "bilateralism" is not always overcome by changes in statutory language. E.g., People v. Foster, 99 Ill.2d 48, 75 Ill.Dec. 411, 457 N.E.2d 405 (1983) (no change in the law will be found in the absence of explicit legislative statement of adopting unilateral view) and Williams v. State, 646 S.W.2d 221 (Tex.Crim.App.1983) (there must still be a meeting of the minds).

Ultimately, is a "unilateral" conspiracy distinguishable from the crime of solicitation? If a jurisdiction has a solicitation statute is there any need or justification for a unilateral conspiracy prosecution? See People v. Foster, supra.

3. A and B are charged with conspiracy to commit grand theft. A pleads guilty. B stands trial and is acquitted. A is then sentenced to imprisonment. Are A's conviction and sentence void? Is the answer dictated by *Regle*? Is judicial responsibility for overseeing the plea bargaining process a basis for intervention? See Eyman v. Deutsch, 92 Ariz. 82, 373 P.2d 716 (1962) (acquittal of one alleged co-conspirator voids prior conviction of other). An opposite and more widely accepted result was reached in United States v. Irvin, 787 F.2d 1506 (11th Cir.1986). Is the issue here the same as the dispute between the "unilateral" and "bilateral" views of conspiracy? When different juries have acted inconsistently on the question of the existence of a single conspiracy the issue is the meaning to be attributed to the prior or subsequent acquittal of the only other alleged conspirators. As has often been noted, juries in our society have the power—although not the lawful authority—to disregard the law and the facts and acquit due to an undue tenderness or prejudice, as well as out of confusion, mistake, or compromise. Although such inconsistent verdicts by the same jury would not be allowed to stand, when done by different juries it would be a windfall to reverse the conviction of the last conspirator who has been found to be such beyond a reasonable doubt by a properly instructed jury. 787 F.2d at 1512–13.

4. A and B are charged with conspiring with each other and with other unknown persons to commit extortion. A is acquitted. May B be convicted? See United States v. Lance, 536 F.2d 1065, 1068 (5th Cir.1976):

[A] person can be convicted of conspiring with persons whose names are unknown as long as the indictment asserts that such other persons exist and the evidence supports their existence. This is true even when co-defendants are known and not prosecuted.

5. Consider an agreement in which all participants other than the defendant cannot be punished for the object offense because legislative intent was to exempt them. Can the defendant be found guilty of conspiracy on the basis that he conspired with them? In Gebardi v. United States, 287 U.S. 112, 53 S.Ct. 35, 77 L.Ed. 206 (1932), a man and a woman had been convicted of conspiring to violate the Mann Act (18 U.S.C.A. § 2421), which prohibits transportation by a man of a woman from one state to another for immoral purposes. The evidence showed only that the woman consented to the transportation and the Court concluded that Congress had not intended to make a woman liable for a violation of the Act merely on the basis of her acquiescence in the transportation. It further reasoned that Congress could not have intended to subject a woman to punishment for conspiracy on the basis of mere acquiescence. Turning to the liability of the man, the Court summarily held, "As there is no proof that the man conspired with anyone else to bring about the transportation, the convictions of both petitioners must be reversed." 287 U.S. at 123, 53 S.Ct. at 38, 77 L.Ed. at 211.

It seems easily understood why the government should not be permitted to thwart the Congressional intention by punishing the woman—the subject of its concern—for conspiracy, but why should the man go free? Insofar as the inchoate nature of conspiracy is concerned, why should the authorities have to wait to intervene until the object offense is committed or attempted? Nevertheless, the *Gebardi* principle continues to be observed, see United States v. Nasser, 476 F.2d 1111 (7th Cir.1973). Would the result be the same under the Model Penal Code? See § 5.04, reprinted page 644, infra, which provides, in part:

" *   *   * it is immaterial to the liability of a person who *   *   * conspires with another to commit a crime that:

(b) the person *   *   * with whom he conspires *   *   * has an immunity to prosecution or conviction for the commission of the crime.

6. A minor yet troublesome aspect of conspiracy law has been the so-called Wharton's Rule or the "concert of action" defense. Francis Wharton's treatise on criminal law first formulated the rule, based upon the author's reading of Shannon v. Commonwealth, 14 Pa. 226 (1850). F. Wharton, Criminal Law 198 (2nd ed. 1852). The current edition of the treatise states the rule as follows:

An agreement between two persons to commit an offense does not constitute conspiracy when the target offense is so defined that it can be committed only by the participation of two persons, or, to use common statutory language, the offense is so defined "that the defendant's conduct is inevitably incident to its commission."

4 C.E. Torcia, Wharton's Criminal Law § 731, p. 545 (14th Ed.1978).

The rule apparently rests upon the assumption that if the object crime necessarily involves a preliminary agreement (i.e., a conspiracy), the preliminary agreement or conspiracy does not constitute a social danger above and beyond the object offense itself and therefore should not be an independent crime. See Gebardi v. United States, 287 U.S. 112, 121–22, 53 S.Ct. 35, 37, 77 L.Ed.2d 206, 209 (1932). The rule is obviously limited by the requirement that the object crime be one that necessarily involves a preliminary agreement. It has traditionally precluded prosecutions for conspiracy to commit adultery, dueling, bigamy, incest, and similar offenses. Thus A, a woman, and B, a man, who engage in sexual intercourse while one is married to another person cannot be convicted of conspiracy to commit adultery, because the act of consensual intercourse involved in adultery necessarily involves a prior agreement to engage in intercourse. The rule has not been applied to conspiracies to commit crimes that often involve preliminary agreements but which do not by definition require such agreements. The Supreme Court has held, for example, that a defendant can be convicted of conspiracy to transport a woman in interstate commerce in violation of the Mann Act, because an agreement between the transporting defendant and the transported woman is not essential to a violation of the Act—the Act can be violated by the transportation of a noncooperating (and therefore nonagreeing) woman. United States v. Holte, 236 U.S. 140, 35 S.Ct. 271, 59 L.Ed. 504 (1915).

Courts have differed in their application of the rule and these variations were discussed by the Supreme Court in Iannelli v. United States, 420 U.S. 770, 95 S.Ct. 1284, 43 L.Ed.2d 616 (1975):

> [S]ome federal courts have differed over whether Wharton's Rule requires initial dismissal of the conspiracy indictment. In [some cases] District Courts sustained preliminary motions to dismiss conspiracy indictments in cases in which the prosecution also charged violation of [the substantive offense. In other cases], however, the courts held that the Rule's purpose can be served equally effectively by permitting the prosecution to charge both offenses and instructing the jury that a conviction for the substantive offense necessarily precludes conviction for the conspiracy.

420 U.S. at 775, 95 S.Ct. at 1288–89, 43 L.Ed.2d at 621–622. The courts have also differed on the existence and application of the so-called "third party exception." Under this aspect of the rule, the prohibition of the rule does not apply to a prosecution for a conspiracy if the conspiracy involved more persons than are logically necessary for commission of the object offense. Thus if A, B, and C enter into an agreement, the object of which is for B (a male) and C (a female) to commit the crime of adultery, this gives rise to an indictable conspiracy because only two-person agreements (between the parties to the intercourse) are inherent in the crime of adultery. Prosecution for three party agreements is thus not barred. See Robinson v. State, 229 Md. 503, 184 A.2d 814 (1962).

In Iannelli v. United States, supra, the Court considered the relationship between Wharton's Rule and a provision of the Organized Crime Control Act of 1970. Petitioners, six codefendants, and seven unindicted coconspirators were charged with both conspiring to violate and with violating 18 U.S.C.A. § 1955, which makes it a crime for five or more persons to conduct, finance, manage, supervise, direct or own a gambling business prohibited by state law. They were convicted on the two charges over their objection that Wharton's Rule applied and prohibited conviction for both. For the first time addressing the "precise role" of Wharton's Rule in federal law, the Supreme Court concluded that the rule "has current validity only as a judicial presumption, to be applied in the absence of legislative intent to the contrary." 420 U.S. at 782, 95 S.Ct. at 1292, 43 L.Ed.2d at 625, 626. The court then analyzed section 1955 in its context as part of the Organized Crime Control Act of 1970 and found a Congressional purpose to make available either or both the crime defined by section 1955 and conspiracy to commit the crime for use in the strategy against organized crime. Congress manifested a clear awareness of the distinct nature of conspiracy and substantive object offenses in drafting the Act, Mr. Justice Powell reasoned for the majority, and defined "gambling activity" in section 1955 and other provisions with pointed avoidance of the reference to conspiracy or agreement. Thus, the majority opinion concluded, had Congress intended to foreclose the possibility of prosecuting conspiracy and the substantive offense it would have specifically so provided. 420 U.S. at 786–791, 95 S.Ct. at 1294–96, 43 L.Ed.2d at 627–631. The Court also noted that the logic of Wharton's Rule as applied to those offenses traditionally invoking it did not apply in the context of section 1955 and the Organized Crime Control Act:

> The classic Wharton's Rule offenses—adultery, incest, bigamy, duelling—are crimes that are characterized by the general congruence of the agreement and the completed substantive offense. The parties to the agreement are the only persons who participate in commission of the substantive offense, and the immediate consequences of the crime rest on the parties themselves rather than on society at large. Finally, the agreement that attends the substantive offense does not appear likely to pose the distinct kinds of threats to society that the law of conspiracy seeks to avert. It cannot, for example, readily be assumed that an agreement to commit an offense of this nature will produce agreements to engage in a more general pattern of criminal conduct.

> The conduct proscribed by § 1955 is significantly different from the offenses to which the Rule traditionally has been applied. Unlike the consequences of the classic Wharton's Rule offenses, the harm attendant upon the commission of the substantive offense is not restricted to the parties to the agreement. Large-scale gambling activities seek to elicit the participation of additional persons—the bettors—who are parties neither to the conspiracy nor to the substantive offense that results from it. Moreover, the parties prosecuted for the conspiracy need not be the same persons who are prosecuted for commission of the substantive offense. An endeavor as complex as a large-scale gambling enterprise might involve persons who have played appreciably different roles, and whose level of culpability varies significantly. It might, therefore, be appropriate to prosecute the owners and organizers of large-scale gambling operations both for the conspiracy and for the substantive offense but to prosecute the lesser participants only

for the substantive offense. Nor can it fairly be maintained that agreements to enter into large-scale gambling activities are not likely to generate additional agreements to engage in other criminal endeavors.

420 U.S. at 782–84, 95 S.Ct. at 1292–93, 43 L.Ed.2d at 625–627. In United States v. Walker, 796 F.2d 43 (4th Cir.1986), the defendant had been prosecuted, under two separate statutes, and convicted of espionage and conspiracy to commit espionage based on his transmittal of United States defense information to Soviet agents. On appeal he complained that the trial judge had erred in refusing to dismiss the conspiracy charge under Wharton's Rule. According to Walker espionage requires only two persons—the one who delivers the information and the one who receives it, and the prosecution had failed to prove the presence of a third conspirator. Therefore, he claimed, the conspiracy charge was duplicative. Does this claim have validity under the principles announced in *Iannelli*?

b. The State of Mind Required

The Supreme Court recently noted:

> In a conspiracy, two different types of intent are generally required—the basic intent to agree, which is necessary to establish the existence of the conspiracy, and the more traditional intent to effectuate the object of the conspiracy.

United States v. United States Gypsum Co., 438 U.S. 422, 443 n. 20, 98 S.Ct. 2864, 2876 n. 20, 57 L.Ed.2d 854, 873 n. 20 (1978). The first of the types of intent distinguished by the Court was treated in Subsection C. 1.a. of this Chapter, supra. This subsection deals with the second type of intent, the state of mind regarding effectuation of the object of the agreement. Perhaps the issue can best be identified in terms of a simple hypothetical: A, aware that B and C are illicitly distilling whiskey, agrees to sell B sugar. This can reasonably be construed as an agreement involving A, B, and C; A has agreed to do something that is part of the scheme, and the production of illicit whiskey is the objective of the scheme. A clearly had that type of "intent" necessary for formulation of the agreement. But what must have been A's state of mind in regard to the object, i.e., the illicit production of whiskey, and did he have it? Must he have desired that whiskey actually be produced? Is it sufficient if he was aware that production of whiskey would result from the scheme? Or might it be sufficient if A was simply aware of a substantial and unjustifiable risk that a result of the venture would be the production of whiskey? Does this end the inquiry? Or might it be necessary to prove that A was aware (or was aware of a risk) that the scheme constituted a *criminal* offense under federal law?

UNITED STATES v. UNITED STATES GYPSUM CO.
Supreme Court of the United States, 1978.
438 U.S. 422, 98 S.Ct. 2864, 57 L.Ed.2d 854.

MR. CHIEF JUSTICE BURGER delivered the opinion of the Court.

This case presents the * * * [question] whether intent is an element of a criminal antitrust offense * * *.

I

Gypsum board, a laminated type of wall board composed of paper, vinyl or other specially treated coverings over a gypsum core, has in the last 30 years substantially replaced wet plaster as the primary component of interior walls and ceilings in residential and commercial construction. The product is essentially fungible; differences in price, credit terms and delivery services largely dictate the purchasers' choice between competing suppliers. Overall demand, however, is governed by the level of construction activity and is only marginally affected by price fluctuations.

The gypsum board industry is highly concentrated with the number of producers ranging from nine to 15 in the period 1960–1973. The eight largest companies accounted for some 94% of the national sales with the seven "single plant producers" accounting for the remaining 6%. Most of the major producers and a large number of the single plant producers are members of the Gypsum Association which since 1930 has served as a trade association of gypsum board manufacturers.

A

Beginning in 1966, the Justice Department, as well as the Federal Trade Commission, became involved in investigations into possible antitrust violations in the gypsum board industry. In 1971, a grand jury was empaneled and the investigation continued for an additional 28 months. In late 1973, an indictment was filed in the United States District Court for the Western District of Pennsylvania charging six major manufacturers and various of their corporate officials with violations of § 1 of the Sherman Act. 26 Stat. 209, as amended, 15 U.S. C.A. § 1.

The indictment charged that the defendants had engaged in a combination and conspiracy "[b]eginning sometime prior to 1960 and continuing thereafter at least until sometime in 1973," App. 34, in restraint of interstate trade and commerce in the manufacture and sale of gypsum board. The alleged combination and conspiracy consisted of:

"A continuing agreement understanding and concert of action among the defendants and co-conspirators to (a) raise, fix, maintain and stabilize the prices of gypsum board; (b) fix, maintain and stabilize the terms and conditions of sale thereof; and (c) adopt and maintain uniform methods of packaging and handling such gypsum board." App. 34.

The indictment proceeded to specify some 13 types of actions taken by conspirators "in formulating and effectuating" the combination and conspiracy, the most relevant of which, for our purposes, is specification (h) which alleged that the conspirators:

> "telephoned or otherwise contacted one another to exchange and discuss current and future published or market prices and published or standard terms and conditions of sale and to ascertain alleged deviations therefrom.

The bill of particulars provided additional details about the continuing nature of the alleged exchanges of competitive information and the role played by such exchanges in policing adherence to the various other illegal agreements charged.

B

* * *

The focus of the Government's price fixing case at trial was interseller price verification—that is, the practice allegedly followed by the gypsum board manufacturers of telephoning a competing producer to determine the price currently being offered on gypsum board to a specific customer. The Government contended that these price exchanges were part of an agreement among the defendants, had the effect of stabilizing prices and policing agreed upon price increases, and were undertaken on a frequent basis until sometime in 1973. Defendants disputed both the scope and duration of the verification activities, and further maintained that those exchanges of price information which did occur were for the purposes of complying with the Robinson-Patman Act [4] and preventing customer fraud. These purposes, in defendants' view, brought the disputed communications among competitors within a "controlling circumstance" exception to Sherman Act liability—at the extreme, precluding, as a matter of law, consideration of verification by the jury in determining defendants' guilt on the price fixing charge, and at the minimum, making the defendants' purposes in engaging in such communications a threshold factual question.

The instructions on the verification issue given by the trial judge provided that if the exchanges of price information were deemed by the jury to have been undertaken "in a good faith effort to comply with the Robinson-Patman Act," verification standing alone would not be sufficient to establish an illegal price fixing agreement. The paragraphs immediately following, however, provided that the purpose was essentially irrelevant if the jury found that the effect of verification was to raise, fix, maintain or stabilize prices. The instructions on verification closed with the observation that

> "[t]he law presumes that a person intends the necessary and natural consequences of his acts. Therefore, if the effect of the

---

4. Defendants contended that the exchange of price information or verification was necessary to enable them to take advantage of the meeting competition defense contained in § 2(b) of the Robinson-Patman Act. 15 U.S.C.A. § 13(b), see Part III, infra.

exchanges of pricing information was to raise, fix, maintain and stabilize prices, then the parties to them are presumed, as a matter of law, to have intended that result."

* * *

[The jury returned verdicts of guilty against each of the defendants.]

II

We * * * consider the jury instructions regarding the elements of the price-fixing offense charged in the indictment. Although the trial judge's instructions on the price fixing issue are not without ambiguity, it seems reasonably clear that he regarded an effect on prices as the crucial element of the charged offense. The jury was instructed that if it found interseller verification had the effect of raising, fixing, maintaining or stabilizing the price of gypsum board, then such verification could be considered as evidence of an agreement to so affect prices. They were further charged, and it is this point which gives rise to our present concern, that "if the effect of the exchanges of pricing information was to raise, fix, maintain, and stabilize prices, then the parties to them are presumed, *as a matter of law,* to have intended that result." App. 1722. (Emphasis added.)

* * *

[W]e hold that a defendant's state of mind or intent is an element of a criminal antitrust offense which must be established by evidence and inferences drawn therefrom and cannot be taken from the trier of fact through reliance on a legal presumption of wrongful intent from proof of an effect on prices. Cf. Morissette v. United States, 342 U.S. 246, 274–275, 72 S.Ct. 240, 255, 96 L.Ed. 288. Since the challenged instruction, as we read it, had this prohibited effect, it is disapproved. We are unwilling to construe the Sherman Act as mandating a regime of strict liability criminal offenses.

A

We start with the familiar proposition that "[t]he existence of a *mens rea* is the rule of, rather than the exception to, the principles of Anglo-American criminal jurisprudence." Dennis v. United States, 341 U.S. 494, 500, 71 S.Ct. 857, 862, 95 L.Ed. 1137. * * *

While strict liability offenses are not unknown to the criminal law and do not invariably offend constitutional requirements, the limited circumstances in which Congress has created and this Court has recognized such offenses, see e.g., United States v. Balint, 258 U.S. 250, 42 S.Ct. 301, 66 L.Ed. 604, attest to their generally disfavored status. Certainly far more than the simple omission of the appropriate phrase from the statutory definition is necessary to justify dispensing with an intent requirement. In the context of the Sherman Act, this generally inhospitable attitude to non-*mens rea* offenses is reinforced by an array of considerations arguing against treating antitrust violations as strict liability crimes.

B

The Sherman Act, unlike most traditional criminal statutes, does not, in clear and categorical terms, precisely identify the conduct which it proscribes. Both civil remedies and criminal sanctions are authorized with regard to the same generalized definitions of the conduct proscribed—restraints of trade or commerce and illegal monopolization—without reference to or mention of intent or state of mind. Nor has judicial elaboration of the Act always yielded the clear and definitive rules of conduct which the statute omits; instead open-ended and fact-specific standards like the "rule of reason" have been applied to broad classes of conduct falling within the purview of the Act's general provisions. Simply put, the Act has not been interpreted as if it were primarily a criminal statute; it has been construed to have a "generality and adaptability comparable to that found desirable in constitutional provisions." Appalachian Coal Co. v. United States, 288 U.S. 344, 359–360, 53 S.Ct. 471, 473–474, 77 L.Ed. 825 (1933).

Although in United States v. Nash, 229 U.S. 373, 376–378, 33 S.Ct. 780, 781–782, 57 L.Ed. 1232, the Court held that the indeterminancy of the Sherman Act's standards did not constitute a fatal constitutional objection to their criminal enforcement; nevertheless, this factor has been deemed particularly relevant by those charged with enforcing the Act in accommodating its criminal and remedial sanctions. The 1955 Report of the Attorney General's National Committee to Study the Antitrust Laws concluded that the criminal provisions of the Act should be reserved for those circumstances where the law was relatively clear and the conduct egregious:

> "The Sherman Act, inevitably perhaps, is couched in language broad and general. Modern business patterns moreover are so complex that market effects of proposed conduct are only imprecisely predictable. Thus, it may be difficult for today's businessman to tell in advance whether projected actions will run afoul of the Sherman Act's criminal structures. With this hazard in mind, we believe that criminal process should be used only where the law is clear and the facts reveal a flagrant offense and plain intent unreasonably to restrain trade." Report of the Attorney General's National Committee to Study the Antitrust Laws 349 (1955).

The Antitrust Division of the Justice Department took a similar though slightly more moderate position in its enforcement guidelines issued contemporaneously with the 1955 Report of the Attorney General's Committee * * *.

While not dispositive of the question now before us, the recommendations of the Attorney General's Committee and the guidelines promulgated by the Justice Department highlight the same basic concerns which are manifested in our general requirement of *mens rea* in criminal statutes and suggest that these concerns are at least equally salient in the antitrust context.

Close attention to the type of conduct regulated by the Sherman Act buttresses this conclusion. With certain exceptions for conduct regarded as *per se* illegal because of its unquestionably anticompetitive effects, the behavior proscribed by the Act is often difficult to distinguish from the gray zone of socially acceptable and economically justifiable business conduct. Indeed, the type of conduct charged in the indictment in this case—the exchange of price information among competitors—is illustrative in this regard. The imposition of criminal liability on a corporate official, or for that matter on a corporation directly, for engaging in such conduct which only after the fact is determined to violate the statute because of anticompetitive effects, without inquiring into the intent with which it was undertaken, holds out the distinct possibility of overdeterrence; salutary and procompetitive conduct lying close to the borderline of impermissible conduct might be shunned by businessmen who chose to be excessively cautious in the face of uncertainty regarding possible exposure to criminal punishment for even a good-faith error of judgment.[17] See P. Areeda & D. Turner, Antitrust Law 29 (1978); Bork, The Antitrust Paradox 78 (1978); Kadish, Some Observations On the Use of Criminal Sanctions in Enforcing Economic Regulations, 30 U.Chi.L.Rev. 423, 441–442 (1963). Further, the use of criminal sanctions in such circumstances would be difficult to square with the generally accepted functions of the criminal law. The criminal sanctions would be used not to punish conscious and calculated wrongdoing at odds with statutory proscriptions, but instead simply to *regulate* business practices regardless of the intent with which they were undertaken. While in certain cases we have imputed a regulatory purpose to Congress in choosing to employ criminal sanctions, see, e.g., United States v. Balint, 258 U.S. 250, 42 S.Ct. 301, 66 L.Ed. 604, the availability of a range of nonpenal alternatives to the criminal sanctions of the Sherman Act negates the imputation of any such purpose to Congress in the instant context.[18]

For these reasons, we conclude that the criminal offenses defined by the Sherman Act should be construed as including intent as an element.

---

17. The possibility that those subjected to strict liability will take extraordinary care in their dealings is frequently regarded as one advantage of a rule of strict liability. See Hall, General Principles of Criminal Law 344 (1960); LaFave & Scott, Criminal Law 222–223 (1972). However, where the conduct prescribed is difficult to distinguish from conduct permitted and indeed encouraged, as in the anti-trust context, the excessive caution spawned by a regime of strict liability will not necessarily redound to the public's benefit. The antitrust laws differ in this regard from, for example, laws designed to insure that adulterated food will not be sold to consumers. In the latter situation, excessive caution on the part of producers is entirely consistent with the legislative purpose. See United States v. Park, 421 U.S. 658, 671–672, 95 S.Ct. 1903, 1911, 44 L.Ed.2d 489 (1975).

18. Congress has recently increased the criminal penalties for violation of the Sherman Act. Individual violations are now treated as felonies punishable by a fine not to exceed $100,000, or by imprisonment for up to three years, or both. Corporate violators are subject to a $1 million fine. 15 U.S.C.A. § 1. The severity of these sanctions provides further support for our conclusion that the Sherman Act should not be construed as creating strict liability crimes. Respondents here were not prosecuted under the new penalty provisions since they were indicted prior to the December 21, 1974, effective date for the increased sanctions.

C

Having concluded that intent is a necessary element of a criminal antitrust violation, the task remaining is to treat the practical aspects of this requirement. As we have noted, the language of the Act provides minimal assistance in determining what standard of intent is appropriate and the sparse legislative history of the criminal provisions is similarly unhelpful. We must therefore turn to more general sources and traditional understandings of the nature of the element of intent in the criminal law. In so doing, we must try to avoid "the variety, disparity and confusion" of judicial definitions of the "requisite but elusive mental element" of criminal offenses. Morissette v. United States, 342 U.S. 246, 252, 72 S.Ct. 240, 244, 96 L.Ed. 288.

The ALI Model Penal Code is one source of guidance upon which the Court has relied to illuminate questions of this type. Recognizing that "*mens rea* is not a unitary concept," United States v. Freed, 401 U.S., [601,] 613, 91 S.Ct., [1112,] 1120 [, 28 L.Ed.2d 356] (BRENNAN, J., concurring in judgment), the Code enumerates four possible levels of intent—purpose, knowledge, recklessness and negligence. In dealing with the kinds of business decisions upon which the antitrust laws focus, the concepts of recklessness and negligence have no place. Our question instead is whether a criminal violation of the antitrust laws requires, in addition to proof of anticompetitive effects, a demonstration that the disputed conduct was undertaken with the "conscious object" of producing such effects or whether it is sufficient that the conduct is shown to have been undertaken with knowledge that the proscribed effects would most likely follow. While the difference between these formulations is a narrow one we conclude that action undertaken with knowledge of its probable consequences and having the requisite anticompetitive effects can be a sufficient predicate for a finding of criminal liability under the antitrust laws.

Several considerations fortify this conclusion. The element of intent in the criminal law has traditionally been viewed as a bifurcated concept embracing either the specific requirement of purpose or the more general one of knowledge or awareness.

"[I]t is now generally accepted that a person who acts (or omits to act) intends a result of his act (or omission) under two quite different circumstances: (1) when he consciously desires that result, whatever the likelihood of that result happening from his conduct; and (2) when he knew that the result is practically certain to follow from his conduct, whatever his desire may be as to that result."

LaFave & Scott, Criminal Law 196 (1972). Generally this limited distinction between knowledge and purpose has not been considered important since "there is good reason for imposing liability whether the defendant desired or merely knew of the practical certainty of the result." LaFave & Scott, supra, at 197. In either circumstance, the defendants are consciously behaving in a way the law prohibits, and such conduct is a fitting object of criminal punishment.

Nothing in our analysis of the Sherman Act persuades us that this general understanding of intent should not be applied to criminal antitrust violations such as charged here. The business behavior which is likely to give rise to criminal antitrust charges is conscious behavior normally undertaken only after a full consideration of the desired results and a weighing of the costs, benefits and risks. A requirement of proof not only of this knowledge of likely effects, but also of a conscious desire to bring them to fruition or to violate the law would seem, particularly in such a context, both unnecessarily cumulative and unduly burdensome. Where carefully planned and calculated conduct is being scrutinized in the context of a criminal prosecution, the perpetrator's knowledge of the anticipated consequences is a sufficient predicate for a finding of criminal intent.

D

When viewed in terms of this standard, the jury instructions on the price-fixing charge cannot be sustained. "A conclusive presumption [of intent], which testimony could not overthrow would effectively eliminate intent as an ingredient of the offense." *Morissette,* supra, 342 U.S., at 275, 72 S.Ct., at 256. The challenged jury instruction, as we read it, had precisely this effect; the jury was told that the requisite intent followed, *as a matter of law,* from a finding that the exchange of price information had an impact on prices. Although an effect on prices may well support an inference that the defendant had knowledge of the probability of such a consequence at the time he acted, the jury must remain free to consider additional evidence before accepting or rejecting the inference. Therefore, although it would be correct to instruct the jury that it may infer intent from an effect on prices, ultimately the decision on the issue of intent must be left to the trier of fact alone. The instruction given invaded this factfinding function.

III

* * *

[Defendants also argued that their conduct was exempt from coverage under the Sherman Act. Section 2(a) of the Robinson-Patman Act, 15 U.S.C.A. § 13(a), prohibits price discrimination by sellers among buyers when the consequence of such discrimination is an injury to competition; section 2(b) of the Act, however, exempts from the prohibition of section 2(a) situations in which discrimination is made in good faith to meet an equally low price of a competitor. Defendants argued that their exchanges of information concerning sale prices were intended to verify information that competing sellers had offered to sell at certain low prices. Since the exchanges were designed to enable the defendants to bring themselves within section 2(b) of the Robinson-Patman Act, the defendants urged, the Sherman Act should be read as exempting the activity from coverage under the Sherman Act's criminal provisions.

The Court first considered the possibility that its decision as to the intent required for criminal liability under the Sherman Act precluded conviction if the defendants believed their actions noncriminal. It concluded that a purpose of complying with the Robinson-Patman Act by exchange of price information was not inconsistent with knowledge that such exchange would have the probable effect of fixing or stabilizing prices. Given that such knowledge is the required mental state for a prosecution such as this, the defendant's purpose for engaging in the prohibited conduct would not be a defense unless it was thought of sufficient merit to justify a general exception from the Sherman Act.

The Court then concluded that the Sherman Act does not exempt from its coverage activity intended to enable sellers to bring themselves within section 2(b) of the Robinson-Patman Act.]

Accordingly, the judgment of the Court of Appeals [reversing the convictions] is

Affirmed.

MR. JUSTICE REHNQUIST concurring in part and dissenting in part.

* * *

I do not find it necessary to decide the intent which Congress required as a prerequisite for criminal liability under the Sherman Act, because I believe that the instructions given by the District Court, when considered as a whole and in connection with the objections made to them, are sufficiently close to respondent's tendered instructions so as to afford respondents no basis upon which to challenge the verdict.

MR. JUSTICE STEVENS, concurring in part and dissenting in part.

* * *

If I were fashioning a new test of criminal liability, I would require proof of a specific purpose to violate the law rather than mere knowledge that the defendants' agreement has had an adverse effect on the market. Under the lesser standard adopted by the Court, I believe MR. JUSTICE REHNQUIST is quite right in viewing the error in the trial judge's instructions as harmless. There is, of course, a theoretical possibility that defendants could engage in a practice of exchanging current price information that was sufficiently prevalent to have had a market-wide impact that they did not know about, but as a practical matter that possibility is surely remote.

PEOPLE v. LAURIA

California Court of Appeal, 1967.
251 Cal.App.2d 471, 59 Cal.Rptr. 628.

FLEMING, ASSOCIATE JUSTICE. In an investigation of call-girl activity the police focused their attention on three prostitutes actively plying their trade on call, each of whom was using Lauria's telephone answering service, presumably for business purposes.

On January 8, 1965, Stella Weeks, a policewoman, signed up for telephone service with Lauria's answering service. Mrs. Weeks, in the course of her conversation with Lauria's office manager, hinted broadly that she was a prostitute concerned with the secrecy of her activities and their concealment from the police. She was assured that the operation of the service was discreet and "about as safe as you can get." It was arranged that Mrs. Weeks need not leave her address with the answering service, but could pick up her calls and pay her bills in person.

On February 11, Mrs. Weeks talked to Lauria on the telephone and told him her business was modelling and she had been referred to the answering service by Terry, one of the three prostitutes under investigation. She complained that because of the operation of the service she had lost two valuable customers, referred to as tricks. Lauria defended his service and said that her friends had probably lied to her about having left calls for her. But he did not respond to Mrs. Weeks' hints that she needed customers in order to make money, other than to invite her to his house for a personal visit in order to get better acquainted. In the course of his talk he said "his business was taking messages."

On February 15, Mrs. Weeks talked on the telephone to Lauria's office manager and again complained of two lost calls, which she described as a $50 and a $100 trick. On investigation the office manager could find nothing wrong, but she said she would alert the switchboard operators about slip-ups on calls.

On April 1 Lauria and the three prostitutes were arrested. Lauria complained to the police that this attention was undeserved, stating that Hollywood Call Board had 60 to 70 prostitutes on its board while his own service had only 9 or 10, that he kept separate records for known or suspected prostitutes for the convenience of himself and the police. When asked if his records were available to police who might come to the office to investigate call girls, Lauria replied that they were whenever the police had a specific name. However, his service didn't "arbitrarily tell the police about prostitutes on our board. As long as they pay their bills we tolerate them." In a subsequent voluntary appearance before the Grand Jury Lauria testified he had always cooperated with the police. But he admitted he knew some of his customers were prostitutes, and he knew Terry was a prostitute because he had personally used her services, and he knew she was paying for 500 calls a month.

Lauria and the three prostitutes were indicted for conspiracy to commit prostitution, and nine overt acts were specified. Subsequently the trial court set aside the indictment as having been brought without reasonable or probable cause. (Pen.Code, § 995.) The People have appealed, claiming that a sufficient showing of an unlawful agreement to further prostitution was made.

To establish agreement, the People need show no more than a tacit, mutual understanding between coconspirators to accomplish an unlawful act. Here the People attempted to establish a conspiracy by showing that Lauria, well aware that his codefendants were prostitutes who received business calls from customers through his telephone answering service, continued to furnish them with such service. This approach attempts to equate knowledge of another's criminal activity with conspiracy to further such criminal activity, and poses the question of the criminal responsibility of a furnisher of goods or services who knows his product is being used to assist the operation of an illegal business. Under what circumstances does a supplier become a part of a conspiracy to further an illegal enterprise by furnishing goods or services which he knows are to be used by the buyer for criminal purposes?

The two leading cases on this point face in opposite directions. In United States v. Falcone, 311 U.S. 205, 61 S.Ct. 204, 85 L.Ed. 128, the sellers of large quantities of sugar, yeast, and cans were absolved from participation in a moonshining conspiracy among distillers who bought from them, while in Direct Sales Co. v. United States, 319 U.S. 703, 63 S.Ct. 1265, 87 L.Ed. 1674, a wholesaler of drugs was convicted of conspiracy to violate the federal narcotic laws by selling drugs in quantity to a codefendant physician who was supplying them to addicts. The distinction between these two cases appears primarily based on the proposition that distributors of such dangerous products as drugs are required to exercise greater discrimination in the conduct of their business than are distributors of innocuous substances like sugar and yeast.

In the earlier case, *Falcone*, the sellers' knowledge of the illegal use of the goods was insufficient by itself to make the sellers participants in a conspiracy with the distillers who bought from them. Such knowledge fell short of proof of a conspiracy, and evidence on the volume of sales was too vague to support a jury finding that respondents knew of the conspiracy from the size of the sales alone.

In the later case of *Direct Sales*, the conviction of a drug wholesaler for conspiracy to violate federal narcotic laws was affirmed on a showing that it had actively promoted the sale of morphine sulphate in quantity and had sold codefendant physician, who practiced in a small town in South Carolina, more than 300 times his normal requirements of the drug, even though it had been repeatedly warned of the dangers of unrestricted sales of the drug. The court contrasted the restricted goods involved in *Direct Sales* with the articles of free commerce involved in *Falcone:* "All articles of commerce may be put to illegal ends," said the court. "But all do not have inherently the same susceptibility to harmful and illegal use. * * * This difference is important for two purposes. One is for making certain that the seller knows the buyer's intended illegal use. The other is to show that by the sale he intends to further, promote and cooperate in it. This intent, when given effect by overt act, is the gist of conspiracy. While it is not identical with mere knowledge that another purposes unlawful action, it is not unrelated to such knowledge. * * * The step from knowledge to intent and agreement may be taken. There is more than suspicion, more than knowledge, acquiescence, carelessness, indifference, lack of concern. There is informed and interested cooperation, stimulation, instigation. And there is also a 'stake in the venture' which, even if it may not be essential, is not irrelevant to the question of conspiracy." (319 U.S. at 710–713, 63 S.Ct. at 1269–1270.)

While *Falcone* and *Direct Sales* may not be entirely consistent with each other in their full implications, they do provide us with a framework for the criminal liability of a supplier of lawful goods or services put to unlawful use. Both the element of *knowledge* of the illegal use of the goods or services and the element of *intent* to further that use must be present in order to make the supplier a participant in a criminal conspiracy.

Proof of *knowledge* is ordinarily a question of fact and requires no extended discussion in the present case. The knowledge of the supplier was sufficiently established when Lauria admitted he knew some of his customers were prostitutes and admitted he knew that Terry, an active subscriber to his service, was a prostitute. In the face of these admissions he could scarcely claim to have relied on the normal assumption an operator of a business or service is entitled to make, that his customers are behaving themselves in the eyes of the law. Because Lauria knew in fact that some of his customers were prostitutes, it is a legitimate inference he knew they were subscribing to his answering service for illegal business purposes and were using his service to make assignations for prostitution. On this record we think the prosecution is entitled to claim positive knowledge by Lauria of the use of his service to facilitate the business of prostitution.

The more perplexing issue in the case is the sufficiency of proof of *intent* to further the criminal enterprise. The element of intent may be proved either by direct evidence, or by evidence of circumstances from which an intent to further a criminal enterprise by supplying lawful goods or services may be inferred. Direct evidence of participation, such as advice from the supplier of legal goods or services to the user of those goods or services on their use for illegal purposes * * * provides the simplest case. When the intent to further and promote the criminal enterprise comes from the lips of the supplier himself, ambiguities of inference from circumstance need not trouble us. But in cases where direct proof of complicity is lacking, intent to further the conspiracy must be derived from the sale itself and its surrounding circumstances in order to establish the supplier's express or tacit agreement to join the conspiracy.

In the case at bench the prosecution argues that since Lauria knew his customers were using his service for illegal purposes but nevertheless continued to furnish it to them, he must have intended to assist them in carrying out their illegal activities. Thus through a union of knowledge and intent he became a participant in a criminal conspiracy. Essentially, the People argue that knowledge alone of the continuing use of his telephone facilities for criminal purposes provided a sufficient basis from which his intent to participate in those criminal activities could be inferred.

In examining precedents in this field we find that sometimes, but not always, the criminal intent of the supplier may be inferred from his knowledge of the unlawful use made of the product he supplies. Some consideration of characteristic patterns may be helpful.

1. Intent may be inferred from knowledge, when the purveyor of legal goods for illegal use has acquired a stake in the venture. (United States v. Falcone). For example, in Regina v. Thomas (1957), 2 All.E.R. 181, 342, a prosecution for living off the earnings of prostitution, the evidence showed that the accused, knowing the woman to be a convicted prostitute, agreed to let her have the use of his room between the hours of 9 p.m. and 2 a.m. for a charge of £3 a night. The Court of Criminal Appeal refused an appeal from the conviction, holding that when the accused rented a room at a grossly inflated rent to a prostitute for the purpose of carrying on her trade, a jury could find he was living on the earnings of prostitution.

In the present case, no proof was offered of inflated charges for the telephone answering services furnished the codefendants.

2. Intent may be inferred from knowledge, when no legitimate use for the goods or services exists. The leading California case is People v. McLaughlin, 111 Cal.App.2d 781, 245 P.2d 1076, in which the court upheld a conviction of the suppliers of horse-racing information by wire for conspiracy to promote bookmaking, when it had been established that wire-service information had no other use than to supply information needed by bookmakers to conduct illegal gambling operations.

* * *

In Shaw v. Director of Public Prosecutions, [1962] A.C. 220, the defendant was convicted of conspiracy to corrupt public morals and of living on the earnings of prostitution when he published a directory consisting almost entirely of advertisements of the names, addresses, and specialized talents of prostitutes. Publication of such a directory, said the court, could have no legitimate use and serve no other purpose than to advertise the professional services of the prostitutes whose advertisements appeared in the directory. The publisher could be deemed a participant in the profits from the business activities of his principal advertisers.

Other services of a comparable nature come to mind: the manufacturer of crooked dice and marked cards who sells his product to gambling casinos; the tipster who furnishes information on the movement of law enforcement officers to known lawbreakers. * * * In such cases the supplier must necessarily have an intent to further the illegal enterprise since there is no known honest use for his goods.

However, there is nothing in the furnishing of telephone answering service which would necessarily imply assistance in the performance of illegal activities. Nor is any inference to be derived from the use of an answering service by women, either in any particular volume of calls, or outside normal working hours. Night-club entertainers, registered nurses, faith healers, public stenographers, photographic models, and free lance substitute employees, provide examples of women in legitimate occupations whose employment might cause them to receive a volume of telephone calls at irregular hours.

3. Intent may be inferred from knowledge, when the volume of business with the buyer is grossly disproportionate to any legitimate demand, or when sales for illegal use amount to a high proportion of the seller's total business. In such cases an intent to participate in the illegal enterprise may be inferred from the quantity of the business done. For example, in *Direct Sales,* supra, the sale of narcotics to a rural physician in quantities 300 times greater than he would have normal use for provided potent evidence of an intent to further the illegal activity. In the same case the court also found significant the fact that the wholesaler had attracted as customers a disproportionately large group of physicians who had been convicted of violating the Harrison Act. In Shaw v. Director of Public Prosecutions, [1962] A.C. 220, almost the entire business of the directory came from prostitutes.

No evidence of any unusual volume of business with prostitutes was presented by the prosecution against Lauria.

Inflated charges, the sale of goods with no legitimate use, sales in inflated amounts, each may provide a fact of sufficient moment from which the intent of the seller to participate in the criminal enterprise may be inferred. In such instances participation by the supplier of legal goods to the illegal enterprise may be inferred because in one way or another the supplier has acquired a special interest in the operation of the illegal enterprise. His intent to participate in the crime of which he has knowledge may be inferred from the existence of his special interest.

Yet there are cases in which it cannot reasonably be said that the supplier has a stake in the venture or has acquired a special interest in the enterprise, but in which he has been held liable as a participant on the basis of knowledge alone. Some suggestion of this appears in *Direct Sales,* supra, where both the knowledge of the illegal use of the drugs and the intent of the supplier to aid that use were inferred. In Regina v. Bainbridge (1959), 3 W.L.R. 656 (CCA 6), a supplier of oxygen-cutting equipment to one known to intend to use it to break into a bank was convicted as an accessory to the crime. In Sykes v. Director of Public Prosecutions [1962] A.C. 528, one having knowledge of the theft of 100 pistols, 4 submachine guns, and 1960 rounds of ammunition was convicted of misprision of felony for failure to disclose the theft to the public authorities. It seems apparent from these cases that a supplier who furnishes equipment which he *knows* will be used to commit a serious crime may be deemed from that knowledge alone to have intended to produce the result. Such proof may justify an inference that the furnisher intended to aid the execution of the crime and that he thereby became a participant. For instance, we think the operator of a telephone answering service with positive knowledge that his service was being used to facilitate the extortion of ransom, the distribution of heroin, or the passing of counterfeit money who continued to furnish the service with knowledge of its use, might be chargeable on knowledge alone with participation in a scheme to extort money, to distribute narcotics, or to pass counterfeit money. The same result would follow the seller of gasoline who knew the buyer was using his product to make Molotov cocktails for terroristic use.

Logically, the same reasoning could be extended to crimes of every description. Yet we do not believe an inference of intent drawn from knowledge of criminal use properly applies to the less serious crimes classified as misdemeanors. The duty to take positive action to dissociate oneself from activities helpful to violations of the criminal law is far stronger and more compelling for felonies than it is for misdemeanors or petty offenses. In this respect, as in others, the distinction between felonies and misdemeanors, between more serious and less serious crime, retains continuing vitality. In historically the most serious felony, treason, an individual with knowledge of the treason can be prosecuted for concealing and failing to disclose it. (Pen.Code, § 38; 18 U.S.Code, § 2382.) In other felonies, both at common law and under the criminal laws of the United States, an individual knowing of the commission of a felony is criminally liable for concealing it and failing to make it known to proper authority. But this crime, known as misprision of felony, has always been limited to knowledge and concealment of felony and has never extended to misdemeanor. A similar limitation is found in the criminal liability of an accessory, which is restricted to aid in the escape of a principal who has committed or been charged with a *felony*. We believe the distinction between the obligations arising from knowledge of a felony and those arising from knowledge of a misdemeanor continues to reflect basic human feelings about the duties owed by individuals to society. Heinous crime must be stamped out, and its suppression is the responsibility of all. Venial crime and crime not evil in itself present less of a danger to society, and perhaps the benefits of their suppression through the modern equivalent of the posse, the hue and cry, the informant, and the citizen's arrest, are outweighed by the disruption to everyday life brought about by amateur law enforcement and private officiousness in relatively inconsequential delicts which do not threaten our basic security. The subject has been summarized in an English text on the criminal law: "Failure to reveal a felony to the authorities is now authoritatively determined to be misprision of felony, which is a common-law misdemeanor; misprision of treason is punishable with imprisonment for life. * * * No offence is committed in failing to disclose a misdemeanor. * * *

" 'To require everyone, without distinction, as to the nature and degree of the offence, to become an accuser, would be productive of inconvenience in exposing numbers to penal prosecutions, multiplying criminal charges, and engendering private dissension. It may sometimes be more convenient that offences should be passed over, than that all should indiscriminately be made the subject of prosecution; and a law would be considered to be harsh and impolitic, if not unjust, which compelled every party injured by a criminal act, and, still more so, to compel everyone who happened to know that another had been so injured, to make a public disclosure of the circumstances. Here, therefore, there is reason for limiting the law against mere misprisions to the concealment of such crimes as are of an aggravated complexion.' " (Criminal Law, Glanville Williams (2d ed.) p. 423.)

With respect to misdemeanors, we conclude that positive knowledge of the supplier that his products or services are being used for criminal purposes does not, without more, establish an intent of the supplier to participate in the misdemeanors. With respect to felonies, we do not decide the converse, viz. that in all cases of felony knowledge of criminal use alone may justify an inference of the supplier's intent to participate in the crime. The implications of *Falcone* make the matter uncertain with respect to those felonies which are merely prohibited wrongs. But decision on this point is not compelled, and we leave the matter open.

From this analysis of precedent we deduce the following rule: the intent of a supplier who knows of the criminal use to which his supplies are put to participate in the criminal activity connected with the use of his supplies may be established by (1) direct evidence that he intends to participate, or (2) through an inference that he intends to participate based on, (a) his special interest in the activity, or (b) the aggravated nature of the crime itself.

When we review Lauria's activities in the light of this analysis, we find no proof that Lauria took any direct action to further, encourage, or direct the call-girl activities of his codefendants and we find an absence of circumstances from which his special interest in their activities could be inferred. Neither excessive charges for standardized services, or the furnishing of services without a legitimate use, nor any unusual quantity of business with call girls, are present. The offense which he is charged with furthering is a misdemeanor, a category of crime which has never been made a required subject of positive disclosure to public authority. Under these circumstances, although proof of Lauria's knowledge of the criminal activities of his patrons was sufficient to charge him with that fact, there was insufficient evidence that he intended to further their criminal activities, and hence insufficient proof of his participation in a criminal conspiracy with his codefendants to further prostitution. Since the conspiracy centered around the activities of Lauria's telephone answering service, the charges against his codefendants likewise fail for want of proof.

In absolving Lauria of complicity in a criminal conspiracy we do not wish to imply that the public authorities are without remedies to combat modern manifestations of the world's oldest profession. Licensing of telephone answering services under the police power, together with the revocation of licenses for the toleration of prostitution, is a possible civil remedy. The furnishing of telephone answering service in aid of prostitution could be made a crime. (Cf. Pen.Code, § 316, which makes it a misdemeanor to let an apartment with knowledge of its use for prostitution.) Other solutions will doubtless occur to vigilant public authorities if the problem of call-girl activity needs further suppression.

The order is affirmed.

MODEL PENAL CODE, COMMENT TO 5.03, 107–10 *
(Tent. Draft No. 10, 1960).

The Requirement of Purpose. The purpose requirement is crucial to the resolution of the difficult problems presented when a charge of conspiracy is leveled against a person whose relationship to a criminal plan is essentially peripheral. Typical is the case of the person who sells sugar to the producers of illicit whiskey. He may have little interest in the success of the distilling operation and be motivated mainly by the desire to make the normal profit of an otherwise lawful sale. To be criminally liable, of course, he must at least have knowledge of the use to which the materials are being put, but the difficult issue presented is whether knowingly facilitating the commission of a crime ought to be sufficient, absent a true purpose to advance the criminal end. In the case of vendors conflicting interests are also involved: that of the vendors in freedom to engage in gainful and otherwise lawful activities without policing their vendees, and that of the community in preventing behavior that facilitates the commission of crimes. The decisions are in conflict, although many of those requiring purpose properly emphasize that it can be inferred from such circumstances as, for example, quantity sales, the seller's initiative or encouragement, continuity of the relationship, and the contraband nature of the materials sold. The considerations are the same whether the charge be conspiracy or complicity in the substantive crime, and the Institute has resolved them, in the complicity provisions of the Code, in favor of requiring a purpose to advance the criminal end. Under the proposed Draft, the same purpose requirement that governs complicity is essential for conspiracy: the actor must have "the purpose of promoting or facilitating" the commission of the crime.

The requirement of purpose would also play a crucial role in the case where a charge of conspiracy is based on membership in an organization having both lawful and criminal objectives, as in the Communist cases. The defendant's membership and dues may encourage and assist the organization in pursuing all its objects, legal and illegal. He would not be guilty of conspiracy, however, unless he had the purpose of promoting or facilitating the attainment of a criminal objective. Of course, knowledge of that objective and conscious assistance may justify an inference of such purpose, but they would not be independently sufficient to establish liability.

* * *

It is worth noting, further, that as related to those elements of substantive crimes that consist of proscribed conduct or undesirable results of conduct, the Draft requires purposeful behavior for guilt of conspiracy, regardless of the state of mind required by the definition of the substantive crime. If the crime is defined in terms of prohibited conduct, such as the sale of narcotics, the actor's purpose must be to promote or facilitate the engaging in such conduct by himself or another. If it is defined in terms of a result of conduct, such as homicide, his purpose must be to promote or facilitate the production of that result.

Thus, it would not be sufficient, as it is under the attempt draft, if the actor only believed that the result would be produced but did not consciously plan or desire to produce it. For example—to use the same illustration as the comments on attempt—if two persons plan to destroy a building by detonating a bomb, though they know and believe that there are inhabitants in the building who will be killed by the explosion, they are nevertheless guilty only of a conspiracy to destroy the building and not of a conspiracy to kill the inhabitants. While this result may seem unduly restrictive from the viewpoint of the completed crime, it is necessitated by the extremely preparatory behavior that may be involved in conspiracy. Had the crime been completed or had the preparation progressed even to the stage of an attempt, the result would be otherwise. As to the attempt, knowledge or belief that the inhabitants would be killed would suffice. As to the completed crime, the complicity draft covers the matter, despite its general requirement of a purpose to promote or facilitate the commission of the crime, by the special provision of Section 2.06(4). This provides that where causing a particular result is an element of a crime, a person is an accomplice in the crime if he was an accomplice in the behavior that caused the result and shared the same purpose or knowledge with respect to the result that is required by the definition of the crime.

A fortiori, where recklessness or negligence suffices for the actor's culpability with respect to a result element of a substantive crime—where, for example, homicide through negligence is made criminal—there could not be a conspiracy to commit that crime. This should be distinguished, however, from a crime defined in terms of conduct that creates a risk of harm, such as reckless driving or driving above a certain speed limit. In this situation the conduct rather than any result it may produce is the element of the crime, and it would suffice for guilt of conspiracy that the actor's purpose is to promote or facilitate such conduct—for example, if he urged the driver of the car to go faster and faster.

Note

In United States v. Feola, 420 U.S. 671, 95 S.Ct. 1255, 43 L.Ed.2d 541 (1975), the defendants were convicted of assaulting federal officers in the performance of the officers' duties, prohibited by 18 U.S.C.A. § 111, and of conspiring to commit that offense, in violation of the general conspiracy statute, 18 U.S.C.A. § 371. The Supreme Court first held that the substantive offense did not require proof of awareness of the fact that the victims were federal officers; this aspect of the case is discussed in note 1 on page 317, supra. The Court then turned to the question whether the Government was nonetheless required under the conspiracy charge to show that the defendants were aware of the victims' status as federal officers:

> [R]espondent relies solely on the line of cases commencing with United States v. Crimmins, 123 F.2d 271 (CA2 1941), for the principle that the Government must prove "antifederal" intent in order to establish liability under § 371. In *Crimmins,* the defendant had been found guilty of conspiring to receive stolen bonds that had been transported in interstate commerce. Upon review, the Court of Appeals pointed out that the evidence failed to establish that Crimmins actually knew the stolen bonds had moved into the State. Accepting for the sake of argument the assumption that such knowledge was not necessary to sustain a conviction on the substantive offense, Judge Learned Hand nevertheless concluded that to permit conspiratorial liability where the conspirators were ignorant of the federal implications of their acts would be to enlarge their agreement beyond its terms as they understood them. He capsulized the distinction in what has become well known as his "traffic light" analogy:

> > "While one may, for instance, be guilty of running past a traffic light of whose existence one is ignorant, one cannot be guilty of conspiring to run past such a light, for one cannot agree to run past a light unless one supposes that there is a light to run past." Id., at 273.

> Judge Hand's attractive, but perhaps seductive, analogy has received a mixed reception in the Courts of Appeals. The Second Circuit, of course, has followed it; others have rejected it. It appears that most have avoided it by the simple expedient of inferring the requisite knowledge from the scope of the conspiratorial venture. We conclude that the analogy, though effective prose, is, as applied to the facts before us, bad law.

> The question posed by the traffic light analogy is not before us, just as it was not before the Second Circuit in *Crimmins.* Criminal liability, of course, may be imposed on one who runs a traffic light regardless of whether he harbored the "evil intent" of disobeying the light's command; whether he drove so recklessly as to be unable to perceive the light; whether, thinking he was observing all traffic rules, he simply failed to notice the light; or whether, having been reared elsewhere, he thought that the light was only an ornament. Traffic violations generally fall into that category of offenses that dispense with a *mens rea* requirement. See United States v. Dotterweich, 320 U.S. 277, 64 S.Ct. 134, 88 L.Ed. 48 (1943). These laws embody the social judgment that it is fair to punish one who intentionally engages in conduct that creates a risk to others, even though no risk is intended or the actor, through no fault of his own, is completely unaware of the existence of any risk. The traffic light analogy poses the question

whether it is fair to punish parties to an agreement to engage intentionally in apparently innocent conduct where the unintended result of engaging in that conduct is the violation of a criminal statute.

But this case does not call upon us to answer this question, and we decline to do so, just as we have once before. United States v. Freed, 401 U.S., at 609 n. 14, 91 S.Ct. at 1118. We note in passing, however, that the analogy comes close to stating what has been known as the "*Powell* doctrine," originating in People v. Powell, 63 N.Y. 88 (1875), to the effect that a conspiracy, to be criminal, must be animated by a corrupt motive or a motive to do wrong. Under this principle, such a motive could be easily demonstrated if the underlying offense involved an act clearly wrongful in itself; but it had to be independently demonstrated if the acts agreed to were wrongful solely because of statutory proscription. See Note, Developments in the Law—Criminal Conspiracy, 72 Harv.L.Rev. 920, 936–937 (1959). Interestingly, Judge Hand himself was one of the more severe critics of the *Powell* doctrine.

That Judge Hand should reject the *Powell* doctrine and then create the *Crimmins* doctrine seems curious enough. Fatal to the latter, however, is the fact that it was announced in a case to which it could not have been meant to apply. In *Crimmins,* the substantive offense, namely, the receipt of stolen securities that had been in interstate commerce, proscribed clearly wrongful conduct. Such conduct could not be engaged in without an intent to accomplish the forbidden result. So, too, it is with assault, the conduct forbidden by the substantive statute, § 111, presently before us. One may run a traffic light "of whose existence one is ignorant," but assaulting another "of whose existence one is ignorant," probably would require unearthly intervention. Thus, the traffic light analogy, even if it were a correct statement of the law, is inapt, for the conduct proscribed by the substantive offense, here assault, is not of the type outlawed without regard to the intent of the actor to accomplish the result that is made criminal. If the analogy has any vitality at all, it is to conduct of the latter variety; that, however, is a question we save for another day. We hold here only that where a substantive offense embodies only a requirement of *mens rea* as to each of its elements, the general federal conspiracy statute requires no more.

* * * Our decisions have identified two independent values served by the law of conspiracy. The first is protection of society from the dangers of concerted criminal activity. * * * That individuals know that their planned joint venture violates federal as well as state law seems totally irrelevant to that purpose of conspiracy law which seeks to protect society from the dangers of concerted criminal activity. Given the level of criminal intent necessary to sustain conviction for the substantive offense, the act of agreement to commit the crime is no less opprobrious and no less dangerous because of the absence of knowledge of a fact unnecessary to the formation of criminal intent. Indeed, unless imposition of an "anti-federal" knowledge requirement serves social purposes external to the law of conspiracy of which we are unaware, its imposition here would serve only to make it more difficult to obtain convictions on charges of conspiracy, a policy with no apparent purpose.

The second aspect is that conspiracy is an inchoate crime. This is to say, that, although the law generally makes criminal only antisocial conduct, at some point in the continuum between preparation and consummation, the likelihood of a commission of an act is sufficiently great and the criminal intent sufficiently well formed to justify the intervention of the criminal law. See Note, Developments in the Law—Criminal Conspiracy, 72 Harv.L.Rev., at 923–925. The law of conspiracy identifies the agreement to engage in a criminal venture as an event of sufficient threat to social order to permit the imposition of criminal sanctions for the agreement alone, plus an overt act in pursuit of it, regardless of whether the crime agreed upon actually is committed. United States v. Bayer, 331 U.S. 532, 542, 67 S.Ct. 1394, 1399, 91 L.Ed. 1654 (1947). Criminal intent has crystallized, and the likelihood of actual, fulfilled commission warrants preventive action.

Again, we do not see how imposition of a strict "anti-federal" scienter requirement would relate to this purpose of conspiracy law. Given the level of intent needed to carry out the substantive offense, we fail to see how the agreement is any less blameworthy or constitutes less of a danger to society solely because the participants are unaware which body of law they intend to violate. Therefore, we again conclude that imposition of a requirement of knowledge of those facts that serve only to establish federal jurisdiction would render it more difficult to serve the policy behind the law of conspiracy without serving any other apparent social policy.

420 U.S. at 689–94, 95 S.Ct. at 1266–69, 43 L.Ed.2d at 555–558.

2. MODEL STATUTORY FORMULATIONS

The Model Penal Code, in the provisions reprinted in this subsection, offers a comprehensive statutory framework for criminal conspiracy law. The particular framework offered by the Code has certain important substantive implications. It is based upon what is sometimes called a "unilateral" approach to conspiracy liability. This unilateral approach focuses upon the conduct that is necessary to establish the culpability of each actor rather than upon the conduct of the entire group of which the actor might be regarded as a part; see the comment to Section 5.03(1), reprinted at page 606, supra.

MODEL PENAL CODE *
(Official Draft, 1985).

Section 5.03. Criminal Conspiracy

(1) *Definition of Conspiracy.* A person is guilty of conspiracy with another person or persons to commit a crime if with the purpose of promoting or facilitating its commission he:

(a) agrees with such other person or persons that they or one or more of them will engage in conduct which constitutes such crime or an attempt or solicitation to commit such crime; or

(b) agrees to aid such other person or persons in the planning or commission of such crime or of an attempt or solicitation to commit such crime.

(2) *Scope of Conspiratorial Relationship.* If a person guilty of conspiracy, as defined by Subsection (1) of this Section, knows that a person with whom he conspires to commit a crime has conspired with another person or persons to commit the same crime, he is guilty of conspiring with such other person or persons, whether or not he knows their identity, to commit such crime.

(3) *Conspiracy With Multiple Criminal Objectives.* If a person conspires to commit a number of crimes, he is guilty of only one conspiracy so long as such multiple crimes are the object of the same agreement or continuous conspiratorial relationship.

* * *

(5) *Overt Act.* No person may be convicted of conspiracy to commit a crime, other than a felony of the first or second degree, unless an overt act in pursuance of such conspiracy is alleged and proved to have been done by him or by a person with whom he conspired.

(6) *Renunciation of Criminal Purpose.* It is an affirmative defense that the actor, after conspiring to commit a crime, thwarted the success of the conspiracy, under circumstances manifesting a complete and voluntary renunciation of his criminal purpose.

(7) *Duration of Conspiracy.* For purposes of Section 1.06(4):

(a) conspiracy is a continuing course of conduct which terminates when the crime or crimes which are its object are committed or the agreement that they be committed is abandoned by the defendant and by those with whom he conspired; and

(b) such abandonment is presumed if neither the defendant nor anyone with whom he conspired does any overt act in pursuance of the conspiracy during the applicable period of limitation; and

(c) if an individual abandons the agreement, the conspiracy is terminated as to him only if and when he advises those with whom he conspired of his abandonment or he informs the law enforcement authorities of the existence of the conspiracy and of his participation therein.

Section 5.04   Incapacity, Irresponsibility or Immunity of Party to Solicitation or Conspiracy

(1) Except as provided in Subsection (2) of this Section, it is immaterial to the liability of a person who solicits or conspires with another to commit a crime that:

(a) he or the person whom he solicits or with whom he conspires does not occupy a particular position or have a particular characteristic which is an element of such crime, if he believes that one of them does; or

(b) the person whom he solicits or with whom he conspires is irresponsible or has an immunity to prosecution or conviction for the commission of the crime.

(2) It is a defense to a charge of solicitation or conspiracy to commit a crime that if the criminal object were achieved, the actor would not be guilty of a crime under the law defining the offense or as an accomplice under Section 2.06(5) or 2.06(6)(a) or (6)(b).

Section 5.05. Grading of Criminal * * * Conspiracy; Mitigation in Cases of Lesser Danger * * *

(1) *Grading.* Except as otherwise provided in this Section, * * * conspiracy [is a crime of] the same grade and degree as the most serious offense that is * * * an object of the conspiracy. * * *

(2) *Mitigation.* If the particular conduct charged to constitute a criminal * * * conspiracy is so inherently unlikely to result or culminate in the commission of a crime that neither such conduct nor the actor presents a public danger warranting the grading of such offense under this Section, the Court shall exercise its power under Section 6.12 to enter judgment and impose sentence for a crime of lower grade or degree or, in extreme cases, may dismiss the prosecution.

* * *

Notes and Questions

1. How should criminal conspiracy be graded for purposes of punishment? Compare the approach of Section 5.05 of the Model Penal Code with that of Section 15.02(d) of the Texas Penal Code, which provides that a criminal conspiracy is graded as one category lower than the most serious offense that is the object of the conspiracy.

2. Traditionally, the crime of conspiracy has included not only agreements to commit felonies and misdemeanors but also combinations to commit "unlawful" acts or lawful acts by "unlawful" means, even if these acts or means were not criminal. It has been said, however, that this has been interpreted to encompass only agreements to engage in conduct that is patently fraudulent, prejudicial to the public welfare, or so oppressive of individuals as to be injurious to the public welfare. Developments in the Law—Criminal Conspiracy, 72 Harv.L.Rev. 922, 942–44 (1959). This approach is still reflected in some state statutes, such as Section 182(5) of the California Penal Code which makes criminal any conspiracy "to commit any act injurious to the public health, to public morals, or to pervert or obstruct justice, or the due administration of the Laws." In Musser v. Utah, 333 U.S. 95, 68 S.Ct. 397, 92 L.Ed. 562 (1948), the Supreme Court indicated that a Utah statute prohibiting conspiracies "to commit any act injurious to the public health, to public morals, or to trade or commerce, or for the perversion or obstruction of justice or the due administration of the

laws" might be unconstitutionally vague. In remanding the case to permit the state court to consider this question, the majority stated:

> [The statute] would seem to be warrant for conviction for agreement to do almost any act which a judge and jury might find at the moment contrary to his or its notion of what was good for health, morals, trade, commerce, justice or order.

333 U.S. at 97, 68 S.Ct. at 398, 92 L.Ed. at 565. The state supreme court found the statute unconstitutional. State v. Musser, 118 Utah 537, 223 P.2d 193 (1950). See also State v. Bowling, 5 Ariz.App. 436, 427 P.2d 928 (1967), holding invalid a similar statute. Compare the Model Penal Code formulation of the crime of conspiracy at page 643, supra.

3. RICO: AN ALTERNATIVE TO TRADITIONAL CONSPIRACY LAW

Among the justifications frequently offered for the continued availability of the crime of conspiracy is the need for an effective means to meet the threat posed by organized crime. The Racketeer Influenced and Corrupt Organizations Act of 1970 (or RICO), Pub.L. 91–452, codified as 18 U.S.C.A. § 1961 et seq. was enacted to facilitate the federal attack on organized crime. Its popularity with federal prosecutors is suggested in the title and content of the article: Tarlow, RICO: The New Darling of the Prosecutor's Nursery, 49 Fordham L.Rev. 165 (1980). The law's purpose is:

> the imposition of enhanced criminal penalties * * * to provide new legal remedies for all types of organized criminal behavior, that is, enterprise criminality—from simple political to sophisticated white collar crime schemes to traditional Mafia-type endeavors.

Blakey & Gettings, Racketeer Influenced and Corrupt Organizations (RICO): Basic Concepts—Criminal and Civil Remedies, 53 Temp.L.Q. 1009, 1013–14 (1980).

RICO aims at "racketeering activity" which is defined as any act chargeable under a vast array of state law, e.g., murder, kidnapping, bribery, drug dealing, gambling, etc., or indictable under specified federal provisions, e.g., statutes relating to certain thefts, bribery, extortion, securities fraud, drug dealing, etc. The statute outlaws, inter alia, the use of income derived from a "pattern of racketeering activity" to acquire an interest in or establish an enterprise affecting interstate commerce, conducting an enterprise through a pattern of racketeering activity, or conspiring to violate any of these provisions.

A "pattern of racketeering activity" requires a showing of at least two acts of racketeering activity with the last being performed not more than 10 years after the prior. An enterprise can be an individual or any association of individuals even though they do not constitute a legal entity. The government's task is to show that the pattern of racketeering activity was conducted through the enterprise. United States v. Turkette, 452 U.S. 576, 592, 101 S.Ct. 2524, 2533, 69 L.Ed.2d 246, 260 (1981). In addition:

there must be a nexus between the enterprise, the defendant, and the pattern of racketeering activity. The mere fact that a defendant works for a legitimate enterprise and commits racketeering acts while on the business premises does not establish that the affairs of the enterprise have been conducted "through" a pattern of racketeering activity. Similarly, a defendant's mere association with a lawful enterprise whose affairs are conducted through a pattern of racketeering activity in which he is not personally engaged does not establish his guilt under RICO.

United States v. Cauble, 706 F.2d 1322, 1332 (5th Cir.1983).

As is suggested by the brief outline above, RICO is a very complex provision. The principal case focuses on the relationship between RICO and traditional conspiracy doctrine. Many of the benefits and problems which have been discussed in connection with conspiracy are obviously present in any RICO prosecution. Most notably, with respect to the benefits, RICO resembles conspiracy in that it also is designed to facilitate the prosecution of persons who are pursuing objectives elsewhere defined as criminal. The court in *Sutherland* argued that RICO represents a Congressional effort to expand the reach of traditional conspiracy charges by establishing a new substantive crime around which a conspiracy might center. As to problems, they are those which inhere in a group trial: the danger of having the words and actions of some defendants tarring others without regard to whether the legal principles authorizing such attribution have been satisfied. Whether the nation needs both RICO and traditional conspiracy charges is an issue that will continue to be the subject of lively debate.

UNITED STATES v. SUTHERLAND

United States Court of Appeals, Fifth Circuit, 1981.
656 F.2d 1181, cert. denied, 455 U.S. 949, 102 S.Ct. 1451,
71 L.Ed.2d 663 (1982).

RANDALL, CIRCUIT JUDGE:

* * *

[The defendants, Glen Sutherland, Grace Walker and Edward Maynard, appeal their conviction for a RICO conspiracy to violate § 1962(c) making it unlawful for any person associated with an "enterprise" affecting interstate commerce to participate in the enterprise's affairs through a "pattern of racketeering activity" (bribery of a state official). Sutherland was an El Paso Municipal Court judge. He, Walker and Maynard were alleged to have agreed that the latter two would collect traffic tickets from their friends and associates, together with the fine and a small ($10) premium, and deliver them to the judge. The judge would have the cases transferred to his docket, favorably dispose of them, and split the funds collected with whichever of the other defendants had brought in the tickets. There was no claim that Maynard and Walker had agreed. The government's evidence did not show that Walker and Maynard knew, or should have known of the other's existence. Rather the evidence indicated there were two unrelated conspiracies with Sutherland-Walker going on between 1975 and 1977, and Sutherland-Maynard being limited to 1979.]

II. THE SUFFICIENCY OF THE EVIDENCE

All three defendants challenge the sufficiency of the evidence to support their convictions under 18 U.S.C. § 1962(d). First, each argues that the government failed to establish a "pattern of racketeering activity" since the evidence does not specifically demonstrate "at least two acts of racketeering activity," as required by 18 U.S.C. § 1961(5).[4] Second, Walker argues that the evidence does not sufficiently establish any agreement between herself and Sutherland. In considering these arguments we must read the evidence in the light most favorable to the government, and must reverse the convictions if we find that any reasonable jury thus reading the evidence must necessarily have entertained a reasonable doubt as to the defendants' guilt.

A. THE REQUISITE "TWO ACTS OF RACKETEERING ACTIVITY"

The government proved that a number of specific traffic tickets were (1) given by traffic violators to either Walker or Maynard, and (2) favorably disposed of by Sutherland in his capacity as municipal judge. Through the testimony of Sally Kalastro (a co-worker with Walker at the time of the events in question), the government identified twenty-five individual tickets that had been accepted by Walker. Through the testimony of several persons who submitted tickets to Maynard (including several bogus tickets prepared for the purpose of the investigation), the government identified fifteen individual tickets that had been accepted by Maynard. In the case of each ticket, the government introduced evidence (primarily from Municipal Court records) to establish its favorable disposition (typically a finding of not guilty) by Sutherland.

[The defendants argued that there was no evidence that any specific ticket was the subject of bribery, or, indeed that a particular ticket and money were delivered by Walker or Maynard to Sutherland

---

4. All parties, as well as the district court, refer to the requisite "two acts of racketeering activity." Strictly speaking, the government need not have proven that two such acts were in fact committed. This case was not brought under the substantive RICO provisions, but is instead based on the defendants' *conspiracy* to violate such provisions. The government need not prove in a conspiracy case that a substantive crime was actually committed, but instead need demonstrate that some "overt act" was taken in furtherance of a conspiracy to commit a substantive crime. In particular, the government need show only that "at least one conspirator committed at least one overt act in furtherance of the conspiracy." *United States v. Fuiman,* 546 F.2d 1155, 1158 (5th Cir.), *cert. denied,* 434 U.S. 856, 98 S.Ct. 176, 54 L.Ed.2d 127 (1977). The overt act need not itself constitute a substantive crime; any act, even if seemingly innocent in itself, is sufficient to support a conspiracy conviction if taken in furtherance of the conspiracy. In this case the government's reliance on specific acts of racketeering activity is understandable, for such evidence constitutes convincing circumstantial evidence of an agreement to violate the substantive RICO provision at issue. Still, however, we find the government's exclusive reliance on these acts for the necessary "overt act" somewhat perplexing in light of the decision (whether made by the government or by the grand jury) not to indict the defendants for a substantive RICO offense.

who, in exchange, favorably disposed of the ticket. The court, however, was satisfied that a conspiracy can be established solely on circumstantial evidence and that the evidence here, although circumstantial, was substantial. There was direct evidence that many tickets were given Walker and Maynard which were later, in a highly irregular manner, the subject of dismissal or acquittal by Sutherland. There were many phone calls and meetings between the judge and each of the other defendants. Walker had confessed the scheme to a co-worker, Kalastro, and Maynard had referred to "fixing" the tickets.]

* * *

B. The Agreement

Walker argues that the government's evidence was insufficient to establish an agreement with Sutherland to violate 18 U.S.C. § 1962(c). Her argument seems similar to that advanced by all the defendants with respect to the requisite two acts of racketeering. In particular, Walker argues that the government advanced no direct evidence of any agreement between Sutherland and herself.

The government was indeed obligated to establish an actual agreement to commit a substantive RICO offense. "To be convicted as a member of an enterprise conspiracy, an individual, by his words or actions, must have objectively manifested an agreement to participate, directly or indirectly, in the affairs of an enterprise through the commission of two or more predicate crimes." [United States v.] *Elliott,* [571 F.2d 880, 903, *cert. denied,* 439 U.S. 953, 99 S.Ct. 349, 58 L.Ed.2d 344 (1978)] (emphasis deleted). In this case, however, we find that the government did introduce direct evidence of such an agreement: Kalastro's testimony as to Walker's admission of a ticket-fixing scheme between herself and Sutherland. Moreover, that agreement, like the predicate crimes discussed above, may be established by circumstantial evidence. In this case an agreement is sufficiently established by the large number (twenty-five) of individual racketeering acts which the jury was entitled to find were committed by Walker and Sutherland. "Where, as here, the evidence establishes that each defendant, over a period of years, committed several acts of racketeering activity in furtherance of the enterprise's affairs, the inference of an agreement to do so is unmistakable." *Elliott, supra,* at 903.

III. The Multiple Conspiracy Doctrine and Rico

A. The Trial of Multiple Conspiracies Under a Single RICO "Enterprise Conspiracy" Count

It is now well settled that a material variance between the indictment and the government's evidence is created by the government's proof of multiple conspiracies under an indictment alleging a single conspiracy.[5] This "multiple conspiracy doctrine" is commonly illustrat-

---

5. In this case the government introduced no evidence from which a jury could conclude that a single conspiracy existed among the defendants. This case should be distinguished, therefore, from cases in which the record contains, in addition to

ed by the Supreme Court's decision in *Kotteakos v. United States,* 328 U.S. 750, 66 S.Ct. 1239, 90 L.Ed. 1557 (1946). The indictment in *Kotteakos* alleged a single conspiracy to obtain government loans by making fraudulent representations, but the government's proof at trial, by its own admission, demonstrated eight separate conspiracies. The common element in these conspiracies consisted solely of one man who had directed each group; aside from this single defendant, there was no connection among the various agreements. Despite their similar objectives and despite their common leadership, none of the *Kotteakos* conspiracies aided or benefited from the others, and no member of the various conspiracies (other than the leader) was aware of the others. As the Court aptly described these multiple conspiracies, the pattern established by the government consisted of "separate spokes meeting in a common center" but "without the rim of the wheel to enclose the spokes." 328 U.S. at 755, 66 S.Ct. at 1243. Absent some connection (the rim) among the various conspirators (the spokes), the government's proof established multiple conspiracies. The Court held that such proof created a material variance with an indictment charging a single conspiracy and, as such, was reversible error unless the defendants' substantial rights had not been affected.[6]

evidence of multiple conspiracies, sufficient evidence to support a finding of a single conspiracy. If the government sufficiently supports its charge of single conspiracy, evidence at trial of multiple conspiracies does not of itself create a material variance with the indictment; at most, such evidence creates a fact question and entitles the defendants to a jury instruction on the possibility of multiple conspiracies.

6. A strong argument can be made that a variance between a single conspiracy indictment and evidence of multiple conspiracies should be treated not as a "variance" problem at all, but rather as a "misjoinder" question under Federal Rule of Criminal Procedure 8(b). Rule 8(b)—which was enacted *after* the Supreme Court's decision in *Kotteakos*—is aimed at precisely the problem faced in that case: the transference of guilt among defendants who should not have been joined together in a single trial. The treatment of the multiple conspiracy doctrine as a variance issue despite the subsequent development of Rule 8(b) arguably creates a serious anomaly in the [law]. If the government indicts several defendants under a single conspiracy count yet proves multiple conspiracies at [trial], a material variance results and the defendants are each entitled to a new trial [if] they can show *that their substantial [rights] were affected by the variance.* If, [howeve]r, the government indicts several [defend]ants under multiple conspiracy counts (or alleges facts in the indictment that amount to multiple conspiracies) and the district court nevertheless refuses to sever the trial, the defendants are each entitled to a new trial *without any showing of prejudice,* for misjoinder under Rule 8(b) is inherently prejudicial. *See, e.g., United States v. Levine,* 546 F.2d 658, 662 (5th Cir. 1977). The end result of the separate development of these two lines of authority— one under variance doctrine and the other under Rule 8(b)—means that the trial of multiple conspiracies is treated differently on appeal depending on whether the government fails to introduce evidence of a single conspiracy at trial (*i.e.,* a variance, requiring reversal if substantial rights are affected) or instead fails in the indictment to allege facts sufficient to constitute a single conspiracy (*i.e.,* a misjoinder under Rule 8(b), requiring reversal in all cases).

As difficult as this anomaly may be to justify, we have no choice but to continue to follow it. In *Schaffer v. United States,* 362 U.S. 511, 80 S.Ct. 945, 4 L.Ed.2d 921 (1960), the Supreme Court held that the propriety of joinder under Rule 8(b) is to be judged according to the language of the indictment, not according to the government's proof at trial. So long as the indictment alleges facts that amount to a single conspiracy, it matters not—as far as Rule 8(b) is concerned—that the government fails to introduce at trial any proof of a single conspiracy. * * *

In this case the government has by its own admission, as in *Kotteakos,* introduced no evidence of a single conspiracy but has instead rested its case on two distinct multiple conspiracies. The government did not attempt at trial to prove an agreement among all three defendants, but instead sought to establish separate conspiracies comprised of (1) Walker and Sutherland, and (2) Maynard and Sutherland. Like the multiple conspiracies in *Kotteakos,* these agreements share a common conspirator and similar objectives, but are otherwise unrelated. The government does not suggest that either bribery scheme was dependent on or benefited from the other, and does not dispute the defendants' contentions that neither Walker nor Maynard knew or should have known of the other. "If there is not some interaction between those conspirators who form the spokes of the wheel as to at least one common illegal object, the 'wheel' is incomplete, and two conspiracies rather than one are charged." *United States v. Levine,* 546 F.2d 658, 663 (5th Cir.1977).

Of course, the government need not always demonstrate an actual agreement among the various conspirators, or even actual knowledge of each other, in order to establish a single conspiracy. In *Blumenthal v. United States,* 332 U.S. 539, 68 S.Ct. 248, 92 L.Ed. 154 (1947), the Supreme Court recognized that in some cases the interdependent nature of the criminal enterprise is such that each conspirator had to have realized that it extended beyond his individual role. This form of conspiracy is often described as a "chain" rather than a "wheel." Since the success of the criminal scheme depends on the success of each link in the chain, "[a]n individual associating himself with a 'chain' conspiracy knows that it has a 'scope' and that for its success it requires an organization wider than may be disclosed by his personal participation." *United States v. Elliott, supra,* at 901, *quoting United States v. Agueci,* 310 F.2d 817, 827 (2d Cir.1962), *cert. denied,* 372 U.S. 959, 83 S.Ct. 1013, 10 L.Ed.2d 11 (1963). The government does not contend that the case at bar is a "chain" conspiracy, and the evidence does not suggest one. Indeed, a chain conspiracy would be difficult to imagine on the facts of this case: while two people may in fact conspire together to bribe a single judge, there is no reason why one who has individually so acted must necessarily have assumed that others have also bribed the same judge.

The government does not defend its joint trial in this case on the basis of traditional conspiracy law, *i.e.,* by arguing either that the evidence connected the spokes of a wheel conspiracy by common knowledge or agreement, or that the evidence demonstrates a chain conspiracy. Instead, the government argues that despite the apparent relevance to this case of the traditional multiple conspiracy doctrine, the defendants were properly tried together for a single "enterprise conspiracy" under RICO. The government contends, in brief, that a single conspiracy to violate a substantive RICO provision may be comprised of a pattern of agreements that absent RICO would constitute multiple conspiracies. The government contends that this is so even where, as here, there is no agreement of any kind between the members of the two separate conspiracies. According to the government, these otherwise multiple conspiracies are tied together by the RICO "enterprise:" so long as the object of each conspiracy is participation in the same enterprise in violation of RICO, it matters not that the different conspiracies are otherwise unrelated. Thus, the government argues that it need not demonstrate any connection between Walker and Maynard because the two conspiracies at issue each involved the same RICO enterprise—the Municipal Court of the City of El Paso.

For this proposition the government relies on *United States v. Elliott, supra.* We held in *Elliott* that a group of defendants who could not have been tried for a single conspiracy to violate any particular predicate crime could nevertheless be tried for a single conspiracy to violate RICO. *Elliott* involved six defendants who had committed a variety of unrelated offenses with no common purpose or agreement as to any of the various crimes. We explained:

> Applying pre-RICO concepts to the facts of this case, we doubt that a single conspiracy could be demonstrated. Foster had no contact with Delph and Taylor during the life of the alleged conspiracy. Delph and Taylor, so far as the evidence revealed, had no contact with Recea Hawkins. The activities allegedly embraced by the illegal agreement in this case are simply too diverse [unrelated acts involving arson, murder, theft, drugs, and obstruction of justice] to be tied together on the theory that participation in one activity necessarily implied awareness of others.

571 F.2d at 902. Despite these facts, we upheld the government's joint trial of the *Elliott* defendants on a single conspiracy count. We defined the RICO enterprise in *Elliott* to consist of at least five persons who joined together to commit crime for profit—"a myriopod criminal network, loosely connected but connected nonetheless." 571 F.2d at 899. Since the defendants had conspired together to participate in that enterprise through a pattern of racketeering activity, we upheld their joint trial despite the absence of an agreement as to any particular predicate crime. We held, in short, that "[RICO's] effect in this case is to free the government from the strictures of the multiple conspiracy doctrine and to allow the joint trial of many persons accused of diversified crimes." 571 F.2d at 900.

Read out of context, without attention to the facts of the case or to the court's rationale, *Elliott* does seem to support the government's position—*i.e.,* that the defendants' participation in the same RICO enterprise is enough to tie otherwise multiple conspiracies together even where, as here, there is no agreement of any kind between the members of the two separate conspiracies.[7] Indeed, *Elliott* has been

---

7. The government's interpretation rests on some admittedly broad language in *Elliott* that suggests that RICO was intended to alter traditional conspiracy con-

cepts. For example, we stated in *Elliott* that

> through RICO, Congress intended to authorize the single prosecution of a multi-

thus read by some courts and commentators (and, as so read, has been uniformly criticized).

To put the *Elliott* holding in its proper perspective, we quote our explanation of that holding at length:

> Under the general federal conspiracy statute, "the precise nature and extent of the conspiracy must be determined by reference to the agreement which embraces and defines its objects. Whether the object of a single agreement is to commit one or many crimes, it is in either case that agreement which constitutes the conspiracy which the statute punishes." *Braverman v. United States,* 317 U.S. 49, 53, 63 S.Ct. 99, 102, 87 L.Ed. 23 (1942). In the context of organized crime, this principle inhibited mass prosecutions because a single agreement or "common objective" cannot be inferred from the commission of highly diverse crimes by apparently unrelated individuals. *RICO helps to eliminate this problem by creating a substantive offense which ties together these diverse parties and crimes.* Thus, the object of RICO conspiracy is to violate a substantive RICO provision—here, to conduct or participate in the affairs of an enterprise through a pattern of racketeering activity—and not merely to commit each of the predicate crimes necessary to demonstrate a pattern of racketeering activity. The gravamen of the conspiracy charge in this case is not that each defendant agreed to commit arson, to steal goods from interstate commerce, to obstruct justice, and to sell narcotics; rather, it is that each agreed to participate, directly and indirectly, in the affairs of the enterprise by committing two or more predicate crimes. Under the statute, it is irrelevant that each defendant participated in the enterprise's affairs through different, even unrelated crimes, so long as we may reasonably infer that each crime was intended to further the enterprise's affairs. *To find a single conspiracy, we still must look for agreement on an overall objective. What Congress did was to define that objective through the substantive provisions of the Act.*

571 F.2d at 902–03 (emphasis added; footnote omitted).

Elliott does indeed hold that on the facts of that case a series of agreements that under pre-RICO law would constitute multiple conspiracies could under RICO be tried as a single "enterprise" conspiracy. But the language of *Elliott* explains that what ties these conspiracies together is not the mere fact that they involve the same enterprise, but is instead—as in any other conspiracy—an "agreement on an overall objective." What RICO does is to provide a new criminal objective by defining a new substantive crime. In *Elliott,* as here, that crime consists of participation in an enterprise through a pattern of racke-

faceted, diversified conspiracy by replacing the inadequate "wheel" and "chain" rationales with a new statutory concept: the enterprise.

571 F.2d at 902. This and similar statements must, however, be read in the context of the balance of the opinion. In context, as discussed below, this language suggests not that the Congress sought in RICO to change traditional conspiracy concepts, but that the Congress sought instead to expand the reach of traditional conspiracy charges by establishing a new substantive crime around which a conspiracy might center.

teering activity. The defendants in *Elliott* could not have been tried on a single conspiracy count under pre-RICO law because the defendants had not agreed to commit any particular crime. They were properly tried together under RICO only because the evidence established an agreement to commit a substantive RICO offense, *i.e.*, an agreement to participate in an enterprise through a pattern of racketeering activity.

To be sure, the government did not prove in *Elliott* that each of the conspirators had explicitly agreed with all of the others to violate the substantive RICO provision at issue. However, the government did prove that, as in a traditional "chain" conspiracy, the nature of the scheme was such that each defendant must necessarily have known that others were also conspiring to participate in the same enterprise through a pattern of racketeering activity. We found the facts sufficient to demonstrate that the defendants knew they were "directly involved in an enterprise whose purpose was to profit from crime," and that each knew "that the enterprise was bigger than his role in it, and that others unknown to him were participating in its affairs." 571 F.2d at 904 & n. 30. The agreement among all of the defendants in *Elliott* was an implicit one, but it was an agreement nonetheless.

This reading of the *Elliott* holding is supported by * * * *United States v. Stratton*, 649 F.2d 1066 (5th Cir.1981). * * *.

Although *Stratton* did not * * * decide whether the government could combine "totally unrelated agreements and overt acts in a single [RICO] conspiracy," we did express serious doubt as to the propriety of such a joinder. Taken to its logical extreme, a rule allowing the joint trial of otherwise unrelated conspiracies solely on the basis of their relationship to a common enterprise—the rule which the government advocates in this case—leads to ridiculous results:

> For example, assuming that our own court—the United States Court of Appeals for the Fifth Circuit—was alleged to be the enterprise (as we assume would be proper under our analysis), we question whether an agreement to bribe a court official in El Paso, Texas could be part of the same conspiracy as an unrelated agreement to use a judicial office for illicit profit-making purposes in Fort Lauderdale, Florida, when neither the El Paso nor the Fort Lauderdale conspirators knew of the existence of the other group.

Id., at 1073 n. 8. This extreme hypothetical problem is not fundamentally different from the case now before us. Although both conspiracies in the case at bar involved the same judge, it is not that fact which the government argues ties the two conspiracies together. Rather, it is each conspiracy's relationship to the same enterprise (the Municipal Court of the City of El Paso) that is said to provide the necessary link. Thus, the theory urged by the government would bring together individual conspiracies to bribe different judges on the same court.

Our review of *Elliott*, * * * and *Stratton*, convinces us that the government has read this authority too broadly. *Elliott* does not stand for the proposition that multiple conspiracies may be tried on a single "enterprise conspiracy" count under RICO merely because the various conspiracies involve the same enterprise. What *Elliott* does state is two-fold: (1) a pattern of agreements that absent RICO would constitute multiple conspiracies may be joined under a single RICO conspiracy count if the defendants have agreed to commit a substantive RICO offense; and (2) such an agreement to violate RICO may, as in the case of a traditional "chain" or "wheel" conspiracy, be established on circumstantial evidence, *i.e.*, evidence that the nature of the conspiracy is such that each defendant must necessarily have known that others were also conspiring to violate RICO.

In this case the government has not attempted to prove that Walker and Maynard agreed with each other to participate in a bribery scheme with Sutherland, nor has it contended that the nature of each defendant's agreement with Sutherland was such that he or she must necessarily have known that others were also conspiring to commit racketeering offenses in the conduct of the Municipal Court. We must conclude, therefore, that the multiple conspiracy doctrine precluded the joint trial of the two multiple conspiracies involved in this case on a single RICO conspiracy count. In accordance with *Kotteakos* and its progeny, we must reverse the defendants' convictions if this error affected their substantial rights.

B. THE PREJUDICIAL EFFECT OF THE VARIANCE IN THIS CASE

We turn next to a consideration of prejudicial effect of the variance involved in this case. As we note above, a variance is fatal only if it affects the substantial rights of the defendants.[9]

Any analysis of the prejudicial effect of a variance between the government's indictment on a single conspiracy count and its proof of multiple conspiracies must begin with the Supreme Court's two seminal cases on this question—*Berger v. United States*, 295 U.S. 78, 55 S.Ct. 629, 79 L.Ed. 1314 (1935), and *Kotteakos v. United States, supra. Berger* announced the rule that such a variance is fatal only if it has affected the substantial rights of the accused, and went on to find no such effect on the facts of that case. The conspiracy charged by the government in *Berger* consisted of four persons who were alleged to have agreed together to utter counterfeit federal reserve notes; what the government proved at trial was the existence of two separate conspiracies, one consisting of two of the defendants and the other consisting of three of the defendants, with one defendant common to both agreements. The Court rested its analysis in *Berger* on the reasons that underlie the prohibition of material variances:

> The general rule that allegations and proof must correspond is based upon the obvious requirements (1) that the accused shall be definitely

---

9. This standard, and the discussion that follows, is premised on the assumption that the multiple conspiracy doctrine should be treated as a "variance" question rather than a Rule 8(b) "misjoinder" question. The distinction is crucial in this case, since prejudice is presumed to follow from misjoinder but not from a variance. *See* note 6 *supra*.

informed as to the charges against him, so that he may be enabled to present his defense and not be taken by surprise by the evidence offered at the trial; and (2) that he may be protected against another prosecution for the same offense.

295 U.S. at 82, 55 S.Ct. at 631. Because nothing in the record suggested that the defendants had been prejudiced in either respect by their joinder, the Court concluded that their substantial rights had not been affected. 295 U.S. at 83, 55 S.Ct. at 631.

In *Kotteakos,* by contrast, the Court did find that the defendants had been sufficiently prejudiced to justify reversal. In reaching this decision, the Court emphasized the size and complexity of the *Kotteakos* conspiracies:

> On the face of things it is one thing to hold harmless the admission of evidence which took place in the *Berger* case, where only two conspiracies involving four persons all told were proved, and an entirely different thing to apply the same rule where, as here, only one conspiracy was charged, but eight separate ones were proved, involving at the outset thirty-two defendants.

328 U.S. at 766, 66 S.Ct. at 1248–49. It was this fact that made the joint trial in *Kotteakos* so serious an error and distinguished it from *Berger:* "The sheer difference in numbers, both of defendants and of conspiracies proven, distinguishes the situation." *Id.* This does not mean, however, that the proper analysis should hinge on numbers alone. A more fundamental distinction between *Kotteakos* and *Berger* can be found in the Court's treatment in *Kotteakos* of the reasons for the prohibition of material variances. When the government tries multiple conspiracies under a single count, an important right is at stake in addition to those cited in *Berger:* "the right not to be tried *en masse* for the conglomeration of distinct and separate offenses committed by others." 328 U.S. at 775, 66 S.Ct. at 1252–53. Prejudice inhered in the *Kotteakos* trial not because of the number of defendants or conspiracies *per se,* but because of "[t]he dangers of transference of guilt from one to another across the line separating conspiracies, subconsciously or otherwise * * *." 328 U.S. at 774, 66 S.Ct. at 1252.

The crucial question before us, therefore, is whether the defendants were substantially prejudiced by the inherent "transference of guilt" that was the focus of *Kotteakos.* Our review of the record convinces us that for several reasons the defendants were *not* so prejudiced. We need not decide whether any one of these reasons would be sufficient to compel such a result; but taken together, the following facts lead us to the conclusion that the defendants' substantial rights were not affected.

First, the number of conspiracies (two) and defendants (three) is small—even more so than in *Berger.* This is not to say that such cases may always be tried together without substantial prejudice to the defendants, but we do think that the danger implicit in the jury's confusion of different defendants and offenses and of the evidence related to each is diminished by the simpler pattern of events involved in a smaller trial.

Second, the evidence as to each conspiracy was clearly distinct. Kalastro's testimony involved only the Walker-Sutherland conspiracy, and the Maynard conversations involved only the Maynard-Sutherland conspiracy. In neither case did the evidence directly implicate the other conspiracy or specifically contradict any portion of the defense as to the other conspiracy. Moreover, the government conceded at trial the independence of these conspiracies, and did not seek to link the evidence on each one to the other. This does not mean that the defendants' joinder in a single trial with evidence of each conspiracy was harmless, for proof at trial of a similar conspiracy to bribe the same judge obviously makes any hypothesis of innocence more difficult to accept. Still we must conclude that prejudice is more difficult to establish where, as here, the evidence as to each conspiracy is so distinct as to render confusion between the different defendants and conspiracies unlikely.

Third, and most importantly, the government introduced overwhelming evidence of guilt as to all three defendants, and this evidence would have been admissible in two separate trials on individual conspiracy counts. * * * This evidence—which would have been admissible in each of two separate trials on the multiple conspiracies involved in this case—most certainly obscured the importance of any potential "transference of guilt" between the two conspiracies. This fact, when considered along with the additional factors discussed above, convinces us that the defendants' substantial rights were not affected by their joinder under a single conspiracy count and that, accordingly, their convictions need not be reversed for variance.

* * *

Affirmed.

Notes

1. A review of Section C.1.a.(2) of this chapter may be helpful to an understanding of the complex issues concerning the "number" of "agreements" which is the subject of *Sutherland*.

2. In enacting RICO, Congress stated:

It is the purpose of this Act to seek the eradication of organized crime in the United States * * * by providing enhanced sanctions and new remedies to deal with the unlawful activities of those engaged in organized crime.

Section 1 of Pub.L. 91–452, 84 Stat. 922.

One of the enhanced sanctions is the forfeiture provision of 18 U.S.C.A. § 1963(a)(1) which provides that a person convicted under § 1962 forfeits to the United States "any interest he has acquired or maintained in violation of section 1962." "Interest" has been interpreted very broadly by the Supreme Court so as to reach any ill-gotten gains of racketeers rather than being limited to interests in the enterprise. Russello v. United States, 464 U.S. 16, 104 S.Ct. 296, 78 L.Ed.2d 17 (1983).

Another form of enhanced penalty lies in the possibility for cumulative sentences. As noted by the court in United States v. Hampton, 786 F.2d 977, 980 (10th Cir.1986):

> An examination of the statutory framework and legislative history of RICO demonstrates that Congress did clearly articulate an intent to permit cumulative punishment for substantive RICO violations and the underlying predicate acts.

That is, a defendant could be separately convicted and punished for a RICO violation which would be established by proof of a racketeering pattern itself shown by underlying or predicate crimes for which the defendant may have already been convicted and punished.

3. Section 1964 of RICO provides for civil remedies, including the recovery of treble damages and attorney's fees if the plaintiff was injured "in his business or property by reason of a violation of section 1962." This has given rise to an explosion of civil litigation because "racketeering activity" can include many fraudulent practices which are commonly alleged in civil litigation although seldom providing the basis for a prosecution. The actions need not include allegations or proof that organized crime, in the sense of the Mafia, be involved. A number of federal courts have expressed dismay at the proliferation of RICO charges being brought against respectable firms, but this has been attributed by the Supreme Court to the breadth and flexibility of the language. Recently, the Supreme Court held that there is no requirement that the defendants have been convicted of the offenses claimed by the plaintiff to represent the pattern of racketeering activity, nor that these offenses be established by proof beyond a reasonable doubt. Sedima, S.P.R.L. v. Imrex Co., Inc., 473 U.S. ___, 105 S.Ct. 3275, 87 L.Ed.2d 346 (1985). In light of the statutory language and decisions such as *Sedima*, many corporate lawyers have had to take crash programs in the criminal law, while urging the Congress to act to limit the scope of this statute.

Chapter XI

GENERAL PRINCIPLES OF CRIMINAL LIABILITY: COMPLICITY

Contents

Traditionally, criminal liability has often extended to persons other than those who actually engaged in the specific conduct amounting to particular offenses. This Chapter deals with the doctrines underlying such liability. Several somewhat overlapping but nevertheless distinct bodies of law are considered. Attention is first focused upon what has traditionally been regarded as the law of "parties" or "aiding and abetting." Next, liability based upon a pre-crime conspiracy is considered. So-called "vicarious" liability is then addressed. Finally, liability for conduct committed after the primary offense has been committed is examined.

One additional matter needs to be considered as a preliminary matter. Under some circumstances, corporations and sometimes other organizations such as partnerships are liable for criminal offenses. It is obvious that an organization itself cannot commit an offense, so organizational liability of this sort must be based upon a rule that makes the organization criminally responsible for certain actions of its employees or agents. While an organization can obviously not be imprisoned, a fine can, of course, be levied upon it. In such cases, some of the burden imposed by the penalty may fall upon persons who did not participate in the offense. If a corporation is fined and convicted, for example, shareholders may suffer financially because of the corporation's need to pay the fine. In a sense, then, the shareholders are penalized for conduct committed by others.

In part because of concern regarding the propriety of penalizing such nonparticipants, courts and legislatures have struggled with the appropriate standard for determining when an organization (and its members) may be punished for an offense committed by only a few employees or agents. Generally speaking, a corporation may be found guilty of certain offenses—usually minor ones—upon a showing that the offenses were committed by a corporate agent or employee acting within the scope of his authority. But more serious offenses—and especially those requiring particular intent or mental states—can give rise to corporate liability only if the offense was directed or acquiesced in by a relatively highly placed corporate officer. See Model Penal Code § 207 (Official Draft 1985); State v. Adjustment Dept. Credit Bureau, Inc., 94 Idaho 156, 483 P.2d 687 (1971); Commonwealth v. Penn Valley Resorts, Inc., 343 Pa.Super. 387, 494 A.2d 1139 (1985).

A. LIABILITY AS AN "AIDER AND ABETTOR"

Editors' Introduction: Parties to Crime, Principals, and Liability for the Crimes of Others

Probably the most commonly-invoked method of imposing criminal liability upon one person for a crime literally "committed" by someone else is the law of "parties" or its modern equivalent. At common law, participants in—or "parties" to—felonies were categorized as follows:

Principal in the First Degree	One who, with the requisite state of mind, performed the criminal act or directly caused the criminal result, either with his own hand, with an instrument or a non-human agent, or by means of an innocent human agent.
Principal in the Second Degree	One who was actually or constructively present at the scene

	of the crime and who, with the required state of mind, aided, counseled, commanded, or encouraged the principal in the first degree.
Accessory Before the Fact	One neither actually nor constructively present at the scene of the crime who, with the requisite state of mind, ordered, counseled, encouraged or otherwise aided and abetted the principal in the first degree.
Accessory After the Fact	One who, with knowledge of the commission of an offense by an offender, concealed the offender or gave him some other assistance to prevent his detection, arrest, trial, or punishment.

The involvement necessary to render one a principal in the second degree or an accessory before the fact was often referred to as "aiding and abetting."

These distinctions were not drawn at common law with regard to misdemeanors. All participants in a misdemeanor—meaning those who would fit in any of the first three categories of felony participants—were guilty of the misdemeanor but all were regarded as principals. Concealment or assistance of a misdemeanant did not give rise to criminal liability at all.

At common law, the law of parties had a number of complex procedural implications. Venue and jurisdictional problems arose because of the rule that an accessory was punishable only at the place where the act of accessoryship was committed and not where the final offense was committed. Strict attitudes towards pleading demanded that a defendant be charged with the specific form of liability that the trial proof would show. One charged as a principal in the first degree could not be convicted if the proof at trial showed that the defendant was an accessory before the fact. Finally, the liability of an accessory was tied to that of the principal. Thus an accessory could not be tried before the principal and anything which prevented the conviction of the principal also prevented conviction of the accessory. This was even expanded to require that reversal of a principal's conviction also result in reversal of the conviction of an accessory. For a general discussion, see Standefer v. United States, 447 U.S. 10, 14–19, 100 S.Ct. 1999, 2003–05, 64 L.Ed.2d 689, 695–96 (1980).

No American jurisdiction still retains unmodified the common law of parties. But the changes have varied widely. Liability for assistance after the commission of a crime—accessoryship after the fact in common law terminology—has generally been separated from liability for the offense itself and made a distinct offense. Such liability is, therefore, treated separately in these materials; see Section D of this Chapter.

Otherwise, American jurisdictions have tended to continue the general common law approach of making all other participants, as defined in the common law categories, liable for the offense itself. But the procedural ramifications of the traditional distinctions and often the distinctions themselves have been abolished. Title 18 of the United States Code Ann., for example, provides:

§ 2. Principals

(a) Whoever commits an offense against the United States or aids, abets, counsels, commands, induces or procures its commission, is punishable as a principal.

(b) Whoever willfully causes an act to be done which if directly performed by him or another would be an offense against the United States is punishable as a principal.

Other statutes provide in more detail for the requirements of liability. Many follow the pattern of Section 2.06 of the Model Penal Code (reprinted at page 682, infra) and address the matter directly in terms of when one person is "liabl[e] for conduct of another." Liability for a crime of persons other than the actual perpetrator is often, even under provisions such as 18 U.S.C.A. § 2 or § 2.06 of the Model Penal Code, referred to as "accomplice" or "aiding and abetting" liability.

Despite the simplification provided by many modern statutes, the task of determining when a person's participation in a crime is sufficient to create liability for that crime is often a difficult one. In resolving particular cases, courts frequently use general language that is of little help in understanding why the case was decided as it was or in predicting how future cases will be decided.

Some distinctions, however, are clearly required by the demands of sound analysis and better articulated judicial discussions. One federal court, for example, has explained:

The seminal [federal] case [on aiding and abetting] is United States v. Peoni, 100 F.2d 401, 401 (2d Cir.1938), in which Judge Learned Hand states that aiding and abetting requires that the defendant "in some sort associate himself with the venture, that he participate in it as in something that he wishes to bring about, that he seek by his action to make it succeed." This suggests two general components of aiding and abetting—an act on the part of a defendant which contributes to the execution of a crime and the intent to aid in its commission."

United States v. Greer, 467 F.2d 1064 (7th Cir.1972). As the cases in this Section demonstrate, however, it is not always easy to separate what "act" the defendant must have performed (and perhaps what impact that "act" must have had) from the "intent" that the defendant must have harbored.

STATE v. WALDEN

Court of Appeals of North Carolina, 1981.
53 N.C.App. 196, 280 S.E.2d 505.

CLARK, JUDGE.

* * *

Defendant was charged and convicted * * * as a principal in the second degree in that she aided and abetted Bishop Hoskins in his assault on young Lamont Walden. The only evidence for the State tended to show that during the assault defendant did absolutely nothing. She did not hinder his actions, but neither did she help. The cases are abundant to the effect that, at least under ordinary circumstances, defendant could not be found guilty of assault on a theory of aiding and abetting for merely standing idly by while another committed the assault.

> "[O]ne who is present and sees that a felony is about being committed and does in no manner interfere, does not thereby participate in the felony committed. Every person may, upon such an occasion, interfere to prevent, if he can, the perpetration of so high a crime; but he is not bound to do so at the peril, otherwise, of partaking of the guilt. It is necessary, in order to have that effect, that he should do or say something showing his consent to the felonious purpose and contributing to its execution, as an aider and abettor."

State v. Hildreth, 31 N.C. (9 Ire.) 440, 444, 51 Am.Dec. 369, 371 (1849) (Ruffin, C.J.).

> "In the case of *S. v. Ham,* 238 N.C. 94, 76 S.E.2d 346, this Court, in substance, held that in order to render one who does not actually participate in the commission of the crime guilty of the offense committed, there must be some evidence tending to show that he, by word or deed, gave active encouragement to the perpetrator or perpetrators of the crime, or by his conduct made it known to such perpetrator or perpetrators that he was standing by to render assistance when and if it should become necessary.

> In *S. v. Birchfield,* 235 N.C. 410, 70 S.E.2d 5, Ervin, J., speaking for the Court, said: 'The mere presence of a person at the scene of a crime at the time of its commission does not make him a principal in the second degree; and this is so even though he makes no effort to prevent the crime, or even though he may silently approve of the crime, or even though he may secretly intend to assist the perpetrator in the commission of the crime in case his aid becomes necessary to its consummation.

State v. Bruton, 264 N.C. 488, 498, 142 S.E.2d 169, 176 (1965) (Denny, C.J.).

A well-noted exception to the rule that a bystander may not be convicted for her mere presence at the crime scene is stated thus: " 'When the bystander is a friend of the perpetrator and knows that his presence will be regarded by the perpetrator as an encouragement and protection, presence alone may be regarded as encouraging.' " *State v. Jarrell*, 141 N.C. 722, 725, 53 S.E. 127, 128, 8 Ann.Cas. 438, 439 (1906).

Because defendant's state of mind is in issue, and a defendant's mental processes are seldom provable by direct evidence, it is the rule in this jurisdiction that "the guilt of an accused as an aider and abettor may be established by circumstantial evidence." *State v. Redfern*, 246 N.C. 293, 297, 98 S.E.2d 322, 326 (1957). In determining whether a person is guilty as a principal in the second degree, evidence of his relationship to the actual perpetrator, of motive tempting him to assist in the crime, his presence at the scene, and his conduct before and after the crime are circumstances to be considered. *State v. Birchfield*, 235 N.C. 410, 70 S.E.2d 5 (1952).

Defendant in this case was more than a mere bystander and more than the mother of the assault victim. There was also evidence that she was very "close" to Hoskins, the perpetrator of the assault, and that he exerted a strong influence over her. The evidence further showed that Hoskins had beaten defendant's children in her presence before, that in the instant case he beat Lamont for an extended period of time, that during this assault defendant had responded to her son's anguished cries by telling him to hush, and that defendant had beaten her children in the past with a lamp cord in Hoskins' presence.

In addition to the above facts, there is the testimony of defendant at trial that it was not Hoskins, but her former husband who beat little Lamont and that she tried to protect the child, but was herself struck when she sought to interfere. This testimony was obviously not believed by the jury and could reasonably be regarded by the jury as tending "to reflect the mental processes of a person possessed of a guilty conscience seeking to divert suspicion and to exculpate herself," *State v. Redfern*, 246 N.C. at 297–98, 98 S.E.2d at 326, and her friend Hoskins as well.

We believe the totality of the circumstances warrants the inference by the jury that defendant knew her silent presence during the beating inflicted upon her son would be regarded by Hoskins as encouragement and support, particularly in light of the testimony that she had witnessed prior beatings by Hoskins (indicating that she was aware of the severity of his treatment of the children); that she had never interfered in the past; that she had herself beaten the children in Hoskins' presence; and that she lied and instructed her children to lie to conceal Hoskins' complicity in the assault.

The Judge's instruction, however, went beyond the scope of the law just explained. The Judge instructed as follows:

"So I charge that if you find from the evidence beyond a reasonable doubt, that on or about December 9th, 1979, Bishop Hoskins committed assault with a deadly weapon inflicting serious injury on Lamont Walden, that is that Bishop Hoskins intentionally hit Lamont Walden with a belt and that the belt was a deadly weapon, thereby inflicting serious injury upon Lamont Walden; and that the defendant was present at the time the crime was committed and did nothing and that in so doing the defendant knowingly advised, instigated, encouraged or aided Bishop Hoskins to commit that crime; or that she was present with the reasonable opportunity and duty to prevent the crime and failed to take reasonable steps to do so; it would be your duty to return a verdict of guilty of assault with a deadly weapon, inflicting serious injury."

In addition to the well-established ground just discussed, the jury was instructed to convict defendant if they found "that she was present with the reasonable opportunity and duty to prevent the crime and failed to take reasonable steps to do so."

This case was tried on a theory of aiding and abetting. The judge charged the jury on the theory of aiding and abetting. We have, however, been unable to discover any law to the effect that failure to prevent a crime by one who is present with the reasonable opportunity and duty to prevent it constitutes aiding and abetting.

A correct instruction would have been that these circumstances could be considered by the jury as bearing on the communication to the perpetrator of defendant's encouragement and support. Both parties knew that the assault victim was defendant's son. The jury could infer from this mutual knowledge that defendant knew that Hoskins would view her refusal to perform her parental duty to protect her child as indicative of her support and encouragement of his actions. Unfortunately, this is not how the charge reads, and not how we think the jury would understand it.

As it appears in the record, the charge allowed the jury to find defendant guilty of assault with a deadly weapon if they found that she was present at the time of the assault and failed to exercise her parental duty to protect her child. The indictment did not charge her with breach of her parental duty, but with assault. Under the law of this State she could only be convicted of assault if she aided and abetted the perpetrator of the offense. The law makes no reference to the failure to perform a legal duty, but rather requires that defendant in some way communicate her encouragement to the perpetrator. The fact that defendant failed to perform her parental duty was relevant as one circumstance that the jury could consider in determining the issue of whether defendant knew that her presence would be regarded by the perpetrator as encouragement or support, but the jury's finding on this question of fact should not have been made dispositive of the case. The issue of defendant's state of mind should have been left to the jury to determine based upon *all* of the relevant circumstances. Defendant is entitled to a new trial in which the significance of her breach of her parental duty is properly explained as it relates to the issue of defendant's state of mind at the time of the crime.

STATE v. WALDEN

Supreme Court of North Carolina, 1982.
306 N.C. 466, 293 S.E.2d 780.

MITCHELL, JUSTICE.

The principal question presented is whether a mother may be found guilty of assault on a theory of aiding and abetting solely on the basis that she was present when her child was assaulted but failed to take reasonable steps to prevent the assault. We answer this question in the affirmative and reverse the opinion of the Court of Appeals which held to the contrary and ordered a new trial.

* * *

The defendant contends that the * * * instructions of the trial court are erroneous in that they permitted the jury to convict her for failing to interfere with or attempt to prevent the commission of a felony. She argues that the law of this State does not allow a conviction in any case for aiding and abetting the commission of a crime absent some affirmative act of commission by the defendant assisting or encouraging the commission of the crime or indicating the defendant's approval and willingness to assist. We do not agree.

It is true, of course, that this Court speaking through Chief Justice Ruffin has stated:

> For one who is present and sees that a felony is about being committed and does in no manner interfere, does not thereby participate in the felony committed. Every person may, upon such an occasion, interfere to prevent, if he can, the perpetration of so high a crime; but he is not bound to do so at the peril, otherwise, of partaking of the guilt. It is necessary, in order to have that effect, that he should do or say something showing his consent to the felonious purpose and contributing to its execution, as an aider and abettor.

State v. Hildreth, 31 N.C. (9 Iredell) 440, 444 (1849). * * * However, this general rule allows some exceptions. Where the common law has imposed affirmative duties upon persons standing in certain personal relationships to others, such as the duty of parents to care for their small children, one may be guilty of criminal conduct by failure to act or, stated otherwise, by an act of omission. Individuals also have been found criminally liable for failing to perform affirmative duties required by statute.

Parents in this State have an affirmative legal duty to protect and provide for their minor children. G.S. 14–316.1. Although our research has revealed no controlling case in this jurisdiction on the question of a parent's criminal liability for failure to act to save his or her child from harm, the trend of Anglo-American law has been toward enlarging the scope of criminal liability for failure to act in those situations in which the common law or statutes impose a responsibility for the safety and well-being of others. *See generally* W. LaFave and A. Scott, Handbook on Criminal Law, § 26, 182–91 (1972). Thus, it has generally been thought that it is the duty of a parent who has knowledge that his or her child of tender years is in danger to act affirmatively to aid the child if reasonably possible to do so. Perkins on Criminal Law, Chapter 6, § 4, 597 (2d Ed.1969).

We find no case from any jurisdiction directly in point on the precise question before us, i.e., whether a mother may be found guilty of assault on a theory of aiding and abetting solely on the ground that she was present when her child was attacked and had a reasonable opportunity to prevent or attempt to prevent the attack but failed to do so. The State has cited numerous cases from various states for the proposition that a mother can be held criminally responsible in such situations. Many of the cases relied upon by the State do, by way of strong *obiter dicta*, indicate criminal liability of a parent in such circumstances. But these statements have been made in cases in which the record would have supported a finding that the parent in one way or another conveyed approval of the criminal act beyond the approval inherent in merely failing to attempt to stop the commission of the crime. * * *

The traditional approach of most American jurisdictions, drawn largely from the English tradition, tends to confine the duty to act to save others from harm to certain very restrictive categories of cases. This approach has frequently been the subject of criticism. Critics have often pointed out the fact that most countries adopt a much more inclusive view in determining what classes of persons shall have a duty to rescue another when they can do so without danger to themselves. The commentators tend to take the view that the duty to rescue another from peril and criminal liability for failure to do so should be based upon "the defendant's clear recognition of the victim's peril plus his failure to take steps which might reasonably be taken without risk to himself to warn or protect the victim." Hughes, Criminal Omissions, 67 Yale L.J. 590, 626 (1958).

Although we are not now prepared to adopt any such general rule of criminal liability, we believe that to require a parent as a matter of law to take affirmative action to prevent harm to his or her child or be held criminally liable imposes a reasonable duty upon the parent. Further, we believe this duty is and has always been inherent in the duty of parents to provide for the safety and welfare of their children, which duty has long been recognized by the common law and by statute. This is not to say that parents have the legal duty to place themselves in danger of death or great bodily harm in coming to the aid of their children. To require such, would require every parent to exhibit courage and heroism which, although commendable in the extreme, cannot realistically be expected or required of all people. But parents do have the duty to take every step reasonably possible under the circumstances of a given situation to prevent harm to their children.

In some cases, depending upon the size and vitality of the parties involved, it might be reasonable to expect a parent to physically intervene and restrain the person attempting to injure the child. In other circumstances, it will be reasonable for a parent to go for help or to merely verbally protest an attack upon the child. What is reasonable in any given case will be a question for the jury after proper instructions from the trial court.

We think that the rule we announce today is compelled by our statutes and prior cases establishing the duty of parents to provide for the safety and welfare of their children. Further, we find our holding today to be consistent with our prior cases regarding the law of aiding and abetting. It remains the law that one may not be found to be an aider and abettor, and thus guilty as a principal, solely because he is present when a crime is committed. It will still be necessary, in order to have that effect, that it be shown that the defendant said or did something showing his consent to the criminal purpose and contribution to its execution. But we hold that the failure of a parent who is present to take all steps reasonably possible to protect the parent's child from an attack by another person constitutes an act of omission by the parent showing the parent's consent and contribution to the crime being committed. *Cf. State v. Haywood,* 295 N.C. 709, 249 S.E.2d 429 (1978) (When a bystander is a friend of the perpetrator and knows his presence will be regarded as encouragement, presence alone may be regarded as aiding and abetting.).

Thus, we hold that the trial court properly allowed the jury in the present case to consider a verdict of guilty of assault with a deadly weapon inflicting serious injury, upon a theory of aiding and abetting, solely on the ground that the defendant was present when her child was brutally beaten by Hoskins but failed to take all steps reasonable to prevent the attack or otherwise protect the child from injury. Further, the jury having found that the defendant committed an act of omission constituting consent to and encouragement of the commission of the crime charged, the defendant would properly be found to have aided and abetted the principal. A person who so aids or abets another in the commission of a crime is equally guilty with that other person as a principal. Therefore, we find no error in the trial court's instructions, the verdict or the judgment on the charge of assault with a deadly weapon inflicting serious injury.

* * *

The defendant has failed to show prejudicial or reversible error occurring in the trial court. The decision of the Court of Appeals is reversed and this cause is remanded to that Court with instructions to remand to the Superior Court, Wake County, for reinstatement of the verdict and the 27 August 1980 Judgment entered in Superior Court.

Reversed and Remanded.

Notes and Questions

1. Liability based upon omissions is discussed in general terms in Chapter V at pages 180–86, supra. If it is clear that Walden can incur criminal liability by virtue of her omission, i.e., her failure to act to protect her child, does that establish that such an omission was, in the case, sufficient to make her liable for Haskins' assault upon the victim? Was it clear to the jury what it would have to find before convicting Walden?

2. Does either *Walden* court make clear its criterion for determining whether a defendant's "act" or "conduct" is sufficient to create liability as an aider and abettor? Must, for example, the aider and abettor's conduct (or omission) have had any particular impact upon the primary offender? Language used by courts seldom provides reasonable answers. See People v. Sims, 136 Cal.App.3d 942, 186 Cal.Rptr. 793, 798 (1983) (aider and abettor must be shown to have "acted in a manner which either directly or indirectly increased the probability that the crime would be completed successfully"); Commonwealth v. Amaral, 13 Mass.App. 238, 242, 431 N.E.2d 941, 944 (1982) (prosecution must show that aider and abettor "somehow participated in the venture to the extent that she sought to make it succeed").

What is necessary under Section 2.06 of the Model Penal Code, reprinted at page 682, infra? If liability were to be sought under § 2.06(3)(iii) on the ground that Walden had "a legal duty to prevent the commission of the offense," did she fail "to make proper effort to do so?" What is meant by "proper effort?"

Where liability as an "accomplice" under § 2.06 of the Model Penal Code is based upon affirmative action rather than an omission, what does the Code require? Note that § 2.06(3)(ii) provides that it is sufficient if the defendant "aids" or "attempts to aid" the other person. When does a person "aid" another? If a person unsuccessfully "attempts to aid" the other person and the other person nevertheless successfully completes the crime, why should the unsuccessful efforts of the first individual render them as liable as if they had been successful? Generally speaking, one who attempts but fails to commit an offense is guilty of a crime but not a crime as serious as would be involved had the attempt been successful; see Chapter X, infra. Why should the law's approach be different where liability as an accomplice is at issue?

In State v. Gelb, 212 N.J.Super. 582, 515 A.2d 1246 (1986), Gelb was prosecuted for a number of crimes (including manslaughter and criminal mischief) committed when a railroad switch was thrown causing a passenger train to derail. Had the switch been thrown before the train reached a particular point—Marlot Avenue—the engineer would have seen a warning light and stopped in time to avoid the accident. Gelb was part of a group of young men gathered around the switch. Although there had been some discussion of throwing the switch, it was not clear that any firm decision to do so had been made. As the train's lights came into view, one Held said, "Throw the switch." Wade began pulling on the switch. Gelb then yelled at Wade to begin "wait until the train passed Marlot Avenue so the engineer doesn't know the switch is pulled." Wade let go of the switch.

Venton, however, reached across and pulled the handle the rest of the way down. The location of the train at this time was unclear. Nor was it clear whether Wade had pulled the switch handle sufficiently to throw the switch. At his trial, Gelb requested that the jury be instructed that if he performed some act designed to aid, abet or incite the commission of the crimes but did so after the switch had been thrown, he did not participate in the offenses so as to be liable for them under a statutory provision, N.J.Stat. Ann. § 2C:2–6, similar to § 2.06 of the Model Penal Code. Finding no error in the trial court's refusal to give such an instruction, the appellate court explained:

> [B]y the very terms of the statute, accomplice liability will attach if an individual merely attempts to aid in the commission of a crime; such an attempt need not actually facilitate the commission of the offense to support a finding of liability.

212 N.J.Super. at 591, 515 A.2d at 1252. Is this result appropriate? Would it have made any difference if the jury concluded that the prosecution failed to show that at the time of Gelb's shout the train had not yet passed Marlot Avenue? Had New Jersey not enacted the statutory provision, would the trial judge have acted properly in refusing Gelb's requested instruction?

3. Courts appear to have had special difficulty determining the amount of involvement necessary for liability where the offense involves sale, particularly sale of controlled substances. In People v. Bryant, 106 A.D.2d 650, 483 N.Y.S.2d 117 (1984), Bryant, while in a bar, was approached by an informant and an undercover police officer. The informer told Bryant that the officer wished to purchase some cocaine and asked Bryant if he had any. Bryant said, "Yea, but not on me." Gesturing towards a man sitting in another area of the bar, Bryan then said, "Go see Michael and tell him I said it's OK to serve you." The two approached Michael, told him that Bryant had said it was okay to serve them, and purchased cocaine and heroin from Michael. Bryant was convicted of criminal sale of a controlled substance. This was reversed:

> Defendant's only link to this transaction was his presence in the bar during the sale and his ambivalent response to the informant's query. The purchase was suggested by the buyer and she paid the seller directly. There is not a scintilla of evidence to establish any previous relationship between defendant and Michael nor to show that defendant stood to profit from the sale. Under the circumstances, the judgment must be reversed * * *

106 A.D.2d at 651, 483 N.Y.S.2d at 118.

But in Beasley v. State, 360 So.2d 1275 (Fla.App.1978), the defendant, an attorney, was approached by a client—Van Landingham—who asked where she could obtain some marijuana. Beasley called Donald Raulerson and told Van Landingham to go to Raulerson's grocery store and to speak only to Charles Rampy who would be able to arrange a delivery of marijuana for her. Van Landingham contacted Raulerson himself and made a purchase of marijuana from him. Affirming Beasley's conviction, the court noted that "he actually aided in setting up the drug transaction." 360 So.2d at 1277.

The matter was discussed in State v. Hecht, 116 Wis.2d 605, 342 N.W. 2d 721 (1984), affirming Hecht's conviction for aiding and abetting a sale of cocaine to a law enforcement agent—Heidecker—by Vollmer:

It is not always an early task to define what degree of conduct is needed to satisfy a charging of aiding and abetting. "Drawing an exact line of sufficient participation, especially in drug distribution cases, is difficult if not impossible." United States v. Winston, [687 F.2d 832, 834 (6th Cir.1982)]. However, once a defendant moves past the point of merely directing the buyer to a potential source, the likelihood that criminal liability will attach begins to escalate.

It is only when the directing or recommending takes on a wider scope or becomes a part of more widespread activities that any real chance of criminality arises. The criminality of such acts begins to form as one moves along a continuum from a single, casual naming of another as a possible source of illicit drugs, through introducing another to the seller, to accompanying another to a meeting with the seller during which the sale takes place, through handling the narcotics and sharing in the proceeds of the sale. Annot., 42 A.L.R.3d 1072, 1075 (1972).

* * *

Although Hecht's conduct was not located at that extreme end of the continuum at which the defendant is present at the transfer, handling the narcotics and sharing in the proceeds, it is clear to us that the defendant's conduct satisfies this court's criteria of aiding and abetting * * *. Hecht undertook conduct which aiding in the execution of the crime. He set up the initial meeting between the agent and Vollmer, a person who he thought could obtain cocaine for the agent or could contact a potential source of the drug. He was present when phone calls were made which worked out the arrangements for the exchange. Hecht acted further to ensure that Heidecker and Vollmer continued their contact, by making telephone calls between the two parties and relaying information, by physically escorting the agents to Vollmer's house for each of the two meetings, and, finally, by accompanying Vollmer to meet the agents just prior to the final sale.

116 Wis.2d at 621–23, 342 N.W.2d at 730–31.

Should it make any difference if the object of the "sale" is something— or someone—other than a controlled substance? In United States v. Garrett, 720 F.2d 705 (D.C.Cir.1983), cert. denied, 465 U.S. 1037, 104 S.Ct. 1311, 79 L.Ed.2d 708 (1984), Garrett was contacted by F.B.I. agent Tuttle, pretending to be a businessman. Tuttle told Garrett he was interested in obtaining a young boy for sexual purposes. Garrett unsuccessfully attempted to interest Tuttle in older males and then indicated he might be able to arrange something. Later, Garrett told Tuttle to call one McNamara and to call Garrett back if McNamara could not "help." When Tuttle had difficulty contacting McNamara, he called Garrett and Garrett indicated he would "see what I can do with [McNamara]." Tuttle finally contacted McNamara and arranged for the provision of a twelve-year old boy for sexual purposes. In response to Tuttle's question concerning Garrett's share of the fee, McNamara responded that Garrett "doesn't want anything." After McNamara brought a youth from Maryland to agent Tuttle in the District of Columbia, Garrett was convicted of aiding and abetting the interstate transportation of a minor for purposes of prohibited sexual conduct for commercial exploitation. On appeal, the conviction was affirmed; the court described Garrett as "a heavily involved go-between." 720 F.2d at 714.

4. If Walden's actions were sufficient for liability, did she have the requisite mental state? What mental state did the North Carolina court require? What should be the necessary mental state? If the North Carolina court had required proof that Walden consciously wished by her action (or inaction) to encourage or facilitate Hoskins' assault, could Walden's conviction have been upheld?

5. A number of American courts have construed accomplice liability law as requiring "intent." The California Supreme Court, for example, recently reviewed that state's law and concluded:

> [T]he weight of authority and sound law require proof that an aider and abettor act with knowledge of the criminal purpose of the perpetrator *and* with an intent or purpose either of committing, or of encouraging or facilitating commission of, the offense.
>
> When the definition of the offense includes the intent to do some act or achieve some consequence beyond the *actus reus* of the crime, the aider and abettor must share the specific intent of the perpetrator. By "share" we mean neither that the aider and abettor must be prepared to commit the offense by his or her own act should the perpetrator fail to do so, nor that the aider and abettor must seek to share the fruits of the crime. Rather, an aider and abettor will "share" the perpetrator's specific intent when he or she knows the full extent of the perpetrator's criminal purpose and gives aid or encouragement with the intent or purpose of facilitating the perpetrator's commission of the crime. * * *

People v. Beeman, 35 Cal.3d 547, 560, 199 Cal.Rptr. 60, 68, 674 P.2d 1318, 1325–26 (1984). See also, Hensel v. State, 604 P.2d 222, 234 (Alaska 1979) ("liability for the crime of another will attach only upon a showing that an individual had knowledge of the criminal enterprise and specifically intended, by his conduct, to aid, abet, assist, or participate in the criminal enterprise").

6. How would *Walden* come out if the intent requirement of Section 2.06 of the Model Penal Code, reprinted at page 682, infra, had applied? The question concerning the mental state that ought to be required for accomplice liability is described in the Comments to that section as "a much debated issue." In explanation, the Comments continue:

> The issue is whether knowingly facilitating the commission of a crime ought to be sufficient for complicity, absent a true purpose to advance the criminal end. The problem, to be sure, is narrow in its focus: often, if not usually, aid rendered with guilty knowledge implies purpose since it has no other motivation. But there are many and important cases where this is the central question in determining a liability. A lessor rents with knowledge that the premises will be used

to establish a bordello. A vendor sells with knowledge that the subject of the sale will be used in commission of crime. * * * An employee puts through a shipment in the course of his employment though he knows the shipment is illegal. A farm boy clears the ground for setting up a still, knowing that the venture is illicit. Such cases can be multiplied indefinitely; they have given courts much difficulty when they have been brought * * *.

Model Penal Code, Comments to Section 2.04, pp. 27–28 (Tent.Draft No. 1, 1953).

A tentative draft of what became Section 2.06 differed from what became the substance of the official draft. It provided for one person to be an accomplice of another in the commission of a crime in the same manner—requiring the "purpose of promoting or facilitating the commission of the offense"—as Section 2.06(3)(a) of the final draft. But, as an alternative, it provided that such liability would also exist if:

> (b) acting with knowledge that such other person was committing or had the purpose of committing the crime, he knowingly, substantially facilitated its commission.

Model Penal Code, § 2.04(3)(b) (Tent.Draft No. 1, 1953). In explanation, the comments offered:

> Conduct which knowingly facilitates the commission of crimes is by hypothesis a proper object of preventive effort by the penal law * * *. It is important in that effort to safeguard the innocent but the requirement of guilty knowledge adequately serves this end— knowledge both that there is a purpose to commit a crime and that one's own behavior renders aid. There are, however, infinite degrees of aid to be considered. This is the point, we think, at which distinctions should be drawn. Accordingly, when a true purpose to further the crime is lacking, the draft requires that the accessorial behavior substantially facilitate commission of the crime and that it do so to the knowledge of the actor. This qualification provides a basis for discrimination that should satisfy the common sense of justice. A vendor who supplies materials readily available upon the market arguably does not make substantial contribution to commission of the crime since the materials would have as easily been gotten elsewhere. The minor employee may win exemption on this ground, though he minded his own business to preserve his job. What is required is to give the courts and juries a criterion for drawing lines that must be drawn. The formula proposed accomplishes this purpose by a standard that is relevant, it is submitted, to all the legal ends involved. There will, of course, be arguable cases; they should, we think, be argued in these terms.

Model Penal Code, Comments to Section 2.04, pp. 30–31 (Tent.Draft No. 1 1953).

Perhaps even this draft did not go far enough. Suppose a person seeks to purchase gasoline from a service station, announcing that he intends to use the gasoline to set fire to a house in which several children are sleeping. If the station operator sells him the gasoline and he uses it to burn the house and kills the children, should the station operator be free from liability because the gasoline could have "as easily" been purchased elsewhere?

5. Another approach to the matter is to provide separately for purposeful and knowing involvement in an offense. The Proposed Federal Criminal Code defined the liability of an accomplice, generally speaking, as requiring "intent that an offense be committed." Section 401(1)(b). But it also proposed the following additional offense:

§ 1002. Criminal Facilitation

(1) Offense. A person is guilty of criminal facilitation if he knowingly provides substantial assistance to a person intending to commit a felony, and that person, in fact, commits the crime contemplated, or a like or related felony, employing the assistance so provided. The ready lawful availability from others of the goods or services provided by a defendant is a factor to be considered in determining whether or not his assistance was substantial * * *

(3) Grading. Facilitation of a Class A felony is a Class C felony. Facilitation of a Class B or Class C felony is a Class A misdemeanor.

The Comment notes that this would provide a solution to the dilemma created by other approaches, which require that any facilitator either be treated as a full accomplice or be completely absolved of criminal liability. Proposed Federal Criminal Code, Comments to § 1002.

Some jurisdictions take this approach. E.g., New York Penal Law §§ 115.00–115.08 (McKinney's 1986 Supp.) (four degrees of criminal facilitation). Under the New York provisions, criminal facilitation consists of aiding another in committing an offense, "believing it probable that he is rendering aid." New York Penal Law § 115.00(1) (McKinney's 1986 Supp.) (aiding commission of any felony is fourth degree criminal facilitation).

Would this provide a more appropriate result in *Walden?* If Walden should incur criminal guilt because of her situation, should her liability be the same as that of Hoskins? Or is it more appropriate that she be found guilty of a less serious offense?

6. Despite the broad phraseology of the general rule, some situations do not permit the imposition of liability on an accomplice basis. The issue was raised and discussed in United States v. Southard, 700 F.2d 1 (1st Cir. 1983), cert. denied, 464 U.S. 823, 104 S.Ct. 89, 78 L.Ed.2d 97 (1983). Southard was tried and convicted of aiding and abetting a violation of 18 U.S.C.A. § 1084(a):

Whoever being engaged in the business of betting or wagering knowingly uses a wire communication facility for the transmission in interstate or foreign commerce of bets or wagers or information assisting in the placing of bets or wagers on any sporting event or contest [commits an offense].

He and two other defendants (Banker and Ferris) urged that the indictment was defective because it alleged both a substantive violation of this section and aiding and abetting violations of it. The Government's theory was that one Brian was in the gambling business and that the other defendants assisted his actions violative of the statute. It showed that the defendants placed bets for Brian with various bookmakers and that they exchanged with Brian various information ("line information") of significance in the wagering business. On the other hand, the defendants urged that the evidence failed to show that they were engaged in the gambling business and therefore they must be considered to have done nothing more than place bets. The court held that on the specific facts of the case, a conviction for aiding and abetting a violation of § 1804(a) was permissible:

[N]ot every substantive crime is susceptible to an aiding and abetting charge. The question is whether section 1084(a) falls within one of the exceptions to the general rule that aiding and abetting goes hand-in-glove with the commission of a substantive crime.

The first exception is that the victim of a crime may not be indicted as an aider or abettor even if his conduct significantly assisted in the commission of the crime. Examples are persons who pay extortion, blackmail, or ransom monies. It is obvious that section 1084(a) does not involve victims; even a compulsive gambler cannot be described as a "victim" of the bookmakers with whom he bets.

The next exception embraces criminal statutes enacted to protect a certain group of persons thought to be in need of special protection. Accomplice liability will not be imposed upon the protected group absent an affirmative legislative policy to include them as aiders and abettors. For example, a woman who is transported willingly across state lines for the purpose of engaging in illicit sexual intercourse is not an accomplice to the male transporter's Mann Act violation. Gebardi v. United States, 287 U.S. 112, 119 (1932). Appellant claims that he was a mere bettor, not one "engaged in the business of betting or wagering," and therefore falls within the same category as the woman transported across state lines. This, of course, is primarily a question of proof. But even if we assume that defendant was only a bettor, he is not helped any. Section 1084(a) was not passed to protect bettors from their gambling proclivities. Its stated purpose was to assist the states in enforcing their own laws against gambling. H.Rep. No. 967, 87th Cong., 1st Sess. reprinted in 1961 U.S.Code Cong. & Ad. News 2631.

The final exception to accomplice liability upon which appellant relies occurs when the crime is so defined that participation by another is necessary to its commission. The rationale is that the legislature, by specifying the kind of individual who is to be found guilty when participating in a transaction necessarily involving one or more other persons, must not have intended to include the participation by others in the offense as a crime. This exception applies even though the statute was not intended to protect the other participants. Thus, one having intercourse with a prostitute is not liable for aiding and abetting prostitution, and a purchaser is not an accomplice to an illegal sale. See generally W. LaFave and A. Scott, Criminal Law, § 65, at 521–22 (1977). Appellant argues that here the legislature has made criminally liable only those "engaged in the business of betting or wagering" and that the other participant are not within the compass of the statute. Therefore, appellant contends, he should only have been charged with the substantive crime, not aiding and abetting.

The flaw in this argument is that it assumes that the other participant is only a bettor who does nothing to assist the principal in carrying on his gambling activities. The question, as the district court recognized, is not whether a mere bettor can be prosecuted as an aider and abettor, but whether a person not "in the business of betting or wagering" can be found guilty of assisting one who is. We think it clear that he can.

We have been unable to find any cases that discuss directly the propriety of an aiding and abetting prosecution in conjunction with a section 108(a) offense. * * *

The evidence, viewed in the light most favorable to the government, establishes clearly that none of the appellants raising this issue was a "mere bettor." The jury could reasonably have found, based on the telephone intercepts, that Banker and Southard were "engaged in the business of betting or wagering," that they exchanged line information with Brian and that they placed bets for him with other bookmakers. Ferris, whose involvement in this prosecution was the most tenuous of all the appellants, placed at least one bet for Brian for another bookmaker. Because the actions of these three appellants exceeded those of mere bettors, we have no difficulty finding they were properly indicted.

700 F.2d at 19–21. The court, however, carefully took no position on whether persons who were "mere bettors" could be held liable as participants in a violation of section 1084(a). 700 F.2d at 20 n. 24.

7. Suppose in *Walden* Hoskins had been acquitted of the assault on Lamont Walden. Would—and should—this have any effect upon the prosecution's ability to try and convict Walden separately? At common law, an accessory could not be convicted without the prior conviction of the principal. Standefer v. United States, 447 U.S. 10, 15, 100 S.Ct. 1999, 2001, 64 L.Ed.2d 689, 695 (1980). But the modern position is that the liability of participants in an offense is independent and is unaffected by the results of any prosecution undertaken of the other participants (or the lack of any such prosecution). The Arizona Supreme Court has explained:

Aiding and abetting is an independent and distinct substantive offense, and it is not necessary to try and convict the perpetrator of a criminal act before an aider and abettor can be tried. * * * But when a principal has been acquitted of a criminal act, can the accomplice, in a separate trial, be convicted of aiding and abetting that criminal act? We hold that he can.

The State is never required to prove more than the allegations contained in [a charge] in order to sustain the conviction of an aider and abettor. * * * What is required at the trial of the aider and abettor is proof, complete and convincing, of the guilt of the principal. Justice demands that the principal crime be fully proved, since the guilt of the aider and abettor depends upon the commission of the principal crime. Thus, whether or not the principal is convicted or acquitted in separate trial can have no bearing on the trial of the aider and abettor, if the evidence shows the latter guilty. Society is no less injured by the illegal acts of the aider and abettor even though the principal himself escapes conviction. In order to convict an aider and abettor, justice demands no more than * * * the evidence convincingly show that a crime was committed by the principal.

State v. Spillman, 105 Ariz. 523, 525, 468 P.2d 376, 378 (1970).

In *Standefer,* the Supreme Court held that the legislative history of 18 U.S.C.A. § 2 (reprinted at page 662, supra) shows a Congressional intention to permit prosecution of an aider and abettor to a federal crime despite the prior acquittal of the actual perpetrator of that offense. 447 U.S. at 18–20, 100 S.Ct. at 2005–06, 64 L.Ed.2d at 697–98. The Court also refused to apply the doctrine of collateral estoppel to bar the Government, in a prosecution of an aider and abettor, from "relitigating" the guilt of the perpetrator where the Government had, in a prior unsuccessful prosecution of the perpetrator, failed to prove his guilt. 447 U.S. at 21–26, 100 S.Ct. at 2006–08, 64 L.Ed.2d at 698–701. In the prosecution of the aider and abettor, of course, the Government must show beyond a reasonable doubt both (a) that the perpetrator actually committed the crime; and (b) that the accused aided and abetted the perpetrator. 447 U.S. at 26, 100 S.Ct. at 1009, 64 L.Ed.2d at 701. But its ability to do this is not, under the general modern rule, affected by its failure to do this in an earlier trial of the perpetrator.

Suppose Hoskins and Walden had been tried together, Hoskins on an allegation that he committed the assault and Walden on an allegation that she aided and abetted Hoskins. If the jury acquitted Hoskins and convicted Walden, would Walden's conviction stand? See People v. Brown, 120 Mich. App. 765, 772, 328 N.W.2d 380, 384 (1982), concluding that such a conviction is valid and explaining, "[J]uries are not held accountable to rules of logic."

STATE v. SMITH
Court of Appeals of Louisiana, 1984.
450 So.2d 714.

WARD, JUDGE.

The State filed a bill of information charging two brothers, Rodney and Haley Smith, with armed robbery. They waived trial by jury and were tried together by Judge Miriam Waltzer of the Orleans Parish Criminal District Court. Judge Waltzer found both guilty of armed robbery. Rodney and Haley Smith have appealed. Rodney Smith contends that the evidence was insufficient to support his conviction for armed robbery. Additionally, both Rodney and Haley Smith ask that we review the record for errors patent.

The trial record shows that at 7:15 on the evening of March 4, 1982, the Smith brothers entered the Athletic Shoes store at 3713 General DeGaulle Drive in Algiers where two employees were on duty in the store, Mindy Crawford and David Berry. Ms. Crawford waited on Haley while Mr. Berry waited on Rodney. Both brothers tried on shoes at the back of the store. When Haley could not be fitted, he and

Ms. Crawford walked to the front of the store to call another store, trying to find the shoes Haley wanted. While Ms. Crawford was on the telephone behind the counter, Haley motioned with his hand inside his jacket, pointed his hand at her and demanded she give him all of the money out of the cash drawer. When she did not respond, Haley reached across the counter and removed the ten and twenty dollar bills from the cash drawer which was under the counter top. When Rodney came to the front of the store, Haley told him to step behind the counter and get the rest of the money. Rodney went behind the counter, and picked up the money from the floor, and a hammer from a shelf under the counter. He then shook it at the clerks, telling them not to move. He put the hammer down, picked up a calculator and a box of shoes, and both fled.

* * *

We have * * * reviewed the record for sufficiency of the evidence to see if each element of the crime was proven, using the [standard] * * * which requires a review of the record to determine if a reasonable trier of fact, after considering the evidence in the light most favorable to the State, could conclude each element of the crime had been proven beyond a reasonable doubt. Thus, to support convictions for armed robbery, the State must prove that each defendant (1) committed a theft, (2) of anything of value, belonging to another, (3) from the person or immediate control of another, (4) by the use of force or intimidation, (5) while the perpetrator is armed with a dangerous weapon. La.R.S. 14:64. A "dangerous weapon" is defined by La.R.S. 14:2(3) as "any * * * instrumentality, which in the manner used, is calculated or likely to produce death or great bodily harm."

The defendants admit stealing money, shoes, and a calculator, and they admit intimidating the clerks to facilitate the theft—facts sufficient to establish a simple robbery. However, each denies that the force or intimidation was accomplished by the use of a dangerous weapon.

As to Rodney Smith, * * * we affirm. As to Haley Smith, we believe it does not, and therefore we reverse his conviction for armed robbery. However, since there is no question but that he committed simple robbery, we remand for the Trial Court to enter judgment of guilty of the crime of simple robbery, and for re-sentencing after the conviction has been made the judgment of the Trial Court.

We hold the proof of Rodney's guilt is sufficient to support a conviction for armed robbery. When Rodney went behind the counter, picked up the hammer, shook it, and threatened the store clerks while picking up money from the floor, he had armed himself with a dangerous weapon while committing the theft. The hammer, in the manner used, can readily be described as an instrumentality calculated or likely to produce great bodily harm. Thus, all the elements of armed robbery were proven. We believe this is consistent with the Legislative intent—to deter robbery with weapons which create a danger of serious physical harm. When Rodney threatened the clerks with it, he created a "highly charged atmosphere" conducive to violence, one that would create a danger of serious physical harm. *State v. Levi*, 259 La. 591, 250 So.2d 751 (1971). Thus, a rational trier of fact, considering the evidence in the light most favorable to the State, could find that Rodney's use of the hammer was the use of a dangerous weapon, creating a likelihood that someone would be injured, bringing the crime within the definition of La.R.S. 14:64.

We have a different situation as to Haley Smith. Although Haley made a motion with his hand inside his jacket while directing Ms. Crawford to give him the money, Haley did not refer to a weapon. While it is true Ms. Crawford believed he had a gun, and while this will suffice as "force or intimidation" to support a conviction of simple robbery, a hand in the pocket is not, of itself, a dangerous weapon[,] and it will not support a conviction of armed robbery. Thus, Haley could not be convicted of armed robbery solely on the basis of his hand motion under the jacket.

We now consider whether Haley is guilty of armed robbery by acting as a principal. The Louisiana statutory law of principals provides:

All persons concerned in the commission of a crime, whether present or absent, and whether they directly commit the act constituting the offense, aid and abet in its commission, or directly or indirectly counsel or procure another to commit the crime, are principals.

La.R.S. 14:24.

These facts show that he was not. The hammer wielded by Rodney was a tool belonging to the store, kept on an open shelf below the cash drawer. The shelf was not visible from the customer's side of the counter where Haley stood during the robbery. There was no evidence that either of the defendants knew of the hammer's existence until Rodney spotted it and decided to use it. The clerks testified that Haley exorted Rodney only to be sure and get all the money, but that Haley did not mention the hammer, either before Rodney picked it up or while he was using it to threaten the clerks.

We find that Haley Smith neither aided or abetted nor counseled or procured Rodney's commission of robbery with a dangerous weapon. He committed a simple robbery and he aided and abetted his brother's commission of simple robbery, but the evidence is insufficient to support the conviction of Haley Smith as principal to armed robbery. And while it is true that Haley continued with the robbery after Rodney threatened the clerks with the hammer, and that he and Rodney both fled with the stolen merchandise, we do not believe these facts are sufficient to conclude that he aided, abetted or counseled Rodney to commit an armed robbery.

All principals to a crime are not necessarily guilty of the same grade of the offense. A principal may be convicted of a higher or lower degree of the crime, depending upon the mental element proved at trial. Hence, we find evidence to convict Haley Smith not of armed robbery, but of the lesser included offense of simple robbery.

We affirm the conviction and sentence of Rodney Smith for armed robbery. We reverse the conviction of Haley Smith and find him guilty of simple robbery in violation of La.R.S. 14:65 and remand his case for sentencing.

Affirmed in Part.

Reversed and Remanded in Part.

SCHOTT, JUDGE, dissenting in part:

I respectfully dissent from that part of the majority opinion which reverses Haley Smith's conviction of armed robbery because he was proved beyond a reasonable doubt to be a principal in Rodney's crime pursuant to R.S. 14:24. * * *

When Rodney threatened the clerks with the hammer Haley was standing but a few feet away. Saying nothing to dissuade Rodney as he made the threat and then continued to pick up the money, Haley's presence constituted an indirect counseling or procurement of the commission of Rodney's crime. Furthermore, after Rodney made the threat, according to Ms. Crawford, Haley "kept telling him (Rodney) to look under the drawer and make sure he got everything." And after Rodney put down the hammer Haley told him to go back for the shoes Haley had tried on. At this point the clerks were still under Rodney's threat to use the hammer on them even though he had put it down. Thus, Haley not only indirectly counseled and procured Rodney's crime by silently lending his moral support but also directly procured the crime by words of encouragement.

I would affirm both convictions and sentence * * *.

Notes and Questions

1. If it is clear that Haley Smith knew Rodney was going to commit a robbery, wanted to assist him in doing so, and did—with this purpose—provide such assistance, should Haley Smith's liability be limited to the robbery? A number of courts define the liability of an aider and abettor more broadly. For example, the Maine court, in a recent case involving a murder committed during a robbery in which the defendant Anderson participated, explained the liability of the aider and abettor as follows:

> [L]iability for a "primary crime" (here robbery) is established by proof that the alleged actor-accomplice intended to promote or facilitate that primary crime of robbery. But * * * liability for any "secondary crime" (here murder) which may have been committed by the principal actor is established as to the alleged actor-accomplice upon a two-fold showing: (a) that the actor-accomplice intended to promote the primary crime (here robbery), and (b) that the commission of the secondary crime (here murder) was a "foreseeable consequence" of the actor-accomplice's participation in the primary crime of robbery.

State v. Anderson, 409 A.2d 1290, 1303 (Me.1979). See also, People v. Croy, 41 Cal.3d 1, 12 n. 5, 221 Cal.Rptr. 592, 598 n. 5, 710 P.2d 392, 398 n. 5 (1985) (aider and abettor's intention to encourage or facilitate a criminal act, see People v. Beeman, discussed at page 672, supra, is "sufficient to impose liability on him for any reasonably foreseeable offense committed by the perpetrator"). Why should liability as an aider and abettor extend to foreseeable but unforeseen and thus unintended crimes once it is established that the defendant intentionally aided and abetted one offense?

If, however, the liability as an aider and abettor does extend to foreseeable but unintended offenses arising out of the events intentionally facilitated, would Rodney Smith's commission of armed robbery have been a foreseeable result of the simple robbery which Haley Smith intentionally aided? In State v. Ivy, 115 Wis.2d 645, 341 N.W.2d 408 (App.1983), the Court of Appeals of Wisconsin held:

> We do not think that armed robbery is a natural and probable consequence of robbery. Therefore, to intentionally aid and abet the commission of armed robbery, an aider/abettor must have some awareness that the principals are armed * * *.

115 Wis.2d at 655, 341 N.W.2d at 413. The Wisconsin Supreme Court, however, reversed:

> [D]epending on the facts and circumstances of a given case, armed robbery could be a natural and probable consequence of robbery; therefore, a defendant could be liable for aiding and abetting the armed robbery even though he or she did not actually know that the person or persons who directly committed the armed robbery were armed with a dangerous weapon. * * * Because threatened or actual force is involved in a robbery, there are myriad factual situations in which it would be reasonable to find that an armed robbery that occurred was a natural and probable consequence of robbery. For example, if a person intends to rob an armored truck, it is likely that the person would have to use a weapon during the robbery to successfully accomplish the robbery. Similarly, if a person intends to rob a bank or business that is guarded by armed security guards, it is likely that the person would have to use a weapon to successfully effectuate the robbery. * * * [W]hether in a given case an armed robbery that was committed was a natural and probable consequence of a robbery that a person charged with aiding and abetting allegedly assisted, and the extent of that person's knowledge, are factual determinations that must be made by the jury in light of the facts of that case.

State v. Ivy, 119 Wis.2d 591, 600–02, 350 N.W.2d 622, 627–28 (1984). On the facts of *Smith*, could a jury find that the armed robbery was a natural and probable result of the simple robbery?

2. If one provides encouragement or assistance to another sufficient to create accomplice liability for any crime the other person may commit, is there any way to escape liability? If, of course, the other person is prevented from committing the offense, there is no offense for which the aiding and abettor party can be liable. But is there any way short of this to prevent liability? It is widely agreed that that such liability can be avoided by undoing the encouragement or assistance earlier provided.

Where only verbal encouragement was provided, it may be sufficient to simply voice disapproval of the plan in a timely fashion. But if more was done, further action may be necessary to avoid liability. If a weapon was provided, for example, reacquisition of that weapon may be necessary. See Commonwealth v. Huber, 15 D. & C.2d 726 (Pa.Q. Sessions 1958). The Model Penal Code (see page 683, infra) and some statutes based on it require that the person "wholly deprive [his complicity] of effectiveness in the commission of the offense" or "[make] proper effort to prevent the commission of the offense."

In State v. O'Neal, 618 S.W.2d 31 (Mo.1981), O'Neal participated with another person in a robbery. He saw that his companion was about to shoot the victims and he turned and walked away. According to his testimony at trial, he was afraid of his companion and therefore did not try to stop him. He did think, according to his testimony, that his walking away might make his companion change his mind about shooting the victims. It did not. At his trial for the killings actually committed by his companion, was he entitled to have the jury instructed on withdrawal? Applying a statute based on the Model Penal Code provision, the Missouri court held that no instruction was required. What would O'Neal have to have done? Is it possible that by letting events progress to the point where his companion was pointing a gun at the victims, he had forfeited any opportunity to withdraw by delaying his effort to withdraw too long?

MODEL PENAL CODE *
(Official Draft, 1985).

Section 2.06. Liability for Conduct of Another; Complicity

(1) A person is guilty of an offense if it is committed by his own conduct or by the conduct of another person for which he is legally accountable, or both.

(2) A person is legally accountable for the conduct of another person when:

(a) acting with the kind of culpability that is sufficient for the commission of the offense, he causes an innocent or irresponsible person to engage in such conduct; or

(b) he is made accountable for the conduct of such other person by the Code or by the law defining the offense; or

(c) he is an accomplice of such other person in the commission of the offense.

(3) A person is an accomplice of another person in the commission of an offense if:

(a) with the purpose of promoting or facilitating the commission of the offense, he

(i) solicits such other person to commit it; or

(ii) aids or agrees or attempts to aid such other person in planning or committing it; or

(iii) having a legal duty to prevent the commission of the offense, fails to make proper effort so to do; or

(b) his conduct is expressly declared by law to establish his complicity.

(4) When causing a particular result is an element of an offense, an accomplice in the conduct causing such result is an accomplice in the commission of that offense, if he acts with the kind of culpability, if any, with respect to that result that is sufficient for the commission of the offense.

(5) A person who is legally incapable of committing a particular offense himself may be guilty thereof if it is committed by the conduct of another person for which he is legally accountable, unless such liability is inconsistent with the purpose of the provision establishing his incapacity.

(6) Unless otherwise provided by the Code or by the law defining the offense, a person is not an accomplice in an offense committed by another person if:

(a) he is a victim of that offense; or

(b) the offense is so defined that his conduct is inevitably incident to its commission; or

(c) he terminates his complicity prior to the commission of the offense and

(i) wholly deprives it of effectiveness in the commission of the offense; or

(ii) gives timely warning to the law enforcement authorities or otherwise makes proper effort to prevent the commission of the offense.

(7) An accomplice may be convicted on proof of the commission of the offense and of his complicity therein, though the person claimed to have committed the offense has not been prosecuted or convicted or has been convicted of a different offense or degree of offense or has an immunity to prosecution or conviction or has been acquitted.

B. LIABILITY UNDER THE COCONSPIRATOR RULE

Editors' Introduction: The "Coconspirator Liability" Rule

A number of jurisdictions provide, in addition to accessorial liability, that under certain circumstances one person is liable for an offense committed by another because the two were both members of a criminal conspiracy.

The leading case adopting the doctrine which accomplishes this result (the "Pinkerton Rule") is Pinkerton v. United States, 328 U.S.

640, 66 S.Ct. 1180, 90 L.Ed. 1489 (1946). Walter and Daniel Pinkerton were convicted of criminal conspiracy to violate the United States Internal Revenue Code and of a number of substantive violations of that Code. There was no evidence tending to show that Daniel participated in the commission of the offenses of which he was convicted. The jury had not been instructed on his potential liability as an aider or abettor but rather had been told that he could be found guilty of crimes committed by Walter if at the time of the offenses both were parties to a criminal conspiracy and Walter committed the offenses in furtherance of this conspiracy. Upholding the convictions, the United States Supreme Court explained:

> We have here a continuous conspiracy. There is here no evidence of the affirmative action on the part of Daniel which is necessary to establish his withdrawal from it. Hyde v. United States, 225 U.S. 347, 369, 32 S.Ct. 793, 803, 56 L.Ed. 1114, Ann.Cas.1914A, 614. As stated in that case, "having joined in an unlawful scheme, having constituted agents for its performance, scheme and agency to be continuous until full fruition be secured, until he does some act to disavow or defeat the purpose he is in no situation to claim the delay of the law. As the offense has not been terminated or accomplished, he is still offending. And we think consciously offending,—offending as certainly, as we have said, as at the first moment of his confederation, and consciously, through every moment of its existence." Id., 225 U.S. at page 369, 32 S.Ct. at page 803. And so long as the partnership in crime continues, the partners act for each other in carrying it forward. It is settled that "an overt act of one partner may be the act of all without any new agreement specifically directed to that act." United States v. Kissel, 218 U.S. 601, 608, 31 S.Ct. 124, 126, 54 L.Ed. 1168. Motive or intent may be proved by the acts or declarations of some of the conspirators in furtherance of the common objective. Wiborg v. United States, 163 U.S. 632, 657, 658, 16 S.Ct. 1127, 1137, 1197, 46 L.Ed. 289. A scheme to use the mails to defraud, which is joined in by more than one person, is a conspiracy. Yet all members are responsible, though only one did the mailing. The governing principle is the same when the substantive offense is committed by one of the conspirators in furtherance of the unlawful project. The criminal intent to do the act is established by the formation of the conspiracy. Each conspirator instigated the commission of the crime. The unlawful agreement contemplated precisely what was done. It was formed for the purpose. The act done was in execution of the enterprise. The rule which holds responsible one who counsels, procures, or commands another to commit a crime is founded on the same principle. That principle is recognized in the law of conspiracy when the overt act of one partner in crime is attributable to all. An overt act is an essential ingredient of the crime of conspiracy under § 37 of the Criminal Code, 18 U.S.C. § 88, 18 U.S.C.A. § 88. If that can be supplied by the act of one conspirator, we fail to see why the same or other acts in furtherance of the conspiracy are likewise not attributable to the others for the purpose of holding them responsible for the substantive offense.

A different case would arise if the substantive offense committed by one of the conspirators was not in fact done in furtherance of the conspiracy, did not fall within the scope of the unlawful project, or was merely a part of the ramifications of the plan which could not be reasonably foreseen as a necessary or natural consequence of the unlawful agreement. But as we read this record, that is not this case.

328 U.S. at 646–48, 66 S.Ct. at 1183–84, 90 L.Ed. at 1496–97.

Some jurisdictions appear to have adopted the same approach but using different terminology. Illinois, for example, follows a "common design" rule which permits the conviction of all participants of a "common criminal design or agreement" of any criminal acts committed by other members of the agreement in furtherance of the common design. See People v. Terry, 99 Ill.2d 508, 77 Ill.Dec. 442, 460 N.E.2d 746 (1984).

If accomplices can be convicted for foreseeable but unintended offenses committed by those whom they aid or encourage (see Section A, supra), does the *Pinkerton* Rule really increase the liability of one who assists another in a criminal enterprise? The existence of *Pinkerton* liability obviously makes a difference in some cases. United States v. Gallo, 763 F.2d 1504 (6th Cir.1985), modified on reh., 774 F.2d 106 (6th Cir.1985), cert. denied, ___ U.S. ___, 106 S.Ct. 826, 828, 1200, 88 L.Ed.2d 798, 800, 89 L.Ed.2d 314 (1986). *Gallo* was a very complex prosecution for a variety of federal crimes arising out of organized gambling and drug activities in Cleveland. In addition to the appellant Fritz Graewe, the events involved, among others, Newman, Odom, and Hoven. Graewe was convicted of a number of substantive crimes, including several violations of the federal "Travel Act," 18 U.S.C.A. § 1952 (aiding racketeering through interstate travel) committed by Newman and Hoven and of possession of cocaine found in a rental car used by Odom. On appeal, his convictions were first upheld on a *Pinkerton* theory. 763 F.2d at 1522. On rehearing, however, the appellate court was persuaded that the jury instructions had not adequately put this theory before the trial jury and therefore the *Pinkerton* Rule could not be used to support those convictions. It nevertheless upheld Graewe's convictions for some substantive crimes on the grounds that the evidence showed he aided and abetted their commission. But with regard to others, the court concluded that without the *Pinkerton* Rule the evidence failed to support Graewe's guilt:

> There is no evidence that [Graewe] knew of, participated in, or otherwise aided and abetted in [the] Travel Act violations. * * * Similarly, * * * [n]o evidence directly linked [Graewe] to [the] rental car, and thus his conviction on [the possession of cocaine charge] also must fall.

774 F.2d at 108–09.

There is still substantial support for the *Pinkerton* Rule. In State v. Barton, 424 A.2d 1033 (R.I.1981), the Supreme Court of Rhode Island noted that it had adopted the same approach as the *Pinkerton* Rule thirteen years before *Pinkerton* and that the rule was "sound and viable" as well as the majority approach. 424 A.2d at 1038. It continued:

> The *Pinkerton* rule has found favor with many states under a variety of theories. Under one view, vicarious liability is supported on the premise that criminal acts, apart from the object of the conspiracy, are dependent upon the encouragement and material support of the group as a whole and therefore justify treating each member of the conspiracy as an agent for the others. * * * Under another view, the *Pinkerton* rule is supported on the theory that group activity presents a greater potential threat to the public than individual action. * * * In a similar vein, others have suggested that conspiracy provides a vehicle whereby criminals will engage in more elaborate and complex schemes than they would attempt if working alone, and therefore such activity should be discouraged via the *Pinkerton* rule.

Id., at 1036–37.

The *Pinkerton* Rule has, however, been rejected by a number of courts. Commonwealth v. Stasium, 349 Mass. 38, 206 N.E.2d 672 (1965); People v. McGee, 49 N.Y.2d 48, 424 N.Y.S.2d 157, 399 N.E.2d 1177 (1979), cert. denied, 446 U.S. 942, 100 S.Ct. 2167, 64 L.Ed.2d 797 (1980); State v. Small, 301 N.C. 407, 272 S.E.2d 128 (1980). In *Small*, the North Carolina Supreme Court observed:

> [T]he erroneous idea that a conspirator automatically becomes liable as a principal to all crimes committed as a result of or in furtherance of the illegal agreement has largely resulted from too broad a reading of case law statements which either (1) discussed the application of the coconspirator rule as a rule of evidence [making the admissions of one conspirator admissible against the others], or (2) applied established principles of accomplice liability to evidence of conspiracy and preconcert.

301 N.C. at 427, 272 S.E.2d at 140. The New York Court of Appeals in *McGee* noted that the legislature had provided in some detail for situations in which one person is liable for crimes committed by another, but made no reference in the statute to conspiracy. Thus the legislature did not intend liability on this basis. Further, the court continued:

> The crime of conspiracy is an offense separate from the crime that is the object of the conspiracy. Once an illicit agreement is shown, the overt act of any conspirator may be attributed to other conspirators to establish the offense of conspiracy and that act may itself be the object crime. But the overt act itself is not the crime in a conspiracy situation; it is merely an element of the crime that has as its basis the agreement. It is not offensive to permit a conviction of conspiracy to stand on the overt act committed by another, for the act merely provides corroboration of the existence of the agreement and indicates that the agreement has reached a point where it poses a sufficient threat to society to impose sanctions. But it is repugnant to our

system of jurisprudence, where guilt is generally personal to the defendant, to impose punishment, not for the socially harmful agreement to which the defendant is a party, but for substantive offenses in which he did not participate.

49 N.Y.2d at 57–58, 424 N.Y.S.2d at 162, 399 N.E.2d at 1181–82.

As is discussed in the principal case in this section, liability under the coconspirator rule may be broader than liability under the law of parties or accessorial liability. On the other hand, liability under the coconspirator rule requires proof of a preliminary agreement, while liability under aiding and abetting doctrine does not. United States v. Beck, 615 F.2d 441, 449 n. 9 (7th Cir.1980). Given the law of conspiracy, however, does this pose much of a task for the prosecution in most cases?

UNITED STATES v. ALVAREZ

United States Court of Appeals, Eleventh Circuit, 1985.
755 F.2d 830.

Before KRAVITCH and HATCHETT, CIRCUIT JUDGES, and HANCOCK, District Judge.

KRAVITCH, CIRCUIT JUDGE:

On December 2, 1982, in a run-down motel in the Little Havana section of Miami, Florida, a cocaine deal turned into tragedy when a shoot-out erupted between the dealers and two undercover special agents from the Bureau of Alcohol, Tobacco, and Firearms (BATF). During the shoot-out, one of the BATF agents was killed and the other agent, along with two of the cocaine dealers, was seriously wounded. Appellants Augustin Alvarez, Mario Simon, Victoriano "Macho" Concepcion, Eduardo Portal, Oscar Hernandez, Ramon Raymond, and Rolando Rios were convicted after a trial by jury on various charges arising from the cocaine deal and shoot-out. All of the appellants were convicted of conspiracy to possess with intent to distribute cocaine, 21 U.S.C. § 846, and possession with intent to distribute cocaine, 21 U.S.C. § 841(a)(1). In addition, Alvarez and Simon were convicted of first degree murder of a federal agent, 18 U.S.C. §§ 1111(a) and 1114, assault on a federal agent by means of a deadly and dangerous weapon, 18 U.S.C. §§ 111 and 1114, and use of a firearm to commit a felony, 18 U.S.C. § 924(c)(1). Portal, Concepcion, and Hernandez were convicted of second degree murder of a federal agent, 18 U.S.C. §§ 1111(a) and 1114, and assault on a federal agent by means of a deadly and dangerous weapon, 18 U.S.C. §§ 111 and 1114.

* * *

On December 1, 1982, at about 6:00 p.m., BATF Special Agents Joseph Benitez, Joseph Tirado, Ariel Rios, and Alex D'Atri, each acting in an undercover capacity, met with appellants Rolando Rios and Ramon Raymond in the parking lot of a convenience store in Homestead, Florida. The purpose of the meeting was to continue previously initiated negotiations for the purchase of two kilograms of cocaine.

Raymond informed the agents that he had obtained a source for the cocaine, but that delivery would be delayed by about a half hour. Raymond attempted to telephone his cocaine source but was unsuccessful. Agent Tirado then asked appellant Rios if he knew when the cocaine would be delivered. Appellant Rios also attempted to telephone the cocaine source but, like Raymond, was unsuccessful. Appellant Rios asked Agents Rios and Tirado to take him to the source's residence. The three men drove to a house about two miles away, but, finding no one there, returned to the parking lot. Meanwhile, Raymond continued to assure the remaining agents that the cocaine would be delivered shortly. At one point, Raymond suggested that the deal be moved across the street because he thought that there were too many cars in the parking lot.

A short time later, appellant Eduardo Portal arrived at the parking lot and began speaking with appellants Rios and Raymond. Portal informed Agents Rios, Tirado, and Benitez that he could make immediate delivery of two kilograms of cocaine. Portal then made a telephone call to appellant Victoriano "Macho" Concepcion. After the call, Portal told the agents that delivery of the cocaine could be made by noon the next day. The agents departed after agreeing to call Concepcion the next morning to arrange the details of the cocaine delivery.

The next day, at about 12:00 noon, Agent Rios telephoned Concepcion and arranged to meet with Concepcion and Portal in the parking lot of a restaurant in the Little Havana section of Miami. Agents Rios and D'Atri met with Concepcion and Portal shortly before 2:00 p.m. D'Atri told Concepcion that he wished to purchase three kilograms of cocaine. Concepcion answered that the cocaine was available at a price of $49,000 per kilogram. The four men left the restaurant parking lot and proceeded, in two separate cars, to the Hurricane Motel on West Flagler Street in Miami. The agents advised their surveillance team of their destination by means of a portable radio concealed in their car.

Shortly after 2:00 p.m., Agents Rios and D'Atri and appellants Concepcion and Portal arrived at the Hurricane Motel. Concepcion advised the agents that only one of them would be allowed inside the motel to complete the deal. The agents refused to proceed under those circumstances, and Concepcion agreed to allow both agents to be present. Concepcion and the two agents entered the motel office, while Portal remained outside. Surveillance agents stationed near the motel observed Portal acting as a "lookout." The agents saw Portal closely watching passing cars and pedestrians, and noticed a handgun-shaped bulge on Portal's left side, under his shirt.

Inside the motel office, Concepcion and the two agents met appellants Augustin Alvarez and Oscar Hernandez. Hernandez was the manager of the Hurricane Motel, and Alvarez and Hernandez shared an apartment that adjoined the motel office. Alvarez told the agents that he was not the cocaine source, but that he would make a telephone call and arrange the cocaine delivery. Alvarez made the call and informed the agents that the cocaine would be delivered shortly. The five men waited in the living room of the Alvarez-Hernandez apartment. While they waited, Alvarez and Agent Rios conversed in Spanish, with Agent Rios translating into English for Agent D'Atri's benefit. According to D'Atri's testimony at trial, Alvarez stated, "In this business, you have to be careful. It's a dangerous business. You have to watch out for rip-offs and Federal agents." Alvarez also stated that he would never go back to prison, and that he would rather be dead than go back to prison. D'Atri answered, "It's always better to be alive than in prison." Alvarez then spoke to Hernandez in Spanish, and D'Atri asked Hernandez what Alvarez had said. Hernandez replied that Alvarez had said that he could never go back.

After twenty or twenty-five minutes, D'Atri decided to make a telephone call to let the surveillance team know that the cocaine deal was still pending. D'Atri asked Hernandez for permission to use the telephone. Hernandez spoke to Alvarez in Spanish, and then indicated that D'Atri could use the telephone in the motel office. After completing the telephone call, D'Atri returned to the living room and joined the other men in general conversation. At one point, Alvarez went into a bedroom, got a sample of cocaine, and asked D'Atri if he wanted to test the sample. D'Atri replied that he wanted to test the cocaine that was about to be delivered, not Alvarez' sample.

After twenty more minutes, D'Atri, who was becoming increasingly concerned about the prolonged delay, announced that he and Agent Rios were leaving. Hernandez said, in English, "Don't worry, he's coming. If he says he's coming, he will be here." At the same time, appellant Mario Simon drove into the motel parking lot. Hernandez said, "He's here," and the men all laughed. Simon entered the living room, and D'Atri asked him whether he had the three kilograms of cocaine. Simon answered, in English, "I have to make a phone call." After making the call, Simon told the agents that he could deliver the cocaine, but that it would take one hour. He also said that he would deliver one kilogram of cocaine at 4:00 p.m., and one kilogram every hour after that. The agents agreed to return to the motel in about one hour.

Agents Rios and D'Atri drove to a nearby restaurant and met with Special Agent Michael Casali, one of the members of the surveillance team. During the meeting, Agent Rios expressed concern about a leather pouch carried by Simon, which Agent Rios thought might contain a weapon. The agents then discussed their plans for effecting the intended drug arrests. The agents decided to place $50,000 in the trunk of their car. Once the cocaine was delivered, Agent Rios would go out to the motel parking lot and remove the money from the trunk. Upon observing this signal, the surveillance and backup agents would wait forty-five seconds to a minute, and then move in to effect the arrests.

At about 4:15 p.m., Agents Rios and D'Atri returned to the motel, but Simon had not yet returned with the cocaine. The agents drove around the area of the motel for several minutes. At about 4:25 p.m., the agents noticed Simon's car in the parking lot of the motel. The agents entered the motel and found Simon, Alvarez, and Concepcion in the living room where the earlier meeting had taken place. Agent D'Atri asked Simon whether he had the cocaine, and Simon replied, "Yes, it is in the car." Simon went out to his car, and returned with a plastic bag. Concepcion took the bag from Simon and removed a cardboard box from the bag. Concepcion handed the box to D'Atri, who opened the box and found another plastic bag containing what appeared to be about one kilogram of cocaine. D'Atri then asked Agent Rios to go out to their car and get the money.

Agent Rios returned to the living room and handed the money, which was in a paper bag, to D'Atri. D'Atri noticed Simon, who was partially seated on and resting against the armrest of a couch, looking out the window and nervously fidgeting with the leather pouch that was suspected to contain a weapon. The other men were all seated on the couch. D'Atri took the money out of the paper bag, stood up, and began to count the money. Again, D'Atri noticed Simon looking out the window and fidgeting with the pouch. At about this time, the surveillance and backup agents began to converge on the motel.

D'Atri heard the surveillance and backup agents arrive at the door of the motel office. Suddenly, Agent Rios shouted, "No," and D'Atri heard a gunshot. D'Atri drew his gun and held it on Concepcion and Alvarez. Meanwhile, out of the corner of his eye, D'Atri saw Simon and Agent Rios engaged in a struggle. D'Atri heard another gunshot, and he turned to help Agent Rios. D'Atri lunged at Simon, but, as he reached Simon, he felt tremendous pain in his forehead and left arm. D'Atri fired several shots at Simon, emptying his weapon in the process. D'Atri then looked up and saw Alvarez aiming a chrome-plated .357 Magnum pistol at him. Alvarez fired one shot at D'Atri, hitting him in the chest. D'Atri saw Alvarez take two steps toward him and fire another shot. The impact of the second shot caused D'Atri to careen into the wall of the living room, where he blacked out.

During this time, the surveillance and backup agents were attempting to force their way into the motel. The agents finally shot the lock off the door of the motel office and entered the living room. The agents found Agent Rios on the couch with a gunshot wound in the face. Agent Rios had also been shot in the finger and the left thigh. Agent D'Atri was lying on the floor in a pool of blood, with four gunshot wounds. Simon, who was covered with blood, was leaning against the wall near a hallway that led to the bedrooms. A carbine rifle was at his feet. Alvarez was running down the hallway toward the bedrooms. Agent Casali yelled, "Freeze, police," but Alvarez ducked into a bedroom. Casali drew his gun and entered the bedroom. Alvarez looked up, saw Casali, and reached for a shotgun that was lying on the bed.

Casali shot Alvarez. Casali then instructed Agent Switzer to watch Alvarez while Casali searched the other bedroom. When Switzer turned his back on Alvarez to help cover Casali's entry into the other bedroom, Alvarez again went for the shotgun, and Switzer shot him.

The surveillance and backup agents tried to administer first aid to Agent Rios, but he died before medical help could arrive. Agent D'Atri, Alvarez, and Simon were taken to the hospital, and eventually recovered from their wounds.

The cause of Agent Rios' death was determined to be the gunshot wound in the face. The bullet had lodged in the back of Agent Rios' skull. Expert testimony at trial indicated that the bullet that killed Agent Rios was fired from Alvarez' .357 Magnum pistol.

* * *

Appellants Portal, Concepcion, and Hernandez contend that their murder convictions under Count III were based on an unprecedented and improper extension of *Pinkerton v. United States,* 328 U.S. 640, 66 S.Ct. 1180, 90 L.Ed. 1489 (1946). Under *Pinkerton,* each member of a conspiracy is criminally liable for any crime committed by a coconspirator during the course and in furtherance of the conspiracy, unless the crime "did not fall within the scope of the unlawful project, or was merely a part of the ramifications of the plan which could not be reasonably foreseen as a necessary or natural consequence of the unlawful agreement." *Id.* at 647–48, 66 S.Ct. at 1184. The three appellants argue that murder is not a reasonably foreseeable consequence of a drug conspiracy, and that their murder convictions therefore should be reversed. We conclude that, although the murder convictions of the three appellants may represent an unprecedented application of *Pinkerton,* such an application is not improper.[21]

1. STANDARD OF REVIEW

We note initially that the scope of our review is limited. The application of the *Pinkerton* doctrine to a particular set of facts ultimately is for the jury to decide. In the instant case, the district court submitted the murder count to the jury with a proper *Pinkerton* instruction,[22] and the jury found the three appellants guilty of murder.

21. The three appellants also contend that their assault convictions were based on an improper application of the *Pinkerton* doctrine. Because drug conspiracies result in assaults at least as frequently as they result in murders, if not more so, our conclusion that murder is a reasonably foreseeable consequence of a drug conspiracy necessarily forecloses the appellants' argument with respect to the assault convictions.

22. The jury was instructed:

If you find that a particular defendant is guilty of conspiracy as charged in Count I of the indictment, you may also find the defendant guilty of either murder as charged in Count III of the indictment or assault as charged in Count IV of the indictment, or both, provided you find the essential elements of murder or assault or both as defined in these instructions have been established beyond a reasonable doubt; and provided you also find beyond a reasonable doubt:

First, that the murder or assault or both were committed pursuant to the conspiracy;

Second, that the murder or assault or both were reasonably foreseeable consequences of the conspiracy alleged in Count I; and

We must determine whether the court erred in deciding to submit the *Pinkerton* issue to the jury. Our standard of review is whether the evidence was sufficient for a reasonable jury to have concluded, beyond a reasonable doubt, that the murder was a reasonably foreseeable consequence of the drug conspiracy alleged in the indictment. In making this assessment, we must view the evidence in the light most favorable to the government, and accept all reasonable inferences and credibility choices made by the jury.

2. REASONABLE FORESEEABILITY

Upon reviewing the record, we find ample evidence to support the jury's conclusion that the murder was a reasonably foreseeable consequence of the drug conspiracy alleged in the indictment. In making this determination, we rely on two critical factors. First, the evidence clearly established that the drug conspiracy was designed to effectuate the sale of a large quantity of cocaine. The conspirators agreed to sell Agents Rios and D'Atri three kilograms of cocaine for a total price of $147,000. The transaction that led to the murder involved the sale of one kilogram of cocaine for $49,000. In short, the drug conspiracy was no nickel-and-dime operation; under any standards, the amount of drugs and money involved was quite substantial.

Second, based on the amount of drugs and money involved, the jury was entitled to infer that, at the time the cocaine sale was arranged, the conspirators must have been aware of the likelihood (1) that at least some of their number would be carrying weapons, and (2) that deadly force would be used, if necessary, to protect the conspirators' interests. We have previously acknowledged the "nexus" between weapons and drugs, *see United States v. Montes-Cardenas,* 746 F.2d 771, 776 (11th Cir.1984), and we have also recognized that weapons have become "tools of the trade" for those involved in the distribution of illicit drugs, *id.* at 777. * * * In light of these observations, and in view of the amount of drugs and money involved in the instant case, the jury's inference was both reasonable and proper.

In our opinion, these two critical factors provided ample support for the jury's conclusion that the murder was a reasonably foreseeable consequence of the drug conspiracy alleged in the indictment. In addition, we note the evidence at trial indicating that at least two of the conspirators were extremely nervous about the possibility of a rip-off or a drug bust. During a lull in the negotiations, Alvarez observed, "In this business, you have to be careful. It's a dangerous business. You have to watch out for rip-offs and Federal agents." Alvarez also stated

Three, that the particular defendant was a member of the conspiracy at the time of the murder or assault or both was committed.

Under the conditions just defined a defendant may be found guilty of a substantive count even though he did not participate in the murder or assault or both.

The reason for this is that a coconspirator committing a substantive offense pursuant to a conspiracy is held to be the agent of other conspirators as to acts which are reasonably foreseeable.

that he would never go back to prison, and that he would rather be dead than go back to prison. Alvarez' statements clearly implied that he contemplated the use of deadly force, if necessary, to avoid a rip-off or apprehension by Federal agents. The evidence also indicated that, immediately prior to the shoot-out, Simon looked nervously out the window while fidgeting with a leather pouch that was suspected to contain a weapon. The jury properly could take this additional evidence into account in reaching its conclusion about the foreseeability of the murder.

Because we find that the evidence in this case was more than sufficient to allow a reasonable jury to conclude that the murder was a reasonably foreseeable consequence of the drug conspiracy alleged in the indictment, we hold that the court did not err by submitting the *Pinkerton* issue to the jury.

3. INDIVIDUAL CULPABILITY

The three appellants also contend that, even if the murder was reasonably foreseeable, their murder convictions nevertheless should be reversed. The appellants argue that the murder was sufficiently distinct from the intended purposes of the drug conspiracy, and that their individual roles in the conspiracy were sufficiently minor, that they should not be held responsible for the murder. We are not persuaded.

It is well established that, under the *Pinkerton* doctrine, "[a] coconspirator is vicariously liable for the acts of another co-conspirator even though he may not have directly participated in those acts, his role in the crime was minor, or the evidence against a co-defendant more damaging." *United States v. Gagnon,* 721 F.2d 672, 676 (9th Cir. 1983). Thus, in a typical *Pinkerton* case, the court need not inquire into the individual culpability of a particular conspirator, so long as the substantive crime was a reasonably foreseeable consequence of the conspiracy.[24]

---

24. A typical *Pinkerton* case falls into one of two categories. The first and most common category includes cases in which the substantive crime that is the subject of the *Pinkerton* charge is also one of the primary goals of the alleged conspiracy. *See, e.g., United States v. Luis-Gonzalez,* 719 F.2d 1539, 1545 n. 4 (11th Cir.1983) (conspiracy to possess with intent to distribute marijuana; substantive crime of possession of marijuana); *United States v. Harris,* 713 F.2d 623, 626 (11th Cir.1983) (conspiracy to distribute cocaine; substantive crimes of possession and distribution of cocaine); *United States v. Tilton,* 610 F.2d 302, 309 (5th Cir.1980) (conspiracy to commit mail fraud; substantive crime of mail fraud).

The second category includes cases in which the substantive crime is not a primary goal of the alleged conspiracy, but directly facilitates the achievement of one of the primary goals. *See, e.g., Shockley v. United States,* 166 F.2d 704, 715 (9th Cir.) (conspiracy to escape by violent means from federal penitentiary; substantive crime of first degree murder of prison guard), *cert. denied,* 334 U.S. 850, 68 S.Ct. 1502, 92 L.Ed. 1773 (1948); *United States v. Brant,* 448 F.Supp. 781, 782 (W.D.Pa.1978) (narcotics conspiracy; substantive crime of possession of a firearm during commission of a felony).

In either of these two categories, *Pinkerton* liability can be imposed on all conspirators because the substantive crime is squarely within the intended scope of the conspiracy.

We acknowledge that the instant case is not a typical *Pinkerton* case. Here, the murder of Agent Rios was not within the originally intended scope of the conspiracy, but instead occurred as a result of an unintended turn of events. We have not found, nor has the government cited, any authority for the proposition that all conspirators, regardless of individual culpability, may be held responsible under *Pinkerton* for reasonably foreseeable but originally unintended substantive crimes.[25] Furthermore, we are mindful of the potential due process limitations on the *Pinkerton* doctrine in cases involving attenuated relationships between the conspirator and the substantive crime.[26]

Nevertheless, these considerations do not require us to reverse the murder convictions of Portal, Concepcion, and Hernandez, for we cannot accept the three appellants' assessment of their individual culpability. All three were more than "minor" participants in the drug conspiracy. Portal served as a look-out in front of the Hurricane Motel during part of the negotiations that led to the shoot-out, and the evidence indicated that he was armed. Concepcion introduced the agents to Alvarez, the apparent leader of the conspiracy, and was present when the shoot-out started. Finally, Hernandez, the manager of the motel, allowed the drug transactions to take place on the

25. The imposition of *Pinkerton* liability for such crimes is not wholly unprecedented. *See, e.g., Government of Virgin Islands v. Dowling,* 633 F.2d 660, 666 (3d Cir.) (conspiracy to commit bank robbery; substantive crime of assault with deadly weapons against police officers, committed during escape attempt), *cert. denied,* 449 U.S. 960, 101 S.Ct. 374, 66 L.Ed.2d 228 (1980); *Park v. Huff,* 506 F.2d 849, 859 (5th Cir.) (liquor conspiracy; substantive crime of first degree murder of local district attorney, committed in attempt to stop investigation of illegal liquor sales), *cert. denied,* 423 U.S. 824, 96 S.Ct. 38, 46 L.Ed.2d 40 (1975). In each of the aforementioned cases, however, vicarious liability was imposed only on "major" participants in the conspiracy.

At trial in the instant case, the government's attorney argued that *Pinkerton* liability for Agent Rios' murder properly could be imposed on all of the conspirators, and expressed the view that prosecutorial discretion would protect truly "minor" participants, such as appellants Rios and Raymond, from liability for the far more serious crimes committed by their coconspirators. We do not find this argument persuasive. In our view, the liability of such "minor" participants must rest on a more substantial foundation than the mere whim of the prosecutor.

26. *See United States v. Johnson,* 730 F.2d 683, 690 n. 8 (11th Cir.), *cert. denied,*

___ U.S. ___, 105 S.Ct. 186, 83 L.Ed.2d 119 (1984); *United States v. Moreno,* 588 F.2d 490, 493 (5th Cir.), *cert. denied,* 441 U.S. 936, 947, 99 S.Ct. 2061, 2168, 60 L.Ed.2d 666, 1049 (1979). We also note the observations of Judge Mansfield of the Second Circuit who, in discussing the analogous issue of aider-and-abettor liability, stated:

[I]t seems to me to place an undue strain on the concept to reason that, once a general conspiracy is shown, a minor or subordinate member who commits some act in furtherance of it thereby becomes an aider and abettor of parallel conduct of which he was unaware on the part of another member whose existence is unknown to him, merely because he should have reasonably foreseen that his conduct might assist others to commit such acts. Although such a foreseeability test might provide a basis for tort liability, the relationship strikes me as too attenuated to support a criminal conviction on the theory of aiding and abetting.

United States v. Blitz, 533 F.2d 1329, 1346–47 (2d Cir.) (Mansfield, J., dissenting) (citations omitted), *cert. denied,* 429 U.S. 819, 97 S.Ct. 65, 50 L.Ed.2d 79 (1976). Judge Mansfield acknowledged that the conviction in *Blitz* could have been upheld under the *Pinkerton* doctrine, but he strongly intimated that he would have disagreed with such a result as well. *See id.* at 1347.

premises and acted as a translator during part of the negotiations that led to the shoot-out.

In addition, all three appellants had actual knowledge of at least some of the circumstances and events leading up to the murder. The evidence that Portal was carrying a weapon demonstrated that he anticipated the possible use of deadly force to protect the conspirators' interests. Moreover, both Concepcion and Hernandez were present when Alvarez stated that he would rather be dead than go back to prison, indicating that they, too, were aware that deadly force might be used to prevent apprehension by Federal agents.

We find the individual culpability of Portal, Concepcion, and Hernandez sufficient to support their murder convictions under *Pinkerton*, despite the fact that the murder was not within the originally intended scope of the conspiracy. In addition, based on the same evidence, we conclude that the relationship between the three appellants and the murder was not so attenuated as to run afoul of the potential due process limitations on the *Pinkerton* doctrine. We therefore hold that *Pinkerton* liability for the murder of Agent Rios properly was imposed on the three appellants, and we decline to reverse their murder convictions on this ground.[27]

Notes and Questions

1. When is an offense a foreseeable consequence of a conspiracy? When is it in furtherance of that conspiracy? In Martinez v. State, 413 So. 2d 429 (Fla.App.1982), the defendant Martinez was charged with robbery and kidnapping. The prosecution's evidence showed that Martinez and one Garcia arranged for a sale of marijuana from Leigh Carracina and Marty Cohen to McConnell. Martinez set up a meeting at which the sale was to be completed. At that meeting (attended by Garcia as well as Martinez and Martinez' girlfriend), the sellers did not produce the marijuana. Instead, they robbed McConnell of the $85,000 he had brought along to pay for the marijuana and tied up Garcia and McConnell. Martinez left with the buyers, drove them to another location, and received $5,000 of the money. He was convicted as a coconspirator of the robbery and kidnapping committed by Carracina and Cohen. Affirming, the appellate court explained:

> A co-conspirator is not responsible * * * for an act in which he did not participate if that act is not the natural and probable outcome of the common design, but is instead an independent act or some of the party, conceived by others and outside the common purpose. It is a question of fact, as to whether * * * the act charged is a natural and probable consequence of [the] conspiracy.

27. Although our decision today extends the *Pinkerton* doctrine to cases involving reasonably foreseeable but originally unintended substantive crimes, we emphasize that we do so only within narrow confines. Our holding is limited to conspirators who played more than a "minor" role in the conspiracy, or who had actual knowledge of at least some of the circumstances and events culminating in the reasonably foreseeable but originally unintended substantive crime.

The trial court acting as trier of fact found that Martinez had entered into a conspiracy with Leigh and Marty to obtain money from McConnell by unlawful means, specifically, that Martinez was a coconspirator for the unlawful sale of controlled substance, namely marijuana. The court also found as a matter of fact that in this case the robbery and kidnapping were a foreseeable consequence of the planned sale of a large quantity of marijuana. Giving appropriate consideration to experience in this community, we think the trial court's second factual finding—that robbery and kidnapping are a foreseeable consequence of a conspiracy to effect a large drug transaction—was legally permissible.

413 So.2d at 430. If Martinez as well as Garcia had been tied and left at the scene of the robbery, would the result have been the same?

2. If the facts of Alverez had been governed by Section 2.06 of the Model Penal Code (reprinted at pages 682–83, supra), how would the liability, if any, of Portal, Concepcion and Hernandez for Rios' murder be analyzed? Note that under Section 2.06(3)(a)(ii), a person may be liable for an offense committed by another person if he "agrees * * * to aid such other person in planning or committing" the offense. But note also that such liability is subject to the requirement in Section 2.06(3)(a) that the defendant act "with the purpose of promoting or facilitating the commission of the offense."

3. The case law often assumes that if a conspirator effectively withdraws from a conspiracy before a crime is committed by a coconspirator, the withdrawal—even if it is not defense to the criminal conspiracy—precludes liability under the *Pinkerton* Rule for the substantive offense committed by a coconspirator. But it is not entirely clear what is necessary to make a withdrawal effective for this purpose. In Collins v. State, 561 P.2d 1373 (Okl.Crim.App.), cert. denied, 434 U.S. 906, 98 S.Ct. 306, 54 L.Ed.2d 193 (1977), Collins was charged with a murder arising out of a burglary-murder episode. Some evidence tended to show that Collins' codefendant (and coconspirator) Prowess held a gun on the victims while Collins bound them. Several times Collins said, "Let's get out of here." When Prowess told him to get the car, Collins ran from the house. Prowess then shot the victims and killed them. The trial court refused to instruct the jury on any possible abandonment by Collins of the venture before the killings by Prowess. Affirming, the appellate court explained:

> [I]n order to successfully abandon the scheme [a] party must communicate to the others involved his intention to do so. * * * [T]he defendant at no point told Jerry Prowess he was withdrawing; he left only upon Prowess' instructions to get the car.

561 P.2d at 1382. Where the defendant's action is sufficient to indicate an intention to withdraw from the venture, it is generally assumed that this "notice" must be actually communicated to all other members of the conspiracy before it becomes effective. See W. LaFave and A. Scott, Criminal Law 486 (1972). In two-person situations such as *Collins,* this is unlikely to be a problem. But in more complex arrangements, involving many individuals, such full communication to all other persons involved may present a difficult or perhaps impossible task.

According to some courts, withdrawal requires more than a communicated notice indicating an intent to withdraw. See United States v. Quesada-Rosadal, 685 F.2d 1281, 1284 (11th Cir.1982), indicating that effective withdrawal requires some affirmative action to defeat or disavow the purpose of the conspiracy. It has also been suggested that a withdrawal must occur before the commission of the crime by the coconspirator "becomes so imminent that avoidance is out of the question." Commonwealth v. Laurin, 269 Pa.Super. 368, 372, 409 A.2d 1367, 1369 (1979).

A recent decision by the Supreme Court suggests that the traditional criterion for determining the effectiveness of efforts to withdraw from a conspiracy may be insufficiently flexible, at least as a matter of federal conspiracy law. In United States v. United States Gypsum Co., 438 U.S. 422, 98 S.Ct. 2864, 57 L.Ed.2d 854 (1978), the defendants were charged with conspiracy to restrain trade in violation of section 1 of the Sherman Act, 15 U.S.C.A. § 1. In light of the five year statute of limitations, no conviction would have been possible if the crime terminated before December 27, 1968. Given the context of the case, the crime committed by the defendants would have terminated when (and if) they effectively withdrew from the conspiracy.

During trial, the defendants introduced evidence that vigorous price competition existed prior to December 27, 1968, and urged that this established that they had withdrawn from any conspiracy before the critical date. Instructing the jury on the defendants' theory, the trial judge told the jurors that withdrawal had to be established by either affirmative notice to each other member of the conspiracy or by disclosure of the illegal enterprise to law enforcement officials. The defendants requested a more expansive instruction which would have specifically permitted the jury to consider resumption of competitive activity, such as intensified price cutting or price wars, as affirmative action showing a withdrawal from the conspiracy; the request was denied. On appeal, the Supreme Court held the instructions on withdrawal to be reversible error:

> The charge fairly read, limited the jury's consideration to only two circumscribed and arguably impractical methods of demonstrating withdrawal from the conspiracy. [In a footnote the Court commented, "In this case the obligation to notify 'each other member' of the charged conspiracy would be a manageable task; in other situations all 'other' members might not be readily identifiable."] Nothing that we have been able to find in the case law suggests, much less commands, that such confining blinders be placed on the jury's freedom to consider evidence regarding the continuing participation of the alleged conspirators in the charged conspiracy. Affirmative acts inconsistent with the object of the conspiracy and communicated in a manner reasonably calculated to reach co-conspirators have generally been regarded as sufficient to establish withdrawal or abandonment.

438 U.S. at 464–65, 98 S.Ct. at 2887, 57 L.Ed.2d at 886.

If *United States Gypsum* establishes the standard for determining whether and when conspirators withdraw from a conspiracy for purposes of determining whether the period of limitations has expired, does the same standard apply when the issue is whether the defendants have effectively withdrawn so as to preclude liability for the crimes committed by cocon-spirators? Courts have tended to apply the same requirements for an effective withdrawal without reference to the context in which the with-drawal issue is raised, although the propriety of a uniform definition of effective withdrawal can be questioned. See Developments in the Law—Criminal Conspiracy, 72 Harv.L.Rev. 922, 959 (1959).

C. VICARIOUS LIABILITY

The term "vicarious liability" is sometimes loosely used in criminal law discussions. For example, the Indiana Supreme Court recently commented:

> When a person hires the commission of murder, he does so for the very reason that he had no desire to be present at the scene or pull the trigger himself. When [an Indiana statute] provides that the person who induces the commission of the offense commits the offense, it is imposing a form of vicarious liability rather than a liability based upon the physical participation in the act which actually constitutes the offense itself.

Kappos v. State, 465 N.E.2d 1092, 1095 (Ind.1984). Of course, one who employs another to commit an offense is clearly a "party" to that offense under the rules discussed in Section A of this Chapter. As the principal case in this section makes clear, there are other situations that in more careful discussion are often characterized as imposing vicarious liability. Is it clear that liability would not exist in these situations without a separate "doctrine" of vicarious liability?

As is also made clear in the principal case, the "vicarious" nature of liability in these situations is often related to what is sometimes the "strict" nature of the liability. Is there—or should there be—a neces-sary relationship between the two matters? Is it possible to impose "vicarious" but not "strict" liability?

STATE v. BEAUDRY
Supreme Court of Wisconsin, 1985.
123 Wis.2d 40, 365 N.W.2d 593.

ABRAHAMSON, JUSTICE.

The jury found the defendant, Janet Beaudry, the agent designated by the corporation pursuant to sec. 125.04(6)(a), Stats.1981–82, of the alcoholic beverage laws, guilty of the misdemeanor of unlawfully re-maining open for business after 1:00 a.m. in violation of sec. 125.68(4)(c), which prohibits premises having a "Class B" license from remaining open between the hours of 1:00 a.m. and 8:00 a.m. The tavern manag-er, not the defendant personally, had kept the tavern open, giving drinks to friends, contrary to his instructions of employment. On the basis of the judgment the defendant was ordered to pay a fine in the amount of $200.00.

The defendant raises two issues on appeal: (1) whether the statutes impose vicarious criminal liability on the designated agent of a corporate licensee for the conduct of a corporate employee who violates sec. 125.68(4)(c), Stats.1981–82, and (2) whether there is sufficient evidence to support the verdict in the case. Before we discuss these two issues, we shall set forth the facts.

I.

The facts are undisputed. The defendant, Janet Beaudry, and her husband, Wallace Beaudry, are the sole shareholders of Sohn Manufacturing Company, a corporation which has a license to sell alcoholic beverages at the Village Green Tavern in the village of Elkhart Lake, Sheboygan county. Janet Beaudry is the designated agent for the corporate licensee pursuant to sec. 125.04(6)(a), Stats.1981–82.

Janet Beaudry's conviction grew out of events occurring during the early morning hours of February 9, 1983. At approximately 3:45 a.m., a deputy sheriff for the Sheboygan County Sheriff's Department drove past the Village Green Tavern. He stopped to investigate after noticing more lights than usual inside the building and also seeing two individuals seated inside. As he approached the tavern, he heard music, saw an individual standing behind the bar, and saw glasses on the bar. Upon finding the tavern door locked, the deputy sheriff knocked and was admitted by Mark Witkowski, the tavern manager. The tavern manager and two men were the only persons inside the bar. All three were drinking. The deputy sheriff reported the incident to the Sheboygan county district attorney's office for a formal complaint.

At about noon on February 9, the tavern manager reported to Wallace Beaudry about the deputy's stop earlier that morning. After further investigation Wallace Beaudry discharged the tavern manager on February 11.

On March 2, 1983, the Sheboygan County Sheriff's Department served the defendant with a summons and a complaint charging her with the crime of keeping the tavern open after hours contrary to sec. 125.68(4)(c), Stats., and sec. 125.11(1), Stats. The tavern manager was not arrested or charged with an offense arising out of this incident.

The case was tried before a jury on May 20, 1983. At trial Janet Beaudry testified that she was not present at the tavern the morning of February 9. Wallace Beaudry testified that Janet Beaudry had delegated to him, as president of Sohn Manufacturing, the responsibilities of business administration associated with the Village Green Tavern; that he had hired Mark Witkowski as manager; that he had informed Witkowski that it was his duty to abide by the liquor laws; and that he never authorized Witkowski to remain open after 1:00 a.m., to throw a private party for his friends, or to give away liquor to friends.

Witkowski testified that he had served drinks after hours to two men. During cross-examination Witkowski confirmed that Wallace Beaudry had never authorized him to stay open after hours; that he had been instructed to close the tavern promptly at the legal closing tie of the offense for which the defendant is determined to be vicariously liable.

* * *

Vicarious liability, in contrast to strict liability, dispenses with the requirement of the *actus reus* and imputes the criminal act of one person to another. LaFave & Scott, *Criminal Law*, section 32 (1972).

Whether the defendant in this case is vicariously liable for the tavern manager's violation of sec. 125.68(4)(c), Stats.1981–82, depends on whether the specific statutes in question impose vicarious liability. We look first at the language of the statutes themselves.

The principal statutory provisions are secs. 125.68(4)(c)1., 125.11(1)(a), and 125.02(14). Sec. 125.68(4)(c), Stats.1981–82, provides that "no premises for which a 'Class B' license or permit has been issued may remain open between the hours of 1 a.m. and 8 a.m. * * *" Sec. 125.11(1)(a), provides that "[a]ny person who violates any provision of this chapter for which a specific penalty is not provided, shall be fined not more than $500 or imprisoned for not more than 90 days or both." Sec. 125.02(14), states that " '[p]erson' means a natural person, sole proprietorship, partnership, corporation or association."

It is apparent that no statute expressly imposes criminal liability upon the designated agent for the illegal conduct of the tavern manager. None of the statutes states, for example, that "whoever by herself or by an employee of the corporation for which she is the designated agent keeps the premises open shall be punished by * * *" or "whoever keeps the premises open is punishable by * * * and any act by a corporate employee shall be deemed the act of the designated agent as well as the act of the employee."

* * *

Nevertheless, as the state correctly points out, over a long period the court has interpreted several statutes regulating the sale of alcoholic beverages as imposing on the natural person licensee vicarious criminal liability for the illegal conduct of an employee.

* * *

[S]ince [these] decisions the legislature has had the opportunity to adopt or to preclude vicarious liability for violations of laws regarding sale of alcoholic beverages. The legislature took neither course of action. Instead the legislature left the statutes in question substantially the same. We read this legislative history to mean that in enacting the current laws the legislature intended to retain the * * * decisional law interpreting the statutes as imposing vicarious liability on the natural person licensee for the conduct of the employee who illegally sells alcoholic beverages.

In addition to the legislative history, another consideration persuades us that the legislature intended the statutes in question to impose vicarious criminal liability on the natural person licensee for an employee's violation of the closing hour law. The purpose of the statute is promoted if the doctrine of vicarious liability is applied.

Several factors influence this court to conclude that the purpose of the statute is promoted by the imposition of vicarious liability. First, the state has imposed numerous restrictions on the sale of alcoholic beverages to protect the public health and safety. The state has been particularly concerned with when and to whom alcoholic beverages may be sold. Statutes regulating the sale of alcoholic beverages have been recognized as creating strict liability "public welfare offenses." *See* Sayre, *Public Welfare Offenses,* 33 Colum.L.Rev. 55, 63 (1933).[13] Second, violation of the closing hours law is a misdemeanor; the penalty is a monetary fine and a relatively short period of imprisonment. Third, in many cases it may be difficult for the state to prove that the natural person licensee or corporate agent was negligent in hiring or supervising the employee, or knew about or authorized the employee's violation of the statute. Lastly, the number of prosecutions may be large so that the legislature would want to relieve the prosecution of the task of proving that the employer knew of or authorized the violation or was negligent. * * *

After reviewing the language of the current statutes, the legislative history of the current statutes, the cases interpreting the statutes, and the purpose of the statutes regulating the sale of alcoholic beverages, we conclude that the * * * line of cases interpreting alcoholic beverage statutes as imposing vicarious criminal liability on the natural person licensee for an employee's violation of an alcoholic beverage sale law have continuing validity under the statutes in question in this case.

Inasmuch as the natural person licensee is subject to vicarious criminal liability for the conduct of her or his employee who illegally sells alcoholic beverages, it logically follows that a corporation licensee should be similarly liable for the illegal conduct of its employee. But in this case the defendant is not the corporation licensee; the defendant is the designated agent of the corporation. The question for the present case, therefore, is whether a designated corporate agent is subject to vicarious criminal liability for the illegal conduct, *i.e.,* remaining open after closing hours, of the tavern manager who is an employee of the corporation. In other words, does the rationale of the * * * cases compel us to conclude that the statutes in issue here impose vicarious criminal liability on a designated agent of the corporate licensee for the illegal conduct of an employee of the corporation?

We agree * * * that the legislature intended to impose such liability on the designated agent. The court of appeals correctly noted that unless vicarious criminal liability was imposed on the designated agent, a natural person licensee could avoid criminal liability by simply incorporating the business. The legislative intent in vesting the desig-

---

13. * * * Many of the same factors that lead a court to interpret a statute as imposing strict liability lead the court to interpret the statute as imposing vicarious liability. LaFave & Scott, *Criminal Law,* sec. 32 (1972).

nated agent with full authority and responsibility for conduct of the business was to treat the designated agent as a natural person licensee for all purposes, including criminal liability. The legislature could not have intended to allow a natural person licensee to avoid criminal liability by incorporating the business.

While legislative purpose and public policy support our holding that a designated agent is vicariously liable for the conduct of the corporate employee who violates the closing hours law, the defendant's final argument is that due process requires blameworthy conduct on the part of the defendant as a prerequisite to criminal liability. Although the imposition of criminal liability for faultless conduct does not comport with the generally accepted premise of Anglo-American criminal justice that criminal liability is based on personal fault, this court and the United States Supreme Court have upheld statutes imposing criminal liability for some types of offenses without proof that the conduct was knowing or wilful or negligent.

The defendant's chief challenge to the constitutionality of the statute in issue in this case appears to be that the defendant could have received a jail sentence of up to 90 days for the violation. As the state points out, the defendant was fined $200, and the due process issue the defendant raises, whatever its validity, is not presented by the facts in this case. A decision by this court on the constitutionality of a jail term where the statute imposes vicarious liability would not affect the judgment of conviction in this case or the sentence imposed on this defendant. *See State v. Young,* 294 N.W.2d 728 (Minn.1980); *Commonwealth v. Koczwara,* 397 Pa. 575, 155 A.2d 825, 831 (1959), *cert. denied,* 363 U.S. 848, 80 S.Ct. 1624, 4 L.Ed.2d 1731 (1960). We therefore do not consider this issue.

* * *

III.

We turn now to the question of whether the evidence supports the verdict that the tavern manager was acting within the scope of his employment. As we stated previously, the jury was instructed that the defendant is liable only for the acts of the tavern manager that were within the scope of his employment. Thus the defendant is not liable for all the acts of the tavern manager, only for those acts within the scope of employment. Neither the state nor the defense challenges this statement of the law limiting the designated agent's vicarious criminal liability.

* * *

The "scope of employment" standard as applied to alcoholic beverage regulation in this state can be traced to *Doscher v. State,* 194 Wis. 67, 214 N.W. 359 (1927). In *Doscher,* the defendant was licensed to conduct a business selling non-intoxicating beverages. Contrary to instructions, an employee brought intoxicating liquor on the premises. The defendant, a natural person licensee, was convicted of unlawfully having intoxicating liquor on his premises. The state urged the court to uphold the conviction on the ground that the conscious possession of contraband liquor by the defendant's employee who was in charge of the licensed premises must be held to be the conscious possession of the defendant. The court reversed the conviction.

The *Doscher* court held that the principle of vicarious liability established in the [earlier] cases was not applicable to the *Doscher* case "because the possession of [intoxicating liquor by Doscher's] agent was not within the scope of his employment. * * *" *Id.* at 70, 214 N.W. 359. The *Doscher* court apparently viewed the employee who acts outside the scope of employment as an interloper for whose illegal conduct the employer would not be liable. The court thus distinguished the facts in that case from the *Conlin* line of cases as follows:

"In the [other] cases * * * the agent was employed to have possession of and dispose of liquor for the defendant. The very employment, therefore, contemplated and covered the field of possession, disposal, and sale of the articles, so that the respective violations by the agents of the specific regulations as to the manner of carrying on such employment could properly be charged against the defendant employers who knowingly furnished the agents with the means and opportunity of violating the law. Here the defendant as employer did not confer upon the one left in charge of the premises any power, authority, or means for any such violation. The act of the employee in going outside of the premises and obtaining the forbidden alcohol was a stepping outside of any express or implied authority given him by defendant. For such an act, entirely independent of and beyond the purpose of the employment, the defendant ought not to stand charged merely because of an existing relationship of master and servant for an entirely different and lawful purpose." 194 Wis. at 70–71, 214 N.W. 359.

The application of the standard of scope of employment limits liability to illegal conduct which occurred while the offending employee was engaged in some job-related activity and thus limits the accused's vicarious liability to conduct with which the accused has a factual connection and with which the accused has some responsible relation to the public danger envisaged by the legislature.

The defendant argues that in this case, as in *Doscher,* the tavern manager went outside his scope of authority. The state concedes that this is a reasonable view of the evidence and that this is a close case. The state argues, however, that the jury's verdict must be upheld under the standard of review applied to jury verdicts.

* * *

The credibility of the bar manager's testimony was a matter for the jury. The bar manager's testimony which supports the defendant's position that the manager was acting outside the scope of employment was based on a statement the bar manager gave defendant's counsel the night before trial. The jury may not have believed this testimony which was favorable to the defendant. Considering that the conduct occurred on the employer's premises and began immediately after "closing time"; that the employee had access to the tavern after hours only by virtue of his role as an employee of the corporate licensee, which role vested him with the means to keep the tavern open; and that the defendant may anticipate that employees may be tempted to engage in such conduct; the jury could conclude that the tavern manager's conduct was sufficiently similar to the conduct authorized as to be within the scope of employment. The jury could view the tavern manager's conduct as more similar to that of an employee to whom the operation of the business had been entrusted and for whose conduct the defendant should be held criminally liable than to that of an interloper for whose conduct the defendant should not be held liable.

For the reasons set forth, we affirm the decision of the court of appeals affirming the conviction.

Decision of the court of appeals is affirmed.

CECI, JUSTICE (dissenting).

* * *

We have previously held that a servant is *not* within the scope of his employment if (a) his acts were different in kind than those authorized by the master, (b) his acts were far beyond the authorized time or space limits, or (c) his acts were too little actuated by a purpose to serve the master. *Strack v. Strack*, 12 Wis.2d 537, 541, 107 N.W.2d 632 (1961), citing *Restatement (Second) of Agency* § 228(2) (1958) * * *.

The first element of the test asks whether Witkowski's acts were different in kind than those authorized by the defendant. Witkowski stated that one of his duties as a manager included closing the tavern at one o'clock. He testified that Wallace Beaudry never authorized him to stay open after the legal closing time. In fact, he was specifically instructed to close promptly at the legal closing time. Additionally, Witkowski testified, "I knew that Wally would not want me to stay open after hours but I decided to do it anyway."

Wally Beaudry also testified at the trial. He confirmed Witkowski's testimony by stating that one of Witkowski's duties was to follow all the liquor laws of this state and that he never authorized Witkowski to remain open after 1:00 a.m., throw a private party for his friends, or give away liquor. * * * I conclude that Witkowski was not within his scope of employment, because his act of keeping the tavern open until 3:45 a.m. was not authorized by Mr. or Mrs. Beaudry.

The second element of the test * * * asks whether Witkowski's acts were far beyond the authorized time or space limits. I conclude that Witkowski's acts were beyond the authorized time limit because, as stated above, there was testimony that Witkowski was not hired to stay open after hours, and, at the time the police arrived at the tavern, it was 3:45 a.m. Witkowski testified that he usually was done with his normal cleanup between 1:15 a.m. and 1:30 a.m. Over two hours passed between the time he should have locked up and left the tavern and the time the police arrived. Although there is no testimony to this fact, it can reasonably be inferred that Witkowski did not expect to get paid for these two hours when he was sitting at the bar and drinking with his friends. It is clear that Witkowski was no longer working at 3:45 a.m. and that his acts were far beyond the time limit authorized by Janet or Wally Beaudry.

The third and final factor to be considered is whether Witkowski's acts were too little actuated by a purpose to serve the defendant. Not only the direct testimony of Witkowski, but also the circumstantial evidence, provide support for the finding that Witkowski's acts were in no way intended to further the defendant's business, but were motivated solely for his own enjoyment and convenience. Witkowski testified that after the other patrons left the Village Green tavern, he was not performing any work duties, but was entertaining his "real good friends." Witkowski stated,

> "I was not trying to benefit Wallace Beaudry by staying open after hours. I was simply using Wally's tavern to have a *private party* for my two friends. By staying open for my two friends I was not trying to benefit Wallace Beaudry in any way, rather I was trying to benefit myself by continuing the conversation I had started with my friends." (Emphasis added.)

The undisputed circumstantial evidence also bears out the fact that Witkowski's acts were not serving the purpose of the defendant.

* * *

In conclusion, I would reverse the judgment of conviction because I conclude that as a matter of law, Mark Witkowski was outside his scope of employment when he kept the Village Green tavern open until 3:45 a.m., and, further, no jury, acting reasonably, could conclude otherwise. It is apparent that the jury did not apply the uncontroverted facts in this case to the law given in the jury instructions.

Notes and Questions

1. In Commonwealth v. Koczwara, 397 Pa. 575, 155 A.2d 825 (1959), cert. denied, 363 U.S. 848, 80 S.Ct. 1624, 4 L.Ed.2d 1731 (1960), the defendant, a tavern licensee and operator, was convicted of permitting minors to frequent the tavern and of selling beer to minors. He was not present at the time of the violations, which were committed by his bartender. The trial court imposed a three-month jail term and a fine of $500 and the costs of prosecution. Concluding that the jail sentence violated due process because it was based upon vicarious liability, the court vacated that portion of the sentence.

2. In Davis v. Peachtree City, 251 Ga. 219, 304 S.E.2d 701 (1983), defendant Davis was president of Kwickie Food Stores, a chain of approximately one hundred convenience stores. Without Davis' knowledge or authorization, an employee of one store sold wine to a minor on a Sunday. Davis was convicted of city ordinance violations barring sale of alcoholic beverages to a minor and sale of wine on Sunday; the ordinance specifically provided that a licensee is responsible for the conduct or actions of

employees while in his employment. Davis was sentenced to a $200 fine and a jail term of 60 days, although the jail term was suspended as long as Davis did not again violate "the laws of Georgia." The Georgia Supreme Court acknowledged that important public interests were served by the vicarious liability imposed but concluded that these interests could be served by the less onerous alternatives of fines and license revocations. As a result, the imposition of vicarious liability on Davis violated due process. Rejecting the *Koczwara* reasoning that vicarious liability was constitutionally acceptable if only a fine was imposed, the court reasoned:

> The damage done to an individual's good name and the peril imposed on an individual's future are sufficient reasons to shift the balance in favor of the individual. The imposition of such a burden on an employer "cannot rest on so frail a reed as whether his employee will commit a mistake in judgment," Koczwara, supra, 155 A.2d at 830, but instead can be justified only by the appropriate prosecuting officials proving some sort of culpability or knowledge by the employer.

251 Ga. at 222, 304 S.E.2d at 704.

3. In United States v. Park, 421 U.S. 658, 95 S.Ct. 1093, 44 L.Ed.2d 489 (1975), the Baltimore warehouse of a national food chain received food shipped in interstate commerce and allowed it to be exposed to rodent infestation. The corporation president, Park, was charged with and convicted of criminal violations of the National Pure Food and Drug Act. Under the applicable case law, a corporate agent could be liable for employee' actions in permitting the infestation if "by virtue of the relationship he bore to the corporation, the agent had the power to prevent the act complained of." The Court continued:

> The theory on which responsible corporate agents are held criminally accountable for "causing" violations of the Act permits a claim that a defendant was "powerless" to prevent or correct the violation "to be raised defensively at a trial on the merits. United States v. Wiesenfeld Warehouse Co., 376 U.S. 86, 91, 84 S.Ct. 559, 563, 11 L.Ed.2d 536 (1964). If such a claim is made, the defendant has the burden of coming forward with evidence, but this does not alter the Government's ultimate burden of proving beyond a reasonable doubt the defendant's guilt, including his power, in light of the duty imposed by the Act, to prevent or correct the prohibited condition. Congress has seen fit to enforce the accountability of responsible corporate agents dealing with products which may affect the health of consumers by penal sanctions case in rigorous terms, and the obligation of the courts is to give them effect so long as they do not violate the Constitution.

421 U.S. at 673, 95 S.Ct. at 1912, 44 L.Ed.2d at 501. Turning to the facts of the case before it, the Court rejected the argument that the jury instructions had been insufficient:

> Viewed as a whole, the charge did not permit the jury to find guilt solely on the basis of [Park's] position in the corporation; rather, it fairly advised the jury that to find guilt it must find [Park] "had a responsibile relation to the situation," and "by virtue of his position * * * had * * * authority and responsibility" to deal with the situation. The situation referred to could only be "food * * * held in

unsanity conditions in a warehouse with the result that it consisted, in part, of filth or * * * may have been contaminated with filth."

421 U.S. at 674, 95 S.Ct. at 1912–13, 44 L.Ed.2d at 502. In *Beaudry,* would the defendant have been permitted to raise defensively a claim that she had been powerless to prevent the violations committed by her employee? Is it constitutionally necessary that a defendant charged with a vicarious liability offense be permitted to raise such claims?

D. LIABILITY FOR ASSISTANCE AFTER THE FACT

As was discussed earlier, the common law of parties made an accessory after the fact a party to the crime and punishable as if he had himself committed it. Most modern criminal codes have abandoned this approach. One who provides post-crime assistance is seldom thereby rendered liable for the crime which was committed by the person assisted. But such a person is often guilty of a separate offense. Title 18 of the United States Code, for example, uses common law "party" terminology but a much different substantive approach than was followed under the law of parties:

§ 3. Accessory after the fact

Whoever, knowing that an offense against the United States has been committed, receives, comforts or assists the offender in order to hinder or prevent his apprehension, trial or punishment is an accessory after the fact.

* * * [A]n accessory after the fact shall be imprisoned not more than one-half the maximum term of imprisonment or fined not more than one-half the maximum fine prescribed for the punishment of the principal, or both; or if the principal is punishable by death, the accessory shall be imprisoned for not more than ten years.

Another approach is that used in following provision of the Model Penal Code:

Section 242.3. Hindering Apprehension or Prosecution

A person commits an offense if, with purpose to hinder the apprehension, prosecution, conviction or punishment of another for crime, he:

(1) harbors or conceals the other; or

(2) provides or aids in providing a weapon, transportation, disguise or other means of avoiding apprehension or effecting escape; or

(3) conceals or destroys evidence of the crime, or tampers with a witness, informant, document or other source of information, regardless of its admissibility in evidence; or

(4) warns the other of impending discovery or apprehension, except that this paragraph does not apply to a warning given in connection with an effort to bring another into compliance with law; or

(5) volunteers false information to a law enforcement officer.

The offense is a felony of the third degree if the conduct which the actor knows has been charged or is liable to be charged against the person aided would be a felony of the first or second degree. Otherwise it is a misdemeanor.

It is sometimes difficult to determine whether assistance was provided at such a time as to render the assisting person a participant in the offense or, instead, liable only under provisions such as 18 U.S. C.A. § 3. This is obviously important. If a person provides assistance *during* the offense, he is guilty of the crime and subject to the full penalty attaching to the offense. If he assists the perpetrator *after* the offense, he is subject to what is generally a much lower penalty. There is agreement that in order to create liability for the offense itself the assistance or encouragement must occur either before the crime or while it is in process. If one assists in the escape of another known to have committed an offense, on the other hand, he is properly convicted as accessory after the fact or under modern statutory equivalents. United States v. Balano, 618 F.2d 624, 631 (10th Cir.1979), cert. denied, 449 U.S. 840, 101 S.Ct. 118, 66 L.Ed.2d 47 (1980).

But despite the technical completion of the offense, for purposes of this analysis offenses are sometimes regarded as having "escape phases." One who assists the perpetrator during this "escape phase" joins the offense. Thus, persons like getaway car drivers are regarded as "entangled in the consummation of the crime itself" and properly charged with complicity in it. Id. See United States v. Willis, 559 F.2d 443 (5th Cir.1977), in which—according to Willis—the evidence showed only that he took the other participants to the bank and, when they ran out after robbing it, drove them away. The court assumed that the facts failed to show Willis' guilty knowledge of the others' purpose until they ran out of the bank and into the waiting car. It held, however, that Willis had been properly convicted of aiding and abetting the robbery because of his role as driver of the getaway car. For purposes of characterizing the involvement of those who join in the "escape phase" only, the court noted, the crime of robbery continues throughout the escape. 559 F.2d at 444 n. 5.

If, on the other hand, the perpetrators had come to Willis' home seeking assistance the day after the robbery and he had assisted them in fleeing to Brazil, he almost certainly would have violated only 18 U.S.C.A. § 3. In part, confusion in this area is due to the use of "escape" in two different senses. The flight of the perpetrators to Brazil in the hypothetical may be referred to as an "escape." But this must be distinguished from the "escape phase" of the robbery itself. Assistance provided to the perpetrators during this "escape phase" creates liability for the robbery itself.

STATE v. CHISM

Supreme Court of Louisiana, 1983.
436 So.2d 464.

DENNIS, JUSTICE.

The defendant, Brian Chism, was convicted by a judge of being an accessory after the fact, La.R.S. 14:25, and sentenced to three years in the parish prison, with two and one-half years suspended. The defendant was placed upon supervised probation for two years. * * *

On the evening of August 26, 1981 in Shreveport, Tony Duke gave the defendant, Brian Chism, a ride in his automobile. Brian Chism was impersonating a female, and Duke was apparently unaware of Chism's disguise. After a brief visit at a friend's house the two stopped to pick up some beer at the residence of Chism's grandmother. Chism's one-legged uncle, Ira Lloyd, joined them, and the three continued on their way, drinking as Duke drove the automobile. When Duke expressed a desire to have sexual relations with Chism, Lloyd announced that he wanted to find his ex-wife Gloria for the same purpose. Shortly after midnight, the trio arrived at the St. Vincent Avenue Church of Christ and persuaded Gloria Lloyd to come outside. As Ira Lloyd stood outside the car attempting to persuade Gloria to come with them, Chism and Duke hugged and kissed on the front seat as Duke sat behind the steering wheel.

Gloria and Ira Lloyd got into an argument, and Ira stabbed Gloria with a knife several times in the stomach and once in the neck. Gloria's shouts attracted the attention of two neighbors, who unsuccessfully tried to prevent Ira from pushing Gloria into the front seat of the car alongside Chism and Duke. Ira Lloyd climbed into the front seat also, and Duke drove off. One of the bystanders testified that she could not be sure but she thought she saw Brian's foot on the accelerator as the car left.

Lloyd ordered Duke to drive to Willow Point, near Cross Lake. When they arrived Chism and Duke, under Lloyd's direction, removed Gloria from the vehicle and placed her on some high grass on the side of the roadway, near a wood line. Ira was unable to help the two because his wooden leg had come off. Afterwards, as Lloyd requested, the two drove off, leaving Gloria with him.

There was no evidence that Chism or Duke protested, resisted or attempted to avoid the actions which Lloyd ordered them to take. Although Lloyd was armed with a knife, there was no evidence that he threatened either of his companions with harm.

Duke proceeded to drop Chism off at a friend's house, where he changed to male clothing. He placed the blood-stained women's clothes in a trash bin. Afterward, Chism went with his mother to the police station at 1:15 a.m. He gave the police a complete statement, and took the officers to the place where Gloria had been left with Ira Lloyd. The police found Gloria's body in some tall grass several feet from that spot. An autopsy indicated that stab wounds had caused her death. Chism's discarded clothing disappeared before the police arrived at the trash bin.

An accessory after the fact is any person, who, after the commission of a felony, shall harbor, conceal, or aid the offender, knowing or having reasonable ground to believe that he has committed the felony, and with the intent that he may avoid or escape from arrest, trial, conviction, or punishment. La.R.S. 14:25.

* * *

[W]e conclude that a person may be punished as an accessory after the fact if he aids an offender personally, knowing or having reasonable ground to believe that he has committed the felony, and has a specific or general intent that the offender will avoid or escape from arrest, trial, conviction, or punishment.[2] See W. Lafave & A. Scott, Criminal Law § 66 at 522–23 (1972); R. Perkins, Criminal Law § 8.4 at 667 (2d ed. 1969).

An accessory after the fact may be tried and convicted, notwithstanding the fact that the principal felon may not have been arrested, tried, convicted, or amenable to justice. La.R.S. 14:25. However, it is still necessary to prove the guilt of the principal beyond a reasonable doubt, and an accessory after the fact cannot be convicted or punished where the principal felon has been acquitted. *Id.* Furthermore, it is essential to prove that a felony was committed and completed prior to the time the assistance was rendered the felon, although it is not also necessary that the felon have been already charged with the crime. La.R.S. 14:25; See Lafave & Scott, *supra.*

Defendant appealed from his conviction and sentence and argues that the evidence was not sufficient to support the judgment. Consequently, in reviewing the defendant's assigned error, we must determine whether, after viewing the evidence in the light most favorable to the prosecution, any rational trier of fact could have found beyond a reasonable doubt that (a) a completed felony had been committed by Ira Lloyd before Brian Chism rendered him the assistance described below; (b) Chism knew or had reasonable grounds to know of the commission of the felony by Lloyd, and (c) Chism gave aid to Lloyd personally under circumstances that indicate either that he actively desired that the felon avoid or escape arrest, trial, conviction, or punishment or that he believed that one of these consequences was substantially certain to result from his assistance.

2. The Louisiana offense, therefore, is a compromise between the traditional common law crime of accessory after the fact, which required actual knowledge of a completed crime plus specific intent to aid the felon avoid justice, and the emerging modern trend, which recharacterizes the offense of accessory after the fact as obstruction of justice, and which dispenses with the requirement of a completed felony and knowledge of that fact by the accessory, allowing for conviction so long as the obstructive purpose is present. See A.L.I., Model Penal Code, part 2, article 242.3 and comment 3 (1980).

There was clearly enough evidence to justify the finding that a felony had been completed before any assistance was rendered to Lloyd by the defendant. The record vividly demonstrates that Lloyd fatally stabbed his ex-wife before she was transported to Willow point and left in the high grass near a wood line. Thus, Lloyd committed the felonies of attempted murder, aggravated battery, and simple kidnapping, before Chism aided him in any way. A person cannot be convicted as an accessory after the fact to a murder because of aid given after the murderer's acts but before the victim's death, but under these circumstances the aider may be found to be an accessory after the fact to the felonious assault. In this particular case, it is of no consequence that the defendant was formally charged with accessory after the fact to second degree murder, instead of accessory after the fact to attempted murder, aggravated battery or simple kidnapping. The defendant was fairly put on notice of the actual acts underlying the offense with which he was charged, and he does not claim or demonstrate in this appeal that he has been prejudiced by the form of the indictment.

The evidence overwhelmingly indicates that Chism had reasonable grounds to believe that Lloyd had committed a felony before any assistance was rendered. In his confessions and his testimony Chism indicates that the victim was bleeding profusely when Lloyd pushed her into the vehicle, that she was limp and moaned as they drove to Willow Point, and that he knew Lloyd had inflicted her wounds with a knife. The Louisiana offense of accessory after the fact deviates somewhat from the original common law offense in that it does not require that the defendant actually know that a completed felony has occurred. Rather, it incorporates an objective standard by requiring only that the defendant render aid "knowing or having reasonable grounds to believe" that a felony has been committed.

The closest question presented is whether any reasonable trier of fact could have found beyond a reasonable doubt that Chism assisted Lloyd under circumstances that indicate that either Chism actively desired that Lloyd would avoid or escape arrest, trial, conviction, or punishment, or that Chism believed that one of these consequences was substantially certain to result from his assistance. After carefully reviewing the record, we conclude that the prosecution satisfied its burden of producing the required quantity of evidence.

* * * Despite evidence supporting some contrary inferences, a trier of fact reasonably could have found that Chism acted with at least a general intent to help Lloyd avoid arrest because: (1) Chism did not protest or attempt to leave the car when his uncle, Lloyd, shoved the mortally wounded victim inside; (2) he did not attempt to persuade Duke, his would-be lover, exit out the driver's side of the car and flee from his uncle, whom he knew to be one-legged and armed only with a knife; (3) he did not take any of these actions at any point during the considerable ride to Willow Point; (4) at their destination, he docilely complied with Lloyd's directions to remove the victim from the car and

leave Lloyd with her, despite the fact that Lloyd made no threats and that his wooden leg had become detached; (5) after leaving Lloyd with the dying victim, he made no immediate effort to report the victim's whereabouts or to obtain emergency medical treatment for her; (6) before going home or reporting the victim's dire condition he went to a friend's house, changed clothing and discarded his own in a trash bin from which the police were unable to recover them as evidence; (7) he went home without reporting the victim's condition or location; (8) and he went to the police station to report the crime only after arriving home and discussing the matter with his mother.

* * *

Therefore, we affirm the defendant's conviction. * * *

DIXON, CHIEF JUSTICE (dissenting).

I respectfully dissent from what appears to be a finding of guilt by association. The majority lists five instances of *inaction*, or failure to act, by defendant: (1) did not protest or leave the car; (2) did not attempt to persuade Duke to leave the car; (3) did neither (1) nor (2) on ride to Willow Point; (5) made no immediate effort to report crime or get aid for the victim; (7) failed to report victim's condition or location after changing clothes. The three instances of defendant's *action* relied on by the majority for conviction were stated to be: (4) complying with Lloyd's direction to remove the victim from the car and leave the victim and Lloyd at Willow Point; (6) changing clothes and discarding bloody garments; and (8) discussing the matter with defendant's mother before going to the police station to report the crime.

None of these actions or failures to act tended to prove defendant's intent, specifically or generally, to aid defendant avoid arrest, trial, conviction or punishment.

Notes and Questions

1. Another means of addressing conduct after the commission of the offense has traditionally been the offense of misprision of felony. This is incorporated into the following provision of Title 18 of the United States Code Ann.:

§ 4. Misprision of felony

Whoever, having knowledge of the actual commission of a felony cognizable by a court of the United States, conceals and does not as soon as possible make known the same to some judge or other person in civil or military authority under the United States, shall be fined not more than $500 or imprisoned not more than three years, or both.

American courts have tended to construe such statutes as requiring some "active" concealment so that, unlike the situation under the English predecessor crime of misprision of felony, mere passive failure to report an offense or the location of an offender does not constitute the crime. See Goldberg, Misprision of Felony: An Old Concept in a New Context, 52 A.M. A.J. 148 (1966). Would it be realistic or desirable to require citizens to report such matters to authorities? Goldberg argues that a properly limited duty of this sort would be desirable:

> It may be * * * objected that a legal duty to report criminal acts to the authorities would be so novel in most American jurisdictions that even responsible citizens would unavoidably break the law. But all Americans are familiar with their legal duty to report serious traffic accidents to the police. It is about time we consider violent assault on persons as important as automobile crashes.

Goldberg, supra, at 150.

3. Many of the offenses governing post-crime assistance have exceptions covering assistance to relatives. A New Mexico statute, for example, provides:

> Harboring or aiding a felon consists of any person, not standing in the relation of husband or wife, parent or grandparent, child or grandchild, brother or sister by consanguinity or affinity, who knowingly conceals any offender or gives such offender any other aid, knowing that he has committed a felony, with the intent that he escape or avoid arrest, trial, conviction or punishment.

N.M.Stat.Ann. § 30–22–4. The rationale for a similar provision in a Florida statute was explained as follows:

> The statute represents a legislatively determined balance between two competing societal interests. The first is society's interest in apprehending suspected offenders. The second is society's interest in safeguarding the family unit from unnecessary fractional pressures. [The statute] achieves a balance between these two goals by restricting its application to a select group of family members and by conferring immunity so that these individuals need never choose between love of family and obedience to the law.

State v. C.H., 421 So.2d 62, 65 (Fla.App.1982).

In State v. Mobbley, 98 N.M. 557, 650 P.2d 841 (1982), the defendant Pam Mobbley was charged with violating the New Mexico statute by aiding one Andrew Needham. The agreed facts were that officers had come to the residence of Pam and Ricky Mobbley, husband and wife, told the defendant that felony warrants had been issued for her husband and Andrew Needham, and asked the defendant if "both were there." Although both men were in the house and the defendant knew it, she denied that they were there. The trial court had dismissed the charge on the ground that these facts could not give rise to the offense. A majority of the New Mexico Supreme Court reversed. It refused to broaden the legislatively-provided exception. Explaining the exception on the ground that the threat of criminal liability cannot realistically be expected to deter persons from assisting their close relatives, the court reasoned that this rationale did not suggest that the exception should be construed to cover the situation at issue. Judge Lopez, dissenting, argued:

> Whether the rationale underlying the legislative exemption is a recognition "that it is unrealistic to expect persons to be deterred from giving aid to their close relatives," LaFave and Scott, Criminal Law § 66 (1972), or an acknowledgement of human frailty, Torcia, Whar-

ton's Criminal Law § 35 (14th ed. 1978), that rationale is ignored by requiring a wife to turn in her husband if he is with another suspect. Such a result requires a proverbial splitting of analytic hairs by attributing the defendant's action, in denying that Needham was at the house, to an intent to aid Needham rather than her husband.

* * *

The practical effect of the majority opinion, which requires a wife to turn in her husband if he is with a co-suspect, is to deny the wife's exemption * * *. The reasons for refusing to force a wife to inform on her husband are the same whether or not he is alone. The statute should not be construed so narrowly as to frustrate the legislative intent to exempt a wife from turning in her husband.

98 N.M. at 559–60, 650 P.2d at 843–44 (Lopez, J., dissenting).

The majority, however, carefully noted that if and when the case went to trial, "a jury could properly determine, on the * * * facts, that defendant lacked the requisite statutory intent to aid Needham." 98 N.M. at 558, 650 P.2d at 842. Is this correct? What would the jury have to determine was the defendant's state of mind in order to find that she lacked the intent required to convict her of aiding Needham?

Chapter XII

"DEFENSES," JUSTIFICATION AND EXCUSE

Contents

To a large extent, the definition of specific criminal offenses and the requirement that the prosecution prove each element of the crime charged serves to define who should be subject to criminal liability. But it is clear that the definitions of the various crimes do not and perhaps cannot be the sole vehicle for defining the scope of criminal liability. The various legal doctrines commonly referred to as "true defenses" to criminal liability, which are the subject of the present chapter, also play an important role in this process.

The doctrines with which this chapter is concerned can be distinguished from those covered in Section E. of Chapter VI by the fact that the present matters are not logically and directly related to the elements of the crime charged. One court recently commented:

> Properly speaking, the description Defense in a criminal case should be reserved for matters in the nature of confession and avoidance where the accused asserts and proves facts in addition to those directly involved in proof or disproof of the ultimate facts alleged in the charge.

Wilson v. State, 284 So.2d 24, 26 (Fla.App.1973), rev'd on other grounds, 294 So.2d 327 (1974). Evidence concerning an alibi, for example, does not go to establishing a defense in the sense in which that word is used by this court; such evidence simply contradicts the proof of the prosecution that tends to show that the defendant committed the acts constituting the crime. A defendant who has produced evidence of an alibi is generally entitled to have the jury instructed that he does not have the burden of establishing an alibi and that if the whole evidence, including that tending to show alibi, leaves the jury with a reasonable doubt of the defendant's guilt, he should be acquitted. State v. Hunt, 283 N.C. 617, 197 S.E.2d 513 (1973).

The definition of "defense" offered in *Wilson* is misleading, however, insofar as it suggests that an inherent characteristic of a defense is placement of the burden of proof on the matter upon the defendant. Since true defenses are not directly related to elements of the crime charged, of course, they need not be negated in the prosecution's pleading. Sometimes the defendant must not only raise defensive matters but must also carry the burden of proof. In other instances, however, local law imposes upon the defendant only the burden of raising the matter by some evidence showing that the defense is an issue in the case. When the matter is so raised by a defendant, the prosecution then has the burden of negating the existence of the defense by proof beyond a reasonable doubt.

Traditionally, distinction has been drawn between doctrines that involve "justification" and those that involve "excuse." The former, under this division, involve a conclusion that the act committed by the defendant was "justified" and thus not wrongful conduct. Doctrines of "excuse," on the other hand, do not go to the justification or acceptability of the conduct but rather establish that the defendant has an "excuse" for engaging in wrongful conduct and thus is not criminally liable. See G. Fletcher, Rethinking Criminal Law 759 (1978). In practice, those doctrines regarded as ones establishing excuses—such as insanity—are ones permitting a defendant to rely on peculiar misperceptions of realty as showing that despite her wrongful conduct the defendant ought not to be held criminally accountable. Although there were formerly important differences in result between establishment of an excuse and of a justification, these no longer exist. J. Miller, Handbook of Criminal Law 255 (1934). But the distinction may still be of value in conceptualizing the impact of the various doctrines discussed in this material.

Professor Fletcher maintains that the conceptual basis on which "defenses" rest ought to affect how some subsidiary issues concerning those defenses are resolved. If a defense is recognized because the conduct is justified, then third persons who assist the actor ought to incur no criminal liability for their assistance. It should not be criminal, he argues, to assist another in performing acceptable conduct. Moreover, if conduct is not criminal because it is justified, resistance to that conduct may itself be criminal. Intentional and forceful interference with the appropriate conduct of another is often—and properly so—made criminal.

On the other hand, if a defense is recognized because the actor's conduct is excused, third persons who assisted the actor may logically be subjected to criminal liability, Professor Fletcher argues. Because the actor's participation is excused does not require or even strongly suggest that the participation of others should also be excused. Moreover, if the actor has an excuse-rationale defense to criminal charges based upon certain conduct, one who forcibly resists that conduct may properly be afforded a defense. One may reasonably be permitted, without incurring criminal liability, to forcibly resist the unjustified conduct of another even if the law exempts the other from criminal liability on excuse-type rationales. Id., at 760–62. Fletcher acknowledges, however, that Anglo-American criminal law has not carefully addressed the rationales for many widely-recognized "defenses" and, of course, has not developed or applied those defenses in ways logically consistent with either an excuse or justification rationale. Id., at 762.

In regard to each area of concern in this Chapter, it is important to consider whether the development of a separate defensive doctrine is necessary or desirable. In some cases at least, it is arguable that the underlying problem can best be accommodated by permitting the defendant to challenge the adequacy of the prosecution's proof of the elements of the crime charged, especially the intent necessary for guilt. If a separate defensive doctrine is appropriate, it is necessary to consider the extent to which it should be specified in narrowly drawn rules applicable to particular fact situations. In resolving this, it is necessary to consider the need to provide a vehicle for preventing or minimizing conviction of nonblameworthy or nondangerous persons. But consideration must also be given to the danger that broad defensive doctrines may be misused by defendants who can falsely persuade judges and juries who may use the flexibility of broad defensive doctrines to acquit defendants who should be convicted.

As with other areas of criminal law, it is necessary to consider the extent to which federal and state constitutional considerations limit the flexibility available to courts and legislatures in regard to defensive doctrines. In each area here, it is necessary to consider whether constitutional doctrines require that a defense be made available to defendants and what if any limitations constitutional doctrines impose upon any such defense as is made available. To some extent, constitutional considerations may define the outer perimeter within which policy choices may be made on the legislative or judicial level.

A. NECESSITY, DURESS, AND JUSTIFICATION GENERALLY

The doctrine of "necessity" has been most widely discussed in regard to situations in which a human life was taken in order to prevent the death of others. One leading case, United States v. Holmes, 26 Fed.Cas. 360 (No. 15,383) (C.C.E.D.Pa.1842), involved an American vessel which struck an iceberg in April, 1842. Nine crew members and thirty-two passengers got into the ship's longboat commanded by the first mate. Twenty-four hours after the ship had sunk, the weather worsened and the longboat appeared about to sink. The mate commanded that some of the passengers be thrown overboard, although he directed his crew not to part man and wife and not to throw over any women. Fourteen men and two women went overboard and perished; the women may have jumped into the sea after their brother was ejected from the boat. After daylight the next morning, two men who had hidden themselves were discovered and thrown into the sea. At no point had the passengers been consulted concerning these actions. All passengers and crew members aboard the longboat were saved the next day when the boat was sighted by another ship.

One of the crew members was indicted and tried for manslaughter. The trial judge instructed the jury as follows:

> Where * * * a case does arise, embraced by [the] "law of necessity," the penal laws pass over such case in silence * * *. For example, suppose that two persons who owe no duty to one another that is not mutual, should by accident, not attributable to either, be placed in a situation where both cannot survive. Neither * * * would * * * commit a crime in saving his own life in a struggle for the only means of safety * * *.
>
> But * * * the slayer must be under no obligation to make his own safety secondary to the safety of others * * *. [On shipboard, officers and sailers have a duty to protect passengers.] Should [an] emergency become so extreme as to call for the sacrifice of life, there can be no reason why the law does not remain the same. The passenger, not being bound either to labour or to incur the risk of life, cannot be bound to sacrifice his existence to preserve the sailor's. The captain, indeed, and a sufficient number of seamen to navigate the boat, must be preserved; for, except these abide in this ship, all will perish. But if there be more seamen than are necessary to manage the boat, the supernumerary sailors have no right, for their safety, to sacrifice the passengers * * *.
>
> But, in addition, if the source of the danger have been obvious, and destruction ascertained to be certainly about to arrive, although at a future time, there should be consultation, and some mode of selection fixed, by which those in equal relations may have equal chance for their life * * *. [T]he selection is [to be] by lot.

26 Fed.Cas. at 366–67. The defendant was convicted and sentenced to six months at hard labor and a fine of $20. After the president refused a pardon, the penalty was remitted.

In July of 1884, three English seamen—Dudley, Stephens, and Brooks—and a seventeen year old youth were forced to abandon an English yacht in an open boat. After twenty days, eight without any food at all, Stephens and Dudley killed the youth over the objections of Brooks. All three fed upon the youth's body and were rescued four days later. Dudley and Stephens were charged with murder. The jury found the basic facts of the case as stated above but disclaimed an ability to determine whether the acts constituted murder. On referral to the court, the facts were held to constitute murder. Regina v. Dudley and Stephens, 14 Q.B.D. 273 (1884). The court explained:

> [T]he temptation to the act which existed here was not what the law has ever called necessity. Nor is this to be regretted. Though law and morality are not the same, and many things may be immoral which are not necessarily illegal, yet the absolute divorce of law from morality would be of fatal consequence; and such divorce would follow if the temptation to murder in this case were to be held by law an absolute defense of it. It is not so. To preserve one's life is generally speaking a duty, but it may be the plainest and highest duty to sacrifice it * * *. It is not needful to point out the awful dangers of admitting

the principle which has been contended for. Who is to be the judge of this sort of necessity? By what measure is the comparative value of lives to be measured? Is it to be strength, or intellect, or what? * * * We are often compelled to set up standards we cannot reach ourselves, and to lay down rules which we could not ourselves satisfy. But a man has no right to declare temptation to be an excuse, though he might himself have yielded to it, nor allow compassion for the criminal to change or weaken in any manner the legal definition of the crime.

14 Q.B.D. at 287–88. The defendants were sentenced to death but this was later commuted by the Crown to six months' imprisonment.

As the following case demonstrates, the doctrine of necessity is closely related to and sometimes indistinguishable from the doctrine of duress, which deals with wrongful pressure by another person to engage in criminal activity.

For a detailed and fascinating account of *Dudley & Stephens* and similar events involving cannibalism in response to maritime disasters see Simpson, Cannibalism and the Common Law (1984). For a general discussions of these matters, see Perkins, Impelled Perpetration Restated, 33 Hastings L.J. 403 (1981); Comment, Necessity Defined: A New Role in the Criminal Defense System, 29 U.C.L.A.L.Rev. 409 (1981).

UNITED STATES v. BAILEY

Supreme Court of the United States, 1980.
444 U.S. 394, 100 S.Ct. 624, 62 L.Ed.2d 575.

MR. JUSTICE REHNQUIST delivered the opinion of the Court.

In the early morning hours of August 26, 1976, respondents Clifford Bailey, James T. Cogdell, Ronald C. Cooley, and Ralph Walker, federal prisoners at the District of Columbia jail, crawled through a window from which a bar had been removed, slid down a knotted bedsheet, and escaped from custody. Federal authorities recaptured them after they had remained at large for a period of time ranging from one month to three and one-half months. Upon their apprehension, they were charged with violating 18 U.S.C. § 751(a), which governs escape from federal custody. At their trials, each of the respondents adduced or offered to adduce evidence as to various conditions and events at the District of Columbia jail, but each was convicted by the jury. The Court of Appeals for the District of Columbia Circuit reversed the convictions by a divided vote * * *. We granted certiorari, and now reverse the judgments of the Court of Appeals.

* * *

I

All respondents requested jury trials and were initially scheduled to be tried jointly. At the last minute, however, respondent Cogdell secured a severance. * * *

The prosecution's case in chief against Bailey, Cooley, and Walker was brief. The Government introduced evidence that each of the respondents was in federal custody on August 26, 1976, that they had disappeared, apparently through a cell window, at approximately 5:35 a.m. on that date, and that they had been apprehended individually between September 27 and December 13, 1976.

Respondents' defense of duress or necessity centered on the conditions in the jail during the months of June, July, and August 1976, and on various threats and beatings directed at them during that period. In describing the conditions at the jail, they introduced evidence of frequent fires in "Northeast One," the maximum-security cellblock occupied by respondents prior to their escape. Construed in the light most favorable to them, this evidence demonstrated that the inmates of Northeast One, and on occasion the guards in that unit, set fire to trash, bedding, and other objects thrown from the cells. According to the inmates, the guards simply allowed the fires to burn until they went out. Although the fires apparently were confined to small areas and posed no substantial threat of spreading through the complex, poor ventilation caused smoke to collect and linger in the cellblock.

Respondents Cooley and Bailey also introduced testimony that the guards at the jail had subjected them to beatings and to threats of death. Walker attempted to prove that he was an epileptic and had received inadequate medical attention for his seizures.

Consistently during the trial, the District Court stressed that, to sustain their defenses, respondents would have to introduce some evidence that they attempted to surrender or engaged in equivalent conduct once they had freed themselves from the conditions they described. But the court waited for such evidence in vain. Respondent Cooley, who had eluded the authorities for one month, testified that his "people" had tried to contact the authorities, but "never got in touch with anybody." App. 119. He also suggested that someone had told his sister that the Federal Bureau of Investigation would kill him when he was apprehended.

Respondent Bailey, who was apprehended on November 19, 1976, told a similar story. He stated that he "had the jail officials called several times," but did not turn himself in because "I would still be under the threats of death." Like Cooley, Bailey testified that "the FBI was telling my people that they was going to shoot me." Id., at 169, 175–176.

Only respondent Walker suggested that he had attempted to negotiate a surrender. Like Cooley and Bailey, Walker testified that the FBI had told his "people" that they would kill him when they recaptured him. Nevertheless, according to Walker, he called the FBI three times and spoke with an agent whose name he could not remember. That agent allegedly assured him that the FBI would not harm him, but was unable to promise that Walker would not be returned to the

D.C. jail. *Id.*, at 195–200.[2] Walker testified that he last called the FBI in mid-October. He was finally apprehended on December 13, 1976.

At the close of all the evidence, the District Court rejected respondents' proffered instruction on duress as a defense to prison escape.[3] The court ruled that respondents had failed as a matter of law to present evidence sufficient to support such a defense because they had not turned themselves in after they had escaped the allegedly coercive conditions. After receiving instructions to disregard the evidence of the conditions in the jail, the jury convicted Bailey, Cooley, and Walker of violating § 751(a).

Two months later, respondent Cogdell came to trial before the same District Judge who had presided over the trial of his co-respondents. When Cogdell attempted to offer testimony concerning the allegedly inhumane conditions at the D.C. jail, the District Judge inquired into Cogdell's conduct between his escape on August 26 and his apprehension on September 28. In response to Cogdell's assertion that he "may have written letters," the District Court specified that Cogdell could testify only as to "what he did * * * [n]ot what he may have done." App. 230. Absent such testimony, however, the District Court ruled that Cogdell could not present evidence of conditions at the jail. Cogdell subsequently chose not to testify on his own behalf, and was convicted by the jury of violating § 751(a).

By a divided vote, the Court of Appeals reversed each respondent's conviction and remanded for new trials. See 190 U.S.App.D.C. 142, 585 F.2d 1087 (1978); 190 U.S.App.D.C. 185, 585 F.2d 1130 (1978). * * *

II

Respondents * * * contend that they are entitled to a new trial because they presented (or, in Cogdell's case, could have presented) sufficient evidence of duress or necessity to submit such a defense to the jury. The majority below did not confront this claim squarely, holding instead that, to the extent that such a defense normally would be barred by a prisoner's failure to return to custody, neither the indictment nor the jury instructions adequately described such a requirement.

2. On rebuttal, the prosecution called Joel Dean, the FBI agent who had been assigned to investigate Walker's escape in August 1976. He testified that, under standard Bureau practice, he would have been notified of any contact made by Walker with the FBI. According to Dean, he never was informed of any such contact. App. 203–204.

3. Respondents asked the District Court to give the following instruction:

"Coercion which would excuse the commission of a criminal act must result from:

"1) Threathening [*sic*] conduct sufficient to create in the mind of a reasonable person the fear of death or serious bodily harm;

"2) The conduct in fact caused such fear of death or serious bodily harm in the mind of the defendant;

"3) The fear or duress was operating upon the mind of the defendant at the time of the alleged act; and

"4) The defendant committed the act to avoid the threatened [*sic*] harm."

Common law historically distinguished between the defenses of duress and necessity. Duress was said to excuse criminal conduct where the actor was under an unlawful threat of imminent death or serious bodily injury, which threat caused the actor to engage in conduct violating the literal terms of the criminal law. While the defense of duress covered the situation where the coercion had its source in the actions of other human beings, the defense of necessity, or choice of evils, traditionally covered the situation where physical forces beyond the actor's control rendered illegal conduct the lesser of two evils. Thus, where A destroyed a dike because B threatened to kill him if he did not, A would argue that he acted under duress, whereas if A destroyed the dike in order to protect more valuable property from flooding, A could claim a defense of necessity.

Modern cases have tended to blur the distinction between duress and necessity. In the court below, the majority discarded the labels "duress" and "necessity," choosing instead to examine the policies underlying the traditional defenses. In particular, the majority felt that the defenses were designed to spare a person from punishment if he acted "under threats or conditions that a person of ordinary firmness would have been unable to resist," or if he reasonably believed that criminal action "was necessary to avoid a harm more serious than that sought to be prevented by the statute defining the offense." The Model Penal Code redefines the defenses along similar lines. See Model Penal Code § 2.09 (duress) and § 3.02 (choice of evils).

We need not speculate now, however, on the precise contours of whatever defenses of duress or necessity are available against charges brought under § 751(a). Under any definition of these defenses one principle remains constant: if there was a reasonable, legal alternative to violating the law, "a chance both to refuse to do the criminal act and also to avoid the threatened harm," the defenses will fail. Clearly, in the context of prison escape, the escapee is not entitled to claim a defense of duress or necessity unless and until he demonstrates that, given the imminence of the threat, violation of § 751(a) was his only reasonable alternative.

In the present case, the Government contends that respondents' showing was insufficient on two grounds. First, the Government asserts that the threats and conditions cited by respondents as justifying their escape were not sufficiently immediate or serious to justify their departure from lawful custody. Second, the Government contends that, once the respondents had escaped, the coercive conditions in the jail were no longer a threat and respondents were under a duty to terminate their status as fugitives by turning themselves over to the authorities.

Respondents, on the other hand, argue that the evidence of coercion and conditions in the jail was at least sufficient to go to the jury as an affirmative defense to the crime charged. As for their failure to return to custody after gaining their freedom, respondents assert that

724 DEFENSES Ch. 12

this failure should be but one factor in the overall determination whether their initial departure was justified. According to respondents, their failure to surrender "may reflect adversely on the bona fides of [their] motivation" in leaving the jail, but should not withdraw the question of their motivation from the jury's consideration.

We need not decide whether such evidence as that submitted by respondents was sufficient to raise a jury question as to their initial departures. This is because we decline to hold that respondents' failure to return is "just one factor" for the jury to weigh in deciding whether the initial escape could be affirmatively justified. On the contrary, several considerations lead us to conclude that, in order to be entitled to an instruction on duress or necessity as a defense to the crime charged, an escapee must first offer evidence justifying his continued absence from custody as well as his initial departure and that an indispensable element of such an offer is testimony of a bona fide effort to surrender or return to custody as soon as the claimed duress or necessity had lost its coercive force.

First, we think it clear beyond peradventure that escape from federal custody as defined in § 751(a) is a continuing offense and that an escapee can be held liable for failure to return to custody as well as for his initial departure. Given the continuing threat to society posed by an escaped prisoner, "the nature of the crime involved is such that Congress must assuredly have intended that it be treated as a continuing one." *Toussie v. United States,* 397 U.S. 112, 115, 90 S.Ct. 858, 860, 25 L.Ed.2d 156 (1970). * * *

The Anglo-Saxon tradition of criminal justice, embodied in the United States Constitution and in federal statutes, makes jurors the judges of the credibility of testimony offered by witnesses. It is for them, generally, and not for appellate courts, to say that a particular witness spoke the truth or fabricated a cock-and-bull story. An escapee who flees from a jail that is in the process of burning to the ground may well be entitled to an instruction on duress or necessity, " 'for he is not to be hanged because he would not stay to be burnt.' " *United States v. Kirby,* 7 Wall. 482, 487, 19 L.Ed. 278 (1869). And in the federal system it is the jury that is the judge of whether the prisoner's account of his reason for flight is true or false. But precisely because a defendant is entitled to have the credibility of his testimony, or that of witnesses called on his behalf, judged by the jury, it is essential that the testimony given or proffered meet a minimum standard as to each element of the defense so that, if a jury finds it to be true, it would support an affirmative defense—here that of duress or necessity.

We therefore hold that, where a criminal defendant is charged with escape and claims that he is entitled to an instruction on the theory of duress or necessity, he must proffer evidence of a bona fide effort to surrender or return to custody as soon as the claimed duress or necessity had lost its coercive force. We have reviewed the evidence examined elaborately in the majority and dissenting opinions below, and find the case not even close, even under respondents' versions of the facts, as to whether they either surrendered or offered to surrender at their earliest possible opportunity. Since we have determined that this is an indispensable element of the defense of duress or necessity, respondents were not entitled to any instruction on such a theory. Vague and necessarily self-serving statements of defendants or witnesses as to future good intentions or ambiguous conduct simply do not support a finding of this element of the defense.[11]

III

In reversing the judgments of the Court of Appeals, we believe that we are at least as faithful as the majority of that court to its expressed policy of "allowing the jury to perform its accustomed role" as the arbiter of factual disputes. 190 U.S.App.D.C., at 151, 585 F.2d, at 1096. The requirement of a threshold showing on the part of those who assert an affirmative defense to a crime is by no means a derogation of the importance of the jury as a judge of credibility. Nor is it based on any distrust of the jury's ability to separate fact from fiction. On the contrary, it is a testament to the importance of trial by jury and the need to husband the resources necessary for that process by limiting evidence in a trial to that directed at the elements of the crime or at affirmative defenses. If, as we here hold, an affirmative defense consists of several elements and testimony supporting one element is insufficient to sustain it even if believed, the trial court and jury need not be burdened with testimony supporting other elements of the defense.

Because * * * the respondents failed to introduce evidence sufficient to submit their defenses of duress and necessity to the juries, we reverse the judgments of the Court of Appeals.

Reversed.

MR. JUSTICE MARSHALL took no part in the consideration or decision of these cases.

---

11. Contrary to the implication of Mr. Justice Blackmun's dissent describing the rationale of the necessity defense as "a balancing of harms," we are construing an Act of Congress, not drafting it. The statute itself, as we have noted, requires no heightened *mens rea* that might be negated by any defense of duress or coercion. We nonetheless recognize that Congress in enacting criminal statutes legislates against a background of Anglo-Saxon common law and that therefore a defense of duress or coercion may well have been contemplated by Congress when it enacted § 751(a). But since the express purpose of Congress in enacting that section was to punish escape from penal custody, we think that some duty to return, a duty described more elaborately in the text, must be an essential element of the defense unless the congres-sional judgment that escape from prison is a crime be rendered wholly nugatory. Our principal difference with the dissent, therefore, is not as to the existence of such a defense but as to the importance of surrender as an element of it. And we remain satisfied that, even if credited by the jury, the testimony * * * could not support a finding that respondents had no alternatives but to remain at large until recaptured anywhere from one to three and one-half months after their escape. To hold otherwise would indeed quickly reduce the overcrowding in prisons that has been universally condemned by penologists. But that result would be accomplished in a manner quite at odds with the purpose of Congress when it made escape from prison a federal criminal offense.

MR. JUSTICE STEVENS, concurring.

The essential difference between the majority and the dissent is over the question whether the record contains enough evidence of a bona fide effort to surrender or return to custody to present a question of fact for the jury to resolve. On this issue, I agree with the Court that the evidence introduced by defendants Cooley, Bailey, and Cogdell was plainly insufficient. Vague references to anonymous intermediaries are so inherently incredible that a trial judge is entitled to ignore them. With respect to Walker, however, the question is much closer because he testified that he personally telephoned an FBI agent three times in an effort to negotiate a surrender. But since he remained at large for about two months after his last effort to speak with the FBI, I am persuaded that even under his version of the facts he did not make an adequate attempt to satisfy the return requirement.

The fact that I have joined the Court's opinion does not indicate that I—or indeed that any other Member of the majority—is unconcerned about prison conditions described by Mr. Justice Blackmun. Because we are construing the federal escape statute, however, I think it only fair to note that such conditions are more apt to prevail in state or county facilities than in federal facilities. Moreover, reasonable men may well differ about the most effective methods of redressing the situation. In my view, progress toward acceptable solutions involves formulating enforceable objective standards for civilized prison conditions, keeping the channels of communication between prisoners and the outside world open, and guaranteeing access to the courts, rather than relying on ad hoc judgments about the good faith of prison administrators, giving undue deference to their "expertise" or encouraging self-help by convicted felons.[8] In short, neither my agreement with much of what Mr. Justice Blackmun has written, nor my disagreement with the Court about related issues, prevents me from joining its construction of the federal escape statute.

MR. JUSTICE BLACKMUN, with whom MR. JUSTICE BRENNAN joins, dissenting.

The Court's opinion, it seems to me, is an impeccable exercise in the undisputed general principles and technical legalism: The respondents were properly confined in the District of Columbia jail. They departed from that jail without authority or consent. They failed promptly to turn themselves in when, as the Court would assert by way of justification, the claimed duress or necessity "had lost its coercive force." Therefore, the Court concludes, there is no defense for a jury to weigh and consider against the respondents' prosecution for escape violative of 18 U.S.C. § 751(a).

It is with the Court's assertion that the claimed duress or necessity had lost its coercive force that I particularly disagree. The conditions

---

8. It would be unwise, and perhaps counterproductive to immunize escapes that would otherwise be unlawful in the hope that they would motivate significant reforms. * * *

that led to respondents' initial departure from the D.C. jail continue unabated. If departure was justified—and on the record before us that issue, I feel, is for the jury to resolve as a matter of fact in the light of the evidence, and not for this Court to determine as a matter of law—it seems too much to demand that respondents, in order to preserve their legal defenses, return forthwith to the hell that obviously exceeds the normal deprivations of prison life and that compelled their leaving in the first instance. The Court, however, requires that an escapee's action must amount to nothing more than a mere and temporary gesture that, it is to be hoped, just might attract attention in responsive circles. But life and health, even of convicts and accuseds, deserve better than that and are entitled to more than pious pronouncements fit for an ideal world.

* * *

Although the Court declines to address the issue, it at least implies that it would recognize the common-law defenses of duress and necessity to the federal crime of prison escape, if the appropriate prerequisites for assertion of either defense were met. Given the universal acceptance of these defenses in the common law, I have no difficulty in concluding that Congress intended the defenses of duress and necessity to be available to persons accused of committing the federal crime of escape.

* * *

I also agree with the Court that the absence of reasonable less drastic alternatives is a prerequisite to successful assertion of a defense of necessity or duress to a charge of prison escape. One must appreciate, however, that other realistic avenues of redress seldom are open to the prisoner. Where prison officials participate in the maltreatment of an inmate, or purposefully ignore dangerous conditions or brutalities inflicted by other prisoners or guards, the inmate can do little to protect himself. Filing a complaint may well result in retribution, and appealing to the guards is a capital offense under the prisoners' code of behavior. In most instances, the question whether alternative remedies were thoroughly "exhausted" should be a matter for the jury to decide.

I, too, conclude that the jury generally should be instructed that, in order to prevail on a necessity or duress defense, the defendant must justify his continued absence from custody, as well as his initial departure. I agree with the Court that the very nature of escape makes it a continuing crime. But I cannot agree that the only way continued absence can be justified is by evidence "of a bona fide effort to surrender or return to custody." The Court apparently entertains the view, naive in my estimation, that once the prisoner has escaped from a life- or health-threatening situation, he can turn himself in, secure in the faith that his escape somehow will result in improvement in those intolerable prison conditions. While it may be true in some rare circumstance that an escapee will obtain the aid of a court or of the prison administration once the escape is accomplished, the escapee, realistically, faces a high probability of being returned to the same prison and to exactly the same, or even greater, threats to life and safety.

The rationale of the necessity defense is a balancing of harms. If the harm caused by an escape is less than the harm caused by remaining in a threatening situation, the prisoner's initial departure is justified. The same rationale should apply to hesitancy and failure to return. A situation may well arise where the social balance weighs in favor of the prisoner even though he fails to return to custody. The escapee at least should be permitted to present to the jury the possibility that the harm that would result from a return to custody outweighs the harm to society from continued absence.

Even under the Court's own standard, the defendant in an escape prosecution should be permitted to submit evidence to the jury to demonstrate that surrender would result in his being placed again in a life- or health-threatening situation. The Court requires return to custody once the "claimed duress or necessity had lost its coercive force." Realistically, however, the escapee who reasonably believes that surrender will result in return to what concededly is an intolerable prison situation remains subject to the same "coercive force" that prompted his escape in the first instance. It is ironic to say that that force is automatically "lost" once the prison wall is passed.

The Court's own phrasing of its test demonstrates that it is deciding factual questions that should be presented to the jury. It states that a "bona fide" effort to surrender must be proved. Whether an effort is "bona fide" is a jury question. The Court also states that "[v]ague and necessarily self-serving statements of defendants or witnesses as to future good intentions or ambiguous conduct simply do not support a finding of this element of the defense." Traditionally, it is the function of the jury to evaluate the credibility and meaning of "necessarily self-serving statements" and "ambiguous conduct."

Finally, I of course must agree with the Court that use of the jury is to be reserved for the case in which there is sufficient evidence to support a verdict. I have no difficulty, however, in concluding that respondents here did indeed submit sufficient evidence to support a verdict of not guilty, if the jury were so inclined, based on the necessity defense. Respondent Bailey testified that he was in fear for his life, that he was afraid he would still face the same threats if he turned himself in, and that "[t]he FBI was telling my people that they was going to shoot me." Respondent Cooley testified that he did not know anyone to call, and that he feared that the police would shoot him when they came to get him. Respondent Walker testified that he had been in "constant rapport," with an FBI agent, who assured him that the FBI would not harm him, but who would not promise that he would not be returned to the D.C. jail. Walker also stated that he had heard through his sister that the FBI "said that if they ran down on me they was going to kill me."

Perhaps it is highly unlikely that the jury would have believed respondents' stories that the FBI planned to shoot them on sight, or that respondent Walker had been in constant communication with an FBI agent. Nevertheless, such testimony, even though "self-serving," and possibly extreme and unwarranted in part, was sufficient to permit the jury to decide whether the failure to surrender immediately was justified or excused. This is routine grist for the jury mill and the jury usually is able to sort out the fabricated and the incredible.

In conclusion, my major point of disagreement with the Court is whether a defendant may get his duress or necessity defense to the jury when it is supported only by "self-serving" testimony and "ambiguous conduct." It is difficult to imagine any case, criminal or civil, in which the jury is asked to decide a factual question based on completely disinterested testimony and unambiguous actions. The very essence of a jury issue is a dispute over the credibility of testimony by interested witnesses and the meaning of ambiguous actions.

* * *

Notes

1. The defense of justification has been found inapplicable in several recent situations. In Commonwealth v. Capitolo, 508 Pa. 372, 498 A.2d 806 (1985), the defendants were charged with criminal trespass, based upon their entry into a nuclear powered electric plant. They asserted as a defense that they believed their entry and refusal to leave the plant was the only available method of shutting down the plant and thus eliminating the danger posed by the emanation of low level radiation from the plant. This was held unavailable, in part because no reasonable person could have foreseen that activity of this sort would halt the operation of the plant. Moreover, at the time the plant was undergoing a two-week shutdown. The defendants could not, then, have reasonably perceived that the plant posed the sort of imminent danger required to bring the defense into play.

In Commonwealth v. Berrigan, 509 Pa. 118, 501 A.2d 226 (1985), the defendants were charged with burglary, criminal mischief, and criminal conspiracy based upon their entry into a manufacturing plant, destroying missile components (apparently bomb shell casings) inside the plant with hammers, and pouring human blood onto the premises. In defense, they offered their belief that this action was necessary to prevent a nuclear holocaust. The Pennsylvania Supreme Court held that as a matter of law the defense was unavailable to them. The action of the defendants was not directed at the use of nuclear weapons but only at the manufacture of one component; the manufacture of these components, then, does not present the sort of imminent danger with which the defense is concerned. Moreover, the actions involved could not reasonably be expected to prevent the evil, i.e., the nuclear holocaust.

A somewhat different situation was presented in State v. Tate, 102 N.J. 64, 505 A.2d 941 (1986). Tate, a quadriplegic, was charged with possession of more than twenty grams of marijuana. A search of his premises revealed this substance plus other evidence (a scale and amounts of money) indicating that he was selling marijuana. As a defense, he asserted "justification" based on "medical necessity," and offered proof that marijuana was the only available method of easing the effects of spastic contractions he regularly suffered because of his condition. A state statute made available permission to use controlled substances under the supervision of physicians, but the program for granting such authorization had apparently not yet been implemented. A split majority of the New Jersey Supreme Court held that the defense was not available to Tate. In part, the court reasoned, the defense is available under the applicable statute only where "a legislative purpose to exclude the justification claimed does not otherwise plainly appear." The overall legislative scheme for regulating controlled substances reveals that the legislature contemplated and provided for possible medical uses of controlled substances. This, in turn, indicates an intention to exclude judicial development of a defense under the doctrine of justification. Moreover, the evidence failed to demonstrate that legal authorization for Tate's use of marijuana was totally unavailable:

> The defendant cannot make a choice to reject a legal alternative on the ground that it is too burdensome. Such a legal alternative was available, the illegal alternative was not "necessary," and resort to it was not justified.

102 N.J. at 75, 505 A.2d at 946–47.

2. There is widespread agreement that duress is no defense to an intentional killing. Some courts say it does not apply to a homicide. State v. Fuller, 203 Neb. 233, 243, 278 N.W.2d 756, 762 (1979). Should it apply to felony murder, especially where the defendant was coerced into participating in the felony and one of the coercing felons caused the victim's death? The Nebraska court uncritically found the duress defense unavailable in such a case without discussion or consideration of the possibility that the rationale for the limitation might not apply to felony murder. State v. Perkins, 219 Neb. 491, 499, 364 N.W.2d 20, 26 (1985). See generally the discussion in State v. Lassen, 679 S.W.2d 363, 369 (Mo.App.1984).

3. Statutes sometimes limit the duress defense even further. Under the Iowa statute, the defense—called "compulsion"—is unavailable for "any act by which one intentionally or recklessly causes physical injury to another." Iowa Code Ann. § 704.10. Under an Indiana statutory provision, the defense is not available to charges of "offenses against the person." Ind.Code § 35–41–3–8. Thus it is no defense to robbery or attempted robbery. Armand v. State, 474 N.E.2d 1002 (Ind.1985).

MODEL PENAL CODE *
(Official Draft 1985).

Section 2.09. Duress

(1) It is an affirmative defense that the actor engaged in the conduct charged to constitute an offense because he was coerced to do so by the use of, or a threat to use, unlawful force against his person or

the person of another, that a person of reasonable firmness in his situation would have been unable to resist.

(2) The defense provided by this Section is unavailable if the actor recklessly placed himself in a situation in which it was probable that he would be subjected to duress. The defense is also unavailable if he was negligent in placing himself in such a situation, whenever negligence suffices to establish culpability for the offense charged.

(3) It is not a defense that a woman acted on the command of her husband, unless she acted under such coercion as would establish a defense under this Section. [The presumption that a woman, acting in the presence of her husband, is coerced is abolished.]

(4) When the conduct of the actor would otherwise be justifiable under Section 3.02, this Section does not preclude such defense.

Section 3.02. Justification Generally: Choice of Evils

(1) Conduct which the actor believes to be necessary to avoid a harm or evil to himself or to another is justifiable, provided that:

(a) the harm or evil sought to be avoided by such conduct is greater than that sought to be prevented by the law defining the offense charged; and

(b) neither the Code nor other law defining the offense provides exceptions or defenses dealing with the specific situation involved; and

(c) a legislative purpose to exclude the justification claimed does not otherwise plainly appear.

(2) When the actor was reckless or negligent in bringing about the situation requiring a choice of harms or evils or in appraising the necessity for his conduct, the justification afforded by this Section is unavailable in a prosecution for any offense for which recklessness or negligence, as the case may be, suffices to establish culpability.

Notes

1. Compare the following provision that appeared in the Proposed Federal Criminal Code (Final Draft, 1971):

§ 610. Duress

(1) *Affirmative Defense.* In a prosecution for any offense it is an affirmative defense that the actor engaged in the proscribed conduct because he was compelled to do so by threat of imminent death or serious bodily injury to himself or another. In a prosecution for an offense which does not constitute a felony, it is an affirmative defense that the actor engaged in the proscribed conduct because he was compelled to do so by force or threat of force. Compulsion within the meaning of this section exists only if the force, threat or circumstances are such as would render a person of reasonable firmness incapable of resisting the pressure.

2. No provision for "justification generally" or "necessity" appeared in the Proposed Federal Criminal Code. § 608 of the Study Draft, which was not included in the final version, provided as follows:

§ 608. Conduct Which Avoids Greater Harm

Conduct is justified if it is necessary and appropriate to avoid harm clearly greater than the harm which might result from such conduct and the situation developed through no fault of the actor. The necessity and justifiability of such conduct may not rest upon considerations pertaining only to the morality and advisability of the penal statute defining the offense, either in its general application or with respect to its application to a particular class of cases arising thereunder.

3. Adoption of the Model Penal Code's justification provisions (including the other "defenses" discussed in this chapter) is examined in Note, Justification: The Impact of the Model Penal Code on Statutory Reform, 75 Colum.L.Rev. 914 (1975).

B. DEFENSE OF PERSONS, PROPERTY AND RELATED MATTERS

Among the most commonly-invoked of the defenses are those based upon claims that what would ordinarily be criminal conduct was engaged in for the purpose of protecting the actor himself, other persons, or property. As a practical matter, these defenses are generally limited to situations in which the defendant is charged with an assaultive crime, such as battery, assault, or one of the homicide offenses.

1. SELF–DEFENSE

There is universal agreement that force used by a person to defend themselves is, sometimes at least, insufficient to give rise to criminal liability. As the court in United States v. Peterson, 483 F.2d 1222 (D.C. Cir.1973), summarized:

Self-defense * * * is as viable now as it was in Blackstone's time * * *. But * * * the right of self-defense arises only when * * * necessity begins, and equally ends with the necessity * * *.

483 F.2d at 1229. Most of the issues in self-defense law concern the proper limits upon the defense in order to reasonably assure that it is available only when sufficient "necessity" existed. Special efforts have been made to limit the defense when the defendant used "deadly force"—force capable of inflicting death or serious bodily harm. This, of course, arises most often in homicide cases when the force used by the defendant in fact caused the death of the victim.

The following case raises issues concerning the defense in the context of a specialized situation—when one kills one's spouse who has over a sustained period of time inflicted psychological and physical harm upon the "killing" spouse. Consider, in connection with the case, whether generally appropriate limitations upon the right of self-defense adequately assure appropriate results in cases of this sort. To the extent that they do not, what remedial action is most appropriate?

The statutory provisions at issue in the case reprinted in this subsection distinguish between conduct which will be regarded as "justified" because of self-defense and other conduct which will be regarded as "excused" for similar reasons. The "justification" defense is based upon the actual existence of a need to use the force at issue to defend oneself. On the other hand, the "excuse" defense is based upon the defendant's belief—which may not have been correct—that the action was needed for self protection. Compare the approach used in Section 3.04 of the Model Penal Code, reprinted later in this subsection. Is any useful purpose served by separating justification from excuse as was suggested by the Proposed Federal Criminal Code and as was done by the North Dakota legislature?

STATE v. LEIDHOLM

Supreme Court of North Dakota, 1983.
334 N.W.2d 811.

VANDE WALLE, JUSTICE.

Janice Leidholm was charged with murder for the stabbing death of her husband, Chester Leidholm, in the early morning hours of August 7, 1981, at their farm home near Washburn. She was found guilty by a McLean County jury of manslaughter and was sentenced to five years' imprisonment in the State Penitentiary with three years of the sentence suspended. Leidholm appealed from the judgment of conviction. We reverse and remand the case for a new trial.

I

According to the testimony, the Leidholm marriage relationship in the end was an unhappy one, filled with a mixture of alcohol abuse, moments of kindness toward one another, and moments of violence. The alcohol abuse and violence was exhibited by both parties on the night of Chester's death.

Early in the evening of August 6, 1981, Chester and Janice attended a gun club party in the city of Washburn where they both consumed a large amount of alcohol. On the return trip to the farm, an argument developed between Janice and Chester which continued after their arrival home just after midnight. Once inside the home, the arguing did not stop; Chester was shouting, and Janice was crying.

At one point in the fighting, Janice tried to telephone Dave Vollan, a deputy sheriff of McLean County, but Chester prevented her from using the phone by shoving her away and pushing her down. At another point, the argument moved outside the house, and Chester once again was pushing Janice to the ground. Each time Janice attempted to get up, Chester would push her back again.

A short time later, Janice and Chester re-entered their home and went to bed. When Chester fell asleep, Janice got out of bed, went to the kitchen, and got a butcher knife. She then went back into the bedroom and stabbed Chester. In a matter of minutes Chester died from shock and loss of blood.

II

Leidholm raises seven issues on appeal, but because of the particular disposition of the case, we do not find it necessary to answer all of them.

The first, and controlling, issue we consider is whether or not the trial court correctly instructed the jury on self-defense. Our resolution of the issue must of necessity begin with an explanation of the basic operation of the law of self-defense as set forth in Chapter 12.1–05 of the North Dakota Century Code.

Our criminal code is the product of a massive revision which began in 1971 and culminated in 1973 with the legislative enactment of Senate Bill No. 2045. Although remnants of the "old code" survived revision and remain in the present code, most of its provisions are in substantial part modeled after the Proposed New Federal Criminal Code [Report of the North Dakota Legislative Council (1973) at 81], which in turn relies heavily on the American Law Institute Model Penal Code. See, generally, Working Papers (1970–1971). Both the Proposed Code and the Model Penal Code are highly integrated codifications of the substantive criminal law which exhibit close interrelationships between their respective parts. Final Report, Foreword at xiii (1971). This integration is especially apparent in Chapter 12.1–05 of the North Dakota Century Code, which is an almost complete adoption of Chapter 6 of the Proposed Code dealing with defenses involving justification and excuse. It is to Chapter 12.1–05, N.D.C.C., that we now turn.

Conduct which constitutes self-defense may be either justified [Section 12.1–05–03, N.D.C.C.] [and Section 12.1–05–07, N.D.C.C.], or excused [Section 12.1–05–08, N.D.C.C.].

[12.1–05–03. Self-defense. A person is justified in using force upon another person to defend himself against danger of imminent unlawful bodily injury, sexual assault, or detention by such other person * * *.

12.1–05–07. Limits on the use of force—Excessive force—Deadly force.

1. A person is not justified in using more force than is necessary and appropriate under the circumstances.

2. Deadly force is justified in the following instances:

* * *

b. When used in lawful self-defense * * * if such force is necessary to protect the actor * * * against death, serious bodily injury, or the commission of a felony involving violence. The use of deadly force is not justified if it can be avoided, with safety to the actor and others, by retreat or other conduct involving minimal interference with the freedom of the person menaced. * * * But * * * no person is required to retreat from his dwelling, or place of work, unless he was the original aggressor or is assailed by a person he knows also dwells or works there.

12.1–05–08. Excuse. A person's conduct is excused if he believes that the facts are such that his conduct is necessary and appropriate for any of the purposes which would establish a justification or excuse under this chapter, even though his belief is mistaken. However, if his belief is negligently or recklessly held, it is not an excuse in a prosecution for an offense for which negligence or recklessness, as the case may be, suffices to establish culpability. * * *

Under North Dakota homicide law, one commits murder if he causes the death of another (1) intentionally, (2) knowingly, or (3) "under circumstances manifesting extreme indifference to the value of human life." Section 12.1–16–01(1), N.D.C.C. Murder is reduced from a class AA felony to a class A felony if "the person causes death under the influence of extreme emotional disturbance for which there is reasonable excuse." Section 12.1–16–01(2), N.D.C.C. One commits manslaughter "if he recklessly causes the death of another human being." Section 12.1–16–02, N.D.C.C. A person commits negligent homicide "if he negligently causes the death of another human being." Section 12.1–16–03, N.D.C.C.] Although the distinction between justification and excuse may appear to be theoretical and without significant practical consequence, because the distinction has been made in our criminal statutes we believe a general explanation of the difference between the two concepts—even though it requires us to venture briefly into the pathway of academicism—is warranted.

A defense of justification is the product of society's determination that the *actual existence* of certain circumstances will operate to make proper and legal what otherwise would be criminal conduct. A defense of excuse, contrarily, does not make legal and proper conduct which ordinarily would result in criminal liability; instead, it openly recognizes the criminality of the conduct but excuses it because the actor believed that circumstances actually existed which would justify his conduct when in fact they did not. In short, had the facts been as he supposed them to be, the actor's conduct would have been justified rather than excused.

In the context of self-defense, this means that a person who believes that the force he uses is necessary to prevent imminent unlawful harm is *justified* in using such force if his belief is a *correct* belief; that is to say, if his belief corresponds with what actually is the case. If, on the other hand, a person *reasonably* but incorrectly believes that the force he uses is necessary to protect himself against imminent harm, his use of force is *excused*.

The distinction is arguably superfluous because whether a person's belief is correct and his conduct justified, or whether it is merely reasonable and his conduct excused, the end result is the same, namely, the person avoids punishment for his conduct. Furthermore, because a correct belief corresponds with an actual state of affairs, it will always be a reasonable belief; but a reasonable belief will not always be a correct belief, viz., a person may reasonably believe what is not actually the case.[3] Therefore, the decisive issue under our law of self-defense is not whether a person's beliefs are correct, but rather whether they are reasonable and thereby excused or justified.

Section 12.1–05–08, N.D.C.C., * * * sets forth the general conditions that excuse a person's conduct * * *.

The first sentence of Section 12.1–05–08, N.D.C.C., in combination with Section 12.1–05–03, N.D.C.C., which contains the kernel statement of self-defense, yields the following expanded proposition: A person's conduct is excused if he *believes* that the use of force upon another person is necessary and appropriate to defend himself against danger of imminent unlawful harm, even though his belief is mistaken.[4] Thus we have a statement of the first element of self-defense, i.e., a person must actually and sincerely believe that the conditions exist which give rise to a claim of self-defense.

From the next sentence of Section 12.1–05–08 we may infer that, besides being actual and sincere, a person's belief that the use of force is necessary to protect himself against imminent unlawful harm must be reasonable. Here, we have the second element of self-defense, namely, a person must reasonably believe that circumstances exist which permit him to use defensive force.

If, therefore, a person has an actual and reasonable belief that force is necessary to protect himself against danger of imminent unlawful harm, his conduct is justified or excused. If, on the other hand, a person's actual belief in the necessity of using force to prevent imminent unlawful harm is unreasonable, his conduct will not be justified or excused. Instead, he will be guilty of an offense for which negligence or recklessness suffices to establish culpability. For example, if a person recklessly believes that the use of force upon another person is necessary to protect himself against unlawful imminent serious bodily injury *and* the force he uses causes the death of the other person, he is guilty of manslaughter. See Sec. 12.1–16–02(1), N.D.C.C. And if a person's belief is negligent in the same regard, he is guilty of negligent homicide. See Sec. 12.1–16–03, N.D.C.C.

We are not the only State to make distinctions like this in the law of self-defense. Other States distinguish between reasonable and unreasonable beliefs when attaching liability for acts assertedly commit-

---

3. For example, a person may reasonably, but mistakenly, believe that a gun held by an assailant is loaded.

4. If the danger against which a person uses force to defend himself is "death, serious bodily injury, or the commission of a felony involving violence," the person may use deadly force [Section 12.1–05–07, N.D. C.C.], which is defined as that force "which a person uses with the intent of causing, or which he knows creates a substantial risk of causing, death or serious bodily injury." Sec. 12.1–05–12(2), N.D.C.C.

ted in self-defense. However, they do not further subdivide the class of unreasonably held beliefs, as our Legislature has done, into the subclass of recklessly held beliefs and the subclass of negligently held beliefs. Still, such interpretations do not significantly differ from our own.

Under both approaches, if a person reasonably believes self-defense is necessary, his conduct is excused or justified. And even though under our view an unreasonable belief may result in a conviction for either manslaughter or negligent homicide, and under theirs an unreasonable belief may result only in a conviction for manslaughter, they are the same to the extent that an honest but unreasonable belief will never result in a conviction for murder.

It must remain clear that once the factfinder determines under a claim of self-defense that the actor honestly and sincerely held the belief that the use of defensive force was required to protect himself against imminent unlawful injury, the actor may not be convicted of more than a crime of recklessness or negligence; but, if the factfinder determines, to the contrary, that the actor did not honestly and sincerely hold the requisite belief under a claim of self-defense, the actor may not appeal to the doctrine of self-defense to avoid punishment, but will be subject to conviction for the commission of an intentional and knowing crime.

As stated earlier, the critical issue which a jury must decide in a case involving a claim of self-defense is whether or not the accused's belief that force is necessary to protect himself against imminent unlawful harm was reasonable. However, before the jury can make this determination, it must have a standard of reasonableness against which it can measure the accused's belief.

Courts have traditionally distinguished between standards of reasonableness by characterizing them as either "objective" or "subjective." E.g., *State v. Simon,* 231 Kan. 572, 646 P.2d 1119 (1982). An objective standard of reasonableness requires the factfinder to view the circumstances surrounding the accused at the time he used force from the standpoint of a hypothetical reasonable and prudent person. Ordinarily, under such a view, the unique physical and psychological characteristics of the accused are not taken into consideration in judging the reasonableness of the accused's belief. See *State v. Cadotte,* 17 Mont. 315, 42 P. 857 (1895).

This is not the case, however, where a subjective standard of reasonableness is employed. See *State v. Wanrow,* 88 Wash.2d 221, 559 P.2d 548 (1977). Under the subjective standard the issue is not whether the circumstances attending the accused's use of force would be sufficient to create in the mind of a reasonable and prudent person the belief that the use of force is necessary to protect himself against immediate unlawful harm, but rather whether the circumstances are sufficient to induce in *the accused* an honest and reasonable belief that he must use force to defend himself against imminent harm.

Neither Section 12.1–05–03, N.D.C.C., nor Section 12.1–05–08, N.D. C.C., explicitly states the viewpoint which the factfinder should assume in assessing the reasonableness of an accused's belief. Moreover, this court has not yet decided the issue of whether Sections 12.1–05–03 and 12.1–05–08 should be construed as requiring an objective or subjective standard to measure the reasonableness of an accused's belief under a claim of self-defense. Finally, the legislative history of our self-defense statutes, as well as the commentaries to the codified criminal statutes which form the basis of the North Dakota Criminal Code, give no indication of a preference for an objective standard of reasonableness over a subjective standard, or vice versa.

We do, however, find guidance for our decision on this issue from past decisions of this court which developed the law of self-defense prior to the adoption in 1975 of Chapter 12.1–05, N.D.C.C. In 1907, the members of this court, confronted with the same issue whether to adopt an objective or subjective standard of reasonableness, unanimously decided to accept the latter standard for judging the reasonableness of an accused's belief because they believed it to be more just than an objective standard. [State v. Hazlett, 16 N.D. 426, 113 N.W. 374, 380–81 (1907)].

Because (1) the law of self-defense as developed in past decisions of this court has been interpreted to require the use of a subjective standard of reasonableness, and (2) we agree with the court in *Hazlett* that a subjective standard is the more just, and (3) our current law of self-defense as codified in Sections 12.1–05–03, 12.1–05–07, and 12.1–05–08 does not require a contrary conclusion, that is to say, our current law of self-defense is consistent with either a subjective or objective standard, we now decide that the finder of fact must view the circumstances attending an accused's use of force from the standpoint of the accused to determine if they are sufficient to create in the accused's mind an honest and reasonable belief that the use of force is necessary to protect himself from imminent harm.

The practical and logical consequence of this interpretation is that an accused's actions are to be viewed from the standpoint of a person whose mental and physical characteristics are like the accused's and who sees what the accused sees and knows what the accused knows. For example, if the accused is a timid, diminutive male, the factfinder must consider these characteristics in assessing the reasonableness of his belief. If, on the other hand, the accused is a strong, courageous, and capable female, the factfinder must consider these characteristics in judging the reasonableness of her belief.

In its statement of the law of self-defense, the trial court instructed the jury:

"The circumstances under which she acted must have been such as to produce in the mind of reasonably prudent persons, regardless of their sex, similarly situated, the reasonable belief that the other person was then about to kill her or do serious bodily harm to her."

In view of our decision today, the court's instruction was a misstatement of the law of self-defense. A correct statement of the law to be applied in a case of self-defense is:

"[A] defendant's conduct is not to be judged by what a reasonably cautious person might or might not do or consider necessary to do under the like circumstances, but what he himself in good faith honestly believed and had reasonable ground to believe was necessary for him to do to protect himself from apprehended death or great bodily injury." *Hazlett, supra,* 113 N.W. at 380.

The significance of the difference in viewing circumstances from the standpoint of the "defendant alone" rather than from the standpoint of a "reasonably cautious person" is that the jury's consideration of the unique physical and psychological characteristics of an accused allows the jury to judge the reasonableness of the accused's actions against the accused's subjective impressions of the need to use force rather than against those impressions which a jury determines that a hypothetical reasonably cautious person would have under similar circumstances.

Hence, a correct statement of the law of self-defense is one in which the court directs the jury to assume the physical and psychological properties peculiar to the accused, viz., to place itself as best it can in the shoes of the accused, and then decide whether or not the particular circumstances surrounding the accused at the time he used force were sufficient to create in his mind a sincere and reasonable belief that the use of force was necessary to protect himself from imminent and unlawful harm.

Leidholm argued strongly at trial that her stabbing of Chester was done in self-defense and in reaction to the severe mistreatment she received from him over the years. Because the court's instruction in question is an improper statement of the law concerning a vital issue in Leidholm's defense, we conclude it amounts to reversible error requiring a new trial.

III

Although we decide that this case must be sent back to the district court for a new trial, there still remain several other issues raised by Leidholm on appeal which must be addressed to ensure a proper disposition of the case on remand.

Expert testimony was presented at trial on what has come to be commonly referred to as the "battered woman syndrome." Such testimony generally explains the "phenomenon" as one in which a regular pattern of spouse abuse [6] creates in the battered spouse low self-esteem and a "learned helplessness," i.e., a sense that she cannot escape from the abusive relationship she has become a part of. See Comment, *The*

---

6. Typically, the pattern begins with a tension-building phase, followed by an intermediate phase where one spouse physically, with undoubted psychological effects, abuses the other, and a final phase where the battering spouse feels remorse for his actions and then attempts to "make up" with the battered spouse.

Admissibility of Expert Testimony on the Battered Woman Syndrome in Support of a Claim of Self-Defense, 15 Conn.L.Rev. 121 (1982).

The expert witness in this case testified that Janice Leidholm was the victim in a battering relationship which caused her to suffer battered woman syndrome manifested by (1) a psychological condition of low self-esteem and (2) a psychological state of "learned helplessness." On the basis of the expert testimony, Leidholm offered the following proposed instruction on battered woman syndrome:

"A condition known or described by certain witnesses as the 'battered wife syndrome' if shown by the evidence to have existed in the accused at the time she allegedly committed the crime charged, is not of itself a defense. However, as a general rule, whether an accused was assaulted by the victim of the homicide prior to the commission of a fatal act by the accused may have relevance in determining the issue of self defense.

"Whenever the actual existence of any particular purpose, motive or intent is a necessary element to the commission of any particular species or degree of crime, you may take into consideration evidence that the accused was or had been assaulted by the victim in determining the purpose, motive or intent with which the act was committed.

"Thus, in the crime of murder of which the accused is charged in this case, specific intent is a necessary element of the crime. So, evidence the accused acted or failed to act while suffering the condition known as the 'battered wife syndrome' may be considered by the jury in determining whether or not the accused acted in self defense. The weight to be given the evidence on that question, and the significance to attach to it in relation to all the other evidence in the case, are for you the jury to determine."

The court's refusal to include the proposed instruction in its charge to the jury, Leidholm contends, was error.

The instruction on battered woman syndrome was designed to support Leidholm's claim of self-defense by focusing the jury's attention on the psychological characteristics common to women who are victims in abusive relationships, and by directing the jury that it may consider evidence that the accused suffered from battered woman syndrome in determining whether or not she acted in self-defense. The instruction correctly points out that battered woman syndrome is *not of itself* a defense. In other words, "The existence of the syndrome in a marriage does not of itself establish the legal right of the wife to kill the husband, the evidence must still be considered in the context of self-defense." [8] [State v. Kelly, 33 Wn.App. 541, 655 P.2d 1202, 1203 (1982)].

---

8. And, if the particular facts of a defendant's case do not fit well with a claim of self-defense, the defendant perhaps should consider abandoning any such claim because the law of self-defense will not be judicially orchestrated to accommodate a theory that the existence of battered woman syndrome in an abusive relationship operates in and of itself to justify or excuse a homicide. When a battered spouse argues that a killing was committed in self-defense, the issue raised is not whether the battered spouse believes that homicide or suicide are the only available solutions to the problems she faces in her relationship with the abusive spouse, nor is it whether

There is nothing in the proposed instruction at issue which would add to or significantly alter a correct instruction on the law of self-defense. The jury's use of a subjective standard of reasonableness in applying the principles of self-defense to the facts of a particular case requires it to consider expert testimony, once received in evidence, describing battered woman syndrome and the psychological effects it produces in the battered spouse when deciding the issue of the *existence* and *reasonableness* of the accused's belief that force was necessary to protect herself from imminent harm. If an instruction given is modeled after the law of self-defense which we adopt today, the court need not include a specific instruction on battered woman syndrome in its charge to the jury.

IV

An inseparable and essential part of our law of self-defense limits the use of deadly force to situations in which its use is necessary to protect the actor against death or serious bodily injury. Sec. 12.1–05–07(2)(b), N.D.C.C. However, the use of deadly force by an actor in self-defense is not justified if a retreat from the assailant can be accomplished with safety to the actor and others. Sec. 12.1–05–07(2)(b), N.D. C.C. Thus, before it can be said that the use of deadly force is "necessary" to protect the actor against death or serious injury, it must first be the case that the actor cannot retreat from the assailant with safety to himself and others. In short, the use of deadly force is not necessary (and therefore not justified) within the meaning of our law of self-defense unless the actor has no safe avenue of retreat.

The practical effect of this statement is that the jury must first satisfy itself that an actor could not safely retreat before it can find that the actor's use of deadly force was necessary to protect himself against death or serious injury. And the way in which the jury determines whether or not the actor could not retreat safely is by considering whether or not the actor honestly and reasonably believed that he could not retreat from his attacker with safety.

The duty to retreat, however, is not a rule without exceptions. Section 12.1–05–07(2)(b), N.D.C.C., provides, in part:

" * * * (2) *no person is required to retreat from his dwelling,* or place of work, *unless he* was the original aggressor or *is assailed by a person who he knows also dwells* or works *there.*" [Emphasis added.]

Included within the trial court's instruction to the jury on the law of self-defense was a statement roughly equivalent to the [emphasized] language above. Leidholm maintains that the principle stated by this language violates the Equal Protection Clause, the Due Process Clause,

the cumulative effect of a series of beatings caused the battered spouse to react violently "under the influence of extreme emotional disturbance" by killing the batterer; under a claim of self-defense the only issue is whether the circumstances surrounding the killing were sufficient to create in the accused's mind *an honest and sincere belief that the use of deadly force is necessary to defend herself against imminent unlawful harm.* See *Kelly, supra,* 655 P.2d at 1203.

and the Privileges and Immunities Clause of Article 14, Section 1, of the Amendments to the United States Constitution. Her argument seems to be that making an individual's duty to retreat from his dwelling dependent upon the status of the assailant unduly discriminates against the accused if the attacker is a cohabitant. We find no merit in this argument.

If the facts and circumstances attending a person's use of deadly force against an assailant who is a cohabitant are sufficient to create in his own mind an honest and reasonable belief that he cannot retreat from the assailant with safety to himself and others, his use of deadly force is justified or excused, and his failure to retreat is of no consequence.

This is a certain corollary to the guiding principle in our law of self-defense that the reasonableness of an accused's belief is to be measured against the accused's subjective impressions and not against the impressions which a jury might determine to be objectively reasonable.

* * *

The judgment of conviction is reversed and the case is remanded to the district court of McLean County for a new trial.

Notes and Questions

1. On remand, if a new trial is held, the jury will probably be barred from convicting Leidholm of murder, since the verdict of guilty of manslaughter in the first trial constitutes an implied acquittal of the charged offense of murder. Under proper instructions, should the jury convict the defendant of manslaughter or negligent homicide or should it acquit her? *If* the jury had the option of convicting her of murder, would that be an appropriate result? Under the North Dakota statute, as well as under most formulations of the defense of self-defense, one may use force only to protect oneself against what is reasonably perceived to be the "danger of *imminent* bodily injury." (emphasis supplied) Could a jury find that Leidholm perceived a danger of imminent bodily injury from the deceased? Could it find that any such belief as she had was "reasonable?" It seems clear that Leidholm used deadly force and under North Dakota law this would be permissible only if she reasonably believed that safe retreat was not possible; see generally note 4, infra. Could the jury find such a belief? Could it find that any such belief as she had was "reasonable?"

In some cases, expert testimony bears more directly on some of these issues. See Note, The Battered Woman Syndrome and Self-Defense: A Legal and Empirical Dissent, 72 Va.L.Rev. 619 (1986). Battering behavior often occurs in cycles. Consequently, although a woman's defensive action may have occurred during a period of "calm," she may nevertheless have reasonably believed that the man presented a threat of imminent harm. Id., at 626. Between the periods of abuse, a man may demonstrate loving behavior that reinforces the woman's hope that the man will reform and thus encourages her to remain in the relationship. Moreover, according to defense experts, women's unsuccessful efforts to secure relief from police and others may reduce them to a state of "learned helplessness" in which they perceive themselves as unable to effectively leave the relationship or take other action short of a violent response. Id., at 629–30. One court summarized:

> [Some] women * * * become so demoralized and degraded by the fact that they cannot predict or control the violence that they sink into a state of psychological paralysis and become unable to take any action at all to improve or alter the situation. There is a tendency in battered women to believe in the omnipotence of their battering husbands and thus to feel that any attempt to resist them is hopeless.
>
> In addition * * *, external social and economic factors often make it difficult for some women to extricate themselves from battering relationships. A woman without independent financial resources who wishes to leave her husband often finds it difficult to do so because of a lack of material and social resources. * * * Moreover, the stigma that attaches to a woman who leaves the family unit without her children undoubtedly acts as a further deterrent to moving out.
>
> [B]attered women, when they want to leave their relationship, are typically unwilling to reach out and confide in their friends, family or the police, either out of shame and humiliation, fear of reprisal by their husband, or the feeling they will not be believed. * * * Case histories are replete with instances in which a battered wife left her husband only to have him pursue her and subject her to an even more brutal attack.

State v. Kelly, 97 N.J. 178, 194–95, 478 A.2d 364, 372 (1984). If such testimony was presented on retrial in *Leidholm,* would it establish the "excuse" of a belief in the right to defend oneself? Perhaps "imminent" should be defined in terms of the defendant's perception of alternatives. Thus if Leidholm reasonably—given her situation and experiences—perceived that she would be seriously harmed by her husband before she was able to secure aid or otherwise take effective preventive steps, the danger of that harm should be regarded as "imminent" within the meaning of self-defense. Cf. State v. Gallegos, 104 N.M. 247, 719 P.2d 1268, 1270–73 (App. 1986), cert. quashed.

2. In *Leidholm,* the admissibility of expert testimony concerning the battered woman syndrome was apparently not contested by the parties. Where challenges have been made to the admissibility of such testimony, the courts have divided although most appear to regard such testimony as admissible. Compare Mullis v. State, 248 Ga. 338, 282 S.E.2d 334 (1981) (holding such testimony inadmissible because the expert's testimony would address matters which are not difficult for jurors to comprehend by themselves) with State v. Kelly, 97 N.J. 178, 478 A.2d 364, 372 (1984) (holding such testimony admissible). If jurors may be reluctant to accept such expert testimony, does the need for accurate application of self-defense standards suggest some special efforts by the court? If so, would the instructions requested by the defense in *Leidholm* adequately perform the task? The Washington Supreme Court found error in a self-defense instruction in a somewhat similar case:

The * * * instruction * * * not only establishes an objective standard, but through the persistent use of the masculine gender leaves the jury with the impression the objective standard to be applied is that applicable to an altercation between two men * * * and, in the context of this case, violates the respondent's right to equal protection of the law. The respondent was entitled to have the jury consider her actions in light of her own perceptions of the situation, including those perceptions which were the product of our nation's "long and unfortunate history of sex discrimination." Frontiero v. Richardson, 411 U.S. 677, 684, 93 S.Ct. 1764, 1769, 36 L.Ed.2d 583 (1973). Until such time as the effects of that history are eradicated, care must be taken to assure that our self-defense instructions afford women the right to have their conduct judged in light of the individual physical handicaps which are the product of sex discrimination. To fail to do so is to deny the right of the individual woman involved to trial by the same rules which are applicable to male defendants.

State v. Wanrow, 88 Wn.2d 221, 240–41, 559 P.2d 548, 558–59 (1977).

3. The law of self-defense is often stated as providing that one can use deadly force in self-defense only if one reasonably believes that he is being assaulted or threatened with deadly force. In State v. Fullard, 5 Conn.App. 338, 497 A.2d 1041 (1985), for example, Fullard had stabbed one Heggs with a knife, killing him. In evaluating Fullard's claim of self-defense, the court commented, a critical question for the jury was whether Fullard "reasonably believed that Heggs was using or about to use deadly physical force, or was inflicting or about to inflict great bodily harm." 5 Conn.App. at 342, 497 A.2d at 1044. Although there is no hard-and-fast rule, this may—as a practical matter—often mean that a defendant can convince a judge or jury that he used deadly force in proper self-defense only if he can show that his assailant was armed with a deadly weapon. In Howard v. State, 390 So.2d 1070 (Ala.Crim.App.) writ denied, 390 So.2d 1077 (Ala.1980), for example, the court approved the following jury instruction:

> [A]n assault with the hand or fist never justifies or excuses a homicide under ordinary circumstances, and it is for you to decide whether the facts in this case are within the ordinary reason or not.

390 So.2d at 1074. And in Biniores v. State, 16 Ark.App. 275, 701 S.W.2d 385 (1985), the trial court rejected Biniores' claim of self-defense to the fatal shooting of Moss. Although there was testimony that Moss kept saying, "These hands can kill!," the court noted no evidence that Moss had a weapon or that Biniores thought he did and held that the trial court could easily have found that Biniores acted too hastily in shooting Moss.

If a victim is attacked with force not amounting to deadly force and nondeadly force would not be effective as a defensive measure, the victim must either submit to the injury or resort to deadly force at the risk of incurring criminal liability. R. Perkins and R. Boyce, Criminal Law 1118 (3rd ed. 1982). Submission, of course, does not bar the victim from pursuing after-the-fact remedies against the assailant, including criminal prosecution. The purpose of this is to "maximize social gain by preserving the life of the aggressor," even if the innocent victim is required to bear the personal cost of injury. LaFond, The Case for Liberalizing the Use of

Deadly Force in Self-Defense, 6 U.Puget Sound L.Rev. 237, 241 (1983). LaFond argues that this state of the law greatly impedes the ability of female, aged and young victims to establish before a judge or jury that they were, in fact, threatened with deadly force by an unarmed adult male assailant and therefore were entitled to use deadly force in self-defense. Moreover:

> Maximizing the preservation of human life by inexorably distributing a significant personal burden of physical harm and psychic scarring to many innocent victims chosen at random by violent aggressors may no longer accord with society's sense of social good. * * * [S]ociety today would not choose to preserve the lives of violent aggressors at the expense of physical and psychic harm to innocent victims.

Id., at 275. He proposes that one who honestly and reasonably believes that he is threatened by another with unlawful violence be permitted to use in self-defense any force—including deadly force—which he honestly and reasonably believes "is necessary to protect himself effectively." Id., at 280.

4. The North Dakota self-defense statute applied in *Leidholm* incorporated the common law position that one may not use deadly force in self-defense if an opportunity to instead retreat existed. This rule was designed to assure that human life was taken only in cases of strict necessity. United States v. Peterson, 483 F.2d 1222, 1234 (D.C.Cir.1973). Most American jurisdictions have rejected it. Id. But it is clear that a defendant's awareness of the availability of an opportunity to retreat may still be relevant to whether a right of self-defense existed. It may bear, for example, on whether the threatened harm was imminent enough to justify the force used and whether the defendant used more force than would reasonably be regarded as necessary under the circumstances. See State v. Jessen, 130 Ariz. 1, 9, 633 P.2d 410, 418 (1981).

Those jurisdictions applying the "retreat rule" generally do not require retreat when one is attacked in one's dwelling. This "castle doctrine" seems to have been based on notions of a special privacy interest in the dwelling and of the likelihood that further retreat would only further endanger the victim. A victim attacked in his dwelling, in other words, is already in the place to which he might otherwise be expected to retreat if attacked. See United States v. Peterson, supra, at 1236. Assuming that one should have a duty to retreat before using deadly force and that this duty should not apply when one is attacked in one's dwelling, do the rationales for the general rule and the "castle" exception suggest that one attacked in one's dwelling by a "co-dweller" should have to retreat? The North Dakota statute governing the situation in *Leidholm* requires retreat in such situations. Explaining its holding that retreat may be required in the face of an attack by a co-dweller, the District of Columbia Court of Appeals stated:

> [A]ll co-occupants, even those unrelated by blood or marriage, have a heightened obligation to treat each other with a degree of tolerance and respect. That obligation does not evaporate when one co-occupant disregards it and attacks another.

Cooper v. United States, 512 A.2d 1002, 1006 (D.C.App.1986). Compare State v. Laverty, 495 A.2d 831, 833 (Me.1985), applying what the court characterized as the majority approach and holding that under the retreat rule one attacked in one's dwelling by a co-dweller need *not* retreat. This position may rest upon the attacked co-dweller's interest in remaining in the home. Cooper, supra, 512 A.2d at 1005. As the New York court remarked early in the century, requiring a dweller to retreat may impose upon him an especially difficult burden. "Whither shall he flee, and how far, and when may he be permitted to return?" People v. Tomlins, 213 N.Y. 240, 244, 107 N.E. 496, 498 (1914), citing Jones v. State, 76 Ala. 8, 14 (1884).

5. In homicide cases, one who killed in the honest belief that the killing was necessary in self-defense but who exceeded the scope of the legal right of self-defense is generally regarded as guilty only of manslaughter. This is often characterized as involving an "imperfect" defense, because the defendant's liability is reduced but he is not exonerated. This applies to one who acted before force was reasonably necessary or who used more force than reasonably could have appeared necessary to prevent the threatened harm. See Sanchez v. People, 172 Colo. 168, 470 P.2d 857 (1970). W. LaFave and A. Scott, Criminal Law 665 n. 5 (2nd ed. 1985) suggest that such killings are best regarded as voluntary manslaughter because they are intentional killings. But if, as *Leidholm* suggests, manslaughter is appropriate because the defendant acted negligently in assessing his right to do what he did, would not involuntary manslaughter be a more appropriate category? The *Leidholm* court indicates that if Leidholm did not, upon retrial, establish a complete defense, the facts might indicate that either manslaughter or negligent homicide was the appropriate verdict. On what basis should the trier of fact choose between these two offenses *if* it determines that the facts do not justify her complete acquittal?

6. Another traditional limitation on the defense of self-defense is the rule that one who provokes an altercation or is the aggressor in it is not entitled to use force in self-defense during the altercation. If, however, he attempts to withdraw and communicates his desire to do so to his initial "victim," his right of self-defense is restored. This rule is based on the proposition that killings in self-defense are permissible only where necessary. "Quite obviously, a defensive killing is unnecessary if the occasion for it could have been averted ∗ ∗ ∗." United States v. Peterson, 483 F.2d 1222, 1231 (D.C.Cir.1973). But what constitutes "aggression" or "provoking the difficulty" has given rise to some dispute. In State v. Deans, 71 N.C.App. 277, 321 S.E.2d 579 (1984), review denied, 313 N.C. 332, 329 S.E.2d 386 (1985), for example, Deans and one Hales engaged in an argument at Hales' auto sales lot; both produced guns during the argument. Hales turned and went into the lot's office. Deans followed and in the office shot and killed Hales when Hales attacked Deans with a hammer. Upholding a verdict convicting Deans of murder, the court explained:

> Taking defendant's version of the incidents as true, he was not entitled to claim [the] absolute defense [of self-defense]. He testified that Hales, after demanding that defendant leave the premises, returned to the office. Defendant intentionally followed Hales into the trailer with

a gun knowing the volatile circumstances. Under these facts defendant "aggressively and willingly entered into the fight" [and therefore was the aggressor].

71 N.C.App. at 234, 321 S.E.2d at 583.

But compare *Deans* with Brown v. State, 698 P.2d 671 (Alaska App. 1985). Brown and one Miller argued, during which threats may have been made by Miller. Miller left for a bar. Brown sought Miller out in the bar, with the intent—according to Brown's testimony—to talk to Miller and convince Miller that he had no basis for his hostile attitude. Specifically, Brown testified he wanted to persuade Miller that Brown had not interfered in Miller's marriage. Brown took along a .22 rifle; he testified he knew Miller was armed and was "afraid of going just barehanded." During a confrontation in the bar, Brown shot and killed Miller. At Brown's trial for murder, the judge refused to instruct the jury on self-defense. This was found error on appeal.

Relying on Bangs v. State, 608 P.2d 1, 5 (Alaska 1980), the state claims that Brown became an initial aggressor and forfeited his right to claim self-defense when he armed himself and sought to confront Miller. * * *

In *Bangs,* a heated exchange took place between Bangs and his eventual victim, Troyer, during which Troyer grabbed Bangs and attempted to choke him. Bangs escaped, walked rapidly to his nearby trailer, grabbed a loaded revolver and returned to the scene of the struggle. Bangs testified that he pointed his gun at Troyer, cocked it, and challenged Troyer to "come on." When Troyer lunged at him, Bangs shot. The Alaska Supreme Court * * * held that * * * he was not entitled to a self-defense instruction, because he had been the initial aggressor.

We do not believe the holding in *Bangs* to be dispositive in the present case. * * * In * * * *Bangs* undisputed evidence established that [Bangs] anticipating resistance, procured [a gun] for the sole purpose of armed confrontation with [his] intended [victim and] challenged [his victim] to physical combat with the apparent purpose of provoking a response. * * * By contrast, in this case there was evidence that Brown * * * did not confront Miller to seek combat or challenge Miller for the purpose of provoking a physical response. * * *

Bangs does not deprive a defendant of the right generally recognized at common law to "seek his adversary for the purpose of a peaceful solution as to their differences." Hunter v. State, 137 Tex.Cr. R. 289, 128 S.W.2d 1176, 1181 (1939) (on motion for rehearing). As noted in State v. Bristol, 53 Wyo. 304, 84 P.2d 757, 765 (1938),

> [N]either the fact of arming himself, nor the fact of going to the restaurant, even if he knew that the [victim] was there, was sufficient to deprive the defendant of the right of self-defense. The criterion is as to what he then did or said when he found the [victim], and whether what he said or did was reasonably calculat-

ed to cause the [victim] to be provoked into attacking the defendant.

* * *

Viewing the evidence in the light most favorable to Brown, we believe that there is some evidence that Brown did not provoke a dispute with Miller under circumstances that he knew or should have known would result in mortal combat. Brown was therefore entitled to have his self-defense claim—weak as it may have been—properly determined by the jury.

698 P.2d at 673–74. Judge Singleton disagreed:

I would hold as a matter of policy that the statutory duty to retreat before resorting to deadly force precludes an assailant from arming himself and seeking out his ultimate victim where he fears a violent confrontation, i.e., he is aware of a substantial risk that a confrontation will be likely to result in the necessity that he use deadly force in self-defense. * * * [Cases holding to the contrary], in my view, encourage violence by authorizing the kind of conduct that Brown engaged in this case. Brown had a right to lead his life unobstructed by Miller. The fact that he knew Miller was armed and could be dangerous did not require Brown to hide in his room. If Brown feared Miller, Brown certainly could arm himself in order to go about his normal business so long as he did not intentionally seek Brown out. In my view, public policy precludes us from holding that Brown may arm himself with a rifle and seek out someone he has substantial reason to fear will shoot him in order to continue a confrontation.

Id., at 675, 677 (Singleton, J., concurring and dissenting).

7. Special problems are presented when the force against which a person defends himself consists of efforts to arrest the "defending" person. What right should one have to resist an arrest which one perceives as unlawful without incurring criminal liability for the resistance itself? The traditional common law rule was that force used to resist an unlawful arrest was a proper exercise of the right of self-defense and thus was not criminal. Regina v. Tooley, 2 Ld. Raymond Rep. 1296 (Q.B. 1709). This rule, however, developed when most arrests were made by private citizens, when resistance to arrests was likely to be effective in preventing the arrest, and when—because of the absence of provisions for pretrial release of accuseds—one arrested might spend years before trial. See Warner, The Uniform Arrest Act, 28 Va.L.Rev. 315 (1942). As a result, American courts have tended to restrict the rule, relying upon several rationales. First, resistance may no longer be effective:

In a day when police are armed with lethal and chemical weapons, and possess scientific communication and detection devices readily available for use, it has become highly unlikely that a suspect, using reasonable force, can escape from or effectively deter and arrest, whether lawful or unlawful. His accomplishment is generally limited to temporary evasion, merely rendering the officer's task more difficult or prolonged. Thus self-help as a practical remedy is anachronistic, whatever may have been its original justification or efficacy * * *.

Indeed, self-help not infrequently causes far graver consequences for both the officer and the suspect than does the unlawful arrest itself.

People v. Curtis, 70 Cal.2d 347, 353, 74 Cal.Rptr. 713, 716–17, 450 P.2d 33, 36–37 (1960). Nor is the need to avoid unlawful arrests, at least by police officers, as great:

In this era of constantly expanding legal protection of the rights of an accused in criminal proceedings, an arrestee may be reasonably required to submit to a possibly unlawful arrest and to take recourse in the legal processes available to restore his liberty. An arrestee has the benefits of liberal bail laws, appointed counsel, the right to remain silent and to cut off questioning, speedy arraignment, and speedy trial. As a result of these rights and procedural safeguards, the need for the common law rule disappears—self-help by an arrestee has become anachronistic. * * *

Commonwealth v. Moreira, 388 Mass. 596, 599–600, 447 N.E.2d 1224, 1227 (1983). Moreover, a rule permitting resistance provides a poor forum for resolving the underlying dispute:

If a police officer is making an illegal arrest * * * the remedy is to be found in the courts. The legality of an arrest may often be a close question as to which even lawyers and judges may disagree. Such a close question is more properly decided by a detached magistrate rather than by the participants in what may well be a highly volatile imbroglio. As the Alaska court wrote in [Miller v. State, 462 P.2d 421, 427 (Alaska 1969)], "We feel that the legality of a peaceful arrest should be determined by courts of law and not through a trial by battle in the streets."

Moreira, supra, 388 Mass. at 600, 447 N.E.2d at 1227. Most American jurisdictions, then, have followed the approach of the Moreira court:

[W]e conclude that in the absence of excessive or unnecessary force by an arresting officer, a person may not use force to resist an arrest by one who he knows or has good reason to believe is an authorized police officer, regardless of whether the arrest was unlawful in the circumstances. * * *

388 Mass. at 601, 447 N.E.2d at 1227. See also, Miller v. State, 462 P.2d 421 (Alaska 1969); State v. Richardson, 95 Idaho 446, 511 P.2d 263 (1973); State v. Koonce, 89 N.J.Super. 169, 214 A.2d 428 (1965). Some jurisdictions have found legislative rejection of the common law rule, relying upon criminal prohibitions against resisting arrest or wounding an officer engaged in official duties. See People v. Hess, 687 P.2d 443 (Colo.1984); State v. Thomas, 625 S.W.2d 115 (Mo.1981).

But as the statement of the "modern rule" by the Supreme Judicial Court of Massachusetts in Moreira suggests, most courts have recognized a person's continuing ability to resist excessive force used in making an arrest. In State v. Mulvihill, 57 N.J. 151, 270 A.2d 277 (1970), the court explained:

If, in effectuating the arrest or the temporary detention, the officer employs excessive and unnecessary force, the citizen may respond or counter with the use of reasonable force to protect himself, and if in so doing the officer is injured no criminal offense has been committed. * * *

There is sound reason for a difference in the rights and duties of the citizen in the two situations. Despite his duty to submit quietly without physical resistance to an arrest made by an officer acting in the course of his duty, even though the arrest is illegal, his right to freedom from unreasonable seizure and confinement can be protected, restored and vindicated through legal processes. However, the rule permitting reasonable resistance to excessive force of the officer, whether the arrest is lawful or unlawful, is designed to protect a person's bodily integrity and health and so permits resort to self-defense. Simply stated, the law recognizes that liberty can be restored through legal processes but life or limb cannot be repaired in a courtroom. And so it holds that the reason for outlawing resistance to an unlawful arrest and requiring disputes over its legality to be resolved in the courts has no controlling application on the right to resist an officer's excessive force.

Two qualifications on the citizen's right to defend against and to repel an officer's excessive force must be noticed. He cannot use greater force in protecting himself against the officer's unlawful force than reasonably appears to be necessary. If he employs such greater force, then he becomes the aggressor and forfeits the right to claim self-defense to a charge of assault and battery on the officer. See Restatement, Torts 2d, § 70, p. 118 (1965). Furthermore, if he knows that if he desists from his physically defensive measures and submits to arrest the officer's unlawfully excessive force would cease, the arrestee must desist or lose his privilege of self-defense.

It has been suggested that the latter qualification is not reasonable because it would require a citizen being subjected to excessive force or attack and defending against it to make a split second determination, amounting to a gamble, as to whether if he terminates his defensive measures, he will suffer further beyond arrest. But application of the rule does not require such action as should follow opportunity for detached reflection. It merely commands that the citizen's conduct be reasonable in the light of all the circumstances apparent to him at the moment. And thus it is a counter-protective measure for the original aggressor officer. Administration of the rule should be no more difficult than those dealing with the duty of an assaulted person to retreat to avoid the attack or the duty not to continue the affray after the original aggressor ceases the assault; once the danger is past, the original victim cannot continue measures that were originally defensive.

57 N.J. at 156–58, 270 A.2d at 279–80.

MODEL PENAL CODE *

(Official Draft 1985).

Section 3.04. Use of Force in Self-Protection

(1) *Use of Force Justifiable for Protection of the Person.* Subject to the provisions of this Section and of Section 3.09, the use of force upon or toward another person is justifiable when the actor believes that such force is immediately necessary for the purpose of protecting himself against the use of unlawful force by such other person on the present occasion.

(2) *Limitations on Justifying Necessity for Use of Force.*

(a) The use of force is not justifiable under this Section:

(i) to resist an arrest which the actor knows is being made by a peace officer, although the arrest is unlawful; or

(ii) to resist force used by the occupier or possessor of property or by another person on his behalf, where the actor knows that the person using the force is doing so under a claim of right to protect the property, except that this limitation shall not apply if:

(A) the actor is a public officer acting in the performance of his duties or a person lawfully assisting him therein or a person making or assisting in a lawful arrest; or

(B) the actor has been unlawfully dispossessed of the property and is making a re-entry or recaption justified by Section 3.06; or

(C) the actor believes that such force is necessary to protect himself against death or serious bodily harm.

(b) The use of deadly force is not justifiable under this Section unless the actor believes that such force is necessary to protect himself against death, serious bodily harm, kidnapping or sexual intercourse compelled by force or threat; nor is it justifiable if:

(i) the actor, with the purpose of causing death or serious bodily harm, provoked the use of force against himself in the same encounter; or

(ii) the actor knows that he can avoid the necessity of using such force with complete safety by retreating or by surrendering possession of a thing to a person asserting a claim of right thereto or by complying with a demand that he abstain from any action which he has no duty to take, except that:

(A) the actor is not obliged to retreat from his dwelling or place of work, unless he was the initial aggressor or is assailed in his place of work by another person whose place of work the actor knows it to be; and

(B) a public officer justified in using force in the performance of his duties or a person justified in using force in his assistance or a person justified in using force in making an arrest or preventing an escape is not obliged to desist from efforts to perform such duty, effect such arrest or prevent such escape because of resistance or threatened resistance by or on behalf of the person against whom such action is directed.

(c) Except as required by paragraphs (a) and (b) of this Subsection, a person employing protective force may estimate the necessity thereof under the circumstances as he believes them to be when the force is used, without retreating, surrendering possession, doing any other act which he has no legal duty to do or abstaining from any lawful action.

(3) *Use of Confinement as Protective Force.* The justification afforded by this Section extends to the use of confinement as protective force only if the actor takes all reasonable measures to terminate the confinement as soon as he knows that he safely can, unless the person confined has been arrested on a charge of crime.

Section 3.09. Mistake of Law as to Unlawfulness of Force or Legality of Arrest; Reckless or Negligent Use of Otherwise Justifiable Force; Reckless or Negligent Injury or Risk of Injury to Innocent Persons

(1) The justification afforded by Sections 3.04 to 3.07, inclusive, is unavailable when

(a) the actor's belief in the unlawfulness of the force or conduct against which he employs protective force or his belief in the lawfulness of an arrest which he endeavors to effect by force is erroneous; and

(b) his error is due to ignorance or mistake as to the provisions of the Code, any other provision of the criminal law or the law governing the legality of an arrest or search.

(2) When the actor believes that the use of force upon or toward the person of another is necessary for any of the purposes for which such belief would establish a justification under Sections 3.03 to 3.08 but the actor is reckless or negligent in having such belief or in acquiring or failing to acquire any knowledge or belief which is material to the justifiability of his use of force, the justification afforded by those Sections is unavailable in a prosecution for an offense for which recklessness or negligence, as the case may be, suffices to establish culpability.

(3) When the actor is justified under Sections 3.03 to 3.08 in using force upon or toward the person of another but he recklessly or

negligently injures or creates a risk of injury to innocent persons, the justification afforded by those Sections is unavailable in a prosecution for such recklessness or negligence towards innocent persons.

Section 3.11. Definitions

In this Article, unless a different meaning plainly is required:

(1) "unlawful force" means force, including confinement, which is employed without the consent of the person against whom it is directed and the employment of which constitutes an offense or actionable tort or would constitute such offense or tort except for a defense (such as the absence of intent, negligence, or mental capacity; duress; youth; or diplomatic status) not amounting to a privilege to use the force. Assent constitutes consent, within the meaning of this Section, whether or not it otherwise is legally effective, except assent to the infliction of death or serious bodily harm.

(2) "deadly force" means force which the actor uses with the purpose of causing or which he knows to create a substantial risk of causing death or serious bodily harm. Purposely firing a firearm in the direction of another person or at a vehicle in which another person is believed to be constitutes deadly force. A threat to cause death or serious bodily harm, by the production of a weapon or otherwise, so long as the actor's purpose is limited to creating an apprehension that he will use deadly force if necessary, does not constitute deadly force.

(3) "dwelling" means any building or structure, though movable or temporary, or a portion thereof, which is for the time being the actor's home or place of lodging.

2. DEFENSE OF OTHERS

Force is generally not regarded as criminal when it is used in defense of a third person. But the courts have shown some inclination to impose more limits upon the right to use force in defense of others than have been imposed upon the right of self-defense. Is there any justification for this? Perhaps it is more reasonable to expect persons to follow legal limits on the use of force when they perceive a risk to others. One who perceives his own safety at risk is, perhaps, unlikely to be influenced by the threat of criminal liability should he act unreasonably. But one who perceives only the safety of another at risk may be more susceptible to the threat of the criminal sanction. Moreover, there may be more of a risk that one acting in defense of another will act improperly, i.e., will use force to assist another who is not in fact entitled to defend himself. While a person will generally be acquainted with those facts that determine whether he himself is entitled to defend himself, a person is less likely to know which party to a fight between two others is at fault and is therefore barred from using protective force. See generally, Model Penal Code, Comments to § 3.05, 32 (Tent. Draft No. 8, 1958).

FERSNER v. UNITED STATES

District of Columbia Court of Appeals, 1984.
482 A.2d 387.

FERREN, ASSOCIATE JUDGE:

A jury, rejecting appellant's claim of self-defense, convicted him of second-degree murder while armed and carrying a dangerous weapon. The trial court sentenced him to consecutive prison terms of fifteen years to life on the murder charge and of three to nine years on the weapon charge. On appeal, he argues that the trial court erred in refusing to give an instruction on the use of deadly force in defense of a third person. We affirm.

I.

On the evening of July 31, 1980, appellant and several of his acquaintances gathered in a parking lot behind the Brentwood Village apartments. The decedent, Maurice Winslow, approached them. Earlier, several of the women in the group, including Winslow's girlfriend, had been together at various bars. Winslow had learned that the women were going to one particular bar, but as it turned out they had stayed only a few minutes and thus apparently were not at the bar where Winslow believed he would find them. Winslow asked one of the women, Diane Aull, why she had lied to him (presumably about where the women were planning to go). One witness testified that appellant's girlfriend, Geraldine Barnes, told Aull she did not have to answer Winslow. Barnes testified that she had said nothing to Aull. In any event, Winslow struck Barnes with his hand or fist.

Barnes then went over to appellant, who was seated in a van a short distance away, and told him that Winslow had hit her for no reason. Appellant then walked toward Winslow, who by this time was engaged in an altercation with another woman in the group, Laverne Reed. Accounts of the altercation varied greatly as to whether Winslow or Reed had instigated the fight, whether Reed struck Winslow, and whether Winslow was slapping, punching, kicking, or stomping Reed. The witnesses agreed, however, that Winslow hit Reed at least once before appellant approached him. Reed suffered facial lacerations as a result of the incident.

After appellant and Winslow had exchanged a few words, Winslow turned around and went to his car to get something, which he then put into his pocket. Appellant returned to his own car and put on his tool belt which contained several tools, including a hatchet. Winslow went back toward Reed and Aull. Appellant then approached Winslow and, soon thereafter, struck him either once or twice on the head with the hatchet. Winslow fell to the ground.

The witnesses disagreed about what Winslow was doing immediately before appellant struck the initial blow. Rosie Johnson testified that Winslow was standing in a threatening posture in front of Diane Aull and having a heated discussion with her. Aull corroborated this account, saying that Winslow had just knocked Reed down but had turned back to Aull before appellant hit him. In contrast, Reed herself testified that Winslow, at the time he was struck, had already knocked her to the ground and was beating her. Similarly, Harry Jenkins testified that Winslow, at the moment of the first blow from appellant's hatchet, was kicking and stomping on Reed, saying he would break her neck. Appellant and William Kenney presented still another story. They testified that Winslow, with knife in hand, was facing appellant at the time Winslow received the first blow. Isaac Batts similarly testified that Winslow, while facing appellant, was beginning to remove an object from his own pocket. Finally, Barnes testified that Winslow had turned away from beating Reed to face appellant, in response to a remark by appellant.

The witnesses agreed that after Winslow fell to the ground, appellant struck him again three to eight times as he lay there. According to the testimony of Johnson, Aull, and appellant, Miles Jenkins told appellant to stop, and he did. Winslow then attempted to get up from the ground. At this point, according to government witnesses, Reed began to hit Winslow with the bicycle frame, then appellant pushed her aside and attacked Winslow again with the hatchet. Appellant also testified that after Winslow attempted to get up, appellant hit him again with the hatchet.

Medical testimony indicated that Winslow had suffered at least 13 hatchet blows to the back of his head. Winslow died of his injuries the next day.

II.

In addition to asking for a jury instruction on self-defense, which the trial court granted (based on Kenney's, Batts', Barnes' and appellant's testimony), appellant requested an instruction on the use of force in defense of a third person, Laverne Reed (based on Reed's and Jenkins' testimony). The court denied this request.[2]

The trial court correctly observed that the right to use force in defense of a third person is predicated upon that other person's right of self-defense. The court went on to say, however, that appellant's right to use force in the defense of Ms. Reed, as well as his right to determine the amount of force necessary, turned exclusively on Reed's own perception—not on appellant's perception—of the situation:

2. Appellant's own testimony supported only a self-defense instruction, since he said he responded with his hatchet when Winslow confronted him with a knife. That testimony does not preclude appellant's request for an instruction on defense of a third person; "a defendant is entitled to an instruction on any issue fairly raised by the evidence, whether or not consistent with the defendant's testimony or the defense trial theory." *Womack v. United States,* 119 U.S.App.D.C. 40, 40, 336 F.2d 959, 959 (1964).

It seems to me the key to the situation with Ms. Reed is her own testimony because it is quite clear that, under the law, that any interven[or] on her behalf only has the same right of self-defense that she does. I cannot find that as a matter of law from Ms. Reed's testimony that she had the right to use deadly or dangerous weapon force. I do not find anything from which anyone could conclude that she was, from her own testimony, in imminent danger of serious bodily harm or death of the type that is needed to justify that defense. I will not give that instruction.

In other words, the court concluded first that Reed—based on her own testimony that Winslow struck her approximately nine times causing facial bleeding—would not have been entitled to use deadly force in self-defense. For that reason, the court next concluded, as a matter of law, that appellant was not entitled to use deadly force in defense of Reed, irrespective of his own reasonable perceptions of what was happening to her.[4]

[T]his court has not resolved, whether one who properly comes to the defense of another can be protected by his or her own perceptions, including a reasonable mistake of fact, about the degree of force necessary. Disagreeing with the trial court, we conclude that when the use of force in defense of a third person is justified, the intervenor is entitled to use the degree of force reasonably necessary to protect the other person on the basis of the facts as the intervenor, not the victim, reasonably perceives them. *State v. Chiarello*, 69 N.J.Super. 479, 487–88, 174 A.2d 506, 514–15 (1961); R. Perkins & R. Boyce, Criminal Law 1146–47 (3d ed. 1982).

We arrive at this conclusion by first examining the factors to be considered in determining whether an act of self-defense is legally permissible and then by applying this analysis to defense of a third person. The right of self-defense, and especially the degree of force the victim is permitted to use to prevent bodily harm, is premised substantially on the victim's own reasonable perceptions of what is happening. Criminal Jury Instructions for the District of Columbia, No. 5.14 (3d ed. 1978) (self-defense—amount of force permissible). The victim's perceptions may include, for example, an enhanced sense of peril based on personal knowledge that the attacker has committed prior acts of violence. Indeed, the victim's personal perceptions are so significant that they may justify the use of reasonable, including deadly, force in self-defense "even though it may afterwards have turned out that the appearances were false." Criminal Jury Instructions, *supra*, No. 5.15. In sum, the victim's subjective perceptions are the prime determinant of the right to use force—and the degree of force required—in self-defense, subject only to the constraint that those perceptions be reasonable under the circumstances.

4. Apparently because deadly force was used against Winslow, the trial court did not address the question whether Reed—or appellant on Reed's behalf—could have used nondeadly force against Winslow.

Given the subjective aspect of the right of self-defense, we find no rational basis for permitting an intervenor to come to the defense of a third person, with all the attendant risks, but conditioning that right on the victim's rather than the intervenor's reasonable perceptions. Obviously, in attempting to determine what the intervenor's perceptions actually and reasonably were, the trier of fact will find relevant the victim's own perceptions. But when it comes to determining whether—and to what degree—force is reasonably necessary to defend a third person under attack, the focus ultimately must be on the intervenor's, not on the victim's, reasonable perceptions of the situation.

It follows that an intervenor may be entitled to use more, or less, force than the victim reasonably could use, depending on their respective perceptions and available resources. For example, an intervenor may reasonably be entitled to use greater force than the victim herself would perceive necessary if the intervenor knows, while the victim does not, that the attacker has killed before. On the other hand, when an intervenor on behalf of a victim of an unarmed assault has strength considerably superior to that of the attacker, the intervenor may reasonably be limited to less force than would a slightly-built victim who has access to a knife. In the present case, therefore, even if Reed herself could not reasonably have perceived that deadly force was necessary in her own self-defense, this does not preclude a finding that appellant reasonably perceived that his use of deadly force was necessary to protect her.

III.

We turn to the facts. An accused is entitled to a requested instruction on the defense theory of the case "if there is 'any evidence fairly tending to bear upon the issue * * *', however weak." *Rhodes v. United States*, 354 A.2d 863, 864 (D.C.1976) (citations omitted). The question, therefore, is whether there is any evidence of record fairly tending to show that appellant reasonably believed there was a need to use deadly force—specifically, enough force to kill Winslow—to prevent death or serious bodily harm to Laverne Reed.

As properly adapted from standard jury instruction 5.14 on the amount of force permissible in self-defense, the requested instruction as to defense of a third person * * * would include two additional explanations. First, the court would have to instruct on the use of deadly force:

A person may use a reasonable amount of force in defense of another person, including, in some circumstances, deadly force. "Deadly force" is force which is likely to cause death or serious bodily harm. A person may use deadly force in defense of another person if [he] [she] actually believes at the time of the incident that that person is in imminent danger of death or serious bodily harm from which [he] [she] can save that person only by using deadly force against the assailant, and if [his] [her] belief is reasonable.

Second, the court would have to put the use of deadly force in perspective by also cautioning the jury about the use of excessive force:

> Even if the defendant was justified in using force in defense of another person, [he] [she] would not be entitled to use any greater force than [he] [she] had reasonable grounds to believe and actually did believe to be necessary under the circumstances to save the other person's life or avert serious bodily harm.

> In determining whether the defendant used excessive force in defending another person, you may consider all the circumstances under which [he] [she] acted. The claim of defense of a third person is not necessarily defeated if greater force than would have seemed necessary to a calm mind was used by the defendant in the heat of passion generated by an assault upon the third person. A belief which may be unreasonable to a calm mind may be actually and reasonably entertained in the heat of passion.

There was some evidence, particularly Reed's testimony that Winslow was "beating" her and Jenkins' testimony that Winslow was "kicking" and "stomping" on Reed and threatening to break her neck, fairly tending to show that Reed in fact was threatened with serious bodily harm at the time appellant intervened. Appellant and other witnesses testified, moreover, that on previous occasions Winslow had threatened others with injury and death and that he had beaten up several persons, including his girlfriend. Finally, there was testimony indicating that Reed, who was intoxicated and lying on the ground, was unable to defend herself effectively. This evidence would be sufficient to support a jury finding that appellant reasonably believed Reed was in imminent danger of serious bodily harm, and thus that appellant was entitled to use deadly force.

The inquiry does not end here, however. In order to provide a basis for the instruction on defense of a third person, appellant also had to point to evidence fairly tending to show that he reasonably believed the particular deadly force he used to avert serious bodily harm to Reed—a hatchet blow to Winslow's head—was necessary, not excessive, under the circumstances.

While we must accept as true, for purposes of evaluating appellant's right to the requested instruction, that Winslow was "kicking," "stomping," or "beating" on Reed [9]—and threatening to break her neck—at the time appellant felled Winslow with one or two hatchet blows,[10] we can easily say on this record, as a matter of law, that

9. Although there was testimony that Winslow earlier had struck Reed with a bicycle frame, no witness testified that he was using any weapon at the time of appellant's intervention. The witnesses who testified that Winslow pulled a knife on appellant did not claim to have seen this knife before or during the altercation with Reed. At most, the evidence could be taken to show that at the time he first struck Winslow with the hatchet, appellant reasonably believed Winslow had concealed some sort of weapon about his person after going to his car.

10. Clearly, after the first two hatchet blows, all other blows occurred after Reed had been rescued. Any justification of those later blows would have to be a matter of appellant's own self-defense, for

appellant did not have "reasonable grounds to believe"—even if acting "in the heat of passion"—that hatchet blows to Winslow's head were necessary to defend Reed. Even if appellant was entitled to use deadly force—*i.e.*, force "likely to cause death or serious bodily harm"—there are, as this definition implies, degrees of deadly force. On some occasions, it may be reasonable only to cause serious bodily harm not threatening life itself. This is such a case. Under the circumstances here, appellant obviously could have saved Reed by striking Winslow with the blunt side of the hatchet elsewhere on the body, with less damaging (here fatal) results. As a matter of law, therefore, appellant used excessive force; it was not necessary for appellant to use an amount of deadly force that was likely to kill Winslow.

Affirmed.

Notes and Questions

1. Probably the leading case for the proposition that one acting in defense of another should have a defense only where the person aided was in fact entitled to act in self-defense is People v. Young, 11 N.Y.2d 274, 229 N.Y.S.2d 1, 183 N.E.2d 319 (1962) (per curiam). Young had come upon two middle-aged men struggling with an eighteen year old youth in the street. He intervened on behalf of the youth, injuring one of the older men. It ultimately turned out that the men were police officers making a valid arrest and the youth was improperly resisting them. But even the officers acknowledged that Young had no way of knowing that the men were officers or that they were making an arrest. Young was convicted of assault, and the New York Court of Appeals, relying upon "[t]he weight of authority," affirmed the conviction. Permitting persons such as Young to intervene on behalf of others without requiring them to act at their own peril, it reasoned, "would not be conducive to an orderly society." 11 N.Y.2d at 275, 229 N.Y.S.2d at 2, 183 N.E.2d at 319. Noting that the assault charge at issue required only that "the defendant knowingly struck a blow," the court observed that the applicable policy might be different "when the felony charged requires proof of a specific intent and the issue is justifiable homicide * * *." 11 N.Y.2d at 275, 229 N.Y.S.2d at 2, 183 N.E.2d at 320.

Should it make any difference whether the situation turned out, as in *Young,* to involve an effort by police officers to make an arrest, or, as in *Fersner,* to involve a purely "private" dispute? If the intervenor had no way of knowing this, how can any difference be justified?

2. In Commonwealth v. Monico, 298 Mass. 373, 366 N.E.2d 1241 (1977), the trial judge instructed the jury that the right to use force in defense of others was limited to defending persons related to the defendant by consanguinity or affinity, unless the force used upon the third person "almost" amounts to deadly force. On appeal, this was held to be error. What might be said in favor of limiting the privilege to situations in which

which he received an instruction that did
not spare him from conviction.

the defendant came to the aid of another person with whom he had a close relationship?

MODEL PENAL CODE *

Official Draft (1985).

Section 3.05. Use of Force for the Protection of Other Persons

(1) Subject to the provisions of this Section and of Section 3.09, the use of force upon or toward the person of another is justifiable to protect a third person when:

(a) the actor would be justified under Section 3.04 in using such force to protect himself against the injury he believes to be threatened to the person whom he seeks to protect; and

(b) under the circumstances as the actor believes them to be, the person whom he seeks to protect would be justified in using such protective force; and

(c) the actor believes that his intervention is necessary for the protection of such other person.

(2) Notwithstanding Subsection (1) of this Section:

(a) when the actor would be obliged under Section 3.04 to retreat, to surrender the possession of a thing or to comply with a demand before using force in self-protection, he is not obliged to do so before using force for the protection of another person, unless he knows that he can thereby secure the complete safety of such other person; and

(b) when the person whom the actor seeks to protect would be obliged under Section 3.04 to retreat, to surrender the possession of a thing or to comply with a demand if he knew that he could obtain complete safety by so doing, the actor is obliged to try to cause him to do so before using force in his protection if the actor knows that he can obtain complete safety in that way; and

(c) neither the actor nor the person whom he seeks to protect is obliged to retreat when in the other's dwelling or place of work to any greater extent than in his own.

Note

In connection with this Section, consider also § 3.09 and § 3.11, reprinted at pages 752–53, supra, in connection with the Code's provision concerning use of force in self-protection.

3. DEFENSE OF PROPERTY

Greater limitations tend to be imposed upon the right to use force in defense of property than are imposed upon either the right of self-defense or defense of others. In large part, of course, this is because the actor's interest—the continued security in his property—is regarded as less important than the interests at issue in the other situations. Are there other considerations? Perhaps it is more reasonable to expect the law to be successful in preventing violence when that violence is—or may be—used to protect "only" property interests.

STATE v. NELSON
Supreme Court of Iowa, 1983.
329 N.W.2d 643.

SCHULTZ, JUSTICE.

This is an appeal by defendant, Gregory Irvin Nelson, from his conviction of false imprisonment in violation of Iowa Code section 710.7 (1981). On appeal, defendant claims that * * * his request for an instruction on the justification defense of "defense of property" should have been given * * *. We hold * * * that the trial court correctly refused to instruct on the defense of property * * *. We therefore affirm.

The facts in this case are rather unusual. Nelson and codefendant, Georgia Stigler, are brother and sister. Reuben Stigler, one of the victims of the alleged false imprisonment, is the husband of Georgia. He, Georgia, and Georgia's twelve-year-old child from an earlier marriage lived together in a house that Georgia owned. Georgia rented a room of this house to Nelson. Nelson, who is single and partially disabled, is a devotee of military training, guns, and shooting, and had an extensive gun collection.

On the night of February 26, 1981, Nelson returned to his room and discovered that four of his guns, $1000, and other miscellaneous items had been stolen. Nelson told Georgia of the theft as soon as she came into the house. Shortly thereafter, Georgia found Reuben and she accused him of being involved in the theft. She told Reuben that the theft would be reported to the police if the items were not returned by morning.

Reuben testified that he and his friend, Russell Hill, went to a tavern where they recovered three of the stolen guns. They then brought the guns to the Stigler house. This partial recovery apparently did little to soothe the indignation of the codefendants.

The State's evidence indicates that when Reuben and Hill entered the house they were held at gunpoint by the codefendants and others. This situation continued for some hours, during which time various phone calls were made in an effort to recover the stolen items. Finally, Reuben and Hill made a dramatic escape from the home; according to Reuben, they upset a table and he dove through a closed window while Hill fled through the rear door. At this time the house was surrounded by police and the codefendants were soon arrested.

The State presented evidence from the victims and from the victims' relatives who had received phone calls that the defendants threatened to kill Reuben and Hill if the remainder of Nelson's property and money was not returned. Nelson testified that although he made threats of bodily injury, he held but did not point his gun at the victims. In regard to the threat to kill, he testified: "I never threatened to kill them. There's a semantic difference there. I said I should."

* * *

Defendant unsuccessfully requested that the trial court instruct the jury on the justification defense of defense of property. On appeal he claims the court's refusal to give such instruction was error. We hold that such instruction was not justified under the facts of this case.

The defense of justification of use of force in defense of property is codified in Iowa Code section 704.4, which in pertinent part states: "[a] person is justified in the use of reasonable force to prevent or terminate criminal interference with his or her possession or other right in property." We must determine, under this statutory definition, whether the defense of justification exists under the facts of this case. If we determine that there are substantial facts which if proved would satisfy this section, then it becomes the province of the jury to determine the validity of these facts.

The issue presented in this division is whether a justification defense exists under section 704.4 for a defendant who has at an earlier time been deprived of possession of his property by a wrongful taking committed out of his presence, and who then attempts by the use of force to recover the property, although the property is elsewhere. We hold that under this fact situation the defense is unavailable.

In interpreting a statute we look to its language, and if its meaning is clear, we are not permitted to search beyond its express terms. *State v. Rich*, 305 N.W.2d 739, 745 (Iowa 1981). The express terms of section 704.4 provide a defense in situations where the defendant attempts "to prevent or terminate criminal interference." If the criminal interference has occurred out of the presence of the defendant at an earlier time, and the property, the reason for the interference, is no longer present, force can no longer be used to prevent or stop the crime. No language in section 704.4 approves of after-the-fact vigilante action.

Another tool of statutory construction is the examination of the statute's purpose. *State v. Newman*, 313 N.W.2d 484, 486 (Iowa 1981). The obvious purpose of this statute is to prevent the imposition of a penalty upon a person who out of necessity is acting to retain his property or to prevent its injury. Thus, the purpose of the statute is not to recover property but to prevent wrongful interference with it. When the injured party is not present at the time of wrongful taking, or the property is elsewhere, there is no necessity or urgency that would call for the use of force to prevent the wrongful activity.

Other authority supports this interpretation of the statute. In a defense based on necessity, a justification defense, it was held in *State v. Marley,* 54 Haw. 450, 472, 509 P.2d 1095, 1108–09 (1973), that elements of a justification defense are (1) that a direct causal relationship must be reasonably anticipated to exist between the defender's action and the avoidance of harm, (2) that the harm to be prevented must be imminent, (3) that there is no alternative available which does not involve violation of the law, and (4) that the criminal act that defendant seeks to prevent or terminate must be committed in defendant's presence. In *Marley* the court, commenting on the element of presence, stated:

> Prevention or termination of the commission of a crime is only one of several "justification" defenses. Some of the others are self-defense, defense of another, and defense of property. Each of these justification defenses obviously and inevitably requires that the criminal act to be counteracted occur in the presence of the actor. * * * To rule that a full justification defense to the prosecution for commission of crime is established even absent a presence requirement would be to create a very dangerous precedent, for it would make each citizen a judge of the criminality of all the acts of every other citizen, with power to mete out sentence.

Marley, 54 Haw. at 470, 509 P.2d at 1108. *See also United States v. Seward,* 687 F.2d 1270, 1276 (10th Cir.1982) (defense of necessity doctrine is based on an emergency); *State v. Ruffin,* 535 S.W.2d 135, 137 (Mo.App.1976) (as general rule only present danger can be a legitimate justification for resort to self defense); W. Lafave & A. Scott *Criminal Law* § 402 (recapture of a chattel by force after an interval has elapsed is not justified); *id.* § 406 (a requirement of justification defense is that the criminal act that defendant seeks to prevent or terminate be committed in defendant's presence).

Applying this construction to the statute, we find no evidence that defendant's acts were for a purpose other than to regain possession of property that had been taken in his absence and had not been returned. After defendant discovered the theft, all that he knew was that the property was gone. He was not present during the taking and he only suspected the identity of the culprit. Nor did the return of part of the property, after threats were made, restart the timetable of the crime so that defendant could "prevent or terminate" its occurrence. Thus, defendant was not entitled to the instruction he requested.

* * *

Affirmed.

Notes and Questions

1. Force is generally regarded as permissible if it used immediately after the dispossession or in "hot pursuit" of the dispossessor:

> If force is allowed to defend possession, it is only a small extension to allow similar force to be used to regain possession immediately after its loss. * * * Moreover, it is an ancient principle of the common law, commended by common sense, that when property is taken on fresh

pursuit it is deemed to be taken at the beginning of the pursuit. The retaking is not any the less immediate because the fresh pursuit turns out to be a protracted chase.

Model Penal Code § 3.06, Comment, at 44 (Tent. Draft No. 8, 1958). In *Nelson,* if Nelson had himself gone to the tavern would he have been entitled to recover the guns there by means of force?

2. If Nelson had confronted Reuben and Hill immediately after the taking of the guns and other items, would he have been permitted to hold Reuben and Hill at gunpoint? Would he have been permitted to threaten to shoot them? Could he have displayed or exhibited a firearm as part of such a threat if he did not point it towards them? It is often said that there is no right to use deadly force, or to "endanger life or inflict serious bodily harm," in order to defend property. State v. Deans, 71 N.C.App. 227, 233, 321 S.E.2d 579, 583 (1984), review denied, 313 N.C. 332, 329 S.E.2d 386 (1985). How far does this limitation go?

In State v. Murphy, 7 Wn.App. 505, 500 P.2d 1276 (1972), the defendant armed himself with a pistol and confronted trespassers on his property with the gun in his hand dropped at his side. In finding no right to engage in such behavior to eject trespassers, the court explained:

> Mr. Murphy's action in arming himself with a revolver was well calculated to excite apprehension of great bodily harm in the minds of the two persons who, he believed, were harassing his business interests. * * * There is a recklessness—a wanton disregard of humanity and social duty—in the threatened use of deadly force to repel what at most could be considered a petty inconvenience, which is essentially wicked and which the law abhors. The law forbids such a menacing of human life for so trivial a cause.

7 Wn.App. at 515, 500 P.2d at 1283.

3. To what extent does—or should—a person have a right to use greater force than would otherwise be available because the confrontation takes place in the person's residence? Although there is widespread recognition in the cases that a doctrine of "defense of habitation" exists, there is substantial disagreement on its scope. Some authorities, especially older ones, suggest that the doctrine gives an occupant the right even to kill to prevent an entry into the residence:

> In Ohio it is the law that where one is assaulted in his home, or the home itself is attacked, he may use such means as are necessary to repel the assailant from the house, or to prevent his forcible entry, or material injury to his home, even to the taking of life. But a homicide in such a case would not be justifiable unless the slayer, in the careful and proper use of his faculties, in good faith believes, and has reasonable grounds to believe, that the killing is necessary to repel the assailant or prevent his forcible entry.

State v. Reid, 3 Ohio App.2d 215, 221, 210 N.E.2d 142, 147, 32 O.O.2d 316 (1965). But the effect of this is diminished by the requirement that the entry justifying a killing be "by force." This has traditionally meant that the trespass must be such as would amount to a breach of the peace; entering premises after being warned not to do so but without force would not make the trespass such a breach of the peace. Carroll v. State, 23 Ala. 28 (1853).

The more modern statement of the doctrine limits the right to kill in defense of the dwelling to situations in which the resident has a reasonable apprehension that the trespasser intends felonious or serious injury to the occupants:

> When a trespasser enters upon a man's premises, makes an assault upon his dwelling, and attempts to force an entrance into his house in a manner such as would lead a reasonably prudent man to believe that the intruder intends to commit a felony or to inflict some serious personal injury upon the inmates, a lawful occupant of the dwelling may legally prevent the entry, even by the taking of the life of the intruder.

State v. Miller, 267 N.C. 409, 411, 148 S.E.2d 279, 281 (1966). What does this add to the right to use force to defend oneself, other persons, and property? If the jurisdiction is one in which retreat is necessary before deadly force is used, the doctrine of defense of habitation dispenses with the requirement of retreat. Law v. State, 21 Md.App. 13, 318 A.2d 859 (1974). In addition, however, it appears to authorize the use of force against one believed to pose a threat to oneself or others before the danger becomes as immediate as is required by the doctrines of defense of self or others:

> [O]ne may [in defense of his habitation] resist with force an unlawful entry by one whose purpose is to assault or to do violence to him, to the extent of taking the aggressor's life, even though the circumstances may not be such as to justify a belief that there was actual peril of life or great bodily harm.

People v. Givens, 26 Ill.2d 371, 375, 186 N.E.2d 225, 227 (1962). See also State v. Gray, 162 N.C. 608, 614, 77 S.E. 833, 834 (1913) (householder need not wait until assailant is upon him but may open his door and shoot). Thus the doctrine arguably permits one to use force before such force would be permitted by the other doctrines.

Suppose a resident discovers an intruder already in the house. Does the doctrine of defense of habitation have any relevance? In State v. Brookshire, 353 S.W.2d 681 (Mo.1962) the court held that it did not:

> It is apparent that the rules pertaining to the defense of habitation authorize certain protective acts to be taken * * * at the time when and place where the intruder is seeking to cross the protective barrier of the house. But once the intruder has crossed that barrier without resistance from the occupant of the house there is no occasion to kill him in order to keep him out because he is already in, and the occupant is not authorized by law to punish for the wrongful entry. Therefore, * * * a homicide then occurring is justifiable only under the usual rules of self-defense or to prevent therein the commission of a felony, except that there is no duty to retreat.

Id., at 691–92. There is, however, authority to the contrary as well. See People v. Stombaugh, 52 Ill.2d 130, 284 N.E.2d 640 (1972).

4. Consider how these matters would be resolved under Section 3.06 of the Model Penal Code, reprinted in this subsection. Consider specifically

the right to use deadly force, as that is defined in § 3.11, reprinted at page 753, supra.

MODEL PENAL CODE *
(Official Draft 1985).

Section 3.06. Use of Force for the Protection of Property

(1) *Use of Force Justifiable for Protection of Property.* Subject to the provisions of this Section and of Section 3.09, the use of force upon or toward the person of another is justifiable when the actor believes that such force is immediately necessary:

(a) to prevent or terminate an unlawful entry or other trespass upon land or a trespass against or the unlawful carrying away of tangible, movable property, provided that such land or movable property is, or is believed by the actor to be, in his possession or in the possession of another person for whose protection he acts; or

(b) to effect an entry or re-entry upon land or to retake tangible movable property, provided that the actor believes that he or the person by whose authority he acts or a person from whom he or such other person derives title was unlawfully dispossessed of such land or movable property and is entitled to possession, and provided, further, that:

(i) the force is used immediately or on fresh pursuit after such dispossession; or

(ii) the actor believes that the person against whom he uses force has no claim of right to the possession of the property and, in the case of land, the circumstances, as the actor believes them to be, are of such urgency that it would be an exceptional hardship to postpone the entry or re-entry until a court order is obtained.

(2) *Meaning of Possession.* For the purposes of Subsection (1) of this Section:

(a) a person who has parted with the custody of property to another who refuses to restore it to him is no longer in possession, unless the property is movable and was and still is located on land in his possession;

(b) a person who has been dispossessed of land does not regain possession thereof merely by setting foot thereon;

(c) a person who has a license to use or occupy real property is deemed to be in possession thereof except against the licensor acting under claim of right.

(3) *Limitations on Justifiable Use of Force.*

(a) *Request to Desist.* The use of force is justifiable under this Section only if the actor first requests the person against whom such force is used to desist from his interference with the property, unless the actor believes that:

(i) such request would be useless; or

(ii) it would be dangerous to himself or another person to make the request; or

(iii) substantial harm will be done to the physical condition of the property which is sought to be protected before the request can effectively be made.

(b) *Exclusion of Trespasser.* The use of force to prevent or terminate a trespass is not justifiable under this Section if the actor knows that the exclusion of the trespasser will expose him to substantial danger of serious bodily injury.

(c) *Resistance of Lawful Re-entry or Recaption.* The use of force to prevent an entry or re-entry upon land or the recaption of movable property is not justifiable under this Section, although the actor believes that such re-entry or recaption is unlawful, if:

(i) the re-entry or recaption is made by or on behalf of a person who was actually dispossessed of the property; and

(ii) it is otherwise justifiable under paragraph (1)(b) of this Section.

(d) *Use of Deadly Force.* The use of deadly force is not justifiable under this Section unless the actor believes that:

(i) the person against whom the force is used is attempting to dispossess him of his dwelling otherwise than under a claim of right to its possession; or

(ii) the person against whom the force is used is attempting to commit or consummate arson, burglary, robbery or other felonious theft or property destruction and either:

(1) has employed or threatened deadly force against or in the presence of the actor; or

(2) the use of force other than deadly force to prevent the commission or the consummation of the crime would expose the actor or another in his presence to substantial danger of serious bodily injury.

(4) *Use of Confinement as Protective Force.* The justification afforded by this Section extends to the use of confinement as protective force only if the actor takes all reasonable measures to terminate the confinement as soon as he allows that he can do so with safety to the property, unless the person confined has been arrested on a charge of crime.

(5) *Use of Device to Protect Property.* The justification afforded by this Section extends to the use of a device for the purpose of protecting property only if:

(a) the device is not designed to cause or known to create a substantial risk of causing death or serious bodily injury; and

(b) the use of the particular device to protect the property from entry or trespass is reasonable under the circumstances, as the actor believes them to be; and

(c) the device is one customarily used for such a purpose or reasonable care is taken to make known to probable intruders the fact that it is used.

(6) *Use of Force to Pass Wrongful Obstructor.* The use of force to pass a person whom the actor believes to be purposely or knowingly and unjustifiably obstructing the actor from going to a place to which he may lawfully go is justifiable, provided that:

(a) the actor believes that the person against whom he uses force has no claim of right to obstruct the actor; and

(b) the actor is not being obstructed from entry or movement on land which he knows to be in the possession or custody of the person obstructing him, or in the possession or custody of another person by whose authority the obstructor acts, unless the circumstances, as the actor believes them to be, are of such urgency that it would not be reasonable to postpone the entry or movement on such land until a court order is obtained; and

(c) the force used is not greater than would be justifiable if the person obstructing the actor were using force against him to prevent his passage.

Note

In connection with this Section, consider also § 3.09 and § 3.11, reprinted at pages 752–53, supra, in connection with the Code's provisions concerning use of force in self-protection.

C. ENTRAPMENT

Editors' Introduction: Development of Federal Entrapment Law

The defense of entrapment has given rise to a great deal of discussion concerning not only the appropriate or acceptable role of undercover police work in law enforcement but also the role that defenses to criminal liability ought to play in regulating law enforcement conduct. Much of the discussion has focused upon the appropriate formulation of the defense. The leading line of cases is undoubtedly the decisions of the United States Supreme Court, developing and applying the defense of entrapment to federal criminal offenses.

As a practical matter, undercover police work involving the creation of "opportunities for crime" has become increasingly commonplace. This is a significant component of the effort to control drug trafficking, as may be suggested by the fact that this is the subject matter of all of the United States Supreme Court cases discussed or presented in this section. However, it should be recognized that there are other crimes which are seen as inherently difficult to detect by reliance on victim complaints. "Sting" operations are also employed to detect such varied criminals as burglars and corrupt public officials. The former are frequently identified by their sale of stolen goods to police-operated "fencing" fronts. The latter have been the target of a number of elaborate purported bribery efforts, the most famous of which was the Abscam operation which resulted in the conviction of several Congressmen. See e.g., United States v. Jenrette, 744 F.2d 817 (D.C.Cir.1984), cert. denied, ___ U.S. ___, 105 S.Ct. 2321, 85 L.Ed.2d 840 (1985); United States v. Kelly, 707 F.2d 1460 (D.C.Cir.1983), cert. denied, 464 U.S. 908, 104 S.Ct. 264, 78 L.Ed.2d 247 (1983), and United States v. Myers, 692 F.2d 823 (2d Cir.1982), cert. denied sub nom. Lederer v. United States, 461 U.S. 961, 103 S.Ct. 2437, 77 L.Ed.2d 1322 (1983).

In Sorrells v. United States, 287 U.S. 435, 53 S.Ct. 210, 77 L.Ed. 413 (1932), the Supreme Court adopted the traditional "subjective" formulation of the entrapment defense. Sorrells had been approached during Prohibition by an undercover police agent who had been a member of Sorrell's military unit during World War I. At several points during their discussion of war experiences, the agent asked if Sorrells could get him some liquor. Sorrells demurred to the first two requests but after the third left and returned with some liquor. He was arrested and tried for possession and sale of the liquor. The trial court refused to instruct the jury on a defense of entrapment or to direct a verdict of acquittal on that basis. Reversing, Chief Justice Hughes formulated the issue for the Court:

> It is well settled that the fact that officers or employees of the government merely afford opportunities or facilities for the commission of the offense does not defeat the prosecution. Artifice and stratagem may be employed to catch those engaged in criminal enterprises. * * * A different question is presented when the criminal design originates with the officials of the government, and they implant in the mind of an innocent person the disposition to commit the alleged offense and induce its commission in order that they may prosecute.

287 U.S. at 441–42, 53 S.Ct. at 212–13, 77 L.Ed. at 416–17. In the latter situations, he continued, Congress must have intended a defense to exist:

> "[G]eneral terms descriptive of a class of persons made subject to a criminal statute may and should be limited, where the literal application of the statute would lead to extreme or absurd results, and where the legislative purpose gathered from the whole act would be satisfied by a more limited interpretation."

We think that this established principle of construction is applicable here. We are unable to conclude that it was the intention of the Congress in enacting this statute that its process of detention and enforcement should be abused by the instigation by government officials of an act on the part of persons otherwise innocent in order to lure them to its commission and to punish them. We are not forced by the letter to do violence to the spirit of the statute.

287 U.S. at 447–48, 53 S.Ct. at 215, 77 L.Ed. at 420. The trial court erred, the majority concluded, in failing to submit the issue of entrapment to the jury.

Sorrells was reaffirmed in Sherman v. United States, 356 U.S. 369, 78 S.Ct. 819, 2 L.Ed.2d 848 (1958). The facts were as follows:

In late August 1951, Kalchinian, a government informer, first met [Sherman] at a doctor's office where apparently both were being treated to be cured of narcotics addiction. Several accidental meetings followed, either at the doctor's office or at the pharmacy where both filled their prescriptions from the doctor. From mere greetings, conversation progressed to a discussion of mutual experiences and problems, including their attempts to overcome addiction to narcotics. Finally, Kalchinian asked [Sherman] * * * to supply him with a source because he was not responding to treatment. From the first, [Sherman] tried to avoid the issue. Not until after a number of repetitions of the request, predicated on Kalchinian's presumed suffering, did [Sherman] finally acquiesce. Several times thereafter he obtained a quantity of narcotics which he shared with Kalchinian. Each time [Sherman] told Kalchinian that the total cost of narcotics he obtained was twenty-five dollars and that Kalchinian owed him fifteen dollars. The informer thus bore the cost of his share of the narcotics plus the taxi and other expenses necessary to obtain the drug. After several such sales Kalchinian informed agents of the Bureau of Narcotics that he had another seller for them. * * *

356 U.S. at 371, 78 S.Ct. at 820, 2 L.Ed.2d at 850–51. At Sherman's trial for sale of narcotics, the jury was instructed on entrapment but nevertheless returned a verdict of guilty. The Supreme Court held that under *Sorrells* entrapment was established "as a matter of law": the Government's evidence showed that, under *Sorrells,* Sherman's criminal conduct "was 'the product of the creative activity' of law-enforcement officials." Relying upon evidence that Sherman had been convicted of sale of narcotics in 1942 and illegal possession of such substances in 1946, the Government urged that Sherman had evinced a "ready compliance" with Kalchinian's request. This was rejected by the majority, which emphasized the age of the prior convictions and uncontested evidence in the record that Sherman was attempting to overcome his drug habit at the time of Kalchinian's approach.

Justice Frankfurter concurred, developing a position previously articulated by Justice Roberts concurring in *Sorrells.* Entrapment, he urged, should not be regarded as resting upon some presumed legislative intention but rather upon the power of courts to exercise supervisory jurisdiction over the administration of criminal justice. Consistent with this, he continued, whether entrapment exists should be regarded as an issue for the judge rather than a guilt-innocence issue to be decided by the trial jury. Under the majority's approach, he emphasized, no entrapment occurs if the evidence shows "a general intention or predisposition to commit, whenever the opportunity should arise, crimes of the kind solicited * * *." 356 U.S. at 382, 78 S.Ct. at 826, 2 L.Ed.2d at 857 (Frankfurter, J., concurring in result). This, he urged, was inappropriate:

> [A] test that looks to the character and predisposition of the defendant rather than the conduct of the police loses sight of the underlying reason for the defense of entrapment. No matter what the defendant's past record and present inclinations to criminality, certain police conduct to ensnare him into further crime is not to be tolerated by an advanced society.

Id., at 382–83, 78 S.Ct. at 826, 2 L.Ed.2d at 857. The proper test, he concluded, would ask whether the officers, in holding out inducements, acted in such a manner as is likely to induce to the commission of crime "those engaged in criminal conduct and ready and willing to commit further crimes should the occasion arise." No entrapment occurs if this is the case. But if the officers act in such a manner as is likely to induce to the commission of crime "those persons * * * who would normally avoid crime and through self-struggle resist ordinary temptations," then entrapment occurs. Id., at 384, 78 S.Ct. at 826, 2 L.Ed.2d at 857.

> This test shifts attention from the record and predisposition of the particular defendant to the conduct of the police and the likelihood, objectively considered, that it would entrap only those ready and willing to commit crime. It is as objective a test as the subject matter permits * * *. It draws directly on the fundamental intuition that led in the first instance to the outlawing of "entrapment" as a prosecutorial instrument.

Id., at 384, 78 S.Ct. at 826, 2 L.Ed.2d at 857–58. As the case reprinted in this Section makes clear, the Court continues to be split on the most appropriate approach to entrapment.

UNITED STATES v. RUSSELL

United States Supreme Court, 1973.
411 U.S. 423, 93 S.Ct. 1637, 36 L.Ed.2d 366.

MR. JUSTICE REHNQUIST delivered the opinion of the Court.

Respondent Richard Russell was charged in three counts of a five count indictment returned against him and codefendants John and Patrick Connolly. After a jury trial in the District Court, in which his sole defense was entrapment, respondent was convicted on all three counts of having unlawfully manufactured and processed methamphetamine ("speed") and of having unlawfully sold and delivered that drug in violation of 21 U.S.C.A. §§ 331(q)(1), (2), 360a(a), (b) (Supp. V, 1964).

He was sentenced to concurrent terms of two years in prison for each offense, the terms to be suspended on the condition that he spend six months in prison and be placed on probation for the following three years. On appeal the United States Court of Appeals for the Ninth Circuit, one judge dissenting, reversed the conviction solely for the reason that an undercover agent supplied an essential chemical for manufacturing the methamphetamine which formed the basis of respondent's conviction. The court concluded that as a matter of law "a defense to a criminal charge may be founded upon an intolerable degree of governmental participation in the criminal enterprise." United States v. Russell, 459 F.2d 671, 673 (CA9 1972). We granted certiorari, 409 U.S. 911 (1972), and now reverse that judgment.

There is little dispute concerning the essential facts in this case. On December 7, 1969, Joe Shapiro, an undercover agent for the Federal Bureau of Narcotics and Dangerous Drugs, went to respondent's home on Whidbey Island in the State of Washington where he met with respondent and his two codefendants, John and Patrick Connolly. Shapiro's assignment was to locate a laboratory where it was believed that methamphetamine was being manufactured illicitly. He told the respondent and the Connollys that he represented an organization in the Pacific Northwest that was interested in controlling the manufacture and distribution of methamphetamine. He then made an offer to supply the defendants with the chemical phenyl-2-propanone, an essential ingredient in the manufacture of methamphetamine, in return for one-half of the drug produced. This offer was made on the condition that Agent Shapiro be shown a sample of the drug which they were making and the laboratory where it was being produced.

During the conversation Patrick Connolly revealed that he had been making the drug since May 1969 and since then had produced three pounds of it.[2] John Connolly gave the agent a bag containing a quantity of methamphetamine that he represented as being from "the last batch that we made." Shortly thereafter, Shapiro and Patrick Connolly left respondent's house to view the laboratory which was located in the Connolly house on Whidbey Island. At the house Shapiro observed an empty bottle bearing the chemical label phenyl-2-propanone.

By prearrangement Shapiro returned to the Connolly house on December 9, 1969, to supply 100 grams of propanone and observe the chemical reaction. When he arrived he observed Patrick Connolly and the respondent cutting up pieces of aluminum foil and placing them in a large flask. There was testimony that some of the foil pieces accidentally fell on the floor and were picked up by the respondent and Shapiro and put into the flask.[3] Thereafter Patrick Connolly added all of the necessary chemicals, including the propanone brought by Shapi-

2. At trial Patrick Connolly admitted making this statement to Agent Shapiro but asserted that the statement was not true.

3. Agent Shapiro did not otherwise participate in the manufacture of the drug or direct any of the work.

ro, to make two batches of methamphetamine. The manufacturing process having been completed the following morning, Shapiro was given one-half of the drug and respondent kept the remainder. Shapiro offered to buy, and the respondent agreed to sell, part of the remainder for $60.

About a month later Shapiro returned to the Connolly house and met with Patrick Connolly to ask if he was still interested in their "business arrangement." Connolly replied that he was interested but that he had recently obtained two additional bottles of phenyl-2-propanone and would not be finished with them for a couple of days. He provided some additional methamphetamine to Shapiro at that time. Three days later Shapiro returned to the Connolly house with a search warrant and, among other items, seized an empty 500-gram bottle of propanone and a 100-gram bottle, not the one he had provided, that was partially filled with the chemical.

There was testimony at the trial of respondent and Patrick Connolly that phenyl-2-propanone was generally difficult to obtain. At the request of the Bureau of Narcotics and Dangerous Drugs, some chemical supply firms had voluntarily ceased selling the chemical.

At the close of the evidence, and after receiving the District Judge's standard entrapment instruction, the jury found the respondent guilty on all counts charged. On appeal the respondent conceded that the jury could have found him predisposed to commit the offenses, 459 F.2d at 672, but argued that on the facts presented there was entrapment as a matter of law. The Court of Appeals agreed, although it did not find the District Court had misconstrued or misapplied the traditional standards governing the entrapment defense. Rather, the court in effect expanded the traditional notion of entrapment, which focuses on the predisposition of the defendant, to mandate dismissal of a criminal prosecution whenever the court determines that there has been "an intolerable degree of governmental participation in the criminal enterprise." In this case the court decided that the conduct of the agent in supplying a scarce ingredient essential for the manufacture of a controlled substance established that defense.

This new defense was held to rest on either of two alternative theories. One theory is based on two lower court decisions which have found entrapment, regardless of predisposition, whenever the government supplies contraband to the defendants. United States v. Bueno, 447 F.2d 903 (C.A.5 1971); United States v. Chisum, 312 F.Supp. 1307 (C.D.Cal.1970). The second theory, a nonentrapment rationale, is based on a recent Ninth Circuit decision that reversed a conviction because a government investigator was so enmeshed in the criminal activity that the prosecution of the defendants was held to be repugnant to the American criminal justice system. Greene v. United States, 454 F.2d 783 (C.A.9 1971). The court below held that these two rationales constitute the same defense, and that only the label distinguishes them. In any event, it held that "[b]oth theories are premised on fundamental concepts of due process and evince the reluctance of the judiciary to countenance 'overzealous law enforcement.' " 459 F.2d, at 674, quoting Sherman v. United States, 356 U.S. 369, 381 (1958). (Frankfurter, J., concurring).

* * *

In the instant case respondent asks us to reconsider the theory of the entrapment defense as it is set forth in the majority opinions in *Sorrells* and *Sherman*. His principal contention is that the defense should rest on constitutional grounds. He argues that the level of Shapiro's involvement in the manufacture of the methamphetamine was so high that a criminal prosecution for the drug's manufacture violates the fundamental principles of due process. The respondent contends that the same factors that led this Court to apply the exclusionary rule to illegal searches and seizures, Weeks v. United States, 232 U.S. 383 (1914); Mapp v. Ohio, 367 U.S. 643 (1961), and confessions, Miranda v. Arizona, 384 U.S. 436 (1966), should be considered here. But he would have the Court go further in deterring undesirable official conduct by requiring that any prosecution be barred absolutely because of the police involvement in criminal activity. The analogy is imperfect in any event, for the principal reason behind the adoption of the exclusionary rule was the government's "failure to observe its own laws." Mapp v. Ohio, supra, 367 U.S., at 659. Unlike the situations giving rise to the holdings in *Mapp* and *Miranda,* the government's conduct here violated no independent constitutional right of the respondent. Nor did Shapiro violate any federal statute or rule or commit any crime in infiltrating the respondent's drug enterprise.

Respondent would overcome this basic weakness in his analogy to the exclusionary rule cases by having the Court adopt a rigid constitutional rule that would preclude any prosecution when it is shown that the criminal product would not have been possible had not an undercover agent "supplied an indispensable means to the commission of the crime that could not have been obtained otherwise, through legal or illegal channels." * * *

The record discloses that although the propanone was difficult to obtain it was by no means impossible. The defendants admitted making the drug both before and after those batches made with the propanone supplied by Shapiro. Shapiro testified that he saw an empty bottle labeled phenyl-2-propanone on his first visit to the laboratory on December 7, 1969. And when the laboratory was searched pursuant to a search warrant on January 10, 1970, two additional bottles labeled phenyl-2-propanone were seized. Thus, the facts in the record amply demonstrate that the propanone used in the illicit manufacture of methamphetamine not only *could* have been obtained without the intervention of Shapiro but was in fact obtained by these defendants.

While we may some day be presented with a situation in which the conduct of law enforcement agents is so outrageous that due process principles would absolutely bar the government from invoking judicial processes to obtain a conviction, cf. Rochin v. California, 342 U.S. 165 (1952), the instant case is distinctly not of that breed. Shapiro's contribution of propanone to the criminal enterprise already in process was scarcely objectionable. The chemical is by itself a harmless substance and its possession is legal. While the government may have been seeking to make it more difficult for drug rings, such as that of which respondent was a member, to obtain the chemical, the evidence described above shows that it nonetheless was obtainable. The law enforcement conduct here stops far short of violating that "fundamental fairness, shocking to the universal sense of justice," mandated by the Due Process Clause of the Fifth Amendment. Kinsella v. United States ex rel. Singleton, 361 U.S. 234, 246 (1960).

The illicit manufacture of drugs is not a sporadic, isolated criminal incident, but a continuing, though illegal, business enterprise. In order to obtain convictions for illegally manufacturing drugs, the gathering of evidence of past unlawful conduct frequently proves to be an all but impossible task. Thus in drug-related offenses law enforcement personnel have turned to one of the only practicable means of detection: the infiltration of drug rings and a limited participation in their unlawful present practices. Such infiltration is a recognized and permissible means of apprehension; if that be so, then the supply of some item of value that the drug ring requires must, as a general rule, also be permissible. For an agent will not be taken into the confidence of the illegal entrepreneurs unless he has something of value to offer them. Law enforcement tactics such as this can hardly be said to violate "fundamental fairness" or "shocking to the universal sense of justice," Kinsella, supra.

Respondent also urges as an alternative to his constitutional argument, that * * * the views of Justices Roberts and Frankfurter, concurring in Sorrells and Sherman, respectively, which make the essential element of the defense turn on the type and degree of governmental conduct, be adopted as the law.

We decline to overrule these cases. Sorrells is a precedent of long standing that has already been once reexamined in Sherman and implicitly there reaffirmed. Since the defense is not of a constitutional dimension, Congress may address itself to the question and adopt any substantive definition of the defense that it may find desirable.

* * *

* * * [I]t [does not] seem particularly desirable for the law to grant complete immunity from prosecution to one who himself planned to commit a crime, and then committed it, simply because government undercover agents subjected him to inducements which might have seduced a hypothetical individual who was not so predisposed. We are content to leave the matter where it was left by the Court in Sherman * * *[.]

Several decisions of the United States district courts and courts of appeals have undoubtedly gone beyond this Court's opinions in Sorrells and *Sherman* in order to bar prosecutions because of what they thought to be for want of a better term "overzealous law enforcement." But the defense of entrapment enunciated in those opinions was not intended to give the federal judiciary a "chancellor's foot" veto over law enforcement practices of which it did not approve. The execution of the federal laws under our Constitution is confided primarily to the Executive Branch of the Government, subject to applicable constitutional and statutory limitations and to judicially fashioned rules to enforce those limitations. We think that the decision of the Court of Appeals in this case quite unnecessarily introduces an unmanageably subjective standard which is contrary to the holdings of this Court in *Sorrells* and *Sherman.*

Those cases establish that entrapment is a relatively limited defense. It is rooted not in any authority of the Judicial Branch to dismiss prosecutions for what it feels to have been "overzealous law enforcement," but instead in the notion that Congress could not have intended criminal punishment for a defendant who has committed all the elements of a prescribed offense, but who was induced to commit them by the government.

* * * It is only when the government's deception actually implants the criminal design in the mind of the defendant that the defense of entrapment comes into play.

Respondent's concession in the Court of Appeals that the jury finding as to predisposition was supported by the evidence is, therefore, fatal to his claim of entrapment. He was an active participant in an illegal drug manufacturing enterprise which began before the government agent appeared on the scene, and continued after the government agent had left the scene. He was, in the words of *Sherman,* supra, not an "unwary innocent" but an "unwary criminal." The Court of Appeals was wrong, we believe, when it sought to broaden the principle laid down in *Sorrells* and *Sherman.* Its judgment is therefore

Reversed.

[The dissenting opinion of Mr. Justice Douglas, with Mr. Justice Brennan concurring, is omitted.]

Mr. Justice STEWART, with whom Mr. Justice BRENNAN and Mr. Justice MARSHALL join, dissenting.

* * *

In my view [the] objective approach to entrapment advanced by the concurring opinions in *Sorrells* and *Sherman* is the only one truly consistent with the underlying rationale of the defense.

In the case before us, I think that the District Court erred in submitting the issue of entrapment to the jury, with instructions to acquit only if it had a reasonable doubt as to the respondent's predisposition to committing the crime. Since, under the objective test of entrapment, predisposition is irrelevant and the issue is to be decided by the trial judge, the Court of Appeals, I believe, would have been

justified in reversing the conviction on this basis alone.   But since the
appellate court did not remand for consideration of the issue by the
District Judge under an objective standard, but rather found entrapment as a matter of law and directed that the indictment be dismissed,
we must reach the merits of the respondent's entrapment defense.

Since, in my view, it does not matter whether the respondent was
predisposed to commit the offense of which he was convicted, the focus
must be, rather, on the conduct of the undercover government agent.
What the agent did here was to meet with a group of suspected
producers of methamphetamine, including the respondent; to request
the drug; to offer to supply the chemical phenyl-2-propanone in exchange for one-half of the methamphetamine to be manufactured
therewith; and, when that offer was accepted, to provide the needed
chemical ingredient, and to purchase some of the drug from the
respondent.

It is undisputed that phenyl-2-propanone is an essential ingredient
in the manufacture of methamphetamine; that it is not used for any
other purpose; and that, while its sale is not illegal, it is difficult to
obtain, because a manufacturer's license is needed to purchase it, and
because many suppliers, at the request of the Federal Bureau of
Narcotics and Dangerous Drugs, do not sell it at all.   It is also
undisputed that the methamphetamine which the respondent was prosecuted for manufacturing and selling was all produced on December 10,
1969, and that all the phenyl-2-propanone used in the manufacture of
that batch of the drug was provided by the government agent.   In these
circumstances, the agent's undertaking to supply this ingredient to the
respondent, thus making it possible for the Government to prosecute
him for manufacturing an illicit drug with it, was, I think, precisely the
type of governmental conduct that the entrapment defense is meant to
prevent.

Although the Court of Appeals found that the phenyl-2-propanone
could not have been obtained without the agent's intervention—that
"there could not have been the manufacture, delivery, or sale of the
illicit drug had it not been for the Government's supply of one of the
essential ingredients," 459 F.2d 671, 672—the Court today rejects this
finding as contradicted by the facts revealed at trial.   The record, as
the Court states, discloses that one of the respondent's accomplices,
though not the respondent himself, had obtained phenyl-2-propanone
from independent sources both before and after receiving the agent's
supply, and had used it in the production of methamphetamine.   This
demonstrates, it is said, that the chemical was obtainable other than
through the government agent; and hence the agent's furnishing it for
the production of the methamphetamine involved in this prosecution
did no more than afford an opportunity for its production to one ready
and willing to produce it.   Thus, the argument seems to be, there was
no entrapment here, any more than there would have been if the agent

had furnished common table salt, had that been necessary to the drug's production.

It cannot be doubted that if phenyl-2-propanone had been wholly unobtainable from other sources, the agent's undercover offer to supply it to the respondent in return for part of the illicit methamphetamine produced therewith—an offer initiated and carried out by the agent for the purpose of prosecuting the respondent for producing methamphetamine—would be precisely the type of governmental conduct that constitutes entrapment under any definition. For the agent's conduct in that situation would make possible the commission of an otherwise totally impossible crime, and, I should suppose, would thus be a textbook example of instigating the commission of a criminal offense in order to prosecute someone for committing it.

But assuming in this case that the phenyl-2-propanone was obtainable through independent sources, the fact remains that that used for the particular batch of methamphetamine involved in all three counts of the indictment with which the respondent was charged—i.e., that produced on December 10, 1969—was supplied by the Government. This essential ingredient was indisputably difficult to obtain, and yet that used in committing the offenses of which the respondent was convicted was offered to the respondent by the government agent, on the agent's own initiative, and was readily supplied to the respondent in needed amounts. If the chemical was so easily available elsewhere, then why did not the agent simply wait until the respondent had himself obtained the ingredients and produced the drug, and then buy it from him? The very fact that the agent felt it incumbent upon him to offer to supply phenyl-2-propanone in return for the drug casts considerable doubt on the theory that the chemical could easily have been procured without the agent's intervention, and that therefore the agent merely afforded an opportunity for the commission of a criminal offense.

In this case, the chemical ingredient was available only to licensed persons, and the Government itself had requested suppliers not to sell that ingredient even to people with a license. Yet the government agent readily offered and supplied that ingredient to an unlicensed person and asked him to make a certain illegal drug with it. The Government then prosecuted that person for making the drug produced *with the very ingredient* which its agent had so helpfully supplied. This strikes me as the very pattern of conduct that should be held to constitute entrapment as a matter of law.

It is the Government's duty to prevent crime, not to promote it. Here, the Government's agent asked that the illegal drug be produced for him, solved his quarry's practical problems with the assurance that he could provide the one essential ingredient that was difficult to obtain, furnished that element as he had promised, and bought the finished product from the respondent—all so that the respondent could be prosecuted for producing and selling the very drug for which the agent had asked and for which he had provided the necessary component. Under the objective approach that I would follow, this respondent was entrapped, regardless of his predisposition or "innocence."

In the words of MR. JUSTICE ROBERTS:

"The applicable principle is that courts must be closed to the trial of a crime instigated by the government's own agents. No other issue, no comparison of equities as between the guilty official and the guilty defendant, has any place in the enforcement of this overruling principle of public policy." Sorrells v. United States, supra, at 459.

I would affirm the judgment of the Court of Appeals.

Notes and Questions

1. In Hampton v. United States, 425 U.S. 484, 96 S.Ct. 1646, 48 L.Ed. 2d 113 (1976), Hampton testified that a federal informant had provided the heroin which Hampton was charged with selling and had initially suggested selling it. The trial court refused to instruct the jury that Hampton should be acquitted if the jury found that the heroin had been supplied to Hampton by a government informer. Hampton was convicted and he appealed. The Supreme Court affirmed. Justice Rehnquist, in the plurality opinion, held that Hampton's predisposition rendered entrapment unavailable to him and even if his testimony were accurate none of his federal constitutional rights had been violated. Justice Powell, joined by Justice Blackmun, concurred but indicated an unwillingness to join some of Justice Rehnquist's language rejecting the likelihood that outrageous police behavior in such situations might offend due process. Justice Brennan, joined by Justices Stewart and Marshall, dissented on the ground that either due process or federal entrapment doctrine should bar conviction where the subject of the charge is the sale of contraband provided to the defendant by a government agent.

2. In State v. Sainz, 84 N.M. 259, 261, 501 P.2d 1247, 1249 (App.1972), the New Mexico Court of Appeals adopted the following formulation of the entrapment defense:

When the state's participation in the criminal enterprise reaches the point where it can be said that except for the conduct of the state a crime would probably not have been committed or because the conduct is such that it is likely to induce those to commit a crime who would normally avoid crime, *or, if the conduct is such that if allowed to continue would shake the public's confidence in the fair and honorable administration of justice,* this then becomes entrapment as a matter of law. (emphasis supplied).

The court further noted agreement with the proposition that as the state's participation in a criminal enterprise increases, the importance of the defendant's predisposition and intent decreases. Id. Does this standard—especially the emphasized portion—go beyond the Model Penal Code formulation? Does it appear to use the entrapment defense to promote interests other than the prevention of criminal acts that would not occur except for government activity? Sainz was overruled by the New Mexico Supreme Court in State v. Fiechter, 89 N.M. 74, 547 P.2d 557 (1976). See State v.

Paiz, 91 N.M. 5, 569 P.2d 415 (App.1977) (state supreme court urged to review *Fiechter's* overruling of *Sainz*).

3. Consider the following proposal made by the American Civil Liberties Union in its Report of its testimony before the Senate Subcommittee on Criminal Law and Procedure on the Final Report of the National Commission on Reform of the Federal Criminal Laws 37–38 (March 21, 1972):

§ 702. Entrapment

(1) *Defense.* It is a defense that the defendant was entrapped into committing the offense.

(2) *Entrapment Defined.* Entrapment occurs (i) when a law enforcement agent induces the commission of an offense, using persuasion or other means likely to cause normally law abiding persons to commit the offense; or (ii) when the criminal design originates with a law enforcement agent and he implants in the mind of an innocent person the disposition to commit an offense and induce its commission in order that the government may prosecute; or (iii) when the law enforcement agent induces the criminal act without reasonable suspicion [probable cause] that the person being solicited to commit an offense or with whom an illegal transaction is initiated is engaged in or prepared to engage in such offense or transaction. Conduct merely affording a person an opportunity to commit an offense does not constitute entrapment.

(3) The defense afforded by this section may be raised under a plea of not guilty. The defendant shall be entitled to have the issue of entrapment decided by the court and to have the fact that the defense has been raised and evidence introduced in support thereof kept from the attention of the jury. Evidence of the defendant's past criminal conduct is inadmissible on the entrapment issue.

(4) *Law Enforcement Agent Defined.* In this section "law enforcement agent" includes personnel of state and local law enforcement agencies as well as of the United States, and any person cooperating with such an agency.

4. It is often held that a defendant may not deny commission of the crime charged and also assert entrapment. This rule may even be applied to require that a defendant take the stand and admit commission of the acts constituting the crime before entrapment will be regarded as having been raised. See State v. Montano, 117 Ariz. 145, 571 P.2d 291 (1977). Although there is no general prohibition against criminal defendants asserting inconsistent matters, the special rule applied to entrapment cases is defended on the ground that denial of the acts constituting the crime and assertion of entrapment is *too* inconsistent to be acceptable. See United States v. Greenfield, 554 F.2d 179, 182 (5th Cir.1977). Can it be argued that there is a reasonable basis for requiring that a defendant who wishes to put entrapment (and therefore his own predisposition) into issue take the witness stand and subject himself to questioning concerning the issues made relevant by his claim of entrapment?

The traditional rule was critically examined and abandoned in United States v. Demma, 523 F.2d 981 (9th Cir.1975). Reading *Sorrells* as establishing that "non-entrapment is an essential element of every federal crime," the court found the prohibition against inconsistent positions contrary to this indication that the government has the burden of establishing the elements of the crime charged. Id. at 983. In addition, the court found a compelling policy reason for refusing to make an exception to the general rule permitting inconsistent defenses for entrapment. The primary purpose of the entrapment doctrine, the court reasoned, is to safeguard the integrity of the law enforcement and prosecution process. The need to accomplish this purpose indicates that the defense should not be weakened by the prohibition against inconsistent positions. Id. at 985. "Of course," the court noted, "it is very unlikely that the defendant will be able to prove entrapment without testifying and, in the course of testifying, without admitting that he did the acts charged." Id.

5. In Shrader v. State, 101 Nev. 499, 706 P.2d 834 (1985), a police informant—Scott—approached Shrader and asked Shrader where Scott could obtain marijuana. Shrader responded that he did not have any, but Scott emphasized that he needed marijuana to relax because of a recent stay in jail. Shrader then sold Scott a quarter ounce of marijuana for $45. About a month later, Shrader took $100 from Scott and obtained an ounce of marijuana. Shrader's conviction for sale of marijuana was reversed because, the Nevada Supreme Court concluded, Shrader had been entrapped "as a matter of law":

Entrapment as a matter of law exists where the uncontroverted evidence shows (1) that the state furnished an opportunity for criminal conduct (2) to a person without the requisite criminal intent.

The entrapment defense is made available to defendants not to excuse their criminal wrongdoing but as a prophylactic device designed to prevent police misconduct. * * * By permitting conviction of only those defendants predisposed to commit the offense, the defense focuses police attention on existing criminal ventures.

Although we recognize that undercover operations are often necessary to detect covert and consensual crimes, those operations must be conducted in a manner consistent with the policy of trapping only the unwary criminal, not the unwary innocent. Therefore, we hold that when the police target a specific individual for an undercover operation, they must have reasonable cause to believe that the individual is predisposed to commit the crime. * * *

In applying this rule to the facts of this case, we conclude that Shrader was entrapped as a matter of law. We are at a loss to discover * * * any evidence in the record of Shrader's predisposition to sell marijuana before he was targeted for an undercover operation. * * *

When questioned by defense counsel as to why Scott targeted Shrader for an undercover operation, Scott testified that he knew marijuana was "available" because he had seen it used at parties at Shrader's apartment. Although an acknowledged user of marijuana, Shrader had no previous criminal record. Evidence of Shrader's previous possession of marijuana does not constitute reasonable cause to believe he was a seller.

* * *

[T]he proper limits of government activity in undercover operations must be made clear to both the police and their agents. We adopt the rule articulated above to guide the police in future investigations and to prevent "the seduction of innocent people into a criminal career." The absence of evidence in the record that Shrader had a predisposition to sell marijuana creates a substantial risk that the criminal intent originated in the mind of the entrapper and not in the mind of the entrapped. * * *

101 Nev. at 501–04, 706 P.2d at 835–37.

MODEL PENAL CODE *
(Official Draft 1985).

Section 2.13. Entrapment

(1) A public law enforcement official or a person acting in cooperation with such an official perpetrates an entrapment if for the purpose of obtaining evidence of the commission of an offense, he induces or encourages another person to engage in conduct constituting such offense by either:

(a) making knowingly false representations designed to induce the belief that such conduct is not prohibited; or

(b) employing methods of persuasion or inducement which create a substantial risk that such an offense will be committed by persons other than those who are ready to commit it.

(2) Except as provided in Subsection (3) of this Section, a person prosecuted for an offense shall be acquitted if he proves by a preponderance of evidence that his conduct occurred in response to an entrapment. The issue of entrapment shall be tried by the Court in the absence of the jury.

(3) The defense afforded by this Section is unavailable when causing or threatening bodily injury is an element of the offense charged and the prosecution is based on conduct causing or threatening such injury to a person other than the person perpetrating the entrapment.

D. "DEFENSES" AND OTHER DOCTRINES RELATED TO MENTAL ILLNESS

Editors' Introduction: Psychological Impairment and Criminal Liability

Perhaps the most perplexing problem of substantive criminal law has been the task of accommodating some offenders' psychological abnormality in the decision as to whether—or to what extent—to hold persons criminally responsible for their conduct. This section explores two possible vehicles for this task. The first is the traditional defense of insanity. The second is the "doctrine" [a] of diminished capacity, under which a defendant's psychological abnormality is considered in determining whether the defendant had the state of mind required by the crime charged.

Both of these doctrines need to be distinguished from another issue often presented in criminal litigation which also involves an inquiry into defendants' mental condition. It is a violation of due process as well as the procedural requirements of virtually all states to place on trial a defendant who is incompetent to stand trial. Pate v. Robinson, 383 U.S. 375, 86 S.Ct. 836, 15 L.Ed.2d 815 (1966). There is widespread agreement that a defendant is incompetent within the meaning of this rule if, because of psychological abnormality, he lacks present ability to consult with his lawyer with a reasonable degree of understanding or if he lacks a reasonable as well as factual understanding of the proceedings. Dusky v. United States, 362 U.S. 402, 80 S.Ct. 788, 4 L.Ed.2d 824 (1960). The competency inquiry, then, focuses upon defendants' mental condition at the time of trial; the questions concerning responsibility considered in this section are concerned with defendants' mental condition at the time of the commission of the acts constituting the alleged offense. There is a far more fundamental difference between the doctrines, however. Incompetency to stand trial is not a "defense" in the sense that it addresses the merits of the charges pending against the accused. Rather, it is simply a bar to trial of the defendant and therefore to disposition of the charges. If, after a determination of incompetency, a defendant is restored to a condition in which he no longer suffers from disabilities rendering him incompetent, he may at that point be tried upon the still pending charges. Both insanity and diminished capacity, on the other hand, are defensive doctrines. If they are successfully asserted by a defendant, the charges are permanently disposed of and there is no danger of a subsequent retrial and conviction.

In discussing the matters covered in this section, it is important to begin with a consideration of what objectives the law is or ought to be pursuing by means of the doctrines at issue. Among those policy objectives which might be considered proper ones are the following:

1. *Exculpation of the Nonblameworthy.* Insofar as criminal liability involves a judgment of ethical reprehensibility, it is desirable to have doctrines that prevent the conviction of those who are

a. Given the existence of a mens rea requirement and the general rule that evidence relevant to issues in the case is admissible, a question might be raised as to why a special "doctrine" is necessary to justify the admission of such evidence. Perhaps the question might be better put as whether there is or should be a special rule barring the admissibility of evidence tending to show that the defendant was psychologically abnormal and therefore lacked the intent required by the crime charged. See generally the discussion at pages 821, 832, infra.

not in fact blameworthy despite their conduct. Not only does exculpation avoid what some argue is the stigmatization resulting from criminal conviction, but it also may prevent the infliction of punishment containing at least an element of senseless revenge.

2. *Channeling Offenders into Appropriate Systems.* To some extent, the insanity defense serves not only to prevent criminal liability but also to channel a defendant who asserts it into the mental health system. This may be seen as desirable for several reasons. It is arguable that it implements society's interest in preventing further offenses by the defendant. Admission to the mental health system may result in an offender being provided with "treatment" that is more appropriate to his needs than any therapy available in the correctional system. Moreover, such action may provide society with the means of retaining the defendant as long as he presents a danger. A defendant sentenced under criminal provisions must usually be released at the expiration of the sentence no matter how dangerous he is believed to be at that time; one committed to psychiatric facilities following exculpation under the doctrines discussed here may sometimes be retained until—and if—it is determined that he no longer poses a danger to society. Further, it is argued that society's interests in protection are accomplished at less cost to offenders, since treatment in the mental health system is less stigmatizing and less disabling in other ways. It may, for example, have less effect upon offenders' employment opportunities.

3. *Reinforcement of General Notions of Responsibility.* Some argue that the concept of criminal irresponsibility and its litigation in occasional cases tends to reinforce the sense of responsibility held by most members of the community. By the process of attempting to identify exceptional cases in which defendants will be regarded as irresponsible, the community reaffirms its belief in the general rule of responsibility and this process of reaffirmance itself tends to cause members of the community to act in a responsible way.

4. *Avoidance of Misuse of Exculpatory Doctrines.* In addition to the general objectives outlined above, it seems clear that there is a strong and legitimate interest in avoiding the misuse of any exculpatory doctrines that might be adopted. For example, an exculpatory rule that might in theory be justifiable on the ground that it would excuse persons who are not in fact blameworthy might be subject to the objection that in practice so many blameworthy defendants would be able to falsely claim the benefits of the rule that the costs of the rule would exceed its benefits. Closely related to this is the danger that a rule might pose questions that, in the context of individual cases, are either impossible of resolution or are so expensive and timeconsuming to resolve that society cannot afford to have the judicial system spend time on efforts to

administer them. Some formulations of the insanity defense or the diminished responsibility rule might be subject to such objections.

It is also important to put the matter in perspective. The National Advisory Commission on the Insanity Defense reported several "myths" relating to the insanity defense, including widespread beliefs that "many criminal defendants plead insanity and most are acquitted" and that "the insanity defense causes major problems for the criminal justice system." Myths and Realities: A Report of the National Commission on the Insanity Defense 14–15 (1983). A public opinion survey conducted after the 1982 acquittal on insanity grounds of John Hinckley, the attempted assassin of President Reagan, found that over 87 percent of those questioned agreed that the insanity defense is a loophole that allows too many guilty people to go free. Hans and Slater, John Hinckley, Jr. and the Insanity Defense: The Public's Verdict, 47 Public Opinion Q. 202, 207 (1983).

In reality, it is clear that defenses based upon mental abnormality are seldom raised and, when raised, most often fail. The National Advisory Commission developed information indicating, for example, that in New York the insanity defense is raised about once in every 600 to 700 cases and is successful in about 25 percent of the cases in which it is raised. The Commission concluded:

> [D]espite the exaggerated attention insanity acquittals receive in the media, in legislatures, and in the legal and psychiatric literature, the consensus of the experts in the field is that the insanity defense is an extremely rare event and a successful insanity defense is even more rare.

> * * *

> It is difficult to imagine how a defense which is invoked so infrequently can be largely responsible for the problems which exist in our criminal justice system. While it is painfully obvious to many Americans that our criminal justice system suffers from various major problems, it should also be apparent that the existence and use of the insanity defense is not one of them. * * * Given the small numbers, the insanity defense event may not even be part of the problem.

Myths and Realities, supra, at 15–16.

Criminal responsibility matters, such as the insanity defense, do, however, pose interesting and difficult questions concerning basic assumptions regarding criminal behavior and the law's potential effect on that behavior. Because of this, the manner in which criminal responsibility issues are resolved often has great symbolic value for those holding strong views regarding these matters. The fact that many members of the public perceive criminal responsibility issues to be a major practical problem for the criminal justice system is itself important, even if that perception is incorrect. Public disenchantment with the system cannot help but have an adverse effect upon the system in many ways.

1. THE DEFENSE OF INSANITY

Editors' Introduction: Development of the Insanity Defense

Traditionally, discussions of the insanity defense have focused upon the appropriate standard to be used for determining which defendants to exculpate on the ground of insanity. While in the ideal world the legal standard *should* be the primary determinant of how specific cases come out, this may not be the result in the imperfect environment of the criminal justice system. How particular trial judges exercise their inevitable discretion to admit or exclude offered expert testimony, for example, may have more effect upon the outcome of cases than does the content of jury instructions. Jurors may, moreover, fail to accurately apply the standard given to them in the judge's instructions because they do not understand it or perhaps because they find it so contrary to their intuitive sense of what "justice" requires. As the American Psychiatric Association recently observed, "the exact wording of the insanity defense has never, through scientific studies or the case approach, been shown to be the major determinant of whether a defendant is acquitted by reason of insanity." American Psychiatric Association Statement on the Insanity Defense, 140 Am.J. Psychiatry 681, 684 (1983).

Nevertheless, consideration of insanity matters must at least begin with the legal criterion and how it should be applied to particular cases. Especially in light of recent changes in insanity standards, it is useful to consider separately whether, and how, the standards should provide for evaluating defendants whose illnesses resulted in cognitive impairment and other defendants whose illnesses arguably gave rise to volitional or "control" disabilities. This is done in the two units of this subsection. First, however, it is necessary to consider the manner in which the current standards developed.

The Benchmark: The "M'Naghten Rule"

Any discussion of insanity must begin with Daniel M'Naghten's Case, 10 Cl. & F. 200, 8 Eng.Rep. 718 (1843), which is the basis for the traditional standard. M'Naghten, in an apparent effort to kill Sir Robert Peel, shot and killed Edward Drummond, Peel's private secretary. At the trial, defense testimony tended to show that the defendant experienced delusions that others were pursuing him and wanted to kill him and that he fired the fatal shot believing that this would bring him peace from his persecution. The jury acquitted. Public outcry was so great that the matter was taken up in the House of Lords and the judges gave an opinion on the question of the nature and extent of unsoundness of mind excusing the commission of a crime of the sort involved. Lord Chief Justice Tindal delivered the opinion, in which all but one of the judges concurred:

> Your Lordships are pleased to inquire of us * * * "What are the proper questions to be submitted to the jury, where a person alleged to

be afflicted with insane delusion respecting one or more particular subjects or persons, is charged with the commission of a crime (murder, for example), and insanity is set up as a defense?" And * * * "In what terms ought the question to be left to the jury as to the prisoner's state of mind at the time when the act was committed?" And as these two questions appear to us to be more conveniently answered together, we have to submit our opinion to be, that the jurors ought to be told in all cases that every man is to be presumed to be sane, and to possess a sufficient degree of reason to be responsible for his crimes, until the contrary be proved to their satisfaction; and that to establish a defence on the ground of insanity, it must be clearly proved that, at the time of the committing of the act, the party accused was labouring under such a defect of reason, from disease of the mind, as not to know the nature and quality of the act he was doing; or, if he did know it, that he did not know he was doing what was wrong. The mode of putting the latter part of the question to the jury on these occasions has generally been, whether the accused at the time of doing the act knew the difference between right and wrong: which mode, though rarely, if ever, leading to any mistake with the jury, is not, as we conceive, so accurate when put generally and in the abstract, as when put with reference to the party's knowledge of right and wrong in respect to the very act with which he is charged. If the question were to be put as to the knowledge of the accused solely and exclusively with reference to the law of the land, it might tend to confound the jury, by inducing them to believe that an actual knowledge of the law of the land was essential in order to lead to a conviction; whereas the law is administered upon the principle that every one must be taken conclusively to know it, without proof that he does know it. If the accused was conscious that the act was one which he ought not to do, and if that act was at the same time contrary to the law of the land, he is punishable; and the usual course therefore has been to leave the question to the jury, whether the party accused had a sufficient degree of reason to know that he was doing an act that was wrong; and this course we think is correct, accompanied with such observations and explanations as the circumstances of each particular case may require.

The [next] question which your Lordships have proposed to us is this:—"If a person under an insane delusion as to existing facts, commits an offence in consequence thereof, is he thereby excused?" To which question the answer must of course depend on the nature of the delusion: but [assuming] that he labours under [a] partial delusion only, and is not in other respects insane, we think he must be considered in the same situation as to responsibility as if the facts with respect to which the delusion exists were real. For example, if under the influence of his delusion he supposes another man to be in the act of attempting to take away his life, and he kills that man, as he supposes, in self-defence, he would be exempt from punishment. If his delusion was that the deceased had inflicted a serious injury to his character and fortune, and he killed him in revenge for such supposed injury, he would be liable to punishment.

Liberalization of Insanity: Loss of Control

The *M'Naghten* Rule was subjected to severe criticism, primarily on the ground that it failed to adequately identify all those impaired persons who could not justly be held responsible for their conduct. As the California Supreme Court explained:

> Principal among [the deficiencies of *M'Naghten*] is the test's exclusive focus upon the cognitive capacity of the defendant ＊ ＊ ＊. As explained by Judge Ely of the Ninth Circuit: "＊ ＊ ＊ This formulation ＊ ＊ ＊ fails to attack the problem presented in a case wherein an accused may have understood his actions but was incapable of controlling his behavior. ＊ ＊ ＊" (Wade v. United States (9th Cir.1970) 426 F.2d 64, 66–67.)
>
>   *M'Naghten's* exclusive emphasis on cognition would be of little consequence if all serious mental illness impaired the capacity of the affected person to know the nature and wrongfulness of his action. ＊ ＊ ＊ Current psychiatric opinion, however, holds that mental illness often leaves the individual's intellectual understanding relatively unimpaired, but so affects his emotions or reason that he is unable to prevent himself from committing the act. ＊ ＊ ＊ To ask whether such a person knows or understands that his act is "wrong" is to ask a question irrelevant to the nature of his mental illness or to the degree of his criminal responsibility.

People v. Drew, 22 Cal.3d 333, 341–42, 149 Cal.Rptr. 275, 278–79, 583 P.2d 1318, 1322–23 (1978). In response to such criticisms of the *M'Naghten* Rule, a number of American jurisdictions modified it or rejected it as the sole determinant of a defendant's right to acquittal on insanity grounds. Often this was accomplished by adding an additional alternative means by which the defense of insanity could be established. In some jurisdictions, this supplementation was by means of an "irresistible impulse" test. In Parsons v. State, 81 Ala. 577, 2 So. 854 (1887), for example, the Alabama court held that juries were to be told that defendants were to be found not guilty by reason of insanity if they were "moved to action by an insane impulse controlling their will or their judgment."

The Supreme Court, however, in 1952 rejected the argument that legislative adoption of "the 'right and wrong' test of legal insanity in preference to the 'irresistible impulse' test" violates due process of law:

> Knowledge of right and wrong is the exclusive test of criminal responsibility in a majority of American jurisdictions. The science of psychiatry has made tremendous strides since that test was laid down in M'Naghten's Case, but the progress of science has not yet reached a point where its learning would compel us to require the states to eliminate the right and wrong test from their criminal law. Moreover, the choice of a test of legal insanity involves not only scientific knowledge but questions of basic policy as to the extent to which that knowledge should determine criminal responsibility. The whole problem has evoked wide disagreement among those who have studied it.

In these circumstances it is clear that adoption of the irresistible impulse test is not "implicit in the concept of ordered liberty."

Leland v. Oregon, 343 U.S. 790, 800–01, 72 S.Ct. 1002, 1008–09, 96 L.Ed. 1302, 1310 (1952).

In 1962, the Proposed Official Draft of the American Law Institute's Model Penal Code proposed a formulation that restated the *M'Naghten* Rule but also added an alternative that permitted acquittal on the basis of volitional impairment:

Section 4.01. Mental Disease or Defect Excluding Responsibility

(1) A person is not responsible for criminal conduct if at the time of such conduct as a result of mental disease or defect he lacks substantial capacity either to appreciate the criminality [wrongfulness] of his conduct or to conform his conduct to the requirements of law.

(2) As used in this Article, the terms "mental disease or defect" do not include an abnormality manifested only by repeated or otherwise anti-social conduct.

The drafters explained:

[The formulation] accepts the view that any effort to exclude the nondeterrables from strictly penal sanctions must take account of the impairment of volitional capacity no less than of impairment of cognition * * *. It also accepts the criticism of the "irresistible impulse" formulation as inept in so far as it may be impliedly restricted to sudden, spontaneous acts as distinguished from insane propulsions that are accompanied by brooding or reflection. * * * [It deems] the proper question on this branch of the inquiry to be whether the defendant was without capacity to conform his conduct to the requirements of law. * * * The application of the principle will call, of course, for a distinction between incapacity, upon the one hand, and mere indisposition on the other. Such a distinction is inevitable in the application of a standard addressed to impairment of volition. We believe that the distinction can be made.

Model Penal Code, Comment to § 4.01, at 157–58 (Tent. Draft No. 4, 1955).

This apparently invigorated the movement for reform of insanity law, because the Model Penal Code's formulation was widely adopted by both courts and legislatures. By 1982, all the federal circuits and at least 29 states defined the defense of insanity so as to provide for acquittal on the basis of volitional impairment of some sort. American Bar Association Standing Committee on Association Standards for Criminal Justice and Commission on the Mentally Disabled, *Report with Recommendations to the House of Delegates* 10, reprinted in *Reports With Recommendations to the House of Delegates, 1983 Midyear Meeting* (1983).

The Movement Away From Volitional Impairment

On June 21, 1982, a Washington D.C. jury found John W. Hinckley, Jr., not guilty by reason of insanity on all charges arising out his efforts the prior year to assassinate President Reagan. The verdict was widely regarded as improper by a public that saw Hinckley as sane. See Hans and Slater, John W. Hinckley, Jr. and the Insanity Defense: The Public's Verdict, 47 *Public Opinion Q.* 202 (1983). The Hinckley acquittal stimulated reconsideration of a number of matters related to criminal responsibility litigation. Among these was proper placement of the burden of persuasion on insanity. The Hinckley jury was instructed that since the insanity issue had been raised, the Government had the obligation of proving sanity beyond a reasonable doubt. Some saw the Hinckley acquittal as confirming that the ready availability of prodefendant expert testimony and the confusing nature of that testimony permits almost any defendant with imagination and financial backing to raise a reasonable doubt as to her sanity in a jury's mind. Hinckley's acquittal, in this view, suggested the need for more widespread adoption of the position taken by some jurisdictions, under which the defendant has the burden of proving—usually by a preponderance of the evidence—that she was insane within the meaning of the defense. This is discussed further, below.

Most importantly, however, the Hinckley verdict provided the impetus for widespread abandonment of volitional impairment as a basis for an insanity defense. Many saw the jury's verdict of acquittal as the result of confusion engendered by large amounts of psychiatric testimony rendered admissible because of Hinckley's ability to challenge his volitional capacity. This perceived risk of jury confusion (and therefore improper acquittals) provided the occasion for a reconsideration of whether expert testimony bearing upon an offender's past ability to control his conduct was as reliable as had been assumed during the "rise" of the defense of volitional impairment. For general discussions, see Dix, Criminal Responsibility and Mental Impairment in American Criminal Law: Response to the Hinckley Acquittal in Historical Perspective, 1 *Law and Mental Health, International Perspectives* 1 (1984); Johnson, The Turnabout in the Insanity Defense, 6 *Crime and Justice* 221 (1985).

Perhaps most amazing was the uniformity with which professional organizations attacked the volitional aspect of many existing insanity standards. The American Bar Association House of Delegates approved "in principle a defense of nonresponsibility for crime which focuses solely on whether the defendant, as a result of mental disease or defect, was unable to appreciate the wrongfulness of his or her conduct at the time of the offense charged." Summary of Action Taken by the House of Delegates, 1983 Midyear Meeting 3 (1983). The American Medical Association urged the abolition of any "special defense" and its replacement by provision for acquittal when, as a result of mental disease or defect, the defendant lacked the state or mind or mens rea required by the offense charged. Insanity Defense in Criminal Trials and Limitations of Psychiatric Testimony, Report of the Board of Trustees, 251 J.Am.Medical Assoc. 2967 (1984).

The American Psychiatric Association indicated a preference for an insanity standard along the lines of that favored by the American Bar Association. In explanation, it noted:

> Many psychiatrists * * * believe that psychiatric information relevant to determining whether a defendant understood the nature of his act, and whether he appreciated its wrongfulness, is more reliable, and has a stronger scientific basis than, for example, does psychiatric information relevant to whether a defendant was able to control his behavior. The line between an irresistible impulse and an impulse not resisted is probably no sharper than that between twilight and dusk. Psychiatry is a deterministic discipline that views all human behavior as, to a large extent, "caused." The concept of volition is the subject of some disagreement among psychiatrists. Many psychiatrists, therefore believe that psychiatric testimony * * * about volition is more likely to produce confusion for jurors than is psychiatric testimony relevant to a defendant's appreciation or understanding.

American Psychiatric Association Statement on the Insanity Defense, 140 Am.J.Psychiatry 681, 685 (1983). It also challenged the apparent assumption that a purely cognitive standard would deprive many volitionally-impaired persons of an opportunity for exculpation:

> In practice there is considerable overlap between a psychotic person's defective understanding or appreciation and his ability to control his behavior. Most psychotic persons who fail a volitional test for insanity will also fail a cognitive-type test when such a test is applied to their behavior, thus rendering the volitional test superfluous in judging them.

Id.

Legislative action has been widespread and generally has involved redefinition of the criterion for insanity along the lines of a "modernized" version of the *M'Naghten* Rule offered by Professor Richard J. Bonnie. See Bonnie, The Moral Basis of the Insanity Defense, 69 J.Am. B.Assoc. 194 (1983). This corresponds to the formulations urged by the American Bar Association and the American Psychiatric Association. Perhaps the most significant legislative action was the federal "Insanity Reform Act of 1984," signed by the President on October 14, 1984. Until this enactment, the substance of the insanity defense as it applied in prosecutions for federal crimes had been left to judicial development. The United States Supreme Court had not addressed the matter, but all of the Courts of Appeal had embraced a version of the Model Penal Code's formulation. As a result of the 1984 legislation, Title 18 of the United States Code now contains the following provision:

§ 20. Insanity defense

(a) Affirmative defense.—It is an affirmative defense to a prosecution under any federal statute that, at the time of the commission of the acts constituting the offense, the defendant, as a result of a severe mental disease or defect, was unable to appreciate the nature and quality or the wrongfulness of his acts. Mental disease or defect does not otherwise constitute a defense.

(b) Burden of proof.—The defendant has the burden of proving the defense of insanity by clear and convincing evidence.

The House Report on the measure explained:

Conceptually, there is some appeal to a defense predicated on lack of power to avoid criminal conduct. If one conceives the major purpose of the insanity defense to be the exclusion of the nondeterrables from criminal responsibility, a control test seems designed to meet that objective. Furthermore, notions of retributive punishment seem particularly inappropriate with respect to one powerless to do otherwise than he did.

* * *

Richard J. Bonnie, Professor of Law and Director of the Institute of Law, Psychiatry and Public Policy at the University of Virginia, while accepting the moral predicate for a control test, explained the fundamental difficulty involved:

Unfortunately, however, there is no scientific test for measuring a person's capacity for self-control or for calibrating the impairment of such capacity. There is, in short, no objective basis for distinguishing between offenders who were undeterrable and those were merely undeterred, between the impulse that was irresistible and the impulse not resisted, or between substantial impairment of capacity and some lesser impairment. Whatever the precise terms of the volitional test, the question is unanswerable—or can be answered only by "moral guesses." To ask it at all, in my opinion, invites fabricated claims, undermines equal administration of the penal law, and compromises its deterrent effect.

H.R.Rep. No. 98–1030, 98th Cong., 2nd Sess. 226–27 (1984), reprinted in [1984] U.S.Code Cong. & Adm.News 3182.

Until 1979, the California Supreme Court had adhered to the *M'Naghten* Rule. In People v. Drew, supra, however, the court adopted the Model Penal Code formulation. But in June, 1982, the California electorate adopted "Proposition 8" which, among other things, established a statutory definition of insanity that embodied a purely cognitive test. See Cal. Penal Code § 25(b). See generally, People v. Skinner, 39 Cal.3d 765, 217 Cal.Rptr. 685, 704 P.2d 752 (1985).

The National Commission on the Insanity Defense, established by the National Mental Health Association, arrived at a conclusion clearly contrary to the trend. The Commission acknowledged that psychiatric testimony on volition might confuse a jury. But, it concluded, if the burden of proof on insanity is placed on the defendant, "the adjudicative difficulties perceived by others in the volitional test ought to be minimized or eliminated." It recommended, therefore, that the insanity test include both cognitive and volitional elements or prongs. *Myths*

& Realities: A Report of the National Commission on the Insanity Defense 36 (1983).

Other Approaches: "Product" or Durham Test

It might be desirable for jury instructions to be less directive than those considered above. Since State v. Pike, 49 N.H. 399 (1870), New Hampshire has submitted insanity cases to juries with a direction to determine whether the defendant was mentally ill and, if so, whether the crime was the product of that mental illness. See State v. Abbott, 127 N.H. 444, 503 A.2d 791 (1985). In a landmark decision, Durham v. United States, 214 F.2d 862 (D.C.Cir.1954), the United States Court of Appeals for the District of Columbia adopted this approach for criminal litigation in the District. Judge Bazelon's opinion seemed to rely heavily upon what the court perceived as the need for a broad rule that, in implementation, would impose no impediment to expert witnesses' efforts to convey to juries all of their information concerning defendants' behavior and its "causes." But administration of the rule proved difficult. In McDonald v. United States, 312 F.2d 847 (D.C.Cir.1962), the court promulgated a definition of the mental disease or defect required. This was defined as "any abnormal condition of the mind which substantially affects mental or emotional processes and substantially impairs behavior controls." 312 F.2d at 851. With this definition, the *Durham* rule arguably differed little in substance from overtly volitional tests, but was less direct and therefore potentially more confusing to jurors.

In United States v. Brawner, 471 F.2d 969 (D.C.Cir.1972), the court abandoned the *Durham* rule in favor of the Model Penal Code formulation (reprinted at page 789, supra). The major difficulty, reasoned the court, was that the *Durham* rule required expert testimony to address the issue of "productivity," i.e., whether the crime charged was the product of the defendant's abnormality. It also required juries to address that question. But neither experts nor jurors had any definition of "productivity." As a result, experts tended to rely upon their own definitions of the term, which inevitably incorporated their own ethical and personal views and values, but to testify as if their conclusions were simply the result of objective application of their professional expertise. Juries would then tend to rely upon this testimony, without awareness that the testimony represented personal value judgments not within the witnesses' area of professional expertise. What the court perceived as the need to reduce, in insanity litigation, "undue dominance by the experts giving testimony," was a major consideration in the court's *Brawner* action. It explained:

> The ALI's formulation retains the core requirement of a meaningful relationship between the mental illness and the incident charged. The language used in the ALI rule is sufficiently in the common ken that its use in the courtroom, or in preparation for trial, permits a reasonable three-way communication—between (a) the law-trained judges and lawyers; (b) the experts and (c) the jurymen—without

insisting on a vocabulary that is either stilted or stultified, or conducive to a testimonial mystique permitting expert dominance and encroachment on the jury's function.

471 F.2d at 983. See also, Bethea v. United States, 365 A.2d 64 (D.C. App.1976).

Other Approaches: General "Justice" Standard

Virtually all of the modern formulations of the insanity defense attempt to focus juries' attention on specific possible effects of a defendant's impairment. It may be that this poses jurors with an impossible task because even with the help of experts such matters as a defendant's prior ability to control his actions simply cannot be resolved. If this is so, perhaps it would be better to make clear to juries that they cannot hope to make specific decisions on "objective" or "scientific" grounds and that they must address the issues as ethical ones. Chief Judge Bazelon so suggested in *Brawner:*

[The ALI test] asks the jury to wrestle with such unfamiliar, if not incomprehensible, concepts as the capacity to appreciate the wrongfulness of one's actions, and the capacity to conform to the requirements of law. The best hope for our new test is that jurors will regularly conclude that no one—including the experts—can provide a meaningful answer to the questions posed by the ALI test. And in their search for some semblance of an intelligible standard, they may be forced to consider whether it would be just to hold the defendant responsible for his actions. By that indirect approach, our new test may lead jurors to
* * * make the "intertwining moral, legal, and medical judgments" on which the resolution of the responsibility question properly depends.
* * *

Our instruction to the jury should provide that a defendant is not responsible *if at the time of his unlawful conduct his mental or emotional processes or behavior controls were impaired to such an extent that he cannot justly be held responsible for his act.* This test would ask the psychiatrist a single question: what is the nature of the impairment of the defendant's mental and emotional processes and behavior controls? It would leave for the jury the question whether that impairment is sufficient to relieve the defendant of responsibility for the particular act charged.

The purpose of this proposed instruction is to focus the jury's attention on the legal and moral aspects of criminal responsibility, and to make clear why the determination of responsibility is entrusted to the jury and not the expert witnesses.

471 F.2d at 1031–32 (emphasis in original) (Bazelon, C.J., concurring in part and dissenting in part).

Other Approaches: The "Mens Rea" Approach

As was discussed above, the American Medical Association urged after the Hinckley acquittal that any special defense of insanity be abolished and replaced by provision for acquittal when a defendant, as a result of mental disease or defect, lacked the state of mind required as an element of the crime charged. This has been done in several states. Montana, for example, has abolished the insanity defense and provided for the jury to return a verdict of acquittal on the ground that "due to a mental disease or defect [the defendant] could not have had a particular state of mind that is an essential element of the offense charged." Mont.Code Ann. § 46–14–201(2). Further, the Montana Code provides:

§ 46–14–311. Consideration of mental disease or defect in sentencing.

Whenever a defendant is convicted on a verdict or a plea of guilty and he claims that at the time of the commission of the offense of which he was convicted he was suffering from a mental disease or defect which rendered him unable to appreciate the criminality of his conduct or to confirm his conduct to the requirements of law, the sentencing court shall consider any relevant evidence presented at the trial and shall require such additional evidence as it considers necessary for the determination of the issue, including examination of the defendant and a report thereof * * *.

§ 46–14–312. Sentence to be imposed.

* * *

(2) If the court finds that the defendant at the time of the commission of the offense suffered from a mental disease or defect as described in § 14–14–311, any mandatory minimum sentence prescribed by law for the offense need not apply and the court shall sentence him to be committed to the custody of the director of the department of institutions to be placed in an appropriate institution for custody, care, and treatment for a definite time not to exceed the maximum term of imprisonment that could be imposed. * * *

(3) A defendant whose sentence has been imposed under subdivision (2) may petition the sentencing court for review of the sentence if the professional person certifies that the defendant has been cured of the mental disease or defect. The sentencing court may make any order not inconsistent with its original sentencing authority except that the length of confinement or supervision must be equal to that of the original sentence.

Although Montana's abolition of the defense came in 1979, before the Hinckley attack and the recommendations of the American Medical Association, the Association's justifications for its position are helpful to an understanding of this approach. In defense of its proposal, the Association explained that an insanity defense could not be an effective device for assuring acquittal of those who cannot be expected to conform to the law and thereby assuring the moral integrity of the law. Assuming that any insanity defense must rest primarily upon psychiatric models, the Association's report continued:

A defense premised on psychiatric models represents a singularly unsatisfactory, and inherently contradictory, approach to the issue of accountability. By necessity, psychiatrists tend to view all human behavior as a product of deterministic influences. This deterministic orientation cannot be reconciled with the concept of free will * * *.

The essential goal of an exculpatory test for insanity is to identify the point at which a defendant's mental condition has become so impaired that society may confidently conclude that he has lost his free will. Psychiatric concepts of mental illness are ill-suited to this task * * *. Because free will is an article of faith, rather than a concept that can be explained in medical terms, it is impossible for psychiatrists to determine whether a mental impairment has affected the defendant's capacity for voluntary choice, or caused him to commit the particular act in question. Accordingly, since models of mental illness are indeterminant in this respect, they can provide no reliable measure of moral responsibility.

* * *

Even under a truncated test of insanity limited to cognitive impairments, the inscrutable cause-and-effect relationship between mental illness and free will remains the central question. * * * Meaningful reform can be achieved only if the focus of the inquiry is shifted away from the elusive notion of free will, and its relationship to mental disease, and back to the relatively objective standards of *mens rea* where it fell traditionally.

Insanity Defense in Criminal Trials and Limitations of Psychiatric Testimony, Report of the Board of Trustees, 251 J.Am.Medical Ass. 2967, 2978 (1984).

Practical difficulties would also be met by the approach, the report argued:

By narrowing the relevancy of defendants' mental conditions, it resolves or avoids many problems of administration that complicate the current use of the [insanity] defense. * * *

Most significantly, perhaps, abandonment of the moral pretense of the insanity defense in favor of a *mens rea* concept may lead to a more realistic appreciation of the relationship between mental impairment and criminal behavior. Some observers of the criminal justice system maintain that this relationship extends far beyond its manifestations in the case of those few offenders aquitted on claims of insanity; recognition of a special defense applicable to these few detracts from the legitimate treatment needs of the many. *Mens rea* proposals seek to correct this myopic focus of the insanity defense by emphasizing considerations of mercy and appropriate treatment for all mentally disordered offenders.

Id., at 2976.

Under this approach, expert testimony of volitional impairment would be inadmissible. Further:

The *mens rea* proposal also would diminish the scope and importance of psychiatric testimony relating to cognitive impairment in the vast majority of cases. Often the defendant's intention is clear and readily may be established by examining his actual course of conduct and other objective evidence. * * * The issue of *mens rea* in such cases would be one that lies within the common experience and knowledge of the community. Accordingly, the jury should be able to resolve the issue without the assistance of expert opinion evidence. Psychiatric testimony, therefore, may be subject to exclusion or limitation under the ordinary rules of evidence relating to the use of expert witnesses. * * *

When such objective evidence of *mens rea* is lacking, as in cases involving bizarre or seemingly inexplicable criminal behavior, expert testimony introduced by the prosecution and defense alike would be relevant to elucidate intent. * * *

Since the *mens rea* elements of crime are defined in terms of the cognitive functions of the conscious mind, expert testimony regarding the defendant's mental impairment also would be relevant to the extent that it negates the minimal functional capacity required to form the requisite intent. Psychiatric testimony describing the defendant's impaired capacity to appreciate the gravity of the act, or to control his behavior, would merely explain rather than negate the existence of this conscious intent, and thus would not constitute admissible evidence. Nor would expert evidence be admissible to show that an actor's consciously entertained *mens rea* was the product of an unconscious disease process. For example, psychiatric testimony would not be permitted to establish that a defendant's conscious premeditation or deliberation was the consequence of a mental disorder or that his intent to kill was motivated by unconscious aberrational influences.

Id.

The constitutionality of the Montana scheme was upheld by the Montana Supreme Court, primarily on the ground that the federal Constitution does not guarantee accuseds a right to have their impairment taken into account before sentencing. State v. Korell, ___ Mont. ___, 690 P.2d 992 (1984). Montana defendants, however, are allowed to offer evidence of impairment at trial insofar as this evidence is relevant to rebutting the prosecution's claim that the defendant possessed whatever state of mind is required for the crime charged. See State v. Watson, ___ Mont. ___, 686 P.2d 879 (1984).

Other Approaches: "Guilty But Mentally Ill" Alternative

Responding to criticisms that the insanity defense forces juries and judges to make a rigid "all or nothing" judgment, some jurisdictions have retained a defense of insanity but, in addition, provided juries with the alternative of finding a defendant "guilty but mentally ill." The following Michigan statute is the prototype of these approaches:

768.36. Guilty but mentally ill * * *

Sec. 36.   (1) If the defendant asserts a defense of insanity * * * the defendant may be found "guilty but mentally ill" if, after trial, the trier of fact finds all of the following beyond a reasonable doubt:

(a) That the defendant is guilty of an offense.

(b) That the defendant was mentally ill at the time of the commission of that offense.

(c) That the defendant was not legally insane at the time of the commission of that offense.

A defendant who is found "guilty but mentally ill" may be sentenced to any punishment that could be imposed upon a defendant who is convicted of the same offense. If the defendant is sentenced to imprisonment, he is to be specially evaluated and any treatment necessary is to be provided, including transfer to a hospital run by the Department of Mental Health. In the event that the parole board considers the defendant for parole, the Board is directed by the statute to obtain information from the facility administering treatment to the defendant. In the event that probation is imposed as a penalty—and if treatment is recommended after an evaluation of the defendant by the Center for Forensic Psychiatry—such treatment is to be made a condition of probation.

The American Psychiatric Association was "extremely skeptical" of this approach:

"Guilty but mentally ill" offers a compromise for the jury. Persons who might otherwise have qualified for an insanity verdict may instead be siphoned into a category of "guilty but mentally ill." * * *

The "guilty but mentally ill" approach may become the easy way out. Juries may avoid grappling with the difficult moral issues inherent in adjudicating guilt or innocence, jurors instead settling conveniently on "guilty but mentally ill." * * *

There are other problems * * *. In times of financial stress, the likelihood that meaningful treatment for persons "guilty but mentally ill" will be mandated and paid for by state legislatures is * * * slight. * * *

Alternatively, whatever limited funds are available for the treatment of mentally ill inmates may be devoted to "guilty but mentally ill defendant," ignoring the treatment needs of other mentally ill but conventionally sentenced prisoners who require mental health treatment in prison.

American Psychiatric Association Statement on the Insanity Defense, 140 Am.J.Psychiatry 681, 684 (1983).

Other Reforms in Criminal Responsibility Litigation

While much attention has been focused upon the criterion for determining insanity, other—perhaps less dramatic—changes may eliminate or at least reduce the problems found by many with the current administration of the defense. If the burden of proof of sanity rests upon the prosecution, expert testimony—even if objectively incredible—may convince many juries that a "reasonable doubt" exists. Thus the federal statute (reprinted at page 791, supra), as well as many others, place the burden on the defendant; the recent federal legislation requires proof by clear and convincing evidence.

Juries may be inappropriately dominated by defense experts for any of several reasons. Such experts may testify solely in conclusory terms that a defendant was insane and, left without any basis on which to evaluate that conclusion, juries may uncritically assume that insanity has been established. In order to address this perceived problem, the federal legislation added the following provision to Rule 704 of the Federal Rules of Evidence:

(b) No expert witness testifying with respect to the mental state or condition of a defendant in a criminal case may state an opinion or inference as to whether the defendant did or did not have the mental state or condition constituting an element of the crime charged or a defense thereto. Such ultimate issues are matters for the trier of fact alone.

There are some who argue that mental health professionals have little, if any, appropriate role in the decision-making process regarding responsibility for criminal conduct. Morse, Failed Explanations and Criminal Responsibility: Experts and the Unconscious, 68 Va.L.Rev. 971 (1982), challenges the scientific validity of psychodynamic explanations of human behavior and argues that its employment leads to misguided decisions and compromises the integrity of the criminal justice system. For a contrary view, see Bonnie & Slobogin, The Role of Mental Health Professionals in the Criminal Process: The Case for Informed Speculation, 66 Va.L.Rev. 427 (1980).

Some and perhaps much of the adverse public reaction to the Hinckley verdict may be attributed to public misunderstanding of the term, "*not guilty* by reason of insanity." To the extent that the verdict suggests a lack of proof that the defendant engaged in the conduct at issue, it of course ran counter to the facts and common sense. As a result, it has been suggested that the term, "not responsible by reason of insanity" be substituted for the term, "not guilty by reason of insanity." *Myths & Realities: A Report of the National Commission on the Insanity Defense* 34–35 (1983). To the extent that a need of this sort exists, would the phrase, "guilty but insane" better serve the need?

Post-Acquittal Confinement and Treatment

Generally, the verdict in a criminal case is either "guilty' or "not guilty." In cases involving an insanity defense, however, the jury is generally told that if it finds the defendant entitled to acquittal on insanity grounds, this should be reflected by the return of a special verdict of "not guilty by reason of insanity." The return of such a verdict usually triggers a procedure for confinement of the acquitted defendant, generally in a high security mental hospital.

These procedures vary from jurisdiction to jurisdiction. The procedure enacted by Congress in 1984, as part of the Insanity Reform Act of 1984, for hospitalization of defendants acquitted on insanity grounds in federal court is reasonably typical. 18 U.S.C.A. § 4243. All such acquitted defendants are to be automatically committed to a "suitable facility." But within 40 days, a hearing is to be held on whether further hospitalization is appropriate. At this hearing, the defendant has the burden of proving that his release "would not create a substantial risk of bodily injury to another person or serious damage of property of another due to a present mental disease or defect." 18 U.S. C.A. § 4243(d). If the crime of which the defendant was acquitted involved bodily injury to another, serious damage to the property of another, or a substantial risk of such injury or damage, the defendant's burden is by clear and convincing evidence. In other cases, it is by a preponderance of the evidence. If the court finds that the defendant failed to meet his burden, the defendant is to be committed for further confinement. Subsequently, the court may hold hearings on whether the defendant should be discharged. At these hearings, discharge is to be ordered only if the defendant establishes—by the same burdens discussed above—that his release would no longer create a substantial risk of bodily injury to another person or serious damage to property of another. If the court finds that the defendant can be safely released only if he continues treatment, the court can order release conditioned upon the defendant complying with such treatment. 18 U.S.C.A. § 4243(f).

In Jones v. United States, 463 U.S. 354, 103 S.Ct. 3043, 77 L.Ed.2d 694 (1983), the Supreme Court considered and rejected several constitutional challenges to such post-acquittal commitment schemes. Jones had been committed following his insanity acquittal on a charge of attempted petit larceny, consisting of attempting to steal a jacket from a department store. Under the applicable law, a defendant was required to prove insanity by a preponderance of the evidence. Had Jones been convicted, his penal sentence could not have exceeded one year. After over a year of hospitalization, Jones sought his release. The Supreme Court found no constitutional deficiency in his commitment:

> A verdict of not guilty by reason of insanity establishes two facts: (i) the defendant committed a criminal act that constitutes a criminal offense, and (ii) he committed the act because of mental illness. Congress has determined that these findings constitute an adequate basis for hospitalizing the acquittee as a dangerous and mentally ill person. * * * We cannot say that it was unreasonable and therefore unconstitutional for Congress to make this determination. * * * We do not agree with [Jones'] suggestion that the requisite dangerousness is not established by proof that he committed a non-violent crime against property. This Court has never held that "violence," however that term might be defined, is a prerequisite for a constitutional commitment.

463 U.S. at 363–65, 103 S.Ct. at 3049–50, 77 L.Ed.2d at 705–06. Nor, the Court reasoned, does the maximum term of incarceration available as punishment upon conviction affect the maximum term of hospitalization that may be required upon an insanity acquittal:

His confinement rests on his continuing illness and dangerousness. * * * There simply is no necessary correlation between severity of the offense and length of time necessary for recovery. The length of the acquittee's hypothetical criminal sentence therefore is irrelevant to the purpose of his commitment.

463 U.S. at 369, 103 S.Ct. at 3052, 77 L.Ed.2d at 708. Justice Brennan, joined by Justices Marshall and Blackmun, argued that an insanity acquittee may, under the Constitution, be confined longer than the maximum penal sentence available for the crime only if the Government affirmatively shows that continued confinement is justified under the standards and procedures used for involuntary civil commitment of mentally ill persons not charged with a crime. 463 U.S. at 386, 103 S.Ct. at 3061, 77 L.Ed.2d at 719 (Brennan, J., dissenting). Justice Stevens agreed. 463 U.S. at 387, 103 S.Ct. at 3061–62, 77 L.Ed.2d at 720 (Stevens, J., dissenting). Under those normal civil commitment procedures, the burden—as a matter of federal constitutional law—is upon those seeking commitment to show by "clear and convincing evidence" that involuntary treatment is justified. Addington v. Texas, 441 U.S. 418, 99 S.Ct. 1804, 60 L.Ed.2d 323 (1979).

a. The Cognitively-Impaired Offender

Under *M'Naghten* and the post-Hinckley aquittal standards, a defendant's claim to acquittal on insanity grounds must be based upon a cognitive rather than a volitional impairment. But under what circumstances will a cognitive deficit entitle an offender to insanity acquittal or its equivilent? Under most formulations, including the original M'Naghten language and the recently-enacted federal statute, a distinction is drawn between an inability to "understand" or "appreciate" what is referred to as "the nature and quality" of the conduct and a similar disability concerning the "wrongfulness" of the conduct. The Virginia Supreme Court recently commented:

[T]he two elements of the *M'Naghten* Rule logically can be separated:

"The first portion of *M'Naghten* relates to an accused who is psychotic to an extreme degree. It assumes an accused who, because of mental disease, did not know the nature and quality of his act; he simply did not know what he was doing. For example, in crushing the skull of a human being with an iron bar, he believed that he was smashing a glass jar. The latter portion of *M'Naghten* relates to an accused who knew the nature and quality of his act. He knew what he was doing; he knew that he was crushing the skull of a human being with an iron bar. However, because of mental disease, he did not know what he was doing was wrong. He believed, for example, that he was carrying out a command from God." 2 C. Torcia, *Wharton's Criminal Law* § 100, at 9 (14th ed, 1979) (footnotes omitted).

Price v. Commonwealth, 228 Va. 452, 459–60, 323 S.E.2d 106, 110 (1984). Is this a satisfactory distinction and definition of the two "prongs" of the test?

The case reprinted in this subsection raises more specifically when an impaired person has, because of mental illness, lost the ability to understand the "wrongfulness" of his actions.

STATE v. CRENSHAW

Supreme Court of Washington, 1983.
98 Wn.2d 789, 659 P.2d 488.

BRACHTENBACH, JUSTICE.

Rodney Crenshaw was convicted by a jury of first degree murder. Finding that the trial court committed no reversible error, we affirm the conviction.

Petitioner Rodney Crenshaw pleaded not guilty and not guilty by reason of insanity to the charge of first degree murder of his wife, Karen Crenshaw. A jury found him guilty. Petitioner appealed his conviction * * *.

Before turning to the legal issues, the facts of the case must be recounted. While defendant and his wife were on their honeymoon in Canada, petitioner was deported as a result of his participation in a brawl. He secured a motel room in Blaine, Washington and waited for his wife to join him. When she arrived 2 days later, he immediately thought she had been unfaithful—he sensed "it wasn't the same Karen * * * she'd been with someone else."

Petitioner did not mention his suspicions to his wife, instead he took her to the motel room and beat her unconscious. He then went to a nearby store, stole a knife, and returned to stab his wife 24 times, inflicting a fatal wound. He left again, drove to a nearby farm where he had been employed and borrowed an ax. Upon returning to the motel room, he decapitated his wife with such force that the ax marks cut into the concrete floor under the carpet and splattered blood throughout the room.

Petitioner then proceeded to conceal his actions. He placed the body in a blanket, the head in a pillowcase, and put both in his wife's car. Next, he went to a service station, borrowed a bucket and sponge, and cleaned the room of blood and fingerprints. Before leaving, petitioner also spoke with the motel manager about a phone bill, then chatted with him for awhile over a beer.

When Crenshaw left the motel he drove to a remote area 25 miles away where he hid the two parts of the body in thick brush. He then fled, driving to the Hoquiam area, about 200 miles from the scene of the crime. There he picked up two hitchhikers, told them of his crime, and enlisted their aid in disposing of his wife's car in a river. The hitchhikers contacted the police and Crenshaw was apprehended shortly thereafter. He voluntarily confessed to the crime.

The defense of not guilty by reason of insanity was a major issue at trial. Crenshaw testified that he followed the Moscovite religious faith, and that it would be improper for a Moscovite not to kill his wife if she committed adultery. Crenshaw also has a history of mental problems, for which he has been hospitalized in the past. The jury, however, rejected petitioner's insanity defense, and found him guilty of murder in the first degree.

A. INSANITY DEFENSE INSTRUCTION

Insanity is an affirmative defense the defendant must establish by a preponderance of the evidence. RCW 9A.12.010. Sanity is presumed, even with a history of prior institutional commitments from which the individual was released upon sufficient recovery.

The insanity defense is not available to all who are mentally deficient or deranged; legal insanity has a different meaning and a different purpose than the concept of medical insanity. *State v. White,* 60 Wash.2d 551, 589, 374 P.2d 942 (1962). A verdict of not guilty by reason of insanity completely absolves a defendant of any criminal responsibility. Therefore, "the defense is available only to those persons who have lost contact with reality so completely that they are beyond any of the influences of the criminal law." *White,* at 590, 374 P.2d 942.

Petitioner assigned error to insanity defense instruction 10 which reads:

> In addition to the plea of not guilty, the defendant has entered a plea of insanity existing at the time of the act charged.

> Insanity existing at the time of the commission of the act charged is a defense.

> For a defendant to be found not guilty by reason of insanity you must find that, as a result of mental disease or defect, the defendant's mind was affected to such an extent that the defendant was unable to perceive the nature and quality of the acts with which the defendant is charged or was unable to tell right from wrong with reference to the particular acts with which defendant is charged.

> What is meant by the terms "right and wrong" refers to knowledge of a person at the time of committing an act that he was acting contrary to the law.

Clerk's Papers, at 27. But for the last paragraph, this instruction tracks the language of WPIC 20.01, which is the *M'Naghten* test as codified in RCW 9A.12.010. Petitioner contends, however, that the trial court erred in defining "right and wrong" as legal right and wrong rather than in the moral sense.

We find this instruction was not reversible error on three, alternative grounds: (1) The *M'Naghten* opinion amply supports the "legal" wrong definition as used in this case, (2) under these facts, "moral" wrong and "legal" wrong are synonymous, therefore the "legal" wrong definition did not alter the meaning of the test, and (3) because Crenshaw failed to prove other elements of the insanity defense, any error in the definition of wrong was harmless.

I

The definition of the term "wrong" in the *M'Naghten* test has been considered and disputed by many legal scholars. *See, e.g.,* A. Goldstein, *The Insanity Defense* 51–53 (1967); H. Fingarette, *The Meaning of Criminal Insanity* 153–157 (1972); S. Glueck, *Mental Disorder and the Criminal Law* 184–85 (1925); H. Weihofen, *Mental Disorder as a Criminal Defense* 77 (1954); Cohen, *Criminal Responsibility and the Knowledge of Right and Wrong,* 14 U.Miami L.Rev. 30, 49–50 (1959); Morris, *Criminal Insanity,* 43 Wash.L.Rev. 583 (1968). Courts from other jurisdictions are divided on the issue. In Washington, we have not addressed this issue previously.

The confusion arises from apparent inconsistencies in the original *M'Naghten* case. In response to the House of Lords' first question, the justices replied that if an accused knew he was acting contrary to law but acted under a partial insane delusion that he was redressing or revenging some supposed grievance or injury, or producing some supposed public benefit, "he is nevertheless punishable * * * if he knew at the time of committing such crime that he was acting *contrary to law; * * * the law of the land.*" (Italics ours.) *M'Naghten's Case,* 8 Eng.Rep. 718, 722 (1843). In this answer, the justices appear to approve the legal standard of wrong when there is evidence that the accused knew he was acting contrary to the law.

This has been characterized as inconsistent with the justices' response to the second and third questions, regarding how a jury should be instructed on the insanity defense:

> If the question were to be put [to a jury] as to the knowledge of the accused solely and exclusively with reference to the law of the land, it might tend to confound the jury, by inducing them to believe that an actual knowledge of the law of the land was essential in order to lead to a conviction; whereas the law is administered upon the principle that every one must be taken conclusively to know it, without proof that he does know it. If the accused was conscious that the act was one which he ought not to do, and if that act was at the same time contrary to the law of the land, he is punishable; and the usual course therefore has been to leave the question to the jury, whether the party accused had a sufficient degree of reason to know that he was doing an act that was wrong: and this course we think is correct, accompanied with such observations and explanations as the circumstances of each particular case may require.

M'Naghten, at 723. This response appears to require both that the accused be "conscious that the act was one which he ought not to do" and that the act be "contrary to the law."

A close examination of these answers, however, shows they are reconcilable in the context of this case. First, the similarities between the hypothetical in the first question and Crenshaw's situation should afford that answer great weight. If, arguendo, Crenshaw was delusional, his delusion was only partial, for it related only to his perceptions of his wife's infidelity. His behavior towards others, *i.e.,* the motel manager and the woman who loaned him the ax, at the time of the killing was normal. Crenshaw also "knew he was acting contrary to law" (*M'Naghten,* at 720), as evidenced by his sophisticated attempts to hide his crime and by the expert, psychiatric testimony. Furthermore, he acted with a view "of redressing or revenging [the] supposed grievance" (*M'Naghten,* at 720) of his wife's infidelity. Thus, the Crenshaw situation fits perfectly into the first hypothetical, and the trial court understandably relied on this passage in approving the challenged instruction.

Second, the answers to the second and third questions certainly do not forbid the additional comment found in instruction 10. The justices expressly provided that the instruction could be "accompanied with such observations and explanations as the circumstances of each particular case may require." *M'Naghten,* at 723. In addition, the justices' hesitance to state the question exclusively with reference to the law stemmed from a fear that "it might tend to confound the jury, by inducing them to believe that an actual knowledge of the law of the land was essential in order to lead to a conviction". *M'Naghten,* at 723. Therefore, in cases such as this where actual knowledge of the law is not an issue, an instruction in terms of legal wrong would not be improper.

In short, *M'Naghten* supports the propriety of the trial court's instruction in several ways: (1) the justices' answer to the first question was more analogous to Crenshaw's fact situation, and that answer referred only to legal wrong, (2) the *M'Naghten* justices provided that in some cases an additional statement by the court would be acceptable, and (3) in this case there was no danger that the jury would be induced to believe that actual knowledge of the law was essential, since Crenshaw demonstrated that he knew the illegality of his acts. Thus, the facts here permit resolution of the inconsistencies in *M'Naghten* in favor of the "legal" wrong standard.

Such an interpretation is consistent with Washington's strict application of *M'Naghten.* This court's view has been that "when *M'Naghten* is used, all who might possibly be deterred from the commission of criminal acts are included within the sanctions of the criminal law." *State v. White,* 60 Wash.2d 551, 592, 374 P.2d 942 (1962).

> [O]nly those persons "who have lost contact with reality so completely that they are beyond any of the influences of the criminal law," may have the benefit of the insanity defense in a criminal case.

State v. McDonald, 89 Wash.2d 256, 272, 571 P.2d 930 (1977), quoting *White,* at 590, 374 P.2d 942. Given this perspective, the trial court could assume that one who knew the illegality of his act was not necessarily "beyond any of the influences of the criminal law," thus finding support for the statement in instruction 10.

II

Alternatively, the statement in instruction 10 may be approved because, in this case, legal wrong is synonymous with moral wrong. This conclusion is premised on two grounds.

First, in discussing the term "moral" wrong, it is important to note that it is society's morals, and not the individual's morals, that are the standard for judging moral wrong under *M'Naghten*. If wrong meant moral wrong judged by the individual's own conscience, this would seriously undermine the criminal law, for it would allow one who violated the law to be excused from criminal responsibility solely because, in his own conscience, his act was not morally wrong. H. Fingarette, *The Meaning of Criminal Insanity* 154 (1972); *see State v. Corley*, 108 Ariz. 240, 495 P.2d 470 (1972); *State v. Malumphy*, 105 Ariz. 200, 461 P.2d 677 (1969) (McFarland, J., concurring specially); *State v. Skaggs*, 120 Ariz. 467, 586 P.2d 1279 (1978). This principle was emphasized by Justice Cardozo:

> The anarchist is not at liberty to break the law because he reasons that all government is wrong. The devotee of a religious cult that enjoins polygamy or human sacrifice as a duty is not thereby relieved from responsibility before the law * * *

(Citations omitted.) *People v. Schmidt*, 216 N.Y. 324, 340, 110 N.E. 945, 950 (1915).

* * *

There is evidence on the record that Crenshaw knew his actions were wrong according to society's standards, as well as legally wrong. Dr. Belden testified:

> I think Mr. Crenshaw is quite aware on one level that he is in conflict with the law *and with people*. However, this is not something that he personally invests his emotions in.

We conclude that Crenshaw knew his acts were morally wrong from society's viewpoint and also knew his acts were illegal. His personal belief that it was his duty to kill his wife for her alleged infidelity cannot serve to exculpate him from legal responsibility for his acts.

A narrow exception to the societal standard of moral wrong has been drawn for instances wherein a party performs a criminal act, knowing it is morally and legally wrong, but believing, because of a mental defect, that the act is ordained by God: such would be the situation with a mother who kills her infant child to whom she is devotedly attached, believing that God has spoken to her and decreed the act. *See People v. Schmidt, supra* at 339, 110 N.E. 945. Although the woman knows that the law and society condemn the act, it would be unrealistic to hold her responsible for the crime, since her free will has been subsumed by her belief in the deific decree. *People v. Schmidt, supra.*

This exception is not available to Crenshaw, however. Crenshaw argued only that he followed the Moscovite faith and that Moscovites believe it is their duty to kill an unfaithful wife. This is not the same as acting under a deific command. Instead, it is akin to "[t]he devotee of a religious cult that enjoins * * * human sacrifice as a duty [and] is *not* thereby relieved from responsibility before the law". (Italics ours.) *Schmidt,* at 340, 110 N.E. 945. Crenshaw's personal "Moscovite" beliefs are not equivalent to a deific decree and do not relieve him from responsibility for his acts.

Once moral wrong is equated with society's morals, the next step, equating moral and legal wrong, follows logically. The law is, for the most part, an expression of collective morality.

Most cases involving the insanity defense involve serious crimes for which society's moral judgment is identical with the legal standard.

Therefore, a number of scholars have concluded that, as a practical matter, the way in which a court interprets the word wrong will have little effect on the eventual outcome of a case. * * *

Society's morals and legal wrong are interchangeable concepts in the context of this case. Petitioner's crime, killing his wife by stabbing her 24 times then hacking off her head, is clearly contrary to society's morals as well as the law. Therefore by defining wrong in terms of legal wrong, the trial court did not alter the meaning of the *M'Naghten* test.

III

We also find that, under any definition of wrong, Crenshaw did not qualify for the insanity defense under *M'Naghten;* therefore, any alleged error in that definition must be viewed as harmless. * * * Here, any error is harmless for two alternate reasons. First, Crenshaw failed to prove an essential element of the defense because he did not prove his alleged delusions stemmed from a mental defect; second, he did not prove by a preponderance of the evidence that he was legally insane at the time of the crime.

In addition to an incapacity to know right from wrong, *M'Naghten* requires that such incapacity stem from a mental disease or defect. RCW 9A.12.010. Assuming, arguendo, that Crenshaw did not know right from wrong, he failed to prove that a mental defect was the cause of this inability.

Petitioner's insanity argument is premised on the following facts: (1) he is a Moscovite and Moscovites believe it is their duty to assassinate an unfaithful spouse; (2) he "knew", without asking, that his wife had been unfaithful when he met her in Blaine and this was equivalent to an insane delusion; and (3) at other times in his life, he had been diagnosed as a paranoid personality and had been committed to mental institutions. A conscientious application of the *M'Naghten* rule demonstrates, however, that these factors do not afford petitioner the sanctuary of the insanity defense.

To begin, petitioner's Moscovite beliefs are irrelevant to the insanity defense, because they are not insane delusions. Some notion of morality, unrelated to a mental illness, which disagrees with the law and mores of our society is not an insane delusion.

Nor was petitioner's belief that his wife was unfaithful an insane delusion. Dr. Trowbridge, a psychiatrist, explained:

A man suspects his wife of being unfaithful. Certainly such suspicions are not necessarily delusional, even if they're ill based. Just because he suspected his wife of being unfaithful doesn't mean that he was crazy.

*　　*　　*　　*　　*　　*　　*　　*　　*

Certainly when a man kills his wife he doesn't do it in a rational way. No one ever does that rationally. But that is not to suggest that every time a man kills his wife he was [sic] insane.

*　*　*

In addition, the preponderance of the evidence weighs against finding Crenshaw legally insane. All of the psychological experts, save one, testified that defendant was not insane at the time of the murder. The only doctor who concluded defendant (petitioner) was legally insane, Dr. Hunter, was a psychologist who had not examined petitioner for a year and a half.

Given the various qualifications of the experts, the time they spent with the petitioner, and the proximity in time of their examinations to the murder, the testimony does not establish by a preponderance of the evidence that petitioner was legally insane at the time of the murder.

Furthermore, in addition to the expert testimony, there was lay testimony that petitioner appeared rational at the time of the killing. After cleaning the motel room, Crenshaw resolved a phone bill dispute with the manager, then shared a beer with him without arousing any suspicion in the manager's mind. * * * Thus, at the same time that he was embroiled in the act of murdering his wife, he was rational, coherent, and sane in his dealings with others.

Finally, evidence of petitioner's calculated execution of the crime and his sophisticated attempts to avert discovery support a finding of sanity. *See State v. McDonald, supra.* Crenshaw performed the murder methodically, leaving the motel room twice to acquire the knife and ax necessary to perform the deed. Then, after the killing he scrubbed the motel room to clean up the blood and remove his fingerprints. Next, he drove 25 miles to hide the body in thick brush in a remote area. Finally, he drove several hundred miles and ditched the car in a river.

Such attempts to hide evidence of a crime manifest an awareness that the act was legally wrong. Moreover, petitioner testified that he did these things because he "didn't want to get caught". * * *

Nevertheless, we do not believe that, in the future, such a comment [as was given to the jury in this case concerning the meaning of "wrong"] should be necessary. As the Legislature has chosen to codify the *M'Naghten* test in statutory form, it would be preferable to have this test presented to the jury without any elaboration. This would permit both parties to argue their theories of the case. It would also prevent the possibility that the jury would presume that ignorance of the law is a defense in cases wherein it may not be as clear as it was here that the person knew the illegality of his act. *See State v. Corley,* 108 Ariz. 240, 495 P.2d 470 (1972). Thus, we hold prospectively, that as a general rule no definition of wrong should accompany an insanity defense instruction.

* * *

Finding no reversible error was committed by the trial court, we affirm the judgment.

WILLIAM H. WILLIAMS, CHIEF JUSTICE (concurring).

I concur in parts 2, 3, 4, and 5, and the result of the majority opinion.

DORE, JUSTICE (dissenting).

* * *

I believe that although at times moral and legal are "synonymous," sometimes they are distinguishable. This is a factual issue to be determined by the trier of the fact, and not by the courts as a matter of law. The submission of instruction 10 constituted prejudicial error. I would reverse for a new trial based on the instruction's erroneous statement of the law on insanity.

The majority has correctly set forth the facts, but I would like to supplement them by adding some pertinent information. Dr. Nathan Kronenberg, the psychiatrist who testified Crenshaw was competent to stand trial, added that in examining Crenshaw he noted tangentiality, loose associations, delusions of grandeur, religiousity (including a belief in his possession of special powers), auditory hallucinations, lack of insight, and extreme emotional liability on the part of the defendant. He further testified that the defendant's ability to assist in his defense was distorted by his paranoia. Report of Proceedings, at 40–43. Dr. Kronenberg further related that the defendant's perception of right and wrong and his capacity to appreciate the consequences of his behavior were very likely distorted at the time of the offense.

Dr. John Mahaffy, another psychiatrist who examined Crenshaw, concluded the defendant was suffering from a paranoid state, and was in remission from former psychotic episodes. Although he testified Crenshaw was competent to stand trial, he qualified his testimony with a statement that the defendant's legal sanity at the time of the offense would be suspect if the defendant at that time was suffering from a psychotic episode. The defendant has a history of mental problems. He was hospitalized in his home state of Texas 15 times between 1970 and 1978, where he was diagnosed as a paranoid schizophrenic.

* * *

This court has previously indicated that the *M'Naghten* test involved the moral definition of right and wrong. Prior to codification of the *M'Naghten* rule into our statutory scheme, we held that a jury was

correctly instructed when it was told that the insanity defense would lie
if defendant "was unable to perceive the *moral qualities*" of his act.
(Italics mine.) *State v. Davis,* 6 Wash.2d 696, 708, 108 P.2d 641 (1940).
The sole question is whether we want to hold a defendant answerable to
our criminal law, notwithstanding the barbaric or cruel nature of the
defendant's acts. A mind which cannot distinguish moral right from
wrong cannot be held accountable for acts performed as a result of that
illness and while suffering under that influence.

The majority surprisingly seems to concede that at times there is a
difference between legal right and wrong and moral right and wrong.
* * * Crenshaw knew if he killed his wife he was violating the law,
but he believed he had a duty to do it under the teaching of his
Moscovite "religious" beliefs. To determine his insanity under
M'Naghten, as codified in RCW 9A.12.010, a determination must be
made as to what was morally right and wrong. The jury had this duty
and responsibility, but to do so it had to be properly instructed.
Instruction 10 wrongly limited the jury to the *legal* right and wrong
test and prevented it from determining whether Crenshaw knew the
difference between *moral* right and wrong at the time he killed his
wife. This constituted prejudicial error.

Notes and Questions

1. In State v. Cameron, 100 Wn.2d 520, 674 P.2d 650 (1983), the court
described the case as follows:

[O]n the morning of June 9, 1980, petitioner stabbed Marie Cameron [,
his stepmother,] in excess of 70 times, leaving the knife sticking in her
heart. The body was left in the bathtub with no apparent attempt to
conceal it. Later that day a police officer saw petitioner in downtown
Shelton wearing only a pair of women's stretch pants, a woman's
housecoat, a shirt and no shoes. He was stopped and questioned.
* * * Having no reason to detain petitioner, the officer released him
to continue hitchhiking. [The next day, petitioner was arrested for the
murder.]

* * *

In [an] oral confession petitioner stated generally that he was
living in or about the home of his father and stepmother. He left
home dressed as he was because his stepmother had become violent.
"[S]he's into different types of sorcery. She's just strictly a very evil
person * * * and she became violent with me, with a knife in her
hand * * *." He indicated that when he walked into the bathroom
he had not expected her. When he saw her, she had the knife which
he was able to take from her easily by bending her wrist back. Then,
as he stated, "I took the knife and really stabbed her."

In describing the stabbing, petitioner related, "I just kept stabbing
her and stabbing her because she wasn't feeling * * *. * * * I feel
that deep inside she was asking somebody to put her out of her misery
* * * she was very symbolic with the 'Scarlet Whore Beast' she was

very much into sorcery very, uh, anti-God, not really anti-God but takes the God's truth and twists it into her sorcery."

Concerning his feelings about the incident petitioner said, "I felt confused * * * I felt no different from the beginning than the end there was no difference. * * * legally I know, that it is against the law, but as far as right and wrong in the eye of God, I would say I felt no particular wrong."

* * *

At trial, [four doctors testified]. All agreed that at the time of the killing * * * petitioner suffered from the mental disease of paranoid schizophrenia. While expressing their views in different ways, they agreed petitioner understood that, as a mechanical thing, he was killing his stepmother and knew it was against the laws of man. They stressed, however, that at the time, he was preoccupied with the delusional belief that his stepmother was an agent of satan who was persecuting him, as were others like Yasser Arafat and the Ayatollah Khomeini. He believed he was being directed by God to kill satan's angel and that by so doing, he was obeying God's higher directive or law. At this time he believed himself to be a messiah and in fact compared himself with Jesus Christ.

100 Wn.2d at 521–25, 674 P.2d at 652–53. The trial court gave the jury the same instruction as was given in *Crenshaw*. On these facts, the Washington Supreme Court held that it was error for the trial court to give the last paragraph of the charge, which precluded the jury from considering Cameron's argument that he believed he was directed by God to kill the victim. This was because *Crenshaw* had created a "deific decree" exception to the general rule that "wrong" means legal wrong. Justice Dore, concurring, suggested that the case was indistinguishable from *Crenshaw*:

Crenshaw performed his dastardly murder believing he had a duty to do it under the teaching of his Muscovite "religious" beliefs. Cameron committed a very similar, vicious murder on the basis that God commanded him to kill his stepmother and that he was obligated to kill the evil spirit [in her]. I frankly don't see much or any distinction, however, in carrying out or executing a murder under the direction of God or Crenshaw's Muscovite religious beliefs, or under the beliefs of a prophet, Buddha, etc.

100 Wn.2d at 534, 674 P.2d at 658 (Dore, J., concurring).

2. As one ground for its holding, the *Crenshaw* court states that Crenshaw failed to establish that his beliefs were "insane delusions." Does this mean that Crenshaw failed to show that he had a mental illness sufficient to serve as a basis for an insanity defense? Or does it mean that he failed to show that his beliefs were sufficiently related to any mental illness that he had? If Crenshaw was suffering from a serious mental impairment, could his beliefs concerning his wife's fidelity and his appropriate response to her lack of faithfulness exist independent of his impairment?

What is a mental illness (or defect) as is apparently required for an insanity defense? Must the defendant's condition come within any particular diagnoses used by mental health professionals? In State v. Coombs, 18 Ohio St.3d 123, 124, 480 N.E.2d 414, 416 (1985), the court commented that the trial court would have erred had it used a standard requiring that a defendant prove a disorder amounting to a psychosis or a neurosis. In its post-Hinckley statement on the insanity defense, however, the American Psychiatric Association made the following recommendation:

> Definitions of mental disease or defect sometimes, but not always, accompany insanity defense standards. * * * Allowing insanity acquittals in cases involving persons who manifest primarily "personality disorders" such as antisocial personality disorder (sociopathy) does not accord with modern psychiatric knowledge or psychiatric beliefs concerning the extent to which such persons do have control over their behavior. Persons with antisocial personality disorders should, at least for heuristic reasons, be held accountable for their behavior. The American Psychiatric Association, therefore, suggests that any revision of the insanity defense standards should indicate that mental disorders potentially leading to exculpation must be *serious*. Such disorders should usually be of the severity (if not always of the quality) of conditions that psychiatrists diagnose as psychoses.

American Psychiatric Association Statement on the Insanity Defense, 140 Am.J. Psychiatry 681, 685 (1983).

Does § 4.01(2) of the Model Penal Code standard (reprinted at page 789, supra) accomplish this? In adopting it, the California Supreme Court recently observed:

> [A]lthough [subdivision 2] was designed to deny an insanity defense to psychopaths and sociopaths, it does not have that precise effect. What it does is prevent consideration of a mental illness if that illness is manifested only by a series of criminal or antisocial acts. If that illness manifests itself in some other way as well, then it can be considered as a "mental disease" under the ALI test, and instances of criminal or antisocial conduct can be ascribed to that disease or cited as evidence of its severity. * * * Whether this requirement denies the insanity defense to a person with an "antisocial personality" will depend upon the individual case, and on the ability of the psychiatrist to base a diagnosis upon facts additional to a list of defendant's criminal or antisocial acts.

People v. Fields, 35 Cal.3d 329, 369–70, 197 Cal.Rptr. 803, 829–30, 673 P.2d 680, 706 (1983). Among the reasons for adopting the subdivision, the court cited:

> If a pattern of antisocial behavior is sufficient basis for an insanity defense, then a substantial proportion of serious criminal offenders would be able to assert this defense. It may be that few would succeed in persuading a jury. But the assertion of the insanity defense by recidivists with no apparent sign of mental illness except their penchant for criminal behavior would burden the legal system, bring the insanity defense into disrepute, and imperil the ability of persons with definite mental illness to assert that defense. * * * To classify persons with "antisocial personality" as insane would put in the mental institutions persons for whom there is currently no suitable

treatment, and who would be a constant danger to the staff and other inmates. Mental hospitals are not designed for this kind of person; prisons are.

35 Cal.3d at 371–72, 197 Cal.Rptr. at 830–31, 673 P.2d at 707–08.

Does the new federal statute, reprinted at page 791, limit the insanity defense more than does subdivision 2 of the Model Penal Code formulation? The House Committee report explained:

> The provision that the mental disease or defect must be "severe" was added * * * as a Committee amendment. * * * The concept of severity was added to emphasize that nonpsychotic behavior disorders or neuroses such as an "inadequate personality," "immature personality," or a pattern of "antisocial tendencies" do not constitute the defense.

H.R.Rep. No. 98–1030, 98th Cong., 2nd Sess. 229 (1984), reprinted in [1984] U.S.Code Cong. & Adm.News 3182.

3. Suppose, in *Crenshaw,* that the defendant's delusional belief that his wife was having an affair had been shown to have been the product of a sufficient mental illness to serve as the basis for an insanity defense. Would his particular delusional beliefs have been sufficient to require acquittal? In Chancellor v. State, 165 Ga.App. 365, 301 S.E.2d 294 (1983), Chancellor was tried for the murder of a woman she believed, because of her mental illness, to be having an affair with her husband. The trial court refused to instruct the jury on "delusional compulsion." Finding no error, the appellate court first concluded that under Georgia law it is no defense to murder that the deceased was an illicit lover of the defendant's spouse. Turning to the insanity issue, it reasoned:

> Before such a defense is available it must appear that the defendant was acting under a delusion which, if true, would justify her act. Since the delusion allegedly suffered by appellant (the adulterous affair between her husband and the victim) does not justify homicide * * *, a charge on delusional compulsion was not authorized.

165 Ga.App. at 367, 301 S.E.2d at 298. Is this an appropriate manner of determining whether a delusional belief justifies holding an offender nonresponsible?

4. The terms used in purely cognitive insanity standards may be interpreted quite broadly. Consider Patterson v. State, 708 P.2d 712 (Alaska App.1985). Under Alaska law, insanity exists only if, because of mental illness, the defendant "was unable * * * to appreciate the nature and quality of [the] conduct." Alaska Stat. 12.47.–030. Evidence showed that defendant Kimberly Patterson was a 23 year old woman with a three year old daughter, both living with her mother. For several months, after being rejected by the child's father, Patterson began to behave strangely, laughing inappropriately, staying up all night, appearing to hear voices, and talking to herself. She believed that three men were in her room and were going to hurt and perhaps rape both her and her daughter. Upon going to a mental health clinic, she was put on antipsychotic medication. Because of the side effects, however, she stopped taking it. She decided that she needed money to enable her to move out of her mother's house and

thus escape the three men she believed were tormenting her. Efforts to borrow from banks failed. She then went to an airport and, using a gun she had recently purchased, attempted to rob the first man she saw in the parking lot. She was subdued by her victim and tried for robbery. Defense experts testified that she was paranoid schizophrenic and her actions were efforts to escape from the men she delusionally believed were trying to harm her. The trial judge instructed the jury:

> A person is "unable to appreciate the nature and quality of her conduct" for purposes of the insanity defense if, because of mental disease or defect, she did not understand that she was performing the physical acts which are part of the crime of which she is charged. * * * [I]f the defendant did in fact understand the basic nature and quality of her conduct—that she was threatening another person in an attempt to obtain his money—then the defendant would not be entitled to a verdict of "not guilty by reason of insanity" * * *.

After reviewing the case law and the legislative history of the statutory provision, the court concluded that the trial court's instruction gave the jury too narrow a meaning of the critical statutory language:

> [W]e believe that the language * * * is to be interpreted broadly rather than restrictively, referring not only to the defendant's basic awareness of the physical acts he or she is performing, but also to his or her appreciation of the nature and quality of that conduct and its consequences.
>
> In reaching this conclusion, we find it particularly noteworthy that the legislature substituted the word "conduct" for the word "act." * * * As defined in the Revised Criminal Code, "conduct" means an act or omission "and its accompanying mental state." AS 11.81.900(b) (5). Applying the statutory definition of "conduct," it becomes apparent that, in order to be sane, it was necessary for Patterson to be aware of more than just the nature and quality of her "acts."
>
> [W]e understand this to mean that she had to have the capacity, at least, to a limited extent to foresee the likely consequences of her acts, and to evaluate the effect those consequences would have on herself and others. We stress that it is Patterson's capacity to foresee and evaluate rather than her exercise of that capacity in a given case that is the issue to be determined by the jury. * * *

708 P.2d at 717. Is this appropriate definition of the statutory terms? Should a jury, so instructed, find Patterson not guilty by reason of insanity? Should those terms be defined so as to increase the likelihood that persons like Patterson are acquitted?

b. The Volitionally-Impaired Offender

As the earlier material made clear, many American jurisdictions have limited their insanity defense criteria so as to preclude the defense from being based upon impairments that cause only so-called volitional impairments. Reconsider the arguments for and against this action in light of the following case. Specifically, consider whether the claim made by the defendant in this case is the sort of claim that the law should entertain.

UNITED STATES v. POLLARD

United States District Court, Eastern District of Michigan, 1959.
171 F.Supp. 474, set aside, 282 F.2d 450 (6th Cir.1960), mandate clarified,
285 F.2d 81 (6th Cir.1960).

LEVIN, DISTRICT JUDGE. The defendant, Marmion Pollard, having waived indictment, the Government instituted this prosecution on a three-count information charging him, under Section 2113(d), Title 18 U.S.C.A., with the attempted robbery of the Chene-Medbury Branch of the Bank of the Commonwealth and the 24th-Michigan Branch of the Detroit Bank & Trust Company on May 21, 1958, and the attempted robbery on June 3, 1958, of the Woodrow Wilson-Davison Branch of the Bank of the Commonwealth. These banks, members of the Federal Reserve System and insured by the Federal Deposit Insurance Corporation, are located in Detroit, Michigan.

On arraignment, the accused pleaded guilty before another judge of this Court. Subsequently, upon advice of counsel, he moved to set aside the guilty plea on the ground that he was insane at the time he committed the acts upon which the prosecution was based. The Court, with the acquiescence of the Government, permitted the defendant to withdraw his guilty plea, and a plea of not guilty was entered. The case was then assigned to me for trial.

Prior to trial, I was advised that a psychiatric report of a psychiatrist retained by the defendant indicated that the defendant was, at the time of the offenses, suffering from a diseased mind which produced an irresistible impulse to commit the criminal acts. Subsequently, a report was submitted to the Government by each of two psychiatrists who had examined the defendant at its request. These reports, which were made available to me, agreed with the conclusion of the defendant's psychiatrist. It then appeared to me that it would be in the interest of justice to secure a psychiatric evaluation of defendant's state of mind based upon more extensive study. I was particularly desirous of having such a study made inasmuch as the psychiatric reports submitted to me were based on interviews that did not exceed a maximum of two hours with each of the three psychiatrists. I, thereupon, on October 10, 1958, entered an order that the defendant be sent to the United States Medical Center at Springfield, Missouri. After a study of thirty days, the Medical Center submitted a report which was introduced in evidence. The gist of the report may be set out as follows:

During the period under inquiry, "a dissociative state may have existed and that his [defendant's] actions may not have been consciously motivated.

"It is, therefore, our opinion that during the period in question, Pollard, while intellectually capable of knowing right from wrong, may have been governed by unconscious drives which made it impossible for him to adhere to the right.

" * * * We readily acknowledge our inability either to marshal sufficient objective facts or formulate a completely satisfactory theory on which to base a solid opinion as to subject's responsibility during the period in question." [1]

The defendant elected to be tried by the Court without a jury. During the trial, the following facts appeared:

The defendant is an intelligent, twenty-nine year old man. In 1949, he married and, during the next four years, three sons and a daughter were born of this marriage. He was apparently a well-adjusted, happy, family man. In 1952, he became a member of the Police Department of the City of Detroit and continued to work as a policeman until he was apprehended for the acts for which he is now being prosecuted. In April, 1956, his wife and infant daughter were brutally killed in an unprovoked attack by a drunken neighbor.

On May 21, 1958, one day before he remarried, at about 11:00 A.M., defendant entered the 24th-Michigan Branch of the Detroit Bank & Trust Company. He paused for a few moments to look over the bank and then proceeded to an enclosure in which a bank official was at work. He told the official, whom he believed to be the manager, that he wanted to open a savings account. He then walked through a swinging gate into the enclosure, sat down at the desk, pulled out a gun and pointed it at the official. He ordered the official to call a teller. When the teller arrived, the defendant handed a brown paper grocery bag to him and told him to fill it with money. While it was being filled, defendant kept the bank official covered. The teller filled the bag with money as ordered and turned it over to the defendant. Thereupon, defendant ordered the bank official to accompany him to the exit. As both the defendant and bank official approached the exit, the official suddenly wrapped his arms around the defendant, who then dropped the bag and fled from the bank and escaped.

About 4:00 P.M., on the same day, he entered the Chene-Medbury Branch of the Bank of the Commonwealth and walked to a railing behind which a bank employee was sitting. He pointed his gun at the man and told him to sit quietly. The employee, however, did not obey this order but instead raised an alarm, whereupon the defendant ran from the bank and again escaped.

After the defendant was apprehended by the Detroit Police under circumstances which I shall later relate, he admitted to agents of the

---

1. Not only is this report, in the light most favorable to the defendant, inconclusive but in part is based upon facts which were not substantiated during the trial. The personal and social history section of the report states that after his wife's death "it was noted by his supervisors that he [defendant] became less efficient, less inter-ested, more withdrawn and a noticeably less effective policeman". However, the police department records introduced in evidence reveal that the defendant's police work covering the period of inquiry, if anything, was more effective than his service prior to the death of his wife.

Federal Bureau of Investigation that after his abortive attempts to rob the two banks, he decided to rob a third bank and actually proceeded on the same day to an unnamed bank he had selected but decided not to make the attempt when he discovered that the bank was "too wide open"—had too much window area so that the possibility of apprehension was enhanced.

On June 3, at about 3:00 P.M., the defendant entered the Woodrow Wilson-Davison Branch of the Bank of the Commonwealth and went directly to an enclosure behind which a male and female employee were sitting at desks facing each other. Defendant held his gun under a jacket which he carried over his right arm. He ordered the woman employee to come out from behind the railing. In doing so, she grasped the edge of her desk. Defendant, in the belief that she may have pushed an alarm button, decided to leave but ordered the woman to accompany him out of the bank. When they reached the street, he told her to walk ahead of him, but not to attract attention. Defendant noticed a police car approaching the bank and waited until it passed him, then ran across an empty lot to his car and again escaped.

On June 11, 1958, he attempted to hold up a grocery market. He was thwarted in the attempt when the proprietor screamed and, becoming frightened, the defendant fled. In so doing, he abandoned his automobile in back of the market where he had parked it during the holdup attempt. Routinely, this car was placed under surveillance and later when the defendant, dressed in his Detroit Police Officer's uniform, attempted to get in it, he was arrested by detectives of the Detroit Police Force.

After his apprehension, the defendant confessed to eleven other robberies, or attempted robberies.

The three psychiatrists who submitted the written reports, all qualified and respected members of their profession, testified that in their opinion the defendant, at the time he committed the criminal acts, knew the difference between right and wrong and knew that the acts he committed were wrong but was suffering from a "traumatic neurosis" or "dissociative reaction", characterized by moods of depression and severe feelings of guilt, induced by the traumatic effect of the death of his wife and child and his belief that he was responsible for their deaths because by his absence from home he left them exposed to the actions of the crazed, drunken neighbor. They further stated that he had an unconscious desire to be punished by society to expiate these guilt feelings and that the governing power of his mind was so destroyed or impaired that he was unable to resist the commission of the criminal acts. In their opinion, however, the defendant was not then, nor is he now, psychotic or committable to a mental institution.

Three of defendant's fellow police officers, called as defense witnesses, testified that during the period in which the defendant committed the criminal acts he had a tendency to be late for work; that at times he was despondent; and that he occasionally seemed to be lost in thought and did not promptly respond to questions directed to him. One of the officers testified that on one occasion, he repeatedly beat the steering wheel of the police car in which they were riding, while at the same time reiterating the name of his murdered wife. However, none of them found his conduct or moods to be of such consequence that they believed it necessary to report the defendant to a superior officer.

Defendant's present wife, who impressed me as an intelligent person, testified that on two occasions defendant suddenly, and for no reason apparent to her, lapsed into crying spells and that he talked to her once or twice about committing suicide. She also testified that during one such period of depression he pointed a gun at himself; that she became frightened and called the police; that the police came, relieved him of his gun, and took him to the precinct police station; and that after his release he appeared jovial and acted as if nothing had happened. Defendant's brother-in-law stated that the defendant had always been a very happy person but that he became noticeably despondent after the death of his wife and child and expressed a desire to commit suicide because he now no longer had a reason for living.

A police lieutenant of the Detroit Police Department testified that the defendant's police work, during the period with which we are now concerned, as evidenced by his efficiency rating and his written duty reports, was, if anything, more effective than his service prior to the death of his wife.

Counsel for defendant contends that since all the medical testimony was to the effect that the defendant was suffering from an irresistible impulse at the time of the commission of the offenses, this Court must accept this uncontroverted expert testimony and find him not guilty by reason of insanity.

* * *

I have great respect for the profession of psychiatry. Vast areas of information have been made available through its efforts. I have found much comfort in having the assistance of psychiatrists in the disposition of many cases on sentence. Yet, there are compelling reasons for not blindly following the opinions of experts on controlling issues of fact. Expert testimony performs a valuable function in explaining complex and specialized data to the untutored lay mind. When the experts have made available their knowledge to aid the jury or the Court in reaching a conclusion, their function is completed. The opinions and judgments or inferences of experts, even when unanimous and uncontroverted, are not necessarily conclusive on the trier of the facts and may be disregarded when, in the light of the facts adduced, such judgments, opinions or inferences do not appear valid. The jury, in determining the probative effect to be given to expert testimony, is not to disregard its own experience and knowledge and its collective conscience. It follows that this is also true of the judge sitting without a jury.

The psychiatrists, as I hereinbefore related, testified that the defendant suffered from severe feelings of depression and guilt; and that in their opinion he had an irresistible impulse to commit criminal acts, an unconscious desire to be apprehended and punished; and that he geared his behavior to the accomplishment of this end. However, his entire pattern of conduct during the period of his criminal activities militates against this conclusion. His conscious desire not to be apprehended and punished was demonstrably greater than his unconscious desire to the contrary. After his apprehension, despite searching interrogation for over five hours by Detroit Police Officers and by agents of the Federal Bureau of Investigation, he denied any participation in criminal conduct of any kind. It was only after he was positively identified by bank personnel that he finally admitted that he did attempt to perpetrate the bank robberies. I asked one of the psychiatrists to explain this apparent inconsistency. In answer to my question, he stated that although the defendant had an unconscious desire to be apprehended and punished, when the possibility of apprehension became direct and immediate, the more dominating desire for self-preservation asserted itself. This explanation may have merit if applied to individual acts. However, the validity of a theory that attempts to explain the behavior of a person must be determined in light of that person's entire behavioral pattern and not with reference to isolated acts which are extracted from that pattern. The defendant's pattern of behavior of May 21, 1958, discloses that the desire for self-preservation was not fleeting and momentary but continuing, consistent and dominant. What, then, becomes of the theory of irresistible impulse? Looking to the events of that day, I am asked to believe, first, that the defendant, acting pursuant to an irresistible impulse, selected a bank site to rob, entered the bank to accomplish that end, purposely failed in the attempt and when the end he sought, apprehension, was in view, escaped because of the dominance, at the moment of ultimate accomplishment, of the stronger drive for self-preservation. I must then believe that when the defendant knew he was apparently free from detection, his compulsive state reasserted itself and that he again went through the steps of planning, abortive attempt and escape. And if I acquiesce in this theory, what other psychiatric theory explains his subsequent conduct—his plan to rob a third unnamed bank and the rejection of that plan because of his subjective belief that the possibility of apprehension would be too great? If the theory remains the same, then it appears that in the latter case, the fear of apprehension and punishment tipped "the scales enough to make resistible an impulse otherwise irresistible." Guttmacher and Weihofen, Psychiatry and the Law, 413. It is a logical inference that, in reality, the other robbery attempts were made as the result of impulses that the defendant did not choose voluntarily to resist because, to him, the possibility of success outweighed the likelihood of detection which is in essence a motivation for all criminal conduct. The impulse being resistible, the defendant is accountable for his criminal conduct.

Psychiatrists admit that the line between irresistible impulse and acts which are the result of impulses not resisted is not easy to trace. Guttmacher and Weihofen, Psychiatry and the Law. To the extent that the line may be traced, the distinguishing motivation of the action, whether the act is performed to satisfy an intrinsic need or is the result of extrinsic provocation, is a determining factor. Admittedly, motivations may be mixed. However, all the facts have clearly established that defendant's criminal activity was planned to satisfy an extrinsic need by a reasoned but anti-social method. The defendant had financial problems of varying degrees of intensity throughout his life. He had financial difficulties during his first marriage. He was now embarking upon a second marriage. He was about to undertake the responsibility of supporting not only a wife and himself, but also four children, three of them the product of his first marriage. In statements given to agents of the Federal Bureau of Investigation admitting his criminal activity, he stated: "Inasmuch as I was about to marry my second wife, I decided that I would not lead the same type of financially insecure life that I led with my first wife. I needed about $5,000 in order to buy a house. My only purpose in deciding to rob a bank was to obtain $5,000 and if I obtained the money, I did not intend to continue robbing." Defendant's entire pattern of conduct was consistent with this expressed motivation.

Life does not always proceed on an even keel. Periods of depression, feelings of guilt and inadequacy are experienced by many of us. Defendant was a devoted husband and loving father. His feelings of despondency and depression induced by the brutal killing of his wife and infant daughter were not unnatural. How else the defendant should have reacted to his tragic loss I am not told. His conduct throughout this crucial period did not cause any concern among his colleagues. All stated unequivocally that in their opinion he was sane. Significant also is the fact that his present wife married him on May 22, 1958, after a year of courtship. It is a permissible inference that defendant's conduct relative to his mental condition, as related by her, did not suggest to her that the defendant was insane.

I am satisfied beyond a reasonable doubt that the defendant committed the acts for which he is now charged and that when he committed them he was legally sane.

I, therefore, adjudge the defendant guilty of the three counts of the information.

Notes and Questions

1. On appeal, the trial judge's decision was reversed. In view of the "unanimous testimony of the government's medical experts * * * and appellant's expert witnesses" and the testimony of the lay witnesses, the presumption of sanity was overcome and the government failed to sustain its burden of proving sanity under the federal rule. Pollard v. United

States, 282 F.2d 450 (6th Cir.1960), mandate clarified, 285 F.2d 81 (6th Cir. 1960).

2. Several federal courts have held that "compulsive gambling disorder" cannot serve as the basis for an insanity defense to a charge of a property acquisition crime. In United States v. Gould, 741 F.2d 45 (4th Cir. 1984), for example, the court held that evidence of such a disorder was properly excluded at Gould's trial for unlawful entry of a bank with intent to rob it. It did not reach whether the disorder was or might be a mental disease for purposes of the insanity defense. Rather it held that the proposition that pathological gambling may deprive some persons of their capacity to conform to legal requirements barring entry of banks with intent to rob had not yet received "substantial acceptance" among mental health professionals. 741 F.2d at 51–52. See also, United States v. Torniero, 735 F.2d 725 (2d Cir.1984), in which the defendant, charged with interstate transportation of stolen jewelry, offered an insanity defense based on the theory that his "compulsive gambling disorder" rendered him unable to resist committing the impulse to steal and transport the jewelry. The appellate court held that the trial judge acted properly in barring the defendant from presenting this "defense" to the jury, since the defense evidence failed to establish a sufficiently firm and accepted relationship between the disorder and offenses such as those charged against the defendant. If judges are this critical of offered expert testimony and exclude testimony where it appears to be of such dubious value, does this significantly reduce the objections to a volitional insanity defense?

3. Perhaps there is no realistic possibility of obtaining "scientific" testimony concerning the extent to which particular offenders were or were not prevented by their impairments from exercising volitional control with regard to antisocial actions in which they were inclined to engage. Recall that the American Medical Association's report on the insanity defense asserted that "[b]y necessity," psychiatrists must view human behavior as determined by "causes" other than free will or volitional choice; see page 795, supra. The matter was recently reviewed by Howard and Conway, Can There be an Empirical Science of Volitional Action?, 41 Am.Psychologist 1241 (1986). The authors concluded that the consensus in psychological research "has been that concepts such as self-determination or volitional behavior are either illusory or unscientific." But they suggested that research can be designed to probe the extent to which choice affects behavior and despite difficulties such research should be undertaken. Why "should [psychologists] * * * take the difficult and risky steps of conducting research on human volition?" Among the reasons identified by Howard and Conway was the need to respond to the disenchantment towards psychology harbored by those in other disciplines—including law as well as philosophy and theology—that often entertain volitional models of human behavior. Id., at 1249.

2. DIMINISHED CAPACITY

The doctrine frequently referred to as "diminished capacity" can be stated with deceptive simplicity—it simply states that in deciding whether a defendant acted with the state of mind required by the offense under consideration, the trier of fact may consider, among other things, any psychological impairment of the defendant and the extent to which that impairment affected his "capacity" to entertain the state of mind at issue.

As the discussion at the beginning of this subsection indicated, such a doctrine is sometimes proposed as a complete alternative to the insanity defense. This, for example, is the essence of the American Medical Association's proposal (see page 790, supra) and the Montana statutory scheme (see page 795, supra). More commonly, however, it is considered for adoption in addition to a defense of insanity. Arguably, the desirability of the doctrine differs, or at least presents different considerations, depending upon whether it is offered as an alternative to, or as a companion of, the "complete" defense of insanity.

JOHNSON v. STATE

Court of Appeals of Maryland, 1982.
292 Md. 405, 439 A.3d 542.

DIGGES, JUDGE.

Lawrence Johnson was convicted, after removal of this criminal cause from Baltimore County, by a jury in the Circuit Court for Calvert County of first degree murder (both premeditated and in the commission of a felony), first degree rape, kidnapping, and use of a handgun during the commission of a felony or a crime of violence. The same jury subsequently sentenced Johnson to death for the murder. * * *

The sordid chronicle of this crime spree was related by the appellant, Lawrence Johnson, at trial. It began on the early morning of February 23, 1980, when he was suddenly awakened by a friend, Amos Batts, while perched on the couch at the home of his cousin, Dwayne Mayers. At the urging of Batts, Johnson followed his friend outside to a car being operated by the cousin. It soon became apparent to Johnson that Mayers and Batts had stolen the vehicle during the night and had abducted its owner, Betty Toulson, in the process. Although Johnson had earlier declined to participate when the other two decided to obtain some money through crime, the defendant this time joined them in the car with the victim. After a brief discussion, Mayers started the vehicle and drove around while the three men smoked "parsley flakes sprayed with some kind of embalming fluid." The victim remained silent throughout this journey "with her head down." Later, after driving to a remote area of Baltimore County, Mayers stopped the car and asked whether his companions "wanted to have sex" with their prisoner. Mayers and the appellant eventually raped the woman on the back seat of her car. The trio then drove the victim to another location nearby where Mayers stripped Ms. Toulson of her coat and pocketbook. After discussing the problem presented by the victim's knowledge of their identities, Mayers returned to the automobile, removed a pistol from under the seat, and presented it to appellant with instructions to kill the woman. Johnson led her into the woods and complied with the directive. Ms. Toulson's snow-covered body was recovered five days later; she had received fatal shots in the head and chest.

Following his trial, convictions, and sentencing, Johnson, because he received the death penalty, appealed directly to this Court * * *.

Johnson * * * asserts that the trial court erred in not admitting certain psychological evidence at trial where he sought to use this information, not to establish his legal insanity, but rather, to demonstrate that he lacked a sufficient mental capacity to form the requisite intent to commit murder in the first degree. As an aid to an understanding of this issue we set out its factual predicate.

At trial, the defense called Dr. Ernest Kamm, a clinical psychologist at the Clifton T. Perkins Hospital Center. Dr. Kamm had conducted a psychological examination of Johnson as part of the court ordered evaluation performed by the Perkins staff and had prepared a report of his findings. Counsel for Johnson proffered that he wished to use Dr. Kamm's entire report and testimony "to go to the mitigation of First Degree Murder and any specific [intent] crimes," rather than to raise the issue of defendant's sanity. The court allowed the psychologist to read to the jury only parts of his report relating to intelligence tests he had administered to Johnson and his conclusion, based on those tests, that the defendant "functions at the borderline intellectual level (I.Q. 72) * * *"[6] Appellant urges that the entire report is relevant to his

---

6. We reproduce here in full Dr. Kamm's psychological report with emphasis indicating the portions read to the jury:

TESTS ADMINISTERED:

WAIS

Bender-Gestalt

Holtsman Inkblot Technique

Color Pyramid Test

TEST BEHAVIOR:

The patient is a 19-year old youth of medium height and build who presented a neat and clean appearance. He was extremely sullen and hostile, and his cooperation for interview and test was poor. In view of this test results have to be considered tentative.

TEST RESULTS:

On the WAIS he earned a Verbal I.Q. of 78, a Performance I.Q. of 68, and a Full Scale I.Q. of 72 which places him within the borderline range of intelligence. His potential, as gauged by his abstract reasoning, is at least within the low average range. Intellectual efficiency is decreased by a combination of educational deprivation and negativism. There are some signs which point in the direction of bizarre thinking and a tenuous hold on reality. E.G. on Card 22 of

the Holtzman he saw "the devil," and on Card 27 he saw "God over water." But these should be interpreted with caution, as they may also be attempts to embarrass and express contempt for the examiner by giving nonsensical answers.

The personality picture is that of an extremely deprived individual who does not expect any affection and emotional support from either parental figure. He perceives the mother figure as domineering, but distant and devoid of warmth and understanding and the father figure as hostile and threatening. Yet he has conjured up the image of an idealized, all wise and all loving father surrogate with whom he will compare any male elder. Since such a person is bound to fall short of his ideal he is apt to equate this person with the real father figure whom he sees in negative terms and reject him. As a result he not only has trouble with authority figures, but perceives the world about him as a cold inhospitable place where he does not have a chance.

CONCLUSION:

The patient functions at the borderline intellectual level (I.Q. 72), but his potential is at least within the low average range. He can be described as a severely deprived individual with a hostile and defense of "diminished capacity"—that is, he did not have sufficient mental capacity to form the requisite specific intent to commit some of the crimes with which he is charged. Consequently, the argument goes, it was error to keep that information from the jury when it determines the guilt issue. In order to decide whether this ruling on the evidence was erroneous, however, we must first examine whether the criminal defense known as "diminished capacity," or as it is sometimes called, "diminished responsibility," is recognized in this State. Only if such a doctrine exists in our jurisprudence is defendant arguably entitled to produce evidence in support of it. Because we here determine, however, that this State does not recognize diminished capacity as a legal doctrine operating to negate specific criminal intent, it was not error to exclude evidence in support of it.

Before expounding on why the principle of diminished capacity has been rejected in Maryland as a criminal defense relevant to the issue of guilt, and why we adhere to that position now, it may prove helpful to explore briefly our understanding of the doctrine and its background. The basic outline of diminished capacity has been summarized as follows:

> [S]ince certain crimes, by definition, require the existence of a specific intent, any evidence relevant to the existence of that intent, including evidence of an abnormal mental condition not constituting legal insanity, is competent for the purpose of [negating] that intent. * * * [T]he actual purpose of such evidence is to establish, by negating the requisite intent for a higher degree of offense, that in fact a lesser degree of the offense was committed. [Annot. 22 A.L.R.3d 1228, 1238 (1969).]

Thus, only after a defendant has been determined to be criminally accountable for his actions (legally sane) has the doctrine been applied to admit expert testimony as to a defendant's mental condition in order to determine the degree of criminality for which the accused will be held responsible.

The states are less than unanimous in their resolution of the question whether application of diminished capacity to criminal trials on the issue of guilt represents a legally sound resolution of the pressing problem of how the criminal law should treat evidence of mental abnormality that does not establish the actor's legal insanity. *Compare, e.g., United States v. Brawner*, 471 F.2d 969 (D.C.Cir.1972) (en banc) (expert testimony admissible to demonstrate diminished capacity) *with Bethea v. United States*, 365 A.2d 64, 83–92 (D.C.App.1976), *cert. denied*, 433 U.S. 911, 97 S.Ct. 2979, 53 L.Ed.2d 1095 (1977) (rejection of diminished capacity doctrine). It is generally recognized, however, that adoption of the concept of diminished capacity as a separate defense involves "a fundamental change in the common law theory of [criminal]

negative orientation and an [sic.] *severe authority problem.* Contact with reality is difficult to evaluate on account of his

poor productivity resulting from extreme negativism.

* * *

responsibility," *Fisher v. United States,* 328 U.S. 463, 476, 66 S.Ct. 1318, 1325, 90 L.Ed. 1382 (1946). This is true because the introduction of expert psychiatric testimony concerning the defendant's mental aberrations when the basic sanity of the accused is not at issue conflicts with the governing principle of the criminal law that all legally sane individuals are equally capable of forming and possessing the same types and degrees of intent. Consequently, an individual determined to be "sane" within the traditional constructs of the criminal law is held accountable for his action, regardless of his particular disabilities, weaknesses, poverty, religious beliefs, social deprivation or educational background. The most that is proper to do with such information is to weigh it during sentencing.

* * *

A review of our prior decisions in this area as they interact with legislative enactments on the subject demonstrates that this State has consistently adhered to the just articulated view that the criminal law as an instrument of social control cannot allow a legally sane defendant's lesser disabilities to be part of the guilt determining calculus. For the purpose of guilt determination, an offender is either wholly sane or wholly insane. In 1888, this Court, following the lead of the celebrated English *McNaughten* case, first enunciated the test for criminal responsibility. An accused was held to be sane and responsible for his act if "at the time of the commission of the alleged offense, he had capacity and reason sufficient to enable him to distinguish between right and wrong, and understand the nature and consequences of his act, as applied to himself. * * *" *Spencer v. State,* 69 Md. 28, 37, 13 A. 809, 813 (1888). Insanity, as defined by Chief Judge Alvey for this Court in *Spencer* was an all or nothing proposition:

> [T]he law is not a medical nor a metaphysical science. Its search is after those practical rules which may be administered without inhumanity for the security of civil society by protecting it from crime, and therefore it requires not into the peculiar constitution of mind of the accused, or what weakness or even disorders he was afflicted with, but solely whether he was capable of having, and did have, a criminal intent. If he had such intent the law punishes him, but if not, it holds him dispunishable. [*Id.* at 41, 13 A. at 814.]

Because the accused in *Spencer* did not offer to establish his insanity as thus defined, the Court declined to accept proffered testimony of the defendant to the effect that he was "nervous and restless * * * haunted with the idea, that so long as the deceased lived, [the defendant] would have no rest or peace of mind, and that he could exercise no power of will or self-control over this idea. * * *" 69 Md. at 35, 13 A. at 812. The *Spencer* court, after reviewing the facts of the homicide, rejected the further use of the proffered testimony "to show such condition of mind as to have rendered the prisoner incapable of forming the wilful and premeditated purpose of killing to constitute * * * murder in the first degree * * *." 69 Md. at 41, 13 A. at 814, and concluded that "[t]he prisoner being criminally responsible, and having thus premeditated the killing, there is no principle that would justify the introduction of such evidence as that proffered for the purpose of reducing the degree of his crime." 69 Md. at 43, 13 A. at 815. * * * In [Armstead v. State, 227 Md. 73, 175 A.2d 24 (1961)], we declined not only to expand the common law concept of insanity so as to encompass diminished capacity but also to recognize the doctrine as an independent defense. This position was reaffirmed shortly thereafter in *Allen v. State,* 230 Md. 533, 188 A.2d 159 (1962).

Upon this common law doctrinal base, the General Assembly passed in 1967 a massive remodeling of the limits of criminal culpability as expressed in the definition of insanity. In that year, Chapter 709 of the Laws of Maryland, Md.Code (1957, 1964 Repl. Vol., 1967 Cum. Supp.), Art. 59, § 9, was enacted replacing the court established *Spencer-McNaughten* test for insanity with a broader rule patterned after that expressed in the American Law Institute Model Penal Code (section 4.01) admitting consideration of a "mental disease or defect." Md.Code 1957 (1964 Repl. Vol., 1967 Cum.Supp.), Art. 59, § 9(a). * * * By thus defining and redefining the limits of criminal culpability as expressed in the definition of legal insanity, the General Assembly has exercised its unique prerogative to balance the interests of the community and the individual accused in this regard. We here reaffirm our position that "the concepts of both diminished capacity and insanity involve a moral choice by the community to withhold a finding of responsibility and its consequence of punishment," *Bethea v. United States, supra,* 365 A.2d at 90, n. 55, and on this basis are indistinguishable. [10] Accordingly, because the legislature, reflecting community

---

10. Given the primary assumption in the criminal law concerning a defendant's criminal culpability regardless of his lesser abilities, whatever they may be, and "recognizing the unique position of the concept of insanity in the framework of criminal responsibility," *Bethea v. United States,* 365 A.2d 64, 86 (D.C.App.1976), we cannot agree with those courts which easily declare that evidence of a legally sane defendant's mental impairment is always probative on the factual question of whether a particular accused entertained the requisite mental state. *See, e.g., State v. DiPaolo,* 34 N.J. 279, 168 A.2d 401 (1961), *cert. denied,* 368 U.S. 880, 82 S.Ct. 130, 7 L.Ed.2d 80 (1961). There is a fundamental difference between evidence demonstrating that the defendant did not *as a fact* possess the requisite mental state, here premeditation and deliberation as opposed to evidence establishing that the defendant was *generally less capable* than a normal person of forming a requisite *mens rea.* Certainly, we recognize the basic proposition that the state must prove every element of a crime beyond a reasonable doubt including specific intent if necessary, and that an

accused is entitled to rebut the state's case. The doctrine of diminished capacity, in our view, however, does not operate to demonstrate that, as a fact, a defendant did not entertain a requisite mental state; rather, the principle is used to establish a legally sane but mentally impaired defendant's diminished culpability for a particular criminal act.

Moreover, facile comparison of the doctrine of diminished capacity with the rule allowing certain evidence of a defendant's intoxication on the issue of *mens rea* does not withstand scrutiny. The degree of intoxication necessary to negate *mens rea* is great and is comparable with that degree of mental incapacity that will render a defendant legally insane. As noted in *State v. Gover,* 267 Md. 602, 608, 298 A.2d 378, 382 (1973):

If the trier of fact determines that at the time the alleged criminal act occurred, the accused had become so inebriated that he possessed no reason or understanding, then he has reached that stage of intoxication that renders him incapable of forming the requisite *mens rea* morals, has, by its definition of criminal insanity already determined which states of mental disorder ought to relieve one from criminal responsibility, this court is without authority to impose our views in this regard even if they differed.

In light of criticism of the *McNaughten* insanity test, diminished capacity has been viewed as a solution to some of the inadequacies of the traditional approach to criminal responsibility, and many decisions allowing evidence of a sane defendant's mental abnormalities arise in jurisdictions which define criminal insanity in terms of the *McNaughten* principle. In fact, some assert that the judicial development of the diminished capacity defense assuaged dissatisfaction with the *McNaughten* test and actually inhibited reform of it. Arenella, *The Diminished Capacity and Diminished Responsibility Defenses: Two Children of a Doomed Marriage,* 77 Col.L.Rev. 827, 854–55 (1977). With the broadening of the concept of criminal insanity beyond the strictures of the *Spencer-McNaughten* test accomplished by section 25(a), however, the arguable need for a doctrine such as diminished capacity to ameliorate the law governing criminal responsibility prescribed by the *McNaughten* rule has been eliminated to the extent the legislature has deemed it advisable to do so.

* * *

What has just been iterated does not mean, however, that evidence of a defendant's mental abnormality which does not establish his insanity has been totally precluded from the consideration of those operating the machinery of our criminal justice system. Such evidence typically constitutes part of the range of data upon which the trial judge, following establishment of guilt, focuses attention when sentencing the individual accused. Such use of this information squares with the practice prevailing in our jurisprudence of permitting the judge wide latitude in making individualized sentencing decisions after consideration of information both in aggravation and mitigation of penalty.

* * *

[The death sentence was held invalid on other grounds, and the case was remanded to the trial court for a new sentencing proceeding.]

ELDRIDGE, JUDGE, dissenting:

* * *

[N]either side raised any issue concerning the general admissibility of [evidence concerning mental condition offered to prove the absence of intent]. Instead, the appellant contended that the trial judge erred in not allowing all of the psychologist's report to be presented to the jury. The State, without disputing the admissibility of the expert testimony, argued that the trial court correctly excluded a portion of the report

which is a necessary element of all specific intent crimes.

Lesser degrees of incapacity, whether produced by intoxication or organic mental impairment will not relieve a defendant of full responsibility for his acts.

because it "was simply not germane to the issue of diminished capacity."

The majority opinion, instead of deciding the issue which was presented, briefed and argued by the parties, now holds that the entire expert testimony and the entire report were inadmissible. On this basis, the majority finds no reversible error in the exclusion of a portion of the psychologist's report. * * * I do question whether, under all of the circumstances, it is appropriate to resolve the issue against the defendant Johnson without first giving him an opportunity to brief and argue the matter.

Turning to the merits of the majority's position, in my view the trial court correctly held that evidence of Johnson's mental condition was admissible for the purpose of showing the absence of certain elements of first degree murder and of the other specific intent crimes with which Johnson was charged. The majority's contrary holding represents an abrupt departure from prior Maryland law as well as from the prevailing view throughout the country. Moreover, it constitutes an unwarranted limitation upon a criminal defendant's constitutional right to present relevant evidence in his own defense.

The majority arrives at its holding by confusing two entirely distinct matters: (1) the existence of criminal conduct when a particular mental state is an element of the crime charged; (2) responsibility for criminal conduct. The confusion is enhanced by the majority's use of the terms "capacity" and "capability" interchangeably with "responsibility" and "culpability."

The defendant Johnson, *inter alia,* was charged with murder in the first degree under Maryland Code (1957, 1976 Repl.Vol.), Art. 27, § 407. In order to constitute first degree murder under § 407, the homicide must be a "wilful, deliberate and premeditated killing." Consequently, the State had the burden of proving the existence of these three elements. The mental condition of the defendant is obviously relevant to willfulness, deliberation and premeditation. * * * Evidence designed to show that a particular defendant was incapable of having the requisite mental state is nothing more or less than evidence designed to show that he did not commit the crime with which he was charged.

On the other hand, under Maryland law criminal *responsibility* due to mental condition is a wholly different matter. Unlike the common law concept of "not guilty by reason of insanity," the Maryland statutory scheme concerning criminal responsibility contemplates an initial determination that the defendant did commit the crime charged before there is an inquiry into his responsibility therefore. * * *

The majority purports to recognize that the State must prove every element of a crime, including mental elements such as specific intent, premeditation and deliberation. Nevertheless the majority asserts, without any reasoning, that "[t]here is a fundamental difference between evidence demonstrating that the defendant did not *as a fact* possess the requisite mental state, here premeditation and deliberation, as opposed to evidence establishing that the defendant was *generally less capable* than a normal person of forming a requisite *mens rea.*" However, I fail to perceive this "fundamental difference" referred to by the majority. A particular individual's abnormal mental capability is a *fact.* It is part of his mental state or condition. * * *

The majority also asserts that "the governing principle of the criminal law [is] that all legally sane individuals are equally capable of forming and possessing the same types and degrees of intent." * * *

The error and confusion in the view adopted today by the majority, was very well described by Chief Justice Weintraub for the Supreme Court of New Jersey in *State v. DiPaolo,* 34 N.J. 279, 294–296, 168 A.2d 401, *cert. denied,* 368 U.S. 880, 82 S.Ct. 130, 7 L.Ed.2d 80 (1961):

* * * * * * * * *

> "The difficulty seems to be that the topic is sometimes explored under the label of 'partial responsibility' or 'diminished responsibility' or perhaps confused with some other concept intended to be so described. Both of those characterizations are misleading since they tend to connote an 'affirmative' defense designed to defeat a case the State has otherwise established and thus to suggest the intrusion of an amendment to the established basis for criminal accountability. Actually the question is simply whether there shall be excluded evidence which merely denies the existence of facts which the State must prove to establish that the murder was in the first degree.

* * * * * * * * *

> "We here are concerned with the category described as a 'willful, deliberate and premeditated killing.' * * * As settled by judicial construction, the first element is premeditation, which consists of the conception of the design or plan to kill. Next comes deliberation. The statutory word 'deliberate' does not here mean 'willful' or 'intentional' as the word is frequently used in daily parlance. Rather it imports 'deliberation' and requires a reconsideration of the design to kill, a weighing of the pros and cons with respect to it. Finally, the word 'willful' signifies an intentional execution of the plan to kill which had been conceived and deliberated upon * * *

> "The three mental operations we have just described are matters of *fact.* The judiciary cannot bar evidence which rationally bears upon the factual inquiry the Legislature has ordered. The capacity of an individual to premeditate, to deliberate, or to will to execute a homicidal design, or any deficiency in that capacity, may bear upon the question whether he *in fact* did so act. Hence evidence of any defect, deficiency, trait, condition, or illness which rationally bears upon the question whether those mental operations did *in fact* occur must be accepted.

* * * * * * * * *

> "It has long been settled that voluntary intoxication or the voluntary use of drugs may be shown for the jury's consideration with respect to whether a defendant did in fact premeditate, deliberate and willfully kill.

*   *   *   *   *   *   *   *   *

"Surely if voluntary intoxication or use of drugs is evidential with respect to the degree of murder, mental illness or deficiency should be accepted as a legally competent 'cause.'"

As Justice Powell stated for the Supreme Court in *Chambers v. Mississippi,* 410 U.S. 284, 302, 93 S.Ct. 1038, 1049, 35 L.Ed.2d 297 (1973), "[f]ew rights are more fundamental than that of an accused to present witnesses in his own defense." By holding that one accused of first degree murder is no longer entitled to present relevant testimony of his mental condition for the purpose of negating the elements of first degree murder, the majority today imposes an unjustified limitation upon the right of a criminal defendant to present evidence in his own behalf.

*   *   *

COLE and DAVIDSON, JJ., have authorized me to state that they concur with the views expressed herein.

Notes and Questions

1. If the Maryland courts had been willing to recognize the "diminished capacity" doctrine, would the evidence offered by Johnson at trial have been sufficient to raise an issue under it? Did the offered evidence really tend to show that he lacked the state of mind required by first degree murder under Maryland law? One criticism of the diminished capacity doctrine is that in its administration triers of fact will often be told to consider evidence that, as a matter of logic, simply does not tend to disprove the state of mind at issue. They may, then, be tempted to adopt a *sub rosa* standard that does not relate to the *mens rea* requirements of the crimes involved but instead bears directly on whether the defendants' responsibility was impaired in the manner placed at issue by the insanity defense but not to such a degree as is necessary for complete exculpation under the insanity defense.

Such an approach might better be called one of "diminished responsibility." It relates to criminal responsibility as that is defined in the law governing insanity, but provides for some legal effect to be given to proof that a defendant's responsibility is diminished but not lacking. American courts, however, sometimes use the phrase "diminished responsibility" to refer to the doctrine at issue in *Johnson.* E.g., State v. McVey, 376 N.W.2d 585, 586 (Iowa 1985).

Would a doctrine of diminished responsibility be desirable? The English Homicide Act, 5 & 6 Eliz. II, ch. 11, § 2 established such a doctrine for purposes of homicide cases. Under this statute, a defendant shown guilty of murder is to be convicted only of manslaughter if the defense shows that at the time of the killing the defendant "was suffering from such abnormality of mind * * * as substantially impaired his mental responsibility for acts and omissions in * * * the killing."

If such an approach is desirable, might it be better provided for by a statute along the following lines:

§ ——. Diminished responsibility

1. An offender shall be regarded as being of diminished responsibility if the trier of fact finds that at the time of the offense he was suffering from a mental disease or defect and that this substantially reduced his ability to appreciate the nature and quality or wrongfulness of his acts [or his ability to conform to the requirements of law], although not to the extent necessary to establish the defense of insanity.

2. Upon a finding of diminished responsibility, [the offense shall be treated for sentencing purposes as one degree lower than would otherwise be the case] [any sentence of imprisonment imposed may not exceed, in minimum and maximum terms, two-thirds of the minimum and maximum that are generally authorized for the offense].

2. Where the doctrine of diminished capacity applies, does it limit defendants to proof that they were unable to form the state of mind required by the charged offense? If so, perhaps it bars efforts to prove that because of mental impairment they failed to form that intent. In State v. Simmons, —— W.Va. ——, 309 S.E.2d 89 (1983), the court found that the instructions requested by the defense did not correctly state the defense:

The [requested] instructions stated that if the defendant was suffering from a mental illness at the time she allegedly committed the crime, then the jury could consider the mental illness on the question of whether she acted "with premeditation, deliberation, and malice." * * * It must be shown by psychiatric testimony that some type of mental illness rendered the defendant incapable of forming the specific intent elements. The instruction should require the jury to determine whether, in light of the mental condition, they believed that the defendant lacked the capacity to form the specific intent.

309 S.E.2d at 99. Is this distinction logical? Does it serve any meaningful purpose?

3. In those jurisdictions in which it has been adopted, the doctrine of diminished capacity is often limited in application. Pennsylvania, for example, appears to restrict it to first degree murder. Commonwealth v. Garcia, 505 Pa. 304, 311, 479 A.2d 473, 477 (1984). More commonly, it is limited to "specific intent" crimes, but the difficulty of adequately defining "specific intent" sometimes makes the substance of this limitation somewhat unclear. State v. Beach, 102 N.M. 642, 699 P.2d 115 (1985) (second degree murder was not "specific intent" offense requiring diminished capacity instructions). Thus courts may use "specific intent," in this context, to refer to the "deliberate and premeditated" formula associated with first degree murder in some jurisdictions. Others may use the term to refer to any mental state requiring "intentionally." These, of course, are different meanings than was suggested in the Editors' Introduction to Section A of Chapter VI, where "specific intent" was defined as mental states having as their object matters which are not elements of the crime charged. Some courts do, however, appear to so define the term. In Dean v. State, 668 P.2d 639 (Wyo.1983), the court held that as arson was defined at the time of the offense (willfully and maliciously burning a dwelling house), it was not a specific intent offense and the trial court did not err in

failing to instruct the jury to consider mental illness in determining intent. But the court noted that the offense had since been redefined as maliciously starting a fire with intent to destroy or damage an occupied structure and suggested that as redefined it was a specific intent offense requiring such an instruction. 668 P.2d at 642 n. 4. Does this make sense?

Limitations imposed upon the defense in some jurisdictions seem designed to limit its application to those situations in which there is a lesser included offense of the crime charged that lacks the specific intent required by the crime charged. This would mean that the doctrine could only be invoked in those situations where its application would result in conviction of the defendant of a lesser offense. Such a limitation, it has been suggested, is necessary to prevent the doctrine from becoming a "complete" defense and thus a substitute for insanity. See State v. Thompson, 695 S.W.2d 154, 159 (Mo.App.1985). If this is the objective, does limiting the defense to "specific intent" crimes reasonably tend to accomplish it?

Such limitations have been found constitutionally unacceptable. Hendershott v. People, 653 P.2d 385 (Colo.1982), cert. denied, 459 U.S. 1225, 103 S.Ct. 1232, 75 L.Ed.2d 466 (1983). At his trial for third degree assault, Hendershott offered psychiatric and psychological expert opinion evidence that because of adult minimal brain dysfunction he lacked the culpability requirement for the offense. The trial court excluded this on the basis of Colo.Rev.Stat. § 18–1–803, which restricts the admissibility of evidence of impaired mental condition offered to show lack of culpability to prosecutions for specific intent crimes. Under § 18–1–501(5), specific intent crimes are those in which the culpability requirement is " 'intentionally' or 'with intent.' " That offense with which Hendershott was charged requires proof that he "intentionally, knowingly, or recklessly cause[d] bodily injury to another." Colo.Rev.Stat. § 18–3–204. The Colorado Supreme Court found error:

> Once we accept the basic principles that an accused is presumed innocent and that he cannot be adjudicated guilty unless the prosecution proves beyond a reasonable doubt the existence of the mental state required for the crime charged, it defies both logic and fundamental fairness to prohibit a defendant from presenting reliable and relevant evidence that, due to a mental impairment beyond his conscious control, he lacked the capacity to entertain the very culpability which is indispensible to his criminal responsibility in the first instance. We therefore disapprove the trial court's ruling as violative of due process of law and hold that reliable and relevant mental impairment evidence is admissible, upon proper foundation, to negate the culpability elements of the criminal charge.

653 P.2d at 393–94.

The Model Penal Code proposed a quite broad and apparently unqualified acceptance of the diminished capacity approach:

Section 4.02. Evidence of Mental Disease or Defect Admissible When Relevant to Element of the Offense * * *

(1) Evidence that the defendant suffered from a mental disease or defect is admissible whenever it is relevant to prove that the defendant did not have a state of mind that is an element of the crime.

* * *

The comments acknowledged that as of the time of the drafting of this provision—1955—"there is a sharp division of authority throughout the country." But they continued:

Some jurisdictions decline for reasons of policy to accord evidence of mental disease or defect an admissibility extensive with its relevancy to prove or disprove a material state of mind. We see no justification for such a limitation of this kind. If states of mind such as deliberation or premeditation are accorded legal significance, psychiatric evidence should be admissible when relevant to prove or disprove their existence to the same extent as any other evidence.

Model Penal Code, Comments to § 4.02 193 (Tent.Draft No. 4, 1955).

4. How much flexibility is there, as a matter of policy or federal constitutional law, in allocating the burdens of persuasion and production of proof in the application of the diminished capacity doctrine? A New Jersey statute provides:

Evidence that the defendant suffered from a mental disease or defect is admissible whenever it is relevant to prove that the defendant did not have a state of mind which is an element of the offense. In the absence of such evidence, it may be presumed that the defendant had no mental disease or defect which would negate a state of mind which is an element of the offense. Mental disease or defect is an affirmative defense which must be proved by a preponderance of the evidence.

N.J.Stat.Ann. 2C:4-2. In State v. Breakiron, 210 N.J.Super. 442, 510 A.2d 80 (1986), the court construed this as follows:

If N.J.S.A. 2C:4-2 were to mean that a defendant has the burden of persuading the trier of fact that he had a mental disease or defect that prevented him from having the mental state which is an element of the offense charged, the statute may be unconstitutional because it would relieve the State of its burden to prove one of the elements of the offense beyond a reasonable doubt. The statute, however, does not have that meaning. The State need not overcome a "diminished capacity" defense until evidence of that defense is admitted. The effect of the statute is to render such evidence admissible only after the trial judge has been persuaded by a preponderance of the evidence that the defense is sound.

The Legislature enacted the [last sentence of the statute] because it was concerned that unlike evidence of the usual affirmative defenses, evidence of "diminished capacity" frequently takes the form of a psychiatric opinion that is not generally shared by experts and is not designed to meet the statutory test of criminal responsibility * * * [The statute] requires the trial judge to determine whether the evidence of "diminished capacity" is of sufficient substance to be admissible. The judge, not the jury, must be persuaded by a preponderance of the evidence that the defendant suffered from a "mental disease or defect which would negate a state of mind which is an element of the offense." If the judge is so persuaded, the evidence is admissible and the State must then overcome it at trial beyond a reasonable doubt * * *.

210 N.J.Super. at 448–49, 510 A.2d at 83–84.

5. The California version of diminished capacity has had an interesting history, composed in large part of efforts by the California Supreme Court to develop the statutory definition of the homicide offenses (reprinted at page 379, supra). The court's objective appears to have been to combine a somewhat revised version of the California law of homicide with the diminished capacity doctrine to create a system of diminished responsibility, as that was distinguished from diminished capacity in note 1, supra. The California doctrine is sometimes referred to as the *Wells-Gorshen* Rule because of the two early cases in which it was recognized, People v. Wells, 33 Cal.2d 330, 202 P.2d 53, cert. den. 338 U.S. 836, 70 S.Ct. 43, 94 L.Ed. 510 (1949) and People v. Gorshen, 51 Cal.2d 716, 336 P.2d 492 (1959). In *Wells*, the court held that it was error—but not reversible error—to exclude psychiatric testimony offered at Wells' trial to prove the absence of the malice aforethought required by the crime charged, serious assault by a prison inmate with malice aforethought. In *Gorshen*, the defendant had been charged with murder. The trial court permitted psychiatric testimony to the effect that despite Gorshen's acknowledged intent to shoot the victim he lacked malice aforethought as required for murder because of sexual hallucinations and other symptoms of abnormality. This was approved on appeal. The California court's subsequent decisions can be read as an effort to redefine the states of mind required by the homicide offenses so as to make diminished capacity an appropriate vehicle for accommodating the seriousness of the offenses for which homicide defendants are convicted and the culpability of their conduct given evidence of substantial psychological impairment.

In People v. Wolff, 61 Cal.2d 795, 40 Cal.Rptr. 271, 394 P.2d 959 (1964), the court addressed the standard for determining whether a defendant engaged in the premeditation required for first degree murder. This, it held, requires that the defendant "maturely and meaningfully reflect upon the gravity of his contemplated act." Psychiatric testimony and the defendant's age in the case (the defendant had been fifteen years old at the time he killed his mother) established the absence of premeditation under this standard:

He knew the difference between right and wrong; he knew that the intended act was wrong and nevertheless carried it out. But the extent of his understanding, reflection upon it and its consequences, with realization of the enormity of the evil, appears to have been materially—as relevant to appraising the quantum of his moral turpitude and depravity—vague and detached.

61 Cal.2d at 822, 40 Cal.Rptr. at 288, 394 P.2d at 976. Thus the conviction for first degree premeditated murder was not supported by the evidence and was reduced by the court to second degree murder.

In several cases, the court considered the meaning of malice aforethought as it related to the nature and quantity of evidence of mental aberration necessary to establish that a killing is manslaughter rather than murder. In People v. Conley, 64 Cal.2d 310, 49 Cal.Rptr. 815, 411 P.2d 911 (1966), the court added a "new" requirement to the state of mind required for murder:

> An awareness of the obligation to act within the general body of laws regulating society ＊ ＊ ＊ is included in the statutory definition of implied malice in terms of an abandoned and malignant heart and in the definition of express malice as the deliberate intention unlawfully to take life.

64 Cal.2d at 322, 49 Cal.Rptr. at 822, 411 P.2d at 918. It then explained *Gorshen* as involving evidence tending to establish that although the defendant premeditated within the meaning of first degree murder, he acted without malice because his abnormality had caused him to forget "about God's laws and human laws and everything else." A defense psychologist testified at trial that at the time of the killing Conley was in a "dissociative state" and because of "personality fragmentation" did not function with his normal personality. Other evidence indicated he was intoxicated at the time of the killings. On the basis of this testimony, the court concluded a jury could find that although Conley deliberated and premeditated the killing, his abnormality (and his intoxication) showed he acted without malice aforethought. The failure to instruct the jury concerning this possibility was therefore error.

Although *Conley* added a new cognitive dimension to the mens rea required for murder, it did not address the extent to which evidence of volitional impairment might be relevant to the absence of malice aforethought. This issue appeared to be dealt with in People v. Poddar, 10 Cal. 3d 750, 111 Cal.Rptr. 910, 518 P.2d 342 (1974). At Poddar's trial for the killing of a woman associate, substantial evidence of his abnormality was introduced. The jury was instructed on second degree murder and manslaughter and was told that diminished capacity could negate the malice aforethought necessary for murder. But the trial judge refused to instruct the jury more specifically on the relationship between impaired mental processes and malice aforethought. Poddar's proposed instructions explaining the need for an understanding of the duty which the law imposed *and* an ability to conform one's conduct to the comprehended duty were refused. The resulting conviction for second degree murder was reversed on appeal. Addressing the question of the relevance of diminished capacity to murder when the prosecution relies upon malice implied from acts committed with a "wanton disregard for human life," the court explained:

> The effect ＊ ＊ ＊ which a diminished capacity bears on malice in a second degree murder-implied malice case is relevant to two questions: First, was the accused because of a diminished capacity unaware of a duty to act within the law? A person is, of course, presumed to know the law which prohibits injuring another. Second, even assuming that the accused was aware of this duty to act within the law, was he, because of a diminished capacity, unable to act in accordance with that duty?

10 Cal.3d at 758, 111 Cal.Rptr. at 916, 518 P.2d at 348. Since the instructions did not apply the evidence to the underlying issues with

sufficient specificity, the court erred in refusing more specific instructions. *Poddar*, then, seems to leave no doubt that impairment of volition can establish the absence of the malice aforethought required for murder, at least in some circumstances.

In 1981, however, legislation responded to these developments. 1981 Cal.Stat. ch. 404. Some modification was also made by 1982 and 1984 legislation. The California Penal Code's definition of malice, necessary for murder, contained in § 188 (reprinted at page 379, supra), was supplemented by the addition of the following paragraph:

> When it is shown that the killing resulted from the intentional doing of an act with express or implied malice as defined above, no other mental state need be shown to establish the mental state of malice aforethought. An awareness of the obligation to act within the general body of laws regulating society is not included within the definition of malice.

The definition of first degree murder, contained in § 189 (reprinted at page 380, supra), was supplemented by the addition of the following:

> To prove the killing was "deliberate and premeditated," it shall not be necessary to prove the defendant maturely and meaningfully reflected upon the gravity of his or her act.

In addition, the following sections were added to the California Penal Code:

§ 21. Manifestation of intent; evidence of lack of capacity or ability to control conduct

(a) The intent or intention is manifested by the circumstances connected with the offense.

(b) In the guilt phase of a criminal action * * *, evidence that the accused lacked the capacity or ability to control his conduct for any reason shall not be admissible on the issue of whether the accused actually had any mental state with respect to the commission of any crime. This subdivision is not applicable to Section 26 [, providing that certain classes of persons (including children, idiots, those acting under ignorance or mistake "which disproves any criminal intent," and persons not conscious of the act) are not capable of committing crimes].

§ 28. Evidence of mental disease, mental defect or mental disorder

(a) Evidence of mental disease, mental defect, or mental disorder shall not be admitted to show or negate the capacity to form any mental state, including, but not limited to, purpose, intent, knowledge, premeditation, deliberation, or malice aforethought, with which the accused committed the act. Evidence of mental disease, mental defect, or mental disorder is admissible solely on the issue of whether or not the accused actually formed a required specific intent, premeditated, deliberated, or harbored malice aforethought, when a specific intent crime is charged.

(b) As a matter of public policy there shall be no defense of diminished capacity, diminished responsibility, or irresistible impulse in a criminal action * * *.

*   *   *

(d) Nothing in this section shall limit a court's discretion, pursuant to the Evidence Code, to exclude psychiatric or psychological evidence on whether the accused had a mental disease, mental defect, or mental disorder at the time of the alleged offense.

§ 29.   Mental state; restriction on expert testimony; determination by trier of fact

In the guilt phase of a criminal action, any expert testifying about a defendant's mental illness, mental disorder, or mental defect shall not testify as to whether the defendant had or did not have the required mental states, which include, but are not limited to, purpose, intent, knowledge, or malice aforethought, for the crimes charged. The question as to whether the defendant had or did not have the required mental states shall be decided by the trier of fact.

*

Index

CONSTITUTIONAL LIMITATIONS

See also Cruel and Unusual Punishment; Defenses; Due Process; Presumptions.

Double jeopardy, 30, 42, 242, 245, 254, 257.

Equal protection, 93, 513, 526, 527.

First Amendment, 93, 105, 137, 318, 555, 575, 579, 584.

Privacy, 136, 140, 152, 514.

Vagueness, 94, 102, 234.

CONSTRUCTION OF STATUTES

Generally, 15, 32, 622.

CONVERSION

See Embezzlement.

CORPORATE LIABILITY

Generally, 660.

CRIMINAL CODES

See Statutes.

CORRECTIONS

Generally, 17.

CRIME

Amounts, 2.

Comparative rates, 6.

CRIMES

See also specific crimes.

Against public authority,
   Interference with arrest or prosecution, 707.
   Misprision, 712.
   Perjury, 11.
   Treason, 10.

Against public health, safety and morals, 10, 28, 136, 140, 307, 316, 525.

Against the habitation,
   Arson, 8, 223.
   Burglary, 8, 223, 228, 496, 544.

Against the person,
   Assault, 7, 230, 269, 536, 640.
   Battery, 7, 230.
   False imprisonment, 8.
   Kidnapping, 8, 231, 232, 241.
   Mayhem, 8.
   Rape, 8, 497.
   Statutory rape, 517.
   Threats against public officials, 555.

Drug related, 152, 168, 175, 307, 538, 589, 606.

Mala prohibita and mala in se, 285, 307, 311–14, 316, 521, 631.

Property offenses,
   Blackmail, 9, 217.
   Claim of right defense, 333.
   Criminal mischief, 223.
   Embezzlement, 9, 194, 204, 295, 300.
   Extortion, 9, 208, 217.
   False pretenses, 198, 205, 208.
   Forgery, 9.
   Larceny, 9, 188, 201, 203, 212, 294, 296, 309, 496, 539.

CRIMES—Cont'd

Malicious mischief, 10.

Robbery, 209, 216, 296, 357, 468.

Theft, 9, 205, 295.

Relationship to alcohol use, 345.

Statistics, 2–8.

"Victimless", 85, 136.

CRIMINAL LIABILITY

Nature of, 66.

CRIMINALIZATION

Generally, 65, 68.

Drug possession, 152.

Homosexual conduct, 140.

Justifications for,
   Generally, 71.
   Deterrence, 75, 121, 279, 792.
   Incapacitation, 80, 279.
   Morality, 85, 87, 136.
   Moralization, 75, 78.
   Retribution, 72, 73, 121, 279.
   Social solidarity, 87, 88.
   Treatment of offenders, 19, 81, 279, 357.
   Utilitarianism, 72, 75, 86.

Legal limits, 136.

CRUEL AND UNUSUAL PUNISHMENT

Death Penalty, 105, 106, 109, 121, 378.

Imprisonment, 125.

Limit upon criminalization, 345.

Public intoxication laws, 345.

CULPABILITY

See Mental State.

DANGEROUS SPECIAL OFFENDERS

Generally, 21.

DEATH

See Homicide.

DEATH PENALTY

See Cruel and Unusual Punishment; Punishment, Capital.

DEFECTIVE DELINQUENCY PROGRAM

Generally, 21.

DEFENSE OF OTHERS

See Defenses.

DEFENSE OF PROPERTY

See Defenses.

DEFENSES

See also Attempts, Impossibility, Renunciation; Battered Spouse Syndrome; Conspiracy, Agreement, "Defenses" based on lack of, Impossibility, Renunciation; Constitutional Limitations; Intoxication; Mistake; Solicitation, Impossibility, Renunciation.

Generally, 320, 716.